D1276481

WITHDRAWN

GENERAL HISTORY OF AFRICA · I

Methodology and African Prehistory

Unesco General History of Africa

Volume I	Methodology and African Prehistory (Editor J. Ki-Zerbo)
Volume II	Ancient Civilizations of Africa (Editor G. Mokhtar)
Volume III	Africa from the Seventh to Eleventh Century (Editor M. El Fasi)
Volume IV	Africa from the Twelfth to Sixteenth Century (Editor D. T. Niane)
Volume V	Africa from the Sixteenth to Eighteenth Century (Editor B. A. Ogot)
Volume VI	The Nineteenth Century until 1880 (Editor J. F. A. Ajayi)
Volume VII	Africa under Foreign Domination, 1880–1935 (Editor A. A. Boahen)
Volume VIII	Africa since 1935 (Editor A. A. Mazrui)

UNESCO International Scientific Committee for the Drafting of a General History of Africa

GENERAL HISTORY OF AFRICA · I

Methodology and African Prehistory

EDITOR J. KI-ZERBO

HEINEMANN · CALIFORNIA · UNESCO

First published 1981 by the
United Nations Educational, Scientific
and Cultural Organization,
7 Place de Fontenoy, 75700 Paris

and

Heinemann Educational Books Ltd
22 Bedford Square, London WC1B 3HH
P.M.B. 5205, Ibadan PO. Box 45314, Nairobi
EDINBURGH MELBOURNE AUCKLAND
HONG KONG SINGAPORE KUALA LUMPUR NEW DELHI
KINGSTON PORT OF SPAIN

First published 1981
in the United States of America by the
University of California Press
2223 Fulton Street, Berkeley
California 94720, United States of America

Heinemann Educational Books	ISBN 0 435 94807 5 (cased)
	ISBN 0 435 94808 3 (paper)
Unesco	ISBN 92-3-101-707-1
University of California Press	ISBN 0-520-03912-2
	LCN 78-57321

Filmset in 11 pt Monophoto Ehrhardt by
Northumberland Press Ltd, Gateshead, Tyne and Wear
Printed and bound in Great Britain by
Richard Clay (The Chaucer Press) Ltd, Bungay, Suffolk

Contents

List of figures ix

List of plates xi

List of tables xv

Preface xvii
AMADOU-MAHTAR M'BOW, Director-General of Unesco

Description of the Project xxiii
B. A. OGOT, President of the International Scientific Committee for the Drafting of a General History of Africa

Note on chronology xxvii

General introduction 1
J. KI-ZERBO

1 The development of African historiography 25
J. D. FAGE

2 The place of history in African society 43
BOUBOU HAMA and J. KI-ZERBO

3 Recent trends in African historiography and their contribution to history in general 54
P. D. CURTIN

4 Sources and specific techniques used in African history: general outline 72
T. OBENGA

5 Written sources before the fifteenth century 87
H. DJAIT

6 Written sources from the fifteenth century onwards 114
I. HRBEK

7 Oral tradition and its methodology 142
J. VANSINA

8 The living tradition 166
A. HAMPATÉ BÂ

9 African archaeology and its techniques including dating techniques 206
Z. ISKANDER

10 History and linguistics 233
P. DIAGNE

Editorial note: theories on the 'races' and history of Africa 261
J. KI-ZERBO

11 Migrations and ethnic and linguistic differentiations 271
D. OLDEROGGE

12 African linguistic classification 292
J. H. GREENBERG

Appendix to Chapter 12: the language map of Africa 309
D. DALBY

13 Historical geography: physical aspects 316
S. DIARRA

14 Historical geography: economic aspects 333
A. L. MABOGUNJE

15 The interdisciplinary methods adopted in this study 348
J. KI-ZERBO

16 Chronological framework: African pluvial and glacial epochs 359
Part I R. SAID
Part II H. FAURE

17 Hominization: general problems 400
Part I Y. COPPENS
Part II L. BALOUT

18 African fossil man 437
R. LEAKEY

19 The prehistory of East Africa 451
J. E. G. SUTTON

20 Prehistory in southern Africa 487
J. D. CLARK

21 The prehistory of Central Africa 530
Part I R. DE BAYLE DES HERMENS
Part II F. VAN NOTEN
with the collaboration of P. de Maret, J. Moeyersons, K. Muya and E. Roche

22 The prehistory of North Africa 568
L. BALOUT

23 The prehistory of the Sahara 585
H. J. HUGOT

24 The prehistory of West Africa 611
C. T. SHAW

25 Prehistory in the Nile valley 634
F. DEBONO

26 African prehistoric art 656
J. KI-ZERBO

27 Origins, development and expansion of agricultural techniques 687
R. PORTÈRES and J. BARRAU

28 Discovery and diffusion of metals and development of social systems up to the fifth century before our era 706
J. VERCOUTTER

Conclusion: from nature in the raw to liberated humanity 730
J. KI-ZERBO

List of Members of the International Scientific Committee for the Drafting of a General History of Africa 747

Biographies of Authors 749

Bibliography 753

Indexes 801

N.B. Mrs Catherine Perlès contributed to the finalization of Chapters 18, 19, 20, 21 and 24.

Mrs Hélène Roche provided some additional items of information to Chapter 19.

List of figures

12.1 Diagrammatic language map of Africa *310*
13.1 Physical map of Africa *317*
14.1 Mineral resources of Africa *332*
16.1 Graphs showing analogies between oxygen isotopes (or temperature variations) and the intensity of the earth's magnetic field *373*
16.2 Graphs showing analogies between temperatures indicated by the microfauna and the magnetic inclination for the last two million years *374*
16.3 Surface water isotherm map of the Atlantic Ocean for February, 18 000 BP *380*
16.4 Map showing differences in surface water temperature of the Atlantic Ocean in the winter, between 17 000 (or 18 000) BP and the present day *381*
16.5 Map showing differences in surface water temperature of the Atlantic Ocean in summer, between 17 000 (or 18 000) BP and the present day *382*
16.6 Comparative evolution of African lakes over the last 30 000 years *384*
16.7 Relative evolution of rainfall evaporation ratio in the Chad Basin (13–18°N) over the last 12 000 years *387*
16.8 Variations in lake level in the Afar Basins *389*
16.9 Map of classical fossil-bearing localities of the Pliocene/Pleistocene era in East Africa *394*
16.10 Chronology and the tempo of cultural change during the Pleistocene, in calibration of hominoid evolution *395*
16.11 Generalized trends in global climate for the past million years *396*
16.12 Radiometric and palaeomagnetic aspects of the Pliocene/Pleistocene time range in eastern Africa, south-western Europe and western North America *398*
17.1 Palaeontological data *416*
18.1 Africa: important hominid sites *438*
19.1 East Africa: important Stone Age sites *461*
19.2 Early Stone Age, first phase: typical Oldowan ('pebble') tools *467*
19.3a Early Stone Age, second phase: typical Acheulian hand-axe *469*
19.3b Early Stone Age, second phase: typical Acheulian pick *470*
19.3c Early Stone Age, second phase: typical Acheulian cleaver *471*
19.4 Middle Stone Age and transitional tools *474*
19.5 Late Stone Age: 'thumbnail' scraper, backed blade and crescent *477*
20.1 Late Pliocene/earlier Pleistocene main faunal and fossil man localities in southern Africa *488*
20.2 Lower Acheulian hand-axe, flake and two core choppers from the Middle Breccia, Sterkfontein *495*
20.3 The distribution of Acheulian sites in southern Africa *497*
20.4 Upper Acheulian tools from Kalambo Falls, Zambia *498*
20.5 Wooden implements from Pleistocene sites in southern Africa *501*
20.6 The distribution of Fauresmith and Sangoan sites in southern Africa *507*

20.7 Artefacts from Sangoan assemblages in the Zambesi Valley, near Livingstone, Zambia *509*
20.8 Upper Pleistocene and some post-Pleistocene fossil man sites in southern Africa *512*
20.9 Tools of the Pietersburg and Bambata Industries from the Cave of Hearths, Transvaal, and Bambata Cave, Zimbabwe *514*
20.10 Middle Stone Age industry from Twin Rivers, typical of the *Brachystegia* woodlands of Zambia *519*
20.11 Middle Stone Age artefacts from Witkrans Cave, typical of the equipment of hunters in the Karroo/Kalahari thornveld *520*
20.12 Tools of the Middle Stone Age Lupemban Industrial Complex from Kalambo Falls, associated with *Brachystegia* woodland and evergreen forest *521*
20.13 Distribution of utilized blades and blade fragments in relation to dolerite boulder structures on a living site at Orangia, Orange Free State *522*
20.14 Tools from Howieson's Poort sites belonging to Group IV of the Middle Stone Age in southern Africa *523*
20.5 Tools of the Later Stone Age Wilton Complex *526*
20.16 Crescent adze-flake or scraper in chert, mounted in mastic, with rhino-horn handle, from a cave at Plettenberg Bay, eastern Cape Province, South Africa *527*
21.1 Central Africa: places mentioned in the text *535*
21.2 Central Africa: vegetation zones *536*
23.1 Principal sites of Saharan paintings and pack engravings *590*
23.2 Pottery from Akreijit, Mauritania *598*
24.1 West Africa: vegetation zones *612*
27.1 Latitudinal zoning of the African continent *690*
27.2 Ecosystems of the African continent *691*
27.3 Cradles of African agriculture *696*
27.4 Geo-cultural sketch map of Africa *702*

List of plates

2.1 Bronze statue representing the dynastic power of the Songhay of Dargol *53*
4.1 Bas-relief from Abomey Museum *86*
5.1 Verso of Arabic manuscript *113*
6.1 Facsimile of Bamum manuscript *140*
6.2 Facsimile of Hausa manuscript *141*
6.3 Facsimile of Vai manuscript *141*
8.1 Valiha player *204*
8.2 Mvet singer *204*
8.3 'Griot hutu' miming the fallen 'mwami' *205*
8.4 Tukulor musician playing the 'ardin' *205*
9.1 X-ray photograph of the frontal chest of the mummy of Queen Nedjemet (twenty-first dynasty) *232*
9.2 Microphoto of a section in a copper staple from the Cheops Boat at Giza *232*
9.3 Glass frit block showing the flat upper surface, lateral sides and a part of the fritting crucible left adhering to the right side *232*
9.4 The bottom part of one of the sandstone columns, Buhen Temple, Sudan *232*
10.1 The serpent king stele *256*
10.2 The Récade dedicated to King Dakodonu, first sovereign of Danxome *256*
10.3 Awe-inspiring lion cub from Abomey Museum *256*
10.4 The Récade showing a gourd, symbol of power, from Abomey Museum *257*
10.5 First page of the first chapter of the *Koran* in Vai *257*
10.6 Phonetic chart of Vai characters *257*
10.7 Sample characters from the indigenous scripts *258*
10.8 The Mum graphic system *259*
10.9 The Egyptian and West African graphic systems *259*
10.10 The Palette of Narmer *260*
11.1 Moroccan *287*
11.2 Algerian woman and baby *287*
11.3 Haratine woman from Idélès, Algeria *287*
11.4 Fulani woman from near Garoua-Boulay, Cameroon *288*
11.5 Fulani woman *288*
11.6 Sarakole woman, Mauritania *288*
11.7 Chief, nomad, Mauritania *288*
11.8 Young Fulani girl from Mali *289*
11.9 Voltaian *289*
11.10 Djerma Songhay woman from Balayera, Niger *289*
11.11 Tuareg child from Agadès, Niger *289*
11.12 Bororo Fulani Woman from Tahoua, Niger *290*
11.13 Twa Pygmy, Rwanda *290*
11.14 Zulu woman *290*

11.15 Pygmy from the Congo *290*
11.16 San group *291*
17.1 One of the oldest stone artefacts in the world, found on the Omo site, Ethiopia *427*
17.2 The Siwaliks excavation, north Pakistan *427*
17.3 Eocene and Oligocene sites, Fayum, Egypt *428*
17.4 Reconstruction of the environment at Fayum, Egypt, 40 000 000 years ago *428*
17.5 Skulls of *Australopithecus robustus* and *Australopithecus gracilis* *429*
17.6 Skull of *Australopithecus boisei*, Omo site, Ethiopia *429*
17.7 Skull of *Homo habilis* *430*
17.8 a & b Skull of *Homo erectus* from Choukoutien, China (reconstruction) *430–1*
17.9 Reconstruction of the environment in which *Homo erectus* lived at Choukoutien, China, 400 000 years ago *431*
17.10 Skulls of *Australopithecus africanus* *431*
17.11 Reconstruction of *Oreopithecus bamboli* *432*
17.12 Skeleton of *Oreopithecus bamboli*, 12 000 000 years old, found on the Grossetto site, Tuscany *432*
17.13 Skull of Cromagnoid from Afalu, Algeria *433*
17.14 Reconstruction of skull of *Ramapithecus* *433*
17.15 The Afar site, Ethiopia *433*
17.16 The Omo sites and palaeontological excavations during the 1969 French expedition *434*
17.17 Olduvai Gorge, northern Tanzania *435*
17.18 An excavation site at Olduvai *436*
17.19 Detail of the surface of the soil at the Olduvai excavations *436*
17.20 Close-up of the surface of the soil at the Olduvai excavations *436*
18.1 *Australopithecus boisei* – lateral view of cranium from Olduvai Gorge, Tanzania *449*
18.2 *Australopithecus boisei* – occlusal view of mandible from Koobi Fora, Kenya *449*
18.3 *Australopithecus africanus* – lateral view of cranium from Koobi Fora, Kenya *449*
18.4 *Australopithecus africanus* – occlusal view of mandible from Koobi Fora, Kenya *449*
18.5 *Homo erectus* – lateral view of cranium from Koobi Fora, Kenya *450*
18.6 *Homo habilis* – lateral view of cranium from Koobi Fora, Kenya *450*
19.1 Olduvai Gorge, northern Tanzania *485*
19.2 Isimila, southern highlands of Tanzania *485*
19.3 Isimila, Tanzania: a concentration of Acheulian hand-axes, cleavers and other tools *485*
19.4 Olorgesailie in the Kenyan Rift Valley *486*
19.5 Apis Rock (Nasera), northern Tanzania *486*
21.1 Upper Acheulian bi-faced tool from the River Ngoere, Upper Sangha, Central African Republic *567*
21.2 Upper Acheulian hand-axe from the River Ngoere, Upper Sangha, Central African Republic *567*
21.3 Flat-bottomed Neolithic vase from Batalimo, Lobaye, Central African Republic *567*

21.4 Megalithic monument in the Bouar region, Central African Republic *567*
22.1 Pebbles fashioned into bi-faced tools and a chopper, from Ain Hanech *581*
22.2 Spherical faceted pebbles from Ain Hanech *581*
22.3 The development of 'Pebble Culture' towards Acheulian shapes *581*
22.4 Hand-axe found on the Acheulian site of Erg Tihodaine, Algerian Sahara *582*
22.5 Bi-faced Acheulian tool, the most advanced implement found on the Ternifine site in western Algeria *582*
22.6 Mousterian pointed tool from El-Guettar, Tunisia *582*
22.7 Aterian tools: pedunculated points, scrapers and Levallois cores *583*
22.8 Typical Capsian industry *583*
22.9 Upper Capsian industry: scalene triangles, trapeziums, saws, grooved knives, burins, micro-burins, drillers, scrapers, etc. *583*
22.10 Upper Capsian industry: geometrical microliths (trapeziums, scalene triangles, crescents and micro-burins) *583*
22.11 Upper Capsian: human fibula fashioned into a dagger, found at Mechta el-Arb, eastern Algeria *584*
22.12 Upper Capsian: engraved limestone plaquette from Khanguet el-Mouhaad, eastern Algeria *584*
22.13 Neolithic-Capsian Tradition: pestle and mortar showing traces of coal ochre and fragments of Helix shells, found at Damous el-Ahmar, eastern Algeria *584*
23.1 Flat notched axe from Gossolorum, Niger *606*
23.2 Cleaver from Ti-n-Assako, Mali *606*
23.3 Chopper tool (Pebble Culture) from Aoulef, Algerian Sahara *606*
23.4 Chopper tool (Pebble Culture) from Aoulef, Algerian Sahara *606*
23.5 Lower Palaeolithic hand-axe from Tachenghit, Algerian Sahara *607*
23.6 Lower Palaeolithic cleaver from Tachenghit, Algerian Sahara *607*
23.7 Large bi-facial double point, Aterian Industry, from Timimoun, Algerian Sahara *607*
23.8 Aterian points from Aoulef, Algerian Sahara *608*
23.9 Aterian bi-facial double point from Adrar Bousv, Niger *609*
23.10 Neolithic pottery from Dhar Tichitt, Mauritania *609*
23.11 Neolithic arrow-heads from In Guezzam, Niger *610*
23.12 Neolithic grooved axe from Adar Bous, Niger *610*
23.13 Neolithic polished axe from the Faya region, Chad *610*
24.1 Industry of Cape Manuel, Senegal *631*
24.2 Stone pendants (basalt) from the Neolithic site at Patte d'Oie *631*
24.3 Neolithic 'Bel Air' pottery from the Diakité site, Senegal *631*
24.4 Pottery of Cape Manuel, Senegal; decorated fragments *631*
24.5 Megalithic circle, Tiekène Boussoura, Senegal *632*
24.6 'Bel Air' polished axes made of dolerite *632*
24.7 Millstone made of volcanic rock, found on the Neolithic site of Ngor *632*
24.8 Iron Age flat-bottomed pot *633*
24.9 Bone smoothing tool, found on the Neolithic site at Cape Manuel, Senegal *633*
24.10 Anthropomorphic statue found on Thiaroye site, Senegal *633*
25.1 Flint javelin heads from Mirgissa, Sudan *655*
25.2 The Valley of the Queens *655*

26.1 Detail from the 'White Lady' cave painting, South Africa *682*
26.2 'Serpent's Track' cave painting *682*
26.3 Engraving of rhinoceros, Blaka, Niger *682*
26.4 Engraving of an elephant, In Eker, Algerian Sahara *683*
26.5 Bovine, Tin Rharo, Mali *683*
26.6 Gazelles, Blaka, Niger *683*
26.7 Cave engraving, Upper Volta *683*
26.8 Close-up of cave engravings, Upper Volta *684*
26.9 Erotic scene, Tassili, Algeria *684*
26.10 Erotic scene, Tassili, Algeria *684*
26.11 Cave painting, Tibesti, Chad *684*
26.12 Cave paintings, Tassili, Algeria *685*
26.13 Cave paintings, Namibia *686*
27.1 Top-soil firing, Futa Djalon *703*
27.2 The 'Soung' or Spade of the Serer Gnominka, Senegal *703*
27.3 Cultivation of land, Kadyendo *704*
27.4 Artificial islands for the cultivation of rice, Guinea-Bissau *704*
27.5 Rice pits, Nyassa, Casamance *705*
28.1 Tomb of Huy, after R. Lepsius *729*
28.2 Tomb of Rekh mi-re at Thebes *729*
28.3 Copper statue of Pepi I (Old Kingdom) *729*
28.4 Razor, Mirgissa *729*
Concl. 1 Laboratory set up at Rosso Bithie for investigating the development of the delta of the River Senegal *745*
Concl. 2 Skull of *Australopithecus boisei* from the Omo site, Ethiopia *745*

List of tables

5.1 Chronological table of principal written sources *102–5*
7.1 Basic forms of oral traditions *145*
12.1 Stages of the Greenberg classification *308*
16.1 The succession of the recognized formations and their chronology *393*
18.1 List of *Homo erectus* materials known from Africa *448*
19.1 Periods and industries in African prehistory *451*
19.2 Prehistory in East Africa *464*
21.1 Climatic variations and prehistoric traditions of the Congo Basin *532*
21.2 The names of the industries, present carbon-14 dating and the evolution of the environment and flora *533*
23.1 Outline of Saharan prehistoric chronology *600*

Preface

AMADOU-MAHTAR M'BOW
Director-General of Unesco

For a long time, all kinds of myths and prejudices concealed the true history of Africa from the world at large. African societies were looked upon as societies that could have no history. In spite of important work done by such pioneers as Leo Frobenius, Maurice Delafosse and Arturo Labriola, as early as the first decades of this century, a great many non-African experts could not rid themselves of certain preconceptions and argued that the lack of written sources and documents made it impossible to engage in any scientific study of such societies.

Although the *Iliad* and *Odyssey* were rightly regarded as essential sources for the history of ancient Greece, African oral tradition, the collective memory of peoples which holds the thread of many events marking their lives, was rejected as worthless. In writing the history of a large part of Africa, the only sources used were from outside the continent, and the final product gave a picture not so much of the paths actually taken by the African peoples as of those that the authors thought they must have taken. Since the European Middle Ages were often used as a yardstick, modes of production, social relations and political institutions were visualized only by reference to the European past.

In fact, there was a refusal to see Africans as the creators of original cultures which flowered and survived over the centuries in patterns of their own making and which historians are unable to grasp unless they forgo their prejudices and rethink their approach.

Furthermore, the continent of Africa was hardly ever looked upon as a historical entity. On the contrary, emphasis was laid on everything likely to lend credence to the idea that a split had existed, from time immemorial, between a 'white Africa' and a 'black Africa', each unaware of the other's existence. The Sahara was often presented as an impenetrable space preventing any intermingling of ethnic groups and peoples or any exchange of goods, beliefs, customs and ideas between the societies that had grown up on either side of the desert. Hermetic frontiers were drawn between the civilizations of Ancient Egypt and Nubia and those of the peoples south of the Sahara.

It is true that the history of Africa north of the Sahara has been more closely linked with that of the Mediterranean basin than has the history of sub-Saharan Africa, but it is now widely recognized that the various civilizations of the African continent, for all their differing languages and cultures, represent, to a greater or lesser degree, the historical offshoots of a set of peoples and societies united by bonds centuries old.

Another phenomenon which did great disservice to the objective study of the African past was the appearance, with the slave trade and colonization, of racial stereotypes which bred contempt and lack of understanding and became so deep-rooted that they distorted even the basic concepts of historiography. From the time when the notions of 'white' and 'black' were used as generic labels by the colonialists, who were regarded as superior, the colonized Africans had to struggle against both economic and psychological enslavement. Africans were identifiable by the colour of their skin, they had become a kind of merchandise, they were earmarked for hard labour and eventually, in the minds of those dominating them, they came to symbolize an imaginary and allegedly inferior *Negro* race. This pattern of spurious identification relegated the history of the African peoples in many minds to the rank of ethno-history, in which appreciation of the historical and cultural facts was bound to be warped.

The situation has changed significantly since the end of the Second World War and in particular since the African countries became independent and began to take an active part in the life of the international community and in the mutual exchanges that are its *raison d'être*. An increasing number of historians has endeavoured to tackle the study of Africa with a more rigorous, objective and open-minded outlook by using – with all due precautions – actual African sources. In exercising their right to take the historical initiative, Africans themselves have felt a deep-seated need to re-establish the historical authenticity of their societies on solid foundations.

In this context, the importance of the eight-volume *General History of Africa*, which Unesco is publishing, speaks for itself.

The experts from many countries working on this project began by laying down the theoretical and methodological basis for the *History*. They have been at pains to call in question the over-simplifications arising from a linear and restrictive conception of world history and to re-establish the true facts wherever necessary and possible. They have endeavoured to highlight the historical data that give a clearer picture of the evolution of the different peoples of Africa in their specific socio-cultural setting.

To tackle this huge task, made all the more complex and difficult by the vast range of sources and the fact that documents were widely scattered, Unesco has had to proceed by stages. The first stage, from 1965 to 1969, was devoted to gathering documentation and planning the work. Operational assignments were conducted in the field and included campaigns to collect oral traditions, the creation of regional documentation centres for oral traditions, the collection of unpublished manuscripts in

Arabic and Ajami (African languages written in Arabic script), the compilation of archival inventories and the preparation of a *Guide to the Sources of the History of Africa*, culled from the archives and libraries of the countries of Europe and later published in nine volumes. In addition, meetings were organized to enable experts from Africa and other continents to discuss questions of methodology and lay down the broad lines for the project after careful examination of the available sources.

The second stage, which lasted from 1969 to 1971, was devoted to shaping the *History* and linking its different parts. The purpose of the international meetings of experts held in Paris in 1969 and Addis Ababa in 1970 was to study and define the problems involved in drafting and publishing the *History*: presentation in eight volumes, the principal edition in English, French and Arabic, translation into African languages such as Kiswahili, Hausa, Fulani, Yoruba or Lingala, prospective versions in German, Russian, Portuguese, Spanish and Chinese, as well as abridged editions designed for a wide African and international public.

The third stage has involved actual drafting and publication. This began with the appointment of the 39-member International Scientific Committee, two-thirds African and one-third non-African, which assumes intellectual responsibility for the *History*.

The method used is interdisciplinary and is based on a multi-faceted approach and a wide variety of sources. The first among these is archaeology, which holds many of the keys to the history of African cultures and civilizations. Thanks to archaeology, it is now acknowledged that Africa was very probably the cradle of mankind and the scene – in the neolithic period – of one of the first technological revolutions in history. Archaeology has also shown that Egypt was the setting for one of the most brilliant ancient civilizations of the world. But another very important source is oral tradition, which, after being long despised, has now emerged as an invaluable instrument for discovering the history of Africa, making it possible to follow the movements of its different peoples in both space and time, to understand the African vision of the world from the inside and to grasp the original features of the values on which the cultures and institutions of the continent are based.

We are indebted to the International Scientific Committee in charge of this *General History of Africa*, and to its Rapporteur and the editors and authors of the various volumes and chapters, for having shed a new light on the African past in its authentic and all-encompassing form and for having avoided any dogmatism in the study of essential issues. Among these issues we might cite: the slave trade, that 'endlessly bleeding wound', which was responsible for one of the cruellest mass deportations in the history of mankind, which sapped the African continent of its life-blood while contributing significantly to the economic and commercial expansion of Europe; colonization, with all the effects it had on population, economics, psychology and culture; relations between Africa south of the Sahara and the Arab world; and, finally, the process of decolonization and nation-building which mobilized the intelligence and passion of people still alive and sometimes still active today. All these issues have been broached with a concern for honesty and rigour which is not the least of the *History*'s merits. By taking stock of our knowledge of Africa, putting forward a variety of viewpoints on African cultures and offering a new reading of history, the *History* has the signal advantage of showing up the light and shade and of openly portraying the differences of opinion that may exist between scholars.

By demonstrating the inadequacy of the methodological approaches which have long been used in research on Africa, this *History* calls for a new and careful study of the twofold problem areas of historiography and cultural identity, which are united by links of reciprocity. Like any historical work of value, the *History* paves the way for a great deal of further research on a variety of topics.

It is for this reason that the International Scientific Committee, in close collaboration with Unesco, decided to embark on additional studies in an attempt to go deeper into a number of issues which will permit a clearer understanding of certain aspects of the African past. The findings being published in the series 'Unesco Studies and Documents – General History of Africa' will prove a useful supplement to the *History*, as will the works planned on aspects of national or subregional history.

The *General History* sheds light both on the historical unity of Africa and also its relations with the other continents, particularly the Americas and the Caribbean. For a long time, the creative manifestations of the descendants of Africans in the Americas were lumped together by some historians as a heterogeneous collection of *Africanisms*. Needless to say, this is not the attitude of the authors of the *History*, in which the resistance of the slaves shipped to America, the constant and massive participation of the descendants of Africans in the struggles for the initial independence of America and in national liberation movements, are rightly perceived for what they were: vigorous assertions of identity, which helped forge the universal concept of mankind. Although the phenomenon may vary in different places, it is now quite clear that ways of feeling, thinking, dreaming and acting in certain nations of the western hemisphere have been marked by their African heritage. The cultural inheritance of Africa is visible everywhere, from the southern United States to northern Brazil, across the Caribbean and on the Pacific seaboard. In certain places it even underpins the cultural identity of some of the most important elements of the population.

The *History* also clearly brings out Africa's relations with southern Asia across the Indian Ocean and the African contributions to other civilizations through mutual exchanges.

I am convinced that the efforts of the peoples of Africa to conquer or strengthen their independence, secure their development and assert their cultural characteristics, must be rooted in historical awareness renewed, keenly felt and taken up by each succeeding generation.

My own background, the experience I gained as a teacher and as chairman, from the early days of independence, of the first commission set up to reform history and geography curricula in some of the countries of West and Central Africa, taught me how necessary it was for the education of young people and for the information of the public at large to have a history book produced by scholars with inside knowledge of the problems and hopes of Africa and with the ability to apprehend the continent in its entirety.

For all these reasons, Unesco's goal will be to ensure that this *General History of Africa* is widely disseminated in a large number of languages and is used as a basis for producing children's books, school textbooks and radio and television programmes. Young people, whether schoolchildren or students, and adults in Africa and elsewhere will thus be able to form a truer picture of the African continent's past and the factors that explain it, as well as a fairer understanding of its cultural heritage and its contribution to the general progress of mankind. The *History* should thus contribute to improved international cooperation and stronger solidarity among peoples in their aspirations to justice, progress and peace. This is, at least, my most cherished hope.

It remains for me to express my deep gratitude to the members of the International Scientific Committee, the Rapporteur, the different volume editors, the authors and all those who have collaborated in this tremendous undertaking. The work they have accomplished and the contribution they have made plainly go to show how people from different backgrounds but all imbued with the same spirit of goodwill and enthusiasm in the service of universal truth can, within the international framework provided by Unesco, bring to fruition a project of considerable scientific and cultural import. My thanks also go to the organizations and governments whose generosity has made it possible for Unesco to publish this *History* in different languages and thus ensure that it will have the worldwide impact it deserves and thereby serve the international community as a whole.

Description of the Project

B. A. OGOT

President, International Scientific Committee for the Drafting of a General History of Africa

The General Conference of Unesco at its 16th Session instructed the Director-General to undertake the drafting of a *General History of Africa*. The enormous task of implementing the project was entrusted to an International Scientific Committee which was established by the Executive Board in 1970. This Committee under the Statutes adopted by the Executive Board of Unesco in 1971, is composed of thirty-nine members (two-thirds of whom are African and one-third non-African) serving in their personal capacity and appointed by the Director-General of Unesco for the duration of the Committee's mandate.

The first task of the Committee was to define the principal characteristics of the work. These were defined at the first session of the Committee as follows:

(a) Although aiming at the highest possible scientific level, the history does not seek to be exhaustive and is a work of synthesis avoiding dogmatism. In many respects, it is a statement of problems showing the present state of knowledge and the main trends in research, and it does not hesitate to show divergencies of views where these exist. In this way, it prepares the ground for future work.

(b) Africa is considered in this work as a totality. The aim is to show the historical relationships between the various parts of the continent, too frequently subdivided in works published to date. Africa's historical connections with the other continents receive due attention, these connections being analysed in terms of mutual exchanges and multilateral influences, bringing out, in its appropriate light, Africa's contribution to the history of mankind.

(c) *The General History of Africa* is, in particular, a history of ideas and civilizations, societies and institutions. It is based on a wide variety of sources, including oral tradition and art forms.

(d) The *History* is viewed essentially from the inside. Although a scholarly work, it is also, in large measure, a faithful reflection of the way in which African authors view their own civilization. While prepared in an international framework and drawing to the full on the present stock of scientific knowledge, it should also be a vitally important element in the recognition of the African heritage and should bring out the factors making for unity in the continent. This effort to view things from within is the novel feature of the project and should, in addition to its scientific quality, give it great topical significance. By showing the true face of Africa, the *History* could, in an era absorbed in economic and technical struggles, offer a particular conception of human values.

The Committee has decided to present the work covering over three million years of African history in eight volumes, each containing about eight hundred pages of text with illustrations, photographs, maps and line drawings.

A chief editor, assisted if necessary by one or two co-editors, is responsible for the preparation of each volume. The editors are elected by the Committee either from among its members or from outside by a two-thirds majority. They are responsible for preparing the volumes in accordance with the decisions and plans adopted by the Committee. On scientific matters, they are accountable to the Committee or, between two sessions of the Committee, to its Bureau for the contents of the volumes, the final version of the texts, the illustrations and, in general, for all scientific and technical aspects of the *History*. The Bureau ultimately approves the final manuscript. When it considers the manuscript ready for publication, it transmits it to the Director-General of Unesco. Thus the Committee, or the Bureau between Committee sessions, remains fully in charge of the project.

Each volume consists of some thirty chapters. Each chapter is the work of a principal author assisted, if necessary, by one or two collaborators. The authors are selected by the Committee on the basis of their *curricula vitae*. Preference is given to African authors, provided they have requisite qualifications. Special effort is also made to ensure, as far as possible, that all regions of the continent, as well as other regions having historical or cultural ties with Africa, are equitably represented among the authors.

When the editor of a volume has approved texts of chapters, they are then sent to all members of the Committee for criticism. In addition, the text of the volume editor is submitted for examination to a Reading Committee, set up within the International Scientific Committee on the basis of the members' fields of competence. The Reading Committee analyses the chapters from the standpoint of both substance and form. The Bureau then gives final approval to the manuscripts.

Such a seemingly long and involved procedure has proved necessary, since it provides the best possible guarantee of the scientific objectivity of the *General History of Africa*. There have, in fact, been instances when the Bureau has rejected manuscripts or insisted on major revisions or even reassigned the drafting of a chapter to another author. Occasionally, specialists in a particular period of history or in a particular question are consulted to put the finishing touches to a volume.

The work will be published first in a hard-cover edition in English, French and Arabic, and later in paperback editions in the same languages. An abridged version in English and French will serve as a basis for translation into African languages. The Committee has chosen Kiswahili and Hausa as the first African languages into which the work will be translated.

Also, every effort will be made to ensure publication of the *General History of Africa* in other languages of wide international currency such as Chinese, Portuguese, Russian, German, Italian, Spanish, Japanese, etc.

It is thus evident that this is a gigantic task which constitutes an immense challenge to African historians and to the scholarly community at large, as well as to Unesco under whose auspices the work is being done. For the writing of a continental history of Africa, covering the last three million years, using the highest canons of scholarship and involving, as it must do, scholars drawn from diverse countries, cultures, ideologies and historical traditions, is surely a complex undertaking. It constitutes a continental, international and interdisciplinary project of great proportions.

In conclusion, I would like to underline the significance of this work for Africa and for the world. At a time when the peoples of Africa are striving towards unity and greater cooperation in shaping their individual destinies, a proper understanding of Africa's past, with an awareness of common ties among Africans and between Africa and other continents, should not only be a major contribution towards mutual understanding among the people of the earth, but also a source of knowledge of a cultural heritage that belongs to all mankind.

Note on chronology

It has been agreed to adopt the following method for writing dates. With regard to prehistory, dates may be written in two different ways.

One way is by reference to the present era, that is, dates BP (before present), the reference year being + 1950; all dates are negative in relation to + 1950.

The other way is by reference to the beginning of the Christian era. Dates are represented in relation to the Christian era by a simple + or − sign before the date. When referring to centuries, the terms BC and AD are replaced by 'before our era' and 'of our era'.

Some examples are as follows:

(i) 2300 BP = − 350
(ii) 2900 BC = − 2900
AD 1800 = + 1800
(iii) 5th century BC = 5th century before our era
3rd century AD = 3rd century of our era

General introduction

J. KI-ZERBO

Africa* has a history. The time has long gone by when maps and portulans had great empty spaces representing the African continent as marginal and subordinate, and the knowledge of scholars on the subject was summed up in the cryptic phrase which perhaps tried to offer its own excuse: 'ibi sunt leones' – here be lions. But then came the discovery of the mines and their profits, and incidentally of the 'native

***Note by the Volume Editor**
The origin of the word '*Africa*' has been difficult to elucidate. It became the accepted term from Roman times onwards in the form 'Africa', replacing the originally Greek or Egyptian word 'Libya', the land of the Lebu or the Lubins in Genesis. From designating the North African coast, the word 'Africa' came to be applied to the whole continent from the end of the first century before our era.

But what was the original meaning of the name?

Starting with the most likely explanations, the following versions have been proposed.

The word 'Africa' is thought to come from the name of a Berber people who lived to the south of Carthage, the Afarik or Aourigha, whence Afriga or Africa to denote the land of the Afarik.

Another derivation of the word Africa is that it comes from two Phoenician terms, one of which means an ear of corn, a fertility symbol in that region, and the other, Pharikia, means the land of fruit.

It is further suggested that the word comes from the Latin adjective *aprica* (sunny) or the Greek *aprikē* (free from cold).

Another origin might be the Phoenician root *faraqa*, which suggests the idea of separation or in other words diaspora. It may be pointed out that the same root is to be found in some African languages, for instance Bambara.

In Sanskrit and Hindi the root *Apara* or *Africa* denotes that which, in geographical terms, comes 'after', in other words the West. Africa is the western continent.

An historical tradition subscribed to by Leo Africanus has it that a Yemenite chief named Africus invaded North Africa in the second millennium before our era and founded a town called Afrikyah. But it is more likely that the Arabic term *Ifriqiya* is the Arabic transliteration of the word 'Africa'.

One version even suggests that Afer was a grandson of Abraham and a companion of Hercules.

tribes' who owned the mines, but who like them were annexed as the property of the colonizing countries. Then, after the 'native tribes', came nations impatient of the yoke, their pulses already beating to the feverish rhythm of liberation struggles.

The history of Africa, like the history of mankind as a whole, is really the story of an awakening. The history of Africa needs rewriting, for up till now it has often been masked, faked, distorted, mutilated, by 'force of circumstance' – i.e. through ignorance or self-interest. Crushed by centuries of oppression, Africa has seen generations of travellers, slave traders, explorers, missionaries, governors, and scholars of all kinds give out its image as one of nothing but poverty, barbarism, irresponsibility and chaos. And this image has been projected and extrapolated indefinitely in time, as a justification of both the present and the future.

It is not our purpose to write a history which will be a mere settling of scores, with colonialist history backfiring on its authors, but rather to change the perspective and revive images which have been forgotten or lost. We must turn once more to science in order to create genuine cultural awareness. We must reconstruct the real course of events. And we must find another mode of discourse.

If these are the goals and reasons, the why and wherefore, of this enterprise, how to set about it, the methodology, is, as always, a more difficult question. And this is one of the matters to be treated in this first volume of the General History of Africa, compiled under the auspices of Unesco.

Why?

This is a scientific undertaking. The shadows and obscurities which still shroud the past of the African continent constitute an irresistible challenge to human curiosity. The history of Africa is practically unknown. Patched-up genealogies; missing dates; structures sketched in a vague and impressionistic manner, or appearing but dimly through a fog; sequences which seem absurd because what goes before them has been destroyed – all these add up to a jerky, incomplete film which reflects only our own ignorance, yet which, with consequences ranging from the irritating to the positively harmful, we have set up as the real history of Africa as it actually happened. Is it surprising, then, that African history should have been accorded such a small and subordinate place in all the histories of mankind and of civilization?

But for some decades now, thousands of research workers, some of them of great and even exceptional merit, have been exhuming whole areas of ancient Africa. Every year dozens of new publications appear, expressing a more and more positive attitude. And discoveries about Africa, sometimes spectacular ones, call in question the meaning of certain phases in the history of mankind as a whole.

But this very proliferation carries with it its own dangers: the risk of contradiction and confusion through lack of co-ordination; squabbles between schools of opinion which tend to ascribe more importance to the research worker than to the object of his research, and so on. It accordingly seemed desirable, for the honour of science, that a survey of unimpeachable quality should be carried out, under the auspices of Unesco, by teams of scholars both African and non-African, under the authority of an International Scientific Committee and with African editors, so as to bring the picture up to date. The number and distinction of the research workers who have collaborated in this great new discovery of Africa make it an outstanding experiment in international co-operation. Perhaps more than any other branch of learning, history is a human science. It emerges red-hot from the busy, sometimes tumultuous, forge of the nations. History, fashioned physically by man in the workshop of life itself, constructed mentally by man in laboratories, libraries and on excavation sites, is also made for man, for the people, to illuminate and motivate their awareness.

For Africans, the history of Africa is not some narcissistic mirror or a subtle excuse for avoiding the tasks and burdens of today. If it were an alienating device of that kind, the scientific objects of the whole enterprise would be compromised. But is not ignorance of one's own past, in other words of a large part of oneself, even more alienating? All the evils that afflict Africa today, as well as all the possibilities for the future, are the result of countless forces transmitted by history. And just as the first step in a rational diagnosis and therapy is the reconstruction of the evolution of the disease, in the same way the first task in any overall analysis of the African continent must be a historical one. Unless one chooses to live in a state of unconsciousness and alienation, one cannot live without memory, or with a memory that belongs to someone else. And history is the memory of nations. This turning back to oneself can act as a kind of liberating catharsis, like the plunging into one's own depths entailed in psychoanalysis, which, by revealing the basic forces that inhibit our personality, at the same time frees us from the complexes by which our consciousness is held fast in the hidden roots of the subconscious. But if we want to be sure of not exchanging one myth for another, we must see that historical truth, the matrix of an authentic and unalienated consciousness, is strictly tested and substantiated.

How?

And thus we come to the formidable question of how, or in other words to the problem of methodology.

In this connection, as in others, we have to steer a middle course between treating Africa as too exceptional a case on the one hand, and on the other, dealing with it too much in terms proper to other parts of the world. Some people say that before we can talk of a real history of Africa we should wait to find the same kinds of evidence as in Europe, the same array of written or epigraphic documents. In short, for them, the problems of the historian are the same everywhere, in the tropics as at the poles. It must be clearly reaffirmed in this connection that there is no question of gagging reason on the pretext that there is a lack of material to present to it. Reason does not become something different because it is exercised in the tropics. Reason is supreme and does not bow to geography. But precisely because reason is not blind, it has, in order to keep an accurate and firm grip on things, to apprehend different realities differently. So the principles of internal and external criticism have to be applied according to a different mental strategy when one is considering, on the one hand, the epic song *Sundjata Fasa*[1] and, on the other, the capitulary *De Villis* or the circulars Napoleon sent to his prefects. The methods and techniques have to be different. And this strategy will not be the same for every part of Africa. The Nile valley and the Mediterranean shores of the continent have, as far as historical reconstruction is concerned, more in common with Europe than has Africa south of the Sahara.

In fact, the difficulties specific to the history of Africa can already be seen when one looks at the facts of the physical geography of the continent. Africa, a lonely continent if ever there was one, seems to turn its back on the rest of the Old World, to which it is joined only by the fragile umbilical cord of the isthmus of Suez. It is to the south, amid the austral waters, that Africa thrusts her solid mass, bound in by coastal ranges through which rivers force their way by means of heroic defiles, in themselves great obstacles to penetration. The only sizeable passage between the Sahara and the Abyssinian mountains is blocked by the vast marshes of the Bahr el-Ghazal. Strong winds and sea currents guard the coast from Cape Blanco to Cape Verde, while in the middle of the continent three deserts add internal barriers to isolation from without: in the south, the Kalahari; in the centre, the 'green desert' of the equatorial forest with all its dangers which man had to overcome before he could make it his refuge; and in the north, the Sahara, desert of deserts, a huge continental filter, a wild sea of ergs and regs which joins with the mountain fringe of the Atlas to separate the lot of the Mediterranean part of Africa from that of the rest of the continent. These ecological forces, though not forming completely watertight compartments, have, especially in prehistory, weighed heavily on every aspect of Africa's destiny. They have also enhanced the value of all the natural loopholes which were from the start to act as gangways or corridors in the exploration of Africa, begun thousands of millennia ago. One paramount example is the great north–south groove of the Rift valley, stretching from the very centre of Africa and across the Ethiopian ridge as far as Iraq. In the east–west direction the valleys of the Sangha, Ubangi and Zaïre must also have

1. In the Malinke tongue, *Praise to Sundjata*. Sundjata, the founder of the Mali Empire in the thirteenth century, is one of the most popular heroes in African history.

acted as a corridor. It is not by chance that the first kingdoms of black Africa developed in those more accessible regions, the Sahels,[2] at once permeable from within, to a certain extent open towards the exterior, and in contact with neighbouring regions of Africa with different and complementary resources. These open areas, with their comparatively rapid evolution, afford, *a contrario,* the proof that isolation was one of the key factors in Africa's slowness in pursuit of certain kinds of progress.[3] As Fernand Braudel wrote, 'Civilizations are made on earth', and he adds, 'Civilization is the daughter of number.' The very vastness of the African continent, with a diluted and therefore readily itinerant population living in a nature at once generous with its fruits and minerals, but cruel with its endemic and epidemic diseases,[4] prevented it from reaching the threshold of demographic concentration which has almost always been one of the preconditions of major qualitative changes in the social, political and economic spheres. Moreover, the slave trade was a severe demographic drain from time immemorial, and especially from the fifteenth to the twentieth century, after the traffic was organized on a large scale, and this can only have helped to deprive Africa of the stability and human dynamism necessary for any outstanding creativeness, even on the technological plane. Neither nature nor man, geography nor history, have been kind to Africa. And it is indispensable that we should go back to these fundamental conditions of the evolutionary process in order to pose the problems in objective terms, and not in the form of such myths as racial inferiority, congenital tribalism and the so-called historical passivity of the Africans. The best these subjective and irrational approaches can do is conceal a deliberate ignorance. As for the worst, the less said the better.

The difficulty of sources

It must be admitted that as far as Africa is concerned the question of sources is a difficult one. There are three main sources for our historical knowledge of Africa: written documents, archaeology and oral tradition. These are backed up by linguistics and anthropology, which enable us to elaborate on and refine the interpretation of data which may otherwise be crude and unyielding. It would be wrong, however, to place these different sources in any preordained and rigid order of importance.

(1) *Written sources,* if not very rare, are at least unevenly distributed in time and space. The most obscure centuries in African history are those which lack the clear and precise illumination that comes from written

2. From the Arabic *sahīl*: shore. Here shore of the desert regarded as a sea.

3. The climatic factor should not be neglected. Professor Thurstan Shaw has stressed the fact that it has not been possible to grow certain cereals adapted to a Mediterranean climate (rain in winter) in the Niger valley because south of 18°N, owing to the blocking of the intertropical front, they cannot be acclimatized. See C. T. Shaw, 1971b, pp. 143–53.

4. See J. Ford, 1971.

accounts – for example, the centuries preceding and following the birth of Christ (here North Africa is an exception). But even when such evidence exists, its interpretation is strewn with difficulties and ambiguities. Thus, on re-examining the travels of Ibn Battuta, and the various ways in which he and al-'Umari transcribed place names, some historians have come to question whether Niani-on-the-Sankarani was the capital of ancient Mali.[5] On the quantitative plane, large masses of written material, archival or narrative, have still not yet been exploited, as is shown by recent incomplete inventories of unpublished manuscripts concerning the history of black Africa which are being found not only in libraries in Morocco,[6] Algeria and Europe, but also in the libraries of Sudanese scholars and leading citizens in towns throughout the Niger bend,[7] and whose titles suggest some promising new veins. Unesco has established the Ahmed Baba centre at Timbuktu to promote the collection of such material. The archives of Iran, Iraq, Armenia, India and China, not to mention the Americas, must hold many scraps of African history awaiting some perspicacious and imaginative researcher. For instance, in the Archives of the Prime Minister in Istanbul, where the records of the decrees of the Imperial Ottoman Dívan are kept and classified, there came to light an unpublished correspondence, dated May 1577, from Sultan Murad III to Maï Idris Aloma and the Bey of Tunis. This correspondence throws quite a new light on the diplomacy of Kanem-Bornu at that period, and on the situation in the Fezzan.[8]

In the African countries deeply influenced by Islamic culture, Institutes of African Studies and Centres for Historical Research pursue an active policy in search of manuscripts. New guides, such as those published by the International Council on Archives under the auspices of Unesco, help to guide researchers through the forest of documents scattered throughout the west.

Only a determined policy of publishing and judicious reprinting, together with translation and distribution in Africa, can bring all these new efforts together and give them a multiplier effect strong enough to enable us to cross a critical new qualitative threshold in the vision of Africa's past. And the new attitude to the new mass of documents will be almost as important in this as the new documents themselves. Many texts which have been in use since the nineteenth century or the colonial era call imperatively for a re-examination free of anachronistic prejudice, and imbued instead with an endogenic approach. In this connection, written sources based on sub-Saharan scripts (Vai, Bamum, Ajami) should not be neglected.

(2) The silent witnesses revealed by *archaeology* are often more eloquent than the official chroniclers. The marvellous discoveries of archaeology have

5. See J. O. Hunwick, 1973. The author risks using the argument *a silentio*: 'If Ibn Battuta had crossed the Niger or the Senegal he would have said so.'

6. See Unesco, 1973, Doc. No. SHC/WS/294.

7. See *Etudes Maliennes*, ISHM, no. 3, September 1972.

8. See B. G. Martin, 1969, pp. 15–27.

already served African history well, especially when, as is the case with several thousand millennia of Africa's past, there is no oral or written chronicle available. Then objects alone, buried with those for whom they bear witness, keep vigil beneath the heavy shroud of the earth over a past without a face and without a voice. Some of these objects are particularly significant as points of reference in the measuring of civilization. These include articles made of iron, together with the technology involved; pottery and its inscriptions, production techniques and styles; objects made of glass; and different graphic styles; the techniques of canoeing, fishing and weaving; foodstuffs; and geomorphological, hydraulic and ecological structures linked to the evolution of climate. The language of archaeological excavation has by nature something objective and irrefutable about it. Thus a study of the typology of the pottery and objects of bone and metal found in the Nigero-Chadian Sahara demonstrates the link between the pre-Islamic peoples (Sao) of the Chad Basin and cultural areas extending as far as the Nile and the Libyan desert. The living ties of the past are revived, beyond the modern landscape with its crushing loneliness and apathy, by the kinship shown in statuettes of baked clay wearing cross-belts, in the decorations on the bodies of figurines, in the shapes of jars and bracelets, harpoons and bones, in arrow-heads or tips, and in throwing knives.[9] The location, classification and protection of archaeological sites in Africa is a matter of prime urgency and importance, which must be undertaken before thieves, irresponsible amateurs or ignorant tourists despoil and disturb them and strip them of any serious historical interest. But such urgent large-scale exploitation of these sites is only possible within a framework of inter-African programmes, backed up by powerful international co-operation.

(3) Besides the first two sources of African history – written documents and archaeology – *oral tradition* takes its place as a real living museum, conserver and transmitter of the social and cultural creations stored up by peoples said to have no written records. This spoken history is a very frail thread by which to trace our way back through the dark twists of the labyrinth of time. Those who are its custodians are hoary-headed old men with cracked voices, memories often dim, and a stickler's insistence on etiquette (*vieillesse oblige!*), as behoves potential ancestors. They are like the last remaining islets in a landscape that was once imposing and coherent, but which is now eroded, flattened and thrown into disorder by the sharp waves of modernism. Latter-day fossils!

Whenever one of them dies a fibre of Ariadne's thread is broken, a fragment of the landscape literally disappears underground. Yet oral tradition is by far the most intimate of historical sources, the most rich, the one which is fullest of the sap of authenticity. As an African proverb has it, 'The mouth of an old man smells bad, but it says good and salutary things.' However useful the written record may be, it is bound to freeze, to dry up its

9. See P. Huard, 1969.

subject. It decants, dissects, schematizes, petrifies: the letter killeth. Tradition clothes things in flesh and blood and colour, it gives blood to the skeleton of the past. It presents in three dimensions what is often crowded on to the two-dimensional surface of a piece of paper. The joy of Sundjata's mother, overwhelmed by the sudden recovery of her son, still bursts forth in the warm and epic tones of the griots of Mali. Of course, we have to skirt many pitfalls in order to winnow the material offered by oral tradition – to separate the wheat of fact from the chaff of words that are only there for the sake of symmetry or polish, and of set phrases that are only the formal wrapping of a message from the distant past.

It has been said that oral tradition does not inspire confidence because it is functional – as if every human message were not by definition functional, including archives, which by their very passiveness, and beneath an appearance of neutrality and objectivity, conceal so many lies by omission, and clothe error in respectability. It is true that the epic tradition in particular is a para-mythical recreation of the past; a sort of psycho-drama revealing to a community its roots and the corpus of values which nourish its personality; a magic passport enabling it to travel back up the river of time to the realm of its ancestors. That is why epic and historical utterance are not exactly the same. The first overlaps the second, with anachronistic projections forward and backward in real time, and with concertina effects like those found in the earth in archaeology. But do not written records suffer from these enigmatic intrusions too? Here as elsewhere we must seek the nugget of sense, try to find the equivalent of a touchstone which identifies pure metal and rejects slag and dross.

Of course, in epic the weakness of the chronological sequence is the Achilles' heel: mixed-up temporal sequences cause the image of the past to reach us, not clear and stable as in a mirror, but like a fleeting, broken-up reflection on the surface of a ruffled stream. The average length of reigns and generations is a highly controversial question, and extrapolations based on recent periods have to be accepted with great reserve, because of demographic and political changes, to name only two factors. Sometimes an exceptional and magnetic dynast polarizes the exploits of his predecessors and successors around his own person, and the others are literally eclipsed. This applies to certain dynasts in Rwanda, or to Da Monzon, King of Segou (beginning of the nineteenth century), to whom the griots attribute all that kingdom's major conquests.

Furthermore, an oral account taken out of its context is like a fish out of water: it dies. Taken in isolation, oral tradition resembles African masks wrested from the communion of the faithful and exhibited to the curiosity of the uninitiated. It loses its significance and life. Yet it is through that life, because it is always being taken over by fresh witnesses charged with transmitting it, that oral tradition adapts itself to the expectations of new audiences; and this adaptation relates mainly to the presentation, though it does not always leave the content intact. Moreover, some modern sharks and mercenaries of oral tradition even serve up rehashes of written texts which they reinject into the oral one!

Even the content of the message is often hermetic or esoteric. For the African, speech is a weighty matter – an ambiguous force which can make and unmake, which can be the bearer of evil. That is why the message is not articulated openly and directly, but wrapped up in fable, allusion, hint, proverbs that are hard to understand for the vulgar but clear for those who possess the antennae of wisdom. In Africa, speech is too weighty to be wasted, and the more authoritative one's position the less one speaks in public. But if someone says to another, 'You have eaten the toad and spat out its head', he understands at once he is being accused of avoiding part of his responsibilities.[10] The hermeticism of this half-speech shows at once the inestimable value of oral tradition, and its limits: it is almost impossible to transfer all its richness from one language to another, especially when that other is structurally and sociologically very remote. Tradition does not stand up well to translation. When uprooted it loses its vigour and authenticity, for language is 'the home of being'. And many errors ascribed to tradition itself are due to incompetent or unscrupulous interpreters.

Be that as it may, the validity of oral tradition has today been amply proved, and confirmed by crosschecking with written and archaeological sources, as in the cases of the Koumbi Saleh site, the Lake Kisale remains and the events of the sixteenth century as transmitted by the Shona, which D. P. Abraham has observed to be in agreement with the writings of Portuguese travellers of the period.

To sum up, the mode of discourse of oral tradition, whether in epic or prose, whether didactic or ethical, has a triple point of view. First, it reveals the values and usages which motivate a people and condition their future acts through representation of archetypes from the past. In doing this, it not only reflects but also creates history. When Da Monzon is addressed as 'master of waters and master of men', this signifies the absoluteness of his power. But the same stories also show him constantly consulting his warriors, his griots and his wives.[11] A sense of honour and reputation is unmistakable in the famous line in the *Song of the Bow* in honour of Sundjata (*Sundjata Fasa*): 'Saya Kaoussa malo yé.'[12] The same idea is also beautifully expressed in the story of Bakary Dian's struggle against the Fulani of Kournari. The valiant Bakary Dian has retired in anger to his village, Dongorongo, and the people come to beg him to return to the head of the Segou army. He gives way finally when they touch the sensitive chord of pride and glory: 'Forget old words exchanged. It is your present name you must think of. For one comes into the world to make a name. If you are born, grow up and die without a name, you have come into the world for nothing, and you have left it for nothing.' Then he cries: 'Griots of Segou,

10. See H. Aguessy, 1972.
11. See L. Kesteloot, 1978.
12. 'Death is better than dishonour.'

since you have come it is not impossible. I will do what you ask, for the sake of my fame. I will not do it for Da Monzon. I will do it for no one in Segou. I will do it just for my reputation. Even after my death, it will be added to my name.'

Similarly – a piece of evidence about both civilization and law – Silamaka says: 'You are fortunate that I am forbidden to kill messengers.'

But the reconstruction of the past is by no means wholly fictional. There are passages of recollection, veins of history which are often more prosaic than the vivid decorations of the epic imagination: 'Thus began this institution of collective herding in Bambara towns. If you were chosen and made a herdsman, you became a public Fula. The public Fulani kept the flocks of the King. They were men of different races, and their chief shepherd was called Bonke.' Again: 'At that time people did not wear slippers, but leather samaras of tanned ox-hide, with a strap round the nose [the big toe] and a strap round the heel.' The epic is strewn with allusions to techniques, and to objects which are not essential to the action but suggest the setting. '[Da Monzon] sent for his sixty Somono paddlers, thirty men at the prow and thirty at the stern. The canoe was richly decorated.' 'Ladders were got ready and set against the wall. The Segou infantry attacked and infiltrated the town . . . The Segou horsemen launched flaming arrows. The houses of the village caught alight.' Saran, the woman in love with Da Monzon, goes and wets the Kore warriors' gunpowder . . . It is only through a careful analysis, sometimes even psychoanalysis, of the very psychoses of the transmitters of the tradition, and of their audience, that the historian can get to the solid substance of historical reality.

The number of different versions transmitted by rival groups – for example, by the various griot-clients of each noble protector (*horon*, *dyatigui*) – far from being a handicap, is on the contrary only a further guarantee for critical history. When accounts agree, as in the case of the Bambara and Fula griots, who belonged to opposing camps, the authenticity of the evidence is reinforced. And as is shown in the case of the Gouro, with whom a liberal and integrationist exoteric tradition, transmitted by the lineage, coexists with the oligarchical and hairsplitting esoteric tradition of the secret society, spoken history contains self-censoring elements because of its very different origins. In fact, it is not private property, but a common fund which derives from and provides for various groups in the community.

The important thing is that internal criticism of these records should be supported by a thorough knowledge of the genre in question, its themes and techniques, its codes and stereotypes, its set phrases of padding, the conventional digressions, the evolution of the language, the audience and what it expected of the story-tellers. Above all, the historian must know about the caste to which these latter belonged – their rules of life, how they were brought up, their ideals, their schools. We know that in Mali and Guinea, for example, there have for centuries been real schools of initiation at Keyla, Kita, Niagassola, Niani, and so on.

This rigid, formal and institutional oral tradition usually has its structure reinforced and supported by court music, which is integral to it and underlines its didactic and artistic portions. Some of the instruments used, such as the Sosso Balla (the Balafon of Sumarro Kante), are so old that they would repay an archaeological investigation in themselves. But the correspondences between types of instrument and music, types of song and dance, make up a minutely ordered world, in which anomalies and later additions are easily detected. Every genre has its own special instrument in each cultural region: the *balla* (xylophone) or the *bolon* (harp-lute) for epic; the *bendre* (a big round one-sided drum made out of a gourd and beaten with the bare hands) of the Mossi for the exaltation (often silent) of the *zabyouya* (*noms de guerre*) of the kings; the *mvet* (harp-zither) for the tropical Nibelungen of the Fang poet-musicians. These instruments, the vehicles of spoken history, are sacred, the object of veneration. In effect they are part of the artist, and their importance in communicating the message is all the greater since, because language is tonal, music has direct meaning; the instrument becomes the artist's voice, and he does not need to utter a word. The triple rhythm of tone, intensity and duration becomes music with meaning, the kind of semantic melodism Marcel Jousse spoke of. As a matter of fact, music is so much a part of oral tradition that some stories can only be told in song. Popular song, which epitomizes the will of the people in a satirical form, sometimes spiced with black humour, which still retains its vitality even in the present age with its election campaigns, is a valuable genre, complementing and counterbalancing the evidence of official records.

What has been said here of music applies equally to the other modes of expression, such as the visual arts. As in the bas-reliefs of the Kingdoms of Abomey and Benin or in Kuba sculpture, we sometimes find a direct expression of historical characters, cultures and events.

So oral tradition is not just a second-best source to be resorted to only when there is nothing else. It is a distinct source in itself, with a now well-established methodology, and it lends the history of the African continent a marked originality.

(4) In *linguistics*, African history has not an auxiliary science but an independent discipline which nevertheless leads history right to the heart of its own subject. A good counter-demonstration of this is Nubia, buried in the double silence of the ruins of Meroe and of the undeciphered Meroitic script just because the language remains unknown.[13] True, much still remains to be done in this field – and what needs doing first is to define scientifically the languages concerned. The descriptive approach must not be sacrificed to a comparative and synthetic one which aims at being typological and genetic. It is only through minute and laborious analysis of the facts of language, 'with its "significants" of consonants, vowels and

13. Unesco organized an international scientific symposium in Cairo in 1974 on the deciphering of this African language.

tones, its wide-ranging diversity of combinations in syntagmatic schemata and its "significatum" in the living experience of the speakers of a given community',[14] that one can extrapolate backwards, an operation often made difficult by a lack of historical depth in knowledge of the languages concerned. In fact, the only way they can be compared in terms of their contemporary strata is by the synchronic method, which is the indispensable foundation of any diachronic and genetic synthesis. It is a difficult task, and one can easily see why learned battle rages in certain areas, particularly over Bantu. Malcolm Guthrie supports the theory of autogenesis; Joseph Greenberg puts up a spirited defence of the idea that the Bantu languages need to be placed in a wider, continental context: this, he says, because of resemblances which are not accidental analogies due to external influence, but derive from an intrinsic genetic kinship, manifested – in similarities in pronouns, basic vocabulary, and grammatical characteristics such as the system of noun classification – in hundreds of languages from Wolof to Baka (Republic of the Sudan). These arguments are not just academic debates as far as the historian is concerned. Anyone who takes, for example, the distribution of groups of analogous words denoting sheep on the edge of the forests in Central Africa, notices that these homogeneous groups do not overlap the edge of the forest, but divide parallel to it. This suggests that the livestock in question spread along the parallels of the two adjoining biotopes of savannah and forest; whereas farther east the linguistic pattern forms vertical belts from East to southern Africa, which suggests introduction at right angles to the parallels of latitude, and illustrates, *a contrario,* the inhibiting role of the forest in the transfer of techniques.[15] But this role was not the same in the case of all techniques. In short, linguistic studies show that the routes and paths of migration, and the diffusion of both material and spiritual cultures, are marked out by the diffusion of related words. Hence the importance of diachronic linguistic analysis and glotto-chronology to the historian who wishes to understand the meaning and dynamics of Africa's evolution. For instance, Greenberg has shown Kanuri's contribution to Hausa as regards cultural terms and terms of military technique, and this brings out the influence of the Bornu Empire in the development of the Hausa kingdoms. In particular, the titles or styles of the Bornu dynasties, including Kanuri terms such as *kaygamma, migira,* etc., spread far into Cameroon and Nigeria. The systematic study of toponyms and anthroponyms can also produce very accurate indications, on condition that the nomenclature is revised according to the endogenic approach. For a large number of names have been distorted by the exotic pronunciation or transcription of non-Africans, or by Africans acting as interpreters or scribes. The hunt for the *mot juste,* even and especially when it has been institutionalized in writing

14. See M. Houis, 1971, p. 45.
15. See C. Ehret, 1968.

for centuries, is one of the most complex tasks to be accomplished by a critical history of Africa.

Let us take an example. The word *Gaoga,* used by Leo Africanus to denote a kingdom of the Sudan, has often been assimilated with the word *Gao*. But if the word *Gaoga* is analysed on the basis of Teda and Kanuri, a kingdom of that name can also be identified between Wadaï (Namena), Darfur (Sudan) and Fertit (Central African Republic).[16] The question of references to the Yemen as the land of origin of numerous Sudanese dynasties has been re-examined in some depth since the time of H. R. Palmer. Should not the word Yemen be interpreted not in the sense of the pious evocations of Muslim chroniclers oriented towards Arabia Felix, but rather as referring to the ancient land of Yam (whence Yaman)?[17] An examination of the Swahili lexicon, full of terms of Arabic origin, and of those of the peoples living along the east coast of Madagascar (Antemoro, Antalaotra, Anosy), also furnishes the historian with a mine of information.

At any rate, linguistics, which has already done African history good service, should discard from the outset the disparaging ethnocentric attitude which characterized the African linguistics of A. W. Schlegel and Auguste Schleicher. According to them, 'the languages of the Indo-European family are at the summit of evolution, and the languages of the Blacks are at the very bottom of the ladder, though it used to be thought that they were interesting in that they revealed a state near to the original state of language, when languages were supposed to be without grammar, speech just a series of mono-syllables, and vocabulary restricted to an elementary inventory.'[18]

(5) The same remark applies *a fortiori* to *anthropology* and *ethnology*. Ethnological discourse[19] has by the force of circumstance been a discourse with explicitly discriminatory premises, and conclusions implicitly political, with, between the two, a 'scientific' exercise which was necessarily ambiguous. Its main presupposition was often linear evolution, with Europe, pioneer of civilization, in the van of human advance, and at the rear the primitive 'tribes' of Oceania, Amazonia and Africa. It asked the question: what on earth was it like to be an Indian, a black, a Papuan, an Arab? The other, whether backward, barbarous, savage to a greater or lesser degree, is always different, and for this reason he is an object of interest to the scientist or an object of greed to the slaver. So ethnology was deputed to serve as a sort of Ministry of European Curiosity *vis-à-vis* 'the natives'. The ethnological outlook, strong on nakedness, misery and folklore, was often sadistic, lubricious and at best paternalistic. Ethnological essays and reports

16. See P. Kalk, 1972, pp. 529–48.
17. See A. and E. Mohammadou, 1971.
18. See M. Houis, 1971, p. 27.
19. The term 'ethnic group' has always been marked by radical prejudice, since from the first it was applied to peoples supposed to possess no writing. Even in the sixteenth century, Clement Marot used the phrase 'idolatrous or ethnic'. Ethnography is the descriptive assembly of material; ethnology, the comparative synthesis.

usually sought to justify the *status quo* and contributed to the 'development of underdevelopment'.[20] Evolutionism *à la* Darwin, despite its other virtues, the one-way diffusionism which has too often regarded Africa as the passive outlet of inventions from elsewhere, or the functionalism of Malinowski and Radcliffe-Brown, which denied primitive societies any historical dimension – all these schools of thought were naturally adapted to the colonial situation, on which propitious soil they duly proliferated.[21] Their approaches, which in fact contributed little to the understanding of exotic societies, were invalidated still further by the fact that they concentrated precisely on those societies which were strangest to them, prototypes of humanity at an elementary stage. But the societies they selected were merely micro-organisms. They had an historical role that was not negligible, that was sometimes even remarkable; but it was usually marginal to the more powerful socio-political ensembles which more deeply influenced the course of history.

Thus the whole of Africa was presented in images which Africans themselves might regard as strange – just as if, at the beginning of this century, Europe was personified by the housing conditions, table manners or technical level of the communities of central Brittany, Cantal or Sardinia. Moreover, the ethnological method based on individual inquiry bearing the stamp of subjective experience, total because it was intensive, but total only at the microcosmic level, led to 'objective' conclusions which proved very fragile as soon as they were used for extrapolation.

Lastly, by an implacable dialectic, the very object or 'other' of ethnology gradually disappeared under the influence of colonialism. The primitive natives who lived by hunting and gathering, if not by cannibalism, were transformed into sub-proletariats of peripheral centres in a world system of production which had its pole of attraction in the northern hemisphere. The colonial system consumed and annihilated its own object, which is why those who had been cast in the role of objects, in this case the Africans, decided to initiate an independent mode of discourse of their own, as subjects of history, daring even to assert that in certain respects the most primitive people are not those who are described as such. At the same time, those who had worked without any preconceived ideas to find original structures in, and a historical thread leading through, African societies, whether political states or not, pioneers such as Frobenius, Delafosse, Palmer and Evans-Pritchard, continued their efforts, which have been

20. See J. Copans and M. Godelier, 1971, p. 45: 'Colonial ideology and ethnology form part of one and the same configuration, and between the two orders of phenomena there is an interaction which determines the development of both.'

21. See J. Ruffié, 1977a, p. 429: 'Le pseudo darwinisme culturel qui inspire la pensée anthropologique du XIXe, légitime le colonialisme qui ne serait pas le produit d'une certaine conjoncture politique, mais celui d'une structure biologique; en somme un cas particulier de la compétition naturelle. L'anthropologie du XIXe donne bonne conscience à l'Europe impérialiste.'

refined and carried further by more recent research workers. This group believes that by using the intellectual tools proper to the human sciences in general, and adapting them to Africa, objective results may be achieved. They thus demolish faulty approaches based either on a supposed material and congenital difference between 'natives' and others, or on the idea that the former occupy a primitive stage on the path of civilization. All that is necessary is to admit that while the 'being' of Africans is the same – that of *Homo sapiens* – their 'being-in-the-world' is different. Once this is done, new instruments can be developed with which to apprehend their particular evolution.

At the same time the Marxist approach, so long as it is not dogmatic, and the structuralist approach of Lévi-Strauss also contribute useful if contrasted views on the evolution of peoples reputed to be without writing. The Marxist method, which is essentially historical and for which history is the collective consciousness in action, lays greater emphasis on productive forces and production relations, on praxis and norms, while the structuralist method aims at unveiling the unconscious but logical mechanisms and coherent ensembles which frame and underlie the actions of minds and of societies. We may hope that anthropology, drawing from these new sources, will be something more than a phoenix risen in response to new needs from the ashes of a certain type of ethnology.[22]

But anthropology will only escape the contradictions which discredited functionalist ethnology if, through the diachronic approach, it includes the temporal dimension, for today's structures are meaningless if they are related only to the point of contemporaneity, which must be integrated with the vector arising in the past and already pointing towards the future. And if it is to be useful to history, anthropology must avoid theoretical reconstructions in which ideology outweighs concrete facts, like 'an apoplectic head on an anaemic body'; such constructions only produce the pseudo-history so hated by the functionalists. Light can be thrown on the historical process only by using structures comparable to the theoretical schemata of evolution. The study of recurrent structural phenomena (genealogies, dynastic lists, age-groups, and so on), in terms of social conceptions of the group, can lead to specially new and fruitful analyses.

Anthropology ought to criticize its own procedures, insist on norms as much as on practices, and not confuse social relations, traceable to experience, with the structures which underlie them. This will result in the mutual enrichment of norms, structures and opinions by making extensive use of quantitative and collective techniques of inquiry and by adopting a rational, objective mode of discourse. Anthropology is concerned not only

22. Sociology would thus be an intra-social science for the modern world while anthropology would represent a comparativist (inter-societal) approach. But this would be tantamount to reviving the highly questionable categories born of the scission between them – ethno-history, ethno-botany, and so on. Indeed, why not ethno-archaeology, ethno-anatomy, and even ethno-mathematics?

with the interactions of general factors, but also with the historical synthesis. For example, there seems to be a correlation between, on the one hand, the existence of trade routes where certain commodities are a royal monopoly and, on the other hand, centralized political forms (in early Ghana and Mali, in the eighteenth-century Asante Empire, in the Lunda Kingdom of Zaïre, and so on), whereas, significantly, unlike the Ngonde and Zulu, peoples like the Nyakusa and Xhosa, with the same language and customs but off such routes, did not reach a monarchical stage.[23] From this one might try to infer a sort of law of anthropology, or political sociology.

Kinship structures can also have a great effect on historical evolution. For instance, when two groups that speak different languages meet, the form of conjugal union between the groups usually determines which language shall predominate: the maternal tongue only prevails if women are taken as wives, not slaves or concubines. So some Nguni groups preserved their original language, while others, who took Sotho wives, lost their own language and were taken over by the Sotho. This has also happened with the Fula shepherds from Macina and Futa Djalon who took Mandingo wives and founded the province of Ouassoulou. All they retain of their Fula origin is the name and certain physical traits. They have lost their original language and speak Malinke or Bambara instead.

So the main sources of African history, as outlined above, cannot be arranged *a priori* according to a scale of values which makes some permanently more important than others. Each case must be judged in itself. It is not really a question of radically differing kinds of evidence. All can be defined as indications which come to us from the past, and which, as the vehicles of messages which are not entirely neutral and objective, contain intentions either open or concealed. So all call for methodological criticism, and each, according to the circumstances, may occupy a predominant position. Each may lead to other kinds of sources. Oral tradition, for example, has often led to archaeological sites, and may even help to place written evidence in perspective. Thus the great Ibn Khaldun writes of Sundjata in his *History of the Berbers*: 'He was succeeded by his son Mansa Uli. *Mansa* in their tongue signifies sultan, and Uli is the equivalent of Ali'. Yet every storyteller still explains that Mansa Uli means 'the King with a fair skin.'

Principles of research

Four main principles must govern research if we want to push forward to a new frontier in African historiography.

To begin with, *interdisciplinarity*. This is so important that it can almost, in itself, be regarded as a source. The application of socio-political anthropology to the oral tradition on the Kingdom of Segou, for example, has considerably filled out a picture which would otherwise be nothing but a

23. See L. Thompson, 1969, pp. 72–3.

bare genealogical tree decked with a few stereotypical deeds, so that the complexity and the interpenetration of structures sometimes modelled on ancient hegemonies (for example, Mali) emerge in all their vivid concreteness. Similarly, in the case of the countries of the Niger delta, oral tradition shows that development was not solely due to the influence of the slave and palm-oil trades, but was also determined by previous endogenic relations in the north–south and east–west directions, reaching as far as Lagos and the Ijebu country – backing up and greatly enriching in this respect the allusions of Pacheco Pereira in the *Esmeraldo*.[24] And was it not a datum of cultural anthropology – the initiatory text of the Fula shepherds[25] – which enabled prehistorians to unravel the enigmas of the Tassili frescoes, such as the legless animals in the picture called the Ox and the Hydra, the magic 'U' of Ouan Derbaouen, and so on? Thus it is that, after an interval of 10 000 years, rituals still performed today enable us to identify the five marvellous dancers in the Jabbaren frescoes as the five mythical sisters of the seven sons of Kiikala.

The expansion of the Bantu, as attested by the concordant sources of linguistics, oral tradition, archaeology, anthropology, and the early written sources, Arab, Portuguese, British and Afrikaaner, becomes a living reality which can be set out in a vivid synthesis. Similarly, while linguistic arguments converge with those of technology to suggest that royal gongs and twin bells spread from West Africa to Lower Zaïre, Shaba and Zambia, archaeological evidence would of course provide invaluable confirmation of this. Such combination of sources becomes all the more imperative when it comes to reducing the difficulties of chronology. Carbon-14 datings are not always to be had, and when they are they need to be interpreted and compared with other evidence from, say, metallurgy or pottery (both materials and styles). Nor do we always have, as in the north of Chad,[26] vast quantities of pottery fragments, on the basis of which we can build up a typology representing a chronological scale of six levels. An excellent example of the coming together of all available sources is Ennedi, where it has been possible to establish a diachronic typology of pictoral and ceramic styles and to draw from them a chronological series extending over eight millennia; and all this supported by stratigraphic excavation, and confirmed by carbon datings and by the study of the flora and fauna, the habitat, and oral tradition.[27]

Maps of the eclipses which are known to have been visible in specific areas at specific times can provide remarkable dating evidence when such eclipses can be identified with particular reigns in dynastic traditions. But, in general, chronology requires the use of several sources, for a variety of reasons: first, the average length of reigns and generations varies;

24. See E. J. Alagoa, 1973.
25. See A. Hampaté Bâ and G. Dieterlen, 1961.
26. See Y. Coppens, 1960, pp. 129ff.
27. A. Bailloud, 1966, pp. 31ff.

secondly, the nature of the relationship between a sovereign and his successor is not always clear; thirdly, the meaning of the word 'son' is sometimes sociological rather than biological; fourthly, one king sometimes has as many as three or four 'strong names'; lastly, as in the case of the Bemba, the list of chiefs sometimes merges with that of the list of candidates to the chieftainship.

Without wishing to minimize the importance of chronology, which is the very spine of history, and without ceasing our attempts to base chronology on solid foundations, we must resist the psychosis of precision at any price – which is in any case a chimera. Why should we be so eager to say Koumbi Saleh fell in the year 1086, instead of just saying the end of the eleventh century? And not all dates are equally important. The degree of accuracy required varies. They do not all need to be placed on a pedestal.

On the other hand, it is very important that the whole course of the historical process should be reintegrated into the context of African time. This latter is not resistant to the ordering of narrative data into a sequence of facts which create one another by means of antecedence and causality. The Africans' idea of time is based on the principle of causality. But this is a causality applied according to particular norms, in which logic is steeped in and diverted by myth; in which the economic stage reached is elementary, and time is not money, so that there is no need for it to be measured numerically; in which the rhythm of works and days is metronome enough for human activity; in which calendars are not abstract or universal, but deal in natural phenomena such as moon and sun, rain and drought, and the movement of men and beasts. Every hour is defined by concrete acts. Thus, in Burundi, *amakama* is the time to milk (7 a.m.); *maturuka* is when the herds are let out (8 a.m.); *kuasase* is when the sun spreads out (9 a.m.); *kumusase* is when the sun spreads out over the hills (10 a.m.), and so on. In this cattle-raising country, time is measured in terms of pastoral and agricultural life. Elsewhere, children's names are derived from the day they were born and events that preceded or followed. In North Africa, for example, Muslims are apt to call their children after the month of their birth – Ramdana, Shābāna, Mulud. Despite the dross of myth, tales and legends are an attempt to apprehend rationally the process of social development. 'And it is since that time that beasts were raised at home . . . that there were smiths . . . that women began to do such work.' That is the moral of history.

This conception of time is historical in several respects. In gerontocratic African societies the idea of anteriority is even more significant than elsewhere, because upon it alone are based such rights as speaking in public, participation in special dances and certain dishes, marriage, the respect of other people, and so on. Primogeniture is not usually a matter of exclusive right to royal succession, and the number of those with potential claims (uncles, brothers, sons) is always high. The fact that age is taken into account in the context of a very open competition again lends significance to chronology. But there is no need to know that one was born in exactly such and such a year: the main thing is just to prove one was born before such and such another person. References to absolute chronology are indispensable only in much larger and more anonymous societies.

This conception of social time is not static: in the context of the African pan-dynamist philosophy of the universe, one should always be adding to one's vital force, which is eminently social and includes the idea of progress in and through the community. As Bakary Dian says: 'Even after my death, it will be added to my name.' In certain languages the same word (*bogna* in Bambara, for example) denotes a material gift, honour and growth.

The reckoning of the seasons is often based on astronomical observation of one series of constellations, such as the Great Bear. Among the Komo of Upper Zaïre, the Pleaides, which they compare to a basket of matchets, signal that it is time to sharpen the knives and clear the fields. If necessary, this conception of time can be made more mathematical: examples include notches in special bits of wood kept as archives in the Dogon caves; the putting of a gold nugget each year into a receptacle in the stool-house of the kings of Bono Mansu, or of a pebble into a receptacle in the king's hut in Manding country; not to mention the great achievements in this respect in pharaonic Egypt and Muslim kingdoms such as that of the Almohads. If one thinks of the difficulty of converting a series of reigns into a series of dates, and the need to find a fixed point of reference, it is clear that the latter is usually provided by some dated external event – for example, the attack on Bono Mansu. The use of writing, the spread of universalist religions with calendars depending on a precise *terminus a quo*, and Africa's entry into the world of profit and the accumulation of wealth, have remodelled the traditional conception of time. But in its day it corresponded to the needs of the societies concerned.

Another imperative requirement is that *African history must at last be seen from within,* not still measured by the yardstick of alien values. There cannot be an independent collective personality without an awareness of self and of the right to be different. Of course, the policy and practice of self-examination do not consist in artificially abolishing Africa's historical connections with the other continents of the Old and New Worlds. But these connections have to be analysed in terms of mutual exchanges and multilateral influences, in which something will be heard of Africa's contribution to the development of mankind. The African historical attitude will not be revengeful or self-satisfied; it will be a vital exercise of collective memory, clearing up the past so as to see its own origins. The brand image of Africa has been shaped by so many interested external attitudes, right up to those of present-day films, that it is time to turn a new look on Africa – one from the inside, one of identity, authenticity, awakening: a 'volte rapatriante' (a return home), as Jacques Berque calls this return to the fountainhead. When one thinks of the power of the word and of names in Africa, and that to name someone is almost to take possession of him, so much so that people who are revered (fathers, husbands, kings) are referred to by nicknames or periphrases rather than by their names, one realizes why the whole series of words and concepts, all the panoply of stereotypes and mental patterns concerning African history, add up to the most subtle form of alienation. A real Copernican revolution is needed, a revolution which would be semantic in the first place, and which, without denying the demands of universal science, would take up the whole historical flow of Africa and guide it into new moulds.[28]

As J. Mackenzie observed as early as 1887, referring to the Tswana (Botswana), many African peoples are known by names which neither they themselves nor any other African peoples have ever used. They have passed through the baptismal font of colonization, and emerged dedicated to alienation. The only road out of this is to write books about African history more and more in African languages. This presupposes other structural reforms. Many books on African history generously accord a tenth of their pages to precolonial history, on the grounds that so little is known about it! With the result that they skip the so-called dark centuries and go straight to some famous explorer or proconsul, the providential demiurge or *deus ex machina* with whom the real story supposedly begins, Africa's independent past being consigned to a sort of disreputable prehistory. Of course there is no question of denying the influxes from outside which have acted as an accelerating or detonating force. For example, the introduction of firearms into the central Sudan in the sixteenth century gave the slave-manned infantry the advantage over the feudal horsemen. This change had repercussions in the power structure throughout the central Sudan, and the *kacella* or *kaīgamma*, originally recruited from slaves, supplanted the noble minister Ciroma in his relations with the king. But mechanical explanations, based on external influences (even in regard to headrests!) and automatic parallels drawn between influxes from without and movements in African history, ought to be banished in favour of a more inward analysis which would aim at revealing endogenous contradictions and dynamisms.[29]

Moreover, this history can only be the *history of the peoples of the African continent as a whole,* seen as a whole including the mainland and neighbouring islands such as Madagascar, according to the definition in the OAU charter. The history of Africa obviously includes the Mediterranean

28. An interesting example of this is furnished by I. A. Akinjogbin (1967). Starting from a comparison between the system of the *ebi* (extended family), the presumed source of Oyo's authority over families, and the Dahomey system of adaptation to the slave trade through authoritarian monarchy exercised over individuals, the author explains the disparity between the two regimes. See also B. Verhaegen, 1974, p. 156.

29. See R. C. C. Law, 1971. The author explains the decline of Oyo as due to internal tensions between social categories dependent on the governing power: slaves, the *alafin*'s (king's) stewards in the provinces, provincial representatives at court and the triumvirate of royal eunuchs (of the middle, right and left).

sector in a unity consecrated by age-long and sometimes bloody links, which make the two parts of Africa on either side of the Sahara the two leaves of one door, the two sides of one coin. It is necessarily a history of peoples, for even the despotism of certain dynasties has always been tempered in Africa by distance, by the absence of those technical means which add to the weight of centralization, and by the permanence of village democracies, so that at every level, from base to summit, the council called together through and for discussion constitutes the brain of the body politic. It must be a history of peoples because, except for a few decades in modern times, it has never been shaped according to the frontiers fixed by colonization, for the good reason that the territorial bases of the African peoples differ everywhere from the frontiers inherited from colonial partition. To take one example among many, the Senufo extend over part of Mali, part of the Ivory Coast, and part of Upper Volta. So in the continental context the emphasis should be on common factors resulting from common origins and age-long inter-regional exchanges of men, goods, techniques and ideas, in other words of both material and spiritual commodities. Ever since prehistory, despite natural obstacles and the low level of techniques, there has been a certain degree of historical solidarity on a continental scale, between the Nile valley and the Sudan on the one hand and the Guinea forest on the other; between the Nile valley and East Africa, including among other things the dispersion of the Luo, between the Sudan and Central Africa, through the diaspora of the Bantu; and between the Atlantic and east coasts, through transcontinental trade across Shaba. Migration, which took place on a large scale in both space and time, is not to be seen as a vast human tide attracted by emptiness and leaving emptiness in its wake. Even the torrential saga of Shaka, the Mfecane, cannot be interpreted only in such terms. The northward movement of the Mossi groups (Upper Volta) from Dagomba and Mamprusi (Ghana) was executed by bands of horsemen who, although they occupied various regions at different stages, could do so only by amalgamating with the people they found there and taking wives locally. The judicial privileges they accorded themselves quickly resulted in the spread of facial scarification, which acted as a sort of identity card. The language and institutions of the newcomers prevailed to the point of ousting those of the other peoples; but other usages, such as those connected with agrarian religion or governing rights of settlement, remained within the province of local chiefs, and 'joking relationship' relations were established with some peoples encountered *en route*. The great 'Mossi' conqueror, Ubri, was himself a 'half-breed'. This osmotic process should almost always be substituted for the romantic but oversimplified scenario of 'nihilistic and devastating invasion', which was how the irruption of the Beni Hilal into North Africa was long and wrongly represented.

The General History of Africa is not a history of one race. The excesses of racially prejudiced physical anthropology are now rejected by all serious authors. But the Hamites and other brown races invented to fit the purpose are still to be found in the mirages and fantasies produced by otherwise scientific minds.

'Such categories,' says J. Hiernaux in an important text,[30] 'cannot be admitted as biological units ... The Fulani are a cultural, not a biological group. Those of south Cameroon, for example, have their closest biological relations in the Haya of Tanzania. As for the biological closeness between the Moors and the Warsingili of Somalia, this derives no more from heredity than from the similar biotope [barren steppe] which conditions both groups.'

Strictly biological factors have for thousands of years been constantly confused by selection and genetic drift, and supply no firm framework for classification, either in terms of blood-groups or in terms of frequency of the Hbs gene which determines abnormal haemoglobin and, in association with a normal gene, strengthens resistance to malaria. This illustrates the crucial role of adaptation to the natural setting. For example, higher stature and wider pelvis coincide with areas of great dryness and heat. The morphology of the narrow, high skull (dolichocephalic) is an adaptation providing for reduction in the absorption of heat. So far as possible the word 'tribe' will be banished from this book, except in the case of certain regions in North Africa,[31] because of its pejorative connotations and the many wrong ideas which underlie it. However much one may stress the fact that a tribe is a cultural and sometimes political unit, some people go on seeing it as a term for a stock which is biologically distinct, and make much of the horrors of the 'tribal wars', which often caused only a few dozen deaths, at most, while forgetting all the real exchanges which have linked the peoples of Africa on the biological, technological, cultural, religious and socio-political levels, and which lend African achievements an undoubted family air.

Moreover, *our* History of Africa *must avoid being too narrative*, for otherwise it would be in danger of according too much importance to external factors and influences. Of course, the establishment of key events is a task of the first importance, indispensable to the task of defining the original outline of African evolution. But the main concern will be with civilizations, institutions, structures: agrarian and metallurgical techniques, arts and crafts, trade networks, the conception and organization of power, religion and religious and philosophical thought, the problem of nations and

30. J. Hiernaux, 1970, pp. 53ff.

31. The Arabic term *Khabbylia* designates a group of persons linked genealogically to a common ancestor and living within a specific territory. Since genealogical filiation is of great importance among Semitic peoples (Arabs, Berbers, and so on), the *Khabbylia* (the English equivalent of which would be 'tribe') has played and sometimes still plays a part not to be disregarded in the history of many North African countries. In order to preserve its full historical and socio-cultural connotation, the original word *Khabbylia* will be retained.

pre-nations, techniques of modernization, and so on. This methodological approach makes interdisciplinarity even more necessary.

Finally, why this return to African sources? While for an outsider this quest for the past could be merely a way of satisfying curiosity, a highly stimulating intellectual exercise for someone eager to solve the riddle of the Sphinx, the real intention of our enterprise should go far beyond these purely individual aims. For the history of Africa is necessary to the understanding of world history, many passages of which will remain impenetrable enigmas as long as the historical horizon of the continent of Africa has not been lit up. Moreover, on the methodological plane, the compiling of a history of Africa according to the norms set out in this volume may furnish information on the validity of the approach advocated by the supporters of total history, history apprehended at all levels and in all dimensions and by means of all the tools of investigation available. History thus becomes a symphonic discipline in which all branches of learning are heard simultaneously, the combination at any particular moment varying according to the subject-matter and the stage reached in research, so as to fit in with the necessities of communication. But the posthumous reconstruction of an edifice once built out of living stones is important above all to Africans themselves. They have a flesh-and-blood interest in it, and enter this area after centuries or decades of frustration, like an exile who discovers the contours of his longed-for homeland, contours that are at once both new and old, because they have been secretly looked forward to. To live without history is to be a waif, or to use the roots of others. It is to renounce the possibility of being oneself a root for those who come after. In the sea of evolution, it is to accept the anonymous role of protozoan or plankton. African statesmen should interest themselves in history as an essential part of the national heritage of which they are custodians, the more so as, through history, they can come to know other African countries than their own, in a context of African unity.

But this history is even more necessary to the African peoples themselves, for whom it constitutes a fundamental right. Teams must be got together by the African states to save, before it is too late, as many historical remains as possible. Museums must be built and legislation passed for the protection of sites and objects. Grants and scholarships must be given, especially for the training of archaeologists. Syllabuses and degree courses need to be completely overhauled and given a properly African perspective. History is a source in which we should not only see and recognize our own reflection, but from which we should also drink and renew our strength, so as to forge ahead in the caravan of human progress. If such is the object of this history of Africa, the weary and difficult task will surely be a fruitful one, and a source of all kinds of inspiration.

For somewhere beneath the ashes of the past there are embers instinct with the light of resurrection.

1 The development of African historiography

J. D. FAGE

The writing of African history is as old as the writing of history itself. The historians of the ancient Mediterranean world and those of the medieval Islamic civilization both took the whole known world as their frame of reference, and this included a considerable part of Africa. Africa north of the Sahara was an integral part of both civilizations, and its past was as much a concern of their historians as was that of southern Europe or the Near East. Indeed North African history continued to be part of the mainstream of western historical studies until the advance of the Ottoman Turkish empire in the sixteenth century. Following Napoleon's expedition to Egypt in 1798, North Africa became again a not inconsiderable field for investigation by historians. With the growth of European colonial power in North Africa following a French conquest of Algiers in 1830 and the British occupation of Egypt in 1882, a European, colonialist standpoint came to dominate the writing of North African history. However, by the 1930s the modernist movement in Islam, the growth of European-style education in the North African colonies, and the rise of North African nationalist movements were all combining to produce indigenous schools of historians, writing in French and English as well as in Arabic, to restore a proper balance to North African historical studies.

This chapter will therefore mainly concern itself with the historiography of West, Central, East and southern Africa. Neither the classical European nor the medieval Islamic historians were uninterested in tropical Africa, but their horizons were limited by the extent of the contacts that were made with it, whether across the Sahara to 'Ethiopia' or the Bilad al-Sudan, or down the Red Sea and Indian Ocean coasts to the limits of monsoon navigation.

The ancient authors' information was scanty and fitful, especially in relation to West Africa. Herodotus, Manethon, the Elder Pliny, Strabo and some others tell us little more than of occasional journeys or raids across the Sahara, or of maritime tentatives down the Atlantic coast, and the authenticity of some of these accounts is often the subject of lively dispute among modern scholars. Classical information concerning the Red Sea and Indian Ocean is more soundly based, for it is plain that Mediterranean, or at least Alexandrian, merchants were developing trade on these coasts. *The*

Periplus of the Erythraean Sea (*c.* 100 of our era), and the accounts of Claudius Ptolemy (*c.* 150 of our era, though the version that has come down to us seems to relate more to *c.* 400) and of Cosmas Indicopleustes (647) are still major sources for the early history of East Africa.

The Arabic authors were much better informed, for in their time the adoption of the camel by the Saharan peoples had facilitated the establishment of regular commerce with West Africa and the settlement of North African traders in the major towns of the western Sudan, while the trade of the western Indian Ocean had also developed to the point at which considerable colonies of merchants from Arabia and nearer Asia had been established along the East African coast. Thus the writing of men like al-Mas'ūdī (*c.* 950), al-Bakrī (1029–94), al-Idrīsī (1154), Yākūt (*c.* 1200), Abu al-Fidā' (1273–1331), al-'Umarī (1301–49), Ibn Battūta (1304–69) and al-Hassan ibn Muhammad al-Wuzza'n (known to Europe as Leo Africanus, *c.* 1494–1552), are of major importance for the reconstruction of African history of the period between about the ninth and the fifteenth centuries, especially the history of the western and central Sudan.

But it is doubtful whether any of these authors or of their classical forebears, however useful their writings are to modern historians, should themselves be counted among the major historians of Africa. Essentially what each of them gives is a picture of those parts of Africa for which information was available at the time he was writing. There is no clear investigation, let alone description, of change over time, which is the true purpose of the historian. Nor in fact is a truly synchronic picture given, for while some of the information given may be contemporary, other parts of it, though still current in the author's lifetime, often originated in reports coming from earlier times. A final disadvantage is that commonly there is no means of assessing the authority of the information; whether, for example, the author gathered it from his own first-hand observation, or from the first-hand observation of a contemporary, or merely from current hearsay or from earlier authors. Leo Africanus provides an interesting example of this problem. Like Ibn Battuta, he himself travelled in Africa; but, unlike Ibn Battuta, it is by no means clear that all his information is derived from his own personal observations.

It is worth recalling, perhaps, that the word 'history' is not unambiguous. Today its common meaning is something like 'a methodological account of events over time', but it can also have the older sense of 'a systematic account of natural phenomena'. It is essentially in this sense that it is employed in the English title given to Leo Africanus' work, *A Geographical History of Africa,* a sense which survives today really only in the obsolescent term 'Natural History' (which, of course, was Pliny's title).

However, there is one major early historian of Africa in the best modern sense. This is Ibn Khaldun (1332–1406), who, if he were better known to western scholars, might well usurp Herodotus' title of 'the father of history'. Ibn Khaldun was, of course, a North African, a native of Tunis. Part of his work is concerned with Africa[1] and its relations with the other peoples of the Mediterranean and the Near East. From his perception of these relations, he evolved a concept of history as a cyclical process in which nomads from the steppes and the desert conquer the sedentary peoples of the arable lands, and there set up major kingdoms which, after about three generations, lose their vitality, and become victims to fresh invasions of nomads. This, indeed, is not a bad model for much of North African history, and a great historian, Marc Bloch,[2] has made use of Ibn Khaldun for his illumination of the history of early medieval Europe. But Ibn Khaldun stands out from his contemporaries not only because he thought out a philosophy of history but also – and perhaps more importantly – because, unlike them, he did not regard all scraps of information about the past as having potentially equal weight and validity; an approach to the truth had to be sought out by processes of criticism and comparison. Ibn Khaldun is in fact a very modern historian, and it is to him that we owe what is almost certainly our earliest surviving fragment of the written history of tropical Africa in any modern sense. As a North African, and also because, however new his philosophy and method, he was also working within the older Mediterranean and Islamic traditions, he was not unmindful of what was going on across the Sahara. Thus one chapter of Ibn Khaldun's work[3] is in effect a history of the Empire of Mali, which was at or close to its peak in his lifetime. This is partly based on the oral tradition then current, and for this reason it still remains an essential base for the history of this great African state.

No powerful state like Mali, or for that matter lesser ones like the early Hausa kingdoms or the city-states of the East African coast, could maintain its identity and integrity if there were not some accepted account of its foundation and subsequent development. When Islam crossed the Sahara and penetrated down the east coast, bringing literacy in Arabic in its train, Negro Africans no longer had to rely on maintaining their histories by oral means, and very quickly took to the production of written histories.

Perhaps the most sophisticated early examples of these histories that are now known are the *Ta'rīkh al-Sūdān* and the *Ta'rīkh al-Fattāsh*, both originally composed in Timbuktu essentially in the seventeenth century.[4] In both cases the authors give us accounts of developments in or just before their own times in considerable detail, and not without analysis and interpretation. But they also preface these with critical accounts of the surviving oral traditions relating to earlier times, so that the end result is not

1. The principal passages relating to Africa are to be found in Ibn Khaldun's most important work, the *Muqaddima* (translated into French by Vincent Monteil), and in the part of his *Universal History*, translated by de Slane under the title *Histoire des Berbères*.

2. See, for example, M. Bloch, 1939, p. 54.

3. In the translation by M. G. de Slane, entitled *Histoire des Berbères*, this appears in Vol. 2, pp. 105–16.

4. The *Tarīkh al-Sūdān* was edited and translated by G. Houdas (1900); the *Tarikh al-Fattash* by G. Houdas and M. Delafosse (1913).

only a history of the Songhai Empire, and of its conquest and domination by the Moroccans, but also an attempt to assess what was significant in the earlier history of the region, notably in the ancient empires of Ghana and Mali. This tends to distinguish the Timbuktu *Ta'rīkhs* from other early African historical works in Arabic, such as those known as the *Kano Chronicle* and the *Kilwa Chronicle*,[5] which are little more than direct written recordings of traditions which earlier were presumably maintained by oral means. While a version of the *Kilwa Chronicle* seems to have been used by the Portuguese historian De Barros in the sixteenth century, there is no evidence to show that the *Kano Chronicle* existed in a written form before about the nineteenth century.

One point of some interest is that Arabic chronicles of this kind are not necessarily limited to those parts of Africa which became thoroughly Islamized. Thus central modern Ghana produced its *Gonja Chronicle* (*Kitab al-Ghunja*) in the eighteenth century, and the recent researches of Ivor Wilks and others have revealed hundreds of examples of Arabic literacy from this and contiguous areas.[6] It must also not be forgotten, of course, that one part of tropical Africa, the modern Ethiopia, had its own Semitic languages, first Ge'ez and later Amharic, in which a continuous literary tradition has been preserved and developed for some two millennia. This tradition was certainly producing historical writing by the fourteenth century, for example, the *Chronicles of the Wars of Amda Sion*.[7] Historical writing in other African languages, such as Hausa and Swahili, as opposed to writing in the imported classical language of Arabic, but using its script, did not develop until the nineteenth century.

In the fifteenth century, Europeans began to become acquainted with the coastlands of tropical Africa. This quickly led to the production of literary works which provide invaluable source materials for modern historians. Four parts of tropical Africa received particular attention: the Guinea coastlands of West Africa, the region of the Lower Zaïre and Angola, the Zambezi valley and the adjacent highlands, and Ethiopia, in the last three of which there was appreciable penetration inland in the sixteenth and seventeenth centuries. But as with the earlier classical or Arabic writers, the result was not always, or immediately, the writing of African history.

The Guinea coastlands were the first part of Africa to be known by Europeans, and from about 1460 (Cadamosto) to the beginning of the

5. A translation of the *Kano Chronicle* is to be found in H. R. Palmer, 1928, Vol. 3, pp. 92–132, and of the *Kilwa Chronicle* in G. S. P. Freeman-Grenville (1962), pp. 34–49.

6. On the *Gonja Chronicle* and the collection of Arabic MSS. in modern Ghana see N. Levtzion, 1968, especially pp. xvii–xxii; I. Wilks, 1963; and T. Hodgkin, 1966.

7. There are a number of translations of this work, including one by J. Perruchon in *Journal Asiatique*, 1889.

eighteenth century (Barbot and Bosman), a whole series of works was written about them. A large amount of this material is of the utmost historical value, providing first-hand and dated evidence to which much other West African history can be anchored. There is also a good deal of historical (as opposed to contemporary) material in these works, especially perhaps in Dapper (1668) who – unlike most of the other authors – was not a first-hand observer, but solely a compiler of others' observations. But all these writers set out essentially to describe a contemporary situation rather than to write history, and, perversely, it is only now that a good deal of West African history has been reconstructed, that the full historical significance of much of what they have to say can be properly appreciated.[8]

The situation in respect of the other areas in which European interest developed in the sixteenth and seventeenth centuries was somewhat different. The explanation may lie in the fact that these were all fields for early missionary endeavour, whereas the prime focus for European activities in Guinea was always trade. So long as Africans delivered the goods which Europeans wanted to buy, as by and large was the case in Guinea, traders felt no imperative to alter African society; they were content simply to observe it. Missionaries, on the other hand, had a positive compulsion to try to change what they found, and perhaps some understanding of African history was a useful asset for them. In Ethiopia, of course, the tools were to hand. Ge'ez was learnt and studied, and chronicles and other writings in it could be used. Historical writing about Ethiopia was undertaken by two notable missionary pioneers, Pero Paez (d. 1622) and Manoel de Almeida (1569–1646), and a full-scale history was written by one of the first of Europe's orientalists, Job Ludolf (1624–1704).[9] In Lower Zaïre and Angola, and also in and around the Zambezi valley, the commercial motive was probably stronger than the evangelistic, but by and large traditional African society could not deliver the goods that Europeans required without considerable pressure. As a result it was changing dramatically, so that even descriptive essays could hardly escape being in part historical. In fact there is a considerable amount of history in the books of men like Pigafetta and Lopez (1591) and Cavazzi (1687), while in 1681 Cadornega produced a *History of the Angolan Wars*.[10]

By the eighteenth century, it would seem that tropical Africa was getting its due share of attention from European historians. It was now possible, for example, to use the earlier, essentially descriptive writers like Leo Africanus

8. G. R. Crone, 1937; J. Barbot, 1732; W. Bosman, annotated edn, 1967.

9. In C. Beccari, 1905–17; Paez's work is in Vols 2 and 3 and Almeida's in Vols 5–7; there is a partial English translation of Almeida in C. F. Beckingham and G. W. B. Huntingford, 1954. Ludolf's *Historia Aethiopica* was published at Frankfurt in 1681.

10. A. de Oliveira de Cadornega, 1940–2.

and Dapper as historical sources, so that the universal histories and geographies of the time, like the *Universal History* produced in England between 1736 and 1765, could give Africa a fair ration of their space.[11] There were also some monographic essays, for example Silva Correia's *History of Angola* (*c.* 1792), Benezet's *Some Historical Account of Guinea* (1772), and the two histories of Dahomey, Norris's *Memoirs of the Reign of Bossa Ahadee* (1789) and Dalzel's *History of Dahomy* (1793). But at this point, caution is necessary. Silva Correia's book was not published until the present century,[12] and the reason why the other three books mentioned were published is that by the end of the eighteenth century there was growing controversy about the slave trade, the mainstay of Europe's connection with tropical Africa for the previous 150 or more years. Dalzel and Norris, both drawing on their experience of slave trading in Dahomey, and Benezet, were all writing history, but their writings were all intended to provide fuel for the argument as to whether or not the slave trade should be abolished.

If it were not for this fact, it is doubtful whether these books would have found a market, because by this time the mainstream of European scholarship was beginning to take an increasingly unfavourable view of non-European societies, and to assert that they had no history worth studying. Essentially this attitude resulted from a conjunction of streams of thought deriving from the Renaissance, the Enlightenment, and the growing scientific revolution. The result was that, building upon what was regarded as a unique Graeco-Roman heritage, European intellectuals persuaded themselves that the purpose, knowledge, power and wealth of their society were so strong that it must prevail over all others; therefore its history was the key to understanding, and the history of all other societies was irrelevant. This attitude was perhaps especially applicable to Africa, since Europeans by now hardly knew Africa or Africans at all outside the context of the slave trade, while the operations of the export slave trade were creating increasing social chaos in many parts of the continent.

Hegel (1770–1831) stated the position very explicitly in his *Philosophy of History,* which contains such statements as that Africa 'is not a historical continent; it shows neither change nor development', and that its Negro peoples were 'capable of neither development nor education. As we see them today, so they have always been.' It is interesting to note that, as early as 1793, the editor who prepared Dalzel's book for publication thought it necessary to justify the appearance of a history of Dahomey. He neatly turned Hegel's attitude on its head, declaring: 'To arrive at a just knowledge of human nature, a progress through the history of the ruder nations is essentially necessary ... [There is no] other way to judge of the value of

11. The folio edition of the *Universal History* has 23 volumes; of these, 16 are devoted to modern history, and these include 2 volumes for Africa.

12. Lisbon, 1937.

cultivation, in the estimate of human happiness, than by this sort of comparison.'[13]

Although Hegel's direct influence on the elaboration of African history may have been small, the view he represented became part of the historical orthodoxy of the nineteenth century, and is not without its adherents even today. A recent Regius Professor of Modern History at Oxford University once declared:

> Perhaps, in the future, there will be some African history to teach. But at present there is none: there is only the history of the Europeans in Africa. The rest is darkness... and darkness is not a subject of history.
>
> Please do not misunderstand me. I do not deny that men existed even in dark countries and dark centuries, nor that they had political life and culture, interesting to sociologists and anthropologists; but history, I believe, is essentially a form of movement, and purposive movement too. It is not a mere phantasmagoria of changing shapes and costumes, of battles and conquests, dynasties and usurpations, social forms and social disintegration ...

He argued that 'History, or rather the study of history, has a purpose. We study it... in order to discover how we have come to be where we are', and that the present world is so dominated by western European ideas, techniques and values, that for the last five centuries at least, in so far as the history of the world has significance, it is only European history that counts. We cannot therefore afford to 'amuse ourselves with the unrewarding gyrations of barbarous tribes in picturesque but irrelevant corners of the globe'.[14]

Ironically enough, it was in Hegel's own lifetime that Europeans entered upon the effective modern, scientific exploration of Africa, and so began to lay the foundations for a rational appraisal of the history and achievements of African societies. In part this exploration was connected with the reaction against slavery and the slave trade, in part with the competition for African markets.

Some of the early European travellers were genuinely interested in finding out what they could about the past of the peoples of tropical Africa, and collected all available material – documents if they were available, if not oral traditions and notes on such antiquities as they saw. The literature produced by the explorers is immense; some of it contains some very good history, and almost all of it contains material of great value for historians. A short list of the major landmarks might include James Bruce's *Travels to Discover the Source of the Nile* (1790); the specifically historical chapters in the accounts of their visits to the Asante capital, Kumasi, by T. E. Bowdich

13. A. Dalzel, *The History of Dahomy* (1793) p. v.

14. These quotations come from the opening remarks of the first lecture of a series by Professor Hugh Trevor-Roper entitled 'The Rise of Christian Europe'. See *The Listener*, 28 November 1963, p. 871.

(*Mission from Cape Coast Castle to Ashantee*, 1819) and by Joseph Dupuis (*Journal of a Residence in Ashantee*, 1824); Heinrich Barth's *Travels and Discoveries in North and Central Africa* (1857–8); M. Guillain's *Documents sur l'histoire, la géographie et le commerce de l'Afrique orientale* (1856), and Gustav Nachtigal's *Sahara und Sudan* (1879–89).

Nachtigal's career, of course, extended into a totally new phase of Africa's history, that when Europeans had embarked on the processes of conquering the continent and of ruling its peoples. These processes seemed to require a moral justification, and here the Hegelian view was reinforced by the application of Darwinian principles. A symptomatic outcome of this was the rise of the new science of anthropology, a non-historical way of investigating and evaluating the cultures and societies of 'primitive' peoples, those who had 'no history worth studying', those who were 'inferior' to the Europeans, and who were usefully distinguishable from them by the pigmentation of their skins.

An interesting case study here is Richard Burton (1821–90). Burton's travels rank him among the greatest of the nineteenth-century European travellers in Africa; he had a restless and inquiring mind and a high order of scholarship and was an outstanding orientalist, and in 1863 he was one of the founders of the London Anthropological Society (which later developed into the Royal Anthropological Institute). Yet, in a much more idiosyncratic way than was the case with Nachtigal, his career marks the end of the period of the dispassionate, scientific exploration of Africa that had begun with James Bruce. There is, for example, in his *Mission to Glele, King of Dahomey* (1864), a remarkable digression on 'The Negro's place in nature' (not, it may be noted, 'The Negro's place in *history*'). In this can be found sentences such as 'The pure Negro ranks in the human family below the two great Arab and Aryan races' (most of his contemporaries would have ranked these last in the inverse order), and 'The Negro, in mass, will not improve beyond a certain point, and that not respectable; he mentally remains a child ...'[15] It was in vain that certain African intellectuals, such as James Africanus Horton, attempted to overcome this attitude in the course of polemical exchanges with the influential members of the London Anthropological Society.

Matters were made worse for the study of African history by the emergence at about this time, and particularly in Germany, of a concept of the historian's craft in which it became less a branch of literature or philosophy than a science based on the rigorous examination and analysis of the original sources. For European history, of course, these were predominantly written sources, and in these Africa seemed remarkably weak and deficient. The matter was put very succinctly when in 1923 Professor A. P. Newton gave a lecture to the (Royal) African Society in London on 'Africa and Historical Research'. Africa, he said, had 'no history before the coming of the Europeans. History only begins when men take to

15. Op. cit., 1893 edn, Vol. 2, pp. 131 and 135.

writing.' Thus the past of Africa before the onset of European imperialism could be reconstructed 'only from the evidence of material remains and of language and primitive custom', and such things were not the concern of historians, but of archaeologists, linguists and anthropologists.[16]

In fact Newton himself was somewhat on the fringe of the historical profession as it had emerged by his time. For much of the nineteenth century, some of the most eminent British historians, for example James Stephen (1789–1859), Herman Merivale (1806–74), J. A. Froude (1818–94), and J. R. Seeley (1834–95),[17] had been vitally concerned with the activities of Europeans (or of their compatriots at least) in the wider world. But Seeley's successor as Regius Professor of Modern History at Cambridge was Lord Acton (1834–1902), who had been trained in Germany. Acton began immediately to plan *The Cambridge Modern History*, the fourteen volumes of which appeared between 1902 and 1910. This is Euro-centric to the point at which it almost totally ignores even European activities in the outside world. Following this, the writing of colonial history tended to be left to men like Sir Charles Lucas (or, in France, Gabriel Hanotaux)[18] who – like Stephen, Merivale and Froude – had themselves once been involved actively in colonial affairs.

In due course, however, colonial or imperial history became an accepted fringe of the profession. *The New Cambridge Modern History*, which began to appear in 1957 under the direction of Sir George Clark, has African, Asian and American chapters throughout its twelve volumes, and by this time the range of the Cambridge Histories had included *The Cambridge History of the British Empire* (1929–59), of which Newton was one of the founding editors. But only a very cursory inspection of this work is needed to show that colonial history, even when applied to Africa, is very different from African history.

Of the *CHBE*'s eight volumes, four are devoted to Canada, Australia, New Zealand and British India. This leaves three general volumes, which are strongly oriented towards imperial policy (of their sixty-eight chapters, only four have a very direct bearing on the British connection with Africa), and one volume which is devoted to South Africa, the one corner of sub-Saharan Africa in which European settlement took firm root. Virtually the

16. 'Africa and historical research', *J. Afr. Soc.*, 22 (1922–3), p. 267.

17. Stephen served in the Colonial Office from 1825 to 1847 and was Professor of Modern History at Cambridge, 1849–59; Merivale was Professor of Political Economy at Oxford before following Stephen as Permanent Under-Secretary at the Colonial Office (1847–59). Froude spent most of his life at Oxford and was Professor of Modern History there in 1892–4, but during the 1870s he served as an emissary of the Colonial Secretary in South Africa; Seeley was Professor of Modern History at Cambridge from 1869 to 1895.

18. Lucas served in the British Colonial Office from 1877 to 1911, rising to Assistant Under-Secretary; he subsequently held a fellowship at All Souls' College, Oxford. Hanotaux (1853–1944) followed two careers, as a politician and statesman who in the 1890s played a leading role in French colonial and foreign affairs, and as a historian who was elected to the Académie Française.

whole of this volume (the largest of the eight) is devoted to the tangled affairs of these European settlers since their first arrival in 1652. The indigenous African peoples, the majority of the country's population, are relegated to an introductory (and largely non-historical) chapter by a social anthropologist, and to two chapters which, though written by the two most perceptive South African historians of their generation, C. W. de Kiewiet and W. M. Macmillan, perforce view them in the perspective of their reaction to the European presence.

Elsewhere, the history of Africa made a timid appearance in certain relatively monumental works: for example, *Peuples et civilisations, Histoire générale,* 20 volumes, Paris, 1927–52; *Histoire générale,* edited by G. Glotz, 10 volumes, Paris, 1925–38; *Propyläen Weltgeschichte,* 10 volumes, Berlin, 1929–33; *Historia mundi: Ein Handbuch der Weltgeschichte in 10 Bänden,* Bern, 1952ff.; *Vsemirnaja Istorija* (*World History*), 10 volumes, Moscow, 1955ff. The Italian C. Conti Rossini published an important *Storia d'Etiopia* in Milan in 1928.

Professional colonial historians, then, like professional historians generally, were wedded to the concepts that the indigenous peoples of sub-Saharan Africa had no history, or no history that they could study or that was worth their studying. As has been seen, Newton regarded this history as the preserve of archaeologists, linguists and anthropologists. Now it is true that archaeologists, like historians, are professionally concerned with the past of man. But for a long time they were little more interested than the historians in applying their skills to discovering the history of human society in sub-Saharan Africa. There were broadly two reasons for this.

First, one major strand in the evolving science of archaeology was that, like history, it is closely directed by written sources. It was devoted to problems like finding the site of ancient Troy, or finding out more about the societies of ancient Greece or Rome or Egypt than were already known from literary sources, and whose major monuments had for centuries been a source for speculation. It was – and sometimes still is – closely allied to the branch of the historical profession known as ancient history, and it is sometimes as much concerned with the finding and elucidation of ancient inscriptions as it is of other evidence. It was only very rarely – as in and around Aksum or Zimbabwe – that sub-Saharan Africa was known to have such major monuments as to attract the attention of this school of archaeology. A second major strand of archaeological research became focused on the search for the origins of man, and so with a spectrum of his past which was more geological than historical in its time scale. It is true that, with the work of scientists like L. S. B. Leakey and Raymond Dart, a major part of this search eventually became focused on eastern and southern Africa. But such men were concerned with a past so remote that society hardly existed, and usually there was a vast conjectural gap between the fossils they discovered and any modern population with whose past society historians might be concerned.

While archaeologists and historians largely held themselves aloof from sub-Saharan Africa before about the 1950s, its enormous variety of physical types, societies and languages inevitably attracted the attention of anthropologists and linguists as their disciplines began to develop. It was for long possible for both to remain armchair sciences, but men like Burton and S. W. Koelle (*Polyglotta Africana*, 1854) had earlier demonstrated the value of fieldwork, and anthropologists in particular became the pioneers of this in Africa. But, unlike historians and archaeologists, neither anthropologists nor linguists have any essential compulsion to discover what happened in the past, and in Africa they found a wealth of data simply awaiting description, classification and analysis – all of which were major tasks. Very often their concern with the past involved nothing more than reconstructing the history that they thought would lie behind and explain their data.

But they were not always aware how speculative and hypothetical these reconstructions were. A classic example is the anthropologist C. G. Seligman who, in his *Races of Africa*, first published in 1930, wrote bluntly: 'The civilizations of Africa are the civilizations of the Hamites, its history the record of these peoples and of their interaction with the two other African stocks, the Negro and the Bushman ...'[19] By inference, these 'two other African stocks' are inferior, and any advances in civilization they have made are due to the extent to which they have been subject to Hamitic influence. (Elsewhere in the book he writes of 'wave after wave' of incoming pastoral Hamites who were 'better armed as well as quicker witted' than 'the dark agricultural Negroes' on whom their influence was exerted.[20]) But there is really no historical evidence whatsoever to support the generalization that 'the civilizations of Africa are the civilizations of the Hamites', or that the historical progress made in sub-Saharan Africa has been due to them alone, or even mainly to them. Certainly no historical evidence is advanced in the book itself, and many of the assumptions on which it is based are now known to be quite without foundation. J. H. Greenberg, for example, has demonstrated once and for all that, if the terms Hamite and Hamitic have any value whatsoever, they are at best categories of linguistic classification.[21] Certainly there is no necessary correlation between the languages which people speak and either their racial stock or their culture. Thus, *inter alia*, Greenberg can cite the marvellous example that 'the Hamitic-speaking agricultural Hausa are under the rule of the pastoral Fulani who speak ... a Niger-Congo [i.e. Negro] language'.[22] He equally demolishes the Hamitic base for much of Seligman's reconstruction

19. Op. cit., 1930 edn, p. 96; 1966 edn, p. 61.
20. Op. cit., 1930 edn, p. 158; 1966 edn, p. 101.
21. J. H. Greenberg, 1963b. In fact Greenberg and most other modern linguists avoid the term Hamitic altogether; they place the so-called Hamitic languages along with the Semitic and other languages in a larger grouping called Afro-Asiatic or Erythraean, and do not recognize any significant Hamitic sub-group.
22. J. H. Greenberg, 1963b, p. 30.

of Negro culture history in other parts of Africa, notably for the Bantu-speaking peoples.

Seligman has been singled out for attention because he was one of the leaders of his profession in Britain (and one of the first to conduct serious fieldwork in Africa), and because his book became something of a standard work, which was often reprinted – as late as 1966 it was still being advertised as a classic of its kind. However, his espousal of the myth of the superiority of light-skinned over dark-skinned peoples was only part of the general European prejudice of the late nineteenth and early twentieth centuries. Europeans thought that their claim to superiority over black Africans had been confirmed by their own colonial conquest, and so in many parts of Africa, especially the Sudan belt and the lacustrine region, they were persuaded that they were merely continuing a civilizing process which other light-skinned invaders, generally labelled Hamites, had begun before them.[23] The same theme runs through many other works of the period from about 1890 to about 1940 which contained much more serious history than can be found in Seligman's little manual. For the most part these were written by men and women who had themselves been involved in the processes of conquest and colonization, and who were not professional anthropologists or linguists or historians. But because they were really interested in the exotic societies they had found, and wanted to find out more about them and to share their knowledge with others, they were amateurs in quite the best sense. Sir Harry Johnston and Maurice Delafosse, for example, both made really major contributions to African linguistics (and to many other fields besides), but the first called his major historical conspectus *A History of the Colonization of Africa by Alien Races* (1899; rewritten and enlarged, 1913), and the theme of the historical sections of the latter's magisterial survey of the western Sudan, *Haut-Sénégal-Niger* (1912), is set when he brings in a 'Judaeo-Syrian' migration to found ancient Ghana. Flora Shaw (*A Tropical Dependency*, 1906) was bewitched by the Muslim contribution to African history (Margery Perham, the biographer and friend of Lord Lugard, appropriately refers to her 'majestic sweep of history from the first Arab conquests of Africa to those of Goldie and Lugard'[24]). A very good amateur historian, Yves Urvoy (*Histoire des populations du Soudan central*, 1936, and *Histoire du Bornou*, 1949), completely mistakes the significance of the interactions between Saharan nomads and Negro sedentaries that he accurately describes; while Sir Richard Palmer (*Sudanese Memoirs*, 1928, and *The Bornu Sahara and Sudan*, 1936), an inspired antiquarian, is always seeking for springs of action in places as remote from his Nigerian themes as Tripoli or the Yemen.

23. It is a remarkable fact that the current revised fourth edition of *Races of Africa* (1966) has on p. 61 a significant phrase that does not occur in the original text of 1930. The Hamites are there defined as 'Europeans, i.e. [they] belong to the same great branch of mankind as the whites'.

24. M. Perham, 1960, p. 234.

However, after Seligman, professional British social anthropologists largely escaped from the shadow of the Hamitic myth. The dominant influences on their training became B. Malinowski and A. R. Radcliffe-Brown, who were very strongly opposed to any kind of conjectural history. In fact the strict functionalist approach to African societies followed by British anthropologists in the 1930s and 1940s tended to discourage any historical interest, even when, through their fieldwork, they were in uniquely good positions to acquire historical data. However, on the continent of Europe (and also in North America, not that many American anthropologists worked in Africa before the 1950s), an older tradition of ethnography continued, in which, *inter alia,* as much attention was paid to material culture as to social structure.

This produced a considerable amount of work of historical importance, as for example Tor Irstam's *The King of Ganda* (1944) or Lars Sundstrom's *The Trade of Guinea* (1965). However, two works deserve especial mention: Hermann Baumann's *Völkerkunde Afrikas* (1940) and the *Geschichte Afrikas* (1952) of Diedrich Westermann. The former was an encyclopedic survey of the peoples and civilizations of Africa in which due weight was given to what is known of their histories, and has still not been superseded as a one-volume handbook. (The more recent *Africa: Its Peoples and their Culture History* (1959), by the American anthropologist G. P. Murdock, suffers in comparison because its author lacks in this field relevant first-hand African experience by which to evaluate his data and because it is wedded to conjectural historical schema as eccentric in its own way – if not as pernicious – as that of Seligman.[25]) Westermann was primarily interested in language (his work of African linguistic classification often foreshadows that of Greenberg, and he contributed a linguistic section to Baumann's book), but his *Geschichte,* unfortunately distorted by the Hamitic theory, is a very valuable compilation of the oral tradition of African peoples as they were available in his day.

To these works one might perhaps add H. A. Wieschoff's *The Zimbabwe-Monomotapa Culture* (1943), if only to introduce his mentor, Leo Frobenius. Frobenius was an ethnologist, a cultural anthropologist and an archaeologist as much as he was a historian, but in his period of activity, corresponding to the first four decades of the twentieth century, he was almost certainly the most productive historian of Africa. He undertook an enormous amount of fieldwork in almost every part of the continent, and presented his results in a steady stream of publications. But these are little read today. He wrote in German, a language which has since become of decreasing relevance to Africa and Africanists. Relatively few of his works have been translated, and their meaning is often difficult to translate because they are encumbered by mystic theories relating to Atlantis, to an Etruscan influence on African culture, and so on.

25. See my review article, 'Anthropology, botany and history', 1961.

To the highly professional historians, archaeologists and anthropologists of today, Frobenius seems a self-taught eccentric whose work is flawed not only by his outlandish interpretations but also by his rapid, crude and often destructive methods of fieldwork. But he did get results, some of which clearly anticipate those of later, more scientific investigators, and others which may now be difficult or impossible to reproduce in modern conditions. It would seem that he had an instinctive flair for winning the confidence of informants and for establishing historical data. Modern historians might be well advised to rescue this data from his works, and to re-evaluate it in the light of modern knowledge and free from the more fanciful interpretations he placed upon it.[26]

The eccentricities of a self-taught, self-inspired genius like Frobenius tended to confirm the academic historians in their view that African history was not an acceptable field for their profession, and to divert attention from a good deal of serious work that was being done during the colonial period. One factor of some importance was that the growth of the European interest in Africa had given Africans themselves a wider range of literacies in which to express their own concern for their own history. This was especially the case in West Africa, where the contact with Europeans had been longest and most consistent, and where – especially perhaps in the zones which became British colonies – a demand for European schooling was established by the early years of the nineteenth century. Just as the Islamized savants of Timbuktu had quickly set to write their *Ta'rīkhs* in Arabic, so by the later nineteenth century Africans who had become literate in the Roman script felt the need to set down what they knew of the histories of their peoples before these were totally engulfed by the Europeans and their history.

Two early classics of this genre, written by Africans who – like the others of the *Ta'rīkhs* before them – had become active in the religion of the incoming culture and had taken their names from it, were Carl Christian Reindorf's *A History of the Gold Coast and Asante* (1895) and Samuel Johnson's *History of the Yorubas* (completed 1897, though not published until 1921). These are very serious works of history indeed; even today, no one can embark on any work on Yoruba history without consulting Johnson. But it was probably inevitable that essays at history on this scale were to become entangled with the writings of the early proto-nationalists, from J. A. B. Horton (1835–83) and E. W. Blyden (1832–1912) to J. M. Sarbah

26. It is impossible in a short chapter such as this to do justice to the immensity of Frobenius' output. His final work of synthesis was *Kulturgeschichte Afrikas* (1933), and his greatest achievement probably the twelve-volume collection *Atlantis: Volksmärchen und Volksdichtungen Afrikas* (1921–8). But account should be taken also of the books reporting his individual expeditions, e.g. (for the Yoruba and Mossi) *Und Africa sprach* (1912–13). See the full bibliography in F. Kretschmar, 1968. Some recent articles in English, e.g. J. M. Ita, 1972, and works there referred to suggest a revival of interest in Frobenius' work.

(1864–1910), J. E. Casely-Hayford (1866–1930) and J. B. Danquah (1895–1965), who touched on many historical matters but usually for purposes of their propaganda. Perhaps J. W. de Graft Johnson (*Towards Nationhood in West Africa*, 1928; *Historical Geography of the Gold Coast*, 1929) and E. J. P. Brown (*A Gold Coast and Asiante Reader*, 1929) belong to both categories. But after them there is a sense that a myth of the African past is being deliberately cultivated to combat the myth of European superiority: for example, J. O. Lucas, *The Religion of the Yoruba* (1948); J. C. de Graft Johnson, *African Glory* (1954). (Some European authors tended to push in the same direction; thus Eva L. R. Meyerowitz's books on the Akan seek to give them a glorious Mediterranean ancestry comparable to that sought by Lucas for the Yoruba.)

On a smaller scale, however, much serious and sound work continued to be done by Africans in recording local historical tradition. The extent and depth of the contact with Christian missionaries seems to have been an important factor here. Thus Uganda has produced a considerable school of local historians from the time of A. Kagwa (whose first work was published in 1906) onwards, while for Yorubaland, R. C. C. Law has noted twenty-two local historians who had published before 1940, often – as also with the Uganda authors – in the vernacular. One work of this kind which has become justly famous is J. U. Egharevba's *A Short History of Benin*, which has passed through a number of editions since its first appearance in 1934.

Secondly, of course, quite a number of the colonialists themselves were intelligent and inquisitive people who sought to find out and to set down the history of those they had come to rule. For such people, African history also often came to have some practical value. The Europeans might be better administrators if they knew something about the past of their subject peoples, and there was some need also for some African history to be taught in the ever-growing number of schools set up by them and their missionary colleagues, even if this was only to serve as an introduction to the more important tasks of teaching English and French history so that Africans could gain school certificates and baccalaureates, and so be enrolled as useful pseudo-European auxiliaries.

Flora Shaw, Harry Johnston, Maurice Delafosse, Yves Urvoy and Richmond Palmer have already been mentioned. Some others wrote serious African history which was relatively free of cultural preconceptions – even if sometimes they (or their publishers) chose remarkably inept titles; for example, Ruth Fisher, *Twilight Tales of the Black Baganda* (1912); C. H. Stigand, *The Land of Zinj* (1913); Sir Francis Fuller, *A Vanished Dynasty: Ashanti* (1921), fully in the tradition of Bowdich and Dupuis; E. W. Bovill, *Caravans of the Old Sahara* (1933); or the numerous scholarly works of Charles Monteil (for example, *Les Empires du Mali,* first published 1929) or

Louis Tauxier (for example, *Histoire des Bambara,* 1942). Perhaps the French were somewhat more successful in writing truly African history than the British, some of whose most solid works (for example, W. W. Claridge's *History of the Gold Coast and Ashanti* (1915) or Sir John Gray's *History of the Gambia* (1940) – though not some of the author's later East African articles) tended to be solidly Eurocentric in their approach. It is also noteworthy that, when they returned to France, a number of the French administrators (for example, Delafosse, Georges Hardy, Henri Labouret)[27] essayed short general histories either of the whole continent or of all sub-Saharan Africa.

Part of the explanation for this may lie in the fact that the French colonial administration tended to evolve more formal structures for training and research than did the British. One notable initiative was the Comité d'Etudes Historiques et Scientifiques de l'AOF (founded in 1917) and its *Bulletin*, which led to the Institut Français d'Afrique Noire, centred on Dakar (1938), and its *Bulletin* and its series of *Mémoires,* and so to works like Raymond Mauny's magisterial *Tableau géographique de l'Ouest africain au Moyen Âge* (1961). But even so, the historians of the colonial period remained amateurs outside the mainstream of the historical profession, and this was just as true of France as of Britain, for although men like Delafosse and Labouret did return home to academic positions, it was as teachers of African languages or of colonial administration, and not as historians.

In 1947, the Société Africaine de Culture and its journal *Présence Africaine* began to promote the idea of a decolonized African history. At the same time, a generation of African intellectuals, having mastered the European techniques of historical investigation, started to work out its own approach to the past of Africa and to seek in it the sources of a cultural identity which colonialism had refused to recognize. These intellectuals also took the opportunity to refine and extend the techniques of historical methodology and rid it of a large number of subjective myths and prejudices. In this connection mention should be made of the symposium organized by Unesco in Cairo in 1974, which enabled African and non-African researchers to engage in a free exchange of views on the problem of the population of ancient Egypt.

In 1948, W. E. F. Ward's *History of the Gold Coast* appeared. In the same year the University of London created a lectureship in African history at the School of Oriental and African Studies, and appointed Dr Roland Oliver to the post. At this point too Britain began a programme of developing universities in its dependent territories: university institutions were founded in the Gold Coast and in Nigeria, and Gordon College in Khartoum and Makerere College in Kampala were promoted to university status. These developments were paralleled in the Belgian and French colonies: in 1950 an Ecole Supérieure des Lettres was set up in Dakar and

27. M. Delafosse, 1921; G. Hardy, 1937; H. Labouret, 1946.

became a fully-fledged French university seven years later; Lovanium, the first university in the Belgian Congo (now Zaïre), opened in 1954.

From the point of view of African historiography the multiplicity of new universities from 1948 onwards was much more significant than the very few institutions which already existed but whose vigour was impaired by lack of funds, such as Liberia College at Monrovia and Fourah Bay College in Sierre Leone, founded respectively in 1864 and 1876.

In South Africa, the nine universities which existed in 1940 were all handicapped by the segregationist policies of the Pretoria government: historical research and teaching were centred on Europe, and the history of Africa was merely that of the white immigrants.

All the new universities, however, quickly established departments of history which, for the first time, attracted a large number of professional historians to work in Africa. At first, most of these historians inevitably came from non-African universities. But Africans rapidly took over: the first African director of a history department was Professor K. O. Dike, who was appointed at Ibadan in 1956. Many African students were trained. Professional historians teaching in Africa felt the need to add more African history to their syllabuses and, when such history was too little known, to explore it through their research.

Since 1948, the historiography of Africa has become increasingly similar to that of any other part of the world. It has its own problems, for example, the comparative scarcity of documentary source materials for early periods and the consequent need to develop other sources such as oral tradition, linguistics and archaeology.

But even if African historiography has made important contributions with respect to the use and interpretation of such sources, it is not fundamentally different from the historiography of other countries, in Latin America, Asia or Europe, which have to face similar problems. Furthermore, the actual provenance of his evidence is not fundamental to the main purpose of the historian, which is to make a critical and comparative use of it in order to produce an intelligent and meaningful description of the past. The important point is that during the last quarter-century groups of African academics have taken a professional interest in history. The study of African history is now a well-established, highly specialized activity and its continued development will be ensured by inter-African exchanges and by relations between the universities of Africa and those in other parts of the world. But it should be stressed that this progress would have been impossible without the process by which Africa threw off the colonial yoke: the armed revolt of Madagascar in 1947, the independence of Morocco in 1955, the heroic war of the Algerian people and the struggles for freedom in all the African colonies contributed powerfully to this process because they gave African peoples the opportunity of renewing contact with their own history and organizing its study. Unesco was quick to recognize this need and initiated or encouraged meetings of specialists; it also rightly insisted on the systematic collection of oral traditions as an essential preliminary. In 1966, in response to the wishes of African intellectuals and states, it launched the idea of a General History of Africa, and the implementation of this major undertaking has been progressing under its auspices since 1969.

2 The place of history in African society

BOUBOU HAMA AND
J. KI-ZERBO

Man is a historical animal, and African man is no exception. Just as everywhere else all over the world, he created his own history, and his own idea of it. On the factual level the proofs and products of this creative ability are there before our eyes in the form of methods of agriculture, cooking, pharmacy, common law, political organizations, the productions of art, religious ceremonies, and highly developed rules of etiquette. Through all the centuries since man first appeared, Africans have shaped an independent society which by its vitality alone bears witness to their historical genius. This history, which came into being empirically, *a priori,* was thought out and interiorized *a posteriori* both by individuals and by social groups. In this way it became an intellectual frame of reference, a spiritual and emotional authority, a reason and a setting for living, a model.

But historical consciousness reflects the society to which it belongs, and even each significant phase in the evolution of that society, so it is clear that the Africans' conception of their own history and of history in general will be marked by their own particular development. The mere fact of isolation is enough to restrict a society's historical vision. Thus the King of the Mossi in Upper Volta used to bear the title of Mogho-Naba, King of the World – a good illustration of the influence of technical and material limitations on people's ideas of social and political reality. One sees, then, that African time is occasionally a mythical and social time. But Africans are also conscious of being the active instruments of their own history, and, as we shall find, African time, as well as being mythical and social, is genuinely historical too.

Mythical time and social time

At first glance, and from many ethnological studies, one gets the impression that the Africans were submerged, almost drowned, in mythical time, a vast ocean without shores and without landmarks, while the other peoples of the world advanced down the avenue of History, a great highway marked out with the milestones of progress. And it is true that myth, the imaginary representation of the past, does often dominate African conceptions of the development of the lives of nations. So much so, that the choice and significance of real events sometimes had to obey a mythical model predetermining even the most prosaic actions of ruler or people. Myth, in the guise of immemorial customs, thus governed, as it also justified, history. From this context emerge two striking characteristics of African historical thought: its intemporality, and its essentially social aspect.

In this situation, time is not duration as it affects the fate of the individual. It is the rhythm of the breathing of the social group. It is not a river flowing in one direction from a known source to a known outlet. In technically advanced countries even Christians make a clear distinction between the end of the world and eternity. This is perhaps because the New Testament differentiates between this fleeting world and the world to come, but it is also because for many other reasons too human time has been to all intents and purposes secularized. But it is generally true to say that traditional African time includes and incorporates eternity in both directions. Bygone generations are not lost to the present. In their own way they remain contemporary, and as influential as they were during their lifetime, if not more so. In these circumstances causality operates in a forward direction, of course, from past to present and from present to future, not only through the influence of bygone facts and events, but through a direct intervention which can operate in any direction. When Mansa Musa, Emperor of Mali (1312–32), sent an ambassador to the King of Yatenga asking him to be converted to Islam, the Mossi ruler answered that he would have to consult his ancestors before taking such a decision. This shows the past in direct connection with the present through religion, ancestors acting as special and direct agents in matters occurring centuries after their death. Similarly, at many royal courts officials responsible for the interpretation of dreams had considerable influence on political action, and might almost be described as ministers of the future. There is the well-known case of the Rwanda king, Nazimpaka Yubi III (end of the seventeenth century), who in a dream saw pale-skinned men coming from the east. He took up his bows and arrows, but before letting fly he tied ripe bananas to the shafts. The interpretation of this dream attitude, at once aggressive and welcoming, and in short ambiguous, imparted a special image to the collective consciousness of the Rwanda people, and may have had something to do with the fact that although they were seasoned warriors they did not put up much resistance to the German columns in the nineteenth century, remembering the pale faces in the king's dream of a couple of centuries earlier.

In this kind of suspended time, the present may even act on what is regarded as the past but in fact remains contemporary. The blood of sacrifices offered up today can help the ancestors of yesteryear. Right up to our own times, Africans have exhorted one another not to neglect offerings made in the name of their ancestors, for those who receive nothing are the poor in the parallel world of the dead, and have to live on the charity of those in whose name generous sacrifices are made.

In a more fundamental way still, some cosmogonies attribute to some mythical time advances which were made in historical time; as the latter is not perceived as such by each individual, it is replaced by the historical group memory. An example of this is the Kikuyu legend about the first making of iron. Ngai (God) had divided up the animals between men and women. But the women were so cruel that their animals ran away and became wild. The men interceded with Ngai on behalf of their wives, saying, 'We wish to sacrifice a lamb in thy honour, but we do not want to do it with a wooden knife lest we run the same risk as our wives.' Ngai congratulated them on their wisdom, and, so that they could have more efficient weapons, told them how to smelt iron.

This mythical and collective conception made time an attribute of sovereignty. The Shilluk king was the mortal repository of immortal power, for he combined in his own person both mythical time (he was the incarnation of the founding hero) and social time, regarded as the source of the group's vitality. The same thing occurs among the Bafulero of east Zaïre, the Banyoro of Uganda, and the Mossi of Upper Volta, for all of whom the chief is the mainstay of collective time: 'The Mwami is present: the people lives. The Mwami is absent: the people dies.' The death of the king is a break in time which halts activity and social order and all expression of life, from laughter to agriculture and sexual union between either people or animals. The interregnum is a parenthesis in time. Only the advent of another king recreates social time, which then comes back to life again. Everything is omnipresent in this intemporal time of animist thought, where the part represents and may signify the whole, and hair and fingernails must not fall into the hands of an enemy lest they give him power over their owner.

Indeed, one has to go as far as the general conception of the world in order to understand the Africans' vision of time and its real meaning for them. We then see that in traditional thought, time in the ordinary sense is only one aspect of another time experienced by other dimensions of the individual. When a man lies down at night on his mat or his bed, to sleep, that is the moment his double chooses to set out and retrace the path the man himself followed during the day, to frequent the places he was in, and to repeat the work and actions he performed consciously during his daily life. It is in the course of these peregrinations that the double encounters the forces of good and evil, both benevolent spirits and the sorcerers who eat up doubles or *cerkos*, as they are called in the Songhay and Zarma languages. It is in his double that a man's personality resides. When the Songhay say of someone that his *bya* (double) is heavy or light, they mean that his personality is strong or weak, and the purpose of amulets is to protect and strengthen the double. The ideal is to succeed in merging into one's double so as to form a single entity, which thus acquires superhuman wisdom and strength. Only the greatest initiate or master (*korté-konynii, zimaa*) can attain this state, in which time, like space, ceases to be an obstacle. Such a one was *Si*, eponymous ancestor of the Songhay dynasty: 'Terrible is the father of the

Si, the father of thunderbolts. When he has toothache he crunches gravel. When his eyes are sore he bursts forth in flame. He strides over the earth. He is everywhere and nowhere.'

Social time, history, experienced in this way by a group, amasses power, and this power is usually symbolized and given concrete form by some object which is transmitted by the patriarch, the head of the clan, or the king, to his successor. It may be a golden ball kept in a *tobal* or war-drum, together with parts of the body of a lion or elephant or panther. Or it may be kept in a box or chest, like the regalia (*tibo*) of the Mossi king. Among the Songhay and Zarma, the object is a rod of iron pointed at one end. Among the Sorko in the old empire of Gao it was an idol in the shape of a big fish with a ring in its mouth. Among those who worked in iron it was a mythical forge which sometimes grew red-hot at night to express its anger. The transfer of such objects constituted the legal transmision of power. The most striking example is that of the Sonianke, descendants of Sonni Ali, who have chains of gold, silver or copper, each link representing an ancestor and the whole chain representing the dynastic line back to Sonni the Great. The chains are produced from the mouths of the celebrants in the course of magical ceremonies, much to the amazement of the onlookers, and when a Sonianke patriarch dies, he disgorges the chain for the last time, and it is swallowed from the other end by his chosen successor. He dies as soon as he has passed the chain over to whoever is to continue the line – a concrete will and testament which well illustrates the strength of the African conception of mythical and social time.

Some people have thought that such a view of the historical process was static and sterile, placing the perfect archetype far back in the past, in the origins of time, and thus seeming to set before succeeding generations an ideal which consisted in stereotyped repetition of the doings and exploits of their ancestors. Myth would then be the motive force of a history which was immobile. But as we shall see, African historical thought cannot be confined to this one approach.

It must also be recognized that a mythical approach lies at the origins of every nation's history. Every history starts off as religious history, and this attitude actually accompanies historical development and reappears from time to time in various marvellous or monstrous forms. One of these is the nationalist myth, by which one famous contemporary head of state addressed his country as if it were a living person. And under the Nazi regime the myth of race, given concrete form in rituals which went back into the mists of time, condemned millions of people to the holocaust.

Are Africans aware of being agents of their own history?

It is true that for some centuries the African has had many reasons for not being conscious of responsibility. He has been accustomed to so many alienating dictates coming from outside that even if he lived far from the slave coast or the seat of the nearest white officer, some part of his soul was bound to be marked with the annihilating brand of the serf.

Likewise, in the precolonial period, many elementary and almost closed African societies give the impression that their members were conscious of making history only to a very limited extent and on a very limited scale, often only within the bounds of the extended family and inside the framework of a customary gerontocratic hierarchy that was strict and oppressive. But even at this level, perhaps especially at this level, the feeling of autonomy, of self-regulation by the community, was vivid and powerful. The Lobi and Kabre peasant in his village, when he was master of the house,[1] felt he had ample control over his own fate. The best proof of this is that it was in such 'stateless' areas, where power was the thing most widely shared, that invaders, and in particular colonizers, had most difficulty in establishing themselves. Here love of liberty was proof of a taste for initiative and a hatred of alienation.

In highly structured societies, on the other hand, the African conception of the chief gave the latter an exaggerated position in the history of nations whose collective fate he literally embodied. So it is not surprising to find oral tradition retracing the whole original history of the Malinke in the *Praise to Sundjata*. Similarly with Sonni Ali, among the Songhay of the Niger bend. This does not represent an ideological conditioning destructive of any critical spirit, although in societies where oral transmission is the only channel of information, the authorities, exercising control over a strong network of griots, had almost a monopoly in the diffusion of official 'truth'. But the griots were not a monolithic and nationalized body.

The later history of precolonial Africa shows that the place accorded to African leaders in the people's mental pictures is probably not an inflated one. A good example is Shaka, who actually forged the Zulu nation in the turmoil of combat.

What both written and oral evidence tells us about Shaka's activity must have been reproduced many times during the course of African history. We are told that the constitution of the Mandingo peoples goes back to Sundjata, and the part played by Osei Tutu and Anokye in the founding of the Asante 'nation' seems to correspond to the Asante's own conception of it right down to the present day. This is all the more so because the idea of a leader who acts as a motive force in history is never reduced to an oversimplified schema crediting the whole of human progress to just one man. Nearly always there is a dynamic group which is famous as such. Nor are the chiefs' companions forgotten (even when they are of inferior status, such as griots, spokesmen and servants). They often enter history as heroes.

The same thing is true of women, who, contrary to what has been repeated over and over again, probably occupy a more important position in the African historical consciousness than their counterparts elsewhere. This is

1. The Bambara expressions *so-tigui*, *dougou-tigui* (head of a village), *dyamanitigui* (head of a canton) and *kele-tigui* (general-in-chief) bring out the force of this authority.

easily understood in the case of matrilineal societies. At the village of Wanzarba, near Tera (Niger), where the succession to the chieftainry was matrilineal, the French of the colonial period tried to bring the people into conformity with the others by appointing a man as chief. But the Sonianke[2] still kept their *kassey* or priestess, who right down to the present is still the repository of spiritual power. But elsewhere too the people see women as having played a role of the highest importance in the historical evolution of the nations.

As daughters, sisters, wives and mothers of kings they were well placed to influence events. Lueji is an astonishing example who was in turn daughter, sister, wife and mother of a king and well deserves her title of *Swana Mulunda* or Mother of the Lunda People. The famous Amina, who in the fifteenth century conquered on Zaria's behalf so many towns and lands in Hausa country which still bear her name, is only one example among thousands of that idea of their own historical authority which women were able to impose on African society. This idea is still alive in Africa today as a result of the part played by women in the Algerian war and within the political parties during the nationalist struggle for independence in the southern Sahara. True, African women have also been used for pleasure and ornament, as is suggested when we see the King of Dahomey presiding at a feast surrounded by ladies wearing imported materials. But in the same ceremony there were also the Amazons who were the spearhead of the royal army against Oyo and against the colonial invaders at the Battle of Cana (1892). African women have always been regarded as playing an eminent role in the history of the people, through the part they play in agriculture, crafts and trade; by their influence over their sons, whether those sons be princes or peasants; and by their cultural vitality. There always have been, and always will be, battles for or by women. Women themselves have often accepted the role of traitress or seductress, as in the case of Sundjata's sister, or of the women sent to his enemies by the King of Segou, Da Monzon.

Despite the fact that they appear to be segregated at public gatherings, everyone in Africa knows that women are omnipresent. Woman is life, and the promise of a fuller life. And it is through her that peoples sanction their alliances. She may speak little in public, but in the privacy of the home she makes and breaks events. As the proverb puts it, 'Women can make or mar anything.'

On the whole it is as if, in Africa, the persistence of elementary community structures throughout historical evolution had made the whole historical process in Africa a remarkably popular one. The smallness of the societies concerned made history the business of everyone. Although – despite telecommunication by talking drums – efficient means of communication were lacking, the limited nature of historical space meant that it was

2. Among these people power is transmitted 'through the milk', though admittedly this is strengthened by the link of blood; but among the Cerko power is handed down only through the milk.

within everyone's mental grasp. Hence the incontestably democratic nature of most Africans' conception of history. Everyone felt he mattered, and that he could in the last resort escape from dictatorship if only by seceding and taking refuge elsewhere. Shaka himself had this experience at the end of his career. This feeling of making history even on the scale of the village microcosm, and on the other hand the feeling of being only an atom in the historical current created at the top by a king seen as a demiurge, are very important factors for the historian. For they in themselves are historical facts, and help in their turn to create history.

African time is a historical time

But can African time be regarded as a historical time? Some people have said it cannot, arguing that the African only sees the world as a stereotyped reproduction of what has gone before. This would make him a stubborn disciple of the past, justifying all his actions by saying, 'That was how our ancestors did it.' If that had really been the case, Ibn Battuta, instead of finding the Empire of Mali, would have found only prehistoric communities living in caves and clothed in skins.

The social nature of the African conception of history itself lends it a historical dimension, for history is the developing life of a group. From this point of view, we may say that, for the African, time is dynamic. Man is not a prisoner marking time, or condemned to do the same things over and over again, either in the traditional view or according to Islamic beliefs.

Of course, in the absence of the idea of a mathematical and physical time made up of homogeneous units added together and measured by special instruments, time remains something pragmatic and social. But that does not mean, in this context, something neutral and indifferent. In the black African overall conception of the world, time is the arena where man can always carry on the struggle against the depletion and for the increase of his vital energy. That is the main feature of African animism,[3] in which time is an enclosed space, a market where the forces that inhabit the world contend or conclude bargains. The ideal of both the individual and the group is to defend themselves against any diminution, to improve their health and strength and the size of their fields and flocks, to increase the number of their children and wives and villages. And this conception is undoubtedly a dynamic one.

The Cerko and Sonianke clans of the Songhay (Niger) are antagonists. The first, which represents the past and tries to reign over the night, attacks society. The second, which is master of the day, represents the present and defends society.

Here is a significant stanza from a Songhay magical invocation:

3. Animism, or rather traditional African religion, is characterized by worship of God and of the powers of intermediary spirits.

It is not from my mouth
It is from the mouth of A
who gave it to B
who gave it to C
who gave it to D
who gave it to E
who gave it to F
who gave it to me
may mine be better in my mouth than in the mouth of the ancestors.

The African is always seeking justification from the past. But this invocation does not signify a static state or contradict the general law of progress and the growth of power. Hence the line, 'May mine be better in my mouth than in the mouth of the ancestors.'

Power in black Africa is often expressed by a word that means force or strength.[4] This synonymy shows the importance the African peoples attach to force, if not violence, in the unfolding of history. But it is not just a matter of crude material force. It is a question of the vital energy which contains various polyvalent forces ranging from physical integrity through chance to moral integrity. Ethical value is regarded as a *sine qua non* of the beneficent exercise of power. Popular wisdom bears witness to this idea in many tales which depict despotic chiefs who are finally punished, thus literally drawing the moral of history. The *Ta'rīkh al-Sūdān* and the *Ta'rīkh al-Fattāsh* are full of praises for the virtues of al-Hajj Askiya Muhammad. It is true that both accounts had material interests in mind, but they systematically relate the ruler's virtues to his being fortunate. The same thought is to be found in Muhammad Bello, who urges Yacuba Baoutchi to meditate on the history of the Songhay Empire. It was thanks to his justice that Muhammad Askiya was able not only to maintain but also to increase the legacy of Sonni Ali. And it was when the sons of Askiya departed from the justice of Islam that their empire disintegrated into a number of weak principalities.

According to the son of Usman dan Fodio, the same principle applied to their own government: 'Look back on the past, on all those who once commanded before us ... Before us there were age-old dynasties in the Hausa country. In them, many peoples acquired great powers, but these crumbled because they departed from their foundation in justice and from their customs and traditions, and because they were weakened by injustice. If we are to endure, our force must be the force of truth and of Islam. The fact that we slew Yunfa[5] and destroyed the work of Nafata,[5] Abarshi,[5] and Bawa Zangorzo[5] may impress present generations even outside the influence of Islam. But the generations that come after us will not see all that. They will judge us by the worth of the organization we leave them, by the permanent force of Islam which we have established, and by the truth and justice we have been able to impose in the state.'

4. *Fanga*, *oanga*, *pan*, in Bambara, Moré and Samo respectively.
5. Princes of Gobir.

This lofty view of the role of ethics in history does not derive solely from the Islamic beliefs of the Sokoto leader. In animist belief too there is the idea that the order of the cosmic forces may be disturbed by immoral deeds, and that the resulting disequilibrium can only harm its author. This vision of the world in which ethical values and requirements form an integral part of the ordering of the universe itself may appear mythical. But it exerted an objective influence on people's behaviour, especially on that of many African political leaders. In this sense one may say that while history is often a justification of the past it is also an exhortation for the future. In pre-state systems, moral authority capable of guaranteeing the conduct of public affairs or of chastizing those who conducted them was vested in special, sometimes secret groups, such as the *lo* of the Senufo or the *poro* of Upper Guinea. These groups often constituted parallel powers which could be appealed to outside the established system. They sometimes ended by clandestinely usurping official power. The people then saw them as occult centres of decision depriving the nation of control over its own history.

In the same type of society, the organization into age-groups is of prime importance for establishing the people's history. This structure, in so far as it conforms to a known periodicity, makes it posssible to trace history back to the eighteenth century. But at the same time it played a specific role in the life of the societies themselves. Even in rural communities which knew no major technical innovation and were therefore fairly stable, conflict between the generations was not unknown. So it had to be controlled, and relations between the generations so structured that the conflict would not degenerate into violent confrontation and sudden change. The generation engaged in action sent one of its members as a delegate to the next generation, the one that would immediately succeed it. The role of the delegate was not to stifle the impatience of the younger group, but to channel their reckless energy so that it was not harmful to the community as a whole and did not impair the younger group's ability to take over public responsibility when the time came.[6]

Africans are vividly aware of time past, but time past, though it greatly influences time present, does not do away with its dynamism, as is attested by many proverbs. The conception of time as one sees it in African societies is certainly not inherent in or consubstantial with some essentially African nature. It is the mark of a certain stage in economic and social development. Proof of this is the striking differences one sees even today between the time-is-money of African city-dwellers and time as it is understood by their contemporaries and brothers in the bush. The essential element in historical time is the idea of a development starting from origins which are to be sought after and examined. Even beneath the crust of tales and legends and the dross of myths, there is an attempt to rationalize social development.

6. For example, the Alladians of Moosou (near Abidjan) are still organized into five generations, each reigning for nine years, even for modern activities such as building, celebrating a diploma or promotion, and so on.

Sometimes even more positive efforts have been made to try to calculate historical time. This may be linked with space, as when a very short time is referred to as the time needed to take a pace. It can also be linked to biology, in references to a breath, in or out. But it is often linked to factors not connected with the individual, and the references then are to cosmic, climatic or social phenomena, especially when these are recurrent. In the savannah of the Sudan, the followers of traditional African religions usually count age by rainy seasons. To indicate that a man is old, one says how many rainy seasons he has lived through, or, more elliptically, that 'he has drunk much water'.

More developed systems of computation have sometimes been attempted,[7] but the decisive step will come only with the spread of writing, though the existence of a literate class is no guarantee that the whole people will become aware of possessing a common history. But at least it makes it possible to establish certain points of reference around which that history is shaped.

The introduction of monotheistic religions rooted in another history has served to provide the mental image of the collective past with another, parallel set of models which can often be glimpsed in the background in various stories. For example, the dynasties are often linked arbitrarily to the sources of Islam, whose values and ideals the black prophets were to make use of to change the course of events in their own countries.

But the greatest upheaval in time comes with the introduction of the world of profit, and the amassing of money. Then acculturation changes the sense of individual and collective time into the mental schemas operative in the countries which influence Africans economically and culturally.

The Africans then see that it is money that makes history. African man, once so close to his history that he seemed to be creating it himself, in micro-societies, is then confronted both with the risk of a colossal alienation and with the opportunity of being a co-author of world progress.

7. Thus Ivor Wilks, in criticizing the book by D. P. Henige, *The Chronology of Oral Tradition: Quest for a Chimera*, shows that the Akan (Fanti, Asante ...) had evolved a complex calendar system, with a week of seven days, a month of six weeks and a year of nine months, which was regularly realigned on the sun by methods that are not yet fully understood. 'The Akan calendar could thus be used to refer, say, to the eighteenth day of the fourth month of the reign of Asantehene Osei Bonsu.' This system of dating was still in use in European countries in the eighteenth and nineteenth centuries. See I. Wilks, 1975, pp. 279 ff.

PLATE 2.1 *Bronze statue representing the dynastic power of the Songhay of Dargol* (A. Salifou)

3 Recent trends in African historiography and their contribution to history in general

P. D. CURTIN

This volume, like the volumes to follow, was planned to show the African past from an African point of view. This is a correct perspective, perhaps the only approach possible to an international effort; it is also the dominant approach among historians of Africa, both in Africa and overseas. For Africans, to know about the past of their own societies is a form of self-knowledge crucial to a sense of identity in a diverse and rapidly changing world. A recovery of African history has been an important part of African development over recent decades, not an expensive frill that could be set aside until more pressing aspects of development were well in hand. This is why historians in Africa and overseas were first concerned to step across the remains of colonial history and begin again with the historical experience of African peoples. Other chapters and other volumes will deal with this recovery, with history as a living tradition that still flourishes, with the role of historical knowledge in building new educational systems for independent Africa. This chapter, however, is concerned with the meaning of African history, first for the international community of historians and secondly for the broader educated public outside Africa.

The fact that African history was seriously neglected until the 1950s is only one symptom of a large phenomenon in historical studies. The colonial period in Africa left an intellectual legacy to be overcome, just as it had in other parts of the world. Europeans conquered and ruled over most of Asia in the nineteenth century, while in the tropical Americas underdevelopment and the domination of the Afro-American and Indian populations by Europeans reproduced the conditions of colonialism, even though the conventions of international law showed a series of independent states. The colonial imprint on historical knowledge emerged in the nineteenth and early twentieth centuries as a false perspective, a Eurocentric view of world history created at a time of European domination. It was then transmitted outward through the educational systems the Europeans had created in the colonial world. Even where Europeans never ruled, European knowledge was often accepted as *modern* knowledge, including aspects of the Eurocentric historiography.

Much of the Eurocentric world view has now disappeared from the best recent historical research, but it is still dominant with many historians and with the broader public in the non-western as in the western world.[1] It has lasted so long because most people 'learned history' in school and found no opportunity to re-learn it in later life. Even research historians sometimes find it difficult to keep up with new research outside their own field of study. Textbooks tend to lag behind the most recent research by ten to twenty years, and other general historical works often carry on the outworn biases of past learning. Every new interpretation, every new datum, has something of a struggle for acceptance.

In spite of these delays between discovery and acceptance as common knowledge, historical studies in the world at large are passing through a dual revolution that began shortly after the Second World War and is not yet finished. One part is the transformation of history from chronicle into the social science concerned with change in human societies; the other involves the replacement of national bias by a broader view based on a world perspective.

Contributions to these new movements have come from all sides – from Europe itself, from historians in Africa, Asia and Latin America, from the overseas Europeans of North America and Oceania. Their effort to extend the scope of history embraced both peoples and regions previously neglected, and aspects of human experience formerly buried under a narrow tradition of political and military history. In this setting, a better knowledge of African history would have been a valuable contribution. But this would have been to let African history appear to be just another parochial history, valuable enough for self-knowledge, as an aid to African development, but not as the most significant kind of contribution to the new view of world history.

Historical parochialism was, indeed, one of the most deeply embedded aspects of the older historical tradition. The best history in the first half of the twentieth century barely began to outgrow an ancient sentiment that considered history to be a semi-private possession, that saw the history of any particular society as valuable to itself but irrelevant to others. Any interest in one's history on the part of foreigners was at best a form of snooping, at worst academic espionage. This emphasis on history as *our* history was especially strong in the European tradition of the early twentieth century. Departments of education tended to define history as national history – not even a general European history, much less a balanced view of

1. The term 'West' is used in this chapter to refer to those parts of the world that are culturally European, or whose culture is dominantly derived from Europe, including the Americas, the USSR, Australia and New Zealand.

world history. History was consciously mythical, designed to build national pride and willingness to sacrifice for the national cause. As Lord Macaulay put it, history was partly narrative art and partly a 'vehicle of ethical and political instruction'.[2] It was supposed to inculcate patriotism, not to give a balanced view of human development, and this attitude is still dominant in most educational systems.

A few historians objected in the name of scholarship, and a few in the name of imperialism, but most accepted the nationalist bias as normal if not desirable. It is still possible in France to earn the title of *agrégé* in history with minimal knowledge of Europe beyond French frontiers, to say nothing of Asia, Africa or America. It is still possible to earn a BA(Hons) degree in several English universities on the basis of English history alone. And the use of *English* not *British* is symptomatic; the English schoolboy is likely to know more Roman history than Welsh, Scottish or Irish history before the eighteenth century. Much the same is the case in eastern Europe, though with different ideological overtones. Only the smaller European countries like the Benelux group or Scandinavia seem to stretch out towards a broader focus on Europe as a whole. Nevertheless, the North American *history of civilization* approach (and its European equivalents) was still ethnocentric, asking 'How did we come to be as we are?' not 'How did mankind come to be as we find it today?'

The task of moving on to a view of world history in which Africa, Asia and Latin America would have an internationally recognized role belonged partly to the historians who sprang from the culture of these continents who gradually overthrew the Eurocentric view of their own history. It belonged more particularly to those historians who crossed the cultural lines in their own work – to the African historians who began to write about Asia or Latin America, to the Europeans or North Americans who began to interpret African or Asian history to their own people, consciously trying to free themselves of the old Eurocentric bias.

The role of historians of Africa, in Africa and overseas alike, was especially important in this general effort if only because African history had been more neglected than that of other non-European regions and because African history had been even more distorted by racist myths. Owing to its protean character, racism is one of the most difficult scourges to stamp out. From the sixteenth century racism found various forms of expression some of which were extreme and led to genocide at certain periods, in particular at the time of the slave trade and during the Second World War. It still survives as a monstrous challenge in South Africa and elsewhere despite what Unesco[3] and other institutions have done to demonstrate its irrational nature. It takes a long time to uproot prejudice. Racism pervades and

2. Thomas Babington Macaulay, Minutes of 2 February, 1835 on Education for India, widely reprinted, most recently in P. D. Curtin, 1971, pp. 182ff.

3. Cf. chapter 11.

permeates school textbooks, biases radio and television programmes and films, and influences the not altogether conscious mental attitudes occasionally transmitted by religious education and even more frequently by ignorance and obscurantism. In this battle, the scientific teaching of the history of peoples is a weapon of overriding strategic importance. Western pseudo-scientific theories of race in the nineteenth century assigned positions on a scale of ability to physical differences, and as the most obvious physical difference was skin colour, they put Africans at the bottom of the scale automatically because they seemed to be most different from themselves. They went on to claim that African history had no importance or value, since Africans could not have produced a true civilization, and any trait worthy of admiration must have been borrowed from their neighbours. Africans were thus made objects of history, never its subjects, since they were held to be capable of receiving foreign influences without contributing anything to the world at large.

Pseudo-scientific racism reached its maximum influence long ago, in the first decade of this century, dwindling among social and physical scientists after the 1920s and virtually disappearing from respectable scientific circles after 1945. But the heritage of pseudo-scientific racism lived on. It was supported at the level of folk knowledge by a rise in urban racial tensions, as migrants of African or Asian descent appeared in greater numbers in western cities – and signs of popular prejudices are still apparent. It was supported by the fact that people remembered their school learning, and those educated in the 1910s, when pseudo-scientific racism was the received doctrine of the biological sciences, only reached the normal age of retirement in the 1960s. A far more insidious survival was the fact that conclusions based on racist evidence could live on after the supporting evidence had died. The proposition that 'Africa had no significant history because Africans are racially inferior' became untenable, but intellectuals in the West still remembered vaguely that 'Africa has no history', even though they may have forgotten why.

In this, as in other attitudes, the heritage of racism reinforced a continuing cultural chauvinism which tended to regard western civilization as the only true civilization. In the late 1960s, the BBC produced a long television series entitled simply 'Civilization' and concerned exclusively with the cultural heritage of western Europe. Some other societies were sometimes credited as civilized, but the common distinction between civilized and uncivilized at the middle of this century was the possession of literacy. This placed African societies that had been mostly non-literate in the precolonial period in the primitive category. But most of Africa was, in fact, literate in the sense that a class of scribes knew how to read and write though not, of course, in the sense of mass literacy, which was a post-industrial phenomenon everywhere. Ethiopia has its ancient writing in Ge'ez. All of Islamic Africa used the Arabic script from the north coast, the Sahara, the northern fringe of the Sudan from Senegal to the Red Sea, and the coastal cities down the east coast to the Mozambique Channel. Even before the colonial period, Arabic had penetrated the tropical forest with the Dyula traders, while Portuguese, English or French were used in written form as the normal language of commerce along the western coasts. Cultural chauvinism plus ignorance nevertheless led western authorities to draw the line between literacy and non-literacy at the edge of the desert, contributing further to the unfortunate tendency to separate North African history from that of the rest of the continent.

But the exclusion of the 'uncivilized' from the realm of history was only one part of a much larger aspect of the western historical tradition. The western masses were also excluded, not, perhaps, through overt class prejudice but because of history's didactic character, where the praise of famous men held out models for emulation. It was hardly chance that the models were usually the rich and powerful, and that history became the account of events within a narrow elite. It played down or left out altogether patterns of behaviour that affected the mass of society. Intellectual history was not the history of what people thought; it was the history of great ideas. Economic history was not the history of the economy or of economic behaviour; it was the history of important government economic policies, private firms and innovations in economic life. If European historians were fundamentally uninterested in a large part of their own society, they were not likely to be much interested in other societies or other cultures.

At this point, the two revolutionary tendencies in recent historical studies ran closely parallel; Eurocentric history and elitist history drew on the same roots. But a working alliance of those seeking a broader coverage of western society and those seeking a broader sweep of historical study beyond the West was slow to emerge. At first, each group moved forward on its own front. Historians of Africa were mainly concerned to beat back the assertion that Africa had no history or no history worth knowing. In the first instance, it was easiest to take the argument on the opponents' terms. If opponents claimed Africa had no history, African specialists could point to kingdoms and large empires that did indeed have a political history that read like early aspects of European history. The bias towards a feeling of superiority of the western public (and the western-trained African public) could be used as a lever to prove that African history was important after all. But this was a weak argument, because it concerned only those aspects of the African past that resemble the western past, without really meeting the problems of cross-cultural misunderstanding. In the early stages of recovering African history, few historians recognized that empires are often cruel and unpleasant institutions and are not necessarily a sign of political progress. Few were ready to acknowledge that, for example, Africa's great achievement in law and politics was probably the stateless society, based on co-operation rather than coercion, not to mention the fact that the African states had been so organized as to preserve genuine local autonomy.

This tendency to accept some aspects of the old historiography as a first stage in decolonizing African history had its most serious effect in the study of the colonial period, where an established 'colonial' history already existed, tending to emphasize European activities and leave out the African factor. At its worst, it showed Africans as barbarians whose will and judgement were weak or ill-directed. Therefore, it implied, superior beings from Europe came in and did what the Africans could not have done for themselves. Even at its best, colonial history allowed Africans only secondary roles on the historical stage.

The first effort to correct this view was simply to change the value judgements, leaving the roles unchanged. Explorers, colonial governors and military officers became cruel exploiters, not heroes in the march of civilization. The Africans became innocent victims, but they were still kept in passive roles. A handful of Europeans were still depicted as the main force making African history what it was. (Europeans sometimes did play crucial roles in the history of the colonial period, but every later revision based on new research at a local level shows the European role to have been much less important than it appeared in the colonial history published before 1960 or so.)

A second step in decolonizing the history of the colonial period came with the rise of nationalist movements demanding independence. Here were African figures playing a role in history, and it was appropriate to give due weight to that role. Political scientists writing at the time of the independence movements were among the first to enter this field.[4] A little later, mainly in the 1960s, scholars began to push back through time to find the roots of resistance and protest movements in the early colonial period, or earlier still in primary resistance to European rule.[5] These accounts of resistance and protest movements were an important corrective, but were still less than a balanced view of African history.

The ultimate decolonization of African history in the colonial period will have to come from a merger of the anti-Eurocentric revolt and the anti-elitist revolt. The behavioural revolution has already begun to influence the historiography of Africa, but that influence is still recent and limited and much of the research is still unpublished. Some historians have adopted an interdisciplinary approach, seeking to use the contribution of other social sciences such as the history of agriculture or the history of urbanization. Others are beginning to look at single, small regions hoping to use microcosmic studies to illuminate larger and still more complex patterns of

4. See, for example, T. Hodgkin, 1956; D. Apter, 1955; J. S. Coleman, 1958; C. A. Julien, 1952.

5. See, for example, G. Shepperson and T. Price, 1958; T. O. Ranger, 1967; J. Iliffe, 1969; R. I. Rotberg and A. A. Mazrui, 1970; Y. Person, 1968–70.

social or economic change.[6] Research is beginning to push vigorously at some of the special problems of economic and religious history, but the true decolonization of African history in these fields has only just begun.

One important step in this direction is the gradual development of analytical history that is also field history, that is, a product of oral interviews and on-the-spot-investigation, not simply immersion in archives. Independence from archival sources is proving to be as important for the colonial period as it is for the precolonial, where archival sources are comparatively rare. The problem with 'colonial' history has been, all along, that those who created the archives and left the records were foreigners. These records necessarily incorporate their biases and attitudes towards themselves, towards those they governed and towards the roles expected of each. This is just as true of government records in Europe or North America, where the bias is simply pro-government. In the colonial world it can lead to disastrous results, especially if the historian neglects to bring in another point of view through oral interviews with living people who experienced colonial rule.

Historians of Africa have been pioneers in the use of oral traditions not so much for the colonial period as for the precolonial, and this work was mostly done in two clusters. Between about 1890 and 1914, a generation of scholar-administrators in the service of colonial governments began the task of recording oral traditions of historical importance. The second cluster occurred in the past fifteen years. The decade of the 1950s ended with G. P. Murdock's dictum of 1959 that 'indigenous oral traditions are completely undependable'.[7] The decade of the 1960s opened with the publication of Jan Vansina's *Oral Tradition; a Study in Historical Methodology*, showing the critical controls that were necessary if oral traditions were to become a dependable source. The recent historical work based on oral tradition, often used in conjunction with other sources, has been an impressive achievement.[8]

The Dakar Seminar organized in 1961 by the International African Institute on the theme of the historian in tropical Africa, and the one held in Dar-es-Salaam in 1965 on a new view of African history, vigorously emphasized the new approaches required, stressing in particular the unique role of oral tradition as a source of African history and all the benefits to be reaped by the historian from linguistics and archaeology informed by oral tradition.

Historians of Africa have already influenced the other social sciences through their work on the precolonial period. This influence made itself felt at several levels. Its most general impact was to force a recognition that

6. See P. Hill, 1963.

7. G. P. Murdock, 1959, p. 43.

8. See, for example, J. Vansina, 1973; R. K. Kent, 1970; D. W. Cohen, 1972; the work of E. J. Alagoa, partly summarized in Alagoa, 1971; A. D. Roberts (ed.), 1968c; D. T. Niane, 1960b.

traditional Africa had not been static. Economists, political scientists and sociologists all have a tendency to discuss modernization by reference to a 'before' and 'after' model, where 'before' was traditional society taken to be virtually changeless and the 'after' was the process of modernization where dynamic change enters the picture. Historians, as students of change, looked for the change that takes place constantly in human societies, and their research of recent decades has shown that African precolonial institutions, social customs, patterns of life, religions and economies were all changing as rapidly as they changed in other societies between the agricultural and industrial revolutions. The rate was not as rapid as it was to become in the post-industrial age, which now affects industrialized Africa, but the assumption of a static 'traditional' past was no longer acceptable.

The problems created by using a static, traditional base or point of departure were most serious for anthropologists. Since the 1920s most anthropologists in the English-speaking world have worked with a model of society which emphasized the way in which each part of the total culture functioned to maintain the whole as a working entity. They recognized that the African societies they were investigating had changed a great deal since the beginning of colonial rule, but they took that fact as an unfortunate aberration in the data. As they saw it, the picture had to be adjusted by focusing on a single temporal plane set somewhere in the not-very-distant past before the European conquest. They assumed that the nature of this traditional society could be discovered by taking present, observed data and subtracting everything that seemed to be an external influence. The result was what they called the anthropological present.

This functionalist approach owed most to Bronislaw Malinowski who dominated British anthropology in the 1920s and 1930s. It went a long way towards understanding how simple societies work, and the functionalists made other important advances by their insistence on prolonged and careful field investigation through participant observation, not simply questioning informants. But it also had some unfortunate corollaries. It led anthropologists to seek out simple societies and isolated cultures. This very selectivity distorted western knowledge of African culture by leaving great gaps in the accounts of large or complex African societies, thus adding to the myth of a primitive Africa.

The effort to abstract the anthropological present from the real present also furthered the assumption that change in Africa must come from an outside influence, since their assumptions made African societies appear changeless till the Europeans arrived. The anthropologists' effort to stabilize the model society in order to describe its functional operations led many to forget that the society they treated as static for analytical purposes was not really static. Most serious of all, the static assumption distracted them from asking how or why the society under scrutiny had changed, which might have produced quite a different picture.

Functionalism would no doubt have run its course in any case, without the influence of history. It was being modified by the acculturation studies of the 1940s and 1950s, while Claude Lévi-Strauss and his followers were moving off in quite a different direction in the postwar decades. Nevertheless, in political anthropology and some aspects of social anthropology the work of precolonial historians helped call attention to the dynamics of change and helped set anthropology on a new path.

The study of African religions and religious organizations also changed through the influence of recent historical research. The earlier students of African religion tended either to be anthropologists in search of a static body of belief and practice, or else missionaries who also accepted the concept of an anthropological present in studying religions they hoped to supplant. They recognized that Islam was dynamic enough, since it had spread even more rapidly than Christianity had during the colonial period; but the most important studies of Islam in North Africa and West Africa were sponsored by the French colonial government as a check to possible dissidence. These studies tended to centre on religious leaders and organizations, not on the process of change within the religion. In recent decades, though, the study of change in African religions was renewed from several sources, not from historians alone. Missionologists were concerned with the development of new African religions with a partly Christian basis, and with the independent churches that split off from the European missions. Anthropologists interested in culture change took up similar studies, and historians have joined in strongly, drawn at first by their concern with the role of religion in colonial rebellion and protest movements. For the precolonial period, they have also come to recognize the obvious and enormous importance of religious reform in the Islamic world as a whole. The result has been an increased awareness that non-Christian, non-Muslim religions were also changing, though social scientists in varying disciplines are only now beginning to study these patterns of change as systematically as they deserve. Another point worth noting is the new interest in the indigenous animist religions and in the associations and societies, sometimes secret, which have often played a decisive role in the development of the African peoples.

While social scientists of many disciplines seem to be able to work comfortably together on African religions, with a broad and mutual interchange of methods and concepts, the study of African economies is sharply divided. Economic historians, like the historians of religion, have shown in recent years that African economies were changing continuously and that economic change was as much a response to internal stimuli as it was to overseas influences. Economists, however, and especially development economists, still go about their business without taking into account the economic culture they are trying to manipulate. They tend not only to ignore the process of change already taking place but also to ignore the static models of the economic anthropologists.

It suited the purposes of development theory, for example, to assume that

Africa was largely made up of subsistence economies where each family unit produced nearly all the goods and services it consumed. This view was especially publicized by Hla Myint in the mid-1960s with the vent-for-surplus theory of economic development based on the liberation of underemployed resources and factors of production.[9] In fact, no community in precolonial Africa was self-sufficient in the sense of having no trade at all, and many African societies had complex patterns of specialized production and export to their neighbours. Many pastoral people along the fringes of the Sahara earned half or more of their annual calorie intake by exchange of animal products for cereals. Many other people regularly produced and sold an agricultural surplus so as to be able to pay for specialized products that came from long-distance trade such as salt, cattle, shea butter, kola nuts or dates. The error underlying the static picture of African economies was, of course, the familiar myth of primitive Africa, reinforced by the anthropologists' tendency to seek out the simplest communities and by their former tendency to suppress time-depth in their data.

Those economists and economic anthropologists who have studied African economies on the spot have, of course, recognized the importance of trade in precolonial Africa, and a few recognized that African economies had been changing quite rapidly before foreigners appeared in force. One group, however, have moved away from the main line of economic thought by emphasizing the differences rather than the similarities of economic cultures. This group – sometimes called substantivists, because of their insistence on studying the substantive nature of production and consumption, trying to relate the way man meets his material needs to the broad patterns of a particular society and not to formal theory – have tended to claim that economic theory is not applicable to their field of research.[10] The result is a broad gap between development economists, who work with macro-economic theory and pay little attention to present economic facts, and the substantivists who avoid cross-cultural theory and stress micro-economic descriptions.

So far, economic historians have not filled the gap, nor have they influenced economic thought about Africa to the same extent that historians have influenced anthropology or religious studies. African history has made great strides in recent years, especially in pioneering some new methods and in filling a large historical gap that had hardly been explored. In the process, however, it has sometimes fallen behind other changes that have taken place in the historiography of other societies. It has not responded as rapidly as some fields of study to the challenge of the behavioural revolution, nor has it kept up with the new and exciting kinds of work that can be done in quantitative history, either in political history or in historical econometrics.

9. H. Myint, 1964.
10. For a convenient summary of the position see George Dalton (ed.), 1968.

Alongside the growth of research about the African past, the influence of the new African history depended on a corps of professional historians principally concerned with African history in their teaching and writing. One reason why African history has lagged behind in the West, even behind the historiography of Asia or Latin America, was the fact that it was mainly the work of non-professional historians – men who did something else for a living, had no established place in the university world, and therefore had little opportunity to influence the historical profession in any western country. Some research on Africa was carried out in research institutes in Scandinavia and in central and eastern Europe even before the Second World War, but that research was almost always marginal to the overall pattern of higher education. It did not lead, therefore, to the training of historians. The only exceptions were in Egyptology and certain aspects of North African history in the Roman period. Otherwise, few of the pre-1950 historians of Africa were professional historians. Some were colonial administrators, some were missionaries. Others were African clerics or clergymen who wrote in one of the international languages – like Carl Christian Reindorf of the Gold Coast, Samuel Johnson for the Yoruba, or Shaykh Musa Kamara of Senegal, whose *Zuhur ul-Basatin fi Ta'rīkh is-Sawadin* is not yet published in its entirety and has only recently begun to be used by other historians.[11] Some anthropologists also dealt with historical themes, but before 1950 no university in Africa offered a concerted programme of specialization in African history at the postgraduate level. In 1950, no professional historian anywhere was exclusively concerned with writing and teaching about African history. Twenty years later, about 500 professional historians with a doctorate or equivalent qualification were principally engaged on African history.

The speed in this change was surprising but explicable enough in retrospect. In Africa, in Europe and in North America – for different reasons on each continent – the political, intellectual and university setting was peculiarly favourable to the emergence of a professional corps of African historians. In Africa the need was obvious from the late 1940s onwards, when a rapid movement towards independence was predictable, at least for most of North and West Africa. By the 1950s new universities were founded, and with them came a demand for a new kind of African history from an African perspective, first at the university level and then percolating down through the teacher training colleges to the schools. Among the pioneers in this broad effort at re-education were K. Onwuka Dike, the first of a new generation of African historians to pass through the normal professional training, in this case at the University of London. Expatriate historians also contributed, like J. D. Fage at the University of Ghana (then the Gold Coast), J. D. Hargreaves at Fourah Bay in Sierra Leone, Christopher Wrigley and Cyril Ehrlich at Makerere College in Uganda.

11. S. Johnson, 1921; C. C. Reindorf, 1889; C. M. Kamara, 1970.

The equivalent shift in francophone Africa came more gradually. In the ex-French territories, the universities continued as a part of the French university system until well after independence, which meant that they kept the French historical curriculum as well. Pioneers nevertheless began working quietly towards an African history. Here, notable contributions came from Amadou-Mahktar M'Bow in Senegal, Joseph Ki-Zerbo in Upper Volta, and Père Engelbert Mveng in Cameroon. Expatriate historians in francophone Africa, who were later to make a major contribution in the universities, were already carrying out research by the early 1950s. Jan Vansina, who later helped to introduce African history at Lovanium University in Zaïre, was already at work at Belgian government research institutes in the Congo and Rwanda. Raymond Mauny, who was later to be a professor of African history at the Sorbonne, was doing research in French West Africa from a base at IFAN in Dakar. Yves Person, still a colonial official, had begun work on the research that was to lead to his *Samori* in 1968 and to his important role in the introduction of African history at the Universities of Abidjan and Dakar. *Présence Africaine,* through its journal and through its two major Congresses of Black Writers and Artists held in Paris and Rome in 1956 and 1959, gave a vigorous impetus to this process.

But all of this had to do with the introduction of African historical studies in Africa. The important step for African history's impact on world history was the development of African historical studies on other continents, a process that began nearly simultaneously with university-based African history in Africa itself. By the early 1950s Roland Oliver had begun teaching African history at the School of Oriental and African Studies at the University of London. In the USSR, D. A. Olderogge and his colleagues at the Ethnographic Institute in Leningrad began a systematic research programme that was to lead in time to the publication of all known documentation for sub-Saharan Africa dating from 1500 or earlier in the original language, with translation and annotation in Russian.[12] In the same decade, the first chair of African history was created at the Sorbonne, where it soon became two, one occupied by ex-Governor Hubert Deschamps and the other by Raymond Mauny. Meanwhile Henri Brunschwig began directing research on African history at the Ecole Pratique des Hautes Etudes, while Robert Cornevin published the first edition of his survey of African history, many times revised and enlarged since then.

Progress was not quite so rapid beyond Europe and Africa, and even in Europe, African history was first admitted into university curricula in those countries that had had colonies in Africa. One might have expected a concern about African history in the Americas where a large part of the population was of African descent, but interest was slight in Brazil and the Caribbean, even though African cultural survivals were strongest there.

12. L. Kubbel and V. Matveiev (in Russian), 1960 and 1965.

Some Haitian intellectuals showed an interest in local African-derived folk culture from the time of Dr Price-Mars's early work in the 1920s, and the influence of cultural Afro-Cubanism was strong with Cuban literary figures like Nicolas Guillen; but there, as in Brazil, the interest in Afro-American culture did not lead on to an interest in Africa, much less in African history. In the British West Indies, decolonization, including the decolonization of West Indian history, had a higher priority, and political pan-Africanism among West Indian intellectuals rarely had historical overtones, even in the 1960s.

Interest was even slighter in the United States before the 1960s – and what interest existed was concentrated on North Africa. A recent compilation listing North American doctoral theses on African history shows seventy-four completed up to and including the year 1960 – quite an amazing total on the face of it, but the total is deceptive. Most were on North Africa, and almost all were done by historians whose professional concentration was on classical history or archaeology, on the history of North Africa and the Middle East, or on European overseas colonization generally. The fact that their doctoral research happened to touch on Africa was almost a matter of chance. Only a few of those who wrote on colonial history became Africa specialists in a broader sense. One of the pioneers was Harry R. Rudin at Yale, who began publishing on German colonial history in Africa during the 1930s and shifted to a broader concern for Africa in the 1950s. Afro-Americans were still more important as a group. W. E. B. Dubois became interested in Africa early in his career, though he had no opportunity to pursue the interest actively until his retirement and emigration to Ghana in 1961. Long before, in 1916, Carter G. Woodson had founded the *Journal of Negro History*. It was more Afro-American than African in focus, but it included African history in its official scope and published occasional articles on the African past. Another advocate of African history was William Leo Hansberry of Howard University, who waged a lonely campaign for the inclusion of African history in the teaching programme of American universities, especially in the then-segregated, predominantly black colleges in the southern states.

To varying degrees, then, a base for the future development of African history outside Africa already existed before 1960. The achievement of independence in North Africa and tropical Africa during a few years scattered on either side of that date, gave Africa a new burst of publicity overseas, aroused popular interest, and some of that interest was directed to the African past – not just to its present and future.

The development of African history over the years since 1960 was disappointing in some places and surprising in others. In North Africa, for example, initial interest was limited to the history of a particular country, at most that of North Africa. In spite of a political emphasis on African unity, North African universities and scholars moved only slightly towards a more continental approach to the study of their own past. The Maghrib belonged to the Mediterranean world, to the Muslim world, and to the francophone intellectual world that still centred in Paris. These three worlds were more than enough for the full attention of the educated public. Egyptian public spokesmen often made much of the fact that Egypt was African as well as Arab and Muslim, but Egyptian historical scholarship was far more parochial, even at a time when the Aswan Dam and the international archaeological teams working in Nubia directed attention up the Nile.

Historical scholarship in southern Africa was still more parochial. The political domination of the Republic of South Africa by overseas Europeans was unrelaxed, and African history was hardly noticed in the universities where history still meant the history of Europe and the history of the European minority in South Africa. *The Oxford History of South Africa* (1969–71) was an important move to broaden its scope so as to include the African majority, but one of the co-editors, Leonard Thompson, no longer practised the historian's craft in South Africa, and the other, Monica Wilson, was a historically-minded anthropologist. Historical studies in Zimbabwe (or Rhodesia) moved towards the inclusion of African history briefly in the early 1960s, but that move was reversed after the white majority's unilateral declaration of independence from Britain. Curiously enough, Zimbabwe has produced more African historical scholars *per capita* than South Africa has done, but most have been forced to pursue professional careers in exile.

The first home of African history on the African continent was tropical Africa, and it was there that the most significant development took place in the first decade of independence. African history was already a part of the curriculum in tropical universities, but the new problem was to readjust to an appropriate balance of local, regional, African and world history. It was a question, in short, of decolonizing the whole history curriculum, not merely adding an African component. The greatest change has been in anglophone Africa, where the rigidity of European standards relaxed more rapidly than they did in francophone countries. The teaching of English and imperial history gave way to new subjects. British imperial history has tended to drop out altogether, while British history merged with European history. Within European history as taught in Africa rethinking has tended to subordinate individual national histories to an emphasis on major themes like urbanization or the industrial revolution, viewed across national lines. Meanwhile African historians have also turned their attention to non-European history – to the history of the Islamic world to the north with special emphasis on its impact on Africa south of the Sahara, to the history of Latin America or south-east Asia which could be seen as a parallel to the African experience, to the history of Asia where the economic growth in Japan was an example from which Africa might learn. The impact of African history was thus to bring about a general reorientation to a view of the world and its past that will be truly Afrocentric – not exclusively concerned with Africa and Africans the way the old European tradition was exclusively concerned with Europeans, but nevertheless a *Weltanschauung* where Africa, not Europe was the point of departure.

This goal is still incompletely realized, even in the most advanced of the anglophone universities. It will inevitably take time as a new generation of innovating African historians are trained and move off in new directions of their own choosing. Francophone universities have lagged behind by about a decade; Abidjan, Dakar and Lubumbashi (as heir to Lovanium in the field of history) represent the oldest francophone universities, and their history staffs came to be largely African only in the early 1970s, a shift that had taken place in the oldest anglophone universities by the early 1960s. With African historians now in place in francophone universities, a similar readjustment of historical world view can be expected. Reformed history curricula were introduced in the secondary schools of the French-speaking countries as early as 1963, however. This was immediately followed by a reform of the university history courses within the framework of the programme of the CAMES (Conseil Africain et Malgache pour l'Enseignement Supérieur).

The impact of African history on the investigation and teaching of history in western Europe is tied with the former colonial relationship. This is one reason why France and England have been the leading European centres of African history. The teaching of African history has nevertheless made some progress elsewhere, especially in Czechoslovakia and Poland, and in the USSR African history is taught systematically at Patrice Lumumba University in Moscow, whose specific role is the education of students from Africa. Elsewhere, research by isolated scholars goes on in scattered university centres, more systematically at research institutes that follow the Germanic tradition of university organization. As a result Africanist research is a little isolated. This may well be part of the reason why African history has not infiltrated history in many European universities outside England and France.

The general tradition of historical studies is equally parochial in those countries, but they had a special responsibility in the first instance for the training of colonial civil servants. After about 1955, these men began to be repatriated, and several of them settled in a new career as historians of the countries they once administered. This was especially the case in France, where Professors Deschamps and Person are notable examples. For France and England alike, the creation and growth of the new African universities of the 1950s meant that employment opportunities existed in Africa. Young historians took up African themes in their training research, or else turned to African history once they found themselves teaching in Africa. Then, in the 1960s and 1970s, those expatriate historians have been gradually replaced by Africans and reabsorbed into the metropolitan educational establishment, often after a period of eight to ten years in Africa. Not all returned to teach African history, but the total numbers were significant – perhaps sixty to seventy historians taken into British universities from African universities from the mid-1960s to the mid-1970s, or about 8 to 10 per cent of history recruitment into British universities over that period. By 1974, three chairs in modern history (which traditionally has meant the history of modern Britain) were held by historians whose main research career has been devoted to Africa. It is still too early to see what impact this re-entry from Africa will have on British historical traditions generally, but it may well be significant.

In France the comparative numbers are somewhat smaller, and those returning from Africa are a smaller proportion of university recruitment, but a similar process has taken place. A new generation of historians began to turn its attention to Africa. In Paris, both in its several universities and in the inter-university Centre d'Etudes Africaines, a number of scholars in history, sociology and archaeology have served in African universities for varying periods of time and still retain close contact with them. It is much the same in Aix, Bordeaux and Lyon.

Meanwhile both British and French universities served as centres for training African historians who were to replace the expatriates.[13] This has tended to give institutions like the School of Oriental and African Studies (SOAS) in London or more scattered sections of the Sorbonne and the specialist graduate schools in Paris a special role. At SOAS, for example, 58 per cent of those who completed PhDs between 1963 and 1973 took up initial teaching posts in Africa; less than 20 per cent of the total were British and only 13 per cent of the total took up initial posts in British universities.[14] This diminished somewhat the direct impact on British education of SOAS, which has the largest staff of Africanist historians to be found in any university in the world. The indirect influence was nevertheless considerable. In addition to SOAS, the universities of Birmingham, Sussex and Edinburgh have created a special niche for African history within the courses offered, and at least eight others have a specialist in African history regularly teaching the subject at the undergraduate level.

This special level of development in Britain was, perhaps, predictable in the light of British colonial and neo-colonial interests in African university structures. The unpredictable development of the 1960s was the enormous growth of Africanist historical scholarship in North America. It was unpredictable in part because historians of the United States had a bad record for dealing fairly with the history of Afro-Americans in their own society. The large minority of African descent had also been there all along without provoking a notable interest in Africa, even from the majority of the Afro-Americans. And the burst of African historical studies came from Canada as well as the United States, even though Canada had neither the

13. I would like to thank Professor J. F. Ade Ajayi of the University of Ibadan, and Professors J. D. Fage and Roland Oliver for information on the impact of African history on history generally in Europe and Africa respectively. Any errors of fact or emphasis that may appear here are nevertheless my responsibility.

14. R. Oliver, 1973.

experience of ruling part of Africa, like Britain, or a large Afro-American minority, like the United States.

Before 1960, African history was hardly taught at all in North America. In 1959, shortly after the foundation of an African Studies Association, only twenty-one of its members resident in the United States or Canada identified themselves as historians. Of these, less than half were in university positions that called for a major commitment of their time to African history. The First International Congress of Africanists, held in Accra in 1962, was attended by some 800 persons in whose presence President Kwame Nkrumah, in an opening address, outlined the responsibilities of historical studies for the new Africa. Then came the explosion. By 1970, the number of North American specialists in African history or archaeology had risen to about 350. Some were historians originally trained in some other field, who moved over and began teaching or research on African history, but the great majority were young scholars who were just emerging from graduate school. North American graduate schools turned out more than 300 PhD degrees in African history between 1960 and 1972. Some were students from Africa who planned to return to Africa. A few were from Europe, but the great majority were North Americans in about the same proportion of Afro- to Euro-Americans as in the population at large, that is, about 10 per cent in the United States, much less in Canada.

The growth of African history in North America was pushed forward by two contrary tendencies in historical studies. From the Afro-American community came the strongly expressed belief that African history was the special possession of African peoples and their descendants on other continents in the same way that European national history has been the special possession of each European nation. The implicit difference between the purposes of African history for Africans and African history in the framework of world history came into the open. Difference, however, is not necessarily conflict. The two kinds of history are not mutually incompatible, though each will emphasize quite different aspects of the past.

As a result the parochial pattern of ethnocentric history was more seriously shaken in North America than it was elsewhere. In many schools, the old 'world' history that was really only a history of western civilization gave way in the 1960s to a new and more genuine attempt to examine history in world perspective, and in this effort Africa entered on equal terms with other major culture-areas like south Asia or east Asia. Many departments of history in North American universities began moving from the old division between American and European history to a threefold division, with the history of the Third World gaining equality as a third branch of historical studies.

These changes are still far from complete, but, taken alongside the spread of African history in Britain and France, and alongside the reorientation of the history curriculum in African universities, they mark a step along the road towards the full impact of African history on history as a whole.

Success in the longer run will depend on the combined efforts of African scholars writing the history of their own societies, on those of non-African historians who interpret African history to other societies, and on a broadening of international social science to the point where scholars in other disciplines will have to consider African data as a relevant basis for any generalization about human society.

Sources and specific techniques used in African history: general outline

T. OBENGA

The general rules of historical criticism that make history a documentary technique, and the historical approach that requires us to study human society in its journey down the ages, are the essential stock-in-trade of any historian in any country. Neglect of this fact meant that the peoples of Africa were for a long time outside the field of interest of western historians, for whom Europe was the whole of history. What lay behind this attitude, though it did not show itself openly, was a persistent belief that, in the absence of written texts and archaeological monuments, Africa did not really have any history.

Hence the first task of a historian is obviously the establishing of sources, which is itself linked to the basic theoretical problem of appraising the techniques of historical research.

A number of research workers, impelled by a great new urge to learn and understand following the advent of the postcolonial era, have laid the foundations of African history once and for all, though the methodology appropriate to it is still being worked out. Huge areas of documentation have come to light and have enabled research workers to ask themselves new questions. As more of African history becomes known, it becomes more varied and develops in new and unexpected directions. During the past fifteen years or so there has been a revolution in the tools of research, and it is now readily accepted that some of these are particularly useful for African history: they include geology, palaeontology, prehistory, archaeology, palaeobotany, palynology, the use of radioactive isotopes to yield absolute chronological data, physical geography and human problems, ethnological and sociological observation and analysis, oral tradition, historical and comparative linguistics, European, Arabic, Indian and Chinese written texts, and economic and demographic documents which lend themselves to computerization.

The sources of African history are still remarkably flexible in scope and therefore new types of intellectual co-operation, which unexpectedly bring together sectors hitherto regarded as distinct, should always be thoroughly explored. The use of a combination of sources emerges as a qualitative innovation. Only the simultaneous application of various categories of sources can ensure any real temporal depth, for an isolated fact tends to remain on the fringe of the general trend. The overall integration of methods and the combination of sources represent an effective contribution by Africa both to knowledge and to contemporary historiographical awareness.

A historian's curiosity ought to follow several trajectories at once. His work is not limited to the establishing of sources: he must use a sound interdisciplinary culture to make himself master of man's past. For history is modern man's view of the whole of time past.

Most of the sources and techniques specific to African history which are drawn from mathematics, atomic physics, geology, the natural sciences and the human and social sciences are amply described in the present volume. I shall therefore concentrate here on aspects and problems not treated elsewhere.

The most decisive methodological advance of recent years is unquestionably the application of modern physics to the study of man's past. The use of radioactive isotopes gives us a chronological gauge to the earliest days of *Homo sapiens* in the case of the carbon-14 method, and to periods more than a million years ago in the case of the potassium-argon method.

These absolute dating methods now considerably shorten discussion on matters of human palaeontology and prehistory.[1] The earliest hominids in Africa have been dated by the potassium-argon method to 5 300 000 before our era, this being the age of a fragment of hominid lower jaw with an intact molar found in 1971 by Professor Bryan Patterson at Lothagam, in Kenya. Again, the hominid teeth discovered in the Villafrancian layers of the Omo valley in northern Ethiopia, by French expeditions under Camille Arambourg and Yves Coppens and P. Clark-Howell's American expedition, are between 2 and 4 million years old. The Zinjanthropus level (Level I) of the famous site at Olduvai Gorge, in Tanzania, has been dated, also by the potassium-argon method, as 1·75 million years old.

Thus thanks to the potassium-argon isotope the birth of East African man (the oldest of all according to the present state of our knowledge) is actually the birth of man as a whole – to the extent that monophyletism is more and more generally accepted in general palaeontology. The African fossil remains now known thus provide the essential ingredients for an answer to the key question of the origins of man, which has been asked in so many different ways throughout the history of mankind: 'Where was man born, and when?'

The old stereotyped ideas which relegated Africa to the fringes of the realm of history have now been completely transformed. Facts brought to light by the use of a variety of sources and methods – in the above-mentioned examples, human palaeontology and nuclear physics – have

1. J. B. Birdsell, 1972, p. 299.

brought out clearly the great span of African history, the origin of which coincides with that of *Homo faber* himself.

Information from other sources, for instance the earth sciences, also throws some light on African history independently of all written documents. The way of life and history of the peoples of the Lake Chad Basin, for example, would be hard to understand were it not for the contribution made by physical geography. It is worth stressing the methodological value of this approach.

Human and other living beings are not distributed at random in the Chad Basin, which may be described in altitude terms broadly as follows: a central accumulation plain at a height of between 180 and 300 metres is surrounded by a somewhat irregular ring of old weathered plateaux, their peneplanation sometimes masked by recent volcanic activity; and linking these plateaux, which are on average 900 metres high, to the lower accumulation areas are (usually steep) slopes affected by active erosion in a humid climate. The highest population density – 6 to 15 inhabitants per square kilometre – is found in the area of very light detrital soils which receives rain. Density is also fairly high in the Sahelian-climate alluvial areas irrigated by seepage or flooding from Lake Chad. On the high plateaux of Darfur and Adamawa to the east and south, where the tributaries of the lake rise, the population is only 1 per square kilometre; and in the north, already Saharan in character, it is lower still. The population pattern of the depression is thus closely linked to and conditioned by questions of physical geography and geomorphology.

As a result, civilization has retreated before the desert, falling back to the area where millet and sorghum can be grown without irrigation, i.e. roughly to the latitude of the neo-Chad (vegetables, tobacco and durum wheat are grown under irrigation on the banks of the Logone and Chari rivers). Farmers, herdsmen and fishermen live in the southern area, where lake and river water irrigates the soil, keeps the pastures green and regularly attracts crowds of fishermen. In the northern desert area, on the other hand, erosion makes the soil unstable and plant life precarious: it is characteristically a thorny xerophilic bush or scrub.

But these geomorphological factors have also conditioned other human activities. For example, invasion has often driven native farmers from the salubrious plateaux and fertile plains to steep mountainous areas unsuitable for stock-breeding. In this way the Fulani drove the Bumi and the Duru back to the least fertile parts of Adamawa, and the Kiroi of north Cameroon back to the granite scree of the Mandara massif. It is admittedly harder and less rewarding for these peoples to work the sloping, previously submerged soils, but their primitive tools give more satisfactory results there. Seasonal or permanent marshland in the alluvial area gives rise to swarms of mosquitoes (*Anopheles gambiae*). Tsetse flies (*Glossina palpalis*) also breed in the low-growing hygrophile masses of *Salix* and *Mimosa asperata* which cover recent silt on the banks of the Logone and Chari rivers. The resulting malaria and sleeping sickness make these into very uninviting areas.

In short, to arrive at a clear understanding of human life in the Chad Basin, which in the past underwent several Quaternary fluctuations due to changes of climate, the historian must investigate a whole range of specific sources and techniques from the earth and life sciences. The present distribution of peoples, their past migrations, their agricultural and pastoral activity and so on are all closely conditioned by the environment.

The Chad Basin is but one example among many. When intellectual inquiry has freed itself from restrictive preconceptions, equally enlightening results have been achieved. Among the Nyangatom or Bumi of the Omo valley, who are related to the Turkana of north-west Kenya, there is a striking difference in the blood of the men tested (300 in 1971 and 359 in 1972). The difference, which is immunological, is observable not between the sexes but between villages (which consist of from 20 to 300 inhabitants). These villages, where the people live by stock-raising, agriculture, food-gathering, hunting and fishing, are organized in accordance with a strict clan system, complicated by division into territorial sections. But in this society there is no chief higher than the eldest son. Thus the differences that arise out of the territorial social organization of the Nyangatom are reflected in serology: a map of serum reactions to arboviral antigens is an exact replica of the territorial distribution of the peoples tested.[2]

This example of active co-operation between the parasitologist and the anthropologist is instructive for the historian, who can put it to very good use. It is important to him to know that such documentary evidence exists and may prove relevant in investigating the sexual behaviour and demographic growth of the Nyangatom.

The basic heuristic and epistemological problem remains the same: the historian of Africa simply must be alert to every kind of analytical procedure, so that his own work may be based on a wide range of knowledge and so be cohesive.

This open-mindedness is particularly important in the case of the early periods, for which there are neither written sources nor even direct oral traditions. We know, for example, that the staple crop of Neolithic man was wheat, barley and millet in Asia, Europe and Africa and maize in America, but we have no way of ascertaining the original agricultural systems of this very remote period. We cannot tell the difference between a population of sedentary predators and a population of farmers; nor do we know how or when the domestication of plants spread in the different continents. Oral tradition and mythology are not much help here. Only archaeology and palaeobotany can give an adequate answer to these important questions about that priceless Neolithic heritage, agriculture.

In a favourable, non-acid soil, the outer skin of the pollen grain is very

2. Cf. the work of François Rodhain, entomologist, and Serge Tornay, ethnologist, both members of the French expedition to Omo led by M. Yves Coppens (1971, 1972).

resistant to time. Palaeopalynology proceeds by microscopic analysis of these botanical remains. Fossil pollens may be recovered by slowly macerating a soil sample in hot hydrofluoric or hydrochloric acid, which eliminates the silica and limestone without harming the pollen, and then the organic humus (potash). The residue is then centrifuged, stained and mounted in gelatine. All that remains is to identify and count the pollen grains, thus arriving at a percentage table which gives the pollen profile of the sediment in question. By this means we may establish whether agriculture was practised on the site, follow the development of the landscape, diagnose the climate through variations in the vegetation, and detect any possible effects of man and animals on the plant life.

Such studies have enabled us to follow the domestication of food plants in Africa; this was focused on several centres, and spread over wide areas. The main plants then cultivated were sorghum (originally domesticated in the savannah that stretches from Lake Chad to the border between Ethiopia and the Sudan), millet, African rice, *Voandzeia* (forage peas), oil-palms (domesticated on the edge of the forests), finger-millet, gumbo and the African yam.

American food plants were introduced comparatively recently, as is attested by specific written sources. Manioc, for example, now the staple food of several peoples in Central Africa, did not reach the Kingdom of Kongo via the Atlantic coast until after the sixteenth century. Among food plants grown on the plateau surrounding Mbanza Kongo, capital of the kingdom, Pigafetta and Lopez's *Relatione* (1591) mentions only *luko*, i.e. the eleusine *Corocana,* whose 'seed comes from the banks of the Nile, in the area where it fills the second lake';[3] *masa ma Kongo,* a grass which is a species of sorghum; maize, called *masango* or *masa ma Mputu,* 'which is the least valued and is fed to the pigs';[4] rice or *loso,* which 'is not much valued either';[5] the banana palm or *dikondo*; and the oil-palm, *ba*.

Less well known is the fact that African food plants also spread abroad. There is no doubt that certain African species spread to India, for example, and to other parts of Asia, though they did so comparatively late. Both kinds of millet (millet and finger-millet) are attested by archaeological evidence in India about 1000 years before our era. Sorghum was only known there later, for there is no word for it in Sanskrit.

All this archaeological and palaeobotanical data helps the historian, in the absence of any written sources or oral tradition, to elucidate the stages by which our Neolithic ancestors moved from a food-gathering economy to a producing one. Moreover the facts themselves bear witness better than any diffusionist theories to the currents of relationship between Neolithic civilizations.

3. F. Pigafetta and D. Lopez, Rome, p. 40: 'Venendo sementa dal fiume Nilo, in quella parte dove empie il secondo lago.'

4. ibid.: 'Ed il maiz che è il più vile de tutti, che dassi à porci.'

5. ibid.: 'il riso è in poco prezzo.'

Remains of dogs, pigs, sheep and goats suggest that the domestication of animals began, in the case of the Neolithic centres of the Middle East, at about the same time as the cultivation of plants, that is, between 9000 and 8000 before our era. On the strength of this, a theoretical chronology for the domestication of the different groups of animals has been put forward. First came scavengers like the dog; then nomadic animals like the reindeer, goat and sheep; and then those for which a sedentary life is required, i.e. cattle and pigs. The last to be domesticated were probably draught animals such as the horse, donkey and llama. But this general chronology does not always apply to Africa.

The horse, which together with the ox and the ass has been a driving force in history down the ages, does not appear in Africa (to be precise, in Egypt) until towards the end of the Hyksos invasion, around 1600 before our era; this is shown by both textual and iconographic sources. About the thirteenth century before our era the horse was transmitted, for use in war, to the Libyans, and later, at the beginning of the first millennium, to the Nubians. Apart from the areas influenced by Roman civilization, the rest of Africa did not make extensive use of the horse until the Arab conquests of the middle ages. Two horses, saddled and bridled and flanked by two rams, were among the emblems of the King of Mali, according to the writer Ibn Battūta (1304–69).

The one-humped camel or dromedary was also no latecomer to African civilization. It appears in a reasonably recognizable form in a rock painting in the Chad Sahara dating from the third century before our era. In 525 before our era Cambyses' men introduced it into Egypt, where it thenceforward played an important part in communications between the Nile and the Red Sea. Only later did it reach the western Sahara: essentially a denizen of the desert, where it often takes the place of ox or ass, it seems to have been taken to the Maghrib by Roman troops of Syrian origin. The Berbers, resisting the *pax romana* and its land tenure arrangements, gained their freedom thanks to the camel, which enabled them to go and settle in the steppes and deserts beyond the *limes*. This resulted in the sedentary blacks of the oases being driven south or reduced to slavery.

All the above leads to the conclusion – in itself a distinct step forward in methodology – that a rich and varied mass of documentary material is to be obtained through the use of sources and techniques derived from the physical and biological sciences. The historian finds himself compelled to be bold in his investigations. All avenues are to be explored. In the new methodology the phrase 'auxiliary sciences' loses its meaning, unless the 'auxiliary sciences of history' are henceforth understood to mean techniques fundamental to the understanding of history which may come from any branch of science and which have not yet all been discovered. Technical investigations are henceforth part of a historian's job, and they shift history a long way in the direction of science.

History also benefits from the discoveries of the earth and life sciences.

However, the biggest contribution to its critical and research equipment comes, in the case of African history, from other human and social sciences, viz. Egyptology, linguistics, oral tradition, economics and political science.

It is worth dwelling a little on Egyptology, because it is a source that has so far not been used for the history of Africa.

Egyptology comprises historical archaeology and the deciphering of texts. In both cases a knowledge of Egyptian is an essential prerequisite. Egyptian, which was a living language for about 5000 years (if we include Coptic), occurs in three different scripts:

(1) Hieroglyphic writing, consisting of signs which fall into two main categories. First, there are ideograms or word-signs (e.g. the representation of a woven basket to denote the word 'basket', in which the main phonetic components are *nb*); and secondly, there are phonograms or sound-signs (e.g. the representation of a basket which only retains the phonetic value *nb*, this sign also serving to convey words other than *basket* which possess the same phonetic value, such as *nb*, 'lord' and *nb*, 'all'. Phonograms are divided into (a) triliterals, that is, signs containing three consonants, (b) biliterals, or signs containing two consonants, and (c) uniliterals, or signs containing only one vowel or one consonant: these constitute the Egyptian phonetic alphabet.

(2) Hieratic writing, a cursive form of hieroglyphics, which appeared in about the third dynasty (2778–2423 before our era). It always runs from right to left, and was written with a calamus or reed pen on sheets of papyrus, potsherds or stone. It had as long a life as hieroglyphics (the most recent hieroglyphic text dates from 394 of our era).

(3) Demotic writing, itself a simplification of hieratic. It made its appearance about the twenty-fifth dynasty (751–656 before our era), and disappeared from use in the fifth century. In terms simply of graphemes, a common origin is accepted for demotic Egyptian script and Nubian Meroitic writing (the latter having not yet been deciphered).

The Egyptian writing system raises interesting methodological questions. Through such a graphic convention, which has its own special character, any historian who learns to decipher a little can as it were capture the state of mind and intentions of men long dead, given that the physical act of writing always reflects a basically human value. To decipher is to converse, involving as it does a constant effort to be accurate and objective. Moreover the diversity, complexity and progressive simplification of the Egyptian graphic system are themselves part of history; and the history of deciphering is one of the essential sources of all historical accuracy. Thus with the Egyptian writing system Africa occupies an important place in general studies of writing as a system of signs and human intercommunication.[6]

The problem of the spread of Egyptian writing within black Africa enlarges still further the scope of the historian's methodological apparatus, and opens up entirely new perspectives in African historical research. The following few facts are relevant. *Gicandi* is an ideographical system formerly in use among the Kikuyu of Kenya and the pictograms of this graphic system show striking analogies with Egyptian pictograms. The structural resemblance between the Nsibidi pictograms of the Efik country (south-eastern Nigeria) and Egyptian pictograms was recognized and reported as early as 1912 by an English scholar, P. Amaury Talbot. Many Egyptian hieroglyphs still show a distinct structural affinity to the signs used in the Mende script in southern Sierra Leone, and the same is true of most of the signs used in the Loma script in northern Liberia. There is also an undoubted causal connection between Egyptian hieroglyphs and several of the signs used in the Vai script in the neighbourhood of Monrovia (Liberia). The writing of the Bamum of Cameroon, which also has more than two graphic systems, shows an equal number of striking analogies, admittedly external ones, with the hieroglyphs of the Nile valley. Just as in Egypt, Dogon, Bambara and Bozo hieroglyphs can be broken down into their components and analysed. But the most significant fact is that these signs from West Africa have the effect of making the things and people they denote aware of themselves; this is an idea typical of the transcendent power of writing, and is found in literal form in Egypt in the way certain texts on the after-life are written.

There is thus still a considerable possibility that we shall see the birth and development of an epigraphy and a palaeography hitherto completely unknown, concerned with the thorough study of black African writing systems and their inter-relationships. Historians will obviously stand to gain, for the history of writing and deciphering throws light on the history of the men who did the writing. The study of writing systems is in itself an invaluable source of history. But historians should always keep a proper sense of the time scale, for many of these writing systems are recent in date and do not throw light on early periods. What their abundance does indicate is the remarkable longevity of the impact of Egypt. Egyptian writing, which supposedly disappeared in 394 of our era, is seen to have had an unbroken series of revivals between the seventeenth and nineteenth centuries. The break between antiquity and Africa's recent past is thus an illusion born of our ignorance: in fact the two are linked by an underground stream.

Knowledge of Egyptian writing and ability to decipher the texts gives direct access to the language of the Pharaohs. It is always advisable for historians to go back as much as possible to the original texts: for translations, even the best of them, are seldom perfect. The historian who knows Egyptian can thus read for himself the many varied texts of ancient

6. E. Doblohfer, 1959.

Egypt: funerary stelae, inscriptions on monuments, administrative documents, hymns, philosophical works, medical and mathematical treatises, and literature (novels, tales and fables).

One series of texts shows clearly that the barrier supposed to have existed between Pharaonic Egypt and neighbouring regions of Africa in this remote period does not accord with the facts. An example to illustrate this is the letter which Nefer-Ka-Rê (Pepi II), a Pharaoh of the sixth dynasty, wrote in about 2370 before our era to Herkhuf, leader of a trading expedition to the remote regions of the south (the Land on the Edge of the World according to the text) probably the area of the African lakes. This far-flung expedition, the fourth of a series, brought a Pygmy back with it.

Another Egyptian text dating from the twentieth century before our era (the very beginning of the twelfth dynasty) gives precise and most interesting information about the life of sailors in those days, navigation in the Red Sea, and trade relations between the Nile valley and the East African coast. This text is *The Tale of the Castaway*.

Queen Hatshepsut, who occupied the throne of Egypt for twenty-one years (1504–1483 before our era), organized several trading expeditions, including one in the ninth year of her reign to the land of Punt on the Somali coast. The expedition is portrayed in the magnificent bas-reliefs at Deir al-Bahri in Upper Egypt.

This suggests a whole new avenue of research, which is bound to interest African historians. We are just beginning to see the importance of introducing ancient Egyptian as a subject in African universities. The latter, after all, have a great responsibility for promoting up-to-date work on Africa's cultural heritage over the whole of its range in both time and space.

As to the linguistic affiliations of ancient Egyptian, the following extract is taken from the final report of an important international symposium on 'The Peopling of Ancient Egypt and the Deciphering of the Meroitic Script' (Cairo, 28 January–3 February 1974): 'The Egyptian language could not be isolated from its African context and its origin could not be fully explained in terms of Semitic; it was thus quite normal to expect to find related languages in Africa' (Final Report, p. 29, para. 5).

In plain language, Pharaonic Egyptian is not a Semitic language, and it were best to abandon the descriptions 'hamito-semitic' or 'Afro-Asiatic' applied to it by certain authors who are often grounded neither in Semitic studies nor in Egyptology.

The fundamental problem that confronts us is to find appropriate techniques for comparing ancient Egyptian with contemporary black African languages, in order, so far as possible, to reconstruct, on the basis of morphological, lexicological and phonetic analogies and affinities, their common ancestors. An enormous task awaits the linguistics expert; and the historian also must be prepared for a radical change of viewpoint when a cultural macro-structure common to Pharaonic Egypt and the rest of black Africa is brought to light. Such a common factor is, properly speaking, a matter of guesswork and awaits formal proof. But here more than anywhere else the historian and the expert linguist must work together, for linguistics has become a historical source – particularly in Africa, where so many languages overlap.

It is mainly a matter of comparative and historical linguistics. The method adopted is comparative and inductive: for the object of the comparison is to reconstruct, i.e. to find the point of convergence of all the languages being compared. This point of convergence will be called the 'common predialectal language'. But we must proceed with great caution. Common Bantu, for example, reconstructed on the basis of suitable studies of the various Bantu languages found today, is neither an ancient language nor a real one fully restored. The expression 'common Bantu' or 'proto-Bantu' denotes only the system of correlations between the known Bantu languages, which supposedly go back to the time when these languages were almost identical. The same is true of, for example, Indo-European. In strictly realistic terms, linguistic archaeology on an extreme view is purely illusory, since no historical or even merely linguistic trace survives of the remote prehistoric period when the reconstructed common language was spoken.

The point of historical linguistics lies not so much in finding a common predialectal language as in appreciating the overall linguistic spread of different, apparently unrelated, languages. A language is seldom enclosed within a clearly defined space, but most commonly overflows its own area by making relationships with other languages of varying degrees of kinship: such relationships being sometimes imperceptible at first. The important underlying problem is obviously that of population movements. A common language does not necessarily go together with racial identity. But it does give relevant information about an essential, indeed the only real, unity, namely, the basic cultural unity of people united by a common language even though sometimes with very different origins and political systems. For example, the Niger–Congo family, if we accept such an entity, indicates that there are very ancient socio-cultural links between the West Atlantic peoples, the Mande, Gur and Kwa peoples, the peoples living between the Benue and the Congo (Zaïre), the Adamawa-Eastern peoples and the Bantu peoples of East, Central and southern Africa.

Historical linguistics is thus a valuable source for African history, as is oral tradition, though the latter was for long despised. But it sometimes happens that oral tradition is the only source immediately available. This is the case, for example, with the Mbochi of the Congo. It is only with the help of oral tradition that it has been possible to reconstruct the history in space and time (admittedly a comparatively short time) of their various chiefdoms. Oral tradition can also settle a point where written records are useless. The chroniclers (Delaporte, 1753, and Proyat, 1776) agree in recording that in the Kingdom of Loanga, in western Central Africa, the kings were buried in two separate cemeteries, one at Lubu and the other at Lwandjili. As to when and why such a distinction was made, the written records so far known are silent. Only the oral tradition of the present-day Vili gives the explanation for the separation. An extremely violent quarrel between the Maloango court and the people of Lwandjili made the king and princes of the day decide to change the burial place and hence, as the result of a conflict between the crown and a rich province of the kingdom, the cemetery at Lwandjili was abandoned in favour of the one at Lubu. In this case oral tradition comes plausibly to the rescue of written evidence. There are countless instances in Africa where it guides archaeological excavation, as well as simultaneously shedding light on written chronicles. The excavations carried out at the end of 1960 at Tegdaoust, a town in the Kingdom of Ghana (western Sudan), by Professors J. Devisse and D. and S. Robert, then of the University of Dakar, used simultaneously and in combination local traditions, medieval Arab chronicles and normal archaeological techniques. Thus a little-known period of African history (the seventh to thirteenth centuries) was restored to the archives. The credit goes of course mainly to archaeology, but also partly to local tradition and written records.

Such examples, which could be multiplied, show that in Africa more than anywhere else oral tradition is an integral part of the historian's basic material and greatly widens its scope. African history can no longer be written, as in the past, by excluding from historical investigation the voice of time represented by oral tradition.

The key points first of how oral tradition presents time itself and secondly of how it presents events in time have not yet been adequately investigated. The crucial question is how the griot presents history. African griots almost never use a chronological framework. They do not set out the sequence of human events with their breaks or accelerations in pace. What they say needs to be heard in perspective, and cannot be listened to in any other way. The point is that they are interested in man only as he is caught up in life, a possessor of values reacting in the world, timelessly. This is why the African griot tends not to synthesize the various moments of the story he is telling. He treats each moment in isolation, as something with its own meaning and having no precise relationship to other moments. The moments of the events reported are disconnected. The correct term for this is absolute history: and absolute history, which sets out stages of development in the round, without dates, is simply structural history. The temporal outcrops known elsewhere as cycles (the idea of a circle), periods (the idea of a space of time), eras (the idea of a pause, or a moment marked by some important event), ages (the idea of duration, the passage of time), series (the idea of a sequence or succession) and moments (the idea of immediacy, of circumstance, of time present) are virtually omitted from the griot's vocabulary. Admittedly he does not neglect either cosmic time (seasons, years, and so on) or man's past, since what is in the past is just what he does recount; but it is not easy for him to make a model of time. He gives at one go the whole fullness of a time.

Still in the realm of the human and social sciences, the contribution of sociologists and political theorists enables us to redefine the elements of cultural and historical knowledge. The notions of kingdom, nation, state, empire, democracy, feudalism, political party, and so on, while certainly appropriate elsewhere, are not always automatically applicable to Africa.

For example, let us consider what exactly is meant by the 'Kingdom' of Kongo. The people themselves use the expression *nsi a Kongo,* literally 'the country (*nsi*) of the Kongo'. We thus have an ethnic group (the Kongo), a region (*nsi*), and the ethnic group's consciousness of living in this region, which thus becomes the country (*nsi*) of the ethnic group in question. Borders and frontiers are extremely fluid, being a function of the way clans and sub-groups of the ethnic group are dispersed. The word 'kingdom' here denotes a territory exclusively peopled by men and women all belonging to one ethnic group. Ethnic, linguistic and cultural homogeneity is essential. The king (*mfumu*) is in fact the eldest son (*mfumu*), the maternal uncle (*mfumu*) of every family (*nzo*) and every matrilineal clan (*makanda*) that recognizes common founder-ancestors (*bankulu mpangu*). If we examine the situation more closely, what the Kingdom of Kongo comes down to is really one huge chiefdom, i.e. a system of government incorporating the small local chiefdoms. The king is the oldest of the eldest sons, the oldest living maternal uncle, and it is this that makes him a *ntinu,* or supreme chief. So the Kingdom of Kongo does not denote a state ruled by a king in the western sense. After all, this western sense (as in, for example, the kingdom of George III) is a late, inappropriate bastard sense – in short, a particular case of the transition from state to national state via absolute monarchy.

The Kingdom of Danxome (Dahomey, in the modern Republic of Benin), on the other hand, comes closer to the pattern of an absolute monarchy, as typified in France by the unfortunate version that prevailed from Henri IV to Louis XVI. Here there is a permanent heart-land and, as Professor Glélé has shown, it had a central authority consisting of the king, his ministers and the ministers' delegates. The king was the very essence of power, and had all the attributes of authority and control. He had the power of life and death over his subjects, the *anato*, the men of the people, from among whom the king, master and owner of all wealth (*dokunno*), chose and recruited *glesi*, i.e. farmers for his estates or to give as presents to the princes and chiefs. Central authority in the villages and regions was exercised by chiefs in the king's name. Thus the Kingdom of Danxome emerges as a highly centralized state organization with the chiefdom system of administrative decentralization operating within it. Thus we have a central authority controlling a people (the Danxomenu) via the chiefdoms. In the course of history, as conquests were made, other countries were annexed and added to the heart-land of the original ethnic group. So from time to time a process of conquest and of acculturation and assimilation was at work among neighbouring and related peoples (the Fon,

Mahi, Alada, Savi, Juda, and so on). The kingdom thus became a multiracial state, organized and centralized through a powerful military and administrative machine, and a strongly controlled economy. In the period immediately preceding colonization the Kingdom of Danxome was a genuine nation-state in which dialogue, the palaver and the consent of the governed (through the chiefdoms) were a principle of government.

Hence, as the examples of Kongo and Danxome make clear, the word 'kingdom' does not mean the same thing throughout Africa and historians should therefore be very careful in their use of the term. It will also have been noted that in Kongo the chieftaincy corresponded to a system of government, whereas in the former Kingdom of Danxome (Abomey) it was a form of administrative decentralization.

In the general context of western Europe (if not always in specific applications), the term 'feudalism' may be understood in the sense used by medievalists of legalistic bent as that which concerns the *fief* (instituted in about the tenth or eleventh century) and the set of relationships (loyalty, homage and dues) linking the vassal to his lord, who owned the estate. This sense of the word excludes peasants, who are not part of the upper classes. Marxists, on the other hand, use the term 'feudalism' in a very wide sense to mean a mode of production characterized by the economic exploitation of the lower classes (serfs) by the ruling classes (feudal lords). Serfs are tied to the land and dependent on the lord. The latter may no longer kill a serf, but may sell him (limited property rights over the workers). Serfdom takes the place of slavery, but many aspects of slavery still survive. Serfs or peasants are not involved in the running of affairs, nor do they hold administrative posts. In the context of the evolution of European society, the feudal system is an intermediate stage in the formation of the capitalist economy. But many Marxists still confuse the political notion of feudalism with the socio-economic notion of seigneury – which, thanks to Marx, historians since 1847 have learnt to differentiate.

But whichever sense of the word is adopted, the question remains whether the regimes of medieval Europe really existed in an identical form in precolonial black Africa. Only comparative sociological studies (of which very few have so far been made) could properly answer this question and supply the necessary distinctions. Attention has already been drawn to the 'feudal' nature of the organization of the Bariba (Republic of Benin), mainly as a working hypothesis. Work on feudalism in black Africa is at such an early stage that the historian should be more cautious; and the so-called feudal tendencies shown by black African societies probably rest not on actual rights arising from the granting of a fief, but on a form of political organization rooted in a particular system of social and economic relationships.

Thus the work of sociologists and political theorists may also provide sources for historians to use. In Africa the historian's archives vary enormously according to period and subject, and also according to the curiosity of the historian himself. The record sequence in Africa is drawn from all kinds of science – exact, natural, human and social. The message of history is now completely transformed in the sense that the methodology consists in using several specific sources and techniques simultaneously and in combination. Data furnished by oral tradition, the rare Arabic manuscripts, archaeological excavations and the carbon-14 dating method have finally restored the legendary Sao people of Chad, Cameroon and Nigeria to the authenticated history of Africa. The mound at Mdaga, in the Republic of Chad, is now known to have had a history of occupation lasting nearly 2500 years, from the fifth century before our era to the middle of our nineteenth century, but such apposite and unexpected conclusions would never have been arrived at without the combined and simultaneous use of a variety of sources.

The classical notions of historical criticism, which speak of 'auxiliary sciences', 'choice of sources', 'prime historical material', and so on, are henceforth banished from African historical research; and this marks an important step forward in contemporary historiography.

The work of a historian of Africa is becoming a continuous interdisciplinary dialogue. New horizons are opening up, thanks to an unprecedented theoretical effort. The idea of combined sources has, as it were, unearthed from the subsoil of general methodology a new way of writing history. The compilation and exposition of the history of Africa may therefore play an exemplary pioneer role in associating other branches of learning with historical research.

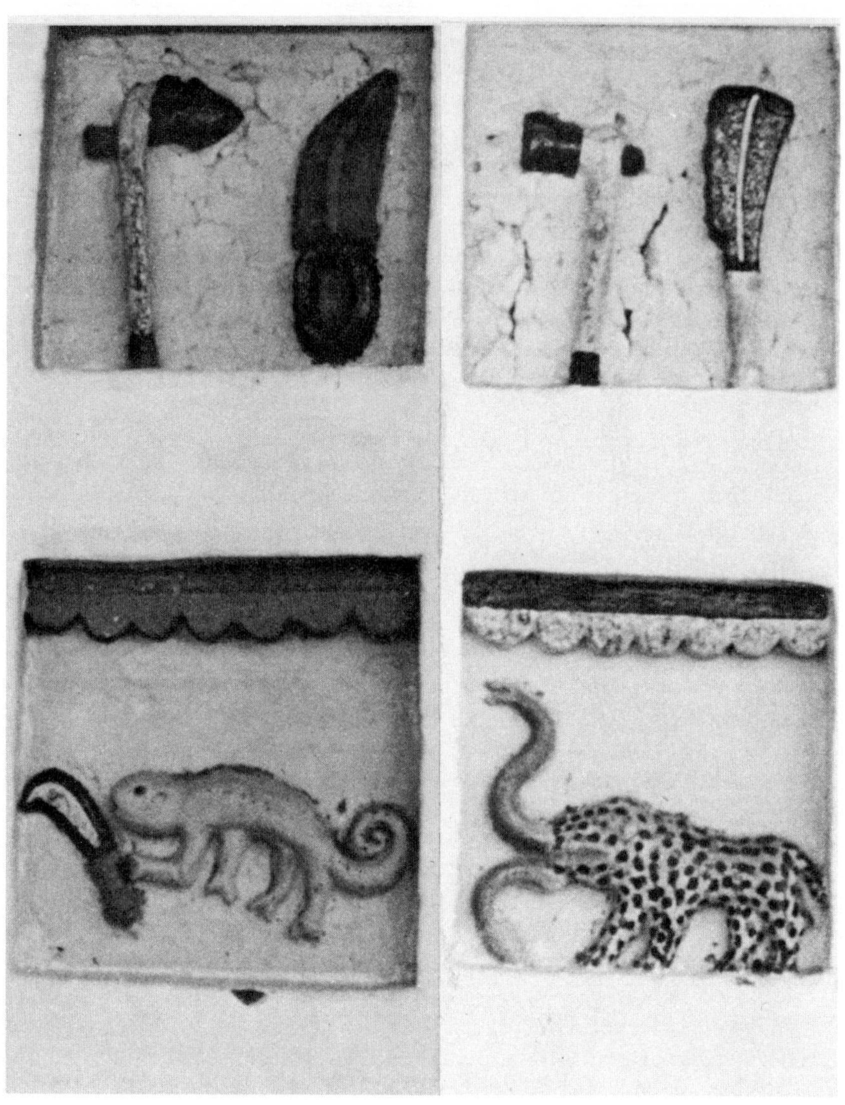

PLATE 4.1 *Bas-relief from Abomey Museum* (photo Nubia)

5 Written sources before the fifteenth century

H. DJAIT

The notion of written source is so broad as to be ambiguous. If we take written to mean all that transmits the voice and sound, then written evidence includes inscriptions carved on stone, gramophone records, coins, in short any message that preserves language and thought, regardless of its medium.[1] Such an extension would mean that this chapter should cover numismatics, epigraphy and other auxiliary studies which have, strictly speaking, become independent of the sphere of the written text. I shall therefore restrict my investigation to what is *drawn* or printed in conventional signs on any kind of support – papyrus, parchment, bone, paper. This still leaves a vast field for research and reflection, first because chronologically it covers a period that begins with the invention of writing and ends on the threshold of modern times (fifteenth century), next because spatially it covers an entire continent, with different civilizations juxtaposed and in succession, and lastly because it includes sources that vary in language, cultural tradition and type.

I am going to consider the general problems that are raised by these sources (analysis by period, by region, by type) before making a critical inventory.

General problems

No comprehensive study of the written sources of African history has so far been made. Because of chronological or regional specialization, the rare studies made have always been associated with compartmentalized fields of scholarly research. Thus Pharaonic Egypt is the field of the Egyptologist, Ptolemaic and Roman Egypt of the classicist, Muslim Egypt of the Islamist: three periods, three specialities, only the first of which stems from what is specifically Egyptian, the other two moving in wider orbits (the classical world, Islam). The same holds true for the Maghrib, though the Punic scholar is both an orientalist and a classicist and the Berber specialist marginal and unclassifiable.

1. A. Dain, 1961, p. 449.

Black Africa made a later appearance both in written history and as a field for modern research. It is varied in itself and study of it cuts across different languages and specialities: there are classical, Arabic and vernacular language sources. These are the same trio we find to the north of the Sahara, but to the south they have neither the same scope nor a similar meaning. There is a huge area where until the fifteenth century the written source is non-existent; and what is a second-rate Arabic source for, say, the Maghrib, takes on prime importance for the Niger Basin. The historian of black Africa studying a document written in Arabic does not approach it like the historian of the Maghrib, and still less like the historian of Islam as a whole.

These compartments and these interferences represent the objective structure of African history, but also the orientation of modern historical studies since the nineteenth century. It is a fact that Egypt was integrated into the Hellenistic world, into the Roman Empire, into Byzantium, and that, once converted to Islam, it became a radiant point in the Islamic world. It is a fact that the classical writers saw *historia Africana* as an illustration of *historia Romana* and that one particular Africa was indeed deeply involved in the destiny of Roman civilization. But it is quite as true that even the modern historian of Roman Africa is a Romanist first and an Africanist second and that the Islamic aspect is out of his epistemological field. To apprehend African history as a whole and look at its written sources as relating to that whole is therefore a delicate and singularly difficult task.

The problem of periodization

What is the justification for placing a caesura at the beginning of the fifteenth century in the study of written sources? Is it that until the fifteenth century the mass of documentation available to us has a certain inner structural unity, whatever the cultural and temporal disparities? Or is it that the development of general history now tends to run antiquity and the middle ages together into one single long stretch of time, cutting them off from a modern age that seems sharply different from anything that went before? The truth is that these two arguments support and supplement each other. The characteristic ancient and medieval sources are literary writings. The evidence they give is for the most part conscious, whether they be annals, chronicles, travels or geographies; whereas from the fifteenth century on archival sources – unconscious evidence – become abundant. For another thing, while until the fifteenth century classical and Arabic sources predominate, after that even our Arabic sources peter out, and we suddenly find evidence from a different provenance: the European document (Italian, Portuguese, etc.) and, for black Africa, the autochthonous document. But this shift in the nature and provenance of sources also represents a change in Africa's real historical destiny. The fifteenth century was the time of European expansion;[2] the Portuguese made their irruption on the coast of black Africa in 1434 and twenty years before (1415) they had settled at Ceuta.[3] For the Mediterranean and Islamic fringe of Africa (the Maghrib, Egypt) the cleavage between two historical eras appears as early as the fourteenth century, when that world was already feeling the effects of the slow expansion of the West and also, doubtless, of internal forces of decay. But the fifteenth century was decisive, because then the Far Eastern sources of Muslim trade ran out, putting an end to its intercontinental role. From that time on Mediterranean–African Islam entered upon a steadily rapid decline. A *terminus ad quem* in the fifteenth century is fully justified, then, if we do not interpret it too rigidly – but perhaps there would be even greater justification for moving it on to the early sixteenth century.

That said, the era we are studying may be broken down into three main periods, in view of the twofold necessity for diversity and unity:

(a) Antiquity, up to Islam: from the Old Kingdom to 622 of our era.
(b) The first Islamic age: from 622 of our era to the middle of the eleventh century (1050).
(c) The second Islamic age: from the eleventh to the fifteenth century.

Here, of course, the notion of antiquity is not the same as obtains in western history, in as much as it is only partly to be identified with classical antiquity. In Africa, antiquity ends not with the barbarian invasions but with the abrupt appearance of Islam. But by the very depth and scope of its impact Islam represents a rupture with a past that might be called ancient, or prehistoric, or protohistoric, according to region. There is also the fact that from the Hellenistic era on most of our ancient sources are in Greek and Latin.

Both because of the structure of our documentation and because of the general course of history, the seventh century, when Islam and Arabic sources appear, must be regarded as the beginning of a new age. But this new, Islamic period should be divided, with a first sub-period stretching from the Conquest to the mid-eleventh century and a second from the eleventh century to the fifteenth. In the history of Africa north of the Sahara the first phase corresponds to the organization of the area on the Islamic model and its attachment to a multicontinental empire (Umayyad, Abbasid, Fatimid caliphates). The second phase by contrast sees the resurgence of autochthonous principles of organization, while civilization is profoundly transformed. For the Maghrib, the mid-eleventh century was the time of the formation of the Almoravid Empire and the reconquest of autonomy by the Zirids, with its corollary – the Hilali invasion. In Egypt, the political

2. Mauny (1965, p. 178) proposes 1434 as the date of Portuguese maritime expansion towards black Africa. See also R. Mauny, 1961, p. 18.
3. A. Laroui, 1970, p. 218.

caesura comes a century later, with the Ayyubids, but it is now that the great centres of trade activity move from the Persian Gulf to the Red Sea and that a worldwide pattern of trade is gradually established, the effects of which are very important.

South of the Sahara, it is likewise in the course of the eleventh century that permanent relations are established with Islam, particularly in the sphere of commerce and religion.

The nature of our documentary material changes. Quantitatively it becomes plentiful and varied; qualitatively, as time passes, we find more and more unconscious sources (documentary records, legal consultations) for Mediterranean Africa and more and more accurate information for black Africa.

Ethno-cultural areas and types of sources

Classifying sources by historical periods is not enough in itself. We have to consider both Africa's articulation into ethnocultural zones characterized by a variety of forces and – above and beyond historical periods and spatial differences – the actual typology of the sources available to us.

Ethno-cultural areas

To begin with the first point: it is rather tempting to make an elementary distinction at the very outset between Africa north of the Sahara – white, Arabic, Islamic Africa, touched to its depths by the Mediterranean civilizations, and by that token distorted from its African origins – and Africa south of the Sahara: black, African to the utmost, endowed with an indomitable ethnohistorical specificity. In reality, without denying the importance of such specific qualities, a more searching historical examination shows lines of cleavage that are more complex and less sharp. For example, the Senegalese and Nigerian Sudan has lived in symbiosis with the Arab-Berber Maghrib, and from the point of view of sources it is much closer to the Maghrib than to the Bantu world. It is the same for the Nilotic Sudan in relation to Egypt and for the Horn of Africa in relation to southern Arabia. Therefore one is tempted to oppose an Africa of the Mediterranean, the desert and the savannah, embracing the Maghrib, Egypt, the two Sudans, Ethiopia, the Horn of Africa and the east coast as far as Zanzibar, to another Africa – animistic, deep, tropical and equatorial: the Zaïre Basin, the Guinea coast, the Zambezi–Limpopo area, the interlacustrine region, and finally southern Africa. And it is true that this second differentiation is in large measure justified by the criterion of exposure to the outside world and the degree of Islamic penetration. This fact of civilization is corroborated by the state of our written sources, where we find an ample supply, with north–south gradations, for one Africa and an absolute void for another Africa, at least during the period we are studying. But with this dual consideration – accessibility to the outside world, and the state of the written sources – there is the risk that value judgements may come in and cast a veil of obscurity over almost half the continent (central and southern Africa). A number of historians have already drawn attention to the danger of 'the resort to Arabic sources' which by their emphasis on the Sudanese zone might create the impression that it was the only centre of an organized civilization and state.[4] I shall come back to this point later. But even here let us recognize that while there is a connection between the state of a civilization and the state of the available sources, we cannot explain the actual course of history simply by that connection. An objective historian has no right to make value judgements on the basis of his documentary material. But neither has he the right to neglect what it has to offer on the grounds that it might possibly be misleading.

While a general history covering the entire historical era and using the whole mass of available documentation may accord as much importance to the Zaïre Basin as to the Niger Basin or to Egypt, a study confined to pre-fifteenth-century written sources cannot. With due allowance for all that has been said above, we can now suggest the following regional divisions:

(a) Egypt, Cyrenaica, Nilotic Sudan.
(b) The Maghrib, including the northern fringe of the Sahara, the zones of the farthest west, Tripolitania and Fezzan.
(c) The western Sudan in the broad sense, that is, extending to Lake Chad to the east and including the southern Sahara.
(d) Ethiopia, Eritrea, the Horn and the east coast.
(e) The rest of the continent, viz. the Gulf of Guinea, Central Africa, southern Africa.

This classification has the advantage of not setting up two opposing Africas; it divides the continent according to African geographical-historical affinities but also pays due heed to the particular nature of the available written sources. In terms of written sources, Central and southern Africa, rich in civilization as it may be, cuts a very poor figure by comparison with the tiniest fraction of the other regional units (Fezzan or Eritrea, for example). For another thing, there can be no doubt that in addition to the general solidarity characterizing the sources for 'known' Africa there is a specific, clearer solidarity in our sources of information for each particular one of the zones delimited above. To make a detailed inventory, therefore, we must review our texts by period and by region, but we must recognize at the outset that through the regions, and to a lesser degree through the historical periods, what we have comes down to sources in a few languages only, of certain limited types, and that they do not always originate in the area they treat of and are not always contemporary with what they describe.

4. I. Hrbek, 1965, Vol. V, p. 311.

Typology of written sources

(a) The languages in which our documents have come down to us are many, but they do not all have the same importance. The African languages most used, the ones conveying the greatest mass of information, are: ancient Egyptian, Berber, Ethiopian languages. The most prolific languages are those of non-African origin: Greek, Latin, Arabic (even if Arabic has been accepted as a national language by a number of African peoples).

If we classify our documents in a pyramid that takes both quantity and quality of information into account, we get roughly the following order: Arabic, Greek, Latin, ancient Egyptian (hieratic and demotic), Coptic, Hebrew, Aramaic, Ethiopic, Italian, Persian, Chinese and some languages of lesser importance.

Chronologically, our first written sources are hieratic Egyptian papyri dating from the New Kingdom but giving texts that were probably first written as far back as the early Middle Kingdom (beginning of the second millennium); in particular the papyrus known as *Instructions for King Merikere.*[5] Then we have New Kingdom papyri and ostraca, still in hieratic Egyptian; Greek sources going back to the seventh century before our era and continuing without a break to a late period roughly coinciding with the expansion of Islam (about 700 of our era); sources in Hebrew (the Bible) and Aramaic (Elephantine Jews) dating from the twenty-sixth dynasty; demotic Egyptian texts dating from the Ptolemaic period; Latin literature; Coptic literature (in Coptic script, using the Egyptian language but the Greek alphabet with a few additional letters), beginning in about 300 of our era; Arabic; Chinese;[6] possibly Persian; Italian; and, later, Ethiopic, the oldest writing in which is of the thirteenth century.[7]

(b) *Generically,* the material we have can be divided into narrative sources and archival sources, the ones deliberately written down so as to leave a record, the others part of the ordinary course of human existence. For Africa – excepting Egypt but including the Maghrib – written documentary material is almost entirely represented by narrative sources until the twelfth century. These therefore cover both antiquity and the first Islamic age. From the twelfth century the archival document makes its appearance – rarely, however – in the Maghrib (Almohad items, *fatwas* or legal consultations of the Hafsid era). In Egypt archival documents become more plentiful under the Ayyubids and the Mamluks (twelfth to fifteenth centuries), while the manuscripts of Ethiopian monasteries contain official documents by way of appendices. But for the rest of Africa this type of text

5. See E. Drioton and J. Vandier, 1962, p. 226.

6. There exists one Chinese text from the latter half of the eleventh century, but mainly the Chinese sources, which are yet to be explored, concern the fifteenth century and the East African coast. The following works may also be mentioned: J. J. L. Duyvendak, 1949; F. Hirth, 1909–10; T. Filesi, 1962; L. Libra, 1963; P. Wheatley, 1964.

7. S. Hable-Sélassié, 1967, p. 13.

remains virtually non-existent during the whole period under consideration.[8]

The features marking this period are a continuing preponderance of narrative sources; the appearance or the relative increase of archival sources from the twelfth century in Mediterranean Africa and the virtual lack of them in black Africa, but generally speaking a substantial increase in documentary material from about 1100 till it reaches a peak in the twelfth to fourteenth centuries.

Our types of sources can be enumerated as follows:

Narrative sources
Chronicles and annals
Geographical works, accounts of travels, works by naturalists
Legal works, religious works (treatises on canon law, devotional books or lives of saints)
Literary works in the strict sense.
Archival sources
Private documents: family letters, business correspondence, etc.
Official documents emanating from the state or representatives of the state: official correspondence, decrees, letters patent, legislative and fiscal texts, juridico-religious documents.

I might point out that the narrative sources begin in the eighth century before our era, with Homer, and include many master works of the human intellect and learning. There are great names among the authors, even if most of them do not treat of Africa in particular but give it a more or less important place against a broader background. Among them are: Herodotus, Polybius, Pliny the Elder, Ptolemy, Procopius, Khwārizmī, Mas'ūdī, Jahiz, Ibn Khaldun. The archival documentation for Africa is the oldest in the world: whereas the Ravenna papyri, the oldest archival records preserved in Europe, date from the early sixth century of our era, the papyri of the Egyptian New Kingdom go back twenty centuries before that. It is true that this type of evidence did not extend beyond the boundaries of Egypt in the first Islamic age and did not extend very much farther even by the end of our period, probably because of the fact that medieval Islamic civilization was to all intents and purposes ignorant of the principle of preserving state documents. In the fourteenth and fifteenth centuries, when archival items are in greatest profusion, it is mostly through encyclopedic works that they are transmitted to us. We have to wait for the modern era, Ottoman and European, for regular respositories of archives to be constituted.

8. We have *mahrams*, letters patent issued by the kings of Bornu probably dating from the late eleventh century: that of Umm Jilmi and that of the Masbarma family. On this subject see R. Mauny, 1961.

Inventory by period

Pre-Islamic antiquity (from the beginnings to 622 of our era)

What characterizes this period by comparison with the one that follows is the predominance of archaeological and, more broadly, non-literary sources. But even if they are secondary written documents they do occasionally provide us with very important information. Moreover, they become more copious and more accurate with the passage of time. From the point of view of zonal distribution, it should be noted that there is a total blank for West and central Africa.

Egypt, Nubia, East Africa

(a) Until the first millennium of our era, written sources for Egypt are exclusively Egyptian. They are hieratic papyri and ostraca which do not go back beyond the New Kingdom in physical form but may, as I have said, record information that is more ancient.[9] 'Papyrus' and 'ostracon' designate the kind of support: the one is a plant, the other a flake of limestone. Hieratic signs differ from hieroglyphic signs in their cursive appearance: they were for drawing on a surface rather than carving. Papyri and ostraca, numerous for the nineteenth and twentieth dynasties of the New Kingdom, or the Ramessid period (1314–1085 before our era), bear on governmental and private life alike: we find civil service and legal reports, accountancy records, private letters, and also stories and novels. The legal[10] and literary[11] papyri have been studied carefully and, from the nineteenth century on, have been published.

Unless new discoveries should be made we can learn nothing of Nubia and the country of Punt from written sources, but must depend on archaeological and epigraphic material (graffiti in particular).

(b) In the first millennium before our era, especially from the sixth century on, there is a diversification and a rearrangement in what our sources have to give. Narrative documents unite with archival ones and at certain moments take their place. Thus the *Book of Kings,* a fragment of the

9. E. Drioton and J. Vandier, 1962, pp. 7–9; J. Yoyotte, 1956.

10. Among legal documents we have the Abbott Papyrus, the Amherst and Mayer Papyri, and the Turin Papyrus, which are the foundation for what we know of the reigns of Rameses IX, X and XI. They have been published: cf. *Select Papyri in the hieratic character from the collections of the British Museum* (London, 1860); P. E. Newberry, 1899; Peet, 1920, 1930.

11. The British Museum collection is rich in literary papyri. It includes for example the tale of Truth and Falsehood and the tale of Horus and Seth. Posener, the great specialist in this subject, made a quasi-exhaustive list of Egyptian literary works and arrived at 58 titles (Posener, 1951). He also published some ostraca (Posener, 1934).

Old Testament, gives us valuable information about the advent of the twenty-second dynasty (*c.* 950 before our era) and remains very useful for the whole of the following period, that is, to the Persian domination (525 before our era). The *Book of Kings* was first written before the destruction of Jerusalem, i.e. before 586,[12] and was reworked during the Exile, but it reproduces traditions that go back to the beginning of the first millennium before our era. Other foreign sources, namely Greek, shed light on the Late Period from the first Saite dynasty (seventh century): Menander, Aristodemus, Philocorus, Herodotus. From the archival point of view, papyri are now written in Greek or in demotic Egyptian – a script even more cursive than the hieratic. In the fifth century the papyri of the Elephantine Jews provide our principal source material, whereas for the fourth and third centuries we have the *Demotic Chronicle*.

(c) The thousand years from the establishment of the Ptolemies in Egypt (late fourth century before our era) to the Arab Conquest (639 of our era) form a period which is distinguished by the importance, quantitatively, of Greek sources and by the Ethiopo-Eritrean zone coming within our ken. Polybius, Strabo, Diodorus and Pliny the Elder speak of this region with a relative accuracy that does not preclude ignorance or *naïveté*. In his *Natural History* the Roman naturalist gives us a great deal of information about the Ethiopian world, especially as regards trade routes and merchandise. It is a compilation of unequal value, certainly, but splendid for various details.

Our information becomes more accurate in the 500 years that follow the appearance of Christianity. Egypt, as is well known, became the chief seat of Hellenistic culture in the second century, and it is quite natural that the country should have produced historians, geographers, philosophers and Fathers of the Church. Politically integrated first into the Roman, then into the Byzantine Empire, Egypt was a topic in many foreign Latin and Greek writings, both narrative and archival (for instance, the Theodosian Code or Justinian's *Novellae*). We may note too that the papyrus tradition was not discontinued. In this mass of documentation, domestic and foreign, a few works of uncommon importance stand out: Ptolemy's Geography[13] (*c.* 140 of our era); *The Periplus of the Erythraean Sea*,[14] an anonymous work once assigned to the first century, now reckoned to have been composed around 230; and the *Topographica Christiana*[15] of Cosmas Indicopleustes (*c.* 535). These writings form the basis of our information on Ethiopia and the Horn

12. A. Lods, 1950, p. 7; E. Drioton and J. Vandier, 1962, *passim*; J. Doresse, 1971, Vol. I, pp. 47–61.

13. For classical and post-classical geographers who dealt with Africa, see the standard work by Y. Kamal, 1926–51. A reissue of this work, augmented by a new and substantial critical apparatus, would be most welcome.

14. Edited by Müller, 1853, Vol. I, and again by Jöns Hjaimar Frisk, 1927. There had been editions of this important work as early as the sixteenth century (1533 and 1577).

of Africa. But on the whole this brief summary shows up two imbalances: imbalance of written sources with respect to other types of documents and of our knowledge of Egypt with respect to our knowledge of Nubia and the Eritrean world.

Ancient Maghrib

The written history of the ancient Maghrib grew out of the collision between Carthage and Rome. It follows that we have nothing important before the second century before our era: some scattered clues in Herodotus, of course, and also in the works of other Greek historians. For the authentically Punic period we depend on archaeology and epigraphy. Moreover, the written sources for the history of Carthage not only before Hannibal but also during its confrontation with Rome, and during its temporary survival thereafter, are almost never Punic. It is now established that the *Periplus of Hanno* (which is in Greek), which describes territory up to the north-west coast of Africa, is spurious and cannot have been written earlier than the first century before our era. This leaves us with the agronomical work ascribed to Mago, of which we have only extracts preserved by Latin authors. But among autochthonous sources mention should be made of the notices of Juba II which Pliny the Elder included in his *Natural History*.

Most if not all of our written sources for the history of the ancient Maghrib – Carthaginian, Roman, Vandal and Byzantine phases – consist of works by classical historians and geographers, that is, historians and geographers writing in Greek or Latin. Generally speaking these authors were foreign to Africa; but as Africa became Romanized autochthonous writers sprang up, particularly among the Church Fathers.

(a) In the period extending from 200 before our era to 100 of our era, which covers the zenith and the fall of Carthage and the organization of the Roman province of Africa under the Republic and the Principate, we have a multitude of well-known Greek and Latin writings as sources: Polybius (200–120), is our chief source; Strabo; Diodorus Siculus; Sallust (87–35); Livy; Appian; Pliny; Tacitus; Plutarch (first century of our era); and Ptolemy (second century of our era), not to speak of the many minor authors.[16]

15. Cosmas was a traveller who visited Ethiopia and the island of Socotra. His work appears in Vol. XXXVIII of Migne's *Patrologia Graeca*, a book which absolutely must be consulted for antiquity, along with the same editor's *Patrologia Latina*. An excellent edition of Cosmas' works, in three volumes, has been published by Editions du Cerf, Paris, 1968–70. For a work which makes an important contribution to our knowledge of the Christianization of Ethiopia, see Rufinus, *Historia Ecclesiastica*, in Migne's *Patrologia Graeca*, which always gives a Latin translation.

16. I might mention Aristotle (*Politics*), Caesar (*Bellum Civile* and *Bellum Africum*), Eutropius, Justinian, Orosius. There are more than thirty textual sources for the story of Hannibal alone.

It would be most helpful if the scattered writings on North Africa were collected. This has been done only for Morocco.[17] At present the student has to go systematically through the great collections of the classics, those collections in which nineteenth-century European erudition put forth all it had by way of criticism and formidable labour: the *Bibliotheca Teubneriana*, the *Loeb Classical Library* (text with English translation), the *Collection G. Bude* (text with French translation), the *Collection des Universités de France*, the *Scriptorum classicorum Bibliotheca Oxoniensis*.

To these narrative sources should be added the more direct sources constituted by texts of Roman law, even though these are of epigraphic origin.[18]

The writings of the Graeco-Latin annalists, chroniclers and geographers are not of uniform value for this whole sub-period. While some of the authors tend merely to compile information provided by their predecessors, others bring us precious original information and occasionally even first-hand testimony. For instance, Polybius was an intimate of the Scipios and seems to have been present at the siege of Carthage in 146 before our era; Sallust's *Bellum Jugurthinum* is a document of the highest order for the Berber kingdoms; Caesar's *Bellum Civile* is the work of an actor in history.

The personality and the work of Polybius dominate this period; Polybius has been called 'a son of the Hellenistic age'[19] and culture. He was born around 200 before our era, that is, at the moment when Rome, on the flood-tide of its imperialism, encountered the Mediterranean world and more especially the Hellenistic East. A prisoner and an exile at Rome, he learned the hard lessons of exile, that 'violent teacher' of historian and philosopher. The Scipios' protection made his sojourn easier and above all gave him the chance to learn a great deal about Roman and Carthaginian history. After sixteen years' captivity he returned to his homeland, Greece, but promptly set off again to travel about the world. We are told that during his stay in Africa he was offered a fleet of ships by Scipio Aemilianus so that he could explore the Atlantic coast of the continent. In other words, here was a man of audacity, experience and tireless curiosity. Polybius is not merely our chief source for everything that touches on the Punico-Roman duel: he is, in a more general way, a first-class observer of the Africa and Egypt of his day. If only the forty books that made up the *Pragmateia* had been left to us we should doubtless know a great deal more than we do, possibly we might even have been given information of an accuracy lacking everywhere else on black Africa. But even as it is, the six books that have come down to us tower over our other sources because of the quality of the information and the intelligent perspective.

(b) After the first century, and throughout the four centuries during

17. M. Roget, 1924.
18. P. F. Girard, 1937.
19. T. R. Glover, 1977, ch. I, p. 1.

which Roman imperial organization took its deepest root in Africa and then entered into a prolonged state of crisis, literary sources are few and far between. There is practically a total void in the second century, and the third and fourth are marked by the preponderance of Christian writings, notably Cyprian's and Augustine's. There are general works that transcend the African frame of reference to pose great religious problems and have no element of direct historical discourse, but there are also polemical and occasional works with a more immediate interest in current events. For instance, our knowledge of the Donatist movement is based on attacks made by its greatest adversary, St Augustine (354–430), and for that very reason we have to tread with extreme caution.

In fact, as far as written sources for the imperial period are concerned, the *Patrologia* is our main instrument of knowledge but a very partial one. Here, too, the student has to turn to great collections such as the *Berlin Corpus* in Greek and the *Vienna Corpus* in Latin. These monuments of German erudition have their French counterpart in Migne's two collections: the *Patrologia Graeca* (Greek text and Latin translation) and the *Patrologia Latina* (Latin text only).

The Vandal interlude, the Byzantine reconquest and the Byzantine presence for over a century led more writers to record events. Minor works abound and archival sources (correspondence, legislative texts) make their appearance. Above all, we are fortunate in having one prolific and talented observer in Procopius (sixth century), whose *De Bello Vandalico* is by far our most fundamental source.

For Greek texts, we can use the *Bonn Byzantine Collection* and, secondarily, the *Fragmenta historicorum graecorum*. The numerous Latin texts can be found either in the *Patrologia Latina* (the works of St Fulgentius have a certain interest for the Vandal period) or in the *Monumenta Germaniae Historica, Auctores Antiquissimi*,[20] another impressive product of German learning, which brings together the minor chronicles of the Byzantine age: Cassiodorus, Prosper Tiro, Hydatius, and above all Victor Vitensis and Corippus. These last two authors are the most noteworthy, Victor for the Vandal period and Corippus for the Byzantine, because they penetrate into the interior of Africa and throw a light on that darkest Africa, so long in oblivion.[21] Charles Diehl, in his classic work on Byzantine Africa, showed how one can use archaeological and textual material conjointly so as to get as close as possible to historical reality. The range of written sources he used was as wide as could be: first of all Procopius, with Corippus, but

20. In Mommsen's *Monumenta*, Vol. 9/1–2 (1892), 11 (1894) and 13 (1898), the text by Victor Vitensis is found in Vol. 3–1 (1879) edited by C. Holm and the text by Corippus is found in Vol. 3–2 (1879) edited by J. Partsch.

21. For Vandal and Byzantine Africa we have two standard modern works that give details of the usable sources: C. Courtois, 1955, and C. Diehl, 1959. S. Gsell's (Paris, 1920–8), though out of date, is still worth consulting.

also Agathias, Gassiodorus, Georgius Cyprius,[22] the letters of Pope Gregory the Great, and legal documents like the *Novellae* and the Justinian Code, so helpful for investigation of economic and social life.

It does not seem likely that our established list of written documents can be enriched by any new discoveries. On the other hand, we can better exploit the documents we do have by studying them more intensively, by applying a rigorous criticism, by collating them with archaeological and epigraphic material (which is not yet exhausted), and above all by using them with greater honesty and objectivity.[23]

Saharan and western Africa

Strictly speaking we have no trustworthy documentation on western black Africa. If we accept with Mauny[24] that the ancients – Carthaginians, Greeks, Romans – did not go beyond Cape Juby and the latitude of the Canaries, as is more than probable, then the information in their writings relates to the extreme southern part of Morocco. They are certainly on the edge of the black world, but they do not penetrate it.

The *Periplus of Hanno* is largely if not entirely spurious.[25] It is a composite work with jumbled borrowings from Herodotus, Polybius, Poseidonius, and the Pseudo-Scylax, and must date from the first century before our era. More serious are the original writings of those same authors. Herodotus reports on the silent trade the Carthaginians carried on in southern Morocco. The Continuer of the Pseudo-Scylax (fourth century before our era) in his turn gives valuable information about their relations with the Libyan-Berbers. But above all Polybius turns out, once again, to be the most accurate source. The snippets of his text interpolated in Pliny the Elder give us the first identifiable place names of ancient times. But his information, too, stops at Cape Juby. It has to be supplemented, for the Canaries archipelago, by the notices of Juba II collected by Pliny. Strabo, Diodorus Siculus and the other historian-geographers of the first centuries before and during our era merely compiled previous authors, save for a few details. Finally, in the second century, Ptolemy, resuming all his predecessors, with special reliance on Poseidonius and Marinus of Tyre, recorded in his *Geography* the most thoroughgoing knowledge antiquity possessed of the contours of Africa.[26] In the map of 'Inner Libya' he also left us, this Alexandrian geographer was able to draw on information the Roman army had obtained in the course of punitive expeditions beyond the *limes* into the Fezzan: the expedition of Balbus in 19 before our era, that of

22. *Descriptio orbis romani*, edited by H. Gelzer, 1890.
23. On distortions caused by a partial reading of texts, A. Laroui's criticism of western historiography is as pertinent as it is well-informed.
24. R. Mauny, 1970b, pp. 87–111.
25. ibid., p. 98; H. Tauxier, 1882, pp. 15–37; G. Germain, 1957, pp. 205–48.
26. Y. Kamal, *Monumenta*, op. cit., Vol. II, fasc. I, pp. 116ff.; R. Mauny, 1947.

Flaccus in 70 of our era, that of Maternus in 86 – the one which pushed deepest into the Libyan desert.[27]

Some names of peoples and regions have survived antiquity: Mauretania, Libya, Garamantes, Gaetulae, Numidians, Hesperides – even Niger, a name advanced by Ptolemy and taken up by Leo Africanus and later on by modern Europeans. This is one thing contributed by our texts which otherwise give us rather the image antiquity had of Africa than any real data. The few data that do crop up here and there concern the Libyan desert and the coast of the western Sahara. Western black Africa remains peripheral in all these texts.

The first Islamic age (*c.* 650–1050)

The Arab Conquest and the establishment of the Caliphate resulted in the unification of previously separate politico-cultural domains (Sassanid Empire, Byzantine Empire), the broadening of man's geographical horizons, the modification of trade routes, and deep penetration into peoples about whom nothing had been known until then. It is not surprising then that for the first time we have increasingly accurate information about the black world, east and west alike. But whereas Egypt and the Maghrib became actual integral parts of the empire, and later of the Islamic community, the black world was only within the Islamic sphere of influence. Hence we have bits and pieces of information, disjointed, sometimes fabulous, and yet, for all that, valuable.

If we except archival sources, the tradition continuing in Egypt and therefore pertaining specifically to that country (Greek and Coptic papyri from Aphrodite, Arabic papyri from Fayum and Ashmunayn[28] and finally a few tenth-century Fatimid items), most of our written sources, whether narrative in the wider sense or indirect, are common to all Africa. This is a conspicuous feature of geographical writings and is visible in many legal texts. Therefore it seems more suitable to inventory our sources from here on by genre, though I shall indicate chronological order and not lose sight of regional structures.

Chronicles

(a) We have no chronicle earlier than the ninth century. In the eighth century oral information was worked into shape, with Egypt as indisputable centre save for the east coast of Africa, which had direct commercial links

27. Referred to by Marinus of Tyre, one of Ptolemy's sources: cf. Y. Kamal, Vol. I, 1926, p. 73.

28. Here A. Grohmann is the authority, 1934–59 and 1955. The Greek and Coptic papyri have been studied by H. Bell. For the Fatimid records see Shayyal, 1958.

with southern Iraq. But Egypt, the Maghrib and *a fortiori* the Sudan were not central to the Islamic world, and the result was that even in the ninth century, when Arabic historiography suddenly began, they received scant attention in the great *ta'rīkhs*[29] (histories) – Tabarī, Dīnawarī, the Balādhuri of the *Ansāb al-Ashrāf* – which focused on the East. Exception must be made for one chronicle which was hardly known until very recently: the *Ta'rīkh* of Khalīfa b. Khayyāt.[30] Not only is this book the oldest Arabic annalistic work (Khalīfa died in 240 AH) but it has preserved ancient materials overlooked by Tabarī: in particular, what it tells us about the conquest of the Maghrib is of the highest importance. Whereas the Medina tradition of the *māghāzī* left the conquest of Egypt and the Maghrib in the shadow – only the barest essentials are given in Balādhurī's *Futūh al-Buldān* – an Egyptian jurist singled it out for study in a word which is the most important document of the ninth century. The *Futūk Misr wa-l-Maghrib*[31] of Ibn 'Abd-al-Hakam, while they resemble a chronicle or *māghāzī* work, are really a collection of legal traditions impinging on history.[32]

(b) After a century of silence[33] (850–950), there appeared a fundamental work which seems not to have been exploited in all its dimensions: the *Kitāb Wulāt Miṣr wa Qudhatuha* of Kindī (d. 961). This biographical work, which is not a chronicle but may be treated like one, not only contains accurate first-hand data on Egypt but, because of the early links between that province and the Maghrib, is one of our soundest sources for the eighth-century Maghrib.[34] The tenth century is the Ismā'ilian century of Islam, and of African Islam first and foremost. Therefore we consult Shi'ite writings like the *Sinat al-Hājib Ja'far*, and above all the Qadi Nu'man's

29. However, it is important to note that one of the very first Arab historiographers, 'Umar b. Shabba, has left us the oldest Arab testimony relating to the black peoples, the text of which is reproduced by Tabarī, *Ta'rīkh*, Vol. VII, pp. 609–14. This was the revolt of the *Sudan* at Medina in 145 AH/762 of our era, which bears witness to the considerable presence of Africans at the height of the period. This text had not been noted or commented on until now.

30. Edited by 'Umari (Najaf, 1965), with a preface by A. S. al-'Ali.

31. Edited by Torrey in 1922, partly translated by Gateau, re-edited by 'Amir at Cairo in 1961. On the caution required in using it, see R. Brunschvig, 1942–7. Brunschvig's hypercritical study does not, I think, impair the contribution made by this text, which is capital for Egypt, useful for Ifriqiya, and important for the black world (possible contacts of 'Uqba with the Fezzan, denied by Brunschvig in another article; the famous Baqt treaty with the Nubians).

32. There is not much to be got from a late compiler, 'Ubayd Allah b. Salih, discovered and magnified by E. Lévi-Provençal, 1954, pp. 35–42, as a new source for the conquest of the Maghrib. Lévi-Provençal's evaluation is followed by Mauny in his *Tableau* (1961), p. 34, where the analysis of Arabic sources, though close and exhaustive, is not overly concerned with rigorous criticism.

33. Except for a few interesting anonymous chronicles like *al-Imān wa' s-Siyāsa*, by the Pseudo-Ibn Qutayba (Cairo, 1904), and the *Akhbar majmu'a* (Madrid, 1867).

34. Edited by R. Guest, 1912, and re-edited at Beyreuth, 1959.

TABLE 5.1 *Chronological table of principal written sources*

	Narrative Sources			
Date before our era	Chronicles, annals	Geography travel, etc.	Legal, religious works	Literary texts
2065				
1580				
800				Homer
			Book of Kings (before 586)	
500				
	Herodotus (485–25)			
300	*Demotic Chronicle*			
200	Polybius (200–120)			
100	Diodorus	Strabo *Pseudo-Periplus of Hanno*		
	Sallust (87–35)			
of our era				
	Pliny the Elder			
100	Tacitus			
	Plutarch			
200		Ptolemy *Periplus of the Erythraean Sea* (230)	St Cyprian (200–58)	
300				
			St Augustine (354–436)	
400				
500	Procopius (492–562)			
		Cosmas Indicopleustes (*c.* 535)		
622				
		Fazarī	Muwattā	
800	Ibn ‘Abd al-Hakam (803–871)	Khuwarizmī (before 833)	Mudawwaza Ahkam as-Suq	Jāhiz
		Ya‘qūbī (d. 897)		

Archival Sources			
Official records	Private documents	Date before our era	Historical context
		2065	Middle Kingdom
Hieratic papyri Ostraca		1580	New Kingdom
		800	Foundation of Carthage Late Egyptian period
	Papyri of the Elephantine Jews	500	
		200	The Ptolemies Roman conquest of Africa (146)
		100	Romanization of Africa
Novellae of Justinian			
		200	Apogee of the School of Alexandria
		300	Aksum and the Christianization of Ethiopia (333)
		400	
Greek and Coptic papyri		500	Byzantine reconquest of Africa (533)
		622	The Hegira Arab expansion Omayyad Caliphate (661–749)
	Aphrodite papyri in Arabic	800	Aghabid Ifrīqiya (800–910) Revolt of the Zandj (868)
Fatimid correspondence in Ifrīqiya			

TABLE 5.1—*continued*

	Narrative Sources			
Date before our era	Chronicles, annals	Geography, travels, etc.	Legal, religious works	Literary texts
900	Kirdi	Mas'ūdī (fl. 947)	Gāothī Nu'mān (Shīte) Abu al-Arab (Sunnite) Ibn as-Saghīr (Kharijīte)	
		Ibn Hawqal (fl. 977)		
1050	al-Raqīq (d. 1028)			
		al-Bakri (fl. 1068)	Mālikī	
1100	Anonymous al-Istibsar	al-Idrīsī	Abū Zakariyā Makhzumi	
1150				al-Qādhi al-Fādhil
1200	Ibn al-Athīr (fl. 1234) Ibn al-'Idhārī	Yāqūt (fl. 1229) Ibn Sa'īd (before 1286) 'Abdarī (fl. 1289)	Hafsid Manāqibs	
1300	al-Muwari ibn Abī Zar' al-Dhahabī Ibn Khaldūn	al-'Umarī (d. 1336) Ibn Battūta Tijanî	Ethiopian monastery manuscripts	
				Safadī
		Cresques, Majorcan Atlas (1375)		
1400	Ibn Taghribardi			
1450	Zurara	Maqrīzī		

Archival Sources			
Official records	Private documents	Date before our era	Historical context
Arabic papyri of Fayum and Ashmunayn		900	
			Establishment of the Fatimids in Egypt (969)
		1050	
Fatimid records in Egypt Geniza			The Hilali in Ifrīqiya
Almoravid letters			Conquest of Ghana by the Almoravids (1076)
Mahram of Umme Jilmi Almohad letters		1100	
	Geniza	1150	Almohads in the Maghrib Ayyubids in Egypt
		1200	Hafsids in Ifriqiya
Italian documents	Italian documents		Marinids in Morocco Mamluks in Egypt
Waf records		1300	
			Mali Empire
	Fatwas		Mansa Musa (1312–35)
al-Qalqashandī			
		1400	Collapse of Mali and emergence of Songhay Capture of Ceuta by the Portuguese (1415) Portuguese discovery of Cape Bojador (1434)
al-Makrīzī		1450	

Iftitah al-Da'wa, a fundamental work which does not give many dates but is full of information about the beginnings of the Fatimid movement.[35]

(c) The first half of the eleventh century saw the writing of the famous *Ta'rīkh* of al-Raqīq (d. 1028), a fundamental source. The work itself is considered as lost, but its main substance was taken up by later compilers like Ibn al-'Idhāri. Not long ago (1968), a fragment treating of the early Ifrīqiyan era, discovered by the Moroccan Mannūnī, was published in Tunis, but the attribution to Raqīq is not certain.[36] In all these chronicles, black Africa has next to no place. Moreover, the historian must be severely critical in approaching any of them, must perpetually compare the data in one with data in the others and with data originating elsewhere. Above all, the historian of the Maghrib and Egypt cannot read these chronicles and stop at that: a thorough knowledge of the East is absolutely necessary, and if he is using these sources he must also do some intensive reading in the classical eastern chronicles.

Geographical sources

These are numerous and important from the ninth century. Whatever category they belong to – the cartographical genre of the *Ṣūrah al-Ardh* made famous by Khwarīzmī, or administrative geography, or itineraries-and-countries (*Masālik*), or simply more or less romanticized travels – Arabic geographical writings illustrate a desire to apprehend the *oikoumene*, the inhabited world, in its entirety. So it is not surprising that black Africa should be represented in them and that they should be the fundamental sources for our knowledge of it. The exhaustive list compiled by Kubbel and Matveiev,[37] which stops with the twelfth century, shows that of the forty authors who speak of black Africa twenty-one are geographers and that their texts are the richest in material. But no real profit can be derived from them without preliminary critical work. The historian of black Africa must put these Arabic geographical works inside their own cultural context. For example, to what extent does a description correspond to reality and to what extent does it merely reflect hackneyed themes from the *Adab* and its various components?[38] What is the share of the Greek heritage, of the Iranian, of the strictly Arabic? How much is compilation and how much original observation? On the other hand, he must also look at the texts from inside – that is, bring to bear a criticism based on a thorough knowledge of African history. Of course, he must be careful not to read that history solely on the basis of essentially geographical sources. But the point of view – a purely ideological one – of those who refuse to make a close study of these

35. Published in Tunis and Beirut by M. Dachraoui.

36. M. Talbi flatly denied Raqiq's authorship in *Cahiers de Tunisie*, XIX (1971), pp. 19ff., but did not succeed in making out a convincing case. The uncertainty therefore subsists.

37. L. E. Kubbel and V. V. Matveiev, 1960 and 1965; see also J. Cuoq, 1975.

38. A. Miquel, 1967 and 1977.

sources because of Islamophobia,[39] because of a misplaced concern for an introverted Africanism, is inadmissible.[40] Of the pleiad of mid-ninth to mid-eleventh-century geographers who gave some space to Africa – and nearly all of them did – only a handful provide original and serious information: Ibn Khurdādhbah, Ya'qūbī (d. 897), Mas'ūdī (fl. 965), Ibn Hawqal (fl. 977).[41] Al Biruni Ya'qūbī travelled in Egypt and the Maghrib and left a substantial account of both regions. In his *Ta'rīkh* and his *Buldān*[42] he tells us a great deal about the black world: Ethiopia, the Sudan, Nubia, the Beja, and Zandj. In the Sudan, he mentions the Zaghawa of Kanem and describes their habitat; he describes the great kingdom of Ghana and in that connection discusses the problem of gold, just as he treats of the problem of slaves when speaking of the Fezzan. Ibn Hawqal's *Kitāb ṣurat al-ard*[43] is still more detailed. He visited Nubia and possibly the western Sudan: his description is especially valuable for the idea it gives of trade relations between the Maghrib and the Sudan. Nearly all the other tenth-century geographers provide notes on black Africa: Ibn al-Faqīh has something on Ghana and Kuku; the traveller Buzurg ibn Shariyar on the east coast and the Zandj; Muhallabī preserved fragments of Uswānī in his treatise. Finally, Mas'ūdī's *Fields of Gold* (965) is dense with information as to the Zandj and the east coast. These texts early attracted the attention of specialists – Africanists and orientalists – like Delafosse, Cerulli,[44] Kramers[45] and Mauny.[46]

Legal and religious sources

Law treatises and hagiographical works of *Ṭabaqāt*, from *Ṣahnūn's Mudawwana* to the Kharijite treatises, are a mine of information on the Maghrib; some of them can be used for the Saharan zone of contact with black Africa. From Ibn as-Ṣaghīr's chronicle of the Rustamid imams of

39. In this connection see the highly critical attitude of L. Frobenius, and J. Rouch, 1953, which mostly denounces the ideological distortion in the Sudanese chronicles.

40. It is true that these texts chiefly concern the Sudanese belt and that therefore a unilateral reading of Arabic sources unaided by archaeology may falsify the perspective. But it is untrue that Arabic authors lacked objectivity. And to reproach them for the fragmentary, disorderly character of their writings is to abandon the point of view of the historian of societies for that of the historian of literature. Properly qualified opinions are expressed by N. Levtzion. A similar approach will be found in I. Hrbek's contribution to the 12th International Congress of Historical Studies held in Vienna (*Actes*, pp. 311ff.). See also T. Lewicki, 1971, and 1969.

41. See the *Unesco Courier*, June 1974.

42. Published by M. J. de Goeje, 1879–94, Vol. VII, as are most of the Arab geographers. G. Wiet's translation, 'Livre des pays', is useful but not always accurate.

43. *Kitāb ṣurat al-arḍ*, ibid., Vol. II; L. E. Kubbel and V. V. Matveiev, 1960 and 1965, pp. 33ff.

44. E. Cerulli, 1931.

45. 'Djughrāfiyā', *Encyclopédie de l'Islam*; L. Kramers, 1938.

46. The first chapter of his *Tableau* is a systematic inventory of geographical sources.

Tahert (early tenth century)[47] we find that there were trade links between the Ibadite principality and Gao by the end of the eighth century. If along with this chronicle we use later compilations like Wisyānī's *Siyar* we can extend that finding to the whole Saharan border of North Africa. But these hagiographical sources disclose information only in an allusive way. They have to be read against a general outline we have already established, and to be constantly crosschecked with other types of sources. They do not, as I see it, authorize constructions and deductions so bold as Lewicki's.

The second Islamic age (1050–1450)

What characterizes this long period is the richness, the excellence and the variety of our information. Archival sources, still secondary to literary writings, are none the less important: Geniza documents, Almoravid and Almohad letters, Waqf records, *fatwas*, Italian documents, official items interpolated in the great compilations. The chroniclers produce works of the highest order, valuable both for their observation of contemporary facts and for reproduction of ancient sources now lost. Finally, for black Africa our knowledge reaches its peak, while new African documents appear in the shape of the Ethiopian manuscripts.

Archival sources

(a) These relate to Egypt and the Maghrib almost exclusively. We now have documents of the Cairo Geniza that cover the whole period under consideration. Most of them, however, are of the Fatimid era, and only a few belong to the Mamluk centuries. These documents are odds and ends of family papers and business correspondence reflecting the preoccupations of the Jewish community in Egypt and elsewhere. Written in the Arabic language and the Hebrew alphabet, and undated, they have to be used with a certain amount of technical caution. But even as they stand they are an inexhaustible mine of information.[48] In the same category of private archives we put the Waqf records, numerous for the Mamluk era, preserved in the Cairo Registry[49] and the *fatwas* of the Hafsid era.

(b) On the other hand the *European* documents of the twelfth, thirteenth and fourteenth centuries concerning Egypt and the Maghrib fall partly in the private, partly in the public category. They are preserved in governmental and private archives in Venice, Genoa, Pisa, Barcelona, and consist of treaties, contracts and letters, usually having to do with business

47. Published in the *Actes du XIVe Congrès International des Orientalistes* (pt III), 1908 and studied by T. Lewicki, 1971.

48. S. D. Goitein is an authority on these: see his article 'Geniza' in the *Encyclopédie de l'Islam*, II, and Goitein, 1960, 1967. See also S. Shaked, 1964; H. Rabie, 1972, pp. 1–3. Many of these documents are in the British Museum and at Cambridge.

49. H. Rabie, 1972, pp. 6–8 and 200.

relations. Amari and Mas-Latrie published only a few of them.[50] Taken as a whole, they form a mass of documentation which may enable us to broaden our field of investigation in economic and social history.

(c) Strictly speaking, we have no state archives for this era. But some Almoravid and Almohad official items have been preserved and published which shed new light on the ideology and institutions generated by the two imperial movements.[51] Laroui says in this connection: 'One begins to see Almohadism from the inside: it is no longer impossible to write a religious and political history of the dynasty.'[52] At a later period, in Egypt, we come on editors of historical-legal encyclopedias who have compiled a good number of official documents; their detailed descriptions of Egypt's fiscal and institutional structures are generally based on the use of state papers. In this half-archival, half-chronicle genre we can place Mammāti's *Qawānīn al-dawāwīn* (Ayyubid period), Qalqashansī's *Ṣubḥ al-A'shā* (fourteenth century), and Maqrīzī's numerous works, among them the priceless *Khiṭaṭ* (fifteenth century).[53] Maqrīzī is a good source not only for the whole history of Islamic Egypt but also for Nubia, Sudan, and Ethiopia.[54]

Narrative sources

(A) CHRONICLES

After a century of silence – the twelfth, during which we find almost nothing but the anonymous *al-Istibsār* and a few minor works – the thirteenth and fourteenth centuries offer us a harvest of chronicles rich from every point of view, from Ibn al-Athīr's *Kamil* to Ibn Khaldūn's *Kitāb al-'Ibar*, passing through Ibn al-'Idhārī, Nuwayrī, Ibn Abī Zar', Dhahabī. Besides telling about their own times, these men undertook to synthesize the events of past centuries. Nuwayrī is as important for the Arab conquest in the Maghrib[55] as for the Mamluks, Ibn al-'Idhārī as important for the whole Ifrīqiyan past as for the Almohads; and Ibn Khaldūn's knowledge of the Berber world makes him the supreme authority for the history of Africa.

(B) GEOGRAPHY

Geographical treatises abound during these four centuries. Their value varies with the writer and the region described. Two geographers stand out from the crowd by virtue of the scope and quality of their information: al-

50. M. Amari, 1863; L. Mas-Latrie, 1866.

51. *Lettres officielles almoravides*, edited by H. Mu'nis and A. M. Makki; *Trente-sept lettres officielles almohades*, edited and translated by E. Lévi-Provençal, al-Baydaq, 1928.

52. A. Laroui, 1970, p. 162.

53. H. Rabie, 1972, pp. 10–20.

54. His *Kitāb al-Ilmām* gives us the list of the Muslim kingdoms of Ethiopia – borrowed, it is true, from 'Umarī. An excerpt was published in 1790, at Leyden, as *Historia regum islamicorum in Abyssinia*.

55. But this fragment is still in manuscript.

Bakrīh (fl. 1068) in the eleventh century, al-'Umarī (d. 1342) in the fourteenth. Idrīsī's well-known work is debatable and debated, but there is original information to be gleaned from less familiar geographical writings: Ibn Sa'īd's, for instance, so interesting on the Sudan.[56]

Al-Bakrīh's *Masālik wa'l-Mamālik*[57] represents the apogee of our geographical knowledge of the Maghrib and the Sudan. He did not travel in those countries himself, but he made intelligent use both of al-Warraq's notes, now lost, and of first-hand information from merchants and travellers. Al-Idrīsī's *Book of Roger* (1154) borrows a good deal from its predecessors. The description, confused for Ethiopia, becomes less inaccurate for West Africa. But here and there an original and sometimes valuable note slips in.

Ibn Sa'īd al-Gharnātī's *Geography* (before 1286) borrows from Idrīsī in its description of Ethiopia, though some new information is to be found in it. Its chief interest lies in the description of the Sudan, largely based on the writings of a twelfth-century traveller, Ibn Fātima.

For the historian of black Africa, the major work of the fourteenth century is al-'Umarī's *Masālik al-Abṣār*.[58] The testimony of an observer of the highest calibre, it is our main source for the study of the Mali Kingdom both in its internal organization and in its relations with Egypt and Islam. But it is also the richest Arabic account we have of the Muslim states of fourteenth-century Ethiopia. Besides giving an interesting description, al-'Umarī poses the problem of the emergence of the state in the black world and the problem of islamization – just as three centuries earlier al-Bakrī posed the problem of the great gold trade. Al-Bakrīh's work suggested the depth of the bonds between the Maghrib and the Sudan: 'Umarī's suggests the movement towards a bond with Egypt. 'Umarī's work is supplemented by that of a direct observer of Sudanese and Maghribian reality, Ibn Battūta.

But there are many minor geographers and many authors of accounts of travels, and they should by all means be consulted. I might mention: al-Zuhrī (twelfth century), Yâqût, Dimashqî (fourteenth century), the so-called 'Mozhafferian Geography', Ibn Jubayr, Baghdadî, Abdarī, Tijanî, Balawî, Himyarî.

(c) SOURCES RELIGIOUS AND LITERARY IN INSPIRATION

The background of the religious sources is varied. There are works of *Ṭabaqāt* and hagiography – Sunnite, Kharijite, Maraboutic and even Christian (from the Coptic community). There are also manuscripts of Ethiopian churches that reproduce official documents in their margins. All these writings prove useful, not only in showing us how the religious

56. For an exhaustive list of geographers see L. E. Kubbel and V. V. Matveiev, 1961, as supplemented by the first chapter of R. Mauny, 1961 the notice by T. Lewicki, 1971 and the introduction to A Miquel's thesis, 1967.

57. Edited and translated by M. de Slane as *Description de l'Afrique septentrionale.*

58. Translated in part by M. Gaudefroy-Demombynes as *L'Afrique moins l'Egypte.*

sensibility and the religious world evolved, but in adding to our knowledge of social life. Works like Mālikī's *Riyādh* or 'Iyādh's *Madārik* have sociological jottings scattered through them. Kharijite sources are of course very important for the whole Saharan zone of the Maghrib, which was the zone of contact with the blacks; the chief representatives are Wisyanī, Darjīnī, Abu Zakariyā, even a late author like Shammākhī. Finally, the whole mass of Arabic and Coptic writing produced in medieval Egypt by the local church illuminates the relations between churches and the relations between the ecclesiastical hierarchy and the state.[59] Literary sources are plentiful during this period; they pertain almost exclusively to the Maghrib and Egypt. In this category the *Rasā'il* of al-Qādhī al-Fādhil and especially Safadī's great dictionary *al-Wafibi-l-Wafayat* hold a special place.

Thus our documentation for this second Islamic age is copious, varied and generally of high quality in contrast to the previous period. In properly Islamic Africa our writers, no longer content with tracing the simple political outlines, now throw a strong light on the working of institutions and the deep undercurrents of history. For black Africa our knowledge reaches its fullest amplitude, until the time when European and autochthonous documents enable us to go deeper and push its limits out to zones that have thus far remained in impenetrable darkness.

Conclusion

It would be wrong to think that the African continent is in a state of hopeless penury as regards pre-fifteenth-century written sources, but it is true that on the whole it is less well supplied than Europe or Asia. Nevertheless, while a great part of the continent is totally devoid of such sources, for the remaining part historical knowledge is possible, and in the case of Egypt is based on a documentation that is exceptionally rich. This means that – failing the discovery of new material, which seems improbable – a meticulous and judicious exploitation of these texts can still contribute a great deal to our knowledge. It is therefore urgent to turn to a full-scale programme of textual criticism, re-edition, collation and translation, a work already begun by a few pioneers, and which must be extended.

Finally, while our sources were written in a framework of universal cultures with focal points outside Africa – classical and Islamic cultures – they have the advantage that they are most of them *common* and can therefore be read in an African context, though we have to be careful when we come up against ideological presuppositions. This is particularly true of Arabic sources, which still form the main basis of our knowledge. Their being relatively or absolutely foreign to their subject takes nothing from

59. *Patrologia Orientalis*, the main collection. Works of concern to us are *inter alia* those of Severus of Alexandria (tenth century) and Ibn Mufrah (eleventh); interesting for Ethiopia: *Kitāb Siyar al-Abā' al-Batāriqa*. Cf. also Michael the Syrian, edited and translated by Chabot, 3 Vols (Paris: 1899, 1910).

their value, except by the fact of distance. Therefore, while socio-cultural differences must be recognized, the fact remains that these sources bring out a certain solidarity in African communication – a solidarity of which, hitherto, Islamic and African scholars have not always been aware.

PLATE 5.1 *Verso of Arabic manuscript* (Bibliothèque Nationale de Paris, MS 2291, fo. 103. *Ibn Battūta* (Second Part) *with a reference to Mali*)

Written sources from the fifteenth century onwards

I. HRBEK

Parallel with the profound changes in the world and especially in Africa at the end of the fifteenth and the beginning of the sixteenth century went changes in the character, provenance and volume of written source materials for African history. As against the previous period a certain number of new trends may be discerned in the flow of this material, some of them touching the whole continent, others only some parts of it, mainly in sub-Saharan Africa.

First, together with the continuous growth of all kinds of narrative sources (travellers' accounts, descriptions, chronicles, and so on) emerge numerous and various materials of a primary character such as official, commercial or missionary correspondence and reports, legal deeds and other items of archival nature, found only sporadically before this period. The increasing abundance of this material offers the historian much greater aid, but at the same time makes a general survey of it more complicated.

We can observe, moreover, a sharp decrease in the volume of external Arabic narrative sources for Africa south of the Sahara. On the other hand this period gave birth to historical literature written in Arabic by autochthones and it is only from this time on that we are able to hear the authentic voice of Africans from south of the Sahara speaking about their own history. The earliest and best-known examples of this local historiography come from the Sudanic belt and from the East African coast, whereas in other parts of tropical Africa similar development took place only later.

In the last 200 years the Africans also started to write in their own languages, using first the Arabic script (e.g. Kiswahili, Hausa, Fulfulde, Kanembu, Dyula, Malagasy, etc.), later in the Latin alphabet. There exist also historical (and other) material in scripts of genuine African origin, such as the Bamum and Vai scripts.

The third trend, a corollary of the preceding one, is the emergence of a literature written in English (and to a smaller degree in other European languages) by Africans, either liberated slaves or their descendants in America, conscious of their African past.

Lastly, the external Arabic sources gradually give way to narratives in various European languages; the amount of this literature shows a steady increase and reaches in the nineteenth and twentieth centuries such volume that the bibliographical reference books alone could be counted in tens.

There was, of course, not only change, but a continuity, too, in the historiography of some parts of Africa, mainly that of Egypt, the Maghrib and Ethiopia. There the chroniclers and biographers kept alive the tradition inherited from the preceding period. While in Egypt and in part in Ethiopia a certain decline befell the quality and even the quantity of such works, the Maghrib and in particular Morocco still produced competent scholars whose contributions to their countries' history are considerable.

The changing situation is reflected also in the geographical area covered by written sources. Whereas before the sixteenth century the fringes of the Sudanese Sahel and the narrow strip of the East African coast formed the boundary of geographical, and thus of historical knowledge, the new epoch was gradually adding new regions, previously untouched by this kind of source. The amount and quality of such sources differ widely, of course, as between the various regions, and the situation changed from one century to another; even more complicated is the distribution according to the languages, character, purpose and origin of these documents.

Generally speaking the expansion progressed from the coast to the interior. But the movement was rather slow and it was not before the end of the eighteenth century that it gained any real acceleration. The African coast and its immediate hinterland were described by the Portuguese in a rough way as early as the fifteenth century; in the following centuries the written sources, now in many languages, started to yield more detailed and abundant information about the coastal peoples. The Europeans penetrated into the interior only in a few regions (on the Senegal and the Gambia, in the Niger delta and Benin, in the realm of the Kongo state and along the Zambezi to the Mwene Mutapa Empire), thus bringing these areas into the horizon of written sources. At the same time some parts of Africa, hitherto practically untouched, became better known, that is, the south-west African coast or Madagascar.

Much more ground was covered by sources written in Arabic. The Sudanese historiographical school, besides itself yielding information about previously unknown regions, spread to other areas, mostly in a southward direction, so that by the nineteenth century the whole belt between the Sahara and the forest – and at some points even as far as the coast – can be considered to be covered by local written sources. But large parts of the interior had to await the nineteenth century before any reliable written accounts were produced.

Even in the coastal regions we encounter wide differences in historical information: on the whole the Atlantic coast is better provided with written documents than the eastern coast, and again, the amount of material available for ancient Kongo, the Senegambia, the coast between Cape

Palmas and the Niger delta is much richer than are the sources for, say, Liberia, Cameroon, Gabon or Namibia. The situation differs also according to periods: there is much more written information for the eastern coast, Benin or Ethiopia in the sixteenth and seventeenth centuries than in the eighteenth and for the Sahara in the first half than in the second half of the nineteenth century.

Owing to this uneven distribution of the source material in space, time and character as well as its various origins and languages, it is preferable to discuss it according to varying criteria and not to stick to one procedure only. Consequently we will present it in some cases according to geographical regions, in others according to its origin and character.

North Africa and Ethiopia

North Africa

Source material for Arab-speaking North Africa, like that for other parts of the continent, underwent some profound changes compared with the preceding period. These changes do not particularly touch local historical writing, which continued as before in its traditional way to chronicle the main events. No outstanding figure comparable to the great Arab historians of the middle ages emerged among the late annalists and compilers and the critical approach to history as preached by Ibn Khaldun was not continued by his successors. It was not until the twentieth century that modern Arab historiography was born.

The changes concern chiefly two kinds of sources, the archival documents of various origins, and the European accounts. It is only from the beginning of the sixteenth century that the primary source material, both in Arabic and Turkish, starts to flow more abundantly. The Ottoman archives are comparable to the most wealthy ones in Europe in volume and importance, but as yet they are only rarely employed and studied by historians of this part of Africa. From the same period originate also the secondary archives in countries that formed part of the Ottoman Empire (Egypt, Tripolitania, Tunisia and Algeria).[1] A special case is that of Morocco whose archives preserved rich historical material throughout its independence.[2] The documents it possesses are chiefly government, administrative and juridical records; less abundant is the material dealing with trade and production, social and cultural life, at least before the nineteenth century. This is partly due to the lack of the private archives that furnish such valuable information for the economic and social history of Europe. For some countries and periods these gaps can be filled: for instance, material on Morocco, found in many European countries, has been collected and published in the monumental work of Henri Castries.[3] The compilation of similar collections, or at least

1. J. Deny, 1930; R. Mantran, 1965; R. le Tourneau, 1954.
2. A. Meknasi, 1953; G. Ayache, 1961.
3. *Les Sources inédites de l'histoire du Maroc*, 24 Vols (Paris, 1905–51).

lists of the pertinent documents, concerning the other North African countries is among the most pertinent urgent tasks for the near future.

Turning now to the narrative sources in Arabic we can discern a steady decline in historical writing, both in quality and quantity, with the sole exception of Morocco. Here the traditional school of chroniclers continued to produce detailed histories of the two Sherifian dynasties up to the present time. Reference may be made by way of example to *Ma'sul* by Mokhtar Sussi in twenty volumes and the *Histoire de Tétouan*, now in process of publication.[4] From among the uninterrupted chain of historians we can indicate only the names of the most distinguished. The Sa'di dynasty found an excellent historian in al-Ufrani (died *c.* 1738),[5] who covered the years 1511–1670; the following period (1631–1812) had the good fortune to be described in detail by the greatest Moroccan historian since the middle ages, al-Zayyani (d. 1833),[6] whereas al-Nasiri al-Slawi (d. 1897) wrote a general history of his country with special emphasis on the nineteenth century, combining traditional and modern methods and using archival documents as well. He is also the author of a geographical work which supplies much material about social and economic life.[7] To these strictly historical works must be added also the narratives of travellers, mostly pilgrims, who described not only Morocco but also other Arab countries as far as Arabia. The two best accounts of this kind are those written by al-Ayyashi from Sijilmasa (d. 1679) and by Ahmad al-Darci from Tamghrut on the Saharan fringes (d. 1738);[8] other interesting pieces are the report of al-Tamghruti, Moroccan ambassador to the Ottoman court in 1589–91, and the *Bihla* of Ibn Othman, Moroccan ambassador to the court of Madrid.[9]

In the countries between Morocco and Egypt the local chronicles were neither so abundant nor similar in quality. For Algeria there are anonymous Arabic and Turkish histories of Aruj and Khayruddin Barbarossa,[10] and a military history up to 1775, by Muhammad al-Tilimsani.[11] Tunisian history can be traced through a series of annalistic works, going from al-Zarkashi (up to 1525)[12] to Maqdish al-Safaqusi (d. 1818);[13] a history of Tripoli has been written by Muhammad Ghalbun (fl. 1739).[14] Ibadite chronicles and biographies, like that of al-Shammakhi (d. 1524), merit

4. E. Lévi-Provençal, 1922; Mokhtar Sussi, *Ma'sul*, 20 Vols published; Daoud, *Histoire de Tétouan*.

5. Edited and translated by O. Houdas (Paris, 1899).

6. Edited and translated by O. Houdas (Paris, 1886).

7. Edited in Cairo, 1894 in 4 Vols. Many partial translations in French and Spanish.

8. Both translated by S. Berbrugger (Paris, 1846).

9. Translated by H. de Castries (Paris, 1929).

10. Edited by Nuruddin (Algiers, 1934).

11. Translated by A. Rousseau (Algiers, 1841).

12. Translated by E. Fagnan (Constantine, n.d.).

13. Published Tunis, 1903.

14. Published by Ettore Rossi (Bologna, 1936). There are also some Turkish chronicles of Tripolitania.

special attention as they furnish much valuable information about the Sahara and the Sudan.[15]

Biographies, or biographical dictionaries, general or particular, mostly of prominent persons (scholars, lawyers, princes, mystics, writers, and so on), often combine biographical material with historical narratives and shed light on many aspects of cultural and social history. This category of writing flourished in all Arab countries, especially in Morocco. Even some poems, sometimes in a vernacular dialect, can serve as historical sources, for example, the satirical poems of the Egyptian al-Hasan al-Hijazi (d. 1719) in which he describes the main events of his times.[16]

For the history of Ottoman Egypt one must depend on chronicles still largely unpublished and unexplored. The country produced in this period only two great historians, one at the beginning of Turkish rule, the other just at its close; Ibn Iyas (d. 1524) recorded day by day the history of his epoch, thus offering a wealth of detail rarely found in other works.[17] Al-Jabarti (d. 1822) is the chronicler of the last days of the Ottoman domination, of the Napoleonic occupation and of the rise of Muhammad Ali, thus covering a crucial epoch of Egyptian history.[18] Although many chronicles and other historical works from Arab countries have been published, the greater number of them are still in manuscript in many libraries both within and outside their countries of origin, awaiting study and publication.

In this period the accounts of European travellers attain an increasing importance. Although the anti-Islamic bias of their authors rarely allows for a fully objective reporting, they contain many interesting insights and observations not to be found elsewhere as the local writers considered many aspects of life as commonplace and thus devoid of interest. The host of European travellers, ambassadors, consuls, merchants and even prisoners (among them Miguel Cervantes) who have left reminiscences and more or less detailed accounts of the Maghrib countries they visited, is endless; the same is perhaps even more true of Egypt which attracted many visitors by her commercial importance and the proximity of the Holy Land.[19] Of particular interest is the monumental work *Description de l'Egypte* (24 volumes, Paris, 1821–24), compiled by the scientific staff of the Napoleonic expedition, an inexhaustible source for every kind of information about Egypt on the eve of a new epoch.

In the nineteenth century the sources for the history of North Africa are as abundant as for any European country: local chronicles and travellers' narratives take second place to more objective archival sources, statistics, newspapers and other direct or indirect evidence, thus permitting historians

15. T. Lewicki, 1961.
16. Referred to by al-Jabarti.
17. G. Wiet, 1960.
18. Many editions; an unreliable translation by Chefik Mansour (Cairo, 1886–96).
19. J. M. Carré, 1932.

to employ the classical methods and approaches elaborated for a fully documented history such as the European.

Two Arab-speaking regions, Mauritania and the eastern Sudan, deserve a separate treatment owing to their particular situation on the outskirts of the Arab world. A common feature of the source material in these two countries is the predominance of biographies, genealogies and poetry over the strictly annalistic form of historical writing, at least until the close of the eighteenth century. For Mauritania various genealogies and biographies were published by Ismael Hamet;[20] this material was augmented by poems and other folklore material collected by René Basset and lately by H. T. Norris.[21] A fruitful and active search for new material is under way by the Mauritanian scholar Mukhtar wuld Hamidun. The first truly historical work originates from the beginning of this century: *Al-Wasit* by Ahmad al-Shinqiti is an encyclopedia of Moorish history and culture past and present.[22] There is a number of local manuscript chronicles of greater or lesser value, in the style of the short chronicles of Nema, Walata and Shinqit.[23] Arabic sources from Mauritania are of particular interest and importance, because in many instances they not only cover Mauritania proper, but also all the adjacent countries of the western Sudan. Owing to the close relations in the past between Mauritania and Morocco, the libraries and archives of the latter must certainly contain precious historical material for the former. In addition to Arabic sources there is also European narrative literature – for the coastal regions beginning in the fifteenth century, for the riverine parts from the end of the seventeenth and from the next century we find diplomatic and commercial correspondence both in Arabic and European languages.

The local historiography in the eastern Sudan seems to have started only in the closing years of the Funj Sultanate, that is, at the beginning of the nineteenth century when oral tradition was put down in the so-called *Funj Chronicle*, extant in several versions.[24] A useful source is the genealogies of various Arab groups[25] as well as the great biographical dictionary of Sudanese scholars, the *Tabaqat*, written by Wad Dayfallah, which is a mine of information on social, cultural and religious life in the Funj Kingdom.[26] The earliest known outside visitor was the Jewish traveller David Reubeni in 1523. Until the nineteenth century there is only a handful of valuable accounts, but among these we find the narratives of such sharp observers as

20. I. Hamet, 1911.
21. R. Basset, 1909–10; T. H. Norris, 1968.
22. A. al-Shinqiti, 1910, and many new editions. Partial French translation, St. Louis, 1953.
23. P. Marty, 1927; Norris, in *BIFAN*, 1962; V. Monteil, in *BIFAN*, 1965.
24. Investigated by M. Shibeika, 1947.
25. Collected by H. A. MacMichael, 1922, together with other historical documents.
26. The most up-to-date commented edition is by Yusuf Fadl Hasan, 1971.

James Bruce (in 1773), W. J. Browne (1792–8) and al-Tunisi (1803), the two last being the first visitors to Darfur.[27] In the first half of the nineteenth century the Sudan was visited by more travellers than any other part of tropical Africa. Their accounts are innumerable and of varied quality as historical sources. Until the 1830s no written sources exist for the upper reaches of the Nile (to the south of 12° latitude); on the other hand the northern part is well covered by Egyptian (Cairo archives) and some European archival documents. Of outstanding importance for the last twenty years of the nineteenth century are the records of the Mahdiyya, consisting of some 80 000 Arabic documents, preserved now mostly in Khartoum.

Ethiopia

The situation in respect to written sources has been not dissimilar in Ethiopia. Here, as in Arab-speaking North Africa, the historian has at his disposal a wide range of documents, both internal and external. For some crucial periods he can even employ material from opposing sources, so the Muslim invasion of Ahmad Gran in the first half of the sixteenth century is covered from the Ethiopian point of view by the *Royal Chronicle* (in Ge'ez) of the Emperor Lebna Dengel and from the Muslim side by the detailed chronicle written in 1543 by the scribe of Gran, Arab-Faqih, not to mention Portuguese records from eye-witnesses.[28]

The writing of royal chronicles had already started in the thirteenth century, and for nearly every reign, even during the period of decline, there is one or more detailed chronicle, recording the main events of the epoch.[29] This tradition continued throughout the nineteenth century and well into the twentieth, as witnessed by the *Amharic Chronicle* of the Emperor Menelik II.[30] Many other kinds of Ethiopian literature yield useful historical material, viz. hagiographies, religious polemics, poetry, legends, histories of monasteries, and so on. A unique document is *The History of the Galla* by the monk Bahrey (1593), an eye-witness of the Galla invasion of Ethiopia.[31] A century later, Hiob Ludolf, the founder of Ethiopian studies in Europe, compiled from the information of a learned Ethiopian one of the first general histories of the country.[32]

Being the only Christian country left in Africa, Ethiopia naturally aroused far more interest in Europe than other parts of the continent even

27. J. Bruce, 1790; W. G. Browne, 1806; Omar El-Tounsy, 1845.
28. Arab-Faqih, 1897–1901; M. Castanhoso, 1548; English translation, Cambridge, 1902.
29. Cf. R. Pankhurst, 1966; H. W. Blundell, 1923.
30. Written by Gabré Selassié and translated into French, Paris, 1930–1.
31. Cf. C. F. Beckingham and G. W. B. Huntingford, 1954. Apart from Bahrey's History, this book contains parts of Almeida's *History of High Ethiopia* (1660).
32. Hiob Ludolf, 1681; English translation, 1682–4.

as early as the fifteenth century. No wonder that the number of foreign travellers, missionaries, diplomats, soldiers, merchants or adventurers who visited this country and recorded it, is very high. They include not only Portuguese, French, Italians and British, but also many people from many other countries, such as Russians, Czechs, Swedes, Armenians and Georgians.[33] And there occasionally emerge Turkish or Arabic records which supplement the other sources in many ways.[34]

From the second half of the nineteenth century onwards, the documents in the archives of all the major European powers as well as in Addis Ababa and even in Khartoum furnish important historical material. The importance of a close study of original Amharic documents for a correct interpretation of history has been demonstrated by the recent brilliant analysis of the Wichale treaty (1889) by Sven Rubenson.[35]

Republic of South Africa

Compared with other parts of the continent (except the Arab-speaking countries and Ethiopia) South Africa offers, for the period under review, a much richer amount of the kinds of material already discussed, both archival and narrative. The lack of sources of genuine African origin before the nineteenth century represents a certain disadvantage, even if many European narratives preserved pieces of the oral tradition of local peoples. The earliest historical information derives from Portuguese or Dutch sailors who were shipwrecked on the south-east coast in the course of the sixteenth and seventeenth centuries.[36] With the establishment of the Dutch colony at the Cape (1652) the flow of material becomes richer and more varied: it consists on one hand of official documents, kept now mainly in archives in South Africa itself, but also in London and the Hague, partially published or made accessible by other means, but for the major part still not readily available.[37] On the other hand narrative literature is represented by books and articles written by white travellers, traders, officials, missionaries and settlers who were first-hand observers of African societies. For a long time,

33. Cf. the monumental collection of C. Beccari, 1903–17. But many previously unknown records have been discovered since Beccari and await publication and study.

34. E.g. the famous Turkish traveller Ewliya Chelebi (d. 1679), the tenth volume of whose *Siyasat-name* (Travelbook) contains descriptions of Egypt, Ethiopia and the Sudan. The Yemeni ambassador al-Khaymi al-Kawkabani left a vivid account of his mission in 1647 to the Emperor Fasiladas for whose reign no Ethiopian chronicle is extant. It is published by F. E. Peiser in two volumes, Berlin, 1894 and 1898.

35. Sven Rubenson, 'The protectorate paragraph of the Wichale treaty', *JAH*, 5, 2 (1964), and the discussion with C. Giglio, *JAH* 6, 2 (1965) and 7, 3 (1966).

36. Cf. G. M. Theal, 1898–1903, and C. R. Boxer, 1959.

37. Extracts of official journals and other documents pertaining to San, Khoi and Bantu-speaking peoples are in D. Moodie, 1960; see also G. M. Theal, 1897–1905.

however, their geographical horizon remained rather restricted and it was not until the second half of the eighteenth century that they penetrated any distance into the interior. It is thus natural that the earliest narratives deal with the Cape Khoi who have now died out; the first detailed account, after some seventeenth-century records,[38] is that given by Peter Kolb (1705–12).[39] During the Dutch period many Europeans visited the Cape Colony but only rarely did they show more than a fleeting interest in Africans or venture into the interior; a great number of their reports has been collected by Godée-Molsbergen and l'Honoré Naber, and many lesser known accounts have been published since the 1920s by the Van Riebeeck Society of Cape Town.[40] A more intimate picture of African societies can be gleaned from the records of missionaries[41] and from some experienced observers from the end of the eighteenth and the beginning of the nineteenth centuries such as Sparrman, Levaillant, Alberti, John Barrow and Lichtenstein.[42] A place of honour belongs to John Philip, whose life and work was dedicated to the defence of African rights and thus reveals aspects not usually found in more official accounts.[43]

With the commercial missionary and colonial expansion in the nineteenth century, more and richer material became available regarding African ethnic groups farther away. Although Namibia was sporadically visited in the late eighteenth century,[44] a more detailed description of the life of San, Nama and Herero only began after the 1830s, when missionaries launched their activities[45] and the country became the target of explorers like J. Alexander, F. Galton, J. Tindall and others.[46]

A similar situation obtains for the areas north of the Orange river: the reports of early traders and hunters give way to an increasing amount of accounts written by explorers and missionaries better equipped for observation through their longer experience and knowledge of African languages, like Robert Moffat, E. Casalis, T. Arbousset and others; the *primus inter pares* is, of course, David Livingstone.[47] Various records (archival documents, correspondence, official acts and deeds, and so on) for

38. I. Shapera, 1668 (1933); Willem ten Rhyne (1686) and J. G. de Grevebroek (1695).

39. P. Kolb (1719).

40. E. C. Godée-Molsbergen, 1916–32; S. L. L.'Honoré-Naber, 1931.

41. Cf. e.g. D. K. Müller, 1923.

42. A. Sparrmann, 1785; F. Levaillant, 1790; L. Alberti, 1811; J. Barrow, 1801–3; H. Lichtenstein, 1811.

43. J. Philips, 1828.

44. A. D. Watts, 1926.

45. H. Vedder's standard work *South-West Africa in Early Times* is compiled mainly from German missionaries' reports.

46. Sir James Alexander, 1836 (1967); F. Galton, 1853; *Journal of Joseph Tindall 1839–1855* (Cape Town, 1959).

47. R. Moffat, 1842 and 1945; E. Casalis, 1859; English edn, London, 1861; T. Arbousset, 1842; English edn, Cape Town, 1846; D. Livingstone, 1957.

the early history of Lesotho were collected by G. M. Theal.[48] A positive feature of this period is the emergence of documents expressing African views, such as letters by Moshesh and other African leaders.

In contrast to the coast, the interior of Natal and Zululand became known to outsiders only in the first decades of the nineteenth century. The early observers such as N. Isaacs or H. F. Fynn[49] were usually untrained, rarely accurate and lacked objectivity when dealing with non-whites. The Zulu had, on the other hand, the good fortune to have their oral traditions collected comparatively early, in the 1880s, although they were published later, by A. T. Bryant, whose book must nevertheless be used with caution.[50]

As with other parts of Africa, the accounts written by Europeans increased enormously in the course of the nineteenth century and there is no need to discuss all its kinds and authors at any length. More interesting are the records of the reactions of the first literate Africans or of some traditional rulers, preserved in correspondence, newspapers, complaints, diaries, deeds or, later, in first attempts to write down the histories of their own peoples.

In addition to the voluminous correspondence between African rulers such as Moshesh, Dingaan, Cetshwayo, Mzilikazi, Lobenguela, Witbooi, the Griqua chiefs and many others, and the colonial authorities, there are such items as the Ancestral Laws (Vaderlike Wete) of the Rehoboth Community from the year 1874, or the *Diary* of Henrik Witbooi,[51] both written in Afrikaans. There are numerous petitions and complaints of Africans, preserved in South African archives or in London as well as many surveys, plans and statistics compiled on the basis of African oral information.

Thanks to the emergence of newspapers in vernacular languages we are able to assess the ideas of the early representatives of a changing society. In the weekly *Isidigimi* (published between 1870 and 1880) appeared the first criticism of European policies and its negative impact on African life, written by the first proto-nationalists like Tiyo Soga (d. 1871) or G. Chamzashe (d. 1896) as well as the collection of Xhosa historical traditions, by W. W. Gqoba (d. 1888). Another forum of African opinion since 1884 was *Imbo Zabantsundu* (The Voice of Black People) edited for many years by John T. Jabawu (d. 1921); shortly before the First World War eleven journals in African languages were being published, but not all of them defended the cause of Africans. An extraordinary figure was Mgnoki (d. 1924), an active participant in the Zulu war of 1879 who later published (in

48. G. M. Theal, *Basutoland Records*, 3 Vols, 1883 (Vols 4 and 5 unpublished MSS.) in Cape Town Archives).

49. N. Isaacs, 1836; N. F. Fynn, 1950.

50. A. T. Bryant, 1929. See also his *A History of the Zulu*, first published as a series of articles in 1911–13 and as a book in Cape Town, 1964. Cf. also J. Bird, 1888.

51. The laws are preserved in Rehoboth and in Windhoek; Witbooi's *Diary* was published in Cape Town in 1929.

the United States) his reminiscences as well as many articles about life in South Africa.[52] It was not until the twentieth century that the first histories written by Africans themselves appeared,[53] thus starting a new epoch in South African historiography. The history of this part of the continent has been for too long viewed from the vantage point of the white community which tends to treat the history of the African peoples as something negligible and without importance. The struggle now going on in South Africa in every field of human activity necessitates also a new approach to the sources; particular attention must be paid to the written evidence of the hard struggle of the Africans for their rights.[54] Only research based on all the evidence and material will allow the writing of a truthful history of South Africa.

External narrative sources

In Arabic and other Oriental languages

Whereas the period between the ninth and the fifteenth centuries is sometimes called 'the era of Arabic sources' owing to the prevalence of written material in this language, the period now under review is marked by a steep decline in this respect. The reasons for this change are connected with the general political and cultural development of the Islamic world and they will be discussed in an appropriate place in a later volume. This does not mean that there are no Arabic narrative sources at all, but their number and quality, with a few exceptions, cannot be compared either with the preceding period or with sources of other origins.

Although the work of Leo Africanus (originally known as al-Hasan al-Wuzzan al-Zayyati) was written in Italian, it arose from the Arab geographical tradition; moreover his travels in the western and central Sudan at the beginning of the sixteenth century were undertaken before his conversion to Christianity and retirement to Italy, consequently as an Arab and Muslim. The work is not free from mistakes, both geographical and historical; it nevertheless supplied Europe for nearly three centuries with its only real knowledge about the interior of Africa.[55]

A very remarkable source is represented by the nautical works of Ahmad ibn Majid (beginning of the sixteenth century), the pilot who led Vasco da Gama from Malindi to India. Among his numerous books on the theory and practice of navigation, the one dealing with the East African coast is the most important as it contains, in addition to a vast amount of topographical

52. Cf. L. D. Turner, 1955.

53. Cf. S. T. Plaatje, 1916 and 1930; S. M. Molema, 1920; J. H. Soga, 1930; idem, 1930; T. B. Soga, 1936.

54. See e.g. D. T. Jabavu, 1920; J. Mahabava, 1922.

55. First published in Rome, 1550; the best modern translation is Jean-Léon l'Africain, *Description de l'Afrique*, by A. Epaulard, annotated by A. Epaulard, T. Monod, H. Lhote and R. Mauny, 2 vols (Paris, 1956).

material and a chart of sea routes, strong opinions about the Portuguese in the Indian Ocean.[56] A few original details about East Africa and the Zanj are to be found in the *Chronicle of the Fortress of Aden*, written by Abu Makhrama (d. 1540).[57] There is a late chronicle bearing on the same region by Salil ibn Raziq (d. 1873) entitled *History of the Imams and Sayyids of Oman*, in which is incorporated an earlier work written in the 1720s by Sirhan ibn Sirhan of Oman.[58]

The eighteenth century did not produce any Arabic external source of great value for the history of sub-Saharan Africa although the beginning of the next century witnessed a certain revival in this respect. Al-Tunisi (d. 1857), whom we have already mentioned, described his visit to Wadai in the first chronicle devoted to that kingdom, and also wrote a valuable report on Darfur.[59] A few decades earlier and at the other end of the Sudanic belt, the Moroccan Abd-al-Salam Shabayni set down information about Timbuktu and the region of Massina before the rise of the Dina.[60]

The history of the Songhay Empire, its fall and the later development of the Niger valley was recorded (in addition to the Sudanese chronicles) by some of the Moroccan historians mentioned above. In recent times many unknown sources for relations between the Maghrib and the Sudan have been discovered in Moroccan libraries and now await publication and study by historians of Africa. There must also be most valuable material, in Arabic and Turkish, scattered throughout other North African countries and in Turkey itself, of whose existence we have so far only extremely scanty information. This situation offers exciting prospects for the historian and the locating, editing and translating of this material are among the most urgent tasks in the near future.

The material in other oriental languages is even scarcer than in Arabic but one must not preclude the discovery of more material in, for instance, Persian or some of the Indian languages. So far the most relevant source remains the Turkish traveller Ewliya Chelebi, who visited Egypt and parts of the Sudan and Ethiopia, but whose knowledge of other parts of Africa was indirect.[61] The same is true of his compatriot the Admiral Sidi Ali who copied and translated from the Arabic parts of Ibn Majid's book, *Al-Muhit*, on the Indian Ocean, adding only some new details.[62] In the early nineteenth century an Azerbaijani scholar, Zain al-Abidin Shirwani, visited Somalia, Ethiopia, the eastern Sudan and the Maghrib describing his travels in a book entitled *Bustanu s-Seyahe* (The Garden of Travels).[63] It

56. T. A. Shumovskiy, 1957.
57. Published by O. Löfgren, 1936–50.
58. Translated by G. P. Badger (London, 1871).
59. *Voyage au Ouaday*, translated by Dr Perron (Paris, 1851).
60. Published by J. G. Jackson, 1820.
61. E. Chelebi, 1938.
62. M. Bittner, 1897.
63. Cf. M. Khanykov, 1859. The parts concerning eastern Africa are being prepared for a translation by V. P. Smirnova in Leningrad.

seems that a vivid interest in Africa, especially Ethiopia, existed in Transcaucasia, mainly among the Armenians. At the end of the seventeenth century two Armenian priests, Astvacatur Timbuk and Avatik Bagdasarian, who later left a description of their travels, journeyed across Africa, starting in Ethiopia and continuing through Nubia, Darfur, Lake Chad and Takrur to Morocco.[64] In 1821 Warga, an Armenian of Astrakhan, crossed the Sahara from the north, visited Timbuktu and arrived on the Gold Coast where his short but highly informative narrative was written down in English.[65] Other material concerning Africa in the Armenian or Georgian languages exists in the libraries and archives of these Soviet Republics.[66]

In European languages

The enormous volume of European narrative literature on tropical Africa since the beginning of the sixteenth century makes an enumeration of even the most important works or authors an impossibility. A survey of the general character and an evaluation of this literature as a source for African history will better serve the purpose of this chapter than an endless list of names and titles.

The change in geographical scope is well known: by the beginning of the sixteenth century the whole coastal line from the Senegal up to Cape Guardafui was known to the Portuguese, who at the close of the same century penetrated into the interior in ancient Kongo, Angola and along the Zambezi. The next two centuries added only little to European knowledge: there were some sporadic attempts to cross the Sahara and more durable contacts were established along the Senegal and the Gambia, and a traveller went from the Zambezi to Kilwa breaking his journey at Lake Malawi. On the other hand the information about coastal peoples, mainly in West Africa, became more detailed and varied. A systematic exploration of the African interior started only at the end of the eighteenth century, which ended with the partition of the continent among the colonial powers.

In terms of national representation it can be said that the sixteenth-century authors were predominantly Portuguese, the seventeenth Dutch, French and British, the eighteenth predominantly British and French, and the nineteenth British, German and French. Other European nations were, of course, represented in the course of all these centuries, for example, the Italians in Kongo in the seventeenth and in the eastern Sudan in the nineteenth century, or the Danes on the Slave and Gold Coasts in the eighteenth and nineteenth centuries. And we find among authors of travel

64. G. Khalatyanc, 1899.

65. Cf. P. D. Curtin, 1967, pp. 170–89: I. Wilks, 'Wargee of Astrakhan'. See also D. A. Olderogge, 1971.

66. A series of documents on the history of relations between Ethiopia and Armenia from ancient times up to the nineteenth century is being published by the Institute of Oriental Studies of the SSR of Armenia, Erevan.

books and descriptions (but mostly in the last century) people from Spain, Russia, Belgium, Hungary, Sweden, Norway, Czechoslovakia, Poland, Switzerland, the United States, Brazil, and sometimes even a Greek, a Romanian or a Maltese. Luckily the majority of the books written in lesser known languages have been translated into a more accessible one.

In evaluating the European material we have to take into account not so much the national origin of the author as the changing attitudes of Europeans towards Africans and their societies in general. It would thus be a simplification to state that the Portuguese writers were more inclined to look with Christian prejudices on the people described than, let us say, the British; or that the Dutch were more prone to objective observation than the members of other nations. Of course, there is a difference between a Portuguese chronicler from the sixteenth century approaching his subject with medieval values and a Dutch scholar or physician of the late seventeenth century who was already a product of a more rational culture. The amount and variety of the material at our disposal does not allow any hasty generalization; a positive judgement could be reached only by analysing it individually, according to its own merits, taking, of course, into consideration both the time when and the purpose for which it was written. We must also avoid the fallacy that over the period there was a gradual improvement in the objectivity of the reporting and that the nearer we come to today the more scientific must be the observations about African reality, thus stipulating in advance the notion that an account by a nineteenth-century traveller has, simply by that fact, a higher credibility than one written three centuries before. Burton and Stanley as observers were prisoners of the allegedly scientifically proved notion of the superiority of white men in the same way as Portuguese authors were of the alleged superiority of their Christian faith. The period of the slave trade was not, in general, favourable to objective reporting about Africans, but the practical necessities of the trade required a close attention to their economic activities and systems of government, so that we have even from this time a series of very valuable records.

Books on Africa and Africans were written by missionaries, traders, officials, naval and army officers, consuls, explorers, travellers, settlers and sometimes by adventurers and prisoners of war. Each had different interest at stake and so the purposes and approaches vary considerably. The travellers' tales, which are typical of a particular class of literature, were concerned with the unfamiliar, exotic and strange world and had to respond to general demands of their readers. This trend in the exotic and adventurous, adorned by more or less fantastic opinions on African peoples or describing the innumerable dangers met by the gallant traveller, persisted far into the nineteenth century.[67]

Missionaries paid some attention to African religion, but they mostly

67. Cf. now R. I. Rotberg, 1971.

lacked the expertise and the goodwill to understand it and were mainly concerned to expose its 'errors' and 'barbarism'; on the other hand they knew local languages and were thus in a better position than others to gain an insight into the social framework. Sometimes they showed an interest in history and started to collect oral traditions.

In the nineteenth century the bulk of narrative literature originates with the explorers. In accordance with the mood of the time they were interested mainly in the solution of great geographical problems and their contribution was towards a greater awareness of the physical geography rather than of African society – 'Most of them were more interested in waterways than in ways of life.'[68] And many of them, being natural scientists, lacked a sense of history or believed in the myth of African non-history. There are, of course, exceptions to this rule, the most famous one being Heinrich Barth.

On the other hand there emerged, even in the course of the eighteenth century, some histories of individual African states or peoples, like Archibald Dalzell's *The History of Dahomy* (London, 1793), which, however, on close investigation proves to be an anti-abolitionist pamphlet.

Having pointed out some deficiencies of the European narrative sources we can now turn our attention to their more positive aspects. Above all they furnish the chronological framework needed so much in African history where dating is one of the weakest points of the oral tradition. Even a single date given by a traveller or other reporter, for example the date of his meeting with some African personality, can form a starting point for an entire chronology of a people and sometimes even for more than one. This is not to say that all dates must be correct simply because they are put down in writing – there are instances when European authors, depending on hearsay or trying to calculate the time-depth from non-controllable sources, made more or less grave errors – but the Europeans had in general at their disposition a more technically developed measurement of time.

The narrative literature is of primordial importance as a source of economic history: trade routes, chief markets, goods and prices, agriculture and crafts, natural resources, all this could be and was observed and described without bias. Moreover, the Europeans needed for their own interests accounts as objective as possible about these matters. It is true that the natural resources or economic possibilities of some regions were painted in too bright colours in order to enhance the merits of the explorer, but the historian is used to such exaggerations and takes them into account.

The Europeans were at their best in observation of the external aspects of African societies, of the so-called manners and customs; they supply rich, accurate and fine descriptions of various ceremonies, dress, behaviour, war strategies and tactics, production techniques, and so on, even if sometimes the description is accompanied by epithets like 'barbarous', 'primitive', 'absurd', 'ridiculous' or other derogatory terms. This in itself does not mean much; it is only a judgement from the standpoint of the writer's own cultural

68. A. A. Mazrui, 1969.

assumptions. Much more significant is the total lack of comprehension of the inner structure of African societies, the complicated network of social relations, the ramification of mutual obligations, the deeper reasons for certain behaviour. In short these authors were incapable of discovering the motivation underlying African activities.

Nevertheless, the writing of African history would be almost impossible without the material furnished by European narrative sources. They may have their shortcomings; many details were not observed at all or treated from a biased viewpoint or interpreted incorrectly. But these are normal risks, inherent in every historiography, and are no reason for discarding this large and enormously important body of information. On the contrary, there is an urgent need to reprint as many accounts of this kind as possible, and to publish them with appropriate commentaries and notes to allow their fresh evaluation and reinterpretation in the light of the new African historiography.

Internal narrative sources

The period under review saw a radical turning-point – the emergence of historical studies written by Africans from south of the Sahara. The means of expression was not at first any of the local African languages but Arabic, whose role in the Islamic world can be compared to that played by Latin in the European middle ages – that is, the means of communication between educated peoples – and, later, also some of the European languages.

It seems that this historiographical tradition started at the same time both in the Sudanic belt and on the East African coast precisely in the two great regions covered until this time by external Arabic sources and in which Islam exercised a prolonged influence. The earliest extant chronicles date from the early sixteenth century although they relate the events of earlier periods. The first, *Ta'rīkh al-Fattāsh*, the work of three generations of the Kati family of Jenne, covers the history of Songhay and adjacent countries till the Moroccan conquest in 1591. More extensive and richer in details is *Ta'rīkh al-Sūdān*, written by the Timbuktu historian al-Sa'di; it covers partly the same period but continues until 1655. Both are works of accomplished scholars with a wide outlook and profound knowledge of contemporary events. More significant is the fact that for the first time we are able to listen to the authentic voice of Africans themselves, even if the authors were biased in favour of Islam and looked on the events from this vantage point. From the eighteenth century originates an anonymous but very detailed history of the Moroccan Pashas of Timbuktu between 1591 and 1751, containing also useful material for neighbouring countries and peoples.[69] Another kind of source is represented by the biographical

69. *Ta'rīkh al-Fattāsh*, ed. and trans. by O. Houdas and M. Delafosse (Paris, 1913; reprint 1964); *Ta'rīkh al-Sūdān*, ed. and trans. by O. Houdas (Paris, 1900; reprint 1964); *Tadhkirat al-nisyan*, ed. and trans. by O. Houdas (Paris, 1899; reprint 1964).

dictionary of the learned men of the western Sudan, compiled by the famous scholar Ahmad Baba of Timbuktu (d. 1627).[70] In the area of the Songhay Empire there is *Ta'rīkh Say*, an Arabic chronicle by Ibn Adwar, said to have been written in 1410. If authentic it would be the oldest extant document written in West Africa, but it seems that the chronicle represents rather a later version of oral tradition.[71]

From Timbuktu and Jenne the tradition of chronicle writing spread to other areas, mainly to the south and west, in the region lying between the Sahel and the tropical forest, and in some cases even further southward. Muslim scholars started to put down in writing, from the mid-eighteenth century or even earlier, local chronicles, clan genealogies, concise biographies and religious books. The most accomplished product is *Kitāb al-Ghunja* written after 1752, which is a history of the Gonja Kingdom, based partly on oral traditions.[72] There are many lesser chronicles and it is to be expected that others will emerge elsewhere in this region which was under the influence of Dyula or Hausa communities. Although the bulk of these works is written in Arabic, many chronicles were also written in Ajami, that is to say, in local languages but with Arabic characters.

A similar situation exists in the Fulfulde-speaking regions too, in the first place in Futa Toro and Futa Djalon. In Guinea itself as well as in Dakar and in libraries in Paris, there are a number of local chronicles in Arabic or Fulfulde (or in both), mostly dating from the eighteenth and nineteenth centuries. It is only in recent times that the Futa Djalon material has been published and used in scholarly work. Reference may be made in this connection to the Gilbert Vieillard collection kept in the IFAN library in Dakar.[73] On the other hand, in Futa Toro the chronicles of the Senegalese Futa by Sire-Abbas Soh, an author of the eighteenth century, were made accessible half a century ago.[74] Another early work, a biographical dictionary by Muhammad al-Bartayili called *Fath-al-Sahkur* (*c.* 1805), is being prepared for publication by John Hunwick; a more modern history of Futa Toro, written in 1921 by Shayk Kamara Musa of Ganguel, entitled *Zuhur al-Basatin* (Flowers of Gardens), remains unpublished.[75]

In northern Nigeria, too, chronicles and other source material in Arabic emerged at a comparatively early date. The Iman Ibn Fartuwa (late sixteenth century) left a fascinating and detailed account of the life and times of Mai Idris and of his wars.[76] Various lists of Bornu rulers and Bornu

70. Published in Fez 1899, Cairo 1912.

71. Cf. V. Monteil, *BIFAN*, 28 (1968), p. 675.

72. See on this and other material I. Wilks, 1963, and T. Hodgkin, 1966.

73. A. I. Sow, 1968; T. Diallo, 1968.

74. Translated by M. Delafosse and H. Gaden (Paris, 1913).

75. Kept in the IFAN library, Dakar; cf. V. Monteil, 1965, p. 540.

76. Edited by H. R. Palmer; trans. in H. R. Palmer, 1928, Vol. I, and in H. R. Palmer, 1929.

chronicles date from a more recent period. An exceptional source is represented by the so-called mahrams, deeds of privileges granted by rulers to families of religious notables that throw light on economic and social conditions.[77] Not much of the pre-jihad historical material is preserved in the Hausa lands, although the state of learning, mainly among the Fulani religious leaders, was relatively very high,[78] but some poems in the Hausa language, like these in Kanuri (Bornu), contain comments on contemporary events.[79]

The beginning of the nineteenth century saw a renaissance of Arabic literature in the central and western Sudan; in addition to works in this language, an increasing number of books was written in local languages like Hausa, Fulfulde, Kanuri, Mandara, Kotoko, and so on, using Arabic characters. The most productive were the leaders of the Fulani jihad in northern Nigeria. Although the bulk of their literary output concerns religious matters, and only a few can be considered as true chronicles,[80] all this literature, be it in Arabic or in one of the African languages, helps to build a more coherent picture of the social and intellectual life in this region. The chronicles of Hausa cities (Kano, Katsina, Abuja, etc.), although of late nineteenth-century origin, are to some degree derived from earlier documents or based on oral tradition.[81] A similar development took place further east, in Baguirmi, Kotoko, Mandara and Wadi. Some chronicles or king-lists have already been published, but many others are still in manuscript and there is hope that more will be discovered in private hands.[82]

A rhymed chronicle in Fulfulde describes the life and activities of the great Tukulor reformer al-Hajj 'Umar Tall,[83] who himself is author of a religious work *Rimah Hizb al-Rahim* (Spears of the Party of Merciful God) which contains also many historical allusions to conditions in western Sudan.[84]

The East African coast can be compared with the Sudan for the number of its chronicles. There are chronicles of individual towns written in Arabic or in Kiswahili (in Arabic script), giving lists of kings and accounts of

77. Collected by H. R. Palmer, 1928 and 1936; cf. also Y. Urvoy, 1941.

78. M. Hiskett, 1957, pp. 550–78; A. D. H. Bivar and M. Hiskett, 1962, pp. 104–48.

79. Cf. J. R. Patterson, 1926.

80. M. Bello, 1951; English translation of Hausa paraphrase by E. J. Arnett, 1922; A. dan Fodio, 1963; H. Sacid, n.d.; also a French translation by O. Houdas, 1899.

81. *The Kano Chronicle*, trans. by H. R. Palmer, 1928, Vol. III; on Katsina cf. op. cit., pp. 74–91; on Abuja see Mallams, Hassan and Shuaibu, 1952.

82. Cf. H. R. Palmer, 1928; various works by J. P. Lebeuf and M. Robinson in *Etudes camerounaises*, 1948, 1951, 1955 and *BIFAN*, 1952 and 1956; M. A. Tubiana on Waday, in *Cahiers d'études africaines*, 2 (1960).

83. M. A. Tyam, *La Vie d'El Hadj Omar – Qasida en Poular*, trans. by H. Gaden (Paris, 1935).

84. *Kitab Rimah Hizb al-Rahim* (Cairo, 1927); new edition and translation is in preparation by J. R. Willis.

political life. Only the chronicle of Kilwa is of any antiquity. It was composed in about 1530 and has come down to us in two different versions, one transmitted by de Barros, and the other copied in Zanzibar in 1877.[85] The majority of chronicles were compiled only in recent times, though some can be traced beyond the second half of the eighteenth century and a number concentrate on events before the arrival of the Portuguese. They are thus, to some extent, recorded oral traditions and should be treated and evaluated as such.[86] A considerable body of manuscripts is still in private hands. Since 1965 more than 30 000 pages of Swahili (and also Arabic) manuscripts have come to light and it is to be expected that when the whole coast has been thoroughly searched, material will be found which will illuminate many unknown aspects of East African history.[87] Besides city chronicles, other literary genres can be profitably employed by historians, for example, Swahili poetry, such as the poem *al-Inkishafi* (composed in the second decade of the nineteenth century) which describes the rise and decline of Pate.[88]

Africans began to write in European languages two centuries after writing in Arabic. As could be expected, the first specimens were produced by individuals from the west coast where contacts with the outside world were more intensive than elsewhere.

Although the names of Jacobus Capitein (1717–47), A. William Amo (*c.* 1703– *c.* 1753) and Philip Quaque (1741–1816), all of Fante origin, should not be forgotten as the first pioneers of African writing in a European language, their contribution to African historiography was negligible. Incomparably more important as historical sources are the works of the liberated slaves from the second half of the eighteenth century: Ignatius Sancho (1729–80), Ottobah Cugoano (*c.* 1745–1800) and Olaudah Equiano (Gustavus Vasa; *c.* 1745–1810?). All three were primarily interested in the abolition of the slave trade and their books are polemical, but at the same time they furnish much biographical material about the conditions of Africans both in Africa and in Europe.[89] From the same period comes a unique document, the diary of Antera Duke, a leading Calabar trader, written in 'pidgin English' and covering a long period; although rather short, this diary throws a colourful light on daily life in one of the important slave ports.[90]

85. Analysed by G. S. P. Freeman-Grenville, 1962.

86. On the Arabic and Swahili chronicles in general cf. Freeman-Granville, 1962; A. H. J. Prins, 1958; J. W. T. Allen, 1959.

87. The most important discovery of this kind in recent years was that of the *Kitab-al-Zanj* (Book of the Zanj) dealing with the history of southern Somalia and northern Kenya; cf. E. Cerulli, 1957.

88. Cf. L. Harries, 1962.

89. I. Sancho, 1781; O. Cugoano, 1787; *The Interesting Narrative of the Life of Olaudah Equiano, or Gustavus Vasa, the African* (London, 1789).

90. D. Forde, 1956. The original manuscript was destroyed in Scotland by bombing during the last war, but extracts for 1785–7 are preserved in copy.

On Madagascar the great Merina King Radama I (1810–28) kept a kind of diary in Arabic script (*sura-be*). Around 1850, two other Merina aristocrats, Raombana and Rahaniraka, wrote in Latin script stories which help to reconstruct a fuller picture of everyday life in nineteenth-century Imerina.[91]

During the nineteenth century many Africans or Afro-Americans participated in exploratory travels or published reflections on African life, combined sometimes with polemics of a general nature. Samuel Crowther, a Yoruba, educated in Sierra Leone and in Britain, took part in the Niger expeditions of 1841 and 1853, leaving a description of his travels.[92] Thomas B. Freeman, born in England of mixed origin, travelled widely in West Africa and described the peoples of the coast and its hinterland with sympathy and insight;[93] two Afro-Americans, Robert Campbell and Martin R. Delany, went in the 1850s to Nigeria in search for a suitable area for a possible colony of Afro-Americans,[94] and a Liberian, Benjamin Anderson, described with many details and accurate observation his trip to the upper reaches of the Niger.[95] Two outstanding African leaders, Edward W. Blyden and James Africanus Horton, belong in a class by themselves. Some of Blyden's books, papers and articles form in themselves a historical source, others have already the character of historical interpretation, but even so they are indispensable for any research dealing with the emergence of African consciousness.[96] The same is true about Horton's work, with the difference that he was more inclined to precise observations of the societies with which he came into close contact.[97]

Both these men belong to the group of Africans who started to write the history of their own countries or peoples. A first attempt, although with more emphasis on ethnography, was undertaken by Abbé Boilat, a St Louis mulatto, in his *Esquisses Sénégalaises*.[98] A greater interest in historical writing, based mostly on oral tradition, was shown in those parts of the continent under British influence, but only at the end of the nineteenth century. C. S. Reindorf, a Gâ, published in 1895 in Basle his *History of the Gold Coast and Asante* and is considered to be the first modern historian of African origin. With him and Samuel Johnson, whose *History of the Yorubas* is contemporary with Reindorf's book, but published only as late as 1921, starts the uninterrupted chain of African historians, at first amateurs (in

91. H. Bertier, 1933; Manuscrit de Raombana et Rahaniraka, *Bull. de l'Académie Malgache*, 19 (1937), pp. 49–76.

92. Cf. *Journals of the Rev. J. J. Schön and Mr. Crowther* (London, 1842); S. Crowther, 1855.

93. T. B. Freeman, 1844.

94. R. Campbell, 1861; M. R. Delany, 1861.

95. B. Anderson, 1870.

96. C. Blyden; cf. H. R. Lynch, 1967.

97. J. A. B. Horton, 1870.

98. Paris, 1853.

majority missionaries), later professionals. Their ideas and works are treated in the chapter dedicated to the development of African historiography.

All these narrative sources, be they written in Arabic or in the various African and European languages, form a vast and rich body of historical material. They do not, of course, cover all aspects of the historical process, and are regionally limited, in some cases offering only a fragmentary picture. Those written by Muslims often show a pronounced Islamic bias that appears clearly in their dealings with non-Muslim societies; the authors of narrative sources in European languages were at the same time polemicists campaigning either against the slave trade or for equality and thus inclined to be one-sided. But these are the quite normal shortcomings of all narrative sources, and while remaining aware of them one must recognize that they have one overwhelming advantage: they are the voice of Africans themselves, revealing to us another facet of history, which has been too little heard amid the flow of outsiders' views.

Archival sources, private papers, confidential reports and other records

Primary sources are essentially those written documents that arose from the need to record various human activities and which were not originally intended for the general public but only for a restricted group of interested persons. They thus comprise mainly correspondence, both official and private, confidential reports, minutes of various dealings, trade accounts and books, statistics, private papers of various sorts, treaties and agreements, ship-logs, etc. This material is the raw meat for the student of history since it offers – in contrast to narrative sources which were composed with a definite purpose – objective evidence innocent, in principle, of any second thoughts destined for a larger public or posterity. This material is mostly to be found in state and private archives or libraries.

The view formerly held that there are not enough written primary sources for the history of Africa has been proved false. There are not only enormously rich collections of documents in the former metropolises and extensive material in Africa itself, created by European states or private institutions in the precolonial and colonial periods, but also the collections of primary material emanating from Africans themselves, written in European languages or in Arabic. Whereas formerly such documents were considered as something exceptional found only in a few privileged places, it is now clear that there exists a mass of written sources of African origin in many parts of the continent and in European and Asian archives as well.

Let us look first at the material written in Arabic. For the pre-nineteenth-century period only isolated items of correspondence, both local and international, have so far come to light, mostly from West Africa. There are letters from the Ottoman Sultan to the Mai Idris of Bornu (in 1578), discovered in Turkish archives, and some correspondence from the Sultan of Morocco to the Askiya of Songhay and the Kanta of Kebbi, also from the end of the sixteenth century. Arabic as a diplomatic language was employed not only by the Islamized courts of the Sudan but also by non-Muslim rulers. The best-known case is that of the Asantehenes who used the services of Muslim scribes, writing in Arabic, to conduct their correspondence with their northern neighbours as well as with Europeans on the coast. A number of such letters was found in the Royal Library in Copenhagen. The Arab chancery of Kumasi functioned well into the second half of the nineteenth century and Arabic was also used for keeping records of administrative and judicial decisions, financial transactions, and so on. An example from the other side of Africa is the treaty, written in Arabic, between the French slave trader Morice and the Sultan of Kilwa in the year 1776.

The nineteenth century saw a considerable development of correspondence in Arabic throughout the continent. The establishment of centralized states in the Sudan necessitated increasing administrative and diplomatic activities and abundant material of this kind has come to light, mainly from the Sokoto Caliphate and its dependent emirates from Gwandu to Adamawa, from the Macina state and from the Bornu Empire. All the Muslim rulers, be their states small or great, were busily corresponding with one another and with the penetrating colonial powers as well. In many archives in West African countries (and sometimes in Europe) there are to be found thousands of archival pieces in Arabic, originating with such personalities as al-Hajj 'Umar, Ahmadu Seku, Ma-Ba, Lat Dyor, Mahmadu Lamin, Samory, al-Bakka'j, Rabih and many lesser leaders and chiefs. The colonial administrations in Sierra Leone, Guinea, Nigeria and the Gold Coast also conducted their correspondence with them in Arabic. There are extant letters exchanged between the Ottoman Pasha of Tripoli and the Bornu Shaykhs, between the Sultan of Darfur and Egypt, between Timbuktu and Morocco. A similar situation existed in East Africa; it seems, nevertheless, that the Zanzibar archives are not so rich in Arabic documents as might reasonably be expected in a city with such large commercial and political interests. There must, of course, be a vast number of documents of varied contents in private hands; their collection and cataloguing will not be an easy task but it is an imperative for the near future.

Many texts were written in the Vai script which was invented about 1833 by Momolu Duwela Bukele and spread very quickly among the Vai people, so that at the close of the century nearly all of them knew the script and employed it currently for private and official correspondence, for keeping accounts and also for writing down customary laws, proverbs, stories and fables. Many neighbouring peoples such as the Mende, Toma (Loma), Guerze (Kpelle) and Bassa adopted and adapted the Vai script and employed it for similar purposes.[99]

99. Cf. D. Dalby, 1967.

At the beginning of the twentieth century Sultan Njoya of Bamum (Cameroon) invented for the Bamum language a special script which he reformed four times during his lifetime; but in contrast with the Vai script, used generally by the majority of the people, knowledge of the Bamum script remained restricted to a small group at the Sultan's court. Nevertheless, Njoya composed a big volume on the history and customs of his people in this script, a book on which he continued to work for many years and which constitutes a real mine of precious information about the past.[100]

To this should be added the texts in Nsibidi[101] from the Cross river valley (south-east Nigeria) consisting of inscriptions in sanctuaries and special forms of language used among members of certain secret societies.

The material in European languages goes from the sixteenth century to today. It is written in a dozen languages, is enormously abundant and is scattered all over the world in a hundred different places, archives, libraries and private collections. This state of affairs makes its use by historians rather difficult, especially in cases where there are no guides or catalogues at their disposal. It was for this reason that the International Council of Archives, under the auspices and with the moral and financial support of Unesco, started to prepare a series of guides to the sources of the history of Africa. The principal object was to meet the needs of students of African history by promoting access to the whole body of available sources. As historical research had long been concentrated on a limited number of archive repositories where the records of the colonial period were housed, it was important to draw attention also to the existence of an extensive and widely dispersed body of material, as yet unused. Whilst the guides are devoted primarily to public and private repositories, they equally take account of material of historical value in libraries and museums. The series should comprise twelve volumes, giving information about archival sources in Africa south of the Sahara, in western European countries and in the United States. So far the following volumes have been published: Volume I – Federal Republic of Germany (1970); Volume 2 – Spain (1971); Volume 3, France – I (1971); Volume 4, France – II (1976); Volumes 5 and 6 – Italy (1973–4); Volume 8 – Scandinavia (1971); and Volume 9 – the Netherlands (1978). Volume 7 is planned for the Holy See. A volume for the United Kingdom and Ireland has already appeared separately (1971), as will volumes for Belgium and the United States, but these follow the same method of presentation.[102] As has been aptly said by Joseph Ki-Zerbo in his Introduction to the series, 'in the battle for the rediscovery of the African

100. *Histoire et coutumes des Bamum, rédigées sous la direction du Sultan Njoya*, trans. by P. Henri Martin (Paris, 1952). The original is kept in the Sultan's palace at Fumban.

101. Cf. E. Dayrell, 1910–11; J. K. MacGregor, 1909, pp. 215, 217, 219.

102. The United States and the United Kingdom volumes list documents relating to the whole continent.

past, the *Guide to the Sources of the History of Africa* forms a new strategic and tactical weapon'.[103]

In addition to this major project there are already some other guides to source material, prepared mostly by regions or according to special criteria. Among the most complete belong the five guides for West African history, published in 1962–73, covering the archives of Portugal, Italy, Belgium and Holland, France, and the United Kingdom.[104]

More ambitious and to a certain extent more advantageous are the editions of archival documents *in extenso* or as catalogues. Until now this kind of presentation has been done mostly for the material in Portuguese archives; apart from Paiva Manso's work in the late nineteenth century,[105] there are now two major collections of missionary documents from Portuguese and some other archives, one by A. da Silva Rego,[106] the other by A. Brasio.[107] A few years ago a monumental collection, prepared by the combined efforts of the Portuguese and Zimbabwe archives, was started, in which all Portuguese documents concerning South-East Africa will be published in the original with an English translation.[108]

There are also collections which deal with subjects restricted in time, scope or matter. This category is represented, on one hand, by British Parliamentary Papers and various Blue and White Books mainly from the colonial period, and on the other hand, by more recent scholarly selections, such as the work of J. Cuvelier and L. Jadin on the Vatican documents for the history of ancient Kongo,[109] or C. W. Newbury's selection on British policy in West Africa and G. E. Metcalfe's documentary survey of relations between Great Britain and Ghana.[110] To this category belongs also the large collection of archival material on Italian policy towards Ethiopia and neighbouring countries, in course of publication by C. Giglio.[111] Many other collections of this kind from various European archives have made accessible documents for some aspect of colonial history. A weakness of these selections lies precisely in their selective character, because each compiler follows, in choosing his material, his own subjective rules, whereas

103. *Quellen zur Geschichte Afrikas südlich der Sahara in den Archiven der Bundesrepublik Deutschland* (Guide to the sources of the history of Africa), Vol. I (Zug, Switzerland, 1970), Preface, p. vii.

104. Guides to materials for West African History in European Archives (University of London at the Athlone Press): P. Carson, 1962; A. F. C. Ryder, 1965a; R. Gray and D. Chambers, 1965; P. Carson, 1968.

105. P. Manso, 1877.

106. A. da Silva Rego, 1949–58.

107. A. Brasio, 1952.

108. The Historical Documents of East and Central Africa, Lisbon-Salisbury, since 1965. It will comprise about 20 volumes.

109. J. Cuvelier and L. Jadin, 1954.

110. C. W. Newbury, 1965; G. E. Metcalfe, 1964.

111. C. Giglio, 1958.

a student doing research requires all the information and complete documentation.

In every independent African state there now exist governmental archives that also keep material inherited from the former colonial administration. Although in some countries printed guides or catalogues have been published, most archives in Africa are still in the process of being systematically arranged and described.[112] A series of guides, such as are now being published for European archives, is at present an urgent necessity for all archives in Africa, state or private.

Government archives in Africa have their useful as well as their negative sides, compared with the deposits in former metropolitan cities. With a few exceptions, the keeping of detailed records began in Africa no earlier than the 1880s and there are many gaps in the material. These shortcomings must be balanced by other sources, the most important being missionary and business records and papers in private hands, and, of course, the archives in European capitals.

On the other hand, the advantages of archives created in Africa over those in the former metropolitan capitals are numerous: the quantitative difference lies in the fact that in the African archives materials and records are preserved which have a more specialized bearing on the local situation, whereas the colonial archives in Europe mainly contain documents on the policy of the colonizing power. They often conserve records from the precolonial period such as reports of the first explorers, information collected by traders, officials and missionaries in the remote interior, reports that were not considered worthy of sending to Europe but which are of unusual importance for local history. These archives contain, too, a much greater number of documents originating with the Africans than those in Europe. Generally speaking, in spite of the amount of material duplicated in archives in Europe and in Africa, any student working only with sources from former metropolitan archives will tend to write a history of European interests in Africa rather than the history of Africans themselves. On the other hand, dependence solely on archives deposited in Africa cannot give a full picture, as many records and documents are missing or are incomplete.

To conclude we should mention some other types of documents. First, there are maps and other cartographic material. Although from the sixteenth century onwards the number of printed maps of Africa increased every year, a great number is still preserved in manuscript in various European archives and libraries, sometimes beautifully decorated and coloured. On these maps we can often find the names of localities no longer existing today or known by another name, but mentioned in other sources, be they oral or written. For instance, a number of eastern Bantu peoples have traditions of migration from an area called Shungwaya; no locality of this name is known at present, but on some of the old maps, for example, that of Van

112. For a survey of the situation on the eve of independence, see P. D. Curtin, 1960, pp. 129–47.

Linschoten (1596) or of William Blaeu (1662) and others, Shungwaya appears under various spellings, first as a town, later as an area, not far from the coast. The old maps furnish also data about the distribution of ethnic groups, about the frontiers or states and provinces, about the various names for rivers, mountains and other topographic features, in short offer very useful toponymic material which in turn yields precious historical information. A working example of how to use cartographic material for historical purposes was demonstrated by W. G. L. Randles in his *South-East Africa in the Sixteenth Century.* [113] The relevance of this material has already been recognized and the historian has at his disposal the great work by Yusuf Kamal, *Monumenta Cartographica Africae et Aegypti*, which contains also many narrative texts in the original and in translation, but stops chronologically just in the sixteenth century.[114] We must thus welcome the appeal of Joseph Ki-Zerbo for publishing a collection of all old maps of Africa in an atlas with commentaries.[115] A first step in this direction, but without sufficient commentary and reproducing only printed material, is the recent Leipzig collection of nearly one hundred maps.[116]

Another category of material found in written sources is linguistic data. Since a special chapter in this volume is reserved for the treatment of linguistics as an associated historical science, we will leave aside the methodological questions and restrict our discussion to indications about the kind of sources in which it can be discovered. From the first contacts with Africa it became fashionable to add to European travel descriptions or other reports shorter or longer lists of words in local languages. The earliest vocabularies go back to the fifteenth century and until the nineteenth we rarely find a book on Africa without such a supplement, sometimes even accompanied by a short grammar. Although the spelling is usually haphazard, it is not difficult to identify the words and languages. The most notable publication of this kind is Koelle's great collection of the vocabularies of about 160 languages;[117] that the value of the work is more than linguistic has been shown by Curtin, Vansina and Hair.[118] Especially lucky in this respect has been the ancient Kongo Kingdom: works dealing with Kikongo have been compiled since the seventeenth century – a grammar by Brusciotto (1659) and a dictionary by De Gheel (d. 1652).[119] In addition to these printed works, others are extant in various libraries and archives (Vatican, British Museum, Besançon, etc.). Their documentary

113. W. G. L. Randles, 1958.

114. Cairo, 1926–51.

115. Cf. note 103 above.

116. *Afrika auf Karten des 12.–18. Jahrhunderts* (Africa in twelfth- to eighteenth-century maps) (Leipzig, 1968).

117. S. W. Koelle, 1854 (reprint Graz, 1963).

118. P. D. Curtin and J. Vansina, 1964; P. E. H. Hair, 1965.

119. *Regulae quaedam pro difficillimi Congenius idiomatis faciliori captu ad Grammatica normam, redactae A. F. Hyacintho Brusciotto* ... (Rome, 1659); J. van Wing and C. Penders, 1928.

value for historians is higher than that of the simple word-lists because they are more complete and thus permit a diachronic study of social and cultural nomenclature.[120]

Written sources, narrative as well as archival, in African, oriental or European languages, represent an enormously rich body of material for the history of Africa. Abundant as are the known documents, records, books and papers, they constitute in all probability only a fragment of the existing material. Inside and outside Africa there must be innumerable places that have been as yet totally untapped for records bearing on African history. These unexplored regions are now the true 'blank spots' on the map of our knowledge of sources for African history. The sooner they disappear the richer will be the picture of the African past.

PLATE 6.1 *Facsimile of Bamum manuscript* (Musée de l'IFAN)

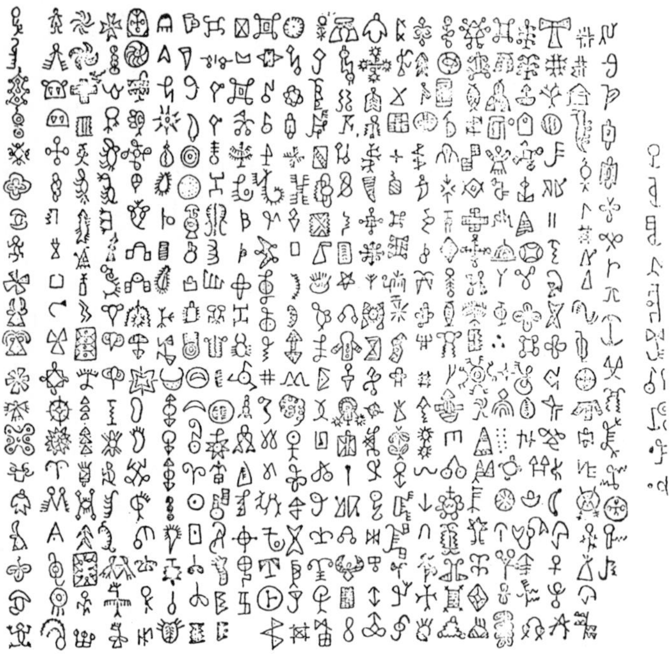

120. Brusciotto's Grammar was studied for these purposes by D. A. Olderogge, 1959.

PLATE 6.2 *Facsimile of Hausa manuscript* (Musée de l'IFAN)

PLATE 6.3 *Facsimile of Vai manuscript* (*from S. E. Holsoe*, 'An Early Vai Manuscript', International African Institute)

Oral tradition and its methodology

J. VANSINA

Oral civilization

The African civilizations in the Sahara and south of the desert were to a great extent civilizations of the spoken word, even where the written word existed, as it did in West Africa from the sixteenth century onwards, because only very few people knew how to write and the role of the written word was often marginal to the essential preoccupations of a society. It would be wrong to reduce the civilization of the spoken word to a merely negative absence of writing and to perpetuate the inborn contempt of the literate for the illiterate which is found in so many sayings, such as the Chinese proverb, 'The palest ink is to be preferred to the strongest word.' To do so would show total ignorance of the nature of these oral civilizations. As a student who had been initiated into an esoteric tradition said, 'The power of the word is terrible. It binds us together and disclosure of the secret destroys us' – by destroying the identity of the society, because the word destroys the common secret.

A scholar who has to work with oral traditions must thoroughly understand and accept the attitude towards speech of an oral civilization. This is completely different from that of a literate civilization which preserves all important records in writing. An oral society recognizes speech not only as a means of everyday communication but also as a means of preserving the wisdom of ancestors enshrined in what one might call key utterances, that is to say, oral tradition. A tradition may be defined, in fact, as a testimony transmitted verbally from one generation to another. Almost everywhere, the word has a mysterious power because words create things. That at least is the attitude in most African civilizations. The Dogon have expressed this nominalism most explicitly, but in all rituals the name is the thing and 'to say' is 'to do'.

The oral approach is an attitude to reality and not the absence of a skill. Traditions are baffling to the contemporary historian who, although so swamped by a mass of written evidence that he has to develop the techniques of rapid reading, can nevertheless rely on constant repetition of the facts in various forms to help his understanding. Traditions call for a continual return to the source. Fu Kiau of Zaïre says with truth that it is ingenuous to read an oral text once or twice and suppose that one has understood it. It must be listened to, learnt by heart, inwardly digested like a poem and carefully examined to make it yield up its many different meanings – at least if it is an important utterance. The historian must therefore learn to work more slowly, to reflect, to work his way into an alien system of ideas and images, since the corpus of tradition is the collective memory of a society which is explaining itself to itself. Many African scholars, such as Amadou Hampâté Ba or Boubou Hama, have expressed this reasoning very eloquently. The historian must learn how the oral society thinks before he can interpret its traditions.

Nature of oral tradition

Oral tradition has been defined as a testimony transmitted orally from one generation to another. Its special characteristics are the fact that it is oral and its manner of transmission, in which it differs from written sources. The oral tradition is complicated and it is not easy to find a definition which covers all its aspects. A written record is an object: a manuscript, a tile, a tablet. But a verbal record can be defined in several ways, because a speaker can interrupt his testimony, correct himself, start again, and so on. A rather arbitrary definition of a testimony might therefore be: all the statements made by one person about a single sequence of past events, provided that the person had not acquired new information between the various statements. In that case, the transmission would be contaminated and we should be faced with a new tradition. Some people, in particular specialists like the griots, are familiar with traditions concerning a whole series of different events. Cases have been known of a person reciting two different traditions to account for the same historical process. Rwandan informants related two versions of a tradition about the Tutsi and the Hutu, one according to which the first Tutsi had fallen from Heaven and had met the Hutu on earth, and the second according to which Tutsi and Hutu were brothers. Two completely different traditions, the same informants and the same subject! That is why the phrase 'a single sequence of events' has been included in the definition of a testimony. Lastly, everyone knows the case of the local informant who tells a composite story, based on the different traditions he knows.

A tradition is a message transmitted from one generation to the next. But all verbal information is not tradition. The eye-witness's verbal testimony must first be singled out. This is of great value because it is an immediate source, not a transmitted one, so that the risks of distorting the content are minimal. Any valid oral tradition should in fact be based on an eye-witness account. Rumour must be excluded, because although it certainly transmits a message, it depends by definition on hearsay. Hence its grapevine character. It becomes so distorted that it can be of value only as expressing a popular reaction to a given event. That too can give rise to a tradition when it is repeated by later generations. Finally there is the true tradition, which transmits evidence to future generations.

The origin of traditions may therefore lie in eye-witness testimony, in a rumour or in a new creation based on different existing oral texts combined and adapted to create a new message. But only the traditions based on eye-witness accounts are really valid. The historians of Islam understood that very well. They developed a complicated technique to determine the value of the different *Hadiths,* or traditions purporting to be the words of the Prophet as recorded by his companions. With time, the number of *Hadiths* became very large and it was necessary to eliminate those for which the chain of informants (*Isnad*) linking the scholar who had recorded them in writing to one of the Prophet's companions could not be traced. For each link the Islamic chronicler worked out criteria of probability and credibility identical with those employed in present-day historical criticism. Could the intermediate witness know the tradition? Could he understand it? Was it in his interest to distort it? Could he have transmitted it and if so when, how and where?

It will be noticed that the definition of traditions given here implies no limitations other than verbalism and oral transmission. It therefore includes not only evidence like the chronicles of a kingdom or the genealogies of a segmentary society, which consciously set out to describe past events, but also a whole oral literature. The latter will give details about the past which are all the more precious for being an unconscious testimony and are also an important source for the history of ideas, values and oral skill.

Traditions are also literary works and should be studied as such, just as it is necessary to study the social environment which underlies the content of every expression of a given culture. That is why the following sections deal successively with literary criticism and with the question of the social and cultural environment before proceeding to the chronological problem and the general evaluation of traditions.

Tradition as a literary work

In an oral society most literary works are traditions and all conscious traditions are oral utterances. As in all utterances, form and literary criteria influence the content of the message. That is the main reason why traditions must be placed in the general framework of a study of literary structures and be critically evaluated as such.

A first problem is that of the actual form of the message. There are four basic forms, resulting from a practical combination of two sets of principles. In some cases the words are learnt by heart, in others the choice is left to the composer. In some cases a series of special formal rules are superimposed on the grammar of the ordinary language, in others no such system of conventions exists. Hence Table 7.1.

TABLE 7.1 *Basic forms of oral traditions*

		content	
		fixed	*free (choice of words)*
form	*set*	poem	epic (poem)
	free	formula	narrative

The term 'poem' is only a label, covering all material learnt by heart and having acquired a specific structure, including songs. The term 'formula' is a label which often includes proverbs, riddles, prayers, genealogies, that is to say, everything which is learnt by heart but which is not subject to rules of composition other than those of normal grammar. In both cases, these traditions comprise not only the message but the actual words in which it is conveyed. Theoretically, therefore, an original archetype can be reconstructed, just as in the case of written sources. Historical arguments can be built on words and not only on the general sense of the message. However, it happens often with formulae, less often with poems, that it is impossible to reconstruct an archetype, because there are too many interpolations. For example, it may be possible to show that the motto of a clan is the product of a series of borrowings from other mottoes without being able to identify the original and specific form of words. It is easy to see why formulae lend themselves so readily to interpolation. In fact, no formal rule exists to impede this process.

On the other hand, fixed sources are in principle the most precious because their transmission is the most precise. In practice, few of them consciously aim to transmit historical information. Moreover, this is where we obviously come up against archaisms – sometimes unexplained. Their meaning can be discovered in the Bantu languages, because there is a good chance that a neighbouring language will have retained a word with the same root as the archaism in question. Elsewhere, we have to rely on the commentary of the informant, who may repeat a traditional commentary or may invent his own. It is especially unfortunate that this type of oral record is cluttered with poetic allusions, hidden images, plays on words with many different meanings. Not only is it impossible to understand anything of such 'hermetic' utterance without a commentary, but also often only the author has understood all the shades of meaning. But he does not include everything in the explanatory commentary of varying quality which accompanies the transmission of the poem. This peculiarity is very widespread, especially in the panegyrical poems or songs of southern (Tswana, Sotho), eastern (the lake region), central (Luba, Kongo) or western (Ijo) Africa.

The term 'epic poem' is a label which means that the composer may choose his own words within a set framework of formal rules, such as rhymes, patterns of tone and syllabic quantity, and so on. This precise case should not be confused with the lengthy literary pieces in the heroic style, such as the narratives of Sundjata, Mwindo (Zaïre) and many others. In this case, the tradition includes the message and the formal framework but nothing else. Often, however, we find here characteristic lines used to fill in spaces or which merely remind the composer of the setting, the formal framework. Some of these lines probably date back to the creation of the epic poem. Do such 'epics' exist in Africa? We think they do and that some Rwandan poetic forms, in particular, as well as the Fang (Cameroon-Gabon) song-fables, fall into this category. It should be noted that it is impossible to reconstruct a true archetype for these epic poems because the choice of words is left to the composer. Nevertheless, the demands of the form are such that it is probable that all the versions of an 'epic' are based on a single original. A study of the variants often shows that this is so.

The last category is that of the narratives, which include most of the time-conscious historical messages. Here, the freedom left to the composer allows for numerous combinations, much recasting, rearranging of episodes, amplifying of descriptions, developments, and so on. It then becomes difficult to reconstruct an archetype. The composer is completely free, but only from the literary point of view. His social environment might sometimes impose a rigid adherence to his sources. Despite these difficulties, it is possible to discover the hybrid origin of a tradition by collecting all its variants – including those which are not considered to be histories and taking account of variants originating among neighbouring peoples. We may sometimes thus pass imperceptibly from the world of history to a wonderland, but we also manage to eliminate those oral versions which are not based on eye-witness accounts. This critical approach is essential.

Every oral literature has its own particular division into literary forms. The historian will not only endeavour to learn the significance of the forms for the culture he is studying, but will also collect at least one representative sample of each of them, because historical information may be found in all of them and the traditions which interest him particularly are easier to understand when taken in the general context. Internal classification provides valuable indications. Thus, we can find out if the propagators of a literary piece make any distinction between, for example, historical and other types of narrative.

Literary forms are also subject to conventions, a knowledge of which is essential in order to understand the true meaning of the piece. Here the question is no longer one of formal rules but of the choice of terms, expressions, unusual prefixes, various types of poetic licence. Closer attention must be paid to words or expressions that have many different reverberations. Moreover, the key-terms which are closely connected with the social structure, the conception of the world, and which are practically untranslatable, need to be interpreted in the light of the literary context in which they appear.

It is impossible to collect everything. The historian is therefore obliged to take practical requirements into account and will consequently not be overambitious once he has a representative sample of each of the literary forms.

Only by cataloguing the various types of narrative belonging to the particular ethnic group being studied, or to other such groups, is it possible to discern not only favourite images or expressions but also the stereotyped episodes, for example, in those narratives which might be called migratory legends (*Wandersagen*). For instance, a Luba narrative from the shores of Lake Tanganyika tells how a chief rid himself of another by inviting him to sit on a mat under which a pit had been dug, containing sharp pointed stakes. The chief sat down and was killed. The same scenario can be found, not only from the Great Lakes to the ocean, but also among the Fula of the Liptako (Upper Volta), the Hausa (Nigeria) and the Mossi of Yatenga (Upper Volta). The importance of these stock narrative themes is obvious. Unfortunately, we possess no useful reference book dealing with them, although H. Baumann mentions a number of stock themes occurring in accounts of the origins of various peoples.[1] It seems high time that practical catalogues were drawn up to enable these stereotypes to be identified. The so-called folk-motif indexes are unwieldy and obscure, because they are based on minor characteristics, arbitrarily selected, whereas in African narratives the episode represents a natural unit – often highly characteristic and wider in scope than a motif – which would thus be easier to identify in a catalogue.

When a stock theme of this kind is encountered, we have no right to reject as invalid the whole tradition, or even the part containing this sequence of events. We should rather explain why the stock theme is used. In the case mentioned, it simply explains that one chief eliminates another and adds a description of how it was done which is imaginary but pleases the listeners. Usually this kind of stock theme builds up explanations and commentaries on a basis of information which may be perfectly valid.

Literary criticism will take into account not only the literal and intended meanings of a tradition, but also the constraints imposed on the expression of a message by formal and stylistic requirements. It will evaluate the effect of its aesthetic distortion, if one exists – and very often one did. After all, even messages from the past must not be too boring! It is here that observation of the social aspect of performances reflecting the tradition is of crucial importance. We say performance rather than reproduction because in most cases an aesthetic element is involved. If aesthetic criteria take precedence over accuracy of reproduction there will be a strong aesthetic distortion which reflects the taste of the public and the art of the person

1. H. Baumann, 1936.

passing on the tradition. Even if this is not the case, arrangements of the recitals are found, which go so far as to clothe traditions having a specific content in the uniform of current artistic standards. For example, in narratives, a series of episodes leading towards a climax form the main plot, whereas others constitute sophisticated parallel repetitions or are only transitions from one stage of the narrative to another. As a general rule, it can be assumed that the more a recital conforms to the standard model of excellence and the more it is admired by the public, the more it is distorted. In a series of variants, the correct variant can sometimes be discerned from the fact that it runs counter to these standards, just as a variant which contradicts the social function of a tradition is more likely to be true than the others. It should not, however, be forgotten that not all oral composers are perfect. There are some bad ones and their variants will always be sorry affairs. But the attitude of the public, like the setting of a performance, is not exclusively an artistic event. It is above all a social event, and this obliges us to consider tradition in its social environment.

The social framework of tradition

Everything a society considers important for the smooth running of its institutions, for a correct understanding of the various social grades and their accompanying roles, for everyone's rights and obligations, is carefully transmitted. In an oral society this is done by tradition, whereas in a society which keeps records in writing, only the least important memories are left to tradition. It is this fact which for a long time led historians who came from literate societies to believe, erroneously, that traditions were some sort of fairy tale, lullaby or children's game.

Every social institution and every social group also has its own identity accompanied by a past embodied in collective performances of a tradition which describes and justifies it. For this reason, every tradition will have its 'social surface', to borrow the expression used by H. Moniot. Without a social surface the tradition would no longer be transmitted and, having no function, would lose its reason for existence and be abandoned by the institution underpinning it.

One might be tempted to follow the lead of some scholars who thought that the nature or profile of a given society's corpus of historical traditions could be deduced in advance on the basis of a classification of collectivities into types, such as states, stateless societies, and so on. Although it is true that the various African societies can be roughly classified under such model headings, it can easily be shown that these types can be split up into an infinite number of subdivisions, because each society is different and the criteria used are arbitrary and limited. No two states are identical or even similar in detail. There are vast differences between the organizational framework of the Masai (Kenya-Tanzania), Embu (Kenya), Meru (Kenya) and Galla (Kenya–Ethiopia) societies, even though they can all be classified as 'age-group' societies and are situated in the same part of Africa. If we wish to take a case of a so-called simple stateless society composed of small groups based on a multiplicity of families, we might think that the Gouro (Ivory Coast) would be a good example. We expect to find a profile of traditions containing only stories of descent and genealogy. And we do find them. But we discover also an esoteric history handed down by a secret society. In the case of the Tonga of Zambia, we again find the story of descent, but also stories of ritual centres run by the rainmakers. Not a single society of this type fails to show us an unexpected major institution. Among the states, the extreme case is certainly that of the kingdom of the Teke (Tio), where the royal tradition does not go back further than two generations, although kingdoms are supposed to have very long-standing traditions. Moreover, we can follow the tradition of the magic symbols of the nobles much further back than we can that of the royal symbol. Hasty generalizations on the value of traditions, the tendency to oversimplify which is still all too prevalent, are completely unwarranted. The profile of a given body of traditions can be determined only *a posteriori*.

It is evident that the functions fulfilled by traditions tend to distort them. It is impossible to draw up a complete list of these functions, partly because a tradition can perform several different functions and can play a role running from the well-defined to the vague in relation to them, but mainly because the word 'function' is itself confusing. It is most often used to describe everything which serves to strengthen or maintain the institution upon which it depends. As the connection is not tangible, the imagination can produce an endless list of functions to be performed and no choice is possible. It is, however, quite easy to distinguish certain precise purposes, manifest or latent, fulfilled by some traditions. For example, there are those 'mythical charters', those histories of dynasties, genealogies, lists of kings which may be considered as being nothing less than unwritten constitutions. We can extend this category by including in it all traditions connected with public legal matters, for example, those which support public rights to property. They are usually *official* traditions in as much as they claim universal validity for the society. *Private* traditions, associated with groups or institutions embodied in others, will be less well preserved because they are less important, but often more true to fact than the others. It should, however, be pointed out that private traditions are official for the group which transmits them. Thus, a family history is private as compared with the history of a whole state and what it says about the state is less subject to control by the state than an official public tradition. But, within the family itself, the private tradition becomes official. For all purposes connected with the family it should therefore be treated as such. We can accordingly see why it is so helpful to use family or local histories to clarify points of general political history. Their testimony is less subject to distortion and can offer an effective check on the assertions made by official traditions. On the other hand, as they concern only sub-groups, their transmission is often lacking in care and depth, as can be seen from the numerous variants which usually exist.

Among other common functions we may briefly mention the religious and liturgical (the performance of rituals); private legal (precedents) as well as the aesthetic, didactic and historical; the function of commentary to an esoteric oral record; and what anthropologists call the mythical function. The functions and the literary form taken together constitute a valid typology which will enable the historian to make a general evaluation of the probable distortions which his sources may have suffered, while also giving indications concerning the transmission. Taking only those types which remain after this process of selection, we can distinguish names, titles, slogans or mottoes, ritual formulae, didactic formulae (proverbs), toponyms, names of persons, genealogies, etc. From their basic form we can classify all these as examples of 'formulae'. Poems – historical, panegyrical, liturgical or ceremonial, religious, personal (lyrical and others), songs of all types (lullabies, working, hunting and canoeing songs, etc.) are 'poems' in this sense. The 'epic poem' as a basic form is represented by some poems which do not correspond to what the term normally connotes. Lastly, 'narrative' includes general narrative, whether historical or other, local, family, epic, aetiological and aesthetic narratives and personal memories. We shall also include here legal precedents which are rarely transmitted by oral tradition, commentaries on oral records and the occasional notes which are essentially short replies to questions such as, 'How did we start growing maize?', 'Where did this dancer's mask come from?', etc.

From this list it can immediately be seen what *may* be the distorting action of an institution on each of these forms. But it must also be shown that such an action actually took place or that the probability of distortion is very great. It is often possible to show that a tradition is valid because it has not suffered the expected distortions. For example, a people says that it is 'younger' than another, a royal chronicle admits a defeat, a particular formula which should explain the physical and human geography of a country no longer conforms to present-day reality. In all these cases analysis shows the validity of the tradition because it has resisted the levelling process.

In their work on the phenomenon of writing (literacy), Goody and Watt assert that an oral society tends constantly and automatically towards a homoeostasis which effaces from the collective memory – hence the expression 'structural amnesia' – any contradiction between the tradition and its social surface. But the cases quoted above show that this homoeostasis is only partial. It therefore follows that the historical value of traditions cannot be rejected in bulk merely because they perform certain functions and that each tradition must be subjected to strict sociological criticism. In the same work, these authors assert that the culture of a verbal society is homogenized, that is to say, that the knowledge-content of the brain of each adult is approximately the same. This is not entirely true.

Craftsmen and political, legal and religious specialists know many things of which their contemporaries in the same ethnic group know nothing. Each ethnic group has its thinkers. Among the Kuba (Zaïre), for example, we met three men who, on the basis of the same system of symbols, had worked out three very different philosophies, and we suspect the same is true of the Dogon. With regard to traditions, we find that in very many groups there are secret *esoteric* traditions, which are the privilege of a restricted group, and public *exoteric* traditions. For instance, the Asante royal family knew the secret story about their origin, whereas the general public knew only the official version. In Rwanda, only the Biiru specialists knew the royal rituals and even then they only knew them all when they were all together, since each group of Biiru knew only part of them. Secret practices and traditions are found in almost all the historical commemorative festivals in Nigeria, and in almost all the rituals for the enthronement of kings throughout Africa. Does this mean that the esoteric tradition is necessarily more accurate than the exoteric tradition? That depends on the context. After all, esoteric traditions too can be distorted for imperative reasons, which are all the more imperative because the group possessing the secret is a key group in the society. It should be pointed out that in actual fact only a very few esoteric traditions are as yet known to us, because the old order in which they have their roots has not completely disappeared. Those which we do know come from societies which have suffered major upheavals and many of these traditions will doubtless vanish without leaving a record. However, from the fragments we do possess, we can affirm that certain Ogboni traditions of the Yoruba country have been so distorted that they no longer constitute a valid message concerning the origins of the Ogboni, whereas the Biiru traditions, for example, seem to be more valid. This is due not to their esoteric character but to their purpose. The former confer legitimacy on the considerable powers possessed by a small group of men, whereas the latter are only reminders of a practical ritual.

Each tradition has its own social surface. To find traditions and to analyse the quality of their transmission, the historian must therefore ascertain as far as possible the kind of society he is studying. He must consider all its institutions in order to isolate traditions just as he will scrutinize all the literary forms for historical information. It is the leading group of a society which retains possession of the official traditions, and their transmission is often carried out by specialists who use mnemotechnical means (often song) to remember the records they have to learn. Sometimes the tradition is checked either by colleagues at private rehearsals or at the public performance which is associated with an important ceremony. The specialists are, however, not always attached to the leading group. This is true in the case of the genealogists, the chiefs' or kings' drummers, the keepers of the tombs[2] and the priests of national religions. But there are also

2. In some countries, however, these persons constitute an integral part of the ruling class, for instance, in the case of the *Bénd-naba* (chief of the drums) of the Mossi.

specialists at other levels. Among the Xhosa (South Africa), there are women specialized in the art of performing amusing *ntsomi* stories. There are also others who know how to do it but do not specialize in it. They usually take part in popular entertainments. Some performers of religious rites are specialists in oral traditions also. The guardians of the Shona *mhondoro* (Zimbabwe) know the history of the spirits entrusted to their keeping. Some, like the griots, are troubadours, who collect traditions at all levels and perform mutually agreed versions before an appropriate audience on certain occasions – marriage, death, a feast in a chief's residence, and so on. It is rare for there to be no specialization, even at the level of the history of the land or of the family. There are always people who are of a higher social status (the *abashinga ntahe* of Burundi for land matters, for example) or who are more gifted and who are entrusted with memorizing and transmitting traditions. One final category of better-informed people – they can hardly be termed specialists – consists of those who live near important historical places. Here the fact of living on the very spot where, for example, a battle was fought, acts as a mnemotechnical aid in the recording of tradition.

An examination of the 'social surface' therefore makes it possible to discover existing traditions, to place them in their setting, to find the specialists responsible for them and to study the transmission. This examination also makes it possible to discover valuable indications of the frequency and form of the performances themselves. The frequency is an indication of the faithfulness of the transmission. Among the Dogon (Mali), the Sigi ritual is transmitted only once every sixty years or so. This leads to forgetfulness, and those who have seen two Sigis and understood enough about what was happening at the first performance to be able to direct the second are very rare. No one under the age of 75 can do so. It can be assumed that the content of the Sigi and the information given will vary more radically than a form of tradition like that of a festival in southern Nigeria which is repeated every year. On the other hand, very frequent performances do not necessarily mean that the transmission is particularly faithful. That depends on the society in question. If it wants a very faithful performance, frequency will help to maintain it. That is the case with magic formulae, for instance, certain formulae to exorcise witchcraft. This explains why some Mboon (Zaïre) formulae to ward off rain are placed in such an archaic geographical context that none of the things mentioned can now be found in the present Mboon country. On the other hand, if the society attaches no importance to the faithfulness of the transmission, very frequent performances will corrupt the transmission more rapidly than less frequent ones would do. Take, for instance, the case of popular songs and especially the best-loved popular narratives. All this can and indeed should be checked by study of the variants collected. Their number is a direct reflection of the faithfulness of the transmission.

It would seem that the changes which occur invariably tend to increase the homoeostasis between the institution and the accompanying tradition; in this Goody and Watt are not entirely wrong. If variants exist and show a well-defined trend, we can deduce that those which are the least in line with the aims and functions of the institution are the most valid. Furthermore, it is sometimes possible to show that a tradition is not to be trusted either where there are no variants, and the tradition has become a stock theme along the lines of 'We have all come from X', and X corresponds perfectly to the needs of the society, or where, as in popular narrative, the variants are so divergent that it is almost impossible to recognize what constitutes a tradition and separates it from another. In this case, it becomes evident that most of the versions are more or less recent fabrications, based on other popular narratives. In these two extreme cases, however, we must be able to show that the absence of variants really corresponds to a powerful motivation of the society or that their proliferation corresponds to aesthetic considerations or to a need to entertain which override all other considerations; or else we should be able to show that the unconscious assumptions of the culture have so homogenized the tradition that it has become a stock theme without variants. This cultural influence must now be examined.

The mental framework of tradition

By mental framework we mean the unconscious collective ideas and images of a culture which influence all its forms of expression and at the same time constitute its conception of the world. This mental framework varies from society to society. At a superficial level, it is relatively easy to discover part of this framework by applying the classical techniques of literary criticism to the content of the whole body of the traditions and comparing that body with the other, mainly symbolic, manifestations of the culture. Tradition always idealizes; this is particularly so in the case of poems and narratives. Popular stereotypes are created. All history has a tendency to establish a pattern and consequently to become mythical, whether its content is 'true' or not. Thus we find models of ideal behaviour and of values. In royal traditions, stereotyped characters like those in a Western are easy to identify. One king is 'the magician', another ruler is 'the just', someone else is 'the warrior'. But this distorts the information; for example, some wars are attributed to the stereotype warrior king when the campaigns were in fact fought by someone else. Moreover, all the kings have common features which reflect an idealized conception of royalty. It is no more difficult to find stereotypes of different characters, especially leaders, in other societies. There is the ubiquitous one of the 'culture-hero', who turns chaos into a well-ordered society, and the stereotyped notion of chaos is then the description of a world literally upside down. We may find more than one stereotype of the founding hero. Among the Igala (Nigeria), some founders are hunters, some are descendants of kings. The former represent achieved status, the latter hereditary or ascribed status. Reflection explains why there are two types of status. Boston suggested that the first stereotype conceals the accession to power of new groups and that the two stereotypes reflect two quite different historical situations.

A wholly satisfactory theory should, however, reveal the entire system of values and ideals linked to the social positions and roles which constitute the very bases of all social action and of every global system. This was not possible until recently when McGaffey discovered that the Kongo (Zaïre; People's Republic of the Congo) possess a simple stereotyped system of the four ideal positions in society (witch-doctor, soothsayer, chief, prophet) which are complementary. It is easy to discover a positive or negative general value: the appreciation of generosity and rejection of jealousy as a sign of witchcraft, or the role of fate – these are values which can immediately be seen in the traditions of the Bight of Benin, as also in the interlacustrine area. But the values are discovered one by one and not as a coherent system which includes all the collective ideas and images. For values and ideals describe only the norms of ideal – or sometimes, more cynically, realistic – behaviour which should guide the actual behaviour and role fulfilment expected of everyone. Roles are linked to social positions and the latter to institutions which, taken together, constitute the society. Theoretically, therefore, a society must be taken to pieces in order to discover its patterns of action, its ideals and its values. Usually, the historian does this unconsciously and superficially. He avoids the obvious traps but unwittingly tends to adopt the assumptions imposed by the system as a whole. He does not succeed in detaching his sources from their environment. We know this very well, having spent eighteen years trying to detect connections of this kind in the distortion of traditions of Kuba (Zaïre) origin.

Among the collective concepts which most influence tradition, there are above all a number of pre-sensual categories. There are those of time, space, historical truth and causality. There are others, such as the division of the spectrum into colours, which are less important. Every people divides time into units, based either on human activities or on recurrent social activities (structural time). Both forms of time are in use everywhere. Day is separated from night, it is divided into parts corresponding to work or meals and activities are correlated with the height of the sun, the cry of certain animals dividing the hours of the night, and so on. The (lunar) months, the seasons and the year are usually defined by the environment and its related activities, but beyond that we must count in units of structural time. Even here, the week is determined by a social rhythm, for instance, the periodicity of markets, which is also associated in many cases with a religious periodicity.

Periods longer than years are counted by initiation to a cult, to an age-group, by reigns or generations. Family history can be calculated by births which form a biological calendar. Reference is made to exceptional events such as great famines, major outbreaks of animal disease, or epidemics, comets and plagues of locusts, but this calendar of catastrophes is necessarily vague and irregular. At first sight, this sort of computation seems to be of little use for chronology; however, it appears that the use of recurrent events should enable relative chronology to be converted into an absolute chronology, once the frequency of genealogies, age-groups, reigns, etc., is known. We shall return to this.

The maximum length of time social memory can comprehend depends directly on the institution which is connected with a tradition. Each has its own temporal depth. Family history does not go back far because the extended family covers only three generations and there is often little interest in remembering earlier events. Consequently, the institutions which cover the largest number of persons are most likely to go back the farthest in time. This has proved true for the clan, the maximum line of descent, the Masai-type age-group and royalty. In the Sudanese savannah, the traditions of the kingdoms and empires of Tekrur, Ghana and Mali, supported by Arab and Sudanese authors, go back to the eleventh century. Sometimes, however, all the institutions are limited by the same concept of the depth of time, as for instance among the Teke (People's Republic of the Congo), where everything is brought forwards to the generation of the father or the grandfather. Everything, including the history of the royal family, is telescoped into odd and even, the odd pertaining to the time of the 'fathers' and the even to that of the 'grandfathers'.

This example shows that the notion of the form of time is very important. In the interlacustrine region, there are cases where time is thought of as a cycle. But as the cycles succeed each other, the concept becomes that of a spiral. In a different connection, the same societies think in terms of eras, above all the era of chaos and the historical era. Nor is time linear elsewhere, for example among the Teke. It oscillates between alternate generations. The consequences for the way in which traditions are presented are obvious.

It is less obvious that the notion of space is of interest in this context. But there is often a tendency to situate the origin of a people in a place of renown or along a significant axis, the direction being either sacred or profane according to whether it is thought that man progresses from the sacred to the profane or vice versa. Each people has imposed a system of directions on its geography. It is often the rivers which give the axis of the cardinal directions. Most societies then fix the direction of their villages, sometimes their fields (Kukuya, People's Republic of the Congo) along this system of axes, as they do their tombs. The consequences are sometimes unexpected. Where the direction of an area lies along a single axis which is part of the geographical relief, it changes with the relative situation of the various features of that relief. Here 'downstream' is westwards, there it is northwards; here 'towards the summit' is eastwards, there it is westwards. Not only do we find that migration is alleged to have come from privileged directions, as is the case with the Kuba (Zaïre) or the Kaguru (Tanzania), which turns this particular narrative into a cosmology rather than a history; we even find variations in points of origin depending on accidents of geographical relief. Only societies which use the movements of the sun to determine the axis of space can give exact information concerning general migratory movements, but unfortunately such peoples are in a minority, except perhaps in West Africa where most of the peoples refer to the east as their place of origin.

The notion of cause is implicit in every explicit oral historical tradition. It is often presented in the form of a separate, immediate cause for each phenomenon. In that case, each thing has an origin which is situated at the very beginning of time. The nature of causality is often best understood by studying the causes attributed to evil. These are very often directly connected with witchcraft, ancestors, and so on, and the connection is immediate. It follows from this kind of notion of causality that change is perceived mainly in some very clearly defined fields, such as war, royal succession, and so on, where stereotypes intervene. It should be noted finally that this sketch of the notion of cause is very summary and must be supplemented by other notions of cause which are more complex though parallel, and which affect only minor social institutions.

As for historical truth, it is always very closely connected with the fidelity of the oral record transmitted. Thus it can mean either the consensus of the rulers (Idoma, Nigeria), or the recognition that the tradition is in conformity with what the preceding generation said.

The cognitive categories combine and join with symbolic expressions of values to produce a record which the anthropologists speak of as a 'myth'. The traditions most subject to a mythical restructuring are those which describe the origin, and consequently the essence, of a people, its reason for existence. Thus a large number of complex Kuba narratives describing their origin and migrations in canoes have finally been explained thanks to the discovery of a latent concept of migration; for the Kuba people migrate in canoes from downstream (sacred) to upstream (the profane). Similarly, many names of migrations and areas of origin have been explained in terms of cosmogony. In the Kuba narrative the idea was not obvious, whereas in the case of many other ethnic groups the correlation is quite clear. This is how many ethnologists, unfortunately following the example of Beidelman, the structuralists or the functionalist sociologists, have ended up by denying that any narrative traditions have any value, because, they say, they are all expressions of the cognitive structures of the world, which underlie all thought *a priori*, like imperative categories. The same judgement should then apply to the text you are now reading or to that of Beidelman himself! Obviously, these anthropologists exaggerate. Moreover, many of their interpretations seem to be very hypothetical. The historian should remember that for each particular case, he must state the reasons there are for rejecting or questioning a tradition and so he must look for these reasons. A tradition can be rejected only when the probability of its having been created to convey a *purely* symbolic meaning is really strong and provable. For, in general, traditions reflect both a myth, in the anthropological sense of the term, *and* historical information. In such circumstances, historical manuals are mythological texts, since every stereotype originating in a system of values and interests is not only a mythical message but also a historical cypher awaiting decoding.

Chronology

If there is no chronology, there is no history, because it is no longer possible to distinguish what preceded from what follows. Oral tradition always gives a *relative* chronology, expressed in lists or generations. In general, this chronology enables the whole body of traditions of the society under study to be placed in the framework of the genealogy or the list of kings or age-groups which covers the broadest geographical area, but it does not enable the relative sequence of events to be linked to those outside the particular region. Important historical movements and even some local evolutions go unnoticed or remain doubtful because the unit on which the chronology is calculated is geographically too restricted. Family genealogy is valid only for the one family and the village or villages it lives in. For example, the chronology of the Embu (Kenya) is based on age-groups which cover only a minute territorial area in which the young men are initiated at the same time. Relative chronologies must therefore be linked together and if possible converted into absolute chronologies. But first there is another problem to be solved, that of ensuring that the information used corresponds to a reality which has not been distorted with respect to time.

It is becoming increasingly clear that oral chronology is subject to distortion acting in two opposite directions: sometimes it shortens and sometimes prolongs the true duration of past events. There is also a tendency to regularize genealogies, successions and sequences of age-groups, to make them conform to the current ideal norms of society. Otherwise, the information would furnish precedents for all sorts of legal disputes. The homoeostatic process is very real.

In certain special cases, for example in Rwanda, the task of regulating tradition falls upon a complex group of specialists whose statements have been borne out by archaeological excavations.

Ethnologists have shown that so-called segmentary societies tend to eliminate 'useless' ancestors, that is to say, those who have not left descendants who still live as a separate group. This explains why the genealogical depth of each group in a given society tends to remain constant. Only the 'useful' ancestors are used to explain the present. This sometimes leads to a very considerable telescoping of the genealogical depth. Furthermore, demographical accidents sometimes reduce a branch of descendants to such a small number, in comparison with the other branches descended from the brothers and sisters of the founder of the first branch, that it cannot any longer exist in parallel with the large neighbouring groups and so is absorbed by one of them. The genealogy will be readjusted and the founder of the diminishing group gives place to the founder of the larger (absorbing) group. The genealogy is thus simplified. The identity of an ethnic group is often expressed by a single ancestor placed at the beginning of a genealogy. This is the 'first man', a founding hero, etc. This will be the father or mother of the first 'useful' ancestor. In this way, the gap between origin and conscious history is abolished. Unfortunately this process has very often led to a situation in which it is practically impossible to go back with any confidence further than a few generations before the present.

It used to be thought that many African societies, and especially the monarchies, had escaped this process. There was no reason why the list of succession of the kings should not be correct, or why their genealogy should be doubtful, except that it was sometimes falsified when one dynasty replaced another and took over the genealogy of its predecessor in order to legitimize itself. The number of kings and generations, however, was apparently still correct. Recent detailed studies show that this position may not be entirely justified. The processes of telescoping, lengthening and regularizing may affect dynastic traditions as much as others. In king-lists, for example, the names of usurpers, that is to say, those who are considered, at present or at any time after their reign, to be usurpers, are sometimes omitted, and so may kings who have not undergone all the initiation ceremonies, which are sometimes very long. The reign of a king who abdicates and later returns to power is sometimes counted as a single reign. All this dislocates the historical process.

Where succession is patrilineal and primogenital, as in the interlacustrine region, the tendency to regularize the facts has resulted in a surprising number of regular successions – i.e. son succeeding father – which are much greater than the average, or even the record, for other parts of the world. This regularization process produces a typical direct-line genealogy from the earliest times up to about the nineteenth century, at which point it branches out laterally. The result is to lengthen the dynasty by increasing the number of generations, since collaterals are shown as fathers and sons. Confusion between people of the same name and between the regnal or titular name and the personal name, as well as other details of this kind, can lengthen or shorten the list. During colonial times, especially in regions under indirect rule, the pressure to lengthen the dynasties was strong because, since European – like so many African – societies have a great respect for antiquity, every ambiguous device and every possible means was used to lengthen the dynasties. All possible names were then used, which were repeated if necessary with the addition of cycles of royal names and collateral branches were pruned in order to lengthen the trunk.

Lastly, and always where kingdoms are concerned, there is often a gap between the founding hero, who belongs to cosmogony, and the first historically 'useful' king. Only a very careful investigation can determine whether or not the processes described actually took place. The presence of irregularities in the succession and in the genealogy is often the best guarantee of authenticity, because they show a resistance to homoeostatic levelling.

Age-group societies have not yet been subjected to this kind of systematic examination. Some cases show that regularization processes are at work to make cycles more orderly or to reduce the confusion produced by people having the same names. But the different kinds of age-group succession have still to be studied. We cannot generalize, except to say that the problem raised is similar to that of the genealogies, because generations are still the unit.

A thorough statistical study, which provided much of the information referred to above, shows that the average length of a dynastic generation is between twenty-six and thirty-two years. The sample was mainly patrilineal, but matrilineal dynasties are not, for example, grouped in the lower segment of the statistical distribution, and the information would be valid for them also. The average length of reign varies so greatly with the system of succession that no generally valid information can be provided. Even in the case of identical types of succession, considerable divergencies are found between different dynasties.

On the basis of the above information, a relative chronology of generations can be converted into an absolute chronology unless the genealogical distortion is such as would make the exercise futile. The average between the first absolute chronological reference provided by a written date and the present is first calculated and that average is projected into the past if it lies between twenty-six and thirty-two years. Averages are, however, only averages. Their probability increases with the number of generations concerned and the calculation provides reasonable dates only for the beginnings of sequences, or at best, say, once a century. Any greater precision leads to error. In any case, absolute dates calculated in this way must be preceded by a siglum to indicate the fact. Thus ±1635 for the foundation of the Kuba Kingdom would indicate that the date was calculated on the basis of genealogies and king-lists.

The same procedure can be applied to determine the average length of a reign. It has been shown why this average is less valid than that relating to generations. One of the reasons is that, when the average is projected back into the past, it is assumed that there was no change in the systems of succession. Yet they could have changed over the years. In fact they probably changed at the time of the founding of a dynasty, because to found is to innovate and the succession no doubt took a certain time to become standardized. In addition account must be taken of changes which may have occurred in the life expectation. Since the margin of error is greater, it follows that it will be particularly useful to possess absolute dates, determined by written documents or by some other means going back as far as possible into the past.

However, continuing in the field of relative chronology, it is possible to try to co-ordinate separate neighbouring different related sequences by studying synchronisms. A battle between two named kings provides a synchronism. It makes it possible to harmonize the two relative chronologies in question and to combine them into one. It has been shown empirically that synchronisms between more than three isolated units are no longer valid. It may be shown that A and B lived at the same time or that A and C lived at the same time because both met B. Therefore A = B = C, but we can go no further. The fact that A's and C's meetings with B might have occurred at any time during B's active life explains why A = C is the limit. In practice, research on the chronology of the ancient Middle East has proved this point. Nevertheless, with a prudent use of synchronisms, reasonably large single fields which possess a common relative chronology can be reconstructed.

After the genealogical data have been examined, an absolute date can be obtained if the tradition mentions an eclipse of the sun. If there is more than one possible date for the eclipse, it must be shown which is the most probable. We can proceed in the same way with other astronomical phenomena or extraordinary climatic phenomena which caused disasters. There is less certainty here than for eclipses of the sun because there are, for example, more famines in East Africa than eclipses of the sun. With the exception of eclipses of the sun, other information of this kind is mainly useful for the last two centuries; even so, few peoples have preserved the memory of much earlier eclipses.

Evaluation of oral traditions

Once sources have been subjected to thorough literary and sociological criticism, they can be assigned a degree of probability. This appraisal cannot be quantified, but it is none the less real. A tradition's accuracy will be greatly increased if the information it contains can be checked against that given in other *independent* traditions or from other sources. Two independent sources which agree transform a probability into something approaching a certainty. But the independence of the sources must be proved. Unfortunately, however, there has been too great a tendency to believe in the purity and watertight quality of transmission from one ethnic group to another. In practice, caravans of merchants such as the Imbangala of Angola, or no doubt those of the Dyula and the Hausa, may bring with them fragments of history which are incorporated into local history because they fit in well. Later on, links were formed between representatives of different groups at the beginning of the colonial period and they exchanged information concerning their traditions. This is strikingly the case for regions under indirect rule, where practical considerations encouraged kingdoms, in particular, to produce their histories. Moreover, all such histories have been influenced by the first histories written by Africans, such as Johnson's book on the Oyo Kingdom (Nigeria) or that of Kagwa (Uganda) for the Buganda. There followed a general contamination of all the histories put into written form subsequently in the Yoruba country and the English-speaking interlacustrine region, with attempts at synchronization in order to make dynastic lists at least as long as those of the models. These two examples show how careful one must be before stating that traditions are really independent. Archives must be searched, precolonial contacts studied and everything carefully weighed before any judgement can be made.

Comparison with written or archaeological data may provide the desired independent confirmation. Here again, the independence must be proved. When the local inhabitants traditionally attribute a visible site to the first inhabitants of the country because there are evident traces of human habitation which are very different from those left by the people currently living there, that does not mean that the site can automatically be attributed to those first inhabitants. The sources are not independent because the site is attributed to those inhabitants by a logical process and *a priori*! It is a case of iconatrophy and gives rise to interesting conjectures, especially concerning the so-called Tellem remains in the Dogon country (Mali) and the Sirikwa sites (Kenya), to mention only two famous examples. None the less, the famous sites of Koumbi Saleh (Mauritania) and at Lake Kisale (Zaïre) show that archaeology can sometimes supply striking proof of the validity of an oral tradition.

It is often difficult to establish a concordance between an oral and a written source, because these two sources speak of different things. A foreigner writing about a country usually restricts himself to economic and political facts, which are often still incompletely understood. The oral source, which is inwards looking, mentions foreigners only casually, if at all. Hence in many cases the two have nothing in common, even if they do relate to the same period. Cases of concordance, above all chronological concordance, are found where foreigners have been settled in the country for long enough to become interested in local politics and to understand them. The Senegal valley has been an example of this since the seventeenth century.

In cases of contradiction between oral sources, the most probable should be chosen. The widespread practice of trying to find a compromise often makes no sense at all. A flagrant contradiction between an oral and an archaeological source is resolved in favour of the latter if it is an immediate datum, that is to say, if the source is an object and not an inference, in which latter case the probability of the oral source can be greater. A conflict between a written and an oral source is resolved exactly as if they were two oral sources. It will be borne in mind that written quantitative information is often more reliable, but that oral information concerning motives is often more accurate than that from written sources. Finally, the historian tries to establish what is most probable. In an extreme case, if only one oral source is available, if it has been proved likely to have suffered distortion, it *must* be interpreted and used with due regard for the probable extent of the distortion.

Finally, the historian often does not feel satisfied with his oral information. He may note that he does not believe it to be really valid but, for lack of anything better, he is bound to use it so long as other sources have not been discovered.

Collection and publication

It follows from all that has been said above that all the elements which enable traditions to be subjected to historical criticism must be collected in the field. This calls for a good knowledge of the culture, the society and the language or languages involved. The historian may acquire this knowledge himself, or he may enlist the help of specialists. But even so, he must himself absorb all the information offered by the ethnologist, the linguist and the translator who are helping him. Lastly, he must adopt a systematic attitude to the sources, all the variants of which must be collected. All this implies long residence in the field, and this stay will be all the longer if the historian is not very familiar with the culture in question. It must be pointed out that the instinctive knowledge acquired by someone who studies the history of his own society is not enough. Sociological reflection is indispensable. The historian must rediscover his own culture. Linguistic experience has shown that sometimes even the man who is a native of the country does not easily understand certain oral records, such as panegyrical poems, or finds himself in difficulties because people speak a dialect different from his own. Furthermore, it is advisable that at least part of the transcriptions made in his mother dialect should be checked by a linguist to ensure that the transcription includes all the signs necessary to the understanding of the account including, for example, the tones.

The collection of traditions therefore requires much time and patience and much thought. After an initial trial period, a well-thought-out plan of campaign must be worked out, taking into account the special features of each case. In any event, the sites associated with the historical processes being studied must be visited. Sometimes it will be necessary to use a sampling of popular sources, but samples cannot be used haphazardly. The rules which determine the birth of variants should be studied in a limited area, and the principles of the sampling to be done established on the basis of these rules. To collect a vast amount of material indiscriminately cannot produce the same result, even if the work is done more quickly. The researcher must take care to examine the ways in which traditions have been transmitted. It is increasingly common to meet informants who have acquired their knowledge from published work on the history of the region, textbooks, newspapers or scientific publications; just as they may from lectures on the radio or on television. The danger will inevitably become more acute with the proliferation of research.

It is now being realized that there is also a more subtle contamination. Some – occasionally very old – manuscripts and above all reports from the early days of colonial administration have been taken over by tradition as ancestral truths. Archival sources must therefore be checked, as well as the possible influence of scientific works, textbooks, radio broadcasts, and so on. For if the fact is noted in the field, these insidious contributions may often be corrected by looking for other versions and by explaining to the informants that the book or the radio is not necessarily right in such matters. Once away from the field, however, it is too late.

Research must be planned with a clear historical idea in view. It is never possible to collect all the traditions and any attempt to do so would produce only a confused mass of information. It is first necessary to decide on the historical problems to be studied and then to look for sources to illuminate them. In order to formulate the problems, it is obvious that the researcher must have absorbed the culture in question. He may then, as is most often the case, decide to pursue the study of its political history. But he can also choose its social, economic, religious, cultural or artistic history, etc. And in each case the strategy used in collecting the tradition will be different. The greatest deficiency in present-day research is the lack of historical awareness. There is too great a tendency to be guided by what one finds.

Lack of patience is another danger. There is a wish to cover as much ground as possible as quickly as possible. In such circumstances, the sources collected are difficult to evaluate; they remain disparate and incomplete. The variants are missing. There is little information about the transformation of a source, its shape and its transmission. The work is badly done. A particularly harmful effect is the impression created among other researchers that this 'area' has already been studied, which lessens the likelihood of better research being done in the future. It should not be forgotten that oral traditions disappear, though happily less quickly than is generally thought. The urgency of the task is no reason for scamping it. It may be and has been said that what we are advocating here is utopian, a counsel of perfection, impossible. None the less, it is the only way of doing good work with the means available in the time available. There are no short cuts. If we find that, in some cases, all this work produces only a very meagre harvest for history, we overlook the fact that at the same time the general knowledge of the language, literature, collective thought and social structures of the civilization studied has been enriched.

Unless it is published, the work is not complete, because it has not been made available to the world of scholars. At least a classification of the sources investigated should be envisaged, with an introduction, notes and an index in order to constitute a body of archives open to all. This work is often combined with the publication of a study based partly or wholly on this corpus of material. No publisher would publish all the material, including the variants and the interpretation of the information. Besides, it is not advisable for a synthesis to be submerged in a vast mass of unprocessed evidence. But each work will explain how the traditions were collected and will give a brief list of the sources and informants, which will enable the reader to form an opinion on the quality of the collection and to understand why the author chose one source rather than another. For the same reason, each oral source should be quoted separately in the work. The work which says 'Tradition has it that ...' makes a dangerous generalization.

There remains a specialized type of publication: editions of texts. Here the same standards are followed as for the publication of manuscripts. In practice, this often leads to collaboration between various specialists. Not everyone is at the same time a historian, a linguist and an etymologist. In fact, the best published texts available to date are nearly all the joint work of two collaborators, at least one of whom is a linguist. The publication of texts is a hard, unrewarding task, which explains why there are so few of them. However, their number is increasing with the help of specialists in African oral literature.

Conclusions

Oral traditions are at present being collected in all African countries. The mass of information collected relates mainly to the nineteenth century and is only one source for historical reconstruction, the other main source for this period being written documents. There are five or six works each year presenting studies based almost entirely on traditions. Typologically they deal chiefly with political history and the history of kingdoms, and geographically they are concentrated mostly in East, Central and equatorial Africa, where traditions are often the only sources. The chronologies rarely date back further than 1700 or become doubtful even before that date. Some scholars believe that the bulk of the information does not even date back further than 1800. However, our increasing grasp of the nature of traditions enables those which were collected earlier to be better evaluated. Thus the exploitation of the traditions recorded by Cavazzi in the seventeenth century became possible only after a study in the field carried out in 1970!

In addition to recent traditions, there exists a vast fund of literary information, such as the epic narratives, and of cosmogonic data which can conceal historical information sometimes relating to very remote eras. The Sundjata epic is one example. Tradition itself does not make it possible to establish dates. For instance, with regard to some historic sites in the inter-lacustrine region, a distorted recollection has been preserved dating back to the first centuries of our era or even earlier, but the oral source is silent as to the date. Only archaeology has been able to solve the problem. Similarly, it appears that Cavazzi's traditions to which we have just referred contain a historical residue which is of the greatest interest for the past of the peoples of Angola. There are succinct references to dynasties which succeeded each other, to forms of government which followed each other; in short, they summarize for the Upper Kwango region social and political changes which may date back several centuries or even to a thousand years before 1500. But there are no dates as landmarks.

There is one final pitfall to be noted. Too often the collection of traditions is still superficial and their interpretation too literal and too closely tied to the culture concerned. This phenomenon contributes to maintaining the image of an Africa whose history consists of nothing but origins and migrations. We know that this is not true. But it must be admitted that that is the image which is reflected by traditions which seek to establish an identity. Superficiality of interpretation and lack of system in the collection of material are moreover the subject of most of the criticisms directed against the use of oral traditions, especially among ethnologists.

Practical experience has proved that the greatest value of traditions lies in their explanation of historical changes within a culture. We find this to be so true almost anywhere that, despite the abundance of written sources for the colonial era, recourse has constantly to be made either to eye-witness accounts or to tradition to complete them and to make the evolution of the people comprehensible. But we find also that traditions are often misleading with regard to chronology and quantitative data. Moreover, any change which is unconscious because it is too slow, a mutation linked to a religious ideology, for example, escapes the memory of a society. Only fragmentary indications of changes can be found in oral records which do not deal specifically with history and even then a complex exposition is necessary. This shows that oral tradition is not a panacea for all ills. But in practice it proves to be a first-class source for the last few centuries. Before that, it has less to contribute and it becomes instead a subsidiary science of archaeology. Its role in relation to linguistic and ethnographic sources has not yet been sufficiently explored, although in principle these three types of sources should together make a considerable contribution to our knowledge of ancient Africa, just as archaeology does.

Traditions have proved their irreplaceable value. It is no longer necessary to convince people that they can be useful sources of information. Every historian knows this. What we must now do is to improve our techniques so that the sources can yield up their full potential wealth. That is the task before us.

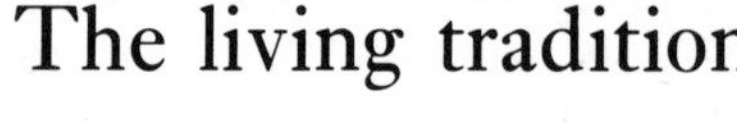

8 The living tradition

A. HAMPATÉ BÂ

> Writing is one thing and knowledge is another. Writing is the photograph of knowledge but is not knowledge itself. Knowledge is a light that is in man. It is the heritage of all that our ancestors have known, and it is in the germ they transmit to us, just as the baobab-tree is potentially in its seed.
>
> Tierno Bokar[1]

When we speak of African tradition or history we mean oral tradition; and no attempt at penetrating the history and spirit of the African peoples is valid unless it relies on that heritage of knowledge of every kind patiently transmitted from mouth to ear, from master to disciple, down through the ages. This heritage is not yet lost, but lies there in the memory of the last generation of great depositories, of whom it can be said: 'they *are* the living memory of Africa'.

In the modern nations, where what is written has precedence over what is spoken, where the book is the principal vehicle of the cultural heritage, there has been a long-standing notion that peoples without writing are peoples without culture. This quite unwarranted opinion has happily begun to wear off since the last two wars, thanks to the work done by certain great ethnologists of every nation. Today the innovative and courageous action of Unesco is raising the veil still further from the treasures of knowledge transmitted by oral tradition, treasures which belong to the cultural patrimony of all mankind.

For some scholars, the whole problem is whether we can place the same trust in the oral as in the written when it comes to evidence of things past. In my view, that is not the right way to put the problem. Written or oral evidence is in the end only human evidence and it is worth what the man is worth.

Does not what is said give birth to what is written, both over the centuries and in the individual himself? The world's earliest archives or libraries were

1. Tierno Bokar Salif (d. 1940) spent his life in Bandiagara (Mali). Grand Master of the Muslim Order of Tijāniyya, he was also a traditionalist in African matters. Cf. A. Hampaté Bâ and M. Cardaire, 1957.

the brains of men. Before he puts his thoughts on paper the writer or the scholar has a private dialogue with himself. Before he writes a story down a man reminds himself of the facts as they were told to him, or as he tells them to himself if it is his own experience.

Nothing proves *a priori* that writing gives a more faithful account of a reality than oral evidence handed down from generation to generation. The chronicles of modern wars serve to show that, as is said (in Africa), each party or nation 'sees high noon from its own doorway' – through the prism of its own passions or mentality or interests, or eagerness to justify its point of view. Moreover, written documents were not themselves always secure against deliberate forgeries or unintentional alterations at the hands of successive copyists – phenomena which *inter alia* gave rise to the controversies over 'Holy Writ'.

What is involved, therefore, behind the evidence itself, is the actual value of the man who is giving the evidence, the value of the chain of transmission he is part of, the trustworthiness of the individual and collective memory, and the price attached to the truth in a given society. In short: the bond between man and the spoken word.

Now it is in oral societies that the function of the memory is most highly developed and, furthermore, the bond between man and the word is strongest. Where writing does not exist, man is bound to the word he utters. He is committed by it. He *is* his word and his word bears witness to what he is. The very cohesion of society depends on the value of and respect for the spoken word. By contrast, with the encroachment of writing we see writing gradually replace the spoken word, become the sole proof and the sole resort; we see the signature become the sole recognized commitment, while the deep sacred bond that used to unite man and word disappears, to be replaced by conventional university degrees.

In African traditions – at least the ones I know, which pertain to the whole savannah zone south of the Sahara – the spoken word had, beyond its fundamental moral value, a sacred character associated with its divine origin and with the occult forces deposited in it. Superlative agent in magic, grand vector of 'ethereal' forces, it was not to be treated lightly.

Many religious, magical or social factors, then, combined to preserve the faithfulness of oral transmission. I think I should give the reader a brief account of these, the better to place African oral tradition in its context, and as it were illuminate it from within.

If a true African traditionalist were asked, 'What is oral tradition?' he would probably be nonplussed. He might perhaps reply, after a lengthy silence: 'It is total knowledge', and say no more.

What does the term oral tradition cover, then? What realities does it convey, what knowledge does it transmit, what sciences does it teach, and who are its transmitters?

Contrary to what some may think, African oral tradition is not limited to stories and legends or even to mythological and historical tales, and the man whom the French call a 'griot' – a wandering minstrel/poet – is far from being its one and only qualified guardian and transmitter.

Oral tradition is the great school of life, all aspects of which are covered and affected by it. It may seem chaos to those who do not penetrate its secret; it may baffle the Cartesian mind accustomed to dividing everything up into clear-cut categories. In oral tradition, in fact, spiritual and material are not dissociated.

Passing from the esoteric to the exoteric, oral tradition is able to put itself within men's reach, speak to them according to their understanding, unveil itself in accordance with their aptitudes. It is at once religion, knowledge, natural science, apprenticeship in a craft, history, entertainment, recreation, since any point of detail can always take us all the way back to primordial unity.

Based on initiation and experience, oral tradition engages man in his total being, and therefore we can say it has served to create a particular type of man, to sculpt the African soul.

Linked with the everyday behaviour of man and community, African culture is not, then, something abstract that can be isolated from life. It involves a particular vision of the world, or rather a particular *presence* in the world – a world conceived of as a whole in which all things are linked together and interact.

Oral tradition is based upon a certain conception of man, of man's place and role within the universe. To situate it the better in its total context before studying it in its various aspects, we must therefore go back to the very mystery of the creation of man and the primordial inauguration of the Word: the mystery which the Word teaches, and in which it originates.

Divine origin of the Word

Since I cannot validly speak of any traditions I have not experienced or studied personally – those of forest countries, especially – I shall take my basic examples from the traditions of the savannah to the south of the Sahara (what was formerly called the Bafour and constituted the savannah zones of former French West Africa).

The Bambara tradition of the Komo[2] teaches that the Word, Kuma, is a fundamental force emanating from the Supreme Being himself – Maa Ngala, creator of all things. It is the instrument of creation: 'That which Maa Ngala says, is!' proclaims the cantor – the singing priest – of the god Komo.

The myth of the creation of the universe and of man which the Komo Master of Initiates (who is always a smith) teaches circumcised youths reveals that when Maa Ngala felt a yearning for an interlocutor he created the First Man: Maa.

The story of genesis used to be taught during the sixty-three-day retreat

2. One of the great initiation schools of the Mande (Mali).

imposed on the circumcised in their twenty-first year, and then twenty-one years were spent in deeper and deeper study of it.

On the edge of the sacred wood, where Komo lives, the first of the circumcised group would chant to a rhythmic beat:

> Maa Ngala! Maa Ngala!
> Who is Maa Ngala?
> Where is Maa Ngala?

The Komo chanter would respond:

> Maa Ngala is infinite Force.
> None can place him in time,
> Nor yet in space.
> He is Dombali (Unknowable)
> Dambali (Uncreated-Infinite).

Then, after the initiation, the recital of the primordial genesis would begin:

> There was nothing except a Being.
> That Being was a living Emptiness,
> brooding potentially over contingent existences.
> Infinite Time was the abode of that One Being.
> The One Being gave himself the name Maa Ngala.
> Maa Ngala wished to be known.
> So he created Fan,
> a wondrous Egg with nine divisions,
> and into it he introduced the nine fundamental
> states of existence.

'When this primordial Egg came to hatch, it gave birth to twenty marvellous beings that made up the whole of the universe, the sum total of existing forces and possible knowledges.

'But alas! None of those first twenty creatures proved fit to become the interlocutor (Kuma-nyon) that Maa Ngala had craved.

'So he took a bit of each of those twenty existing creatures and mixed them; and then, blowing a spark of his own fiery breath into the mixture, he created a new Being, Man, to whom he gave a part of his own name: Maa. And so this new being, through his name and through the divine spark introduced into him, contained something of Maa Ngala himself.'

Synthesis of all that exists, pre-eminent receptacle of the supreme Force and confluence of all existing forces, Maa, Man, received as his legacy a part of the divine creative power, the gift of Mind and the Word.

Maa Ngala taught Maa, his interlocutor, the laws according to which all the elements of the cosmos were formed and continue to exist. He installed him as guardian of his universe and charged him with watching over the maintenance of universal harmony. That is why it weighs heavy, being Maa.

Initiated by his creator, Maa later passed all that he had learned on to his descendants; and that was the beginning of the great chain of initiatory oral transmission of which the order of Komo (like the orders of Nama, Kore, and so on, in Mali) claims to be a continuator.

Once Maa Ngala had created his interlocutor Maa he spoke to him, and at the same time endowed him with the faculty of replying. A dialogue was begun between Maa Ngala, creator of all things, and Maa, symbiosis of all things.

As they came down from Maa Ngala towards man, words were divine, because they had not yet come into contact with materiality. After their contact with corporeity they lost something of their divinity but took on sacredness. Hallowed in this way by the divine Word, corporeity in its turn gave out sacred vibrations which established relations with Maa Ngala.

African tradition, then, conceives of speech as a gift of God. It is at once divine in the downward direction and sacred as it rises upwards.

Speech in man as creative power

Maa Ngala, it is taught, deposited in Maa the three potentialities of ability, willing and knowing contained in the twenty components of which he was composed. But all the forces to which he is heir lie dumb within him. They are static, till speech comes and sets them into motion. Then, vivified by the divine Word, they begin to vibrate. At a first stage they become thoughts, at a second sound, and at a third words. Speech – spoken words – is therefore regarded as the materialization or externalization of the vibrations of forces.

Let me point out, though, that at this level the terms 'speaking' and 'listening' refer to realities far more vast than those we usually attribute to them. It is said: 'The speech of Maa Ngala is seen, is heard, is smelled, is tasted, is touched.' It is a total perception, a knowing in which the entire being is engaged.

In the same way, since speech is the externalization of the vibrations of forces, every manifestation of a force in any form whatever is to be regarded as its speech. That is why everything in the universe speaks: everything is speech that has taken on body and shape.

In Fulfulde, the word for 'speech' (*haala*) is derived from the verbal root *hal*, the idea of which is 'to give strength' and by extension 'to make material'. Fulani tradition teaches that Gueno, the Supreme Being, conferred strength on Kiikala, the first man, by speaking to him. 'It was talking with God that made Kiikala strong', say the Silatiqui (the Fulani Master Initiates).

If speech is strength, that is because it creates a bond of coming-and-going (*yaa-warta*, in Fulfulde) which generates movement and rhythm and therefore life and action. This movement to and fro is symbolized by the weaver's feet going up and down, as we shall see later in connection with the traditional crafts. (In fact the symbolism of the loom is entirely based on creative speech in action.)

In the image of Maa Ngala's speech, of which it is an echo, human speech sets latent forces into motion. They are activated and aroused by speech – just as a man gets up, or turns, at the sound of his name.

Speech may create peace, as it may destroy it. It is like fire. One ill-advised word may start a war just as one blazing twig may touch off a great conflagration. In Malian adage: 'What puts a thing into condition [that is, arranges it, disposes it favourably]? Speech. What damages a thing? Speech. What keeps a thing as it is? Speech.'

Tradition, then, confers on Kuma, the Word, not only creative power but a double function of saving and destroying. That is why speech, speech above all, is the great active agent in African magic.

Speech, active agent in magic

It must be borne in mind that in a general way all African traditions postulate a *religious vision of the world*. The visible universe is thought of and felt as the sign, the concretization or the outer shell of an invisible, living universe, consisting of forces in perpetual motion. Within this vast cosmic unity everything is connected, everything is bound solidly together; and man's behaviour both as regards himself and as regards the world around him (the mineral, vegetable, animal world and human society) is subject to a very precise ritual regulation – which may vary in form with the various ethnicities and regions.

Violation of the sacred laws was supposed to cause an upset in the balance of forces which would take expression in disturbances of different kinds. That is why magic action, that is, the manipulation of forces, generally aimed at restoring the troubled balance, re-establishing the harmony of which, as we have seen, man had been set up as guardian by his creator.

The word 'magic' is always taken in a bad sense in Europe whereas in Africa it simply means management of forces, a thing neutral in itself which may prove helpful or harmful according to the direction it is given. It is said: 'Neither magic nor fortune is bad in itself. It is use of them that makes them good or bad.'

Good magic, the magic of initiates and 'masters of knowledge', aims at purifying men, animals and objects so as to put forces back into order. This is where the force of speech is decisive.

For just as Maa Ngala's divine speech animated the cosmic forces that lay static in Maa, so man's speech animates, sets into motion and rouses the forces that are static in things. But for spoken words to produce their full effect they must be chanted rhythmically, because movement needs rhythm, which is itself based on the secret of numbers. Speech must reproduce the to-and-fro that is the essence of rhythm.

In ritual songs and incantatory formulae, therefore, speech is the materialization of cadence. And if it is considered as having the power to act on spirits, that is because its harmony creates movements, movements which generate forces, those forces are then acting on spirits which themselves are powers for action.

In African tradition, speech, deriving its creative and operative power from the sacred, is in direct relation with the maintenance or the rupture of harmony in man and the world about him.

That is why most traditional oral societies consider lying as an actual moral leprosy. In traditional Africa the man who breaks his word kills his civil, religious and occult person. He cuts himself off from himself and from society. Better for him to die than to go on living, both for himself and for his family.

The singer of the Komo Dibi at Koulikoro, in Mali, in one of his ritual poems, sang:

Speech is divinely accurate,
one must be accurate with it.

The tongue that falsifies the word
taints the blood of him that lies.

Here blood symbolizes the inner vital force whose harmony is disturbed by the lie. 'Who spoils his word spoils himself', says the adage. When a man thinks one thing and says another he cuts himself off from himself. He breaks the sacred unity, the reflection of cosmic unity, creating discord in and around him.

Now we can better understand the magico-religious and social context of respect for the word in societies with an oral tradition, especially when it comes to transmitting words inherited from ancestors or elders. The thing traditional Africa holds dearest is its ancestral heritage. Its religious attachment to all that has been passed down comes out in phrases like 'I have it from my Master', 'I have it from my father', 'I sucked it at my mother's breast.'

The traditionalists

The great repositories of this oral heritage are the persons who are called 'traditionalists'. They, the living memory of Africa, are the best witness of it. Who are these masters?

In Bambara, they are called *domas* or *somas*, the 'knowers', or *donikebas*, 'makers of knowledge'. In Fulfulde, they are called, according to region, *silatiquis*, *gandos* or *tchioriknes*, words which have this same sense of 'knower'.

They may be Master Initiates (and Masters of Initiates) in one particular traditional branch (initiations of the smith, the weaver, the hunter, the fisherman, etc.) or may possess complete knowledge of the tradition in all its aspects. Thus there are *domas* who know the blacksmith's science, the shepherd's, the weaver's, as well as of the great initiation schools of the savannah – in Mali, for instance, the Komo, the Kore, the Nama, the Do, the Diarra Wara, the Nya, the Nyawarole, and so on.

But let us make no mistake. African tradition does not cut life into slices and the knower is rarely a specialist. As a rule he is a generalist. For example, one and the same old man will be learned not only in plant science (the good or bad properties of every plant) but in earth sciences (the agricultural or medicinal properties of the different kinds of soil), and water sciences, and astronomy, cosmogony, psychology, and so on. What is involved is a *science of life* in which knowledges can always be turned to practical use. And when we speak of initiatory or occult sciences, terms that may confuse the western reader, traditional Africa always understands by this an eminently practical science which consists in knowing how to enter into the appropriate relationship with the forces that underlie the visible world and can be made to serve life.

Keeper of the secrets of cosmic genesis and the sciences of life, the traditionalist, usually gifted with a prodigious memory, is often also the archivist of the past events, transmitted by tradition, or of contemporary events.

Therefore a history intended to be essentially African must necessarily depend on the irreplaceable testimony of qualified Africans. 'You cannot dress a person's hair when he is away', says the adage.

The great *domas,* those with total knowledge, were known and venerated, and people came from afar to appeal to their knowledge and wisdom.

Ardo Dembo, who initiated me into things Fulani, was a Fulani *doma* (a 'silatiqui'). He is dead now.

Ali Essa, another Fulani *silatiqui,* is still alive.

Danfo Sine, who used to come to my father's house when I was a child, was a well-nigh universal *doma*. Not only was he a grand Master Initiate of the Komo, but he possessed all the other knowledges of his time – knowledge pertaining to history, initiation or natural sciences. He was known to everyone in the region between Sikasso and Bamako, that is, the old kingdoms of Kenedugu and Beledugu.

His younger brother Latif, who had experienced the same initiations, was also a great *doma*. He had the additional advantage of reading and writing Arabic and of having done his military service (in the French forces) in Chad, so that he was able to pick up a great deal of knowledge in the Chadian savannah which proved to be similar to what was taught in Mali.

Iwa, of the *dieli* caste, is one of the greatest Mande traditionalists now alive in Mali, as is Banzoumana, the great blind musician.

Here I should make it plain that a *dieli* is not necessarily a traditionalist knower but may become one if his aptitudes lie that way. But he cannot gain access to the Komo initiation, from which *dielis* are barred.[3]

3. For the *dieli*, see below, pp. 187–92.

Generally speaking, the traditionalists were brushed aside if not actually proceeded against by the colonial power, which needless to say sought to uproot local traditions in order to implant its own ideas; for, as they say, 'Neither in a planted field nor in a fallow does one sow.' For that reason initiation usually took refuge in the bush and quit the large towns, which were called *tubabu-dugus* or 'towns of the whites' – meaning the colonizers.

Yet in the different countries of the African savannah that make up the old Bafour – and doubtless elsewhere too – there still exist knowers who continue to transmit the sacred heritage to those who consent to learn and listen and show themselves worthy of receiving instruction by their patience and their discretion, basic rules required by the gods.

In ten or fifteen years all the last great *domas*, all the last old men who have inherited the various branches of the tradition, will probably have vanished. If we do not make haste to gather their evidence and their teaching, the whole cultural and spiritual patrimony of a people will go down into oblivion with them and a rootless younger generation be abandoned to its own devices.

Authenticity of transmission

More than all other men the traditionalist-*domas*, great and small, are bound to respect the truth. For them lying is not merely a moral blemish but a *ritual interdict*, violation of which would make it impossible for them to fulfil their function.

A liar could not be an initiator or a master of the knife, still less a *doma*. And if the unheard-of happened and a traditionalist-*doma* proved to be a liar, no one would ever turn to him again for anything, and his function would vanish on the spot.

Generally speaking African tradition has a horror of the lie. It is said: 'Take care not to cut yourself off from yourself. Better for the world to be cut off from you than for you to be cut off from yourself.' But the ritual ban on lying affects more particularly all officiants (or sacrificers, or masters of the knife, and so on)[4] of all degrees, beginning with the father of a family who is sacrificer or officiant for his household, going on through the smith, the weaver, the traditional craftsman – practice of one's craft being a sacred activity, as we shall see. The prohibition strikes at all who have to carry out some magico-religious responsibility and perform ritual acts and are thereby in a way intermediaries between common mortals and the tutelary forces; at the summit are the sacred officiant of the country (for example, the *hogon,* among the Dogons) and eventually the king.

This ritual prohibition exists, to the best of my knowledge in all the traditions of the African savannah.

The reason for the ban on lying is that if an officiant lied he would vitiate

4. Not all ritual ceremonies necessarily involved the sacrifice of an animal. The sacrifice may consist of an offering of millet, milk or some other natural product.

ritual acts. He would no longer fulfil all the ritual conditions necessary for performing the sacred act, the chief one being that he himself be in harmony before he manipulates the forces of life. For let us not forget that all African magico-religious systems aim at preserving or re-establishing the balance of forces on which the harmony of the surrounding world, material and spiritual, depends.

More than all others, the *domas* are bound by this obligation, for as Master Initiates they are the great *holders of the Word,* the principal active agency of human life and of spirits. They are the heirs of the sacred incantatory words passed on down by the chain of ancestors, words which can be traced back to those sacred first vibrations emitted by Maa, the first man.

I shall cite the case of a Dogon Master of the Knife from the Pignari country (Bandiagara district) whom I knew in my youth and who had once been led to lie in order to save the life of a hunted woman whom he had hidden in his house. After that incident he voluntarily resigned his office, deeming that he no longer fulfilled the ritual conditions which would make his tenure valid.

When religious and sacred things are concerned the traditional grand masters are not afraid of the unfavourable opinion of the masses, and should they happen to make a mistake they acknowledge their error publicly, without calculated or evasive excuses. For them, confessing any faults they may commit is an obligation, for it is a purification from defilement.

If the traditionalist or knower is so respected in Africa it is because, to begin with, he respects himself. Inwardly in good order, since he must never lie, he is a well-regulated man, master of the forces that inhabit him. Round about him things fall into line and disturbances subside.

Even aside from this prohibition against lying, he disciplines his speech and does not utter it recklessly. For if speech, as we have seen, is regarded as an externalization of the vibrations of inner forces, conversely inner force is born of the internalizing of speech.

If the traditionalist-*doma* is the holder of speech, other men are the depositories of small talk.

Given this way of looking at things, the importance traditional African education attaches to self-control can be better understood. To speak sparingly is the mark of a good education and the sign of nobility. Very early the young boy learns to master the expression of his emotions or his suffering, to contain the forces that are in him, in the image of the primordial Maa who with him, submissive and orderly, contained all the forces of the cosmos.

Of a respected knower or a man who is master of himself people will say: 'He's a Maa!' (or, in Fulfulde, a Naddo): that is, a complete man.

We must not confuse the traditionalist-*doma*, who know how to teach by amusing and by putting themselves within their audience's reach, with minstrels, story-tellers and public entertainers, who are usually of the *dieli* and *woloso* (house-captive)[5] castes. For these, the discipline of truth does not exist; and as we shall see later tradition recognizes their right to travesty or embellish the facts, even grossly, so long as they contrive to divert or interest their public. 'The *dieli*', people say, 'is allowed to have two tongues.'

By contrast, no African from a traditionalist background would dream of questioning the veracity of what a traditionalist-*doma* says, especially when it is a matter of passing on knowledge inherited from the line of ancestors.

Before speaking, the *doma* out of deference addresses the souls of former men and asks them to come to his aid and save him from a slip of the tongue or a lapse of memory that would make him leave something out.

Danfo Sine, the great Bambara *doma* whom I knew in my childhood at Bougouni and who was the Komo chanter, used to say before embarking on a story or a lesson:

> O Soul of my Master Tiemablem Samake!
> O Souls of old smiths and old weavers,
> first initiating ancestors come from the East!
> O Jigi, great man who first blew
> on the trump of Komo,
> when he came on the Jeliba [Niger]!
> Come all of you and harken to me.
> In accordance with your sayings, I am going
> to tell my hearers
> how things have happened,
> from you in the past to us here present,
> so that what is said may be guarded as something precious
> and faithfully transmitted
> to the men of tomorrow
> who will be our children
> and the children of our children.
> Hold the reins of my tongue well, O you Ancestors!
> Guide my words as they come forth
> that they may follow and respect
> their natural order.

Then he would add:

'I, Danfo Sine, of the clan of Samake [the male elephant], am about to tell you the tale as I learned it, in presence of my two witnesses Makoro and Manifin.[6]

5. The *wolosos* (literally, ones born in the house) or house-captives were servants or servant families attached for generations to one household. Tradition allowed them complete freedom of gesture and speech as well as considerable material rights over their masters' possessions.

6. Makoro and Manifin were his two co-disciples.

'They both know the warp as I do.[7] They will serve me both as surveillants and as props.'

If the storyteller made a mistake or forgot something, his witness would take him up: 'Man! Mind your manner of opening your mouth!' To which he would reply: 'Excuse it, my ardent tongue has played me false.'

A traditionalist-*doma* who is not a smith by birth but knows sciences relating to the forge will say before talking of it: 'I owe that to So-and-so, who owes it to So-and-so, etc.' He will pay homage to the ancestor of the smiths, crouching in token of allegiance, with the tip of his elbow on the ground and his forearm raised.

The *doma* also may cite his master and say: 'I render homage to all the intermediaries back to Nunfayri ...'[8] without having to mention all the names.

Always there is reference to the chain in which the *doma* himself is but one link.

In all branches of traditional knowledge the *chain of transmission* is of supreme importance. If there is no regular transmission there is no magic, only conversation or story-telling. Speech is then inoperative. Transmitted through the chain, it is supposed to convey, from the original transmission on, a force that makes it operative and sacramental.

This notion of respect for the chain or respect for transmission means that an African who has not been influenced by European culture will generally tend to report a story in the very form in which he heard it, aided by the prodigious memory illiterate persons have. If contradicted, he will merely answer: 'So-and-so taught it to me like that!' – always naming his source.

Beyond the traditionalist-*doma*'s personal integrity and their attachment to a chain of transmission, an additional guarantee of authenticity is provided by *permanent control by the peers or elders* who surround them, who keep a jealous guard on the authenticity of what they transmit and take them up on the slightest error, as we have seen in the instance of Danfo Sine.

In the course of his ritual excursions into the bush, the Komo chanter may add meditations or inspirations of his own to the traditional words he has inherited from the chain and sings for his companions. His words, new links, then serve to enrich the words of his predecessors; but he gives the warning: 'This is what I am adding, this what I am saying. I am not infallible, I may be wrong. If I am, do not forget that like you I live on a handful of millet, a mouthful of water, and some whiffs of air. Man is not infallible!'

The initiates and the neophytes who accompany him learn these new words, so that all the Komo songs are known and kept in their memories.

The degree of a Komo disciple's evolution is measured not by the

7. A traditional story always has a thread or immovable base which must never be modified but on which one may embroider developments or embellishments as inspiration or the attention of one's auditors suggests.

8. Ancestor of smiths.

quantity of words he has learned but by the *conformity of his life* to those words. If a man has only ten or twelve Komo words and *lives* them, then he becomes a valuable adherent of the Komo within his association. To be a Komo chanter, then a Master Initiate, one must know the inherited words in their totality – and live them.

Traditional education, especially when it concerns knowledge associated with an initiation, is linked with experience and integrated into life. That is why the researcher, European or African, who wants to get close to African religious facts condemns himself to remaining on the outer edge of the subject unless he consents to live the initiation that corresponds to them and accept its rules, which presupposes at the very least a *knowledge of the language*. For there are things that are not to be explained but are experienced and lived.

I remember that in 1928, when I was serving in Tougan, a young anthropologist arrived in the country to make a study of the sacrificial hen at a circumcision. The French Commandant went to the headman of the indigenous canton and asked that everything be done to satisfy the anthropologist, insisting that he be told everything.

In his turn the headman assembled the leading citizens. He laid the facts before them, repeating the Commandant's words.

The leading man of the assembly, who was the Master of the Knife in that particular place and therefore responsible for circumcision ceremonies and the corresponding initiation, asked him: 'He wants us to tell him everything?'

'Yes', replied the canton headman.

'But has he come to be circumcised?'

'No, he has come for information.'

The old man turned his face away from the headman. 'How can we tell him everything', he demanded, 'if he does not want to be circumcised? You know well, perfectly well, Chief, that that's impossible. He will have to live the life of those who are circumcised, for us to teach him all the lessons.'

'Since we're obliged by force to give satisfaction', the canton headman returned, 'it's up to you to find us a way out of the difficulty.'

'Very well', said the old man. 'We shall get rid of him without appearing to, by putting him in the straw.'

This 'putting in the straw' or hoodwinking, which consists of deceiving a person with some made-up tale when you don't want to tell him the truth, was invented when the colonial power sent its agents or representatives to do anthropological research without their consenting to live under the requisite conditions. Many anthropologists were unwitting victims of this policy later – and many others, without actually having been led up the garden path, imagined that they understood a thing completely when, not having lived it, they could not truly know it.

Beyond the esoteric instruction given in the great initiation schools like the Komo or the others mentioned above, traditional education actually begins in each and every family, where the father, the mother or the older persons are at once masters and teachers and constitute the first cell of the traditionalists. They are the ones who give the first lessons in life, not only through experience but through the medium of stories, fables, legends, maxims, adages, and so on. Proverbs are missives bequeathed to posterity by the ancestors. Their number is legion.

Certain children's games have been worked out by initiates with an end to conveying certain cyphered esoteric knowledge through the ages. I might mention for example the Banangolo game, in Mali, which is based on a numeral system related to the 266 *siqiba* or signs that correspond to the attributes of God.

Moreover, education is not systematic but is tied in with the circumstances of life. This manner of proceeding may seem chaotic, but in fact it is very practical and very live. The lesson given on the occasion of some special event or experience is deeply graven on a child's memory.

If an old teacher comes upon an ant-hill during a walk in the bush, this gives him an opportunity for dispensing various kinds of knowledge according to the kind of listeners he has at hand. Either he will speak of the creature itself, the laws governing its life and the class of being it belongs to, or he will give children a lesson in morality by showing them how community life depends on solidarity and forgetfulness of self, or again he may go on to higher things if he feels that his audience can attain to them. Thus any incident in life, any trivial happening, can always be developed in many ways, can lead to telling a myth, a tale, a legend. Every phenomenon one encounters can be traced back to the forces from which it issued and suggest the mysteries of the unity of life, which is entirely animated by Se, the primordial sacred Force, itself an aspect of God the Creator.

In Africa, everything is history. The grand history of life includes the history of lands, lakes and rivers (geography), the history of plants (botany and pharmaceutics), the history of the sons of the womb of the earth (mineralogy, metals), the history of the stars (astronomy, astrology), the history of water, and so on.

In savannah tradition, particularly in the Bambara and Fulani traditions, the sum total of the manifestations of life on earth is divided into three categories or classes of being, each subdivided into three groups:

(1) At the bottom of the scale, inanimate, the so-called 'mute' beings, whose language is considered occult, since it is incomprehensible or inaudible to common mortals. This class of beings includes everything that lies on the surface of the earth (sand, water) or resides within it (minerals, metals, etc.). Among the mute inanimates we find solid, liquid and gaseous (literally, smoking) inanimates.

(2) In the middle degree, immobile inanimates, beings that are living but do not move. This is the class of plants, which can stretch

or open out in space but cannot move their feet. Among the immobile animates we find creeping, climbing and upright plants, the last class being the highest.

(3) Finally, mobile animates, which include all animals, up to man. The mobile animates include land animals (with and without bones), aquatic animals and flying animals.

Everything that exists can therefore be placed in one or another of these categories.[9]

Of all the histories, the greatest and most meaningful is that of man itself, the symbiosis of all of them, since according to myth he was made up of a bit of everything that existed before him. All the kingdoms of life (mineral, vegetable and animal) are found in him, conjoined with multiple forces and higher faculties. Teachings about man are based on myths of the cosmogony which determine his place and role in the universe, and they reveal what his relationship with the world of the living and the dead ought to be. They will explain both the symbolism of his body and the complexity of his psyche. 'The persons of the person are many in the person', say the Bambara and Fulani traditions. Man will be taught how he ought to behave towards nature, how to respect its equilibrium and not disturb the forces that animate it, and of which it is only the outward and visible show. Initiation will show him his relationship with the world of these forces and lead him little by little towards self-mastery, the ultimate goal being to become, like Maa, a complete man, interlocutor of Maa Ngala and guardian of the living world.

The traditional crafts

The traditional artisanal crafts are great vectors of oral tradition.

In the traditional African society, often human activities had a sacred or occult character, particularly those activities that consist in acting on matter and transforming it, since everything is regarded as alive.

Every artisanal function was linked with an esoteric knowledge transmitted from generation to generation and taking its origin in an initial revelation. The craftsman's work was sacred because it imitated the work of Maa Ngala and supplemented his creation. Bambara tradition, in fact, teaches that creation is not yet finished and that Maa Ngala, in creating our earth, left things there unfinished so that Maa, his interlocutor, might supplement or modify them with a view to leading nature towards its perfection. The craftsman's activity in operation was supposed to repeat the mystery of creation. It therefore focused an occult force which one could not approach without respecting certain ritual conditions.

Traditional craftsmen accompany their work with ritual chants or sacramental rhythmic words, and their very gestures are considered a

9. Cf. A. Hampaté Bâ, 1972, pp. 23ff.

language. In fact the gestures of each craft reproduce in a symbolism proper to each one the mystery of the primal creation, which, as I indicated earlier, was bound up with the power of the Word. It is said:

> The smith forges the Word,
> The weaver weaves it,
> The leather-worker curries it smooth.

Let us take the example of the weaver, whose craft is linked with the symbolism of the creative Word deploying itself in time and space.

A man who is a weaver by caste (a *maabo,* among the Fulani) is the repository of the secrets of the thirty-three pieces that are basic to the loom, each of which has a meaning. The frame, for example, is made up of eight main pieces of wood: four vertical ones that symbolize not only the four mother elements (earth, water, air, fire) but the four main points of the compass, and four transverse ones that symbolize the four collateral points. The weaver, placed in the middle, represents primordial Man, Maa, at the heart of the eight directions of space. With his presence, we obtain nine elements which recall the nine fundamental states of existence, the nine classes of being, the nine openings of the body (gates of the forces of life), the nine categories of men among the Fulani, etc., etc.

Before beginning work the weaver must touch each piece of the loom, pronouncing words or litanies that correspond to the forces of life embodied in them.

The movement of his feet to and fro as they go up and down to work the pedals recalls the original rhythm of the creative Word, linked with the dualism of all things and the law of cycles. His feet are supposed to speak as follows:

> *Fonyonko! fonyonko!* dualism! dualism!
> When one goes up the other goes down.
> There is the death of the king and the coronation of the prince,
> the death of the grandfather and the birth of the grandson,
> quarrels over divorce commingled with the sound of
> a marriage feast ...

For its part, the shuttle says:

> I am the barque of Fate.
> I pass between the reefs of the threads of the warp
> that stand for Life.
> From the right bank I pass to the left,
> unreeling my intestine [the thread]
> to contribute to the fabric.
> And then again from the left bank I pass to the right,
> unreeling my intestine.
> Life is a perpetual to and fro,
> a permanent giving of the self.

The strip of cloth accumulating and winding around a stick resting on the weaver's belly represents the past, while the reel of thread still to be woven, unwound, symbolizes the mystery of tomorrow, the unknown what-is-to-be. The weaver always says: 'Oh tomorrow! Hold no unpleasant surprise in store for me.'

In all, the weaver's work represents eight movements to and fro (movements of his feet, his arms, the shuttle and the rhythmic crossing of the thread of the fabric) that correspond to the eight pieces of wood in the loom-frame and the eight legs of the mythical spider which taught its science to the weavers' ancestor.

As for the smith, he is the depository of the secret of transmutations. He is pre-eminently the Master of Fire. His origin is mythical and in Bambara tradition he is called the First Son of the Earth. His skills go back to Maa, the first man, whom his creator Maa Ngala taught amongst other things the secrets of metal-working. That is why the forge is called Fan, by the same name as Fan the primordial Egg from which the whole universe issued forth and which was the first sacred forge.

The elements of the smithy are linked to a sexual symbolism, itself the expression or reflection of a cosmic process of creation.

Thus the two round bellows worked by the smith's assistant are likened to the male's two testicles. The air they are filled with is the substance of life, sent through a kind of tube that represents the phallus into the furnace of the forge, this representing the womb where the transforming fire works.

The traditional smith may enter the smithy only after a ritual purifying bath prepared with a decoction of certain leaves or barks or roots of trees chosen according to the day. For plants (like minerals and animals) are divided into seven classes corresponding to the days of the week and linked by the law of analogic correspondence.[10] Then the smith garbs himself in a special way, since he may not penetrate the forge dressed in just any sort of clothes.

Every morning he purifies the smithy by means of special fumigations based on plants he knows of.

These operations over, cleansed of all outside contacts he has had, the smith is in a sacramental state. He has become pure once again and is equivalent to the primordial smith. Only now can he create in imitation of Maa Ngala, by modifying and fashioning matter. (In Fulfulde the name of the smith is *baylo*, a word which literally means 'transformer'.)

Before beginning work he invokes the four mother elements of creation (earth, water, air, fire), which are necessarily represented in the forge: there is always a receptacle filled with *water*, *fire* in the furnace, *air* sent by the bellows, and a little pile of *earth* beside the forge.

During his work, he pronounces special words as he touches each tool. Taking his anvil, which symbolizes feminine receptivity he says: 'I am not Maa Ngala, I am the representative of Maa Ngala. It is he who creates and

10. On the law of analogic correspondence see A. Hampaté Bâ, 1972, pp. 120ff.

not I.' Then he takes some water or an egg and presents it to the anvil, saying: 'Here is your bride-price.' He takes his hammer, which symbolizes the phallus, and strikes the anvil a few times to sensitize it. Communication established, he can begin to work.

The apprentice must not ask questions. He must only look and blow. This is the mute phase of apprenticeship. As he advances in knowledge, he blows in rhythms that are more and more complex, each one having a meaning. During the oral stage of apprenticeship, the master will gradually transmit all his skills to the pupil, training him and correcting him until he acquires mastery. Then, after a liberation ceremony, the new smith may leave his master and set up his own forge. A smith usually sends his own children to another smith to serve their apprenticeship. The adage goes: 'The master's wives and children are not his best pupils.'

Thus the traditional artisan, imitating Maa Ngala, repeating the primal creation by his gestures, used to perform, not work, in the purely economic sense of the word, but a sacred function that brought the fundamental forces of life into play and engaged him in his entire being. In the secrecy of his workshop or his smithy he partook of the renewed mystery of eternal creation.

The smith must have knowledge covering a vast sector of life. With his repute as an occultist, his mastery of the secrets of fire and iron make him the only person entitled to perform circumcision; and, as we have seen, the grand Master of the Knife in the Komo initiation is always a smith. Not only is he learned in all that pertains to metals; he is expert also in the classification of plants and their properties.

The operator of a high furnace, who both smelts and casts the metal, is the man who is furthest advanced in knowledge. In addition to all his knowledge of metallurgy, he has a perfect knowledge of the Sons of the womb of the Earth (mineralogy) and the secrets of plants and the bush. Indeed, he knows what kind of vegetation covers the earth, where it contains a particular metal, and he can detect a lode of gold merely by examining plants and pebbles.

He knows the incantations to the earth and the incantations to plants. Nature being regarded as living and as animated by forces, any act that disturbs it must be accompanied by a ritual behaviour designed to save and safeguard its sacred equilibrium, for everything is connected, everything echoes everything else, every action agitates the life-forces and sets up a chain of consequences the repercussions of which are felt by man.

The relationship of traditional man with the world was therefore a living relationship of *participation,* not of pure utilization. It is understandable that in this *all-inclusive vision of the universe,* the role of the profane is negligible.

For example, in the old Baule country, gold, in which the earth was rich, was viewed as a divine metal and was not exploited to excess. It was used above all for the making of royal or religious objects, and also served as a means of exchange and for the making of gifts. Anyone could extract it but no one could keep nuggets of over a certain size for himself; any nugget over the standard weight was given back to the god and went to swell the royal gold, a sacred store which the kings themselves had no right to draw from. In this way certain royal treasures were handed down intact until the European occupation. Since the earth was supposed to belong to God, a man could not own land; he only had rights of usufruct.

To return to the traditional craftsman: he is the perfect example of how knowledge can be embodied not only in one's gestures and actions but in one's entire life. He has to respect a set of prohibitions and obligations associated with his function which constitutes a regular code of behaviour towards nature and his fellow-men.

Thus there is what is called the way of the smiths (*numusira* or *numuya,* in Bambara), the way of the farmers, the way of the weavers, and so on; and, on the ethnic plane, the way of the Fulani (*lawol Fulfulde*). These are true moral, social and legal codes peculiar to each group, faithfully handed down and observed by means of oral tradition.

The craft or the traditional function can be said to sculpt man's being. The whole difference between modern education and oral tradition lies there. What is learned at the western school, useful as it may be, is not always *lived*; whereas the inherited knowledge of oral tradition is embodied in the entire being. The instruments or tools of a craft give material form to the sacred words; the apprentice's contact with the craft obliges him to live the word with every gesture he makes.

That is why oral tradition taken as a whole cannot be summed up as transmission of stories or of certain kinds of knowledge. It *generates and forms a particular type of man.* One can say that there is the smiths' civilization, the weavers' civilization, the shepherds', and so on.

Here I have examined in depth only the examples of the smiths and the weavers, who are especially typical examples; but in a general way every traditional activity constitutes a great initiatory or magico-religious school, a way of access towards the Unity of which, for initiates, it is a reflection or a peculiar expression.

Usually, in order that secret skills and the magic powers deriving from them be kept within a certain lineage, each group had to observe strict sexual prohibitions against outsiders and practise endogamy. Endogamy, then, is due not to an idea of untouchability but to the desire to keep ritual secrets inside the group. Once we know this, we can see how these narrowly specialized groups relating to sacred functions gradually led to the notion of caste as it exists today in the African savannah. 'War and the nobleman make the captive', says the adage, 'but it is God who made the craftsman (the *nyamakala*)'.

The notion of higher or lower castes, therefore, is not based on a traditional sociological reality. It made its appearance in the course of time, in certain places only, probably in consequence of the appearance of particular empires in which the warrior function reserved to noblemen conferred a kind of supremacy on them. And in the distant past the notion of nobility was probably different: spiritual power took precedence over temporal. In those days it was the *silatiqui* (Fulani Master Initiates) and not the *ardos* (headmen, kings) who governed Fulani communities.

Contrary to what some have written or supposed, the smith is much more feared than scorned in Africa. First Son of Earth, Master of Fire, manipulator of mysterious forces, he is dreaded above all for his power.

At any rate, tradition made it obligatory on the nobles to provide for the maintenance of the caste or *nyamakala* classes (*nyamakala* in Bambara; the Fulfulde word is *nyeeno*, pl. *nyeebe*). These classes enjoy the prerogative of being able to obtain goods (or money) not by asking to be paid for work but by claiming a privilege which the noble cannot refuse.

In Mande tradition, which centres in Mali but covers more or less the whole territory of the old Bafour (that is, former French West Africa with the exception of the forest zones and the eastern part of Niger), the persons belonging to a caste, or *nyamakala*, include:

(1) The smith (*numu* in Bambara, *baylo* in Fulfulde).
(2) The weaver (*maabo*, in both Fulfulde and Bambara).
(3) The woodworker (both woodcutter and joiner; *saki* in Bambara, *labbo* in Fulfulde).
(4) The leather-worker (*garanke* in Bambara, *sakke* in Fulfulde).
(5) The public entertainer (*dieli* in Bambara; in Fulfulde he is designated by the general name for a *nyamakala* or member of a caste, that is, *nyeeno*). He is better known, perhaps, by the French name for him, 'griot'.

Although strictly speaking there is no notion of superiority, the four craftsmen classes of *nyamakala* have precedence over the *dieli* class, because they each involve initiation and a special skill and field of knowledge. The smith ranks highest, followed by the weaver, their crafts being the most initiatory. Members of these two classes may intermarry, since the women in both are traditional potters and therefore share the same women's initiation.

In the Mande classification the craftsmen-*nyamakalas* always go by threes:

There are three kinds of smith (*numu* in Bambara, *baylo* in Fulfulde):

(a) The mining smith (or smelting smith) who extracts mineral ores and smelts metal. The great initiates among these smiths can also work at the forge.
(b) The blacksmith, who works at the forge but does not extract ore.
(c) The worker in precious metals or jeweller, who is usually attached to a chief or a noble and so may be found in the outer courtyard of his palace.

There are three kinds of weaver (*maabo*):

(a) The wool weaver, the most highly initiated. The designs on blankets are always symbolic and are associated with the mysteries of numbers and of cosmogony. Every design has a name.
(b) The *kerka* weaver, who weaves huge blankets, mosquito nets and cotton hangings that may be six metres long, with an endless variety of motifs. I have seen some with 165. (Each motif has a name and a meaning. The name itself is a symbol that stands for many things.)
(c) The common weaver, who makes simple lengths of white cloth and is not involved in a high degree of initiation.

It sometimes happens that ordinary weaving is done by noblemen. For instance, certain Bambara work lengths of white cloth without being of the weaver caste. But they are not initiates and may not weave *kerka*, wool or mosquito nets.

There are three kinds of woodworker (*saki* in Bambara, *labbo* in Fulfulde):

(a) The maker of mortars, pestles and sacred statuettes. The mortar, in which sacred medicines are pounded, is a ritual object made only from particular kinds of wood.
    As in the smithy, the two fundamental forces are symbolized here: the mortar, like the anvil, represents the feminine pole and the pestle, like the hammer, the masculine.
    Sacred statuettes are made at the command of a *doma*-initiate who will charge them with sacred energy for some particular use. Besides the charging ritual, the choosing of the wood and the cutting, too, must be carried out under special conditions known only to the woodcutter.
    The craftsman in wood cuts the wood he needs himself. Therefore he is also a woodcutter, and his initiation is linked with knowledge of the secrets of plants and the bush. Since the tree is regarded as alive and as inhabited by other living spirits, it may not be felled or cut up without particular ritual precautions known to the woodcutter.
(b) The maker of wooden household utensils or furniture.
(c) The maker of dug-out canoes.
    The canoe-maker must further be initiated into the secrets of water.
    In Mali, the Somono, who have become fishermen without belonging to the Bozo people, have also begun to manufacture dug-outs. They are the men one sees working on the banks of the Niger between Koulikoro and Mopti.

There are three kinds of leather-worker (*garanke* in Bambara, *sakke* in Fulfulde):

(a) The one who makes shoes.
(b) The one who makes straps, reins, bridles, etc.
(c) The one who makes saddles, horse collars, etc.

Leather-work, too, involves initiation; and the *garanke* often has the reputation of being a witch.

Hunters, fishers and farmers correspond not to castes but rather to ethnic groups. Their activities are among the most ancient in human society. Gathering (of plants) and hunting (whether on land or water) represent yet other great schools of initiation; for the sacred forces of Mother Earth and the powers of the bush, where animals live, are not to be approached in a random way. Like the smelting smith, the hunter usually knows all the bush incantations and must be thoroughly versed in the science of the animal world.

Healers (healing either through plants or through the gift of speech) may belong to any class or ethnic group. They are often *domas*.

Often a people will have a heritage of particular gifts handed down from generation to generation through initiation. Thus the Dogon of Mali are reputed to know the secret of leprosy, which they can cure very quickly without a trace being left, and the secret of the cure for tuberculosis. They are furthermore excellent bonesetters who can reset broken bones even in cases of serious fracture.

Public entertainers (*dieli* in Bambara)

If the occult and esoteric sciences are the prerogatives of the master of the knife and the chanter of the gods, on the other hand the music, lyric poetry, and tales which enliven popular recreation, and often history as well, are the province of the *dieli*, a sort of troubadour or minstrel who may wander about the country or may be attached to a family.

It has often been wrongly supposed that the *dieli* were the only possible traditionalists. Who are they?

They can be divided into these categories:

(1) The *musicians*, who play every instrument (monochord, guitar, cora, hand-drum, and so on). Often wonderful singers, they are preservers and transmitters of ancient music, and composers too.
(2) The *ambassadors* and courtiers responsible for mediating between great families when differences exist. They are always attached to a royal or noble family, sometimes to one particular person.
(3) The *genealogists*, historians or poets (or men who are all three in one), who are usually also storytellers and great travellers, and not necessarily attached to a family.

Tradition confers a special social status on the *dieli*. Unlike the *horon* (nobles), they have the right to be shameless, and they enjoy a very great freedom of speech. They may act uninhibitedly, even impudently, and they sometimes joke about the gravest, holiest things without its mattering. They are under no compulsion either to be discreet or to hold the truth in absolute respect. They can sometimes tell brazen lies without being held to account. 'That's what the *dieli* says! So it isn't the true truth, but we take it as it is.' This maxim shows well enough how, without being gulled by them, tradition accepts the fabrications of the *dieli* – who, the maxim adds, has 'a crooked mouth'.

In all Bafour tradition, the noble or the chief is not only prohibited from performing music in public gatherings but is bound to be moderate in expression and speech. 'Too much talk ill beseems the mouth of a *horon*', says the proverb. And so the *dieli* attached to families quite naturally come to play a role as go-betweens, or even ambassadors, when great or small problems spring up. They are their master's tongue.

When attached to a family or a person, they are usually charged with the negotiations called for by any customary occasion, especially marriage negotiations. For example, a young nobleman will not address a woman directly to tell her of his love. He will make his *dieli* his spokesman, and the *dieli* will get in touch with the girl, or the girl's female *dieli*, so he can speak of his master's feelings and praise his merits.

Since African society is fundamentally based on dialogue between individuals and discussion between communities or ethnic groups, the *dieli* are the natural active agents in these exchanges. Authorized to have 'two tongues in their mouth', they can if need be unsay what they have already said without being held to strict account. This would be impossible for a noble, who is not allowed suddenly to go back on his word or change his decision. A *dieli* will even shoulder responsibility for a fault he has not committed in order to remedy a situation or save face for the nobles.

It is the old wise men of the community at their secret conclaves who have the grave duty of 'looking at things through the right spectacles': but it is up to the *dieli* to make what the wise men have decided and ordained actually *work*.

Trained to gather and give out information, they are the great carriers of news – but frequently scandal-mongers also.

Their Bambara name, *dieli,* means blood. And indeed like blood they circulate in the body of society, which is cured or falls ill accordingly as they temper or exacerbate conflicts with their words and songs.

I should say at once, though, that all this is a matter of general characteristics only and that the *dieli* are not all necessarily impudent or shameless. Far from it. Among them there are men who are called *dieli-faama* – *dieli*-kings. These are in no way second to noblemen when it comes to courage, morality, virtues and wisdom; and they never abuse the rights they have been granted by custom.

The *dieli* used to be a great active agent of human commerce and culture.

Often highly intelligent men, they played a very important part in the traditional society of the Bafour because of their influence over nobles and chiefs. Even now, at every opportunity, they stimulate and excite the nobleman's clan pride with their songs, often for the sake of presents but often, too, to encourage him in some difficult situation.

For example, during the night of vigil before the circumcision rite they encourage the child or youth to show himself worthy of his forebears by remaining impassive. 'Your father,[11] so-and-so, who was killed on the field of battle, swallowed the gruel of flaming iron [bullets] without blinking. I hope that tomorrow you will not let yourself be afraid of the edge of the blacksmith's knife', they sing among the Fulani. At the stick or *Soro* ceremony among the Bororo Fulani of Niger, the songs of the *dieli* sustain the boy who has to prove his courage and patience by smiling, without a quiver of his eyelids, as he receives stinging lashes from the stick on his breast.

The *dieli* took part in all the battles in history at the side of their masters, whose courage they whipped up by recalling their high pedigree and the great deeds of their forefathers. For the African, the evocation of his family name has great power. Even today one greets him and gives him praise by repeating the name of his lineage.

The influence of the *dieli* on the course of history was good or bad depending on whether their words spurred the leaders to vainglorious excesses or, as was often the case, recalled them to a sense of their traditional duties.

It is clear that the *dieli* are an inseparable part of the history of the great African empires of the Bafour, and their role deserves a thoroughgoing special study.

The secret of their power and influence over the *horon* (nobles) resides in their knowledge of genealogy and family history. Some of them have been real specialists in this. Such *dieli* seldom belong to a household, but travel the country in quest of more and more extensive historical information. They can therefore be sure of having an almost magical ability to touch off the enthusiasm of a noble when they come and declaim his genealogy, heraldic devices and history – and, as a matter of course, receive liberal presents from him. A nobleman is capable of stripping himself and his house and handing over everything he possesses to a *dieli* who has managed to stir his feelings. Wherever they go, then, these genealogist *dieli* are sure to make a good living.

But it must not be thought that this is a matter of pay. The idea of remuneration for work done is contrary to the traditional notion of the right of the *nyamakala* over the noble classes.[12] Whatever their fortune,

11. 'Your father', in African languages, can quite as well be an uncle or a grandfather or a forefather. It means the whole paternal line, collaterals included.

12. 'Noble' is a very rough translation of *horon*. In actual fact any person is a *horon* who does not belong either to the *Nyamakala* class or the *jon* (captive) class, the latter having evolved from prisoners taken in time of war. The duty of the *horon* is to ensure the defence of the community and give his life for it, and to ensure the maintenance of the other classes.

noblemen are traditionally obliged to make presents to the *dieli* or to any *nyamakala* or *woloso*[13] – even the poorest noble, and even if the asker is infinitely richer than the giver. Generally speaking it is the *dieli* caste that does the most soliciting. But whatever his gains, a *dieli* is always poor, for he is a lavish spender, counting on the nobles for his sustenance. 'Oh!', sing the questing *dieli*, 'A nobleman's hand is not stuck to his neck with avarice; it is always ready to dig into his pocket to give to him who asks.' And if by any chance the present is not forthcoming, the noble had better beware of trouble from the 'man with a crooked mouth' whose 'two tongues' can ruin many a project, many a reputation!

From the economic point of view, therefore, the caste of *dieli*, like all the *nyamakala* and *woloso* classes, is a great burden on society, and especially on the noble classes. The gradual change in economic conditions and *mores* has somewhat altered this state of affairs, with former nobles or former *dieli* accepting remunerative functions; but the custom continues notwithstanding, and people still ruin themselves on the occasion of baptisms or marriages by giving presents to the *dieli* who come to enliven the feasts with their songs. Some modern governments have tried to put an end to the custom but, to my knowledge, have not yet succeeded.

The *dieli*, being *nyamakala*, must in principle marry within the *nyamakala* classes.

It is easy to see how the genealogist *dieli*, specializing in family history and often endowed with prodigious memories, have quite naturally become as it were the archivists of African society and, occasionally, great historians. But let us keep in mind that they are not the only persons with such knowledge. The historian *dieli* can, it is true, be called traditionalists; but with this reservation, that theirs is a purely historical branch of tradition and that tradition has many branches.

The fact of being born a *dieli* does not necessarily make a man a historian, though it gives him a certain inclination in that direction. Nor does it make him learned in traditional matters, one who has knowledge – far from it. Generally speaking the *dieli* caste is the one farthest removed from the realms of initiates – these requiring silence, discretion and control of one's speech.

The opportunity of becoming masters of knowledge is not closed to them, however, any more than to anyone else. Just as a *doma*-traditionalist (the traditional master of knowledge in the true sense of the term) can be at the same time a great genealogist and historian, so a *dieli*, like any member of any social category, can become a traditionalist-*doma* if his aptitudes permit and if he has gone through the corresponding initiations (with the exception, though, of the Komo initiation, which is forbidden him).

Earlier in this chapter I mentioned the example of the two *dieli* masters of knowledge now living in Mali: Iwa and Banzoumana, the latter being at once a great musician, a historian and a *doma*-traditionalist.

13. For *woloso*, house-captive, see above, p. 176, n. 5.

The *dieli* who is also a *doma*-traditionalist constitutes an absolutely reliable source of information, for his being an initiate gives him a high moral value and makes him subject to the prohibition against lying. He becomes another man. He is the *dieli*-king I spoke of earlier, whom people consult for his wisdom and his knowledge and who, albeit able to entertain, never abuses his customary rights.

When a *dieli* tells a story he is usually asked, 'Is it a *dieli* story or a *doma* story?' If it is a *dieli* story, people say, 'It's what the *dieli* say!' and they expect a few embellishments of the truth intended to play up the role of such and such a family – embellishments which would not be added by a *doma*-traditionalist who cares above all for truthful transmission.

We have to distinguish: when we are in the presence of a historian *dieli* we have to ascertain whether he is an ordinary *dieli* or a *doma-dieli*. And yet it has to be admitted that the factual basis is hardly ever changed; it serves as a springboard for poetical or panegyrical displays which, if they do not falsify, at least decorate it.

A misunderstanding which still has its sequel in some French dictionaries ought to be cleared up. The French took the *dieli,* whom they called a griot, to be a witch (*sorcier*), which was not the case.[14] It can happen that a *dieli* is a *korte-tiqui*, caster of a bad lot, just as it can happen that a *dieli* is a *doma*, traditional knower – and that not because he was born a *dieli* but because he has been initiated and gained his proficiency, good or bad, at the school of some master of his art.

The misunderstanding probably arises from the ambivalence of the word 'griot', which the French sometimes use for all *nyamakala* (who include the *dieli* among others) and, more often, for the *dieli* caste only.

Tradition has it that the *nyamakala* are all *subaa*, *subaa* meaning a man versed in hidden knowledge known only to initiates, a sort of occultist. Tradition excludes from this designation the *dieli*, who do not lead the life of proper initiates. Therefore it is the craftsmen-*nyamakala* who are *subaa*. Among these the *garanke*, the leather-worker, does have the reputation of being a *subaa*: a witch, in the bad sense.

I am inclined to think that the first European interpreters confused the two terms *subaa* and *subaga* (which are close in pronunciation) and that the ambivalence of the term 'griot' did the rest.

Since tradition declares that 'All *nyamakala* are *subaa* [occultists]', these

14. Translator's note: 'Griot' is given in the standard French dictionary, Robert (1969), as a word of unknown origin meaning 'a West African Negro belonging to a special caste. The griots, often chosen by princes to be their advisers, are at once poets, musicians, singers and witches.' English-language works on the people of former French West Africa occasionally use griot, but it remains a rare and foreign word. (It is in neither the *OED* nor Webster.) Griot is a familiar word in France, and Mr. A. Hampaté Bâ, who wrote this chapter in French, uses it throughout. But since, as he explains, it is misleading, and since it is quite as strange to the general English reader as the African word *dieli*, the latter is used to this English version.

interpreters must have understood 'All *nyamakala* are *subaga* [witches]', which – because of the double usage, collective or particular, of the word griot – became 'All griots are witches.' Hence the misunderstanding.

Be that as it may, the *dieli*'s importance lies not in any powers of sorcery he may have but in his part in managing speech – which, if one comes down to it, is another form of magic.

Before leaving the *dieli*, let us note some exceptions that may cause confusion. Certain weavers can be found who have abandoned their traditional craft and became guitar players. The Fulani call such a man *bammbaado*, literally one who is carried on the back, because his expenses are always borne by another man or by the community. These *bammbaado*, who are always story-tellers, can also be poets, genealogists and historians.

Certain woodcutters, too, may exchange their tools for a guitar and become very good musicians and genealogists. Bokar Ilo and Idriss Ngada, who were among the great genealogists I know of in the Upper Volta, were woodcutters turned musicians. But these are exceptions.

Again, certain *déclassé* nobles may become popular entertainers – not musicians, though[15] – and they are called *tiapourta* (in Bambara and Fulfulde alike). They are then more impudent, more shameless, than the most impudent of *dieli*, and nobody takes their remarks seriously. They will ask the *dieli* for presents, to the point where the latter make their escape when they see a *tiapourta* coming.

While generally speaking music is the *dieli*'s great speciality, there is also a ritual music played by initiates and accompanying ritual ceremonies or dances. The instruments of this sacred music are then true cult objects which make it possible to communicate with invisible forces. Accordingly as they are string, wind or percussion instruments they are in rapport with the elements of earth, air and water.

Making music for incantations to the spirits of fire is the prerogative of the association of fire-eaters, who are called *kursi-kolonin* or *donnga-soro*.

How one becomes a traditionalist

In the Africa of the Bafour, as I have already suggested, anyone could become a *doma*-traditionalist, that is, a master of knowledge in one or more traditional subjects. Knowledge was open to everyone (initiation being omnipresent in one form or another) and acquisition of it depended simply on individual aptitude.

Knowledge was so highly esteemed that it had precedence over everything else and conferred nobility. The master of knowledge in any field could sit in the council of elders which governed the community, regardless of his social category – *horon* (noble), *nyamakala* or *woloso*. 'Knowledge

15. We must remember that Fulani or Bambara *horon* (nobles) never play music, at least in public. The *tiapourta* have in general kept up this custom.

knows neither race nor the paternal doorway [the clan]. It ennobles its man', says the proverb.

African education was not systematic like European schooling. It was dispensed throughout life. Life itself was education. In the Bafour, until he was 42, a man was supposed to be at the school of life and had no right to speech in meetings, save exceptionally. He was supposed to be still listening and deepening the knowledge he had been receiving since his initiation at the age of 21. At 42, he was deemed to have assimilated and deepened the instruction received from youth on. He acquired the right to speak in assemblies and became a teacher in his turn, to give society back what he had received of it. But that did not prevent his continuing to learn from his elders, if he so wished, and soliciting their advice. An old man can always find an older or wiser man than himself, to ask for additional information or for an opinion. 'Every day', they say, 'the ear hears what it has never yet heard.' Thus education could last a whole lifetime.

After learning his craft and following the relevant initiation, the young craftsman-*nyamakala,* ready to fly with his own wings, would usually go from village to village, to increase his sum of knowledge by learning from new masters. 'He who has not travelled has nothing seen', people say. So he would go from workshop to workshop, covering as much of the country as he could. Men from the hills would come down to the plain, those of the plain went up into the mountains, those of the Beledugu came to the Mande, and so on.

On his travels the young smith would always wear his bellows slung across his back in order to be recognized; the woodcutter would have his axe or his adze; the weaver carried his loom on his back, dismantled, but held his shuttle or his spool shouldered high. The leather-worker held his little pots of dye. When the young man arrived at a big village where craftsmen lived in separate groups, by guilds, people would automatically lead him towards the leather-workers' quarter, or the weavers' etc.

How much he learned in the course of his travels and investigations depended on his dexterity, his memory, and above all his character. If he was polite and attractive and obliging, old men would give him secrets they would not hand over to others, for it is said: 'The old man's secret is bought not with money but with good manners.'

As for the young *horon,* he would spend his childhood in his father's court and in the village, where he would attend all the meetings, hear everybody's stories and retain as much as he could. In the evening sessions of his age-set each child would retell the stories he had heard, whether historical or initiatory (but in the latter case without grasping the full implications). From 7 on he was automatically part of his village initiation society and began to receive its instruction, which, as I have said, concerned all aspects of life.

When an old man tells an initiatory tale in an assembly, he develops its symbolism so as to suit the nature and understanding of his audience. He can make it a simple tale of wonders with a moral, for children, or he can make it a profound lesson in the mysteries of human nature and man's relation with invisible worlds. Each person retains and understands according to his aptitudes.

It is the same with the historical tales which give life and spirit to meetings, tales in which the great deeds of the men of old, the country's heroes, are evoked in the most minute detail. A stranger passing through will tell stories of distant lands. And so the child is immersed in a particular cultural ambiance which he absorbs as well as his memory permits. His days are marked by history, stories, fables, proverbs and maxims.

As a rule the young *horon* does not go abroad, since he is destined for the defence of his country. He works with his father, who may be a farmer or a garment-maker or be in any other activity reserved for the *horon* class. If he is a Fulani, he moves about with his parents' camp, soon learns to tend the herd all alone out in the bush, night and day, and receives the Fulani initiation associated with the symbolism of cattle.

Generally speaking, one does not become a *doma*-traditionalist by staying in one's village.

A healer who wants to deepen his knowledge has to travel so as to learn about the different kinds of plants and study with other masters of the subject.

The man who travels discovers and lives other initiations, notes the differences or similarities, broadens the scope of his understanding. Wherever he goes he takes part in meetings, hears historical tales, and lingers where he finds a transmitter of tradition who is skilled in initiation or in genealogy; in this way he comes into contact with the history and traditions of the countries he passes through.

One can see that the man who has become a *doma*-traditionalist has been a seeker and a questioner all his life and will never cease to be one.

The African of the savannah used to travel a great deal. The result was exchange and circulation of knowledge. That is why the collective historical memory in Africa is seldon limited to one territory. Rather it is linked with family lines or ethnic groups that have migrated across the continent.

Many caravans used to plough their way across the country using a network of special routes traditionally protected by gods and kings, routes where one was safe from pillage or attack. To do otherwise would have meant exposing oneself either to a raid or to the risk of violating, unawares, some local taboo and paying the consequences dearly. Upon arrival in a strange country travellers would go and 'entrust their heads' to some man of standing who would thereby become their guarantor, for 'to touch the stranger is to touch the host himself'.

The great genealogist is necessarily always a great traveller. While a *dieli* may rest content with knowing the genealogy of the particular family he is attached to, for a true genealogist – *dieli* or no – to increase in knowledge he has to travel about the country to learn the main ramifications of an ethnic group and then go abroad to trace the history of the branches that have emigrated.

Thus Molom Gaolo, the greatest genealogist I have been privileged to know, possessed the genealogy of all the Fulani of Senegal. When his great age no longer allowed him to go abroad he sent his son Mamadou Molom to carry on his survey of the Fulani families that had migrated through the Sudan (Mali) with al-Hajj ‘Umar. At the time when I knew Molom Gaolo, he had succeeded in compiling and retaining the past history of about forty generations.

He had the habit of going to every baptism and every funeral in the leading families so as to record the circumstances of deaths and births, which he would add to the list already filed in his astonishing memory. So he was able to declaim to any important Fulani: ‘You are the son of So-and-so, born So-and-so, the descendant of So-and-so, offspring of So-and-so ... Each of them died at such and such a place of such a cause and was buried in such and such a spot’, and so on. Or else: ‘So-and-so was baptized on a certain day at a certain hour by the Marabout So-and-so ...’ Of course all this information was and still is orally transmitted and recorded by the genealogist's memory alone. People have no idea of what the memory of an ‘illiterate’ can store up. A story once heard is graven as if on a die and can then be reproduced intact, from the first word to the last, whenever the memory calls on it.

Molom Gaolo died at the age of 105, around 1968 I believe. His son Mamadou Gaolo, now 50, lives in Mali, where he is carrying on his father's work by the same purely oral means, being himself illiterate.

Wahab Gaolo, a contemporary of Mamadou Gaolo, also still alive, has carried out a survey of Fulfulde-speaking groups (Fulani and Tukulor peoples) in Chad, Cameroon, the Central African Republic, and even in Zaïre, in order to learn the genealogy and history of families that emigrated to those countries.

The Gaolos are not *dieli* but a Fulani-speaking group equivalent to the *nyamakala* class and enjoying the same prerogatives. Talkers and declaimers rather than musicians (except for their women, who sing to their own accompaniment on rudimentary instruments), they can be story-tellers and entertainers, and there are many genealogists among them.

Among the Marka (Mande group) genealogists are called ‘Guessere’ from the name their group has among the Marka.

Genealogist means historian; for a good genealogist knows the history and exploits of every person mentioned, or at least the most outstanding ones. This science is at the very base of history in Africa: for if people are so much interested in history it is not on account of dates but on account of genealogy – so as to be able to trace a given family, clan or group as it spreads out through time and space.

So everyone is a bit of a genealogist in Africa, and capable of going fairly far back in his own family tree. If not, it would be as if he had no identity card. In old-time Mali there was no one who did not know at least ten or twelve generations of his forebears. Among all the old Tukulor who came to Macina with al-Hajj 'Umar there was not one who did not know his genealogy in the Senegalese Fouta (their country of origin) and his relationship to the families that were still there. These were the people whom Mamadou Molom, son of Molom Gaolo, came to Mali to consult to continue his father's inquiry.

Genealogy is therefore at once a sense of identity, a means of exalting family glory and a resort in case of litigation. For example, a dispute over a piece of land could be settled by a genealogist – who would state exactly what ancestor had cleared and cultivated the land, to whom he had given it, under what conditions, and so on.

Even now, one finds any number of people who belong neither to the *dieli* nor the Gaolo class but are well up in genealogy and history. In them, we have an important source of information on the history of Africa, at least for a while to come. Each patriarch is a genealogist for his own clan, and the *dieli* and Gaolos will often come to him for information to supplement what they already know. Generally speaking, every old man in Africa is a master of knowledge in some historical or traditional field.

Dieli and Gaolos, then, have no monopoly over genealogical knowledge; but it is only they who specialize in declaiming genealogies in front of nobles for the sake of obtaining gifts.

Influence of Islam

The peculiarities of the African memory and the modalities of its oral transmission have not been affected by the widespread islamization of the savannah countries, the old Bafour. In fact, as Islam spread, it nowhere adapted African tradition to its own thought but rather adapted itself to African tradition whenever – as was often the case – this did not violate its fundamental principles. The symbiosis that came about was so great that it is occasionally hard to make out what belongs to the one tradition and what to the other.

The great Arab-Berber family of the Kunta islamized the region well before the eleventh century. As soon as they learned Arabic, the autochthones began to use their ancestral traditions for transmitting and explaining Islam.

Great Islamic schools that were purely oral taught the religion in the vernacular tongues (except for the Koran and the texts that form part of canonical prayer). I might mention, among many others, the oral school of Djelgodji (called Kabe), the school of Barani, Amadou Fodia's school in Farimake (Niafounke district, in Mali), Mohamed Abdoulaye Souadou's school at Dilli (Nara district, Mali), and Shaykh Usman dan Fodio's school in Nigeria and Niger, where all teaching was in Fulfulde. Closer to us there was Tierno Bokar Salif's *Zawiya* in Bandiagara and the school of Shaykh Salah, the great Dogon marabout, who is still alive.

To give an idea of what the African memory is capable of: most children leaving the Koranic schools knew the entire Koran by heart and could recite it all, in Arabic and in the desired psalmody, without understanding what it meant!

In all these schools the basic principles of African tradition were not repudiated but on the contrary used and explained in the light of Koranic revelation. Tierno Bokar, who was a traditionalist both in African matters and in Islam, became famous for his intensive application of this educational method.

Quite apart from their having a common vision of the universe as sacred, and the same conception of man and the family, we find in both traditions the same concern for always citing one's sources (*isnad*, in Arabic) and never changing anything in the master's words, the same respect for the chain of initiatory transmission (*silsila* or chain, in Arabic), and the same system of initiatory ways of life that make it possible to deepen through experience what is known through faith (in Islam, the great Sufi congregation or *tariqa*, plural *turuq*, the 'chain' of which goes back to the Prophet himself).

To the existing categories of traditional masters of knowledge were now added those of the marabouts (widely read in Arabic or in Islamic jurisprudence) and the great Sufi Shaykhs, although the structures of society (castes and traditional crafts) were preserved even in the most islamized environments and continued to convey their particular initiations. Knowledge of Islamic subjects constituted a new source of ennoblement. Thus Alfa Ali (d. 1958), a Gaolo by birth, was the greatest authority on Islamic subjects in the Bandiagara district, like his whole family before him and his son after him.[16]

How a body of oral material was collected

To give a practical illustration of how historical or other stories live and are preserved with strict fidelity in the collective memory of an oral tradition society, I shall tell how I managed to assemble, solely on the basis of oral tradition, elements that enabled me to write the *History of the Fulani Empire of Macina in the Eighteenth century*.[17]

As I belonged to the family of Tidjani, ruler of the province, from childhood on I had ideal conditions for hearing and retaining. My father Tidjani's house at Bandiagara was always full of people. Night and day there were great gatherings at which everyone would talk about a great variety of traditional matters.

My father's family having been closely involved in the events of their day,

16. Generally speaking Islam, coming from the north and the east, affected more particularly the savannah countries, whereas Christianity, coming by sea, touched the coastal forest regions more. I cannot speak of the encounter between tradition and Christianity, having no information on the subject.

17. A. Hampaté Bâ and J. Daget, 1962.

the stories were often about history; and each person would relate a well-known episode of some battle or other noteworthy occurrence. I was always present at these gatherings; I lost not one word: and my memory, like virgin wax, recorded everything.

It was there that, from early childhood, I knew Koullel, the great Fulfulde-speaking story-teller, genealogist and historian. I followed him about everywhere and learned many tales and stories which I would proudly tell over again to the boys in my age-set – to the point where they nicknamed me Amkoullel, which means 'little Koullel'.

As the result of circumstances beyond my control I went with my family to many countries, where I was always able to be in touch with great traditionalists. Thus when my father was obliged to live in Bougouni, where Koullel had followed us, I made the acquaintance of the great Bambara *doma* Danfo Sine, and later of his younger brother Latif.

Later on, at Bamako and at Kati, my father Tidjani's court was practically reconstituted, and traditionalists from all countries flocked to it, realizing that there they would meet other masters of knowledge in whose company they could control or even increase their own knowledge, for one always finds someone more learned than oneself.

That was where I began to learn a good deal about the history of the Fulani Empire of Macina, both in the Macinanke version (that is, the version of people originating in Macina, partisans of the Sheikou Amadou family) and in the version of the Tukulor, their antagonists – and also in the version of other peoples (Bambara, Marka, Sarakole, Songhay, and so on) who had taken part in what happened, or been present.

Starting, then, from a well-prepared personal position, I set out to collect information systematically. My method consisted of recording stories first of all without caring about truthfulness or possible exaggeration. Next, I compared the Macinanke stories with those of the Tukulor or the other peoples involved. One can always do this, find groups in every region whose stories will provide a control for statements made by the principals.

It was a long task. Gathering information took me over fifteen years; it meant journeys that took me from the Fouta Djalon (Senegal) to Kano (Nigeria) so that I could retrace the routes both Sheikou Amadou and al-Hajj 'Umar had followed in all their travels.

In this way I recorded the stories of at least a thousand informants. In the end I kept only those statements that agreed, those that were congruous with both the Macinanke and Tukulor traditions and also with those of the other peoples concerned (the sources for which I cited in my book).

I found that on the whole my thousand informants had respected the truth of events. The thread of the story was everywhere the same. The differences, which affected only minor details, were due to the quality of the reciter's memory, or his particular spirit. Depending on what ethnic group he belonged to, he might tend to minimize certain defeats or try to find some excuse for them. But he did not change the basic data. Under the influence of the musical accompaniment, a story-teller might let himself be a trifle carried away by his enthusiasm, but the general outline remained the same: places, battles, victories and defeats, meetings and parleys, things said by the chief characters, and so forth.

That experience proved to me that oral tradition was perfectly valid from the scholarly point of view. Not only is it possible to compare the versions of different peoples, as I did, to exercise a control, but society itself exerts a permanent auto-control. No reciter could allow himself to change the facts, for there would always be comrades or elders in his entourage who would immediately pick up the error and call him a liar to his face – a gravely injurious accusation.

Professor Monteil once mentioned me as having reported in the *History of the Fulani Empire of Macina* stories which his father had collected fifty years earlier and not one word of which had varied. That gives some idea of the fidelity with which data are preserved in oral tradition.

Characteristics of the African memory

Among all the peoples of the world, it has been found that those persons who do not write have the most highly developed memory.

I have given the example of genealogists able to retain an unbelievable mass of data, but one could also adduce the example of certain illiterate businessmen (I still know many such), handling deals that may involve tens of millions of francs, lending to many persons as they travel about, and keeping in their head the most accurate account of all these movements of merchandise and money without the slightest written note and without making the slightest mistake.

The datum to be remembered is incribed on the traditionalist's memory at one stroke as on virgin wax, and there it remains, constantly available, in its entirety.[18]

One peculiarity of the African memory is its restoring the recorded event or story *in its entirety*, like a film that unreels from beginning to end, and restoring it *in the present*. It is a matter not of remembering, but of *bringing up into the present* a past event in which everyone participates – the person who is reciting and his audience.

The whole art of the storyteller lies in that. No one is a storyteller unless he can report a thing as it happened 'live' in such a way that his hearers, like himself, become new living, active witnesses of it. Now every African is

18. This phenomenon might be related to the fact that man's senses are most highly developed wherever he has to make intense use of them and are atrophied in modern life. For example, the traditional African hunter can hear and identify certain noises from several kilometres away. His sight is particularly keen. Certain persons can 'feel' water, like diviners without wands. The desert Tuareg has a sense of direction that is close to miraculous. And so on. Whereas modern man, submerged in noise and information, sees his faculties gradually atrophy. It is medically proven that city-dwellers hear less and less well.

to some extent a storyteller. When a stranger arrives in a village he bows and says: 'I am your stranger.' They reply: 'This house is open to you. Enter in peace.' Then they say: 'Give us news.' Then he relates his whole history from the time he left home: what he has seen and heard, what has happened to him, and so on, and that in such a way that his hearers are with him on his travels and relive them with him. That is why the tense of a story is always in the present.

In general African memory records the whole scene: the setting, the characters, their words, even their clothing to the smallest detail. In the Tukulor war stories we know what embroidered *bubu* the great hero Oumarel Dondo wore in a given battle, who his groom was and what became of him, what the name of his horse was and what became of *him,* and so on. All these details give colour to the story and help make the scene come alive.

That is why the traditionalist cannot summarize, or can only do so with great difficulty. If he is asked to summarize a scene, for him that is the same thing as making it disappear. Now by tradition he has no right to do that. Every detail has its importance for the truth of the picture. He tells the story in its entirety or not at all. He will answer such a request with: 'If you haven't time to listen to me, I'll tell the story some other day.'

In the same way, he is not afraid of repeating himself. No one gets tired of hearing the same story told over in the same words, as he has perhaps told it many times over already. Each time the whole film unreels again. The event is there, restored. The past becomes the present. Life is not to be summarized. At most, one can shorten a story for children if one has to, telescoping certain sequences; but then it will not be taken for true. When dealing with adults one relates a fact or one refuses to speak.

This peculiarity of the traditional African memory, bound up in a context of oral tradition, is in itself a guarantee of authenticity.

As for the memory of the traditionalists, especially the *doma*-traditionalists or masters who encompass vast fields of traditional knowledge, this is a veritable library in which the archives are not classified but are completely inventoried.

For a modern mind it is chaos; but for traditionalists if there is chaos it is in the manner of molecules of water that mingle in the sea to form one living whole. In that sea they move with the ease of a fish.

The intangible catalogue-cards of oral tradition are maxims, proverbs, tales, legends, myths, etc., which may be skeleton-outlines to be developed further or subject-entries for didactic stories, old or improvised. For example, stories, especially initiation stories, have a basic thread which never varies but to which the narrator may add flourishes, developments or teachings suited to the understanding of his listeners. It is the same with myths, which are digests of knowledge in synthetic form which the initiate may always elaborate or go into more deeply for his pupils.

We must pay attention to the contents of myths and not catalogue them too quickly. Realities of very various orders are often concealed in them;

sometimes they are even to be understood at several levels simultaneously.

While some myths refer to esoteric knowledge and veil what they teach even as they pass it on down through the centuries, others may bear some relation to actual events. Take the example of Thianaba, the mythical Fulani serpent. Legend traces its adventures and its migration through the African savannah from the Atlantic Ocean. Around 1921 the engineer Belime, who was in charge of building the Sansanding Dam, was curious enough to follow the trail of the geographical clues in this legend, which he had learned from Hammadi Djenngoudo, a great Fulani knower. The result was that to his surprise he discovered the path of the former bed of the river Niger.

Conclusion

For Africa the present era is one of complexity and commotion. In Africa different worlds, different mentalities, different periods are superimposed, interfering with one another, sometimes influencing one another, not always understanding. The twentieth century is cheek by jowl with the middle ages, the West with the East. Cartesianism, a particular way of 'thinking' the world, brushes against animism, a particular way of living it and experiencing it in the whole being.

The modern young leaders govern with mental patterns and systems of law or ideologies directly inherited from foreign models, peoples, and realities which depend on other laws and other mental patterns. For instance, in most of the territories of former French West Africa, the legal code worked out on the morrow of independence by our young jurists, fresh out of French universities, is purely and simply copied from the Napoleonic Code. The result is that the population hitherto governed by sacred inherited ancestral customs which had ensured social cohesion does not understand why it is being judged and condemned in the name of a custom that is not its own, that it does not know, and that does not square with the fundamental realities of the country.

The whole drama of what I shall call 'basic Africa' is that it is often being governed by an intellectual minority who no longer understand it, along principles that are incongruous with it.

For the new African intelligentsia, trained in western university disciplines, tradition very often has ceased to live. Tradition is a matter of old men's tales! However, it must be said that for some time now a great many cultivated young people have felt a growing and urgent need to turn back towards ancestral traditions and disengage the fundamental values in them, in order to find their own roots and the secret of their own innermost identity.

By contrast, in 'basic Africa', which is usually far from the big towns – those western islands – tradition has remained alive and, as I have indicated, a very great number of its representatives or repositories can still be found. But for how much longer?

The great problem of traditional Africa is in fact the *break in transmission*.

In the former French colonies, the first great break came with the war of 1914, most of the young men having enlisted to go and fight in France, whence many of them never returned. These young men left the country at the age when they ought to have been undergoing the great initiations and deepening their knowledge under the guidance of their elders.

The fact that it was compulsory for important men to send their sons to 'white schools', so as to cut them off from tradition, also fostered this process. The major preoccupation of the colonial power was, understandably, to clear away autochthonous traditions as far as possible and plant its own conceptions in their place. Schools, secular or religious, were the essential instruments of this undermining.

The modern education our young men have received since the end of the last war finished off the process and created a true phenomenon of acculturation.

Initiation, fleeing the large towns, took refuge in the bush, where, because of the attraction of the large towns, and because of new needs, the 'old men' found fewer and fewer 'docile ears' to which they could transmit their teaching. For, in the stock phrase, teaching can only be given 'by the sweet-smelling mouth to the well-cleaned ear' (that is, the keenly receptive ear).

For oral tradition and all that bears on it, therefore, we stand today in the presence of the last generation of great repositories. That is why the work of collecting must be intensified over the next ten or fifteen years, after which the last great living monuments of African culture will have vanished, and with them the irreplaceable treasures of a peculiar education – at once material, psychological and spiritual, based on a feeling for the unity of life – the sources of which are lost in the mists of time.

To succeed in this great work of collection, the researcher must arm himself with great patience and remember that he must have 'the heart of a dove, the skin of a crocodile, and the stomach of an ostrich'. 'The heart of a dove', so as never to become heated or angry even if disagreeable things are said to him. If people refuse to answer his question, it is pointless to insist: he may as well go sit on another branch. A dispute here will have repercussions elsewhere; whereas a discreet departure will make him regretted and often lead to his being summoned back. 'The skin of a crocodile', so as to be able to lie down anywhere at all, on anything at all, without a fuss. And 'the stomach of an ostrich', so as to be able to eat no matter what without being disgusted or falling ill.

But, most important condition of all, the researcher must be capable of renouncing the habit of judging everything according to his own criteria. To discover a new world one must be able to forget one's own; otherwise one merely carries that along with one and does not 'keep one's ears open'.

The Africa of the old initiates warns the young researcher, through the mouth of Tierno Bokar, the sage of Bandiagara:

> If you wish to know who I am,
> If you wish me to teach you what I know,
> Cease for the while to be what you are
> And forget what you know.

PLATE 8.1 *Valiha player. The instrument is wooden with steel strings* (Musée de l'Homme)

PLATE 8.2 *Mvet singer* (Documentation Française)

PLATE 8.3 *'Griot hutu' miming the fallen 'mwami'* (B. Nantet)

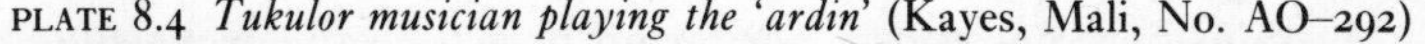

PLATE 8.4 *Tukulor musician playing the 'ardin'* (Kayes, Mali, No. AO–292)

African archaeology and its techniques including dating techniques

Z. ISKANDER

Introduction

When an archaeologist discovers an artefact he usually starts studying it by purely archaeological means such as recording the stratum in which it was found, reading the text found on it, describing its shape, finding its dimensions, etc. The data obtained will then be studied stratigraphically, philologically and typologically, and sometimes important archaeological information may be obtained as regards its date, origin, etc. In most cases, however, the archaeologist may not be able to find any data which answer his questions or help him draw any conclusion from the information available. In such cases he has to submit his find to other disciplines for scientific investigation. This investigation is supposed to give useful information about its material, origin, technique of manufacture, date, purpose for which it was used, etc. It might be stressed, however, that this investigation should only be considered as another criterion by which the archaeologist can tackle a particular problem; the scientific evidence should be taken together with such points as stylistic, philological and stratigraphic considerations.[1]

Other scientific techniques which may assist archaeology are field surveys of archaeological sites underground without digging and the conservation of the antiques and monuments discovered.

The scientific techniques used apply to all archaeology. They apply to African archaeology in the same way as to European, Asian or American archaeology, but sometimes the methods of application differ. The subject is very wide, and therefore we shall deal with the following items in a general way without entering into much laboratory detail:

(1) Analytical techniques used in archaeometry
(2) Aims of archaeometric investigation and analysis
(3) Dating techniques
(4) Techniques used in archaeological prospecting
(5) Techniques of conservation.

1. E. T. Hall, 1970.

Analytical techniques in archaeometry

The techniques of analysis have increased to such a degree that it is sometimes difficult to decide what technique to use on a particular sample to get the information needed. In the following section, this question is discussed from all its aspects.

Choice of the method of analysis to be used

Archaeological samples are exceptionally valuable for two reasons. The first is that the quantity of material available is usually so small that it may be hardly sufficient for one complete analysis, and if completely used up it may not be possible to replace it. The second is that a part of the sample has to be kept for future reference or display. Accordingly, great care has to be taken to ensure that the greatest amount of information may be obtained from an archaeometric analysis. The criteria determining the method of analysis to be adopted can be summarized as follows.[2]

Availability of material

If the amount of available material is big enough, wet chemical analysis is preferable for determining the percentages of the *principal* constituent elements in the sample since this method gives the most accurate results. Atomic absorption analysis can be applied to determine the percentages of the alkali metals such as sodium, potassium and lithium. For trace elements and compounds, however, X-ray fluorescence and X-ray diffraction analyses are to be preferred although they will give results which may be only within 10–20 per cent of the correct answer.

If only a very small amount of the sample is available and several elements have to be estimated it can be best analysed by spectrophotometric methods or by X-ray diffraction methods. If the archaeologist is not willing to provide a piece, however small, of the object, the material can be analysed by emission spectrometry or by X-ray fluorescence, provided the size and shape of the object permit the apparatus in question to be used.

Kind of material to be analysed

Archaeological materials vary greatly in kind. Some of them are wholly or partly organic such as foods, ointments, resins, oils, waxes, etc. Others are inorganic such as metals, pigments, ceramics, glass, plaster, etc. The organic materials are usually submitted to ignition, saponification, solvent extraction, infra-red survey, thermal analysis or chromatographic analysis. The inorganic materials are submitted to ordinary wet chemical analysis, emission spectrometry, X-ray fluorescence, X-ray diffraction or neutron activation, according to the information needed.

2. loc. cit.

Kind of information needed

To save time and expense the analysis must be performed according to a well-planned programme designed in co-operation with the archaeologist to answer specific questions. For example, ancient copper and bronze look superficially similar, so in order to differentiate between them only tin is tested for. This is usually done by treating a small part of the sample with concentrated nitric acid followed by dilution with distilled water when a white precipitate of metastannic acid is formed. This test can even be carried out by the archaeologist himself. Also lead minerals were used at one time for glazing ceramics in Egypt, therefore only lead need be tested to determine roughly the date at which a glazed object was made.

Presentation of results

Since the archaeologists who are going to study the results of scientific investigation and use them for their commentary and conclusions are not usually themselves scientists, the results should be presented to them in an easily understandable manner. Thus they should not, for example, be expressed as gramme equivalents of a certain constituent per 100 grammes of sample. It will be more helpful to express all results as percentages so that they may be universally understood. Moreover, this will make comparison of results between different laboratories easier.

Methods of examination and analysis

In the light of these considerations, we can list the most important analytical techniques used in archaeometry as follows.

Microscopic examination

To get a preliminary idea about an ancient material or artefact, an examination with a simple magnifying glass (10 × or 20 ×) is often very useful. A better device for such an examination is a binocular pattern having a magnification of 7 ×, 10 × or 20 × and a long 'working distance' between object glasses and focal plane. This latter feature permits observation of the bottom of deep cavities into which magnifying glasses cannot enter.

To obtain a clearer idea, the sample can be examined with a compound microscope 100 ×, 200 ×, 400 × and 1250 × with oil immersion. Microscopic examination can be applied for the following purposes:

(a) *Identification:* In most cases it is possible to identify a given sample, whether pure or composed of a heterogeneous mixture by studying microscopically its grain size or the crystalline forms of its constituents.

(b) *Qualitative analysis:* Techniques are now available for precipitation, dissolution, observation of gas evolution and other processes which can be carried out on a minute part of the sample.[3] For example, if a small part of the sample is put on a slide and a drop of water is added to it, it can be observed whether it dissolves or not. If a drop of silver nitrate solution is added to this solution and a white precipitate insoluble in nitric acid is formed, a chloride anion is present.

(c) *Quantitative analysis:* Microscopic methods are particularly valuable in the quantitative analysis of complex heterogeneous mixtures which are not readily amenable to ordinary chemical methods.[4] This is usually done by counting the number and determining the size of the different components of a powdered sample. The volume percentages of the components in the mixture can be converted into approximate weight percentages if the density of each component is known.[5]

Radiography

Radiography is essential in the examination of works of art to detect whether there are any objects stuffed, for instance, inside a wrapped mummy or whether there is any decorative inlay hidden under layers of corrosion. Such information is necessary to decide on the correct procedure to follow in unwrapping mummies or conserving metallic artefacts. Taking X-rays of the royal mummies in the Cairo Museum, for example, revealed that some of even the unwrapped ones still have jewellery which has escaped detection because it lies under thick layers of resin[6] (Plate 9.1).

Specific gravity determination

Gold in antiquity usually contained silver or copper. Gold objects are so precious that in most cases no samples, however small, can be spared from them for analysis. Caley, therefore, thought of applying the method of specific gravity determination, which is a completely non-destructive method, to find out the percentage of gold in artefacts.[7] This method is very easy and is conducted by using Archimedes' Law. If the weight of the object in air is W gm, and its weight in water is X gm, its specific gravity (S.G.) will be equal to $\frac{W}{W-X}$.

Since the S.G. of gold (19·3) is nearly double that of silver (10·5) or of copper (8·9), the presence of small amounts of silver or copper can be detected. Assuming that platinum is absent, that the alloying component is defined (silver or copper) and that no contraction occurs in alloying, the

3. G. W. Ewing, 1954, p. 411.
4. E. M. Chamot and C. W. Mason, 1938, p. 431.
5. I. M. Kolthoff, E. B. Sandell, E. J. Meehan and S. Bruckenstein, 1969.
6. J. W. Halpern, J. E. Harris and C. Barnes, 1971, p. 18.
7. E. R. Caley, 1949, pp. 73–82.

likely error in determining the gold content is of the order of 1 per cent.

Ordinary chemical analysis by wet methods

These methods are indispensable in archaeological work for the study of the material of the artefact as well as for deciding a suitable method for its conservation. They are usually used for the qualitative and quantitative analyses of mortars, plasters, corrosion products of metallic artefacts, food-stuffs, cosmetic materials, refuse of embalming materials, etc.

A description of the methods used for such analyses is not included in this work. All chemists working in the field of archaeology are well acquainted with them. They are described in detail in analytical chemistry textbooks such as those of Kolthoff *et al.*[8] for inorganic materials, and in the work of Iskander[9] and Stross[10] for organic and inorganic materials. Iron objects discovered at Niani (Guinea) and dating from about the thirteenth to the fifteenth centuries of our era have been chemically analysed and proved to contain copper, phosphorus, nickel, tungsten, titanium and molybdenum as impurities probably present in the ores used.[11]

Emission spectrometry

This technique is used for the analysis of ancient bronzes, ceramics, mortars, pigments, etc. There are several factors which make emission spectrometry particularly useful when compared with other methods of trace analysis. The sensitivity achieved is generally adequate and it permits the detection of a high proportion (up to 20 per cent) of most of the elements present. Moreover, all the proportions of the elements present in the sample can be recorded by lines on a photographic plate in one exposure and so provides a permanent record which can be referred to at will. A new variation in emission spectrometry has been provided by the development of the 'Laser milliprobe spectrometer'.[12] Spectrographic analysis of the naturalistic Nigerian Ife 'bronzes' showed that they are made not of bronze but of brass.[13]

Atomic absorption analysis

This method is suitable for samples of any inorganic material such as metals, cements, solders, glass, glaze, salts, etc. The advantages of this method in archaeometry are that 'a high degree of accuracy can be achieved (about 1 per cent error) using samples of 5 to 10 mg, that major, minor and trace elements can be determined in the same sample, and that the technique is

8. I. M. Kolthoff, E. B. Sandell, E. J. Meehan and S. Bruckenstein, 1969.

9. N. Farag and Z. Iskander, 1971, pp. 111–15; Z. Iskander, 1961; Z. Iskander and A. E. Shaheen, 1964; A. Zaki and Z. Iskander, 1942.

10. F. H. Stross and A. E. O'Donnell, 1972, pp. 1–16.

11. A. Muzur and E. Nosek, 1974, p. 96.

12. E. T. Hall, 1970.

13. F. Willet, 1964, pp. 81–3.

a standard one so that inter-laboratory comparisons can be made with confidence, as the possible sources of experimental error can be more easily controlled'.[14]

X-ray fluorescence

Excitation of a specimen by X-rays provides a useful method for analysis. The principle is that when an atom is bombarded with X-rays of high-energy, an electron is removed from an inner orbit of the atom, and the vacancy thus created is filled by an electron from an outer orbit. The difference in energy between upper and lower level appears as secondary or fluorescent X-rays characteristic of the elements composing the specimen.[15] Since the depth of penetration of the X-rays is limited, this method can only be used on the surface of objects, and accordingly it would only be suitable in the analysis of such objects as glass, faïence and pottery glazes, obsidian and most kinds of stone. Ancient metal objects, however, suffer depletion, since the less noble metals partly migrate towards the surface, and therefore a surface analysis of such objects by this method may give very different results from that obtained if the whole object were analysed.[16]

Neutron activation analysis

In this technique a group of samples and chemical standards of known composition are placed in a nuclear reactor and irradiated with thermal-energy neutrons. Some of the isotopes so produced will have suitable half-lives and will emit γ-rays. Since each radio-isotope emits γ-rays having wavelengths characteristic only of that isotope, the analysis of these rays enables us to identify the elements present in the specimen and to determine the concentration of both the main elements and the trace elements in it.

Neutrons and γ-rays have a much greater penetrating power than X-rays. This allows an analysis from a greater thickness of specimen and hence decuprification effects in metals can be ignored.[17]

In performing such an analysis, however, it has to be borne in mind that if the specimen has to be returned to the museum, the residual radioactivity must decay to a low level in a reasonable time. Radio-silver, for example, has an isotope of 225 days' half-life, and if too high an irradiation dose is given to a silver object it might not be possible to return it to the museum for hundreds of years.[18] In such a case, therefore, an extremely small amount of the silver is taken from the specimen by rubbing it against a small disc of roughened quartz. This streaked quartz is then irradiated in the reactor

14. A. E. A. Werner, 1970.
15. I. M. Kolthoff, E. B. Sandell, E. J. Meehan and S. Bruckenstein, 1969.
16. E. T. Hall, 1970.
17. loc. cit.
18. loc. cit.

and analysed for silver, gold, copper, antimony and arsenic in the usual way.

This method has been applied very recently to the study of glass beads in African archaeology, subjecting them to two neutron activations. The first bombardment was brief and the samples were analysed immediately after for short-lived isotopes. The second bombardment was intense and continued for eight hours. The samples were set aside for a few days and analysed for medium-lived isotopes, set aside again, and later analysed for long-lived isotopes.[19]

A survey of the many applications of this technique in archaeometry is given by Sayre and Meyers.[20]

Aims of archaeometric analysis

The most important aims of scientific investigation and analysis in archaeometry are the following.

The exact identification of materials

An exact identification of archaeological material is essential to ensure an accurate description because a significant interpretation of the object concerned usually depends on knowing the exact nature of the material it comprises. Errors of identification are, unfortunately, not infrequent in the older archaeological literature and have caused a lot of perplexity. Copper is sometimes confused with bronze, although the discovery and use of bronze posits a certain cultural revolution. Bronze is sometimes confused with brass, and hence a wrong conclusion may be reached as to the date of the object since brass was first made at about the middle of the first century before our era, while bronze had been known and used some twenty centuries earlier.[21]

Since most inaccurate identifications arose from a dependence on visual appearance, it must be emphasized that the identification of archaeological material must be based upon chemical examination or X-ray diffraction analysis so that misleading interpretations may be avoided.

Translation of unknown ancient words

Accurate identification serves sometimes to clarify the meaning of unknown words. For example, two pots were found in the tomb of King Hor-'Aha (first dynasty, about 3100 before our era) at Saqqara in Egypt. On each of these pots is written in hieroglyphic the word *seret* whose meaning was not known. Chemical analysis showed that the contents were cheese and

19. C. C. Davison, 1973.
20. E. V. Sayre and P. Meyers, 1971.
21. E. R. Caley, 1948.

it was therefore concluded that *seret* meant 'cheese'.[22] Another example is the hieroglyphic word *bekhen* written on some stone statues. Since the stone had been identified as greywacke (schist) in some other cases and this word was used in texts connected with Wadi-Hammamat, it was concluded that most probably *bekhen* meant the greywacke of Wadi-Hammamat.[23]

Detection of the sources of materials

The presence of numerous specimens of a material of foreign origin at an archaeological site is a clear indication of the import of such a material through trade or commerce. If the source of this material can be located, then the path of the trade can be established. For example, it is known that obsidian does not occur in Egypt; nevertheless, it was used in Egypt as early as Predynastic times (before 3100 before our era). Some objects made of this obsidian were examined and compared with the obsidian found in neighbouring countries. It was found to be very similar to the obsidian of Ethiopia, hence it is concluded that it was imported from Ethiopia and that there had been trade relations between the two countries from very early times.[24]

Determination of trace elements in pottery by neutron activation or X-ray fluorescence can afford a means of studying trade routes both locally and between different countries.[25] Trace impurities in copper ores and artefacts can help also in establishing the relationship between the artefacts and the kind of ore from which the material of the object was derived.[26]

Determination of nickel in an ancient iron artefact affords a means of deciding whether it is meteoric iron or man-made iron, since meteoric iron always contains nickel in the ratio of 4–20 per cent. The famous iron dagger of Tutankhamun has been examined for the author by emission spectral analysis and it has been shown that the iron of the dagger contains a good quantity of nickel, thus proving that the iron is of meteoric origin.

Finding out the purpose for which a material was used

Sometimes it is difficult to know for what purpose a certain material was meant to be used. In this respect chemical analysis may be of great help. For example, in the tomb of Neferwptah (about 1800 before our era) which was discovered in the Fayum in Egypt in 1956, a very large alabaster jar was found to contain 2·5 kg of a strange material. Chemical analysis showed it to be composed mainly of 48·25 per cent galena (natural lead sulphide) and

22. A. Zaki and Z. Iskander, 1942.
23. A. Lucas, 1962, pp. 416, 419–20.
24. loc. cit.
25. I. Perlman and F. Isaro, 1969.
26. P. R. Fields, J. Milsted, E. Henricksen and R. W. Ramette, 1971.

51·6 per cent resin, i.e. of galena and resin in the ratio of 1 : 1 approximately. Such a composition had never been found before, and therefore the reason why it had been put in the tomb was completely obscure. However, on consulting the prescriptions given in the Ebers Papyrus, it was found that prescription No. 402 states: 'another [remedy] for the removal of white spots which have arisen in the two eyes: black kohl [galena] and Khet-'wa [resin] are ground fine and put in both eyes'. From this text and the chemical composition of the material contained in the jar, it was concluded that this was a medicament for the eyes; that Neferwptah most probably had leucoma in one or both of her eyes and that is why she was provided with a great quantity of this medicament for use in the hereafter.[27]

Determination of the details of ancient technical processes

The examination of ancient objects by scientific methods can yield information about the techniques utilized by ancient people in their chemical arts and industries. This can be shown by the following examples:

Manufacture of Egyptian blue

Specimens of this blue pigment have been examined chemically, microscopically and by X-ray diffractometry, as well as a similar blue frit which has been reproduced experimentally. These studies proved that Egyptian blue was made in ancient times by heating to 840°C a mixture of sand or powdered quartz, powdered limestone, malachite and a flux of common salt or natron.[28]

Microscopic examination of metal objects

Metallographic examination of metal objects can show whether they were produced by casting or by hammering or by a combination of both. For example, a copper staple from the Cheops Boat discovered in 1954 behind the Great Pyramid at Giza has been examined metallographically and it was revealed that the metal has a fragmented dendritic character (Plate 9.2), thus proving that it had been shaped by hammering.[29]

Examination of the refuse of embalming materials

Examination of samples of the refuse of embalming materials discovered in Saqqara, Luxor, and Mataria in Egypt proved that they contain a small proportion of soaps of solid fatty acids which were formed as a result of the saponification of the fats of the body by the action of natron during mummification. From this it was concluded that in the process of mummification such materials had been used for the temporary stuffing of

27. N. Farag and Z. Iskander, 1971, pp. 111–15.
28. A Lucas, 1962, pp. 416, 419–20.
29. Z. Iskander, 1960.

the body cavities prior to its dehydration in a heap of natron on the bed of mummification.[30]

Glass-fritting crucibles

The scientific investigation of some of the remains of a glass factory in Wadi-El-Natrun showed that glass was manufactured in two stages in Egypt during the Roman period. The first stage was to prepare the glass frit by heating together a mixture of silica quartz, calcium carbonate and natron or plant ash or both, in a special kind of crucible, the fritting crucible, at a temperature less than 1100°C. The clay of which this crucible was made contained a high proportion of sand and finely chopped straw. Such a mixture would produce a highly porous pottery when baked, a characteristic which was clearly intended by the ancient glass maker so that he could easily release the frit block (Plate 9.3) by breaking the crucible. So it was used only once.

The second stage was to obtain a good quality glass of various colours. The frit blocks were ground into a fine homogeneous powder and divided into small batches. To each batch certain colorant oxides, opacifiers or decolourizing agents were added and reheated until complete fusion in order to obtain the kind of glass required.[31]

Testing of authenticity

For many years, the historic and aesthetic approach was the only method of judging authenticity. In more recent years great progress in scientific examination has made it possible to judge the genuineness of an object with greater certainty. The most effective scientific methods used for testing authenticity are the following.

Examination under ultra-violet light

This technique is particularly useful for the examination of ivories and marbles. Under ultra-violet light different marbles fluoresce different colours, and the surface of ancient marble frequently has a characteristic fluorescent colour which is very different from that of fresh stone of the same kind. On this basis also, alterations or repairs in an ancient marble or ivory object or a painting, which are not visible in ordinary light, may become strikingly conspicuous when the object is scrutinized under ultra-violet light. Similarly, infra-red light and X-rays have been found useful in the detection of forgery.[32]

Examination of the surface corrosion crust

Ancient metals usually corrode slowly, and a coherent corrosion layer or

30. Z. Iskander and A. E. Shaheen, 1964.
31. S. A. Saleh, A. W. George and F. M. Helmi, 1972.
32. E. R. Caley, 1948.

crust is formed in the course of time. In metal fakes, an artificial crust is usually applied to the surface to give it an ancient appearance. This crust is found to be comparatively loose and can be removed by solvents such as water, ethyl alcohol, acetone or pyridine. Moreover, on copper and bronze objects, this artificial crust will in most cases be composed of one layer and can easily be distinguished from the naturally formed crust which is always composed of at least two layers, the inner of red cuprous oxide and the outer of green basic copper carbonate or basic sulphate or chloride. Such an arrangement cannot be intentionally imitated in such a way as to deceive an experienced chemist in an archaeological museum.

Analysis of the material of the object

A very striking example of such a technique is the analysis of the core of ancient Egyptian faïence. While the core of the genuine ancient Egyptian faïence is made up of quartz frit, the body core of modern faïence fakes is usually made of kaolin or china clay and this affords a quick and reliable test of authenticity. Another example is that ancient metals contain certain impurities such as arsenic, nickel, manganese, etc., since the ancient metallurgical techniques did not adequately refine metals. Therefore, if a small sample taken from an inconspicuous place on the artefact is analysed by neutron activation or X-ray fluorescence and proves to be free of such trace elements, the object is most probably a fake.

Identification of pigments and media in painting

By microchemical techniques it is possible to identify the pigments used in a painting with reasonable accuracy. If the pigment proves to be among the recently discovered ones, the painting is a fake. For example, a painting, purportedly a fifteenth century profile portrait, was examined by Young. The blue pigment proved to be synthetic ultramarine which was not discovered and used as a pigment before the nineteenth century. The white pigment was found to be titanium oxide which was not used in painting before 1920. The painting proved, therefore, to be a forgery.[33]

Examination of surface patina and polish

Most stones acquire in the course of time a surface patina or desert varnish. This is formed as a result of the migration of iron and manganese salts to the surface where they are deposited as oxides which form a kind of epidermis or patina. Since this patina forms a part of the stone, it is coherent to the surface and cannot easily be removed by washing with a neutral solvent or by scraping. It is consequently possible to distinguish an authentic aged surface from a freshly carved surface even if it is artificially patinated.

Apart from the naturally formed patina, the marks of ancient carving and polishing may afford means of deciding authenticity. These marks still show themselves as irregular intersecting lines under the surface patina of stone or

33. W. J. Young, 1958.

metal and are easily distinguishable from the regular parallel lines due to recent polishing, since the ancient people did not use coarse files in carving, nor fine files or emery paper for polishing.

Testing the thermoluminescence of pottery

In pottery as well as in the soil in which it is buried, there exists a very small percentage of radioactive elements. These emit a certain amount of radiation which causes an accumulation of electrons over thousands of years in the body of the pottery. On heating such pottery to a temperature above 500°C, the accumulated electrons are released as thermoluminescence which varies according to the age of the pottery. Thermoluminescence, therefore, provides museum curators with very powerful evidence as to whether a pottery object is imitation or genuine. The sample for testing is obtained by drilling a small hole in an inconspicuous position and the powder obtained is heated to above 500°C in darkness. If thermoluminescence is produced the pottery is genuine, if not, it is a forgery.[34]

Dating techniques

Science affords several techniques for dating ancient materials. The main techniques used in this respect are the following.

Rough dating by archaeometric analysis

An analysis of specimens of the same groups of materials – such as mortars, glass, faïence, metals and pigments – but of different known dates may give results which can be used as a clue to indicate roughly dates for other specimens of unknown dates. The following examples illustrate this.

Dating by analysis of glass beads from West Africa

Dichroic 'Akori' beads, which appear blue by reflected light and greenish-yellow by transmitted light, were subjected to X-ray fluorescence analysis. They were found to fall into two groups. Group A was found to be much poorer in lead (less than 0·05 per cent) and arsenic (less than 0·05 per cent) than group B in which lead is about 27 per cent and arsenic is about 2 per cent. There is also a smaller difference in the manganese content (group A 0·3 plus or minus 0·1 per cent, group B about 0·05 per cent). Other elements determined were iron, cobalt, copper, zinc, rubidium, strontium, tin, antimony and barium, but no striking differences were noted. Group A beads are found in West Africa in relatively old inland sites (430 to 1290 of our era) while group B is found only in younger contexts. The finding of such beads in a tomb or a stratum can afford, therefore, a means for indicating roughly its date.[35]

34. M. J. Aitken, 1970.
35. C. C. Davison, R. D. Giauque and J. D. Clark, 1971.

Dating of southern African paintings by analysis of albuminous binders

Paintings may be dated by determining the number of amino acids in their albuminous binders after hydrolysis. This method has been used to determine the ages of 133 rock paintings from southern Africa with 20 per cent accuracy. The 'White Lady' of Brandberg proved to be 1200–1800 years old. Limpopo paintings ranged from 100 to 800 years in age. Drakensberg samples ranged from 60 to 800 years in age. The number of amino acids which could be identified decreased with the age of the painting from 10 in the binders 5–10 years old to one in materials 1200–1800 years old.[36]

Dating by analysis of mortars

Analysis of various mortars used in Egypt showed that lime mortar was not used before the time of Ptolemy I (323–285 before our era).[37] Any monument whose bricks or stones were bound together with lime mortar would, therefore, belong to a period later than 323 before our era.

Radio-carbon dating

Basic principle

When cosmic rays strike the atoms in the upper layers of the atmosphere, they cause them to disintegrate into tiny fragments among which is the neutron. The neutrons produced bombard the most abundant atom in air, namely nitrogen of mass 14, converting it into carbon of atomic weight 14. This newly formed carbon-14 is radioactive and combines with oxygen from the air forming $^{14}CO_2$ and is mixed with the ordinary carbon dioxide which contains mainly non-radioactive carbon atoms of masses 12 and 13 in abundances of 99 and 1 per cent respectively. This carbon-14 enters into the plants together with the ordinary $^{12}CO_2$ and $^{13}CO_2$ forming their tissues by the process of photosynthesis. Since animals feed on plants, 'all the living animal and vegetable world should be very weakly radioactive owing to the presence of a minute proportion of carbon-14 (approximately one atom of carbon-14 to a million million atoms of ordinary carbon). Atmospheric carbon dioxide also enters the oceans as dissolved carbonate, so this too should be weakly radioactive and any shells and deposits formed from it.'[38]

At death, the ancient organic matter is supposed to have had the same radioactivity as living organic material at the present time. But after death isolation occurs, i.e. further uptake or exchange of radio-carbon would cease and the carbon-14 starts to decay, or as Professor Libby expressed it, 'the radio-carbon clock starts ticking'.[39] If the radioactivity of an ancient sample

36. E. Denninger, 1971.
37. A. Lucas, 1962, pp. 416, 419–20.
38. M. J. Aitken, 1961.
39. W. F. Libby, 1970, pp. 1–10.

is measured and compared with the activity of a modern sample, it is possible, knowing the half-life of carbon-14,[40] to calculate the age of the ancient sample by applying a radioactive decay equation.

Materials most suitable for radioactive dating

The materials suitable for this technique must be of organic nature such as wood, charcoal, bone, leather, cloth, grasses, food-stuffs, shells, etc., but the best suited are those derived from plants growing within a single year such as reeds, cereals, grass or flax. The samples should not be treated with any chemicals when first collected, and should be put directly into glass containers or nylon bags to eliminate contamination with any new organic matter. The procedure in general consists of four steps, namely, purification of the sample, combustion, purification of the carbon dioxide gas obtained and, finally, counting of the particles emitted.

Results and prospects

In order to test the accuracy of this method, a comparative study of historically well-dated samples and radio-carbon dates has been undertaken.[41] Since the oldest and best understood historical sequence is the chronology of Egypt, it was decided internationally to measure the radio-carbon content of a long series of archaeologically precisely dated Egyptian samples belonging to the time period from the first dynasty (about 3100 before our era) to the thirtieth dynasty (378–341 before our era). The dating was carried out in several laboratories at the same time using both 5568 year half-life as well as the newer and physically more correct value of 5730 ± 40 years. The results of these laboratory tests showed that radio-carbon dates, using the 5730 year half-life, match well with the historical chronology back to the time of King Senusret III, i.e. to about 1800 before our era, but there are wide divergences between the two dates for the earlier samples. If, however, a correction factor, the Stuiver-Suess correction, is applied to the samples which antedate 1800 before our era, the results will be found to be in agreement with the archaeological dates to within 50 to 100 years at most.[42] For example, reeds taken from the mastaba of Qaa' at Saqqara, first dynasty, were dated in the British Museum research laboratory. The radio-carbon date obtained is 2450 ± 65 before our era. On applying the correction factor, its date was calculated as 2928 ± 65 before our era, which is very close to its historical date, 2900 before our era.[43]

40. The period of carbon-14 (duration of the disintegration of half of the radioactive body) was first assessed at 5568 years; later, more precisely, at 5730 ± 40 years.

41. R. Berger, 1970; I. E. S. Edwards, 1970; H. N. Michael and E. K. Ralph, 1970; E. K. Ralph, H. N. Michael and M. G. Han, 1973.

42. R. Berger, 1970; H. N. Michael and E. K. Ralph, 1970; E. K. Ralph, H. N. Michael and M. G. Han, 1973; M. Stuvier and H. E. Suess, 1966.

43. I. E. S. Edwards, 1970.

The speculation at the moment is whether the main deviation is due to a weakening of the Earth's magnetic field[44] or to variations in the intensity of the solar wind which fends off cosmic rays.[45] Moreover, the actual half-life of radio-carbon is not entirely certain. Some other causes are under consideration and research is being carried out in many laboratories on this problem.

If all these questions were answered, it would be possible to date with greater precision on periods earlier than 1800 before our era. Until then conventional radio-carbon measurements of ancient organic samples from these periods must be corrected as indicated above.

Potassium-argon dating

The limitation of radio-carbon dating to about 70 000 years leaves a long gap in the chronology of biological and geological development, extending from this date to about 10 million years earlier. For this very early period it would be possible to apply established geological radioactive methods based on the rates of change in certain substances such as the change of uranium-235 to lead-207 which has a half-life of 710 million years, or rubidium-87 to strontium-87 which has a half-life of 13 900 million years. The gap can be filled to some extent by applying the technique of potassium-argon dating.[46] In fact, this method is used particularly for the dating of lower geological ages, but by using large samples of a substance of comparatively small grain size (but not less than 100 μ) and containing only little atmospheric argon, it is possible to apply it to comparatively more recent periods which may even overlap with carbon-14 results.[47]

Basic principle

Potassium as we find it now in nature contains 93·2 per cent potassium-39, 6·8 per cent potassium-41 and 0·0118 per cent potassium-40. At the time of the formation of the Earth the abundance of potassium-40 was about 0·2 per cent but most of it decayed into two daughter products: calcium-40 and argon-40. Since potassium-40 has a very long half-life (1330 million years), a small amount of it amounting to 0·0118 per cent is still present. For 100 atoms of potassium-40 which decay, 89 become calcium-40 by beta decay and 11 become argon-40 by capture of beta particles. Argon is a gas and is retained between the grains of the mineral.[48]

The potassium-argon dating has found a number of applications for the following reasons:

44. V. Bucha, 1970.
45. S. Z. Lewin, 1968.
46. M. J. Aitken, 1961.
47. W. Gentner and H. J. Lippolt, 1963.
48. loc. cit.; E. I. Hamilton, 1965.

(a) Potassium exists in the Earth's crust to the extent of 2·8 per cent by weight and hence it is one of the most abundant elements and is contained in almost all materials.

(b) Argon-40 can be measured more easily than most other elements even in very small concentrations.

(c) The half-life of potassium is long enough for appreciable amounts of argon-40 to be formed in potassium minerals within geologically interesting periods. By measuring the concentration of the radiogenic argon-40 and the total content of potassium of a mineral, it is possible to determine the age of the mineral by applying a radioactive decay equation.[49]

Problems to be solved by potassium-argon dating

Potassium-argon dating has recently been applied to calculate the *in situ* first-order rate constant for the racemization of aspartic acid in old bones. Once the racemization reaction has been calibrated for a site, the reaction can be used to date other bones from the deposit. Ages deduced by this method are in good agreement with radio-carbon ages. These results provide evidence that racemization is an important chronological tool for dating bones which are either too old or too small for radio-carbon dating. As an example of the application of this technique for dating fossil man, a piece of Rhodesian Man from Broken Hill, Zambia, was analysed and tentatively assigned an age of about 110 000 years.[50] The problems which can be solved with the help of potassium-argon dating of the Pliocene and Pleistocene periods include the determination of an absolute time-scale dating the origin of Man, the coincidence in time of fossils in the different parts of the Earth, and the origin of tektites as well as other special geological problems.

Potassium-argon dating has been used to determine the ages of the basalt layers and the overlying tuff layers in Olduvai with the aim of determining the absolute age of the Zinjanthropus remains which were found near the bottom of Bed I of tuff. Curt and Evernden concluded that the basalts at Olduvai are at least 4 million years old, but are unreliable for dating purposes because of chemical alterations visible in thin sections of all dated Olduvai basalts except those associated with the older pebble-tool industry. Gentner and Lippolt comment on the different results obtained by reporting that 'as no further inconsistency exists between the dates of the overlying tuff and the basalts, an age of 2 million years for Zinjanthropus seems to be possible'.[51]

Archaeomagnetic dating

In order to give a simplified idea about this technique, we shall deal with the following items.

49. W. Gentner and H. J. Lippolt, 1963.
50. J. L. Bada, R. A. Schroeder, R. Protsch and R. Berger, 1974, p. 121.
51. W. Gentner and H. J. Lippolt, 1963.

Palaeomagnetism

This term signifies the study of the remnant magnetism of archaeological remains. It is based on the fact that the magnetic field of the Earth is changing continuously in direction and intensity. Observations over the past fifty years indicate that the changes in direction are at the rate of 0·2° of longitude westward per year.[52] Archaeomagnetic investigations based on the measurement of remnant magnetization in baked archaeological objects and in rocks show that the Earth's magnetic intensity during the past 8500 years had its maximum around 400–100 before our era when the field reached 1·6 times its present intensity, and its minimum around 4000 before our era when the field dropped to around 0·6 times its present intensity.[53] These effects or variations in direction and intensity are termed 'secular variation'. This is of a regional nature, and it is the basis of magnetic dating since the changes in the Earth's magnetic field leave their record in baked pottery as thermo-remnant magnetism (t.r.m.).

Application of the t.r.m. for archaeological dating

For magnetic dating of baked clay which has remained *in situ* since firing, it is necessary first to establish the behaviour of the geomagnetic field direction by measurements on archaeological structures of known age for the region in which dating application is to be made. The results are plotted in a curve showing the secular variation in that region over a long period of time. Knowing the direction of the magnetic field recorded in a baked clay of unknown date in the same region, it is possible to determine its date of firing by reference to this secular variation curve.

The most suitable samples for magnetic dating are baked clays from kilns, ovens and hearths which have remained in their original places until now. Since a portable magnetometer has not yet been produced to measure their geomagnetic field direction *in situ,* samples must be removed for measurement in a fixed magnetometer in a laboratory. It is essential that each sample should be marked with its original orientation to serve as a reference for the direction of its own remnant magnetism. This is done in practice by capping it with plaster of Paris, taking care that the top surface is horizontal and marking the direction of the geographic North on the horizontal surface of the mould before the sample is detached. In this way the ancient declination (D) and the ancient angle of inclination (I) can both be determined.[54] To compensate for anomalies, six or more samples should be taken, preferably from different parts of the structure and in a symmetrical pattern.[55]

52. M. J. Aitken, 1961; R. M. Cook, 1963.
53. V. Bucha, 1970; V. Bucha, 1971.
54. M. J. Aitken, 1970.
55. R. M. Cook, 1963.

Archaeomagnetic results for D and I have been obtained for England, France, Japan, Iceland and Russia. As far as I know, the method has not yet been tried in Africa. It is hoped, however, that it may be applied very shortly for dating in African archaeology, especially since the method has been appreciably improved in the last few years.

Thermoluminescent dating

Thermoluminescence is the emission of light when a substance is heated. It is quite different from red-hot glow and it is due to the release of energy which has been stored as trapped electrons in the heated material.

Origin

All pottery and porcelain contain small proportions of radioactive components (a few parts per million of uranium and thorium and a few per cent of potassium). In addition, there are radioactive impurities in the surrounding burial soil, as well as cosmic rays which can penetrate the soil to the burial place of the pottery. These will emit radiations which will bombard the crystalline materials such as quartz in the pottery. The resultant ionization will produce electrons which may become trapped within the crystal structure. These 'electron traps' are metastable, and when a sample of the ceramic is heated the traps will be dissipated and the excess energy appears as a photon of light. The intensity of this light or thermoluminescence will be directly related to the age. It is also dependent on the particular thermoluminescence constituents in the pottery sample and surroundings.[56] By measuring the amounts of uranium, thorium and potassium present in the pottery fragment and in the soil, the radiation dose received by the fragment each year can be calculated. In principle the age is then directly calculated using the following relation:[57]

$$\text{Age} = \frac{\text{accumulated radiation dose}}{\text{dose per year}}$$

Accuracy of results and prospects

At present an absolute accuracy of around plus or minus 10 per cent is achieved. This is somewhat poorer than is obtainable with radio-carbon dating, and is attributed to many difficulties which have arisen such as the uncertainty about the burial circumstances, and the uncertainty about the degree of wetness of the burial place which affects the dose-rate due to radio-isotopes in the pottery fragment. It is hoped, however, that further research will solve such difficulties but, for various practical reasons, it is not likely to improve this result to a greater precision than plus or minus 5 per cent error.[58]

56. M. J. Aitken, 1970; E. T. Hall, 1970.
57. M. J. Aitken, 1970.
58. loc. cit.

Despite this low accuracy, however, this technique has the advantage over radio-carbon dating that pottery is much more abundant in more archaeological sites than organic material, and that the event dated is the actual firing of the pottery, whereas in the case of radio-carbon dating of wood or charcoal the event dated is the cutting of a tree and not the date of using it in antiquity.

This technique will have a very important application in Egypt. Neolithic and predynastic cultures in Egypt have so far been mainly dated by the types of pottery characteristic of these cultures according to the Sequence Dating System first invented by Flinders Petrie.[59] Now it will be possible by thermoluminescence dating to determine the absolute dates of these cultures.

Techniques used in archaeological prospecting

The basic aim of scientific techniques in field prospecting is to discover information on buried archaeological sites either before or instead of excavations. This saves much time, effort and expense. Archaeological prospecting by scientific methods includes the following techniques:

Air photography

This technique is basically used for the recognition of a feature by its geometrical pattern. It has two main applications. The first is that it gives a more distant and thus a clearer view fitting the individual surface traces together into more meaningful patterns.[60] The aerial photographs can then be used to identify the areas which have to be excavated to give a complete picture of the whole archaeological complex. This method has been applied for the study of the Karnak temples at Luxor in Egypt, where the area of the site is about 120 hectares.

The second application is that it reveals the existence of buried archaeological structures in cultivated land from *crop marks*. Crop marks result from different moisture conditions in the soil. The crop above a buried stone wall will be weak showing up as a lightened line, while above a buried ditch the crop is richer and therefore darker in appearance. From the geometrical layout of these traces, the buried structures can be recognized and excavated.[61]

Soil analysis

Remains of ancient inhabited cities and ancient cemeteries can usually be located by an analysis of the soil. Since calcium phosphate is the main constituent of bones and man's other waste materials, its percentage will

59. W. M. F. Petrie, 1901.
60. R. E. Linington, 1970.
61. M. J. Aitken, 1961.

naturally be much higher in areas of occupation or burial. Therefore, the limits of such archaeological zones can be found by analysing soil samples taken at regular intervals from the zone and measuring their phosphate content.

Pollen analysis

Pollination in flowering plants usually takes place by the action of birds, insects or wind. Flowers pollinated by wind produce large quantities of pollen grains most of which fall to the ground without being fertilized. These pollen grains usually decay, but if they happen to fall on suitable soil, such as mud or peat-bogs, they may become fossilized and can easily be examined under the microscope. The identification and enumeration of the various types of pollen present in a sample is of potential value in archaeology as a means of providing information about the ecological environment in which human remains and artefacts are situated, and a knowledge of the ecological environment may in turn point to the kind of life which prevailed at that time.

Pollen analysis is only useful as a technique for dating, however, if the pollen spectra can be related to a time scale based on some direct dating method such as radio-carbon dating.

For further details of this technique, see Faegri and Iversen,[62] and Dimbleby.[63]

Electrical resistivity surveying

This was the first geophysical technique to be adapted to archaeology. In this technique, an electrical voltage is applied to the ground and the resistance to the flow of electric current is measured. The resistance depends upon the nature of the ground, the quantity of water retained in its pores and its content of soluble salts. Hard compact rocks such as granite and diorite have a very high resistivity compared with clay soil. Therefore resistivity surveying will mainly apply to the detection of stone-built structures buried in mud soil and earth-field features cut into rock.[64]

The normal system used in this method is to insert four metal probes into the ground, pass the current between the two outer probes and measure the resistivity between the inner two. The value of the resistance obtained is a rough average for the material beneath the inner probes down to a depth of approximately 1·5 times the distance between them, as long as it is fairly uniform.[65]

Normally almost all the applications of resistivity surveying consist of making lines of reading, keeping the same contact arrangement and

62. K. Faegri and J. Iversen, 1950.
63. G. W. Dimbleby, 1963.
64. M. J. Aitken, 1961.
65. R. E. Linington, 1970.

separations in order to locate changes in the measured resistivity values. Often these lines will be combined to give an overall rectangular grid of values, and the location of buried features will be indicated by the parts which give abnormal readings.

This technique has now been somewhat replaced by magnetic prospecting. This is mainly due to some disadvantages, mainly the slow survey speed and dependence on long-term climatic effects coupled with the fact that the interpretation of results tends to be difficult except in the simplest cases.[66]

Magnetic surveying

This is the most common technique used now in archaeological prospecting. In this technique the intensity of the Earth's magnetic field is measured at points above the present ground surface in the site to be prospected. The variations in these measurements can reveal the presence of archaeological features. By this technique it is possible to detect buried remains of iron, baked pottery structures such as kilns and furnaces, soil-filled pits cut into rock, or rock structures buried in clay soil.

The variations due to buried iron objects are very large, but those due to the other categories are very much weaker. Consequently, the technique of magnetic surveying cannot be of any use unless the detecting instrument is sufficiently sensitive to detect very small variations, besides being speedy and simple to operate.[67] The Archaeological Research Laboratory of Oxford University has succeeded in developing a proton magnetometer which meets all these requirements.[68] It is composed of two parts, the detector bottle and the counter. The detector bottle is carried on a wooden tripod and moved by one operator from point to point over the area to be surveyed. A second operator controls the counter and records the readings in plan form. The interpretation of the plan should identify the situation and outlines of buried archaeological structures.[69] Other forms of magnetometers have been developed, namely, the differential proton magnetometer, the fluxgate gradiometer,[70] the caesium magnetometer, the electron spin resonance pumped magnetometer.[71] Every one of these has advantages, but the most useful form for almost all cases is, however, the differential proton magnetometer.

The magnetic method has several advantages over the resistivity method since it is simpler and faster, and its results are easier to interpret.[72]

66. loc. cit.
67. M. J. Aitken, 1963.
68. M. J. Aitken, 1961.
69. loc. cit.
70. E. T. Hall, 1965, p. 112.
71. I. Schollar, 1970.
72. R. E. Linington, 1970.

Probing the Egyptian pyramids with cosmic rays

Cosmic rays consist of a stream of electrically charged particles known as 'μ-mesons' or 'muons'. These rays reach the earth with equal intensity from all points in the sky. A square metre is struck by some 10 000 muons per second, whatever its direction may be. Cosmic rays have a very high penetrating power and are much more penetrating than X-rays and their velocity is almost equal to the velocity of light.

Probing with these rays is useful because the muons lose energy as they pass through matter. The loss of energy (or absorption of muons) is proportional to the density and thickness of the matter through which they pass. The intensity or quantity of cosmic rays which passes can be estimated by a device known as the spark chamber, which in the case of the pyramids was placed inside a subterranean chamber. Muons which have passed through a void (or an unknown chamber or passage) would be slowed down to a lesser degree than those which traverse the solid rock, and therefore the cosmic rays which pass through voids would have a greater intensity, and this will be shown by the spark chambers. With two spark chambers oriented horizontally, and about 0.3 metres apart from each other in the vertical direction, it would be possible not only to detect any hidden chamber, but also to indicate its location to within a few metres. Excavation would then be conducted to reach the predicted void or chamber.

Probing started in the Second Pyramid which belongs to King Chephren of the fourth dynasty (2600 before our era). The data were analysed by means of a computer and the results were announced on 30 April 1969, indicating two important facts. The first is that the burial chamber of the king does not fall exactly in the centre of the base of the pyramid but lies a few metres towards the north. This finding agrees with the surveying results, thus proving the validity of this technique for probing the pyramids. The second fact is that the upper third of this pyramid does not contain any unknown chambers or corridors.

The experiment had to be repeated using another apparatus which was designed in such a way that it would be able to probe the whole pyramid. The analysis of the recorded data indicated that the whole pyramid does not contain any unknown voids, a fact which agrees with archaeological expectations.

Techniques of conservation

It is not intended here to describe the technical methods used in the conservation of artefacts made of various materials, such as pottery, faïence, glass, ivory, bone, wood, leather, papyrus, woven fabrics, metals, etc., since these are very varied and need much more space than is allowed for this chapter. For their conservation, reference is made to the more specialized books[73] and periodicals, particularly *Studies in Conservation*, the journal of the International Institute for Conservation of Historic and Artistic Works, London.

The most serious problems of conservation in Africa, however, are the great fragility of materials and the violent deterioration of stone monuments.

Great fragility of materials

Owing to the excessive heat and dryness of many countries in Africa, artefacts made of organic materials, such as parchment, papyrus, leather, wood, ivory, etc., have become extremely fragile. Such materials should be handled with great care, lest they should crumble into tiny fragments. They have at first to be kept for some time in a closed wet system, wrapped in damp blotting-paper sheets, or treated with steam in a steam box, to restore their malleability wholly or partly. They can then be safely unrolled or unfolded without their breaking into pieces.

After regaining their malleability, such artefacts should be exhibited or kept in air-conditioned museums or store-houses at a temperature of 17° ± 2°C and relative humidity of 60–65 per cent, so that they may not become brittle again as they would if exposed to dry climatic conditions.

Violent deterioration of stone monuments

This grave problem will be discussed in more detail.

Main causes of deterioration

The main agencies which cause the severe decay of stone in African monuments are:

(a) *Migration of salts:* soluble salts migrate in the presence of water or moisture from the saline soil into the stone monuments by capillary action. In dry conditions, these salts pass in the form of aqueous solutions from the inside of the stone to its outer surface, and may crystallize under the surface causing it to flake out. These effects are more pronounced on the surface itself, causing its disintegration, or may crystallize at the bottom of walls or columns where the stone meets the saline soil, as can be seen in some of the columns of the Buhen temple, Sudan (Plate 9.4).

(b) *Drastic atmospheric agencies:* In Africa, the stone is badly affected by the great variations in temperature and humidity. These lead to the gradual flaking out of the surface layers of most kinds of stone.

In many places, especially in coastal regions, both factors of decay act together, leading to very serious deterioration of the monuments, as can be seen very conspicuously in the Roman temples at Leptis Magna and Sabratha in Libya.

73. R. M. Organ, 1968; H. J. Plenderleith, 1962; E. Payddoke, 1963; G. Savage, 1967.

Surface treatment and its inadequacy

Extensive trials have been made to consolidate deteriorated stone surfaces by treating them with organic preservatives or inorganic silicates. Such treatment proved not only to be ineffective, but also to be deleterious, since it accelerates deterioration and flaking out of the stone. The failure of these trials has been stressed by the international symposia on the conservation of stone monuments which declared that the problem of strengthening stone is still far from solved and that this difficult problem must be approached with care.

International efforts to solve the problem

The difficulty of the problem and its seriousness led ICOM, ICOMOS and the International Centre for Conservation to form in 1967 a committee of ten specialists in stone conservation to study the problem. The group has made many studies and presented several reports and continued its activities up to the end of 1975 to draft a series of standard tests to evaluate the degrees of deterioration of stone and the efficiency of various conservation treatments.

New hope

Professor Lewin has developed a new method for the strengthening of limestone and marble surfaces.[74] It comprises the treatment of the deteriorated parts with a hot concentrated solution of barium hydroxide (about 20 per cent) containing some urea (about 10 per cent) and glycerol (about 15 per cent). The method depends chemically on the replacement of the calcium ions in the decayed stone with barium ions. The treatment causes the stone to become markedly harder and more resistant to the action of deteriorating agents. Since the newly formed barium carbonate forms a continuous part of the body of the stone and does not form a surface coat which has different properties from those of the inside, this method offered a new hope that the treated surfaces would not scale off and would protect the underlying layers from attack by weathering agents.

This treatment was applied in July 1973 for strengthening the disintegrating surface of the neck of the limestone statue of the Sphinx at Giza. The result is satisfactory up to the time of writing, but we shall have to keep the neck under observation for ten more years at least before we can report on the validity of this technique for the conservation of deteriorating limestone.

Remedial measures

Despite the hope we have in Lewin's technique, the problem of conserving stone monuments by chemical treatments has to be considered still unsolved. Certain mechanical measures, however, are recommended to

74. S. Z. Lewin, 1968.

protect the monuments from the action of deteriorating agencies, namely:

(a) The surfaces of outdoor monuments which are exposed to direct sun rays should not be treated with any preservative solutions which close the pores of the stone, otherwise the surface layers will scale off.

(b) The soil in which the monuments are constructed must be desalinated periodically by washing with water drained off by a well-designed drainage system.

(c) Whenever possible, the stone monument is to be insulated from the salty soil to cut off the migration of the soluble salts from the soil to the stone. The insulation can be done by introducing a lead sheet or a thick layer of bitumen under the statue, wall or column, etc.

(d) If the monument contains soluble salts which cause efflorescence or cryptoflorescence, these salts have to be extracted by washing with water and/or by coating the salt-infected parts with wet sandy clay several times until the stone becomes almost completely free from soluble salts.

(e) If the monument is fairly small, it can be removed from the open air to a museum or a shelter in order to protect its surfaces from the deleterious effects of atmospheric agencies. An alternative solution is to keep it in its original place and construct a shelter over it.

(f) A missing roof should be rebuilt to protect interior mural paintings or reliefs from the action of direct sunlight and rain and decrease to some extent the deterioration due to great variations in temperature and humidity.

Recommendations for restoration

Since an erroneous treatment of artefacts or monuments may cause more damage or even complete deterioration, some of the important rules of restoration which have been recommended in international conferences may be quoted.

(a) The patina of old monuments should not be washed off or removed in any way to show the original colour of the stone. The cleaning of the façades should be confined to dust removal so as to keep the patina untouched since it is the most important archaeological character a monument possesses.

(b) In the restoration of ancient monuments, only the falling parts have to be rebuilt in their original places. Replacements and additions should be avoided unless they are needed for supporting the fallen parts or for protecting the old surfaces from being attacked by weathering agents.

(c) In all cases of rebuilding, a mortar should be intercalated between the stones so that their weights may be evenly distributed to prevent strains or cracks in the structure.

(d) The mortar used for the renovation of walls should, as a rule, be identical with the original mortar unless the latter is of gypsum. The use of cement is not to be recommended in the case of buildings constructed of sedimentary rocks such as limestone or sandstone.

(e) The mortar most recommended in all cases of rebuilding is salt-free lime-putty mortar since it is fairly malleable and porous and would not therefore prevent slight movement of stones due to changes in temperature, and consequently no strains or cracks would occur.

(f) As regards methods for distinguishing the surfaces of the added stones, the following are worth noting:

(i) The new facing can be slightly inset from the vertical surface of the original stonework.

(ii) Different materials could be used but the dimensions of the original blocks be restored.

(iii) Alternatively, the same type of material could be used but the form and dimensions of the blocks could be made different from those in the original parts.

(iv) The alignment of the stone courses and all the joints could be conformed to, but new blocks moulded using a conglomerate of stone chips of uneven sizes.

(v) Identification marks carrying the date of restoration could be incised on all new stones.

(vi) The surface of the new stones could be made entirely distinct from that of the old by pecking it with a pointed tool to give a certain grain or engraving it deeply with a graver to let it acquire a certain geometrical design, preferably of parallel or intersecting lines.

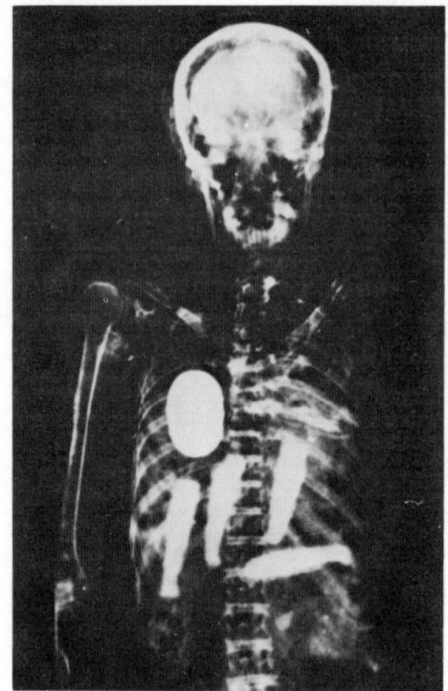

PLATE 9.1 *X-ray photograph of the frontal chest of the mummy of Queen Nedjemet (twenty-first dynasty). It shows that a large scarab and four small statuettes representing the Four Sons of Horus still remain in the thoracic cavity after unwrapping the mummy* (Cairo Museum)

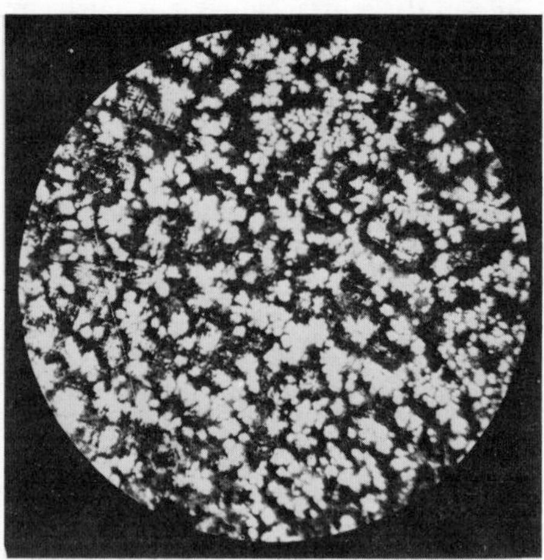

PLATE 9.2 *Microphoto of a section in a copper staple from the Cheops Boat at Giza showing the fragmented dendritic character due to hammering*

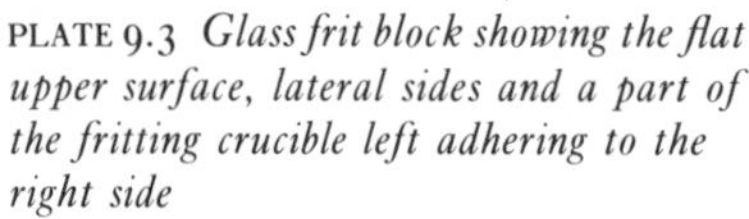

PLATE 9.3 *Glass frit block showing the flat upper surface, lateral sides and a part of the fritting crucible left adhering to the right side*

PLATE 9.4 *The bottom part of one of the sandstone columns, Buhen temple, Sudan. This illustrates the flaking away of the surface layer due to efflorescence*

10

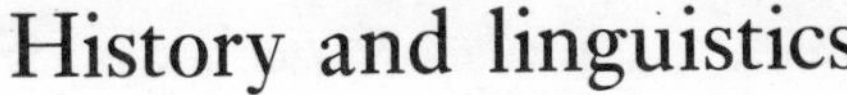

History and linguistics

P. DIAGNE

> *Aada koy demgna woni* (Fulfulde)
> *Lammii ay dekkal demb* (Wolof)
> Speech is what gives shape to the past

The African sees a link between history and language. This view is common to Bantu, Yoruba and Mande. But that is not its originality.

Indeed, an Arab or a Greek before the time of Thucydides would certainly agree with the Fulani dictum that 'narrative is where we meet the past': *Hanki koy daarol awratee*.

What is special about the link between history and language in the African tradition lies in the view of history and language to which that tradition, on the whole, has adhered.

Language and thought are often identified, and history is seen not as science but as wisdom and as an art of living.

History aims at knowledge of the past. Linguistics is a science of language and speech. Historical narrative and historical works are contents and forms of thought. Language itself is the medium and prop of such thought.

Thus, obviously, linguistics and history each have their domain, their particular subject-matter and their methods. Nevertheless, there is interaction between them, at least from two points of view.

Language as a system and tool of communication is a historical phenomenon. It has its own history. As the medium of thought, and that of the past and knowledge of the past, it is the channel and the most important source of historical evidence. Thus linguistics, used here in its widest sense, covers an area of research which supplies history with at least two kinds of data: first, linguistic information properly speaking; and secondly, evidence which might be termed supra-linguistic. Linguistics can be used to see beyond the evidence of thought, beyond the conceptual apparatus used in a language and the oral or written evidence, to the history of men and their civilizations.

Once the problem is thus defined, it is easier to see what common ground there is between the historian and the linguist working on Africa.

The linguistic sciences and history

All the sciences that take language and thought as their subject-matter can contribute to historical research. However, some have a more direct connection with history.

This is the established view, though it may, on further reflection, be questionable. Thus it is usual to say the study of relationships between languages is the cross-roads between linguistics and history; it is not so easy to say the same of an analysis of the development of material furnished by written or oral texts and by the vocabulary of a language. Yet both types of research are concerned with the facts of language or thought, and thus with the facts of history.

Here, European historiography has suggested a separation between historical science properly speaking and literary history or the history of ideas. This distinction is justifiable only in certain contexts.

The Kongo of the Bantu civilization, the Ibo of Guinea or the Susu of the Sudan have left few, if any, texts which meet the norms of modern historical science. On the other hand, as far as sources of information are concerned, they did produce an abundant oral literature, divided more or less clearly into *genres* and works which one might nowadays be tempted to classify under the heading of short stories, narratives of various kinds, chronicles, historical epics, legends, myths, philosophical or cosmogonic works, or technical, religious or sacred thinking.

In them, the historically true is mingled with fiction and the purely imaginary with events that can be precisely dated. In order to reconstruct the history of the Kongo, the Ibo or the Susu, use is made not only of the critical analysis of such literature and oral tradition, but also of the critical analysis of their discourse, their techniques and knowledge through the deciphering of the languages, concepts and vocabulary which they used, and which still, taken together, reveal the history of each of the groups.

We shall refer to various sciences and methods which can be used to guide the African historian. But the list will not be exhaustive. This may be a good thing from the point of view of clarity. The linguist sets reasonable limits to his study, and this enables him to study particular areas in detail. He thus leaves the study of the history of ideas, the sciences, economics or literature to the appropriate experts, who then take into account the linguistic dimension of their investigations.

The science of classification and the history of the African peoples

To classify languages is to uncover the relationships between the peoples who speak them, and the history of those peoples. Several types of classification may be distinguished.

Genetic classification
This classification establishes relationships and affiliations within a linguistic family, and thus helps at least to some extent to re-establish the historical unity of peoples and cultures using languages derived from a common stock.

Typological classification
This method of classification groups together languages having obvious structural or systemic similarities and affinities. Languages of identical or quite different origin may have the same kinds of lexical structure, as regards nouns, verbs or pronouns, whilst at the same time being genetically, historically or geographically far removed. The tendency to use the same noun and verb form is found both in Wolof and English:

liggeey	*liggeey bi*
to work	*work* (n.)

But despite this typological similarity the two idioms are far removed, both genetically and geographically. Moreover languages may belong to the same family but be of different types. Their kinship rests on their possession of a convincing amount of a common vocabulary even though they have developed along different structural lines. Sometimes, owing to lexical borrowings and losses, the differences may be revealed in the lexicon itself. The classifications of African languages so far drawn up do not, for example, group together some members of the so-called Chadic or the so-called Senegal-Guinea families of languages. Yet, on further consideration their phonological systems, morphology and syntactical structure suggest that typologically the majority at any rate of these languages in fact belong together.

Geographical classification
This method of classification is mainly the result of an instinctive tendency to compare and group together languages which at the present time exist in any one setting. It is often founded on inadequate data.

Where Africa is concerned, this classification, though based on evident geographical considerations, leaves out of account such phenomena as migrations and overlappings of peoples. Koelle, Delafosse, Westermann and Greenberg mainly use topological and geographical denominations and groupings: they thus categorize languages as being West Atlantic, Niger-Congo, Senegal-Guinea, Niger-Chad, and so on.

A valid classification of African languages requires procedures which ensure that the forms, vocabulary and linguistic structures which it is proposed to use as elements in a comparison are not only representative of the languages to be compared, but also belong to the original heritage of those languages. Any resemblance should be due neither to borrowing nor to earlier or more recent contacts.

For historical reasons which are familiar, Arabic and the Semitic languages and also French, Portuguese, Afrikaans and English have been depositing a considerable amount of vocabulary in many African languages for several centuries, sometimes for thousands of years. Some variants of Kiswahili contain more than 60 per cent of lexical borrowings from Arabic. It is easy to go one step further, out of religious enthusiasm or lack of scientific care, and conclude that Kiswahili belongs to the Semito-Arabic group. This conclusion has, indeed, sometimes been drawn.

Forms which were originally common to more than one language may in the course of time have undergone phonetic, morphological or structural changes. This development, which is bound by philological rules, is a well-known and analysable phenomenon. Even the meanings of these forms, the meanings of the words in the vocabulary to be compared, may have varied within the limits of a semantic field which it is possible to some extent to define. The modern form of Wolof, for instance, shows the failure of the final vowel after a geminate: 'Bopp' or 'fatt' replacing 'Boppa' or 'fatta', which are still preserved by the Gambians and Lebu. The ancient Egyptian form 'neds' has become 'neddo' in modern Fulfulde, and 'nit' in Wolof. The Bantu says 'Mutumuntu', the Hausa 'Mutu', the Mande 'mixi' or 'moxo', the Fon 'gbeto', the Mina 'agbeto', etc. The Egyptian 'xemit' once meant 'burnt' or 'black'. Today it is used in the sense of ashes, burns, etc.

The historical reconstruction of a language as a method of rediscovering the vocabulary and common structural heritage takes account of these changes. The reconstruction method makes it possible to retrace the history of a language or a language family; it helps to establish the original proto-language, and to date the times at which the various branches split off. To this extent reconstruction is an invaluable taxonomic aid.

Various criteria and techniques are used to reconstruct a language and reinvent its original components. Sound shifts play an important part in the reconstruction of a proto-language or the establishment of a family relationship. When it is known, for example, that in one variant the *p* becomes *f* and in another the *u* becomes *o*, it is possible, by positing *Fa* = *Pa*, *Lu* = *Lo*, to reconstruct the original phonetic system and forms.

Phonological reconstruction

This is a step in the reconstruction of the lexical base and the original vocabulary. The phonemes are not the only things that change: the *morphology* and *structure* also develop. The subject function in Latin is indicated by an inflexion called the nominative, whereas in languages of Latin origin or influenced by Latin, this function is indicated mainly by word order:

Homo vidit = vidit homo = l'homme a vu = the man saw

In reconstructing proto-languages (proto-Bantu, proto-Chadic, etc.), reference is always made to the *vocabulary*, the *common lexical stock*. It is thus possible to make a lexical count and work out percentages of words in common. J. H. Greenberg's[1] classification mainly relies on this technique, and D. Sapir in his work on the West Atlantic group[2] also uses this method. He concludes that Serer and Fulani, which he places in the same group, have 37 per cent of words in common, Baga, Koba and Temne have 79 per cent, Temne and Serer have only 5 per cent and Basari and Safen also 5 per cent. Yet he groups all these languages together in the same family. But the extent of common vocabulary (something that may easily be borrowed) is not enough to prove or disprove a historical link. We therefore take other factors, for example, similarity of typological features or *identity of structure*, into account by comparing, for example, pronominal, verbal or nominal systems, and so on.

The typological component, taken together with the data furnished by lexical and phonological analysis, makes it possible to arrive at results which are all the more convincing in that history and outside influence have been taken into account. Reconstruction also aims to date the period when this common heritage was shared within a proto-language and taken over by related languages then in the process of differentiation. It is concerned to establish the character of the original language that gave rise to the various languages traceable to a single proto-language.

Reconstruction and dating can also be used to determine the age of lexical and structural material collected in the course of the study of the languages and, through comparison, to define with varying degrees of certainty the level at which the languages in question are related. These techniques also provide precise landmarks in the history of the separation of peoples who originally belonged to the same cultural and linguistic world. At the same time, they shed light on the history of ethnic groups and multinational or multi-ethnic civilizations.

In research concerned with a recent age and written languages, the task is relatively simple. But in research which goes back 4000 years or more before our era, the scarcity of evidence makes for difficulties. The task, however, simply becomes one of working out the history of decisive periods of linguistic change. The processes of change in vocabulary or structure which are examined with this purpose, as we shall see, are very slow and difficult to grasp. To make up for this scarcity of information, there are techniques of varying effectiveness.

Glottochronology is one of the most recent of such techniques which has been applied in the African field. Its principle is that of dating the lexical development of a language from the rate of change of its vocabulary; its cultural vocabulary (philosophical concepts, techniques, etc.) and basic vocabulary (names of parts of the body, numbers from one to five, the words for natural phenomena, etc.). Glottochronology, as a technique, is intended

1. J. H. Greenberg, 1963a.
2. D. Sapir, 1971b.

to provide information on the age and the stage and state of development of lexical terms and forms. The fundamental or basic vocabulary develops relatively slowly in early societies, at least when there are no catastrophic historical changes of influences. In black Africa, in particular, the work of Delafosse has enabled us to form an idea of this rate of development by using lists of words recorded in writing since the eleventh century. Delafosse's work deals with the vocabulary of the languages of the Sudan collected in Arabic texts. Such vocabulary remains almost unchanged over a thousand years of history. Not only is the development of the basic vocabulary slow, it is also suggested by proponents of glottochronology that the rate is constant in all languages. This is the view of Swadesh, who has sought to apply this theory to African languages. Tests carried out in some specific contexts seem to confirm this hypothesis. Glottochronology postulates a rate of change among the items of the basic vocabulary which can be measured in percentages. The ratio of vocabulary retention, the theory goes, varies between 81 ± 2 and $85 \pm 0{\cdot}4$ per cent for a given period of 1000 years. On this basis, glottochronology has provided a number of conclusions by applying the following equation:

$$t = \frac{\log c}{1{\cdot}4 \log r}$$

(t=duration, c=percentage of terms common to the languages being compared, r=ratio of retention). The question is whether, on the basis of the results obtained, glottochronology can be considered a valid time gauge, a sort of historical time-clock. In fact the findings fall short of expectations for one simple reason: in a context of linguistic overlapping and lexical interference, the extent of which it is difficult to determine, and with no precise evidence from written or other sources, it is not easy in the present state of research to arrange the data in series, to distinguish between normal change and changes due to borrowing, even within the basic lexicon.

In the future, however, a classificatory science which applied all these techniques would provide the key to ethnic and linguistic relationships.

Linguistic classifications and ethnocultural relations

Despite some remarkable studies, the problem of linguistic and ethnical relationships in Africa is far from being solved. In many areas, intuition still takes precedence over scientifically established proof in the detection of such relationships.

The idea and the notion of a Bantu community uniting the vast majority of central and southern African peoples were born in the nineteenth century with the work of W. H. I. Bleek. In his famous book published in 1862, Bleek established the close relationship between the languages and dialectal variants spoken over a vast area inhabited by ethnic groups differing in various degrees from one another, and using languages which showed various degrees of inter-comprehensibility. Similarities of language and culture are obviously most apparent in a situation where the ethnic groups concerned are living side by side, as in the case with the so-called Bantu peoples.

In some cases, distance in space and time creates problems. The Fulani are a good example of this. From the Senegal basin to the Nile valley they live in groups which are often isolated within the areas inhabited by very different peoples. The Duala of Cameroon speak a Bantu language which in practice may be considered to belong to the same Bantu sub-group as Lingala, just as are the languages of Mbandaka or Kinshasa, despite the distance which separates it from the communities which speak the last two languages, and despite its relative isolation from them.

Pharaonic Egyptian, which was spoken 5000 years ago, offers some striking resemblances to Hausa, Wolof and Songhay.[3]

There are also phenomena of overlapping. Major universal, unifying languages continue for various reasons (political, economic, cultural, etc.) to serve as a basis for the integration of different ethnic groups. As they advance, they wipe out languages and cultures through their social pressure and their historical weight, often leaving only remnants behind.

Lingala, Hausa, Swahili, Yoruba, Twi, Ibo, Bambara-Dyola, Fulfulde, Arabic and Wolof are spoken by millions or even tens of millions of speakers of different origins. As vehicles of communication, they have greatly outgrown their original ethnic and geographical framework, to become languages of civilization common to peoples whose origins were often very different.

The Fulani and the Serer constitute the great majority of Wolof speakers in Senegal. Wolof was originally the language of a Lebu ethnic group, traces of which are found on the frontier between Senegal and Mauritania. Nowadays, the Lebu are only a small minority living in the Cape Verde peninsula.

With the urbanization of Senegal, however, Wolof culture and language are effacing many dialects before our very eyes: Serer, Lebu, Fulani, Dyola, Noon, etc., belong to the ethnic groups of the same names which a few centuries ago were playing a very important part in the history of the area.

This is a general development. Kiswahili, which is spoken by tens ot millions of Bantu-speakers, arose from a Zanzibar dialect used initially by a few villages. It spread very quickly over a relatively homogeneous Bantu linguistic area, until it now constitutes, together with Lingala, central and southern Africa's main language of communication. Between 50 and 60 million people speak one of these two languages, or a closely related language

3. On this question reference should be made to the works of Mlle Homburger, the chapters by Professors Greenberg and Obenga in this *History*, and the proceedings of the Cairo Symposium.

in this area (Zaïre, Congo, Central African Republic, Uganda, Tanzania, Kenya, Zambia, Malawi, South Africa, Sudan, Ethiopia, etc.).

Traditional African thinking has often shown a great awareness, not only of such overlapping, but also of the role that linguistics can play in explaining and elucidating history. In African tradition, many anecdotes tell of the relationship between different languages or of the more or less mythical origin of their differentiation. Often, the observations are correct. This is true of the similarities between Fulfulde and Serer whose speakers almost intuitively assert the close ethnic and linguistic relationship existing between them. Mande, Bantu-speakers, Akan and Fulani, who think of themselves as people of the same language, sometimes intuitively feel themselves to be members of groups, or sub-groups, of the single, common family.

In most cases, however, the observable relationships exist only because of a need to assimilate with or coexist with a community which has a position of some influence within the ethnic group. For a traditional saga will only command allegiance if the peoples concerned accept the fact of their kinship whether this is founded in reality or myth.

However, the traditional linguistic knowledge of African societies does not provide any clear indications of the existence of an ancient science or of systematic thinking on such relationships. This contrasts with what may be noted in other spheres, for example, in etymological science, in linguistic analysis itself or even in relation to lexical phenomena. The Fulani, Bantu or Wolof master of speech and eloquence is often very consciously interested in and well informed about the origin of words. The historian of Kayor, for instance, will amuse himself picking out borrowings or breaking down a word to show its origin. *Barjal,* says the guardian of the Kayor tradition, comes from *Baar* and *Jal.* He goes on to explain both the formal contraction which the constituent parts of the word undergo, and its context and meanings. In an article by A. Tall[4] there are some examples relating to such work by traditional etymologists among the Mossi and the Gurmanche.

The application of classificatory science to linguistics begins with S. W. Koelle, W. H. I. Bleek and European research. The beginnings of that science were the works of the nineteenth-century Indo-European comparativists and research into African linguistics began with their disciples.

In regional studies, there has been much work of considerable importance, if not for the originality or adequacy of its interpretations, at least for the quantity of data collected.

W. H. I. Bleek[5] was one of the first to set out to establish that the Bantu languages were related, and in this field he preceded authors like Meinhof or

4. 'La tradition orale', Centre régional de documentation pour la tradition orale de Niamey, 1972.

5. W. H. I. Bleek, 1862–9.

Johnston. The contribution made by Delafosse[6] to the study of West African languages is well known.

The same is true of the contributions made by C. R. Lepsius,[7] A. N. Tucker[8] and G. W. Murray[9] to the study of the Nilotic languages, and Basset to that of the Berber languages. The study of ancient Egyptian, so essential for African research, and of the Semitic or Indo-European languages of North Africa and even the Punic and Graeco-Latin languages, has also been of great value.

As is stressed by J. H. Greenberg,[10] the author of the most recent and now most controversial classification of the African languages, the most noted modern writings on the continent as a whole are those of Drexel[11] and Meinhof.[12] These are neither the first nor the only books in the field. Koelle[13] as early as 1856, and Migeod[14] in 1914, proposed methods and types of classification. Bauman and Westermann,[15] in 1940, propound an interesting system for the same purpose.

This work, however, remains controversial and is questionable for two main reasons.

The first reason is that African linguistics has not escaped ethnocentric ideology. In this connection, the criticisms recently voiced by J. H. Greenberg himself are in perfect agreement with those expressed by Cheikh Anta Diop twenty years ago in *Nations nègres et cultures* and repeated with the addition of more up-to-date information by T. Obenga in his paper to the 1977 Lagos Festival.

The second reason is purely scientific. Almost all linguists feel that attempts at classification are premature. Indispensable methodological precautions are not being taken. The properly analysed and processed material which is necessary for a genetic or even a typological comparison between African languages has not been assembled.

The need for more research

Even the task of simply listing all African languages is fraught with difficulties. Work on such a list has not yet achieved any very precise results. At a rough estimate there are in Africa between 1300 and 1500 systems of

6. M. Delafosse, 1924; L. Homburger, 1941. Among writers who put forward classifications, we should mention A. Werber, 1925 and 1930.

7. C. R. Lepsius, 1888.

8. A. N. Tucker, 1940.

9. G. W. Murray, 1920.

10. J. H. Greenberg, 1957b. See the critical analysis in Greenberg, 1957b and also in Greenberg, 1963.

11. Cf. J. H. Greenberg.

12. C. Meinhof, 1904, 1906, 1912 and 1932.

13. S. W. Koelle, 1854 (1963 edn).

14. F. W. Migeod, 1911.

15. H. Baumann and D. Westermann, 1962.

speech which may be classified as languages. Progress has certainly been made in recent years, though the right climate does not yet exist for a really thorough work of synthesis since some languages have still to be precisely identified and accurately analysed, and until this has been done they can hardly be classified.

A few specific examples will serve to illustrate the depth of the controversy and the extent of the uncertainty.

The first two examples concern the dialects to be found on the present geographical frontier of the Hamito-Semitic family and the black African family. The third concerns the West Atlantic (or Senegal-Guinea) group.

From the work of Meinhof,[16] Delafosse,[17] Meek,[18] Lucas,[19] and Cohen,[20] to that of Greenberg in 1948, A. N. Tucker and M. A. Bryan in 1966,[21] and the recent criticisms of T. Obenga,[22] it emerges that there is no complete agreement either on the data, the method of classification, the members of the groups or the genesis and character of the relationships of the languages between the Nile and the Chad basin. Yet geography, in particular, and proximity unquestionably give these languages a real unity. The age-old parallel existence of black African and Semitic languages has led to a large stock of mutual borrowings. These two-way contributions make it difficult to draw the line between the original stock and outside acquisitions. The problem is to know whether the vocabulary proper to ancient Egyptian, Hausa, Coptic, Baghirmian, Sara and the Chadic languages that occurs in Berber and in Semitic languages such as Arabic and Amharic is evidence of a family relationship or simply of borrowing.

Data for ancient Egyptian goes back 4000 years and that for Semitic 2500 years. Comparable analysis of Chadic, Berber and Cushitic does not exist for times prior to the nineteenth or twentieth centuries of our era.

In 1947 M. Cohen published his *Essai comparatif sur le vocabulaire et la phonétique du Chamito-sémitique*, in which he compares Egyptian, Berber, Semitic, Cushitic and Hausa (to which he makes occasional reference). In 1949 Leslau[23] and Hintze[24] began to challenge Cohen's findings and even to question his methods. J. H. Greenberg, having in mind that the very notion of a Hamito-Semitic group was disputed, widened the range of its components. He suggested a separate fifth member, Chadic, and renamed the whole group Hamitic, and later, Afro-Asiatic. These conclusions

16. C. Meinhof, 1912.
17. M. Delafosse, 1924.
18. C. Meek, 1931.
19. J. Lukas, 1936.
20. M. Cohen, 1947; J. H. Greenberg, 1948: 'Hamito Semitic', *SJA*, VI, pp. 47–63.
21. A. N. Tucker and M. A. Bryan, 1966.
22. T. Obenga, paper delivered at the Lagos Festival, 1977.
23. W. Leslau, 1949.
24. F. Hintze, 1951.

provoked controversy from the moment of their publication. Polotsky[25] doubted whether it was possible at present to accept the existence of five branches. Greenberg, be it noted, repeated (still without carrying conviction) the predominantly geographical thesis about Chadic and its connections which he put forward in an article in *Languages of the World*. One only needs to refer to the contradictory classifications of Greenberg, Tucker and Bryan, constantly brought into question even by the authors themselves, to gain an idea of the inconclusive nature of their proposals.

Recent work gives substance to the notion of a Chadic family, the borders of which extend far beyond the shores of the lake. Newman and Ma[26] in 1966 and Illie Svityè[27] in 1967 have improved our knowledge of proto-Chadic. The work of Y. P. Caprille[28] has charted its expansion in Chad itself. On the basis of systematic observation, a genetic link might be suggested between the Sara and Chadic groups and several languages classified as West Atlantic (Serer, Fulfulde, Wolof, Safen, etc.).[29] These attributions alone cast doubt upon the whole attempt at classification, as is emphasized by C. T. Hodge in an excellent article.[30] The major problem of the nature of the links between the languages of the frontier between the black African and the Hamito-Semitic languages remains unresolved. The sheer volume of published work that identifies the world of African culture with Semitic is a further problem.

There is still a problem of the membership and even of the identity of the black African language family. The symposium on 'The Peopling of Ancient Egypt', organized by Unesco in Cairo in 1974, emphasized this. On this occasion Professor S. Sauneron recalled, by way of illustrating these uncertainties, that 'The Egyptian language could not be isolated from its African context and its origin could not be fully explained in terms of Semitic' (Final Report, p. 29).

Cushitic is another example of the present uncertain state of research and classification. Greenberg, Tucker and Bryan and the Soviet scholar Dolgopoljskij have recently put forward three differing, not to say contradictory, classifications for the complex of languages (Somali, Galla, Sidamo, Mbugu, etc.) that goes by the name of Cushitic. Dolgopoljskij's classification hinges upon a phonological type of reconstruction based on a limited number of examples. In particular, he compares the labials (p, b and f) and dentals (t and d) in the languages, and classifies them in ten sub-groups, whereas his colleagues identify from three to five.

Greenberg ignores the phonological, morphological and grammatical data and concentrates mainly on a comparison of vocabulary. But here

25. H. Polotsky, 1964.
26. P. Newman and R. Ma, 1966.
27. Illie Svityè, *The History of Chadi Consonantism*; cf. C. T. Hodge, 1968.
28. Y. P. Caprille, 1972.
29. Cf. P. Diagne, 1976.
30. C. T. Hodge, 1968.

borrowing plays an important part. Tucker and Bryan, who criticize Greenberg's method, offer a classification based on a comparison of the pronoun system and the verb structure. They themselves regard the inclusion of some of the languages that they group together as doubtful, and emphasize the purely tentative nature of their approach. One can only observe that the outstanding feature of the classifications set forth here is their provisional nature.

The same difficulties arise as regards the languages geographically bounded on the west by the Atlantic and extending along the coast from southern Mauritania to Sierra Leone. In 1854 Koelle, in his *Polyglotta Africana*, classified them under the heading West Atlantic, basing his identification on their changes of prefix or initial or final inflexion. This is a typical feature of Bantu but is not enough to define a group. Moreover Koelle later came to regard all these languages as unclassified. Delafosse in 1924[31] and Westermann in 1928 asserted that the West Atlantic languages constituted a genetic group, and in 1963 Greenberg[32] gave his whole-hearted approval to this: he called them the extreme western group of the Niger-Congo family.

In the same year Wilson[33] and Dalby,[34] while noting the internal typological similarities of the group, completely rejected the idea of regarding these languages as a homogeneous and related group. In details of morphology, syntax and vocabulary, wrote Wilson, the 'West Atlantic' or 'Senegal-Guinea' group is by no means an entity. Indeed, recent work by D. Sapir,[35] published in 1974, shows that there is no more than 5–10 per cent common vocabulary between the great majority of these languages, the only unifying factor in most cases, as has been suggested elsewhere, being geography. Here as in the Nile-Chad area, migration intermingled peoples of different origins; they are bracketed together, perhaps too hastily, in the absence of precise information that would enlighten history and the historian.

It is here, moreover, that linguistics as a tool of historical research suffers at present from serious limitations. The research worker is faced by the twin obstacles mentioned above. Research has met with no success because it remains incomplete and embryonic. In the second place, the tentative results of research can often not be used because they are falsified by distortions of approach and ideology.

Ideological distortions

History is the favourite haunt of ideology. Ideology develops around and within it. The earliest works on the African past and on African languages

31. M. Delafosse, 1924.
32. J. H. Greenberg, 1963b.
33. W. Wilson, 1966.
34. D. Dalby, 1905.
35. D. Sapir, 1971b.

coincided with the European colonial expansion. Such works were strongly tainted with the contemporary notions of racial supremacy.

The ethnocentric viewpoint was the natural expression of the need to judge the value of any civilization by internal reference. It led men to appropriate to themselves the most distinctive points of any civilization in order to legitimize their world dominance in thought and power. The theories of the primacy of the civilizing Indo-European, Aryan or white man are evidence of excesses which still today leave profound reverberations in a number of works on African history and linguistics.[36]

Egypt was for a long time set on one side by comparison with the rest of the continent, or rejuvenated for the benefit of Mesopotamia or other centres of civilization which were assumed, on the basis of unsupported speculation, to be Indo-European or Semitic. Benin art was allotted imaginary founders. A systematic theory of Hamitization[37] was worked out, so as to explain by external influences any interesting cultural features in black Africa.

Whilst seeking to promote a strictly scientific methodology, Greenberg (whose contribution, though not entirely beyond dispute, remains very fresh and important) sometimes echoes the negative aspects of ethnocentric ideology.

Seligman and Meinhof, and also after them authors as important as Delafosse, Baumann, Westermann and Müller, put forward some staggeringly unscientific arguments, based as they are on prejudices of the kind expressed by Meinhof when he wrote: 'In the course of history one phenomenon has constantly recurred, namely that the Hamitic peoples have subjugated and ruled over the black-skinned peoples.'

Such an observation shows how careful we must be today when using any material which linguistic research makes available to historians or human scientists in general.

'The vagueness of the use of the term Hamite', wrote Greenberg, 'as a linguistic term, together with its extension as a racial term for a type viewed primarily as Caucasoid, has led to a racial theory in which the majority of the native population of Negro Africa is considered to be the result of a mixture between Hamites and Negroes.' Thus in *Races of Africa*, C. G.

36. Cf. J. H. Greenberg on this point.

37. The words 'Hamite' and 'Hamitic' have been used to excess in the learned language and everyday speech of the western world for centuries. This usage originated in a garbled and tendentious reading of the Bible and was responsible for the myth of the curse on the black descendants of Ham. Although the term took on a seemingly less pejorative meaning and at least lost its religious connotations as a result of the researches of nineteenth-century linguists and ethnologists, it has still continued to be used as a criterion for discriminating between certain black peoples who are regarded as being superior, and the rest. In any event, the International Scientific Committee is giving encouragement to the critical studies being conducted into the historical uses of the term, which can only be used with express qualifications.

Seligman calls the speakers of 'Nilo-Hamitic' languages racially 'half-Hamites', while the Bantu are also supposed to be another variety of Hamiticized Negroes. And this, Greenberg continued, 'on the basis of the speculations of Meinhof (for which he never produced the slightest proof, for the very good reason that no proof is possible) to the effect that, as Seligman says, Bantu is a mixed language, so to speak, descended of a Hamitic father and a Negro mother'.

The east/west and north/south migrations of the African peoples have confused the ethnic, racial and linguistic map of the continent. This has been shown in many studies of the evidence of personal names, place names and purely linguistic facts about the basic vocabulary itself. The languages of Senegal like Wolof, Dyola, Fulfulde and Serer show considerably more similarities to the Bantu languages of South Africa, Tanzania, Cameroon and Zaïre than to the languages of the Mande family, by which they are geographically surrounded. The lexicon, the structure and the essential principles of written ancient Egyptian, as we shall see below, are closer to corresponding phenomena in languages such as Wolof or Hausa, or to the Dahomeyan graphic tradition, than to the Hamito-Semitic linguistic systems to which they have been incautiously assimilated.

Ancient Egyptian, Hausa and the languages of the Rwanda pastoralists, the Abyssinians, the Fulani and the Nubians are baptized Hamito-Semitic on the strength of obviously flimsy data or of an utterly unconvincing methodology and choice of criteria.

The Fulani are perhaps of mixed blood just as the Luba, the Susu, the Songhay, and many black peoples in their former or present habitat had contacts with white peoples, although this interbreeding hypothesis is now distinctly questionable as a result of recent discoveries about the process of pigmentation mutation.

In its phonology, vocabulary and structure, Fulfulde bears a closer resemblance to Serer than to any other known language: so much so that the Serer and the Fulani themselves suggest that their relationship is not only linguistic but ethnic. This has not deterred scholars such as Müller, Jeffreys, Meinhof, Delafosse and Westermann from seeking to establish a white origin for the Fulani on the grounds that Fulfulde is a proto-Hamitic language.[38] W. Taylor goes as far as to write: 'From its wealth of vocabulary, its sonorous diction and the delicate shades of meaning it can express, I certainly do not think it [Fulfulde] belongs to the [black] Sudanese family.' All these comments show how widespread the confusion is between categories as different as language, way of life and 'race', not to mention the concept of ethnic group which is used according to taste to refer to one or more of these categories.

As Greenberg has pointed out, the simple equation of Hamites with cattle-ownership and conquest must be abandoned. In West Africa there is a one-hundred per cent negative correlation, for the Hausa agriculturalists

38. J. H. Greenberg, op. cit.

who speak a 'Hamitic' language were conquered by cattle-owning Fulani, speaking a black African (Sudanic or Niger-Congo) language. Another inversion of the stereotype which one might note is that of the great age and continuity of rule by the Sudanic-speaking Mande or Wolof over peoples so hastily assimilated to 'Hamitic' as the so-called pre-Hamitic Fulani or the Berbers.

None of the classifications drawn up for the whole or parts of Africa can so far be considered unquestionably sound from a scientific point of view. Ethnocentricity has gone a long way to distort analysis of the material. In many cases all we are left with is guesswork, the begging of questions and quick overall surveys.

A number of conditions must be fulfilled if we are to study African languages according to strictly scientific principles such as will help to clarify the history of the peoples and civilizations of Africa.

First, such work must be free from obsession with irrelevant ideas, derived from the study of Semitic or Indo-European languages, which are part of European history.

Furthermore, if we are to establish the relationships between the African languages, we must cite early linguistic evidence, and not geographical distribution, early or late influences, explanatory schema chosen *a priori* or linguistic features which are marginal in relation to the main facts of the language-systems.

Auxiliary sciences

Analyse acculturaliste, or typological analysis[39] as it is called in English, is part of a science which studies the origin and spread of cultural features (ideas, techniques, and so on). German scholars were first in the practical application of this method, with the study of cultural cycles by Frobenius, Westermann and Baumann, and so on.

Such studies have often been concerned with the spread of crops and agricultural techniques, pastoral methods, the invention and spread of iron-working and other metal-working techniques, the use of the horse and the development of ontological notions of the pantheon of the gods or of artistic forms.

On occasion, however, typology has exceeded its brief. In particular, it has introduced many errors into classificatory linguistics. Many extremely incautious writers have felt bound to infer linguistic relationships from cultural features alone when such phenomena are often due to borrowing, contact or convergence.

Onomastics is the science of names: place names (*toponyms*), personal names (*anthroponyms*), names of water courses (*hydronyms*), and so on.

Onomastics is closely connected with vocabularies. Ethnic communities which have for a time remained relatively homogeneous, as well as ethno-

39. Cf. M. Guthrie, 1969.

linguistic groups which are more heterogeneous in their membership and have a language in common, create their names mainly by reference to the realities of their languages. They provide the territorial or geographical milieu which they inhabit or have inhabited with characteristic names. Equally it is possible, by personal names, to establish the ethnic make-up of a community. In general, the Serer are called Jonn, Juuf, Seen, Ture, Jara, etc., while the Berbers and the Bantu-speakers each have their own sets of names.

Anthroponymy plays an important part in the history of ethnic groups in political or cultural communities. The study of the names in use among the Tukulor of Senegal, for instance, shows that we are dealing with a very heterogeneous ethno-linguistic community. This Fulfulde-speaking group, established along the river Senegal, and on the borders of Mali and Mauritania, is culturally very homogeneous. They have a highly developed national sentiment. In fact, the community is a combination of Fulani – who supplied the language – and of Mande, Serer, Lebu-Wolof and Berber.

Toponymy and hydronymy are also essential for the study of the migration of peoples. Using the names of former or existing villages, precise maps can be drawn up showing the movements of the Mande, whose villages have names containing *dugu*. In the same way, we can draw up a toponymic map of the former or present habitation of the Fulani who use the term *Saare* for their settlements. A similar map can be drawn for the Wolof using the term *Ker*, for the Arabo-Berbers using *Daaru*, for the Hausa, and so on.

Semantic anthropology

Semantic anthropology or ethno-linguistics is a new approach which attempts to discover man's culture from his language. It is based on an overall analysis of all the data which can be culled from the language of an ethnic group or heterogeneous linguistic community possessing a common language to express its culture, thought and history.

This method goes beyond the mere collection of written and oral traditions and literature. It involves reconstruction of the whole set of ideas in a language, not necessarily in relation to a systematic work or systematic discourse. Such research thus operates at both infra- and supra-linguistic levels to establish from vocabulary, thought-patterning, procedures of formalization, of conceptualization and structuring of a language, the various types of knowledge within which the specific world-view and history of the community speaking a given language are crystallized. Ethno-linguistics uncovers systems: metaphysical conceptions, ethics, ontology, aesthetics, logic, religion, knowledge of techniques, and so on.

Thus, the written and oral literature relating the past of the Hausa, together with their religious documents, fables, legal, medical, metallurgical and educational practices, sheds light both on the development of the content of Hausa thought and on their history and culture.

In predominantly oral civilizations in which written texts are rare, diachronic interpretation based on the comparison of texts from different periods is virtually impossible. In such cases, linguistics becomes an invaluable means for the rediscovery of the intellectual heritage – almost a sort of time machine.

The oral cultures which are traced through semantic anthropology provide us not only with works to be collected and recorded, but also with authors and with the specialities of those authors. Any African oral or written culture, such as that of the Wolof, has left its philosopher, like Ndaamal Gosaas, its political historian, like Saa Basi, its master of speech and eloquence, its master of epic and story, like Ibn Mbeng,[40] and also its inventors of pharmaceutical, medical and agricultural or astronomical techniques.[41] These works and their authors are excellent sources for analysing the evolutionary dynamism of the culture of a society in all its various forms.

Bantu ontology can be deciphered, and even interpreted and systematized, simply by reference to Bantu words relating to the human being in the world, and also on the basis of the process of elaboration and conceptualization which, working through Bantu words and utterances, gives form to the views that the Bantu languages have of such phenomena.

Language being as it were the crystallizing point for all the intellectual and material tools fashioned by succeeding generations, we may think of a people's historical experience as being deposited in stratigraphic layers within the very tissue of the language.

An adjunct to records and historical thought

Nowadays the importance of oral tradition in African history is readily admitted. Traditionalist griots are even asked to scholarly conferences. There have been suggestions that university posts should be created for them and even that historical research and teaching should be entrusted to them.

On the whole, the pre-eminence of spoken over written material is still a fact today, in Africa, as elsewhere in predominantly rural traditional cultures.

Oracy has its own methods of elaborating and defining the results of thought. While written and oral forms of thought cover the same ground, the means and methods of their conception and transmission are not always the same.[42]

We shall simply note that written thought, literature in the narrow sense,

40. All these are historical figures famous in the history of Wolof thought.

41. The works of Johnston on the Yoruba, Tempels on the Bantu, Griaule on the Dogon, Traore on African medicines, Guthrie on metallurgy, etc., with the 'fixed literary classics', make up an important contribution to semantic anthropology. Cf. P. Diagne, 1972.

42. Cf. P. Diagne, 1972.

has a greater tendency to become fixed for all time, as it is set down. This distinguishes it from oral tradition, which offers greater latitude for invention and myth creation. On the level of language, the spoken word has also greater potential for dialectalization because there is less control over its development. A language used mainly for oral expression remains closer to the people and more exposed to the distortions which regular use brings about in its structure, in its sounds and even in the forms which it borrows.

A literary language, on the other hand, tends more towards unification. In addition, it has a more important visual side to it, because it has, among its means of expression, graphical features which give it a particular character: an orthography which conflicts with its phonology, a system of punctuation, etc.

Oral language, on the other hand, makes greater use of sound as a means of signifying thought through cadence, rhythm, assonance or dissonance and other vocal tricks. The importance of the role played by memory, to compensate for the absence of the written medium, also affects the character of the spoken word and the forms it uses. It consciously submits to the restraints of mnemonic techniques, a specific science for the memorizing of texts. Written records and oral tradition thus become complementary, and unite their respective virtues.[43]

Moreover oral accounts, once they are transcribed, become literary texts.[44]

The graphical tradition – African writing

The nature and origin of the needs which are met by the invention of writing differ according to context and have not always been clearly brought out. Writing as an instrument of commerce and administration is a phenomenon of urban civilization, but this is not necessarily the origin of all writing. In Africa, not only in the age of the Pharaohs but also under the kings of Dahomey or the Mandinga *Mansas*, writing served mainly non-material needs. Egyptian writing and that of the Dahomey bas-reliefs or the Bambara or Dogon ideograms had, in their original context, two purposes. The first was to materialize thought and to enshrine something of religious or sacred significance. According to legend, Egyptian writing was invented by the god Thot, and long remained confined principally to temples and the use of priests. It served to record secrets designed for the use of initiates or as a medium for a type of thought conceived as an active substance to be materialized in the word or writing itself.

43. Cf. P. Diagne, 1972.

44. Cf. the many publications on this theme: A. Hampaté Bâ, A. Ibrahim Sow, Mufuta, E. Dampierre, K. Moeene, F. Lacroix, M. Griaule, G. Dieterlen, Whiteley, E. Norris, L. Kesteloot, T. Niane, M. Diabate, J. Mbiti have written classic works on this subject, published by the Oxford University Press, Julliard, Gallimard, Cenre de Niamey etc.

The second great function assigned to literary records in civilizations of purely African origin coincides with the need to perpetuate history. Both Egyptian writing and that of the palaces of Abomey are used to glorify sovereigns and peoples who are concerned that their feats should be remembered. The same purpose preoccupied the Bambara or Dogon as they carved their ideographs on the walls of Bandiagara.

There are more than affinities between the *Récade* of King Glélé, which was a message-carrying ceremonial axe, and the *Palette* of Narmer. Not only is the spirit the same, but also the principles and techniques of writing.[45]

Egyptian writing, as we have said, is attributed to the god Thot, who also invented magic and science, as did the jackal-headed god of the Dogon, who is himself the guardian of the word, knowledge and effective speech.

The few experts who have studied, often most minutely, the systems of writing originating from Africa have all without exception ignored the seemingly obvious and technically demonstrable link between the best known Egyptian hieroglyphs and the writing systems of black Africa.

The Egyptian hieroglyph remained fundamentally pictographic in its original function as an instrument of the temples. Like its Dahomeyan counterpart, it makes as strong as possible a reference to the image. It is a deliberately realistic writing concerned to materialize living beings, objects and ideas in the most concrete and substantial manner, rather as if to store or conserve their natural qualities.

It is not by chance that the distortion of pictographic writing by the use of a cursive script, which alters and disfigures the objects represented, is allowed only outside the temples. Hieratic writing, which was used principally for secular purposes (despite the implications of its Greek etymology), and popular demotic writing, with its even more simplified signs, are non-sacred, utilitarian systems.

To the Egyptian priest, the hieroglyph has, in addition to its other qualities, as M. Cohen so rightly emphasizes, 'a power of magical evocation' and this explains, in his opinion, why images of maleficent creatures are either omitted or mutilated. Here we have an ontological viewpoint which is deeply rooted and steeped in the Negro-African tradition. For thousands of years, this tradition remained incapable of secularizing thought and its oral or graphic media, as the Indo-Europeans and especially the Greeks had done. The Bambara, the Yoruba, the Nsibidi and the Dogon priests have exactly the same view of the writing systems which they use in their temples or their divination ceremonies.

The unity of the writing systems originating from Africa lies not only in the ideological presuppositions which give those systems their functions and nature, but in the technique of transcription itself.

Continually throughout the history of African writing systems, three techniques for the graphic recording of thought are relevant – the use of the image, through pictograms depicting the creature or the object; the use of

45. M. Glélé, 1974.

the symbol to represent an entity through ideograms, which are signs with no direct link of physical resemblance to the concept they symbolize; and finally the use of phonograms, each representing one whole set of homophones, that is, of entities denoted by the same sound or group of sounds. This is the principle of picto-phonographic writing.

It is revealing to compare the *Palette* of Narmer and the *Récades* of Glélé or Dakodonu. Both transcribe thought on the same principles.

On the *Palette,* we have the image of a king seizing a defeated enemy by the hair in order to dispatch him, while the rest of the conquered army flees beneath the feet of the gigantic Pharaoh. The pictograms are clear and eloquent. The other signs are ideograms. One such distinct sign is an oval 'ta', symbolizing the earth. Above is a group of signs and a square as the emblem of the Pharaoh's name, Horus. A fish and a bird make up the name of the Pharaoh. The two images are picto-phonograms.

The *Récade* of Gezo shows the Dahomey sovereign in the form of a buffalo, as Pharaoh is symbolized by a falcon. His teeth are bared, meaning that he sows panic among his enemies from earliest youth. In this case, we have an example of a symbolic representation. Others are more significant.

The *Récade* of King Dakodonu or Dokodonu, which is older (1625–50) and is described by le Herissé, shows even more clearly the principle of the Dahomey hieroglyph. The text on the axe blade can be read as follows: there is a pictographic symbol representing a silex 'da', with below the symbol of the earth, 'ko', having a hole in the middle, 'donon'. These signs are pictograms used here as picto-phonograms. By combining them, as in the case of the Pharaoh's name in the Narmer *Palette,* we get the name of the Dahomey King Dokodunu. Dahomey writing bears the strongest possible likeness to the Egyptian hieroglyphs and the principles and spirit of that system. It reveals the three techniques used by Egyptian graphics: the pictographic image, the ideographic symbol and the picto-phonographic sign.[46]

The Soviet scholar Dmitri A. Olderogge, in an article outstanding for the synthesis it presents, has reasserted that, as Cheikh Anta Diop first pointed out, the hieroglyphic system survived until recently in black Africa.

In his *Historical Description of the Three Kingdoms of Congo, Matamba and Angola*, published in 1687, Cavazzi de Montecudolo asserts that hieroglyphic writing was used in these areas.

In 1896, a hieroglyphic inscription was discovered on the rocks at Tete in Mozambique, beside the Zambezi. The text of the inscription was published at the time. Cheikh Anta Diop notes elsewhere the use of a late pictographic writing system in Baol, where recently traces of hieroglyphs have been discovered on 1000-year-old baobabs. The Vai of Liberia for many years used a pictographic writing system on strips of bark.

Meroitic writing, which grew up on the southern limits of ancient Egypt, is unquestionably a continuation of ancient Egyptian writing. The latter

46. See Chapter 4 above.

inspired the former; or else the former gave rise to the latter, or shares a common origin with it.

The ideographic systems of writing, however, seem to have been more durable on western black African soil than were the hieroglyphs.

In practice, the vast majority of African peoples are familiar with the use of ideograms either in divining techniques or in their use by priests of religion and engravers of works of art, and so on.

The Gurma have a very elaborate system of divination. The diviner, the *tambipwalo*, draws signs in the sand and interprets them. Then he issues a kind of prescription consisting of abstract signs carved with a knife on a piece of calabash to denote the altars, the places where the client must go to make sacrifices, what kind of animal must be sacrificed, how many times, and so on. It is in fact a system of coded writing.

The Ifa divination system, which is found all along the coast of the Gulf of Benin, is also remarkably rich. The diviner shuffles palm-nuts from one hand to the other eight times, and according to the number of nuts remaining in his left hand he writes a figure on a tray sprinkled with dust or on the ground. Tables (to a possible maximum of 256) are thereby drawn up, of which the sixteen most important constitute the *odu* (threads) or words of the gods ruled by Ifa the god of destiny. Everyone must sacrifice to his *odu* but at the same time take account of those of his relatives and ancestors, his country, and so on. The permutations are legion, and the multiplicity of *odu* are combined in a sort of mythological strategy which is also a graphological technique.

The collection of ideographic systems[47] has given a rich yield, especially in savannah countries which have retained their traditional religion and are relatively little affected by Islam. This is no coincidence. Experts, of which Migeod was one of the first, have uncovered some of these systems.

Dogon ideographic writing has been described by M. Griaule and G. Dieterlen, who analysed the Bambara graphic system and made a good survey of the area's systems.

Nsibidi ideography, which is used by the Ibo of southern Nigeria, was discovered by Europeans at the end of the last century. It is based on transcribing principles that were very widespread throughout the Guinea coastlands.

Phonetic writing,[48] which systematizes the use of phonograms, represents simple or complex sounds by regular signs; such systems, in the opinion of the author, appear in Africa as a late development. The hieroglyphs of ancient Egypt and of Dahomey represent many sounds with signs.

But purely phonetic systems based on the word, the syllable or the single

47. Cf. G. Niangora Bouah, 'Recherches sur les poids à peser l'or', doctoral thesis, Abidjan, 1972.

48. D. Dalby puts forward interesting new ideas on this topic in Dalby, 1970.

phoneme – the latter being alphabetic transcription – mark a new stage.[49]

Berber writing, which is used among the Tuareg of the Sahara and which is still known by the name of Tafineq, is said to have developed under Punic influence through contact with Carthage.

The Nubian writing system was formed in the tenth century through contact with Coptic writing, which in turn grew up under Greek influence. The alphabet used for Amharic and Tigriniya in Ethiopia is derived from the Sabean writing of southern Arabia.

The West African syllabic and alphabetic writing systems that were very widespread on the Guinea coast and in Sudanese areas from the end of the eighteenth century may have arisen by internal developments, or may have taken on their final form under the distant or not so distant influence of an outside element of European or Arab origin.[50]

Vai writing became known in Europe in 1834 through the discoveries of Eric Bates, and in 1849 through those of Koelle; it developed in an area where traces of the hieroglyphic system had been noted. Momolu Masakwa, a nineteenth-century Liberian Consul in England, described the principles of the hieroglyphic system used in his area at that time.[51]

Momolu reports that, to express victory over an enemy, the Vai drew on a strip of bark (instead of papyrus) the outline of a man running with his hands on his head. A dot is placed alongside the image to indicate large numbers of fleeing men, a routed army. In this use of a dot to denote the plural instead of the dashes used in the Nile valley in antiquity we find features of Pharaonic script.

Thus the Vai may have altered their earlier system in the direction of phonetic transcription. Today, we have instances similar to that of Vai writing among many West African peoples: the Malinke, Mande, Bassa, Guerze, Kpelle, Toma, etc. Wolof and Serer have also recently been provided with graphical systems based on these principles.

Contrary to the commonly held view, the use of writing has been a permanent feature of African history and thought, from the *Palette* of Narmer to the *Récade* of Glélé. The wealth of writing systems and of evidence of their use bears witness to this fact.

Post-Pharaonic African writing systems followed a normal development, and there are many reasons for this. Quite simply, this development was adapted to the historical context and the historical requirements of an affluent rural society and economy. Its members were not forced by the pressures of poverty to consolidate in their own age their material or intellectual acquisitions, because these were not continually threatened. An

49. E. Hau, 1959.

50. Sudanese writing systems combine pictograms (realistic images) with ideograms (signs with symbolic meanings). Cf. M. Griaule and G. Dieterlen, 1951. The combination of these signs serves to transcribe and fix speech in a manner decipherable for the initiate, from the writing and the knowledge which the writing conveys.

51. Cf. D. Olderegge's excellent survey article, 1966.

ecology providing an easy balance between resources and population gave most African civilizations and their cultural features the power to wax and wane geographically while always preserving their essence: their principles. From the point of view of internal equilibrium, there was no great risk. But external forces and the growing effects of progress made such fragility a handicap.

Conclusion

Linguistics is absolutely essential to the development of an African science of history. However, it will be able to make its contribution only if a great effort is undertaken. So far its contribution has been relatively slight and, in many instances, scientifically unsound. Research is under way. The precision of its methods has increased, and the area of its investigations has broadened considerably. In this context, we can expect the analysis of African languages to contribute in the near future to the clarification of important points of the history of the continent.

PLATE 10.1 *The serpent king stele* (Musée du Louvre)

PLATE 10.2 *The Récade dedicated to King Dakodonu, first sovereign of Danxome* (Nubia)

PLATE 10.3 *Awe-inspiring lion cub from Abomey Museum* (photo M. A. Glélé, Nubia)

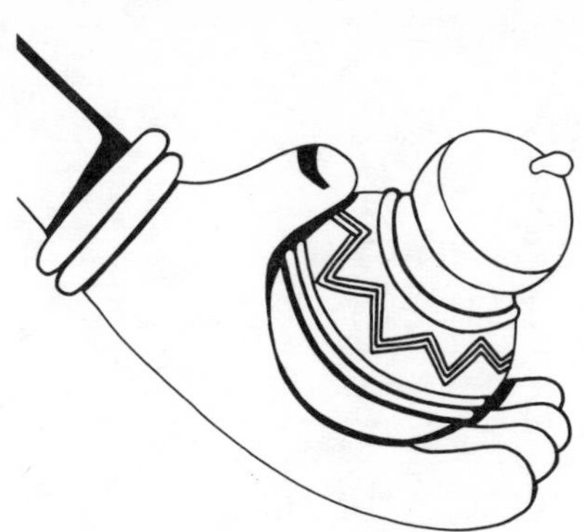

PLATE 10.4 *The Récade showing a gourd, symbol of power, from Abomey Museum* (Nubia)

PLATE 10.5 *First page of the first chapter of the* Koran *in Vai* (from T. Obenga, 1973, Présence Africaine)

PLATE 10.6 *Phonetic chart of Vai characters* (from T. Obenga, 1973, Présence Africaine)

a*	ga	la	ra	wa
é	gé	lé	ré	wé
ĕ	gĕ	lĕ	rĕ	wĕ
ī	gī	lī	rī	wī
ō	gō	lō	rō	wō
ŏ	gŏ	lŏ	rŏ	wŏ
ū	gū	lū	rū	wū
ba	ha	ma	sa	ya
bé	hé	mé	sé	yé
bĕ	hĕ	mĕ	sĕ	yĕ
bī	hī	mī	sī	yī
bō	hō	mō	sō	yō
bŏ	hŏ	mŏ	sŏ	yŏ
bū	hū	mū	sū	yū
da	ja	na	ta	za
dé	jé	né	té	zé
dĕ	jĕ	nĕ	tĕ	zĕ
dī	jī	nī	tī	zī
dō	jō	nō	tō	zō
dŏ	jŏ	nŏ	tŏ	zŏ
dū	jū	nū	tū	zū
fa	ka	pa	va	
fé	ké	pé	vé	
fĕ	kĕ	pĕ	vĕ	
fī	kī	pī	vī	
fō	kō	pō	vō	
fŏ	kŏ	pŏ	vŏ	
fū	kū	pū	vū	

cha	kpa	nda	nya	zha
ché	kpé	ndé	nyé	zhé
chĕ	kpĕ	ndĕ	nyĕ	zhĕ
chī	kpī	ndī	nyī	zhī
chō	kpō	ndō	nyō	zhō
chŏ	kpŏ	ndŏ	nyŏ	zhŏ
chū	kpū	ndū	nyū	zhū
dha	lba	nga	sha	*Miscellaneous.*
dhé	lbé	ngé	shé	faa
dhĕ	lbĕ	ngĕ	shĕ	hn
dhī	lbī	ngī	shī	kpna
dhō	lbō	ngō	shō	nwa
dhŏ	lbŏ	ngŏ	shŏ	nwo
dhū	lbū	ngū	shū	whew
gba	lda	nja	tha	ahn
gbé	ldé	njé	thé	*Punctuation and other Signs.*
gbĕ	ldĕ	njĕ	thĕ	bridge
gbī	ldī	njī	thī	comma
gbō	ldō	njō	thō	question
gbŏ	ldŏ	njŏ	thŏ	period
gbū	ldū	njū	thū	exclamation
hna	mba	nkpa	wha	accent
	mbé	nkpé	whé	detraction
hnĕ	mbĕ	nkpĕ	whĕ	nasal
hnī	mbī	nkpī	whī	continuation of sound
	mbō	nkpō	whō	
hnŏ	mbŏ	nkpŏ	whŏ	
hnū	mbū	nkpū	whū	

* These vowels have the sounds of — *a* as ah, *é* as in they, *è* as in net, *ı* as in pin, *ō* as in old, *ŏ* as in not, *ū* as in tube.

(We print this chart as received, but we suspect that the sound denoted by *ū* is really the *u* in « rule » — not that usually heard in « tube », which is a combination of *y* and *u*. — Ed.)

	ka	*kε*	*ke*	*ki*	*ku*	*ko*	*kɔ*
Vai (1849)							
(1962)							
Mende							
Loma							
Kpelle							
Bassa							
Bamum (1906)		*kεt*	*ket*				
(1916)							
Obεri Ɔkaimε							
Djuka							
Manding							
Wolof							
Fula *Dita*							
Fula (Ba)							
Bete			*keu*				

The Bagam and Guro scripts (no record available), the Yoruba 'holy' script and the Gola script (both undeciphered) are excluded from this chart.

PLATE 10.7 *Sample characters from the indigenous scripts* (from D. Dalby, 1970, 110–11, Frank Cass and Co. Ltd.)

a) *Pictographic system*

Mum word	Meaning	Signs collected in 1900 (Clapot)	Signs collected in 1907 (Göhering)
pè	kola nut		
fom	king		
ntab	house		
nyad	ox		

b) *Ideographic system*

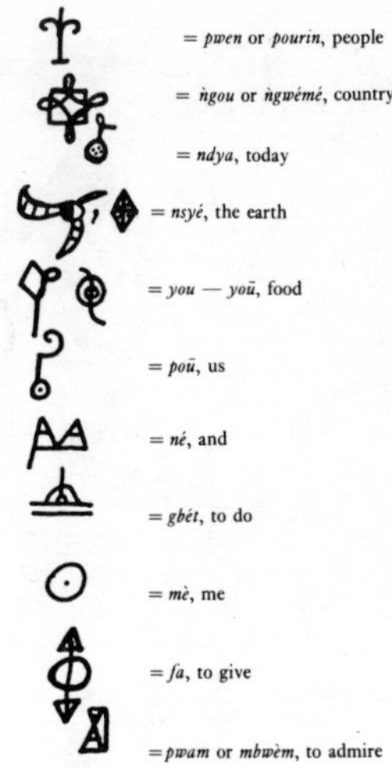

c) *Phonetic-syllabic system*

= syllable *ba*, from *iba* meaning: two

= *ben*, from *ben*: dance (a kind of —)

= *bé*, from *byét*: to circumsize, or *byé*: to hold

= *cha*, from *ncha*: fish

PLATE 10.8 *The Mum graphic system* (from T. Obenga, 1973, Présence Africaine)

PLATE 10.9 *The Egyptian and West African graphic systems* (from T. Obenga, 1973, Présence Africaine)

	Egyptian pictograms (about 4000 before our era)	*Nsibidi pictograms*[34]
A_{21}	man running, an arm outstretched inw = messenger	Dayrell$_{107}$, man running an arm outstretched Macgregor (p. 212), a messenger
F_{32}	mammal's stomach; *ḫ.t.* = stomach, body	Dayrell$_{127}$, symbol containing fish bones
I_1	lizard; *'ś ȝ* = numerous, rich	Talbot$_{51}$, lizard
I_{14}	woman or snake (*h f'w*); worm (*ddft*)	Macgregor (p. 212), snake; Dayrell$_{104}$, very long snake; *uruk —ikot*, snake in Efit and *shaw*, in Uyanga.
N_8	*wbn* : to rise	Talbot$_{35}$, sc sun shining, nant, *ūtinn* sun in Efik and in *dūawng*, in Uyanga.
N_{11}	lunar crescent; *i' h* = moon	Talbot$_{36}$, lunar crescent; *ebt* = moon, in Uyanga.

34. For the *nsibidi* signs, cf. especially: J. K. Macgregor, op. cit., p. 215, p. 217, p. 219: the signs are numbered from 1 to 98. E. Dayrell, op. cit., pl. LXV–LXVII: in total 363 signs: P. A. Talbot, op. cit., Appendix G: 'Nsibidi signs', pp. 448–461: 77 signs and 8 texts.

PLATE 10.10 *The Palette of Narmer* (from C. A. Diop, 1955, Présence Africaine)

Editorial note: theories on the 'races' and history of Africa

J. KI-ZERBO

The concept of race is one of the most difficult to define in scientific terms. If we agree with most scholars since Darwin that mankind is a single stock,[1] the theory of 'races' can only be developed scientifically within the context of evolution.

Raciation is part of the overall process of evolutionary differentiation. As J. Ruffié has pointed out, it requires two conditions: first, breeding isolation (often partial), which gradually produces a special genetic and morphological situation. Raciation thus arises from a difference of gene stock, caused either by genetic drift (that is, the random transmission of genes allows a given gene to be transmitted more often than another, unless of course the allele is more widespread), or by natural selection. The latter leads to adaptive differentiation, by which a group tends to preserve the genetic equipment that best adapts it to a given environment. In Africa both processes have clearly gone on. Genetic drift, which works most powerfully within small groups, will have operated within limited populations, which are in any case liable to undergo a social process of binary fission at times of territorial and succession disputes – and also because of the great expanses of virgin land available to them. The genetic inheritance of endogamous and forest-dwelling peoples will have been particularly affected by this process; while natural selection will have operated in environments as diverse as desert, dense forest, high plateaux and mangrove coasts. What it amounts to in biological terms is that the members of one 'race' share certain genetic factors which in another 'racial group' are replaced by their alleles, whilst in half-breeds both gene types exist together.

As was to be expected, 'races' were originally identified according to visible criteria, but deeper realities gradually came to be taken into account. Indeed, outward features and inward phenomena are not completely unrelated, for although the colour of the skin is determined by hereditary mechanisms which depend on certain genes, it is also affected by the environment. A positive correlation has been noted between stature and the highest temperature of the hottest month, and a negative correlation

1. For polycentric theories with their variants, see the works of G. Weidenreich and Coon and the disproofs of Roberts.

between height and humidity. Similarly, a narrow nose warms the air better in a colder climate and humidifies dry air. This is why the nasal index of peoples south of the Sahara shows a marked tendency to rise as one passes from the desert through the savannah to the forest. Although they have the same number of sweat glands as whites, they perspire more and this keeps their body and skin at a lower temperature.

There are therefore several stages in the scientific investigation of races.

The morphological approach

Reickstedt defines races as 'natural zoological groupings of forms belonging to the hominid family whose members display the same typical set of standard and hereditary characteristics from the morphological and behavioural points of view'.

A whole arsenal of observations and measurements now exists, ranging from data concerning skin colour and hair form or quantity of body hair to those concerning metrical and non-metrical features, or even including the anterior femoral flexure and the cusps and grooves of molars. Special attention has been given to the cephalic index because it relates to the part of the head which houses the brain. Dixon, for example, establishes various types on the basis of three indices combined in various ways, namely, the horizontal cephalic index, the vertical cephalic index and the nasal index. But out of the 27 possible combinations only 8 (those occurring most often) have been accepted as representative of fundamental types, the other 18 being considered to be mixtures. Morphological characteristics, however, are merely a more or less distorted version of the genetic stock. They are seldom all found combined in a perfect prototype; it is a matter, rather, of particularly striking features of the interaction between man and his environment – which is to say that they are much more acquired than innate.

This illustrates one of the most serious weaknesses of the morphological and the typological approach in which the exceptions are eventually found to be more important and more numerous than the rule. In addition, we should not overlook the academic disputes over the methods of measurement (how, when, and so on) which make it impossible to draw valid comparisons. Multivariate distance data and coefficients of racial resemblance 'format' and 'shape' data, the generalized distance of Nahala Novis – all these lend themselves to processing, but a race is a real biological entity which has to be examined as a living whole and not as a dissected specimen.

The demographic or population approach

Accordingly this method concentrates from the outset on group factors (gene pool or genome) which are less prone to variation than the genetic structure of individuals in varying circumstances. Indeed, it is the frequency of characteristics observed in a race, rather than the characteristics themselves which are significant for the identification of a race. Now that the morphological method has been practically abandoned,[2] serological or genetic factors can be classified according to more objective rules. According to Landman, a race is 'a group of human beings who (except in a few cases) display more genotypical similarities, and also very often more phenotypic similarities, to one another than to members of other groups'. Alexseev also follows a demographic approach to the question of race using purely geographical names (north Europeans, southern Africans, and so on). Schwidejzky and Boyd have emphasized genetic systematics: distribution of blood groups A, B and O, combinations of the Rhesus factor, the gene of the saliva secretion, and so on.

Blood-group specialists also take anatomy into account, but at the molecular level. They are concerned with describing the minute structure of those human cells whose antigen structure and enzyme systems are differentiated, the most convenient tissue for this purpose being the blood. Blood markers have made possible a historic qualitative advance in the scientific identification of human groups. They have decisive advantages over morphological criteria, starting with the fact that they are almost always monometric, that is, their presence depends on a single gene, whereas the cephalic index, for instance, is the product of a number of factors that are not easy to pinpoint.[3]

Again, while morphological criteria are translated into figures which lead up to arbitrary and ill-defined distinctions, as for instance between the typical brachycephal and the typical dolichocephal, with blood markers it is a case of one thing or the other. A person is either Group A or not, Rh-positive or Rh-negative, and so on. Furthermore blood factors are almost completely unaffected by environmental influences, the haemotype being permanently fixed at the time of the formation of the zygote. Hence blood markers are free from the subjectivism of morphological typing: individuals are described in terms of genotypes, and populations in terms of genotype frequencies. The high degree of precision of these factors makes up for the fact that they represent only a small part of the mass of genes that go to make up a genome. This has made possible the compilation of an atlas of the traditional 'races'.

Three categories of blood factors have been established. Some, such as the blood-groups in the ABO system, occur in all the traditional races without exception, and hence no doubt antedate hominization. Others, such as the variants in the Rh system, are omnipresent but preponderate in certain 'races': thus the r chromosome is mainly found in whites, while the Ro chromosome (the so-called 'African chromosome') has a particularly high frequency of occurrence in blacks south of the Sahara. These are therefore certainly systems dating from the time when man began to move into a variety of ecological niches. Another category of variants indicates

2. Cf. K. Wiercinsky, 1965.
3. Cf. J. Ruffié, 1977a.

even clearer racial demarcation lines, as for instance the Sutter and Henshaw factors, found almost only in blacks, and the Kell antigen, found mainly in whites. Though never completely exclusive, they have been termed 'racial markers'. Lastly, some factors are very localized geographically, as for instance haemoglobin C among the peoples of the Volta plateau.

Though blood factors have no direct value as adaptations, they are not unrelated to the infective and parasitic aspects of the environment: the latter may operate selectively on blood factors with survival value, thus leading, for instance, to the presence of characteristic haemoglobins. An example is the S haemoglobins, associated with the presence of sickle cells or drepanocytes among the red corpuscles, which have been detected in the blood of blacks in Africa and Asia. Haemoglobin S (Hb S), which is dangerous only in the case of homozygotes, represents an adaptation to the presence of *Plasmodium falciparum,* the malaria parasite.

The study of blood-groups over wide areas makes it possible to construct isogenic curves showing the geographical distribution of blood factors throughout the world. Together with the computation of genetic chronology, it gives us some idea of the inter-relationships between different populations; and the direction of the gene flows makes it possible to reconstruct the earlier stages in their evolution.

But the blood-group and population method, despite its remarkable achievements, comes up against difficulties. For one thing, its parameters are multiplying at a tremendous rate, and are already producing results which are odd to the point of being regarded by some as aberrant. Thus L. L. Cavalli-Sforza's phylogenic tree of the peoples of the world departs from the anthropometric classification. The latter puts African Pygmies and San on the same anthropometric branch as the aborigines of Australia and New Guinea, whereas on the phylogenic tree Pygmies and San are closer to the French and English, and Australian aborigines are closer to the Japanese and Chinese.[4] In other words, anthropometric characteristics are more affected by the climate than genes are, so that morphological affinities are more a matter of similar environments than of similar heredities. The work of R. C. Lewontin, based on blood-group research, shows that for the world as a whole over 85 per cent of variations occur *within* nations. There is only a 7 per cent variation between nations belonging to the same traditional race, and only 7 per cent between the traditional races. In short, there is more difference between individuals in the same racial group than there is between 'races'.

This is why more and more scientists are adopting the radical position of

4. Quoted by J. Ruffié, 1977a, p. 385. Again, on the basis of certain genetic characters (the Fy^a antigen in the Duffy system, the Ro allele, etc.), the percentage of white admixture in American blacks resulting from the crossbreeding that goes on in the United States is put at 25 to 30 per cent. Some scientists have concluded from this that what we have here is a new racial group, somewhat hastily labelled 'North American coloured'.

denying the existence of race altogether. According to J. Ruffié, in the early days of mankind small groups of individuals, living in very different, widely separated ecological areas, became differentiated in response to very powerful selective pressures – their technical resources being extremely limited – and gave rise to the variants *Homo erectus, Homo neanderthalensis* and the earliest *Homo sapiens*. The facies, for instance, which is the part of the body most exposed to specific environments, evolved differentially; black pigmentation in the skin developed in tropical regions, and so on. But this differentiating tendency was soon halted, and remained embryonic. Man everywhere began to adapt himself to his environment not morphologically but culturally (that is, in clothing, habitat, food, and so on). Man born in the tropics – a hot climate – evolved for a long time as *Australopithecus*, and *Homo habilis* and even *Homo erectus*. 'It was only during the second ice age, thanks to his efficient control of fire, that *Homo erectus* opted to live in cold climates. The human species is moving from polytypic to monotypic, and this process of racial standardization seems to be irreversible. The whole of mankind must be regarded nowadays as a single pool of intercommunicating genes.'[5]

In 1952, Livingstone published his famous article on 'The non-existence of human races'. In view of the enormous complexity and therefore the inconsistency of the criteria adopted for the description of races, he recommended that the Linnean classification system should be abandoned and suggested a 'genealogical tree' instead. In areas which are not isolated, the frequency of certain traits or genes changes gradually in various directions, and the differences between two populations are proportional to the physical distance between them, following a kind of geographical gradient (cline). By relating each distinctive trait to the selection and adaptation factors that may have contributed to its development, we find frequency rates apparently linked far more closely to technological, cultural and other factors which do not at all coincide with the distribution map of 'races'.[6] Whenever a different criterion is adopted (colour of the skin, cephalic index, nasal index, genetic characteristics, and so on), a different map is obtained. That is why some scientists have come to the conclusion that 'the whole theory of races is unconvincing and can be regarded as mythical'.

'In the light of the most recent advances in human genetics, no biologist nowadays any longer admits the existence of races within the human species.'[7] Biologically speaking, skin colour is a negligible element in relation to the genome as a whole. Bentley Glass considers that the white race differs from the black by no more than six pairs of genes. In terms of numbers of genes there are often greater variations than this among whites, and among blacks likewise. On the strength of this, Unesco, having held a

5. E. Mayr, quoted by J. Ruffié, 1977a, p. 115.
6. Cf. M. F. A. Montagu, 1952.
7. J. Ruffié, 1977a, p. 116.

conference of international experts, issued a declaration to the effect that 'race is not so much a biological phenomenon as a social myth'.[8] The truth of this is demonstrated by the fact that in South Africa a Japanese is regarded as an 'honorary white' and a Chinese as 'coloured'.

Hiernaux compares mankind to a network of genetic territories, of collective genomes forming peoples that resemble each other in varying degrees, the qualitative distance of which is expressed by a quantitative estimate (numerical taxonomy). The boundaries of such territories, as defined on the basis of climatic gradient, fluctuate, in fact, with all the changes which affect the visible features (phenotypes) and the serological data (genotypes) of communities.

This bears out Darwin's brilliant intuition that any 'race' seems, in the last analysis, to be identified with an endless process similar to those observed in fluid dynamics, and all peoples have been and are becoming hybridized. In fact, whenever one people come together with another the result can be analysed in scientific terms as a genic migration, and a gene flow affects the biological capital of both.

But even if this was a more scientific approach, even if these shifting genetic territories were really accepted by the communities concerned, could we say that 'racial' feelings would thereby be eradicated? For their visible and tangible differences would still be in evidence in the form of phenotypical features.

Ever since the assertion by Nazis – and by other pseudo-intellectuals as well as Hitler – that Mediterranean man represents an intermediate level between the Aryan, 'Prometheus of Mankind', and the black, 'half ape by descent', the racial myth dies hard. Impenitent morphologists still feebly foster the wretched idea.[9] Linnaeus, writing in the eighteenth century, subdivided the human species into six races, American, European, African, Asiatic, savage and monstrous: we may be sure that racialists fall into one or other of the last two categories!

From all these theories, theses and hypotheses let us therefore single out for closer scrutiny the dynamic character of 'racial' phenomena, bearing in mind that we are dealing with slow and complex processes of change occurring at many different levels among which variations in the colour of the skin – even if measured by an electro-spectrophotometer – and the shape of the nose rank so low as to be almost negligible. Two interacting factors in 'racial' dynamics deserve special attention, namely, the genetic heritage which can be regarded as a gigantic biological data bank in action, and the

8. Four declarations on the racial question, Unesco, Paris, 1969.

9. J. Ruffié quotes a French dictionary of medicine and biology which in 1972 still upheld the concept of race, stating that there are three main groups, white, black and yellow, on the basis of morphological, anatomical, sociological (and also psychological) criteria. At the turn of the century Charles Seignobos wrote in *Histoire de la civilisation:* 'The men that people the earth also differ in language, intelligence and feelings. These differences make it possible to subdivide the earth's inhabitants into a number of groups known as "races".'

environment in the broadest sense of the term since in this context it starts with the foetal environment.

The changes resulting from the interaction of these two basic factors may occur either in the form of selection and genic migration (crossbreeding) which is difficult to verify, or in the form of genetic drift or gene mutation which is a matter of chance. In short, it is the entire history of a population that accounts for the different aspects of its present racial facies, including group attitudes, religion and dietary, clothing and other customs.

In this context what can we say about race where the African continent is concerned? A historical analysis of the subject is difficult since human fossils are not well preserved owing to the humidity and the acidity of African soils. It can be said, however, that contrary to the European theories which sought to explain the peopling of Africa by migrations from Asia,[10] the population of Africa is for the most part indigenous. Several writers think that the colour of the skin of the earliest inhabitants of the continent living in tropical latitudes must have been dark (Brace, 1964), since the colour black is a natural protection against harmful rays, and against ultra-violet rays in particular. The pale skin and light-coloured eyes of the peoples of the north are held to be secondary characteristics caused by mutation or selective pressure (Cole, 1965).

Today, although we cannot draw hard and fast boundaries, we can identify two major 'racial' groups on the African continent living on either side of the Sahara. In the north there is the Arab-Berber group which derives its genetic heritage from the 'Mediterranean' peoples (Libyans, Semites, Phoenicians, Assyrians, Greeks, Romans, Turks, etc.), and in the south there is the Negro group. A point to note is that climatic changes which have sometimes obliterated the desert have resulted in much mixing population groups over thousands of years.

Nei Masatoshi and A. R. Roycoudhury carried out a study[11] of the genetic differences within and between the Caucasoid and Mongoloid groups, using several dozen blood markers. They used correlation coefficients to establish the approximate dates when these peoples diverged and came into being as distinct groups. The negroid grouping seems to have become distinct 120 000 years ago, whilst the Mongoloids and Caucasoids only separated 55 000 years ago. According to J. Ruffié, 'this chronology fits in with the greater part of our basic-group data'.[12] From that period onward, much interbreeding took place on the African continent.

Attempts have even been made to bring out the biological distances between populations by statistical analysis of their main components. Jacquard set out to do this, using five blood-group systems comprising

10. The Hamitic theory (Seligman *et al.*), which can be partly attributed to the proponents' ignorance of certain facts and partly to their desire to justify the colonial system, is the most racialist of these pseudo-scientific explanations.

11. N. Masatoshi and A. R. Roy Coudhury, 1974, 26, 421.

12. J. Ruffié, 1977a, p. 399.

eighteen factors, for twenty-seven populations extending from the Mediterranean region to south of the Sahara.[13] He obtained three main groups comprising four aggregates: one to the north, the caucasoids, consisting of Europeans, the Regueibat, the Saudi Arabs and the Kel Kummer Tuaregs; a southern aggregate consisting of the Negro groups of Agades; and intermediate aggregates including some Bororo Fulani, the Aïr and Tassili Tuaregs, the Ethiopians, and so on, but also the Harratin, who are traditionally regarded as blacks. It would therefore be a mistake to take this subdivision as supporting the traditional classification into races, for quite apart from what has been said above, the general shape of the subdivision depends on the amount of data taken into account: if it is very small, the points may be all clustered together.

As regards the men living south of the Sahara, it should be noted that the original name given them by Linnaeus was *Homo afer* (African). They were then called 'Negroes', and later still 'blacks', and sometimes the broader term 'negroid' was used to include all persons resembling the blacks who are found on the fringes of the continent or on other continents. Today, except for a few dissenting voices, the large majority of scholars agree on the basic genetic unity of peoples south of the Sahara. According to Boyd, the author of the genetic classification of human races, there exists only one negroid group, which spreads over the whole of the sub-Saharan part of the continent, and is also found in Ethiopia, and it differs significantly from all the other major groupings. Research by Hiernaux has yielded remarkably convincing evidence to support this proposition. Without denying that variations are apparent at local levels, he has produced the findings of an analysis of 5050 distances between 101 populations to show the uniformity of the peoples of the sub-Saharan hyperspace which embraces the 'Sudanese' as well as the 'Bantu', the inhabitants of coastal regions and those of the Sahel, the 'Khoisan', Pygmies, Nilotic, Fulani and various minor groups such as those akin to the 'Ethiopians'. On the other hand, he also shows the great genetic distance that separates 'Asian blacks' from African blacks.

Even in the field of linguistics, which has nothing to do with 'race' but which has been used in racist theories to invent a language hierarchy reflecting the so-called 'racial' hierarchy, with the 'pure Negroes' on the bottom rung of the ladder, new systems of classification are shedding more and more light on the basic unity of African languages.

Somatic variations can be explained scientifically by the causes of the changes discussed above. In particular biotopes may give rise at one time to amalgamations of more composite populations (Nile valley), and at other times to pockets of peoples which develop relatively atypical characteristics to be found in mountainous country, forests, marshlands, and so on. Lastly, history accounts for other anomalies which have resulted from invasions and migrations, particularly in outlying areas. The biological influence of the

13. A. Jacquard, 1974.

Arabian peninsula on the Horn of Africa is also evident in the peoples of that region, such as the Somali, Galla and Ethiopians, but also, no doubt, in the Teda, Fulani, Tukulor, Songhay, Hausa, and so on. I have seen Marka (Upper Volta) with very typically 'semitic' profiles.

To sum up, the remarkable variety of African phenotypes is a sign that this continent has been evolving over a particularly long period. Such prehistoric fossil remains as are available indicate that the type found south of the Sahara settled over a very vast area stretching from South Africa as far as the northern part of the Sahara, the Sudan region having apparently been at the crossroads of these population movements.

It is true that the history of Africa is not a history of 'races'. But the pseudo-scientific myth of the superiority of certain races has all too often been misused to justify a certain historical record. Even today a half-breed is considered to be a white in Brazil and a black in the United States of America. The science of anthropology, which has already amply demonstrated that there is no connection between race and the degree of intelligence, has found on the other hand that such a connection does sometimes exist between race and social class. One may well ask when the historical primacy of culture over biology, which has been evident since Man emerged, will finally prevail in thinking on this subject.

Glossary to Chapter 10

Allele Either of a pair of genes.

Selection Differential reproduction of genotypes from one generation to another.

Genic migration Crossing-over of reproducing individuals from their original population to an adopted population (cross). Crossbreeding, regarded by racialists as deleterious for the superior race, in fact in this context represents an enrichment of the human gene pool. It is thus a positive factor in biological terms – though it may give rise to social problems.

Genetic drift A change in the composition of the genetic heritage which occurs by chance in a small and isolated human group, resulting in a drop in gene frequency or the disappearance of an allele.

Mutation The appearance of a change in a hereditary characteristic through the modification of one or more genes.

Studies undertaken at Unesco's request as a part of the General History of Africa project:

J. Hiernaux, *Rapport sur le concept de race*, Paris, 1974.
J. P. Rightmire, *Comments on Race and Population History in Africa*, New York, 1974.
E. Strouhal, *Problems of Study of Human Races*, Prague, 1976.

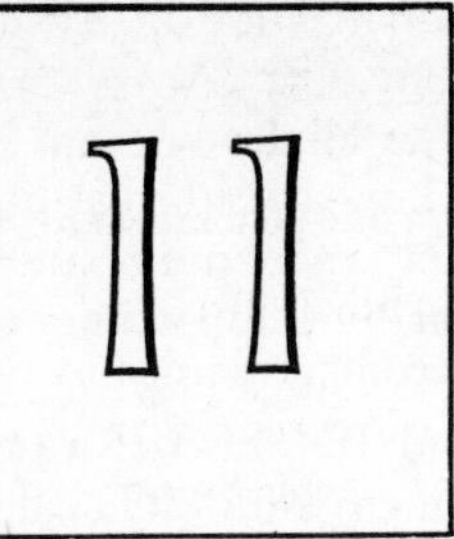

Migrations and ethnic and linguistic differentiations

D. OLDEROGGE

Historians were long convinced that the peoples of Africa had never had any history of their own, nor any evolution that was peculiarly theirs. Everything in the nature of a cultural achievement was thought to have been brought to them from elsewhere, by waves of immigrants coming from Asia. Such convictions are reflected in the works of many nineteenth-century European scholars. They were systematized and crystallized in the form of doctrine in the works of German ethnographers and linguists writing at that period. At that time, Germany was the main centre of Africanist studies. Shortly after Africa had been divided up by the great colonial and imperialist powers, works describing the life and customs of the peoples of the colonized countries began to make their appearance in England, France and Germany. It was in Germany that the potential of the scientific study of the African languages was first recognized. The year 1907 saw the establishment in Hamburg of the Colonial Institute, which subsequently became a great centre of scientific research and was responsible for the publication of the most important theoretical works of the German school of African studies. Germany was far in advance of the other colonial powers in this field, for in England it was not until 1917 that the School of Oriental Studies began to teach African languages, whilst in France, at that time, the Ecole des Langues Orientales Vivantes paid little attention to them. It was only in 1947 that the School of Oriental Studies in London was renamed the School of Oriental and African Studies. In France, too, the systematic teaching of these languages was not introduced until slightly later.

The theories of the German school and recent discoveries

All this explains why Germany played a predominant role in research into the history, ethnography and languages of Africa in the period immediately preceding the First World War and also why work which appeared in England, France and Belgium was based on the theories of German scholars. Thus western European ethnographers continued to maintain, at the beginning of the twentieth century, the view propagated by German scholars that the peoples of Africa had never had a history of their own, and these views provided linguists with a basis for what is known as the Hamitic theory, according to which the development of civilization in Africa was influenced by the Hamitic peoples who came from Asia.

An examination of these thoughts shows that they all derive from Hegel, who divided the peoples of the world into two kinds: historical peoples, who had contributed to the development of mankind, and non-historical peoples, who had taken no part in the spiritual development of the world.

According to Hegel, there was no historical evolution in Africa proper. The destinies of the northern fringes of the continent could be said to be linked to those of Europe. Carthage, being a Phoenician colony, he considered formed part of Asia and he saw nothing of the African spirit in Egypt. Hegel's ideas exercised a considerable influence over almost all the scientific research done on Africa in the nineteenth century, in particular on the first attempt at a history of the peoples of Africa by Schwarz, who compares the history of the races of Europe to the events of a fine sunny day and that of Africa to a heavy dream which the sleeper, on awakening, soon forgets.

It was in Asia, Hegel said, that the light of the spirit dawned and the history of the world began. This was considered to be beyond dispute, and European scholars regarded Asia as the cradle of mankind from which emerged all the peoples who invaded Europe and Africa. It is interesting to note that the English ethnographer Stow thought it quite certain that the oldest inhabitants of Africa – the San – came from Asia in two separate migratory waves: the first consisting of rock painters, the second of rock engravers, who took another, quite different route. They were said to have crossed the Red Sea by the Bab el-Mandeb Strait and then traversed the equatorial forests, reaching the southernmost tip of the continent.

The fullest account of the thesis propounded by the German school, fortified by its historical and cultural basis, regarding the progressive occupation of the African continent by successive waves of immigrants is to be found in the works of the German geographer and traveller, Fr. Stuhlmann. In fact, at the end of the nineteenth and the beginning of the twentieth century, a vigorous offensive was launched against the doctrine of evolution, which constituted the theoretical basis of the works of R. Taylor, L. H. Morgan, Lubbock, and others. The cultural and historical school of thought repudiated the theory of a uniform, overall development of mankind and advanced a diametrically opposed theory, postulating the existence of different cycles of civilization, differentiated by intrinsic elements derived from a mainly material culture. According to these writers, the spread of cultural achievements was due mainly to migrations. The first to put forward this view was the German scholar Leo Frobenius, and Ankermann subsequently described the progress of the cycles of civilization across Africa. But it was Stuhlmann who gave the most detailed account of the development of African cultures. He maintained that the original population of Africa consisted of small people – the Pygmies and the San – possessing virtually no elements of culture. Then arrived in migratory waves from south-east Asia dark-skinned, fuzzy-haired Negro peoples who spread all over the Sudanese savannah and penetrated into the equatorial forest, bringing with them the beginnings of agriculture, the cultivation of bananas and root-crops, the use of wooden implements and bows and arrows, and the building of round and square huts. These people spoke isolating languages. They would have been followed by waves of proto-Hamites, also from Asia, but in this case from regions further north than those which were the homeland of the Negroes. The newcomers spoke agglutinative languages with noun classes and they taught the indigenous peoples of Africa the use of the hoe in agriculture, the cultivation of sorghum and other cereals, the rearing of small-horned cattle, and so on. The crossbreeding of the proto-Hamites with the Negro peoples gave birth to the Bantu peoples. They were followed by invasions of waves of fair-skinned Hamites, coming into Africa, some through the Suez isthmus and some across the Bab el-Mandeb Strait. They were said to have been the ancestors of the Fulani, Hausa, Masai, Bari, Galla and Somali peoples, and also of the Khoi-Khoi. The latest arrivals brought further elements of culture to Africa, large-horned cattle, spears, many uses of leather, shields, and so on. These fair-skinned Hamites, Stuhlmann maintained, came originally from the steppes of western Asia. They were followed by a wave of Semitic peoples, who provided the basis for the development of the culture of ancient Egypt. They brought with them the cultivation of cereals, the use of the plough and of bronze. They were followed, in Egypt, by the arrival of the Hyksos and the Hebrews and, in the Ethiopian highlands, by that of the Habashat and the Mehri. The last to come were the Arabs, in the seventh century of our era. All these peoples brought with them to Africa new elements of civilization that were quite unknown before their arrival. Stuhlmann's work was published in Hamburg in 1910, not long before the First World War, but his ideas on the gradual building-up of African civilization by alien races were developed later by other ethnographers, such as Spannus and Lushan in Germany, Seligman in England, and Honea in Austria.

In linguistics, the Hamitic theory began to emerge parallel with the theories of the cultural-historic school. The initiator of this theory, Meinhof, held that the ancestors of the present-day San were the oldest autochthones of Africa, and that they were a race quite distinct from all others, and speaking languages which had click consonants, while the Negroes – considered to be autochthonous in the equatorial and Sudanic zones – spoke tonal and isolating languages with monosyllabic roots. Subsequently Hamitic peoples entered the Sudan from Arabia by way of North Africa. These newcomers spoke inflected languages; they engaged in cattle-breeding and, from the cultural point of view, were on a much higher level than the Negroes. Some of the Hamitic invaders, however, traversed the savannahs of East Africa and interbred with the indigenous population to produce the Bantu-speaking peoples.

In short, this pattern can be reduced to a film in four sequences. At the outset, there were the click languages and these were followed by the highly rudimentary isolating languages spoken by the Sudanic Negroes. The mixture of these languages with the Hamitic languages produced the Bantu group of languages of the superior agglutinative type. Finally, the languages spoken by the Hamitic conquerors introduced the inflected languages which were eminently superior. The Hamitic theory was upheld by many linguists and spread from Germany throughout western Europe and beyond.

In the period between the two world wars, however, all these theories collapsed. The first blow they suffered came from the discovery of the Australopithecines in 1924 in South Africa. Other discoveries followed and are still constantly being made, not only in the southern part of Africa, but also in North Africa and, more particularly, towards the east, in Tanzania, Kenya and Ethiopia. All these discoveries combined to show, without any possibility of error, that the development of man in all his racial variety took place in Africa. Thus, any theories according to which Africa was populated by consecutive waves of immigrants are untenable. As the celebrated palaeoanthropologist, Arambourg, so rightly points out, Africa is the only continent where there is evidence, in unbroken chronological sequence, of all the stages in the development of man. In fact, specimens of the Australopithecine age, pithecanthropoid man, Neanderthal man and *Homo sapiens* succeeded one another, each with their implements, from the most distant eras right through to the Neolithic age. This bears out Darwin's theory that the remote ancestors of man lived on the African continent. Furthermore, these discoveries proved that it would be totally wrong to deny their endogenous cultural development. In this respect, the rock paintings and petroglyphs in the Atlas mountains, in southern Africa and in the Sahara provide striking evidence with far-reaching implications.

There is no longer the faintest shadow of doubt about the great depth of the cultural archaeological evidence, since relative chronology (based on the form and treatment of objects and their stratigraphical position) has now been supplemented by absolute dating based on such scientific methods as carbon-14 and potassium-argon. The picture of the pattern of the cultural evolution of the African peoples has been completely transformed. For instance, it has been found that the Neolithic era in Saharan and Sahelian latitudes dates back much further than had been thought. This discovery completely alters the relationship between cultural development in Africa and in the Mediterranean world and, in particular, the Near East.

The remains discovered in Tassili N'Ajjer and also at Tadrart-Acacus in the borderland between Algeria and Libya are quite conclusive. Examination of hearths and ceramics discovered here shows that the people were already using pottery from 8000 before our era onwards. At Acacus, a negroid-type skeleton bearing traces of skin clothing was discovered. The materials examined date to 9000 before our era. A similar date applies to remains, discovered in the Ahaggar mountains, which were subjected to analysis in three separate laboratories. From these findings we may conclude that the Neolithic age in Tassili N'Ajjer and Ennedi is apparently older than the Neolithic age in the countries of the Maghrib and is contemporary with that of southern Europe and Cyrenaica.

Of particular significance are the results of research done on organic remains found in Neolithic camps in Lower Nubia. From the results obtained it has been possible to draw the conclusion that people already gathered and prepared grain from wild cereals in the thirteenth millennium before our era, radio-carbon tests on the remains found in the Ballana district having indicated the date 12 050 ± 280. The same method of examination applied to remains from the Tuskha region gives the date 12 550 ± 490. This proves that the gathering of grain from wild cereals was practised in the Nile valley 4000 years earlier than in the Near East.

According to a firmly entrenched historical tradition any account of the history of Africa should start with Egypt. Today, however, there are good grounds for revising this view. The American Egyptologist Breasted, who wrote in the early years of this century, described the area made up of Egypt, Palestine and Mesopotamia as the Fertile Crescent and indeed this zone does form a kind of crescent in which the Pharaonic civilization took shape and the city-states of Sumer and Akkad developed. But these date back only to the sixth or fifth millennium before our era whereas, much earlier than that, the existence of climatic conditions suitable to the development of stock-raising and rudimentary agriculture throughout the whole of the area lying between the valley of the Indus and the Atlantic Ocean had favoured the emergence of a primitive form of class society and state.

Thus, the Fertile Crescent represents only a terminal development in a large region teeming with life where, little by little, men grew familiar with wild cereals and began to cultivate them, and also began to domesticate large-horned cattle, sheep and goats. Proof of all this is furnished by the study of rock paintings in the Sahara and by radio-carbon dating, together with the analysis of fossil pollens, etc. We may expect that some chronological schema may subsequently be made more precise. However, the theory about the peopling of Africa from Asia is already completely discredited. Instead, Africa must be recognized as the centre from which men and techniques were disseminated in one of the key periods in the development of mankind (the Early Stone Age). In later eras we find evidence of a reversal of this trend with migratory currents flowing back to the continent of Africa.

Anthropological and linguistic problems

Comparison of the information furnished by the anthropological, linguistic and cultural research done on the ancient history of Africa shows that anthropology certainly provides the most important and the most reliable data. Anthropological characteristics persist for a very long time, whereas languages undergo rapid changes, sometimes in the course of a few generations, as we see when a people emigrates to another linguistic area or when it is invaded by conquerors speaking a different language. So we see that the black population of North America has retained its original anthropological type unchanged by climatic and geographical conditions very different from those in their continent of origin but that its language and culture do not now differ from those of the white population of the United States. The only traces of its ancient African cultural and spiritual background remain in songs, music, dances and religious beliefs. A parallel case is that of the Siddi descended from the Africans who were taken to India centuries ago from the east coast of Africa. As late as at the beginning of the nineteenth century these people still retained their own language, but they now speak the languages of the Hindu people amongst whom they live – Gujarati, Urdu and others – so that all that remains to indicate their African origin is their physical type.

In both these cases, the language the Africans took with them to a foreign land was lost in the course of a generation or two. The history of the languages spoken by the aboriginal inhabitants of North Africa may also be cited.

After the conquest of the countries of the Maghrib by the Arabs and more particularly after the invasion by Arab tribes in the eleventh century, the population of the countries of North Africa became Arab so far as language and civilization are concerned. Their original languages survive only in parts of Morocco, and in Kabylia, Jebel Nefusa and the oases. According to the anthropologists, however, the main characteristics of the original physical type have remained unchanged, which shows that anthropological features, while subject to the influence of the biotope on the physical character, are more stable than language or culture. It may be stated on the data at present available that, on the whole, the distribution of modern racial types throughout Africa reproduced the ancient pattern of the major anthropological groups which are sometimes rather hastily termed 'races'. The various types of the Mediterranean race have been represented in North Africa since a very distant era. East Africa was inhabited by peoples of an Ethiopoid type, as confirmed by the finds of palaeoanthropologists in Kenya, and the whole of the extreme southern part of the continent by San groups. The tropical and equatorial forests formerly occupied a much larger area than at present and it was probably there that the Pygmies appeared. They were a separate race whose physical type developed in the special environment of an extremely humid climate and the virtual absence of light in the forest. The negroid race, called Sudanic or 'Congolese', developed to meet the conditions of tropical latitudes, in West Africa in particular. Probably because the acidity of tropical soils is not favourable to the preservation of fossils, few skeletal remains have been found for identification and dating. None the less, after the first discoveries made during the excavations at Asselar, negroid-type skeletons of various, sometimes extremely ancient, periods have been found not only in the Sahara, but also in southern Nigeria, which probably indicates that it was here that this particular human type evolved. The problem of the early peopling of the Sahara has been keenly disputed. But it is quite clear from a study of the rock paintings that a black population predominated in this area, although other types can also be detected, such as the groups with Afro-Mediterranean features which were also early inhabitants. In Egypt, documents and monuments dating back to the Old Kingdom refer to Temehu Libyan peoples with fair skin and blue eyes and also to darker-skinned Tehenu peoples. Greek historical sources, too, speak of fair-skinned Ethiopians as well as of darker-skinned more southerly Ethiopians. It seems therefore that the ancient population of Libya was made up of different races. Thus we find one Roman author saying that 'some of the Libyans resemble Ethiopians, whilst others are of Cretan stock'.[1] The ethnical composition of the population of the Nile valley seems to have been very complex. As the Sahara dried up, its peoples retreated towards the humidity of the valley. The Ethiopoid and the Afro-Mediterranean groups mingled with Negro groups of the Sudanic type. The same kind of intermingling probably took place in all the fluvio-lacustrine basins adjoining the desert, such as the lower Senegal, the middle Niger and Lake Chad. Since, as has already been stressed, the anthropological profile displays remarkable constancy, often over many thousands of years, it might not be entirely wrong to project some of the main features of the present-day ethnic pattern backwards into prehistory. In any event, a race is formed from the interaction of a great variety of factors progressively creating different inherited characteristics but also transmitting these different characteristics through heredity. These characteristics derive from the need of a people to adapt itself to its environment: to the conditions of sunlight, temperature, vegetation cover, humidity, and so on.

As a general rule – which is naturally subject to many exceptions – anthropologists suppose that the forest African is rather small in stature and light-skinned, whereas the African of the savannah and the Sahel is taller, lean and slim, and darker-skinned. However, things should never be viewed from only one angle, since many factors are at work simultaneously. For instance, the migration of groups bearing different genetic heritages immediately brought two possible sources of mutation into play: the first was the change of biotope, and the second the meeting of different groups,

1. *Scriptores Physiognomici*, ed. R. Foerster, 1893, Vol. I, 389.

with the possibility of crossbreeding. Whenever a remarkable somatic resemblance is observed between two ethnic groups that are very remote from each other in space, such as that existing between the Dinka along the upper reaches of the Nile and the Wolof of Senegal who look alike because they are both dark-skinned and tall, the fact that they live at the same latitude may provide the clue to a perfectly adequate explanation. However, the combination of factors brought into play by the actual march of history should always be borne in mind.[2] In this regard, the highly controversial case of the Pygmies and the San deserves to be studied in greater detail.

In the past, it was assumed that there was a racial link between the Pygmies of Africa and those of southern Asia, but that theory now appears to have been discarded.

There seems to be every reason for believing that these peoples are the outcome of the adaptation of a certain physical type to its environment and that this process took place over a very long period of isolation. At the present time, Pygmies are to be found in the forests of Cameroon, Gabon, some parts of the Central African Republic, Zaïre and Rwanda. It seems certain, however, that in the past they inhabited a much larger area. The oral traditions of some of the peoples of western Africa contain references to groups of dwarfs who lived in the forest before the arrival of people of taller stature.

The legends of some peoples of western Europe speak of gnomes versed in the working of metals and living in the mountains. African traditions about dwarfish peoples are, however, to be taken more seriously in view of the fact that we possess historical evidence indicating the existence in the past of Pygmies in regions where no trace of them can be found today.

The earliest mention of Pygmies is found in Egypt in inscriptions dating from the sixth dynasty of the Old Kingdom. Inscribed on the walls of the tomb of Herkhuf[3] at Aswan is the text of a letter from the Pharaoh Pepi II in which the young king thanks him for bringing him, as a present, a dwarf named Deng, a word found in the modern languages of Ethiopia – for instance, in Amharic and its various dialects, and also in the languages Tigrinya, Galla, Kambatta and others in the forms *denk, dank, dinki, donku, dinka*.[4] The letter states that a similar dwarf had been brought a hundred years earlier to the Pharaoh Isesi, that is to say, during the fifth dynasty. In this connection it is worth recalling the report of an English traveller who spoke of the presence of dwarfs called *doko* in some regions of southern Ethiopia. There is thus evidence that, in the past, there were dwarfs living in what is now the Republic of the Sudan and in present-day Ethiopia.

The Pygmies living in the equatorial forest were gradually supplanted by in-coming peoples of tall stature speaking Bantu languages. The Pygmies were driven into the densest and most distant parts of the forests of

2. Cf. J. Hiernaux, 1970, Vol. I, pp. 53 and 55.
3. The exact transliteration of this name is *Hrw-hwif* (R. Herzog, 1938, p. 93).
4. W. Leslau, 1963, p. 57.

the Ituri and the Uele, as recounted in the Nsong-a-Lianja, the epic cycle of the Mongo dealing with the peopling of the valley of the Zaïre. Similar legends exist also amongst other Bantu-speaking peoples. Thus the isolated groups of Pygmies which now exist can be considered as the surviving enclaves that prove the existence of a more extensive population which once inhabited the equatorial and tropical forests of Africa.

The San are another very specific group living in the continent of Africa. They are of small stature, with copper-coloured or yellowish skin, and their hair grows in tufts. In anthropological studies, they are still put together with the Khoi-Khoi in a 'Khoisan race'. This no doubt comes by extrapolation from the linguistic classification which places the languages of the San and the Khoi-Khoi in a single family characterized by the use of phonemic clicks. The term 'Khoisan', suggested by Shapera and now adopted in many works, is a combination of two Khoi-Khoi words: *khoi* meaning man, and *san*, the root *sa* of which means to gather edible plants, pull up roots, collect fruits, and also to capture small animals. A human group is accordingly styled by its way of life, its mode of production. In point of fact, however, the San and the Khoi-Khoi have very few common characteristics. Account may be taken of the light colour of their skin, and also the presence of click consonants in both their languages. It should be recalled, however, that this is not a specific characteristic; such clicks exist also in the south-eastern Bantu languages, such as Zulu, Xhosa, Sotho, Swazi.

Examination of the anthropological features of these two groups shows, however, that Khoi-Khoi and San differ in many respects, for instance, in stature, the Khoi-Khoi being distinctly taller than the San. They differ also in regard to cranial characteristics,[5] type of hair, and steatopygia, which is very common among the women, whereas the presence of epicanthus is specific to the San. Furthermore, the Khoi-Khoi and San languages differ as regards both grammatical structure and vocabulary. E. O. J. Westphal, a leading specialist in this field, showed that pronouns, the oldest and most stable part of speech, have remarkably highly developed forms in the Khoi-Khoi languages. They have two genders and three numbers – singular, dual and plural: there are inclusive and exclusive forms, whereas in the San languages nothing similar exists.[6] There are therefore not sufficient grounds for classifying the San and Khoi-Khoi languages in one group. As to the culture of these peoples, they differ in every way. This was, moreover, noted by the first travellers who visited southern Africa in the seventeenth century, such as Peter Kolb. The Khoi-Khoi lived in kraals, worked metals and raised cattle, whereas the San lived by hunting and gathering and had no fixed dwellings. Thus, neither anthropologists nor linguists can provide sufficient grounds for assuming the existence of a Khoisan group consisting of Khoi-Khoi and San.

5. In regard to craniological differences between the two groups, cf. K. Alexseev, 1973.
6. E. O. J. Westphal, 1962.

These two groups of peoples have completely different histories. The San are certainly the remnants of the original population of the extreme south of the African continent. They are now confined to the inhospitable and waterless regions of Namibia and the Kalahari. Isolated clusters of them are to be found also in Angola. In former times, they inhabited the savannahs of southern and East Africa as far as the borders of Kenya, as the toponymy and hydronymy of these regions bear witness, the local names of rivers and mountains being borrowed from the languages of the San. The click-sounding consonants which are characteristic of the San languages have been borrowed by several Bantu languages. Finally, the rock paintings of the high veld of southern Africa show scenes of armed combat between short, light-skinned San and tall, dark-skinned warriors whose ethnic origin can easily be discerned from the shape of the shields they carry. A small ethnic group, the Hadzapi, living in the region of Lake Eyasi in Tanzania, is a further indication of the extent of former San settlement throughout Africa. The language of the Hadzapi has not yet been studied in sufficient detail, but there are grounds for thinking that it is related to those of the San. Sometimes support for the thesis that the San once occupied a much larger area than they do today is sought in the presence of round stones, pierced in the centre, throughout East Africa. These ring-shaped stones, called *kwe* by the San, were used for weighting a stick for digging up edible roots. However, it is not proved that this technique was diffused by the San group. Thus, for instance, among the Galla in southern Ethiopia and in the region of Harrar men dig the soil with long stakes called *dongora* and these stakes are almost always fitted with such ring-shaped stones. The same device is used to weight the pestle for crushing tobacco. Thus it is not possible to uphold the view that the San formerly wandered everywhere where ring-shaped stones of the *kwe* type are found.

The earliest population of southern Africa should not, however, be considered solely in terms of the Pygmies in the forests and the San in the savannahs. Other peoples may have existed alongside these. There is, for instance, the fairly recent discovery in Angola of the Kwadi group, which closely resembles the San in its style of life and probably also in language. At the beginning of the twentieth century, Vedder studied the Otavi, who are the remnants of former groups. These people are of small stature and live by hunting and gathering. Unlike the San, they have a very dark skin and thick lips. The name by which they call themselves is Nu-Khoin, which means 'black people', as opposed to the Khoi-Khoi, whom they called 'red people'. An extremely interesting feature of this group is their system of counting. It differs sharply from the system used by the Khoi-Khoi, who count in tens. Groups such as these, which probably exist also in other areas, throw precious light on the very complex problem of the earliest peoples of the forests and savannahs of central and southern Africa. The complexity of the problem is illustrated in the vocabulary and phonetics of the Bantu languages, for example when the presence of click sounds indicates very early contacts between ethnic groups. It follows that discrepancies exist between Bantu languages sometimes to the extent of differences in the word root structure, as in the case of the Dzing group in the north-west of the Bantu language area. These differences can only be the result of the influence of a pre-existing linguistic substratum.

The Pygmies and the San, who have been considered above, today constitute numerically minute groups compared with the predominant 'Negro' groups and even with the Afro-Mediterranean race of North Africa.

The linguistic map of Africa today does not coincide with that of the distribution of 'racial' types, though it may have done so in the remote past. But as the early ethnic groups multiplied, migrated and crossbred over a long period, the development of languages and the formation of 'racial' types no longer coincided in time. By the process of forming 'racial' types is meant the genetic heritage and gradual adaptation to the environment. At present there is no longer any correlation between racial and linguistic distribution. This is particularly evident in the peoples of the Sudan, a convergence zone for two different types of language families.

North Africa, including Mauritania and Ethiopia, belongs to the vast Hamito-Semitic area of languages. This is an inapposite term in that it suggests that the languages of this family fall into two groups – Semitic and Hamitic. In the nineteenth century, indeed, linguists considered that this linguistic family was composed, on the one hand of the Semitic languages spoken in the Near East, and on the other hand, the Hamitic languages spoken in Africa. But the French Semitist and linguist M. Cohen stated quite rightly that there were no grounds for dividing these languages into two groups. In fact, it is now generally agreed that the languages of this family fall into five groups: Semitic, Cushitic, Berber,[7] ancient Egyptian[8] and the Chad language group. Hence the languages of this great linguistic family are spoken by several races, both Semitic and black.

In the extreme south of the African continent, the San languages, to which the Kwadi languages of Angola and Hadzapi in Tanzania have to be added, would seem to belong to a specific group possessing the two general characteristics of the presence of click sounds and an isolating type of structure. The wisest course would perhaps therefore be to classify these languages as palaeo-African, in the same way as the term palaeo-Asian is used for the languages of the peripheral regions of north-east Asia.

The Khoi-Khoi languages, whose grammatical structure is different, should not be included in this group. The Khoi-Khoi were cattle-breeders

7. According to some authors, Berber forms part of the Semitic group.

8. In the view of some African Egyptologists, ancient Egyptian is one of the African 'Negro' languages.

who came south with their herds from north-east Africa and settled in the midst of San indigenous population. Some groups of San adopted the Khoi-Khoi language, for instance, the ethnic groups found in the Otavi mountains. It is quite possible that this is also the history of the San central nucleus, especially the Naron. The view that this route may indeed have been taken by the Khoi-Khoi as they spread from the upper reaches of the Nile in the north across the savannahs of East Africa is supported by the existence, not far from Lake Eyasi, in Tanzania, of the small Sandawe group whose language appears to be related to the Khoi-Khoi languages. The history of the Khoi-Khoi is, generally speaking, one of the most puzzling problems in the ethnic evolution of Africa. In this connection it may be noted that Westphal thought it possible that the click sounds in the Khoi-Khoi languages may have been taken from the San languages. This would seem to be an interesting theory, but so far no evidence has been produced in its support.

No doubt the savannahs of East Africa were the first part of the continent to be inhabited by human beings. This region is inhabited today by peoples of Negro race speaking Bantu languages, but they were preceded by San and Khoi-Khoi groups, whose survivors are the Sandawe and the Hadzapi. Other peoples in the same region speak Cushitic languages or languages belonging to other linguistic families, Iraqw, for instance. These languages are those of peoples who lived in these parts before the arrival of the speakers of Bantu languages some of whom made their appearance in comparatively recent times.

Between the zone of the Semito-Hamitic languages spoken in the north and the zone of the palaeo-African languages which are spoken in the south of the continent, there is a vast zone inhabited by peoples speaking languages that Delafosse called Negro-African languages, Meinhof and Westermann called Sudanic and Bantu, and which Greenberg now calls languages of the Congo-Kordofanian and Nilo-Saharan families.

As early as 1963, I recognized the unity of these languages, proposing that they be called the Zindj languages. Within this general category linguistic families or groups could have been distinguished, by further research.

The term 'Negro-African languages' is unsatisfactory. The first part of the term seems to confuse the concepts of race and language. Black inhabitants of the Americas, and sometimes even of parts of Africa itself, speak totally different languages. The second part of this term – African – is also inappropriate because all the languages spoken by the inhabitants of Africa, including Afrikaans, are African languages.

Furthermore, the division of the 'Negro-African' languages into two major groupings, Sudanic and Bantu, also appears to be an error, for Westermann's work shows that the languages of the western Sudan, as regards both structure and vocabulary, have many features in common with the Bantu languages. It was his work which prepared the way for a general revision of the classification of African languages which the German school of linguists had launched in so unfortunate a manner.

The classification proposed by Greenberg is based on the method of mass comparison. Whilst taking account of the basic features of grammatical structure, he concentrates attention mainly on vocabulary. Applying this method, in 1954 Greenberg distinguished sixteen linguistic families and then narrowed these down to twelve. This number was again subsequently reduced in 1963 to only four. So rapid a reduction in the number of language families is sufficient indication that the method has not been adequately refined, and it also suggests excessive haste to produce a classification at all costs.

Of the four families retained by Greenberg, the Afro-Asiatic group is, in fact, none other than the Semito-Hamitic family. As for the so-called click-language family, later called Khoisan, this comprises the languages of the San and Khoi-Khoi peoples. As has already been stated, this combination is mistaken. In addition to the Niger-Congo family, to which Greenberg later added the Kordofan languages, he distinguishes a fourth group formed by the Nilo-Saharan languages, but their structure has so far been very little studied. In 1972 Edgar Gregersen, using Greenberg's method, came to the conclusion that all languages of both families constituted but a single language family, for which he proposed the name Congo-Saharan.

This opinion is in line with my own proposal to bring all these languages together under the heading of the Zindj group. This group is characterized by the use of varying tones and noun classes, as opposed to the Semito-Hamitic or Erythrean languages with their specific accentuation and grammatical gender. It is not impossible that further studies will reveal the specific character of particular languages or groups of languages within the Zindj or Congo-Saharan family, but this already displays the same type of coherence as does, for instance, the Indo-European family.

Within the great Zindj family, the Bantu languages undoubtedly display a significant homogeneity, as shown by the research of Bleek, Meinhof and Guthrie. Among the sub-groups detected by Westermann in the Sudanic linguistic groups, Mande is quite clearly that with the most positive identity.

To the west and the east of the Mande group are the languages which Westermann called the West Atlantic and the Gur languages respectively. However, the West Atlantic languages are not as homogenous as the Mande languages: thus British linguists have seen within the West Atlantic languages a distinct group which they called the Mel languages. In point of fact, this extreme western region of Africa was a place of refuge where successive waves of small peoples were telescoped together under pressure from newcomers. Some of these languages still retain traits characteristic of the Bantu languages, the most striking case being that of Bulom. The earlier hypothesis that the Gur languages constituted a single unit has been disproved by the work of Manessy, an eminent authority in this field. The presence in these languages of noun classes formed in a great variety of ways by the use of prefixes, suffixes and even affixes, is an indication of the ethnic complexity of the area, which has served as a refuge for many of the so-called palaeo-Nigritic groups, who may be found in mountain areas throughout the Sudan from Senegal to Kordofan. The theory was that they were remnants of the oldest autochthonous inhabitants of the Sudan. This reasoning seems, however, to be entirely without foundation. The composition of this mosaic of groups who have been crowded together in these inhospitable areas is extremely varied as regards both language and physical type. The Sudanese chronicles report on some of these events, thus showing that the process involved was not of very ancient origin. Hence, linguistic fragmentation in Africa has to be linked primarily to historical causes which triggered off waves of migration.

Of all the languages of Africa, those of the eastern Sudan appear to have received the least attention. Among these Sudanese languages, the Nilotic languages form a separate group, or perhaps even a linguistic family; that is to say, a family of genetically related languages developed over a long period of isolation. The extreme complexity of the ethnic and linguistic composition of the peoples of the eastern Sudan is shown in the remarkable work of the English linguists M. A. Bryan and A. N. Tucker, who devised a very interesting method for differentiating languages on the basis of the significance of a few characteristic linguistic features. This led to the division of the languages of the eastern Sudan into two groups, the T/K and the N/K languages.

Among the linguistic groups of this great Congo-Saharan family, the Bantu languages display so striking a genetic relationship that this must be regarded as being a relatively recent phenomenon. Of all the Zindj language groups, only the Bantu languages form a well-established unit. They undoubtedly constitute a genetically related family. The problem of elucidating 'the Bantu genesis' is one to which not only linguists but also historians and archaeologists are devoting considerable research. But there are a number of theories. Some consider that the Bantu-speaking peoples came from the north and, more precisely, from the Cameroon region or, in the case of those who think they came from a wider area, the Chad Basin. The migration is presumed to have skirted the forest to the north, so as to outflank it on the east side, and then to have passed through East Africa to spread into southern Africa. Other scholars, like H. H. Johnston, believe that the Bantu came directly from the central African region through the Zaïrean forest. Lastly, some scholars, in line with the theories of the linguist Malcolm Guthrie, who situate the prototype linguistic core of the Bantu among the Luba and Bemba on the upper Zaïre, visualize their original homeland as being in that region.

Going even further, the Bantu-speaking peoples are even presented as being a biological and cultural unit, overlooking the point that the term

Bantu has only a linguistic reference. However, some archaeologists link the spread of the use of iron in the southern part of the continent with the migration of the Bantu, who are presumed to have brought with them a superior technology. However, when the Portuguese landed on the island of Fernando Po, they found that the population spoke Bubi, a Bantu language, but knew nothing about the use of iron. This mistake of confusing languages and life-styles or modes of production had already been made by the ethnographers who conceived of 'Hamite' as involving a unity of race, language and civilization. When historical development is being traced, it is most important not to set about trying to find pure types.

It must be remembered that the peoples speaking Bantu languages vary greatly in their anthropological features – the colour of their skin, their height, their physical build, and so on. The Bantu-speaking people living in the forests have different somatic characteristics from the peoples living in the savannah. There are also great variations in the patrilineal domestic economy and social structure. Some Bantu-speakers are matrilineal, while others have a patrilineal system; some use masks and form secret societies, others have nothing of the sort. The only thing all these peoples have in common is a similar language structure based on noun classes, the class indices having always a similar phonetic structure derived from a common base.

In the savannah of the Sudan, there were apparently groups of peoples who lived side by side for a long time and who spoke languages with noun classes in which differences in tonality played an important part. As the Sahara dried up, these peoples withdrew to moister areas: to the mountains to the north, the valley of the Nile to the east, and the great palaeo-Chad lake. These groups of hunters and cattle breeders drove out the indigenous groups, who were forced to withdraw towards the south, either into the forest or round it to the east. These migrations were not necessarily connected with the beginning of the diffusion of iron-working, but it is certain that the knowledge of metallurgy possessed by some of the newcomers gave them the advantage over other peoples.

It so happens that copper deposits and ancient workings are located in the same region as that identified by Guthrie as being the nuclear Bantu area, where the Luba and Bemba languages contain the greatest percentage of words belonging to 'a common Bantu vocabulary'. The swift development of copper production was bound to be an incentive for the subsequent expansion of the civilization. The greater the distance from the nucleus, the less pure the Bantu linguistic type became for, as they moved away from the centre, the Bantu-speakers mixed increasingly with peoples speaking other languages.

This particular case shows us that the concepts of language, anthropological type and civilization must never be confused, but that, in the gradual settlement of the continent by many kinds of population movement, the mode of production presumably often acted as a principal vector of linguistic expansion and even for the predominance of particular biological features.

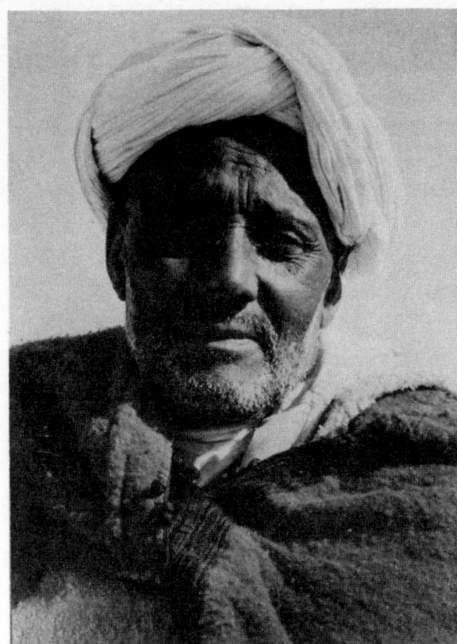

PLATE 11.1 *Moroccan* (Hoa-Qui, photo Richer)

PLATE 11.2 *Algerian woman and baby* (A.A.A. Photo, Géhant)

PLATE 11.3 *Haratine woman from Idélès, Algeria* (A.A.A. Photo, Naud)

PLATE 11.4 *Fulani woman from near Garoua-Boulay, Cameroon* (Hoa-Qui photo)

PLATE 11.5 *Fulani woman* (Archives outre-mer)

PLATE 11.6 *Sarakole woman, Mauritania (Soninka group from the River area)* (B. Nantet)

PLATE 11.7 *Chief, nomad, Rkiz, Mauritania* (B. Nantet)

PLATE 11.8 *Young Fulani girl from Mali* (A.A.A. Photo, Naud)

PLATE 11.9 *Voltaian* (A.A.A. Photo, Naud)

PLATE 11.10 *Djerma Songhay woman, from Balayera, Niger* (B. Nantet)

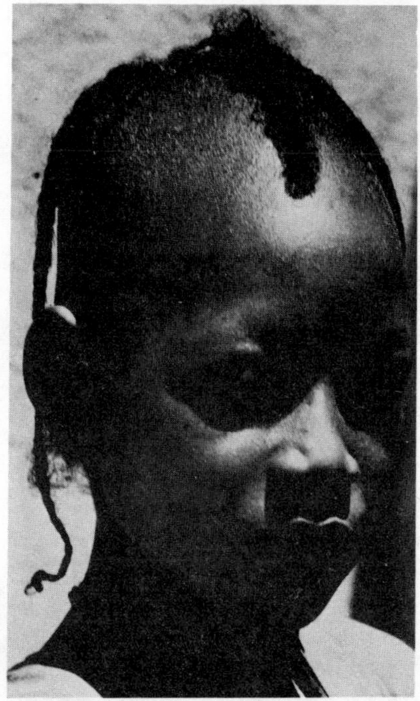

PLATE 11.11 *Tuareg child, from Agadès, Niger* (B. Nantet)

PLATE 11.12 *Fulani woman, Bororo, Tahoua, Niger* (B. Nantet)

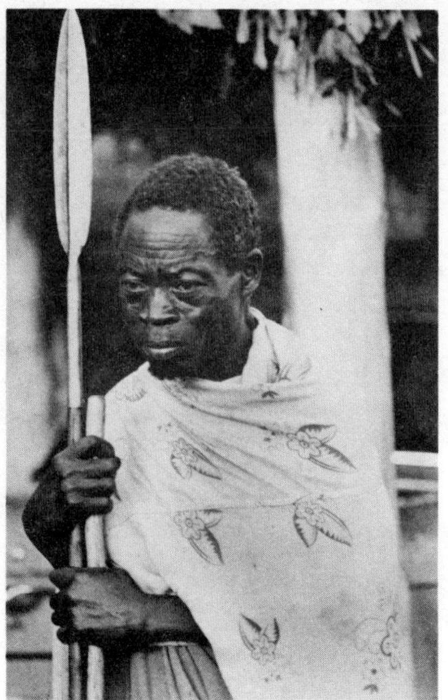

PLATE 11.13 *Twa Pygmy, Rwanda* (B. Nantet)

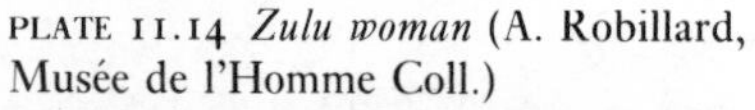

PLATE 11.14 *Zulu woman* (A. Robillard, Musée de l'Homme Coll.)

PLATE 11.15 *Pygmy from the Congo* (Congo Press, Danday, Musée de l'Homme Coll.)

PLATE 11.16 *San group* (F. Balsan photo, Musée de l'Homme Coll.)

African linguistic classification

J. H. GREENBERG

The nature and purposes of linguistic classification

Like any other set of entities, languages can be classified in an indefinitely large number of ways.

One particular method, however, commonly called genetic classification, has certain unique and important characteristics so that when the term 'classification' is employed without further specification in relation to language, it is this type of classification which is meant. It will, accordingly, form the basis for the detailed classification to be set forth in later sections of this chapter.

A genetic classification takes the form of sets of hierarchical units with the same logical organization as a biological classification into species, genera, families, and so on, in which the members of the set at each level are included in those of a higher level. It could in fact be set forth in the form of a genealogical tree. For languages to have an immediate common ancestor in such a tree means that they are all the later differentiated continuations of what were once dialects of the same language. We may illustrate this by the well-known example of Indo-European. Since Indo-European has not yet been shown to belong to any higher grouping this will be our highest level. The Indo-European family is divided into a number of branches, for example, Germanic, Celtic, Slavic, Indo-Iranian and others. This is another way of saying that the original Indo-European speech community eventually divided into a certain number of dialects – Germanic, Celtic, and so on. In turn Germanic, for example, split into three dialects, Gothic, West Germanic and Scandinavian. Of these Gothic is extinct but known from earlier records, while West Germanic differentiated into Anglo-Frisian, Low German and High German. Each of these constitutes a group of present-day local dialects some of which have become the basis of standard languages, for example, German (a High German dialect), Dutch (a Low German dialect) and English (an Anglo-Frisian dialect).

The importance of such classifications is that they reflect the actual history of ethnic differentiation in respect to language. Secondly, they form the basis for the application of the methods of comparative linguistics by means of which much of the linguistic history of individual groupings can be reconstructed. Finally, such knowledge of linguistic history provides the essential basis for inferences regarding the non-linguistic cultural history of the groups concerned.

The history of African linguistic classification

It is obvious that without an adequate accumulation of empirical data regarding the languages of Africa, it would not be possible to undertake a comprehensive classification of the languages of the continent. Even minimal satisfaction of this requirement was not present until the earlier part of the nineteenth century. However, even previous to this period, certain observations relevant to classification had been made, based on an accumulation of data that begin essentially in the seventeenth century when the first grammars and dictionaries of African languages began to appear.[1] For example, Luis Moriano, early in the seventeenth century, noted that the Malagasy language was 'very similar to Malay, which proves in an almost certain manner that the first inhabitants came from the ports of Malacca'.[2] At a similarly early period several Portuguese investigators noted the similarity between the languages of Mozambique on the east coast of Africa and Angola and the Congo on the west, thus foreshadowing the notion of a Bantu family of languages covering most of the southern third of the continent. Another example are the descriptions of Ge'ez and Amharic by Job Ludolfus in the seventeenth century who showed that these Ethiopian languages were related to Hebrew, Aramaic and Arabic.

The eighteenth century saw only very modest additions to our knowledge of African languages but towards the end of that period we find that the basic concept of genetic classification begins to come into clearer focus in the form of specific hypotheses regarding the existence of certain language families. It was such hypotheses that formed the basis in the nineteenth century of the development of linguistics as a comparative-historical science.

Works on the history of linguistics commonly cite a statement by William Jones in 1786 to the effect that the relationship of Indo-European languages was the decisive event in regard to these developments. That such ideas were in the air can be seen from the fact that five years earlier Marsden had, with at least equal clarity, enunciated a similar hypothesis in regard to the

1. For more detailed information on the history of African linguistics see C. M. Doke and D. T. Cole, 1961; D. T. Cole, 1971. There are occasional words from African languages in the works of medieval authors. For these see M. Delafosse, 1912–14, pp. 281–8, and C. Meinhof, 1919–20.

2. 'Relation du voyage de découverte fait à l'Ile Saint-Laurent dans les années 1613–14', a Portuguese manuscript published in French translation in A. and G. Grandidier, 1903–20, p. 22.

Malayo-Polynesian languages and likewise Gyarmathy for the Finno-Ugric languages.

These developments were accompanied by a virtual mania for collecting comparative materials on large numbers of languages. The earliest of these was the *Glossarium Comparativum Linguarum Totius Orbis* of 1787 sponsored by Catherine the Great of Russia, which included data from thirty African languages in the revised edition of 1790–1.

The early nineteenth century was marked by a great acceleration in the production of grammars and dictionaries of African languages as well as the publication of comparative word lists of considerable numbers of African languages such as those of Kilham (1841), Norris (1841) and Clarke (1843).[3] By far the most important of these in its extent, systematic organization and consistency of phonetic symbolization was the classic *Polyglotta Africana* compiled in Freetown (Sierra Leone) by S. W. Koelle.[4]

This accumulation of data in the first part of the nineteenth century was paralleled by the first attempts at overall classification, for example, by Balbi and in successive editions of Prichard's *Inquiry into the Physical History of Mankind*.[5]

In spite of differences in details, certain generally accepted conclusions emerged during the first half of the nineteenth century. Some of these have stood the test of subsequent research, while in other instances they at least raised the fundamental questions to which subsequent classifiers had to address themselves. The results which had thus been attained by 1860 may be summarized as follows:

(1) The term Semitic, introduced by Schlözer in 1781, was already understood in approximately its present form.[6] The existence of an Ethiopian branch of this family was well established, including Ge'ez (classical Ethiopic) and such modern languages as Amharic and Tigrinya.

(2) The resemblances and probable relationships of certain other languages to Semitic were already noted. These included ancient Egyptian, Berber and the Cushitic languages. These latter are spoken mainly in Ethiopia and Somalia. Hausa in West Africa was by some included in this category. These languages were sometimes called Sub-Semitic. The name Hamitic was proposed by Renan in 1855.[7]

(3) In southern Africa Lichtenstein is credited with making the first clear distinction between the Khoi-Khoi and San languages on the

3. H. Kilham, 1828; E. Norris, 1841; J. Clarke, 1848.

4. S. W. Koelle, 1963.

5. A. Balbi, 1826. The last edition of Prichard was edited and enlarged by E. Norris: J. C. Prichard, 1855.

6. A. L. von Schlözer, pt 8, 1781, p. 161.

7. E. Renan, 1855, p. 189.

one hand and the Bantu on the other.[8] The identity of this latter group of closely related languages was by this time clearly recognized. It was variously called the Kaffrarian or South African family of languages. The name Bantu, from the word for 'people' in many of these languages, was first proposed by W. H. I. Bleek, the founder of comparative Bantu studies in 1851, and is the name under which it has been known ever since.

(4) There remained a very large group of languages embracing most of those spoken in the western and eastern Sudan which could not be assigned to the groups just mentioned, that is, those which were not Semitic, Hamitic, San or Bantu. These were generally called Negro languages and provided the greatest problem for classifiers. Norris in his 1855 revision of Prichard's work admitted that they 'eluded classification' and that 'the Negroes hitherto have been considered as constituting one race rather from physiological than philological evidence'.[9]

Although all the overall classifications of African languages up to the recent period completely separated Bantu from 'Negro' languages, a few observers noted that some or many of the languages considered to be 'Negro', especially those in West Africa, showed relationship to Bantu. Apparently the first was Bishop O. E. Vidal in his introduction to Samuel Crowther's grammar of Yoruba.[10] A comprehensive statement is that of Bleek who extended the name Bantu to 'the greater part of Western Africa as far as 13° northern latitude, extending in that region from the lands of Senegal to those of the Upper Nile'.[11] This basic idea was revived in modified form much later by Westermann and in a more explicit way by Greenberg in the now current classification.

(5) The affiliation of Malagasy to Malayo-Polynesian and hence its non-relationship to the languages of Africa had been already noted as early as the seventeenth century, as has been seen, and was generally accepted.

The decade of the 1860s was noteworthy for two comprehensive classifications which were destined to dominate the field until about 1910. The first of these was that of Lepsius which appeared in two versions in 1863 and 1880 respectively.[12] The other was that of Friedrich Müller which likewise had two versions, that of 1867 and 1884.[13] The work of Müller provided the basis of the important study of R. N. Cust, which helped to popularize his work in the English-speaking world. Cust's essay is an

8. H. Lichtenstein, 1811–12.
9. J. C. Prichard, 1855, Vol. 1, p. 427.
10. O. E. Vidal in S. A. Crowther, 1852.
11. W. H. I. Bleek, 1862–9, Vol. I, p. viii.
12. R. Lepsius, 2nd edn 1863 and 1880.
13. F. Müller, 1867 (1876–84). For African languages see I, 2 (1877) and III, 1 (1884).

extremely valuable source for the bibliography of African linguistics up to that period.

Both Lepsius and Müller excluded Malagasy from consideration as linguistically non-African. For the rest, the main problem to which they addressed themselves was that of the 'Negro' languages and their position in relation to Bantu, since the latter was the one well-established and extensive grouping of languages spoken by Negro peoples. In both Müller's and Lepsius' classifications, racial considerations played a large role although in different ways.

The basis of Lepsius' classification was the criterion of types of noun classification. This approach derived from the earlier work of Bleek (1851).[14] Bleek was impressed by what he considered the fundamental difference between the Bantu languages, which had complex systems of noun classes in which sex gender played no part, and the Semitic and Hamitic languages which had sex gender as their principle of noun classification. Pursuing this distinction, Bleek assigned Khoi-Khoi to Hamitic because it had sex gender, in spite of its basic similarities in virtually all other respects to the San languages.

Lepsius, taking Bleek's general idea as his point of departure, considered that among languages spoken by black populations, Bantu with its non-sex noun classification was fundamental, while the remaining languages were mixed, having undergone Hamitic influence. He classified the languages into four groups: (1) Bantu; (2) Mixed Negro; (3) Hamitic; (4) Semitic. Fundamentally there were, however, two sets of languages: (a) Bantu and Mixed Negro (class languages) and (b) Semitic and Hamitic (gender languages). Ultimately the latter should be shown to be related to Indo-European which also has sex gender. In fact Indo-European, Semitic and Hamitic were called by him the Noahite family with its three branches representing the three sons of Noah, Japhet, Shem and Ham. The superiority of the gender languages is explicitly stated. 'It seems, however, unquestionable that the three great branches of gender languages were not only in the past the depositories and the organs of the historical process of human civilization, but that to them, and particularly their youngest branch, the Japhetic, belongs the further hope of the world.'[15] The intellectual line of descent of the 'Hamitic theory' from Bleek through Lepsius to the theories of Meinhof at a later period is evident.

In Müller's comprehensive work of 1884 the world's known languages are classified on the assumption of a fundamental agreement between physical type and language. His basic divisions are 'the languages of the straight-haired peoples', 'the languages of the woolly-haired peoples', and so on. This assumption leads him, for example, to classify Khoi-Khoi not with Hamitic, like Lepsius, but with Papuan among the languages of the frizzy-

14. W. H. I. Bleek, 1851.
15. C. R. Lepsius, 1880, p. 90.

haired races. The majority of 'Negro' languages are divided into African Negro and Bantu. His hypothesis on this question is the exact opposite of Lepsius', since he considers the former basic and the latter derivative. A number of languages spoken by black populations are considered to belong to a more culturally advanced group called Nuba-Fulah whose speakers were physically related to Mediterraneans and Dravidians as curly-haired. In Cust's popularizations of Müller for the English-speaking world, the languages of Africa are divided into the following six groups: (1) Semitic; (2) Hamitic; (3) Nuba-Fulah; (4) Negro; (5) Bantu; (6) Khoisan.

For some time questions of classification were in abeyance as interest concentrated on the vast scientific task of African language description. Westermann's work on the Sudanic languages (1911) and Meinhof's on Hamitic (1912) usher in the modern period.[16]

The former of these, whose basic thesis was apparently developed by Westermann under Meinhof's influence, introduced the term Sudanic to embrace virtually all the languages of Africa not included in Semitic, Hamitic (in the extended sense given it by Meinhof), Bantu or San. It thus embraced essentially all those languages which had earlier been called 'Negro languages.' Westermann selected from this vast assemblage eight languages (nowhere is a complete listing given), of which five were from the western Sudan and three from the eastern Sudan, and sought to establish their relationship by a series of etymologies and reconstructed ancestral forms.

Meinhof, already famous for his basic work on comparative Bantu, in his book on the languages of the Hamites sought to extend the membership of Hamitic beyond generally accepted bounds to include such languages as Fulani, Masai and, following Lepsius, Khoi-Khoi, basically on the criterion of gender. This work contained definite overtones of Hamitic racial superiority.[17]

From the joint work of Meinhof and Westermann there thus emerged a fivefold scheme (Semitic, Hamitic, Sudanic, Bantu, San). These results were popularized in the English-speaking world by the writings of Alice Werner and became standard in anthropological and linguistic textbooks.[18]

This classification did not remain unchallenged during its period of dominance (approximately 1910–50). Though not reflected in the usual textbook treatment, the most significant criticism came from Westermann himself in his important study of 1927 on Western Sudanic languages.[19] In this work he limited his former conception of Sudanic languages to those of West Africa and distinguished by means of detailed lexical and grammatical documentation a number of distinct sub-groups within West Sudanic (e.g.

16. D. Westermann, 1911; C. Meinhof, 1912.

17. The Hamitic hypothesis became the basis for much culture-historical interpretation. On this, see E. R. Sander, 1969.

18. A. Werner, 1915 and 1930.

19. D. Westermann, 1927.

West Atlantic, Kwa, Gur). Even more significantly he pointed to detailed resemblances in vocabulary and grammatical structure between West Sudanic and Bantu, without ever stating their relationship in a fully explicit manner. In fact Sir Henry Johnston in his vast work on Bantu and Semi-Bantu had considered many West African languages as affiliated with Bantu.[20] In his terminology they were 'Semi-Bantu'. However, he adhered to the typological criterion of noun classification, so that of two closely related languages if one had noun classes it would be Semi-Bantu while the other would not.

Brief mention should also be made of several other classifications of the period 1910–50 of which only that of Delafosse attained any currency. One of these was proposed by A. Drexel who sought to establish an agreement between African language families and cultures, a relationship which was posited by the *Kulturkreislehre*. The French Africanist M. Delafosse, in contrast to the German investigators of the period, limited Hamitic to Berber,[21] Egyptian and Cushitic and treated all other non-Semitic and non-Khoisan languages as forming a vast Negro-African family.[22] In addition to sixteen non-Bantu branches, many of which were established on a geographic rather than a purely linguistic basis, Delafosse apparently considered that Bantu was to be included as Negro-African. Part of Delafosse's terminology is still current among Africanists of French expression. Mention should also be made of Mlle Homburger who likewise, starting from the notion of African linguistic unity but even more broadly conceived, espoused the theory of an Egyptian source as the explanation of this unity and even, without considering it to be contradictory, an ultimate derivation from the Dravidian languages of India.[23]

In 1949–50 in a series of articles in the *Southwestern Journal of Anthropology*, the present writer outlined what was in many respects a new classification and one which ultimately won broad acceptance.[24] It differed from previous classifications methodologically in a number of ways. It was

20. H. H. Johnston, 1919–22.

21. Note added at the request of a member of the Committee: this classification runs counter not only to the views of German scholars but indeed to the scientific facts. North African linguists have shown up the political motivations which prompted the colonial school of French Berber scholars to classify the Berber languages among the Hamito-Semitic languages. The fact is that Berber is a Semitic language and is even one of the oldest of that family of languages, together with Akkadian and Hebrew. Hence, it is neither Hamito-Semitic nor Afro-Asiatic, as stated elsewhere in this chapter. See, in particular, in Arabic: M. El Fasi, 1971.

22. M. Delafosse, 1924, pp. 463–560.

23. L. Homburger, 1941.

24. For the most recent version of the Greenberg classification see J. H. Greenberg, 1966. A bibliography of the controversial literature on this subject is found in D. Winston, 'Greenberg's classification of African languages', *African Language Studies*, 7 (1966), pp. 160–70. For a different viewpoint see Chapter 11 above by Professor Olderogge.

strictly genetic in the sense described in the introductory section of this paper. Hence massive resemblances among groups of languages involving sound and meaning simultaneously, whether involving roots (vocabulary) or grammatical formants, were viewed as probative. Resemblances involving sound only, without meaning – for example, agreement in having tone or resemblances extending to meaning only without sound, for example, grammatical gender where the phonetic form of the markers did not agree – were considered irrelevant. Such typological features had, as we have seen, figured largely in previous classifications. Thus the mere possession of sex gender was not considered as evidence for relationship since, for example, sex gender may and does arise independently in different parts of the world. On the other hand the existence of a feminine gender marker *t* in all branches of Afro-Asiatic (Hamito-Semitic) is a piece of positive evidence for relationship. Similarly the absence of gender through loss of the category is not in itself negative evidence. This is generally accepted in areas where the comparative method is well established, for example, Indo-European. Persian, Armenian and Hittite among others do not have sex gender whereas most other languages of the family do.

Earlier classifications, for example, that of Lepsius, did not use and cite any concrete evidence for groupings. Westermann in his work on Sudanic did provide etymologies but only for eight languages out of the hundreds involved. The only previous work which did this in detail was Westermann's later work on Western Sudanic and this only for part of Africa. In the present writer's classification, etymological and specific common grammatical features were presented for all major groupings based on an exhaustive review of the literature.

The most important concrete proposals, some of which have produced a fairly extensive controversial literature, are the following:

(a) The relationship of Bantu to Western Sudanic based in Westermann's data is accepted. Moreover Bantu became not a separate branch of the larger family but merely a sub-group within what Westermann called the Benue-Congo ('Semi-Bantu') sub-group of his Western Sudanic. Further, many other languages farther east (Adamawa-Eastern branch) are part of the family which was renamed Niger-Congo.

(b) Of the proposed extensions of Hamitic by Meinhof, only Hausa was accepted. Further, Hausa is but one member of an extensive branch (Chadic) of Hamito-Semitic. Semitic is included but merely as a single branch co-ordinate with the others. Hence Hamitic becomes merely an arbitrary name for non-Semitic branches of the larger family now renamed Afro-Asiatic and viewed as consisting of five branches: (1) Berber; (2) ancient Egyptian; (3) Semitic; (4) Cushitic; (5) Chadic.[25]

25. J. Lukas, 1938, pp. 286–99; M. R. Cohen, 1947.

(c) 'Negro' languages not included in Niger-Congo were shown to belong to another major grouping called Nilo-Saharan.
(d) Khoi-Khoi was classified as a San language belonging to the Central group of South African Khoisan.

The overall result is that African languages are classified into four major families (excluding Merina) as described in the following sections in which each one of these families is considered in detail.[26] In this exposition recent proposals modifying or extending the original classification are mentioned where appropriate as well as more drastic criticisms.

The Afro-Asiatic languages[27]

These languages, also called Hamito-Semitic, cover all of northern Africa, almost all of the eastern Horn of Africa (Ethiopia, Somalia); some languages of the Cushitic branch are spoken as far south as Tanzania. In addition, the Semitic branch includes languages which at present or in former times included almost the entire Middle East. Afro-Asiatic is generally analysed as consisting of five about equally differentiated divisions: Berber,[28] ancient Egyptian, Semitic, Cushitic and Chadic. However, Fleming has recently proposed that the languages which had been hitherto classified as West Cushitic, a group including Kaffa and other languages in south-western Ethiopia, in fact constitute a sixth branch for which the names Omotic and Ari-Banna have been proposed.[29]

The Berber branch of Afro-Asiatic has less internal differentiation than any other branch of Afro-Asiatic except Egyptian. Its main division seems to be between the language of the various Tuareg groups in the Sahara and the Berber proper of North Africa and Mauritania. It is probable that the extinct language of the Guanches of the Canary Islands was affiliated with Berber. In addition mention should be made of the existence of Old Libyan inscriptions which are imperfectly understood but possibly represent an earlier form of Berber.

A second branch of Afro-Asiatic, the Egyptian, is documented in the earlier period by hieroglyphic inscriptions, hieratic papyri and in the latest

26. For more detailed listing of languages than is possible given the length limitation on this chapter see J. H. Greenberg, 1963b, the volumes of the series *Handbook of African Languages* and the provisional *Language Map of Africa* (by D. Dalby, 1977) published by the International African Institute, London; and C. F. and F. M. Voegelin, 1973.

27. At the Cairo Symposium on the Peopling of Ancient Egypt, African scholars recalled that Professor Greenberg's classification overlooked the fundamental fact of the establishment of phonetic rules. Their view is shared by Professor Istvan Fodor. The same African scholars put forward arguments to prove the genetic linguistic relationship existing between ancient Egyptian and modern African languages.

28. Cf. note 21 above.

29. H. C. Fleming, 1969.

period also by documents in the demotic script. All these scripts represent the same spoken language. In the Christian period this language continued to be spoken and developed an extensive literature written in an alphabet adapted from the Greek. In this later or Coptic form there were a number of literary dialects of which Bohairic still survives in liturgical use in the Coptic church. After the Arab conquest of Egypt, the ancient Egyptian language gradually lost ground and became extinct as a spoken language probably in the seventeenth century.

The Semitic branch of Afro-Asiatic has far more internal differentiation than either Berber or Egyptian. It is usually assumed that the most fundamental division within Semitic is between East Semitic and West Semitic. The former is represented only by the long extinct Akkadian written in cuneiform. It has two basic regional dialects, southern (Babylonian) and northern (Assyrian). West Semitic is in turn divided into North-West Semitic and South-West Semitic. The former of these includes Canaanite (Hebrew, Moabite, Phoenician and, probably, Ugaritic) and Aramaic. Of these only Hebrew, revived as a spoken language within the past century as the language of Israel, and a few dialects of Aramaic still survive. The modern forms in Aramaic represent survivals of West Aramaic in the Antiliban of Syria, and East Aramaic chiefly in northern Iraq.

South-East Semitic likewise has two divisions, northern and southern. The northern branch contains most of the dialects of the Arabian peninsula and their modern descendants, dominant in a vast area embracing North Africa, the Middle East and parts of the Sudan (i.e. Arabic proper). The southern division consists on the one hand of South Arabic and on the other of the Semitic languages of Ethiopia. South Arabic is known in its earlier form from Minean, Sabean and Qatabanian inscriptions and in its contemporary form of Mehri and Shahri in south Arabia and Soqoṭri, the language of the island of Soqotra in the Indian Ocean.

The Ethiopian Semitic languages divide into a northern group (Tigrinya, Tigre and Ge'ez or classical Ethiopic) and a southern group (Amharic, Gurage, Argobba, Gafat and Harari).

The fourth group of Afro-Asiatic languages, the Cushitic, contains a large number of languages which fall into five strongly differentiated branches, the Northern, Central, Eastern, Southern and Western. Northern Cushitic consists essentially of a single language, that of the Beja. The Central Cushitic languages are sometimes called the Agau languages. They were probably once spoken over a continuous area but their former speakers have largely adopted Ethiopian Semitic languages. The Falasha, or Ethiopian Jews, formerly spoke an Agau language. The Central Cushitic languages include a northern group (Bilin, Khamir, Qemant) and Awiya in the south. Eastern Cushitic includes the two Cushitic languages with the largest number of speakers, Somali and Galla. The Eastern Cushitic languages fall into the following groups: (1) Afar, Saho; (2) Somali, Baiso, Rendille, Boni; (3) Galla, Conso, Gidole, Arbore, Warazi, Tsamai, Geleba,

Mogogodo; (4) Sidamo, Alaba, Darasa, Hadiya, Kambatta, Burji. Of these the last or 'Sidamo-Burji' is probably to be grouped as a single branch against the three others. The Southern Cushitic languages are spoken in Tanzania. They included Burungi, Goroa, Alawa, Ngomvia (Asu), Sanye and Mbugu. This southern group is linguistically closest to Eastern Cushitic and is quite possibly to be classified as merely a sub-group of the latter. One Southern Cushitic language, Mbugu, has been extensively influenced by Bantu both grammatically and lexically so that some investigators consider it to be a mixed language.

The Western Cushitic languages are extremely divergent from the other languages traditionally considered to be Cushitic. At the very least Cushitic would fall into two groups, Western versus the remainder. As noted earlier, Fleming has proposed that it be considered a separate sixth branch of Afro-Asiatic. The Western Cushitic languages may be divided into two groups, Ari-Banna (for Ari, the term Bako was used in the earlier literature) and the remainder. These in turn may be grouped as follows: (1) Maji, Nao, Sheko; (2) Janjero; (3) Kaffa, Mocha, Shinasha, Southern Mao; (4) Gimira; (5) the Ometo group ('Western Sidamo') including Chara, Male, Basketo, the Welamo cluster, Zaysse and Koyra-Gidicho.

The last branch of Afro-Asiatic to be considered is Chadic. It includes Hausa, the most widely spoken language in West Africa, and perhaps as many as a hundred other languages spoken by much smaller populations. In Greenberg (1963b) the Chadic languages were divided into nine sub-groups as follows: (1) (a) Hausa Gwandara, (b) Bede-Ngizim, (c) (i) Warjawa (northern Bauchi) group, (ii) Barawa (southern Bauchi) group, (d) (i) Bolewa group, (ii) Angas group, (iii) Ron group; (2) Kotoko group; (3) Bata-Margi; (4) (a) Musgoi group, (b) Marakam group; (5) Gidder; (6) Mandara-Gamergu; (7) Musgu; (8) Masa-Bana group; (9) Eastern Chadic, (a) Somrai group, (b) Gabere group, (c) Sokoro group, (d) Modgel, (e) Tuburi, (f) Mubi group.

Newman and Ma have suggested that of the above sub-families (3) and (6) are particularly close to each other and likewise (1) and (9). For the former of the groupings the name Biu-Mandara is proposed and for the latter Plateau-Sahel.[30] Nothing is asserted by them regarding the other sub-groups.

Niger-Kordofanian

This family has two branches, very unequal in numbers of speakers and geographical extent. The first, Niger-Congo, covers a very considerable portion of sub-Saharan Africa including almost all of West Africa and parts of the central and eastern Sudan, and its Bantu sub-branch occupies most of central, East and southern Africa. Kordofanian, the other branch

30. P. Newman and R. Ma, 1964.

of Niger-Kordofanian, is confined to a limited area in the Kordofan region of Sudan.

The basic division with Niger-Congo is that between the Mande languages and the rest. In addition to lacking many of the most common lexical items found in the rest of Niger-Congo, Mande has no convincing traces of the noun classification generally found both in Kordofanian and in the remainder of Niger-Congo. There are, of course, many individual languages in Niger-Congo which have lost this system. Because of this divergence of the Mande language, Mukarovsky has proposed that Mande is really a branch of Nilo-Saharan, the other large family of Negro African languages, but the well-known expert on Mande languages, William E. Welmers, disagrees.[31]

Within Mande it is now universally agreed that the division between Mande-tan and Mande-fu based on the word for 'ten' first proposed by Delafosse is invalid.[32] The Mande languages may be classified as follows: (A) Northern-Western Division: (1) Northern including Susu-Yalunka, Soninke, Hwela-Numu, Ligbi, Vai-Kono, Khasonke and Maninka-Bambara-Dyula; (2) South-western: Mende-Bandi, Loko, Loma, Kpelle. (B) Southern-Eastern Division: (1) Southern: Mano, Dan, Tura, Mwa, Nwa, Gan, Guro; (2) Eastern: Samo, Bisa, Busa. A single language Sya (Bobo-fing) remains unassigned. It is clearly Mande but it should perhaps be considered the earliest offshoot within the stock so that genetically it represents one of two branches, the other being Mande proper.

The remaining Niger-Congo languages are classified in Greenberg (1963c) into five branches: (1) West Atlantic; (2) Gur; (3) Kwa; (4) Benue-Congo; (5) Adamawa-Eastern. However, of these groups (2), (3) and (4) are particularly close and form a kind of nuclear group within which in particular the boundary between Benue-Congo and Kwa is not clear.[33]

The West Atlantic languages, a term introduced by Westermann in 1928 and substantially identical in its membership with the Senegalo-Guinéen of Delafosse and subsequent French investigators, falls into two clearly marked groups, a northern and a southern. This and the internal diversity, particularly in the northern group, has led Dalby to suggest the abandonment of the concept of West Atlantic and to the assertion of the independence of the southern sub-group, consisting of Greenberg's southern West Atlantic minus Limba. For this group he proposes the term Mel.[34] However, in a more recent study David Sapir, buttressed by glottochronological evidence, reasserts the basic unity of West Atlantic as traditionally conceived and includes Limba within the southern branch.[35]

31. H. G. Mukarovsky, 1966.
32. M. Delafosse, 1901.
33. On this question see J. H. Greenberg, 1963c, pp. 215–17.
34. D. Dalby, 1965, pp. 1–17.
35. See D. Sapir, 1974b; Sapir, however, expresses some reservations regarding the conclusions cited in the text.

The chief innovation that he proposes is that Bijago, the language of the Bijago Islands, should be considered a separate branch co-ordinate with the northern and southern. This corresponds with my own impression of the divergence of this language. It should be noted that the classification of Fula, considered to be Hamitic by Meinhof and the subject of much controversy, is now by general agreement included within West Atlantic. The classification of West Atlantic is then as follows: (A) Northern Branch: (1) (a) Fula, Serer, (b) Wolof; (2) Non group; (3) Dyola, Manjak, Balante; (4) (a) Tenda, Basari, Bedik, Konyagi, (b) Biafada, Pajade, (c) Kobiana, Banhum, (d) Nalu; (B) Southern Branch: (1) Sua (Kunante); (2) (a) Temne-Baga, (b) Sherbro-Krim, Kisi, (c) Gola; (3) Limba; (C) Bijago.

Another major grouping within Niger-Congo is Gur. An alternative name is Voltaic, a designation which is particularly common in the French literature. The most recent suggestions regarding subclassification within Gur is that of Bendor-Samuel which is followed here in outline. It is noted that the great majority of languages which have been considered to be Gur belong to one very large sub-group called Central Gur by Bendor-Samuel.[36] This corresponds to the Mossi-Grunshi group of earlier investigations. Central Gur may be divided into three sub-groups: (1) More-Gurma; (2) Grusi group; (3) Tamari. The remaining sub-groups of Gur are: (1) Bargu (Bariba); (2) Lobiri; (3) Bwamu; (4) Kulango; (5) Kirma-Tyurama; (6) Win; (7) Senufo group; (8) Seme; (9) Dogon.

Even granted the validity of a Kwa group as distinct from Benue-Congo, as mentioned earlier, there are two sub-groups, Kru in the extreme west and Ijo in the extreme east, whose assignment to Kwa may be considered doubtful. With these reservations the basic sub-groupings of Kwa are as follows, stated in approximately west to east order: (1) Kru languages; (2) Western Kwa which includes the Ewe-Fõ, the Akan-Guang (now sometimes called Volta-Camoe), Gã-Adangme and the so-called Togo Remnant languages; (3) Yoruba, Igala; (4) Nupe group; (5) Edo group; (6) Idoma group; (7) Ibo; (8) Ijo. Benue-Congo is essentially the same sub-group of Niger-Congo which was called Benue-Cross or Semi-Bantu by Westermann, with the addition of Bantu within the Bantoid subdivision. There are four basic divisions within Benue-Congo: (1) Plateau languages; (2) Jukunoid; (3) Cross River, containing as its largest language community Efik-Ibibio; (4) Bantoid, consisting of Bantu, Tiv and a number of smaller languages in the middle Benue area.

A number of languages in Nigeria formerly considered Semi-Bantu in the broad sense are now generally agreed to be Bantu. Included here are the Bamileke, Ekoi and Jarawa groups. The most fundamental division within Bantu itself may be between such languages and Bantu in its conventional acceptation. Within Bantu in this latter sense the basic division appears to be

36. I am following here in the details of sub-grouping J. T. Bendor-Samuel, 'Niger-Congo, Gur' in T. A. Sebeok (ed.), *Linguistics in Sub-Saharan Africa* (Paris/The Hague: Mouton), pp. 141–78.

between Eastern and Western Bantu. For finer sub-groupings the division by Guthrie into zones indicated by letters, but variously modified by different specialists, is current.[37]

The assignment of the Bantu grouping as a whole to a sub-group of Benue-Congo, itself a branch of the large Niger-Congo family, has been one of the most controversial aspects of Greenberg's classification. Guthrie in particular espoused the notion that Bantu is genetically independent and that the extensive resemblances to Bantu found in the other Niger-Congo languages is the result of Bantu influences on a fundamentally different group of languages. He has argued on this basis that the original Bantu point of origin is the 'nuclear' area of southern Shaba. Greenberg places it in the middle Benue valley in Nigeria because the most closely related languages of the Bantoid sub-group of Benue-Congo are spoken there.[38]

The final grouping within Niger-Congo is the Adamawa-Eastern branch. The Adamawa group consists of many relatively small language communities, among whom the Chamba and Mbum may be mentioned as examples. The Eastern branch contains a number of languages of major importance, for example, Gbeya in the Central African Republic and Zande.[39]

In contrast to the vast Niger-Congo family just discussed, the other branch of Niger-Kordofanian, namely the Kordofanian languages, contains no language of major importance and shares the Korodofan hills with various languages of the Nilo-Saharan stock. It may be divided into five highly differentiated sub-groups of which one (the Tumtum group) is the most divergent of all. These sub-groups are: (1) Koalib; (2) Tegali; (3) Talodi; (4) Katla; (5) Tumtum (also called Kadugli-Krongo).[40]

The Nilo-Saharan family

The other major Negro-African language stock is Nilo-Saharan. In general it is spoken north and east of the Niger-Congo languages and is predominant in the upper Nile valley and the eastern parts of the Sahara and Sudan. It has however a western outlier in Songhay of the Niger valley. It has one very large branch, Chari-Nile, containing the majority of the languages of the entire family. In essentially west to east order, the branches of Nilo-Saharan are as follows: (1) Songhay; (2) Saharan, (a) Kanuri-Kanembu, (b) Teda-Daza, (c) Zaghawa, Berti; (3) Maban; (4) Furian; (5) Chari-Nile (see

37. For this classification see M. Guthrie, 1948.

38. On the Bantu controversy see M. Guthrie, 1962, pp. 273–82; R. Oliver, 1966, pp. 361–76; J. H. Greenberg, 1972, pp. 189–216.

39. For a detailed listing of the Adamawa-Eastern languages see J. H. Greenberg, 1966, p. 9.

40. For more detailed information on the Kordofanian languages see J. H. Greenberg, 1966, p. 149.

the following sections for further details); (6) Coman (Koma, Ganza, Uduk, Gule, Gumuz and Mao).

The Chari-Nile languages include two major groups, Eastern Sudanic and Central Sudanic, and two individual languages, Berta and Kunama.

Eastern Sudanic is the largest single unit within Nilo-Saharan. It contains the following ten sub-groups: (1) Nubian, (a) Nile Nubian, (b) Kordofan Nubian, (c) Midob, (d) Birked; (2) Murle-Didinga groups; (3) Barea; (4) Ingassana (Tabi); (5) Nyima-Afitti; (6) Temein, Teis-um-Danab; (7) Merarit group; (8) Dagu (Dajo group); (9) Nilotic divided into (a) Western Nilotic: Burun, Luo group and Dinka-Nuer, (b) Eastern Nilotic: (i) Bari group, (ii) Karamojong, Teso, Turkana, Masai; (c) Southern Nilotic: Nandi, Suk, Tatoga; (10) Nyangiya, Teuso (Ik).

Considerable controversy exists concerning the classification of two sub-groups of Nilotic, namely Eastern and Southern. Meinhof in classifying Masai as Hamitic evidently intended to include other languages of these two groups in spite of their close resemblance to the languages classified here as Western Nilotic, for example, Shilluk, Luo, Dinka. His separation of such otherwise similar languages as, for example, Shilluk and Masai was carried out primarily because of the possession of sex gender by the latter. Westermann attempted a compromise position, calling the languages of the Eastern and Southern Nilotes Nilo-Hamitic, presumably on the assumption that they are mixed languages. He reserved the term Nilotic for Western Nilotic. Tucker at first adopted a view of this sort but later moved these languages closer to Nilotic, calling them Paranilotic.[41] Other divergent views in the recent period have been those of Hohenberger who compared Masai to Semitic, and Huntingford who apparently sought to revive the earlier views of Meinhof that these languages are Hamitic.[42]

The other extensive sub-group of Chari-Nile is Central Sudanic. It may be divided into six sub-groups as follows: (1) Bongo-Bagirmi; (2) Kreish; (3) Moru-Madi; (4) Mangbetu; (5) Mangbutu-Efe; (6) Lendu.

The Khoisan family

All of the Khoisan languages have click sounds and the majority of their speakers belong to the physically distinctive San type.

The bulk of the Khoisan languages are spoken in southern Africa. However, there are two small populations much farther north in Tanzania, the Hatsa and Sandawe, with languages differing considerably both from each other and from those of South Africa. Accordingly the family is divided into three branches: (1) Hatsa; (2) Sandawe; (3) South African Khoisan. South African Khoisan consists of three groups of languages: (1) Northern, containing the Northern San languages of the Auen and Kung; (2) Central

41. See A. N. Tucker and M. A. Bryan, 1966.

42. On these developments see G. W. B. Huntingford, 1956; I Hohenberger, 1956; J. H. Greenberg, 1957b.

Khoisan, divided into two groups, (A) Hiechware, (B) Naron, Khoi-Khoi; (3) Southern San, the internally most differentiated group with a considerable number of individual San languages.[43]

As was noted in the section of this chapter dealing with the history of classification, a number of linguists, Bleek, Lepsius and later Meinhof, separated Khoi-Khoi from San and assigned it to Hamitic. A modified form of this theory is espoused at the present time by E. O. J. Westphal.[44] He divides Khoisan as described here into two independent families. One is Sandawe-Khoi-Khoi consisting of Sandawe and the Central Khoisan languages. All these languages except Hiechware have sex gender. Nothing is asserted concerning a possible connection with Hamito-Semitic. Westphal's other group, Hadza-San, consists of Hatsa and the Northern and Southern San languages. However, he considers the connection between Hatsa and the San languages not to be completely established.

The Merina language, which has come to dominate the languages of African origin spoken in some regions of the island of Madagascar, is not included in the foregoing classification. Its status as an Austronesian (Malayo-Polynesian) language has never been disputed. Its closest relative within Austronesian is probably the Maanyan language of Borneo.[45] Another language not mentioned in the classification is Meroitic,[46] an extinct language written in an alphabet which takes two forms, hieroglyphic and cursive. It became extinct about the fourth century of our era and is known only from archaeological remains covering approximately an area from Aswan in southern Egypt to Khartoum in Sudan. While the phonetic values of the letters are known, because of the absence of bilingual inscriptions our knowledge of lexicon and grammar is limited and uncertain. The earliest theory was that it was Nubian (Griffith). A Hamitic hypothesis (Meinhof, Zyhlarz) was refuted in an important article by Hintze. More recently the Nubian hypothesis has been revived in a broadened form by Trigger who suggests that it belongs to the Eastern Sudanic sub-branch of Nilo-Saharan to which Nubian also was assigned in the Greenberg classification.[47]

Finally, mention should be made of European and Indian languages of recent importation which in some cases are now spoken by populations born in Africa. English, besides being spoken in South Africa and Zimbabwe, is the language of the descendants of the American blacks who founded Liberia and is also spoken in creolized form (Krio) in Freetown, Sierra Leone. Afrikaans, closely related to Dutch, is spoken in South Africa. There

43. See the conflicting opinion of Professor D. Olderogge, Chapter 11.

44. E. O. J. Westphal, 1966.

45. The evidence for this hypothesis is presented in O. C. Dahl, 1951.

46. It should be remarked that the important symposium held in Cairo in January–February 1974 reviewed the research conducted into the deciphering of the Meroitic script (see Volume 2).

47. On this question see F. Hintze, 1955; B. G. Trigger, *Kush*, 12, pp. 188–94.

is a substantial French, Spanish and Italian population in North Africa. A creolized form of Portuguese is the first language of some thousands of speakers in Guinea and elsewhere. Finally, some languages native to India are spoken in East Africa. These include both Aryan and Dravidian languages, most importantly Gujarati.

TABLE 12.1 *Stages of the Greenberg classification*

I (1949–50)

1	Niger–Congo	9	Mimi of Nachtigal
2	Songhay	10	Fur
3	Central Sudanic	11	Temainian
4	Central Saharan	12	Kordofanian
5	Eastern Sudanic	13	Koman
6	Afroasiatic (Hamito-Semitic)	14	Berta
7	Click	15	Kunama
8	Maba	16	Nyangiya

II (1954)

1	Niger–Congo	7	Maban (I. 8 Maban; I. 9 Mimi of Nachtigal)
2	Songhay	8	Fur
3	Macro-Sudanic (I. 5 Eastern Sudanic; I. 3 Central Sudanic; I. 14 Berta; I. 15 Kunama)	9	Temainian
		10	Kordofanian
4	Central Saharan	11	Koman
5	Afroasiatic	12	Nyangiya
6	Click		

III (1963)

1 Niger-Kordofanian (II. 1 Niger-Congo; II. 10 Kordofanian)
2 Afroasiatic
3 Khoisan (formerly II. 6 Click)
4 Nilo-Saharan (II. 2 Songhay; II. 4 Saharan (formerly Central Saharan); II. 7 Maban; II. 8 Fur; II. 11 Koman; Chari-Nile including II. 3. Macrosudanic, II. 9 Temainian, II. 12 Nyangiya)

References

I *South-western Journal of Anthropology*, 1949, 1950
II *South-western Journal of Anthropology*, 1954
III *Languages of Africa*, 1963

Appendix to Chapter 12: the language map of Africa

D. DALBY

Africa, although less densely populated than the world as a whole,[1] has a greater degree of linguistic complexity than any other continent.[2] As a result, there has until now been no detailed charting of the continental language map of Africa, even though it is a map so badly needed by historians and others. The Soviet ethnodemographic map of Africa is probably the best substitute to date,[3] although it suffers from the blurring of linguistic and ethnic distinctions, from the overloading of the map with demographic as well as 'ethnolinguistic' data, and from the rendering of all African names in the Cyrillic alphabet. Other continental maps, of ethnic groups rather than of languages, are in general too grossly oversimplified to be of much scientific value.[4]

Some degree of oversimplification is of course inevitable in any attempt to arrive at a continental view of language distribution and relationships in Africa. The only truly accurate map would need to represent every person on the continent with a separate illuminated spot, which would move as the person moved and which would light up in any of up to 2000 different colours according to the language that person was speaking at the moment. Since such a map is a physical impossibility, we must satisfy ourselves with something less perfect, although hopefully more detailed and accurate than the documents previously available. For the last ten years, work has been proceeding on a specifically linguistic map of Africa (as opposed to ethnic),

1. While representing approximately 20 per cent of the total land surface of the world, Africa accounts for just below 10 per cent of the total population of the world.

2. New Guinea (little more than one-fortieth the size of Africa) has an equal – or even greater – degree of linguistic complexity, but nowhere in the world is there such a geographically extensive area of linguistic 'fragmentation' as in sub-Saharan Africa.

3. *Narodni Afriki* (Moscow, 1960) and *Karta Narodov Afriki* (Moscow, 1974).

4. E.g. G. P. Murdock 'Tribal map of Africa' (1959), or the 'Map of the tribes and nations of modern Africa' by Roy Lewis and Yvonne Foy, published by *The Times* in the early 1970s.

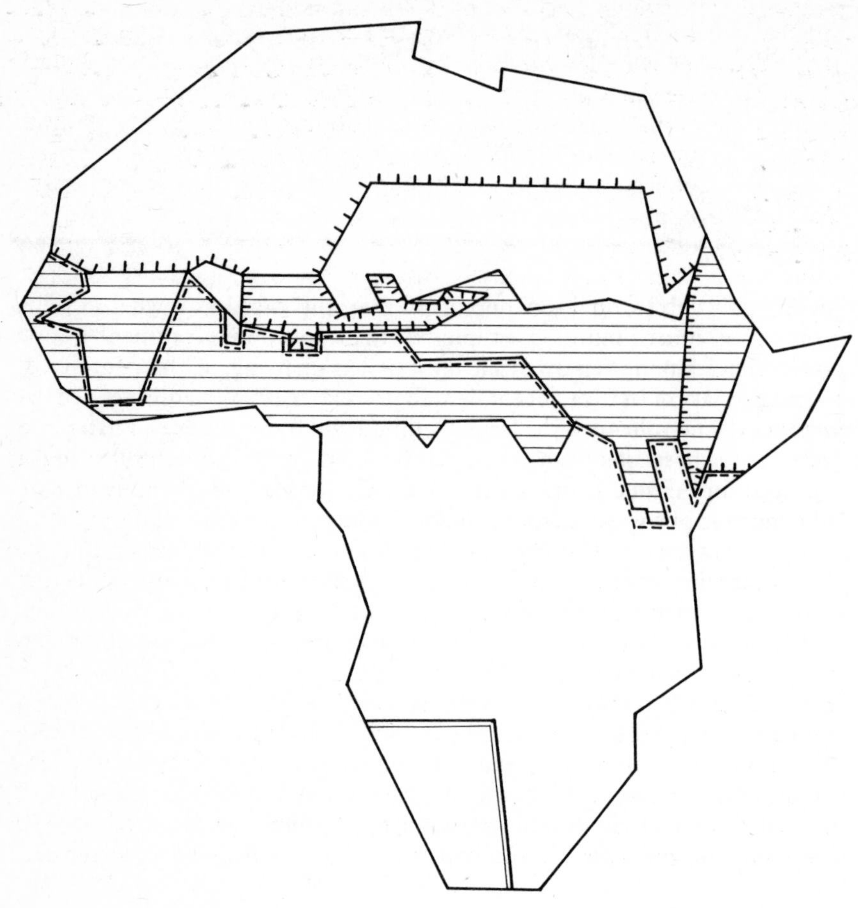

FIG. 12.1 *Diagrammatic language map of Africa*

and the present article draws attention to aspects of this work which are relevant to the history of Africa.[5]

Despite its technical appearance, the comparative study of African languages has often been oversimplistic. There has been a tendency to assume that the complex language map of today has evolved from a much simpler language map in the past, and that linguistic relationships can be expressed in terms of 'family trees', with a descending hierarchy of levels ('families', 'sub-families', 'branches', and so on). A belief that the many hundreds of modern languages in Africa may be traced back in regular order to a handful of 'proto-languages' has led comparative linguistics to examine the possible ultimate and most distant relationships of African languages before establishing on a sound basis their immediate relationships. It has led them to concentrate on the historical process of divergence among languages with an assumed common origin, to the exclusion of the process of convergence among related languages or of re-convergence among related languages. The ill-effects of this approach have been compounded by the fact that the pseudo-historical classifications arrived at by these means have been used also as frameworks of reference (not only for African languages, but even for African peoples), and have consequently exercised an undue influence on historical thinking about Africa.

A major priority must therefore be the unscrambling of the linguistic jigsaw of the African language map, reducing it to its immediate components (that is, language-groups with a close, overall relationship and with external as well as internal unity[6] = 'complex units'; or individual languages which cannot be included within any such group='simple units').Such treatment reveals an important characteristic of the language map which has been obscured by previous classifications, namely, the fact that from a total of around 120 complex and simple units in Africa as a whole, over 100 are confined entirely to a single belt extending across Africa from the coast of Senegal in the west to the Ethiopian and East Africa highlands in the east.[7] Expressed in terms of individual languages,[8]

5. *Language Map of Africa and the adjacent islands*, in compilation at the School of Oriental and African Studies and the International African Institute (IAI). The map is designed to show the modern distribution, and linguistic relationships, of 'home' or 'first' languages at a basic scale of 1 : 5 000 000 with insets of more complex areas at scales of 1:2 500 000 and 1:1 250 000. A provisional edition, with a classified list of African languages, was published in 1977 by the IAI (leading to a subsequent finalized edition, to be published later by Longmans).

6. If a relationship is established among languages 'A', 'B' and 'C', they may be considered as having 'internal unity'. This grouping has no significance, however, unless the languages in question also possess an 'external unity', i.e. where the relationship of 'A' to 'B', of 'A' to 'C', or of 'C' to 'B' is in each case closer than between any of the three languages and any language excluded from the group.

7. Of the remainder, no less than nine units include languages spoken on the fringes of the Fragmentation Belt (leaving only the few, 'non-Bantu' units of southern Africa and Madagascar).

approximately two-thirds of the total for the continent are spoken within this belt, some 5600 kilometres in length but only 1100 kilometres in average width. The belt runs immediately to the south of and parallel to the Saharan desert, and, in terms of its location and linguistic complexity, may be usefully termed the sub-Saharan *Fragmentation Belt*. Its limits may be determined by reference to physical as well as linguistic geography, being roughly coterminous with the desert fringe in the north, the highland ranges in the east, the forest fringe in the south and the Atlantic coast in the west. Areas of maximal fragmentation, in spatial terms, are located along the north-eastern, central and western margins of the Fragmentation Belt, at the southern tip of its East African salient, and in a block covering a large part of West Africa. In terms of overall structural and lexical relationships, the most fragmented area is probably in and around the tip of the East African salient, where representatives of all four of Greenberg's postulated African 'families' are spoken within a radius of only 40 kilometres. In this case, and in the case of the Togo Hills, Jos Plateau, Cameroon highlands, Nabu Hills and western Ethiopian highlands, there appears to be some correlation between mountainous country and intense linguistic fragmentation.[9] It should also be observed that the internal relationship of certain complex-units, represented by languages outside as well as by languages within the Fragmentation Belt, becomes increasingly blurred at the points where they enter the Fragmentation Belt.[10]

The linguistic and historical importance of the Fragmentation Belt has been obscured by the superimposition of a network of language 'families' and 'sub-families', postulated by European and American linguists. Among these, the two most extensive 'families' can be singled out as having more substance and undisputed validity than the two other major 'families' of Greenberg's classification, or even than several of the 'sub-families' into

8. In the case of many clusters of more or less closely related speech-forms in Africa, only arbitrary distinctions can be made between 'languages' and 'dialects' of 'languages'. If one treats clusters of more or less inter-intelligible speech-forms as single 'languages', then the total for Africa is in the order of 1250. If one treats each speech-form as a separate language where it is regarded as such by its speakers, and where it has a separate name, then the total would be nearer 2050. The latter method, if applied to Europe, would count Swedish, Norwegian, Danish as separate languages, but the former method would count them together as a single language. It is proposed that an 'order of magnitude' for the number of languages in Africa be arrived at by taking the average of these two assessments, i.e. approximately 1650 languages in Africa, of which approximately 1100 (arrived at by the same process) are spoken within the 'Fragmentation Belt'.

9. As a point of comparative interest, it is worth noting that there is a similar 'Fragmentation Belt' among North American Indian languages. This largely mountainous belt, over 3000 kilometres long and approximately 300 kilometres wide, runs parallel to the Pacific coast from South Alaska to the Mexican border, and includes an area of maximal fragmentation in North California (where representatives of six out of eight major postulated families of North American Indian languages have been situated within a radius of around 150 kilometres).

10. Viz. Semitic, East 'Cushitic' and Bantu (including Bantoid).

which they have themselves been traditionally 'divided'. Since the term 'family' implies a more human or biological sequence of descent than is appropriate to the phenomenon of language, the term 'area of wider affinity' may be suggested as a suitable label for each of these two 'families', especially as they each cover a more or less contiguous area within the African continent. The first of these, the *Northern area of wider affinity,* has been traditionally known as 'Hamito-Semitic' and more recently as 'Afro-Asiatic' (Greenberg) or 'Erythraic' (Tucker). The second or *Southern area of wider affinity*, has been known recently under the labels 'Niger-Congo' and 'Congo-Kordofanian' (Greenberg), or 'Nigritic' (Murdock).[11] There has been no dispute about the overall validity of these two areas of wider affinity, which have been apparent to European linguists since the seventeenth century[12] and presumably to African observers for very much longer. The relative importance of these two areas of wider affinity is expressed by the fact that they include between them *over 80 per cent* of the languages spoken in Africa, the Southern area of wider affinity itself including approximately 66 per cent of the individual languages of the continent. In the conservative classification employed for the current language map, the languages of the Northern area of wider affinity are treated within a total of seventeen complex and simple units (twelve being confined entirely to the Fragmentation Belt) and the languages of the Southern area of wider affinity within a total of 58 complex and simple units (57 of these being confined entirely to the Fragmentation Belt).[13]

There is an important reason for not establishing intermediate levels of relationship between the ultimate areas of wider affinity at the continental level, and the immediate complex or simple units at the relatively local level. This is the fact that such intermediate levels of linguistic relationship are, for an as yet indeterminate reason, much less obvious and difficult to define than the ultimate and immediate levels. Thus it is that the unity of 'West Atlantic' or 'Kwa' or 'Gur' or 'Benue-Congo', within the Southern area of wider affinity, or the unity of 'Cushitic' or 'Chadic', within the Northern area, has never yet been adequately demonstrated. Although attention was drawn some years ago[14] to this major area of weakness in the traditional European and American classification of African languages, these

11. Greenberg's 'Congo-Kordofanian family' covers his 'Niger-Congo family' plus a small group of more distantly related class-languages in the Kordofan. 'Nigritic' is an older classificational term revived in 1959 by Murdock.

12. See Greenberg's chapter in this volume (pp. 292–308 above): Greenberg also draws attention to the fact that the relationship between Malagasy and Malay was likewise observed in the seventeenth century.

13. Within the Southern area of wider affinity, the only complex-unit lying (largely) outside the Fragmentation Belt is Bantu. On the other hand, this one complex-unit accounts for almost as many languages (around 500) as the combined total of the other 57 units in that area of wider affinity.

14. See D. Dalby, 1970.

intermediate levels of classification continue to figure importantly in the literature. The imposition and maintenance of these arbitrary divisions on the language map of Africa may in some ways be compared to the history of arbitrary colonial divisions on the political map of the continent.

Greenberg performed a service to African linguistics in drawing attention to the arbitrary use of the term 'Hamitic', as an intermediate level of classification,[15] but was unfortunately responsible for perpetuating the arbitrary use of many other intermediate levels of classification. Doubts by linguists about several of these have already been referred to,[16] but more recently Professor Stewart has published an even clearer rebuttal of 'Benue-Congo', the largest of Greenberg's supposed 'sub-families':

> One important result of all this [recent] work on the Benue-Congo languages was to raise serious doubts about the validity of Benue-Congo as a genetic unit. At first it had been taken for granted that Greenberg was correct in his claim that many common innovations could be cited as evidence, even though in fact he cited only one, the word for 'child'. Williamson reports, however, that when regular sound correspondences are taken into consideration this item turns out not to be confined to the Benue-Congo languages and therefore not to be valid evidence: she further reports that in the whole of Volume I of the *Benue-Congo Comparative Wordlist* there is not one item which is valid evidence.[17]

When Stewart points out the long-standing doubts which had already existed regarding the external unity of Benue-Congo, one cannot but wonder why comparative linguists have been so reluctant to abandon its use as part of their classificational framework. Tragically, the whole object-lesson of 'Benue-Congo' appears to have been lost, and – rather than abandon this and other unproven levels of intermediate classification – Stewart prefers to perpetuate Greenberg's scheme by amalgamating 'Benue-Congo' with 'Kwa' and 'Gur' (two equally arbitrary concepts), to form yet another arbitrary subdivision of 'Niger-Congo',[18] now known as 'Volta-Congo'. We shall no doubt have to wait for the outcome of more comparative linguistic work before Stewart's 'Volta-Congo' is further enlarged to include the whole of 'Niger-Congo' or the Northern area of wider affinity, the one ultimate level of external and internal unity which is clear and undisputed.

15. See Greenberg's chapter in this volume (pp. 292–303 above).

16. See D. Dalby, op. cit., p. 160.

17. J. M. Stewart, 1976, p. 6.

18. Ironically, the only intermediate 'sub-family' of Greenberg's 'Niger-Congo' which is itself clear and undisputed is Mande. The clarity of this division reflects the fact that it is the only one of his putative 'sub-families' whose ultimate membership of 'Niger-Congo' is itself in any doubt!

Historians should note that the 'broad acceptance' of Greenberg's standard classification rests largely, in respect of Niger-Congo, on his own acceptance of Westermann's *Gruppen* or 'sub-families' of West African languages. As has already been pointed out, Westermann did *not* establish the external unity of his *Gruppen*,[19] while their clear internal unity demonstrates only that their constituent languages belong to the Northern area of wider affinity.

Although current classifications of African languages deserve to be treated by historians with reservation, one cannot overemphasize the importance of the language map of Africa as a source of information on the prehistory of the continent. Much more detailed work remains to be undertaken, and one awaits a new generation of historical linguists who are themselves speakers of African languages. They will be in a position to reinforce the essential groundwork of a close and detailed comparison of neighbouring and closely related languages. From this stage, it will then be possible to move back to the wider strategic interpretation of the African language map as a whole. Despite its greater degree of linguistic complexity than any other continent, Africa is notable for the fact that two-thirds of its languages belong to a single area of wider affinity, and that a differently composed two-thirds should be confined to the sub-Saharan Fragmentation Belt. Bantu-speaking Africa is the one region of the continent which has already seen an intensive debate on the prehistorical interpretation of linguistic data. The key to the prehistorical interpretation of such data on a continental scale, however, will be our better understanding of linguistic relationships within the Fragmentation Belt, although the scale of the task can scarcely be overestimated.

19. D. Dalby, op. cit.

Historical geography: physical aspects

S. DIARRA

Introduction

It is, of course, hard to separate African history from its geographical setting. But it would be fruitless to rely on determinist concepts in order to establish the full complexity of the relationships that have been established between African societies and their respective environments. Each community has reacted in its own way to its surroundings. The attempts made, with varying degrees of success, to order the environment bear witness to the degree to which men are organized and to the efficacy of their techniques for making the best of local resources. But for a changing Africa it is important to look at certain geographical peculiarities which can throw light on the major events of the continent's long geographical and political history. Here the architectural features of Africa as a whole, its extraordinary climatic zonality and the originality of its natural environments have been the inheritances impeding or promoting human activity, while in no way determining its development. In a word, there is nothing simple about the intimate relationships between African nature and the men that live in it, exploit, develop and transform it in accordance with their political structures, technical possibilities and economic interests.

Architectural features of the African continent

It is generally agreed that Africa belongs to a very ancient continent which, before breaking up and slowly drifting apart, included America, southern Asia and Australia. This continent, Gondwana, is said to have been the result of the earliest orogenic efforts of the earth's crust, which threw up powerful mountain ranges, generally running south-west/north-east. These plications, greatly eroded by long denudation, were reduced to peneplains, of which the largest are to be found in Africa.

Geological originality of Africa

Africa's originality can be seen first of all in the exceptional size of the pre-

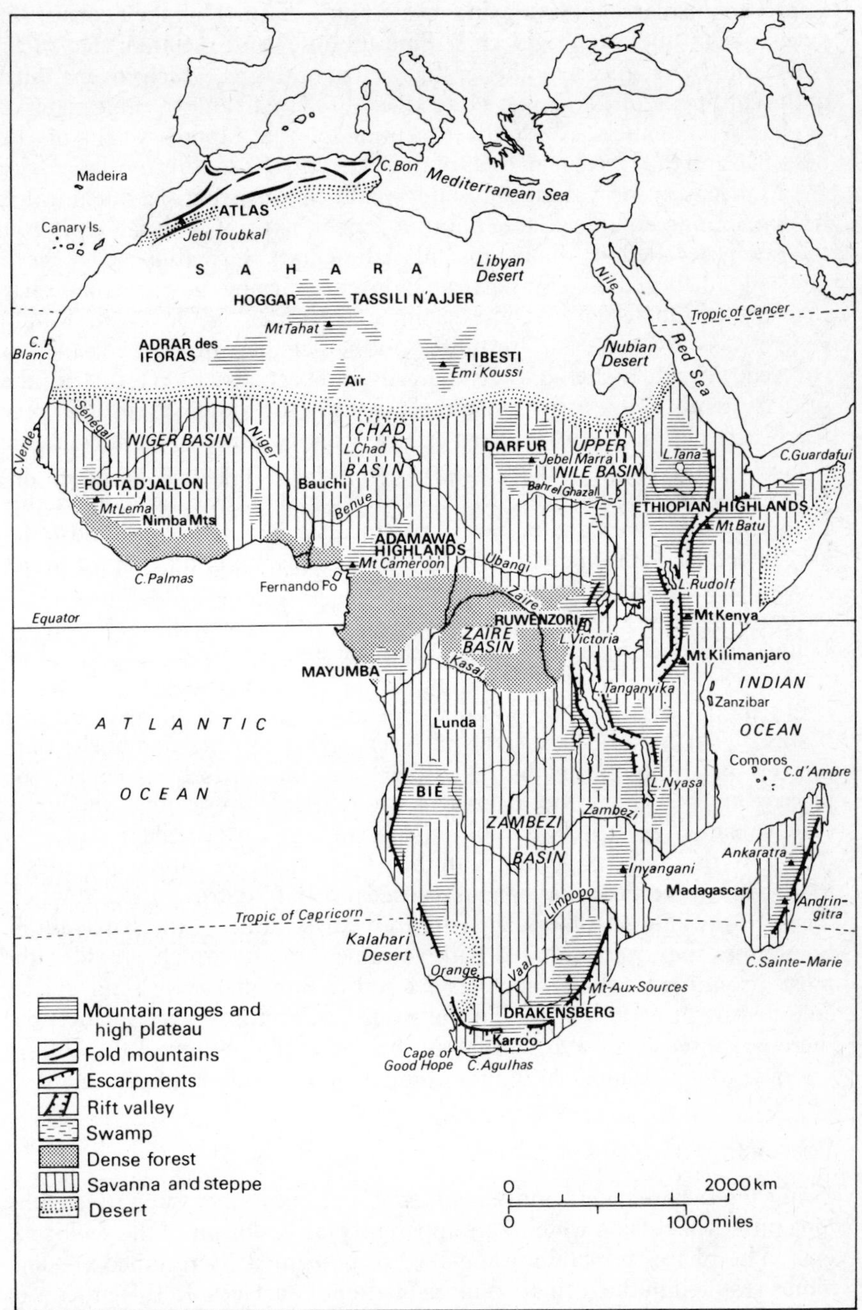

FIG. 13.1 *Physical map of Africa (after J. Ki-Zerbo, 1978)*

Cambrian insular shelf occupying most of its surface. This shelf consists of very ancient and very rigid crystalline (granite) and metamorphic rocks (shale, quartzite, gneiss), either in the form of outcrops, which cover a third of the continent, or else covered by a layer of sediment and volcanic material of varying thickness. With the exception of the Alpine system of the Maghrib and the Hercynian folds of the Cape and the southern Atlas, Africa and Madagascar form an ancient stable platform consisting of a shield which has undergone no appreciable plication since the pre-Cambrian era. Over the shelf, levelled by long erosion, sedimentary formations have been unevenly disposed in sub-horizontal layers, varying in age from early Primary to Quaternary. These sedimentary series, made up of rough, generally sandy material, are more continental than marine, for the sea covered the insular shelf only temporarily and partially. In West Africa the primary sandstones form an aureola within the outcrops of the pre-Cambrian platform. In southern Africa large continental permo-triassic deposits make up the Karoo system, in which the sandstone series are sometimes 7000 metres thick. In the northern part of the continent, notably in the eastern Sahara and in Nubia, the Jurassic and cretaceous sandstones are 'intercalary continental'. But in the Secondary period, marine series accumulated from the Jurassic to the Eocene in the coastal regions and the basins of the interior. They can be seen in the gulfs of Senegal-Mauritania, Benin, Gabon and Angola, the Chad Basin and the coastal plains of East Africa, from Somalia to Mozambique. From the Eocene onwards, 'terminal continental' fluviatile and wind deposits accumulated in the great interior basins of Africa. All these series of layers, lying on the rigid shelf, were affected not by plications but by widely sweeping distortions which took place from the Primary up to a recent era. Regional upwarpings and large-scale subsidences explain the fold-and-basin structure so characteristic of Africa. In the Tertiary period, with the paroxysm of the Alpine orogenesis, more violent vertical movements caused great fractures in East Africa. These form long sub-meridian rifts framed by faults – the Rift valleys. Sometimes they were coupled with volcanic outflows which provided the most prominent reliefs, such as Mount Kilimanjaro with its glacier culminating at 6000 metres. To the west, the fractures were smaller; but there was intense volcanic activity in the one at the bottom of the Gulf of Guinea, which resulted in the imposing Mount Cameroon (4070 metres).

Palaeoclimatic influences

Following the orogenetic movements the African continent was affected by long phases of erosion which were apparently fairly slow in all the geological eras. The phases of stabilization were accompanied by resumed erosion, which resulted in the formation of vast flattened surfaces. In this process of evolution the most important factor was climatic variation, and the most remarkable of such variations took place in the Quaternary. Alternating humid and semi-arid climates resulted in phases during which rocks were weathered and erosion in linear or sheet form took place. The low-lying areas were filled in and hard rocks made to project, often forming isolated reliefs emerging abruptly from the flattened surfaces. There are a great many of these inselbergs in the regions south of the Sahara. In the Quaternary, climatic changes and variations in sea levels were coupled with considerable adjustments to the pattern produced by successive cycles of denudation and accumulation during previous periods. Palaeoclimates are responsible for the Sahara, whose numerous stone artefacts and equatorial-type fossil fauna prove that in ancient times it had a humid climate favourable to human settlement. But during the Quaternary, increased or diminished rains resulted in an extension of the existing climatic zones either north or south. Thus pluvial periods considerably increased the proportion of the total surface of the continent suitable for human life. Arid periods, on the other hand, brought about an extension of desert regions beyond their existing limits and made the Sahara a climatic hiatus between the Mediterranean and tropical worlds. Nevertheless, the Sahara, which covers nearly a third of the continent, extending over some 15 degrees of latitude, has never been an absolute barrier between north and south. Inhabited by nomads, it has been crossed by caravan routes for centuries. It has not prevented communication between tropical Africa and the Mediterranean from ancient times to our own, but it has acted as a filter limiting the penetration of Mediterranean influences, especially in agriculture, architecture and crafts. So the widest desert in the world has played a vital role in geographically isolating a large part of Africa.

Massiveness of the African continent

The vigour and definition of Africa's physical features distinguish it from all the other continents. Africa's massiveness and heavy relief are the result of a long geological history. A glance at the map shows that Africa, with its 30 million square kilometres, stretches over nearly 72 degrees of latitude, from Ras ben Sakka (37°21′N, near Bizerta), to Cape Agulhas (34°51′S). There are some 8000 kilometres between these two extremities of the continent; laterally there are 5700 kilometres between Cape Verde and Cape Gardafui. The greater part of the continent – some two-thirds – lies above the equator; the continent dwindles in the southern hemisphere. Africa's massive nature is underlined by its lack of the deep coastal indentations present in Europe and Central America, for instance. Moreover, islands are not a significant part of the continent, whose sculpted form is vigorously enhanced by its simple outline and weakly developed continental platform. Any lowering of the sea level would have little effect on Africa's shape, since the 1000-metre bathymetrical contour is generally close to the coast. The continent seems even more massive because of the heavy relief, often in the form of plateaux, the edges of which rise to form coastal folds, which river complexes cross with difficulty. Despite its few plicated ranges, Africa has a remarkable average altitude of 660 metres because of the orogenic pressures which in the Pliocene were characterized by vigorous fractures and upthrusts in the shelf. Beneath an apparently simple relief, however, there are considerable regional differences. The Maghrib, for instance, has a marked individuality, being related to Europe through its mountain ranges and partitioned relief. It has two major mountain areas: the Tell and northern Rif ranges, and the southern Atlas. These ranges form long east–west bands between Mediterranean and Sahara.

There is another family of reliefs in the enormous region of north-east Africa, West Africa and the Zaïre Basin. Here the predominant features are plains, basins and low plateaux surrounded by mountainous folds. The largest basins in this area, the heart of the continent, are the Niger, Chad, Zaïre and Bahr el-Ghazal basins.

Eastern and southern Africa are the continent's highland regions, with altitudes exceeding 1500 metres in many places. The southern highlands are bounded by a marginal fold, the Great Escarpment, dominating the coast with a rocky wall 3000 metres high in places. But the originality of East Africa lies in its powerful reliefs caused by Tertiary tectonic movements. The shelf was violently raised and deep cuts were made by faults and fractures. At the same time it was affected by a violent volcanic movement. The summit of the Abyssinian massif, consisting of a great upwarping surmounted by over 2000 metres of lava, rises to more than 4000 metres. Rift valleys stretch over 4000 kilometres from the Red Sea to Mozambique. The Rift valleys, which have played a remarkable role in the movement and settlement of peoples, contain a series of lakes, including lakes Nyasa, Tanganyika, Kivu, Edward, Mobutu (former Albert), Victoria and Turkana (Rudolf), and are bordered by gigantic volcanic mountains, the most famous of which are Mounts Kenya and Kilimanjaro.

Geographical isolation

Because of its massiveness and heavy relief, Africa has been isolated until recent times. Apart from North Africa, which looks towards the Mediterranean world, the rest of the continent remained for centuries outside the major flows of trade. True, this isolation was never absolute, but it had a great deal of influence on many societies which developed in geographical isolation. Detached from the Old World when the continents drifted apart, Africa nevertheless has one point of contact with Asia in the Suez isthmus, which was the corridor for great prehistoric migrations. The greater part of the African coastline borders two oceans which until modern times were not used to an equal degree. The Atlantic was not used before the fifteenth century when the great seafaring explorations began from Europe. Before that time, the techniques of navigation under sail did not allow Arab seamen, for instance, to travel beyond the Sahara coasts, for their ships could not sail into the trade winds which blew southwards all the time. The Indian Ocean, however, had long helped to promote contacts between East Africa and southern Asia. Arab and Indian sailing ships were able to sail to Africa and return to their home ports, aided by the alternating monsoon winds of the Indian Ocean. The intensive relationships established between East Africa and the world of the Indian Ocean were restricted to the coast, for the seafaring peoples of Asia wished to trade rather than to colonize the interior. The influence of the maritime civilizations of other continents did not penetrate very far into the interior of tropical Africa, most of which remained outside the Old World.

Traditionally the inhospitable character of Africa's coasts has been put forward as the reason for its isolation. The lack of indentation means that there are few harbours along the coastline, which is low lying and sandy. Rocky coasts are few and far between in West Africa but there are more of them in the Maghrib, in Egypt along the Red Sea and at the southern tip of South Africa. In West Africa, the coasts from southern Senegal to Guinea and the Cameroon and Gabon coasts are characterized by rias. These are vast estuaries resulting from the submersion of ancient fluvial valleys, but most are silted up. Some of the low-lying coasts, swept by tides, have mangrove swamps, especially in the region of the 'Rivières du Sud' reaching to Sierra Leone, in the delta of the Niger and along the coast of Gabon. Elsewhere, offshore bars border the continent, in places isolating lagoons like those in the Gulf of Guinea. Finally, there are coral reefs along the Red Sea, the Mozambique Channel and the coast of Madagascar. The inhospitable nature of the African coast has been largely attributed to the heavy surf, breaking in powerful, regular waves, which made it hard to land in some coastal regions. But coastal inhospitability has been exaggerated: the Mediterranean coast did not prevent centuries-long trading between North Africa and the interior. The lack of natural harbours is also put forward in explanation of tropical Africa's isolation until recent times. But one need only list the sites attractive to sailors for navigation to see how rich Africa is in this respect, both on the Atlantic and on the Indian Ocean coasts. In any case these have never been insurmountable obstacles, for Asian and, later, European influences have left a strong impression on the peoples of Africa: their isolation was only relative. Human factors doubtless explain better why the African coastal peoples have taken so little interest in major seafaring ventures.

Climatic zonality of Africa

Living conditions in Africa depend in the main on climatic factors. The symmetry and great size of the continent on either side of the equator, its massiveness and relatively uniform relief combine to give the climate a zonality unparalleled elsewhere in the world. Africa is highly unusual in its successive climatic bands parallel to the equator. In both hemispheres,

African rainfall conditions gradually worsen towards the higher latitudes. Because Africa is widest in the intertropical zone, it is the most uniformly hot of all countries. This heat is coupled with increasingly dry conditions towards the Tropics or with a generally higher degree of humidity in the lower latitudes.

Cosmic factors

In this eminently intertropical continent, climatic differences depend much more on rainfall than on temperature, which in any case is high all the year round in most regions. Rainfall and heat are in any case primarily connected with cosmic factors, namely, the latitude and the apparent movement of the sun. The sun reaches the zenith twice a year in all intertropical regions, but reaches the Tropics of Cancer and Capricorn only once, on 21 June, the date of the summer solstice, and 21 December, the date of the winter solstice in the northern hemisphere. It reaches the zenith twice a year at the equator, at the spring equinox (21 March) and the autumn equinox (21 September). The sun in its apparent movement never goes very low on the horizon: this is why temperatures are high all the year round in the intertropical zone. In the regions near the equator, where the sun's apparent position oscillates round the zenith, there is no hot season, for there are few seasonal variations in temperature. There are some 3 to 4 degrees of difference every year. But as we near the northern and southern Tropics there is an increasing contrast in temperature. In the Sahara there are wide variations – some 15 degrees – between the average January and July temperatures. The northern and southern tips of the continent, which belong to the temperate zones, have contrasting thermal regimes, with wide annual variations resulting from the contrast between cold winters and hot summers. Moreover, daily variations can be as high in the Mediterranean region as in the intertropical zone. Cosmic factors determine two major types of thermal regime: regular in the equatorial latitudes and increasingly varied closer to the Tropics.

Rainfall mechanism

The reason for the seasonal variations in the African climate is the existence of major centres of atmospheric activity which set in motion air masses of tropical or equatorial, maritime or continental types. There are permanent Tropical anticyclones, or high pressure centres over the Atlantic, one in the northern hemisphere (Azores anticyclone), the other in the southern hemisphere (St Helena anticyclone). There are two further anticyclone cells, one over the Sahara, the other over the Kalahari. These continental anticyclones are seasonal and play an important part only in the northern and southern winters. In summer they are weaker and are flung back to the tips of the continent. Another major atmospheric activity is the low-pressure zone centred on the thermal equator, oscillating from latitude 5°S in January to latitude 11°N in July. Surface winds flow out from the anticyclones towards the equatorial low pressure zone – the trade winds which sweep the intertropical area. The Azores anticyclone sends out fresh, stable winds – the north-east Atlantic trade winds – affecting only a narrow fringe of the Sahara coast as far as Cape Verde. The high anticyclone over the Sahara is the source of steady north-easterly continental winds which are dry and relatively cool, but warm up as they move further south. The easterly harmattan, burning and dry, blows with great regularity over the whole of the Sahel from Chad to Senegal. It is accompanied by sand- or dust-storms bringing dry mists. In the southern hemisphere during the winter, there are also relatively dry hot winds in some parts of the Zaïre Basin. But above all in the southern winter – corresponding to the northern summer – low continental pressures centred south of the Sahara attract maritime trade winds from the St Helena anticyclone which bear north-east after crossing the equator. This is the Guinean monsoon, which thrusts beneath the harmattan, flinging it northwards and upwards. At the point where these air masses of different direction, temperature and humidity meet, there is a zone of intertropical convergence, or an intertropical front, which gives rise to the rainy seasons.

During the northern summer (May–September) the intertropical front, running east–west, moves from latitude 10° to 20°N, thus allowing the southerly trade winds to bring humid air masses towards the Guinea coast, thus beginning the rainy season. In winter, the convergence zone occurs in the Gulf of Guinea, touching the coast in Cameroon and cutting across the southern half of the continent to the Mozambique Channel and north-west Madagascar. North of the equator, West Africa is dominated by dry continental winds. South of the equator, the convergence of the southern continental trade winds with air masses from the maritime trade winds coming from the northern Indian Ocean brings rain.

The general mechanism of the climate may be modified by geographical factors such as marine currents, relief and coastal orientation. The constant cold currents on the Atlantic side of Africa are symmetrical on either side of the equator. In the north, the Canaries current, set in motion by winds from the Azores anticyclone, follows the coasts from Gibraltar to Dakar, bringing lowered temperatures and fog. Around latitude 15° the Canaries current turns west. Its counterpart in the southern hemisphere is the Benguela current, set in motion by winds from the St Helena anticyclone. This brings low temperatures and dense mists all along the coasts of south-western Africa, before it turns west at the level of Cape Frio. This is the reason for the coastal deserts of Mauritania and Namibia. Between the two cold Atlantic coastal currents of the Atlantic façade is the equatorial Guinea counter-current, which displaces warm water masses from west to east, increasing atmospheric humidity and instability and hence the possibility of rain along the coast from Conakry to Libreville.

The circulation of marine currents on the Indian Ocean side takes a different form. The equatorial waters pushed towards the continent by south-easterly winds from the anticyclone centred east of Madagascar form the warm Mozambique current flowing southwards and continuing further as the Agulhas current. This brings humidity to the south-east coast of Africa. North of the equator, the marine currents reverse with the change in wind direction. In summer, for instance, a hot north-easterly current flows along the Somali coast; in winter a cold current flows from Arabia towards the equator.

The relief of Africa, despite its relative uniformity, has an influence on the climate, for it acts like a draught-excluder, a veritable screen impeding access by the humid maritime air masses to the central basins, interior plateaux and rift valleys where varying degrees of aridity prevail.

The lie of the coast in relation to the direction of the rain-bearing winds also affects the climate. Sectors directly exposed to the south-westerly monsoon, especially when they are mountainous, have the highest rainfall in West Africa (nearly 5000 mm in the Republic of Guinea). In southern Africa and Madagascar, the coasts perpendicular to the direction of the maritime trade winds receive heavy rainfall. But coastal sectors parallel to the direction of the winds and without notable relief, such as those between Cotonou and Accra and in Somalia, receive less rain.

In Africa, seasonal climatic patterns are in the main determined by the amount of rainfall. The amount of rainfall decreases gradually from the equator to the Tropics, and the Sahara and Kalahari deserts have less than 250 mm of rainfall a year. Decreasing precipitation totals are coupled with increasingly marked contrasts in seasonal rainfall patterns as we go north. In the regions near the equator with permanently low atmospheric pressure, rain falls all the year round, but there is considerably less at the solstices. Further north and south, rainfall is concentrated in a single period corresponding to summer in either hemisphere. A rainy season is thus contrasted with a dry season which becomes increasingly long as we approach the Tropics. But the two tips of the continent – the Maghrib and the Cape Province – are unique in that they have winter rains. These regions have a middling rainfall irregularly distributed over the land.

Climatic zones

The variations in total annual rainfall and seasonal distribution of rainfall divide Africa into major climatic zones.

(1) *Equatorial climates* characterize the central regions on either side of the equator which see two equinoctial passages of the intertropical front bringing heavy rains. From southern Cameroon to the Zaïre Basin there is abundant rainfall all the year round. The air is saturated with water-vapour all the year round. The annual total rainfall generally exceeds 2000 mm. In this humid atmosphere there is little monthly variation in temperature: the yearly average is 25°C.

To the east, in the equatorial regions under the climatic influence of the Indian Ocean, we find the same rainfall patterns, but with an annual total of less than 1500 mm. The annual variations of temperature are more marked than on the Atlantic side of the equatorial zone. Diurnal temperatures are higher in the regions which, climatically speaking, belong to the Indian world.

(2) *Tropical climates* are found in the wide areas influenced by the movements of the intertropical front north and south of the equatorial zone. North-west Africa, between latitude 4° and the Tropic of Cancer has a variety of climates, ranging from two equinoctial passages in the south to a single solsticial passage in the north. On the coast of the Gulf of Guinea, the climate is subequatorial or Guinean, without a dry season but with heavier rains when the sun reaches its zenith twice a year. The orographical effect of the coastal screen condenses the strong humidity borne by the south-westerly monsoon. The coastal fringe from the Republic of Guinea to Liberia has over 2000 mm of rainfall a year.

The Sudan region further north displays several aspects of the intertropical climate. There is a humid variety and a dry variety associated with the proximity of the desert. At higher latitudes the two passages of the intertropical front are less and less distinguishable. This means that two seasons – wet and dry – alternate in the intertropical zone. Between the two extremes of the heavy equatorial rains and the aridity of the Tropic of Cancer, we find the following gradations:

In the first sub-zone with annual rainfalls between 1500 and 2000 mm, rain falls more than six months in the year. Annual temperature ranges are higher than those of the equatorial zone.

The central sub-zone is drier: rain falls only three to six months a year, totalling 600–1500 mm. Here temperature ranges show a marked increase.

The northern sub-zone, known as the Sahel in West Africa, has less than 600 mm of rain, falling in less than three months. Rainfall is increasingly irregular and there are wider variations in temperature.

South of the equator there is a similar latitudinal distribution of tropical climatic variations. But the gradations are more marked because southern Africa is less massive and because of the height and size of the relief dominating the coastal plains bordering the Indian Ocean. The convergence of the equatorial maritime air from the north-west and the Tropical maritime air from the east brings abundant rains to the coasts of Mozambique and eastern Madagascar. The Atlantic coast, however, is dry because of the cold Benguela current which is responsible for the Namib desert.

(3) *Desert climates* characterize the regions on either side of the Tropics. Rainfall is less than 250 mm and highly irregular. The whole of the Sahara, the largest hot desert in the world, has less than 100 mm of rain a year. But there are gradations because of the oscillation of the Sahara anticyclone which between the solstices moves up to the Mediterranean or descends to low latitudes. In the former position it helps monsoon

infiltrations to penetrate; in the latter it brings polar air. These oscillations distinguish the northern Sahara, with its Mediterranean rains in the dry season, from the central Sahara, with practically no rain, and the southern Sahara, with tropical rains in the hot season.

At the Tropic of Capricorn, the Kalahari desert is more open than the Sahara to oceanic influences from the south-west, for here the continent is narrower and the influence of the anticyclonic cell on the climate is accordingly reduced. Thus there is greater humidity and less heat.

(4) The originality of the *Mediterranean climates* in the Maghrib and at the southernmost tip of Africa lies in the fact that the winters are cool and rainy and the summers very hot and dry. The Mediterranean climate with temperate-zone winds is characterized by the passage in winter of humidity-bearing ocean cyclones. Sometimes there are invasions of polar air with intense cold, frost and snow, notably in the mountain ranges of the Maghrib. The dryness and heat of the summer are caused by the winds blowing from the neighbouring deserts – the Sahara in the northern hemisphere, the Kalahari in the southern hemisphere.

African bioclimatic environments

In Africa probably more than anywhere else, human life has been organized in natural contexts which are above all bioclimatic environments. Climate and relief combine to determine major regions, each of which has its own hydrological, soil and botanical characteristics.

Outflow of continental waters

The climatic diversity is reflected in hydrography. But in Africa the flow of water to the oceans is far smaller than rainfall would suggest. More than half the continent's surface is composed of regions either with no drainage at all or only draining internally. Moreover, river systems find obstacles in their way. Their profiles consist of gently sloping stretches connected by abrupt rapids, falls and cataracts. Hence much of the water that they drain undergoes permanent infiltration and intensive evaporation through stagnation in the basins, rifts and depressions of the plateau.

Organization of hydrological networks

Vast areas of the continent with little or no rainfall have no permanent water courses. But the dry Mediterranean area receives some violent rains which trickle into sheets of water and sometimes concentrate in wadis. These are finally emptied through water evaporation and infiltration. In regions with sufficient rainfall, in Tropical or equatorial climates, the major rivers and their principal tributaries form organized networks which collect part of the water from the basins and empty it, often under difficult conditions. The basins in which most of Africa's river systems are formed have peripheral ridges which are not conducive to good drainage to the sea. The continental waters are evacuated through the coastal folds by deep narrow gorges, with frequent changes in gradient on the lower reaches of some of the major rivers. The Zaïre has thirty-two rapids between Stanley Pool and the estuary. The Zambezi falls 110 metres at the Victoria Falls before plunging into the Kariba Gorge and passing over several basaltic cataracts. Downstream from Khartoum the Nile passes through six rapids, the Cataracts, before it reaches the Mediterranean. All the other large rivers – Niger, Senegal, Orange, Limpopo – have stepped profiles, notably in their lower reaches. It is easy to understand why it is so hard to navigate the rivers of Africa, which appear to be very poor channels of communication. Nevertheless, in the past they have encouraged fruitful contacts between different peoples of the continent.

Between the major river systems there are jumbled networks of streams, pools and swamps, ill-organized and with no regular drainage to the outside. Sometimes these waters are stagnant or are the outcome of the seasonal flooding of adjacent rivers; sometimes, on the other hand, they feed such rivers, which in the geological past developed in subsidence basins at the bottom of which lakes were formed and alluvium accumulated. Exterior drainage became possible as a result of tectonic movements, the hitherto enclosed lakes draining through rift valleys or faults. River captures, resulting from these tectonic movements or morphological change, have also doubtless contributed to the present shapes of the hydrological systems. But internal drainage can also be seen in the Chad and Okovango basins, occupied by shallow lakes and marshes which become impressively large when the seasonal streams make their contribution. There are, however, other subsidence basins with outlets to the ocean with a similar tendency towards internal drainage. These are the marshes of Macina or the inner Niger delta, those of the Bahr el-Ghazal in the Sudan and the Zaïre Basin.

African river regimes

All over Africa rainfall patterns regulate the hydrological regimes: seasonal variations in the amount of water in the rivers depend on the annual rainfall. Water courses in the equatorial regions are regular, with abundant water all the year round. Nevertheless they do have two high-water periods, corresponding to the times of the equinoctial rains.

In the Tropical zone a high-water period corresponding to the rainy season – the summer solstice – is followed by a period of sparse rains during the dry season. The regime is thus one of strong contrast. Moreover there is a gap between the times when the rains fall and the waters rise, because the waters flow slowly down the slopes, which are mostly gentle.

In the sub-arid regions, the wadis flow intermittently when rare but violent rains cause sudden spates which are, however, shortlived since the waters are lost downstream. In the Mediterranean zone, the violent downpours and the presence of mountains turn the rivers into torrents.

These rivers are highly irregular, in spate in winter and at a very low level in summer. Many water courses in this climatic zone are wadis with an intermittent flow.

The great African rivers with networks extending over several climatic zones fall outside this simple general scheme of things. They are characterized by complex regimes, with seasonal variations in flow changing from one end of the river to the other.

The major African rivers

There are a few great rivers, among the largest in the world, which drain vast basins almost all of which are in the intertropical zone. Their regimes depend on the rainfall supply on the slopes of their basins.

The Zaïre is the most typical example of an equatorial river with two equinoctial maxima. The Zaïre river system extends over nearly 4 million square kilometres between latitudes 12°S and 9°N. Through the intermediary of the Kasai and the Lualaba, it crosses the southern regions with maximum rain at the solstices. Its principal tributary in the northern hemisphere is supplied by rainfall at the northern solstice, and through much of its course it runs through regions with two equinoctial maxima. The combination of different intumescences gives Kinshasa a hydrological regime with two maxima (March and July). The Zaïre is a full, regular river whose annual average flow of 40 000 m^3/s is exceeded only by that of the Amazon.

The Nile which, through its parent branch, the Kagera, rises in Rwanda and Burundi, receives equatorial waters which spread out into the swamps of the Bahr el-Ghazal. After passing through Lake Victoria, it is re-inforced by tropical affluents from the Ethiopian mountains. The Blue Nile and the Atbara, with their solsticial maximum regime, enable the Nile to cross a huge desert area before reaching the Mediterranean. Although, with 6700 kilometres, it is the longest river in Africa, the Nile is not very powerful: its average annual flow is less than 3000 m^3/s. Nevertheless from Antiquity it has been one of the world's most useful rivers.

The Niger, whose basin stretches from latitude 5°N to latitude 16°N, has a more complex regime. It flows in a large, unusual loop. It rises in the mountain fringe of the Atlantic, flows towards the Sahara, then turns towards the Gulf of Guinea, into which it flows through a vast delta. Its upper and lower reaches cross southern regions with a humid tropical climate. The middle reach flows through an interior delta with a Sahelian climate, and with difficulty it curves inwards in the sub-desert region of Timbuktu before receiving an increasingly large volume of water downstream. The rainy season brings two simultaneous floods: one in the upper and one in the lower reach. But the former, visible as far as Nigeria, gradually declines because of evaporation and infiltration in the dry tropical zone. The second, which is visible from north-western Nigeria onwards, continues downstream because of the local solsticial maximum rains. The

Niger receives and is swelled by the Benue, its major tributary, in its lower reaches.

African soils

The geographical distribution of the soils follows a zoning influenced by climate. The various soil formations are in the main the result of the action of water and temperature on the local rocks. In the Tropical regions, warm, abundant, acid rains wash the rocks, dissolving basic minerals and carrying them deep down. In the very humid, low latitudes, up to 10°N or S of the equator, the chemical decomposition of the rocks results in the formation of ferrallitic soils. These are generally of loose reddish clay, several metres thick. They come from transformation of the matrix into colloidal elements, including kaolin, haematite and a proportion of silica (about 30 per cent of the whole). The ferrallitic soils are protected by the forest covering from erosion, and contain little organic matter or humus.

In the Sudanese regions with a marked dry season there are tropical ferruginous soils, which are much shallower. These are rich in iron oxide, with a sandy surface and clay at lower levels. They are very unstable and are sensitive to water and wind erosion. Their structure deteriorates very rapidly on the surface when plant cover is lacking. These soils are frequently caked or plated in West Africa, where the process of gullying during the rainy season alternates with intense desiccation in the dry season, especially when the harmattan blows. In some regions to the north of the coastal fringe of the Gulf of Guinea, there are ancient denuded erosion surfaces, plated or with hard pan, called *bowe*. These are characterized by large accumulations of iron oxide and alumina, with hardening at shallow levels. But many of these ancient *bowes* date from the Tertiary era. Their hardened surfaces broke through after the erosion of the loose upper levels. Everywhere such soils are of very limited value in farming. Similar soils are found in Madagascar on the *tampoketsa* to the north-west of Tananarive. Further north in the northern hemisphere, brown structured soils, of great agricultural value, have formed in a climate with contrasting seasons under a herbaceous cover. Despite their sensitivity to gullying, they permitted the evolution of agrarian cultures associated with the great Sudanese empires of the precolonial era.

South of the equator, in the countries watered by the Zambezi, lightly gullied soils resembling podzolic formations were constituted under cover of the dry forest.

In the north and south, in the sub-arid regions near the Sahara and the Kalahari, there are brown steppe-like soils consisting of more or less fixed dune sands with clay-sand formations in the depressions. Light and loose, they are good for farming, but to allow them to regenerate, long periods of bush or grass fallow are necessary. In the arid regions where mechanical forms of erosion are predominent, there are wide variations in temperature in which the rocks tend to break up and the violent action of the wind and the sparse rains cause sheet erosion. In these regions there are sterile sands forming ergs, gravel or regs covering vast expanses, with clay crusts in the plains. Apart from the oases, the deserts have no soil for farming.

In the Mediterranean environments, the action of water and the contrasted seasons brings less chemical weathering to the rocks than in the humid Tropical zone. The soils are like those of the dry Tropics, with red, grey or chestnut-coloured surfaces. They are generally rich in salts. Some, such as the steppe-like soils, are rich in calcium, thus heralding the temperate environments. Others, formed of calcium or gypsum crusts, are characteristic of the Mediterranean zones.

Biogeographical areas

Climatic and soil factors account for the diversity of the mesological conditions in which the botanical landscapes are formed.

Dense moist forests

The most imposing of the botanical landscapes is in the centre of the continent, between latitude 5°N and 5°S. Here the characteristic vegetation is the high, dense, moist forest. This is divided into several layers, while creepers and epiphytes accentuate the obscurity caused by the superposition of evergreen leaves. There are, however, gradations: marshy thickets on wet clay soils, or the clearings which herald the change to drier conditions. The species found in the moist forest are so diverse and mixed that their exploitation is difficult. With constant heat and humidity, exuberant vegetation thrives and micro-organisms, worms and insects abound. This environment is hostile to man; despite its silence it is inhabited by a wide variety of animals such as the hippopotamus, the elephant, the bush pig and the leopard. But it is the tree-dwelling birds, reptiles and mammals that can move easily and multiply despite morbidity factors such as the many parasites. Outside the equatorial zone, the great moist forest can exist on high land long exposed for much of the year to moisture-bearing winds, for example, on the eastern slopes of the high Madagascan plateau.

Savannah and open forests

The rain-forest zone is bordered by the dry deciduous forest characteristic of regions with rainfall concentrated around the solstices. It is often open, with the trees only partly covering bush and plant undergrowth. When overexploited by man, this landscape gives place to grassland characteristic of regions with a more marked dry season. Tropical savannah emerges as the low latitudes are left behind. This vegetation associated with areas with seasonal climates contains some elements of the more or less humid plants of the Tropical climates.

At the edge of the forest, in the woodland savannah, there are still large trees, but they are less frequent than bushes, and the grass cover becomes more important. Gallery forest, in strips of varying widths, borders the rivers. In the savannah parkland there are wooded spaces next to areas with less cover, which are populated mainly with tall grasses. There are grassland savannahs devoid of trees, doubtless because of man's deforestation and the caking of the soil. Further away from the dense forest, the grassland savannah composed of a continuous carpet of tall plants gradually gives way to scrub savannah where the soil is often bare between patches of plant cover. Herbivorous wild-life finds favourable living conditions in the different kinds of savannah. Hunting is good and stock-raising possible. Man finds it easy to farm in these lands, which are not hard to clear.

Steppe lands

Steppe, consisting of grass tufts and prickly thorn bushes, notably acacia, is typical of regions with a long dry season. This open landscape is found in the northern parts of West and East Africa, and more sporadically in South Africa, in the Kalahari and south-western Madagascar. Sub-desert vegetation of poor steppe is found in regions with less than 200 mm rainfall.

Mediterranean vegetation

At the tips of the African continent there are bushy or grassy steppes in the driest regions. But in the more humid zones, notably the mountain ranges of the Maghrib, there are dry forests of green oak, cork-oak, pine and cedar. These trees have evergreen leaves dominating a bushy undergrowth.

Conclusion

Africa is an old continent which, from very ancient times, has been occupied by a people that very early developed splendid cultures. Africa's geography, in its structural features as well as in its natural environment, displays vigorous characteristics inherited from a long geological past. Africa is more massive and continental than any other continent. Vast regions in the heart of the continent, more than 1500 kilometres from the sea, long remained outside the major circulatory flows which explains the importance for human settlement, since prehistoric times, of great meridian troughs like the Rift Valley of East Africa. This geographical isolation was strengthened near the Tropics because of climatic variations in the Tertiary and Quaternary eras.

For thousands of years the humid Sahara was one of the world's oldest centres of human settlement. Later, dry phases helped to form huge deserts such as the Sahara and the Kalahari. Exchanges of all kinds between the different cultures of the continent suffered but were not interrupted. Climate, then, is an essential factor for an understanding of Africa's past. Moreover, rainfall patterns and the bioclimatic environment have a real influence on the life of man today. African societies have in fact taken advantage of the complementarity of climatic zones to establish between themselves long-standing and vigorous flows of trade. Finally, the history of Africa has been markedly influenced by its mineral wealth, one of its most powerful attractions for conquering peoples. The gold of Nubia and Kush was exploited by the dynasties of ancient Egypt. Later, the gold of tropical Africa, notably of the Sudanese region and Zimbabwe, became a source of prosperity for the societies of North Africa and the Near East, and the mainstay of the great African empires south of the Sahara. Iron was traded in ancient times between the forest and the Tropical regions of Africa. The salt mines on the edge of the Sahara played an important role in relations between the black states of the Sudan and the Arabo-Berber peoples of North Africa. Recently, Africa's mineral wealth has been exploited on behalf of colonial powers. Today it is still mainly exported as raw material.

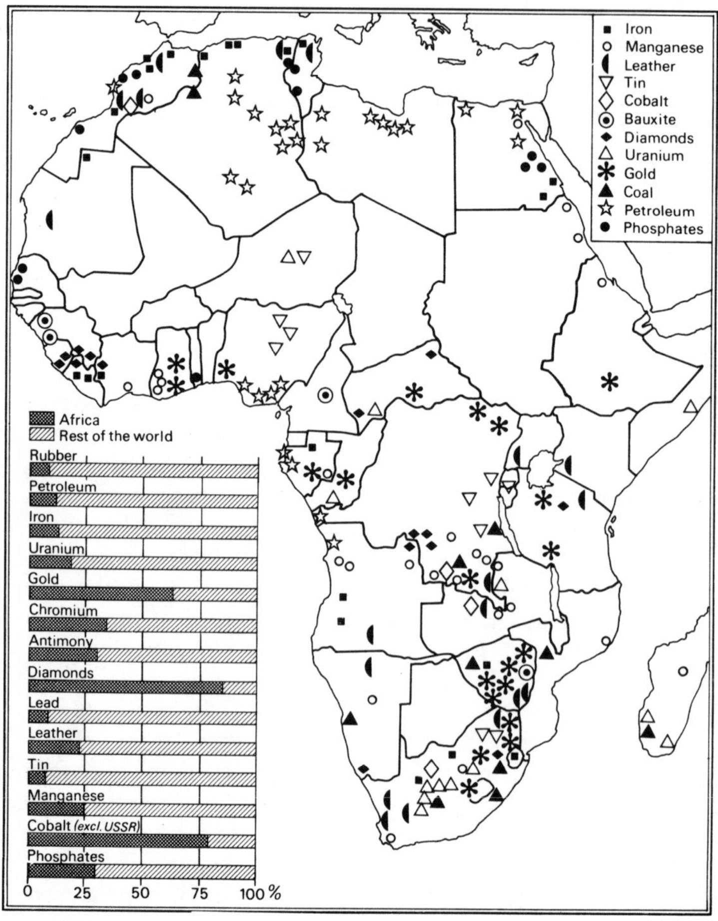

FIG 14.1 Mineral resources of Africa (*after Journaux, 1976*)

Historical geography: economic aspects

A. L. MABOGUNJE

According to Gilbert, 'the real function of historical geography is to reconstruct the regional geography of the past'.[1] In a volume such as the present, such a definition would imply an attempt to present a regional geography of African prehistory with special emphasis on the economic aspects. Such an attempt clearly would involve a comprehensive review of both physical and human conditions in the distant past and is sure to overlap with many other chapters in the volume. In the circumstances, the emphasis in this chapter is to consider the natural resource base especially in terms of how this was perceived and utilized in prehistoric Africa. Such a consideration, while emphasizing the broad spectrum of the continent's natural resources as known to us today, will seek to underline which of them were appreciated as such in the distant past, where they were found, how they were used and to what extent they aided or hindered man's control of large areas of the continent.

Minerals and the development of human technology

Perhaps the most significant of natural resources for the human mastery of his environments are minerals. Minerals are the material of which the world is made. In general, they are formed by processes which are extremely slow and which may run into millions of years. In consequence, compared to the human occupancy of the earth, which goes back barely 3 million years, the geological time scale is extremely long, covering well over 5000 million years.

Large parts of Africa are underlain by rocks, which are some of the oldest in the world. These ancient, crystalline rocks, which are referred to as basement complex rocks, cover at least a third of the continent. They are comprised largely of granites as well as highly metamorphosed rocks such as schists and gneisses. Some of these rocks are highly mineralized. Among the most important of such formations are those found in the copper belt of Shaba (Zaïre) and Zambia which extend for a distance of over 300 kilometres. Besides containing the largest deposits of copper in the world, this belt also

1. E. W. Gilbert, 1932, p. 132.

has some of the most complex deposits of radium and cobalt. The Bushveld igneous complex in Transvaal (South Africa), an area of 95 000 square kilometres, as well as the Great Dike that runs through Transvaal into Zimbabwe, a distance of 530 kilometres, forms another highly mineralized zone. The minerals here include platinum, chromite and asbestos. The African diamond zone has no equal in the world and shows its greatest concentration in South Africa although smaller deposits are found in Tanzania, Angola and Zaïre. Gold fields also exist in South Africa, Ghana and Zaïre and tin is to be found in Zaïre and Nigeria. There are also rich deposits of iron-ore such as those in Sierra Leone, Liberia and Guinea in West Africa.

The ancient basement complex of Africa has also suffered frequent volcanic disruptions going back even to the pre-Cambrian times. These disruptions have given rise both to granitic intrusions with which gold and tin are associated and to the intrusions of basic and ultra-basic rocks. They have also produced eruptive or effusive rocks, many of more recent age, which, apart from weathering down into good, fertile soils, have provided minerals and rocks such as the obsidian basalt in Kenya of real significance for the history of the continent.

Over much of the remaining two-thirds of the continent are found old, sedimentary rocks of pre-Cretaceous age. Because of their age, these rocks also contain notable mineral deposits. Along the northern rim of the continent, for instance, in an area extending from Morocco through Algeria to Tunisia is the great phosphate rock belt associated with which are iron deposits of considerable importance. Similarly, important iron-ore deposits of sedimentary origin are found in the Karoo region of South Africa and in the Damara Systems of Namibia. Coal deposits are, by contrast, notable by their virtual absence in Africa except for a few isolated occurrences in the high veld of South Africa and the Wankie field of Zimbabwe. As if to compensate for this deficiency, the younger sedimentary rocks of post-Cretaceous age in the Sahara and coastal areas of West Africa have been found to contain vast deposits of petroleum and natural gas.

These sources of mineral wealth provided much of the economic underpinning for human organization and exploitation over a long period of history. It has been suggested, for instance, that the control of the trade in gold between West and North Africa across the desert was one of the major reasons for the rise and fall of empires and kingdoms in the western Sudan during the medieval period. The trade in gold and iron-ore certainly attracted the Arabs to East Africa from the last millennium onward. The Europeans, on the other hand, were initially distracted by the mineral wealth of Latin America, but in the last hundred years they have concentrated on Africa as a colonial reserve of mineral raw material to stoke their industrial growth.

Yet in the prehistoric period, the minerals that were of fundamental importance for the gradual technological development of man were of more modest types and their distribution more diffused. The most important of these were those lithic or stone minerals which are homogenous in structure, high rating in their quality of hardness and with good flaking properties.[2] Of these, the best are the volcanic glasses which are found, for instance, in the volcanic regions of East Africa, particularly around the Gregory Rift valley and which formed the basis of the Palaeolithic Kenya Capsian industry for the production of long blades and various microlithic tools.

Other good quality material includes the chalcedonic forms of silica, flint, chert and jasper, siliceous rocks such as quartzite, and the fine-grained silica-indurated rocks such as silcrete, indurated shales and tuffs. Chalcedony was used extensively in the Mesolithic Bambata industry of Zimbabwe whilst Eocene flint and chert were particularly important on the Tunisian plateau and in Egypt, where they are believed to have been imported. Quartzites are more widespread in Africa, especially as pebbles in river channels, and form the basis of the oldest stone-age industries referred to as the Acheulian. In places such as in the middle reaches of the Orange river in South Africa, indurated shales were used for much the same purpose as quartzite.

Of rather inferior lithic property are the fine-grained amphibole rocks known as greenstone, basis and intermediate igneous rocks like basalt, dolerite and diorite, all of which provide suitable material for the manufacture of axes and adzes. They are also useful for making weapons such as throwing-stones and stone arrow-heads. Basalt is perhaps the most commonly used igneous rock for making stone vessels, although virtually all available rock types can be and were used. Of other igneous rocks, granites, diorite and porphyzite are also known to have been locally important. Softer rocks such as limestones were not unrepresented and in Egypt even very soft rocks such as steatite and serpentine were used. Besides, all over Africa, clay provided the basis for a widely dispersed and highly diversified pottery industry from the Mesolithic period.

The importance of minerals in the development of human technology in prehistoric times goes beyond the making of tools, weapons and vessels. It certainly includes the construction of dwelling places, for which simple mud served as important plaster. Major public buildings or monumental masonry such as the pyramids in Egypt also required large amounts of hard granitic rocks or quartzite. Minerals provided the pigment for rock paintings some of which, in the Sahara and in southern Africa, have been remarkably preserved until today. Such pigment was obtained from grinding various kinds of rock such as haematite, manganese and kaolin and mixing the powder with some fatty or resinous medium.

But without any doubt the mineral which had the greatest significance for development in the later part of the prehistoric period in Africa is iron-ore. Although modern technology with its elaborate mechanization

2. A. Rosenfeld, 1965, p. 158.

and huge economic investment requires the use of deposits of relatively high ore content which are very localized in their occurrence, the position was less restrictive in prehistoric times. Ferruginous laterite or ferricrete covers quite extensive areas in the grassland savannahs of Africa and is typical of old upland plains over many kinds of rocks. Some types are so rich that they formed the basis of the earliest iron-working activities on the continent. Once the technique was discovered in the continent, it spread quickly throughout it. This was in sharp contradiction from the situation with copper and tin which were so localized in their distribution that, apart from a few prehistoric copper-using communities such as the plateau-dwellers of north-eastern Ethiopia and the Luba groups in the Shaba, they failed to provide Africa with a widespread bronze culture. It should be recalled, however, that a copper age flourished in Mauritania five centuries before our era.

Vegetal resources and population growth

The vegetal resources of Africa had a very direct relationship with the capacity of the continent to support an ever-increasing density of population. As already pointed out, Africa is predominantly a grassland continent with grasses of various types occupying over 50 per cent of its total area, followed by desert occupying some 30 per cent and forest less than 20 per cent. In terms of human occupancy these varied environments have had significance related to their capacity to support game animals, provide edible fruits or roots, yield material which can be used to construct tools, clothing and shelter, or furnish cultigens which can be domesticated into agricultural crops.

The grassland zone was pre-eminently the rich game region of Africa with its wide variety of antelope, gazelle, giraffe, zebra, lion, buffalo, hartebeeste, elephant, rhinoceros and hippopotamus as well as numerous small game. It is thus no wonder that, as Clark noted, some of the earliest sites of human occupation are to be found along streams and river courses, round lakes and on the seashore in country that is today grassland, woodland savannah, Sahelian semi-desert or desert proper.[3] Such sites were generally absent from the forest zones, although with time, both the increase in man's number and the greater improvement of his hunting techniques encouraged him to occupy all kinds of country from the sea coasts to the high mountain plateaux and from what is now waterless desert well into the forest lands.

It is, however, important to bear in mind that today's vegetal zones do not necessarily correspond with the situation during prehistoric times. A succession of periods of great climatic variation have marked the Sahara desert which was, during the early Quaternary, more humid and carried savannah type vegetation which supported animals such as the ox, the wild boar, warthog, antelope and hippopotamus. By contrast, the equatorial

3. J. D. Clark, 1970c, pp. 93–4.

forest is believed to have experienced more arid conditions at about the same period.

Contemporaneous with resources deriving from the wild game-carrying capacity of different vegetal zones is the exploitation of these zones by man for edible fruits and roots. In this regard, the presence of gallery forests along river banks in grassland zones meant that Acheulian man had the advantage of fruits, seeds and nuts of both forest and savannah environments. According to Clark, many of the wild savannah fruits, nuts and plants available to the late Palaeolithic Nachikufan population in northern Zambia, such as the fruits of the *mubuyu* and *musuku*, are still regularly collected and eaten by the Bantu-speaking peoples today.[4] When the population grew such that virtually all types of environments were occupied, the range of food gathered for human consumption must have widened considerably. It is believed, for instance, that it was the greater emphasis which came to be placed on cereal grasses by food-gathering communities in the Nile valley that anticipated the intentional planting of grain and ushered in the era of agricultural expansion which has had such decisive effect on the human occupancy of Africa.

Apart from hunting and gathering, the vegetal resources were of tremendous importance in the provision of tools, clothing and shelter. Wooden tools have been well preserved in the area around the Kalambo Falls at the southern end of Lake Tanganyika. Here were found several single and double-pointed wooden implements and short, obliquely truncated sticks that probably served as digging sticks, all of which date back to the early Palaeolithic period. Although elsewhere such wooden tools have not survived, there are indications that they were widely used. In the equatorial forest, for instance, the Lupemban industrial complex of the Palaeolithic period reflects the importance of wood-working in its bifacially trimmed core-axe. Similarly, the presence of many heavy kinds of scrapers among the stone tools of the Nachikufan populations of the late Palaeolithic period in the woodland savannahs of Zambia and Malawi suggests extensive use of wood and its by-products, no doubt for making game fences, game stakes and traps of various kinds.

Where, as in the woodland regions, large game was not so numerous that their skins could provide clothing, the barks of trees were often used. It is probable that hafted edge-ground axes such as those found in the Mwela rocks area of nothern Zambia were used to strip and prepare bark for clothing, containers and rope. Especially from the Mesolithic period onward, vegetal products began to be used in the construction of shelters in place of caves. Branches of trees, thatch or matting were used, for instance, to construct the Mesolithic wind-break whose collapsed remains were found at Gwisho Springs and which dated from the middle of the third millennium before our era. By the Neolithic period and especially in those areas where agriculture had been discovered, shelters made of plant material or

4. ibid., p. 178.

sometimes of plant-and-mud material were to increase in number and spread. They marked man's initial steps in putting unequivocally his cultural stamp on the landscape everywhere.

But if the presence of such humble dwellings marked the beginnings of man's effective occupancy of the earth's surface, it was his ability to domesticate new plants out of the abundant wild species around him that ensured his eventual dominance. The conditions which enabled man to create new cultivable species (cultigens) from their wild varieties remain a matter of some controversy among scholars. Controversies also shroud the assessment of Africa's contribution to this great event. In the present state of knowledge, it is generally accepted that this has not been great, certainly nothing as impressive as the contribution of Asia. More recent researches after the monumental work of Vavilov, the Russian botanist who did not consider that there was any important centre of crop domestication in Africa outside the Ethiopian highlands, are starting to provide a more informed perspective on the native contribution of Africa to its stock of cultivated crops.[5] In this regard, there is no gainsaying that the savannah has been by far more important than the forest land. It was here that in the period between the fourth and the second millennium before our era many of the cultivated varieties of the African indigenous crops were domesticated. Many of these cultigens were of the seed agriculture complex and were characterized by the sowing of grain as the preparation for cultivation.[6]

By contrast, the few cases of domestication in the forest region belonged to the vegeculture complex, involving the planting of cuttings, rhizomes, tubers or shoots as the preparation for cultivation. The most important crop domesticated in this region was the yam (*Dioscorea* spp.), various species of which are now cultivated. The other domesticated plant in this region is the oil-palm (*Elaeis guineensis*).

In spite of the limited number of domesticated crops, the discovery of cultivation implied a new productive relation between man and his biotope. In particular, it meant a certain receptiveness to innovations involving the diffusion of cultigens from other centres, and Africa has received a large number of such new crops, notably from Asia and South America. In terms of the natural vegetal resources, this declared preference for a limited number of plants both indigenous and foreign has meant not only that man derived sustenance from the natural environment, but also that he was now set on a path of major biotic modifications. The need to clear land for the new crops and to suppress other plants competing with them for soil nutrient has resulted in drastic changes to the character of vegetation everywhere in Africa.

Perhaps the most potent agency used by man for this purpose has been fire. Evidence of the use of fire by man in Africa dates from the later part of the lower Palaeolithic and has led to the conclusion that as far back as 60 000

5. N. I. Vavilov, 1935. See Chapter 27 of this volume.
6. R. Portères, 1962, pp. 195–210; in this connection, see Chapter 27 of this volume.

years ago man was regularly using fire in Africa. Initially, however, it would appear that he used it for protection, for tool making and perhaps for hunting animals through setting fire to the grass and driving them out. Once he had attained the knowledge of cultivation it was only natural that he should use the same means to remove unwanted vegetation. This burning of vegetation for purposes of cultivation had different effects on grasses and trees. Grass, especially during the dry season in the savannah zone, burns down to ground level but is not destroyed because of its underground root stocks. Trees, on the other hand, unless protected by thick bark may be killed. Where they are not killed, they become twisted and gnarled.

The implication of the introduction of fire to the natural environment has thus been that man in Africa over the ages has significantly moulded the appearance of the landscape. As the frequent firing kills off the fire-tender tree species of the humid forest, conditions are created which favour the gradual extension of grassland. In West Africa, for instance, this process has been so vigorous as to create an extensive zone of derived savannah which is found locally as far south as 6°N latitude.[7] Within the savannah itself, it is notable that under the impact of the annual fires the vegetation alters in character with minor features of the landscape, changing from grassland on the open plains to a more woody cover over rocky sites. Indeed, the survival of such woody groves on rocky sites has led to the suggestion that the climax vegetation over a large part of present-day grassland must have been forest.[8]

Whatever the situation, the grassland regions of Africa proved of greater resource value to early man since not only were they easier to clear for cultivation but they were also easier to traverse. This factor of easy traversability was decisive in the peopling of the continent. Africa is *par excellence* the continent of large human movements, some of which are now being delineated by archaeological, ethnographical, linguistic and historical evidence. These large movements of people have been important for the rapidity of the spread of new ideas and especially of tools and techniques. So rapid sometimes is the rate of spread that it often creates great difficulties for researchers concerned with identifying the source region of the diffusion of various innovations.

Easy traversability has also been a vital factor in the spatial organization of groups of people to form political entities. The grassland regions of Africa have thus been notable for providing conditions conducive to the emergence of states in Africa. Once such states possessed the means of coercion, it was natural to expect that they would seek to bring under their domination other groups with inferior organization or implements of war. Such groups, once their resistance was broken, had the option of either becoming assimilated or retreating into less accessible or hospitable areas. In short, the corollary of the emergence of states in the grassland areas has been the further dispersal of weaker, less well-organized groups into more difficult environments such

7. W. B. Morgan and J. C. Pugh, 1969, p. 210.
8. S. R. Eyre, 1963.

as highly broken, mountainous areas, arid wastes or heavily forested regions.

The vegetal resources of Africa can thus be seen to have played a very vital role in the historical evolution of man in Africa. Not only have they provided man with an abundant supply of fruits and roots, but they have enabled him to create crops which can be nurtured and protected to provide him with new and richer sources of sustenance. The increase in food supplies facilitated the steady growth of African population. Up to 1650, the continent, according to Carr-Saunders, was only less populous than Asia, its population of 100 million representing over 20 per cent of the world total.[9] An important factor in the growth of population was the greater security offered by the better organized socio-political entities. Because of their greater distribution within the savannah zone, it is easy to appreciate why this zone probably accounted for a large proportion of the continent's population at this time – a fact which, especially in West Africa, came to be gradually reversed with slave raiding and the eventual foreign colonization of the continent from the sixteenth century onwards.

Animal resources and cultural diversification

Closely related to the vegetal resources is the pattern of distribution of the animal resources. Africa has attracted attention from as far back as records go as the continent with large mammalian resources. Indeed, it is claimed that, excluding bats, the African mammalians consist of as many as thirty-eight families.

The distribution of these animals over the continent has varied both in time and space. Fossil remains indicate that all regions of the continent carried at one time or the other an assortment of even the larger wild life. The North African Mediterranean region, for instance, was the home of animals such as the lion and the elephant, many of which were believed to have been driven out in the periods of great aridity during the Pleistocene. Most of those left behind were overexploited in our era to meet, for instance, the large demands of Roman amphitheatres. Indeed, as late as the middle of the nineteenth century, the army of the French Duc d'Aumale discovered great numbers of wild animals, including lions, wherever they went in Algeria, from the precipitous rocks of Constantine to the plains of Oran.

The desert still preserves a remarkable range of wild life. These include the dorcas and dama gazelle, the addax, the scimitar-horned oryx or oryx algazel. In much earlier and wetter times, its resources are known to have been more considerable and to have included animals such as the elephant, rhinoceros, hippopotamus, giraffe, the now extinct giant buffalo, and many of the larger antelopes.

But it is the grassland plains of Africa which are the true home of the

9. A. M. Carr-Saunders, 1964. At the present time, the population of Africa represents barely 10 per cent of the world total.

majority of African game.[10] Within these zones in West, East, central and southern Africa are found beasts of prey such as the lion, the leopard, the African tiger-cat and the hyena. It is here also that we find the bubal hartebeests, the topi, the red-fronted gazelle, the wart-hog, the roan antelope, the zebra, the giraffe and the ostrich. Here is the natural habitat of the elephant, the buffalo and the black rhinoceros as well as of the Derby and Cape eland, the bushbuck, waterbuck and reedbuck. The extent of territory covered by each of these has changed over the centuries. All of the animals have suffered great depredations at the hands of man or have lost to other species in the great competition for survival as environmental conditions changed. The absence of the white rhinoceros between the Zambezi and the upper White Nile, for instance, is ascribed to the competitive advantage which the change in climate and vegetation during the Pleistocene gave to the more aggressive black rhinoceros.

Although most of the wild game frequent the forest of tropical Africa, this region is on the whole less endowed with animal resources. Some of the more notable forest animals include the bush pig, the giant forest hog, the bongo, the great apes such as the gorilla and champanzee and the okapi. Even here environmental changes have affected the extent of the territory available earlier. The intermittent presence of the bongo is due to the reduction of what must once have been a continuous forest cover across equatorial Africa.

These abundant animal resources certainly served man over the long period of his existence as primarily a hunter. So inexhaustible did these resources appear that some African communities have remained in this hunting stage of development right up to the present day. A special category of animal resources is represented by fish, which have also been caught from as far back as the Mesolithic. Not only the rivers but also freshwater lakes such as Turkana (Rudolf), Nakuru and Edward in East Africa and the Chad in West Africa attracted early human population because of their fish resources.[11] Of the rivers, the Nile was obviously of special importance. Here were found waterside communities who used harpoons and fish-hooks of bone and, in addition, hunted and ate the hippopotamus and the crocodile. The use of simple dugout canoes for fishing in inland waters is still pervasive throughout Africa. Only a few fishing communities, however, developed canoes large enough to attempt coastal sea fishing. Everywhere until recently, inadequate technological development prevented the exploitation of the rich fish resources in the sea around the continent.

The singular richness of variety among land animals, however, provided a tremendous reserve of potential domesticates. Now, domestication of animals in Africa was virtually limited to the ass, the cat, the guinea fowl, the sheep and the cow.[12] One reason for this state of affairs is that Africa

10. F. Sommer, 1953, p. 64. In this connection, see Chapter 20 of this volume.
11. Cf. Putton; in this connection, see Chapter 20.
12. J. D. Clark, 1970c, p. 204.

during the Neolithic was influenced by an earlier and more successful experiment in south-west Asia. It was at this time that the continent was introduced to pastoralism. According to Clark, 'the first Neolithic pastoralists appear in the Sahara in the fifth millennium before our era, perhaps earlier. They drove herds of long and short-horned cattle and goats and flocks of sheep and continued there until the increasing desiccation after two thousand five hundred years before our era forced some of them to move out.'

Pastoralism was, however, not diffused uniformly in all the environments of the continent. Whilst most communities came to own the smaller varieties of stock, only a few mastered the skill of tending the larger ones. Among these the Tuareg of the Sahara, the Fulani of the West African savannah and the Masai of the East African grassland remained overwhelmingly committed to animal husbandry, and have eschewed any attempt at combining this skill with that of plant husbandry. Constantly following their herds in search of water and pasture, these communities have maintained till today the nomadic way of life in its purest form. Some Bantu groups in East Africa, however, have managed to combine animal husbandry with cultivation to the mutual advantage of both.

Perhaps one of the factors inhibiting the spread of pastoralism in Africa was the proliferation of other zoological species which had a negative impact on resource development of the continent. Prominent among these is the tsetse fly. This large, bustling brown fly is the main, but not the only, vector of trypanosomiasis, a disease which causes sleeping sickness in man and spells death for his animals. This fly is found today in a belt running across Africa between latitudes 14°N and S of the equator. The only exceptions are the highlands rising to levels above 1000 metres which are relatively cold, and the open short-grass country where the dry season is too hot and desiccating for the fly to breed.

Tsetse fly has been present in Africa since very remote times. Given the fact that fossil impressions of this fly have been found in the Miocene beds in North America, it would appear that the fly must have had a far wider distribution in prehistoric times.[13] Its disappearance from various areas in Africa and in parts of it may be the result of a combination of climatic changes, natural barriers and glaciation. Indeed, within Africa, the climatic alternations of the Pleistocene must have had a tremendous influence not only on the distribution of various species of the fly but also on their infection rates.

Belts of land infested by these flies have constituted effective barriers to the development of animal husbandry. Herders must have realized at an early stage that their herds would face heavy losses when travelling through infested country. As such, the penetration of cattle from North Africa to the south was subject to the existence of natural fly-free corridors as well as those created by densely settled agricultural communities. Of the

13. T. D. A. Cockerell, 1907, 1909, 1919.

latter, a good example is provided by the migration of cattle owners some nine centuries ago creating, through the merging with other peoples, the Tutsi and Hutu society of present-day Rwanda and Burundi.

The history of Africa would have been very different if the continent had been free of tsetse. Instead, with the fly effectively keeping large livestock out of the reach of settled agricultural communities, the use of such animals for draught purposes never occurred nor was opportunity created for discovering the great importance of the wheel. On the other hand, some of the larger livestock provided some peoples with riding animals whose fleetness of foot encouraged them into aggression and political domination of the sedentary peoples.[14]

Among other adverse zoological factors, we find the malarial mosquito and the locust. Of the several species of mosquito capable of transmitting malarial parasites of one kind or another, some are more attracted to human blood than others. The most prevalent in Africa is *Anopheles gambiae* which, because it also feeds on animals, is very difficult to eradicate as it can survive even if temporarily prevented from feeding on man. The mosquito usually breeds in standing water and is most numerous near swamps and rivers. Its breeding places increase with increasing rainfall, and high temperatures boost both the development of its larvae and that of the plasmodium cycle in the adult mosquito. By the same token, cooler temperatures encountered at higher altitudes curtail the incidence of the mosquito. Thus, endemic malaria tends to disappear above 1000 metres even though transmission may persist beyond this level.

How long the mosquito has been part of the human environment in Africa is not known. The very high incidence of the sickle-cell trait found in many African populations would seem to suggest a long-standing and intimate relation between it and the evolution of the African populations. This trait is certainly the product of age-long selection pressure favouring the survival of these populations in conditions of hyper-endemic malarial infections. The malarial mosquito, to the extent that it greatly impairs the survival chances of non-adapted human groups, has also been a major factor in the history of the continent. Certainly, until the twentieth century, it effectively discouraged European settlement in the hot and humid climate of West Africa and saved the region from those thorny inter-racial problems that have plagued the history of the more elevated regions in North, East, central and southern Africa which had fallen victim to settler colonization.

Locusts are amongst the traditional plagues of Africa. They are large grasshoppers living normally in single, solitary state or in small groups. They are found in areas of vegetational transition at the desert margins or near woodland and grassland savannahs. Three main kinds of locust are found in Africa south of the Sahara. These are the red locust, the African migratory locust and the desert locust. All three need two kinds of habitat:

14. This may be seen in the role played by mounted warriors in the creation of African states, particularly north of the Equator.

bare ground for laying their eggs and vegetated country for feeding. Occasionally when, for various reasons, their feeding ground is restricted to a small area they congregate into large swarms to invade areas far and near. Examples of such invasions are not easy to identify from the distant past, although the Old Testament does refer to the locust as one of the plagues from which Egypt suffered at the time of Moses. From about the nineteenth century records of invasions become more abundant. Central Africa, for instance, suffered invasions from the red locust at different times between 1847 and 1854, 1892 and 1910, and more recently between 1930 and 1944. For settled agricultural populations, the depredations of such invasions, especially just before harvest, can make all the difference between abundant food and famine. Where, in the past, other conditions such as drought coincided with locust invasion, the stage was set for considerable social and political upheaval on the continent.

Water resources and human mobility

The significance of water resources in the evolving history of Africa can hardly be overestimated. Although the continent has within it areas with some of the highest annual rainfall figures in the world, it also has areas with some of the lowest. The extensive regions of the Sahara and the Kalahari are a standing testimony to the acute aridity of large parts of Africa. But besides the deserts, the broad savannah zone has only marginally adequate rainfall and human lives in these regions depend greatly on the fluctuating vagaries of rain-bearing winds. This fact would not be a matter of serious concern if it were possible to exploit other sources of water such as surface streams, lakes and groundwater.

However, over large parts of the continent, especially in the relatively hot, lowland regions, the river valleys are infested with debilitating insects and are therefore unsuitable for human settlement. The river regimes also closely parallel that of the rain and thus bring little relief in periods of rain failure or prolonged dry seasons when the river beds are themselves bare of water. Traditional technology except along the lower Nile valley had no means of storing water against rainless days. Poorly developed technology also meant that groundwater could not be tapped below certain depths even in areas such as the artesian basins where the geological structures have helped to imprison vast reserves of water. In large parts of the continent underlain by basement complex rocks, little water storage capability is found and human settlement cannot depend on other than the annual rainfall.

Water shortage resulting in serious drought conditions has thus always been a fact of life in Africa. The climatic history of the Pleistocene period shows that for different parts of the continent there may be a cyclical pattern of long periods of more or less rainfall. But whatever the situation, drought represents an environmental pressure on human groups, forcing them to respond in various ways. Characteristic of virtually all of these ways is the element of movement, a search for better-watered areas either on a temporary or a permanent basis. Such human migratory movements can be peaceful but very often they tend to be aggressive, depending on their organization and their leadership. The histories of many communities in Africa record their migratory movements from one area to another, or the incursions of more powerful migrant groups who conquered and re-organized their societies.

Where water is adequate, however, whether from rainfall or groundwater sources, and where the art of agriculture has been developed, a settled population grows up with the potentiality of gradual social evolution along the arduous road towards controlling nature. Rich and varied crops ripen and the rhythm of their maturation comes to dictate the rhythm of social life. The harvesting season becomes a special occasion and rituals are developed to give appreciative sanctity to an event that is inexplicable except in terms of a benign natural force. Whether this settled population rises higher in the ladder of social evolution depends on a number of other factors, not least of which is the abundance of food resources to encourage a division of labour within the community and facilitate the emergence of groups with specialized skills. This possibility depends not only on the adequacy of water supply but also on the fertility of the soils.

Soil resources and the social evolution of communities

To a large extent, the geological characteristics of large parts of Africa determine the quality of its soils. Because of the variety of rock types within the basement complex, the character of soils developed on this parent material is highly variable and their fertility is no more than moderate. Such rocks, however, tend on the whole to have an adequate reserve of most plant mineral nutrients although their variability means that conditions may change rather sharply within a short distance. Soils developed on sedimentary rocks tend, on the other hand, to be more uniform in character over large areas, but they do not form anything approaching the wide tracts of highly productive soil as do the chemozems of the wheatlands of the Ukraine or the prairies of North America.

The interaction between soil characteristics and climatic factors has been crucial for soil fertility and its capacity to support dense population over the long run. In humid regions, for instance, the illusion of fertility produced by the luxuriant growth of vegetation hides the fragile nature of the soils. Once the natural vegetation is cleared, the organic matter in the soil rapidly disintegrates as a result of intensive bacterial action stimulated by the generally high temperatures. In no time, the fertility drops, crop yields diminish and the human population is constrained to shift elsewhere.

In the subhumid regions, on the other hand, soil fertility is much better. However, the periodic oscillation in the pattern of movement of soil moisture encourages the development of extensive areas of lateritic ironstone crust which are completely unsuitable for cultivation. The presence of such crusty surfaces means that moderately fertile soils are scattered and their capacity for supporting dense human population greatly impaired. Such soil conditions are characteristic of western Africa north of the forest zone and of the central African plateaux at the margins of the Zaïre Basin. In semi-arid lands with lower rainfall similar surfaces, known here as duricrusts, are also to be found, although their occurrence is more scattered. The result is that the brown sandy soils of this region are more valuable and in years of good rainfall give moderately good harvests. Further north, the desert soils are shallow, have poorly developed profiles and lack organic matter.

A striking fact of the geography of Africa, therefore, is that really fertile soils are limited in extent and highly scattered in their distribution. They include the deep loamy clayey soils derived from basalts and other volcanic rocks of Pliocene and later ages which are found particularly in parts of East Africa. Under high forest, these soils are chocolate brown in colour at high altitudes but red at lower levels. Of equal significance are the rich alluvial soils derived from the same type of rocks and found in the flood plains of rivers such as the Nile. The abundant yields of crops from both types of soils have facilitated the growth of dense human populations. Where, as in the Nile valley, this concentration is combined with a high degree of social and environmental management such as was provided from the predynastic Neolithic period, the stage is set for the emergence of a more highly evolved society. This later society with its growth of an urban civilization, its class differentiation, fine craftsmanship and monumental architecture as well as its use of writing, was the outcome not only of increasingly regular interaction with Mesopotamia but also of the possibility of supporting a dense population composed of a variety of social groups by an agricultural surplus which in those distant periods must have been very impressive.

Such conditions were later to be reproduced in a few areas of Africa such as the Bend of the Niger at the time of the emergence of the Ghana Empire in the early medieval period. But although there are other areas of fairly good soils, wide tracts of the continent, above all the upland plains where weathering has continued for millions of years, have soils that are thin, lack adequate plant nutrients or essential minerals, and are even today still of limited value for agriculture. In such areas, from as far back as the Neolithic, man has only succeeded in depending on shifting cultivation to eke out a living. This form of economy is profligate in its use of land and thus discourages the emergence of densely settled communities. The sparsity of population over large parts of Africa, with its inhibiting effect on social evolution, must thus be seen as a critical factor in its history. It is, of course, now known that the fertility of any area is as much a function of effective soil management as it is of natural characteristics. Indeed, other areas of the world where societies have today attained a higher level of social evolution have also passed through a phase of development in which their economy depended as much on shifting cultivation. For Africa, therefore, soil management constitutes a matter of vital importance for societal evolution. It was a determining factor in the past and points to the path that will have to be taken if a serious effort is to be made to embark on a process in which progress will be decisive.

Conclusion

The historical geography of Africa especially in its economic aspects yields a picture of a continent in which nature has been unusually kind, at least on the surface. The superficiality of natural bounteousness, so well exemplified in the fragile luxuriance of the tropical forest, has been something of a trap for the human population in Africa. Finding existence so easy to achieve, communities have side-stepped the agonizing demands of social evolution. It is true that some far-sighted individuals or groups of individuals have emerged here and there to urge their communities forward, but their impact has failed to be cumulative. No doubt external interference, particularly the long history of slave raiding, has had a pernicious effect on the general state of development on the continent. But the fact that such interference was possible is a grim reminder of the dangers for any human group of failing to engage in the continuous struggle of fashioning stronger, larger and more cohesive social organizations to face possible challenges.

The history of Africa will have availed us nothing if it does not strongly emphasize this fact. As in the prehistoric period, the geography of Africa today reveals a continent with still abundant natural resources. Its recent colonial past has, however, helped to create a situation where much of these resources are exploited largely as exportable raw materials to serve the needs of other societies. Moreover, exploitation with its high technological requirements demands the organization of the African peoples in large integrated communities to develop these resources for genuine development. The history of a decade of political independence of African countries leaves an ambiguous impression that the importance of fashioning such communities in competition with other similar communities is still far from being grasped. The purpose of this sketch of a historical, economic geography of the continent, if it serves any purpose at all, should be to stress that nature in Africa, as elsewhere, determines neither the destiny of a people nor the route it will take. Its role is at best permissive. Peoples, like individuals, have been and will continue to be the architects of their own fortunes.

The interdisciplinary methods adopted in this study

J. KI-ZERBO

Introduction

The interdisciplinary approach to historical research is a fashionable idea. But when it comes to putting it into practice, difficulties arise: there are great differences in method of work between different disciplines; and research workers are deeply imbued with the habit of specialization, and jealous of the territorial integrity of their own subjects. The same tendency appears even in presenting the results of research: the life of a community is still dealt with under quite separate headings covering, for example, economic, social and cultural aspects. Any suggestion of interdisciplinary working is thought of in terms of take-over bids. In this struggle for territory and leadership, history is in an ambivalent position. It is essential to all disciplines; but having (unlike other subjects) no esoteric vocabulary of its own for its practitioners to take refuge behind, it runs the risk of becoming devalued – acquiring universality, as it were, at the cost of respectability.

If history is an orchestra, its conductor has traditionally been the written record. But the history of Africa, particularly south of the Sahara, is characterized by a relative dearth of written sources, especially before the sixteenth and even more before the seventh century of our era. There is an African proverb which says, 'When your mother is not there, you suck your grandmother.'[1] Failing written source material, African history must combine all other available sources in order to recreate the past. The deficiency may in the last analysis become something of an advantage: it makes possible an escape from the overriding influence of the written word and the consequent implicit devaluation of other sources.

Historical and anthropological research in Africa has long suffered from two contradictory evils. One is the weakness of historians for regarding the process of social change as a mere string of dates. Hence the obsessional urge to construct a chronology that will make human development intelligible, to the neglect of everything else – economics, social structure and culture.

1. Lactation appears to be a reflex process, but the African pharmacopoeia included recipes for making grandmothers lactate.

Hence the linear approach aimed at producing a genealogy or a succession of events – the bare bones of history, in short, without the flesh and blood. The other even more pernicious aberration may come partly from applying to the real African preconceived ideas of the primitive condition drawn from sketchy concepts of evolution; it analyses structures as though they were timeless, disregarding the historical depth which alone gives them meaning, subjective or objective.

Again, some scholars are taken with the notion of the self-sufficiency of their own subjects: there are linguists allergic to any suggestion of cultural interaction, and functionalist anthropologists who reject the idea of historical depth. Happily, watertight compartments of this sort are being progressively broken down. 'The realization', writes J. Desmond Clark, 'that archaeologists, linguists and cultural anthropologists or ethnographers are faced with many of the same problems and that the best way of solving them is by interdisciplinary teamwork, is one of the most encouraging and exciting factors in African studies today.'[2]

The pseudo-history characterized by an exclusive preoccupation with chronology, and the delusion of a purely static, formal structural analysis, are on the wane. This is demonstrated by those schools of thought which are introducing diachrony and conflict into their methods of work, either integrating cultural data with linguistic data (for example, Calame-Griaule and Houis) or abandoning the sociologists' static approach for a dynamic one that takes movement and comparison as its tools (Balandier). Contradiction is, after all, an integral part of reality. What is certain is that no single discipline can tackle alone the dense jungle of the reality of Africa. The Gordian knot is not to be sliced through with a cutlass.

Some workers claim to have found the essential explanation of a particular African society in a single factor, for example, in a structural analysis of kinship, or in the complex of representations, beliefs, myths and symbols considered as a logical entity in itself, independent, for instance, of productive relations.[3] In fact a study of kinship shows us systems less 'pure' and more complex in Africa than, say, in Australia, with structures which Lévi-Strauss admits are conditioned by economic and political factors as well as the mere mechanism of kinship rules.

African history is less well equipped than any other subject to thrive in a vacuum, even (indeed, especially) when it comes to what might be regarded as history's special preserve: establishing the chronology. The correct solution to a problem of chronology often calls for the use of four different sources: written records, archaeology, linguistics and oral tradition. Thus the historian following time backwards is like a motorist with several instruments at his disposal for measuring distances: his mileometer, his

2. J. D. Clark, 1970.
3. See M. Griaule and G. Dieterlen, 1965.

watch, the milestones and, conceivably, information from a local inhabitant. This essential co-operation helps to ensure that the picture of the past is re-created with a clarity and completeness that no one source alone could give. The description of Koumbi Saleh given by Al-Bakrī would still be sadly incomplete were it not for the mass of supplementary information furnished by archaeological excavation. Even oral tradition made its contribution here, leading as it did to the discovery of the site of Koumbi Saleh. Hence it seems inappropriate to classify sources in order of importance, with written records at the top and oral tradition at the bottom. The value of a source is not absolute, but varies according to the subject of research. In any given case the mass of available data will include a master source, which will vary according to the topic. For African prehistory or for Pygmy societies, written records are obviously not the best source: there are none. For different periods and areas the range of historical evidence is dominated by different master sources, the others playing subsidiary roles. The master source is not the same for an obscure Gaetulian tribe, Jugurtha's kingdom, the Kirdi of northern Cameroon, the Asante of Ghana, the Kabre of northern Togo and the Gao Empire described in the *Ta'rīkh al-Fattāsh*. Moreover, it may well be that the master source will be identified only after the research is complete: for though the source conditions the results, it is the results that vindicate the source. So it is safe to say that in the field of African history the interdisciplinary approach, far from being a luxury, is one of the essential factors. There is in fact no alternative to it.

How sources complement one another

The sources of African history are manifestly complementary. Any single one on its own will be defective and give a blurred image of reality which can only be brought into sharp focus by means of other sources.

Archaeology by itself may yield little more than a dry-as-dust description or a sterile conclusion incautiously arrived at on the basis of a small number of samples; and if waiting for further excavations were the only way of confirming or exploding hypotheses, the pace of progress would become intolerably slow. But replaced in the many-faceted living context which it is its purpose to explore, archaeology does much for other disciplines and receives much from them in return. Finds are often explained from outside archaeology, as at Zimbabwe, where it is the gold mines and their defence, plus religion, that make sense of most of the structures above and below ground level. Grave-goods, and the positioning of bodies in tombs, can be explained only in terms of a people's beliefs and its ideas of the hereafter. Conversely, when excavation in northern Ghana brings to light architectural features identical with those of the Sudanic Sahel, archaeology sets or solves an interesting problem of cultural influence.

African art, again, can only illuminate history if it is illuminated by it. Art, and particularly prehistoric art, is conditioned by a multiplicity of factors, from geology through social and political structure and kingly ambition to religion, mythology and cosmogony. Aesthetics is closely governed by ethics, while at the same time serving it. Moreover, by recording ritual, scarifications, hair styles, costumes and scenarios, art often acts as a museum of social (and even physical) anthropology.

Art defined as craft plus inspiration cannot be understood without history. Social organization often explains points of style: for instance, at Benin the same artists (*Igbesanvan*) carve wood and ivory, while others work in pottery and bronze. The manufacture of ivory and bronze objects is in large part explained by a switch from one material to the other, just as the outline and external decoration of pots from prehistoric periods is only to be explained by their descent from plaited straw baskets. Then there are masks, on the making of which Africans have lavished such boundless imagination. Bobo masks, for instance, especially the three main types, *kele* (ancestor-mask), *kimi* (head of marabout crane) and *tiebele* (buffalo skull), are real personalities, familiar in the village: they are not only evidence of history, but contribute actively to the making of it.[4]

The cowries described by Ibn Battūta in 1352 at the court of Mali were originally intended for use as coinage, but they also served as adornments, artistically strung together, and were specially important on social occasions and at religious ceremonies. Here art is an integral part of a whole complex pattern which gives it meaning and which at the same time it endows with life. To embark on the history of certain African societies without a knowledge of the rich language of cowries and masks would be like going into a library without being able to read: it would inevitably produce a defective version of their evolution.

The same is true of oral tradition, which is discussed at length elsewhere. Oral tradition is history from life and transmitted by the collective memory, with all the garbling and lack of sophistication that this entails – but also all the freshness and vigour. Certainly it has its flaws: for example, it is often silent about economic and social factors. But even with its flaws it can point us to other sources which are often more relevant, such as manuscripts or archaeological sites: indeed, before embarking on any programme of excavations it is wise to set to work to collect oral traditions. It is also a help in correcting errors of interpretation that may arise from a purely external approach and it makes it possible to limit the number of hypotheses,

4. 'The great oracle mask or "spirit of God" is Go Ge, and is guarded by a high priest called a Gonola. The great mask plays an important part in the political system of these societies, which is virtually an extension of ancestor-worship, operating at night in the closest secrecy. For meetings of the Poro the great mask is brought to the sacred wood beforehand, covered with a white cloth. The Gonola acts as headman and priest, and dispenser of ancestor-sanctified truth. Go Ge is also a legislator: its decisions are promulgated in the village and have the force of law.' Translated from M. Houis in *Etudes Guinéennes*, 1951, G. W. Harley, 1950.

to narrow the spectrum of alternatives.[5] Where there are several versions of the same tradition, some other source (e.g., reference to a map showing the areas affected by an eclipse) will make it possible to decide between them.

Drums, which have their roots in tradition, are one of Africa's great living books. Some drums are oracles; others are broadcasting stations, war cries inciting to heroism, or chroniclers recording landmarks in the life of the community. Their language is essentially a message replete with history. In this connection some divide ethnomusicology into internal, technical musicology and external musicology, which is part of the social and cultural fabric.[6] The greatest epics and chronicles are often sung by groups organized for the purpose, and in a manner peculiar to Africa, in which the whole audience join, for music is never passively listened to, but it is performed by everyone who is present. What is happening is a collective celebration: the song, dance and music become a synthesis to which linguistics, history, botany, psychology, social psychology, physiology, psychoanalysis, religion, etc., may all contribute. Without exaggerating the importance of musico-chronology, the comparative study of music and musical instruments by arithmetical means and statistical analysis can provide clinching evidence on the question of the spread and development of cultures.

The world of African music is giving ground in the face of an invasion by other types of music, often less rich even if introduced by richer economic systems. Is the drum that has made history destined to end up in the near future itself as a museum exhibit?

Linguistics is becoming more and more the partner of history – and a young, reliable, productive partner it is. For languages are a living museum in which tradition is preserved, and to extract the real essence of them it is necessary to possess the science of language. Every language is both a psychological entity and a social phenomenon. Its vocabulary, for instance, reflects the impact of history on a people. But conversely it is the language, the 'word', that instils a system of concepts and behavioural rules into a people's mentality and motivations. Some concepts are difficult to express properly in a language geared to a different overall context; as for instance that of *sanakuya* (in Mande) or *rakire* (in Mole), roughly translatable as 'joking relationship', which plays such an important historical role in the

5. Obviously oral tradition must be placed in context. An interesting tabular analysis of tales and legends sets out in nine columns data internal to the tale (e.g. semantic and stylistic) and external data, some within the context of culture and civilization and some outside it. See 'Littérature orale Arabo-Berbère', *4e Bulletin de Liaison*, 1970, Centre d'études maghrébines, Musée de l'Homme, Paris.

6. Working on these lines, it is possible to advance into many more specialized areas, such as the relationship between music and speech, the social and philosophical symbolism attaching to music, the links between rhythm and possession-phenomena, the relationship between music and economic and ecological environment, and the relationship between the musics of different ethnic groups. Simha Aron and D. Constant in D. Martin and T. Yannopoulos, 1973.

Sudan and Sahel; or that of *dyatigui* (in Mande), which by no means coincides with the simple notion of 'landlord', or of *tengsoba*, rendered literally 'master of the land' or 'earth-priest' – though these do not convey the meaning. The historian will be continually using linguistic evidence along with other source material. Thus for instance the date and origin of the circular ruins in the Lobi area were determined by the conjunction of several pieces of mutually conflicting and supporting evidence. A hypothetical Portuguese origin, based on a text by de Barros, was ruled out by the line of the road supposedly used and by examination of the pebbledash coating, which turned out to be too fresh to justify an early dating; then the Wiili and Birifor name for these ruins, *kol na wo* or 'stables for foreigners' cows', was noted; the foreigners were identified as the Koulango on the strength of the style of pottery found in the ruins; and finally an estimate of date was made taking into account the migration traditions of the peoples of the area. This is a practical demonstration of the decisive role of linguistics in interpreting a particular historical fact.[7]

It would be a great mistake to confuse the phenomenon of language, which is cultural, with tribalism or the biological factor of race. The language of the Dagomba horsemen who invaded the Volta Basin in the fourteenth century is probably lost, having been supplanted by that of the local Kusase women whom they took as their wives and who became the mothers of their children. Here we see an example of linguistic contamination at the expense (as sometimes happens) of the political ruling class.

Ethnohistory, in the shape of the quasi-static ethnographic present of the functionalist anthropologists, is not real history. It has nothing to contribute to our team of sources, each of which is not static but a variable carried along by the tide of history. Besides, functionalist ethnohistory too often ignores material cultures and that general movement of produce which Leroi-Gourhan described as the matrix of civilization. Barter trade across the Sahara, on the basis of salt for gold from the Sudan (superseded some centuries later by that of slaves for guns), may well have been the main factor underlying the rise of the kingdoms and empires of West Africa.

Thus we see that a dynamic sociology must also form one of the principal strands in African historical research. It is not a matter of blindly shifting one's effort from one socio-political workface to another, either in time or space: that would create more problems than it solved. For instance, to calculate the average length of reign it will not do simply to extrapolate backwards from an average length established for a known contemporary period: the political and social stability or instability are not necessarily the same. Again, the preferential collateral succession – from brother to brother – in the Mossi kingdom of Yatenga would not produce the same average values as in the kingdom of Ouagadougou, where succession was preferentially in the direct line from father to son. In the case of Ouagadougou the

7. See P. Parenko and R. P. J. Hebert, 1962.

average length of reign would tend to be longer and the number of generations greater. There are also religious factors to be taken into account. For the dynasties of the Gan kings (Gan-Massa), who were regularly chosen from among the youngest full-grown men, the average length of reign would be greater again. In other words, the chronological horizon cannot be determined independently of data from the political sociology of a given country. But even the concept of stability itself is not an invariant ready-made model for all periods and countries. Stability may be merely apparent, or be bought at a high social cost. In Ethiopia and the kingdom of Ouagadougou the elimination or deportation of unsuccessful candidates and of collaterals produced a certain stability, but at a high price in human resources which must be accounted for in terms of instability if a true historical account is to be given of the development of these countries.

The natural sciences will also be brought into play to help crystallize the picture of Africa's past and bring it into focus. We have computers for processing certain numerical data; there are technological, physical, chemical and biochemical methods of dating, of analysing metals, plants and foodstuffs and of investigating livestock and its heredity; and there is epidemiology and the study of natural disasters, a branch of climatology. It is no accident that famines occupy an important place in African tradition, serving as historical landmarks in the same way as wars. Violence has no doubt played the same sort of part in the historical development of Africa as in that of other continents; but there are differences. On the one hand the low level of technological development has lessened its absolute impact; whilst on the other its relative impact has been greater because even a slight lead by one people over another in this field had heightened significance. Disparity in armament was probably the deciding factor in enabling the Assyrians in Egypt, the early kings of ancient Ghana and Shaka the Zulu to establish their hegemonies.

Statistics also has a major contribution to make, if only in helping to quantify facts that would otherwise be subject to qualitative distortion: for there is a threshold beyond which a qualitative change in social phenomena may be said to take place. A population of 10 000 will not have the same sort of structure as one of 10 million. When we speak of invasions by fourteenth-century African armies, the anachronistic pitfall is to think of these forces in twentieth-century terms. Recourse to statistical data, even if only in the form of rough estimates, will help to show events more nearly on the scale on which they really happened.

The study of African wars, moreover, is only of use to African history if taken together with that of religion, with which they are intimately bound up: for the art of war was partly an exercise in magic. To be convinced of this, one has only to look at Al Boury N'Diaye's fighting dress, covered in amulets. This custom continued down to the African riflemen of the First and Second World Wars.

Physical anthropology too can help in the compilation of true history.

This field has long been bedevilled with racialist myths based on outward appearances, such as the 'Hamitic' theory. The only cure is the interdisciplinary approach, which brings together different types of evidence in the search for the truth. Clues to certain identification are furnished by prehistoric rock paintings, though it is important not to confuse life-style as portrayed on a rock face with race. We must not forget that certain types of skeletal deformation, such as the lengthening of the skull practised by the Mangbetu, are related to culture and life-style. Haematology can help to clear up some misconceptions; it indicates, however, that even blood-groups adapt to environment, thus demonstrating the decisive effect of habitat on race. Race can be understood only by regarding it (like most of history) as compounded of nature and culture, with biology as the link. African nature has indeed left its mark on history; and consequently, while we must avoid mere mechanistic determinism, we should never lose sight of environmental factors.[8] The specificity of the cultures and prehistoric development of Central Africa, as de Bayle des Hermens has pointed out, is understandable only if we bear in mind the lack of daylight in the jungle – a reminder to us of the influence of space on time.[9] Nor can we usefully consider the earliest inhabitants of the Nile valley without reference to geomorphology and palaeoclimatology.[10]

Method

Thus the historian of Africa must take account of a wide range of interlinked and overlapping disciplines. How is he to organize this united front of heterogeneous allies in the battle for the face of Africa that was?

It is possible to envisage a loose association, amounting to no more than agreeing to common objectives, each member of the group then being left to work according to the techniques of his own discipline, with a meeting at the end to collate results. This does not seem a satisfactory method; it leaves intact all the drawbacks of individual disciplines without taking advantage, if not of all their virtues, at least of the beneficial effect of their close association one with another. A better way is the interdisciplinary method under which different disciplines, instead of merely working alongside, are grafted on to one another. Not only the overall research strategy but also the tactical details must be settled jointly. First the essential questions are agreed in rough list form, then they are split into groups according to the

8. 'Nature proposes and man disposes', wrote Vidal de la Blache; but as P. Teilhard de Chardin put it, 'Is not what a bird's-eye view of history shows us the most recent chapter in natural history?'

9. See H. Lefebvre, 1974 – a forceful work in which the author discusses a unitary theory of space (physical, psychological and social).

10. Chemical tests on calcium, phosphate, pollens and proteins can help to reconstruct dietary habits, which in turn may throw light on demographic aspects and the period over which sites were occupied. Palynologists are aiming to build up a bank of African pollens.

disciplines likely to be involved. Checks or collation of results must be carried out at regular intervals, or even when necessary at the request of one of the parties involved in the work; the problems are then restated in revised form in the light of the overall progress to date. Snags or bottlenecks that come to light as a result of the checks are dealt with by crash programmes or concentration of effort. This sort of continuous association or teamwork needs a director for the whole project or programme; but separate leaders may be designated in advance for the various stages of the investigation – one of which will call for a linguist, another for a sociologist, and so on. This sort of interdisciplinary working may well result in improving each discipline's techniques and making its attack on the joint research topic more effective. Journeying down blind alleys can be quickly stopped, and the maximum of useful routes and short-cuts can be opened up. Team research of this kind, in which archaeologists took historians, social anthropologists, art specialists and botanists with them to their sites, would act like a gigantic trawl-net, dipping both wide and deep into world history. This presupposes, of course, that Institutes of African Studies (of which a considerable number already exists) can adapt their structure to this way of working; and it presupposes above all a new attitude of mind on the part of the research workers themselves.

What, then, is the object of the exercise? It is to give back to Africans a conspectus and an awareness of their past. This cannot be a photocopy of the original: but, in somewhat the same way as in Plato's allegory of the cave, it must convey an impression of scenes that were real in days gone by.

Now life is essentially integration and coherence, the grouping of differing forces for a common purpose. Death, by definition, is disintegration and non-coherence. Life, whether individual or collective, is neither linear nor one-dimensional: it is dense, compact tissue. The re-creation of the past, a feat rarely achieved by historians, is occasionally attempted with success (admittedly under easier conditions) by historical novelists. Teachers of history, economics, sociology and so forth would find a fruitful subject for joint study in such slices of life as John Steinbeck's *The Grapes of Wrath*, André Malraux's *La Condition humaine* and Thomas Mofolo's *Chaka*.

Without turning to the writing of novels, we must aim at reconstructions of this order of density: for real life was even more action packed than novels. Truth is stranger than fiction. Every historical process partakes at one and the same time of all aspects of social reality, and any reconstruction that fails to take them all into account will be, if not non-history, at any rate a different history: incomplete and therefore one-sided. We can, of course, concentrate on a single dot on the surface of the historical picture and make an enlargement from it, always provided that we remember that it is part of the picture – without which it cannot be completely understood, even as a dot. This is even truer of the picture as a whole. Major historical facts like the Mande expansion in West Africa are the result of a conjunction of factors, including technology, material equipment, trade, linguistic advantages, appropriate political organization and religious fervour. To seek (as is often done) to give undue prominence to a single prime cause, before endeavouring to portray in all their teeming profusion the parts played by all the factors, is to set up a conceptual structure instead of trying to re-create the past in one's mind. This view of history in the round is even more essential in the case of simple and relatively unified societies than in countries divided on class lines. A distinction (perhaps somewhat facile) has been drawn in Africa between societies with a state structure and those without – the latter, of course, being defined according to the rules of one's own collective experience.[11] This is perhaps to overlook the case of an empire such as Mali: it had no metalled roads and no bureaucracy, and its rulers deliberately opted for the decentralization that the facts dictated; and the result of all this was that the real life of the majority of the population went on outside the state. It went on, that is, in the villages, which had been independent for centuries and were connected with the centre neither by the juridical link of a feudal fief, the physical link of railways and motorways, nor the functional link of income tax returns and central or local government regulations. To ignore this is to condemn oneself to a simplistic approach based on lists of kings and princes, many of whom may be known only for one or two high points in a reign of ten or twenty years, and who are set up as arbitrary landmarks in the real life of the people. The overwhelming majority of African peoples lived as unitary if not totalitarian societies, in which everything was of a piece, from tool-making to fertility rites, including the ceremonies of love and death on the way. In this sense a society ruled by animism is as highly integrated as one governed by Islam. In many respects this was not a secular society, and to think of it as such is to jettison a large part of the facts. It is quite true that centralization also exists in such countries, but it is not the type found in the modern state,[12] where it is as it were the price paid (and the antidote) for pushing the division of labour to extremes. For instance, among the Senufo, where the men's secret society is the Poro, the Lobi, who have the Dyoro, and the Dyola of Senegal, initiation often played a key role, the whole life of the community being organized around it. Again, whole federations of villages may be built round a common altar or cult, as in the Samo area of Upper Volta and in the Ibo country.

While productivity in Africa has remained relatively low, there has, on the contrary, been a tremendous flowering of folk art. For people almost totally dependent on nature, any clothing was finery. The meanest tool or pot was covered with decoration. Again, bodily scarification to produce

11. On this see J. J. Maquet, 1961. The author analyses economic, sociological and political aspects in turn in an attempt to define a model applicable to Soga society.

12. The episode related by Ibn Battuta about the people of Bouré illustrates this very clearly. The Emperor of Mali, having unsuccessfully attempted to assimilate them, in the end recognized their cultural independence.

sunken or raised designs fulfils the dual function of denoting ethnic identity and satisfying an aesthetic urge. Similarly with the iron coins (*guinze*) used by the Loma (Toma), Kissi, Konianke, Mende and Kouranko in Guinea, Sierra Leone and Liberia: they were at the same time coins, protectors of houses and land, and the resting-places of the spirits of the departed and the ancestors, and it would be a mistake to see them as limited to any one of these functions. To portray unitary societies of this type clearly calls for a correspondingly all-embracing history, the kind of interdisciplinary teamwork exemplified in the study of the Konkomba carried out jointly by the anthropologist David Tait and the historian J. D. Fage. A similar synthetic approach was adopted by J. Berque for his work on the social history of an Egyptian village.[13]

The global approach means taking into account all external factors as well as purely local ones. It means looking beyond the frontiers of Africa and integrating contributors from Europe, Asia, America and Indonesia into the fabric of Africa's personality. A perfunctory diffusionism is not, of course, enough: even when there is outside influence, it is modified by internal forces. As the schoolmen's adage has it, *quidquid recipitur, ad modum recipientis recipitur*, 'whatever is received is received in the light of and according to the form of the recipient'. Thus Asiatic rice was domesticated in areas where the indigenous African strain already existed, and similarly manioc where the yam already grew. African culture is a subtle blend of factors: it cannot be reduced to the arithmetical total of these factors, since they are not packets of groceries to be lined up and counted. African culture subsumes and sublates its constituent parts; and the object of African history must be to give full weight to all the parts and so portray the dynamic development of the whole. In other words, the interdisciplinary method should eventually lead to a transdisciplinary approach, one in which all disciplines are represented with equal right.

13. J. Berque, 1957.

16 Chronological framework: African pluvial and glacial epochs

Part I R. Said

Our purpose here is to give a general account of some of the changes in the physical aspects of the African continent during the Pleistocene and early Holocene or recent epoch. During this approximately 2 million years the climates and environments of the world fluctuated considerably. The series of momentous climatic events which occurred during this epoch subjected the northern latitudes of the globe on four successive occasions to the advances and retreats of ice sheets (known as Günz, Mindel, Riss and Würm in the Alps); river valleys and terraces were formed, the present coastlines were established, and great changes were induced in the fauna and flora of the globe. The earliest proto-human forms had diverged from the ancestral primate stock by the beginning of the Pleistocene, and the oldest recognizable tools are found in horizons of lower Pleistocene age. In large measure, the development of culture since man's appearance as a tool-using mammal seems to have been profoundly influenced by the environmental factors that characterized the successive stages of the Pleistocene epoch.

The idea that during several episodes of the Pleistocene epoch the glaciers were formerly far more extensive than at present had become well established in Europe, and it soon became obvious that these European episodes of climatic deterioration were of more than local character. Work in Africa, for example, has shown that the continent underwent during the Pleistocene climatic changes of far-reaching dimensions and, although these have not yet been correlated conclusively with the events occurring in the northern part of the globe, they are to a large measure tied to these events in a manner which has yet to be deciphered.

The prospects for the establishment of a time scale for the late Conozoic and Pleistocene have greatly improved during the last decade. Deep sea drilling programmes have given extremely valuable information on a more or less continuous sedimentary record of the events of the latter part of the earth's history. The detailed and multidisciplinary studies carried out on the cores raised from these programmes, the advances in geophysical and particularly palaeomagnetic studies, and the perfection of the techniques of radiometric measurements – have all contributed to a reasonably well-established time scale for this latter part of the earth's history. Much remains to be done in this field as the events of any one area have not yet been finally correlated with events in other areas. However, the chronology of the later part of the earth's history is better established than that of many other parts, and even though authors still differ in drawing the limits of the Pleistocene epoch, due to the great confusion arising from placing the classical stratotypes of the Pliocene and Pleistocene epochs within the sequence established from the sea bed, the following is the classification used in this chapter. The geomagnetic time scale of the last 5 million years shows that the earth's magnetic field has been alternately changing from normal to reversed. These epochs were interrupted by minor events in which a reversal of the general pattern of that particular epoch took place. The epochs are, from the youngest to the oldest: Brunhes (0·69 million years to present); Matuyama (2·43–0·69 million years); Gauss (3·32–2·43 million years); and Gilbert (5·4–3·32 million years). The Gilbert–Gauss magnetic interval was characterized by a great deterioration of the climate noticeable in many areas of the world (see for a review on this subject Hays *et al.*, 1969). This cool episode corresponds with the base of the continental Nebraskan glaciation (as recorded in the Gulf of Mexico), the onset of ice-drafted detritus in the northern Atlantic, and the middle Villafrancian continental fauna. According to several authors who would determine the Pliocene/Pleistocene boundary at the first onset of climatic deterioration, this episode marks the advent of the Pleistocene. However, the adoption of such a boundary would be inconsistent with the boundary as defined at the International Association for Quaternary Research (INQUA) Congress in 1955 as it would imply that the faunal assemblages of the classical section of Castellarquato, Italy, should be excluded from the Pliocene. Since this section has had worldwide use in biostratigraphic correlations, the consensus is to keep it in the Pliocene. The boundary is rather fixed at 1·85 million years b.p. corresponding with the base of the Calabrian and the Olduvai magnetic event of the Matuyama epoch. Recent work has shown that this was a period of warming rather than cooling. The first great Pleistocene glaciations in temperate latitudes occurred *c.* 700 000 years b.p. at the Brunhes-Matuyama boundary. This glaciation may correspond to the Alpine Günz. The Pleistocene, therefore, can be divided roughly into two parts, the later representing the glacial era and the earlier a preglacial Pleistocene. The Alpine Riss occurred around 120–130 000 years b.p., while the Würm started at 80 000 b.p. The latter glacial is perhaps the best dated and studied. It lasted up to the Holocene fixed at around 10 000 years b.p.

As stated earlier, this chapter attempts to review the most salient physical changes that set over the African continent in response to the climatic changes of the Pleistocene. A continent of the size of Africa includes a number of distinct environments, none of which need have responded in similar fashion or degree to the great palaeoclimatic changes of the

Pleistocene. The approach, therefore, is to review these changes within the framework of the present-day major climatic regions of the continent. These regions may be classified under two headings: equatorial and sub-equatorial belts, and the tropical and sub-tropical belts.

Equatorial and sub-equatorial belts

The equatorial belt covers today the hot and humid Zaïre basin of western Africa characterized by slight fluctuating winds, slight seasonal fluctuations of temperatures and humidity, and frequent cloudbursts and thunderstorms. This belt is covered today by typical rain forests. The sub-equatorial belt covers most of the middle parts of Africa. It is characterized by the prevalence of equatorial type air masses in summer, and tropical type air masses in winter. Winter is dry and only slightly cooler than summer. Most of this belt includes areas with abundant moisture to support a tropical savannah vegetation. The northern and eastern fringes, however, today support a tropical steppe vegetation.

As a result of the fluctuations in rainfall in these belts during the Pleistocene, this epoch may be subdivided on the basis of a succession of pluvial and interpluvial stages. The pluvials known as Kageran, Kamasian, Kanjeran and Gamblian are believed to represent the sub-equatorial equivalents of the four major glacial stages of the northern hemisphere, but this has not yet been proved. Two subpluvial phases, the Makalian and Nakuran, have been recognized in the Holocene.

The effect of the pluvials can be seen in bigger wadi alluviation and in the higher lake sediments or shorelines left behind in several closed basins as a result of the expansion of the existing lakes. The interpluvial stages are characterized by the expansion of aeolian activity when wind-borne sands were deposited or redistributed well to the south of the present-day southern limit of mobile dunes and when radical changes in vegetation took place. Several volcanic peaks in these belts show glacial features at lower elevations than the present snow line indicating cooler climates in past episodes. In the following paragraphs examples are given of these changes in some selected areas in equatorial and sub-equatorial Africa.

Lake basins of East Africa

East Africa, and in particular its lake basins, provides the type area of the pluvials and interpluvials proposed for sub-equatorial Africa. The lakes of East Africa lie within the African Rift system. Those which fill the lows of the eastern branch of this rift, with the exception of Lake Victoria, lack surface outlets and are situated in much drier climates. In contrast, the major lakes of the western branch of the Rift valley are filled to their overflow levels.

It must be obvious from the outset that evidence of higher lake levels in a highly seismoactive zone like East Africa must be considered as suggestive rather than conclusive. Possibilities of tectonic displacement of shorelines, modification of lake overflow levels and tilting of lake basins must be taken into consideration in this extremely unstable area. For this reason the concept of early to middle Pleistocene pluvials has fallen into disuse (Cooke, 1958; Flint, 1959a; Zeuner, 1950). Recent studies on East African lake basins have limited the use of this climato-stratigraphic evidence to the Gamblian pluvial where in places tectonically underformed sediments are recorded.

However, abundant geological evidence proves beyond doubt that the boundaries of the main rain forests have fluctuated considerably in the past. The great forests of the western drainage basins have been a major factor in conditioning human life throughout the archaeological record. The famous stratified site of Olduvai Gorge in northern Tanzania includes at its base a magnificently preserved vertebrate fauna of undoubted lower Pleistocene age. The climatic associations indicate a period of markedly high rainfall (Kageran or Olduvai I). Above these are two formations, indicating respectively a drier interval followed by relatively high rainfall (Olduvai II–IV). In this particular locality a stratigraphical succession is known which carries the most complete evolutionary series for the handaxe, from the earliest primitive forms to all the main specialized variants of this tool-type of the lower Palaeolithic as known in Europe and western Asia.

The pluvial evidence for the Gamblian in East Africa is primarily based on high strandlines and fossil lacustrine deposits of three formerly contiguous lakes lying to the north-west of Nairobi (Nakuru, Elmenteita and Naivasha). Naivasha has one high beach level of slightly pre-upper Palaeolithic age which indicates that the lake had a maximum depth of 200 metres and probably overflowed across a nearby watershed. Since the catchment area of the lake is small and the modern lakes do not exceed 10 metres in depth, this surface is taken as an indication of past wetter climates in East Africa.

In a rock shelter overlooking the modern Nakuru and Elmenteita lakes, a well-stratified site with a true large-scale blade industry was found by Leakey in Gamble's Cave in Kenya. The lowest deposit is described as a lake beach shingle resting on the rock floor of the shelter at a height of about 200 metres above the present lake level. The implementiferous deposits lie unconformably upon this shingle, and consist of a loose deposit of 'ash, dust, bone and obsidian'. The associated fauna is obviously of modern type. According to Leakey the implementiferous levels belong to the end of a period of high rainfall (which he calls the Gamblian after the site in question), the first to follow that of the latest levels at Olduvai which contained Acheulian implements and a highly distinctive extinct fauna.

The classic work of Nilsson (1931, 1940) on the East African lake basins presents one of the best documented studies of the past fluctuations of their levels. This author describes high shorelines from Lake Tana (surface level 1830 metres), the source of the Blue Nile, and records five major shorelines to

+125 metres with a less distinct level at +148 metres. Nilsson also shows that four lakes of the Rift valley (Zwai, Abyata, Longana and Shala) were linked up and temporarily overflowed northward into the Awash river.

Palaeoclimatological records of Lake Victoria show that the lake was low and without an outlet for a period of undetermined length prior to 14 500 b.p., at which time open savannah vegetation prevailed. The lake began to rise 12 000 years b.p., at which time forest vegetation first appeared around the northern lake margins, but for a short time around 10 000 years b.p. the level may have fallen to 12 metres below the present level. Lake Victoria was full between 9500 and 6500 years b.p. with an evergreen forest near its shores. The level of Lake Victoria has, in part, been affected by incision of its outlet, but the former low lake levels as well as the pollen sequence were certainly independent of this factor.

Butzer and others (1972) carried out a detailed study of the East African lake basins and gave the radio-carbon dates of some of the sediments of their former beaches. The events and dates of the late Quaternary of lakes Turkana (Rudolf) Nakuru, Naivasha and Magadi coincide to a large extent. Lake Turkana with a contemporary surface area of 7500 square kilometres is the largest non-outlet lake in East Africa. Situated in a downwarped zone adjacent to the East African Rift, the lake is fed primarily by the Omo river which takes its source from the western Ethiopian highlands. Butzer's work shows that the littoral, deltaic and fluvial beds associated with this lake had a level of about 60 metres higher than the present level at a period about 130 000 years b.p. and again 60–70 metres higher than the present level about 13 000 years b.p. Between this latter time and 9500 years b.p. the lake became smaller than at present and the climate more arid. Starting from this latter date, the lake rose again and fluctuated between 60 and 80 metres above the present level until 7500 years b.p. when Lake Rudolf shrank to smaller dimensions. This was followed by further higher levels at 6000 b.p. Starting from about 3000 b.p. the lake fell to its present dimensions.

The evidence from other East African lakes as studied by Butzer and others, 1972, shows a similar late Quaternary history.

The Chad and Sudd basins

The Chad Basin deserves special attention because of its location on the southern edge of the Sahara and the great surface area of the inland sea that filled the entire basin during the Pleistocene. The present-day Lake Chad is a relic of this old inland sea (see Monod, 1963 and Butzer, 1964 for references). The basin derives its waters from Central African savannahs.

The present lake surface stands at 280 metres with an area fluctuating between 10 000 and 25 000 square kilometres, a mean depth varying between 3 and 7 metres, and a maximum depth of 11 metres. The lake is separated from two large depressions, the Bodele and Kjourab, by a low divide, breached by the dry valley of the Bahr el-Ghazal. The lowest strandline of the present Lake Chad, at 4–6 metres, would permit water to overflow into the 500 kilometres distant Bodele depression. At its highest stand at 332 metres, the Pleistocene lake ancestral to Chad formed conspicuous shorelines at 40 to 50 metres and so occupied an area of 400 000 square kilometres. Intermediate, less continuous shorelines are also recorded. Grove and Pullan (1963) show that the great loss of the present lake by evaporation is largely balanced by the inflow of the Logone and Shari from the south. These authors estimate that evaporation from the Pleistocene lake may have been sixteen times greater, so that it must have received annually a volume of water equal to one-third the annual discharge of the Zaïre.

Butzer (1964) states rightly that the ancient Chad Sea represents, therefore, an excellent piece of evidence in favour of greater precipitation in subhumid tropical latitudes. Unfortunately the shorelines of the different parts of the basin have not been correlated. The 600 metres thick Pleistocene section which underlies parts of the basin shows the complexity and long history of this inland sea. In the case of Nigeria, Grove and Pullan (1963) suggest that a 52 metre lake stage during the upper Pleistocene was followed by a dry climate, with extensive dune formation on the former lake plain. Re-establishment of a stream network at a later date was followed by another wetter period with a rise of lake level at least 12 metres during the Holocene. It can thus be stated that two poorly resolved positive lake movements appear to have occurred prior to 21 000 years b.p.; they were followed by a long interval of desiccation and aeolian activity until shortly before 12 000 years b.p. when the lake began to expand again. The lake reached a maximum level with at least intermittent overflows at around 10 000 years ago. This high level lasted until about 4000 years b.p.

The upper Pleistocene–Holocene history of this internal sea, therefore, seems to coincide almost in detail with those of the East African basins.

The Sudd of southern Sudan represents, in the opinion of the present author, another great internal sea which probably had a similar history to the Chad Basin. The Sudd is a defunct lake which is assumed to have covered the Sudd region of the upper reaches of the Nile and to have extended beyond to the White Nile, parts of the Blue Nile and Bahr el-Ghazal. The idea of the existence of this former lake stemmed from the irrigation engineers working in Egypt (Lombardini, Garstin and Willcocks) and was elaborated by Lawson (1927) and Ball (1939). All were impressed with the flatness of the plains of central and southern Sudan and recognized that a small increase in the levels of the Niles would flood extensive areas. The Sudd Lake was estimated by Ball to have occupied an area of 230 000 square kilometres (the area within the 400 metre contour, the elevation of Shambe where the present Sudd growth of the Bahr el-Gebel begins to spread widely over the alluvial plains). This area is covered by the Um Ruwaba formation which has been recently mapped and which is made up of a long series of fluviatile, deltaic and lacustrine deposits. The highest point in this formation exceeds 500 metres in elevation and this far exceeds the lowest overflow point of the Sabaluka ridge to the north of Khartoum (434 metres), which is supposed to have formed the northern boundary of the lake. As has been pointed out by Said (MS.) this ridge lies in one of the major fault lines which bounds the southern edge of the highly seismic Nubian massif. This elevation, for this reason and for reasons pertaining to incision of Sabaluka Gorge by later erosion, cannot be taken as representing the height of the ridge during the filling of the lake. Further complications arise from the fact that during high floods the Blue Nile waters rush into the Nile, causing a damming effect on the waters of the White Nile. Even though the history of Lake Sudd is not known in detail, evidence of its extensive reach is obvious from the 382 metre beach skirting large areas of the White Nile. Like the Chad Basin it seems to have been very extensive between 12 000 and 8000 years b.p. To the north it must have been 50 kilometres wide (Williams, 1966). The lake thereafter shrank, and at about 6000 years b.p. annual rainfall had diminished to about 600 millimetres near Khartoum, and the level of the White Nile had fallen to 0·5–1 metre above its present mean high level.

Glacial phenomena

The former glaciation of Africa is closely related to the glaciers of the present day which, in turn, are dependent chiefly on the distribution of very high land. With one exception, the Atlas mountains, all known glaciated highlands lie in East Africa within a few degrees of the equator. Altitudes range from nearly 3900 metres to 6100 metres. Flint (1947, 1959a) gives a summary of the significant data of these glaciated areas and states that the snowfall that nourished the glaciers was probably the orographic precipitation of moisture brought by maritime air masses moving eastward from the south Atlantic and, to a lesser extent, moving westwards from the Indian Ocean.

The altitude of Mount Kenya (lat. 0°10′S; long. 37°18′E) is 5199 metres and the present snowline is at 4600 metres; the maximal Pleistocene snowline is estimated at 900 metres (Flint, 1959a). Mount Kilimanjaro in Tanzania (lat. 3°05′S; long. 37°22′E) has an altitude of 5895 metres and seems to lie at present just above the climatic snowline; the lowest Pleistocene snowline was above 1300 metres (Flint, 1959a). Mount Elgon, Uganda (lat. 1°08′N; long. 34°33′E) has an altitude of 4321 metres and lies at present well below the climatic snowline. During the Pleistocene it was glaciated. Mount Ruwenzori (lat. 0°24′N; long. 29°54′E) has an altitude of 5109 metres and its modern snowline lies at 4750 metres on the western (Congo) side and 4575 metres on the eastern (Uganda) side. Pleistocene glaciers extended down to 2900 metres on the western side and to about 2000 metres on the eastern side.

The Ethiopian highlands are not glaciated today but the Semien mountains (lat. 13°14′N; long. 28°25′E) seem to have been glaciated during the Pleistocene. Nilsson (1940) demonstrates two former glaciations in some of the peaks of this range (altitude *c.* 4500 metres) with climatic snowlines at 3600–4100 metres and 4200 metres. A glacial retreat correlated with the late Pleistocene corresponds to a snowline at 4400 metres. Nilsson (1940) also describes a late Pleistocene glaciation at Mount Kaka (lat. 7°50′N; long. 39°24′E) with a snowline elevation estimated at 3700 metres. Glaciations from other volcanic peaks in Ethiopia which at present lie well below the snowline have also been reported: Mount Guna (lat. 11°43′N; long. 38°17′E); Amba Farit (lat. 10°53′N; long. 38°50′E) and Mount Chillalo (lat. 7°50′N; long. 39°10′E).

The evidence is convincing that the equatorial and sub-equatorial belts of Africa were glaciated at least twice and that they were considerably cooler during the Würm. In addition to the glacial phenomena of some of the peaks of this belt, solifluction and soil frost activity have been found in Ethiopia (4200–9300 metres). According to Buedel (1958) the lower limit of solifluction during the Würm reached 2700 metres. Glacio-fluvial deposits have also been recorded in many areas of equatorial Africa. The deposits of Mount Ruwenzori have been studied by de Heinzelin (1963) and were found to grade into the Gamblian terraces of the Semliki river. The Semliki, joining lakes Edward and Albert on the Zaïre–Uganda border, possesses massive beds of cobbles, gravel, sands and red soil sediments which were alluviated together by colluvial deposits. De Heinzelin shows that the Sangoan–Lupemban terraces are contemporary with the glacio-fluvial deposits of Mount Ruwenzori.

Tropical and sub-tropical zones

The modern tropical zone of Africa has easterly prevailing winds and noticeable seasonal fluctuations of air temperature. The western part of this belt, which lies on the Atlantic coast, has stable trade winds, relatively cool temperature, high air humidity and is almost rainless. The remainder of this belt covers the great deserts of the north and south of the continent. These are hot arid regions with a great daily range of temperature and absolute maximum air temperature. The sub-tropical zone covers the northern and southern fringes of the continent and is characterized by having tropical air masses prevailing in summer and moderate type of air masses prevailing in winter. The seasonal temperature and rainfall differ considerably. Those regions with Mediterranean climate possess clear calm weather in summer and are rainy in winter.

The Sahara

The Sahara represents perhaps the most salient fact of this zone. Stretching for more than 5500 kilometres from the Red Sea to the Atlantic and having an average width from north to south of more than 1700 kilometres, it covers almost one-quarter of the area of the entire African continent. Across the whole of this area, the rainfall, though very unevenly distributed, is in places over 100 mm/annum, and on an average very much less. As a result no perennial streams are known in the Sahara with the exception of the Nile which derives its waters from sources far beyond the desert. Such ephemeral and permanent pools as do result from surface drainage are of no more consequence to present-day human life than are the wells and springs deriving their water from subterranean sources.

The Sahara consists of a rigid nucleus of pre-Cambrian rocks overlapped by Palaeozoic to Cenozoic sediments which remained stable for most of the Phanerozoic. It is only in the Atlas range from the Gulf of Gabes to Morocco and in the Red Sea hills east of the Nile that a certain degree of crustal warping and folding took place. A similar crustal disturbance is also noted in Cyrenaica and in the subsurface of coastal North Africa. These folding movements belong to the Alpine system of mountain building of late Cenozoic and Quaternary age. The Red Sea range, on the other hand, is connected with the crustal movements and the spreading of the great African Rift valley.

The greatest area of relief is that of the Atlas massif which has the highest rainfall. Minor elevations exist in Cyrenaica and in the Ahaggar and Tibesti massifs of the central Sahara. These latter form two regions of mountainous topography joined by the low saddle-back ridge of Tummo. The area has an average elevation of 2000 metres although peaks as high as 3600 metres are known. Most of the peaks are made up of volcanic rocks which formed during a long and protracted period of volcanic activity extending well into the Pleistocene. Smaller areas of volcanic rocks are seen in the massifs of Aïr, south-west of the Ahaggar, the Oweinat which rises abruptly halfway between Tibesti and the Nile, Mount Ater and others. At the present time these high massifs have an insignificant effect on the climate, but there is abundant geological evidence that the Sahara region was far less arid during several episodes of the Pleistocene than at present.

The greatest force of erosion in the desert today, as it always has been during the long periods of aridity, is wind erosion which is responsible for the formation of the great pediplain of the Sahara. The wind-borne coarse sands resulting from this erosion accumulate in fields which are known as *erg* or *reg*, while the finer materials are carried high up in the air where they remain in partial suspension for long periods of time. The bare rock surfaces which result from the processes of desert erosion are known as the *Hammada*. Basins and depressions occur on these surfaces. These range from small shallow basins to enormous depressions reaching in places as low as 134 metres below sea level (Qattara depression). These depressions became, in times of pluvials, the site of alluviation, and when they were lowered down to the ground water level, the sites of spring activity and lacustrine sedimentation. The large depressions lie mostly on the edge of escarpments but are seldom encircled by scarps on all sides. Because they form internal basins with no outlet they were certainly formed by wind action.

Views differ as to the geological history of the Sahara. Certain authors claim that it was a desert for as long a period as the entire Phanerozoic, wet periods representing abnormal fluctuations in an otherwise continuous history of aridity. Others claim that the desertification is a recent phenomenon pertaining to the present-day pattern of distribution of air masses.

Evidence that the desert in the recent past enjoyed wetter climates is overwhelming. The evidence ranges from the pattern of distribution of animals to sedimentary features that cannot be explained except by assuming a wetter climate in the past. Certain indigenous central African animals are known to have lived in the desert, and these could not have migrated there except via corridors of vegetation or water. Central African crocodile species have been found in water-holes in deep ravines of the Ahaggar and Tibesti massifs; the African mudfish has been recorded as far north as the oasis of Biskra in southern Tunisia. The drainage features of the desert indicate previous greater rainfall. West of the Ahaggar, a huge plain extends to a few hundred kilometres from the Atlantic, sloping gently from the margins of the El Juf depression. In the past, this clearly formed the evaporation basin of an extensive system of streams. The lines of drainage leading from the southern slopes of the Atlas southward, of which Wadi Saoura has been traced for more than 500 kilometres, are significant. Here is a valley which in the past carried sufficient volume of water to remove the aeolian sands that today choke its middle reaches.

From the Red Sea hills some wadis are as much as 300 kilometres long and they drain areas close to 50 000 square kilometres. One of these, Wadi Kharit debouching in the Kom Ombo plain to the north of Aswan, is fringed by alluvial thinly bedded fine-grained silts of more than 100 metres in depth. These must have certainly been deposited by an active perennial river of considerable volume.

The extensive work on the climato-stratigraphic divisions of the Sahara is reviewed by Monod (1963). He cites the work of Alimen, Chavaillon and Margat (1965) on the classic basin of the Saoura, for which the following periods have been suggested, from the oldest to the most recent:

(1) Villafrancian pluvial (= Aidian): sand, gravel, conglomerate deposits of red-pink colour resting upon older rocks.
(2) Arid post-Villafrancian: talus breccias, sandy loess, etc., topped by a red-brown palaeosoil. Crudely worked pebble tools have been reported from one site in Algeria.
(3) First Mazzerian pluvial (Q/a): conglomerates and sands.
(4) Arid post-Mazzerian: sandy clay deposits, aeolian sands, scree.

(5) Second Taourirtian (or Ougartian I) pluvial (Q/b): conglomerates, very evolved pebble culture possibly of the middle Acheulian.
(6) Arid post-Taourirtian: erosion.
(7) Third pluvial (or Ougartian II): varicoloured pebbles and sands or a red-brown palaeosoil.
(8) Arid post-Taourirtian: erosion.
(9) Fourth Saourian pluvial (Q^{I}): grey-green sands, rubble, black fossil soils – Neolithic.
(10) Post-Saourian pluvial: sandstone crust: Neolithic.
(11) Guirian wet episode (Q^{2a}): Neolithic.

According to Arambourg (1962), the four main pluvials – the Mazzerian, Ougartian I, Ougartian II and Saourian – of the north-west Sahara may correspond to the East African pluvials – the Kageran (Olduvai I), the Kamasian, the Kanjeran and the Gamblian. The Guirian of north-west Africa may correspond to the post-Gamblian humid stages.

The Nile

The Nile has attracted the attention of scholars for a long time and the literature dealing with its various aspects is enormous. The prehistory and the geological evolution of this river have been recently subjected to intensive study by Wendorf (1968), Butzer and Hansen (1968), de Heinzelin (1968), Wendorf and Schild (MS.), Giegengack (1968) and Said (in press). The following notes are the result of a study by the last author based on field mapping of the fluviatile and associated sediments of the Nile valley and the examination of a large number of boreholes, both deep and shallow, which were drilled in the search for water or oil. It is possible to conceive of the Nile as having passed through five main episodes since it cut its channel in the upper Miocene. Each of these episodes was characterized by a river which drew the larger part of its waters from sources outside Egypt. Towards the end of the first four episodes (the last is still current) the river seems to have declined or ceased entirely to flow into Egypt. These major recessional phases were accompanied by important physical, climatic and hydrological changes. In the first of these recessions, the sea seems to have advanced inland forming a gulf which occupied the excavated valley as far as to the south of Aswan. During the second recessional phase, which started with the advent of the Pleistocene and continued for more than 1 100 000 years, a hyperarid climate developed over Egypt which was converted into a veritable desert. During this episode wind action was most effective, the great depressions of the desert started forming and the carpet of vegetation which covered Egypt for almost all the Pliocene was destroyed. There is evidence that during the early part of this episode there occurred for a relatively brief period an intensive pluvial phase. During this pluvial there occurred ephemeral torrential rivers which drew their waters solely from Egypt. The five rivers which occupied the valley of the Nile since its excavation in upper Miocene times are termed: the Eo-Nile (Tmu); Paleo-Nile (Tplu); Proto-Nile (Q_1), Pre-Nile (Q_2) and Neo-Nile (Q_3).

The climatic fluctuations thus recorded in Egypt may be summarized in the following table from the most ancient to the most recent:

(1) Pliocene pluvial (Tplu), 3·32 to 1·85 million years b.p. The sediments of the Paleo-Nile are mostly in the form of fine-grained thinly bedded clastics and clays, known in the subsurface in the valley and also in outcrop along the wadi fringes. The sources of the Paleo-Nile were in Egypt as well as in equatorial and sub-equatorial Africa. There was an important carpet of vegetation, intensive chemical disintegration and a reduced run-off. Rainfall was probably evenly distributed over the year.

(2) Lower Pleistocene hyperarid phase (Tplu/Q_1 Interval), 1·85 to 0·70 million years b.p. Egypt became desert, the Nile valley became seismically active and wind action was at its maximum. It was interrupted by a short pluvial (Armant) resulting in the formation of gravel beds alternating with graded-sand or marl beds embedded in a yellow-red matrix and topped by a cemented red breccia. No tools are found in these deposits.

(3) Idfu pluvial (Q_1), ?700 000 to 600 000 years b.p. The climate of the Paleo-Nile returned, the Proto-Nile, with recurrence of Paleo-Nile climatic conditions; the Proto-Nile with similar sources to that of its predecessor broke into Egypt and cut its course on bedrock in a westerly and parallel direction to that of the modern Nile. River sediments took the form of gravel beds made up of quartz and quartzite pebbles embedded in a matrix of red-brick soil. Sediments were derived from a deeply disintegrated and highly leached terrain. In the deserts comparable sediments of wadi conglomerates are known in the form of inverted channels. Rolled implements, of possibly Chellean tradition, are recorded from these deposits.

(4) Pre-Nile arid phase (Q_2),? 600 000 to 125 000 years b.p. An effective new river broke into Egypt deriving its waters from the Ethiopian highlands. The mineral composition of the sediments of the Pre-Nile shows the presence of the mineral augite (characteristic of modern Nile sediments derived from the Ethiopian highlands) as well as an abundance of the mineral epidote, which distinguishes these deposits from those of the succeeding Neo-Nile and modern Nile. There were conditions of minor pluvial in the early phases of this interval.

(5) Abbassia pluvial, 125 000 to 80 000 years b.p. The Pre-Nile stopped flowing into Egypt, the sources of the river being cut by the

elevation of the Nubian massif. This pluvial is characterized by polygenetic gravels derived from Egyptian Red Sea hills whose surface was deeply disintegrated but little leached. Abundant late Acheulian tools are found in these gravels.

(6) Abbassia/Makhadma arid phase, 80 000 to ?40 000 years b.p. Erosion.

(7) Makhadma subpluvial, ?40 000 to 27 000 years b.p. Sheet wash with implements of Sangoan-Lupemban tradition are known on several slopes of the eroded bed of the Pre-Nile. In the deserts implements of Mousterian and later of Aterian tradition are ubiquitous.

(8) Neo-Nile arid phase (Q_3), 27 000 to present. A river (Neo-Nile) with similar sources and regimen to the modern Nile broke into Egypt. The Neo-Nile passed through recessional phases which formed subpluvial maxima: Deir el Fakhuri subpluvial (15 000 to 12 000 b.p.); Dishna subpluvial (10 000 to 9200 b.h.) and Neolithic (7000 to 6000 b.p.).

It can thus be stated that the sediments of the Nile valley are not very different from those recorded from the Sahara. It is possible, in fact, to generalize and state that the Egyptian Armant pluvial may correspond to the north-west Saharan Villafrancian pluvial, the Idfu to the Mazzerian, the Abbassia to the Ougartian, the Makhadma to the Saourian and the Deir el Fakhuri, Dishna and Neolithic to the Guirian.

It must be noted, in conclusion, that the African pluvials must have been due to world climatic fluctuations that, in theory, should correspond to the glacials of Europe and North America. Even though this has not been proven, it is possible to state that, in general, the Ougartian (of north-west Africa), the Abbassia (of north-east Africa) and the Kanjeran (Olduvai IV) of East Africa can be correlated with the Alpine Riss. Further work, particularly in the fields of palaeomagnetic and radiometric measurements, is needed before any definite conclusion can be drawn.

Part II H. Faure

Introduction

The last few million years of the past of our globe have been marked by a repetitive pattern of extreme climatic changes. The most outstanding phenomenon, one which has been well known for more than a century, is undoubtedly the extraordinary advance and recession of the glaciers at high latitudes and altitudes. This phenomenon reflects the considerable glaciations which had a profound influence on the environment and life of hominids. In Africa the most spectacular aspect of the Quaternary climatic variations was the extension of lacustrine areas in zones which are now arid, and the development of great stretches of dunes in regions which now have a more humid climate.

Over the past decade considerable progress has been made in the dating of climatic events occurring during the last 30 000 years, thanks to the systematic use of carbon-14. In regard to those occurring during the last few million years, the dating of magnetic reversals, based on radiometric measurements by the potassium-argon method, allows of correlation with other regions at a distance where such methods are also used, particularly ocean regions.

Before these methods of chronological correlation came into use, Quaternary stratigraphy was based mainly on the succession of climatic events, regarded as a chronological framework. Correlations from one region to another were established by paralleling successive epochs characterized by similar climates. For instance, a rather arbitrary correspondence had been suggested between the European glacial periods and the African pluvial epochs. This suggestion was opposed by several authors (among others, Tricart, 1956; Balout, 1952a).

The answer to this question of correlation has proved to be much more complex in reality, and it is only beginning to be glimpsed now that the mechanisms of global climatology are better known and a detailed climatic chronology has been established for the last few thousand years.

Magnetostratigraphy and radiometric dating

In addition to the comments made above by Rushdi Said, lithostratigraphic, biostratigraphic and chronostratigraphic units have frequently been confused, with the result that the lack of precision in definitions has produced a nomenclature which is often difficult to use in a more exact chronological framework.

Then again, certain features of the magnetic field, such as slope or intensity, seem to be very closely related to climatic features (Figs 16.1 and 16.2, from Wollin *et al.*, 1974).

Quaternary glaciations and dating

It is likely that at least twelve considerable cold changes have been recorded in the continuous deposits accumulated at the bottom of the oceans during the Quaternary (see Fig. 16.2). Only about eight have been recognized in the continental deposits of northern Europe. The fluvial terraces and glacial deposits of the alpine region are related to four (or six) generally accepted glaciations: Günz, Mindel, Riss, Würm (and Donau, Biber), each of which may comprise a number of stages.

The discontinuous nature of the continental evidence makes it difficult, and often illusory, to correlate glacial periods in distant regions when they are not situated with certainty on a magnetochronological or radiometric

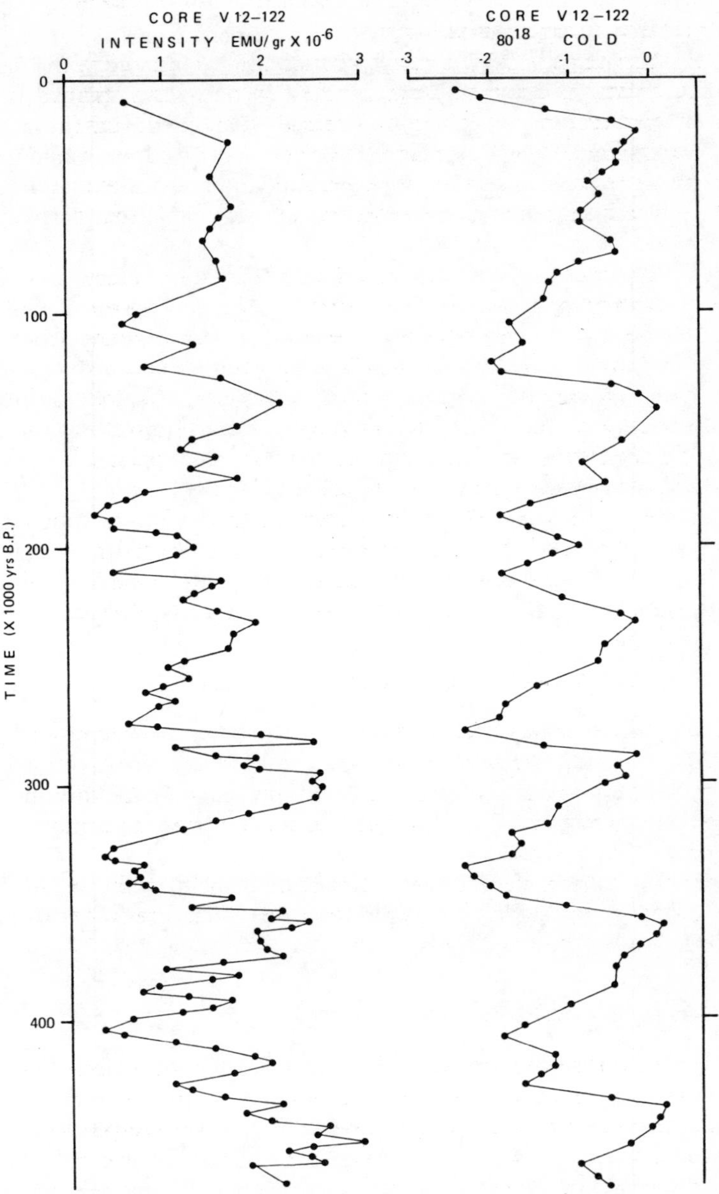

FIG. 16.1 *Graphs showing analogies between oxygen isotopes (or temperature variations) and the intensity of the earth's magnetic field, in a deep-sea core, for the last 450 000 years (after Wollin, Ericson & Wollin, 1974)*

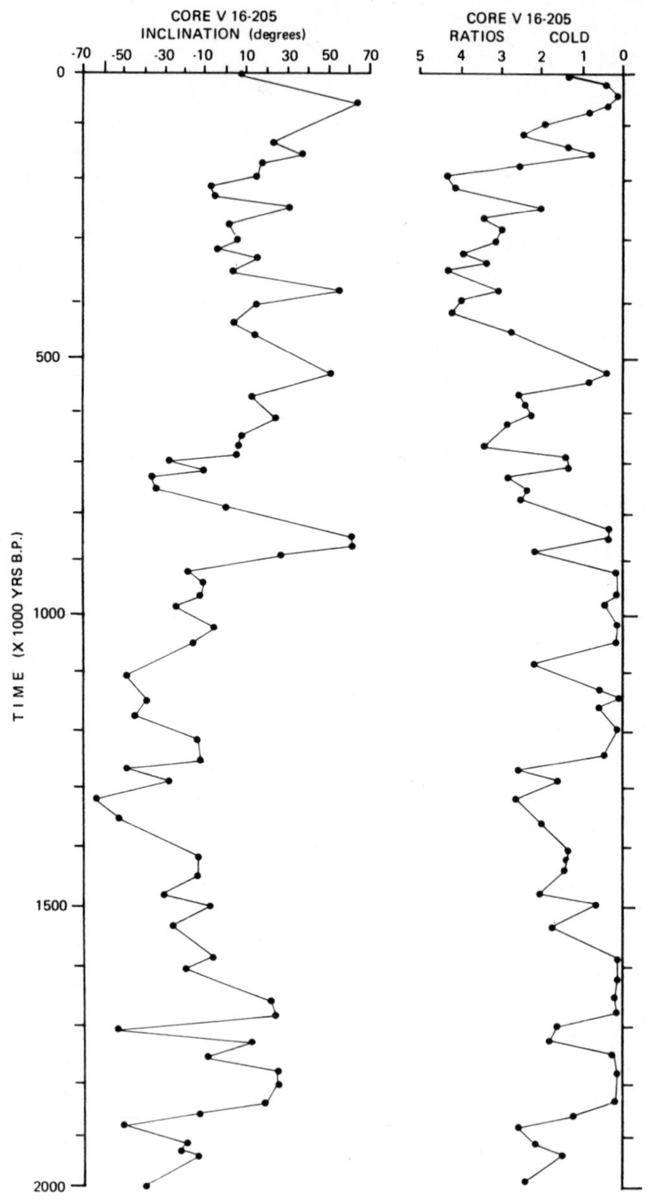

FIG. 16.2 *Graphs showing analogies between temperatures indicated by the microfauna and the magnetic inclination for the last two million years (after Wollin* et al., *1974)*

scale. In point of fact the accepted chronology for the alpine glaciations is vague. The terms Günz, Mindel, Riss, Würm and Biber have been used in various regions to denote formations which are not synchronous. Thus, according to the potassium-argon dating of the volcanic rocks intercalated in the Rhine terraces, the formations known as Mindel I and II appear to be 300 000 and 260 000 years old and the terraces known as Günz I and II 420 000 and 340 000 years old. But the same term Günz is sometimes applied to the cold period preceding the Cromerian, which would therefore be from 900 000 to 1 300 000 years old, coinciding with the cold period preceding the Jaramillo event in the undersea cores. According to the latter interpretation, the Donau, the preceding cold period, should include the Gilsa event and be the equivalent of the Eburonian.

It will be understood from this example how dangerous it is to transfer from one region to another a chronology based on continental climatic successions: if one retraces the number of cold occurrences identified and reviews the arbitrary nomenclature attributed to them, the divergences render precarious any correlation of evidence of alpine glaciations with the successive cold changes measured in ocean cores.

Complete and continuous recording of all climatic phenomena, on the one hand, and of magnetostratigraphic and radiometric references, on the other, is essential if a stratigraphic scale is to be worked out even approximately and if valid comparisons between two regions are to be made possible.

The Matuyama-Brunhes magnetic reversal (690 000 years) was identified in the Cromerian stage by means of palynology, and the Gilsa occurrence (1 790 000 years) in the Eburonian stage (Van Montfrans, 1971).

Quaternary transgressions and dating

Each glaciation brings about a glacio-eustatic regression of the sea, which may amount to a hundred metres or so. Marine regressions brought about by the melting of ice therefore make it possible in littoral zones to link climatostratigraphic chronology with the chronology of marine cycles.

In regions where the marine formations are coralline (Barbados, Bermudas, New Guinea, the Red Sea), dating by methods based on the disequilibrium of uranium applied to the aragonite of corals has made it possible to ascertain the age of marine transgressions from the last interglacials (200 000; 120 000; 105 000; 85 000 years b.p. approximately). Within the margin of physical error of the various radiometric dating methods, it is observed that these high sea levels correspond fairly well with the higher temperature phases indicated by the marine microfauna, pollens and oxygen isotopes.

Mechanisms of global climatology

Climate does not constitute a simple means of chronological correlation. Owing to the complexity of the factors entering into it at any given moment (or over a period lasting centuries or millennia) there can be no question of using data which have not been properly dated as stratigraphic or chronological criteria.

The facts leading to these observations are of two kinds:

(1) A knowledge of the global evolution of climate over a few decades (or a few centuries, on the basis of historical data) shows how complex the problem is on a global scale. One has to know the evolution of all factors: the solar constant, ocean circulation, the situation of polar fronts, distribution of temperatures, rainfalls (not only their averages but their variability).

(2) A knowledge of the variations of certain climatic factors over the past 25 000 years or so (end of the Pleistocene and Holocene), obtained by means of radiometric measurements, shows us, on the one hand, the rapidity of the changes concerning which reliable evidence exists, and, on the other hand, the complexity of correlations on a global scale. The time scale taken into consideration then plays a major role.

The climatic system, as defined by the National Academy of Sciences, Washington (1975), is made up of the properties and processes which are responsible for the climate and its variations (thermal properties: temperature of air, water, ice, soils; kinematic properties: wind, ocean currents, ice movements, etc.; aqueous properties: humidity of the air, clouds, surface water or groundwater, ice, etc.; static properties: pressure, density of the oceans, salinity, etc.; as also the geometric limits and constants of the system). All the variables in the system are interconnected by the physical processes which occur in it: precipitation, evaporation, radiation, transfer, convection, turbulence.

The physical components of the climatic system are: atmosphere, hydrosphere, cryosphere, lithosphere, biosphere. The physical processes responsible for climate may be expressed quantitatively by dynamic equations of movement, the equation of thermodynamic energy and the equation of continuity of mass and water.

Climatic variations will be complex in as much as there may be considerable interaction between the elements in the climatic system. So the causes of climatic changes are many and varied, particularly having regard to the time scale involved and the interaction mechanisms (feed back). Oceans play a considerable part in climatic changes through the processes at the air–water interface, which govern exchanges of heat, humidity and energy.

These preliminary considerations go to show that the climatostratigraphy of the Quaternary has been a stage, a necessary approximation, but that it is gradually making way for an attempt to understand the mechanisms involved in particular situations over different periods of time. For this reason several examples of recent results bearing on the present era, the Holocene, the Pleistocene and the Plio-Pleistocene will be examined.

Climatology in Africa today and in the recent past

In Africa the annual rhythm of alternation of a dry season and a rainy season in the intertropical zone is bound up with the displacement of the intertropical convergence zone (ITCZ).

As summed up recently by J. Maley (1973) and L. Dorize (1974), the ITCZ represents the place where the monsoon (humid air coming from the equatorial regions or the maritime trade-wind from the southern hemisphere) and the harmattan (dry air from the Sahara) meet. The ITCZ, which lies approximately west–east, moves from the south to the north during the spring and the first two months of summer, then from north to south. This seasonal oscillation occurs between 4°N and 20–23°N. The surface of discontinuity between the humid air and the dry air slowly rises north to south. The humid bank of the monsoon is only a very thin cold corner towards the north in summer, not giving much precipitation. The humid air has to be from 1200 to 1500 metres thick for precipitations of any importance to occur. These conditions are found only from 200 to 300 kilometres south of the ITCZ (L. Dorize, 1974). The position of the ITCZ varies considerably, not only from one season to another, but also from day to day, as a result of the field of pressure of the whole of Africa and the Atlantic Ocean. As shown by P. Pedelaborde (1970), the original thrust from the southern Atlantic combined with the activity of the south polar front represents the essential motive force pushing the convergence zone northwards. The southward withdrawal of the ITCZ (in September) would then be due to the weakening of the south Atlantic anticyclone and the influence of the northern hemisphere. The occasional intervention of northern air dried after its transit over the Sahara gives only a little rain on the Sahara mountain ranges. Conversely, the southerly air, after crossing the ocean, brings potential humidity.

The present climatic crisis in the Sahel zone is due to the fact that the ITCZ has remained from 3° to 4° farther south than its average position. During the wet decade of 1950–9, on the other hand, the Sahara shrank. As J. Maley has shown (1973), the humid phase coincided with a drop in the maximum temperatures on its southern borders.

Now, the colder the polar air, the stronger the polar fronts and the farther they extend towards the equator. In this connection, Maley (1973) distinguished two mechanisms, namely, that of the glacial periods and the one made evident in our own time. In the former case the area of the ice sheets in the northern hemisphere increased considerably, while the

Antarctic ice sheet would appear to have varied little. The north polar front then had a preponderant influence, driving the monsoon far south in summer. Aridification then went hand in hand with glacial expansion. With the warmer temperatures of the Holocene period before 5000–4000 b.p. the centre of polar action weakened. During the northern summer the regression of the north polar front favoured the extension of the monsoon north of the equator, while the south polar front drove the subtropical anticyclones towards the equator. During the northern winter the polar front could again extend its action over the Sahara and bring rain. The occurrence of rain both in summer and in winter would explain the humid climate which prevailed in the southern Sahara and the receding of the desert during the first half of the Holocene.

Over the past 5000 years the regression of the Arctic ice sheet has reduced the strength of the north polar front, while the centre of action in the Antarctic has also diminished in strength. The thrust of the monsoon and the diminishing effects of the northern polar air on the Sahara at the same time, would thus explain the gradual aridification of the Sahara.

These meteorological mechanisms may help us to understand the climatic changes which occurred in Africa during the Quaternary.

Dating and climates over the past 25 000 years

The last 25 000 years of the Quaternary (end of the Pleistocene and Holocene) afford a recent and now well-documented example of a vast glacial advance and of the ensuing recession up to the present interglacial. During the same period the intertropical regions underwent extreme aridity, followed by a humid phase, then aridification again. This is the only climatic fluctuation which can be studied over a period of several centuries or several millennia, permitting comparison of the elements of the climatic system and its variations in many regions of the globe situated at nearly all latitudes. In addition, for this period the indications supplied by pollen, diatoms and fauna identical to the modern species allow of quantifying the magnitude of the variations of the geographical environment with precision. Besides, the average sea level is well enough known for us always to be able to have some idea of the general volume of the ice and the isotopic relationships of the oxygen in the principal reservoirs (oceans, ice) (see Morner, 1975).

As regards the African Sahara, since the first comprehensive surveys based on radio-carbon dating (Butzer, 1961; Monod, 1963; Faure, 1967 and 1969), the most recent studies which can serve as a basis for a detailed chronology of climatic variations are those of M. Servant and S. Servant, in the Chad and Niger; F. Gasse, in Afar; and of the teams of Van Zinderen Bakker and Livingstone, of Richardson, of Williams, of Wickens, and so on in East Africa. Their findings are comparable with those of many surveys in regions in high latitudes, in particular those of Velitchko, Dreimanis, and so on. The Atlantic Ocean region is known as a whole through the work of the CLIMAP[1] group and McIntyre, while the southern hemisphere is known through the publications of Van der Hammen, Williams, Bowler and others.

To situate the evolution of the climate of Africa over the past 25 000 years in a global perspective, several chronological stages may be distinguished.

25 000 to 18 000 years b.p.

High Latitudes

The period of time covered by the years 25 000 to 18 000 b.p. corresponds to the end of the maximum extension of the ice sheets in the northern hemisphere. This last extension of the Würm glaciation (Wisconsin–Weichselien–Valdaï) covered with ice an area representing from 90 to 95 per cent of that covered during all the previous Quaternary glaciations (Flint, 1971). It is thus a very representative model of a glaciation.

In periglacial zones the permafrost (soil permanently frozen all the year round) seems to have been more extensive than it was during other glaciations (Velitchko, 1973 and 1975). The presence of this extensive permafrost on the continents would appear to have been associated with sea ice, also very extensive in the arctic oceans, which was a factor in reducing evaporation at the air–sea interface.

Oceans

Combined with the reduction of free surface due to sea ice, the lowering of mean sea level, going down from about −50 to about −100 metres, contributed to reducing the area of the oceans by a further 10 per cent or so. At the end of the period under consideration nearly all the continental shelves had emerged.

Research workers in the CLIMAP group (McIntyre *et al.*, 1974 and 1976; Hays, in CLIMAP, and so on) have been able to construct charts of the temperatures of the surface waters of the Atlantic Ocean for the time of the glacial maximum (18 000 b.p.) (Fig. 16.3). On comparison with charts for existing situations (which are those of an interglacial), these charts show a general average of temperature differences which is only 2·5° between the glacial maximum and the present interglacial. However, the distribution of temperature differences shows a maximum at medium latitudes (differences of from 6° to 10°) and much smaller differences (less than 3°) at intertropical latitudes (Figs 16.4 and 16.5). For instance, at the point 50°N 30°W, the surface temperature was from 7·3° to 12·7° lower in winter 18 000 (or 17 000) years ago than it is at present. In summer the difference dropped, from 1·2 to 6·6° (CLIMAP, 1974).

In both hemispheres the migration of polar waters was the dominant factor in this glacial epoch. In the northern Atlantic, the polar waters came

1. CLIMAP (Climatic Long-Range Interpretation, Mapping and Prediction) of the International Decade of Ocean Exploration (IDOE).

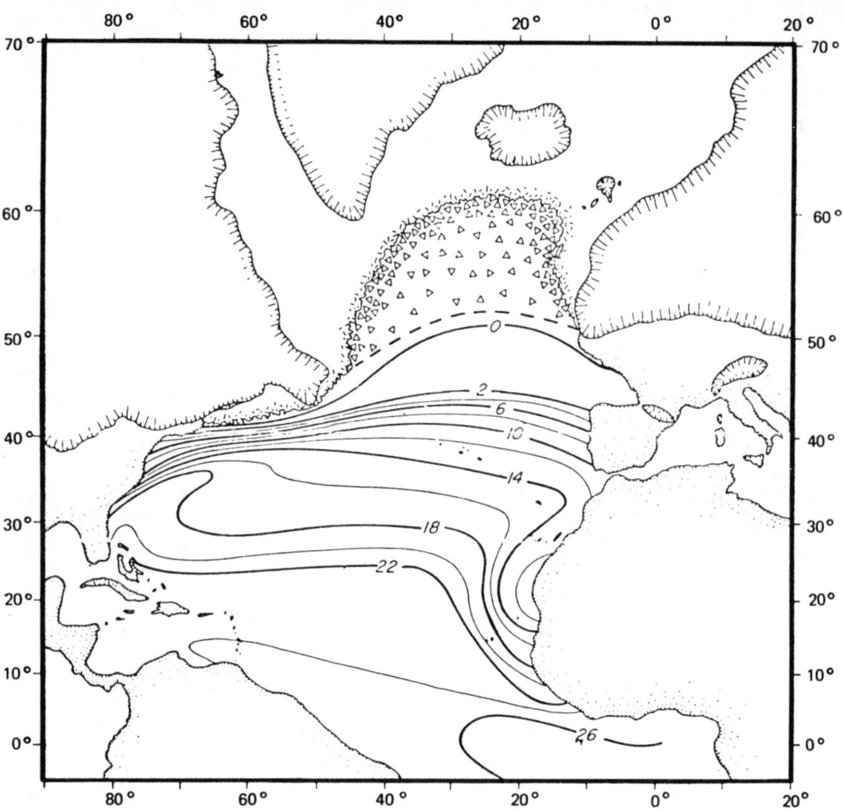

FIG. 16.3 *Surface water isotherm map of the Atlantic Ocean for February, 18 000 b.p. The dashed isotherms are interpretative. The major continental ice-masses are delineated by hatched borders, the permanent pack-ice by granulate borders. The glacial shoreline is drawn to a sea-level of −85 m from today (after McIntyre* et al., *1975*)

down as far as the 42nd parallel (from a position near the present one, about 60°N), giving rise to a rapid temperature gradient south of the 42nd parallel, which was therefore the probable axis of the westerlies in the glacial epoch. South of this limit the pattern was much the same as it is now, but it is observed that the isotherms, running parallel to the coasts of Africa, reveal the existence there, particularly in winter, of relatively cool waters due to an increased upwelling (Gardner and Hays, 1975).

The polar fronts and the axis of the westerlies moved more than 2000 kilometres towards the equator in the north Atlantic and only 600 kilometres in the south Atlantic. (In the Pacific Ocean the polar fronts seem to have moved very little in glacial periods.) This would explain the diminished penetration of the monsoon over the Sahara (see Maley, 1973, pp. 7–8) and the arid state of the Sahel zone at the end of the glacial period.

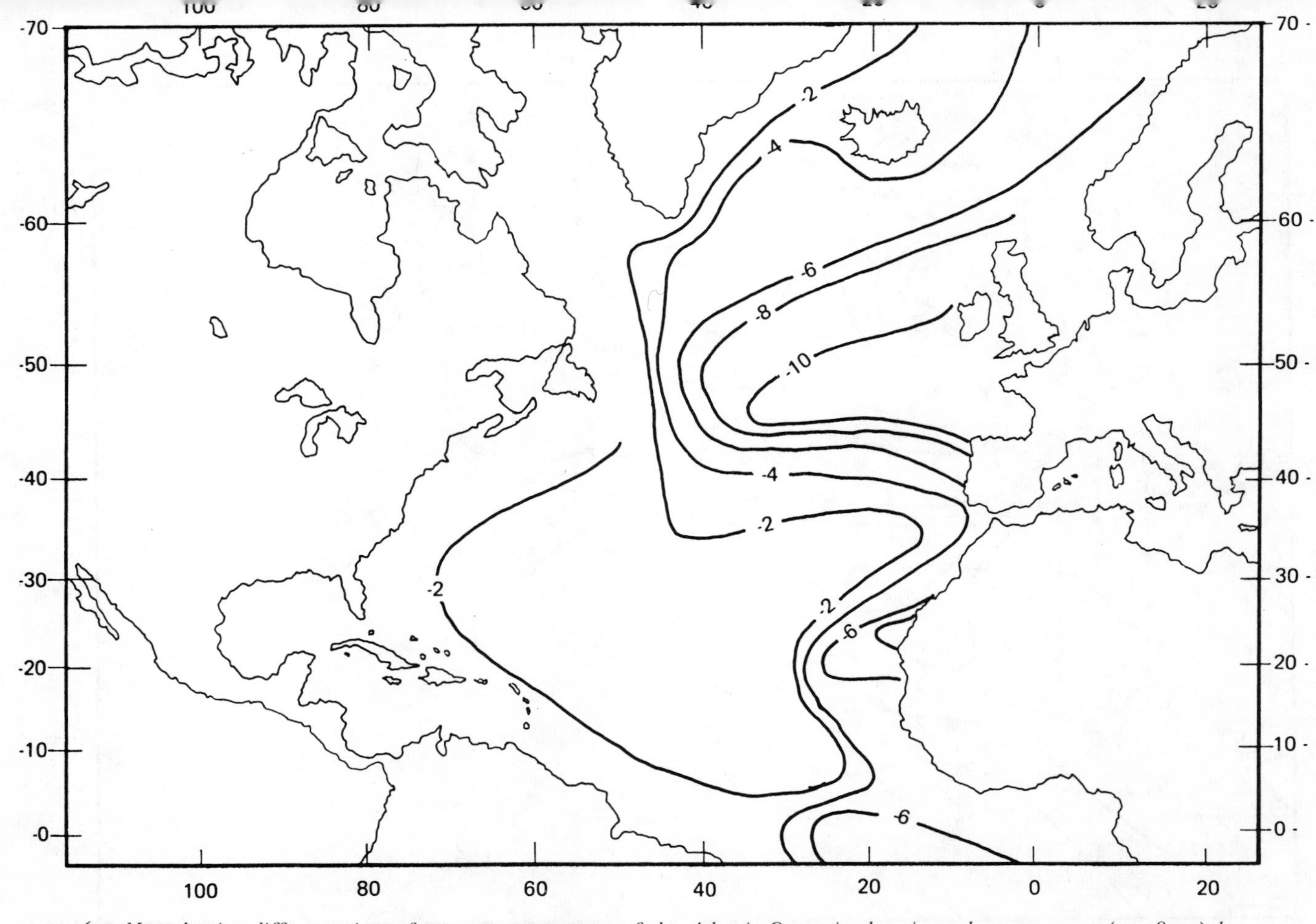

FIG. 16.4 *Map showing differences in surface water temperature of the Atlantic Ocean in the winter, between 17000 (or 18000) b.p. and the present day (after McIntyre, 1974) (CLIMAP)*

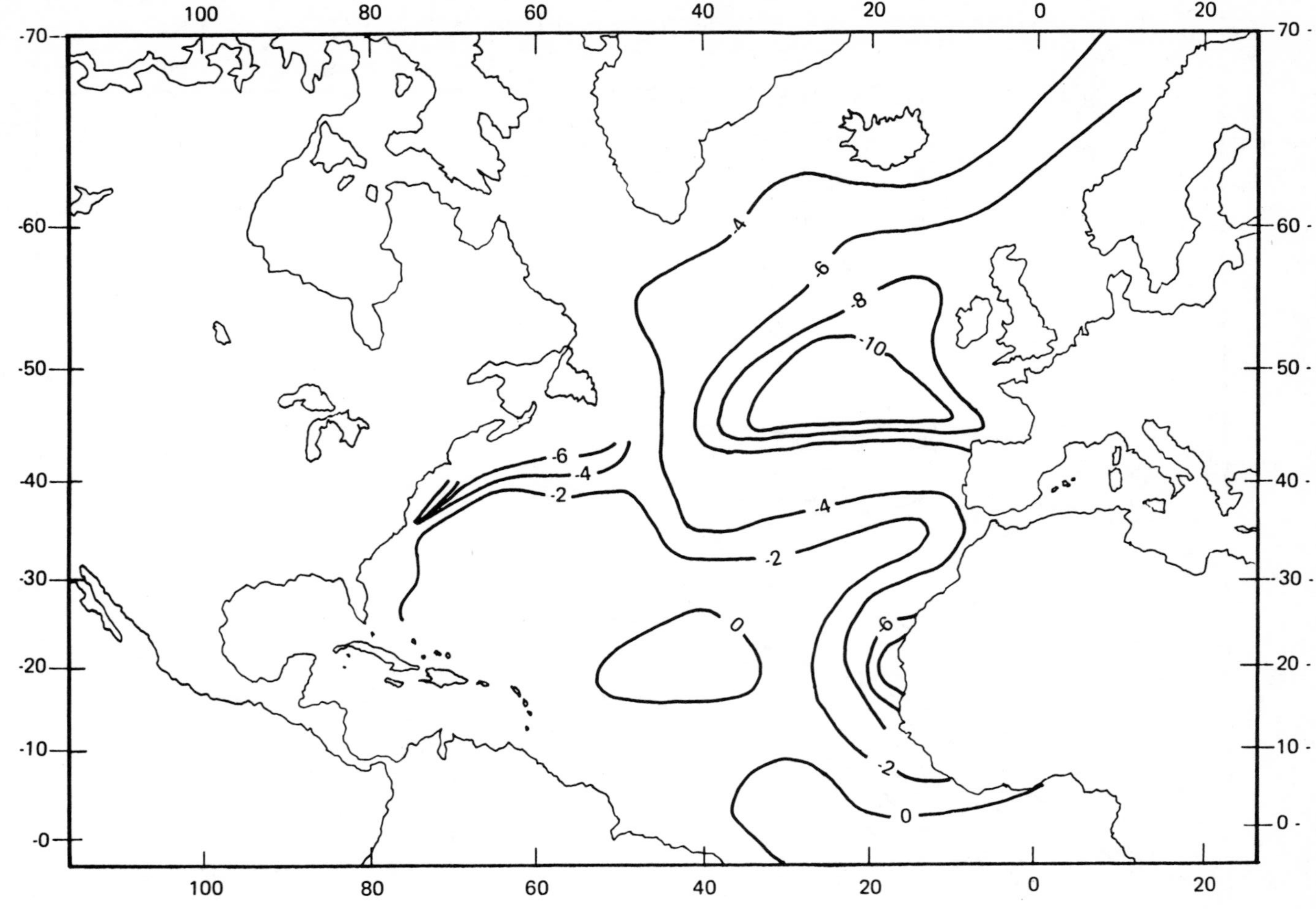

FIG. 16.5 *Map showing differences in surface water temperature of the Atlantic Ocean in the summer between 17,000 (or 18,000) b.p. and the*

Africa

In the southern Sahara and the Sahel regions the general evolution of the climate over the past 25 000 years shows a fairly similar trend from the Atlantic coasts to the Red Sea. This period of time comprises the end of a humid epoch of the upper Pleistocene (which lasted from about 30 000 to 20 000 years b.p.) and the beginning of an arid epoch, which ended around 12 000 b.p.

The study of lacustrine deposits in the Chad Basin has shown that the relationship between precipitation and evaporation (P/E) was sufficient to enable quite extensive lakes to remain in existence from 40 000 years b.p. to about 20 000 years (M. Servant, 1973). During the ensuing eight millennia the arid zone extended, spreading more than 400 kilometres farther south than its present limits.

This transition from a lacustrine episode to a very arid epoch is also observable in the deposits of the Afar lakes, where F. Gasse showed the existence of three lacustrine epochs in the upper Pleistocene. Between 20 000 and 17 000 years b.p. the lacustrine environment deteriorated and the dried-up bed of Lake Abay was occupied by *Gramineae* (Gasse, 1975).

Reviewing the most recent literature, M. Servant (1973) and F. Gasse (1975) note a quite comparable evolution in the case of other East African lakes at various altitudes and latitudes: the work of Richardson, Kendall, Butzer and others, Grove and others, Livingstone, on lakes Turkana, Nakuru, Naivasha, Magadi, Albert, etc. This comparison is summed up in Fig. 16.6, which shows a fairly parallel evolution for twelve African lakes.

18 000 to 12 000 years b.p.

High Latitudes

In regions at high latitudes this period corresponds to the end of the glacial maximum and to the deglaciation. The ice caps which covered eastern North America and Scandinavia and which reached their greatest extent between 22 000 and 18 000 years b.p. began to melt immediately after that time. That of the North American cordillera reached its maximum only 14 000 years b.p. and disappeared around 10 000 years b.p. The general deglaciation began, therefore, around 14 000 years b.p. In the southern hemisphere, on the other hand, the continental ice cap in the eastern Antarctic seems to have varied little, while the one in the western Antarctic, with its base below sea level, seems to have dwindled quite considerably (National Academy of Sciences, Washington, 1975).

Oceans

The huge surfaces covered with sea ice certainly disappeared with the very rapid rise of the sea level following deglaciation. This rise attained 1·5 metres per century on the average between 15 000 and 12 000 years b.p., by

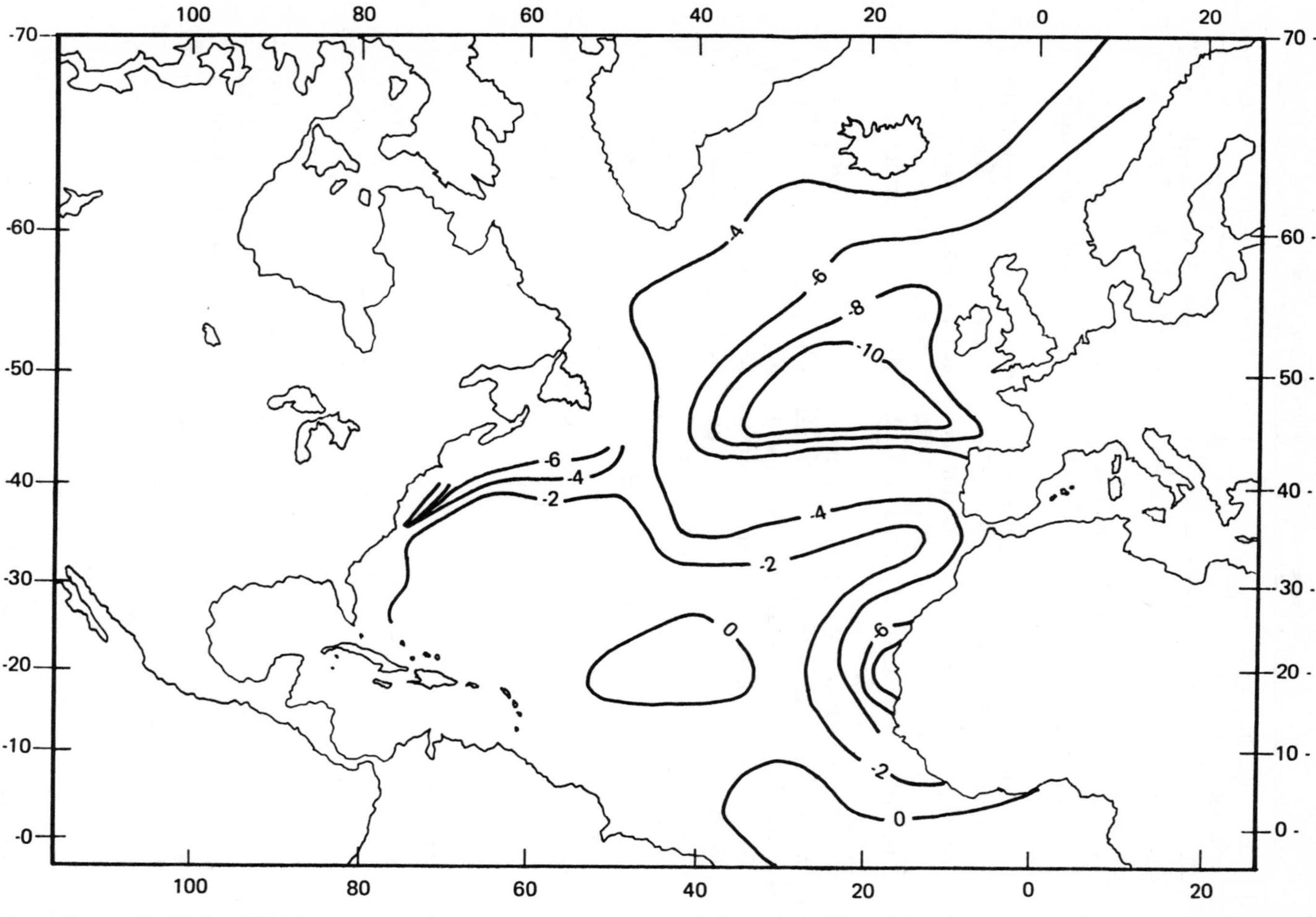
100
80
60
40
20
0
20
-70
-60
-50
-40
-30
-20
-10
-0
70
60
50
40
30
20
10
0
-4
-6
-8
-10
-6
-4
-2
-4
-2
0
-6
-2
0

which time half, if not two-thirds, of the rise had occurred. At the same time the polar waters of the Atlantic returned to more northerly latitudes.

Africa

The great aridity of the period comprised between 18 000 and 12 000 years b.p., which extended over a large part of Africa, is the best documented phenomenon. It is well evidenced by the graphs showing the evolution of lake levels in Niger and Chad (Servant, 1973), in Afar (Gasse, 1975), in Sudan (Williams, 1975; Wickens, 1975), and so on. The disappearance of vegetation enabled the winds to drive the dunes forward from 400 to 800 kilometres in the direction of the equator and on the emerged continental shelves. There is no doubt that over several millennia the Sahara, thus extended, constituted a more formidable barrier to man than does the Sahara of today. This aridification seems to have been extremely general and there are many indications that the intertropical zones as a whole dried up to some extent in Africa (de Ploey, Van Zinderen Bakker, etc. in Williams, 1975) and in Asia, particularly India (Singh, 1973).

Williams (1975) recently reviewed the literature concerning this arid epoch and showed its exceptional and approximately synchronous extension.

Mediterranean Basin

Although the evolution of the climate during the last glaciation (some 100 000 years ago) seems fairly complicated in the Mediterranean Basin (see p. 392 below), palynological findings (Bonatti, 1966) and pedological findings (Rohdenburg, 1970) indicate that at the glacial maximum the climate was dry and cool. The Mediterranean zone was occupied by a very dry steppe between 16 000 and 13 000 years b.p. and calcareous crusts developed on the soils.

Southern Hemisphere

In Australia, the study of pollens indicates that there was a gradual drop in temperatures until about 18 000 or 17 000 years b.p., while drought conditions became established and dunes extended over the emerged continental shelf (Bowler *et al.*, 1975). The glaciation occupied Tasmania and the Snowy Mountains while the South Australian lakes dried up around 16 000 years b.p. Warmer conditions, indicated by a rise in altitude of the treeline, set in around 15 000 years b.p., but the South Australian lakes only began to fill up again after 11 000 years b.p. (Bowler *et al.*, 1975).

Van der Hammen (1974) and Williams (1975) have drawn attention to the analogies which characterize the climates of both hemispheres during the last glacial maximum around 18 000 years b.p. A general aridity persisted during several millennia in all regions of the globe lying at low latitudes, with the exception of the south-west of the United States.

12 000 years b.p. to the present

High Latitudes

This period is characterized by the end of the glaciation and a distinct rise in temperatures culminating between 7500 and 4500 years b.p. (the climatic optimum, still referred to in Europe as the Atlantic period). The ice cap on the Cordillera melted very rapidly and disappeared around 10 000 years b.p. The one in Scandinavia disappeared shortly afterwards (9000 years b.p.). Distinct rapid fluctuations at intervals of about 2500 years (as, for instance, the cooler conditions of the new Dryas between 10 800 and 10 100 years b.p.) have been noted.

The situation in respect of glaciation began to be comparable with that prevailing at present around 8500 years b.p. in northern Europe and around 7000 years b.p. in North America (Nat. Acad. Sci., 1975). At that time, too, the ice sheet in the west of the Antarctic receded.

Oceans

The rise in sea level, which reflects the average melting state of the world's glaciers, was still very rapid between 12 000 and 7000 years b.p. (more than one metre per century on the average, but with a considerable deceleration or a fall around 11 000 years b.p.). The oceans seem to have reached a level very close to the existing level after 6000 years b.p. and to have oscillated only a few metres above and below it ever since. In addition to this general trend, sea level fluctuates in accordance with general climatic variations (Morner, 1973).

The zones in which marine sedimentation was reasonably rapid, zones studied by Wollin and Ericson, also enable us to follow changes in the distribution of *Foraminifera*, in particular, the variation of the percentage of sinistral *Globorotalia truncatulinoides*. According to Morner (1973), the peaks in the corresponding curves could reflect the peaks in the curves of climatic changes recorded by means of isotopic surveys of ice in Greenland, palynologic scales and fluctuations in sea level. However, the limit of precision of the radiometric dating method is reached here and linear interpolations are required between the dates, the variations in the sedimentation rates being taken into account. Besides, the distortion of the chronological scale of carbon-14 in relation to the time scale makes corrections necessary, and it is tricky to correlate phenomena which existed for only a century or two.

Africa

After the extreme aridity of the period extending from 16 000 to 14 000 years b.p. and from 12 000 years b.p. onwards, the lakes in the Saharan regions expanded in a remarkable fashion from the Atlantic coasts to the Red Sea. In nearly all the low-lying regions, lacustrine deposits, often consisting of diatoms, are to be observed.

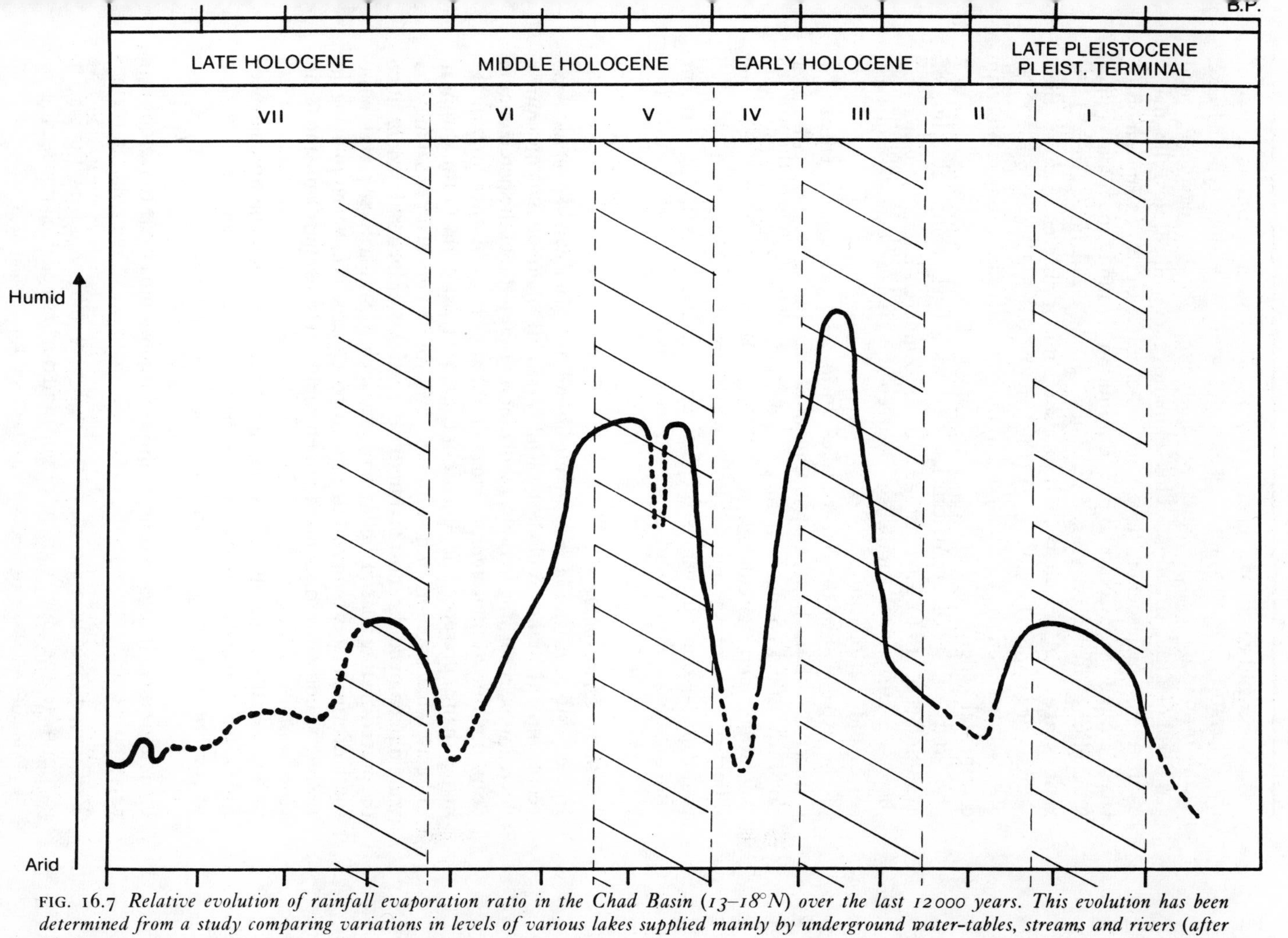

FIG. 16.7 *Relative evolution of rainfall evaporation ratio in the Chad Basin (13–18°N) over the last 12000 years. This evolution has been determined from a study comparing variations in levels of various lakes supplied mainly by underground water-tables, streams and rivers (after M. Servant, 1973, pp. 40–52)*

In Niger and Chad, M. Servant (1973) worked out a continuous curve of the P/E ratio (Fig. 16.7) on the basis of a study of various types of lake, taking into account their source of supply and their hydrogeological and geomorphological situation. This climatic curve illustrates the major oscillations, which seem to have a general character; great expansion of the lakes around 8500 years b.p.,[2] diminution around 4000 and minor fluctuations after 3000 years b.p. These major oscillations affected the various lakes in Afar, too, though with some minor differences due to their sources of supply (Gasse, 1975) (Fig. 16.8). A definite analogy is to be observed between the Chad curve and the humidity curve for the Siberian continental zone.

A study of the other African lakes shows a fairly comparable line of evolution (Fig. 16.6). Livingstone and Van Zinderen Bakker consider that there is a fairly close parallelism between the climatic evolution of East Africa and that of Europe.

The expansion of the Sahara lakes up to 8000 years b.p. seems to be connected with the better distribution of rainfall throughout the year and a cloud cover thick enough to reduce evaporation. M. Servant (1973) suggests that atmospheric circulation was different then from what it is now. The presence of several levels of cold climate diatoms leads him to postulate possible intrusions of polar air over the Sahara. The present climatic mechanism would appear to have become established only after 7000 years b.p.

Southern Hemisphere

In the north of Australia and in New Guinea the glaciers disappeared 8000 years b.p. (Mount Wilhelm), while rainfall increased, with minor fluctuations, according to Bowler and others (1975). Between 8000 and 5000 years b.p. the average temperature would appear to have been 1° or 2° higher than at present. The climatic optimum (Hypsithermal) would appear to be a global phenomenon, while the rain forest between 7000 and 3000 years b.p. enjoyed the most favourable conditions for its development since the preceding interglacial, before 60 000 years b.p. Similarly, the lakes in the south of Australia, which had dried up 15 000 years b.p., began to fill again around 11 000 years b.p. and attained high levels around 8000 and 3000 years b.p.

It seems likely that in general temperatures rose and humidity increased in low latitude zones during the first half of the last 12 000 years, leading to conditions characteristic of the present interglacial.

Conclusion with regard to the climatic chronology of the past 25 000 years

This period gives us a picture of the climatic evolution during the glacial maximum (at the end of a glacial period) and during a deglaciation leading to

2. Diminution just before 7000 b.p., another expansion around 6500.

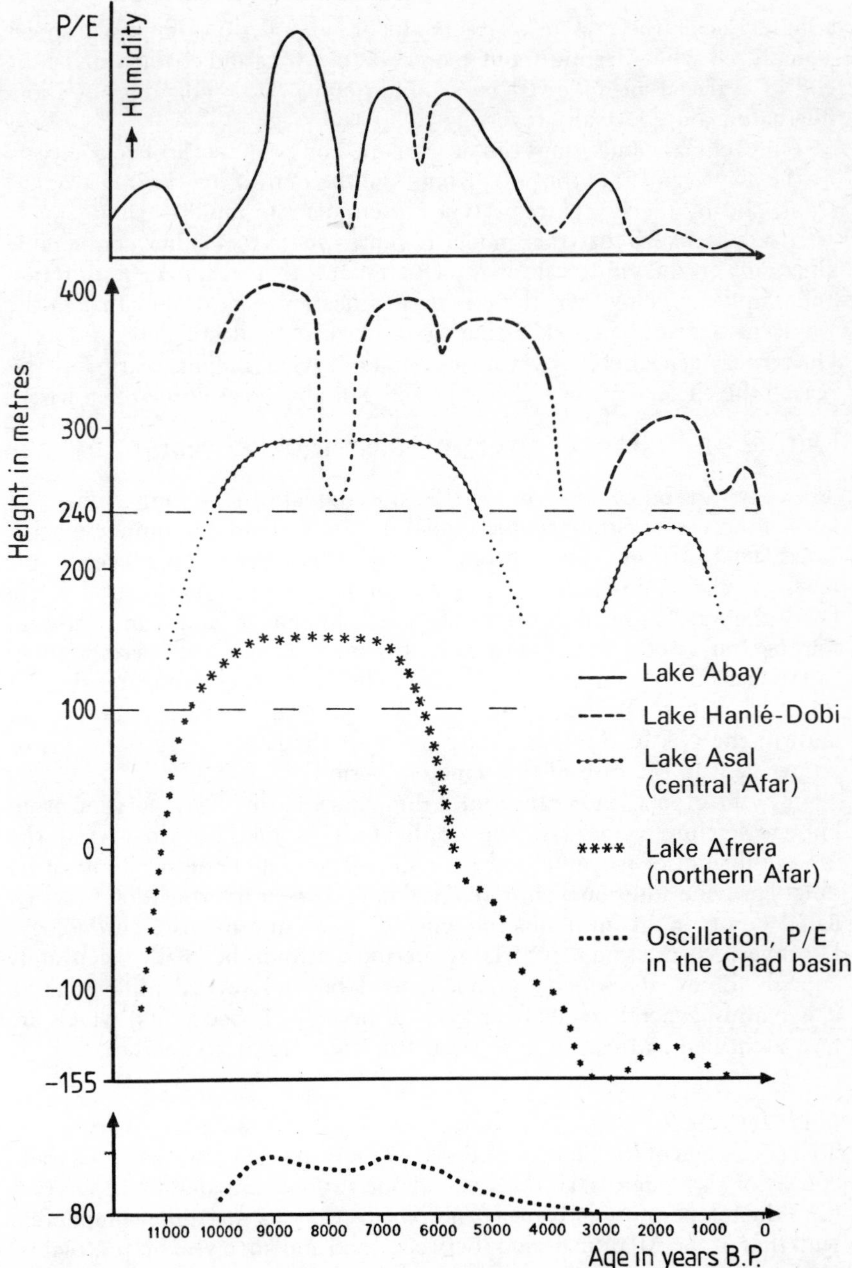

FIG. 16.8 *Variations in lake level in the Afar Basins. The curves for Lake Abay, Lake Hanlé-Dobi and Lake Asal, situated in central Afar, are represented on the top part of the graph. The curve for Lake Afrera is separate. Comparison could be made with the curve in variation of the P/E in the Chad Basin (after F. Gasse, 1975)*

an interglacial (the present). This model of half a deglaciation cycle shows generalized aridity lasting about 5000 years in Africa and characterizing the end of a glaciation, followed by a humid epoch of comparable duration, fluctuating but gradually reverting to an arid stage.

These climatic pulsations can be explained on a time scale of 20 000 years by the displacement of the polar fronts and their effects on the intertropical front, and by the two extreme types of circulation: rapid or slow.

It is also likely that this model is representative of other comparable situations on the same scale as the Quaternary, that is, similar in duration and amplitude. However, there is no justification for extrapolating to the whole of a glacial period lasting 100 000 years, and still less to all the Quaternary glaciations, covering a period of several million years. For this reason the chronology of a glacial period will now be examined as a whole.

Dating and climates over the past 130 000 years

The past 130 000 years (upper Pleistocene) afford an opportunity of studying a climatostratigraphic model on the scale of a complete glacial/interglacial period. The chronology of this period far exceeds the reach of the radio-carbon dating which has enabled us to establish a fairly accurate succession (to within a century or at least a millennium) for the last 25 000 years. However, this interval of time, corresponding to the last major interglacial (Eemian) before the present one and the last major glaciation (Würm, Wisconsin, Weichselien, Valdaï), is fairly well known, the risk of error in dating being of the order of 10 per cent, or 20 per cent in the case of the remotest period.

In point of fact, in oceans and sedimentary basins, extrapolation from known settling velocities, the application of methods involving the disequilibrium of uranium and potassium-argon at the upper limit of its range, provide additional chronological data. Linear interpolation between dated points in a continuous sequence gives an approximate chronology. However, correlations over large periods cannot be made accurately enough for events which did not extend beyond several millennia. So it is mainly general trends over average periods (10 000 years) which are best identified and can be compared from one region to another.

High Latitudes

The vegetation of the Eemian interglacial indicates that during the warmest epochs of that interglacial (between about 125 000 and about 80 000 years b.p.) the temperature in Eurasia and North America was quite comparable with that of the Atlantic period (between 7000 and 5000 years b.p.), that is, not much different from what it is now. Both these interglacials occurred suddenly after a considerable drop in temperatures (the last very cold stage of the Riss, 135 000 years b.p., and the last very cold stage of the Würm, 20 000 years b.p.).

Oceans

Variations in the level of the oceans reflect the two glacial maxima fairly well, dropping considerably (−110 metres ± 20 metres for the second maximum around 20 000–18 000). The highest levels reached during the Eemian interglacial and the present one are comparable (to within 5 per cent). Rises in sea level during the interim stages (45 000 and 30 000 years) may have attained from 60 to 80 per cent of the maximum rise (the Inchirian in Mauritania, for instance). They confirm that an equivalent mass of ice melted during the interim stage.

Africa

As in the case of the oceans, the repercussion of glacial phenomena was probably attenuated towards the intertropical latitudes. The differences between the temperatures of a glacial stage and those of an interglacial stage, from 5° to 10° at average latitudes, may have been only from 2° to 3° between the tropics. In Africa the effects on the distribution and quantity of rainfall constitute the most readily observable phenomenon.

Few regions in Africa possess a well-established radiometric chronology for the past 130 000 years. However, by sounding Lake Abay, F. Gasse (1975) was able to find evidence of three lacustrine stages in the upper Pleistocene, before the aridification from 20 000 to 14 000 years b.p. These lacustrine stages were as follows: the period from 30 000 to 20 000 years b.p. (temperate humid tropical climate), separated from another expansion of the lakes from about 40 000 to 30 000 years b.p. by a considerable regression around 30 000 years b.p., and earliest of all, the lacustrine stage from 50 000 to 60 000 years b.p. (or perhaps from 60 000 to 80 000), corresponding to a cooler period, as indicated by the diatoms.

A further indication concerning a climatic variation of uncertain date in the upper Pleistocene was yielded by a study of pollens in the upper valley of the Awash (Afar), where R. Bonnefille (1973, 1974) found evidence of a climate distinctly more humid than the present climate, and perhaps colder, characterized by a steppe vegetation on high tablelands.

Mediterranean Basin

Situated between the two geographical zones studied above, the Mediterranean Basin is an important climatic field, the evolution of which seems complex. In particular, the glaciations can no longer be considered as a simple cause for the establishment of a humid climate.

Analysing the palynological, micropalaeontological and isotopic studies made in the eastern Mediterranean, in Greece and in Israel, by Emiliani (1955), Vergnaud-Grazzini and Herman-Rosenberg (1969), Wijmstra (1969), Van der Hammen (1971), Rossignol (1969), Issard (1968) and Issard and Picard (1969), Farrand (1971) reached the conclusion that the drop in temperature during the last glaciation might have been 4° in the case of the air and from 5° to 10° in the case of the sea. In Greece the drought was more marked during the glacial period, whereas the reverse was true on the coasts of Israel.

On the other hand, a study of fragments of mammals (rodents), made by Tchernov (1968, in Farrand, 1971) seems to indicate a gradual evolution of humid conditions in the direction of arid conditions during the past 80 000 years. Around 20 000 years b.p. the level of Lake Lisan, in Israel, dropped by 190 metres in a thousand years as a result of dryer conditions (combined with a tectonic movement in the Dead Sea rift) and, as we have seen (p. 386), the end of the maximum extension of Würmian cold was accompanied by cold and arid conditions throughout the Mediterranean Basin.

As with Africa, the complexity of the geoclimatic situation in the Mediterranean Basin is such that further very detailed studies will be required to enable us to have a clear idea of the climatic evolution in the Würm period.

Conclusion with regard to dating and climates over the past 130 000 years

The last glacial period gives us a model of a complete climatic cycle on the scale of 100 000 or so years (interglacial – glacial – interglacial) with its fluctuations during and between those stages lasting something like 10 000 years. In Africa it is characterized by stages of lake expansion (of comparable duration) separated by stages of desiccation.

Given our present state of knowledge, dating is not exact enough to allow of correlating cold or warm periods with any certainty with humid or dry periods in Africa. It is to be hoped that the work under way, supported by sections and samplings yielding a continuous succession of events, will enable us to answer this question in the future.

Dating and climates over the past 3 500 000 years

The slow trend towards lower temperatures which is a feature of the Quaternary began nearly 55 million years ago ('Cenozoic climatic decline') (Nat. Acad. Sci., 1975). The Antarctic ice sheet, which had already formed about 25 million years ago, increased considerably about 10 million years ago, then again about 5 or 4 million years ago, when it nearly attained its present volume. The Arctic ice sheet over the continents neighbouring the north Atlantic appeared about 3 million years ago. The first big drop in the temperatures of the oceans generally began about 1 800 000 years ago (Bandy, in Bishop and Miller, eds, 1972), shortly before the lowest level of the Calabrian marine stage, around the same time as the occurrence of the Gilsa (1 790 000 years ago).

In Africa several regions (Chad, East Africa, and so on) have yielded a wealth of vertebrate fauna, first ascribed to the Villafrancian (between

3 300 000 and 1 700 000 or 1 million years ago). Some associations of mammals presuppose much more humid conditions than those which are a feature of the present environment of the deposits. They have therefore been regarded as marking 'pluvial periods' in Africa.

The most detailed stratigraphies, based on potassium-argon and palaeomagnetic dating, are those of the East African Rift deposits. In this type of sedimentary filling the effect of the climate is more difficult to discern than that of tectonic and volcanic activity and the topographical changes which they produce, so that present authors have abandoned the attempt to establish a detailed climatic succession. On the other hand, the chronostratigraphy is well established and constitutes a world reference.

In the various deposits of vertebrates and hominids in East Africa (Figs 16.9 and 16.10), dated sedimentary successions are as follows:

Omo (*Ethiopia*)

The Shungura formation about 1000 metres thick, extending from 3 200 000 to 800 000 million years ago; the Usno formation, from 3 100 000 to 2 700 000 years ago (according to de Heinzelin, Brown and Howell, 1971; Coppens, 1972; Bishop and Miller, 1972; Howell, 1972; Brown, 1972, 1975). A study of pollens in the Shungura formation has revealed a considerable climatic change in the direction of drier conditions nearly 2 million years ago with the development of a grassy savanna (Bonnefille, 1973, 1974). This change is confirmed by a study of the fauna. The suggestion might be made that it be paralleled with a world drop in the temperatures of the oceans (1 800 000 years ago).

Olduvai (*Tanzania*)

The succession of the recognized formations and their chronology is as shown in Table 16.1.

TABLE 16.1 *The succession of recognized formations and their chronology*

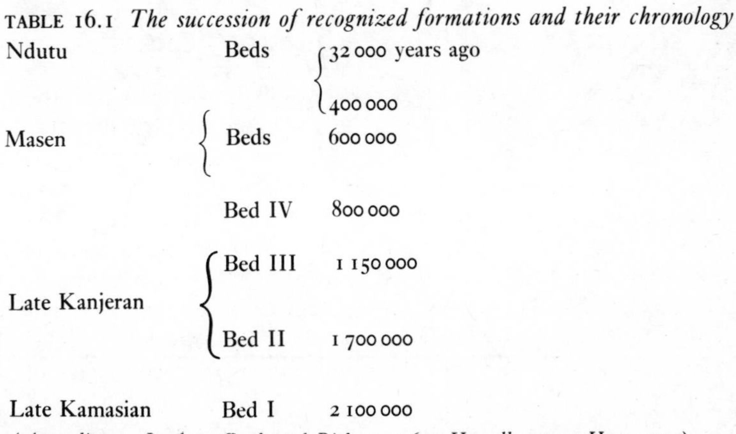

Formation	Beds	Age
Ndutu	Beds	32 000 years ago – 400 000
Masen	Beds	600 000
	Bed IV	800 000
Late Kanjeran	Bed III	1 150 000
	Bed II	1 700 000
Late Kamasian	Bed I	2 100 000

(*According to Leakey, Cook and Bishop, 1967; Howell, 1972; Hay, 1975*)

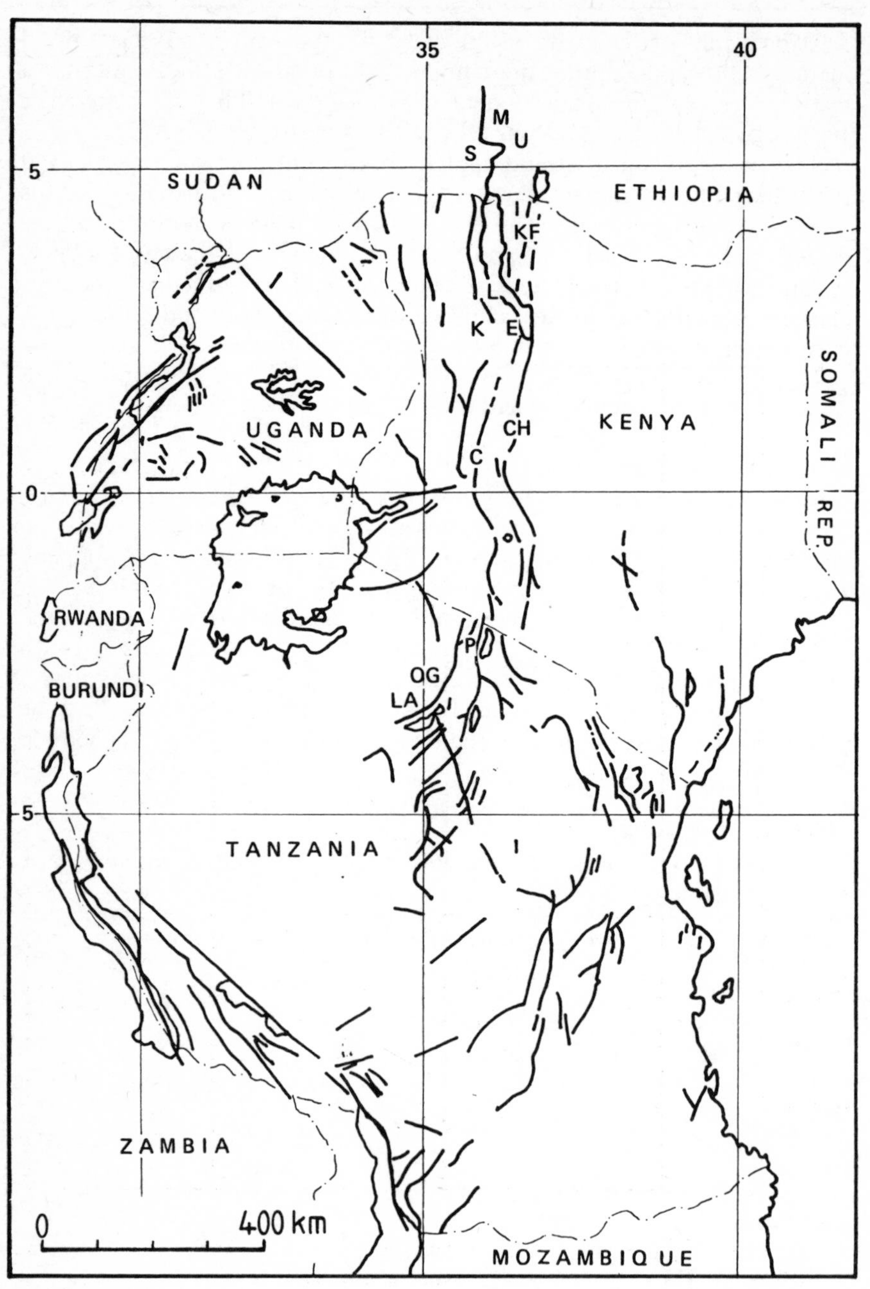
35
40
5
0
5
M
U
S
SUDAN
ETHIOPIA
KF
L
K
E
SOMALI REP.
UGANDA
CH
KENYA
C
RWANDA
P
OG
LA
BURUNDI
TANZANIA
I
ZAMBIA
0
400 km
MOZAMBIQUE

FIG. 16.9

FIG. 16.9 *Map of classical fossil-bearing localities of the Pliocene/Pleistocene era in East Africa: M, Mursi; U, Usno; S, Shungura formations, lower Omo basin; I, Ileret; KF, Koobi Fora, eastern sectors of the Rudolf area; L, Lothagam; KE, Kanapo & Ekora, of the lower Kiero drainage; C, Chermeron; CH, Chesowanga localities, Baringo basin; K, Kanam, Kavirondo Gulf; P, Peninj, Natron basin; OG, Olduvai Gorge; LA, Laetolil, Serengeti plains. Base map largely after 1 : 4 million East African Geology, Survey of Kenya (after F. Clark Howell, 1972)*

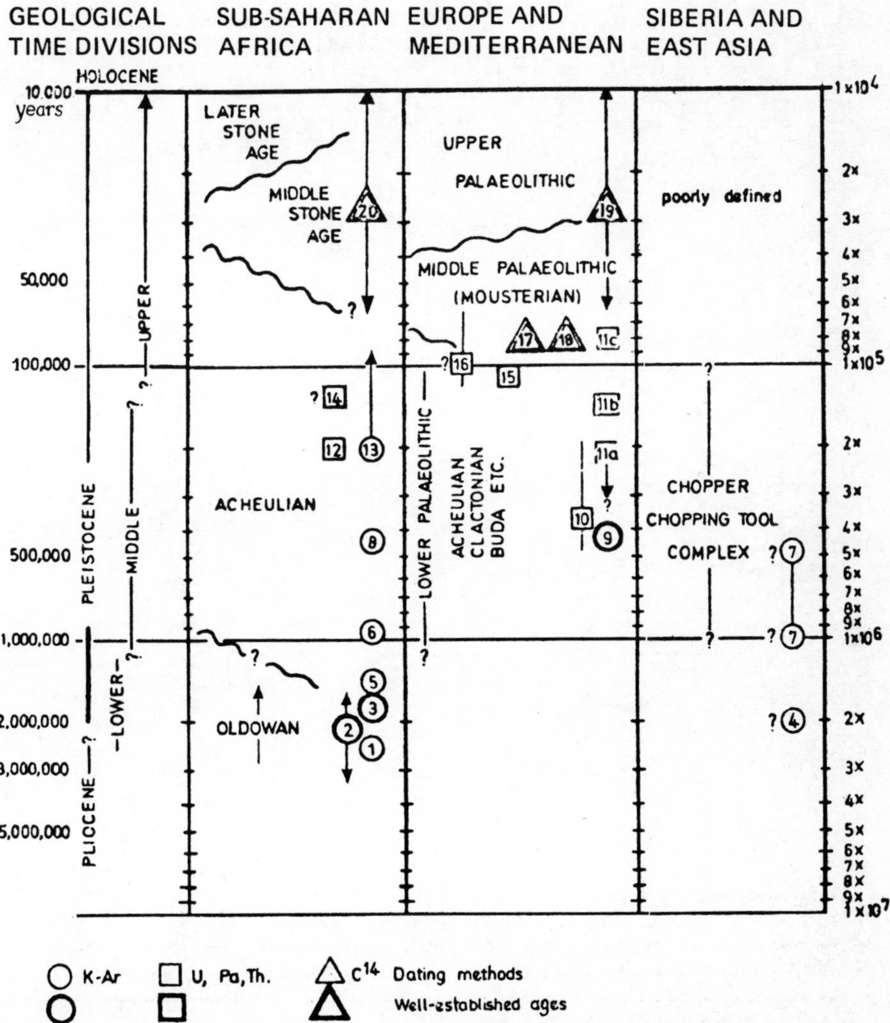

FIG. 16.10 *Chronology and the tempo of cultural change during the Pleistocene, in calibration of hominoid evolution. Gross culture-stratigraphic entities are shown in relation to a logarithmic time scale (after G. L. Isaac in Bishop & Miller (eds), 1972, pp. 381–430)*

East Turkana (Rudolf) (Kenya)

The stratigraphy summed up in Fig. 16.10, which is due to Brock and Isaac (1974), concerns 325 metres of deposits spread over a period extending from about 3 500 000 to 1 500 000 years (according to Bowen, Brock, Isaac and Vondra, 1975).

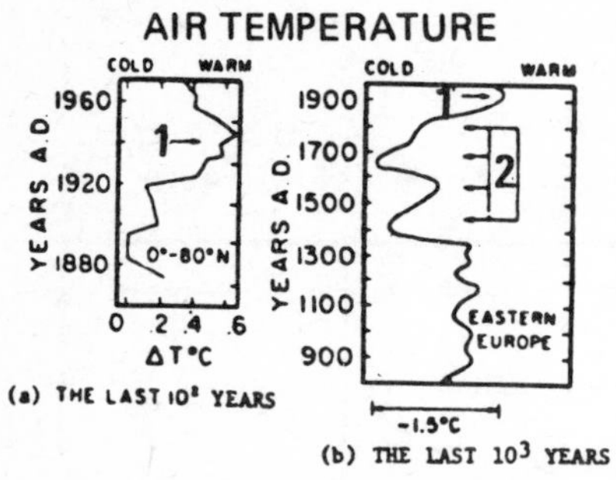

LEGEND
1. THERMAL MAXIMUM OF 1940s
2. LITTLE ICE AGE
3. YOUNGER DRY AS COLD INTERVAL
4. PRESENT INTERGLACIAL (HOLOCENE)
5. LAST PREVIOUS INTERGLACIAL (EEMIAN)
6. EARLIER PLEISTOCENE INTERGLACIALS

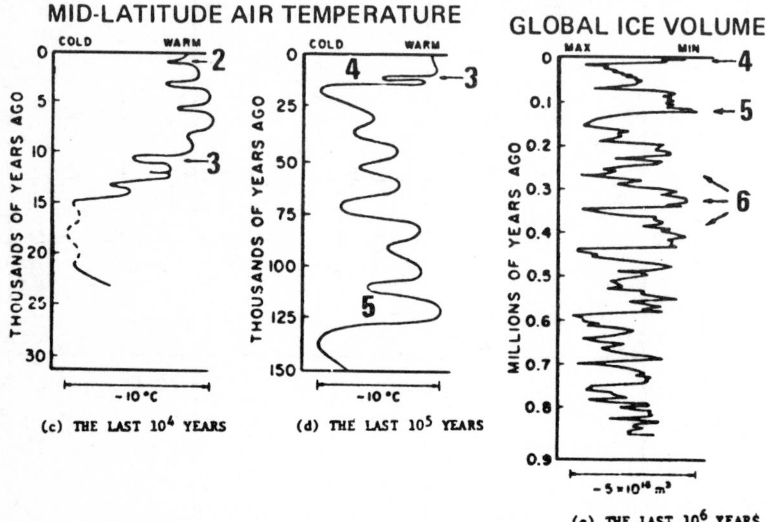

FIG. 16.11 *Generalized trends in global climate for the past million years. (a) Changes in the five-year average surface temperatures over the region 0–80°N during the last 100 years (Mitchell, 1963). (b) Winter severity index for eastern Europe during the last 1 000 years (Lamb, 1969). (c) Generalized midlatitude northern hemisphere air-temperature trends during the last 15 000 years, based on changes in tree lines (LaMarche, 1974), marginal fluctuations in alpine and continental glaciers (Denton and Karlen, 1973), and shifts in vegetation patterns recorded in pollen spectra (Van der Hammen* et al., *1971). (d) Generalized northern hemisphere air-temperature trends during the last 100 000 years, based on midlatitude sea-surface temperature and pollen records and on worldwide sea-level records. (e) Variations in global ice-volume during the last 1 000 000 years as recorded by changes in isotopic composition of fossil plankton in deep-sea core V28–238 (Shackleton and Opdyke, 1973)*

Hadar, Central Afar (Ethiopia)

Finally, the formations at Hadar in central Afar, which contain hominids and a wealth of fossils and which have been studied by the International Afar Research Expedition (IARE), are 3 million years old according to Johanson and Taieb and others (1974, 1975).

In a few years' time the work actively pursued in these parts of East Africa will make it possible to suggest another theory of climatic evolution based on sedimentology and plant and animal ecology, and taking into account the intervention of tectonic and volcanic factors.

Intensive studies have been made of other parts of Africa, such as the Saoura (Alimen *et al.*, 1959; Alimen, 1975b), the Nile valley (Wendorf, 1968; Butzer and Hansen, 1968; de Heinzelin, 1968; Giegengak, 1968; Said, in press), Chad (Coppens, 1965; Servant, 1973) and North Africa. The climatic variations proposed are based on the succession of sedimentations and bed lowerings of the nuers, or the successions of mammal fauna. Failing a radiometric or magnetostratigraphic dating, it is not yet possible to correlate these variations with the European glacial fluctuations.

Conclusion

A feature of the upper Cenozoic over the past 5 million years is the accentuation of the thermal gradients of the globe combined with considerable climatic changes in the course of time. This accentuation has led to considerable variations in temperature at high latitudes and hence to glacial and interglacial periods. At intertropical latitudes thermal fluctuations were somewhat attenuated, but atmospheric circulations, disturbed by the strengthening or weakening of the polar fronts, brought about considerable variations in the distribution and quantity of rainfall, which helped to change profoundly the environment of the different climatic zones, periodically modifying the geographical and plant environment in which the fauna lived and in which hominids developed. These climatic variations establish the rhythm of the evolution of Africa more clearly than do the glaciations in Europe.

What should be borne in mind in this brief survey of the state of our knowledge concerning climatic variations and dating in Africa is the need for continuing observations and measurements before fitting our heterogeneous knowledge into the rigid framework of a theory. On the other hand, we see the importance of the time scales of the various manifestations of climatic change. Care should be taken to place each observation and each phenomenon within the correct time scale. By way of conclusion, this is illustrated in Fig. 16.11 taken from the volume of the National Academy of Sciences (1975) in which five examples of climatic variations are given for time scales ranging from a century to a million years.

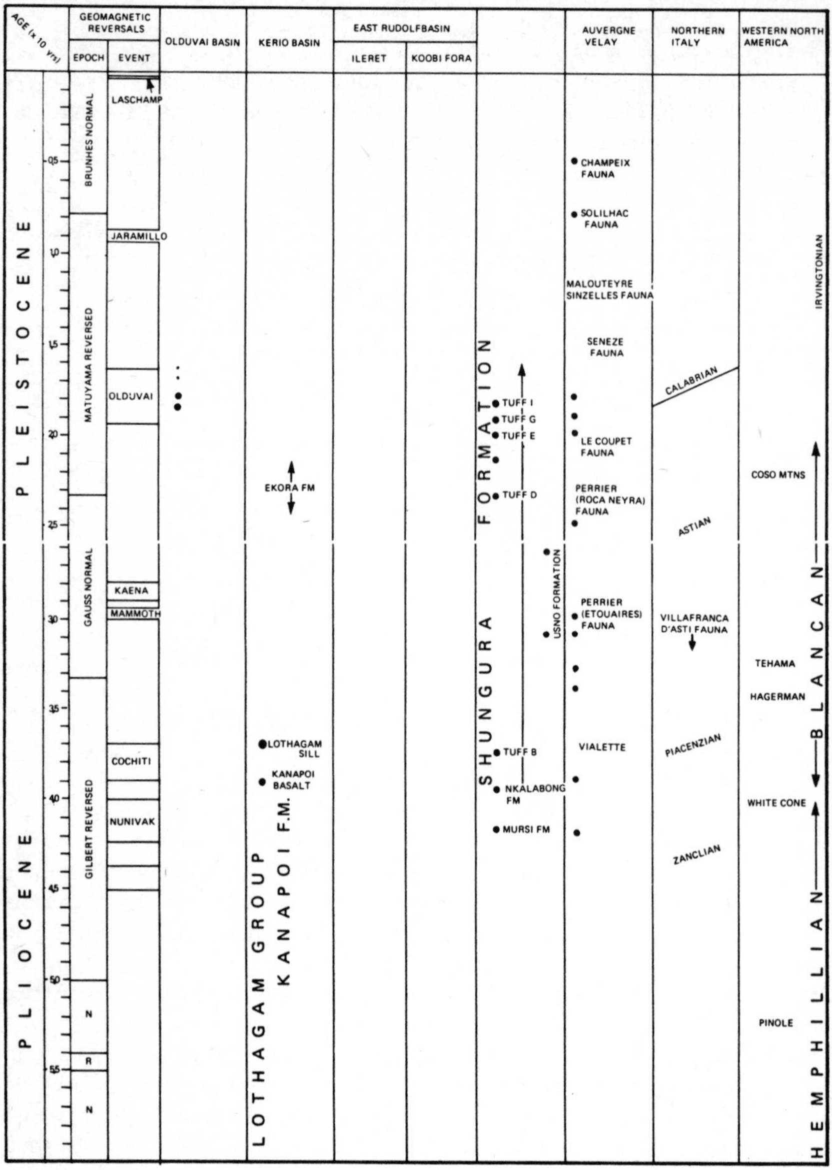

AGE (x 10 yrs)	GEOMAGNETIC REVERSALS: EPOCH	GEOMAGNETIC REVERSALS: EVENT	OLDUVAI BASIN	KERIO BASIN	EAST RUDOLF BASIN: ILERET	EAST RUDOLF BASIN: KOOBI FORA		AUVERGNE VELAY	NORTHERN ITALY	WESTERN NORTH AMERICA

PLEISTOCENE

PLIOCENE

Age scale: 0.5, 1.0, 1.5, 2.0, 2.5, 3.0, 3.5, 4.0, 4.5, 5.0, 5.5

Epochs: BRUNHES NORMAL; MATUYAMA REVERSED; GAUSS NORMAL; GILBERT REVERSED; N; R; N

Events: LASCHAMP; JARAMILLO; OLDUVAI; KAENA; MAMMOTH; COCHITI; NUNIVAK

Kerio Basin: EKORA FM; LOTHAGAM SILL; KANAPOI BASALT; LOTHAGAM GROUP; KANAPOI F.M.

SHUNGURA FORMATION: TUFF I; TUFF G; TUFF E; TUFF D; TUFF B; NKALABONG FM; MURSI FM; USNO FORMATION

Auvergne Velay: CHAMPEIX FAUNA; SOLILHAC FAUNA; MALOUTEYRE SINZELLES FAUNA; SENEZE FAUNA; LE COUPET FAUNA; PERRIER (ROCA NEYRA) FAUNA; PERRIER (ETOUAIRES) FAUNA; VIALETTE

Northern Italy: CALABRIAN; ASTIAN; VILLAFRANCA D'ASTI FAUNA; PIACENZIAN; ZANCLIAN

Western North America: IRVINGTONIAN; COSO MTNS; TEHAMA; HAGERMAN; BLANCAN; WHITE CONE; PINOLE; HEMPHILLIAN

FIG. 16.12 *Radiometric and palaeomagnetic aspects of the Pliocene/Pleistocene time range in eastern Africa, south-western Europe and western North America. The very important successions afforded by exposures in the Ileret and Koobi Fora areas, East Rudolf Basin, are still under investigation and, as the results are incomplete, their respective columns have been left blank (after F. Clark Howell, 1972)*

Hominization: general problems

Part I Y. Coppens The palaeontological data

Man is a Mammal; to be more precise, a placental mammal.[1] He belongs to the order of the Primates.

Palaeontological criteria

The Primates, of which Man forms part, differ from other placental mammals on account of their precocious brain development, improved stereoscopic vision and reduced face size, the replacement of claws by flat nails, and the opposability of the thumb to the other fingers. Among the Primates, which are divided into Prosimians and Simians, Man comes under the second category, which is characterized by increased stature, the displacement of the eye-sockets on the face with the resulting improvement of vision, and the independence of the temporal cavities.

There was a sudden proliferation of forms among these Simians in the upper Oligocene about 30 000 000 years ago, which suggests that the differences occurring in the *Hominidae* family may date back to that epoch. In order to be able to write the history of these *Hominidae,* we accordingly have to search among the Simian fossils of the past 30 million years, in a bid to identify those whose evolutionary tendencies point towards the features which typify us as the genus *Homo,* as bipeds with all that this implies by way of changes in the feet, legs and pelvis, the orientation of the skull, the proportions of the spinal column, the development of the brain case, the reduction of the face, the rounding of the dental arch, the reduction in size of the canine teeth and the hollowing of the palate.

The *Propliopithecus* of the upper Oligocene displays discrete signs of some of these tendencies, which is why some authors have been prematurely enthusiastic in regarding him as being akin to ourselves.

The tendencies that can be observed in *Ramapithecus* are more relevant,

1. The Mammals are the highest of the five classes of the *Vertebrata* and placental Mammals are the highest of the Mammal class. They have a new organ, the placenta, which enables the foetus to breathe and be fed.

in that the brain appears to have grown in volume to 400 cc, the face is reduced in size, the dental arch is rounded and the incisors and canines are likewise smaller and are implanted vertically. Since another Primate, *Oreopithecus,* for which we have a complete skeleton, has the same skull features and the pelvis of an occasional biped, it can be presumed that the postcranial skeleton of *Ramapithecus,* which we do not yet possess, may also bear the same first signs of adaptation of the body to the upright posture.

However, there can be no ambiguity about the evolutionary tendencies of the Australopithecines, since these permanent bipeds have human feet, very modern hands, a distinctly larger capacity brain, small canines and a smaller face, and can accordingly only be regarded as *Hominidae.*

At the end of the chain, the genus *Homo* differs from the Australopithecines by his increased stature, improved erect stance, increased brain capacity, which may be as much as 800 cc in the very earliest species, and a change in dentition, with a relative growth of the front teeth compared with the side teeth as a result of the change from a vegetarian to an omnivorous diet.

It can be seen that the palaeontological approach involves a study of anatomy which is at once comparative and dynamic. Since palaeontologists know that evolution always moves from the simplest to the most complicated and from the undifferentiated to the specialized, they have to find fossils that are both sufficiently comparable and, with due regard to their geological age, are sufficiently different from Man whose ancestors they are seeking.

The oldest Primates are the Prosimians. At the present time, this group is represented by the lemurs of Madagascar, the tarsiers of the Philippines and Indonesia, and a small galago of tropical Africa.

From the Eocene[2] onwards, the Simians divided into two main groups: the *Platyrrhina*[3] or New World Monkeys, with a broad nasal septum and thirty-six teeth, and the *Catarrhina* or Old World monkeys, with a narrow nasal septum and thirty-two teeth.

The *Catarrhina* are divided in their turn into a number of families: the *Cercopithecidae,* the *Pongidae,* the *Hominidae,* the *Hylobatidae,* the *Oreopithecidae,* the *Gigantopithecidae,* and so on.

20 to 40 million years ago

Lack of evidence makes it difficult to see what was afoot in the Eocene and

2. We recall that geological time is divided into the Primary, Secondary, Tertiary and Quaternary eras. The Primates, which emerged at the end of the Secondary era some 70 million years ago, developed during the Tertiary and Quaternary eras. The Tertiary is divided into five main stages, these being, from the oldest to the most recent, the Palaeocene, the Eocene, the Oligocene, the Miocene and the Pliocene. The Quaternary has only two stages, the Pleistocene and the Holocene.

3. This chapter has a Glossary giving the meaning of the different scientific terms used.

Oligocene ages, between 20 and 40 million years ago, but a rich site at Fayum, about sixty miles south of Cairo, investigated by numerous expeditions, has yielded up signs of an incredible variety of Primates: *Parapithecus*, *Apidium*, *Oligopithecus*, *Propliopithecus*, *Aeolopithecus*, *Aegyptopithecus*.

Parapithecus and *Apidium* are notable as having three premolars, that is, thirty-six teeth like the Prosimians and the Platyrrhines (New World monkeys). *Amphipithecus,* a third type, found in Burma, with a similar morphology, belongs to the same group.

But many other traits cause this group of Primates to belong rather to the Catarrhines (characterized by thirty-two teeth). They are in fact ancestors of the Catarrhines, or Protocatarrhines.

Thus our first look backwards reveals an introductory stage, the Protocatarrhine, with thirty-six teeth and existing in three types (*Parapithecus, Amphipithecus, Apidium*).

Oligopithecus, Propliopithecus, Aeolopithecus and *Aegyptopithecus* have two premolars and are true Catarrhines with thirty-two teeth.

Oligopithecus is a small Primate about a third of a metre high, with primitive-type molars, regarded as the ancestor of the Cercopithecines. It is the oldest known Primate with thirty-two teeth.

Aeolopithecus has huge canines and molars with independent tubercles and may be a forerunner of the gibbons. Closely related are the *Pliopitheci* of the European Miocene and the Limnopithecines of the Kenyan and Ugandan Miocene.

Aegyptopithecus also has large canines and heteroform premolars.[4] It is the ancestor of the Dryopithecines found all over the Old World, and perhaps also of the chimpanzees.

Propliopithecus has less robust molars and a front lower premolar with one and a half tubercles. This has been seen as foreshadowing the homomorphy of the two lower premolars which is characteristic of the *Hominidae*. Is this, then, the ancestor of the group, or, more modestly, the common ancestor of the large monkeys and of men, or is it already a member of the *Pongidae* family?

Whatever the pattern of relationships, this period is interesting as proof that in north-east Africa, 30 million years ago, there was a great variety of small Primates foreshadowing all the Primates of today (*Cercopitheci, Pongidae, Hyloleatidae* and *Hominidae*). The guidelines had been laid down.

4. Premolars and molars have crowns which are divided by bridges into small bumps which are called cusps or tubercules. Among the large monkeys (*Pongidae*), the first lower molar resembles a canine and has only one cusp. Among the *Hominidae*, this tooth resembles the second premolar and has two cusps. In the first case, we speak of the heteromorphism of the premolars, and in the second of their homomorphism.

10 to 20 million years ago

In this period other steps forward were taken. In Kenya and Uganda L. S. B. Leakey discovered a small Primate, *Kenyapithecus Africanus*, which he classified as a member of the *Hominidae*. It is 20 million years old, with a rounded dental arch, diverging upper cheek teeth[5] and slightly protruding jaws.[6] Its incisors and canines are vertical, the crowns of the premolars and molars low. Many commentators, however, have seen characteristics here of the large monkeys.

Leakey also discovered, at Fort Ternan in Kenya, what he considers another species of the same type, *Kenyapithecus wickeri*, dated as 14 million years old.

Other experts, interpreting its characteristics differently or basing their opinion on other characteristics than those selected by Leakey, class this specimen also as one of the *Pongidae*.

But Leakey has brought cultural arguments to bear, too, in support of his new candidate. At the Pan-African Conference at Dakar in 1967 he showed fragments of basalt whose natural cutting edges bore traces of use. And at Addis Ababa in 1971 he affirmed that most of the animal bones discovered in association with *Kenyapithecus wickeri* had been artificially broken. The imagination is certainly very struck by the thought of this little African Primate selecting sharp or pointed stones with which to prepare his food. Theoretically, at least, it is not impossible.

Since 1934 we have known about another Primate, *Ramapithecus punjabicus*, 8 to 14 million years old, discovered in the Mio-Pliocene formations of north India and Pakistan.

Simons of Yale has re-examined it and connected it with remains attributed to *Bramapithecus*. It (i.e. *R. punjabicus*) is a small Primate weighing from about 18 to 36 kilogrammes. Its face is squat, its lower jaw thick with a vertical attachment, it has small incisors and small canines vertically set, with late-growing molars and premolars similar to each other in the lower jaw. Because of all these things, many – though not all – experts classify *Ramapithecus punjabicus* as belonging to the *Hominidae*.

Simons has even taken it, together with *Kenyapithecus* from East Africa and a few scattered discoveries in China and Europe, as evidence for a prehominid Miocene area covering the whole of the Old World.

He was not wrong, in fact, since searches in the past three years have led to the discovery of the same *Ramapithecus* in Turkey (I. Tekkaya) and Hungary (M. Kretzoi), while considerable information on this Primate has been obtained from new material from Pakistan gathered by the D. Pilbeam expedition.

5. Premolars and molars are known as cheek teeth.

6. Prognathism means protrusion of the jaw and refers to the projection of all or part of the face beneath the nose.

China and India have produced an enormous Primate, *Gigantopithecus*. It is called *Gigantopithecus blacki* in China and *Gigantopithecus bilaspurensis* in India, where its age is estimated at several million years. Its incisors are small; its canines, while not large, are not hominid. The first lower molar has two cusps, the cheek teeth are big and strong and show considerable wear. The face is squat, the lower jaw powerful with a long vertical attachment. But today most scholars reject it as a possible ancestor of Man.

Searches in Greece under the direction of L. de Bonis have brought to light a 10-million-year-old Primate, *Ouranopithecus macedoniensis,* which could be the ancestor of *Gigantopithecus.*

Finally, 12 million years ago, another Primate, *Oreopithecus,* used to swing from branch to branch in the forests of Tuscany and also perhaps of Kenya.

It was discovered by Gervais in 1872, and described by a gifted Swiss palaeontologist, Johannes Hürzeler, who took over some excavations at Grossette in Tuscany and had the good fortune to find an almost complete skeleton of *Oreopithecus bambolii.* This had a squat face, with a nose that stands out in profile. It has small incisors and canines and two cusps on the first lower premolar. Its pelvis is that of a biped, but its forelimbs are extremely long.

Oreopithecus may possibly be a small hominid, but it is one of the brachial type of Primates,[7] adapted to life in the trees.

So we have *Kenyapithecus Africanus, Kenyapithecus wickeri, Ramapithecus punjabicus, Gigantopithecus blacki, Gigantopithecus bilaspurensis* and *Oreopithecus bambolii.* For the moment, the important thing is not to know who is whose ancestor. Several different lines are in any case represented here. But, taken together, these four types from the Miocene and Pliocene epochs give a picture of a forest-dwelling Primate who seems for the first time to come and seek some of his food in the open areas around lakes and on the banks of rivers. This emergence from the forest will naturally entail new modes of life. And at the same time there occurs a reduction in the size of the fore teeth and of the face, and a tendency for the first premolar, no longer hampered by the canine, to develop two cusps instead of one. This is a foreshadowing of the conquest of the plain, and, at the same time, of bipedalism, walking on two feet.[8]

10 to 1 million years ago

From the Pliocene to the Pleistocene epochs, between 10 and 1 million years ago, we find ourselves in the presence of the Australopithecines, a group at

7. Brachiation is a mode of locomotion in trees consisting of moving from branch to branch suspended by the forelimbs.

8. Bipedalism is a mode of locomotion on land consisting of moving in an erect posture on the two hind limbs.

once very varied in form and very localized. A brief account of their discovery will help us to see both their history and their geography.

Chronology

It was in 1924 that Professor Raymond Dart described and named the first *Australopithecus*. It was the skull of a child of about 5 or 6 years old, found in the breccia of a cave at Taung in Bechuanaland. From 1936 on, this discovery was followed up by many others made by Professor Dart and Professor Philip Tobias in four caves in the Transvaal – Sterkfontein, Swartkrans, Kromdraai near Johannesburg, and Makapansgat near Potgietersrust.

In 1939 a German Professor, L. Kohl Larsen, extended the distribution of *Australopithecus* to East Africa by discovering a jawbone at Garusi or Laetolil to the north-east of Lake Eyasi in Tanzania.

Work has recently been resumed on this deposit by Mary Leakey with considerable success, since she has discovered a very interesting series of fossil *Hominidae* which can probably be related to the *Australopithecines*.

Then came the celebrated researches of the Leakey family in the gorge at Olduvai in Tanzania. Since 1955 they have produced nearly seventy specimens attributable to the *Hominidae*, some of them very remarkable.

In 1964, R. Leakey and G. Isaac brought the number of sites in Tanzania up to three when they found an *Australopithecus* jaw near Lake Natron. Then the finds shifted towards the north.

In 1967 an international expedition resumed excavations at palaeontological sites in the west of the lower Omo river valley in Ethiopia. There were three teams: a French team led by Professor C. Arambourg and Y. Coppens; an American one under Professor Clark Howell; and a Kenyan one directed by L. S. B. Leakey and his son Richard. These sites, discovered by French travellers at the beginning of this century, had been excavated in 1932 and 1933 by an expedition from the National Museum of Natural History in Paris, led by C. Arambourg. During its very first month the new expedition was fortunate enough to find the first *Australopithecus* jaw that the sites had produced. Numerous other finds followed: in the course of nine seasons, the French and American missions made exceptional discoveries: the remains of about 400 *Hominidae*.

The Kenyan team left Omo in 1968 to explore the east banks of Lake Turkana in Kenya under the leadership of R. Leakey. In the course of ten seasons this team collected more than 100 hominid fragments, some of them very important.

Meanwhile, on the south-west shores of the same lake, an American expedition from Harvard, under the leadership of B. Patterson, was excavating three small sites of which two produced hominid remains.

A team from Bedford College, London, whose aim was to draw up a geological map of the basin of Lake Baringo in Kenya, discovered five sites containing palaeoanthropological remains.

In four seasons, starting in 1973, an international expedition led by Maurice Taieb, Yves Coppens and Donald C. Johanson to Hadar in the Ethiopian Afar region, discovered more than 300 palaeoanthropological fragments belonging to one or two hominid forms in an exceptional state of preservation. A second mission to the Afar region, as a follow-up to the first, subsequently collected a skull which can be attributed to a *Pithecanthropus*.

Lastly, in 1975 and 1976, after nine years' painstaking excavations, Jean Chavaillon uncovered three interesting fragments in association with Oldowan and Acheulian industries at Melka Konture near Addis Ababa.

All these discoveries, taken together, limit the distribution of *Australopithecus* to the eastern and southern parts of Africa.

Age

The oldest of these sites is N'Gorora, 9 to 12 million years old, in the basin of Lake Baringo in Kenya. So far it has yielded only an upper molar belonging to a hominid of unidentified type, but high hopes are entertained for the results of future excavations. The molar is low-crowned like those of *Ramapithecus*, but the structure of the cusps is like that found in the Australopithecines and it may be a *Sivanpithecus*.

A molar has also been discovered in another deposit in the Baringo Basin, at Lukeino, which is dated to between 6 and 6·5 million years. In this instance the find consists of a rearmost lower molar very similar to that of *Australopithecus*.

At Lothagam, south-west of Lake Turkana in Kenya, Patterson discovered a fragment of lower jaw with a tooth embedded in it; the form suggests an Australopithecine, and related vertebrates also found point to a Pliocene age that may be placed from 5 to 16 million years ago.

Two other sites in Kenya – Chemeron in the basin of Lake Baringo and Kanapoi in that of Lake Turkana – have yielded a hominid temporal bone and humerus respectively.

The Laetolil deposit in Tanzania was dated from at least 3 500 000 years ago. Its fossil *Hominidae* are remarkably comparable to those collected at Hadar in the Ethiopian Afar, which are dateable to between 2 800 000 and 3 200 000 years ago.

The Omo sites consist of sedimentary strata nearly a mile in depth, made up of a succession of fossil-bearing sands, clays and volcanic deposits which can be dated with certainty. It has been worked out that the strata range from over 4 million years old at the bottom to less than 1 million years old at the top. The hominid remains are found from the 3 200 000 level to the top – in other words, continuously over more than 2 million years.

The hominid-yielding sites east of Lake Turkana stretch over the period between 3 and 1 million years ago.

Comparison of fauna has recently given an estimated age of 2·5 million to more than 3 million years for the oldest caves in South Africa (Makapansgat, Sterkfontein) producing Australopithecine remains, but this date is still much disputed.

The Olduvai gorges in Tanzania produce remains of *Hominidae* and their activities throughout the hundred yards or so of the deposit, dated as being 1 800 000 years old at the base.

Two other late South African caves with Australopithecine remains, Swartkrans and Kromdraai, are about the same age as the oldest levels at Olduvai, or even a little older (2 to 2·5 million years).

Probably the youngest Australopithecines have come from Chesowanja in the Baringo Basin in Kenya, the Lake Natron site in Tanzania and perhaps the Taung breccia in South Africa: they are scarcely more than a million years old.

The Australopithecines therefore seem to appear about 6 or 7 million years old, and to disappear about a million years ago. What have these sites given us, then? Several kinds of hominid, some contemporary with one another. One is called *Australopithecus robustus*, or *Paranthropus*, or *Zinjanthropus*. Another is called *Australopithecus gracilis*, or *Australopithecus* proper, or *Plestanthropus* or *Paraustralopithecus*. A third is called *Homo habilis*, or *Australopithecus habilis*. A fourth is called *Homo erectus*, or *Telanthropus*, or *Meganthropus*.

Australopithecus robustus

This has been found in caves in South Africa from 2 to 2·5 million years old, in Omo in Ethiopia and east of Lake Turkana in Kenya, at Olduvai about 1 800 000 years ago, and at Chesowanja 1 100 000 years ago. It is called *robustus* because it is in fact larger and stronger than the others.

The form of the skull corresponds to a powerful set of masticatory equipment, and the molars and premolars are very large. There is a strong lower jaw, well-set muscles for chewing, a powerful zygomatic arch,[9] and a marked sagittal ridge for the temporal muscles.[10] There is no forehead. The face is high and flat and the fore teeth small to facilitate lateral chewing movements. The lower jaw has therefore a very high attachment, to augment the masticatory action of the masseter and pterygoid muscles.

The body is stronger than that of the other species of *Australopithecus*. It is about 1·5 metres tall, and its weight is estimated at between about 36 and 66 kilogrammes.

It was not perfectly adapted to walking on two feet: the apophysis of the femur is small and its neck long.

Brain size is estimated at 530 cc both for the Swartkrans and for the Olduvai

9. The zygomatic arch is the skull bone joining the forehead to the face.

10. The sagittal ridge is a bone growth on the top of the skull forming a ridge similar to the crest of a helmet.

specimens. The development of the cerebellum is to be noted: it may indicate increased control of movement (for example, manipulation and locomotion).

Australopithecus gracilis comes from Makapansgat and Sterkfontein in South Africa, and is also thought to have been found at Omo in Ethiopia, Garusi or Laetolil in Tanzania and Lothagam in Kenya.

It is said to have been just over 1·2 metres tall and to have weighed from just under 18 to just over 32 kilogrammes.

The face is more prominent than in *Australopithecus robustus.* The eyebrow ridges[11] are fairly developed and support a comparative developed forehead.

The incisors are spatulate and set vertically, the canines small and similar to incisors. The cheek teeth diverge to form a parabolic dental arch, and are large, with round cusps and thick enamel, and worn right down.

Even if this *Australopithecus* had a more varied diet than *Australopithecus robustus,* it must still have been basically vegetarian: the thickness of the lower jaw and the enamel, the wearing of the teeth down to the gums, the shortness of the face and the size of the premolars and molars all indicate a powerful masticatory system.

The teeth are late in cutting, and this, together with the thickness of the enamel, signifies adaptation to a longer adolescence and to a longer life altogether.

Brain size varies from 428 to 485 cc – the mean of the South African form.

The long bones, especially the humerus and scapula, are reminders of ancestors who swung from branch to branch. But *Australopithecus gracilis* is a permanent biped.

Homo habilis was described at Olduvai in Tanzania in 1964, and may have been encountered again at Omo in Ethiopia, to the east of Lake Turkana, and at Kanapoi in Kenya.

The cheek teeth are flatter than in the examples of *Australopithecus gracilis* found in South Africa. They are also longer and narrower.

Estimates based on the parietal bones give *Homo habilis* a brain capacity of 680 cc, while a skull for east Lake Turkana has a capacity of almost 800 cc.

The evolutionary tendencies of teeth and brain thus place it nearer to us than *Australopithecus.* Apart from the skull, however, the rest of the skeleton[12] is reminiscent of *Australopithecus gracilis*: the clavicle in particular suggests ancestors who swung from branch to branch, as in the case of *Australopithecus gracilis.*

The height of *Homo habilis* is estimated at between about 1·2 and 1·4 metres.

11. The eyebrow ridges are the bony upper edges of the eye-sockets.
12. Postcranial skeleton is the term used for the whole skeleton minus the skull.

Homo erectus

Finally, at Swartkrans in South Africa (2·5 million years old), at Olduvai in Tanzania (1·5 million years) and east of Lake Turkana in Kenya (1·5 million years), at Melka Konture, at Bodo, in Omo in Ethiopia between 500 000 and 1 500 000 years, excavators have discovered what they call *Homo erectus,* that is, *Hominidae* more advanced in the scale of evolution than any of those that went before.

In 1949, at Swartkrans, Broom and Robinson isolated some bones which they attributed to a more hominid form called *Telanthropus capensis.*

In 1957 Robinson had the idea of attributing it to the Pithecanthropines and labelling it *Homo erectus.*

In 1969 Ron Clarke, Clark Howell and Brain, handling the Swartkrans specimens, noticed that the skull of the *Australopithecus robustus*, SK 847, fitted perfectly on the upper jaw of *Telanthropus.* This combination produces an interesting picture confirming Robinson's suppositions: a prominent eyebrow ridge[13] is surmounted by a receding forehead, corresponding to the lack of forehead in *Australopithecus robustus*; the skull has large frontal sinuses;[14] postorbital constriction[15] is fairly marked; the bones of the nose are prominent; the dental arch is short, indicating a small mandible with lower vertical attachment; and finally the dentition and structure of the facial skeleton bring this specimen close to *Homo,* and in particular to *Homo erectus.*

At Olduvai, Hominid 13 has dental equipment 20 per cent smaller than *Homo habilis* and a smaller lower jaw. Hominid 16 has a prominent eyebrow ridge, and Leakey and Tobias speak of *Homo erectus.* However, while the status of these two fossils is uncertain, the same is by no means true of Hominid 13, which undoubtedly represents the skull cap of *Homo erectus.*

To the east of Lake Turkana in Kenya, a large number of discoveries can be related to this progressive species of the genus *Homo.* In particular, the recent crop of three skulls from different dates is a very fine illustration of the growth of evolutionary tendencies in this species.

It is worth recalling that a recent dating of the oldest Javanese Pithecanthropine, the skull of a child found at Modjokerto, gives an age of 1 900 000 years, but it is arguable whether it is really an *Homo erectus.*

Tobias and Von Koenigswald, having compared the original remains from Java and Tanzania at Cambridge, concluded that the oldest *Homo habilis* is morphologically the same as *Meganthropus palaeojavanicus* and perhaps as *Hemianthropus peii* from China, and that the most recent *Homo*

13. When the eyebrow ridge is surmounted by a bony protraction, it is known as a supra-orbital torus.

14. Sinuses are cavities.

15. The skull is compressed laterally behind the eye-sockets. This is what is known as postorbital constriction.

habilis (Hominid 13) is morphologically the same as *Pithecanthropus IV*, *Sangiran B* and *Telanthropus capensis*.

Industries

For the first time in the history of Primates, such remains are found in association with artifacts.

The French expedition to the Omo site in 1969 turned up several tools of stone and bone over 2 million years old. The following year the Kenyan expedition east of Lake Turkana discovered a comparable production of stone and bone tools in a volcanic stratum dated as 2 000 000 years old. In 1978 the French and American expeditions at Omo found similar archaeological remains over 2 million years old. So in three years, through the discoveries made in the Pleistocene basin of Lake Turkana, the age of the first manufactured tools had been pushed back to more than 2·5, perhaps even 3 million years, thus adding over a million years to the time in which such activity is known to have existed.

The first manufactured articles in the world consist of a large number of fragments deliberately chipped and used for their cutting edge; pebbles on which a point or sharp edge has been chipped at and improved; and bones and teeth either shaped in some way or used as they stood if they lent themselves to direct use, as in the case of the canine teeth of Hippopotamus or *Suidae*, for example.

These tools may be divided into a number of types, each represented by several examples. This indicates that the shape had been deliberately worked out and sought after; it was the fruit of experience transmitted from one generation to another, implying a certain degree of social life. This means not that we are 2·5 million years away from the actual origin of the tool, but rather that we are here approaching the limits of awareness of it. Further in the past, it is indistinguishable from natural objects.

At Makapansgat in South Africa an industry of tools made of bone, horn and teeth has been brought to light. This production has been named Osteodontokeratic because of the materials it uses, and if recent attempts to correlate the South African caves with the great East African sites prove successful, it too may turn out to be very ancient. At any rate one can make the same observations as in the Lake Turkana basin: the various types of tool are mass-produced, which shows that the process was no longer in its early stages.

At Hadar H. Roche recently uncovered a shaped pebble industry, similar to that at Olduvai, at a level which it is not impossible to date to 2 500 000 years ago.

From the oldest deposits at Olduvai onwards (1 800 000 years), tools are to be found everywhere, in large quantities and always the same; the particular frequency of pebble implements has earned the industry the name of 'Pebble Culture' or Oldowan (formed from the place name Olduvai).

One day, working in the oldest level at Olduvai, Dr Leakey noticed a large accumulation of basalt pebbles. As the dig progressed, he saw that instead of being scattered about at random they were arranged in little heaps forming a circle. Each heap probably served to wedge a post into the ground. Imagine a ring of posts or hoops with skins or vegetation stretched between them, and one is naturally tempted to see here the remains of some kind of building. One would therefore be in the presence of a dwelling some 2 million years old!

In the oldest Oldowan level (1·5 million years) at Melka Konture, near Addis Ababa, Jean Chavaillon recently came upon a rather similar structure. Right in the middle of an inhabited area strewn with tools, he suddenly uncovered a round surface about 2·5 metres in diameter, without any tools and raised about a third of a metre above the surrounding level, with a trough or gutter some 1·8 metres long. A few heaps of stones again suggest the presence of posts.

It has been suggested that *Australopithecus robustus* might be the male of *Australopithecus gracilis*; that *Homo habilis* was an *Australopithecus gracilis* somewhat younger and more developed than the one found in South Africa; that *Telanthropus* or *Homo erectus* from Swartkrans might come within the lower limits of the variations found in *Australopithecus robustus* at the same site; that *Meganthropus javanicus* was an Australopithecine; even that certain Australopithecines (e.g. at Olduvai and Swartkrans) were Pithecanthropines.

From this apparent confusion one clear argument nevertheless emerges, namely that it is in the midst of the Australopithecine area, at first limited to East and South Africa and subsequently extending (with *Australopithecus* in the same or a more advanced form) to Asia south of the Himalayas, that there appear the genus *Homo* and the deliberately fabricated tool.

The latter very quickly becomes the hallmark of its maker; various types of tools are quickly developed for particular purposes; tool-making is taught. Finally, dwelling-places are constructed. It is in this sense that the human race may be said to have its origins in Africa.

Conclusion

Man thus emerges, at the end of a very long history, as a Primate who one day improves on the tool he has already long been using. Deliberately fabricated tools, together with dwellings, suddenly reveal a thinking being, a being with foresight who teaches and transmits, who creates the first society and endows it with the first culture.

A date of over 2 million years has recently been advanced for certain hominid fossil remains in Java. Worked pebbles from several sites in the south of France have sometimes been said to be equally old. But in the present state of our knowledge, the victory lies with Africa because of the amount and the importance of the very early evidence discovered in the continent.

It is as if, 6 to 7 million years ago, in the south-eastern quadrant of the African continent, a group of *Hominidae* called Australopithecines came into being, and as if from this polymorphous group there emerged, 2·5 to 3 millions years ago, a creature, *Australopithecus* himself or what may already be called Man, capable of shaping stone and bone, of building huts and of living in small societies. This being, in all his manifestations, thus represents the origin, properly speaking, of *Homo faber*, tool-making Man.

The last million years

The last million years have seen the birth of *Homo sapiens*; the last few hundreds of years his alarming proliferation. It took 115 years for the world's population to rise from 1 to 2 thousand million; in a further 35 years it rose from 2 thousand million to 3; in the last 15 years from 3 to 4 thousand million and the acceleration continues.

Part II L. Balout The archaeological data

The prehistorian approaches the problem of hominization in Africa from a point of view somewhat different from that of the palaeontologist. For him, hominization is the gradual cerebralization that enables man to conceive of, and, by means of ever more elaborate techniques, to equip himself with tools (in the widest sense of the term) so diversified and efficient, in order to further his development, as to have had down the ages a cumulative impact on the natural environment sufficient to overthrow all kinds of biological equilibrium. The palaeontological evolution leading up to man does not allow us to point to any definite threshold of hominization: a chipped stone is enough to show the threshold has already been crossed. In a justly famous passage Teilhard de Chardin says: 'Man made his entrance in silence . . . He moved so quietly, in fact, that when we first begin to notice he is there, revealed by the indelible stone implements providing multiple evidence of his presence . . . he already covers the entire Old World.'

The prehistorian's attitude is understandable. The real missing link is not the intermediate form between Australopithecines and Pithecanthropines, Neanderthal man and *Homo sapiens*, but what comes between shaped stones and bones, and these fossils. The prehistoric industries which have been attributed with absolute certainty to *Homo sapiens* from the early Palaeolithic on, and somewhat doubtfully to Neanderthal man in the middle Palaeolithic, can be ascribed only hypothetically to the Pithecanthropines and Australopithecines. True, this is perhaps the only scientific hypothesis possible here. But the industry associated with Peking man is not the same as that found with the Pithecanthropines, and it is again different in Java (Pithecanthropine), Algeria (Atlanthropine) and East Africa. As for the Australopithecines, they are a heterogeneous group among whose members it is still difficult to say which were the probable, or even possible, authors of the Osteodontokeratic and Pebble Cultures.

If, however, there is for the palaeontologist a threshold of hominization, the cerebral Rubicon which Professor Vallois has defined as a brain capacity of 800 cc, the prehistorian has a technical threshold which, once crossed, opens the path of progress right down to our own times. But before we can define this threshold we have to solve two problems: how? and when? The first problem entails eliminating all natural causes and identifying, in the tool, the hand of man. For the second, we need to establish a chronological framework enabling us to date, to within an acceptable degree of approximation, the most remote evidence of human activity.

Up till now, only Africa has provided anything like a positive solution to these two problems.

And, since the theory of monogeny, or a common origin for the whole of the human race, is universally accepted, Africa is currently regarded as the cradle of mankind. This cradle on wheels, as the Abbé Breuil called it, so long whisked to and fro from the peaks of the Pamir to the plains of the Euphrates, has settled down for the moment, then, in East Africa, where, according to theory, everything happened 3 million years ago at least. The Old Testament *Book of Genesis* placed the earthly Paradise, Eden, in a landscape of gardens and cultivation. God dedicated Adam to a life of agriculture and stock-raising, a Neolithic mode of life in a region that was gradually to reveal the Palaeolithic. All chronologies drawn from the Scriptures date the creation between 6484 and 3616 years before our era. The Near East may well have been one of the most ancient, if not actually the oldest, centre of Neolithization. But it is no longer possible to call it the cradle of mankind.

Man made his entrance in silence, and it was the stones he shaped that long afterwards betrayed his existence. The human race 'made no disturbance in nature when it first appeared ... we see it emerge phyletically, exactly like any other species' (Teilhard). So the prehistorian's responsibility is an enormous one: by identifying the earliest perceptible traces of human activity, he does what palaeontology is powerless to do – through tools, he identifies Man.

The prehistorian of Africa must begin by answering three questions:

(1) Are tools the true criteria of hominization?
(2) Do they enable us to locate the beginning of hominization?
(3) In so far as they have survived at all, can they be identified with certainty?

(1) The data for the solution of this problem come largely from Africa. The Abbé Breuil, struck by the behaviour of certain animals, told me towards the end of his life that he doubted whether tools really marked the

crossing of the threshold of hominization, and if it might not be better to take art as a criterion. This would amount to distinguishing *Homo* truly '*sapiens*', the painter of Lascaux, our direct ancestor, from an earlier series of diligent beings, known as *Homo faber*.

As Madame Tetry has shown, the use of tools other than the natural tools which form part of the body is not peculiar to Man, or even to the Primates in general. This is proved by the digger wasp and the tailor ant among the insects; the Galapagos finch, the gull, the vulture, the buzzard, and the song thrush among the birds; by the beaver and the sea otter; and by many other examples. Among the Primates the chimpanzee is closest to Man. In its daily life it uses tools and weapons to defend itself against such enemies as snakes, and a fear or defence reflex will lead it to pick up sticks and brandish them.[16] This behaviour, already observed in zoos and other forms of captivity, was also studied, between 1964 and 1968, in game reserves in Tanzania. There chimpanzees, living in groups of more than thirty individuals, select twigs with which to dig out termites, use sticks for breaking nests or reaching honey, leaves for scooping up water from hollows in trees, branches as crooks for hooking down bananas. They use stones for breaking fruit and, thrown over or under arm, as an alternative to sticks for chasing off rival predators. And, lastly, they communicate with one another by means of audible signals. Similar observations have been made on gorillas in Rwanda.[17]

Thus, if tools are to be considered a criterion of hominization, the mere use of something other than the 'natural tools' of the body is not enough. There has to be a deliberate transformation of the object used, a concept which makes possible an affirmative answer to our third question, though not to our second.

(2) Tools do *not* make it possible for us to locate the beginnings of hominization. In the first place, only fossilized bones and stones have come down to us. Without going out of our way for far-fetched ethnographical examples, we may remind ourselves that a human group can perfectly well get all its implements from the vegetable world. The classic example are the Menkopis of the Andaman Islands. And it is as probable as it is incapable of proof that on the wooded plains of the African plateaux, trees provided the first hominids with their first tools. Even as regards fossil bones and teeth, Dart antedated these by attributing to the Australopithecines of the Transvaal an industry based on bones, teeth and horn, which he called the Osteodontokeratic Culture and which was long disputed; we shall return to it. Within the Pebble Culture, R. Van Riet Lowe distinguished between split and trimmed pebbles, the first of which – pebbles that have merely been broken – have come to be generally regarded with scepticism. Certainly, if a pebble picked up and thrown by a human hand retains no discernible trace of its being put to this use, a split pebble can easily be just the work of nature.

16. *CA*, June 1967.

17. *Nat. Geog. Soc.*, Washington, DC, October 1971.

Waterfalls and waves produce stones that are indistinguishable from those split open by man. The supposed Kafuan industry did not survive scrutiny of this kind.

The text already partly quoted from Teilhard de Chardin contains some big mistakes and a very serious omission. The passage reads, more fully: 'Man made his entrance in silence ... He moved so quietly, in fact, that when we first begin to notice he is there, revealed by the indelible stone implements providing multiple evidence of his presence, he already covers the entire Old World from the Cape of Good Hope to Peking. Already, certainly, he speaks and lives in groups. Already he makes fire. And isn't this, after all, exactly what we ought to have expected? Every time some new living form arises before us out of the depths of History, do we not know it arises fully formed and that it is already legion?' But *Homo loquens* does not really seem to have appeared until the time of the Pithecanthropines; nor, before them, at least not in Africa, is there any reliable evidence of the fire mistakenly attributed to *Australopithecus Prometheus*; and the indelible stone implements from Olduvai certainly do not indicate a beginning. The variety of form, their number, the deliberateness with which they are reproduced, suggest the completion of a process rather than a beginning. It was the prehistorians of Africa who wanted those extra million years before Bed I at Olduvai which Omo and Koobi Fora have recently made available to them. And even that does not satisfy us!

(3) So we must apply ourselves to solving the third problem which is to prove human intention in the most rudimentary and simple tools. Only Africa provides material abundant enough for this. There are two main areas of inquiry – bone and stone.

(a) *The Osteodontokeratic industry*. The hypothesis suggested by Dart in 1949 was examined by Donald F. Wolberg in *Current Anthropology*, February 1970. The Abbé Breuil, examining the bones found with the Sinanthropines at Choukoutien, had previously supposed that the Stone Age might have been preceded by a bone age. A 'Prelithic' was supposed to have gone before the Palaeolithic. Before 1955, when relevant remains were found in South Africa, and before 1959–60 (Olduvai, Tanzania), 1969 (Omo, Ethiopia) and 1971 (Lake Turkana, Kenya), there was no evidence of stone manufacture in association with Australopithecine sites. Instead, Dart proposed an Osteodontokeratic culture based on bones, teeth and horn. Unfortunately, there is no reliable chronology, either relative or absolute, for the Australopithecines of South Africa, though usable chronologies do exist for those of Ethiopia, Kenya and Tanzania. Dart, who maintained the existence of his bone industry from 1949 to 1960, based his argument on the examination of baboon and Australopithecine skulls (selection rather than chance having seemingly accounted for the collection of bones found at Makapansgat – there were, for example, 336 humerus bones to 56 femurs) and on cervical vertebrae, which, with cattle skulls, represented 56 per cent of the total collected. According to Dart the animal bones found in the

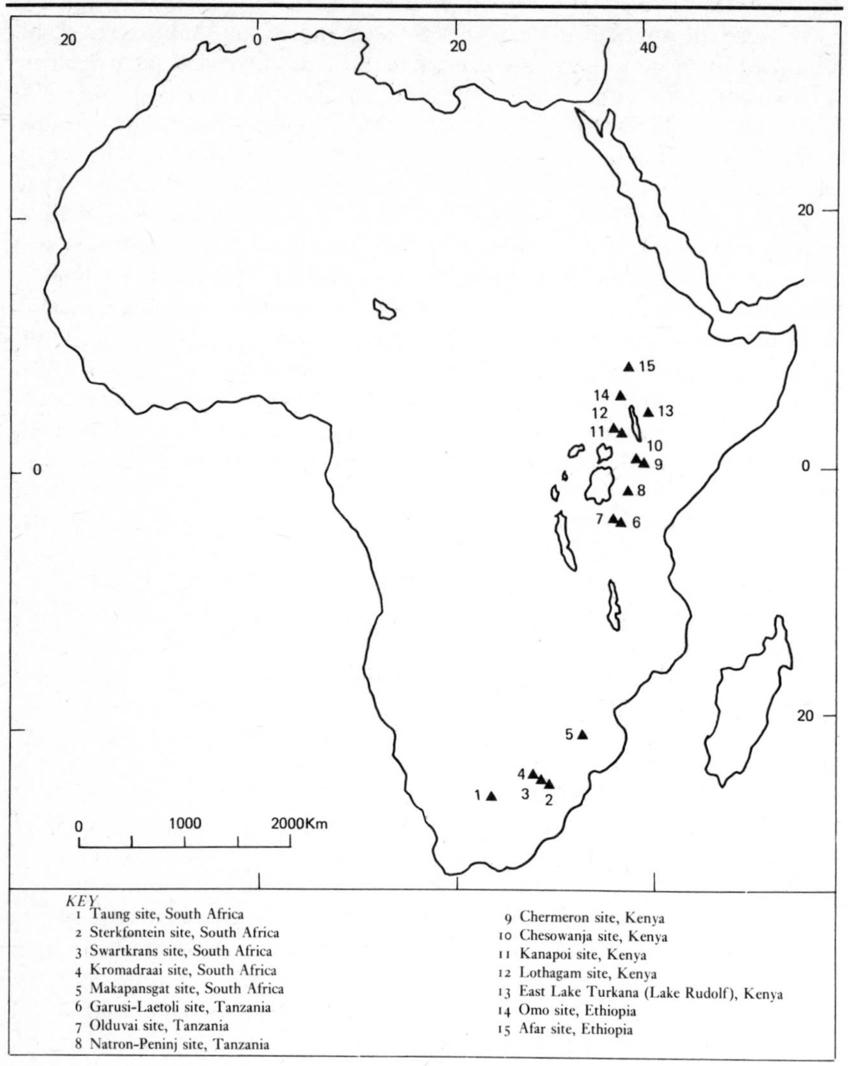

FIG 17.1 *Palaeontological data*

breccia of the caves in which Australopithecine was found were refuse, debris from the kitchen of a hunter-predator who now that he stood upright could use his hands to wield tools and weapons. After examining fifty baboon skulls and six Australopithecine skulls, Dart declared that 80 per cent showed traces of lesions, caused by blows. The blows were usually struck from in front, and some were dual, indicating two-headed weapons. At Makapansgat many ungulate humeruses bore traces of having been worn down before fossilization while the other long bones were intact, from which Dart concluded that the typical weapon of the Australopithecine was a bone club, preferably an ungulate humerus. The hunter also used jawbones. Spiral fractures in humerus or shin-bones were held to be due to torsional stress and also to imply the agency of the human hand. This had already been suggested by Breuil and Teilhard de Chardin in connection with the Sinanthropine sites at Choukoutien. A fossilized *Gazella gracilior* horn embedded in an antelope's femur and fixed there by calcite thus indicated human action of some kind, whether it was a tool used to split the femur or a tool of which the femur formed the handle. A similar interpretation was given to a hyena skull with the heel-bone of an antelope thrust between the brain-pan and the zygomatic arch.

All this presupposed an Osteodontokeratic stage, first Prelithic, then Palaeolithic, leading first to the Pebble Culture and then to biface industries. This would certainly constitute a beginning of a 'cultural implemental activity'.

Such a theory was bound to give rise to heated arguments as to which was the hunter and which the hunted. Some experts considered all the bones, including those of the Australopithecines themselves, to be mere remains left over from the gorgings of carnivores. Others thought they were refuse that had accumulated in hyenas' lairs, though this does not correspond to that animal's habits. Others attributed it all to porcupines. But out of 7159 bone fragments found at Makapansgat before 1955 only 200 had been gnawed. Moreover, hyenas live surrounded by the bones of other hyenas. A site assigned to the Riss-Würm period was to show that out of a total of 130 animals, 110 were hyenas, whereas at Makapansgat, out of 433 specimens, only 17 were hyenas. In the Australopithecine cave, 47 out of 729 separate teeth belonged to hyenas; at the Riss-Würm site they accounted for 1000 out of 1100.

But gradually a consensus in favour of the Osteodontokeratic industry emerged, though without prejudice to the type of Australopithecine that was to be considered the hunter. The theory received support from the coexistence of a stone industry (Sterkfontein, 1955). But clinching proof came from the bone industry at Olduvai, excellently described by Mary Leakey.[18] This discovery is beyond dispute, and prepares the way for the similar industry attributed to the Pithecanthropines of Africa, Asia (Choukoutien) and Europe (e.g. Torralba and Ambrona). Throughout prehistoric times there was a kind of bone industry just as there was a stone industry. It is more difficult to analyse but it exists just the same. And it is nowhere more ancient than in Africa, even if a prelithic stage has not yet been proved.

(b) *The stone industry*. Since the theory of eoliths was abandoned, the fashioned pebbles of what has long been known as the Pebble Culture have represented the oldest recognized stone industry. It was E. J. Wayland

18. Olduvai Gorge, Vol. III.

who, in 1919, when he was director of the Uganda Geological Service, noticed there the sort of chipped pebbles that had been discovered in Ceylon before 1914. In 1920 he invented the terms Pebble Culture and Kafuan culture (the latter from the name of the river Kafu), and by 1934 had distinguished four successive stages. It was Wayland who in 1936 suggested Oldowan as a name for the advanced Pebble Culture of the Olduvai Gorge in Tanzania. In 1952 Van Riet Lowe attempted the first technical and morphological classification of the Pebble Culture. But it was from H. Movius, and from Asia, that the first real definition of forms came, in 1944, with the introduction of the terms chopper, chopping tool and handaxe. Gradually the prehistorians of all Africa, though not always those of Europe, were convinced: Algeria (C. Arambourg), Morocco (P. Biberson), the Sahara (H. Hugot, H. Alimen, J. Chavaillon), Shaba (Mortelmans), and so on. Morphological classifications based on chipping techniques were put forward by such experts as L. Ramendo and P. Biberson. Two things emerged immediately: first, the Pebble Culture was too complex, with forms too varied, rigid and systematic, to represent the actual beginning of stone industries; secondly, the Pebble Culture contained, in potential, all the possibilities which would lead to the classic biface and handaxe industries of the lower Palaeolithic in Africa. We shall dwell on the first point only.

Because of the complexity of the Pebble Culture and its distribution, the prehistorians of Africa wished to establish a longer chronology than that, itself arrived at with such difficulty, which allocated a million years to the Quaternary. The dating of the Olduvai industry by the potassium-argon method (1 850 000 to 1 100 000 years for Bed 1) was backed up first by the dating of the Omo chopping-tool (between 2 100 000 and 2 500 000), and soon after by that of the site at Lake Turkana (2 600 000). But this last, though it did include a great number of chipped pebbles, did not all belong to the Pebble Culture. It was an industry of fragments. In 1972 other fragments, perhaps less conclusive ones, were found at Omo. One may therefore wonder whether the fashioning of pebbles into pebble tools was not preceded by the use of fragments knocked off some block of raw material. But at that point we come to the last possible non-natural explanation; if the marks of working are not clear, if we have to put the emphasis on improvement, we come face to face once more with the old problem of eoliths.

So we come to what is inexplicable except by the intervention of a hominid. But then where do we stop? The boldest limit has been reached by Louis Leakey, who attributes 'bone-bashing activities' to *Kenyapithecus*, suggesting that he employed a 'lump of lava' battered and bruised by use, and a long bone with a depressed fracture.[19]

At this point, at their origin, the problem of the bone industry and that of the stone industry become the same. No further technological or morphological proof is possible. There is no classic mark of human action.

19. L. S. B. Leakey, 1968.

The only positive argument is in fact the inexplicable presence of flakes with the remains of *Kenyapithecus*; but even if *lusus naturae*, a sport of nature, is eliminated, that does not rule out the possibility of use by some prehominid anthropoid. As we have seen, the observed behaviour of chimpanzees may support such a possibility.

For the prehistorian of Africa, the tools of bone and stone bear witness to a cerebral process of hominization that was in progress two and a half million years ago. But that was not when it began.

Glossary

Abbevillian Industrial complex defined by H. Breuil at Abbeville, in the Somme valley, northern France. It is characterized by the existence of bifacial tools which have been chipped with a hard hammer-stone to remove large flakes. This complex was defined in Europe, where it corresponds to the beginning of the lower Palaeolithic. See also Chellean.

Acheulian From Saint-Acheul, in the Somme valley, northern France. This is the main cultural complex of the lower Palaeolithic, and it lasted from the Mindel glaciation to the end of the Riss-Würm interglacial stage. The most typical feature is a bifacial tool that is more regular than the Abbevillian and is chipped with a soft hammer made of wood or antler.

Aeneolithic (From the Latin *aeneus*: bronze, and the Greek *lithos*: stone.) Prehistoric period in which copper was first used.

Amazonite A green-coloured variety of microline.

Amirian Moroccan continental cycle contemporary with the Mindel stage in Europe.

Anfatian From Anfa, in Morocco. The third Quaternary marine transgression in Morocco.

Aterian From Bir el Ater, in eastern Algeria. North African Palaeolithic industry between the Mousterian and the Capsian. It consists of tanged points and scrapers and a few foliate points. The Aterian developed throughout part of the Würm period and is probably partly contemporary with the upper Palaeolithic in Europe.

Atlanthropus Fossil of the Archanthropus group defined by C. Arambourg at the Ternifine site in Algeria. The remains are dated to the end of the lower Pleistocene.

Augite Natural silicate of calcium, magnesium and iron entering into the composition of basalt.

Aurignacian From Aurignac, on the upper Garonne, France. Prehistoric industry dating from the beginning of the lower Palaeolithic. This name, which was coined by H. Breuil and E. Cartailhac in 1906, is used to designate industries that are situated chronologically between the Mousterian and the Perigordian. It is characterized by reindeer-antler spear-heads, thick scrapers, long blades with continuous flat and flaky retouching, and some burin-chisels. It witnessed the emergence of the first works of art, consisting of rudimentary animal figurines and summarily engraved signs on limestone blocks. It is dated to some 30 000 years ago.

Australopithecus (From the Latin *australis*: southern, and the Greek *pithêkos*: monkey.) Genus name coined by Dart in 1924 to designate several fossils from South Africa displaying Simian characteristics but heralding some human features. Similar discoveries were subsequently made in eastern and southern Africa.

Basalt A volcanic rock.

Biface A stone tool chipped away on both faces to produce an almond shape. They were first called 'choppers' and then 'handaxes', and seem to have been used for cutting purposes and, to a lesser extent, for scraping. They are the typical tools of the Lower Palaeolithic.

Breccia Rock of regular stones cemented together by lime etc.

Calabrian From Calabria, southern Italy. The oldest stage of the marine Quaternary identified by M. Gignoux in 1910.

Calcite A crystallized natural carbonate of calcium found in chalk, white marble, limestone, alabaster, etc.

Capsian From Capsa, the Latin name for Gafsa, in southern Tunisia. Late Palaeolithic African industry identified by J. de Morgan. Upper Palaeolithic tools are found in association with a large number of microliths and small thick borers which were probably used for drilling holes in ostrich eggshell fragments to make necklaces. It is dated to about 11 000 years ago.

Carnelian Red chalcedony.

Catarrhines Old World monkeys, with thirty-two teeth and a narrow septum.

Cenozoic Synonym for Tertiary and Quaternary, starting with the Eocene 65 million years ago and followed by the Oligocene (40 million years ago), the Miocene (25 million years ago), the Pliocene (11 million years ago), the Pleistocene, and the recent period.

Cercopithecus (From the Greek *kerkos*: tail, and *pithêkos*: monkey.) An African long-tailed monkey.

Chadanthropus (Chad man.) Hominid fossil situated anatomically between the *Australopithecus* and *Pithecanthropus* stages.

Chalcedony A fibrous variety of silica composed of quartz and opal.

Chellean From Chelles, France. Industrial complex of the lower Palaeolithic described by G. de Mortillet. Former name of the Abbevillian.

Clactonian From Clacton-on-Sea, Great Britain. Lower Palaeolithic industry described by H. Breuil in 1932 and characterized by flint flakes with a smooth and broad striking surface. The Clactonian appears to be contemporary with the Acheulian.

Cleaver Massive flake tool with a sharp cutting edge produced by striking two surfaces against each other. It is typical of the African Acheulian but is also found in early and middle Palaeolithic industries at several sites in southern France and Spain.

Diabase Rock of the gabbro and diorite family, often green.

Diorite Coarse-grained rock.

Discoid Late Acheulian disc-shaped stone tool chipped on both edges.

Dolerite Rock of the gabbro family with the constituent minerals visible to the naked eye.

Eocene First period of the Tertiary era, dating to 65 to 45 million years ago.

Epidote Natural hydrated silicate of aluminium, calcium and iron.

Fauresmith Place name in the Orange Free State, South Africa. Lithic industry comprising scrapers and points with single-edge trimming, bifaces and small axes, and corresponding to the Middle Palaeolithic in Europe.

Galena Natural sulphide of lead.

Gamblian Fourth African fluvial defined around lakes Nakuru, Naivasha and Elmenteita in Kenya. Contemporary with the Würmian period, but the term is no longer used.

Günz From the name of a river in Germany. The earliest Quaternary Alpine glaciation.

Haematite Natural ferric oxide.

Handaxe An almond-shaped stone tool trimmed on both edges, used for digging and skinning purposes. A synonym is *biface*.

Harounian The fourth Quaternary marine transgression in Atlantic Morocco.

Holocene The most recent period of the Quaternary beginning 10 000 years ago.

Hominid Zoological family of the Higher Primates represented by fossil and present-day man.

Homo Genus name in the zoological classification given to fossil and present-day man.

Homo faber 'Tool-making man'.

Homo habilis Name coined by Leakey, Tobias and Napier to designate fossils whose degree of anatomical evolution stands midway between that of the Australopithecines and the Pithecanthropines.

Homo sapiens Term coined by C. Linnaeus in 1735 and now used to designate the modern or neanthropic forms of Man who, through intelligence, has reached a state of adaptation to the environment which enables him to think and introspect freely.

Ibero-Maurusian Cultural complex of the Late Palaeolithic and epi-Palaeolithic in the Maghrib, the development of which was marked by the greatly increased number of microliths and which lasted from 12 000 to 7000 years ago.

Jadeite Natural alumino-silicate of sodium, with small quantities of calcium, magnesium and iron.

Jasper Impure chalcedony with generally red-coloured veins or patches.

Kafuan From the Kafu river in Uganda. Industrial complex from the beginning of the Lower Palaeolithic in East Africa, characterized by flat pebbles which have been summarily chipped but not trimmed. There is some controversy as to whether it is of human origin.

Kageran From the Kagera river in Tanzania. First African pluvial, identified by E. J. Wayland in 1934. Contemporary with the Günz Alpine glaciation. The term is no longer used.

Kamasian From Kamasia in Kenya. Second African pluvial, commonly known as Kamasian I. Contemporary with the Mindel glaciation in Europe, but seldom used.

Kanjeran From Kanjera in Kenya. Third African pluvial defined by L. S. B. Leakey. Commonly known as Kamasian II. This corresponds to the period of the Riss glaciation in the Alps, but the term is no longer used.

Lapis Lazuli Azure-blue stone used in mosaics, the powdered form being used for ultramarine pigment.

Laterite (From the Latin *later*: brick.) Bright red or reddish brown soil rich in iron oxide and alumina, formed by leaching in hot climates.

Levallois (technique) From Levallois-Perret, France. Stone-making technique enabling large flakes of predetermined shape to be obtained from a prepared core.

Levalloisian Industrial complex defined by H. Breuil in 1931, characterized by flakes struck from Levallois-type cores, with little or no subsequent trimming. It is no longer acknowledged as being a genuine industry.

Lupemban From Lupemba, Kasai, Zaïre. Industrial complex of the Late Palaeolithic, characterized by the combined presence of massive chipped stone tools (picks and chisels) and leaf points trimmed on both edges, dating from about 8000 years before our era.

Lydianite Hardened shale.

Maarifian From the Maarif, Morocco. Second Quaternary marine transgression of Atlantic Morocco.

Magosian From Magosi, in Uganda. Stone industry discovered by Wayland in 1926, situated between the Gamblian and the Makalian, and combining objects of Mousterian appearance such as cores, discoidals and points, foliate pieces trimmed on both edges, and geometrical microliths.

Makalian From the Makalia river in Kenya. Wet stage of the Quaternary in southern Africa, contemporary with the postglacial period in Europe. No longer used.

Malachite Green-coloured natural base carbonate of copper.

Mazzerian First Saharan pluvial, equivalent to the Kageran.

Mesolithic (From the Greek *mesos*: in the middle of, and *lithos*: stone.) This word was long used to designate all the cultural complexes which it was possible to situate between the Palaeolithic and the Neolithic. These are now more commonly related to an epi-Palaeolithic stage.

Micoque A prehistoric site situated to the north of Les Eyzies, 25 kilometres to the north-west of Sarlat, in central France, which produced the Micoquian industry, a very evolved form of the Acheulian contemporary with the Würm glaciation.

Mindel Name of a river in Bavaria. Second Quaternary Alpine glaciation which appears to have been situated between 300 000 and 400 000 years ago.

Miocene (From the Greek *meiôn*: less, and *kainos*: recent.) In other words, it contains fewer recent forms than the system following it. It is a period of the Tertiary era between 25 and 10 million years ago.

Moulouyan From the Moulouya valley, Morocco. Term used by Biberson. The Middle Villafrancian of Morocco.

Mousterian From Moustier, Dordogne, France. Prehistoric industry of the Middle Palaeolithic, which was widespread in the second half of the last interglacial period. It was identified by E. Lartet in 1865 and is characterized by the very large number of points and scrapers obtained by trimming flakes from only one of their faces.

Nakuran Wet stage defined by the deposits in the shoreline sediment below the 102-metre level, at Lake Nakuru, Kenya. These layers have revealed Neolithic-style industries dating back some 3000 years.

Neanderthal From the name of the valley in the Düssel Basin in Germany where the first specimen was discovered by Dr Fuhlrott in 1856. Representative of a particular group of the genus *Homo* which lived in western Europe in the Upper Pleistocene and died out suddenly without leaving any descendants.

Neolithic (From the Greek *neos*: new, and *lithos*: stone.) Stone age with food production (agriculture, stock-raising). Term coined in 1865 by J. Lubbock.

Obsidian Compact vitrous volcanic rock resembling dark-coloured glass.

Oldowan From the Olduvai Gorge in northern Tanzania. Ancient lithic tool complex (Pebble-tools) discovered by Katwinkel in 1911. Complex in which Leakey identified eleven levels of Oldowan I, corresponding to the Old Chellean, and Oldowan XI corresponding to Acheulian VI, with Levalloisian tools.

Oligocene Second period of the Tertiary, from 45 to 25 million years ago.

Osteodontokeratic Prehistoric industry based on bones (Greek *osteon*), teeth (Greek *odous, odontos*) and antlers (Greek *keras, keratos*), discovered at Makapansgat in South Africa by R. A. Dart.

Ougartian I Second Saharan pluvial, equivalent to the Kamasan.

Ougartian II Third Saharan pluvial, equivalent to the Kanjeran.

Palaeolithic (From the Greek *paleos*: old, and *lithos*: stone.) Term used to designate the Stone Age with no food production. Term coined by J. Lubbock in 1865.

Palaeozoic A synonym for Primary.

Paranthropus Robust *Australopithecus* discovered in 1948 in the Plio-Pleistocene deposits at Kromdraai in the Transvaal = *Zinjanthropus* = *Paraustralopithecus*. This ancient type displays many simian characteristics but possesses, particularly in its dental structure, features which situate it closer to Man than to the anthropoids.

Pebble Culture The oldest known stone tool-making industry, composed essentially of pebbles on which a cutting edge was created by striking off one or more flakes.

Pithecanthropus (Monkey-man.) Fossil displaying features close enough to present-day man to belong to the genus *Homo*, and other somewhat different characteristics representative of another species. The first specimen was discovered by E. Dubois in Java in 1889. Belongs to the species *Homo erectus*.

Platyrrhines New World monkeys with thirty-six teeth and a broad septum.

Pleistocene (From the Greek *pleistos*: much, and *kainos*: recent.) A geological subdivision of the Quaternary period comprising the beginning and the greater part of that period. This term, which was coined by C. Lyell in 1839, corresponds to the periods of the great Quaternary glaciations and preceded the Holocene period, which started 10 000 years before the present.

Pliocene Terminal period of the Tertiary era, beginning 5·5 million years ago and ending 1·8 million years ago.

Pongid Family of anthropoid monkeys typified by the orang-utang and also comprising the gorilla, the gibbon and the chimpanzee.

Pre-Cambrian The oldest geological configuration. It lasted from the formation of the Earth (estimated to date to 4000 million years ago) until the Primary era (500 million years ago).

Pre-Soltanian Moroccan continental period corresponding to the end of the Riss stage and coming prior to the Soltanian (from Dar es Soltan).

Ramapithecus; Ramapithecus wickeri. Omnivorous primate of the Miocene which may be the ancestor of the hominids, dating to 12–14 million years ago. Discovered in the Siwaliks range in northern India. Other specimens have been found in China, Turkey, Africa (Fort Ternan) and Europe (Austria, France, Germany, Greece, Hungary and Spain).

Riss Name of a river in Bavaria. Penultimate Quaternary Alpine glaciation, situated between 200 000 and 120 000 years ago.

Sangoan Eponymous site at Sango Bay on Lake Victoria in Uganda. It is a stone-tool complex discovered by Wayland in 1920 and is characterized by the existence of flaked objects produced by the Levallois technique, massive points, bifacial tools and crude core axe forms. The site belongs to the period between the Kamasian and the Gamblian.

Saourian From Saoura, a wadi in the Algerian Sahara. Fourth Saharan pluvial, equivalent to the Gamblian.

Serpentine Hydrated silicate of magnesium.

Shale Foliated silico-aluminous sedimentary rock breaking down easily into thin flakes.

Sinanthropus (From the Latin *sinensis*: Chinese, and the Greek *anthrôpos*: man.) Fossil displaying features close enough to present-day man to belong to the genus *Homo,* and other somewhat different characteristics representative of another species. The Choukoutien site, south-west of Peking, was worked from 1921 to 1939 by Dr Pei, M. Black, Father Teilhard de Chardin and F. Weidenreich. Belongs to the species *Homo erectus.*

Solutrian From Solutré, Saône et Loire, France. Prehistoric industry of the Upper Palaeolithic, characterized by very thin flint blades. The typical tools owe their appearance to the fact that they were shaped by a process of flat parallel retouching which cut into the two faces of the piece.

Stillbay From Still Bay, Cape Province, South Africa. Stone industry rich in foliate pieces trimmed on both edges reminiscent of the laurel leaves of the French Solutrian. Contemporary with the Gamblian.

Tektite Natural glass rich in silica and alumina, most probably of meteoritic origin.

Telanthropus Generic term given by Broom and Robinson to two jaw fragments found in 1949 in the Swartkrans deposit in South Africa, with a morphology reminiscent of certain Archanthropines.

Tensiftian From Wadi Tensift, in western Morocco. Moroccan continental stage corresponding to the first part of the Riss glaciation.

Tschitolian Term coined to denote a stone-tool complex discovered at Tschitolo, Kasai, Zaïre. Epi-Palaeolithic industrial complex characterized by the continued existence of massive tools, although smaller in size than the Lupemban, and by the large number of arrow-heads trimmed on both faces.

Tuff Lightweight and soft porous volcanic rock.

Villafrancian From Villafranca d'Asti, Piedmont, Italy. Sedimentary formation corresponding to the transition between the Tertiary and Quaternary eras.

Wilton From the Wilton site, in western Cape Province, South Africa. Stone industry dating to some 15 000 years ago, consisting of small groin-shaped scrapers, 'lunate' and trapezoidal microliths, borers and pieces with denticulated edges. This was a late culture which persisted until the introduction of iron.

Würm From the name of a lake and river in Bavaria. The most recent of the Quaternary Alpine glaciations, beginning 75 000 years ago and ending 10 000 years before our era.

PLATE 17.1 *One of the oldest stone artefacts in the world, found on the Omo site, Ethiopia; excavations led by J. Chavaillon* (Musée de l'Homme Coll.)

PLATE 17.2 *The Siwaliks excavation, north Pakistan; excavations led by D. Pilbeam* (photo H. Thomas, Musée de l'Homme Coll.)

PLATE 17.3 *Eocene and Oligocene sites, Fayum, Egypt* (photo E. Simons, Musée de l'Homme Coll.)

PLATE 17.4 *Reconstruction of the environment at Fayum 40 000 000 years ago. Drawing by Gaillard and Bertoncini* (Musée de l'Homme Coll.)

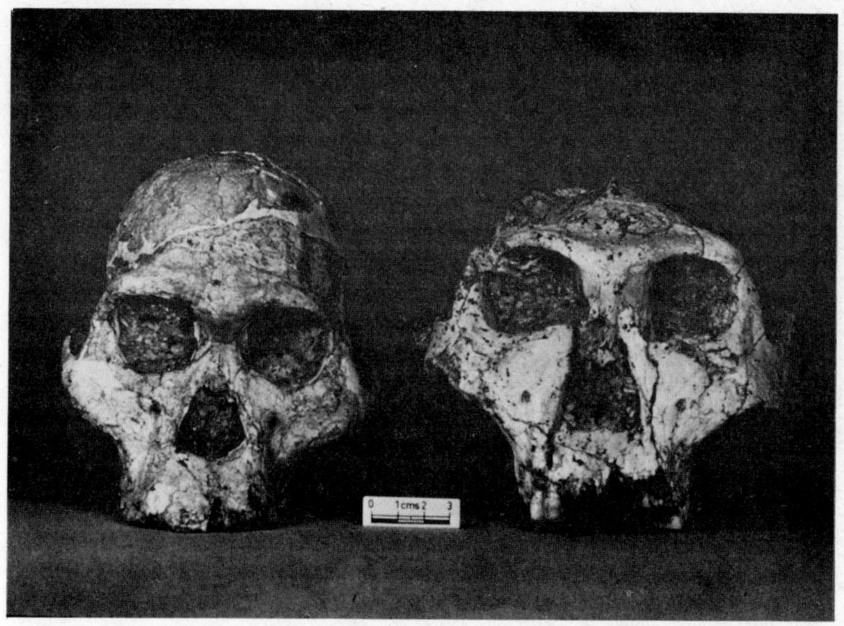

PLATE 17.5 *Skulls of* Australopithecus robustus (*on the right*); Australopithecus gracilis (*on the left*) (photo J. Robinson, Musée de l'Homme Coll.)

PLATE 17.6 *Skull of* Australopithecus boisei, *Omo site, Ethiopia; excavations led by Y. Coppens* (photo J. Oster, Musée de l'Homme Coll.)

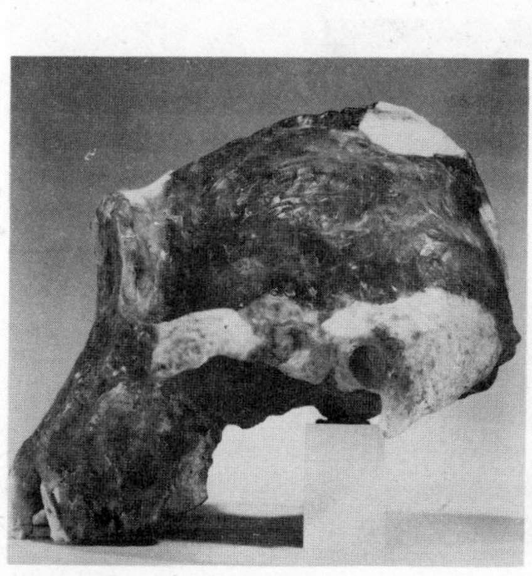

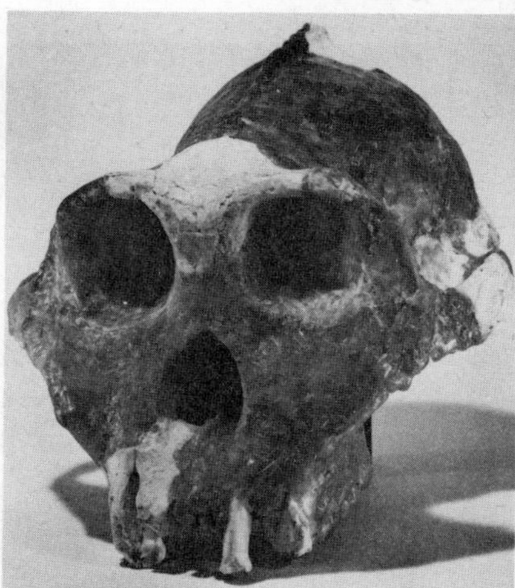

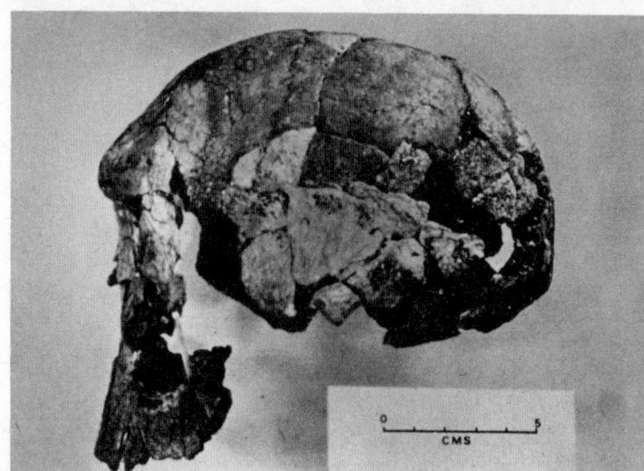

PLATE 17.7 *Skull of* Homo habilis (National Museum of Kenya)

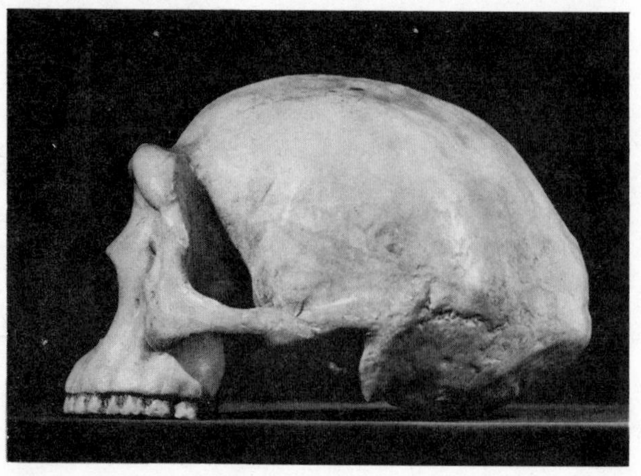

PLATE 17.8a *Skull of* Homo erectus *from Choukoutien* (*reconstruction*) (photo J. Oster, Musée de l'Homme Coll.)

PLATE 17.8b *Skull of* Homo erectus (*see Plate 17.8a*)

PLATE 17.9 *Reconstruction of the environment in which* Homo erectus *lived at Choukoutien, China (40 000 000 years ago). Drawing by Gaillard and Bertoncini* (Musée de l'Homme Coll.)

PLATE 17.10 *Skull of* Australopithecus africanus – *young person on the right* (*Taung, Botswana*), *adult on the left* (*Sterkfontein, Transvaal*) (Photos Y. Coppens, Musée de l'Homme Coll.)

PLATE 17.11 *Reconstruction of* Oreopithecus bamboli

PLATE 17.12 *Skeleton of* Oreopithecus bamboli, *12 000 000 years old, found on the Grosseto site, Tuscany, by Johannes Hürzler in 1958* (photo J. Oster, Musée de l'Homme Coll.)

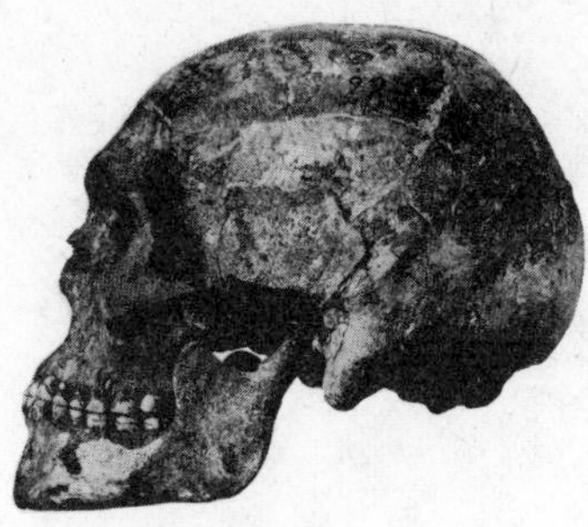

PLATE 17.13 *Skull of* Cromagnoid *of Afalu, Algeria* (photo J. Oster, Musée de l'Homme Coll.)

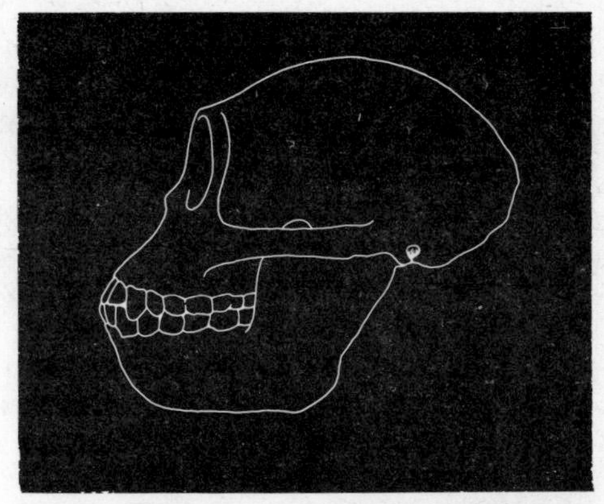

PLATE 17.14 *Reconstruction of skull of* Ramapithecus (photo J. Oster, Musée de l'Homme Coll.)

PLATE 17.15 *The Afar site, Ethiopia; expedition led by M. Taieb, Y. Coppens & D. C. Johanson* (photo M. Taieb, Musée de l'Homme Coll.)

PLATE 17.16 *The Omo sites and palaeontological excavations during the 1969 French expedition led by Y. Coppens* (photos Y. Coppens, Musée de l'Homme Coll.)

PLATE 17.17 *The Olduvai Gorge, Tanzania; excavations led by L. and M. Leakey* (photos Y. Coppens, Musée de l'Homme Coll.)

PLATE 17.18 *An excavation site at Olduvai* (photo J. Chavaillon, Musée de l'Homme Coll.)

PLATE 17.19 *Detail of the surface of the soil at the Olduvai excavations* (photo J. Chavaillon, Musée de l'Homme Coll.)

PLATE 17.20 *Close-up of the surface of the soil at the Olduvai excavations; the bone of a hippopotamus and some polyhedrons are visible* (photo J. Chavaillon, Musée de l'Homme Coll.)

18 African fossil man

R. LEAKEY

Africa, the cradle of mankind

Charles Darwin was the first scientist to publish important scientific comments on the study of evolution and he made remarks about the ancestry of man. It was Darwin who first pointed to Africa as the home of man, and during the past hundred years research has shown how correct he was. Many aspects of Darwin's pioneering work have been substantiated and to consider evolution merely as a thory is no longer realistic.

The evidence for man's development in Africa is incomplete, but over the past decade there has been a substantial increase in the number of fossil specimens available for study and interpretation. There is good evidence to suggest that Africa was the continent on which man made his first appearance and later developed upright, bipedal gait as a component of his technological adaptation. There is considerable interest in the question of when and by what processes man was able so to adapt. The evolutionary period is long and many phases in the evolution of man may not in fact be represented by fossil specimens because these occur only in quite specific conditions.

For a fossil to be formed, there have to exist geological conditions where sedimentation is rapid and where the chemical composition of the soils and ground water is such that mineral replacement can occur. Fossils so formed lie buried deep in the accumulated sediments and may never be found by modern man except where nature has taken a hand through erosion and earth movements. Such sites are few and far between and while new fossil-bearing localities are being reported each year, much of Africa will never produce fossil evidence of the appearance of man.

It is of interest to comment on the reasons why parts of Africa are so rich in prehistoric evidence. There are several points here and the first of these reflects the diversity of habitat in Africa. The continent is vast, spanning the equator and extending into temperature zones to the north and south. This fact alone accounts for the variety in climates but Africa offers a further dimension of high lands in the equatorial region. The land mass rises from a coastal belt through a series of plateaux up to mountain ranges and peaks, some of which still hold snow despite the fact that the climate is quite dry and hot.

These various elevations provide different environments since they are progressively cooler as altitude is increased. These factors have always existed in Africa and while climatic changes certainly occurred, Africa seems always to have offered a suitable habitat. When a particular area became too warm or too cold, migration to more propitious environments was possible. In contrast, in the temperate area of the world, the onset of cold weather conditions in a glacial period resulted in vast tracts of land being ice-bound and thus inhospitable to life with only a few specialized exceptions.

It has been suggested that the glacial (ice age) periods of the northern

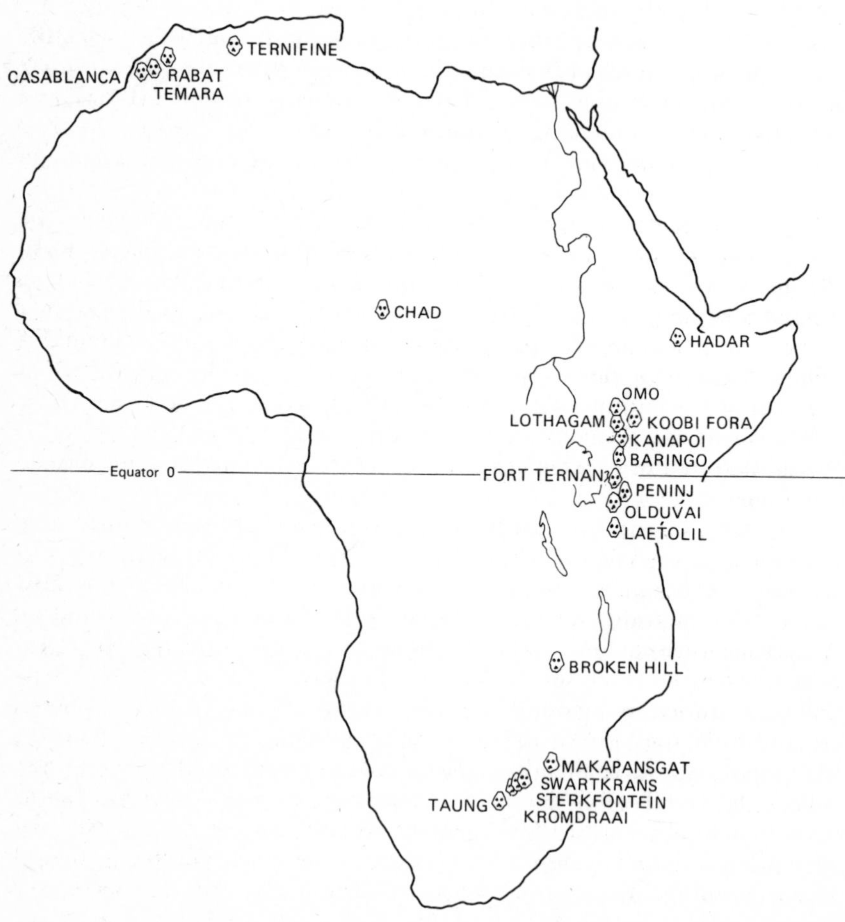

FIG. 18.1 *Africa: important hominid sites*

hemisphere can be correlated with wet periods in Africa since there appear to have been major fluctuations in the lake levels which reflect variations in rainfall. There has been considerable research into this in recent years and while a glacial advance would presumably have a global effect on weather, a specific correlation seems unlikely.[1] Despite this, the accumulation of sediments in African lake basins during the period known as the Pleistocene supports the view that Africa enjoyed heavier rain during that period.

This high rate of sediment deposition has been important. Many of the lakes in the African Pleistocene were small and shallow, probably seasonal in character with water level fluctuations each year reflecting the tropical weather patterns where, for a few months, rain is heavy and the remainder of the year dry. These lakes were ideal for sediment catchment and the annual flooding of the shallow basins provided conditions for sedimentation to stretch over the flat shores and around the mouths of inflowing rivers that overspilled their banks during high water. Remains of animals that had died, from whatever cause, near the lake shores were thus often buried in the sands and silts deposited during flooding. This process was continuous for millions of years and animal remains were trapped at different levels in sediment accumulations that might eventually exceed 500 metres in thickness.

As the lakes silted up and rainfall patterns changed, some basins dried up while new ones were formed. The process of fossilization is slow but the Pleistocene extends over more than 2 million years of time and throughout this long period, as well as before and since, animal remains were being embedded in sediments suitable to the formation of fossils.

The location of these remains is of course a major problem for the palaeontologist but here again factors in Africa, especially eastern Africa, have contributed in such a way as to mitigate the difficulty. During the Pleistocene, and in particular during the latter part of this period, eastern Africa experienced a period of earth movements associated with a weakness in the earth's crust that is today called the Rift valley. These earth movements caused faulting and, in many places, the uplifting of blocks of sediment. Subsequent erosion has exposed strata in which fossils were formed and the search for fossil remains is usually concentrated in ancient lake basins where sedimentary formations have been faulted and exposed as badlands.

There are exceptions and the very important collection of hominid remains from southern Africa is a case in point. These fossils were formed in limestone caves where the accumulation of bones was buried in cave-fill and collapsed cave-fill and collapsed cave roof. The bones were brought into the caves by several agencies and the most likely were scavengers and predators such as leopards and hyenas. There is some evidence to show that early man also occupied the caves and would therefore be responsible for some of the

1. See Chapter 17 above.

bone debris subsequently fossilized. The problem of cave sites of this kind is that there is virtually no detail of stratification and it is consequently difficult to determine the relative age of the fossils recovered.

In many parts of Africa during the Pleistocene, conditions were not suitable for the fossilization of animal remains. Consequently, while there may be no evidence for the existence of early man in most parts of Africa, there is no reason to suppose that he did not range widely on the continent. Continued search may yet reveal new sites.

More common than fossil remains are stone implements. These are generally more durable and stone does not have to be rapidly buried in appropriate sediments to ensure its preservation. Consequently, archaeologists have assembled a wealth of data on early human technology in Africa that tells us a great deal about the appearance of man.

Man, or more specifically, the genus *Homo*, might well be considered the only animal able to make stone implements but here, as in other areas of research related to the origin of man, there are various professional opinions which differ.

The study of man's origin relies heavily on the interdisciplinary approach – investigation into more than fossil bones. Geology, palaeoecology, palaeontology, geophysics and geochemistry are important and, in the later stages where man had begun to use artefacts, archaeology becomes of major importance. The study of living primates, including man, is often useful to a more complete understanding of the prehistory of this planet.

Fossils of the family of man, the *Hominidae*, can be shown as distinct and separate from the apes, the *Pongidae*, from the present day all the way back in time to the Miocene period more than 14 million years ago. This earliest evidence of man is incomplete and there remains a large gap in our knowledge of man's development between 14 million and a little more than 3 million years ago. It was during this period that the final stages of adaptation appear to have started because from 5 million years ago onwards several forms of fossil hominids are known.

The fossil record of animal groups other than man is sometimes better known with more complete material. This record is important and it is possible to attempt the reconstruction of early huminid ecology during the early evolutionary periods. Major adaptive changes may reflect a response to cataclysmic events affecting the environment, and there is already an indication of several important periods when many animals underwent fairly rapid change, presumably as a response to environmental pressures.

It has been shown that man passed through various stages before becoming large-brained and fully bipedal as he is today. At certain points in time, there existed more than one type of men and each seems to represent a specific adaptation. The changes from the very early ape-like form of the Miocene hominid must reflect specialization or adaptation of some kind and our concern is to understand the nature of these changes. The available evidence is far from complete but some details of the complex situation are known. We shall start by examining the most recent fossils and work our way backwards to the oldest.

Contemporary man and *Homo sapiens*

A typical dictionary definition of man is far from satisfactory – 'Human being, the human race, adult male, individual (male) person'. One of the problems in definition is that modern man is perhaps the most diverse single species known. There are so many differences – behavioural and physical – to be documented between extant populations around the world. Are these important? In some matters they may be, but the purpose here is to stress that regardless of superficial differences, man today is of one species and all men have a common origin and a common early developmental history. It is probably only in the past few thousand years that man has been influenced by superficial differences, and let us hope that this knowledge will speed up his recognition of his common identity and purpose.

Man belongs to the *Homo sapiens* species, and can today exist in a remarkable variety of habitats. In each instance this has been made possible by the technological extension to behaviour. Life in crowded cities contrasts with nomads who herd camels in the desert, as do both with hunting people living deep in the rain forests of West Africa. Man can live for long periods under the sea in submarines and is capable of orbiting the earth in space capsules. Adaptation through technology is the key in each instance. A large, complex brain together with fully manipulative hands which are freed from any locomotor function are the basic physical requirements. Evidence for the large brain, manipulative hands and bipedal gait can be traced back in time, as can the durable elements of man's technological activity. The degree of brain expansion, manipulative skill and bipedalism may well prove to be the best yardstick to use when tracing our species to its origins.

In Africa, there have been several important discoveries that illustrate the presence of primitive *Homo sapiens* on the continent for more than 100 000 years. There is every indication that our species has been present in Africa as long as elsewhere and further research may enable a precise date to be placed on the earliest record which may prove to be close on 200 000 years ago.

In 1921, a skull and some skeletal remains were found at Broken Hill, Zambia, and because the country was formerly known as Northern Rhodesia, the specimen became known as Rhodesian Man or *Homo sapiens rhodesiensis*. A date of about 35 000 years ago has been suggested and the specimen is certainly within the range for our species. This important fossil may perhaps be much older but it is not possible to date the skull itself. It bears close affinities with the Neanderthal material from Europe and it is most likely an African example of this morphospecies. Even earlier evidence for *Homo sapiens* has been recovered from East Africa.

In 1932, the late Dr L. S. B. Leakey recovered parts of two skulls from a site called Kanjera in western Kenya. The fossils seemed to be associated with a late Middle Pleistocene fossil fauna and this implies an age of close to 200 000 years. The site has not yet been accurately dated, which is unfortunate, as the two skull parts and a fragment of femur appear to be examples of *Homo sapiens* and may well represent the oldest evidence known at present for the species in Africa.

In 1967, parts of two individuals were recovered from a site in the Omo valley of south-west Ethiopia. The specimens consist of a partial skull and a fragmented skeleton and the calotte of a second skull. Both fossils were from strata that suggest an age of a little more than 100 000 years. The locality of the Omo valley is probably better known for earlier fossils but there are extensive fairly recent deposits which hold promise of a further wealth of information on early *Homo sapiens* in Africa. In addition, there are sites reported in the same area from which early pottery has been noted, and in view of the prehistoric link between the Omo and the Nile river systems, further research may result in further information on the early use of earthenware vessels.

While early *Homo sapiens* is poorly represented in the fossil collections, it seems reasonable to assume that the species was widely scattered both in Africa and elsewhere on the globe.

Pre-*Homo sapiens*

There is always a tendency to relate early species to modern species and this must be confined to the terms of a broad relationship. It is proposed here to consider the origin of *Homo sapiens* within a lineage that can be traced back in time for several million years. At different points in time, there probably existed several morphologically distinct models within the lineage, and the genetic composition of modern man must reflect, in part, elements from this diverse heritage.

The naming of fossil species is difficult and often confusion arises from the need to give a label to a particular specimen. The usual practice is to place similar specimens into one species, minor differences providing a basis for species differentiation while major differences are grounds for generic differentiation. The palaeontologists' problem is to consider, over a period of time, evolutionary changes which have affected a particular species which may have experienced rapid adaptation. In this account, the term morphospecies will be used to describe fossils that are alike in physical characteristics. It should here be noted that much of the controversy that is associated with the study of man's origin results from differing views on the use of terminology.

Within the *Hominidae* at least two genera and several species have been identified in the fossil record of the past 3 million years and these forms are the basis for understanding the origin of our own species. Until recently it was thought that evolution had occurred at a uniform rate, but it now appears that local populations of a given species may have responded to selective pressures differently. Apparently primitive forms can be found contemporary with advanced or progressive forms. The identification of primitive characters in a species that is recorded over a long period of time is less difficult than the same exercise in a limited sample. It is possible to identify trends and adaptations which help to explain the process by which survival through progressive modification has occurred.

The fossil record of man in Africa shows two major groupings of characters. It is proposed to consider these as lines of development or evolutionary lineages in which one lineage represented by the genus *Homo* can be traced through to the present, the other, represented by the genus *Australopithecus,* apparently becoming extinct approximately 1 million years ago.

It is also possible to consider primitive forms recorded from deposits in which more advanced forms previously known from older deposits are not recorded. This might be seen as evidence for a retrogression, but it is more probable that the continuation of a progressive species is not represented in the specimens available for study for no other reason than that it occupied areas where remains were not preserved through fossilization.

For the purpose of this chapter, it is proposed to consider man prior to *Homo sapiens* on the basis of the two lineages. The form which was ancestral to both cannot be readily identified since the fossil evidence is so fragmentary. The earliest African evidence for the family *Hominidae* is from Fort Ternan in Kenya where a number of fragments of upper jaw, a part of a lower jaw and some dental fragments have been recovered. This site has been dated at 14 million years. The fossil evidence shows that at this time the differentiation between the *Hominidae* and the *Pongidae* had already occurred. The Fort Ternan fragments show that the reduction of the canine, a diagnostic feature of the *Hominidae*, had progressed some way from the typical ape situation.

The fossil record between 14 and 3·5 million years is very incomplete since there are only four specimens which can be related to this period. These are a very badly damaged fragment of mandible from Kanam in Kenya, recovered by the late Dr L. S. B. Leakey in 1932, a fragment of mandible with one tooth crown preserved from Lothagam, Kenya, and an isolated molar tooth from Ngorora, Kenya. The first three specimens are from deposits dated at between 4 and 5·5 million years while the isolated tooth is considered to be from deposits dated at 9 million years. None of these specimens throws much light on the problem because they are too fragmentary. The mandibular fragment from Lothagam has been related to *Australopithecus,* but at this stage any degree of positive identification is considered unwarranted by a number of anthropologists.

The sample of fossil hominid remains is considerably larger from the onset of the Pliocene era, and between about 4 million years ago to the first appearance of *Homo sapiens,* there exist substantial data on human evolution in Africa. Since 1973, new work has been initiated at two localities where large numbers of fossils have been recovered from deposits dating between 3 and 4 million years. These sites, Laetolil (Tanzania) and Hadar (Ethiopia) deserve some specific comments in relation to the fossil evidence for the earliest record of *Homo*.

The Laetolil site is situated some 50 kilometres south of the famous Olduvai Gorge, on the slopes of the Lemagrut hills overlooking the northern end of Lake Eyasi. The date for this locality is about 3·5 million years which is of particular interest because the various fossils of early hominid from here have been proposed as falling within the category of *Homo*. The material consists of jaws and teeth and the occasional element of limb.

The Hadar site in the Afar region of Ethiopia is about the same age or slightly younger. A wealth of material has been recovered from this site since 1973 and includes excellent specimens of both the cranial and post-cranial skeleton. A distinction can be made between three types relating to *Homo habilis*, *Australopithecus gracilis* and *Australopithecus robustus*.

While we know virtually nothing of the early hominid forms prior to 3·5 million years, since those that are recorded do not provide any important answers to the origin of either *Homo* or *Australopithecus*, the period of time between 3 and 1 million years is relatively well represented in the fossil record in Africa.

The relatively large sample of material now available from sites dated from less than 3 million years shows that there were two distinct genera of early hominids, often occupying the same area. These two forms, *Homo* and *Australopithecus*, presumably occupied different ecological niches and while their physical territory may have overlapped, the competition for food was apparently not sufficient for one form to exclude the other. There remains a great deal to be learnt about the adaptation of each hominid and, at present, the coexistence of the two genera for a period in excess of 1·5 million years has been established and attests to the distinctiveness of the two.

Was *Australopithecus* ancestral to *Homo*? This question used to be answered in the affirmative but with the new data it is no longer certain, and some workers (including the author) tend towards a view in which both forms have a common ancestor distinct from both. To establish such a contention, it is necessary to examine the two genera in terms of their special adaptations and consider the rate of change, if any, in each group. Before this can be done, it is essential to define clearly the characteristics that are diagnostic of each, and that are consistent through time.

Lastly, we may note that some researchers group all these fossils under the same genus, which could be said to display significant intra-generic variability and marked sexual dimorphism.

The genus *Homo* (*pre-sapiens*): *Homo erectus*

The best known *pre-sapiens* form of *Homo* is that which has been attributed to a wide-ranging, diverse morphospecies known as *Homo erectus*. This species was first recognized from material recovered from sites in the Far East and China, but in comparatively recent years the same form has been collected in North and eastern Africa and maybe in southern Africa. There are no firm dates for the Asian collections although an inferred age for some material has been published, and it would seem that *Homo erectus* is recorded from sites that are between 1·5 million and 0·5 million years old. The dating of the North African sites that have yielded *Homo erectus* is also inferred and terms such as Middle Pleistocene have been used. The material from East Africa has been recovered from sites where dating is possible and the earliest example is placed at just over 1·6 million years. The very early record of this form in eastern Africa is indicative of an African origin, and many scholars accept the contention that the *Homo erectus* populations beyond the African continent are migrant populations that originated in Africa during early Pleistocene times. Nevertheless, there are a number of extremely early new dates for the *Homo erectus* of Java.

At the present time, there is not an abundance of material upon which comprehensive studies can be made. There is, however, sufficient data to show that this species was widely distributed in Africa as well as occurring in Asia and in Europe. The limb material indicates upright posture with adaptation for striding, bipedal gait that was close in character to that seen in modern man. The degree of intelligence can be roughly assessed by estimating the cranial capacity (the volume of the brain case). From the known material, the endocranial volume can be shown to range from some 750 cc to a large 1000 cc for *Homo erectus,* while the average *Homo sapiens* is significantly greater at 1400 cc.

The technology used by *Homo erectus* can be inferred from his remains. It seems that *Homo erectus* made and used stone implements and lived as a hunter/gatherer on the open savannahs of Africa. The consensus of professional opinion links the handaxe or Acheulian industry to *Homo erectus*; this type of stone tool industry is distinctive and represented by sites in Africa, Europe and to a lesser extent in Asia. Whether *Homo erectus* was the final stage of development leading to *Homo sapiens* remains uncertain and it is probably wise to leave the matter open pending further information on this species.

Before leaving *Homo erectus,* the characteristics of the species should be briefly discussed. The most diagnostic features are seen in the skull: the heavy, protruding eyebrow ridges, the low forehead and the shape of the back part of the skull. The teeth may be diagnostic but it is possible that different morphospecies within the *Homo* lineage might have very similar dental morphology. Similarly, the mandibular morphology may be less distinctive than presently thought and some alleged *Homo erectus* specimens that consist only of teeth and jaws might, in fact, represent a different morphospecies within the same genus.

The genus *Homo* (*pre-sapiens*): *Homo habilis*

Material attributed to the *Homo* lineage but distinctive and occurring earlier than *Homo erectus* ia confined to eastern Africa. The earliest forms are those from Hadar and Laetolil which have yet to be studied in detail but which almost certainly are ancestral to later species. The intermediate species, if that is what it is, could perhaps be termed *Homo habilis* and is based upon material from Olduvai and, more recently, from Koobi Fora on the east side of Lake Turkana.

The principal characteristics of *Homo habilis* would be the relatively large brain, the cranial capacity value exceeding 750 cc, thin-bonded skulls which are high-vaulted and show minimal postorbital contraction. The anterior teeth are relatively large with moderately large molars and premolars and the mandible shows external buttressing. The postcranial elements show morphological features that are very similar to modern man.

The best examples of *Homos habilis* are from Koobi Fora where several cranial specimens, mandibles and limb bones are known. The most complete skull is that referred to as KNM-ER 1470 (Plate 18.4).

Australopithecus

The problem of species definition with *Australopithecus* is far from settled, but I am of the opinion that evidence for two species of this genus can be established with some conviction in the Koobi Fora Formation. The most obvious, *Australopithecus boisei,* is very distinctive, being characterized by hyper-robust mandibles, large molars and premolars relative to the anterior dentition, cranial capacity values less than 550 cc, and sexual dimorphism manifested in superficial cranial characters such as sagittal and nuchal crests in males (Plate 18.1). The known postcranial elements, such as the femur, humerus and talus, are also distinctive. This widespread species has been reported from other localities, such as Chesowanja, Peninj and Olduvai Gorge in the southern Rift valley of East Africa. *A. boisei* may require reconsideration as a full species and should instead perhaps be ranked as a sub-species as a deme of the South African form of *A. robustus*. Additional data are needed if we are going to solve the problems that are always associated with such refined systematics in vertebrate palaeontology. Consequently the retention of two allied but spatially separate robust species seems desirable for the moment.

The case for a gracile East African species of *Australopithecus* is less secure, but there seems to be too great a degree of variation if all the material is included as a single species. The best example of the gracile form from East Africa would be the specimen from Koobi Fora Formation – OH5 (Plate 18.1). Various mandibles and some postcranial elements might also be included, keeping in mind the difficulty of classifying mandibles. No detailed proposal for such a classificatory scheme for the East African fossils has been put forward, but the typical characteristics would include gracile mandibles with small cheek teeth, cranial capacity values at 600 cc or less and sagittal crests rare or non-existent. The postcranial morphology appears to be similar to that seen in *A. boisei*, although on a smaller and less robust scale. In both species, one of the most distinctive features is the proximal region of the femur; a long femoral neck is compressed from front to back, and there is a small, subspherical head. There are other features, but very little is known about variation, and the sample is not impressively large at present.

I consider this species to be closely allied to the gracile *A. africanus* from South Africa; it may be a more northern deme of that species. The innominate bone is known for *A. africanus* and for *A. robustus* in South Africa, and slight differences have been noted between the two forms. No innominate remains are attributable to *Australopithecus* from East Africa, but *Homo* is represented by two specimens that are equivalent in time and they illustrate marked differences between the two genera that are greater than would reasonably be expected for a single, albeit spatially extended species.

Tools and habitations

The most impressive records of tools and habitation sites are from Lake Turkana in Kenya, Melka Konture in Ethiopia and Olduvai Gorge in Tanzania, where numerous localities have been excavated over the past thirty years. The progression from simple pebble tools to intricate and perfect bifacial implements is well documented in this area. There are also inferences to be drawn on the probable social organization, in the sense of community, size and hunting preferences. At one locality, in Olduvai, remains of a stone structure – perhaps the base of a circular hut – were uncovered; there is an excellent date of 1·8 million years for this. At Melka Konture a raised platform, likewise circular, has been uncovered. The threshold of technological ability is difficult to pinpoint exactly, and at best one could only suggest that it occurred during the Pliocene, perhaps in relation to the adaptive response embodied by the differentiation of *Homo*.

During the early Pleistocene, *c.* 1·6 million years ago, bifacial tools such as crude handaxes make their appearance. The development can be traced *in situ* at Olduvai and is supported by findings from other East African sites. Until recent times the first record of stone implements in Europe was of handaxes. In my opinion, the evidence available could suggest a migration of the handaxe people from Africa into Europe and Asia, during the early Pleistocene, or a little earlier. The subsequent development of stone implements is complex, with impressive records from most parts of the world. It is not proven but can be postulated that the post-Acheulian, or handaxe technologies can be related to the emergence of *Homo sapiens*. The association of stone implements with early hominid remains is rare, and many mid-Pleistocene and subsequent sites contain only one or two specimens, with certain impressive exceptions.

It is clear that extraordinary advances have been made in recent years in the information recorded and continuing investigations will presumably provide further evidence. There is now obvious evidence for considerable morphological diversity in the Plio/Pleistocene hominids of Africa, which has been interpreted as a consequence of a Pliocene differentiation with different evolutionary trends persisting into the early Pleistocene. The presence of at least three contemporary species in East Africa may be established on both cranial and postcranial material, and any review must incorporate the analysis of the entire fossil collection.

TABLE 18.1 *List of* Homo erectus *materials known from Africa*

Region	*Country*	*Site*	*Specimen details*
North-west	Algeria	Ternifine	3 mandibles and fragment of skull
North-west	Morocco	Sidi Abderrahmane	2 fragments of mandible
North-west	Morocco	Rabat	Mandible fragment and skull
North-west	Morocco	Temara	Mandible
East	Tanzania	Olduvai	Skull, some postcranial remains and a possible mandible
South	South Africa	Swartkrans	An incomplete skull and some fragments of mandible

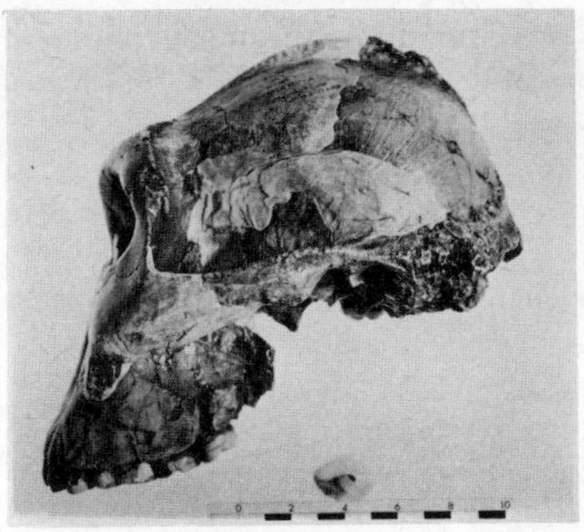

PLATE 18.1 Australopithecus boisei. *Lateral view of cranium from Olduvai Gorge, Tanzania (OH5)* (Kenya National Museums)

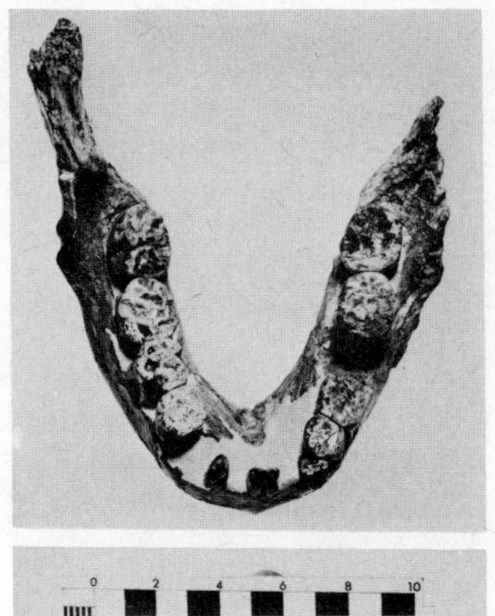

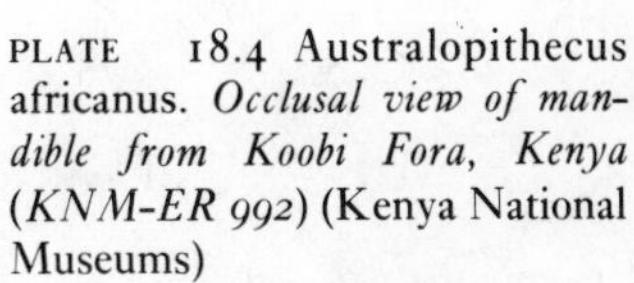

PLATE 18.2 Australopithecus boisei. *Occlusal view of mandible from Koobi Fora, Kenya (KNM-ER 729)* (Kenya National Museums)

PLATE 18.3 Australopithecus africanus. *Lateral view of cranium from Koobi Fora, Kenya (KNM-ER 1813)* (Kenya National Museums)

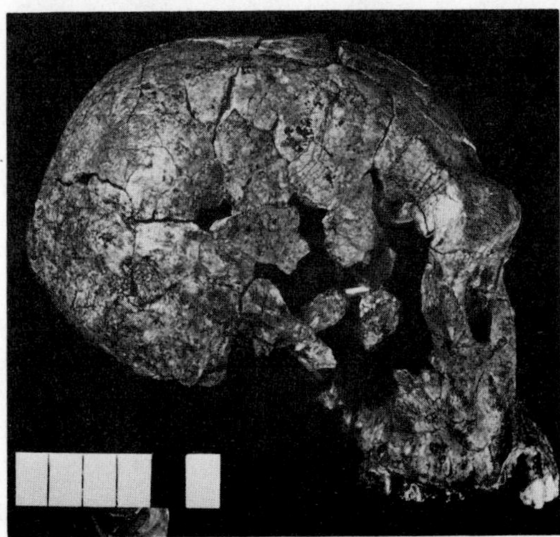

PLATE 18.4 Australopithecus africanus. *Occlusal view of mandible from Koobi Fora, Kenya (KNM-ER 992)* (Kenya National Museums)

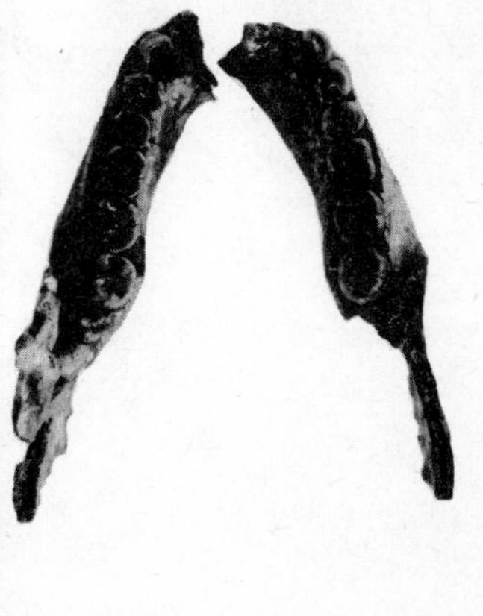

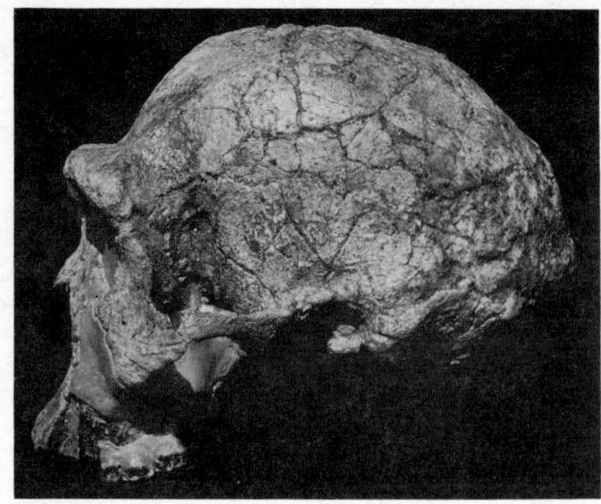

PLATE 18.5 Homo erectus. *Lateral view of cranium from Koobi Fora, Kenya (KNM-ER 3733)* (Kenya National Museums)

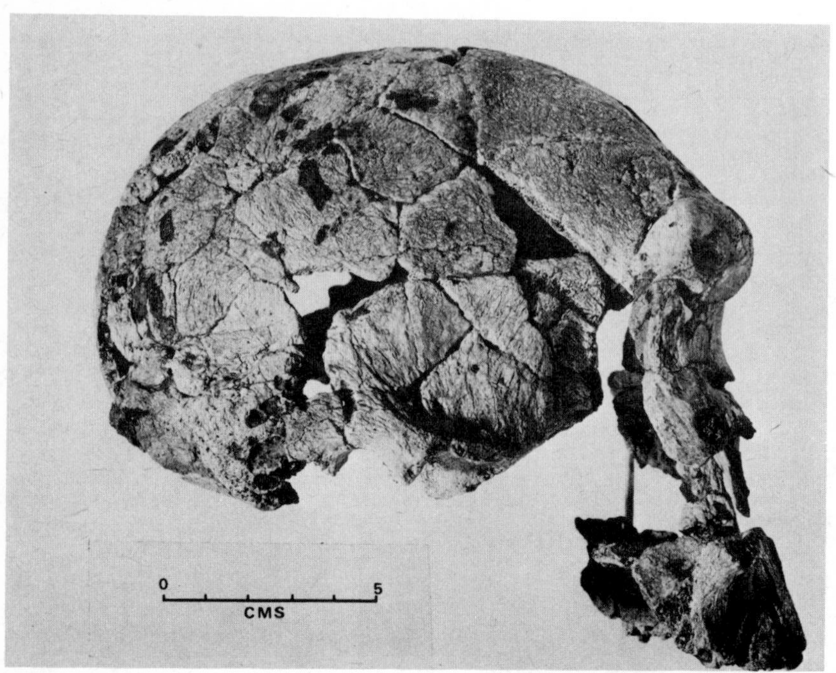

PLATE 18.6 Homo habilis. *Lateral view of cranium from Koobi Fora, Kenya (KNM-ER 1470)* (Kenya National Museums)

TABLE 19.1 *Periods and industries in African prehistory: table of equivalents drawn up by H. J. Hugot*

	Maghrib	*East Africa*	*Western Sahara*	*Southern Sahara*	*Industries*	*English archaeological equivalents for corresponding levels*	*Europe*
Holocene	Rharbian		Present	Present	Age of Metals	Late Stone Age	Present
			Guirian	Desertification	Neolithic		Post-glacial
		Makalian Pluvial		Pluvial Recurrence	Epi-Palaeolithic	Second Intermediate	
Upper Pleistocene	Soltanian	Arid post-Gamblian	Soltanian	Arid			Würm
		Gamblian Pluvial		Last great lakes	Aterian Mousterian	Middle Stone Age	
Middle Pleistocene	Tensiftian	Arid post-Kanjerian	Ougartian	Arid			Riss-Würm
		Kanjerian Pluvial		Sahara of the great lakes		First Intermediate	Riss
		Arid post-Kamasian			Lower Palaeolithic with bi-facial tools	Early Stone Age	Mindel-Riss
	Amirian	Kamasian					Mindel
	Saletian	Arid post-Kageran	Taourirtian				Gunz-Mindel
Lower Pleistocene	Moulouyan	Kageran	Moulouyan		Archaic Lower Palaeolithic with Pebble Culture	(Earlier Stone Age)	Gunz
							Donau-Gunz
							Donau

The prehistory of East Africa

J. E. G. SUTTON

Research on prehistory: introduction to methodology

It was on the eastern side of Africa that man emerged as an erect and tool-making animal around 3 million years ago. For this reason the history of this part of the world has been longer than elsewhere, and in particular the Stone Age here was more extended than in other continents and other parts of Africa. It began when the first hominids started to make recognizable tools of stone of predetermined shapes and patterns as a regular activity. This combination of bodily and mental powers to produce tools, in other words to improve biology, and the growing dependence on these extra-biological, that is, cultural, abilities and activities are what distinguish man from other animals and define humanity. Man's evolution as a ground-living animal able to stand and move on two feet (unlike the apes, monkeys and other quadruped or quadrumanous mammals) facilitated tool use and tool manufacture through freeing the arms and hands for holding, carrying, gripping and manipulation. More than that, these were essential developments for survival and success in the world, and especially to obtain and prepare food. Each new generation had to learn the accumulated cultural and technological skills and knowledge of its parents. Now, it is likely that the very earliest humanly fashioned tools remain unknown, since they were so crude or indistinguishable from natural objects as to be unrecognizable. It is probable that other materials which have decayed beyond trace, such as wood, leather and bone, were used and worked at least as early as stone. (However, advances with other materials must have been limited until man had mastered the basic skill of how to produce a sharp-edged practical cutting tool through striking and breaking a selected stone with precision with another stone or suitable hard object.) Tool making – and humanity – may thus have begun somewhat before the date for which we have convincing evidence for these crucial developments. Our evidence consists then of the first recognizable stone tools; and this we must take as the beginning of the Stone Age, as it is called for convenience.

This Stone Age lasted from about 3 million years ago down to that very recent phase of human history when stone was superseded by metal as the essential material from which to develop a technology and make tools and produce sharp edges. This transition from a stone (or lithic) technology to a metal one took place at slightly different times all over the world. In western Asia techniques of working copper began 6000 to 9000 years ago. In East Africa, iron, the first and only metal used regularly, was worked about 2000 years ago.

One may wonder whether the term 'Stone Age' is a really satisfactory one for a period which includes all but one-thousandth part of the long stretch of time during which men have lived in East Africa and which, in any case, emphasizes the technological rather than the economic or cultural aspects of human development. It may be objected that it is much too broad in terms of time and too restricted in terms of culture. But there are answers to these objections and Stone Age, as a term and concept, remains useful provided that certain things are understood. This very long period of time is known to us only from archaeological evidence (mostly stone artefacts) and since these are practically the only things which have survived from a period which had no written records or any oral tradition known to us, it was reasonable to choose for it a name which reflected its chief characteristic.

The Stone Age was not a static period. That techniques evolved during the Palaeolithic and Neolithic periods is readily demonstrated by the changes and diversity in the range of stone tools, their efficiency and their methods of manufacture. We must therefore subdivide the Stone Age both chronologically and geographically. Collections of stone tools (if skilfully selected and displayed) can be fascinating to look at, but they tell us little unless arranged with a sense of chronology and development. Popular expressions such as 'living in the stone age' or 'stone age man' are also unhelpful if they are based on the false assumption that man and his way of life remained the same throughout that long period of time. For the tool-kits of Stone Age populations differed from period to period and region to region, and the populations themselves developed culturally and physically. The stone age witnessed mutations and differentiations in the human physique and brain, in the economy, social organization and culture, hand in hand with the advances in technique revealed by the archaeological evidence. One other observation to make at this point is that, while change in all periods of the Stone Age was very slow by modern standards, it was slowest of all in the earlier periods. The closer we come to the present age, the quicker the changes have been. The later periods saw regional specialization and diversification, which meant that from time to time features which had slowly developed in one region were carried in that particular form into another region, either by migration or by cultural contact, and could thus produce the illusion that a revolution had occurred. So, in terms of development, two or three generations at the end of the Stone Age might be equivalent to half a million at an early period.

Hence, the study of the Stone Age is not simply concerned with stones or tools. Occasionally the archaeologist is fortunate in recovering other finds.

These occur most commonly on living sites dating from the very end of the Stone Age where direct evidence of cooking and eating may be preserved in the form of charcoal fragments from the hearths and broken animal bones. Early organic remains are extremely rare in Africa, except at a few sites where favourable mineral conditions caused fossilization of bones before they rotted. But even where he has only stones to work with, the archaeologist should attempt broader deductions from his evidence and wider interpretations, over much wider-ranging areas.

In the first place, it is not the individual tools found that matter, but the tool-kits, the whole range and variety recoverable from a site, be it a living-place of a group, a temporary hunters' camp, or a workshop where tools were made. Usually far commoner than the finished tools are the waste flakes and stone cores (being the chips and lumps struck off the raw material during manufacture and the unusable remnants); these need to be studied together with the actual tools made since they indicate the manufacturing techniques and the level of expertise. Also these waste products were not always simply discarded: often, especially in the earlier years of the Stone Age, many of these flakes happened to have knife-sharp edges and would, if their size and shape were convenient for handling, have supplemented the heavier finished tools and thus have formed an essential part of the kit. Merely to collect and study the more spectacular finished handaxes and cleavers leads to a sadly limited and grossly distorted picture of the technology and activities of prehistoric populations. By the later periods of the Stone Age, heavy core tools of the handaxe type had given way to smaller, more delicate and more precise stone implements, often intended for hafting into wooden shafts or bone handles, the stone pieces produced by expert preparation of the core or intricate reworking of the flake or blade struck off. Here it is equally essential – for analysis and deductions – to have as complete as possible an assemblage of the finished pieces together with the waste material.

The range of stone tools with their various kinds of edges and points, for cutting, paring, skinning, scraping, boring, grooving, striking, chopping and digging, will (even allowing for some obvious uncertainties in interpreting the actual purposes and uses) suggest other tools fashioned from perishable animal and vegetable materials used by that community. For instance, these tools suggest the preparation of animal skins which, once scraped clean of fat, dried and tanned, could be cut into leather ropes and thongs. In the catching, killing and skinning of animals, as well as in the preparation of the hide and the making of ropes and thongs, a variety of stone and wooden tools and weapons would have been required. Ropes and thongs could have been combined with stone tools to tie and bind missiles used in hunting or to secure, with the help of a vegetable gum, a stone blade or a point to the tip of a wooden spear or arrow-shaft. Apart from such weapons it is possible to reconstruct the common composite tools, consisting of small intricately fashioned stone flakes and blades neatly fixed and gummed into shafts and handles prepared from wood and bone, from the study of the lithic finds of the end of the Stone Age, although direct evidence of the wooden and bone parts rarely exists. But even earlier, before wooden and stone implements were combined and were therefore clumsier, they were none the less interdependent. A spear-shaft, for instance, might or might not have had to be cut to the required length with a stone knife, yet it would certainly have needed planing or smoothing with a stone scraper or dressing tool and perhaps with a thong of leather or vegetable fibre before it could be suitable for holding and throwing. The preparation of the spear's point, moreover, would have required sharp stone tools, after which it could have been hardened by fire, as some of the specimens found indicate. In the later part of the Stone Age the successful hafting of a stone point to a wooden spear-shaft depended on delicate paring and grooving with precision tools.

These are a few illustrations of what can be gained by intelligent and imaginative study of stone tools, to make them in fact less stony and more lively. It would be possible to expand the argument on the uses of prepared wood and skins to include tents and wind-breaks. Here, as with the tools and weapons just discussed, we are moving beyond a consideration of techniques towards a more general economic and cultural interpretation of the evidence and to reconstructions of the lives of the different hunting and food-gathering communities of the various periods of the Stone Age.

One particular point to be made here is that throughout the Stone Age the majority of tools, even stone tools were not weapons. Although hunting was always essential to provide protein (except in those places where fish were plentiful and the means of catching them were known), the collecting of vegetable foods, and in particular the digging up of starchy roots and tubers, would have been equally important and would normally have contributed the larger part of the diet. The bulk of the tools were for these activities together with general domestic use and wood-working. Inability or difficulties in carrying water would have restricted the choice of camp sites very significantly. A seasonal camp for a family group had to be close to a stream or lake. Such a site would, naturally, have been further blessed with richer vegetation and variety of foods and thus more attractive to game.

A study of the techniques of the Stone Age periods can, with common sense and imagination, lend itself to the reconstruction of economic and cultural conditions. But it cannot be denied that the evidence, even for the latest part of the Stone Age in East Africa, is very scarce and that attempts at a broader interpretation are inevitably speculative. It is, indeed, necessary to resist wild theoretical conjectures. But, that accepted, there is no use bemoaning the lack of remains: rather what there are need to be faced shrewdly and imaginatively to see what facts and ideas can be deduced from them. Thus new approaches and the search for new evidence are stimulated. The remainder of this chapter considers some of the ways by which more information could be obtained and more interesting conclusions reached.

Occasionally fossilized animal bones have been found on certain early sites and also unfossilized food bones in Late Stone Age living places, notably under rock-shelters. This provides direct evidence of the type of animal hunted and eaten. Sometimes, moreover, an examination of the bones for tool-marks and fractures and even of the pattern in which the debris was found may suggest the methods by which the animal was butchered and consumed. But even such direct evidence can represent only a part of the story. For instance, small mammals and reptiles, birds and insects may have been caught but there is no trace of them, either because their bones or hard parts were too fragile to survive or because the hunter devoured such small prey at the place of kill instead of carrying it to the camp. In the same way there is no trace of the honey, fruit, berries, nuts and even birds' eggs which would, similarly, have been eaten in the wild rather than brought home, with few, if any, stone tools needed for their collection and preparation. In fact, evidence of prehistoric remains of vegetable foods is very rarely obtained. Nevertheless, the diets of early hunter-gatherer populations must have been reasonably balanced, and a plausible reconstruction of them has also to be balanced by an intelligent assessment of both the actual archaeological finds and the food resources provided by the local environment.

For certain regions (e.g. central Tanzania) the archaeological evidence for the hunter-gatherer way of life at the very end of the Stone Age is supplemented in a remarkable way by surviving examples of rock-painting. Quite aside from the technical skill and artistic sense and maturity which many of these paintings demonstrate, they provide valuable information on the kind of animals hunted for food as well as on the methods of hunting them with spears, bows and arrows, and various types of traps. More rarely other food-getting activities seem to be shown, such as digging up roots and collecting honey. All this is most enlightening and vastly expands our vision of prehistoric life, especially since some of the activities portrayed in the paintings can be compared with the recent or current practices of the peoples of East Africa.

The evidence provided by the paintings has to be considered along with the technological material which could serve an economic or cultural purpose. Once the pattern begins to emerge, we can start asking further questions about hunting, trapping and collecting methods and the size of the hunting band, and still further about the community as a whole, its territorial range and the type of social organization it created to maintain itself. The testing of conjectures of this kind is still at an experimental stage, so that the answers to these questions are rarely expressed with entire confidence. Nevertheless, definite progress is being made, and since progress depends on primary archaeological evidence, it must be collected by the most careful, systematic and, if possible, sophisticated methods available.

Sites with stone tools are not rare in East Africa. They began to be recognized very early in the twentieth century and, following the pioneer survey work of the late Dr Louis Leakey in Kenya in the 1920s, increasing numbers of sites of all periods of prehistory have been discovered in the region. Many discoveries can be expected. They are usually revealed by erosion or the disturbance of the land – the tools or waste flake are washed out of gulleys, river-beds or steep hillsides, or they are brought to the surface by cultivation, cattle hoofs or building activities. It is not only professional archaeologists who discover these sites and remains; more commonly amateurs, including farmers and students, come across them and collect the finds. Any site is worth noting and should be reported to the relevant educational or antiquities authority. All tools and other archaeological material collected should be deposited in a museum, where they can be available for study and comparison with other local collections. The practice of foreign archaeologists of removing their finds to museums in their home countries was never very prevalent in the case of East Africa, and has now, happily, ended. However, a few collections of East African material made early in this century are kept in European museums, though by far the greater and most valuable part of the East African archaeological record is housed in the national museums of the countries concerned.

By itself a surface collection tells us little since the tools and waste pieces have been removed from their original positions. In addition the collection itself is usually selective. Nevertheless, even a small surface collection is likely to contain clues, in the form of certain types and sizes of tools or of manufacturing methods, relating to the period of the Stone Age to which it belongs and of its cultural relationship to other known sites. This will help in determining whether a more detailed investigation and full-scale excavation would be worthwhile.

Excavation needs to be planned and undertaken by archaeologists experienced in the type of site in question. However, as just shown, expert archaeologists depend on local information provided by amateurs and students. Moreover, the latter can often assist in an excavation and learn the skills. Only through correct methods, up-to-date techniques of excavation and examination of the finds, both in their original place and after their recording and removal, can the archaeologist recover the maximum amount of information from a site and provide the fullest possible, if not exhaustive, picture of what went on there. It deserves to be noted here that some of the revealing excavation work on Earlier Stone Age sites in East Africa undertaken in recent years has helped set the style, in method, analysis and interpretation, for research in other parts of the world.

The excavating archaeologist, then, is concerned not so much with *finding* individual specimens as with *finding out* as much as possible about the way of life of a former community, through identifying and exhaustively studying as much as possible of the cultural assemblage and gaining all available information on the environmental setting. This may demand very slow and meticulous excavation methods, if all the objects are to be recovered and all the features of a living floor, including slight irregularities in the surface or colour changes in the soil which might indicate fire or some other activity, are to be recognized. Where small objects, including stone flakes, bone splinters and even vegetable seeds, are expected or likely to occur, it is commonly necessary to sieve the soil. This is a very frequent practice in Late Stone Age rock-shelters where the deposits tend to be very soft and ashy. Usually in a rock-shelter, and frequently in open sites, the materials do not represent a single occupation but successive ones, each leaving its rubbish on top of that of the last and requiring separate study. The excavator has therefore to pay very careful attention to the stratigraphy; for, if an object of one period of occupation should be muddled with those of another, the interpretation will be sadly distorted.

While the responsibility for identifying, recording and studying all finds lies with the excavator himself, he will still need the assistance of other scientists. Some of this assistance, such as the identification of animal bones, may be undertaken later in a laboratory. Similarly, should the excavator, through the luck of preservation, come across vegetable remains (for instance carbonized seeds and nuts or pieces of wood) he will need to dispatch them to a botanical expert after specially treating them on the spot. The identification and study of samples of this kind will add to information on the diet and economy of the community. But equally important will be what they reveal about the environment at that time. If by chance ancient pollen should have been preserved, a palynological examination may illustrate the vegetation which then existed and changes which have occurred in it. Similarly revealing can be soil samples containing microscopic organisms or snail-shells. These also help to identify the type of vegetation which prevailed, and hence the climate of the time. Studies of the geology, geomorphology and soil structure are also useful in reconstructing the ancient environment and the resources which a prehistoric community could have exploited. Clearly much of this environmental investigation, if it is to be at all thorough and reliable, benefits from the presence of these various experts at the excavation site at least for part of the time. For it is not just the samples collected and taken to the laboratories which contain the clues. The samples have to be carefully selected and controlled in the context of the site. Big changes may have taken place in the landscape between the period under study and the present day, either because of climatic change or geological action, or more frequently because of human activities, notably cultivation and associated forest- or bush-clearance in recent times. But the approach to the past must always be through an intelligent study of the situation of the site as found and of all the clues, archaeological and other, which it contains.

There are other studies which are relevant, for, even if they provide no direct evidence, they throw valuable indirect light on the prehistoric period.

The first of these is anthropological research among the few existing hunter-gatherer societies in the world, and especially those in Africa. In fact, a number of suggestions outlined above were prompted, explicitly or implicitly, by the way of life of modern hunter-gatherers, such as the Hadza of northern Tanzania and the San of the Kalahari, to which researchers have been turning attention in recent years. Now, the ways of the Hadza and San provide many useful insights on the probable viability, organization and constraints of the hunting and gathering mode of life, and suggest many points which would otherwise have eluded the archaeologist's mind. Nevertheless, we would be sadly mistaken in regarding these communities as exact replicas of Stone Age societies or as mere survivals from that age.

It is true, of course, that certain of the present-day hunter-gatherer groups, notably the San of southern Africa, still reflect the conditions of Late Stone Age populations, and can therefore shed light on some of the problems of that period. For instance, a not infrequent find in late stone age contexts is a stone with a circular hole bored through it. The San today sometimes use these bored stones as weights for sharpened wooden sticks for digging up edible roots and there are apparently rock paintings in South Africa which illustrate this use. But specific correlations of this sort are rare. Also, changes have taken place in San society for various reasons, including contact, close or distant, with peoples using iron and living in a food-producing economy. Very few San continue to work stone regularly, for iron is obtainable from trade or scrap and this inevitably causes modifications at technological and cultural levels. Other surviving hunter-gatherer groups have intermixed more intimately with food-producing populations: while others again are barely aboriginal, having reverted in recent times to this way of life in the backwoods and maintaining themselves by exchange of forest products with their agricultural and pastoral neighbours. This reciprocal dependence has been the case with many of the groups known as Dorobo which still exist in the highlands of Kenya and northern Tanzania. These examples show the dangers of drawing parallels between modern hunter-gatherer populations and those of recent prehistory, dangers multiplied when considering the remotest ages. Yet, in spite of the dangers, the insights provided on the food resources of the land and the organization necessary for exploiting them are valuable.

Another invaluable source of information is to be found in the lives and societies of primate animals, notably of man's nearest living relatives, the two African apes (chimpanzee and gorilla), as well as those of baboons. The latter are monkeys and much less closely related to man biologically, but behaviourally they are of special interest for the study of human society since, more than most other primates, they live in groups much of the time on the ground. They are consequently easy to observe. Now, as explained elsewhere, man did not descend from these apes and monkeys, and it is not suggested here that any prehistoric communities, not even the earliest ones, were significantly closer to them than modern men are. Yet, in reflecting on the basic behaviour of primates and the habits which man inherited from his pre-human ancestors, and also in trying to understand how these immediate ancestors of man, who lacked the ability of making and using tools, got their vegetarian living, there are numerous ideas to be gleaned from these field studies, a large number of which have been carried out in East Africa.

Prehistory, as we have stressed, was enormously long and the human populations of the end of it were vastly advanced and quite distinct from those of early men at the opening of prehistory. Moreover, the Late Stone Age inhabitants of eastern Africa, some of whom remained in existence till very recent times, were distinctively African. Some were related to the San, others have been assimilated into the modern negroid iron age populations. By contrast, the people of the early stone age and especially those of its earliest stage, though well represented in East Africa and for a long time confined to this part of the world, were also ancestral to mankind as a whole. For these earliest stone tool makers, whose bones have been found in the lowest layers at Olduvai Gorge in northern Tanzania and in the Lake Turkana region of northern Kenya and southern Ethiopia, are usually classified as *Homo*. However in both body and brain they were distinct from modern men (*Homo sapiens sapiens*). The early history of East Africa is thus also the history of mankind, and it is this element which gives it a worldwide significance. Since it contains such invaluable information on early man and his culture, as well as on primate ecology, East Africa has very properly become the world centre for research into the life, environment and origin of man.

Chronology and classification

Whereas in most of Asia, Europe and northern Africa the stone age is divided conventionally into Palaeolithic, Mesolithic and Neolithic, in Africa south of the Sahara this system has been abandoned by most modern writers. Here the Stone Age is usually viewed and studied in three broad periods – Early, Middle, Late – distinguished largely by important and recognizable changes in technology (which have of course broader cultural and economic implications). These differences in classification are *not* two ways of saying the same things conceptually; and chronologically, too, the criteria of classification are completely different. (See Table 19.2, p. 464, and the notes related to it.)

The three African periods are dated very approximately as follows.

> Early Stone Age: from the time of the earliest stone tools (say, 3 million years ago) till about 100 000 years ago.
> Middle Stone Age: from around 100 000 to 15 000 years ago.
> Late Stone Age: from about 15 000 years ago until the beginning of the Iron Age (which occurred in most regions 2000 years ago).

The approximate nature of this dating must be emphasized and also the fact of its being subject to some controversy. Hitherto rather later dates have

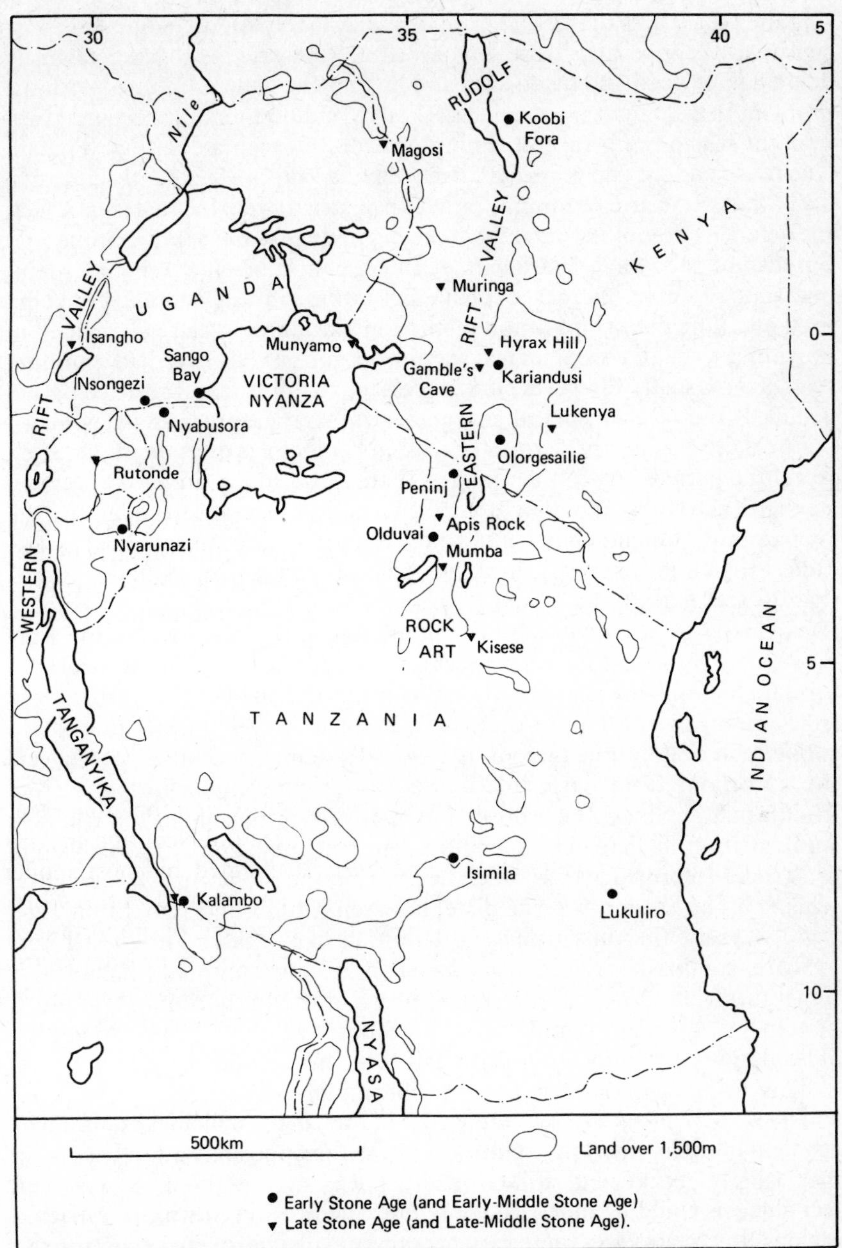

FIG. 19.1 *East Africa: important Stone Age sites*

usually been suggested for the transition from the Middle to the Late Stone Age and more particularly that from the Early to the Middle Stone Age. This conservative approach arose in part from the scarcity of satisfactorily defined, described and dated sites and lithic collections, combined with the problem that the first transition (Early to Middle Stone Age) occurred at a time for which radio-carbon testing provides no accurate dating. Though dates of 50 000–60 000 years have been obtained and are frequently cited, it is likely that these are minimum, rather than strictly reliable, dates. (In fact, the detailed chronology not only of the beginnings of the Middle Stone Age, but also of the whole latter part of the Early Stone Age, remains highly uncertain. New techniques, explained elsewhere in this volume, are being tried out. The potassium-argon method in particular has already helped in providing a rough chronological framework for periods over half a million years ago. Usually, however, it is necessary to fall back on relative dating deduced from archaeological and geological stratigraphies and typology.)

For these reasons the datings suggested here for the division of the Stone Age into periods are rather longer than those found in most previous standard accounts. But they are not so radical as some students of the subject now contend they should be. (Even the revisionist school is less radical than it may appear, since the issues raised relate more to definitions than to real dates.)

The dates for the division of the Stone Age into Early, Middle and Late periods are imprecise and controversial. In addition it would be wrong to imagine that they were internally static or unvariegated or that the changes from one to the next were necessarily sudden. Developments took place *within* each of the three periods as well as from one to another. Moreover, the transitions from Early to Middle Stone Age technologies, and from Middle to Late Stone Age, were complex. In recognition of this some writers speak of Intermediate periods. The recent tendency, however, has been to drop these Intermediates as official periods in the Stone Age chronological scheme. (The Second Intermediate, between Middle and Late Stone Age, was always a rather unsatisfactory definition in any case. The First Intermediate, comprising the industries known as Fauresmith and Sangoan, is sometimes viewed now as a terminal phase of the Early Stone Age; but is here included in an expanded Middle Stone Age. This helps explain the older dating of the opening of the latter in this account.)

This dropping of the term Intermediate is merely a matter of convenience and does not betoken a more simple view of human technological, cultural or economic development in prehistory. Quite the opposite view is becoming increasingly recognized. First, in all epochs of the Stone Age variant technologies could be practised contemporaneously, even within restricted regions. In certain cases these variants can be explained by differences in the environment, with one technological tradition emerging in, say, woodland or waterside situations and a distinct, contemporary one in drier or more open areas, where the food resources and methods of obtaining them would have dictated a different cultural adjustment and technology.[1] But the probable explanation may not always be so neat: sometimes the various activities undertaken by a single community (hunting of larger or smaller game, trapping, digging roots and tubers, working wood and leather), some of which were seasonal, appear sufficient to account for different types of tool-kits of similar date in a particular locality. On the other hand, there may be differences indicating much deeper cultural divergences and economic specializations, maintained conceivably by distinct communities or races – or, in Early Stone Age times, different species of *Homo*. This is a controversial subject. Nevertheless, the most recent discoveries in East Africa show that what were once regarded as two essentially discrete sub-periods of the Early Stone Age – the Pebble-tool (or Oldowan) culture succeeded by, or evolving into, the handaxe (or Acheulian) culture overlapped for a very long time lasting at the very least half a million years. It is difficult to stretch the activity-pattern theory to embrace this evidence satisfactorily, and some scholars would interpret it as representing the distinct cultural traditions of two quite separate populations existing side by side but exploiting different food resources.

Furthermore, overlapping is discernible between the arbitrary divisions into Early, Middle and Late Stone Age. One may find Early Stone Age tool-types or evidence of early manufacturing techniques in an essentially Middle Stone Age assemblage. A mixture of innovatory and conservative features may be a sign of gradual change. But signs of transition do not always exist: on some sites with clear stratigraphic successions it can happen that a new technology appears suddenly in developed form without any trace of local evolution. This suggests cultural diffusion from one region to another, possibly but not necessarily resulting from the movement of populations. Climatic change which affected the environment was also a stimulus to cultural adjustment and technological advance; but here the archaeologist has to beware of adducing simplistic determinist interpretations.

This rather arbitrary periodization of the Stone Age is therefore a useful scale of reference in the present state of knowledge, but one which must be kept flexible in order to accommodate constant modifications. Some day it may outlive its uses. Though that day has probably not arrived yet, the scale's usefulness is in danger of being undermined by those who would apply it too formally or rigorously to achieve results for which it was never designed.

In Table 19.2 a more detailed scale is presented to illustrate how the various Stone Age cultures and lithic industries recognized by archaeologists in East Africa should fit into this tripartite periodization. This is offered as a guide to current knowledge and the main studies and makes no pretence of being a correct interpretation or one that will survive the results of further research or revaluations of older work. It must be seen simply as a guide and as a flexible one at that. Certain of the cultures named here (and others

1. See in particular the account of the Middle Stone Age, pp. 472–5.

TABLE 19.2 *Prehistory in East Africa*

Years ago (approx.)	Divisions		*Diagnostic technological features*	*Main lithic industries* (watersides – forests)	*Main lithic industries* (highlands – savannahs)	*Rough equivalents in Mediterranean and Eurasian regions*	*Geological periods (approx. correlations)*
3 million	EARLY STONE AGE (ESA)	FIRST PHASE	chopper-tools and flakes	Oldowan (pebble-tool industry)		Lower Palaeolithic	Lower Pleistocene
1 million		SECOND PHASE	bifacially flaked tools, cleavers, etc.	Acheulian (biface industry)			Middle Pleistocene
100 000	MIDDLE STONE AGE (MSA)	FIRST PHASE	flaked tools made from prepared cores	Sangoan	Fauresmith	Middle Palaeolithic	Upper Pleistocene
40 000		SECOND PHASE	hafting; smaller, finished tools	Lupemban	Stillbay		
15 000	LATE STONE AGE (LSA)		blades and microliths with retouch; composite tools	Tschitolian	(Magosian) Wilton	Upper Palaeolithic	Holocene
				Kenya Capsian 'stone bowl' cultures ('terminal LSA')	Kenya highlands	epi-Palaeolithic or Mesolithic Neolithic (in some parts)	
of our era	IRON AGE						

deliberately omitted) may have been given a separate identity on the basis of inadequate research or descriptions, occasionally with only one site well investigated or described so that their validity as units may be in doubt. Others are enormously extensive, whether temporally or geographically or both. The Acheulian of the Early Stone Age spans more than a million years in eastern Africa, and it extends not only right across the continent but also into a large part of southern and western Eurasia. In the first phase of the Middle Stone Age, the Sangoan stretched from parts of eastern and southern Africa to the far west of the continent. Among later industries represented in East Africa, Stillbay and Wilton were first described and named in the Cape province of South Africa. Experts on these may prefer to give the East African variants new and distinct names. But in this account a more comprehensive approach is preferred, some obvious problems and likely revisions being noted at the appropriate points. Those so wishing can follow up the new developments and debates beginning with the works listed in our bibliography – and can then proceed to try to apply more sophisticated terminologies.

Notes to Table 19.2

Table 19.2 is devoted to terminology. Terminology by itself tells one nothing and to set too much store by it would be a disservice to understanding. But the Stone Age as a prehistoric period can only be known to us and sensibly discussed and studied through terms and symbols invented by archaeologists. Any serious attempt to understand this period and its vast literature, therefore, whether viewed as a whole or analysed in detail, demands a grasp of the terminologies used by various writers, inconsistent and injudicious though some may be.

The two right-hand columns, showing rough correlations with geological periods and with the Mediterranean, northern African and Eurasian system of periodizing the Palaeolithic, are included merely for reference, especially in relation to other chapters in this volume and other publications (including old works on East African archaeology). These two columns are not necessary for a reading of this chapter by itself.

The terms Lower, Middle and Upper, in which Lower is the earliest, follow normal geological practice based on stratigraphic sequences. In most geological, and many archaeological, works, therefore, such tables are set out in logical succession from bottom to top. The present table is ordered from top to bottom to conform with historical time-charts.

As the table shows, the term Palaeolithic (or Old Stone Age) is *not* the equivalent of the African Early Stone Age. Palaeolithic, as first used in Europe and still used, means Stone Age without food production, in contrast to Neolithic (or New Stone Age) meaning Stone Age with food production (i.e. agriculture and/or pastoralism before the use of metals). A somewhat different interpretation of Neolithic, which is occasionally encountered, prefers the criterion of advanced material culture, notably pottery or ground stone, to specific evidence of food production. In some parts of the world a transitional period (or cultural backwater, as some would see it) is recognized and called Mesolithic. This is not relevant here, except to note that it has no connection whatever with the African Middle Stone Age (an all too frequent error in general writings on African history).

In almost all of Africa south of the equator, as in most of East Africa, there was no equivalent of the Neolithic of other parts of the world, since food production did not spread until the opening of the Iron Age.[2] However, in the highlands of Kenya and northern Tanzania there is evidence of food production (herding, if not a little agriculture too) in the terminal Late Stone Age 2000–3000 years ago. This, with its pottery and stone bowls (see the end of the chapter), is labelled Neolithic in some studies.

A1: Early Stone Age (first phase)

The earliest known humanly fashioned tools date from between 2, if not 3, million years ago and less than 1 million and have been found by the edges of former lakes and marshes close to the Rift valley in northern Tanzania and Kenya. These were hand-size pebbles and stone chunks from which a few flakes were struck off (with another stone) to produce crude but usable cutting implements. Heavy work such as cutting through an animal's skin or breaking or crushing tough vegetable material would normally have required the use of the main tool held in the fist. Many flakes (commonly, but incorrectly, described as waste), being thinner and hence sharper, would have been suitable for lighter and more precise work such as preparing the kill for food, making wooden weapons or in domestic work in the camp. In fact, more intense studies of these so-called chopper- or pebble-tool industries, notably by Dr Mary Leakey at Olduvai Gorge where they occur in the lowest levels, reveal greater variety of tool-types and technological sophistication than has been assumed hitherto. The description chopper-tool does not do real justice to the implement, nor is the term Pebble-tool culture, frequently used for this phase of the Early Stone Age, accurate, especially since the stones chosen for manufacturing the choppers, flakes and other tools were not always pebbles. Moreover, bones, and doubtless wood too, were used. Most archaeologists prefer therefore to call this phase Oldowan, after Olduvai in northern Tanzania where such tools were first recognized and described (Fig 19.2). This does not mean, of course, that they were first made at Olduvai.[3]

At one time it was thought that the makers of these pebble-tools were able to hunt and kill only small game, such as birds, lizards, tortoises and hyrax,

2. Many authors do not share this opinion.

3. The strange spelling 'Oldowan' is derived from the German form of the name Oldoway, found on early maps. The place name is a Masai one in origin, more correctly rendered Oldupai.

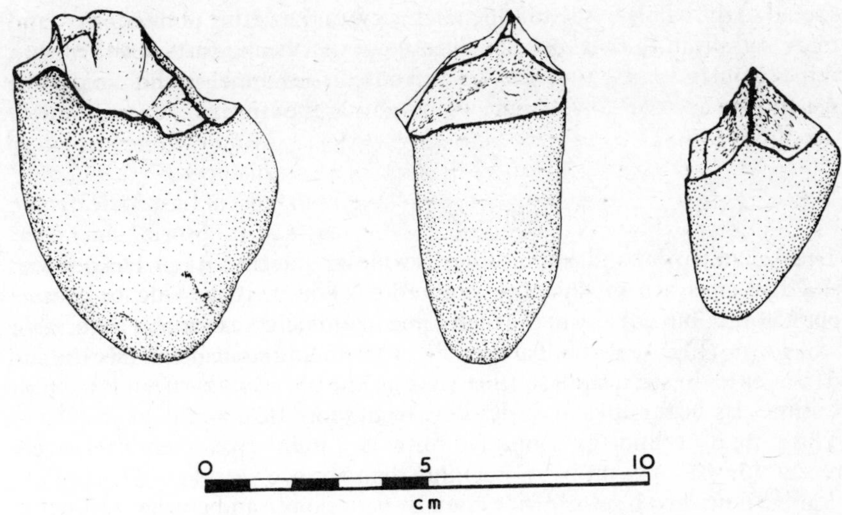

FIG. 19.2 *Early Stone Age, first phase: typical Oldowan ('pebble') tools*

to supplement their fruit, vegetable and insect collecting. It is now evident that they butchered large animals too. Among the fossilized bones found with the tools at or close to camp sites are those of elephants and large antelopes. Some of these beasts may have died naturally or been crippled by accident or killed by lions or other predators, but it is likely that others were at this early stage caught in traps or driven into waterside mires by hunting parties which would have completed the kill with wooden spears and clubs, and perhaps stone missiles.

Part of the meat was doubtless consumed by the hunters at the place of kill. But some of it must have been carried back to the camp to be shared by the rest of the group including women and children. For the rubbish which has survived often includes the bones of several different animals together with a variety of cutting, scraping and pounding tools, thus constituting most remarkable evidence that in this, the earliest, stage of humanity the idea of a home base already existed. Furthermore, study of the scatter patterns of the rubbish suggests that actual wind-breaks were set up, while at Olduvai a rough circle of stones is believed to have been the base for a wooden frame of a hut or shelter perhaps covered with skins. At Melka Konture, an artificial platform may have served the same purpose.

Besides being known from several East African former lakesides extending from Olduvai to Lake Turkana, where the earliest sites yet known exist, 'pebble-tool' deposits have been discovered from South Africa right up to the shores of the Mediterranean. They may date from a more evolved stage than the earliest in East Africa. It is likely then, but not absolutely certain, that this tool making began in central or eastern Africa and then spread to the whole of the continent. In view of the dating of these tools, and more significantly their occasional discovery in East Africa together with actual human bones, they can be attributed to the earliest hominids, the Australopithecines – or, as some would now argue strongly, to *Homo habilis* specifically.[4]

A2: Early Stone Age (second phase)

The Acheulian or handaxe culture is as widespread in Africa as the Oldowan and the sites are much more numerous. This may be due to greater populations, but equally to the increasing manufacture of large recognizable tool-forms (Fig 19.3). Unlike the Oldowan, the Acheulian extends beyond Africa into western and southern Asia and also southern and western Europe. Its beginnings in Africa date from more than a million years ago. This type of technology continued for over a million years until relatively recent times, that is, probably not more than 100 000 years ago. This million years was marked by worldwide climatic variations,[5] and it is not likely that all the regions in which Acheulian tools have been found were continuously occupied. Eastwards of India, moreoever, true Acheulian industries are rare or non-existent, and it appears that eastern Asia persisted with a distinct stone technology more akin to the advanced pebble-tool type. This may represent an important cultural divergence between East and West. These Acheulian industries, in which the handaxe is the best-known tool, are usually associated with *Homo erectus,* a form of man intermediate between the Australopithecines and modern man. However, by the end of the Acheulian phase, the evolution from *Homo erectus* to early types of *Homo sapiens* was already in train.

Africa was one of the places where *Homo erectus* emerged. His appearance was accompanied by a cultural evolution shown by the improved Acheulian tool-making techniques and the more efficient way of life they introduced although, no doubt, older cultural traditions (and probably the earlier physical types) persisted for some time alongside the new. This point is best illustrated in the successive layers of ancient lake-beds at Olduvai, where for several hundreds of thousands of years either side of a point 1 million years ago discrete Oldowan and Acheulian tool-kits were being made and used. The Acheulian, moreover, contains numerous stages and variations, but for general purposes only the main division is significant, that is, the division between the cruder or simpler Early Acheulian and the evolved Acheulian to which belong the most beautifully manufactured handaxes and cleavers. Selections of these tools are displayed in the East African museums, those from Isimila in the southern highlands of Tanzania being among the world's finest. Clearly, evolved Acheulian must have begun by developing at some

4. See Chapter 17 above.
5. See Chapter 16 above.

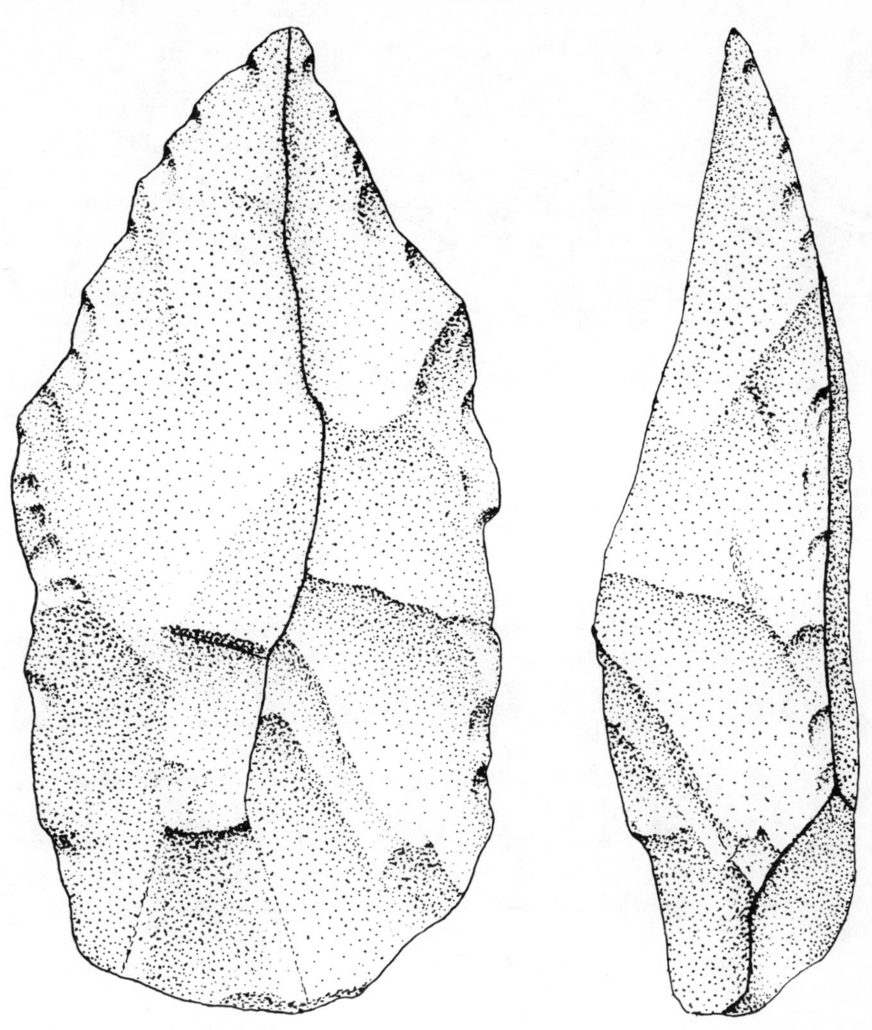

FIG. 19.3a *Early Stone Age, second phase: typical Acheulian hand-axe, front and side views*

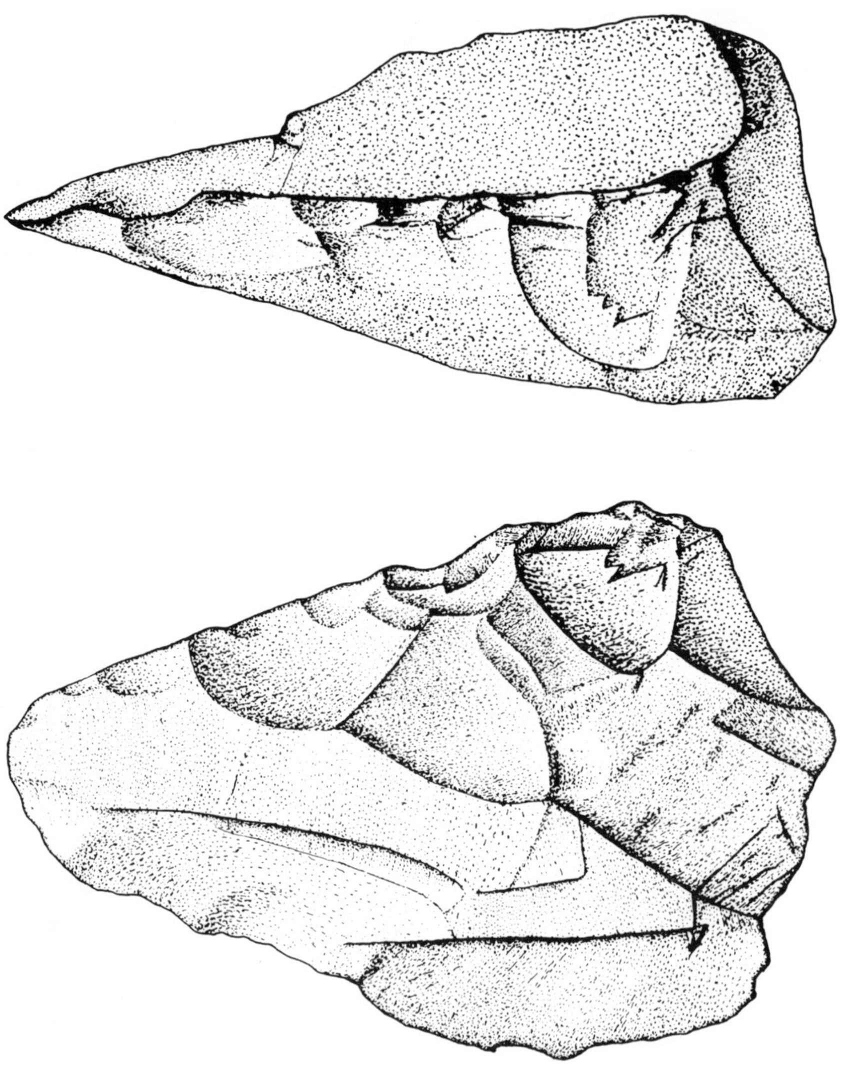

FIG. 19.3b *Early Stone Age, second phase: typical Acheulian pick, front and side views*

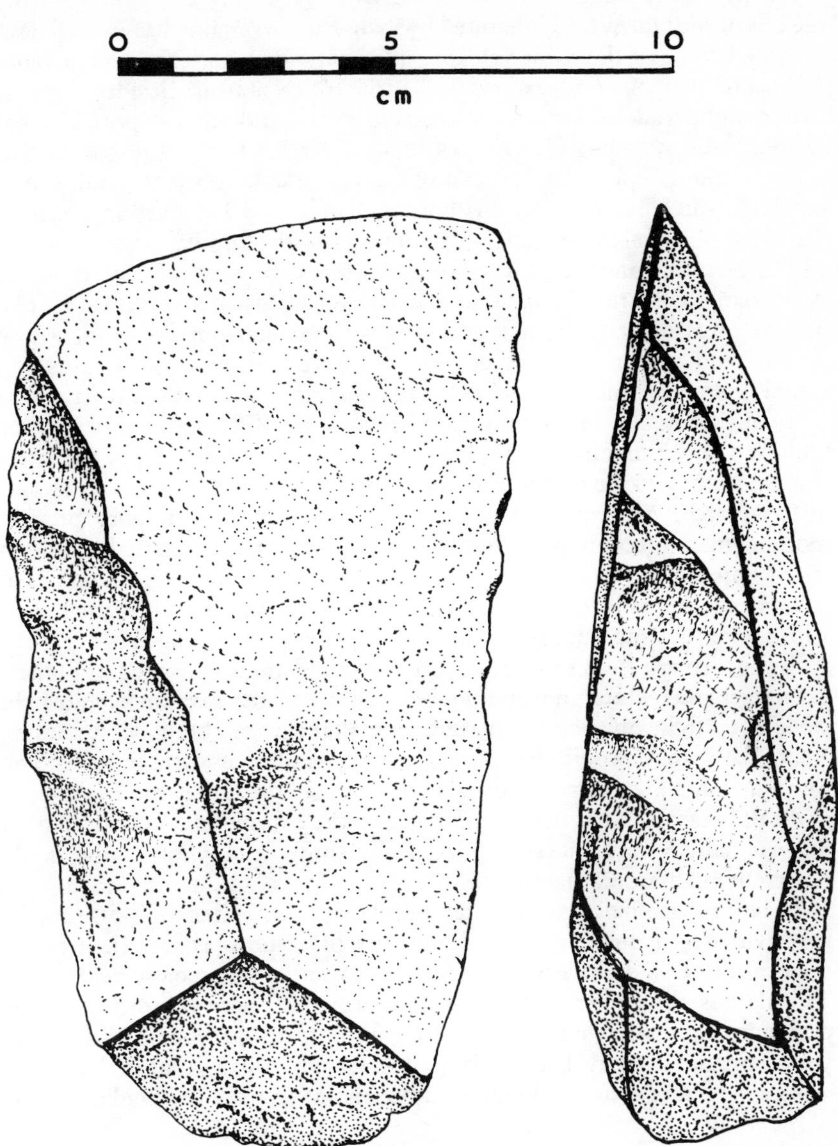

FIG. 19.3C *Early Stone Age, second phase: typical Acheulian cleaver, front and side views*

point from Early Acheulian but, once this had occurred, the new techniques and the old tradition went on side by side for some time.

So, in this Acheulian phase, East Africa was only one among many regions of the Old World inhabited by man. But it contains sites which have provided some of the most valuable information on both the technologies and economies of *Homo erectus* and early *Homo sapiens*. Besides Olduvai (with its unparalleled series of successive layers) and other deposits in that region, these sites include Olorgesailie and Kariandusi in the Kenya Rift valley, several deposits to the east of Lake Turkana, Nsongezi and others nearly on the Uganda–Tanzania border, Isimila and Lukuliro in southern Tanzania and Kalambo Falls on the border with Zambia.

The names handaxe and cleaver for the two most typical types of Acheulian tools are of course archaeological terms of convenience. The handaxe was not an axe, it was doubtless a general-purpose tool, whose pointed end and long cutting edges could have been used for digging and skinning among other things. The cleaver with its squarish cutting end is especially suitable for skinning animals. The difference between the Oldowan and Acheulian technologies is largely one of degree: in the latter stages, both the kits and the individual tool-types are more clearly differentiated. Moreover, the Acheulian techniques with more precise, more regular and more persistent flaking on both faces, executed less often with a hammerstone (as in the Oldowan) than with a cylindrical hammer of wood or an animal's long-bone, allowed for the production of bigger tools with longer cutting edges, as well as sharper flakes for knives.

Right through the Early Stone Age the populations consisted of hunter-gatherer bands which moved about seasonally in the savannahs and light woodlands following the fluctuating animal and vegetable food resources. Very likely they would have split up to wander at certain times and combined into bigger groups by lakes or other rich grounds towards the end of the dry season. It has been suggested that the enormous concentrations of fine Acheulian tools at such places as Isimila and Olorgesailie could represent such annual jamborees.

It is in archaeological sites containing evolved Acheulian tool-kits that the first evidence of fire has been discovered in eastern Africa. In previous publications this discovery is usually placed some 50 000 or so years back. This date is almost certainly much too cautious. There is said to be good evidence of fire and cooking by *Homo erectus* in eastern Asia half a million years ago; and it seems highly likely, if so far not proven, that in Africa fire was known and roasted food enjoyed during much of the Acheulian phase.

B: Middle Stone Age

The populations of the Middle Stone Age belonged to the species *Homo sapiens,* though maybe at first to sub-species of *Homo sapiens* somewhat different from modern man. By the end of the Middle Stone Age, however, not only would modern man (*Homo sapiens sapiens*) have emerged, but the distinctive physical characteristics of the races which now exist would also have been fairly well developed in Africa as elsewhere.

In technology, the Middle Stone Age saw significant advances (Fig. 19.4). The basic stone tool making was no longer a matter of knocking flakes off a core until it was reduced to a reasonably standard shape with useful edges. Instead, the more complex technique of preparing the core by precise flaking to a required shape and size, and then finally striking off the finished tool, came increasingly into use. At the same time, the technique was perfected of breaking off random flakes which were subsequently shaped by retouching. This permitted the production of smaller, more perfectly shaped and refined tools, usually thinner than those of the Early Stone Age and consequently more efficient. In the second phase of the Middle Stone Age, this was followed by an innovation with far-reaching implications – the fitting of worked stone pieces into a haft of wood or other material. The leaf-shaped point distinctive of the Stillbay industries, neatly worked down by pressure-flaking, was doubtless often gummed into a slot at the end of a wooden shaft to form a spear. Many domestic tools would similarly have been hafted into convenient handles. This involved not only the preparation of gums from tree-resins, but also the more intricate shaping, paring and grooving of wood, no doubt also tempered in fire.

Keeping pace with these technological developments of the Middle Stone Age were economic or at least environmental adjustments. There are two interrelated issues here. The first is climatic changes.[6] The details, dating and links of changes in climate with archaeological evidence are still rather poorly known, and it would be rash to try to explain the one by facile reference to the other. Moreover, climatic changes – fluctuations from drier to wetter and vice versa, which affected the expansion and contraction of the forest, the frequency and sizes of lakes and rivers and thus the distribution and richness of different food resources – were nothing new; and we must ask why climatic changes had not led to an earlier Middle Stone Age technological and economic breakthrough. At the present stage of research, this question cannot be answered satisfactorily, though one might conjecture that increasing population forced more efficient and varied ways of exploiting the environment. For, whatever the cause, this is what certainly did happen in the Middle Stone Age.

Our second issue is regional specialization. Men began to populate new territories. Throughout the world *Homo sapiens* was exercising his innate versatility and pushing back the boundaries of his places of settlement. In Africa there emerged a clear cultural division between the peoples of the grasslands and the more lightly wooded savannahs on the one hand, and those who now penetrated the wetter and more thickly forested regions. In the former big game hunting with the spear was developed (not, though, to the exclusion of gathering); whereas in the latter the collecting of vegetables

6. See Chapter 16 above.

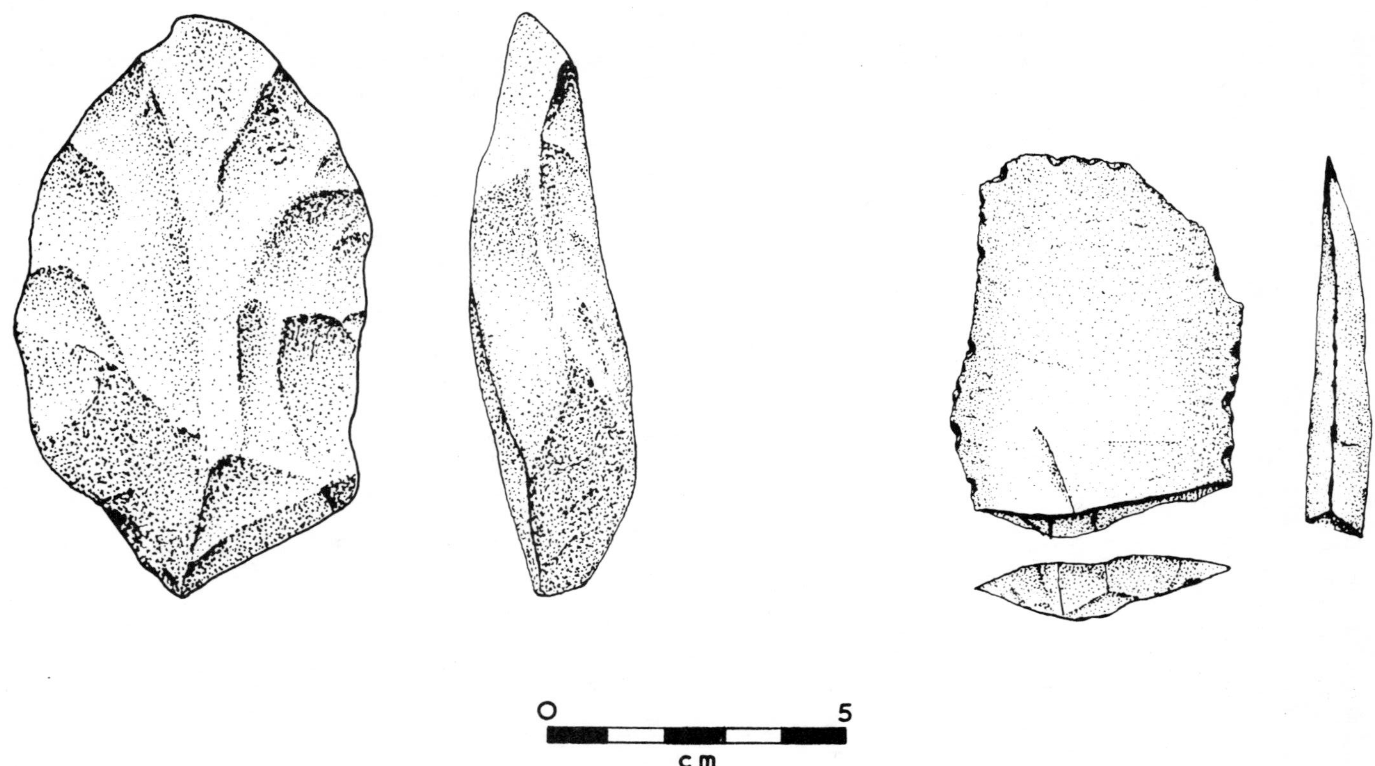

FIG. 19.4 *Middle Stone Age and transitional tools: the right-hand example is a fine point suitable for hafting perhaps as a spear-head*

and fruits, fishing and waterside catching, with lances and doubtless various kinds of trap, were emphasized.

In the first phase of the Middle Stone Age this regional specialization was not so extreme as is sometimes assumed. In the Kenya highlands, close to, if not inside, the forest, tools known as Fauresmith have been collected. This is in many respects a refined Acheulian technique. It has the same basic range of tools, but they are generally smaller and are produced by new manufacturing techniques. In contrast to this are the more widespread Sangoan industries, the best East African examples of which occur around Lake Victoria and the western Rift valley, in southern Uganda, Rwanda and western Tanzania. These industries are also a mixture of some Acheulian types of tool and new techniques, but the emphases are different from the Fauresmith type. One's first impression of Sangoan tools is their crudity; but this is probably not a sign of cultural retrogression but a more varied technological activity. For many of these crude-looking implements were most likely tools with which to make other tools, especially of wood; while the heavy picks would have been useful for digging up roots which were part of the woodland diet.

The Sangoan industries are first encountered in East Africa in a developed form and this suggests that their origin and evolution from an Acheulian source occurred somewhere else, to the centre or west of the continent. It is possible that they were introduced into the westerly parts of East Africa during a wet period when the equatorial forest extended its bounds. But this point may be over-argued. It is likely that camp sites were in woodlands and forested watersides rather than in the densest continuous forest. It is noticeable that in the Zaïre Basin the distribution of recorded Sangoan sites shows barely more penetration into the equatorial forest than had occurred in Acheulian times. However, in the second phase of the Middle Stone Age the makers of the Lupemban industries, which were essentially evolved and refined forms of the Sangoan and which were famous for their exquisitely fashioned stone lance-heads, belonged more decidedly to the forest and its waters.

The Lupemban is also found around Lake Victoria and other westerly parts of East Africa as well as in the Zaïre Basin, contrasting with the Stillbay of the high grasslands bordering the Rift valley with its leaf-shaped spear-points. In other regions, notably south-eastern Tanzania, there prevail different types of Middle Stone Age industries, less distinctive or rather awaiting proper classification. Some of these may have a general Sangoan-Lupemban appearance. But probably there were a number of regional traditions, whose origins may be explained as adjustments to local environments, but which, once entrenched, would have maintained many of their distinctive characteristics for reasons of cultural attachment as much as environmental or economic pressures. Such regional cultural factors may have an important bearing on the variability which is evident in East Africa once Late Stone Age technological innovations were adopted.

C: Late Stone Age

Ten to twenty thousand years ago these even more intricate techniques of stone tool manufacture became common. Instead of the Middle Stone Age emphasis on producing flakes from prepared cores, the main concentration in the Late Stone Age was on blades – striking (or indirectly punching) long, delicate, parallel-sided pieces from a suitable stone (Fig. 19.5). Such blades could then be trimmed (or retouched) for a variety of shapes and purposes. Usually the trimmed pieces were very small – microliths, sometimes less than a centimetre in length. A common form is one which archaeologists call the crescent or lunate with a straight sharp cutting edge and a curved blunted back. These were designed, not for holding and use as a complete instrument in the hand, but for hafting and gluing into handles of bone and wood. Hafting was now an evolved and regular practice. Frequently, moreover, several microliths would be fixed together in sequence slotted into a wooden handle to make a composite tool, such as a knife or saw. In regions where the stone was suitable for blade production, notably chert or better still the opaque volcanic glass (obsidian) which occurs in places close to the Rift valley in northern Tanzania and Kenya, beautiful crescents, backed blades, awls, burins for grooving, scrapers and other distinctive tools could be manufactured. But there were other regions where only quartz or some inferior type of stone with less regular flaking properties was available. Though efficient tool-kits were made from these, the first impression they give is of crudity and irregularity. Sometimes archaeologists recover thousands of quartz flakes and chips in a Late Stone Age living site, but only 2 or 3 per cent of them can be classified as recognizable tool-shapes.

On the basis of these technological innovations, a number of cultural and economic ones can be recognized or deduced. It was probably at this period that the bow and arrow began to be used in hunting. One or two microliths could be fixed at the end of the wooden shaft of an arrow to make a point, and others placed farther down could serve as barbs. The preparation of poisons to tip such arrows probably dates back to these times. This, as well as the use of nets in wooded areas, is suggested by the practices of existing or recent hunter-gatherer populations among which some of the Late Stone Age traditions are maintained. Bone was doubtless put to more uses, and the recognition of awls from both bone and stone is an indication that skins were sewn, either for clothing or for tentage. Beads made of seeds, bone, ostrich eggshell and, in time, of stone may have been sewn on to such clothing or strung to make necklaces. Grindstones, which occur in some Late Stone Age series, were used for crushing red ochre but probably served a more basic economic purpose in pounding vegetable foods.

Some Late Stone Age camps were in open country by streams or lakes, where wind-breaks or huts made of poles, grass and possibly skin covers have to be imagined. Also common at this time was the occupation of rock-shelters (sometimes inaccurately described as caves). These natural shelters

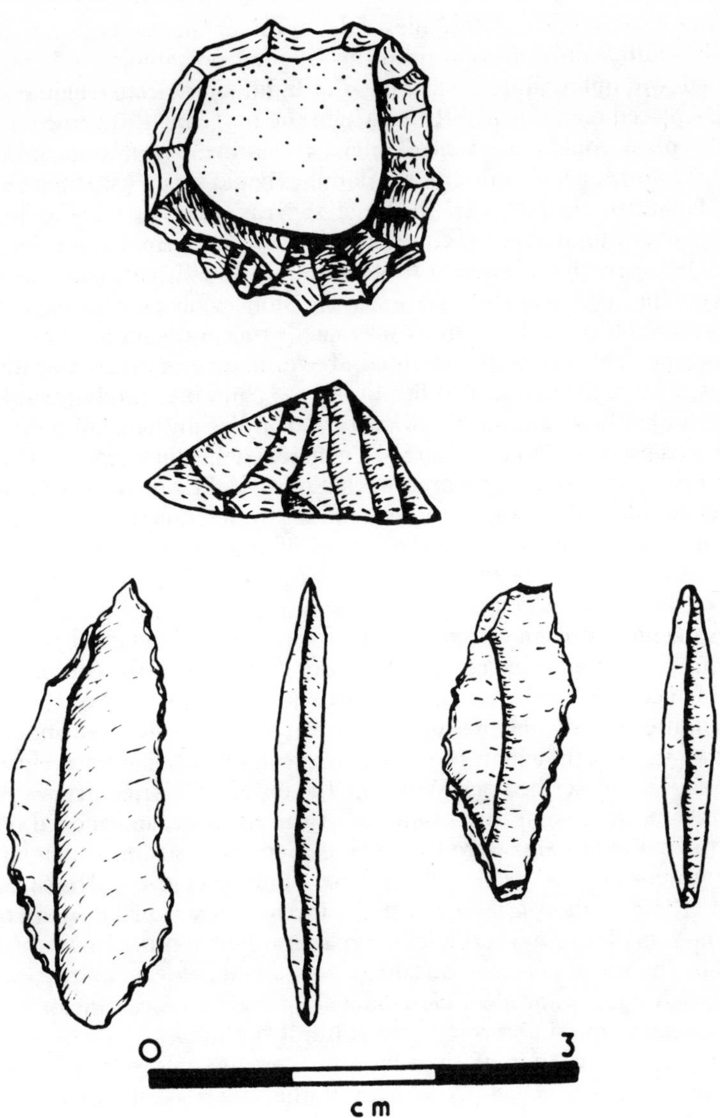

FIG. 19.5 *Late Stone Age: 'thumbnail' scraper (top), backed blade (left) and crescent (right), made from obsidian in the Kenya Rift valley.*

were found below cliffs, along valley-sides or under enormous granite rocks, wherever sufficient protection from the rain and prevailing wind could be provided without unduly restricting the light. Some rock-shelters were usefully placed on eminences from which the movement of game on wide areas of plain could be watched. Here a hunting party could make an overnight stop or a family or group of families could set up base for a season. Some favourite shelters were resorted to year after year or at least at intervals over hundreds or even thousands of years of the Late Stone Age. Hence the layers upon layers of rubbish found, usually consisting of ashes from cooking, bones of the animals eaten, stone tools and waste.

In one region of north-central Tanzania the rock walls at the rear of many of these rock-shelters were, as noted above, decorated with paintings of animals, hunting scenes and other designs. While it is rarely possible to connect individual paintings with particular layers in the Late Stone Age sequence represented in the shelters, a general connection between the two is perfectly clear. It is likely moreover that most of the surviving art belongs to recent millennia, towards the end of the Late Stone Age, some of it overlapping with the period of the spread of Iron Age communities. The origin of this hunter art – and of the beliefs and cosmology behind it – must, however, be much more ancient.

The likelihood of an ancient fund of tradition, stretching back many millennia to the beginning of the Late Stone Age if not to the Middle Stone Age, may account for the general similarities which exist between the Tanzanian hunter art and that of southern Africa. Similarly, the lithic industries of the two regions, though by no means identical, share some general features (often loosely described as Wilton). In southern Africa it has been demonstrated that some late examples of the rock art, and indeed of the Wilton stone industries, were the work of San groups some of whom still lead a hunter-gatherer life in certain regions. Their San physical features and Khoisan (or click) languages are both distinctive. Now, in East Africa there is only one small region where click languages are spoken and this is the very region of the north-central Tanzanian rock art. These Khoisan-speakers, besides betraying some possible evidence of San physical ancestry, still retain a very strong hunter-gatherer cultural tradition.[7]

This certainly cannot be explained as a result of a relatively recent migration of San out of southern Africa. Rather, there must once have been a continuum of such hunter-gatherers from northern Tanzania to the Cape of Good Hope, a continuum broken by the arrival in the region during the last 3000 years of peoples with different languages, cultures and pastoral or agricultural economies. The origins of this cultural continuum in the savannahs of eastern and southern Africa clearly belong well back in the Late Stone Age – if not with the Stillbay phase of the Middle Stone Age. However, the question of time-depth must be left open until this second phase of the Middle Stone Age, as well as the transition to Late Stone Age with the

7. See Chapter 11 above.

inadequately defined Magosian industries, is better recognized and understood in the intervening regions.

This notion of a long tradition for the savannah cultures of the Late Stone Age may account for some of the regional variability contained in the general category of Wilton industries. In this category archaeologists have in the past tended to include almost all industries in both eastern and southern Africa with a marked microlithic element and it may be that some of these, in the more northerly parts of East Africa, are related in only a very tenuous way and may have nothing to do with the San populations of the south. In the westerly parts of East Africa, moreover, one might expect to find a distinct tradition connected with the Zaïre Basin where Tschitolian industries flourished, derived from the Sangoan-Lupemban woodland and forest culture of the Middle Stone Age. But this is not especially evident, except in Rwanda.

The one region which does contain some strikingly contrasting features lies in the Kenya highlands and Rift valley. Here are found some Late Stone Age industries with Wilton affinities; but also others in which tools made on long blades rather than microliths predominate. These, known as Kenya Capsian, made from local obsidian sources, date from between about 10 000 before our era and 5000 before our era. The best series is that which Dr Leakey found at Gamble's Cave near Makuru in the 1920s. Related or derived industries continued until the very end of the stone age. This Kenya Capsian belongs to an older blade tradition widespread over much of north-eastern Africa and the Mediterranean region. But the comparison of the lithic industry is not the only consideration which matters. More important, the Kenya Capsian and its makers represent the south-western extremity of the Negro aquatic civilization which extended right across Africa in the southern Saharan belt and up the Nile valley to East Africa. These areas appear to have been occupied during a temporary wet period in which lake-levels were high and rivers swollen. This civilization was at its zenith about 7000 before our era. The riparian peoples caught fish and aquatic animals with typical bone spears and harpoons manufactured with stone tools. They are found at Lake Edward in the western Rift valley and on the former shoreline of Lake Nakuru. Basket and pottery making was known, and the latter represented one of the earliest uses of pottery-firing anywhere in the world. This all points to a sedentary society with the principal habitat situated at the water's edge.

D: The Neolithic

Only a few years ago, for want of archaeological evidence, stock-raising and, above all, agriculture were regarded as not having been very advanced prior to the first millennium, except in the sites along the Nile valley related to the Khartoum Neolithic. It is still a matter of speculation whether the fishermen groups (which were partly sedentary living beside the great lakes and rivers from the seventh and sixth millennia onwards) were at the origin of pastoralism, and perhaps also of agriculture. This change in their way of life was due partly to the pressures exerted by the environment (the sudden increase in the drying up of the Sahara from the beginning of the third millennium) and partly to their advanced technology, since, as we know, they already had pottery. However, it is thought that these people were receptive to the notion of collective food production, particularly of animal and plant domestication, which was to spread throughout the region from the third millennium onwards and to soften the impact of the change of climate on natural resources.

The best-known site from this period is Esh Shaheinab, in the Sudan, which is situated on an old terrace slightly to the north of the confluence of the Blue and White Niles. In addition to the discovery there of a lithic industry consisting of geometrical microliths, A. J. Arkell found harpoons perforated at the base and fish-hooks made of shells, both of which testify to the existence of fishing as a permanent activity, rhyolite adzes, gouges, small polished bone axes, and pottery with a wavy-lined and dotted decorative motif. The bone remains included wild species, many of them fish, but also goats and occasionally sheep. The Esh Shaheinab site dates from the second half of the fourth millennium. At the Kadero site, which is located nearby and is very similar in the type of material discovered, nine-tenths of the remains collected are from domesticated species, including members of the *Bovidae* family.

At Agordat in the Eritrea province of Ethiopia, traces have been found of four villages which were inhabited on a semi-permanent basis. Although study has been confined to the surface layers, the site has produced axes, polished stone hammers, stone discs and bracelets, pottery with an embossed or grooved herring-bone pattern, pearls, lip ornaments and necklaces. The presence of grinding-stones, mortars and a stone figurine representing a cattle species similar to those raised by the C-Group populations centred on Nubia and to the west does not necessarily prove that there was an agricultural and pastoral economy, but suggests that there might have been. In the Godebra shelter near Aksum dating from the third millennium, grains of the *Eleusine coracana* variety of millet have been found in conjunction with a geometrical microlith industry and pottery. No trace has yet been found in Ethiopia of the ancient cultivation of tef (*Era grostis tef*) which is still the staple and highly nutritious cereal consumed by many ethnic groups in northern Ethiopia, or of the Abyssinian banana (*Ensete edule*), which is more widespread in the south, or of wheat or barley.

In Kenya, although evidence of the existence of agriculture is still lacking, there are ample vestiges of pastoralism throughout the Rift valley as far down as Tanzania, as well as in the highlands. These vestiges are found either in burial places, such as the cremation sites at the Njoro River Cave near Nakuru and the Keringet Cave near Molo, or in the cairn-covered grave in the Ngorongoro crater in northern Tanzania, where the skeleton is in the folded position. All these sites provide a range of archaeological artefacts such as grinding-stones and pounders; or else of settlement sites, such as Crescent Island near Lake Naivasha and Narosura in southern Kenya. At Narosura, 95 per cent of the fauna identified are of domestic animals and consist of 57 per cent goats and sheep and 39 per cent cattle. A study of the bone remains has shown that large animals were slaughtered when they reached old age, while goats and sheep were killed when they were much younger. The conclusion we can draw is that cattle were raised more for their milk – and perhaps for their blood, as among the present-day Masai – than for their meat. Here, again, the presence of grinding stones and pounders are only indirect evidence for the existence of some kind of agriculture.

The introduction of pastoralism and agriculture, which were very frequently linked in a mixed economy, has often been presented, in the case of East Africa, as being the outcome of two influences, one flowing from what is now the southern Sahara towards the Sudanese region, and the other from Egypt towards Nubia (Khartoum). The process of Neolithization may have reached the Ethiopian highlands and then been carried southwards by small-scale movements of Cushitic-speaking peoples. However, as is often the case, the change to a production economy was gradual, and the archaeological evidence shows that the existing substratum continued to play an important economic and technological role. Hunting and fishing went on as in the past, and there was no break in continuity with the material culture of the small fishermen groups which had become partly sedentary well before the third millennium, or even with the hunter-gatherers, who did not know the use of pottery (the Kenya Capsian-Elmenteitian). While there is as yet little evidence that agriculture was very advanced, it is known to have existed and the raising of sheep, followed by goats and cattle, developed very rapidly from the third millennium onwards and above all during the second millennium. When the Iron Age began, these East African peoples had probably already advanced beyond the pre-agricultural stage.

E: The aquatic tradition of middle and eastern Africa

Eight to ten thousand years ago the climate of Africa was unusually wet, so that the lakes were bigger and more numerous, the swamps more extensive, the rivers fuller and longer and the seasonal streams longer lasting. In this situation there spread right across the continent, from the Atlantic coast to the Nile Basin, in a broad belt lying between a much shrunken Sahara and an enlarged equatorial forest, a very distinctive way of life intimately connected with the waters, their banks and their food-resources, and especially with advanced techniques of boat-building and fishing. This aquatic civilization, as we might call it, is known from numerous archaeological sites in the Saharan highlands and the southern fringe of the desert from the upper Niger, through the Chad Basin to the middle Nile, and thence southward as far as the East African Rift valleys and the equator. In the western rift it has been recognized at Isangho on the Zaïre shore of Lake Edward, whereas in the eastern rift sites are found along the ancient high shorelines of lakes Turkana and Nakuru, the former low-lying, the latter farther south in the Rift valley's elevated stretch. The most important site lying by this greater Lake Nakuru is called Gamble's Cave: it is in fact a rock-shelter which was excavated by Dr L. S. B. Leakey in the 1920s. The lowest occupation layer was found to contain Late Stone Age remains of the type called Kenya Capsian. However, the presence of distinctive pottery and bonework and the recent dating of this layer to 6000 or so enable us now to see the Kenya Capsian as the local expression of the great African aquatic tradition.

Fish-bones and mollusc-shells, as well as bones of aquatic mammals and reptiles (reed-rats and turtles, and sometimes hippos and crocodiles), occurring at these old waterside camps and settlements, provide useful economic insights. But land animals were hunted too; and very probably nutritious plants of the waters and marshes were gathered and eaten, maybe quite systematically. The technology for obtaining and preparing food had some remarkably advanced features – harpoon heads carved from bone (by means of precious stone tools) and pottery vessels. The harpoons were fixed into the ends of wooden spears with line attachments and thus used for catching fish and other aquatic animals either from boats or from the water's edge. The pots were large and decorated, often by means of fish-bones or shells, in patterns known as wavy-line and dotted wavy-line. Though it has its variations, the wavy-line/dotted wavy-line tradition is distinct enough to prevent confusion with other and later pottery types in these broad regions. Some of the decorative patterns, as well as the large open shapes of these pottery vessels, may be derived from those of baskets, such as may well have been used to hold the catch of fish.

Along the East African lake-shore sites, as well as along the middle Nile and in the Sahara, the forerunner of this aquatic civilization has been dated to 8000–5000 before our era. Its zenith and full extent were reached in the seventh millennium. The first harpoons were probably carved a little earlier while the discovery of how to make pottery occurred no later than 6000 before our era. These pottery vessels are not only the most ancient in Africa, but among the earliest manufactured anywhere in the world. There can be little doubt that this was an invention occurring independently somewhere in this middle African belt.

There is nothing to suggest that these aquatic people practised any agriculture between 7000 and 10 000 years ago, whether in East Africa or in other parts of their vast range. Nevertheless, this very expansion and the rapidity with which it occurred, together with the technological sophistication of this new way of life, demonstrate its cultural prestige and dominance for as long as this very wet period lasted. To consider it as just one other variant of the Late Stone Age hunter-gatherer cultures is, therefore, to miss completely its distinctiveness and achievements. These people may not have lived in permanently settled villages, but, with assured food supplies from the great lakes and rivers and a technology geared to exploit this situation effectively, they were able to maintain community settlements bigger and more stable than had any previous populations. Not only did this encourage population increase; it also provided a new social and intellectual climate, of which both the complex craftsmanship involved in making boats and harpoons, baskets and pots, and the more sophisticated style of living which made use of these things, are equally diagnostic.

The role of pottery is especially important – more so than historians, and even archaeologists, have usually appreciated. Being fragile, pottery vessels are of limited usefulness to mobile societies lacking fixed bases, and thus to most hunter-gatherers. But for settled communities, pots have a civilizing and home-drawing significance in allowing versatility and new sophistication in the preparation and cooking of food.

These aquatic people of West and East Africa may have varied somewhat in their physical type. But the few skeletal remains which have been recovered indicate that the stock was basically negroid.[8] In fact, it seems that it was this very spread and success of the aquatic culture and economy 9000 or 10 000 years ago which established the dominance of a definitely negroid type right across the Sudan belt, the middle and upper Nile Basin and the northerly part of East Africa. Very likely this was associated with the geographical expansion and consequent break-up and differentiation of the big language family (or phylum) which Greenberg calls Nilo-Saharan. This is now extremely fragmented and reaches all the way from the upper Niger to central Tanzania: such fragmentation is itself a sign of an antiquity of several thousand years for this so widely distributed family, an antiquity greater than that of other language families (that is, Niger–Congo and various branches of Afro-Asiatic) which have intruded into this middle African zone. Among the regions where Nilo-Saharan held its own, including its easterly division known as Chari-Nile, are those with lakes, swamps and rivers, that is, those where the old aquatic way of life, intimately associated with Nilo-Saharan speech, one might imagine, was able to persist longest even if in modified form.

This discussion of the great aquatic civilization and the Nilo-Saharan languages has roamed much farther in both time and space than might seem appropriate in this chapter and volume. But it is a highly important and hitherto neglected aspect of the history of the African peoples, and one which has left important marks on the subsequent populations, their culture and economies, across a large part of the continent, including East Africa.

From about 5000 years before our era, the effects of the widespread drying-out of the climate began to be felt. Lake-levels fell and the economy

8. The frequent statement that the 'Kenya Capsian' people were caucasoid is based on misinterpretation of Leakey's work at Gamble's Cave and elsewhere: see *J. Afr. Hist.*, XV (1974), p. 534.

based on harvesting aquatic resources went into decline. However, it continued for some time longer in the Rift valley in Kenya. Over a period from 2000 to 1000 before our era, new populations arrived in the region from Ethiopia, bringing cattle and perhaps some agricultural practices with them.

PLATE 19.1 *Olduvai Gorge, northern Tanzania. The gorge, cut more than a hundred metres through the plain, reveals a succession of layers (mostly old lake-beds). The lowest layers, which are about 2 million years old, contain the remains of some of the earliest inhabitants, their tools (Oldowan type) and food waste. The upper layers contain handaxes and other implements of the Acheulian tradition* (J. E. G. Sutton)

PLATE 19.2 *Isimila, southern highlands of Tanzania. A view along the erosion gully revealing the beds in which Acheulian tools have been found* (J. E. G. Sutton)

PLATE 19.3 *Isimila. A concentration of Acheulian handaxes, cleavers and other tools. (The small trowel in the centre is for scale)* (J. E. G. Sutton)

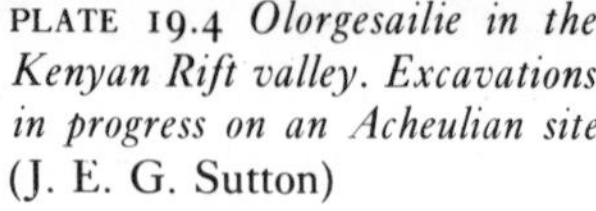

PLATE 19.4 *Olorgesailie in the Kenyan Rift valley. Excavations in progress on an Acheulian site* (J. E. G. Sutton)

PLATE 19.5 *Apis Rock* (*Nasera*), *northern Tanzania. Excavations have revealed a succession of Late Stone Age occupations under the shelter, clearly visible on the right* (J. E. G. Sutton)

20 Prehistory in southern Africa

J. D. CLARK

The earliest hominids

Darwin and Huxley considered the tropics, and within them perhaps the African continent, as being the habitat in which man had his origins, for it is here that the chimpanzee and the gorilla, man's closest relatives among the primates, are to be found. These pongids, like the common ancestor of apes and man, are forest-dwellers and their morphological characteristics show that they must have evolved over a very long period of adaptation to living in the tropical lowland and montane forests. Man, on the other hand, evolved, not in the forest, but in the savannah lands, and the earliest hominid fossils, from eastern and southern Africa, are found in the semi-arid grasslands and deciduous woodlands where the ancestral form has been faced with an entirely different set of problems for successful survival and with infinitely greater potential resources than those available to the anthropoids.

There is as yet no general agreement as to when the hominid and pongid lines diverged. The palaeontological evidence has been interpreted as indicating that it was possibly sometime in the earlier Cenozoic, the lower Miocene, about 25 million years ago, that that divergence took place. On the other hand, the recent calibration work on the comparative biochemistry of primates (chromosomes, serum proteins, haemoglobin and immunological differences between man, apes and Old World monkeys) suggests that the separation took place no earlier than 10 and perhaps as late as 4 million years ago. It might be thought that the evidence provided by the fossils themselves would be the most reliable, but unfortunately this is not so as, if the long chronology is correct, the crucial period when the hominids can be expected to have already become significantly differentiated from the lineage of the great apes – the late Miocene/earlier Pliocene (12–5 million years ago) – is one from which there is at present very little fossil primate evidence. It is only towards the close of the Pliocene that fragmentary fossil material becomes available again and there can be no doubt that fossil hominids were present in the record by that time.

The late Miocene fossil *Ramapithecus wickeri,* recovered from Fort Ternan in the Lake Victoria Basin, is some 12–14 million years old. It is,

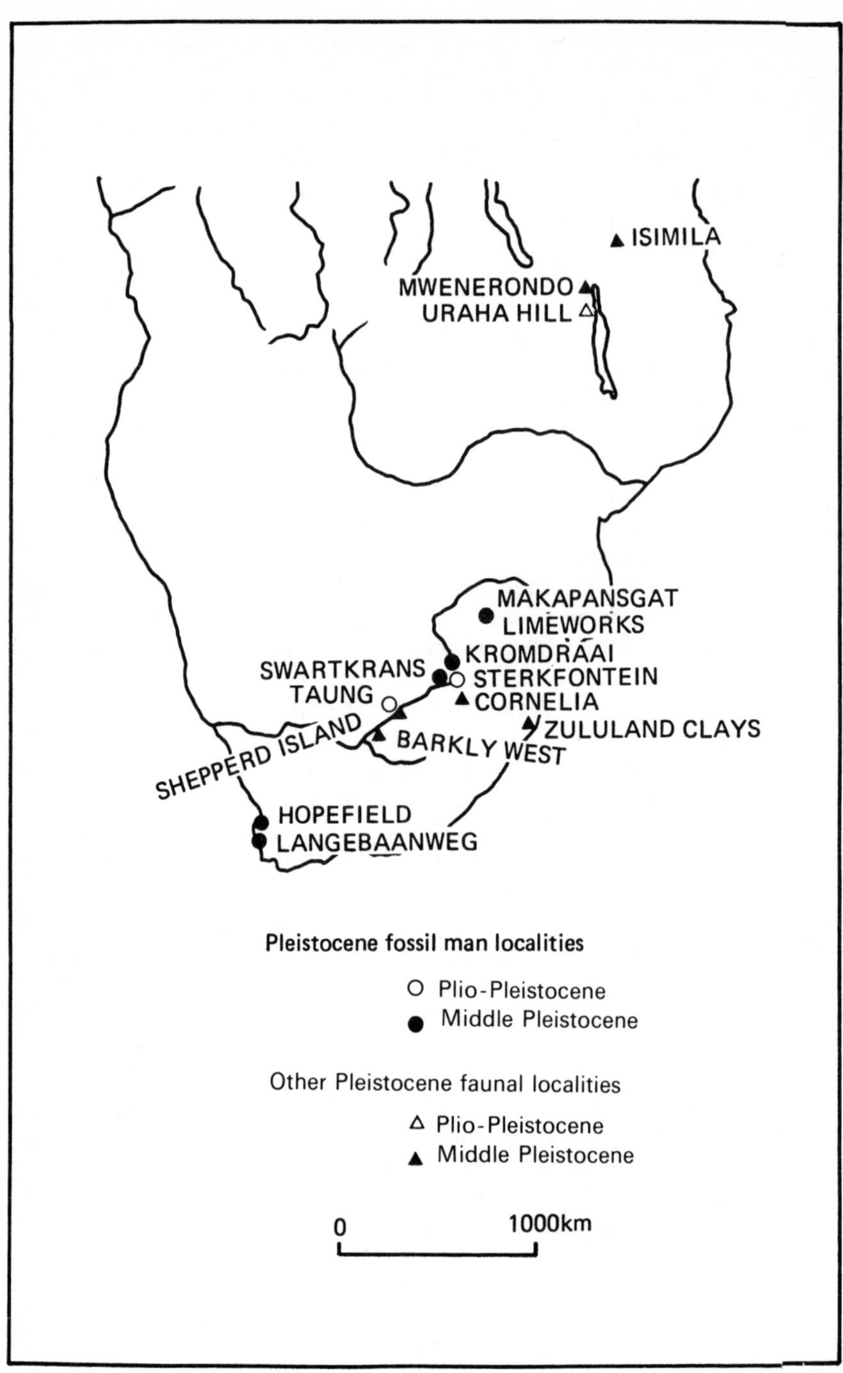

FIG. 20.1 *Late Pliocene/earlier Pleistocene main faunal and fossil man localities in southern Africa (after J. D. Clark, 1970)*

unfortunately, known only from portions of the face and teeth but these show characteristics that suggest classification as a hominid. To be certain, however, that the rest of the anatomy and the form of locomotion were not very different from those of hominids, less fragmentary remains are needed and particularly post-cranial bones. It is unfortunately necessary, therefore, to reserve judgement for the present as to whether this form was already differentiated as a hominid. *Ramapithecus* occupied a habitat dominated by gallery forest, streams and savannah at a time when the evergreen forests that now survive only south of the Great Escarpment in South Africa were much more extensive in southern Africa than they are today. Since *Ramapithecus* was present in both East Africa and north-western India, it was probably present also in the southern African savannahs.

The earliest unequivocal evidence for hominids dates from about 5 million years ago, by which time the Australopithecines or Man Apes had already made their appearance in the East African part of the Great Rift valley. These Australopithecines occupied the southern savannah lands as well as those of eastern Africa and the fossils from South Africa are believed to date from the late Pliocene/earliest Pleistocene time-range some 2·5–3·0 million years ago.

Most of the Pliocene geological period was a time of relatively stable climate which facilitated the development and spread of biologically adapted species in the savannah. This period of comparative stability was brought to an end by the general lowering of world temperature and by major tectonic movements and volcanicity, in particular throughout the length of the Great Rift valley. The drainage pattern of a number of the African river systems and lake basins also underwent – often drastic – modification at this time through tectonic warping of the earth's crust. The lowered temperatures that mark the beginning of the Pleistocene period were also accompanied by decreasing rainfall and increasing desiccation so that the arid Karroo bush spread extensively in southern Africa at the expense of the grasslands and forests.

These major changes in climate and environment necessitated significant readjustments on the part of the hominids and an attendant greater diversification in their morphology, probably dictated by adaptative responses to the new environmental pressures.[1] By this time it is certain that the ancestral form of the hominids (whether a knuckle-walker or more persistently bipedal) which had moved out of the forest into the savannah some time during the Pliocene, or perhaps before, had undergone fairly

1. The only important locality in southern Africa yielding fossils of this period is that of Langebaanweg in the western Cape. The site is not far from the coast and the environment is estuarine and terrestrial, preserving a rich fauna of archaic forms of African mammals indicating an age of *c.* 3–5 million years. Although no hominid remains have yet been found here, primate fossils are present and there is every possibility that continuing work at Langebaanweg may produce evidence of hominids for comparison with those of this age from East Africa.

rapid genetic change in response to adaptation to more than one new ecological niche, so that by the Lower Pleistocene in southern Africa there appear to have been at least three forms present that were also, most probably, interspecifically fertile.

The first Australopithecine fossil, a juvenile, was found in 1924 in a lime-cemented breccia in a cave at Taung in the north of the Cape Province in South Africa. The first adult individual was discovered in 1936, again in old cave deposits, this time in the Krugersdorp region of the Transvaal. Since then a large number of Australopithecine and other hominid fossils have been recovered as a result of intensive teamwork studies at the level of the waterlaid sediments in the trough of the East African Rift and in the deep caves of the interior limestone plateau regions of South Africa where the conditions are favourable to the preservation of fossils of this age.

Apart from these regions, the only other fossil ascribed to the Australopithecine comes from the Lake Chad Basin at Korotoro. However, this specimen is now considered as being more recent. Hence, although a very large number of Australopithecine fossils are now known, these come from a limited number of localities, mostly from South African caves and the Rift valley sites, since it is comparatively rarely that favourable conditions exist for the preservation of fossil bone. In many regions of Africa, acid soils, erosion and other phenomena have precluded the preservation of fossils, in the dense West African forest region, for example; there is, none the less, good reason to believe that several differential hominid forms were widespread in the tropical savannah lands some 2–3 million years ago. In eastern Africa, the fossils are becoming increasingly well dated by radiometric methods and by the palaeo-magnetic reversal time-scale. As yet, the fossils from South Africa can be dated only relatively by palaeontological and geomorphological comparisons. Latest assessments based on the studies of pigs, elephants and hyenas, suggest that the earlier Transvaal fossils are about 2·5 million years old at least. The cave breccias yielding these fossils, at Makapan Limeworks and the Sterkfontein type site, contain a few mammalian forms in common with those of the East African faunal assemblages that show morphological features comparable with those of the Plio–Pleistocene boundary.

The earlier South African Australopithecines were mostly of gracile build (*A. africanus*), on an average 1·4 m tall with an erect gait, the lower limbs adapted to fully bipedal locomotion and the forelimbs adapted to tool use. The head was centrally placed on the vertebral column which was supported by the essentially human and basin-like pelvis. The cranial capacity was more like that of a gorilla (450–550 cc) than of a modern man, though the post-cranial skeleton and the dentition show essentially a human form. The face, however, is more ape-like, the lower part protruding, the cheek bones pushed out and with heavy ridges above the orbits. The areas for the attachment of the masticatory and neck muscles show these to have been very powerful.

In the later cave sites, Swartkrans and Kromdraai (and most probably also, it is now thought, Taung), the predominant form is much more robust (*A. robustus*). This is a much heavier individual weighing about 68 kilos and the large males were furnished with bony crests, one running over the top and another round the back of the skull for the attachment of the very powerful neck and masticatory muscles. It was generally thought that the earlier forms were all gracile (*A. africanus*) and the later all robust (*A. robustus*) but recent anthropometric studies are showing that the differentiation is not as clear-cut as was at first thought and both robust and gracile forms have now been shown to occur together in at least one of the South African sites (Makapan). Similarly, both robust and gracile forms are found together in the Lower Pleistocene in East Africa and the evidence from this region suggests that their differentiation from a common, more gracile, ancestor may have taken place as early as 5 million years ago.

Recently, in 1972, from the north-eastern part of the Lake Turkana Basin and dating between 3·0 and 2·6 million years ago, a fossil cranium (with a cranial capacity of about 810 cc), long bones and other fragmentary cranial and post-cranial fossils have been found that show many close affinities with *Homo* although also exhibiting features (in particular about the face and dentition) that link them with the Australopithecines. Other related fossils with enlarged cranial capacities and classified either as advanced Australopithecines or early *Homo* (*H. habilis*) are known from other sites in East Africa, notably from the Olduvai Gorge in northern Tanzania, and date from between 2·0 and 1·75 million years ago.[2] It is most probable that an early *Homo* form was also present in southern Africa at this time although characteristic fossils remain to be found.

This likelihood is borne out by the discovery in 1975, in the Hadar, in the Ethiopian part of the Rift valley known as the Afar Triangle, of hominid fossils dating from some 3 million years ago. Dr D. Johanson suggests that the twelve individuals discovered could belong to three different taxa: a gracile hominid represented by a very well preserved skeleton, a robust form comparable to *A. robustus,* and a third form identified by the lower and upper maxilia, which is closer to *Homo sapiens.* If this were confirmed, it would follow that the *Homo* lineage was already differentiated from the Australopithecines 3 million years ago.

Early hominid way of life

Although a large number of Australopithecine hominid fossils have been found in the South African caves, it seems unlikely, indeed improbable, that the contexts in which they occur there represent their home-bases or the

2. The robust Australopithecine facial fragment and palate from Chesowanja in the Lake Baringo Basin is now believed to be 3.0 million years old and, since this also shows some features that link it to *Homo sapiens indet*. It may belong close to the time when the *Homo* lineage began to become differentiated from the Australopithecines.

places where they lived. At one time it used to be thought that the deep limestone caves in the Transvaal were the living places of the hominids and that the fossil animal bones they contained were the various parts of the animals preyed upon that had been carried back by the hominids for making into weapons and other equipment. This Osteodontokeratic culture, as it was called, can, however, more reliably be interpreted as the food waste of some carnivore, since careful study of the faunal remains from the Swartkrans site shows that the accumulation of Australopithecine and other mammalian fossils might have resulted from several different causes, the most significant, at that site, being predation by large carnivores, most probably leopards or tigers. However, there is no consensus regarding this point (cf. Chapter 17, pp. 415–17).

Since most other materials are destroyed fairly rapidly, other than in exceptional circumstances, the earliest of man's artefacts that have survived are made from stone. However, no generally accepted stone artefacts occur in the cave breccias that have yielded the older hominid fossils from South Africa (Makapan, Sterkfontein), although stone tools are known from three sealed East African hominid sites which are 2·5 million years or more old. As the East African evidence shows us, occupation sites there were situated close to a lake-shore or the bank of a stream draining into a lake and are identified by a limited concentration of bones and stone artefacts. There can be no doubt, from the various species and numbers of individual animals represented by the deliberately broken faunal remains on these sites, that these bones are the remains of the collective hunting/scavenging activities of the hominids who used the stone tools, amongst other activities, to process the meat and bone as well as the plant foods that must have made up the major part of their diet. The diversity of the remains and their varying state of preservation suggests that these home-bases were occupied over a period of several days at least and not simply on a single occasion, although so-called kill sites are also known where the remains of a single large animal had been butchered by a group. The generally small area covered by the occupation waste on the living sites suggests that the group was probably small and perhaps consisted of no more than two or three families. The extent to which these early hominids were the predatory killers they have sometimes been made out to be is debatable and it seems much more likely that, while they derived an increasing proportion of their sustenance from meat, they were no more aggressive than other large carnivores and probably appreciably less so because they were not dependent on meat alone but used also an abundance of plant resources. Clearly, however, it was the organization of the hunt that provided the stimulus for early man to develop a more rigidly structured socio-economic pattern which was made possible by his ability to manufacture tools for specific purposes. The evidence of the East African home-bases, to which the products of the hunting and collecting activities were regularly brought back, shows that the late Pliocene/Lower Pleistocene hominids were probably organized in open social groups, the composition of which may have changed frequently. These groups were held together by the practice of food-sharing and the length of time during which the young were dependent upon their parents for food and instruction (i.e. much the same as the human child today). The significant activities that most probably led to the making of stone tools for obtaining flakes for cutting were hunting and meat eating. Hunting required efficient organization and communication among the participants and this, in time, led to the development of language. Differentiation of activities as between males and females can be expected to have begun about this time also, the males now concentrating on hunting and the females on collecting and the care of the young.

If, however, the Transvaal caves were not the living places of the hominids but the larders of some other large carnivore, to which the hominids themselves at times fell victim, it seems likely that the Australopithecines were not, in fact, living too far away for, in the later breccias in the Sterkfontein group of caves (Swartkrans, Sterkfontein extension site and Kromdraai) which could be about 1·5 million years old, simple stone artefacts have been found in association with the fossils. They are made from rocks foreign to the immediate area of the cave – cobbles of quartzite, quartz and diabase – and they presumably came from a nearby camp.

Because most of the hominid remains from the later cave breccias of Swartkrans and Kromdraai represent the robust Australopithecine, it has been assumed that this form was the tool maker, as also at the nearby Sterkfontein extension site. However, a fragmentary cranium and face with some post-cranial bones representing an early *Homo* species are present in the same deposit at Swartkrans and this form is more likely to be that associated with the tools. This does not, however, preclude the possibility that the Australopithecines also made tools, since a recent experimental study at Bristol has graphically demonstrated the ability of a young orang-utang to strike flakes for securing food after the process had been demonstrated to him and he was able to observe the use to which these flakes could be put. Since both Australopithecine and *Homo* fossils are found in East and South Africa in the same localities and relate to very similar or identical ecological niches, it is even more likely that *Australopithecus robustus* had the ability to make simple tools such as those that belong to the earliest known industrial complex, the Oldowan, though the invention of tool-making appears to be more specifically related to the appearance of early *Homo* forms (e.g. *H. habilis* and others) about 2·5 million years ago.

The earliest stone tools: the Oldowan Industrial Complex

Although the earliest of man's artefacts that have survived are made from stone, it needs to be remembered, nevertheless, that a number of other materials – wood, bark, bone, horn, hide, and so on – could also have been used.

A very long period of tool *using*, during which suitably shaped artefacts received minimal or no modification, can be expected to have preceded intentional tool *making*, behind which lies the express intention of producing a small number of distinctive kinds of tools from some quite different material. After flaking or other modification, these would then sometimes be further shaped by retouching or trimming. From the very beginning the stone artefacts demonstrate the ability of the hominids to strike flakes and to understand the principles of stone technology.

The earliest stone tool complex of which we have evidence from anywhere in the world has been named the Oldowan – from the Olduvai Gorge in Tanzania – and the earliest examples of it from East Africa date from 2·6 million years ago.[3] It is possible that some of the finds made in ancient river gravels (those of the Vaal or the Zambezi), or lying on high-level marine platforms around the coasts in southern Africa, may also belong in this time-range. However, since these artefacts have not yet been found sealed in circumstances where they can be dated, judgement as to their antiquity has to be reserved as they could be appreciably younger. It might have been expected that the Malawi rift, like the East African rift, would have preserved artefacts from this time as well as hominid fossils. While the northern end (Malawi) has yielded a Plio–Pleistocene faunal assemblage that forms the only important link between those of East and South Africa, this area was not, for some reason, favoured for occupation by early man until much later and primates in general are only rarely found in the sediments of these deep southern rift basins.

The tools from the later Australopithecine sites (Swartkrans, Sterkfontein extension site and Kromdraai) near Krugersdorp are of several distinctive kinds: choppers made by flaking a cobble or chunk from one or both faces to form an irregular chopping edge; polyhedral stones which often show evidence of bruising and use for heavy battering; flat-based and rounded-backed tools with a steep scraping edge worked on part of the circumference; flakes suitable for cutting and skinning and the cores from which such flakes were intentionally struck. Flakes and waste from flaking are generally uncommon at the Sterkfontein extension and Swartkrans sites which is another reason for supposing that they were not living places. However, as systematic excavation of the breccias at these two sites progresses, and more complete assemblages become available, we can expect to know considerably more regarding the tool-kit of these early hominids.

3. The KBS tuff tools of Koobi Fora had been dated from 2.6 million years ago by the potassium-argon method. However, recent results and faunal correlations with the Shunguna formation of the Omo Basin and the Koobi Fora formation of Lake Turkana suggest that their age may have been overestimated and that the more likely date may be 1.8 million years ago.

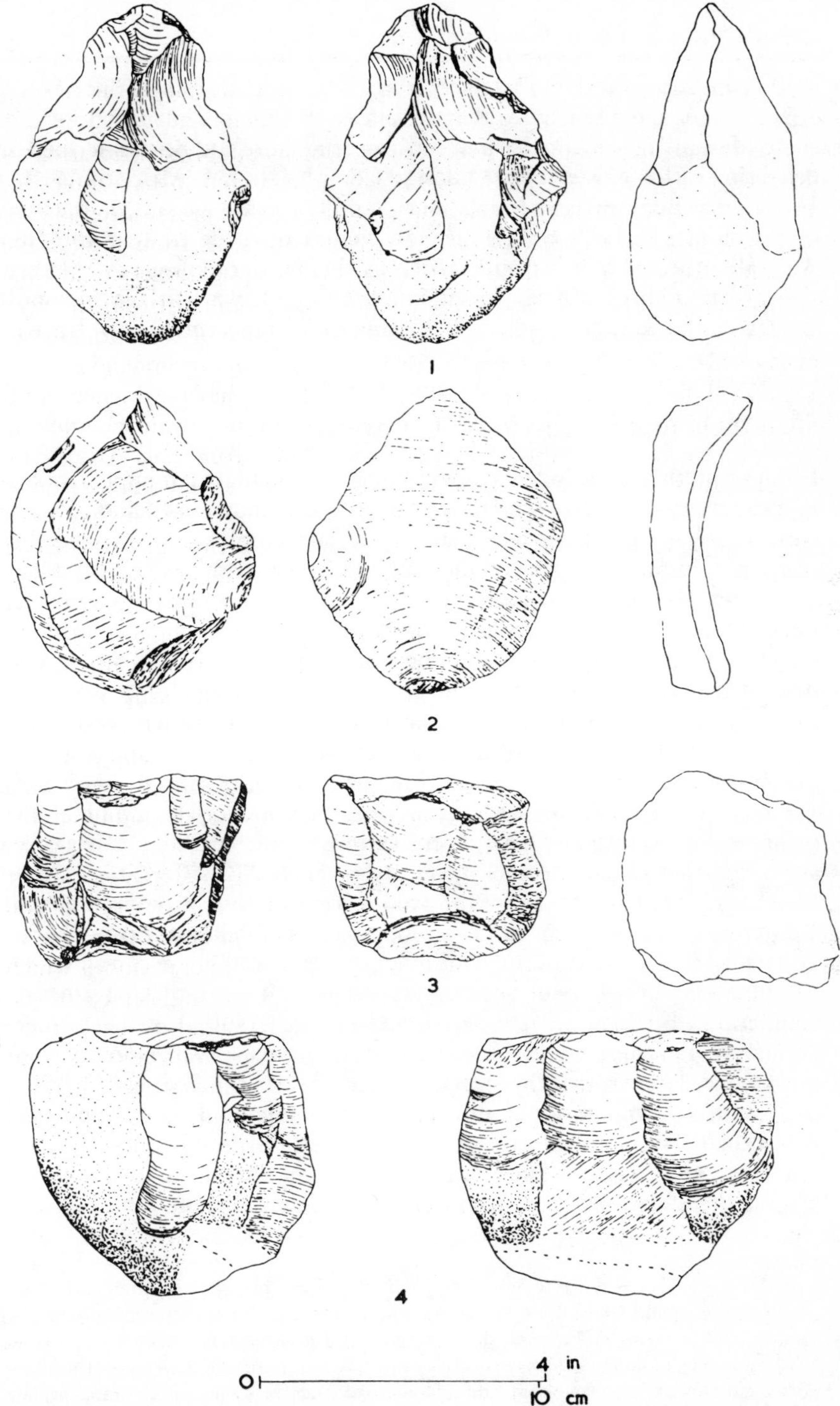

FIG. 20.2 *Lower Acheulian hand-axe, flake and two core/choppers from the Middle Breccia, Sterkfontein (after R. Mason, 1962)*

On comparison with the artefacts from the East African sites, these South African tools show attributes that are closer to the more advanced form of the Oldowan than to the earlier and can, therefore, be best described as belonging with the Developed Oldowan Complex. In East Africa the earliest Developed Oldowan dates from about 1·5 million years ago and, on the basis of the faunal remains also, it is now generally accepted that the later Australopithecine sites in South Africa also belong in this range of time.[4] By then also there appear to be two fairly clear hominid lines – that of the robust Australopithecine and another comprising early representatives of the true *Homo* line.

The Acheulian Industrial Complex

From about this time also a second industrial entity makes its appearance. It is characterized by large bifacial cutting tools known as handaxes and cleavers and is named the Acheulian Industrial Complex. It is distinguished from the Oldowan by a general increase in size and by the fact that the tools are often made from large flakes, both force and skill being required to break up the blocks and boulders that furnished such flakes. By contrast, the Oldowan tools are all such as can be held in the palm of the hand or, for more delicate work, with the precision grip between finger and thumb. The Developed Oldowan and the Acheulian Complexes have been represented as two contemporary evolving entities that are sometimes found either as purely Oldowan or purely Acheulian, or sometimes mixed together in varying proportions on the same occupation horizon. These two technological traditions have been variously interpreted. It has been suggested that they were each made by a genetically different species of hominid or, again, that they are the products of different activities requiring a different set of tools related to varying patterns of behaviour (see Chapter 19). These two traditions continue and are found in innumerable combinations up to about 200 000 years ago, that is, until long after the competition between *A. robustus* and *Homo* had resulted in the former's extinction. For these reasons, the explanations for these two distinctive tool-kits favoured here is that they relate to different sets of activities or patterns of resource exploitation, influenced by individual and traditional preferences and manufactured by a single hominid population as circumstances dictated. The relatively sudden appearance of the Acheulian shows, therefore, that new resources were being exploited or improved

4. Dr C. K. Brain recently announced that the oldest breccia containing remains of *Australopithecus* and *Homo* could be divided into two levels. The older level I produced *A. robustus* and *Homo* sp. and a single definitely identifiable stone tool, while the more recent level II is said to contain *Homo* sp. (*Telanthropus*) and a pebble industry featuring two Acheulian handaxes. Level II probably dates to 500 000 years ago. C. K. Brain, personal communication.

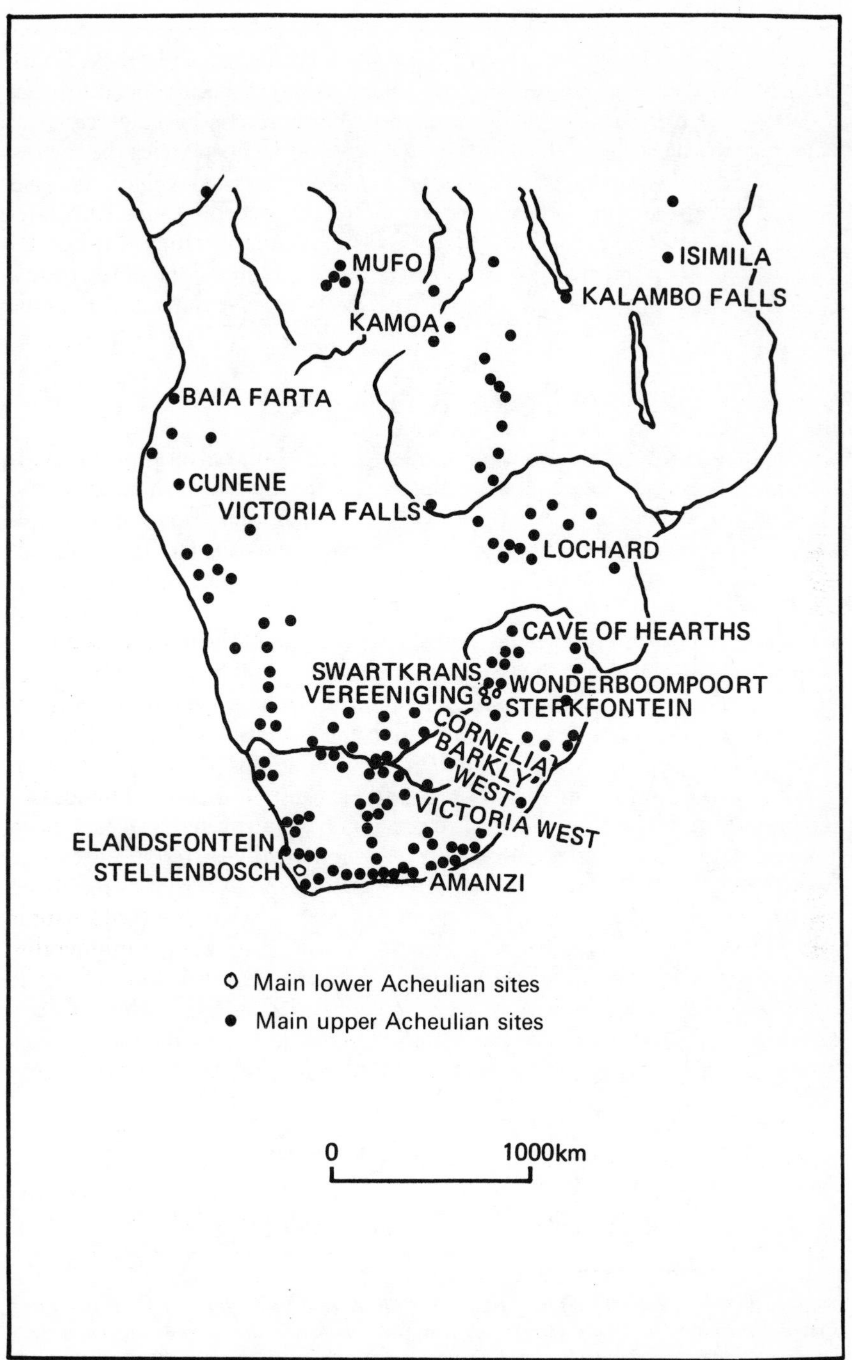

FIG 20.3 *The distribution of Acheulian sites in southern Africa (after J. D. Clark, 1970)*

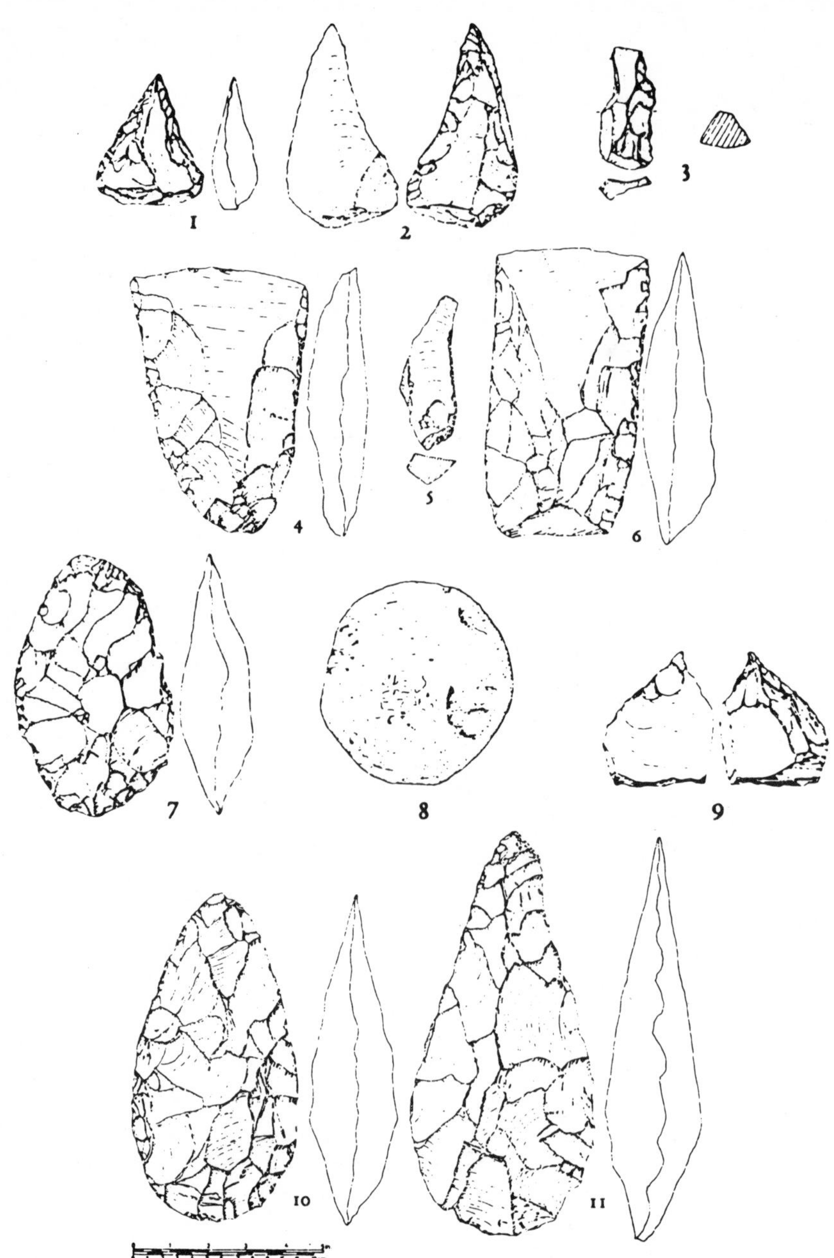

FIG. 20.4 *Upper Acheulian tools from Kalambo Falls, Zambia (after J. D. Clark, 1970), dated to more than 190 000 years b.p. (large tools quartzite, small tools chert): 1, convergent scraper; 2, concave side scraper; 3, denticulated side scraper; 4, divergent edged cleaver; 5, flake knife with marginal retouch; 6, parallel edged cleaver; 7, ovate hand-axe; 8, spheroid; 9, awl or bec; 10, elongate ovate hand-axe; 11, lanceolate hand-axe*

methods had been invented for dealing with those already being processed with the Oldowan-type tool-kit.

The earliest assemblages that belong to the Acheulian and that may be nearly contemporary with the hominids, *Homo* sp. and *A. robustus* from Swartkrans, come from two adjacent sites at the junction of the Vaal and its tributary the Klip river near Vereeniging. They are contained in a gravel terrace 10 metres above the present river and the artefacts are mostly abraded and so are derived and not in their original context. A range of tools is represented – pointed handaxes made by the removal of a very few large flakes, cleavers, polyhedral stones, choppers, core-scrapers and a number of minimally modified flake tools as well as cores and waste. These all exhibit hard hammer technique and in this respect are the equivalent of the Abbevillian of Europe. The presence of two handaxe-like forms at the Sterkfontein extension site lends credence to the suggestion that it is not far removed in time from the Klip river sites (Three Rivers and Klipplaatdrif). Occasional finds of other early-looking assemblages have been made from different parts of southern Africa – for instance, from old river terraces at Stellenbosch in the Cape Province or from near Livingstone in Zambia – but they are incomplete and even less satisfactorily dated.

Somewhere between 1 million and 700 000 years ago, the early *Homo* stock (represented by the hominid 1470 skull from Koobi Fora, East Turkana, and by *Homo habilis* fossils from the Olduvai Gorge, the Omo basin and other sites) was replaced by a more robust, larger-brained form known as *Homo erectus*. Roughly at the same time or somewhat earlier, there had been a rapid dispersal of hominid groups into North Africa and out of Africa into Europe and Asia, and *H. erectus* fossils and cultural remains are found in several widely separated parts of the Old World. In Africa, a large-brained form of *H. erectus* fossil is now known from the upper part of Bed II at the Olduvai Gorge, from the discoveries at Melka Konture in Ethiopia and from coastal and inland sites in north-west Africa and the Maghrib where they are associated with earlier Acheulian assemblages. *H. erectus* was most probably the member of the Acheulian in southern Africa, but no fossil discovery has so far been made.

It is with the appearance of the later, or more advanced, Acheulian that we begin to find a proliferation of sites in southern Africa – as in the whole of the continent – that strongly suggests an overall increase in the number and size of the hominid groups. The scarcity of sites belonging to earlier times may, in part, be due to the comparative sparseness of preserved sediments belonging to those times, but this is not likely to be the main reason to account for the marked increase in the number of recorded sites belonging to the later Acheulian and for the more extensive area that many of these cover. Although many sites are known, however (389 are recorded for South Africa in the *Atlas of African Prehistory*, most river systems that have been investigated having yielded assemblages of characteristic handaxes and cleavers), only a very few have been excavated and not many are in a primary context[5] which preserves the distribution scatter of artefacts and other evidence of habitation after the site has been abandoned by the occupants.

The excavated sites show the varied nature of the habitats and some of the behavioural practices of Acheulian man. None of these sites is as yet accurately dated because they all lie well beyond the range of radio-carbon dating and the rocks and sediments with which they are associated are unsuitable for potassium-argon or the palaeo-magnetic reversal chronology methods. The most northerly site is that of the Kalambo Falls on the Zambian–Tanzanian border in Central Africa, however, where a unique series of events has preserved wood in association with six or more stratified occupation floors. This wood can be dated and some from one of the later horizons has given a date by the amino-acid racemization method of more than 190 000 before our era (J. Bada, personal communication). Such a date is in agreement with that from Isimila in central Tanzania where a somewhat similar stratified Acheulian sequence is dated to about 260 000 years by the uranium/thorium method. It is unlikely that any of these assemblages is older than 700 000 years when the last major palaeo-magnetic reversal epoch (the Matuyama epoch) ended or earlier than 125 000 years ago when the last interglacial (Eemian) period began and more advanced industries were being practised. They belong essentially, therefore, to that time-range defined as the Middle Pleistocene.

The Kalambo Falls occupation concentrations were situated on sandbanks close to the river and presumably within the riparian forest that lined the banks at that time. Pollen evidence shows that the temperature at the beginning of the Acheulian sequence was warmer and the rainfall rather less than the present day, but the swing towards more arid conditions was insufficient to change markedly the pattern of the vegetation community which, then as now, was one of evergreen, riparian forest close to the river, of shallow, grass-filled, seasonally flooded valleys (*dambos*) and, on the higher slopes, *Brachystegia* woodland. Towards the end of the Acheulian sequence, however, there is evidence from the pollens and macroscopic plant remains of lowered temperatures and some increase in rainfall that enabled some species of plants now living as much as 300 metres higher to descend to the altitude of the local Kalambo Basin. The living horizons are each believed to represent one or two seasons' occupation at the most, after which the surface was covered by deposits of river sand, silt and mud on which subsequent and similar occupation then took place. These horizons were discrete concentrations with fairly sharply defined boundaries and they yielded a large number of handaxes and cleavers, many retouched flake tools and core-scrapers and a lesser number of picks, polyhedrals and spheroids.

5. For example, large quantities of Acheulian artefacts are present in the western part of the valley of the Vaal river and many of its tributaries but, while some of these assemblages show interesting technological changes, all of them appear to be in geological context and derived.

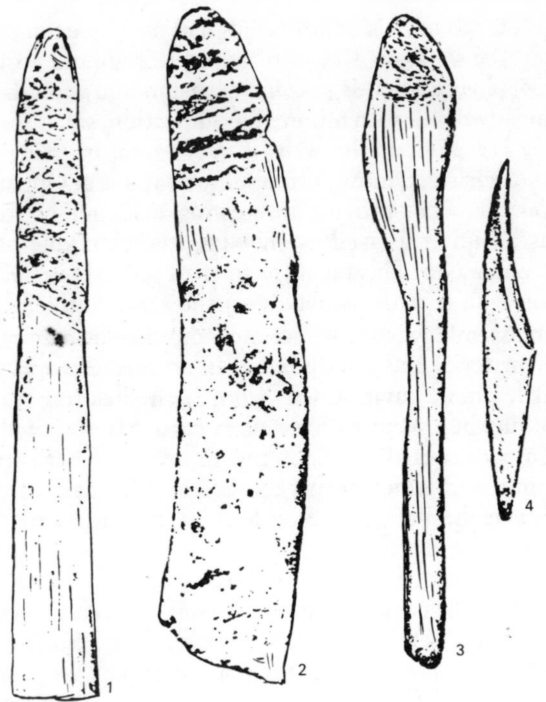

FIG. 20.5 *Wooden implements from Pleistocene sites in southern Africa (after J. D. Clark, 1970): 1, The grip end of a throwing stick from Peat 1, Florisbad Mineral Spring, age* c. *48 000 b.p. for comparison with 2, the grip end of an Australian throwing stick showing the cut marks made to prevent the hand from slipping; 3, club and 4, double pointed tool from Acheulian occupation floor at the Kalambo Falls, Zambia, age 190 000 b.p.*

Associated with the stone tools were several wooden implements – a club, digging-sticks, short pointed sticks (also, perhaps, used for digging), a thin, blade-like wooden tool and fragments of bark which may have served as carrying trays. Some of these occupation horizons provided ample evidence for the use of fire in the form of charred tree-trunks, charcoals, ash and oval, basin-shaped, concentrations of carbonized and compressed grasses and woody plants which may, perhaps, have been lined sleeping places. In addition, there were a number of carbonized seeds and fruits belonging to genera and species of edible plants that are still growing in the Kalambo Basin today. As these become ripe in the closing part of the dry season (September and October) it is thought that these Acheulian living floors represent dry season camp sites.

There were no fauna preserved at the Kalambo Falls but at Mwanganda's, near Karonga at the north-west end of Lake Malawi, is another site dating from the Middle Pleistocene where an elephant had been butchered close to a stream running eastwards to the lake-shore. At least three groups of individuals, it appeared, had taken part in these butchering activities as three separate groups of bones were found each together with the stone tools made for this specific occasion and then discarded. These tools were mostly flakes with minimal modification, small scrapers and a few choppers – a Developed Oldowan, in fact – and in them is reflected the butchery kit of earlier, Oldowan times. Excavations at Oppermansdrif, near Bloemhof on the Vaal, provide interesting evidence of Acheulian man's efficiency as a hunter as well as showing his technique of butchery and disposal of bone waste. This takes the form of several piles of bones adjacent to the stream course with handaxes on the same horizon.

Acheulian assemblages are sometimes found associated with outcrops of suitable raw material and incorporated in scree and workshop debris. We can learn little about environment from such sites (e.g. Gwelo Kopje in Zimbabwe) but they seem to have been regularly revisited – for instance Wonderboompoort near Pretoria in the Transvaal, where up to 3 metres of waste are found and which seems to have been associated with one of the gaps in the Magaliesberg range on a game migration route between the middleveld and the highveld.

The favoured living places in Acheulian times were, however, always close to water such as, for instance, *dambos* where the game is usually concentrated and where water is always available. Such a site is that at Kabwe (Broken Hill) adjacent to the famous kopje that produced the skull and other remains of *Homo rhodesiensis*. Here a small assemblage of large cutting tools was found associated with spheroids and a number of small tools in quartz. Another fossil *dambo* site, not yet excavated, is that of Lochard on the Zambezi/Limpopo divide in Zimbabwe which has produced many handaxes and cleavers. The locality of Cornelia in the northern Orange Free State (South Africa) is another example. Unlike the first two sites, Cornelia has produced much fauna, some of which is believed to be associated with an industry comprising a few handaxes and cleavers and a number of polyhedrals, choppers, core-scrapers and small tools. The animals, in particular giant hartebeeste, may have been driven into the mud in the *dambos* and then butchered. There is reason to believe that the highveld at this time was well watered and covered by short grassland with scattered groves of trees and riverine forest – not greatly different from the present day. In the dry Karroo bush of the northern Cape Province and Botswana, the Acheulian population settled around pans and shallow lake sites that abounded in the region at that time. One such is Doornlaagte near Kimberley where a concentration of artefacts, apparently in primary context, is found cemented and sealed by calcrete. It shows repeated occupation over a longish period of time but no fauna are present.

Round the pools or *vleis* in the troughs between old stabilized sand-dunes at Elandsfontein in the western Cape Province close to Hopefield, was a favourite place for Acheulian man to hunt large mammals. The fauna are Middle Pleistocene and, in general, characteristic of the historic Cape fauna with elephant, rhino, giraffe, hippo, large and medium-sized antelopes, *Equus* and pigs. Again, the animals may have been killed by being driven into swampy ground and there is a suggestion that poisoning of water-holes may also have been practised. This site yielded the skullcap of a hominid closely comparable to that from Kabwe (Broken Hill) and unmistakably more advanced than *H. erectus*. Again, there is nothing to suggest that the environment of the western Cape Province was generally different from that of the present day.

Yet another habitat favoured by Acheulian man – the shoreline – is shown by the large Acheulian site found farther south on the narrow coastal plain at Cape Hangklip, False Bay, in consolidated dune sands overlying the 18-metre beach. There are no fauna but the site has yielded a large number of well-made handaxes and a smaller number of cleavers as well as many flake-scrapers, core-scrapers, spheroids and small tools. It is, however, important to note that at this time in Atlantic Morocco and the Mediterranean basin, no marine mammals or fish feature in the diet, only land mammals being represented.

Spring localities were also occupied, such as the site of Amanzi in the winter rainfall belt south of the Great Escarpment near Port Elizabeth, where there is a ridge with several springs which have built up a stratified sequence of sands when they were active, and peaty layers during times of quiescence when reeds and other vegetation grew over the site. These springs were visited regularly by Acheulian man who camped round the periphery where his discarded tools were trampled by elephants and other game that also came there to water. Several discrete assemblages have been excavated and wood, plant remains and pollens have been found in association, suggesting a vegetation not significantly different from the Cape Macchia of today.

Lastly, caves were sometimes occupied by Acheulian man in southern Africa and two must be mentioned. The first, the Cave of Hearths, is situated at Makapan in the bushveld of the northern Transvaal and contained some 9 metres of deposit with Acheulian occupation layers and interbedded hearths. Sediment analysis suggests that the rainfall then was greater than at the present time; the fauna are generally Middle Pleistocene and similar to the bushveld fauna of historic times. A human jaw fragment was also associated – a juvenile that may show affinities with the neanderthaloid and so, perhaps, with the rhodesioid fossils. The range of artefacts is similar to those from the Kalambo Falls, Hangklip and other sites where large cutting tools are found together with an important small tool element. The second cave, that of Montagu in the southern Cape Province, is close to a permanent spring and stream and in the midst of macchia vegetation. It too contained a number of superimposed occupation layers of later Acheulian form but, unfortunately, no fauna.

These various sites are good examples of the different types of habitat favoured and the range of variation present in the Middle Pleistocene

Acheulian assemblages. All the habitats have certain features in common. They are all in open country ranging from deciduous woodland (e.g. Kalambo Falls and Kabwe – Broken Hill) to open grassland/parkland (e.g. Lochard and Cornelia) or macchia (e.g. Montagu and Amanzi). All are in close proximity to water, where trees provided shade and edible fruits and where the game would tend to concentrate as the dry season advanced. They are all situated in localities where today there exist several distinct vegetation communities (i.e. in ecotone areas) and, if the general pattern was the same in the past – as the available evidence would seem to suggest – then all these several vegetation communities would have been exploitable at no great distance from the sites. Where fauna are preserved, the sites show that there was a predilection for the large game animals – elephant, hippo, giraffe, the larger bovids and *Equus* – but many smaller bovids, pigs, etc., are also represented in the food waste.

A variety of raw materials was used for stone tool making, depending on what was available locally and showing that Acheulian man possessed no small versatility and skill in flaking many of the rocks by both hard and soft hammer techniques and making very shapely, refined tools. It also shows his ability to select from several different techniques the one most suited to the material being used. Where cobbles of chert or quartzite were the raw material, a handaxe was flaked directly from the cobble; but where boulders or large blocks had to be used, several ingenious methods[6] were developed by preparing and striking a large core to obtain big flakes from which the handaxes and cleavers were made.

The later Acheulian in southern Africa probably covers much the same length of time as it does in eastern Africa, where it lasted, perhaps, from about 700 000 to 200 000 years before our era, but as yet there exists no sufficiently precise method of measuring the age differences between the various Acheulian occurrences. When such precision does become available, and when more sealed context occurrences have been excavated, it should prove possible to see whether any general trends in artefact technology can be quantitatively established and whether a relationship can be shown to exist between any of the different variants identified within the Acheulian complex and the palaeo-ecology of a site at the time it was occupied.

As this necessarily brief summary has shown, the Acheulian assemblages form certain broad patterns that are reproduced throughout the Acheulian world. There are assemblages that consist mostly of handaxes and cleavers, others that comprise choppers and smaller tools of the Developed Oldowan pattern, others again that show various combinations of both these traditions and yet others where picks, core-scrapers and other heavy-duty equipment predominate. While, therefore, there is an infinite variety in the

6. For example, pseudo-Levallois, proto-Levallois, Levallois, Techengit and Kombewa. See M. W. Brézillon, 'La dénomination des objets de pierre taillée', *Gallia Préhistoire*, Suppl. IV (Paris), pp. 79–96 and 101–2.

composition of the industries and in the nature of the habitat and its resources, there is a certain broad patterning common to the Acheulian as a whole which suggests that the overall way of life did not vary greatly from one end of the handaxe world to the other. The general picture of Middle Pleistocene hominid behaviour that emerges is thus one of hunting and gathering groups with a generally similar life-style and the ability to communicate moderately efficiently. They were living in larger groupings than in earlier times and paying more regular visits to favoured sites, following an established seasonal pattern. The social structure must still have been an open one allowing for free movement of individuals and ideas. Large areas of the continent, however, including the forests, remained unoccupied, and the sparseness, in absolute terms, of the overall population, must have meant that each group probably lived fairly isolated from the next.

The Final Acheulian or Fauresmith

Certain assemblages have for long been known to exist on the high interior plateau. They are characterized by generally smaller-sized and well-made handaxes, a wide range of flake tools, core-scrapers and comparatively few cleavers and are probably, but not certainly, later in time than the Acheulian that we have been considering. If this is so, then these assemblages probably represent a final stage of the handaxe tradition. Most of the assemblages are, however, surface collections and for that reason may be mixed with later material. The raw material used was generally lydianite (indurated shale) in the regions where that rock abounds, but elsewhere quartzite was more commonly used.

There are only a very small number of excavated samples of these assemblages which may, perhaps, be taken as representative. One of these lies in a former pan at Rooidam west of Kimberley where the industry is contained within some 5 metres of sediments capped by a massive steppe lime; these sediments represent a steady accumulation of colluvial fill deposited by rainwash. The bifaces are sometimes diminutive and rather poorly made and the greater number of tools are small scrapers and other small, retouched artefacts all in lydianite. In this assemblage, a method of core preparation known as disc-core technique, yielding several small flakes, is well represented, while another technique, the Levallois, yielding one larger flake to each preparation of the core, appears to be absent. Two other sealed sites (on the Vaal river near Windsorten and in the Verwoerd Dam area on the Orange river) preserve a similar industry but with both Levallois and disc-core techniques present. It would, therefore, seem that traditional usage and perhaps other factors, as well as time, may be a partial explanation for this kind of variability in flake and core forms.

These industries have been termed Fauresmith after the locality in the Orange Free State where the characteristic almond-shaped handaxes were first found on the surface in large quantities. It remains unclear, however, whether these industries represent an entity sufficiently distinct from the Acheulian to warrant the retention of a specifically distinctive name. They are more usually found in the grasslands, Karroo bush and macchia of South Africa and Namibia. The only indication of their possible age is a uranium/thorium date on the carbonate from Rooidam which gave a determination of 115 000 ± 10 000 years b.p.[7] The time when Fauresmith industries were superseded by a new technological complex or tradition emphasizing flake and blade tools and marking the beginning of the Middle Stone Age is unknown but may have been between 100 000 and 80 000 years ago.

In the heavier rainfall, more closed vegetation regions of Central Africa, the late Acheulian was replaced, not by the Fauresmith, but by industrial entities with a high proportion of heavy-duty equipment – picks, core-axes, choppers and core-scrapers. This kind of equipment was present, of course, in Acheulian assemblages but, except in the little-known Heavy-Duty Variant, it never at that time predominated over the other categories of tools. Such heavy-duty equipment now becomes significant, however, in the areas of higher rainfall and temperature where it is found together with a range of light-duty tools made of flakes and fragments. Such occurrences are found in Zambia, Zimbabwe, parts of south-east Africa (in particular on the Mozambique plain) and in the coastal regions of Natal, and belong to what is termed the Sangoan Industrial Complex. Sangoan assemblages are mostly undated except in a relative, stratigraphic way and it is not known for certain whether they are broadly contemporary with or later than the final Acheulian (Fauresmith) of the open grass savannah lands.

At the Kalambo Falls the local manifestation of the Sangoan (Chipeta Industry) is dated, on twelve radio-carbon results, to between 46 000 and 38 000 years b.p. A comparable stage from Mufo in north-eastern Angola dates from about 38 000 years b.p. In Zimbabwe, the local Sangoan (Gwelo Industry) resembles, but is believed to be older than, assemblages at one time described as proto-Stillbay.[8] The difficulty of correlation of these Sangoan-like industries is compounded by ecological and other factors for, where habitat, tradition or idiosyncratic considerations together favoured the use of this heavy-duty equipment, it can be expected at an early stage to have become significant and to have remained so as long as the underlying reasons for its use persisted. The correlation of this tool-kit with higher

7. b.p. = before present, this being 1950, the year in which the carbon-14 method was used for the first time.

8. The composition of these proto-Stillbay assemblages in Zimbabwe can best be seen from sealed cave sites such as Pomongwe and Bambata and from an open site on the Chavuma plateau, after which the industrial entity has now been renamed the Chavuma Industry. Although no finite dates are available, the Chavuma industry is older than 42 000 b.p. so that the Gwelo Industry is thought to be still earlier.

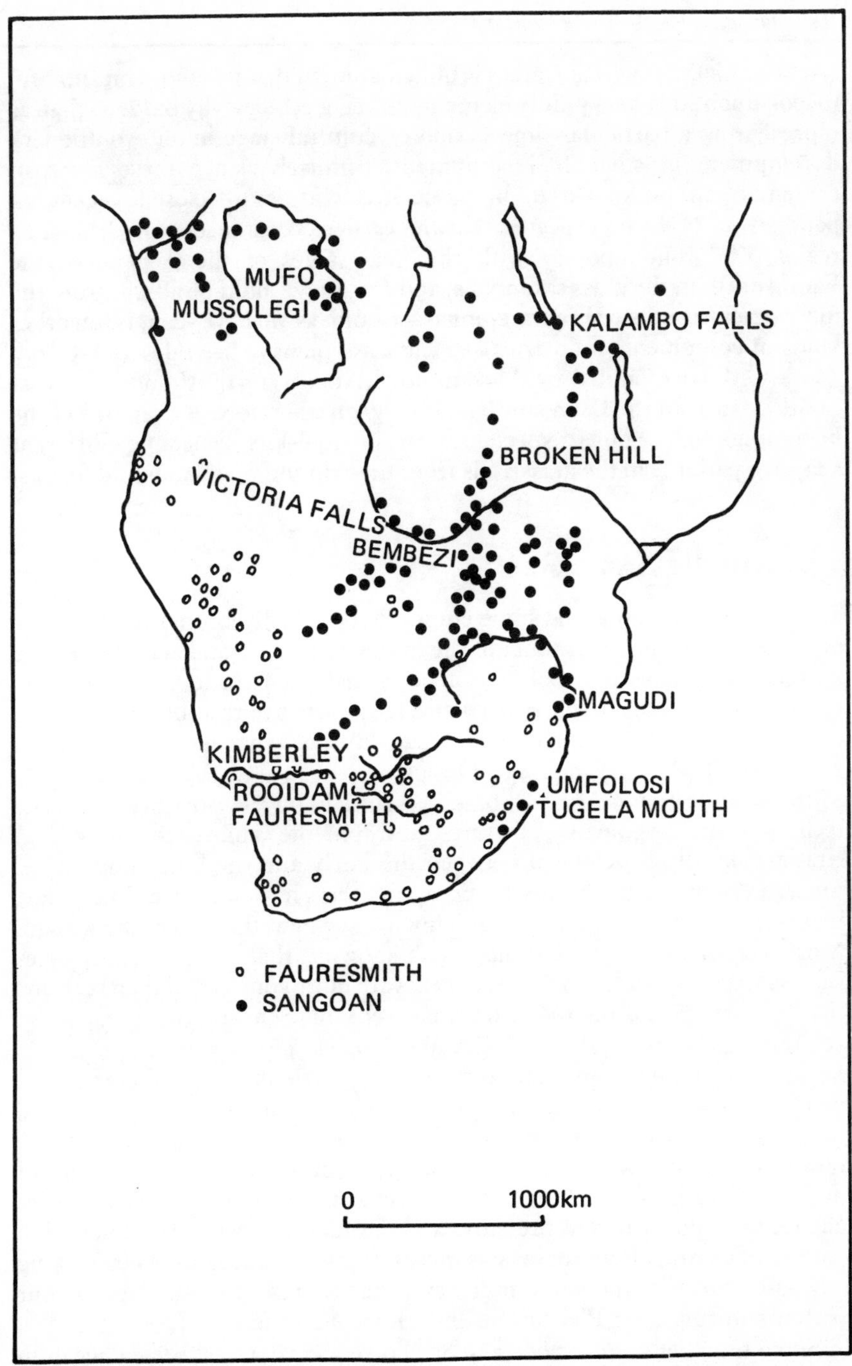

FIG. 20.6 *The distribution of Fauresmith and Sangoan sites in southern Africa (after J. D. Clark, 1970)*

rainfall, thicker vegetation areas is undeniable, so that it is more meaningful to look upon such heavy-duty elements as being ecologically induced than as representing a particular time-period or cultural stage in an evolutionary development of stone tool equipment. Similarly, since these Sangoan elements can be shown to be associated with more closed vegetation patterns, it might be expected that the earlier occurrences would, in such regions, be contemporary with the final stages of the Acheulian (the Fauresmith) in the grass savannahs, and that they would be absent from the more open habitats where the emphasis would, as we have seen, be on other kinds of equipment. Industries of Sangoan type have been described from Zambia, Malawi, Zimbabwe, Mozambique, Angola and north and south-east South Africa. In the Fauresmith and Sangoan, therefore, we can detect the beginnings of regional specialization in tool-kits reflecting different adaptive patterns in the grasslands from those in the woodlands and forests.

The Middle Stone Age

The need to look upon the stone equipment – usually all that remains – of prehistoric man as the product of the immediate needs and activities of the makers and not as the tool-kits of necessarily genetically and ethnically distinct populations becomes particularly apparent in relation to the varied components of the regional assemblages during what has for long been known as the Middle Stone Age. Designation of an assemblage as belonging to the Middle Stone Age was based essentially on the presence of certain technical and typological features and on the ability to show that stratigraphically it belonged between the Early and the Late Stone Ages. Such developmental, chrono-stratigraphic terms have little meaning today, however, as they remain as ill-defined as when they were first used. Moreover, radio-carbon chronology is showing that technological stages such as were postulated in these concepts are more conjectural than real, and that techniques and the tool types that were their end-products transcend such artificial horizontal boundaries. Working closely with stone artefacts, as he does, the prehistorian sometimes tends to overlook the fact that these are merely the sole remaining part of an extensive range of equipment and materials that have not survived. Had these been available for study, however, they would surely have dramatically modified our conceptions of prehistoric technology. Moreover, wherever the need exists, technologies change in response to new pressures and the adaptive, selective exploitation pattern of a group. Both these facts must be taken into account when making any assessment of the stone industries that represent cultural behaviour patterns during later Pleistocene and Holocene times.

Some time between 100 000 and 80 000 years ago, the sea-level began to drop from the 5–12 metre highstand that is well represented by the raised beach remnants at a number of localities round the southern shores of the

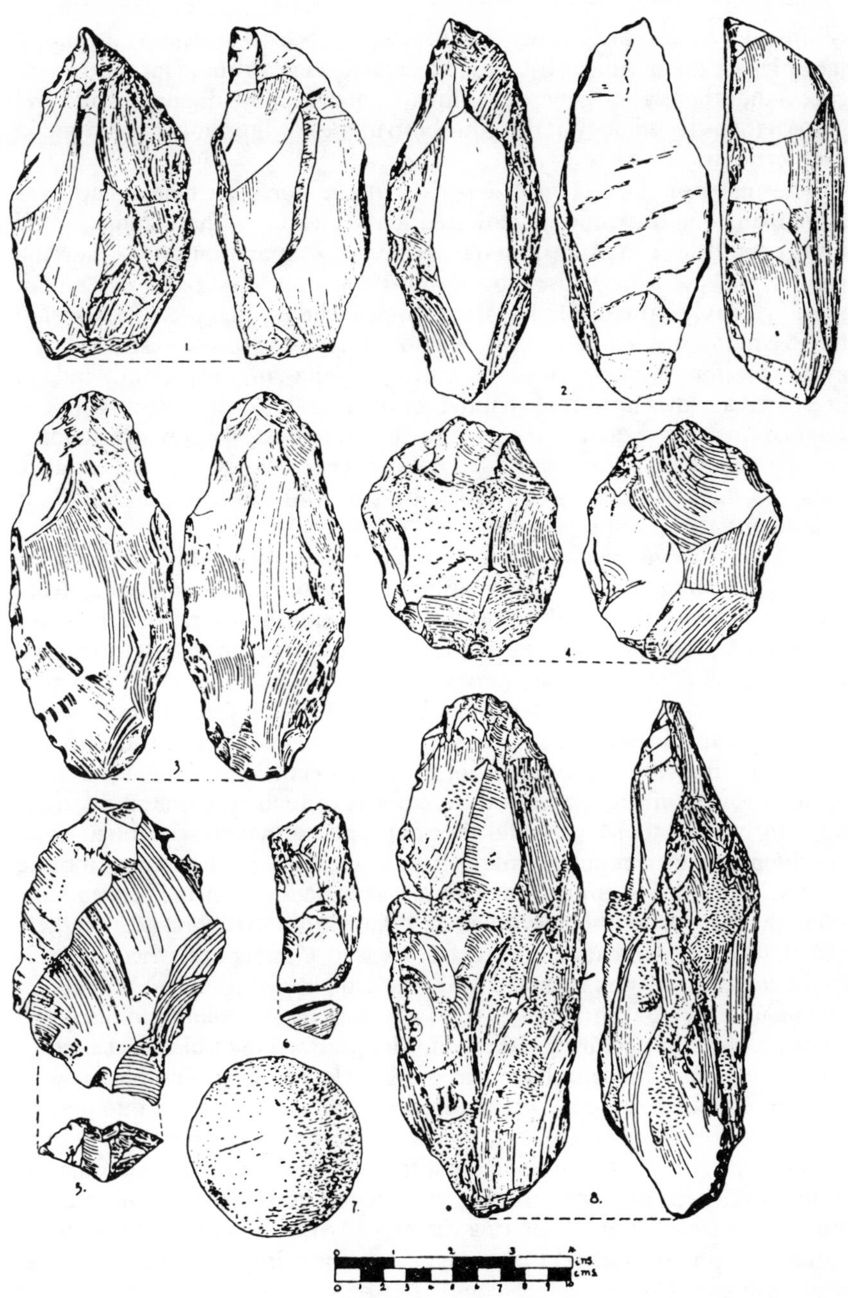

FIG. 20.7 *Artefacts from Sangoan assemblages in the Zambezi Valley, near Livingstone, Zambia (after J. D. Clark, 1950): 1 and 2, picks; 3 and 8, core axes; 4, disc core; 5 and 6, modified flakes; 7, spheroid*

continent[9] and, shortly after this time, man began to occupy favoured localities on the recently abandoned beaches. Some of these localities were caves and there is a generally similar, though individually distinctive, pattern to the technology of this time both in the Mediterranean basin and in southern Africa.

The onset of the last glacial period in the northern hemisphere was accompanied in the tropics by lowered temperatures (perhaps about 6–8°C lower) and drier conditions, though decreased evaporation rates ensured a regular and even, perhaps, more extensive supply of surface water than there is today. At the same time, the semi-arid climate that then pertained in the basin of the Zaïre in the equatorial region greatly restricted the evergreen forest or replaced it with grassland and woodland and so presented a highly favourable habitat for man and gregarious game animals. Populations now began to move into this previously largely unoccupied country. Similarly, during the later Pleistocene, the Namib desert also, today so inhospitable, was occupied by bands of hunters who left their equipment at the camp sites.

The stratigraphic sequence in each major region during the Middle Stone Age appears to show a consistent pattern of technological development from less elaborate to more evolved end-products and, in general, the artefacts also show a progressive diminution in size. However, the cultural sequence in one region is not necessarily comparable with that in another, although some overall trends and patterns can be traced. Many factors – ecological, technological and social – were probably responsible for the regional variability that is characteristic of these Upper Pleistocene industries. Different ways of life required different sets of tools or dictated different uses to which tool-kits could be put and, although continent-wide developments in technology might have played a part in determining the time at which any seemingly new trait was introduced, it is likely to have been the nature of the resources and the traditional methods of their exploitation that were the deciding factors as to whether and when any new technological trait was accepted and adapted.

The underlying techniques of this time were the Levallois and disc-core methods for manufacturing flakes, and the production of blades at first by direct percussion and later by means of a punch. The flakes and blades were made into a range of light-duty equipment that was retouched into points, scrapers, knives, burins (chisels), borers and a number of other types of tool. In southern Africa, these regional entities can be grouped, on the basis of technology, into three major units, that are in large part, but not entirely, also chronological units. For this reason they can best be referred to as groups or phases rather than stages – which imply a chronological relationship.

9. This last highstand is believed to be the equivalent of the last interglacial (Eemian) high sea-level in the Mediterranean Basin where it is usually found at a comparable level – between 6 and 8 metres.

The first of these groups or phases (Group I) is characterized by large, radially prepared flakes made by the Levallois method and by long blades struck by direct percussion. Only a few discrete assemblages are known.[10] At the few sites where a stratified evolutionary sequence exists, the technically more evolved occurrences are found in the overlying strata and the group I assemblages are the earliest (e.g. at the Cave of Hearths and the Kalambo Falls); but there appears to be no chronological consistency between the different regions. For example, the 'Middle Stone Age' I at Klassies river is believed to be close to 80 000 years old while the Nakasasa industry at the Kalambo Falls, on the other hand, dates between *c.* 39 000 and 30 000 years b.p.: the other assemblages have not yet been found in datable contexts.

Other assemblages that belong to the earlier part of the Upper Pleistocene, that is, before 40 000 years b.p., but do not fall into Group I, show a different set of characteristics. For instance, an industry of informal flakes, cores, core-scrapers, polyhedrals, anvils and grindstones in dolerite comes from Peat I at Florisbad in the Orange Free State. These tools are largely undiagnostic and may well not represent the full range of equipment being made at the site at this time but it is also possible that a single, long, trimmed blade might be associated. Peat I also yielded what appears to be the grip end of a curved wooden throwing-stick and a fragmentary hominid cranium. This Florisbad horizon dates from more than 48 000 years b.p. Another industry that differs from but is probably contemporary with those in Group I is the Chavuma Industry from Zimbabwe referred to above as being older than 42 000 years b.p. It is characterized by picks and rare handaxes and an important light-duty element comprising, amongst other tools, points, scrapers and utilized blades. It is made from a variety of raw materials – chalcedony, opaline breccia, quartzite, quartz, and so on. The industry from Twin Rivers in Zambia (dated to 22 800 ± 1000 years b.p.) resembles that from Chavuma although the date, if correct, emphasizes that basic technological method is now of little value as a means of correlating assemblages between regions.

Many assemblages from both caves and surface sites fall into a second group of industries (Group II).[11] They date generally between about 40 000 and 20 000 years b.p. but may sometimes continue later as, for example, on

10. The Lower Pietersburg from Bed 4 in the Cave of Hearths, Makapan; the 'Middle Stone Age' I from immediately above the 6–8 metre beach in Klassies river mouth; an open site in the Orange river scheme area (Elandskloof); and one in the central Transvaal (Roedoesrand). In addition the Nakassa Industry from the Kalambo Falls is characterized by similar forms although it also has certain bifacial, heavy-duty tools such as we have seen are to be expected with entities from the *Brachystegia* woodlands.

11. Examples of group II assemblages are those from Bed 5 in the Cave of Hearths; from Bed I at Mvulu's Cave in the Transvaal; the 'Middle Stone Age' II from Klassies river; assemblages from Mossel Bay and Skildergat Cave in the southern Cape; and the Stillbay Industry from Mumbwa Cave in Zambia.

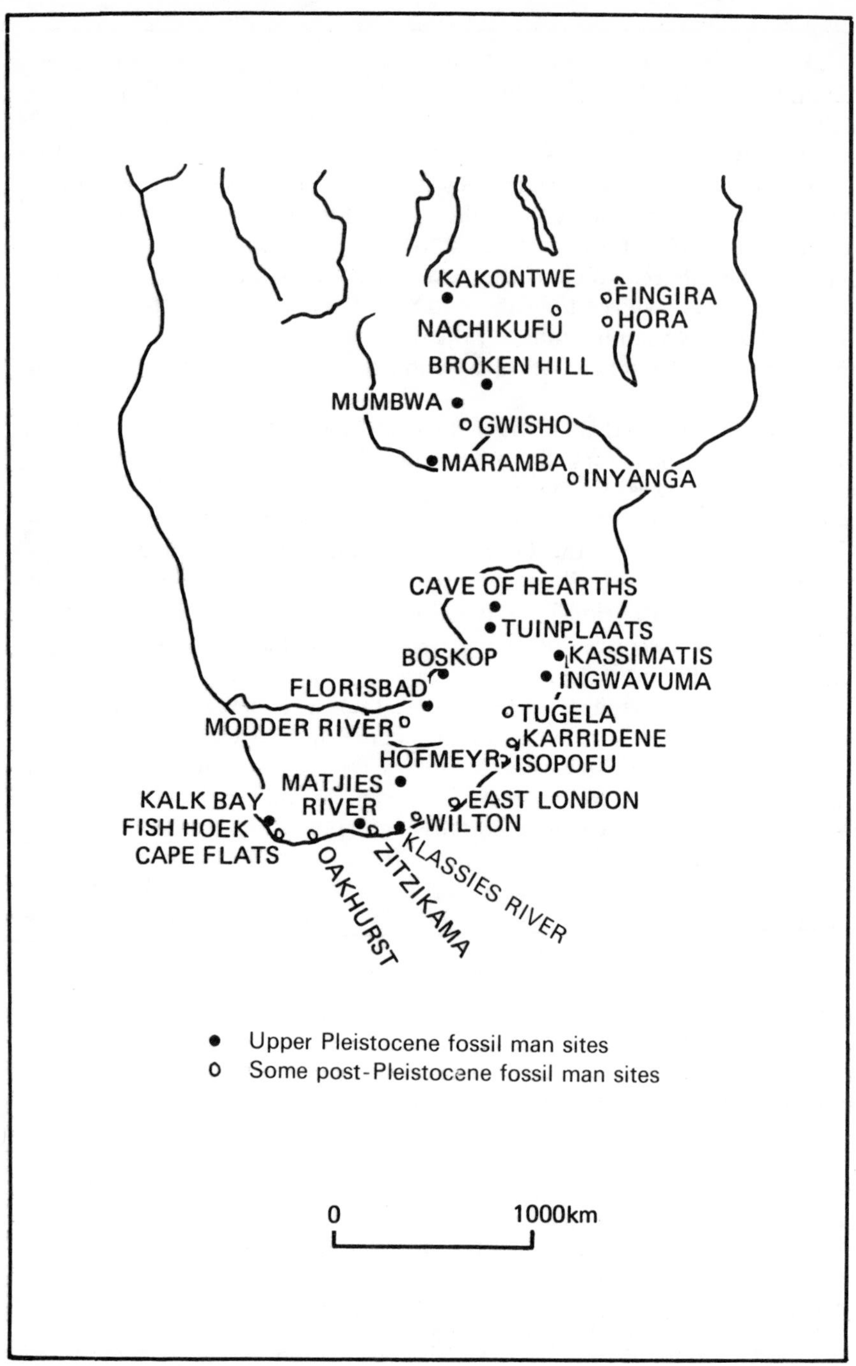

FIG. 20.8 *Upper Pleistocene and some post-Pleistocene fossil man sites in southern Africa (after J. D. Clark, 1970)*

the south coast. These industries are characterized by varying use of the disc-core and Levallois techniques, in particular for the production of triangular flakes, and by an important blade element. Blades and triangular flakes, made predominantly from quartzite and lydianite, are common in the winter rainfall areas south of the Great Escarpment; in south-west Africa and on the highveld in the Orange Free State and Transvaal. Retouch or trimming on these Group II tools is never extensive; it is usually confined to the margins and not infrequently takes the form of denticulation. In the tropical woodlands north of the Limpopo, where quartz was more generally used, the emphasis was on shorter flakes worked into various scraper and other forms with similar, restricted retouch. A small but significant part of the tool-kit here is composed of heavy-duty tools, occasioned, it is believed, by more extensive use of wood and its by-products.

A third group of industries (Group III)[12] ranges in age from about 35 000 to about 15 000 years b.p. and is distinguished by many more extensively retouched artefacts. Scraper retouch is semi-invasive and strangulated forms are not uncommon; foliate points may be retouched over the whole of one or both faces; borers and upper grindstones are characteristic. In general the tools have smaller dimensions and show a refinement in retouch that is not found in the earlier groups.

In addition to the three groups just described, there is a fourth (group IV) that shows some significant differences from them. This is what used to be known as the Magosian or Second Intermediate Complex. It combines an evolved and often diminutive expression of the disc-core and Levallois techniques with the manufacture of delicate, often ribbon-like blades struck from cores by means of a punch of bone, horn or hardwood. The raw materials selected were often crypto-crystalline rocks and foliate and triangular points, side- and end-scrapers made from these, often by the disc-core and Levallois methods, are finely finished, sometimes, it is believed, by pressure-flaking. With these, more traditionally Middle Stone Age, tools are found others made on blades and blade segments, often of diminutive proportions, that have been blunted, or backed, or utilized and trimmed in various ways, as well as several burin or chisel-like tools, notably a carinated or polyhedral form. This type of assemblage appears to be restricted to certain parts of the subcontinent – to Zimbabwe and Zambia, the eastern Free State, the southern Cape Province and parts of Namibia, for example – but it is apparently absent from most of the central portion of the interior plateau where lydianite was the main raw material used. If such a distribution has an ecological basis, it behoves us to try to determine what there was in common between the regions where these Group IV industries are found.

It used to be considered that these evolved industries represented a fusion of middle stone age prepared core and upper Palaeolithic punched blade

12. The Upper Pietersburg Industry from the Cave of Hearths and Mvulu's Cave or the Border Cave in Natal; the upper part of the Stillbay from Peer's Cave at the Cape; the Bambata Industry from the cave sites and from Khami in Zimbabwe are examples.

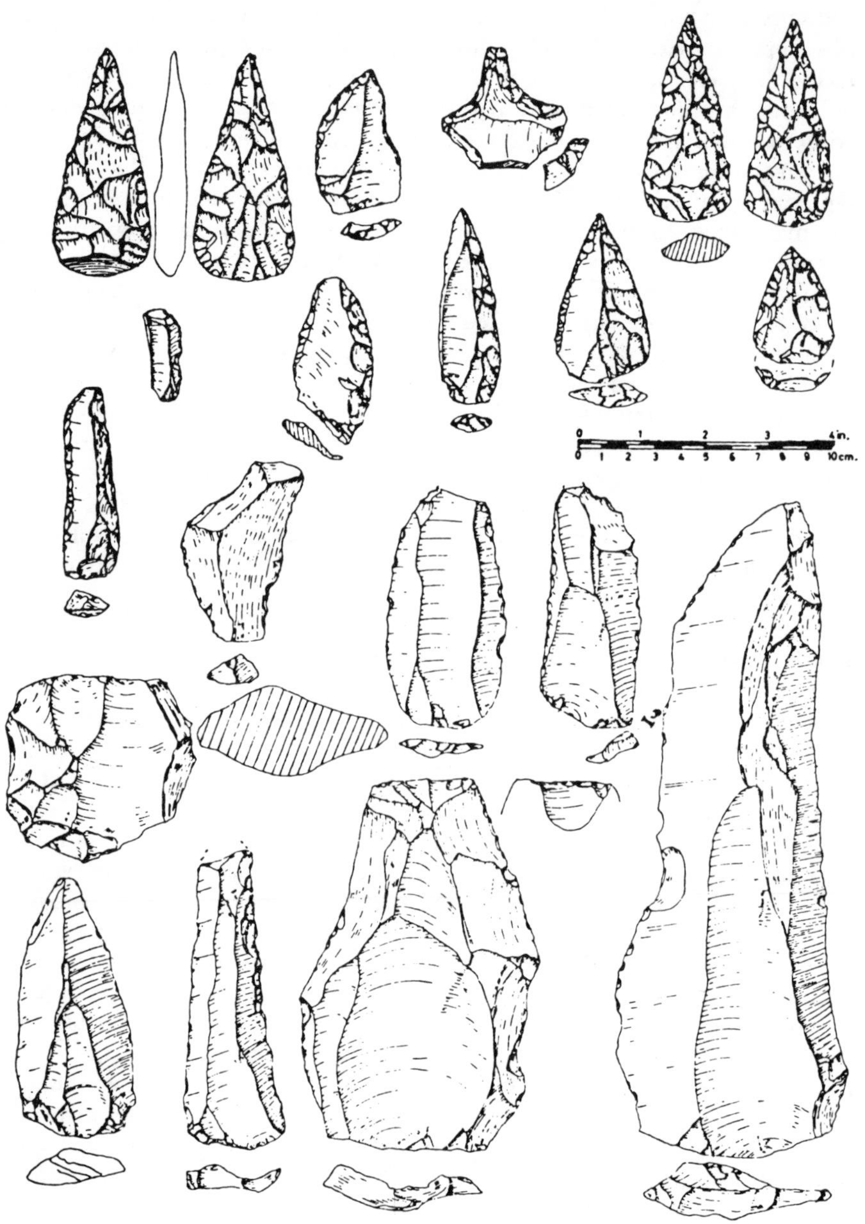

FIG. 20.9 *Tools of the Pietersburg and Bambata Industries from the Cave of Hearths, Transvaal, and Bambata Cave, Zimbabwe, typical of the open thornbush and bushveld country (after J. D. Clark, 1970)*

technologies and that they were probably not much older than 15 000–20 000 years b.p. (and, indeed, a number of age determinations fall within this range). More recently, however, several much older ages[13] have been obtained for Group IV industries – those which had been termed Magosian or, in South Africa, Howieson's Poort (after the site near Grahamstown where the first characteristic assemblage was found). Unfortunately, with the exception of Montagu Cave at the Cape and the Tshangulan industry from Zimbabwe no detailed information on the composition of these occurrences is yet available, so that it is uncertain whether each of these assemblages is homogeneous or whether more than one industrial entity is represented.

Assuming for the present that the assemblages are homogeneous, these early dates now show that a developed blade technology was present in southern Africa contemporaneously with prepared flake technologies of traditional Middle Stone Age.

The situation is not dissimilar from that in North Africa where two contemporaneous industrial complexes – the Dabban and the Aterian – are found regionally differentiated. Changes and replacements of stone tool-kits have, in the past, usually been explained by postulating movements of genetically discrete ethnic populations. This migration hypothesis finds little or no support from other lines of evidence, however, and the extent to which tool-kits were adopted and spread among hunting-gathering populations is more likely to have been dependent upon any advantages or superiority they possessed over the traditional equipment, especially where the exploitation of new resources was thereby facilitated. Long-distance migration, unless it involves the occupation of empty regions such as the New World or the Zaïre Basin and West African forest zones after the end of the Middle Pleistocene, is probably minimal at the hunting-gathering level and relates more particularly to food-producing populations. Independent invention among fairly isolated communities in regions using similar resources and similar exploitation methods is a more probable explanation for the changes exhibited by contemporaneous tool-kits which can better be explained as stimulus diffusion than as due to wide-scale ethnic migration.

By way of explanation, it is necessary to review briefly the fossil evidence from southern Africa after the end of the Acheulian with which the Saldanha skull is believed to be associated. Since the skull from Kabwe (Broken Hill) so closely resembles that from Saldanha, it is likely that they were not separated by any very great interval of time. The small number of

13. Group IV industries have been dated at Montagu Cave to −23 200–> −48 850 at Klassies river, in the southern Cape Province dates cluster round ±36 000 b.p.; at Rose Cottage Cave in the Orange Free State the date is over 50 000 and over 46 300 for the Epi-Pietersburg at Border Cave. The regional group IV industry in Zimbabwe the Tshangulan, dates between 21 700 ± 780 and 25 650 ± 1800 years b.p.

light-duty artefacts and the spheroids from Kabwe, believed to be associated with the hominid fossils, are undiagnostic and might belong in time anywhere between a late Acheulian and an early Middle Stone Age. Stratified occupation horizons ascribed to this time-range are present at the immediate locality so that, while it may be suspected that this virtually complete skull and other remains are representative of the kind of hominid responsible for the local Sangoan or final Acheulian, this cannot be proved to be so until some more precise method of dating the fossil itself is devised. Since, however, there are resemblances between the Saldanha and Kabwe (Broken Hill) fossils, the fragmentary cranium (H.12) from Bed IV at the Olduvai Gorge and that from Njarassi in the Lake Eyasi rift in East Africa, it would seem that these rhodesioid and related forms of *Homo sapiens* replaced *H. erectus* during the later part of the Middle Pleistocene, as did Neanderthal man in Eurasia and, by the beginning of the Upper Pleistocene, were widely spread within the tropical parts of sub-Saharan Africa.[14]

The climatic changes which pollen, limnological and other studies are showing took place in Africa at the same time as those accompanying the last glaciation in Eurasia, and the general sparseness and near-isolation of the hominid populations, can be expected to have brought about changes and development in several different directions as the hominids became more efficiently adapted genetically and culturally to the several diverse environments which they now successfully occupied.

Whatever were the causes – full language, improved social structure, advanced technology, or others – that gave modern man (*H. sapiens sapiens*) such an undeniable advantage over the other hominid forms, it is clear that they lie behind the genetic interchange which resulted in the comparatively rapid replacement of the neanderthaloid, rhodesioid and other less well adapted forms. Modern man (represented by the skulls from the Kibish Formation in the lower Omo Basin and from the Lake Victoria Basin at Kanjera) was present in East Africa by about 200 000 years b.p. In South Africa, the skull from Florisbad, which is more than 48 000 years old, represents an early, robust form close to modern man. A number of later but, as yet less securely dated fossils, most of them probably falling within the 35 000–20 000 b.p. time-range (from Boskop, Border Cave, Tuinplaats, Skildergat – Peer's Cave, Mumbwa and elsewhere) represent more than one regionally differentiated and early modern population responsible for one or other of the Middle Stone Age cultural variants.

By the end of the Pleistocene, about 10 000 years ago, genetically related but regionally distinct populations, ancestral to some of the present-day peoples, had become differentiated – the large and small Bushman stock in South Africa and east-central Africa; the negroid in equatorial and West Africa; and the nilotic form in East Africa. The fossil evidence is fragmentary and usually confined to a single specimen; rarely are there

14. New racemization determinations for two of the Kabwe hominid fossils fall between 100 000 and 200 000 years b.p. (J. Bada, personal communication).

sufficient individuals in a sample to give much indication of the range of variation that can be expected within any one population. It is none the less clear, however, that the indigenous African 'races' have a very considerable antiquity in the continent, where they may be seen as having evolved during the Upper Pleistocene and earliest Holocene by means of a long period of adaptation and selection in the major bio-geographical regions.

As stated above, the punched blade element and various small, backed and truncated blade tools found with the group IV (Howieson's Poort) tool-kits have in the past been identified as evidence of population movements with the further implication that these kits were introduced by immigrant groups of modern man. Whether this ethnic hypothesis will later be substantiated, or whether these tool-kits reflect the acceptance of new techniques transmitted by stimulus diffusion and adopted because they permitted more efficient exploitation of the favoured local resources, or whether, again, they are the products of quite other factors, must await the outcome of more definitive studies of the excavated sites. There can be little doubt, however, that whatever the cause, the introduction of the small or micro-blade technology is related to the development of the composite tool in which two or more parts and/or materials are combined to make an improved, more efficient implement. Hafting stone or other material for more effective use probably begins during Group II times, and the fluting scars on the dorsal faces of the Mossel Bay points or the removal of the platform by retouch on the ventral face of an artefact are believed to be evidence of modification associated with hafting. The most readily available medium for mounting, for example, a stone knife or a projectile point, in Africa is likely to have been various forms of mastic (resin, gum, latex, and so on) with binding where necessary of sinew or bast.

The appearance of modern man in the prehistoric record is associated with a series of innovative cultural practices and traits. The deep, accumulated sediments in caves and rock-shelters and in some stratigraphically favoured open sites show that regular seasonal occupation was the general rule from this time onwards. We appear to be dealing with much more closely structured groups, though clearly these were still open and their composition is likely to have changed frequently.

The multiplicity and standardization of different types of tool, intentional burial and the placing of artefacts and food with the dead for use in the after-life, the employment of pigment for decoration and possibly ritual – even a liking for music is represented in North Africa – these are all indications of the immeasurably superior genetic advantages of *H. sapiens sapiens*. One aspect of the more regionally specialized nature of the tool-kits can be seen in regional preferences for certain kinds of game animals and the increasing use being made of certain plant foods, the processing of which required grinding and pounding. Grinding equipment makes its first regular appearance with the Group III and IV occurrences and more particularly after about 25 000 before our era. A significant heavy-duty component accompanies the light-duty tools in north and north-west Zambia and reflects a similar exploitation pattern of much the same kind of resources as those in the Zaïre basin and Angola.

The traditional view of the Middle Stone Age as being composed of several discrete regional variants (Stillbay, Pietersburg, Mossel Bay, Howieson's Poort, and so on) all more or less contemporary and distinguished by a few *fossiles directeurs* can now be seen to be excessively oversimplified. Middle Stone Age industries are better, therefore, regarded as the products of a steadily developing adaptation to bio-geographically distinct regions or zones where the requirements and activities of the groups dictated the preferences and the extent to which the different raw materials for artefacts might be used. An understanding of the relative importance to the group of these different materials – wood, stone, bone, horn, and so on – can best be obtained from a comparison of palaeo-ecological data with those obtained from site catchment analysis studies.[15] An assemblage of informal stone tools does not necessarily indicate dimness nor does a refined stone tool assemblage represent superiority. Stone artefacts alone can only provide a minimal amount of information concerning the behaviour of the makers. It is the association of these artefacts with all other surviving products and features of a single occupation that is significant. Fewer features are known from Middle Stone Age sites than from those of Acheulian and earlier times. We have evidence of hearths from the Cave of Hearths and the discrete scatter of artefacts associated with hearths on single horizons is well documented at Montagu Cave. The stone foundations of several small wind-breaks are known from Orangea I site and evidence of a single large screened activity area at Zeekoegat 27 in the Orange River Scheme area. The piling of bones from one or more successful hunts has been recovered from the bushveld site at Kalkbank in the central Transvaal and there is evidence from Lions Cave in Swaziland that haematite began to be extracted for pigment as early as 28 000 years ago. Anvils wedged in position for flaking stone are present on the Rubble I horizons at the Kalambo Falls dating from about 27 000 years b.p., where also small circles of stones may delineate former hearths, while the sparse scatter of artefacts from a single camp of Bambata Industry hunters has been found on the Nata river in Botswana. Faunal remains representing food waste show that it was mostly the larger game animals that were the sources of supply and some, such as buffalo, wildebeeste, hartebeeste, zebra and pig were among the commonest species carried back to the living sites. In general there appears to be a rather greater

15. Site catchment analysis is a method developed by Vita Finzi and Higgs (1970) to establish the resource potential of a region exploited from a given prehistoric site. This calls for identification of the limits of the territory and of the extent to which the habitat and biome differed from those of the present day. Vita Finzi and E. S. Higgs, 'Prehistoric economy in the Mount Carmel area of Palestine: site catchment analysis', *Proc. of the Preh. Soc.*, 36, 1970, pp. 1–37.

range of species represented on Middle Stone Age than on Acheulian sites. The evidence suggests, however, that, while better hunting weapons appear to have led to more efficient hunting, the bag remained a very varied one, only assuming a more selective character with the Late Stone Age.

In sum, no longer can the so-called Middle Stone Age occurrences be looked upon as a simple progression towards a more refined or evolved technology from beginning to end but rather, if the dating is correct, they show several different techniques with an essentially economic basis. These interact to varying degrees and may change as the economy changes. The different variants that have been identified probably reflect regional resource and extraction preferences though most of these variants remain to be precisely defined. Within some regions certain stratified sites (e.g. the Cave of Hearths) exhibit a clear developmental sequence, while at others (e.g. Klassies river on the South African south coast and Zombepata Cave, Zimbabwe) the stratigraphic succession shows a pattern not unlike that of the Mousterian traditions in western France and different group occurrences may follow each other in no apparently consistent pattern.

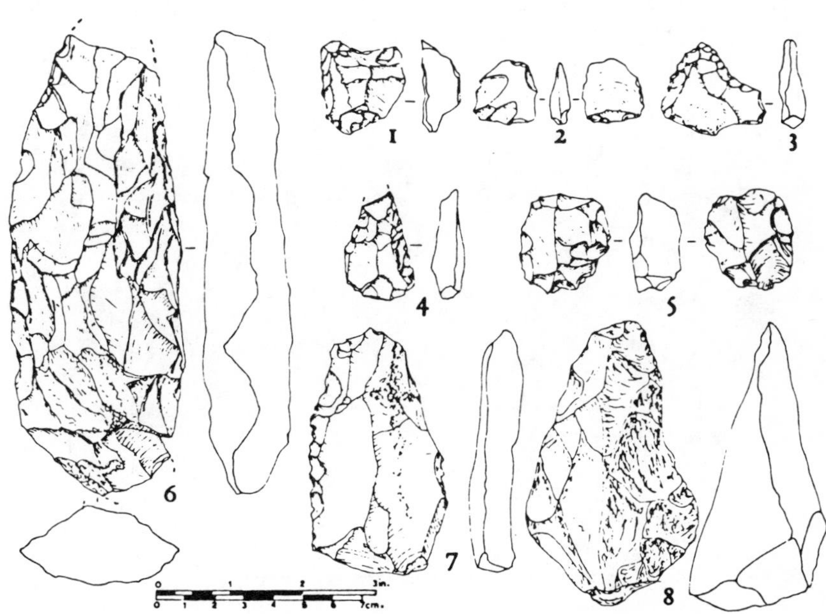

FIG. 20.10 *Middle Stone Age industry from Twins River, typical of the Brachystegia woodlands of Zambia (after J. D. Clark, 1970), dated between 32 000 and 22 000 years b.p.: 1, angled scraper; 2, utilized flake from diminutive disc core; 3, convergent scraper; 4, convergent scraper with point missing; 5, diminutive side scraper; 6, 7, bi-facial heavy-duty tools; 8, hand-axe (3 chert, 8 dolerite, all others quartz)*

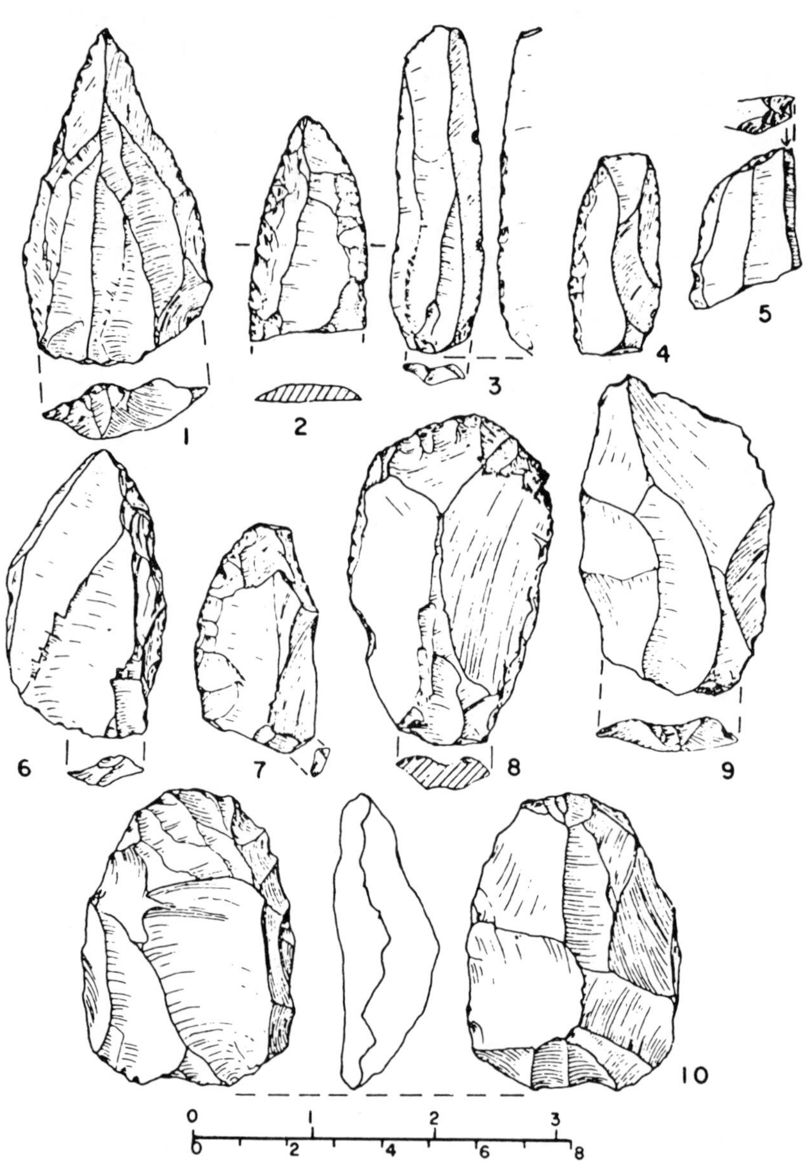

FIG. 20.11 *Middle Stone Age artefacts from Witkrans Cave, typical of the equipment of hunters in the Karroo/Kalahari thornveld (after J. D. Clark, 1971), all in chert, except no. 6 in shale: 1 and 2, unifacial points; 3, utilized blade; 4, 6 and 7, singleside scrapers; 5, burin on truncation; 8, end scraper; 9, Levallois flake; 10, Levallois core*

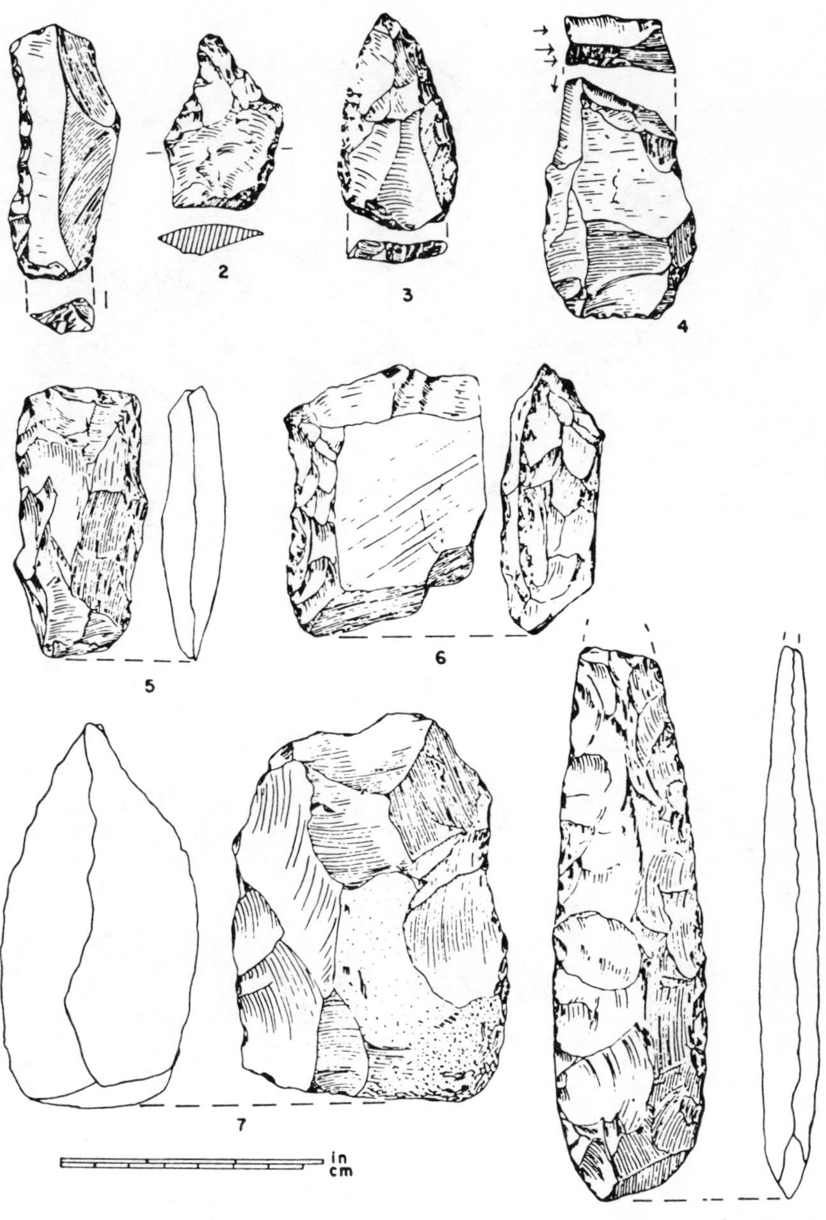

FIG. 20.12 *Tools of the Middle Stone Age Lupemban Industrial Complex from Kalambo Falls, associated with* Brachystegia *woodland and evergreen forest (after J. D. Clark, 1970) Rubble 1, Site B1, 1956: 1, single concave side scraper (chert); 2, denticulate, convergent and nosed scraper (chert); 3, unifaced point (chert); 4, dihedral burin (silcrete); 5, core axe (chert); 6, core scraper (chert); 7, chopper (quartzite); 8, lanceolate (chert)*

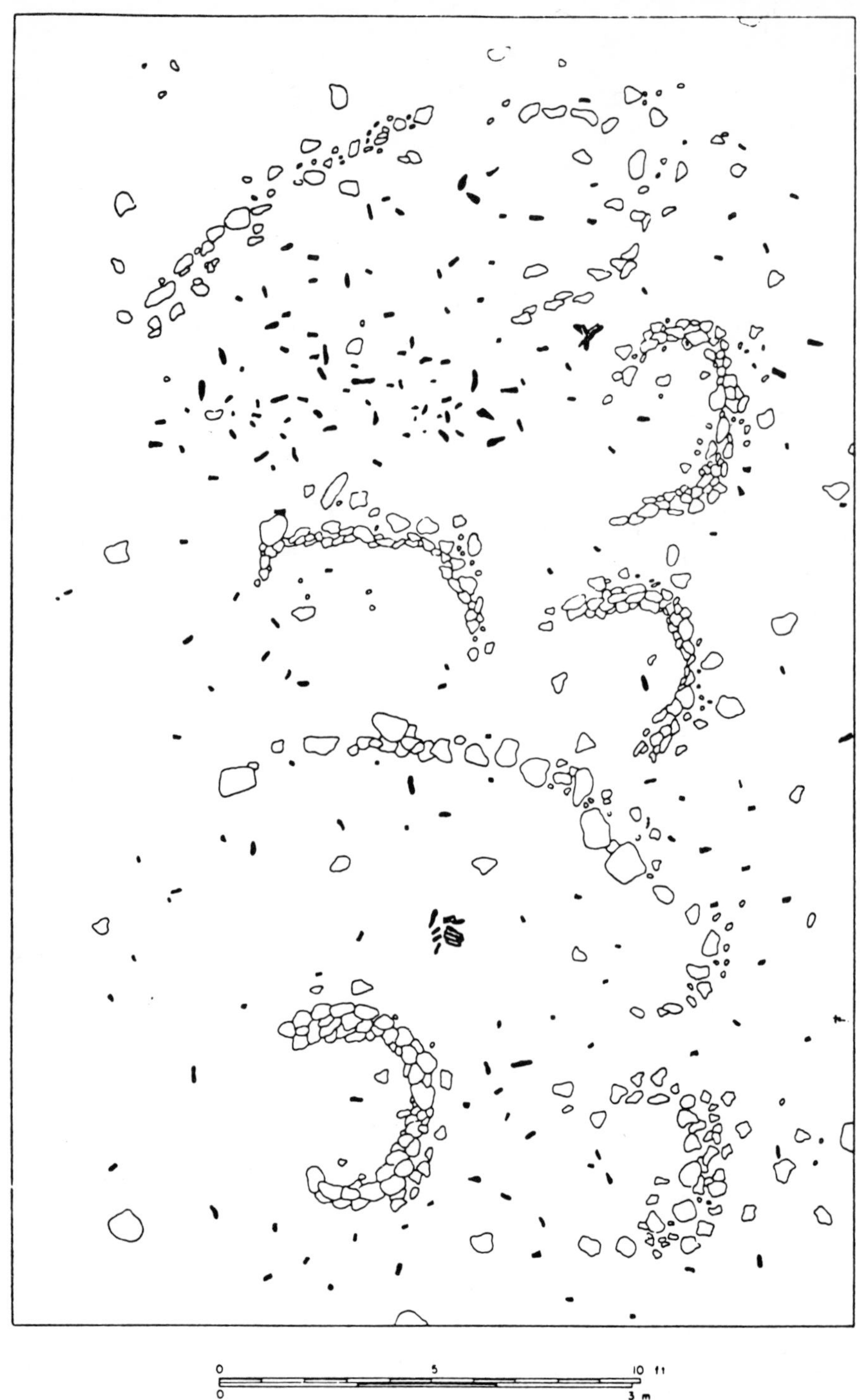

FIG. 20.13 *Distribution of utilized blades and blade fragments in relation to dolerite boulder structures on a living site at Orangiea, Orange Free State (after C. G. Sampson, 1974)*

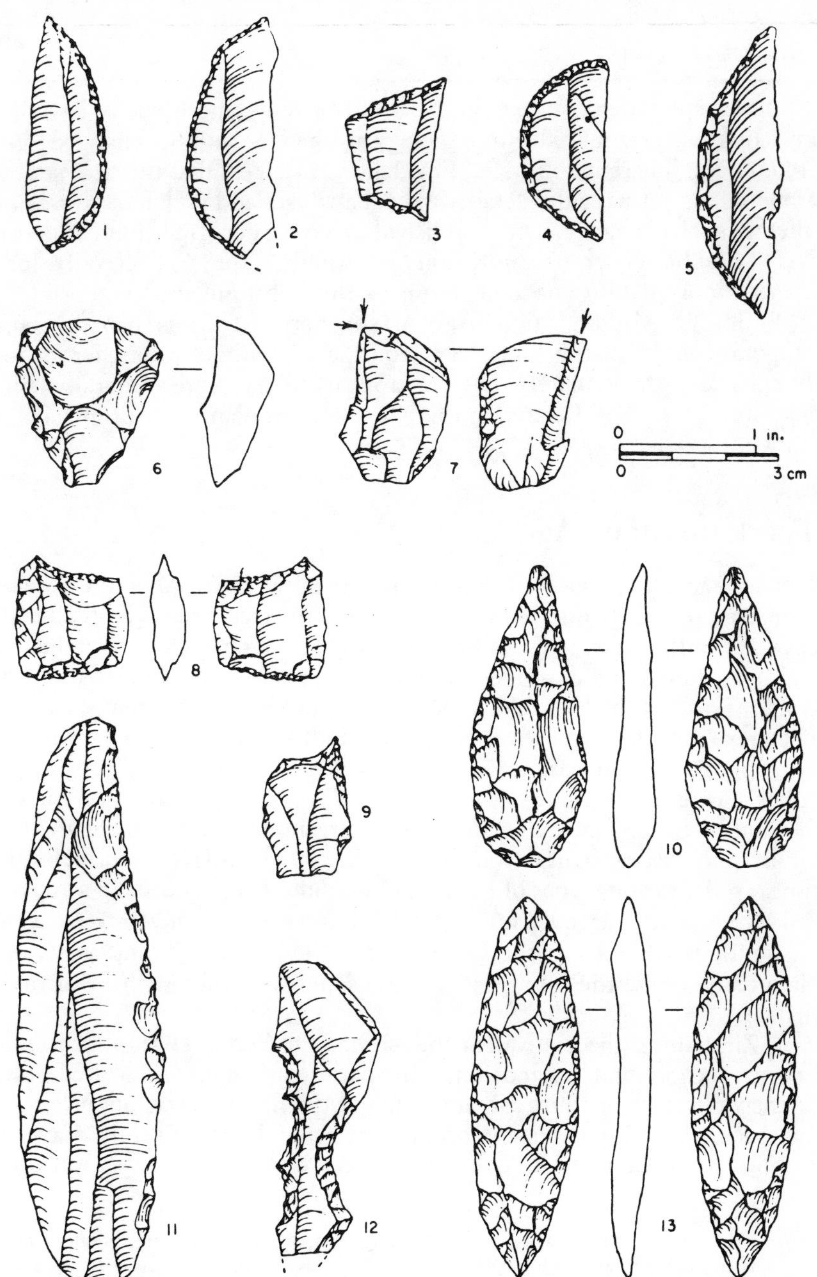

FIG. 20.14 *Tools from Howieson's Poort sites belonging to Group IV of the Middle Stone Age in southern Africa, found in a range of environments from macchia to parkland and dry woodland (after C. G. Sampson, 1974): 1, 2, 4, 5, backed crescents; 3, backed trapezium; 6, utilized Levallois core; 7, burin; 8,* outil écaillé*; 9, borer; 10, 13, bifacial points; 11, sidescraper; 12, double sidescraper. Specimens 2, 3 and 5 are from Howiesonspoort; all others are from Tunnel Cave*

These replacements of one group occurrence by another may have had an economic origin, reflecting ecological changes and so changed food preferences. There is some slight evidence to suggest that this was so, but we do not as yet have the detailed faunal analyses and pollen data to know whether such changes can be established as having occurred simultaneously over wide bio-geographical regions or whether they reflect only local changes in availability of food resources through time at a single site.

While the Middle Stone Age of southern Africa is broadly contemporaneous with the Upper Palaeolithic in Europe, its earlier stages, though very inadequately known, appear to be more generally contemporary with the Mousterian there or the Jabrudian/pre-Aurignacian in the Middle East.

The Late Stone Age

In southern Africa, the conventional picture of the Late Stone Age is one of industries of largely microlithic tools usually referred to as Wilton after the cave site in the western Cape Province, where the characteristic industries were first found and described, and of Smithfield scraper industries in the lydianite area of the highveld. In some parts of the subcontinent, however, what have come to be known as pre-Wilton industries have been recognized. These make their appearance shortly after 20 000 years ago and represent a radical change in the stone tool technology. The prepared core techniques of the Middle Stone Age are replaced by occurrences with informal cores and the irregular flakes struck from them. The only consistently formal tools appear to be various types of larger scraper, both flakes and steep scrapers, and several smaller, convex forms. Such occurrences are known from sites at the south coast,[16] from the Orange Free State,[17] the Transvaal[18] and Namibia[19] where the occurrence is associated with the butchery of three elephants.

In Zimbabwe, the equivalent industry is the Pomongwan which dates from ± 9400 and 12 200 b.p. In particular, it is associated with extensive hearths of white ash and some of the first bone points belong to this time. A possible related occurrence from Leopard's Hill Cave in Zambia dates between 21 000 and 23 000 b.p. Other as yet undated

16. Nelson's Bay Cave, dating from 18 000 to 12 000 b.p.; Matjes river, dating from 11 250 to 10 500 b.p.; and Oakhurst. At Nelson's Bay Cave an industry overlying the as yet unnamed steep scraper industry dates between 12 000 and 9000 b.p. The majority of the artefacts are large flake tools and there are no microlithic forms. A similar pre-Wilton industry is found at other sites in the southern mountain region, e.g. at Melkhoutboom, where it dates from 10 500 ± 190 years b.p.

17. A Smithfield, e.g. Phase I industry from Zeekoegat 13.

18. Uitkomst, dating from 7680 b.p.

19. Windhoek, dating from ± 10 000 b.p.

occurrences of this kind are known from Pondoland (Umgazana Cave), the middle Zambezi valley in Zambia (Lukanda) and other regions. The distribution suggests that this radical, technological change may have been fairly general between about 20 000 and 9000 years ago. Why it should have come about is unclear but, again, this writer suspects that it may have been caused by a combination of the environmental changes believed to be recorded at a number of sites in southern Africa at this time (e.g. Nelson's Bay Cave, Zombepata Cave, and so on) and the independent development or diffusion or more efficient equipment and techniques, in particular with respect to new hunting methods.

There is some evidence to show that these pre-Wilton industries are associated with the exploitation of large ungulate fauna – hartebeeste, wildebeeste, blue antelope and quagga. In addition, at Nelson's Bay Cave, they appear to be associated with an ecological change shortly after 12 000 b.p. when the grassland flora were replaced by evergreen forest forms and the appearance of a quantity of marine animals in the faunal remains indicates that the rise in sea level in the closing stages of the Pleistocene had made it possible to exploit sea foods directly from this cave.

Small blade industries with a high percentage of microlithic backed forms are now seen to have made their appearance in south-central Africa much earlier than used at one time to be thought. One of the first of these is represented by the earliest stage of the Nachikufan Industrial Complex (Nachikufu I) from Zambia where the oldest date recorded is 16 715 ± 95 b.p. The local Wilton industry begins in Zimbabwe about 12 000 b.p. (Tshangula Cave) and somewhat later in South Africa (e.g. 8000–5000 b.p.). These and other early occurrences in south-central Africa are paralleled by fully microlithic backed blade industries from sites in East Africa – from Uganda (Munyama Cave, Buvuma Island, 14 480 ± 130 b.p.), from the Nakuru/Naivasha Rift in Kenya (Prolonged Drift, 13 300 ± 220 b.p.) and from central Tanzania (Kisese Rock-Shelter, 18 190 ± 300 b.p.). A related but regionally distinctive development was that of the Tschitolian in the Zaïre Basin (12970 ± 250 b.p.).

The microlithic tradition is associated with the development of more efficient forms of composite tools, one of the most significant of which was the bow and arrow. It is not known when this weapon made its first appearance in Africa – probably during the closing stage of the Pleistocene – but of equal importance with the lunates and other small backed forms of stone tool used for the heads of the arrows were the various forms of bone point and linkshaft also believed to be the heads of arrows. Some of these may be as old as 12 000 years b.p.

It is believed that development sequences can be recognized in these microlithic industries in many different parts of southern Africa but, in other regions, as in the north-west of Zambia, the disc-core apparently continued until the second millennium before our era, while in other parts (e.g. the Orange Free State) the Wilton microlithic element seems to

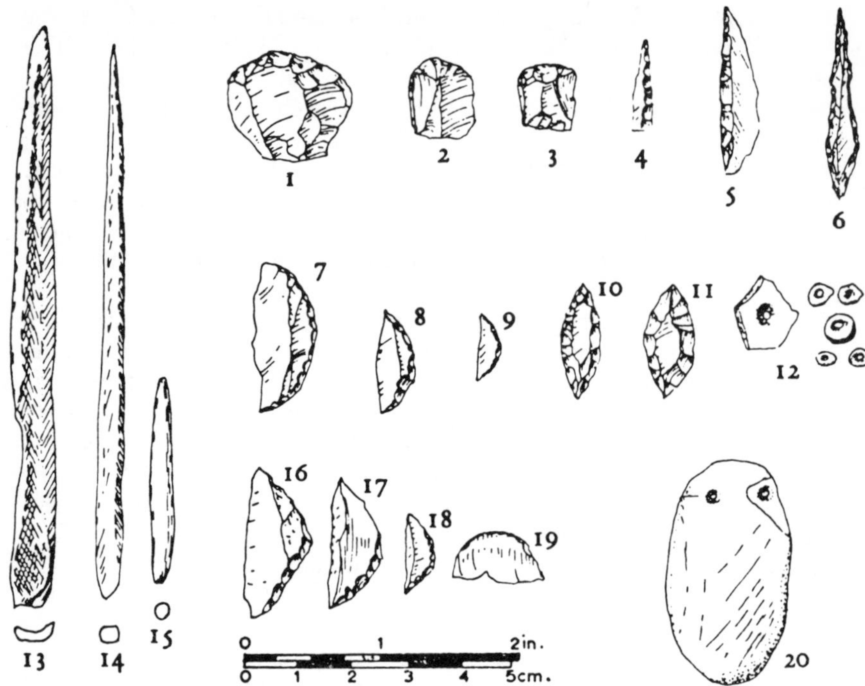

FIG. 20.15 *Tools of the Later Stone Age Wilton complex (after J. D. Clark, 1970). 1–12, of chert and chalcedony, Cape Province, South Africa (after M. C. Burkitt, 1928): 1–3, short endscrapers; 4, 5, straight backed microliths; 6, awl; 7–9, lunates; 10, 11, 'double crescents'; 12, ostrich eggshell beads; 3, 4, 12 from Wilton Rock-shelter, others from the Cape Flats. 13–20, Matopan (= 'Rhodesian Wilton') Industry tools from Amadzimba Cave, Matopo Hills, Zimbabwe (after C. K. Cooke and K. R. Robinson, 1954): 13, spatulate bone awl; 14, bone point with bevelled butt; 15, link shaft; 16–19, lunates and deep crescents, quartz; 20, slate pendant*

disappear and to be replaced later by scraper-dominated industries (Smithfield B.).

There are many more Late Stone Age than Middle Stone Age sites known and there is reason to believe that the early Holocene was a period of population increase. From this time also (i.e. about 10 000 b.p. onwards) caves and rock-shelters began to be more extensively occupied. Local resources were exploited more intensively than previously, and faunal assemblages found at occupation sites show that greater emphasis was now placed on the hunting or trapping of specific animals. The pattern of exploitation was probably not greatly different from that of the Kalahari San and other hunter-gatherers in the dry tropics today.

The movements and range of a group would have been regulated by the seasonal availability of water, plant and animal resources, and regular interaction between neighbouring groups is to be expected. Those living

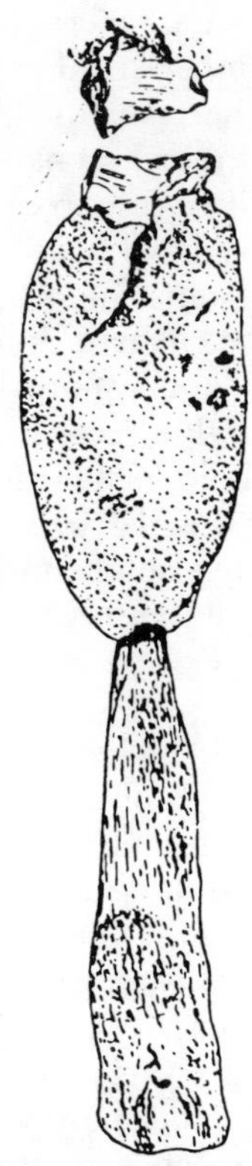

FIG. 20.16 *Crescent adze-flake or scraper in chert, mounted in mastic, with rhino horn handle, from a cave at Plettenberg Bay, eastern Cape Province, South Africa (after J. D. Clark, 1970)*

within range of freshwater sources and the sea now exploited the fish, shellfish and aquatic mammal fauna. Others concentrated on the huge herds of antelope and others again on small game. In the interior southern mountain region of the Cape Province, the commonest forms of stone tools are small scrapers of various kinds and the food waste is mostly from smaller mammals, perhaps secured by trapping and snaring. On the other hand, in Zimbabwe, Zambia and elsewhere in the grasslands and woodlands, the industries contain large numbers of microlithic lunates and backed blades associated with a food waste of large mammals. These tools suggest that the chief weapon was most probably the bow and arrow, the microliths being hafted singly or in pairs to form the broad cutting-heads, similar to the dynastic Egyptian and the few historic San arrows of this type that have survived. Territorial ranges of the bands would have depended upon a number of different ecological factors but, in the western Cape Province (De Hangen) it has been shown that the late prehistoric San groups spent the winter at the coast living mostly from sea foods and the summer in the mountains about 140 kilometres inland where the diet consisted of various plant foods, hyrax, tortoises and other small game.

The Late Stone Age hunter-gatherers in the highly favourable regions of southern Africa occupied some of the richest natural resource areas of plant and animal foods in the world. Where resources for hunters were virtually inexhaustible, as here, there must have been plenty of opportunity for indulging intellectual interests, some of which are manifest in the magnificent rock art of the Drakensberg mountains, Zimbabwe and Namibia. While much of the art may not be more than 2000–3000 years old, it nevertheless provides an incomparable record of the way of life of these prehistoric hunter-gatherers which, in many respects, is perpetuated today in the life of the San of the central Kalahari.

The origins of this art are clearly also of considerable antiquity and the earliest paintings yet known from southern Africa come from the Apollo 11 Rock-Shelter in Namibia where they occur on rock slabs in a horizon dated to 28 000 years b.p.

In the first few centuries of our era, the Late Stone Age hunting-gathering populations were replaced over much of southern Africa by agricultural peoples with a knowledge of metallurgy. These populations are most likely to have been an advance guard of Bantu-speaking groups that migrated into the subcontinent from a homeland somewhere, it is thought, in the north-west (Chad and Cameroon). There is, therefore, in southern Africa no evidence of a Neolithic stage of culture, by which is implied that there were no food-producing peoples making pottery but using only stone tools, in particular ground and polished axes. It is, however, necessary to qualify this by saying that, while there is no evidence for the cultivation of any plants before the coming of the Early Iron Age peoples, it is quite certain that some of the Late Stone Age groups in the south-west had acquired sheep and, later, cattle, at least by the first century before our era and almost certainly earlier. Some of these people can be identified with the historic Khoi Khoi and were nomadic pastoralists who grew no crops but who made a distinctive kind of pottery. No certainly identified pastoral occupation sites have yet been excavated, however, so our knowledge of these groups must be drawn from historic sources and not yet from archaeology. There is also debate as to whence they obtained their stock. Some suggest, on linguistic data, that it was from Eastern and Central Sudanic-speakers, others favour Early Iron Age migrants. Whatever the original source, this pastoral phase can hardly have begun before about 300 before our era at the earliest and it came to an end in the eighteenth century of our era.

The record provided by prehistoric studies in southern Africa shows, therefore, the high interior plateau lands to have played a leading part in the evolution of man the tool maker. The increasing ingenuity and efficiency with which succeeding hominid populations developed patterns of behaviour and the cultural equipment with which to exploit ever more intensively the resources of these eco-systems in which they lived help to explain the racial and cultural differences that distinguish the indigenous peoples of southern Africa today (San, Khoi-Khoi, BergDama, OvaTjimba, Twa and Bantu) as well as demonstrating the great antiquity and continuity of many behavioural traits which still persist up to the present time.

21 The prehistory of Central Africa

Part I R. de Bayle des Hermens

Introduction

Geographically, the Zaïre basin extends from the Gulf of Guinea in the west to the great lakes zone in the east and approximately from the 10th parallel south of the equator in Angola and Shaba (ex Katanga) to the watershed of the hydrographic basins of the Chad and the Zaïre in the north.[1]

It lies mainly in the equatorial zone and its plant cover consists of some of the densest forest to be found in Africa. This forest zone is known to have extended much farther north during certain very wet periods than it does at present. In the course of thousands of years the forest has retreated, and now exists only in galleries of varying width along the rivers. We emphasize the importance of this plant cover because it has been of the first importance in the development of prehistoric cultures in this region. It is thought, in the light of recent research, that prehistoric cultures and, it seems, more particularly those coming after the Acheulian, developed locally, conditioned by the primeval forest and without any contact with the inhabitants of zones where the vegetation was less dense. In the north, the great Neolithic migrations moving from east to west skirted the forest without penetrating it, as if it were a formidable barrier and a world into which peoples accustomed to living in the savannah and wide open spaces did not venture. Nothing in the industries of the Middle and Upper Palaeolithic, nor in the Neolithic, nor in cave art – which was moreover uncommon in the Zaïre Basin – gives ground for belief that there were contacts with the peoples living in a Sahara which was not then the great arid desert we know today. To find traces of contacts, we must turn to the east and south of Africa, where the starting-point of the migrations of the human groups which peopled the great equatorial forest in the west must likewise be sought.

1. The term Central Africa is taken to include the following countries: Zaïre, Central African Republic, People's Republic of Congo and Gabon, and parts of Angola, Rwanda and Burundi.

In the Quaternary, the Zaïre basin would seem to have had a climate very similar to that of East Africa, allowing for local variations due to the high altitude of the mountain regions. According to G. Mortelmans (1952) there were four pluvials and two humid periods:

Nakuran	2nd humid
Makalian	1st humid
Gamblian	4th pluvial
Kanjeran	3rd pluvial
Kamasian	2nd pluvial
Kageran	1st pluvial[2]

The settlement of people depended to some extent on these alternations of relatively dry periods with periods of high rainfall, which modified what is now called the environment.

The fact that the forest was dense and therefore difficult to penetrate has led several prehistorians to think that this zone was thinly populated from the Lower Palaeolithic to the Neolithic periods. We do not share this opinion and the myth about the difficulty of peopling this region should be abandoned. If relatively few stone tools have been found it is because research workers have hesitated to undertake lengthy investigations under difficult conditions. The results obtained recently by several expeditions in Angola, the Central African Republic and Zaïre and the large number of flaked stones they have collected indicate that the tropical forest was as thickly populated as other parts of Africa in prehistoric times.

Finally, it should be noted that in the humid equatorial zone the acidity of the soils impedes the preservation of organic remains. Consequently, human fossils, remains of fauna and bone tools are not found, with very rare exceptions which, moreover, relate to very recent, even historical, periods.

History of research

The prehistory of the equatorial forest of the Congo Basin remained unknown for a long time because of its extremely thick vegetation and

2. Nakuran: humid phase named after the deposits of the terrace below the 102-metre limit at Lake Nakuru in Kenya.

Makalian: humid phase recognized in the 114-metre and 102-metre terraces at Lake Nakuru.

Gamblian: fourth pluvial identified around Lakes Nakuru, Naïvaha and especially Elementeita (Gamble's Cave) in Kenya.

Kanjeran: third pluvial named by L. S. B. Leakey after a fossil-bearing deposit discovered at Kanjera on the Kavirondo Gulf.

Kamasian: second pluvial, which owes its name to the diatomite deposits studied by Gregory at Kamasia in the Kenya Rift valley.

Kageran: first pluvial, so named after a system of terraces on the river Kagera in Tanzania, discovered by E. J. Wayland in 1934.

TABLE 21.1 *Climatic variations and prehistoric industries of the Congo Basin after G. Mortelmans (1952)*

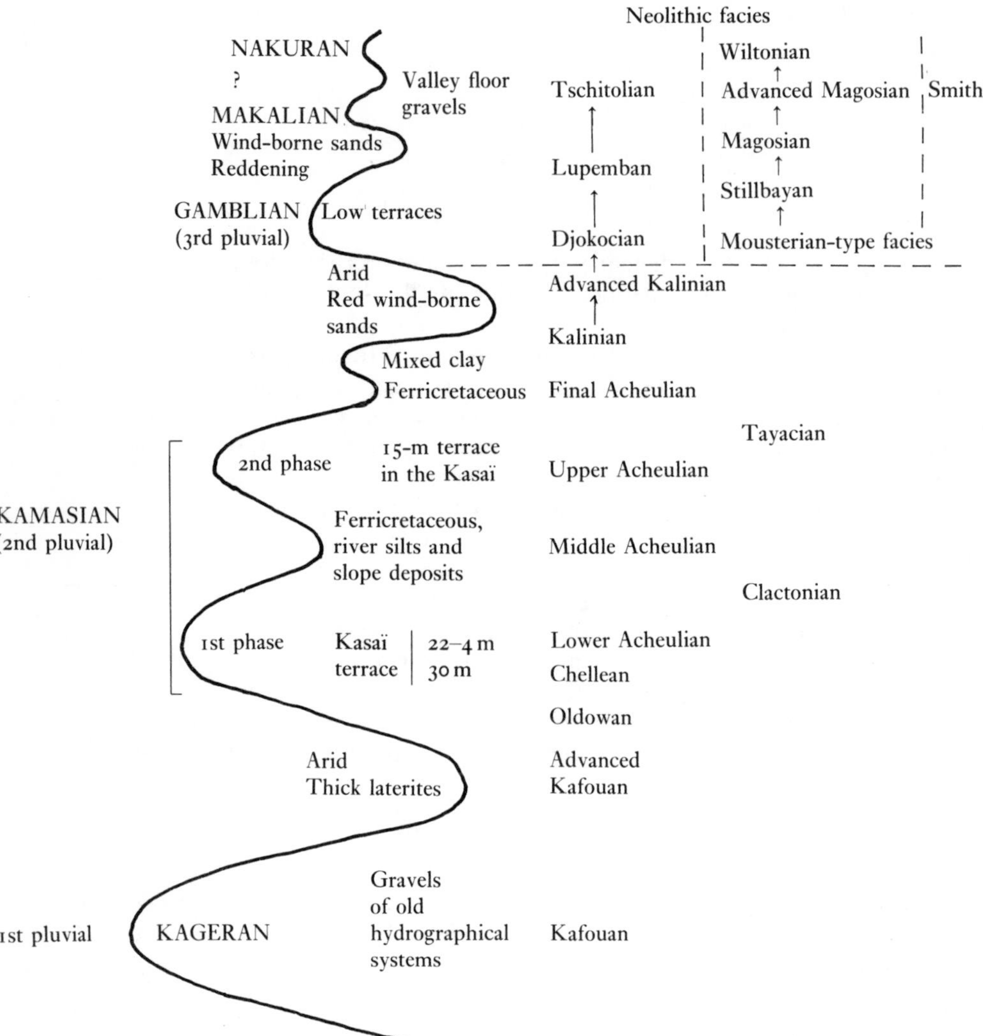

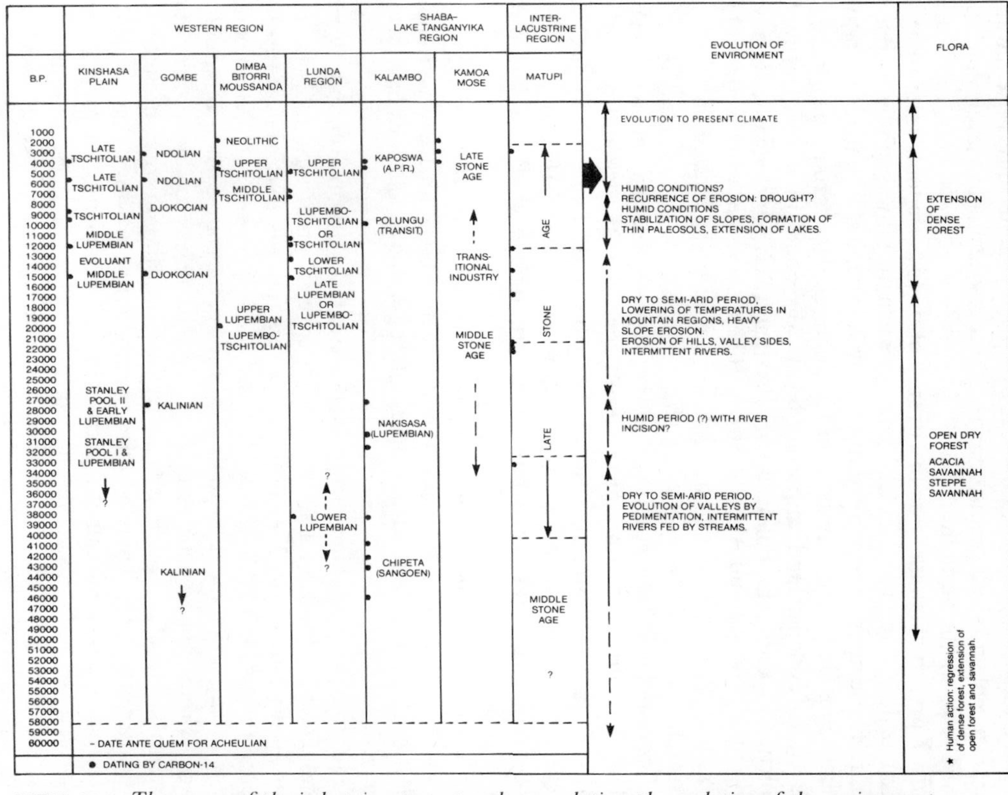

TABLE 21.2 *The names of the industries, present carbon-14 dating, the evolution of the environment and flora*

because of the massive laterite formations in which the industries of several prehistoric civilizations were deeply embedded.

The first attempts to study its prehistory had to wait until major public works were undertaken (the construction of railway lines, roads, bridges and sanitary canals) and the region was prospected for its mineral deposits, for then geologists and prehistorians had access to geological levels in which stone tools might be found.

In Zaïre, the first sporadic discoveries of prehistoric tools seem to have been made by Commandant Cl. Zboïnsky when the railway lines were being built. These finds were studied in 1899 by X. Stainier, who made tentative conclusions despite the absence of stratigraphic data. From 1927 to 1938 research developed and important work was done, in particular by J. Colette, F. Cabu, E. Polinard, M. Becquaert; G. Mortelmans, Rév. P. Anciaux de Favaux and Abbé H. Breuil. The most recent work is that of H. van Moorsel, F. van Noten and D. Cahen, who are all engaged on further research.

Less work has been published on the People's Republic of the Congo, whose territory lies mainly in the forest zone. Mention should be made, however, of the research and studies of J. Babet, R. L. Doize, G. Droux, H. Kelley, J. Lombard and P. Le Roy, which relate particularly to the discoveries made along the railway line running from Pointe-Noire to Brazzaville.

The prehistory of Gabon is known through the work of Guy de Beauchène, B. Farine, B. Blankoff and Y. Pommeret, but there again our knowledge is rather limited and no firm stratigraphic conclusions have been reached.

The first investigations made in the Central African Republic were conducted by Professor Lacroix, who discovered prehistoric tools in the alluvial deposits of the Mouka plateau rivers towards 1930. These results were published in 1933 by Abbé H. Breuil and in the same year Félix Eboué drew attention to some stone tools unearthed in the course of various public works. From 1966 to 1968 R. de Bayle des Hermens was able to carry out systematic research which gave a fairly exact idea of the prehistoric industries of a region where practically nothing had previously been found.

Little was known about the prehistory of Cameroon until very recent years and we had to wait for the work of N. David, J. Hervieu and A. Marliac to give us the first general picture of the situation in a part of Africa which archaeologically has still to be fully explored.

Research in Angola is associated with the names of J. Janmart, H. Breuil and J. D. Clark, who took as their hunting-ground the rich alluvial deposits of the diamond workings.

Chronological bases

For this section we shall use the chronology of the Quaternary era

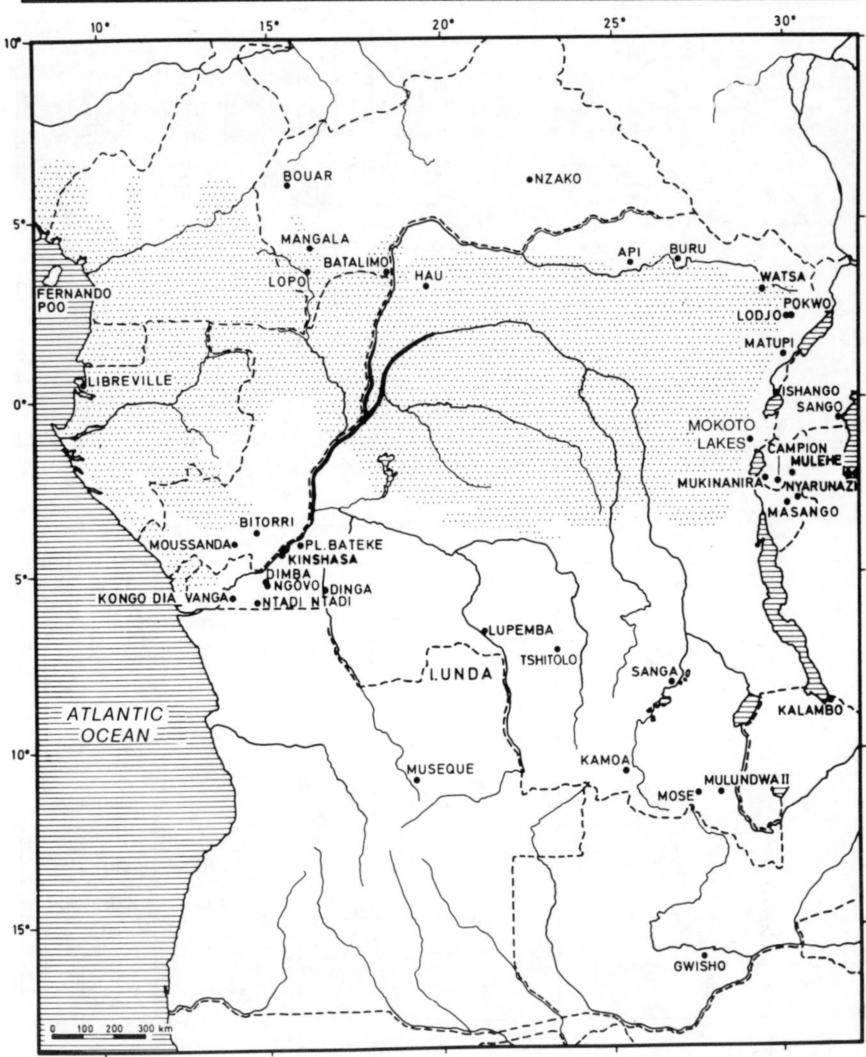

FIG. 21.1 *Central Africa: places mentioned in the text*

established by G. Mortelmans (1955–7) for the Zaïre basin, which is the most acceptable one in the light of present knowledge (Fig. 21.1).

The Kageran pluvial

This seems to be the most important of the four successive pluvials. It was a period of intensive valley excavation and in which very old gravel terraces containing the oldest industries of the Zaïre basin were formed. These industries, consisting almost entirely of roughly worked pebbles, are classified as pre-lower Acheulian (G. Mortelmans' Kafuan). A long arid

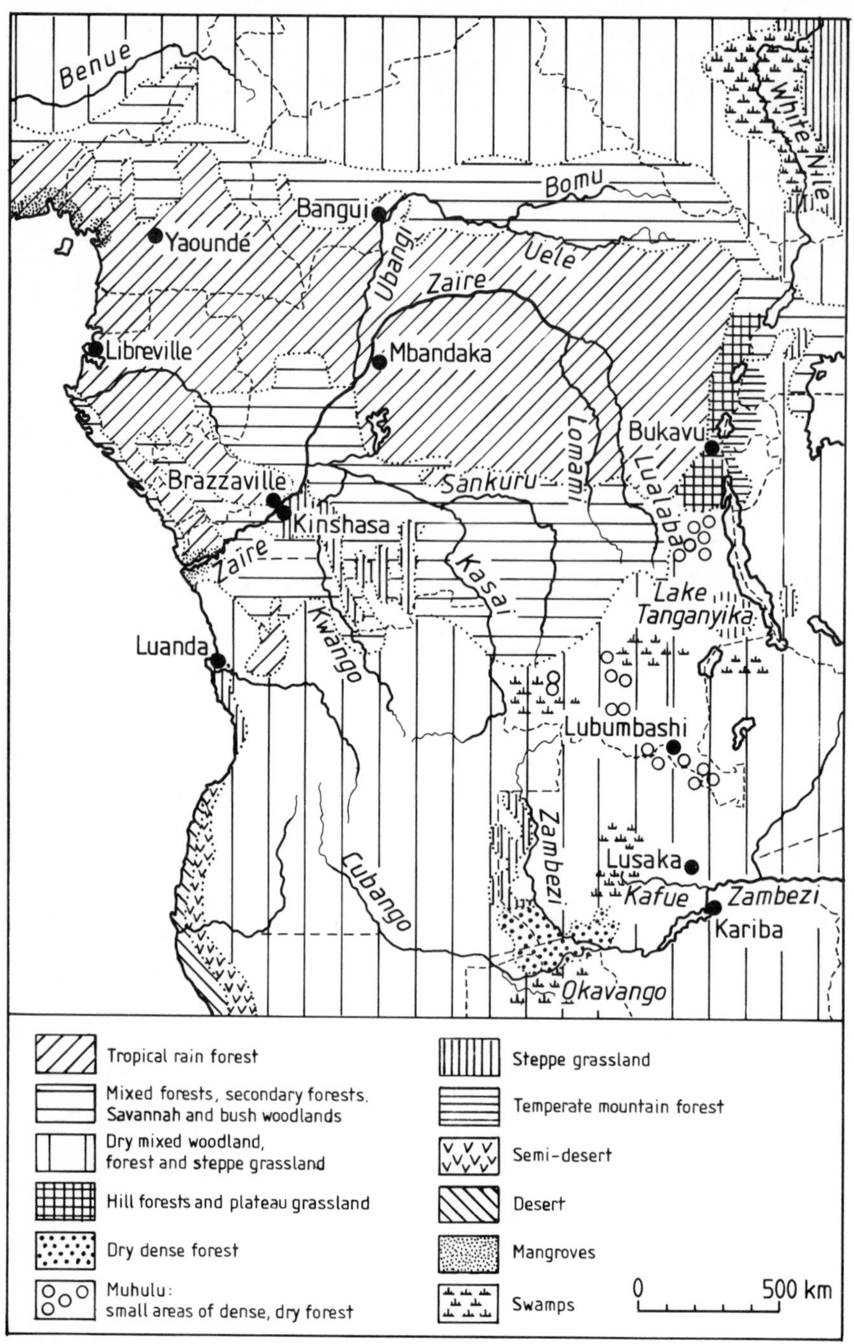

FIG. 21.2 *Central Africa: vegetation zones*

period followed the Kageran pluvial and the old terraces were covered with a thick mantle of laterite. Here pre-Acheulian industry has been found which is lacking in chronological definition owing to the lack of stratigraphic evidence.

The Kamasian pluvial

This pluvial occurred at the final stage of the Lower Pleistocene and lasted for the whole of the Middle Pleistocene. It consisted of two phases separated by a drier period. In the Kasai basin the 30-metre and 22–4-metre terraces date back to this period; in Shaba and, it seems, in the west of the Central African Republic it is represented by gravel terraces, valley-floors and fossil-beds of streams. During this pluvial in regions with moderate relief, some river-beds were entirely filled in and the water then cut out a new course. In the lower strata of these fossil river-beds, pre-Acheulian tools have been found which are more highly developed than those discovered in the old Kageran terraces. A few bifacial artefacts begin to appear but they too are difficult to date with any certainty.

After the climax of the Kamasian pluvial the roughly flaked pebble industries were superseded by the Lower Acheulian. This Lower Acheulian still comprised many flaked stone artefacts but new tools began to appear: bifacial implements and handaxes in particular. The latter, rather rare to begin with, soon came to occupy an important place among the tools of this civilization.

The first Kamasian climax was followed by a moderately dry phase in the course of which new laterite formations developed, slopes crumbled and river silt was deposited. A Middle Acheulian industry is associated with this period. Its artefacts were generally made by flaking, usually from the side of a core by what is called the Victoria West I technique.[3]

With the second Kamasian climax,[4] which was less pronounced than the first, new gravels were deposited and the 15-metre terraces of the Kasaï were laid down. The new dry period resulted in new laterite formations. The Acheulian industry continued to evolve with a new flaking technique known as Victoria West II, and the development of a new tool, the pick, which was to occupy a prominent place among the objects produced by post-Acheulian industries in the forest zone.

The post-Kamasian arid period is the most important known in this region. The Sahara spread southwards and the Kalahari desert northwards. Some writers believe that the equatorial forest practically disappeared, only surviving in narrow belts of woodland. Red desert sand accumulated in layers, sometimes of considerable depth. The Acheulian industry died out,

3. Name given to two Levallois flaking techniques observed especially in the industries discovered in the vicinity of the Victoria Falls on the Zambezi.

4. Some writers hold this second Kamasian climax to be the Kanjeran. This gives four humid periods instead of three, including one with two quite distinct phases.

or rather it seemed to develop locally into a new industry called the Sangoan, particularly in equatorial Africa and the forest zones.

Tools were transformed. Handaxes became rare and finally disappeared; bifacial artefacts became thicker and more massive; picks abounded and new tools totally unknown in the Acheulian period made their appearance – long bifaces of large size. These tools would seem to be suited to forest life. This conclusion is not, however, consistent with the environment in which the Sangoan developed, if it is assumed that the equatorial forest had practically disappeared by the post-Kamasian arid period from which this industry is dated. It must be recognized that at present the Sangoan is one of the African industries about which we know very little.

The Gamblian pluvial

In the course of the Gamblian pluvial the equatorial forest was reconstituted, the rivers hollowed out valleys and deposited silt which formed low terraces – this silt being composed of the wind-borne sands accumulated during the preceding arid period. In western Zaïre and Kasaï, the Sangoan tended to develop into a new and less massive industry known as the Lupemban, which was also regarded as a forest culture. In the south-eastern regions, industries akin to those of South Africa and Kenya developed. Characterized by flakes and blades with Mousterian features, and denoted Middle Stone Age, they are as difficult to identify typologically as stratigraphically – stratigraphical evidence being frequently non-existent.

Post-Gamblian humid phases: the Makalian and Nakuran

These two periods were much less extreme than the pluvials which preceded them. They were separated by a short dry phase and the Nakuran is not very clearly differentiated in the Zaïre Basin. In the Makalian the rivers hollowed out shallow beds and these were then filled in again. The Lupemban industry evolved locally, the tools becoming smaller and smaller while chisels and arrow-heads became very numerous in the Tschitolian, which was a culture of hunters. In eastern Zaire, Shaba and Angola, several aspects characteristic of the Late Stone Age developed. This assemblage should be thoroughly re-examined, for it embraces several different and seemingly incompatible industries which cannot, at present, be fitted into a definite place in the chronological sequence.

During and after the Nakuran humid period, Neolithic industries, including the Tschitolian, spread over the whole of equatorial Africa, where they seem to have lasted much longer than they did elsewhere. The copper and Iron Ages did not penetrate into this relatively inaccessible region until a much later date, which again tends to indicate that its prehistoric cultures developed locally.

The prehistoric industries of the Zaïre Basin

Pre-Acheulian industries

Very early prehistoric industries consisting of worked pebbles are to be found in practically the whole of the Zaïre Basin. They are generally buried under old laterites as in the upper Kafila Basin in Zaïre, and in the laterite formations of the Salo plateau in upper Sangha in the Central African Republic, where they are also encountered in the deep alluvial deposits of fossil river-beds. In Angola they exist in the deep beds of coarse alluvial deposits found in many great rivers.

These ancient prehistoric cultures, usually known as Pebble or Earlier Stone Age cultures, bear various names according to the localities where they were found or to the prehistorians who reported them first. In point of fact they are all part of a slow evolution of flaking techniques which lasted nearly 2 million years.

KAFUAN

The eponymous site is in the Kafu valley in Uganda. This industry was discovered by E. J. Wayland in 1919 and consists of river pebbles from which three flakes were struck off in three directions or, very rarely, in one only, to make a crude cutting tool. Today the Kafuan is subdivided into four stages: Archaic Kafuan, Early Kafuan, Late Kafuan and Advanced Kafuan. Traces of these four stages are found at Nsongesi (in the south of Uganda) in 82- and 61-metre terraces. The Advanced Kafuan is very close or even identical to the Oldowan. Some prehistorians hold that the early stages of the Kafuan cannot be regarded as evidence of human workmanship and that the chipped pebbles were produced by natural processes.

OLDOWAN

The eponymous site is at Olduvai in the Serengeti plain in Tanzania. It was discovered by Katwinkel in 1911 and became famous in 1926 because of the researches and finds of L. S. B. Leakey.

The Olduvai Gorge cuts deeply through the deposits of a lake which once existed during the Middle and Upper Pleistocene periods. Eleven Chelleo-Acheulian levels have been identified above a pre-Acheulian level constituting the Oldowan.

The Oldowan is an industry of artefacts made with river pebbles, most of which are less flat than the Kafuan ones. Flaking was more highly developed and the curved cutting edge was obtained by working alternate sides. In the final stage of this industry, the pebbles were shaped to a point which is an early forerunner of the bifacial artefacts of later cultures. The Oldowan industry has been found in Shaba, in the west of the Central African Republic (in the upper Sangha alluvial deposits), and it seems to have existed in the north-east of Angola. On the other hand, although a few widely scattered specimens of roughly worked pebbles have been found in Cameroon, Gabon and the People's Republic of the Congo, this industry has not been identified with any certainty in the three last-mentioned countries bordering on the Gulf of Guinea.

The Acheulian industry

The Acheulian culture is particularly well represented in the Zaïre Basin and some alluvial terrace deposits are exceptionally rich in artefacts. The division of the Acheulian into four stages, or five, according to which author is consulted, is chiefly a matter of classifying different flaking and retouching techniques. The distinctions are more typological than stratigraphical. The Acheulian deposits are found mainly in the alluvium of early watercourses, which formed terraces; in the gravels and sands of valley-floors; and in the fossil-beds of streams which have changed course. Consequently the industries are not found in their place of origin: running water has moved and accumulated them, and in the process they have become worn. Consequently, the study of the Acheulian artefacts of these deposits is based chiefly on typology and not on stratigraphy, as it is at Olduvai where the lake deposits containing the industries are some 100 metres deep.

The Acheulian industry was characterized by a fairly wide range of tools which were much more developed than in the pre-Acheulian cultures. Worked pebbles continued to be used, but they became rarer as the industry progressed without, however, disappearing entirely. New tools assumed great importance – first of all the biface which, as the name indicates, was made of a pebble flaked on both sides. It was oval or pear-shaped, with a more or less sharp point; the base was often rounded, the section usually lentiform and the dimensions were very variable. Another important tool was the cleaver, knapped from a flake and with a cutting-edge opposite the base. In addition there were picks, not very numerous during the Lower and Middle Acheulian periods but very plentiful in the final stage of this culture. As well as these four tools, many varieties of flakes of very different sizes were used untrimmed or were retouched to form side-scrapers, end-scrapers and other less refined tools such as the notched implements.

There are five subdivisions of the Acheulian based on typology and working techniques.

ACHEULIAN I [TERMED ABBEVILLIAN OR EARLY CHELLEAN BY SOME WRITERS]

The tools comprise very large flakes made from blocks of stone by percussion on a striking platform. These Clactonian flakes were sometimes used untrimmed, but were usually transformed into bifaces and cleavers – heavy, massive tools with markedly curved cutting-edges. Pebble flaking did not disappear. On the contrary, we know that this pre-Acheulian skill was perfected, for some of the so-called unworked-base bifaces are the finest specimens of flaked pebbles.

This stage is represented in Shaba in the Kamoa and Luena deposits discovered by Fr. Cabu. Examples also come from northern Angola, where they have been found in the Luembe Basin. Some deposits in the west of the Central African Republic also belong to this stage. Acheulian I tools recovered from alluvial terrace deposits or fossil river-beds are very often found to have been much worn by the action of the water. This is particularly typical of the Lopo and Libangué deposits in the Central African Republic.

ACHEULIAN II (LATE ABBEVILLIAN OR LOWER ACHEULIAN)

This industry is very like the preceding one, and is equally found in the gravels of the rivers of Angola and Shaba but the tools are less water-worn and, above all, the secondary flaking is more finished than is the case with the Acheulian I tools. The edges of bifaces and of handaxes are straighter, apparently as a result of reworking with a flaking tool of soft material such as wood or bone.

ACHEULIAN III (MIDDLE ACHEULIAN)

The tools of this stage are found near the surface of the gravels of the Luena and the Kamoa where they are incorporated in river silts. At this period a real revolution occurred in working techniques, namely the preparation of a core with a view to obtaining large flakes. This technique, well known in southern Africa, is called Victoria West I. It marks the beginning of a proto-Levallois technique. The preparatory work on the core produced a multi-faceted striking platform. The flake was removed laterally and then carefully retouched to make a biface, a cleaver, or a side-scraper. The flaking was done with a soft percussion implement. The tools are very regular and symmetrical and the side edges are practically straight. The side edges of the cleavers have been trimmed to make them lozenge-shaped in section.

ACHEULIAN IV (UPPER ACHEULIAN)

At this stage, working techniques remained basically the same but were improved (Victoria West II technique). The core was much rounder, with a faceted striking platform from which large curved flakes were removed. They had a narrow base instead of the very wide base characteristic of the Victoria West I technique. The flakes were used to make tools – bifaces, side-scrapers and cleavers – which were all very carefully retouched. The section of the handaxes is trapezoidal or lentiform. This upper Acheulian industry is found at Kamoa in silts of the Kamasian II age and in the 15-metre terraces of the Kasaï.

ACHEULIAN V (ADVANCED AND FINAL ACHEULIAN)

The final Acheulian stage saw the beginning of a cultural change which introduced regional forms better adapted to the climatic and vegetational environment. At this time human settlements developed on the now dry middle and low terraces. The Levallois technique began to be used as well as the earlier techniques. Otherwise the tools varied little from those of the preceding stages, except for a general improvement, more finished work in particular, and for the appearance of very large bifaces and cleavers, some of which were over 30 centimetres long. One tool greatly developed during this period was the pick. It was robust and heavy, triangular or trapezoidal in section, and was perhaps intended for use with large oblong bifaces for wood-working. It is thus a forerunner of the Sangoan complex. We also find stone balls perfectly shaped and comparable to the South American *bolas*. A particularly large collection of these balls was discovered in the Mangala river deposits in the west of the Central African Republic. This final Acheulian industry is found in Shaba, Kamoa and around Kalina in Zaïre. It is also represented in Angola, perhaps around Brazzaville and, in the Central African Republic, in the rich deposits of the Ngoere river in upper Sangha.

Unfortunately, nothing is known about the people of this culture, for no organic remains have been preserved in any part of the Zaïre basin owing to the acidity of its soils.

The Sangoan industry

The eponymous site which gave this culture its name is Sango Bay on the west bank of Lake Victoria in Tanzania. It was discovered by E. J. Wayland in 1920.

The Sangoan industry stems directly from the local Acheulian technique without any trace of external influence. It was contemporary with the end of the Kanjeran pluvial and lasted during a transition phase between this pluvial and the major arid period which followed. It is a relatively little-known industry which displays several local characteristics. These seem to have evolved in isolation and were adapted to a forest environment, or rather to lightly wooded environment, since the industry coincided with the beginning of an arid period. Five stages have been distinguished in this culture: Proto-Sangoan, Lower Sangoan, Middle Sangoan, Upper Sangoan and Final Sangoan.

The Sangoan stone tools – for only the stone ones have survived – are very different from those of the final Acheulian industry which preceded them. At the beginning of the Sangoan industry, the bifaces followed the Acheulian tradition but they gradually became heavier, wider and shorter, while at the same time other bifaces, akin to picks and with two pointed ends, began to be produced. Cleavers, on the contrary, died out very quickly, the rare surviving examples are small and the edges of both sides, shaped by removing broad flakes, are wavy. Roughly flaked pebbles are still found but not in very large numbers. The picks which began to appear at the end of the Acheulian became an important tool. They were large, with a triangular, lozenge-shaped or trapezoidal section, and since they are found in association with many side-scrapers, one can conclude that they were designed for working wood. The most spectacular development was the creation of long, narrow bifaces, percussion-flaked and often very finely worked. These implements sometimes account for almost a quarter of the Sangoan tools discovered in a deposit. They have been classified into various types of tool: picks, planes, chisels, gouges and daggers. They are often combined to produce multi-purpose tools such as chisel-picks, plane-picks, gouge-picks, dagger-picks. Some of the implements were exceptionally large, being over 25 centimetres long. As the Sangoan industry evolved, these tools, which scarcely varied at all in type, became smaller while the flaking technique was brought close to perfection.

The products of Sangoan industry are found in great quantities in the Zaïre basin. The industry is known in the Kinshasa plain in Zaïre, and in upper Shaba, where it differs from that of the western zones in the absence of daggers and leaf-shaped points. On the other hand, the industry includes many *bolas,* faceted polyhedrons or balls carefully finished by a hammering technique, and large numbers of discarded flakes. Examples have been found in the alluvial deposits of the river Luembe, at Candala, and in Lunda in the north-east of Angola, where they are mingled with those of industries of other periods because they were lying in gravels which had been disturbed. They have also been found in the People's Republic of the Congo, on the right bank of Stanley Pool and in Gabon, where they were recently identified. In the Central African Republic, the industry is represented by exceptionally rich deposits situated on the eastern side of the central part of the country, where the alluvium of the Nzako diamond workings at Ambile, Téré, Tiaga and Kono has yielded thousands of remarkably well preserved tools which can be classified as belonging to the Middle or Upper Sangoan stage.

Up till now the Sangoan has not been certainly identified in Cameroon and this raises the problem of its extension towards West Africa. Some authorities have reported it in Senegal. In point of fact, the industries in question possess bifaces which are identical or very close to the Sangoan but they have not so far been dated with any certainty in the chronology of prehistory. Groups of people may conceivably have moved westwards in the equatorial forest zone but at present we have no means of identifying them or their influence.

Like the Acheulian before it, the Sangoan evolved locally, without much contact with the world outside the forest environment. It was followed, under conditions still imperfectly understood, by an industry called the Lupemban.

The Lupemban industry

According to the classification recommended at the 1955 Pan-African Congress, the Lupemban[5] is a Middle Stone Age industry. However, the

5. Lupemban: the name comes from the prehistoric site of Lupemba in the Kasaï. The term was first used by Abbé H. Breuil.

term Middle Stone Age should be used with caution, for a whole group of heterogeneous tools whose position on the time-scale has not as yet been properly established has been placed under this head.

The Lupemban developed at a time when the rainfall was at normal levels at the beginning of the fourth or Gamblian pluvial. It reached its peak during the second part of this very humid period and absolute dating techniques indicate that it lasted some 25 000 years. Like the final Acheulian in the course of its local development, the Sangoan became more refined and acquired new flaking techniques which were perfected in the Lupemban period without trace of outside influence though naturally adapting to the forest environment. At the beginning of the Lupemban period, the industry still included a few bifaces, but these were discarded very quickly. No cleavers have been found. The Levallois technique predominated in the production of blades and flakes, which were trimmed by flaking. At a later stage, the Levallois technique was still used for obtaining flakes, but a much more advanced technique known as pressure-flaking was used for producing handsome blades from which long, narrow and admirably retouched implements were made.

Five stages of the Lupemban industry have been identified.

LUPEMBAN I

Examples of this stage are found throughout the western basin of the Zaïre, where the industry seems to be a local development of the Sangoan. Acheulian characteristics have disappeared entirely and flaking and polishing were carried out by the percussion technique. Sangoan tools were still produced, but gradually became smaller. The maximum length of picks, plane-picks and flat-edged picks was 15 centimetres. Gouges, chisels, cutting-tools and saws shaped from blades made their appearance. Alongside these finely made implements, the basic tools continued to be crude flakes. At the end of Lupemban I, points, daggers and true arrow-heads began to appear.

LUPEMBAN II

This stage was identified at Pointe Kalina by J. Colette, but specimens have also been found at Stanley Pool. The leaf-shaped chisels of Lupemban I were improved and became axes. Straight-edged chisels and a new type of tranchet with a slanting blade replaced the Sangoan types. Weapons included daggers from 15 to 35 centimetres long with very thin, finely flaked, leaf-shaped points.

LUPEMBAN III

This industry has been identified in surface deposits at Stanley Pool and at some deposits in Angola. At this stage stone-shaping skills reached the peak of perfection with the pressure-trimming technique. Flakes obtained by means of an advanced Levallois technique were triangular, rectangular or oval. Hafted tools appeared, developed and became very widespread. Tools of the early Lupemban type are also found here, but smaller in size: picks, chisels, small bifaces, a few side-scrapers, files, tranchets with straight or slanting cutting edges, backed blades. Daggers sometimes attained considerable size, even up to 46 centimetres long. The points were denticular, thus forming lethal weapons. Axes became more common, without, however, being very numerous. The important development was the arrow-head of various types, some highly refined: some leaf-shaped, some lozenge-shaped, hafted or otherwise, some with denticulated edges.

In Angola a late stage of the Lupemban industry has been dated by the carbon-14 method at 14 503 ± 560 years before our era.

LUPEMBAN IV

Very little is known about the Lupemban IV industry. Its main feature would seem to be a flaking technique, very close to the Levallois.

LUPEMBO-TSCHITOLIAN

This final stage seeems to have occurred, according to stratigraphical evidence, during the arid phase which terminated the Pleistocene in central and eastern Africa and just before the first Makalian humid period. The known deposits are situated on beds of gravelly alluvium or at the bottom of the humid layer covering them and in many cases on river islands.

The flaking technique employed during the other stages of the Lupemban industry remained unchanged. It was still Levallois in type. Retouching, on the other hand, was done by a new technique, partly percussion and partly pressure. This was the abrupt trimming which is characteristic of the Mesolithic period. The tools still included chisels, gouges and bifaces, but no more side-scrapers or backed blades were produced. To the tranchets was added a small tranchet with steeped trimmed edges, which can be regarded as a weapon with a transverse cutting-edge. Arrow-heads were more diversified – leaf-shaped, lozenge-shaped, barbed, more rarely denticulated and hafted.

In Angola, an industry classified as Lupembo-Tschitolian has been dated from 11 189 ± 490 years before our era.

The Lupemban industry has not yet been found in the Central African Republic or in Cameroon. On the other hand, it has been reported in the People's Republic of Congo and Gabon. However, as the deposits are situated in regions which are not easily accessible, very few details are available at present.

Prehistoric cultures in non-forest environments

While the Lupemban industry continued in the forest zone in the west of the basin, cultures in non-forest environments were developing in Shaba and eastern Angola: the proto-Stillbayan, Stillbayan and Magosian. These cultures became widespread in eastern and southern Africa.

PROTO-STILLBAYAN

The eponymous site is Still Bay, on the coast of Cape Province. The proto-Stillbayan industry is characterized by unifacial points, end-scrapers, arrow-nocks, hurling stones, and a few small bifaces, thick semi-foliate points, crudely retouched, and a few burins. These tools were produced by relatively abrupt retouching.

STILLBAYAN

The Stillbayan tools were not appreciably different from those of the preceding stage, but they display great mastery of Levallois-type flaking techniques. An important development was pressure-trimming, used chiefly in the shaping of unifacial or bifacial weapons and points of the Mousterian type which often retained a faceted heel. At the final stage, known only in Kenya, the tools included backed blades, burins and circle segments.

The proto-Stillbayan industry is prevalent in Shaba; the Stillbayan is less common. The oldest human remains discovered in Zaïre belong to the Stillbayan period. These are two molars found along with specimens of flaked quartz and a bifacial point by Rév. P. Anciaux de Favaux in the bone-bearing breccias of Kakontwe.

MAGOSIAN

The eponymous site of this industry is at Magosi in Uganda. It was discovered by Wayland in 1926. The Magosian culture continued to use the principal Stillbayan-type methods. The industry includes microliths: backed blades, circle segments, triangles, U-shaped end-scrapers, micro-burins and also beads made of ostrich eggshell. The Magosian may have existed in Shaba but no site has yet been identified with any certainty.

A mesolithic industry: the Tschitolian

At the end of the Pleistocene, two relatively dry periods caused the equatorial forest to recede, particularly at high altitudes. It was on soils thus freed from dense vegetation, in the vicinity of springs, and often at the top of tablelands or on mountain passes that Tschitolian man settled.[6] Deposits of this type are known on the Bateke plateau, at Stanley Pool, in the Kinshasa plain and in the north-east of Angola. The tools vary from one deposit to another. They still include a fairly large proportion of implements for working wood though these are now very small. New tools or tools little known in the preceding industries have been found: planes, blades with trimmed points, backed knives and above all geometrically shaped microliths such as trapezes, triangles, orange segments and small tranchets. Arrow-heads vary widely in type and shape, being leaf-shaped, lozenge-

6. Tschitolian: this term was coined when a deposit of stone tools was found at Tschitolo in the Kasaï.

shaped, oval, triangular, barbed, tanged, denticulated or transversal. They were shaped almost entirely by pressure-trimming which gave them a very keen cutting-edge.

Because the weapons of the Tschitolian industry are limited to arrow-heads, it may be regarded as a pre-Neolithic culture without pottery or polished axes. It emerged as a late form of African forest culture prior to the development of the Neolithic culture of western Zaïre, which seems to have been intrusive.

The Neolithic industry

The prehistoric cultures we have mentioned, which existed throughout the Zaïre basin from the pre-Acheulian period to the Tschitolian, represent the successive stages of a vast cultural complex which developed in a forest environment without receiving any appreciable contributions from the outside.

Aspects of the Neolithic – for it must be at once understood that there are several of these, sometimes very different from one another – developed during the short last pluvial, the Nakuran. At that time, the climate was much the same as it is today. The forest was denser, as it had not yet suffered from the inroads made by man. The plant species were those which exist today.

So it was in dense tropical forest that the people of a Neolithic culture known as Western Congo gradually invaded the region from the north and crossed the river near the Isanghila rapids. These people brought with them techniques which merged to some degree with local techniques. The distinguishing feature of this Neolithic industry is the almost exclusive use of rocks which are very difficult to work, such as schists, quartz and jadeite, so that poorly made flakes were produced, resulting in very mediocre tools. These tools vary with the site. They comprise crudely made picks, chisels, very small roughly flaked pebbles, perforated stones of various shapes, weights and materials and, above all, a large number of axes. The latter were first shaped and partly polished, then pecked and finely polished. In Zaïre many rubbing-stones have been found. They were undoubtedly used for polishing axes. Arrow-heads are not lacking, but they are generally of poor workmanship and in many cases they are made of flakes of quartz. In some sites, especially at Isangho, the industry includes bone tools, and in particular, harpoons with one, then two, rows of barbs. Along with these stone and bone tools, some deposits were rich in very well decorated pottery.

Neolithic sites have been found in western Kwango, in association with the Tschitolian, on both banks of the river Zaïre between Stanley Pool and Congo dia Vanga, and at several points in the People's Republic of the Congo. A site with a large number of haematite axes, particularly carefully polished, has been found in the Uele Basin in the north of Zaïre. Various aspects of the Neolithic have been found in Cameroon, Gabon and the Central African Republic. In the latter, the Batalimo deposit in Lobaye has yielded a jadeite industry in which large numbers of flaked axes are associated with very fine pottery. The date indicated for this industry by the thermo-luminescence method is 380 ± 220 of our era. This date may at first glance seem abnormal, but on reflection and in the light of present knowledge, it would seem that the Neolithic did indeed last much longer in the equatorial forest than it did in other regions, surviving into historical times. The introduction of metals seems to have occurred very late in this zone. According to some authorities, iron came in around the ninth century of our era.

Megalithic monuments

Megalithic cultures developed in various forms throughout Africa, more especially in North Africa and the Sahara. Such cultures did not exist in the Zaïre basin, except in the north-west of what is now the Central African Republic. In Angola, Zaïre, Gabon and the People's Republic of the Congo no megalithic monuments have been found, and in Cameroon only a few standing stones exist.

The Central African Republic, on the other hand, possesses quite spectacular megaliths in the Bouar region. These monuments are situated in a tract of land 130 kilometres long and some 30 kilometres wide on the watershed of the Zaïre and Chad basins. They do not seem to exist in Cameroon or in other parts of the Central African Republic, so this culture was undoubtedly confined geographically to the north-west of the country.

The monuments are in the form of tumuli varying in size, crowned with standing stones ranging in number from just a few to several dozen, and rising in some cases 3 metres above the ground. Several of these monuments have been excavated and their internal structure revealed, but very little archaeological material has been found apart from specimens of flaked quartz, pottery and some metal objects embedded in the upper strata. However, the charcoal recovered has made it possible to apply the carbon-14 dating method.[7] This has yielded some extremely important dates, one group lying in the lowest strata of the monuments: 7440 ± 170 b.p., that is, 5490 before our era and 6700 ± 140 b.p., that is, 4750 before our era; and a second group: 1920 ± 100 b.p., that is, 30 of our era and 2400 ± 110 b.p., that is, 450 of our era. The earlier of these two groups of dates indicates when the megaliths were erected and the later when they were re-utilized. The fact that they were re-utilized is confirmed by the handful of metal objects recovered from the upper strata. At the present stage of research, we cannot be certain where the Bouar megaliths should be placed in the Neolithic period, but the culture which erected them can at least be said to be contemporary with the Neolithic.

Rock art

Lying as it does between the two great regions of rock art, the Sahara and

7. R. de Bayle des Hermens and P. Vidal, 1971.

South Africa, the Zaïre basin also has its rock art, but not as rich an art as might be expected in view of its position.

In Chad, at Ennedi and Borkou, a rock art developed which belongs to the great Saharan complex. In Cameroon there is a site in the north, at Bidzar, with engravings on horizontal slabs of rock, polished and worn by erosion. Most of the figures are geometric, representing circles and loops. They are found separately or in groups.

In Angola there are engravings in the Calola region. They appear on horizontal slabs of rock and the designs are geometric as in Cameroon. Paintings which appear to be more recent have been reported from the same area. In Zaïre there are a number of sites dating from various periods. Shaba seems to be the province which is richest in rock art, belonging to the same group as Zambia and eastern Angola. The art of this group is characteristically abstract and not naturalistic like that of South Africa. In 1952, Abbé Henri Breuil published the incised and dotted figures in the Kiantapo Cave[8] and G. Mortelmans a tentative synthesis of research on the Shaba rock drawings[9] in which he stressed the difficulty of dating the different styles owing to the lack of arachaeological evidence. Engraved rock slabs have been discovered in the lower Zaïre basin, where rock art continued to be practised up to quite recent times. A series of engravings at Mount Gundu in the Uele basin seem to have been connected with water and fire rites.

In the Central African Republic, the rock art which has so far been discovered is situated in the north and east of the country. In the north, the Toulou, Kiumbala and Djebel Mela shelters contain paintings done with white, black and red ochre, in which human beings are represented, along with various signs, but no animals. In the east, the Lengo and Mpatou sites near Bakouma include engravings on horizontal slabs of laterite, which appear to be relatively recent and were the work of people already familiar with iron, judging from the numerous throwing-knives and lance-heads represented.

The rock art of the Zaïre basin bears no resemblance to that of the Sahara. It is to South and East Africa that we must look to find its origins. This art is very close to that found in Bantu lands, so it is recent, belonging even to historical times. However, it is important for the study of migrations and population movements during a period of the protohistory or even the history of tropical Africa of which we know very little.

Conclusions

From the foregoing account of the prehistory of the Zaïre basin it is apparent that right up to the Upper Acheulian the prehistoric industries differed very little from what is known in the other regions of south

8. Abbé H. Breuil, 1952.
9. G. Mortelmans, 1952a.

equatorial Africa. It was from the Sangoan complex onwards that there began a great regional diversification of the cultures of the forest zone. This has one remarkable feature, namely the almost total isolation in which the men of the forest region lived until the arrival of the Neolithic people who came from the north, perhaps already fleeing the Saharan zones as these became more arid.

The great equatorial forest acted as a natural barrier restricting contact with the areas north and south of the equator. Neolithic cultures lasted in this zone much longer than they did elsewhere, for they were isolated and protected up to a time when other regions had long since entered the historical period with the introduction of metals and iron-working.

Part II F. Van Noten with the collaboration of P. de Maret, J. Moeyersons, K. Muya and E. Roche

Introduction

For the purposes of this section of the chapter, Central Africa comprises Zaïre and some of the countries bordering on it: the People's Republic of the Congo, Gabon, Rio Muni, the Central African Republic, Rwanda, Burundi and Angola.

This part of the continent has attracted the attention of archaeologists since the end of the nineteenth century, but research in it has been very sporadic.

The earliest research workers to take an interest in Central Africa sought initially to identify periods there similar to those that had been described in Europe. X. Stainier attempted an early comprehensive study in 1899, but the distinction of having undertaken excavations as far back as 1925 belongs to J. Colette (Bequaert, 1938). Scientific research only really got under way, however, after the Second World War. Since then, systematic studies have been carried out by J. D. Clark in Zambia and Angola, R. de Bayle des Hermens in the Central African Republic, J. Nenquin in Rwanda and Burundi, G. Mortelmans, J. de Heinzelin and H. van Moorsel in Zaïre, and the Société Préhistorique et Protohistorique Gabonaise in Gabon. In Zaïre, the amount of research work has shown a notable increase since the establishment in 1970 of the Institut des Musées Nationaux.

Our knowledge still remains very patchy, however. Although Colette led the way in carrying out the first chrono-stratigraphical study, his example was all too rarely followed and for many parts of the area our knowledge is based entirely on surface finds.

It must be realized, however, that archaeology in Central Africa has many difficulties to contend with. Some areas, such as the northern part, are unsuited for excavation because of the thick laterite crust, while in the forest itself prospecting is anything but easy. Other factors further complicate the task. Climatic conditions and the acidity of the soil have in general militated against the preservation of bones, which is why at most of the sites investigated none have been found. There are exceptions, however, notably Isangho and Matupi, where skeletal material was well preserved due to the calcareous soil.

The nomenclature has undergone continual revision, and the subdivisions have been repeatedly called in question. The sequence Early, Middle and Late Stone Age separated by intermediate periods is no longer really acceptable either in chronological or even in typological terms. After a period in which exact classification was attempted, opinion is now coming round to the view that these broad categories are extremely relative and provisional.

This view is borne out by work on sites that have been recently excavated and systematically dated. To take the Late Stone Age as an example, in 1959 J. D. Clark put the beginning of this period at about 7500 b.p. In 1971 we obtained a date of about 15 000 b.p. for Munyama Cave, Uganda (van Noten, 1971), and six years later the microlithic industry at Matupi was dated at about 40 000 b.p. (van Noten, 1977). Thus there are obvious contradictions between the old classification and recent discoveries.

Whereas everywhere else in the world archaeologists are beginning to be interested primarily in the way prehistoric man lived, studying his environment and his relationships with it, Central African prehistory has for long remained the study of topology and chronology, and in all this concentration on nomenclature, very little attention has been paid to man himself.

Rather than drawing up an exhaustive list of sites, most of which comprised only a few surface finds, we propose to concentrate on the all-too-rare systematic excavations that have provided some indication of dating, namely, Ishango, Gombe, Bitorri, Kamoa, Matupi and Kalambo. These widely separated sets of data will of course need to be filled out with additional information from the study of other localities.

We are more than ever convinced that it is impossible to establish large, well-defined cultural areas. We must be content to note the presence of man at given times, without as yet being able to tell whether he evolved *in situ* or came from elsewhere. He certainly adapted himself very early to well-defined habitats, each with its own particular climate, flora and fauna. The primitive hunter-gatherer needed to explore these habitats if he was to survive, and when it came to tool making his course of action was dictated by the raw materials available. Man must obviously have reacted in different ways to the disparate conditions produced by environmental variations in Central Africa. The result is distinguishable areas, sometimes with certain features in common but also showing regional and even local variations not explicable simply by the influence of different ecological conditions. It would be premature, however, to think of them as cultural areas.

Geographical background

The main morphological features of the enormous area known as Central Africa are the result of a series of tectonic movements that had already started at the beginning of the Tertiary and are probably not yet complete.

The central basin, which does not rise more than 460 metres above sea-level, is surrounded by a ring of plateaux, ridges and mountains formed on the geological layers covering the crystalline Precambrian substratum. The latter outcrops at the periphery. It is very mountainous, especially in Kivu where it has undergone upheaval, sometimes reaching heights of over 3048 metres, and is deeply scoured by erosion. The substratum is topped in places by very high relief features such as the basalt plateau south-east of Lake Kivu (about 3048 metres), the Adamawa mountains (about 2440 metres), the volcanic peaks of the Virunga mountains (4507 metres), the horst of the Ruwenzori range (5119 metres) and the Huambo plateau (2610 metres). The tectonic movements that gave rise to the highlands also produced faulting such as the Great Rift Valley to the east of Central Africa, and the Niger–Benue trough.

Apart from the coastal area of southern Angola and the Cubango–Zambezi Basin, Central Africa has plentiful rain. In the central basin, rainfall is regular all the year round, amounting to over 1730 millimetres a year. On the coasts of Gabon, Rio Muni and Cameroon it may be as high as 4060 millimetres. Elsewhere, in areas with a dry season (3–7 months), annual rainfall still amounts to 810–1220 millimetres.

The dense rain forest that has developed in the rain belt of Central Africa between lat. 5°N and lat. 4°S covers the Zaïre basin, the greater part of the People's Republic of the Congo, Gabon, Rio Muni and southern Cameroon. To the east, this forest gives way to transitional forest, and then to the dense mountain forest that covers the peaks and high-rainfall slopes of eastern Zaïre, Rwanda and Burundi between lat. 2°N and lat. 8°S. Where the dense forest has been cleared, new growth and secondary forest make their appearance.

The equatorial forest is bordered by thick semi-deciduous forest, often very degraded, yet capable of surviving a two- or three-month dry season. On the north side this constitutes a narrow fringe, running from Cameroon via the southern part of the Central African Republic and the area between the Bomu and the Uele rivers to Lake Victoria. To the south, together with man-made savannah, it forms a patchwork of vegetation covering part of the People's Republic of the Congo, lower Zaïre, the lowlands of the Kwango, Kasaï-Sankuru and Lomami.

In an arc around the dense forest region of Guinea, open woodland and Sudano-Zambezi savannah cover an area where the dry season may last for seven months of the year: namely, central Cameroon, the Central African

Republic, southern Sudan, eastern Rwanda and Burundi, Shaba in Zaïre, Zambia and Angola.

Great marshy depressions occur along the course of the rivers, particularly on the White Nile in the southern Sudan, in the central basin and the Lake Upemba depression in Zaïre, and in the Zambezi basin in Angola and Zambia.

The evolution of the environment

The reconstruction of prehistoric man's environment has become an important factor in archaeological research. The first work in this field was carried out in East Africa. Various workers, including E. J. Wayland (1929, 1934), P. E. Kent (1942) and E. Nilson (1940, 1949), had observed, in the Quaternary, alternations of humid periods, called pluvials, with dry periods (interpluvials). The pluvials were considered to be contemporary with the glaciations of the northern hemisphere and were named (proceeding from the earliest to the most recent) the Kageran, the Kamasian and the Gamblian. Two humid periods at the beginning of the Holocene were subsequently observed, the Makalian and the Nakuran. L. S. B. Leakey (1949), J. D. Clark (1962, 1963a) and others subsequently sought to extend the use of these names, which had acquired a specific stratigraphical connotation in East Africa, to other parts of Africa. Authors such as T. P. O'Brien (1939), H. B. S. Cooke (1958), R. F. Flint (1959a, b), F. E. Zeuner (1959) and W. W. Bishop (1965), on the other hand, expressed reservations about the general applicability of the theory, and research in Central Africa has shown that considerable intervals of time separated the pluvial phases in one region from those in another.

J. De Ploey (1963) was the first to recognize the existence in Central Africa of a semi-arid period in the upper Pleistocene, contemporary (or largely so) with the Würm glaciation in Europe. This dry phase has been found in Shaba by various authors (Alexandre and Alexandre, 1965; Moeyersons, 1975). A more humid fluctuation about 6000 b.p. was found in lower Zaïre by J. De Ploey (1963), at Mose in Shaba (Alexandre, personal communication) and at Moussanda in Zaïre (Delibrias *et al.*, 1974, p. 47). Work on the Kamoa has shown that this phase was preceded by another fluctuation between 12 000 b.p. and 8000 b.p., separated from the 6000 b.p. fluctuation by a short period of erosion associated with a recurrence of drought. The humid fluctuation between 12 000 b.p. and 8000 b.p. is contemporary with the extension of the East African lakes, found by K. W. Butzer and others (1972). The work of J. De Ploey (1963, 1965, 1968, 1969) in lower Zaïre, and of J. Moeyersons (1975) on the Kamoa, indicates that the drier periods were characterized by an intensification of the morphogenetic process. Thus in the Kinshasa region during the Leopoldvillean, the hills were greatly denuded with much consequent sedimentation in the plain. Similarly, on the Kamoa, this period saw marked changes in the slopes, taking the form of a narrowing of the valleys. All this goes to confirm H. Rhodenburg's (1970) view about the alternation of morphodynamic phases, corresponding with the dry periods, the stable humid phases.

The evolution of the environment in Central Africa has thus been much influenced by the climatic conditions of the last fifty millennia. Studies of the present-day vegetation forms and their equilibrium within the climate, and also pollen analysis from various sites, have made it possible to reconstruct the ancient plant cover and the climatic conditions that gave rise to it.

It is in the mountainous areas to the east that climatic changes can best be deduced from the movements of the vegetation stages. Pollen diagrams from the high peat bogs show a succession from a cold flora to a warm, humid flora, and then to a dry flora. This is especially clear at the Kalambo Falls site, 1140 metres above sea-level in Zambia, where J. D. Clark and E. M. van Zinderen Bakker (1964) found a long dry phase between 55 000 b.p. and 10 000 b.p., with two humid fluctuations about 43 000 b.p. and 28 000 b.p. and the beginnings of a longer humid phase about 10 000 b.p. During the arid periods, the temperature fell considerably in the highlands overlooking the Great Rift Valley, as previously reported by J. A. Coetzee and E. M. van Zinderen Bakker (1970) from Mount Kenya, where they provided evidence for the Mount Kenya glaciation of 26 000–14 000 b.p.

J. D. Clark and E. M. van Zinderen Bakker (1962) also studied the evolution of the plant cover in the Lunda area. This area was occupied 40 000–10 000 b.p. by *Brachyṣtegia* dry woodland savannah, which gave way to thicker forest during the 10 000–5000 b.p. humid phase. According to the pollen analysis of the Kamoa site, carried out by E. Roche (1975) by way of complementing J. Moeyersons's (1975) geomorphological study, there seems to have been a dry period from the final Acheulian until 15 000 b.p. There is an observable progressive evolution of steppe savannah into woodland, and then the establishment of thicker forest, with extension of the forest galleries after the climate became wetter from 12 000 b.p. onwards.

According to M. Streel (1963), a great extension of dry woodland and *Acacia* savannah took place 50 000–20 000 b.p. This extension, which is thought to have started in the eastern Zambezi area, had the effect of pushing back the tropical forest towards the central basin. According to P. Duvigneaud (1958), Shaba may be regarded as a crossroads, that is, its vegetation shows the influence of several regions – Zaïre and Guinea, Zambezi and East Africa.

On the basis of Milankovitch's theory of the mobility of the thermal equator, A. Schmitz (1971) considers that a southwards movement of 8 degrees by the latter during a hot, humid phase occurring 12 000–5000 b.p. brought about a considerable extension of the tropical forest. This is thought to have covered the whole of Zaïre and even part of Angola, as witness the presence of strips of dry tropical forest in present-day woodland savannahs. The forest also extended farther north, covering most of Cameroon and the Central African Republic.

During this humid phase, savannah and woodland savannah survived in situations favourable to them, that is, on the plateaux and on poor soils. It is quite likely that the plateaux of southern Zaïre and Angola have never known really dense vegetation, and that it was from there that the woodland savannah started to extend again when the climate became drier after 5000 b.p. A. Schmitz (1971), however, thinks that it is primarily human activity that has brought about the retreat of the tropical forest during the last thousand years.

To recapitulate, from 50 000–10 000 b.p. Central Africa passed through a long dry phase, contemporary with the Würm glaciation, whilst the humid phase that started about 12 000 b.p. could correspond to the climatic fluctuations of the early Holocene. During this long dry period, probably interrupted by a humid fluctuation about 28 000 b.p., there was much morphodynamic activity and a great extension of the woodland savannah. During the humid period at the beginning of the Holocene, the tropical forest spread to cover most of Central Africa, and its retreat in modern times is attributable to human activity.

The peopling of Central Africa

In the absence of human bones it is generally accepted that the first sign of human presence is represented by chipped or flaked pebbles. These are comparable to the Oldowayan artefacts from the eponymous site at the Olduvai Gorge in Tanzania. Similar objects are to be found pretty well all over Central Africa – in the Kasai basin and Shaba in Zaïre, in Cameroon, Gabon, Zaïre and the Central African Republic, and in north-east Angola, where they occur in alluvium. It is nevertheless not always easy to be sure whether the flaking of the pebbles is to be ascribed to man or to natural agencies. We feel it a mistake (and it is a common one) to regard as tools all pebbles which definitely show signs of deliberate working. For the most part, these are cores from which flakes have been knapped, and it was the flakes that were either used as they were, as all-purpose tools, or trimmed for use as side-scrapers or end-scrapers.

No living-site dating from this period has so far been discovered, neither do we have any of the wood and bone artefacts that must have accounted for a substantial proportion of the tools used. We may suppose the flaked pebbles to be the work of Australopithecines or *Homo habilis* who, according to observations made elsewhere in Africa, definitely led a necrophagous existence. Some form of social organization must, however, have started at about this time. The beginnings of this period in human history date back more than 2 million years, and it continued until about half a million years ago.

It is, however, only with Acheulian tools that we come to the first indisputable proof of human presence in Central Africa. Its oldest phase, the

Lower Acheulian, is known only from the Lunda area (Clark, 1968b). Upper Acheulian, usually found in arid environments, has been discovered at various points around the periphery of the central basin. J. D. Clark has described it in Angola, J. Nenquin in Rwanda and Burundi, and R. de Bayle des Hermens in the Central African Republic. The best reference sites are Kalambo in Zambia and the Kamoa in Zaïre.

The Acheulian is characterized by bifaces and cleavers. Various attempts have been made to classify them by shape (Cahen and Martin, 1972, and others), and some authors have sought to trace a gradation from an archaic stage to a more advanced one, with a succession of five stages from Acheulian I to Acheulian V; but these typological distinctions do not always have much chronological significance. A biface, as the name implies, is an artefact produced by trimming a pebble or a large flake on both sides. It characteristically has a fairly definite point, and nearly always a rounded base. The other very characteristic tool found with the biface is the cleaver, which ends, unlike the biface, in a cutting edge. Alongside these tools other, less characteristic, artefacts are found, such as trihedrals, picks, knives, spheroids and various small tools. Although Acheulian finds are plentiful, the sites at which this industry can be regarded as archaeologically in context, or even as homogeneously represented, remain rare. One of the few stratified sites where the Acheulian has been found is on the banks of the Kamoa river, in Shaba (Cahen, 1975). It is a very large site, covering several acres. Its hunter-gatherer inhabitants left their tools behind, and also the waste chippings produced in manufacturing them. We may therefore reasonably assume that we are dealing here with some sort of workshop-cum-living area. In view of the homogeneity of the industry, in which no development is to be distinguished, it may well be that it represents an accumulation resulting from a season's occupation. The raw material was brought from a place 1·6 kilometres from the site, where huge bedrock cores are to be found. The flakes were transported to the site, where the cutting and finishing of the tools must have taken place. The advanced or final Acheulian of the Kamoa is analogous to the industries found in the Sahara and South Africa. The date of 60 000 b.p. suggested for it must be considered a *terminus ante quem,* the actual date in our view being much earlier.

In the light of finds in other parts of Africa, we know that this industry is to be attributed to *Homo erectus,* a hominid who depended for his livelihood on hunting and food-gathering. It must be assumed that the organization of society continued to evolve, and that man had acquired the mastery of fire.

Adaptation and technological development

Post-Acheulian industries from a number of areas, though differing from each other, nevertheless give the impression of a certain unity. Let us for practical purposes divide Central Africa into an eastern half and a western half, the former of which may again be subdivided into two; though in view of the lack of data for the regions to the north and south of the area in question, these subdivisions must be largely conjectural. In the western half, which extends from Angola to Gabon, the area about which most is known comprises lower Zaïre, Kinshasa, the Lunda area, the Kwango and the Kasai, that is, the south-western Zaïre basin. The eastern half covers the interlacustrine area and the Shaba–Lake Tanganyika area.

In the western half, a series of industries has been tentatively identified, usually described as forming a chronological and typological sequence: first the Sangoan, then the Lupemban and, last, the Tschitolian. The Sangoan supposedly represents the transition between the Acheulian and the Lupemban, and is attributed to the First Intermediate Period. The Lupemban would constitute the Middle Stone Age, and the Lupemban–Tschitolian the Second Intermediate Period, leading to the Tschitolian proper which is considered as contemporary with the Late Stone Age of East and southern Africa. All these industries are characterized by bifacial flaking, as though they represented prolongations of the Acheulian technique. The Levalloisian technique remains rare.

The eastern half of Central Africa displays a much greater variety of industries. They are comparable with those of the western half, but bifacial flaking is less common. On the other hand, the so-called Mousterian and Levalloisian flaking techniques are highly developed and blades and laminar flakes are common. From the Second Intermediate Period onwards, great changes are discernible and the tradition dies out completely, being replaced by microlithic industries apparently unrelated to the earlier industries. The Sangoan and Lupemban industries in this area are quite typical, and make it possible to distinguish two different parts of the area. One, which probably covered the northern part, that is, the interlacustrine area, is characterized by daggers and leaf-shaped and lanceolate biface points. The other, covering the southern part, that is, Shaba and the shores of Lake Tanganyika, is distinguished by the absence of points and the presence of chisel- and gouge-type biface tools which, strangely enough, are almost entirely lacking in the interlacustrine area. This clearly illustrates the absurdity of differentiating on the basis of these remains between forest industries and savannah industries. Furthermore, it seems that in the period in question no one area was any more wooded than another. On the contrary, the climate must have been distinctly drier than today, and it was only towards the end of the period that the extension of the forest took place. The Masanga site is a good example of the type of industry in this area, there being a wide range of biface points along with clumsier items such as picks. Levalloisian features are very well represented (Cahen, Haesaerts and van Noten, 1972). A sequence of stone industries running from the Sangoan to the Late Stone Age has apparently been discovered at Sanga, but has not yet been studied in detail (Nenquin, 1958).

Let us now look at the western area more closely. Its industries cover the whole range of types found in the eastern areas, which gives them greater typological variety and brings them closer to the generally accepted picture of the Sangoan and the Lupemban. There are crude picks such as were already found in the Acheulian and persist right up to the Tschitolian. This artefact, regarded as the *fossile directeur* of the Sangoan, thus, in fact, has no chronological significance. Also associated with them, however, are very finely worked tools, including some beautiful leaf-shaped lance-points and long daggers. One also finds arrow-heads subsequently making their appearance, showing that man had discovered the use of the bow. These adaptations are probably the work of *Homo sapiens,* even though up to the present no human remains have been recovered.

The sites at which several levels are found in stratigraphy are rare. It was at Gombe that J. Colette discovered the first sequence of these Central African industries, providing evidence of four, the Kalinian, the Djokocian, the Ndolian and the Leopoldian, followed by traces of the Iron Age. The First Pan-African Congress of Prehistory, held at Nairobi in 1947, ignored Colette's nomenclature and adopted the terms Sangoan and Lupemban, which rested on no proper archaeological foundations. The new names passed into the literature and have since been used indiscriminately not only in Central Africa but even far beyond. Gombe, the only known site offering any hope of establishing a chronology, was re-excavated by D. Cahen in 1973 and 1974 (Cahen, 1976) with the object of clarifying and dating the sequence discovered by J. Colette. Apart from some items reminiscent of the Acheulian, the sequence begins with the Kalinian, which is characterized by crude picks made from pebbles or flakes, massive scrapers, large serrated tools and planes of considerable size. There are also lanceolate bifaces, convergent scrapers and narrow bifacial and unifacial tools with more or less parallel edges. In addition, there are numerous flake tools with transverse cutting-edges (small skinning-knives), and Mousterian-type circular cores. The chippings include Levalloisian-type flakes and some blades of poor quality. The bigger items are reminiscent of the Sangoan, while the delicate tools are reminiscent of the Lupemban or even the Tschitolian. The next level, the Djokocian, is characterized particularly by tanged or leaf-shaped arrow-heads, often trimmed by pressure-flaking; the flakings are the same as in the Kalinian. The Djokocian is reminiscent of the late Lupemban of the Kinshasa plain (Moorsel, 1968) and the Lupembo–Tschitolian – that is, the late Tschitolian as defined by G. Mortelmans (1962) and J. D. Clark (1963). The third level, the Ndolian, is represented only in small concentrations. Small leaf-shaped arrow-heads are typical of it. The bipolar flaking was carried out *in situ,* which explains the presence of splinters. This industry is somewhat similar to late Tschitolian (Moorsel, 1968; Cahen and Mortelmans, 1973).

One of the dates obtained for the Kalinian coincides with the age estimated for the Sangoan (Clark, 1969, p. 236), and another with the early phases of the Lupemban (Clark, 1963, pp. 18–19; Moorsel, 1968, p. 221).

The dates obtained for samples from the Djokocian level differ little from dates calculated elsewhere for similar industries. Of the dates associated with the Ndolian, one corresponds to the dates of the late Tschitolian as previously obtained in the Kinshasa plain and the Lunda area.

By and large, we can say that the industries found in stratigraphy in the Lunda region, at Gombe and in the Kinshasa plain are typologically comparable and correlate well chronologically. The Lower Sangoan-Lupemban is put at 45 000 and 26 000 b.p., the Upper Lupemban and the Lupembo–Tschitolian at 15 000 and 10 000 b.p., the Lower Tschitolian at 10 000–7000b.p., and the Upper Tschitolian at 6000–4000 or 3500 b.p. (see Table 19.1).

A sample trench excavated by P. de Maret at Dimba Cave yielded a sequence of fifteen archaeological strata and a date of 20 000 ± 650 b.p. for an industry of the Upper Lupemban of Lupembo-Tschitolian type. This should probably be put further back to about 25 000 b.p. This date would fill the gap in datings between 27 000 b.p. and 15 000 b.p. noted by D. Cahen (1977).

Hau Cave, the only site that may have been in equatorial forest at the time of its occupation, where F. van Noten found traces of a 'Lupemban' industry followed by a Late Stone Age one, has yielded no acceptable radio-carbon datings.

J. P. Emphoux (1970) excavated Bitorri Cave in 1966 and found twenty levels of Stone Age occupation. One level gave a radio-carbon date of 3930 ± 200 b.p., and a lower level a date of 4030 ± 200 b.p. The stone artefacts, which show no development between one level and another, may be regarded as a typological entity, the industry being reminiscent of the upper Tschitolian. The same research worker dated at 6600 ± 130 b.p. a middle Tschitolian level at Moussanda (Delibrias *et al.*, 1974, p. 47). (Delibrias *et al.*, 1974, p. 47).

In Gabon, supposedly Lupemban industries have been found on several occasions (Blankoff, 1965; Hadjigeorgiou and Pommeret, 1965; Farine, 1965).

Specialized hunter-gatherers

At a given moment, probably between 50 000 and 40 000 b.p., geometrical microliths make their appearance: segments of circles, triangles, rectangles and trapezoids. The most typical are probably the segments, although in South Africa these are found as early as the end of the Middle Stone Age when they were probably used as barbs fixed below lance-points.[10] In the Late Stone Age, on the other hand, these microliths were used by themselves, as arrow-heads, lance-points and harpoon-points, and chisel-blades and knife-blades.

10. F. Carter, personal communication.

As in the case of the previous period, the area studied may be subdivided into two distinct parts. In the western part, covering northern Angola, the Kasai, the Kwango, lower Zaïre and the People's Republic of the Congo, the so-called Lupemban tradition is found to persist, as though it had evolved *in situ* and given rise to the Tschitolian. Geometrical microliths become numerous but without predominating in the way they do in the eastern part where they represent the basic element in the tools. S. Miller (1972), who carried out a survey of the Tschitolian and summarized previous results, defines this industry by the presence of biface tools of the chisel-pick type, leaf-shaped points, tanged points, small skinning knives and geometrical microliths. The Lunda region produced an industry combining all these features, although they are usually incompletely represented at individual sites. Thus a valley style has been distinguished with large numbers of small skinning knives as at Dinga, and a plateau style in which the tools consist mainly of tanged points (Bequaert, 1952). A site on the Bateke plateau, where G. Mortelmans carried out a rescue dig in 1959 (Cahen and Mortelmans, 1975), yielded an industry said to be comprehensive, like that described in the Lunda region. The polymorphous sandstone, which is virtually the only material to have been used for the tools discovered, comes from deposits the nearest of which are some 9·6 kilometres from the site. This industry is characterized by a high proportion of flakes and waste chippings (96·1 per cent), together with some cores (1·4 per cent) and some implements (2·4 per cent). Along with leaf-shaped and tanged arrow-heads, a large number of geometrical microliths were recovered, and also a large flake with a polished cutting edge. Most of the cores are of the circular or lamellar type; there are also many small cores, completely used up. The chippings, consisting mostly of waste fragments from retouching, contain a few Levalloisian flakes and some blades and lamellae. These are the typical features of a late Tschitolian. The site is very likely to have been a hunting camp because, although the Bateke plateau is definitely steppe-like in character, it is broken by forest galleries that must have attracted prehistoric man in quest of game. Though the raw material used was brought in, many of the tools must have been fashioned *in situ*, and it is conceivable that the latex and copal resins found during excavation were used as mastic to fix the microliths to the shafts of arrows and lances. The scrapers, chisels and axes were undoubtedly employed to make composite tools which made use of oblique cutting edges and tanged biface arrow-heads.

The Lunda region studied by J. D. Clark yielded a Tschitolian dating of 13 000–4500 b.p. (Clark, 1963b, pp. 18–19), but this industry is thought to have continued up to the beginning of our era (Clark, 1968b, pp. 125–49). The Tschitolian of the Kinshasa plain, on the other hand, dates from 9700 to 5700 b.p. (Moorsel, 1968, p. 221).

We may perhaps pause here to consider the significance of the different styles found in the Tschitolian. The question is whether they were adaptations to different environments, as for instance specialized hunting methods, or whether they simply represent cultural differences.

In the eastern part, on the periphery of the equatorial forest from the Central African Republic to Shaba, so-called Late Stone Age industries are found. The earliest of these industries are typologically undifferentiated since more specialized tools did not make their appearance until later. This was observed at Matupi Cave, where two consecutive seasons of excavation, in 1973 and 1974, revealed traces of very long human occupation, beginning well before 40 000 b.p. and continuing without a perceptible break until 3000 b.p. (van Noten, 1977). The material so far studied comes from one single square metre of soil, which has yielded 8045 artefacts, nearly all made of quartz by the bipolar technique, a process characteristic of purely microlithic industries. Waste chippings account for 90 per cent of the material, tools proper representing only 5·4 per cent, to which must be added items which, though showing signs of use, cannot count as fully finished tools. These account for 5 per cent. The industry is typically microlithic, the maximum length of the flakes being 17·7 millimetres. All the stone implements must have been used for making composite tools. The tools proper (in order of frequency) consist of notched scrapers, borers, gravers, flakes and lamellae with chamfered edges, retouched flakes, truncated pieces and a few geometrical microliths (segments, half-circles and triangles). The macrolithic implements, made out of quartzite, sandstone or schist, consist of grindstones, pestles, anvils, hammerstones, concave scrapers and a few chisels. A fragment of pierced stone with incised decoration has been dated at about 20 000 b.p.[11] The animal bones are well preserved, and point to a drier environment than today. The animals hunted by the occupants of the cave were, in descending order, bovines (antelopes and buffaloes), hyraxes, rodents (particularly cane rats), pigs, and to a lesser extent cercopithecine monkeys and porcupines. Though now in the equatorial forest, this cave must have been in savannah for nearly the whole of its occupation, but according to the evidence of pollen analysis it was not far from forest galleries. It was occupied continuously over a period during which the industry, initially very atypical, changed to a more classical one yielding geometrical microliths, occasional bone tools, red haematite used as a pigment, and disc beads made out of ostrich eggshell. In view of the very small number of items capable of use as implements or weapons, particularly in the earlier strata, we take the view that the tools must have been very largely made of wood, as we found to be the case at Gwisho (Fagan and van Noten, 1972).

J. de Heinzelin's 1950 excavations at Ishango revealed three microlithic industries (Heinzelin, 1957). Though the earliest contains no geometrical microliths, there are some in the next one, and in the most recent they are plentiful. Typologically the industry is mostly very rough; the flaking

11. Also known as *kwe*, the pierced stones found in Late Stone Age industries were probably used as weights for digging-sticks.

represents a combination of all techniques, and is influenced by the consistency of the quartz of very poor quality used as raw material. These features are definitely reminiscent of the development observed at Matupi. Ishango yielded a series of harpoons, presumably used for hunting and fishing, which show a distinct development, running from a type with two rows of barbs in the lower strata to a type with only one row in the more recent strata. One of the most spectacular finds is a small bone rod with a scratched decoration, used as the handle for a quartz flake. The Ishango industry has been dated at 21 000 ± 500 b.p., which at the time when the monograph about the site was published seemed on the early side; but in the light of the dates obtained at Matupi, this finding now seems much less improbable.

The inhabitants of Ishango lived by fishing and hunting, mainly hippopotamus and topis but also other mammals, some of which are now extinct. Birds also served as game. The fish consisted principally of catfish, lungfish and cichlids. The human remains, found among the cooking debris, were studied by F. Twiesselman (1958) and indicate that the site was inhabited by a population with rugged, atypical anthropometric features bearing no direct relation to any modern population.

Along with these purely microlithic industries, industries typologically intermediate between the pure microlithic and the typical industries of the western part of Central Africa make their appearance in the interlacustrine area, and also in Shaba and on the shores of Lake Tanganyika. It is possible that the unusual character of these industries is due to the fact that they represent a continuation of the middle stone age tradition described above. J. Nenquin had to coin the term 'Wilton-Tschitolian' to describe the Late Stone Age in Rwanda and Burundi (Nenquin, 1967), where unfortunately very few sites have been dated. The age of the transitional industry of the Kamoa, which can be compared with the Lupembo-Tschitolian of the western region, has been put at 15 000–12 000 b.p. At the same site the Late Stone Age, which is poor and uncharacteristic, has been dated at approximately 6000–2000 b.p. (Cahen, 1975). Thus it certainly seems as though different traditions were able to last for a long time alongside one another and indeed, side by side with industries of mixed character, or, purely microlithic ones such as are found at Mukinanira (van Noten and Hiernaux, 1967) and the Mokoto lakes (van Noten, 1968a).

Central Africa has not so far yielded a site rich enough to make possible a detailed reconstruction of these hunters' way of life which must have been comparable to that still followed to this day by the San of the Kalahari. The site at Gwisho, in Zambia, gives a very complete picture of Late Stone Age life in the fifth millennium b.p. By a remarkable stroke of luck, along with polished tools, a large number of wooden and bone objects were found there, which prove the importance of wood-working even in orchard savannah (Fagan and van Noten, 1971).

The end of the Stone Age

The abundance of polished tools in some areas has meant that they have come to be regarded as the hallmark of the Neolithic, but we have seen that such tools are found in the Late Stone Age, and that in the Uele river area they were still being made and used in the nineteenth century (van Noten, 1968b). Hence the discovery of polished tools outside any archaeological context is of no particular significance. The distribution of those artefacts, however, is not without interest, for they have only been reported on the periphery of the central basin. In the east such finds are extremely rare. At the most, two polished axes and a cave with some rubbing stones are known from Burundi (van Noten, 1969; Cahen and van Noten, 1970). The number of finds increases somewhat towards the south-east, where a few polished axes and some rubbing stones have been reported from Shaba whilst in the Kasai, though some rubbing stones are still found, polished tools are virtually non-existent (Celis, 1972).

North of the great equatorial forest, on the other hand, such items make up the key element in archaeological finds. In the Uele Basin and into Ituri, more than 400 implements have been recovered, including some splendid haematite axes, meticulously polished, and a great many polishing grooves. Only one distribution map of these tools has so far been compiled (van Noten, 1968b). To some extent at least, the Uele Neolithic technique may not go back beyond the seventeenth century, and hence forms part of the Iron Age, as the excavations at Buru (van Noten and van Noten, 1974) seem to suggest.

Farther west, where the Ubangi river penetrates into the forest, another concentration of polished axes is found. They are much less well finished than those from the Uele, being mostly only partially polished. An exploration of this area failed to bring to light any similar tools in an archaeological context, but on the other side of the river, at Batalimo in the Central African Republic, R. de Bayle des Hermens (1975) found, for the first time in an excavation, an axe with a polished edge associated with a non-microlithic industry and with some pottery. The latter is flat-bottomed and usually has an all-over decoration made by a combination of grooving, incising and imprinting generally with a comb. Dated by thermo-luminescence, this pottery turns out to be no earlier than the fourth century of our era, which seems very late for an industry of this sort. Though some other isolated polished axes have been recovered at various points in the Central African Republic, there is not, as far as we know, a single rubbing stone in this region.

Before passing on to the last area of concentration, we should mention that on the island of Fernando Po, off the coast of Cameroon, polished axes associated with pottery have been dated to the seventh century of our era (Martin del Molino, 1965) and were still in use until recent times.

The last area is the one running parallel to the Atlantic coast from Gabon to north-west Angola. The so-called Neolithic tools found in this enormous area are generally rough-hewn, only the cutting-edges being polished.

In Gabon the axes have wavy edges forming a characteristic tenon (Pommeret, 1966b). A pot unearthed during large-scale building operations contained a fragment of a polished tool and some charcoal, which unfortunately was not dated (Pommeret, 1965). In the People's Republic of the Congo and in Angola (Martins, 1976) only surface finds are known. At Gombe, on the other hand, J. Colette earlier discovered a polished axe apparently associated with flat-bottomed pottery (Bequaert, 1938); he coined the term Leopoldian Neolithic for it and the term was subsequently used to describe the many polished axes found in lower Zaïre. Mortelmans (1959) found polished axes, atypical trimmed quartzes and crude-flat-bottomed pottery on the surface at Congo dia Vanga. This same pottery occurs again in the Ntadi-ntadi, Dimba and Ngovo caves, associated at the two latter sites with polished axes. On four occasions charcoal found close by has been dated to the last two centuries before our era (Maret, 1977a). Unfortunately the samples are too small for an Iron Age origin to be absolutely ruled out, especially since fresh excavations have shown that Gombe Leopoldian may perhaps fall within the Iron Age (Cahen, 1976). This site has been very much disturbed, however, and it may simply be a case of contamination from upper layers.

At Dimba and Ngovo, the only site at which bones were preserved, analyses of the associated fauna have not so far revealed the presence of domestic animals. In the absence of any other socio-economic data, it is premature to assume a true Neolithic, with a population using pottery and polished tools whilst at the same time keeping cattle and engaging in agriculture. The same goes for all the other Neolithic-style industries so far found in Central Africa. We know nothing about the people who used them, their period or their economic system. The hypothesis has, however, recently been advanced that some of the remains in question may belong to a final phase of the Stone Age, possibly corresponding to the early stages of the expansion of the Bantu-speaking peoples around the first millennium before our era, that is, before they had acquired the mastery of iron (Phillipson, 1976; Maret, 1977b; van Noten, 1978).

We should also mention here the megaliths found in the Bouar area; they probably date either from the fifth or the first millennium before our era, though it may be a case of their having been re-used (Bayle des Hermens, 1975). Judging by their size, these monuments must surely have been the work of sedentary populations: that is, we may assume that they had passed the hunting and food-gathering stage. The megalithic pavement at Api is a natural phenomenon and not man-made at all (van Noten, 1973), and the same is true of all the other so-called megalithic constructions so far reported in Zaïre.

The search for a perfect sequence

At the Pan-African Congress at Dakar in 1967, J. D. Clark attempted to introduce some order into the nomenclature of the Zaïre basin (Clark, 1971a). D. Cahen has summarized the history of the various nomenclatures used to describe the post-Acheulian industries of the area dealt with here, and has clearly shown what an extraordinary jumble they are (Cahen, 1977).

Recent excavations at Gombe have made it possible to re-establish and date the archaeological sequence first laid down by J. Colette. But the connections between pieces from different levels indicates that the site has been very much disturbed and that the industries are not homogeneous (Cahen, 1976). The objects have shifted in the soil, as has been confirmed by laboratory experiments (Moeyersons, 1977). It is therefore possible that a similar process may have taken place at other sites where archaeological remains are deposited in shifting Kalahari sands, as in north-east Angola, lower Zaïre, the Kasaï, Shaba and the Congo (Cahen and Moeyersons, 1977). We cannot tell, however, in what proportion the various industries have been affected by these soil movements. There is, furthermore, a striking typological and chronological convergence between the various prehistoric sites in the southern Zaïre Basin, and to a lesser extent in Central Africa. D. Cahen (1977) has suggested consolidating these convergent prehistoric groupings into a single post-Acheulian Central African Industrial Complex, initially covering the whole of Central Africa but contracting in the course of time until it was finally limited to the south-west Zaïre basin. This author also considers that none of the terms such as Sangoan, Lupemban and Tschitolian correspond to any scientifically established facts. Nevertheless, as we have endeavoured to demonstrate in this section of the chapter, it seems to us possible to distinguish regional variants among post-Acheulian stone industries and to trace their evolution. Diagrammatic and debatable though these distinctions may be, they reflect a certain reality, though it now seem to us to be a far more complex reality than was at first supposed. Refining our taxonomy on the basis of new excavations will be the best way of arriving at an understanding of the extraordinary diversity of Central Africa during the Stone Ages. The existing nomenclature, in our view, may as well be retained for the time being as a working tool.

Conclusions

Central Africa's past is still little known since scholars have only very recently set about studying it systematically. Nevertheless, archaeology is already yielding some preliminary findings. Thus in the space of a few years the number of radio-carbon datings has almost quintupled (Maret, van

Noten and Cahen, 1977), and the first syntheses can be drafted (van Noten, in preparation).

The primary object of the new research was to carry out a series of excavations covering different areas and periods, in the hope of establishing within a reasonable space of time an overall chronological and stratigraphical framework for Central Africa. This ambitious project must for the time being take second place. A key site such as Gombe has thrown doubt not only on the existing nomenclature but even on the validity of stratigraphical observations, and other sites, such as Matupi, have yielded new industries whose dating raises doubts about their place in an overall scheme of things in which industries and cultures must be allocated their correct niches once and for all.

The more new sites are discovered, the clearer it becomes that something original and unexpected comes to light every time. This fits in with one of our working hypotheses, namely, that great diversity is to be expected within each 'industry' or culture. Faced with a particular micro-environment, man had to adapt his tools to his habitat. We like to think of him leading a rather more settled existence, within the confines of his territory, than the wholly nomadic life too often ascribed to hunter-gatherers. So, far from tirelessly hunting game, these people must have evolved a culture of their own, a harmonious synthesis of environmental factors and ancestral traditions (we do not believe that environmental influence is absolutely paramount). Once ecological equilibrium was established, tools could remain unchanged for very long periods. They no doubt fully met the demands of the habitat and of its inhabitants, and so long as this delicate balance was maintained, man was under no particular pressure to evolve rapidly.

PLATE 21.1 *Upper Acheulian: bi-faced tool from the River Ngoere, Upper Sangha, Central African Republic* (Muséum National d'Histoire Naturelle)

PLATE 21.2 *Upper Acheulian: hand-axe from the River Ngoere, Upper Sangha, Central African Republic* (Muséum National d'Histoire Naturelle)

PLATE 21.3 *Flat-bottomed Neolithic vase from Batalimo, Lobaye, Central African Republic*) (Muséum National d'Histoire Naturelle)

PLATE 21.4 *Megalithic monument in the Bouar region, Central African Republic* (R. de Bayle des Hermens)

22 The prehistory of North Africa

L. BALOUT

The nearness of the countries of the Maghrib to Europe and their Mediterranean seaboard made them an early target for prehistoric research, some of it dating back to over a century ago. A substantial bibliography resulted, the reliability of which was highly variable. It was subsequently clarified and narrowed down (1952, 1955, 1974), but research into the prehistory of this part of North Africa did not keep the lead it had gained for long; it has, on the contrary, fallen behind in two important respects: excavation methods apart from all-too-rare exceptions, and absolute chronology, here essentially limited to radio-carbon dating. In East Africa, infinitely greater progress has been made in these respects.

The result is that the lack of Lower Pleistocene human fossils, of dates for Palaeolithic occupation sites obtained by the potassium-argon dating method, has meant that we are only able to date hominid settlements in the Maghrib and the Sahara through hypothetical correlations of the fauna and the typology of stone industries.

Without more and fuller stratigraphical material it has been difficult to establish the continuity of human occupation, highly probable though it was. Type sites are isolated both in time and in space: Ternifine (*Atlanthropus*) in Algeria is an example. The problems of the Mousterian, of its connection with the Aterian, of the human type that was the bearer of the latter culture, of the transition from the Aterian to the Ibero-Maurusian, of Capsian stratigraphy and of the stages of Neolithization, are largely unsolved. Prehistoric research has provided important insights into the Quaternary era – stratigraphy, palaeontology – and has made it possible to establish a typology reaching beyond the confines of the Maghrib; it should henceforth adopt a palaeo-ethnological approach: Man *in* his environment rather than Man *and* his environment.

The earliest human industries: the pre-Acheulian

There is no lack of evidence, but it is difficult to interpret other than typologically. Interpretation has been based on the stratigraphy of the coastal Quaternary in Morocco (Biberson), animal palaeontology in Algeria

(Aïn Hanech, near Setif, excavated by C. Arambourg) and in Tunisia (Aïn Brimba, near Kebili), and solely on typology in the Sahara (Reggan, In Afaleh, etc.). A somewhat tenuous link-up with the Tanzanian, Kenyan and Ethiopian sites can thus be inferred: tenuous because the Atlantic coast of Morocco provided the only evidence for the evolution of the pebble tools used by P. Biberson as the basis for his conclusions, some of which are now challenged; because the fauna are not necessarily contemporary; because we are confronted with an archaeological *presence* on the one hand, and with archaeological *structure* on the other; because the methods of typological analysis vary from French-speaking to English-speaking Africa, and so on.

It seems unlikely at this stage of our knowledge that hominids were present in the Maghrib and the Sahara as early as in eastern and southern Africa. There has been no identification of the flake industries preceding the pebble tools, there is no trace of an Osteodontokeratic culture, nor are there remains of Australopithecines. We do, however, have every reason to believe that the Pebble Culture of Morocco, Algeria and the Sahara coincides chronologically with the Olduvai industries, that is, that it dates back to between 2 and 1 million years ago ($2\frac{1}{2}$ million if the Omo bifacially flaked pebble is taken into consideration).

Investigations have therefore necessarily concentrated on correlating the chronostratigraphy and typological evolution. It has given rise to a compilation of 'typological lists' with chronological implications, as is testified by the work of P. Biberson in Morocco, H. Hugot and L. Ramendo in the central Sahara, H. Alimen and J. Chavaillon in the western Sahara. Their analyses are founded on technical characteristics, the repetition of which has made it possible to establish systematic patterns. The order of classification proceeds from the simple to the complex: unifacial, bifacial, polyhedrical flaking. This classification corresponds in all probability to a chronological sequence. Patterns of at least regional validity have been reconstructed by P. Biberson for the Quaternary beaches of the Moroccan Atlantic seaboard, and J. Chavaillon for deposits in the Saoura. Palaeontology provided the basis for placing the Aïn Hanech faceted spheroids in the evolutionary process of Villafrancian fauna as it is known from Morocco (Fouarat), Algeria (Aïn Boucherit, Aïn Hanech), Tunisia (Lake Ischkeul, Aïn Brimba).

Generally speaking, we base our assumptions on a stratigraphical analysis of the Villafrancian based largely on animal palaeontology. It is in this sequence that human industries appeared, and their evolution towards the bifacial tools and handaxes of the classical lower Palaeolithic can be proved; but nowhere is there an archaeological structure, and hence a palaeethnological frame, as there is in Tanzania (Olduvai), Kenya, or Ethiopia.

The Acheulian industries

Since the Burg Wartenstein Symposium (1965) and the Dakar Pan-African Prehistoric Conference (1967), the entire Lower Palaeolithic has been grouped together as the African Acheulian, which coincides in western Europe with the Abbevillian and the Acheulian, but also the Clactonian and the Levalloisian, both of which are the subject of a great deal of controversy.

Examples of the Acheulian in the Maghrib are plentiful. Apart from surface sites, it is to be found in three characteristic types of site:

(1) Those relating to the coastal, continental and even marine Quaternary. This is the case particularly on the Atlantic coast of Morocco, where P. Biberson has been able to suggest an Acheulian sequence starting from the pebble tools of the pre-Acheulian Pebble Culture through to the Middle Palaeolithic (Aterian). For reasons connected with its coastal geomorphology, Algeria has not proved so well endowed, but deposits have been located on the Kabylian coast (Djidjelli) and near Annaba (Bône). I am not aware of any Acheulian sites of this kind on the Tunisian coast.

(2) Sites in riverine and lacustrine alluvial deposits. The former are far scarcer and poorer than in Europe, and their stratigraphical and palaeontological relations are more often than not extremely imprecise. This is true of a number of Moroccan (Oued Mellah) and Algerian sites (Ouzidane, near Tlemcen, Champlain, near Medea, Tamla (Oued Sebaou), Mansourah (Constantine), Clairfontaine (north of Tebessa), S'Baïkia, and, particularly, El-Ma El-Abiod (south of Tebessa). In Tunisia there is the Acheulian of Redeyef (Gafsa). Lake-shore sites scarcely bear mentioning beside the spectacular examples in East Africa (e.g. Olorgesailie, Kenya), although there is Lake Karar (Tlemcen) where excavations were conducted rather too long ago, and badly, by Boule, and Aboukir (Mostaganem), which is even less well known. There is only one site which stands out amidst this uncertainty, and that is Sidi Zin (Le Kef, Tunisia), where a layer containing handaxes was found between two other layers containing bifaceted artefacts but no handaxes. On the other hand, Acheulian assemblages in lacustrine deposits are common from Mauritania to Libya.

(3) Sites associated with former artesian springs, which appear to have attracted man from the Acheulian to the Aterian. Examples are Tit Mellil (Casablanca) and Aïn Fritissa (south of Oudja) in Morocco, Lake Karar, which we have already mentioned, in Algeria, as well as Chetma (Biskra) which we know almost nothing about, and above all Ternifine (Mascara). Only the last-named has been excavated recently (1954–6) and thoroughly, by Professor C. Arambourg, commissioned by the Algerian authorities. But we

should not draw over-hasty conclusions. The industry is extremely interesting, the fauna are exceptionally rich, and it was here *Atlanthropus* was discovered; but the stratigraphy of this remarkable site presents a problem, leaving too broad a chronological span in which to place the finds; possibly the very nature of the site, with the constant disturbance of the sand by the artesian upwellings, made it impossible to establish a chrono-stratigraphy. It has not been proved. A study of the tools would suggest that what was here was not tool making workshops but more probably the regular hunting of animals coming to water.

The Maghribian and Saharan Acheulian is not fundamentally different from the Acheulian as it was formerly defined in France. The methods of analysis (Bordes, 1961 and Balout, 1967) do not indicate any basic difference in the bifacial tools. The same is true of trihedral implements. The presence of flakes and of a small industry, at Ternifine for instance, comes as no surprise. The soft hammer came into use towards the end of the early Acheulian (for shaping or reshaping); only one specimen has been found at Ternifine (bifacial). We also find the characteristic tranchet marks in the shaping of the working tips of trihedrons. The most original feature, which has long been emphasized, is the importance of flaked cleavers. It is stretching a point to suggest that it was a strictly African implement (a sort of chopping tool). In fact, it is not always present in the African Acheulian (and has not been found in the admirable El-Ma El-Abiod assemblage, to take only one example, in Algeria); but it does exist from the Near East to the Indian peninsula. Its presence in Spain (Rio Manzanares, near Madrid) and across the Pyrenees has led H. Alimen in a very recent investigation (1975a) to reconsider the question of how the Straits of Gibraltar were crossed well before Neolithic navigation. It has been concluded that there was an isthmus, caused partly by shallow water conditions, which became practicable during the Riss regressions.

The most relevant typological analysis of the Maghribian handaxes is that made by J. Tixier. Two conclusions are of crucial importance. The first is the appearance, from as far back as the early Acheulian, of the Levallois stone-working technique, leading to the incredibly widespread standardization of the so-called Tabelbalat-Tachenghït cleavers (western Algerian Sahara). The second is the technique of flaking from a core, which made it possible to produce bifacial flakes with a perfectly sharp cutting edge (the Kombewa technique of southern Africa). Were these highly elaborate techniques transmitted from Africa to Europe, where the first of the two, at least, played a significant role up to the Middle Palaeolithic?

The definition of the Acheulian has always been expressed in archaeological terms. The industries associated with bifacial tools span two glaciations (Mindel, Riss), the interglacial between them and the interstadials into which they are subdivided. Biberson has sought to equate them with marine transgressions and regressions: Amirian = Mindel,

Anfatian=Riss, Tensiftien=Riss. These correlations are still speculative. A prolongation into the Riss–Würm interglacial is perfectly plausible.

For want of absolute dating, we must base our theories on palaeontology. The fauna lose their remaining Upper Villafrancian components and become, in Arambourg's words, the 'great Chado-Zambezian fauna', although we might add that we know nothing yet of the microfauna or the flora of Ternifine.

The *Atlanthropus* found at Ternifine, and those discovered in Morocco (Rabat Man) (?) and Sidi Abderrahmane (Casablanca Man), belong to the genus *Homo erectus*. It is difficult to date these specimens of *Pithecanthropus*, which are in fact close to *Sinanthropus pekinensis*, with any accuracy: at least 400 000–500 000 years ago seems the most plausible hypothesis. Elsewhere, they had mastered the use of fire and possibly had a crude form of language. The Maghrib supplies us with no additional data in this field.

Mousterian–Aterian

In 1955, I wrote that I doubted the existence of an autonomous Mousterian in North Africa. Dr Gobert took me up sharply on this, and he was right in doing so. I subsequently (1965) modified my judgement appreciably; but the problem was not solved, it was merely shifted. There were undoubtedly truly Mousterian sites in the Maghrib, but their geographical distribution was extraordinary, quite contrary to any accepted conception of prehistoric ethnic unity. Six sites beyond dispute in Tunisia: Sidi Zin (Le Kef); Aïn Mhrotta (Kairouan); Aïn Metkerchem (Dj. Chambi); Sidi Mansour de Gafsa; El-Guettar (Gafsa); Oued Akarit (Gabes). Only one in Algeria: Retaïmia (Chelif valley); three in Morocco: Taforalt (Oudja); Kifan bel Ghomani (Taza); Djebel Irhoud (Safi). None in the Sahara. There are, however, hundreds of pre- or post-Mousterian sites. This does not reflect the state of research, for the discovery of the Mousterian was a central preoccupation of prehistorians trained in France, where it abounds, as it does in the Iberian and Italian peninsulas, as far south as Gibraltar for example. Sidi Zin (Le Kef) is 800 kilometres from Retaïmia, the latter 360 from the Taforalt Cave, and Taforalt another 700 from the Djebel Irhoud. Yet we have here typical Mousterian, comparable to the European facies, and in particular to the Levalloisian flaking technique. And at each geographical extreme we have the human evidence: the Neanderthals of Djebel Irhoud and the earliest ritual monument yet discovered – the cairn or 'Hermaion' of El-Guettar, of which only the summit emerges from the spring to which it was no doubt dedicated. With the exception of the Oued Akarit, no indisputably Mousterian site is near the coast. But where was the shore of the Gulf of Gabes at that time? The Maghribian Mousterian can only have come from the east. But the most remarkable thing is that this Mousterian developed in a very short time in a most original manner: it gave way to the Aterian *in situ*. Basing my deductions upon a rigorous application of geological rules of classification, I had regarded as Aterian those Mousterian industrial complexes in which Aterian peduncular points were found (El-Guettar, Aïn Metkerchem, and so on). I do not think that this is proof that Mousterian and Aterian were contemporary; I believe that the Maghribian Mousterian developed differently from all the other Mousterian traditions. J. Tixier has shown beyond doubt that it was not a matter of adding peduncular points or scrapers, but of transforming some thirty Mousterian tool-forms into Aterian forms by making a peduncular base. In Europe, especially in France, the Mousterian tradition developed differently. The Maghribian development is so original that a distinct definition was adopted, but this is no longer tenable: the Aterian is only an evolved facies of the Mousterian characteristic of a part of Africa, and it coincides with the Mousterian, even chronologically. R. Vaufrey's definition of an 'Upper Palaeolithic' Aterian is, in essence, no longer valid. Some of the early writers had already suggested the existence of a 'Mousterian with peduncular artefacts' just as we today use the term 'Mousterian with denticulated artefacts'. And; since the industry from the eponymous site of the Aterian (Oued Djebbana, near Bir el Ater, south of Tebessa) was never thoroughly analysed by its discoverer, Aterian is still, as M. Antoine put it, a *nomen nudum*. Since, moreover, it is an early development from the Mousterian, covering an extremely broad lifespan and spreading through the Maghrib and from the northern to the southern Sahara, it coincides chronologically with part of the Middle Palaeolithic and at least the beginning of the Upper Palaeolithic.

But there is still very little precise chronological evidence to go by. G. Camps' proposition concerning a possible correlation with McBurney's dating in Cyrenaica is tenuous, for there is no positive evidence that the industries are related. The Aterian is 'highly debatable' (Camps) and the Ibero-Maurusian 'non-existent' (Tixier). Stratigraphical relations with the continental or marine Quaternary have been established both in the Sahara and the Maghrib, and both in relative and absolute chronology. The fortieth millennium before our era is doubtless not the earliest date to which the beginning of the Aterian can be assigned. The difficulty arises over the limits of the reliability of carbon-14 dating. But the dates produced in the Maghrib and the Sahara are between 37 000 and 30 000 before our era and constitute a coherent, plausible sequence. In its beginnings, the Aterian is thus early Middle Palaeolithic. It is subsequently contemporary with the Castelperronian and the Aurignacian, that is, the early stage of the Upper Palaeolithic, in France at least. Its relationship with Quaternary formations is consistent. There are cases where Aterian implements have been found, in their original condition, in the neo-Tyrrhenian beaches which had just emerged as a result of the beginning of the last great regression (for example, at Karouba, near Mostaganem, western Algeria). The end of this Würmian interstadial (Würm 1/2) had occurred around 48 000 before our era. The continental, generally rubefied, formations, rich in Aterian, under which these beaches now lie, are below the present sea-level; they date back to the regression which probably reached some 150 metres.

Assigning a date to the end of the Aterian is a far more complicated task. That it spread over the entire Sahara is an established fact. Another fact is the technological development of the industry towards forms that more or less heralded the Neolithic. According to Hugot, the Aterian spread no farther than the great diatomaceous lakes which were full until the seventh millennium before our era. There is no positive evidence of this 'pre-Neolithic' Aterian, however attractive the proposition may be. However, no trace of an intermediate industry has yet been discovered, and the main obstacle, one of palaeo-anthropology, is in the process of disintegrating: very recent finds in Morocco give weight to the theory that Aterian Man was not Neanderthal Man like the Mousterians of Djebel Irhoud, but already *Homo sapiens*.

Upper Palaeolithic and epi-Palaeolithic

Whatever the ramifications of the Aterian may have been in the Sahara, in the Maghrib the sequence was different. It is unnecessary here to go back over the refutation of R. Vaufrey's theories which for decades were regarded as being authoritative. Let us rather recapitulate the current state of our knowledge. Four key ideas emerge:

(1) The Ibero-Maurusian, which I had already been partly responsible for distinguishing from the Capsian for anthropological and palaeo-ethnological reasons, is much older than was previously thought. It coincides with the French Magdalenian and is therefore an Upper Palaeolithic culture.

(2) The controversy over the 'Collignon horizon', in which R. Vaufrey was opposed to Dr Gobert and myself, is now settled. This blade industry, closer to the Iberomaurusian than to the Capsian, is appreciably earlier than the latter.

(3) Vaufrey's definition of a typical Capsian displaced by an upper or developed Capsian has been superseded by the theory of a *floruit* of Capsian industries based on a very large number of radiometric dates, not all of which are readily accepted.

(4) The 'Neolithic of Capsian tradition' proposed by Vaufrey on very meagre evidence but nevertheless extended by him to include a large part of Africa, must be confined to its original geographical limits, leaving the vast areas unjustifiably attributed to it to a number of other facies of the African Neolithic.

The Ibero-Maurusian

The definition once put forward by Pallary (1909), and which is still in use, is no longer tenable. He had stressed the widespread use of one particular technique, the backed blade technique, which was characteristic of almost all the stone artefacts. J. Tixier's highly detailed typological analyses finally made it possible to substitute a set of precise forms for the idea of an overall technique, as had in fact been sensed more or less strongly, by a number of prehistorians, particularly Dr Gobert in Tunisia. Fresh excavations by E. Saxon on the Tamar Hat site (Bejaia Corniche, Algeria) revealed extremely early specimens, isotopically dated, and provided more ample information on these mouflon-hunters and cave-dwellers living on the coast but separated from the sea by marshes and an emerged continental shelf abounding in shellfish. The Ibero-Maurusian is in fact a culture occupying the coast and the tell but which nevertheless penetrated here and there inland, the last questionable evidence of which is afforded by the Columnata site (Tiaret, Algeria). However, singularly little trace of it can be found in the Tangiers region and on the coast of the Tunisian Sahel. This absence of the Ibero-Maurusian from Tunisia south of Oued Medjerda can be attributed to a separate development there, which we shall discuss below.

Even a detailed analysis reveals little of note among the Ibero-Maurusian artefacts. A few hundred micro-burins collected some time after the original excavations in the type-site of La Mouillah (near Marnia, Algeria) confirmed that they were associated with the manufacture of points with a trihedral working tip (called La Mouillah points) and not geometrical microliths, as in the Capsian industries. The bone industry is extremely mediocre, with only one particularity: the tranchet. There is no personal or mural art, even though it coincided in time with Altamira and Lascaux, and Cromagnoid men of the Mechta El-Arbi type were present both to the north and the south of the Mediterranean.

There is no satisfactory evidence to support the traditionally held view that this culture originated in the east, splitting into two branches, the European Cromagnons spreading along the northern Mediterranean and Mechta El-Arbi Man along the African coast to the south. Anthropologically, they may perhaps be thought to descend from the Neanderthals through Aterian Man. But, however attractive this theory is, it does not explain the development of an industry which has nothing in common with the Mousterian or even the Aterian which preceded it. To suggest that the Ibero-Maurusians were not the bearers of this culture is hardly conceivable, since it had no roots locally. And this is not the only problem. The vocation and destiny of these Maghribian Cromagnons were diametrically opposed to their European counterparts. Their stone industry, which coincided, at least in its early stages, with the Magdalenian, was Mesolithic to the extent that it was formerly described as a Berber Azilian; their bone industry was far removed from the Magdalenian equivalent; and there was no personal or mural art, in spite of assertions to the contrary in Morocco. They did, however, survive until the Neolithic, even colonizing the Canary Islands, towards the end of the third millennium before our era at the earliest. Many other distinctive features are characteristic in the Maghrib: dental mutilation, cemeteries in caves or rock-shelters (Afalou-bou-Rhummel, Algeria; Taforalt, Morocco), funeral monuments (Columnata).

The 'Collignon horizon' and the other pre-Capsian blade industries

It has now been proved on the basis of stratigraphy and geomorphology that the blade industries of pre-Saharan Tunisia (Gafsa, Lalla, Chotts region, and so on) were earlier than the entire Capsian sequence. At Gafsa (Sidi Mansour), the 'Collignon horizon' is stratified in the alluvial fill; the final stage of lagoon sedimentation is marked by substantial gypsiferous formations. Sedimentation resumed and was then halted by the subsidence of the Gafsa Basin, causing renewed erosion. The typical, developed Capsian occupies the level surfaces of this erosion as its mounds bear witness. No precise chronology can be established apart from the fact that there is some Mousterian in the lowermost layer of the sediment. These blade industries can only be associated with the Ibero-Maurusian in that they are specifically different from the Capsian. Their typology is different, with the exception of the backed blade technique. Their origin can no doubt be sought towards the east (Cyrenaica, Egypt, Near East).

Other distinctive epi-Palaeolithic industries can be placed locally between the Ibero-Maurusian and Capsian facies. The seventh millennium site of Columnata, with its cemetery, is characterized by its abundance of microliths. Other sites have been discovered, the largest of which is that at Koudiat Khifene Lahda (Aïn M'lila, eastern Algeria) where the pre-Capsian industry also dates back to the seventh millennium before our era. The term 'elassolithic' has been proposed to describe this ultra-microlithic complex which is doubtless related to an as yet undefined way of life. Other facies have been located in western Algeria, in particular the Keremian and the Kristelian, which appear to date back to the eighth millennium before our era, on the Oran coast. This list is by no means exhaustive. There was in fact a proliferation of industries between the largely Palaeolithic Ibero-Maurusian and the Capsian, comparable to the Mesolithic in Europe.

The Capsian facies

The Capsian sequence was the keystone of R. Vaufrey's theories: 'typical Capsian', 'Upper Capsian' and of 'Capsian tradition'. Although this oversimplified structure has been criticized, and justifiably, with the support, more particularly, of a large number of radiometric dates, it must be conceded that research into this series has not made the headway one might have expected over the past twenty years. With a few rare exceptions, excavations in shell middens have not produced a means of identifying the stratigraphy or archaeological structure. Until such time as a sufficient number of sections enable us to observe the superimposed layers of the various Capsian facies, we shall have to base our assumptions regarding contemporaneity and sequence on the carbon-14 dates which are incomparably less reliable than a sound stratigraphy.

With positive evidence in several places of the superimposing of 'Upper Capsian' on 'typical Capsian', this remains the basis of all classification. In both cases, the sites are heaps of miscellaneous waste matter: a mixture of ashes and charred stones, hundreds of thousands of snail-shells, skeletal fragments of animals eaten by man, his lithic and bone industry, objects of ornamentation and personal art, human remains, and so on. We can allow ourselves some speculation on the hut-dwellings which were the origin of these heaps of refuse: possibly they were reed huts held together with clay, if we can judge by a find made – unfortunately before exact dating techniques were possible – in the region of Khenchela (eastern Algeria).

The 'typical Capsian' stone industry is usually remarkable in quality. Truncated angle burins are exceptionally frequent. Less frequent, but just as characteristic, are the long, backed blades, sometimes known as 'knives', the blunt edge often tinted with ochre. The backed blades make up a quarter to a third of the stone tool-kits and were sometimes made by retouching burin offcuts (Gobert's 'aiguillons droits'). Micro-burins were already in existence, produced not as a result of the manufacture of La Mouillah points, as in the Ibero-Maurusian, but of the true geometric microliths (trapezes, scalene triangles). The bone industry is poor. Typical Capsian has only been found within a fairly well-defined area, on either side of the Algero-Tunisian border, to the south rather than to the north of the 35th parallel. To judge by the radiometric dates, it coincided with the seventh millennium before our era but did not outlast it. It would therefore appear to coincide, within this area, with the 'Upper Capsian'; but this is at variance with known stratigraphy. I shall believe it when 'Upper Capsian' is found stratified below 'typical Capsian'. And in that case, where does the generally accepted definition of 'developed Capsian' come in? Furthermore, we know virtually nothing of the bearer of 'typical Capsian' culture.

The developed Capsian is found in a *floruit* of facies which spread over western Africa and at least part of the Sahara. But we should be careful not to commit the error made by R. Vaufrey in asserting the diffusion of his 'Neolithic of Capsian tradition' over a large part of Africa on the basis of a succession of scattered finds.

With the exception of what I have termed the 'Tebessan facies', still encumbered with the heavy-duty implements of the typical Capsian, the developed Capsian is an industry of small-sized artefacts, rich in geometrically shaped microliths of generally outstanding technical quality, especially the triangular and some of the trapezoid tool-forms. Definitions based on statistical data are meaningless for they are taken from museum collections, material usually inexactly selected and sorted, sporadic excavations, and artificial strata of varying thicknesses according to the whim of the excavators. One 'shell midden' I studied at Aïn Dokkara was occupied by man for a thousand years, from the middle of the seventh to the middle of the sixth millennium before our era. Can one justifiably define its industry in terms of overall statistics?

The upper Capsian, or at least its southerly branch, lasted down to the fifth millennium before our era and survived until the process of Neolithization which itself covered a very long period. It is therefore tenable that typical and upper Capsian industries coincided with the 'Neolithic of Capsian tradition' in different areas.

Capsian culture thus lasted nearly 2000 years, only a few centuries less than Egypt of the Pharaohs. Even if we are unable to record its history, we can at least grasp its essential ethnological elements. Capsian Man did not belong to the Cromagnoid type of Mechta-Afalou: he was a Mediterranean, and the most intact, best-preserved specimen, found in unquestionable stratigraphical conditions, is the Man of Aïn Dokkara (Tebessa), who dates back to the middle of the seventh millennium before our era. Hundreds of Capsian dwellings have been found, all of which survived for centuries, and some for over a millennium. The sedentary life of these people, prior to pastoralism and agriculture, is worthy of note. Yet their dwellings were no more than huts made of reeds and branches daubed with clay or covered with hides. Hunting did not play a significant role, to judge, not by the variety of animal remains, but by their small quantity. The importance of land molluscs should not be minimized; but plant-gathering played an appreciable role, and although it is tempting to draw further inferences, neither the Columnata sickles nor the perforated stone balls, nor the stone mullers, nor the 'harvest lustre' on some sickles afford proof of agriculture.

Capsian man practised a variety of burial rites, and the corpses were often found lying on their side in the foetal position. The frequent use of ochre remains a mystery. More surprising is the use of human skeletal fragments, such as the unexpected trophy skull, possibly used as a mask, discovered at Faid Sonar (Aïn Bieda, Algeria). The Capsians had already practised dental mutilation on the living, specifically on women, up to the eight incisors.

They were nevertheless the first artists in the Maghrib – ornaments, engraved ostrich eggshells from the typical Capsian onward, small engraved slabs, sculpted stones – which may have foreshadowed rock art.

Neolithization and Neolithics

From as early as 1933 we were given a neat, systematic, uniform picture of the Neolithic by R. Vaufrey. His 'Neolithic of Capsian tradition', which he claimed had been diffused over the whole of the Maghrib, the Sahara and part of sub-Saharan Africa, became generally accepted theory, to the point that the initials 'NTC' (standing for *Néolithique de tradition capsienne*) came into common use. However, Dr Gobert and myself expressed strong doubts about what we regarded as the artificial product of a piecemeal reconstruction of data which to us seemed unrelated.

In fact, we had not grasped the thread of Vaufrey's deductions. Why did he take the extremely mediocre site of the Table de Jaatcha (Tunisia) as his frame of reference? In his thesis (1976), C. Roubet describes how Vaufrey arrived at his conclusions. He was not interested in the Neolithic for its own sake, but wished to establish the persistence of a 'Capsian tradition' which tailed off gradually as it moved farther away from its original source. The Neolithic was therefore no more than an epi-phenomenon of the Capsian. He justified his claim regarding the broad diffusion of the NTC by superimposing a series of cultural elements which he regarded as Neolithic. This gave rise to a typological conception of the Neolithic, and did not take into account the overlying, explanatory factor in technological revolutions, the disruption of a way of life. But, in fact, the strong persistence of the Capsian tradition disproves the theory of the development of a Neolithic culture. And the projectile tips, arrow-heads, found in such quantity in the Sahara, afford positive evidence of the persistence of a hunting-gathering mode of life which cannot remotely be regarded as Neolithic.

In these circumstances, the 'Neolithic of Capsian tradition' must be confined to its original frontiers. And this is what C. Roubet has done, basing his investigations on the Capeletti Grotto excavations (Aures, Algeria). Next to the essential typological factors, ecology, that is, knowledge of the environment in which men lived, is of fundamental importance. It is therefore possible to identify a pastoral, pre-agricultural economy in which transhumant migration was practised, which represents not the final stage of prehistory but the beginning of what are today the mountain peoples of the Aures, the Chaouis, who are small-scale shepherds and goatherds.

Thus between the fifth and the second millennium before our era there were a number of forms of neolithization in the Maghrib other than the NTC *sensu stricto*. In the first place, the areas untouched by the Capsian influence developed separately, with certain distinctive features: the Ibero-Maurusian was superseded, and they soon came into contact with Mediterranean Europe, from as early as the fifth millennium before our era. This raises the issue of navigation. There are several coastal facies of the Neolithic, completely independent of the Capsian tradition, which give evidence of contacts with Europe by their pottery and imported obsidian. The same applies to the Moroccan Atlantic coast.

On the other hand, the 'Neolithic of Capsian tradition' cannot be extended, as Camps has suggested, to the northern Sahara, and even less to the more southerly regions of the Sahara, where we have the rock art of Ahaggar and Tassili N'Ajjer.

The association of rock art with the Neolithic, as proposed by Vaufrey, is, however, extremely plausible, however debatable the attribution of the 'Neolithic of Capsian tradition' may be. Even so, this association is only valid for part of the engravings, the remainder dating to protohistoric times. These early naturalistic works cannot be connected with either Europe or the Sahara, and their origin should be placed in the neolithization of the Capsian, although the connection between the industry and the art remains to be proved.

Despite the wealth of prehistoric remains in the Maghrib, its prehistory is still imperfectly understood. Progress will be made only with large-scale excavations conducted in accordance with modern scientific methods.

PLATE 22.1 *Pebbles fashioned into a bi-faced tool and a chopper, Ain Hanech* (M. Bovis)

PLATE 22.2 *Spherical faceted pebbles, Ain Hanech* (M. Bovis)

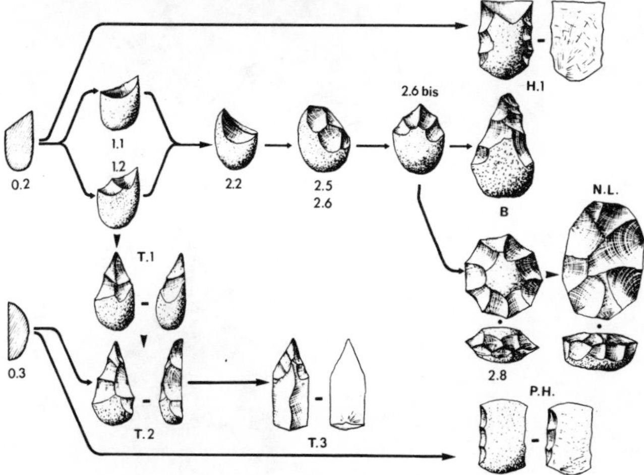

PLATE 22.3 *The development of 'Pebble Culture' towards Acheulian shapes: the numbers and figures refer to the system of classification used for the African Pre-Acheulian industry* (M. Bovis)

PLATE 22.4 *Hand-axe found on the Acheulian site of Erg Tihodaïne, Algerian Sahara* (M. Bovis)

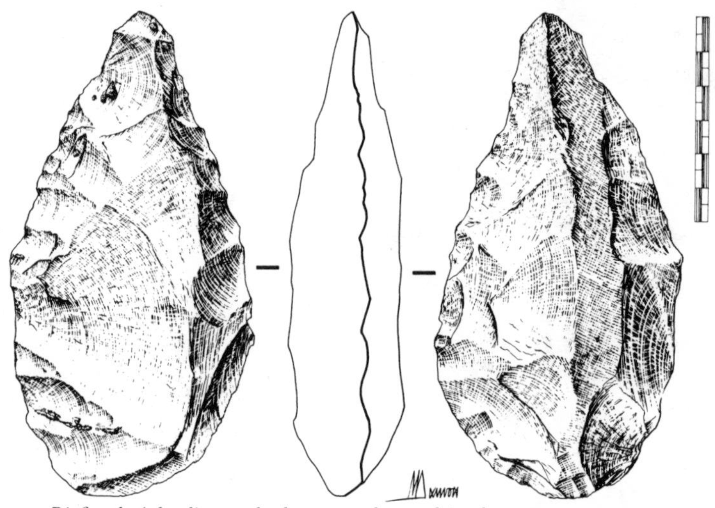

PLATE 22.5 *Bi-faced Acheulian tool, the most advanced implement found on the Ternifine site, Western Algeria* (M. Bovis)

PLATE 22.6 *Mousterian pointed tool, El-Guettar, Tunisia; excavations led by M. Gruet* (M. Bovis)

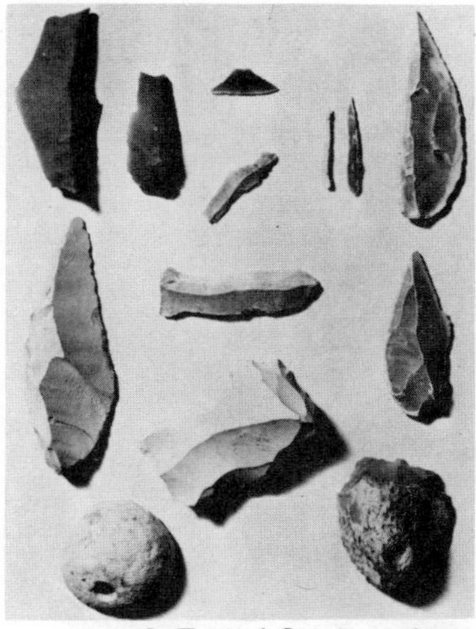

PLATE 22.8 *Typical Capsian industry* (M. Bovis)

PLATE 22.7 *Aterian tools – pedunculated points, scrapers and Levallois cores, Oued Djouf-el-Djemel, eastern Algeria* (M. Bovis)

PLATE 22.9 *Upper Capsian industry: scalene triangles, trapeziums, saws, grooved knives, burins, micro-burins, drillers, scrapers, etc.* (M. Bovis)

PLATE 22.10 *Upper Capsian industry: geometrical microliths (trapeziums, scalene triangles, crescents and micro-burins)* (M. Bovis)

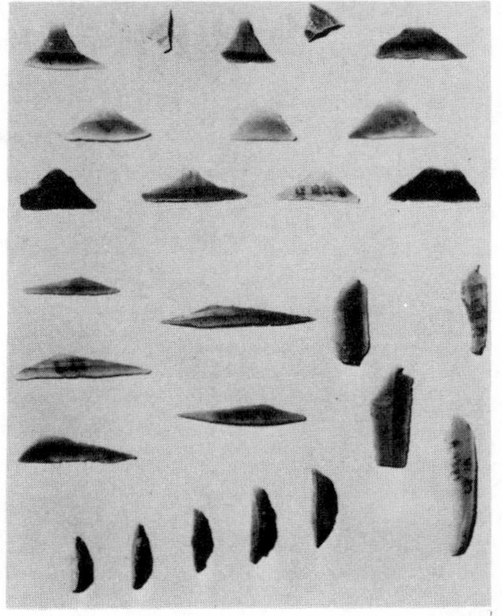

PLATE 22.11 *Upper Capsian, human fibula fashioned into a dagger found at Mechta el-Arbi, Eastern Algeria, during excavations in 1952* (M. Bovis)

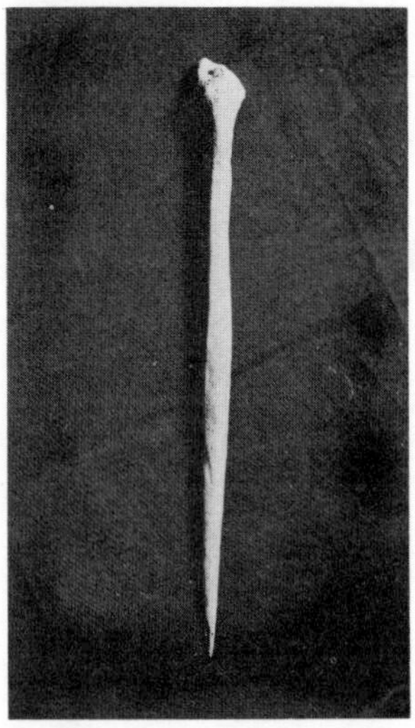

PLATE 22.12 *Upper Capsian: engraved limestone plaquette from Khanguet el-Mouhaad, Eastern Algeria* (M. Bovis)

PLATE 22.13 *Neolithic-Capsian Tradition: pestle and mortar showing traces of coal ochre and fragments of* Helix *shells, found at Damous el-Ahmar, Eastern Algeria* (M. Bovis)

23 The prehistory of the Sahara

H. J. HUGOT

The Sahara is an immense desert that covers the greater part of North Africa. It is not easy to define either its limits or its characteristics, but aridity is the factor common to all its various regions. Stretching 5700 kilometres from east to west, between the Red Sea and the Atlantic, and 1500 kilometres from north to south, between the pro-Saharan Atlas and the Sudanese Sahel, desert conditions now cover an area of nearly 8·6 million square kilometres. Yet the Sahara as we know it today has changed considerably since prehistoric times.

The unifying factor in the different regions of the Sahara is the remarkably low hygrometric level, one of the lowest in the world. Apart from the extreme shortage of water, its other characteristics are wide differences between day and night temperatures and an abundance of sand, continually blown before the wind, that is fast eroding the ageing relief.

Although the Sahara is a desert now, it was populated extensively in several earlier periods. The departure of its last inhabitants is attributable to the increasing dryness and heat of the climate, which led to rarer rainfall and to the drying-up of springs and rivers. This in turn brought about the disappearance of the plant life and the animals on which man lived, and he was forced to retire to the fringes of the desert, where conditions were more clement.

Many experts have considered the problem of the transformation of the Sahara into a desert and the causes and consequences of this change, among them E. F. Gautier,[1] T. Monod,[2] R. Capot-Rey,[3] J. Dubief,[4] L. Balout,[5] K. Butzer[6] and S. A. Huzayyin,[7] to mention only a few. We now know in theory why the monsoon of the Gulf of Guinea and the cold polar front no longer brought to the Sahara the two opportunities for rainfall that governed

1. E. F. Gautier, 1928.
2. T. Monod, 1945; Burg Wartenstein Symposium, 1961.
3. R. Capot-Rey, 1953.
4. J. Dubief, 1959.
5. L. Balout, 1952a.
6. K. W. Butzer, 1958.
7. S. A. Huzayyin, 1936, pp. 19–22.

its fertility, making it, in prehistoric times, a smiling and populous land. However the evolution of the Saharan climate is still open to debate. We still do not know whether the deterioration of the climate has reached its peak, has still to reach it, or has perhaps passed it. Moreover, the way the desert grows is not clear: does it spread out round a centre, or do the fringes of the Sahara shift alternately between the north and the south?

We are still a long way from being able to reconstruct an exact chronology for the various climatic periods which from time to time made the Sahara habitable by man. Although extensive research has been carried out in one or two directions, such works are rare and no serious effort has been made to develop them. Yet they are of capital importance, not only from the scientific point of view, but also for a better understanding of a phenomenon that affects all human life; an understanding of the climatic changes that have taken place in the Sahara during the Quaternary era is essential for the study of ecological change and soon, when each square metre of the earth's surface will become vital for mankind, the better the past of the 'Great Desert' is known the more important its role will be.

The historical progress of research

Since the journals listing research on the prehistory of the Sahara as a whole have ceased publication, it is not easy to draw up a schedule of the work already done. We do in fact possess such lists for the colonial period, but they are incomplete and often widely scattered. Some important discoveries have, for example, been described in military reports, which are somewhat difficult of access. The political division of the Sahara also accounts for the dispersal of works devoted to its prehistoric wealth, for not only the British, French, Italians and Spaniards, but also later the Germans, Japanese, Russians and others, have all made important scientific contributions to the discovery of the Sahara's past.

Yet the desert has only relatively recently been penetrated. The first serious work on the prehistory of the Sahara was probably that published by the Abbé Richard in 1869[8] on the Algerian Sahara. Research in Egypt began at almost the same time with a letter from A. Arcelin dated February 1867.[9] But research in the western Sahara had hardly begun by the beginning of this century. The expeditions led by Foureau from 1876 on[10] contributed greatly to work on the central Sahara, particularly the important expedition of 1898–1900.[11] Meanwhile O. Lenz[12] had remarked on the presence of prehistoric objects at Taudenit in 1886. Thenceforth the study

8. Abbé Richard, 1868, pp. 74–5.

9. A. Arcelin, in a letter to the editor of the journal, *Matériaux pour l'histoire primitive de l'Homme*, published in Vol. V, 1869.

10. F. Foureau, 1883.

11. F. Foureau, 1905.

12. O. Lenz, 1884.

of Saharan prehistory attracted a fair amount of attention, and its progress was hardly impeded even by two world wars.

Many scientists have, naturally, been attracted by the wealth of prehistoric remains in the Sahara. It would be impossible to give a complete list here, but one is struck by the valuable contributions made by the earlier authorities. The work of G. B. M. Flamand,[13] Frobenius[14] and Miss G. Caton-Thompson,[15] for example, is indispensable for any serious study of Saharan prehistory.

Prehistoric research in the desert has been more affected than any other kind of research by momentary preoccupations. Moreover, an understanding of its particular needs was for many years obscured by the fact that it was regarded as only subsidiary to the main interests of the various trans-Saharan expeditions. So the work was entrusted to amateurs or to specialists in some other subject who could not provide the required expertise. Moreover, in such a difficult environment, where lives may depend on every pound of baggage, the bulk, weight and cumbersomeness of prehistoric evidence led to its often being left behind. It should also be added that the Sahara is not an ideal place for travellers to wander in; still less does it allow the time or the means of making detailed investigations. This probably explains the many references to 'non-existent industries', 'complete absence of stratigraphy', '*nomen nudum*', and so on. In fact the prehistory of the Sahara is as rich as that of any other region.

As soon as time and money enabled specialized expeditions to investigate the Sahara, the situation changed rapidly. This occurred after the Second World War, and resulted in a number – unfortunately small – of excellent monographs that deal principally with Ahaggar, the Saoura, Chad, Mauritania, the Libyan desert, the Fezzan, and so on. A joint venture between science and industry even made possible the remarkable results recorded in the *Documents scientifiques des missions Berliet-Ténéré-Tchad*.[16]

Yet despite the desirability of investigating Saharan prehistory and the rich evidence available, it will be a long time before any kind of textbook is prepared. There is not even a popular account in this age – which has seen man reach the moon. All one can point to in Saharan prehistory are the many studies in detail and a few chapters in general works, in particular those of H. Alimen,[17] H. J. Hugot[18] and R. Vaufrey.[19]

13. G. B. M. Flamand, 1902, pp. 535–8; 1921, pp. 114–15; R. Perret, 1937: list of the sites studied.
14. L. Frobenius, 1937.
15. G. Caton-Thompson and E. W. Gardner, 1934.
16. H. J. Hugot, 1962.
17. H. Alimen, 1960.
18. H. J. Hugot, 1970.
19. R. Vaufrey, 1969.

Attempt at a chronological account

From the very beginning Saharan prehistory took its points of comparison from Europe and, in particular, from France. Such terms as 'Clacto-Abbevillian', 'Chelles-Acheulian', 'Mousterian', 'Aurignacian flakes' and 'Solutrean foliate arrow-heads' were current. The errors bred by this simplistic point of view still infect Saharan studies today. Saharan prehistory, like all prehistory, grows from the analysis of detailed monographs on particular industries, and monographs of this kind have not yet been written. Another regrettable consequence of the lack of order which reigns in Saharan research is the light-hearted attribution of precise social organizations to vanished ethnic groups without any real assurance that the evidence on which they are founded is valid.

Two remarks should be made on the subject of chronology.[20] First, nowhere in the Sahara has a sufficiently comprehensive stratigraphy[21] been found to enable us to establish a precise prehistoric succession. Secondly, apart from the Neolithic period, we have no dates that would enable us to establish an absolute chronology. However, despite these difficulties we possess such excellent studies as those of J. Chavaillon on the Saoura,[22] H. Faure on Chad,[23] P. Chamard on Mauritania,[24] backed up by

20. *Quaternary chronology*: a succession of varying climatic phases. In most cases we only hope to establish a relative chronology for the Sahara as it is stratigraphically so poor. One of the best comparative chronologies has been suggested by J. Chavaillon (*Quaternary Formations of the Western Sahara*, Paris: CNRS, 1964). From the base to the top of the Saoura terraces in the north-west Sahara that author distinguishes:

Upper Quaternary (Villafrancian)	Aïdian
	Mazerian
Middle Quaternary	Taourirtian
	Ougartian
Recent Quaternary	Saourian
	Guirian
Holocene	

21. *Stratigraphy*: the study and interpretation of the layers successively deposited in one place. It is easy to understand that a region subject to such climatological cataclysms as the Sahara should not contain much stratigraphic evidence. Sufficient stratigraphic sites do exist, however, to show that in many places there is a series of three terraces, old, middle and new, which testify to the existence of three long climatic periods. We should not overschematize, however, for when we take micro-climates into account the problem of the climatic periods that can be deduced from stratigraphy becomes extremely complex. Stratigraphy shows that by about 1000 before our era the Sahara was already a desert.

22. J. Chavaillon, 1964.

23. H. Faure, 1962.

24. P. Chamard, 1969–70.

solid peripheral studies on Algeria,[25] Morocco,[26] Libya,[27] and so on.

In the light of such studies we can get a fairly accurate idea of the outlines of Saharan prehistoric chronology. But there are too few palaeontological data and, in general, too little organic material that can be used for radiocarbon dating for us to take an absolute chronology any further back than the Neolithic (see Table 23.1, p. 600).

Of course Table 23.1 is drastically simplified, and in particular it does not account for an important complex of large flakes, often made by the Levallois technique, found on top of a collection of thin, bifacial flakes, small in size and light in weight, that probably date from the end of the Acheulian. Such complexes have been found at Tiguelguemine,[28] at Broukkou,[29] and other places. Finally we should point out that up till now nothing has been found that would enable us to speak of an upper Palaeolithic[30] period in the Sahara, since the term is not borne out by the facts. Still less is it possible to talk of a Mesolithic period, although in any case that particular term is going out of use.

Table 23.1 may perhaps give rise to a more detailed chronology. It correlates what is known of climatic trends and population densities in prehistoric times.

Although very few skeletons have been found together with industries which will allow of classification, yet those that have been found indicate the very great antiquity of man in the Sahara.

The appearance of man in the Sahara; the 'Pebble Culture' industry

On the banks of extinct rivers it is often possible to see terraces that were formed when the waters were still flowing. Such terraces form three distinct levels, called, for the sake of convenience, old, middle and late terraces. At Djebel Idjerane,[31] 120 kilometres east of In Salah in the Algerian Sahara, pebble tools have been found in the old terrace. We know that such pebbles are the first tools to bear recognizable marks of having been worked by man. In most cases they are simply river pebbles from which a few flakes have been struck to fashion a rough, uneven cutting edge. It has been postulated

25. L. Balout, 1955b.
26. P. Biberson, 1961b.
27. C. B. M. McBurney and R. W. Hey, 1955.
28. H. J. Hugot, 1962.
29. ibid.
30. *Palaeolithic*: the recognition of *Homo habilis* as the probable ancestor of present-day man has necessitated a new chronological division of this period, but this has not modified the problems relating to the Sahara. It appears at present that there was no Middle Palaeolithic or epi-Palaeolithic period in the Sahara, but rather a terminal Palaeolithic that is represented by the Aterian, therefore post-Mousterian and separated from the Neolithic by only a brief gap.
31. A. Bonnet, 1961.

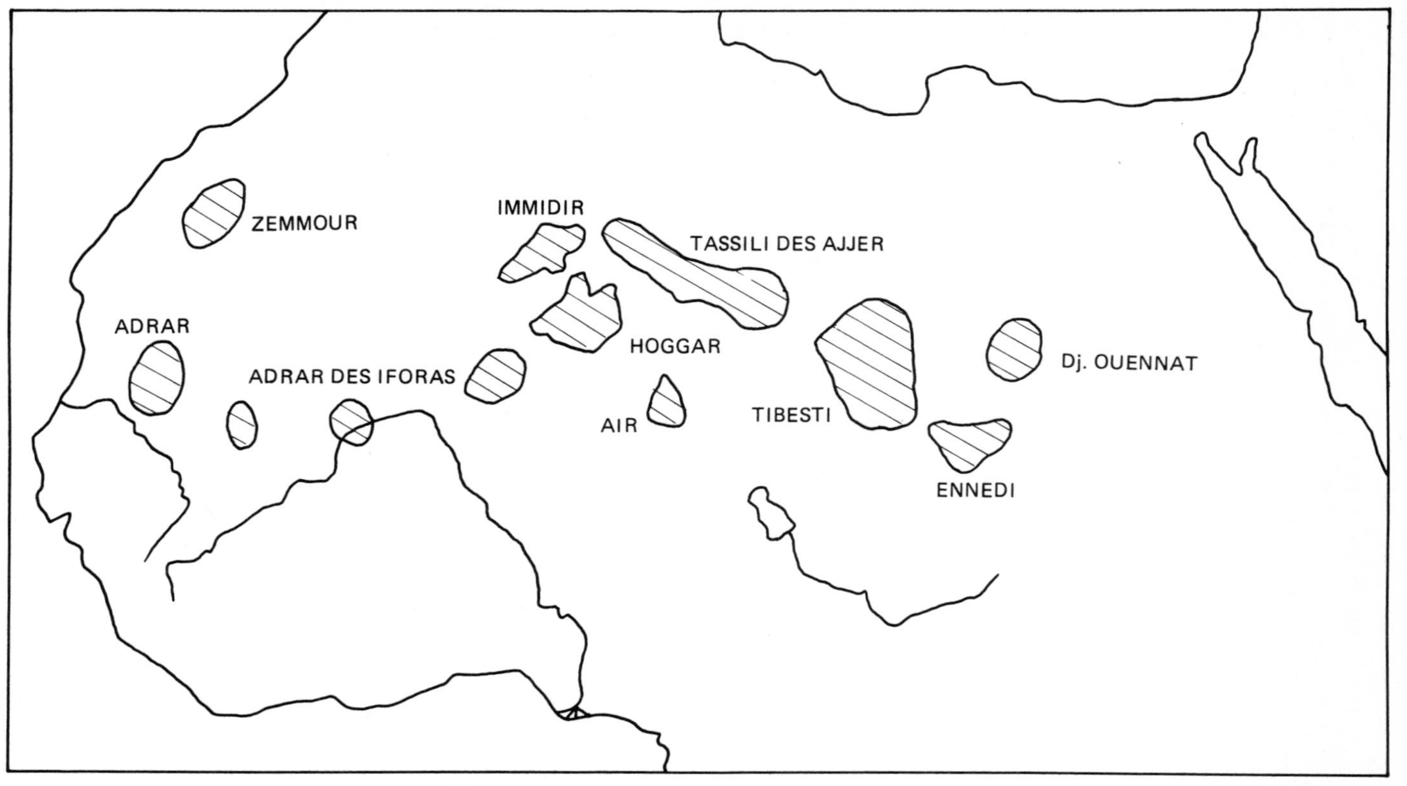

FIG. 23.1 *Principal sites of Saharan paintings and rock engravings*

that such objects belonged specifically to the industries of *Homo habilis*.

In the Saharan region of Niger, on the banks of the Teffassasset,[32] an ancient tributary of Lake Chad, large quantities of pebble tools have also been found, but in a less significant situation than in Idjerane. Other collections, as in Aoulef,[33] have been scattered or destroyed, while the series found in the Saoura[34] is too small to provide sufficient material for study. But we can say for certain that the Pebble Culture was widely found throughout the Sahara, which at that time was humid and very different from the desert we know today. Unfortunately no animal or human fossils from this period have been discovered, and all we can do is to put forward the hypothesis that these very rough tools, which are found more or less throughout the Sahara as well as at sites where large quantities remain, really are those that were fashioned and used by our most distant ancestors.

Homo erectus, maker of bifacial tools

At the close of the Pebble Culture a technical change appears leading to the evolution of tools which were still in use at the beginning of the Lower Palaeolithic. The mystery surrounding this great human and technical advance remains complete. In the Sahara no skeleton of the makers of this remarkable tool (and of the derivative form, the cleaver, which suggests a forest environment at that period) has been found. But although we know nothing of the ecology of the Pebble Culture, we are slightly better informed on that of *Homo erectus*. The Sahara was then a region of great lakes with high water-levels and sufficient rainfall to maintain a type of vegetation indicative of an almost cool climate. The large animals now found only south of the desert then lived throughout the Sahara. One remarkable fact is that the torrential downpours typical of the following period destroyed or severely damaged the deposits of sediment which accumulated almost everywhere in the great lakes, and moreover the very dry spell between the preceding period and the period under discussion may well have hastened the process of destruction.

Because of the widespread disturbance of these deposits, reliable stratigraphic evidence is extremely rare, although the number of bifacial tools found in the Sahara is enormous.

We shall not go so far as to say that the fossil man of Chad[35] made bifacial tools. Vaufrey[36] puts him at the beginning of his chapter in the Lower and Middle Palaeolithic in the Sahara, but since we have no knowledge as to

32. H. J. Hugot, 1962, pp. 151–2.
33. H. J. Hugot, 1955b.
34. J. Chavaillon, 1956.
35. Y. Coppens, 1962, pp. 455–9.
36. R. Vaufrey, 1969, p. 21.

whether this venerable ancestor made tools, we can only describe him as an extremely interesting palaeontological discovery. Tihodaïne was first mentioned by Duveyrier in 1864[37] and was visited by E. F. Gautier and M. Reygasse in 1932.[38] An Acheulian industry has been found there with remains of rhinoceros, elephants, hippopotamuses, bovines, buffalo, wart-hogs, zebra, crocodiles, gazelle, and so on. All the material in Tihodaïne is late Acheulian, and it often includes carved bone or wood, so that it was at advanced stage of the Acheulian and does not follow directly from the culture already described.

Not far from Tihodaïne there are two very fine Acheulian deposits with a variety of bifacial tools, often very small and almost 'S'Baïkian', and of cleavers. This is the Admer Erg deposit,[39] discovered by a soldier in 1934 and first published by H. Lhote and H. Kelley in 1936.[40] This surface deposit, like the one at Wadi Teffassesset[41] discovered by the Berliet-Ténéré expedition, is not easily dated, but their importance has not inspired the research necessary to get full value from the material.

Tabelbala and Tachenghit[42] are well known for their bifacial tools in reddish quartzite sandstone, and more especially for their impressive range of cleavers that show a highly developed technique.

In the same part of Africa J. Chavaillon and H. Alimen have found an undisturbed deposit of a developed Acheulian culture which either immediately preceded the flake industry or else should be included in the Middle Acheulian. This is the case at Mazer, Beni Abbes and Kerzas.[43]

At Chebket Mennouna (Saoura in the Algerian Sahara)[44] there would be a significant series of artefacts except that, unfortunately, they are very few.

At In Ekker, Meniet and Arak,[45] the middle Acheulian is buried under sediment containing scattered objects of the Aterian.

A large number of Acheulian objects have also been found at Aoulef,[46] at Sherda,[47] at El Beyes,[48] at Esh Shaheinab, [49] in the western Sahara at

37. H. Duveyrier, 1864.
38. E. F. Gautier and M. Reygasse, 1934.
39. H. Lhote and H. Kelley, 1936, pp. 217–26.
40. This surface stratum is a good illustration of the difficulties of distinguishing between a dominant industry and later contamination by more recent objects.
41. H. J. Hugot, 1962.
42. B. Champault, 1953.
43. H. Alimen, 1960, pp. 421–3.
44. J. Chavaillon, 1956, p. 231; 1958, pp. 431–43.
45. H. J. Hugot, 1963.
46. W. P. Pond *et al.*, 1938, pp. 17–21.
47. M. Dalloni, 1948.
48. P. Biberson, 1965, pp. 173–89.
49. A. J. Arkell, 1954, pp. 30–4.

Kharga,[50] and in the Libyan desert.[51] We may conclude that the Acheulian is present in the whole Sahara, but we are unable to date it for, apart from four or five sites, no stratigraphic deposits have been found. The most important work (careful excavations and observations) remains to be done.

An obscure point: the flake industries

Both in Europe and in the Sahara the Lower Palaeolithic is characterized by the basic bifacial tool, which began in extremely rough forms that were at first called Chellean, and developed into elegant, balanced, perfectly chipped and finished pieces like those found at Micoque. In the Sahara the precursors of bifacial tools are small worked pebbles, but we soon find a radical change in the techniques used in stone flaking, and to this new mastery of the difficult art of stone preparing the refinement and perfection of form is partly due. In Europe and the Sahara such progress was made possible only by the discovery of the virtues of using a more pliable striker, made of bone or wood, rather than a stone hammer, which could not be used with great precision because of the force of impact it required.

But although the bifacial tool is in a sense the characteristic, or *fossile directeur* of the Lower Palaeolithic, it is far from being the only object made by *Homo erectus*. We have many reasons for believing that as soon as the technique was evolved flakes were used too, and also a large number of the many chips that came off the core. That is why it is quite normal to find a preponderance of flake tools at the dawn of the Middle Palaeolithic.[52] The flake tool is thus a development rather than a discovery, a development which also takes the form of reducing bifacial tools in size as well as using them more and more as weapons. On the other hand what is revolutionary is the widespread use of the Levallois technique. It appears very early in the Sahara, and influenced the techniques used in the making of certain bifacial tools from Tachenghit,[53] as well as at Broukkou and Timbrourine. But despite the very early appearance of the Levallois technique, it does not seem to have changed the style of life of its inventors, who were certainly not Neanderthal men, or they would have adopted a different style of life requiring lighter tools and weapons, quite opposite in conception to the heavy bifacial tool and cleaver. The really striking fact, although it has hardly been noticed, is not so much the absence of any Mousterian or Mousteroid period in the Sahara, but that the Aterian period that takes its place, and which in fact has a Mousterianizing influence, is above all an industry providing weapons for hunting. The ability to make a tanged weapon implies not only that the concept of a shaft was known, but also

50. M. Almagro-Basch, 1946.

51. G. Caton-Thompson, 1952.

52. However we should not forget that the real mutation is human, and is marked by the appearance of Neanderthal Man, the instigator of the Mousterian industries.

53. J. Tixier, 1957.

those of the assegai and the *bolas*. In brief, it is the industry of a migratory people, which is why its implements are so light compared with those of preceding cultures.

At the present stage of research it would appear therefore that in the Sahara the Aterian[54] takes the place occupied elsewhere by the Mousterian, and shares several of its features such as the use of the Levallois technique, which appears not only in the style of retouching but also in the typology of the finished objects. However the Aterian differs from the Mousterian in two essential characteristics:

(1) the presence of tanged objects that might serve as boring instruments, either retouched or in a rough form, scrapers, awls or even drills;
(2) noticeable statistical differences from the classical Mousterian industry.

Apart from this, however, the idea of a Mousteroid substratum remains strong, and although we have no Aterian skeletons it is quite usual to attribute this interesting industry to a relation of Neanderthal Man.

We know that the Aterian is a North African industry that was diffused southwards[55] and stopped roughly along the banks of the great lakes of the southern Sahara. As it progressed southwards it gradually changed until it produced such works as the dazzling culture of Adrar Bous,[56] where as well as the classical collection of cores, blades, flakes, scrapers, notches, double foliated arrow-heads made by the bifacial technique and stone balls, we find very fine hafted arrow-heads also made by the bifacial technique, one of which is nearly 19 centimetres long.

The Aterian culture is extremely widespread. We find it in Tunisia,[57] Morocco,[58] Algeria,[59] Saoura, Tidikelt (where it uses an Arancaria fossil successfully as a basic material),[60] and Mauritania where Adrar roughly marks its limits.[61] We find it everywhere, in Ahaggar[62] at the Admer

54. *Aterian*: an industry of North African origin, with an essentially Mousterian basis and in addition a series of hafted objects. The Aterian is a later culture than the Mousterian. The stone tools, which show a marked influence of the Levallois technique, become more highly developed as it moved across the Sahara. The southernmost limit of the Aterian seems to have been the great southern lakes that are now found only in Chad. On the north-west borders of Chad sites dating from 9000 to 8000 before our era have been found. This industry dates from the Late rather than the Middle Palaeolithic.
55. H. J. Hugot, 1967, pp. 529–56.
56. H. J. Hugot, 1962, pp. 158–62.
57. M. Gruet, 1954.
58. M. Antoine, 1938.
59. M. Reygasse, 1922, pp. 467–72.
60. E. F. Gautier, 1914: Minette de Saint-Martin, 1908; M. Reygasse, 1923.
61. R. Guitat, 1972, pp. 29–33.
62. H. J. Hugot, 1962, pp. 47–70.

Erg,[63] at Tihodaïne,[64] at Adrar Bous,[65] and also in the Fezzan, in Zumri, and at its most easterly point at Kharga in Egypt.[66]

It is very difficult to place the Aterian in a chronological sequence. It may have begun *c.* 35 000 before our era. On the borders of Chad its progress seems to have been arrested by the last high water-level, and if that were the case then it would have lasted till 9000–7000 before our era. But all this is mere hypothesis.

It seems logical that an industry so obviously influenced by the Mousterian should be succeeded by an Upper Palaeolithic period, but two questions then arise. First, can we really put the Aterian, which did after all come very late, in a Middle Palaeolithic? In his masterly thesis, L. Balout thought it would be wrong to succumb to such a temptation. Secondly, what do we know of a true epi-Palaeolithic in the Sahara? Very little really, and the industry discovered by R. Mauny at Wadi Eched[67] has not yet yielded up its secrets. The Capsian-style collections of stone tools found on the southern border of the Tademaït[68] are still a matter of much debate. Only the series at Merdjouma (Wadi Mya on the Tademaït plateau in the central Algerian Sahara), which was found long ago, gives any proof of the presence of a true Capsian ensemble in the region now covered by the Sahara, and that is hardly enough to carry conviction.

In order to provide a chronological solution it has therefore been suggested that the Aterian should be placed under the uncontroversial heading of terminal Palaeolithic.

The hiatus

In order to describe a developed post-Aterian industry of Adrar Bous (Niger), J. D. Clark recently used the word Mesolithic. This term which is, fortunately, gradually falling into disuse, has no meaning generally speaking, and does not correspond to anything known in the Sahara. Its use can only reinforce Arkell's error,[69] which was quite understandable at the time when he was working on the Nile. In the current state of research, French prehistorians prefer not to use this term.

But this does not mean that the problem of the epi-Palaeolithic does not exist, for the Egyptian Sebilian III, with its intrusive geometric microliths,[70] precedes the Neolithic A without merging with it, and there are some

63. J. Bobo, 1956, pp. 253–68.
64. L. Balout, in C. Arambourg and L. Balout, 1955, pp. 287–92.
65. H. J. Hugot, 1962, pp. 158–62.
66. G. Caton-Thompson, 1952, 1946.
67. An unpublished monograph has been given to the Department of Prehistory of the IFAN of the University of Dakar.
68. H. J. Hugot, 1952, 1955a.
69. A. J. Arkell, 1949a, 1953.
70. E. Vignard, 1923, pp. 1–76.

indications, though these are rare, that it may have spread farther than the zones where its presence has been recognized.

The Neolithic

We know little or nothing of the genesis of the Neolithic peoples.[71] They seem to have spread through the Sahara from different points. According to M.-C. Chamla,[72] one factor in the Neolithic peopling of the Sahara is crossbreeding, with Blacks at one extreme and Middle Eastern peoples, ordinarily grouped under the name 'Mediterranean', at the other.

The Neolithic population of the Sahara was far from homogeneous. If we take the waves of settlement in order, the oldest seems to be that which formed on the banks of the Nile, near Khartoum and Esh Shaheinab, and then spread westwards along the banks of the great lakes. This wave does not seem to have spread farther than the eastern fringes of Aukar, nor to have penetrated into the forests, but it did send out two feelers northwards, one into the Ahaggar as far as the northern edge of the mountains before Tassili N'Ajjer, and the other from Tilemsi towards the Saoura. This brilliant civilization is easily recognized from the distinct character and the richness of its pottery decoration. Its industries, however, are very difficult to describe precisely, as the 'Neolithic of Sudanese tradition' made use of all that came to hand. The first inhabitants of the Sahara were fishing, hunting, food-gatherers, who were fond of hippopotamus and the berries of the nettle-tree (*Celtis* sp.), but who did not disdain fish from the lakes, freshwater turtles, or water-melons. The fact that they made adzes, hoes, grinders, grindstones and similar objects does not mean at all that they engaged in any form of agriculture.[73] Though they constantly filled jars

71. *Neolithic*: descriptive of new techniques (in particular pottery, stone-polishing, the beginnings of domestication, agriculture and urbanism) that supplemented the highly developed lithic industry of the epi-Palaeolithic. The oldest Neolithic sites in the Sahara can, it seems, be attributed to the fifth and sixth millennia before our era. The term Neolithic does not necessarily presuppose a knowledge of all the techniques mentioned above. However one of the most remarkable phenomena, which merits some consideration, is the cooking of food; the chemical changes resulting from this had a decisive influence on the physiological development of man. The Saharan Neolithic in its various forms is a technical explosion, rather than a revolution as it has often been called.

72. M.-C. Chamla, 1968.

73. *Agriculture*: 'The deliberate cultivation of selected plants on areas of land worked specifically for that purpose'. We may deduce that a culture had a knowledge of agriculture from the following:

(1) Statistically valid palynological proof.
(2) The existence of traces of cultivated land.
(3) The discovery of identifiable vegetable fossils.

The presence of a so-called agricultural range of tools is not in itself significant, as hoes may have been used to dig up clay for pottery, grindstones may have been used for grinding pigments, wild grains, medicines, etc. 'Agricultural' is therefore a term that can only be applied in accordance with fixed rules and not on the basis of unverified hypotheses.

with nettle-tree berries, and though imprints of gourd seeds are often found during the excavation of sites, this gives rise at most to the hypothesis of a proto-cultivation. There was a division of labour for specialized pursuits divided up into specialized tasks. Stone polishing was widespread, and the range of weapons was extensive. Hunters used bows and/or throwing-spears; bone harpoons and fishhooks were used. Polished stone axes, hoes and adzes formed an important part of their equipment. They were adept at making beads from hard stones such as amazonite, chalcedony, haematite and carnelian; specialists had perfected very clever drilling equipment,[74] consisting of burin splinters, needles and drills used with resins and fine sand. A lot of grinding equipment has been found, and it is often very fine; it proves that even if there was no true milling at least the art of grinding was known. The product that they ground was certainly ochre, but also perhaps wild grains, berries, dried grasses, vegetable dyes, or medicines. Their pottery deserves special mention, not only for its richness of decoration but also for its beauty of form. It should be noted that conical dimple bases and elongated amphora-shaped vessels are not found, though there are a few pouring lips, handles and knobs.

We are quite well informed, therefore, on the first wave of settlers. It was followed, farther to the south, by another African people which spread into the forests, where it was so well hidden that despite its importance this Neolithic culture remained for long undiscovered. It has been identified quite clearly in Guinea, hence its name of Guinean Neolithic, though in fact it probably originated in central Africa.[75]

A little later the 'Neolithic in the Capsian tradition', the result of the Neolithization of the old North African Capsian culture, began moving southwards. It reached Mauritania from the north-east, and got as far as Ahaggar, since at Meniet it has been found just below the surface on Sudanese Neolithic sites. We are less certain of its eastern limits, as there are no usable monographs for Libya. The Capsian Neolithic tradition is more austere than the Sudanese Neolithic. Its pottery has little, if any, decoration. But while the Sudanese lithic industry is often hackneyed, the Capsian uses a very rigorous technique and in the Sahara is enriched with a dazzling proliferation of weapons and arrow-heads. The polished stone is often very beautiful, and the bowls made from hard stone and zoomorphic statuettes[76] are masterpieces that quite make up for the bad impression made by their pottery. In this facies of Neolithic culture we find small beads pierced for threading that are sometimes fragments of encrinite, but more often discs made out of small pieces of ostrich eggshell. Whole eggs have been blown to make containers, and some have been engraved with line drawings.

74. M. and J. Gaussen, 1965, p. 237.

75. R. Delcroix and R. Vaufrey, 1939.

76. *Collections préhistoriques. Musée d'Ethnographie et de Préhistoire du Bardo (Alger), Album No. 1* (Paris: AMG, 1956), Plates 107–10.

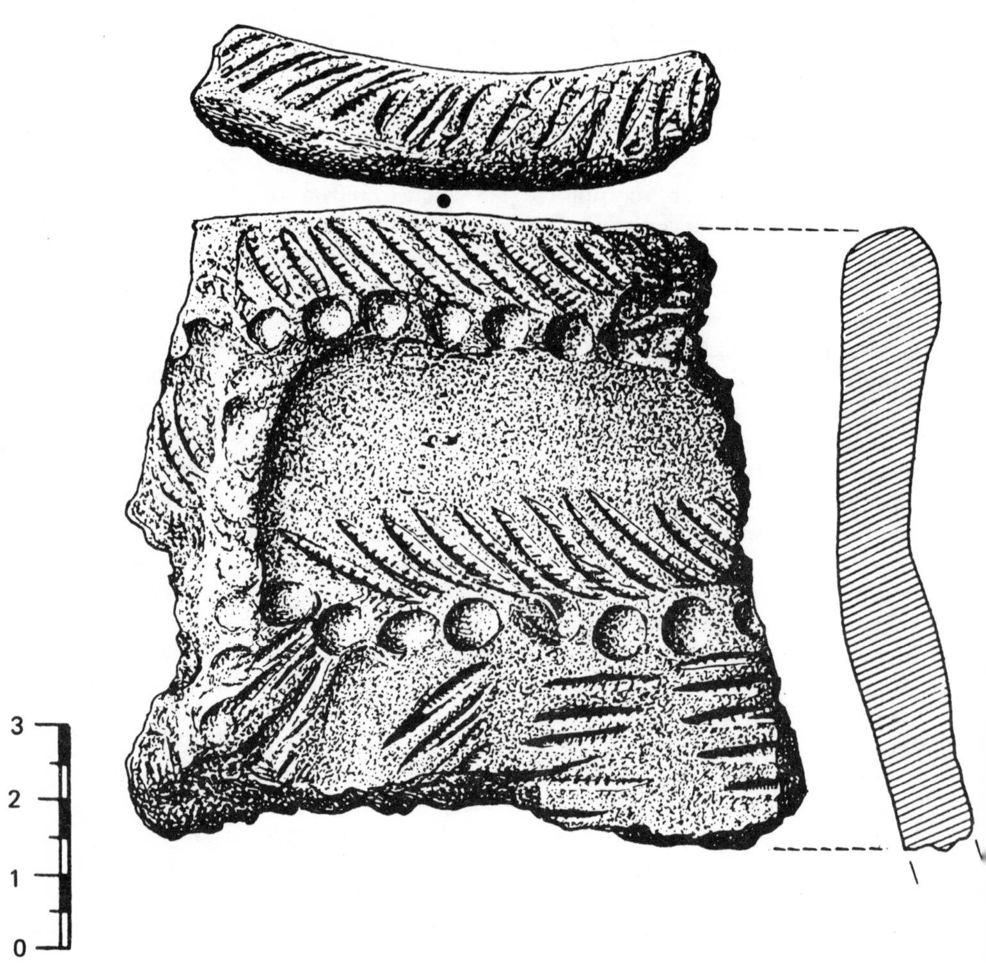

FIG. 23.2 *Pottery from Akreijit, Mauritania*

We know that the Ibero-Maurusians and the Capsians were not the same people. The latter lived mainly on the high Algerian plateaux where they left those strange heaps of shells known as *escargotières*. The Ibero-Maurusians settled on the shores of the Mediterranean, from Tunisia to Morocco, but we do not know for certain how these Cromagnoids settled in North Africa, nor how the two peoples were distributed. What is certain is that both underwent Neolithization in North Africa. The Ibero-Maurusian Neolithic people, living as they did near the sea, could not but be influenced by it, and if one continues south down the Atlantic coast of Morocco one finds mounds of mussel and oyster shells, and farther on of *Arca senilis*, which are still eaten in Senegal. The whole coast of the Moroccan Sahara and of Mauritania was occupied by a strange Neolithic industry that has been studied little if at all, and is characterized by rough pottery with little decoration, hearthstones and occasional stone tools. It would be very interesting to know how this industry was formed and where it came from, for although it was influenced by the Ibero-Maurusian culture in Morocco we know nothing of its constituent elements.

There is a fifth stream of Neolithic culture that has since drawn the attention of specialists, the one discovered at Adrar Bous and called Tenerean for that reason. J. D. Clark, who has actually seen the site, suggested that it might be representative of the 'Saharan Neolithic', but this is quite impossible unless 'Saharan' is taken merely to mean a very extensive area.

The Tenerean, discovered by Joubert in 1941,[77] is characterized by lotus-shaped projectile points, thick concave scrapers, elementary saws and hafted axes as well as by its typology and statistical composition, and it is, again, impossible to call it a classical Saharan Neolithic culture as that term is reserved exclusively for the two cultures, Sudanese and Capsian, which cover most of the Sahara. Vaufrey, who was often tempted to relate everything to the Capsian Neolithic,[78] says that 'the Egyptian influences that can be recognized in the Algerian Sahara spread, in their most highly perfected form, as far as the Ahaggar', and, further on, 'the Tenerean sites represent the apex of the Saharan Neolithic industry and evoke irresistibly the pre-Dynastic Egyptian culture'.[79] We should however point out that outside Ténéré there is no clear Egyptian influence to be found, despite Vaufrey's assertion.

We still have to find out, therefore, how the obvious outside influences reached the magnificent Tenerean industry with its characteristic beautiful green jasper artefacts.

One should however be careful not to take the notion of a facies too far. We now know with what varied exuberance a particular people may respond to the different limitations placed on it by such factors as the

77. G. Joubert and R. Vaufrey, 1941–6.

78. R. Vaufrey, 1938, pp. 10–29.

79. R. Vaufrey, 1969, p. 66.

TABLE 23.1 *Outline of Saharan prehistoric chronology*

−1000 to +1000	Last wet period.	So-called pre-Islamic monuments.
−1000 to −2000	Silting up of tributary beds. Drying up of springs. First wells. Subsidence of alpine micro-climates.	Recent Neolithic. Tichitt. Fadelian. Borkou.
−2000 to −5000	Last glacial erosion of valleys. Reeds growing in lakes.	Early Neolithic. Meniet. In Guezzam. Tilemsi.
−5000 to −7000	Ancient dunes, type II. Aukar.	?
−7000 to −15000	Final level of great lakes containing diatoms. Silurus, elephant, hippopotamus, rhinoceros. Torrential rainfall.	Aterian. Saoura. Tidikelt. Mauritania. Aïr.
	Ancient dunes, type I. Volcanic activity.	Acheulian III–VIII as established by Biberson (1961).
	Ferruginization of conglomerates. End of erosion. Formation of Teffassasset terraces. Flowing of great rivers. Formation of great lakes. Violent erosion.	Pebble Culture.

ecology, the subsoil and the minerals which are found in it, and where the presence of jasper and flint may result in masterpieces in stone, quite different results will be obtained where the only material is a fragile sandstone. Adrar Bous and Gossolorum[80] are the same, but one has to study the pottery, the discs and the axes in order to realize this, for all that the two industries have in common is the quality of the stone-working.

A few words remain to be said on a very fine Neolithic facies found in south-east Mauritania along the course of the Dhar Tichitt.[81] Extensive excavation in this region has shown that this rather late industry is linked

80. H. J. Hugot, 1962, pp. 154–63 and 168–70.
81. H. J. Hugot *et al.*, 1973.

to an exceptional group of dry-stone villages which are of great interest because of the extent of urbanization[82] and the skill in fortification which they show. Here at last we have proof that from 1500 before our era the local communities ate millet, and so for once we see some sense in the enormous amount of grinding equipment found in the ruins of these villages. The Dhar Tichitt culture is African, as can be seen from its pottery and other characteristics. It may have come from the east, most likely from neighbouring Tilemsi, but that is only a working hypothesis. It may thus be seen that the Neolithic involved a number of influential secondary currents acting on a common foundation which can be identified in the pottery and less often from the particular techniques used in their stone or bone industries.

The Neolithic can be regarded as lasting from 5000 before our era to about the beginning of the first millennium before our era, during which period the level of the lakes constantly sank, until eventually the varied large fauna retreated to the edges of the desert, especially to the south, the flora dwindled, and man in his turn emigrated with his herds.

The fauna of this period were inherited from the Aterian, which ended when the lakes were at their last high level. On the shores and in the waters of these lakes were found the so-called 'Ethiopian' fauna, which included rhinoceroses, crocodiles (*Crocodilus niloticus*), hippopotamuses, elephants, zebra, giraffes, buffaloes and wart-hogs. Catfish (*clarias*) and Nile perch (*Lates niloticus*) teemed in the waters, as did freshwater turtles (*Trionyx*) while the pastures were grazed by goats and antelopes. The only surprising thing about such a catalogue is that it applies to the Sahara. The flora is even more staggering. At the beginning of the Neolithic the hazel, the limetree, the willow and the ash were still to be found. A limicolous shell found at Meniet (at Mouydir in the Algerian Sahara) indicates an annual rainfall of at least 500 millimetres, and that heather covered parts of the mountains. However this vegetation soon dwindled and was replaced by one characteristic of a more arid zone with cedars, Aleppo pines, junipers, olives and the gum and nettle trees that were such an important feature in the diet of the population.

The lakes were also well provided with shellfish, and in some places the remains of enormous collections of *Unio* shells are found.

One of the characteristics of the Sahara at the beginning of the Neolithic culture was the string of lakes all isolated from each other. The Sudanese Neolithic populations tended to migrate along the shores of the lakes, which offered suitable sites for settlements as well as varied food resources.

82. *Urbanism*: the study of the layout of a group of dwellings, usually occupied by a sedentary population and precisely organized according to the division of labour and religious ideas of the occupants. The only Saharan group that conforms to this definition is Dhar Tichitt in Mauritania, a settlement that began in about 2000 before our era.

The Sahara, a cradle of agriculture

The idea that the Sahara was a cradle of agriculture has been put forward on a number of occasions, often without considering that this might be a misuse of such a significant term. Agriculture cannot be said to be proved by the presence of tools or other objects of possible agricultural application; proof is provided only when fossil grains or pollens bear out the hypothesis put forward concerning the application of tools or objects. Collections of millet grains found at Tichitt in Mauritania confirm Munson's[83] and Monod's[84] ideas on this subject.

Apart from that we know that the Saharan Neolithic people collected large quantities of berries (*Celtis* sp. and nettle-tree berries) which they certainly used for food, and at Meniet and Tichitt *Curcurbitaceae* seeds (probably of water-melons though not *Citrulus colocinthis*) have been found. These two plants provide the staple of food-gathering or, at the most, indications of protocultivation, but not of agriculture which means preparing the soil deliberately in order to grow selected plants.

On this definition we do not have much evidence to offer. At Meniet,[85] palynological analysis of Neolithic deposits has thrown no precise light on the existence of any form of agriculture. At Adrar Bous a summary analysis gave no results either, not at Ti-n-Assako, nor at any of the many sites studied from this point of view. The only remains found in Neolithic sites that show for certain that vegetable products were eaten are seeds of *Ziziphus lotus*, *Celtis* sp., and various types of wild grain. To these we should also add the imprints of *Pennisetum* found by Munson and the millet grains discovered at Tichitt in fossilized turf.

But before any conclusions can be drawn we must await a systematic analysis of the Neolithic deposits. Despite its enormous potential, palynology has been little used in the Sahara, but even if some plants were cultivated there it seems unlikely that it was the spot where conditions favoured the development of the cereals commonly consumed in North Africa.

It was, almost everywhere, stock-raisers who, long ago, succeeded the hunter-gatherers and the fact that stone tools such as hoes, grindstones, grinders, weights for balancing digging-sticks, and picks have been found more or less everywhere does not *ipso facto* imply that agriculture in any real sense existed. In Egypt, where agriculture was extensively developed, very precise traces are found, and in such places as Tichitt in Mauritania, where the sedentary population may well have practised agriculture, such traces are also to be found. But, according to the present state of know-

83. P. J. Munson, 1968, pp. 6–13.
84. T. Monod, 1963.
85. G. B. M. Flamand, 1921.

ledge, the situation is unlikely to have been the same elsewhere, and we should not forget that by 1000 before our era the Sahara was almost completely desert. But although the ending of the wet period hardly encouraged agriculture, this does not mean that all protocultivation, or the selective food-gathering that preceded it, were unknown. Moreover, we may be certain that experimenting with vegetable foods must have stimulated the search for particular species, which, in itself, was an early form of selection. But cultivation is only possible among a population that is sedentary, or at least seasonally fixed, and in most of the Sahara the Neolithic period at its height is more reminiscent of nomad encampments than of organized villages, though some of these certainly existed.

The origins of domestication and the Sahara

The Neolithic Sahara had its own way of life. The stock-raisers of Tassili N'Ajjer were contemporaries of the artists of the 'flying gallop' chariots. Although their exact period is not known, they probably lived at about the time when the invading 'Peoples of the Sea' were repulsed when they tried to conquer Egypt. In any event, these stock-raisers developed the art of herding to such an extent as often to surprise the uninitiated for, at its height, this civilization had developed such skilful methods of managing stock as to presuppose a long experience. The Egyptians seem to have tried to domesticate many kinds of animal, but we can only tell this from bas-reliefs. Without them we would never have known that they tried to tame members of the feline and canine families, gazelles and even hyenas. What was the situation in the Sahara? The Sudanese saluki, that invaluable helper of the Nemadi hunters, seems to be of very ancient stock and it is probably the saluki that is depicted in the paintings of the stock-raising peoples. There are also other indications, but none of them conclusive. We know that in 2000 before our era both cattle and dogs were found in Aukar, but the rock-paintings do not show which animals man might have attempted to domesticate in earlier periods.

The Neolithic way of life

We know that the people of the Sudanese Neolithic were endlessly curious about new techniques. They continued working stone and produced a marvellous range of arrow-heads and tools, usually very light, made of flint flakes that had been retouched in various ways, awls, several forms of scraper, geometrical microliths, saws, and so on. What is new is the subtle stone-polishing technique used for axes, hoes, gouges and chisels. Hard-stone vessels, amazonite, cornelian and quartz beads and small balls that may have been used in sling-shots were added to their range of artefacts. We also find a profusion of fixed grindstones and grinders, which are not necessarily a proof of a knowledge of agriculture, and of *kwes*, the stones once used for weighing down digging-sticks that are still in use in South Africa and among the Pygmies. The collection is completed by a dazzling series of pottery vases, already typical of the later art of Africa south of the Sahara in shape and decoration. Bone was also worked and was used for making harpoons, awls, needles, potters' combs, smoothers and maybe daggers. The people of the Sudanese Neolithic made the best possible use of the lithic resources wherever they lived, and this led to the idea that they came from several different ethnic stocks. But in fact theirs was a stable and united culture, as is proved by the unity of inspiration in their pottery decorations if by nothing else. We should also add that these peoples, already moulded by certain types of social organization, must have known how to manage boats, and it is not impossible that they may have sailed on the lakes in reed boats like those still found in Chad and called *kaddeii*.

The people of the Capsian Neolithic differ in many ways from their Sudanese counterparts and predecessors. The latter left the Sudan in several waves, going westward but not, it seems, reaching the Atlantic coast. They were black-skinned, often true Africans. But the people that set out from the high plateaux of Algeria were more Mediterranean, and they had inherited from their Capsian ancestors a real gift for flint-working. They had an astonishing range of tools. Fine flakes on which the working is hardly visible are often reminiscent of jewellery. Awls, sharp points and little scrapers are found along with geometrical microliths made from the 'waste' of the flaking process in the shape of trapezes, rectangles, triangles and segments of circles. They were not ignorant of hunting, since they made innumerable arrow-heads that have now unfortunately become the object of a large-scale tourist trade. There is an abundance of polished axes, but they are not compact and squat as is usual in the Sudanese Neolithic. The Capsian culture had a wider range of stone tools than the Sudanese, and also used far more varied techniques. They too knew how to polish hardstone bowls and to make marvellous sculptures like the bull of Silet, the ram of Tamentit and the gazelle of Imakassen. But their pottery is far less rich in form and decoration, not because the artists lacked imagination – their skill in decorating ostrich eggs which they used, whole, as containers and, broken into bits, to make innumerable beads proves that this is not the case. Many fragments of ostrich shell exist decorated with fine line drawings. They also, of course, had fixed grindstones and grinders and we know for certain that some of these were used for grinding pigments, probably for painting their bodies.

The Neolithic of the coast is little known. The work done on this subject has not yet been published, but we do know that all along the Atlantic coast from Morocco southwards countless shell mounds have been found – some of them veritable 'tells' – mixed up with ashes and potsherds. This is true as far down as Senegal, at which point a protohistoric ethnic movement seems to have taken over. It still remains to be explained why at the frontier between Mauritania and the Rio de Oro the round- or flat-bottomed pottery common in the Sahara is replaced by a marvellous pottery with distinctly conical bases; as yet, however, nothing has been published on this problem.

Farther east, at Adrar Bous in Aïr, there is a stratum that cuts right through all the other known aspects of Saharan Neolithic cultures, whatever their origin. This is the Tenerean. Using bright green jasper to make quite magnificent tools, many of the shapes found are reminiscent of the Egyptian Neolithic. It is true that common forms such as flat discs, lotus-shaped projectile points, nicked scrapers known as 'crescents', and hoes polished by use might just be coincidental, but they occur so often that this seems unlikely. Certain fixed grindstones associated with this brilliant culture are similar to those found in Egyptian bas-reliefs, so that one is almost led to believe that Adrar Bous was colonized by people who had close links with the Nile, although it is strange that they used pottery similar in all respects to the Sudanese Neolithic. We should not forget, however, that the latter has its archetypes at Esh Shaheinab.

During an epoch that was more humid than today, the forests south of the line of lakes must have been greener and denser than they are now, and this may explain the fact that the people of the Sahara never crossed this barrier. The study of the Neolithic culture of these forests has hardly begun. For purposes of convenience and precedence it has been called 'Guinean', but in fact it seems to have originated much farther afield, maybe even in Zaïre.

Conclusion

The fascinating study of the past of the Sahara is still taking its first halting steps, and it offers to specialists and to men of goodwill an opportunity that should be quickly seized, before the exploitation of its last natural resources destroys for ever our chances of solving problems which, in the long run, concern the past of the whole of mankind. It is only by becoming aware of his past that Man can determine his future; our experience comes not only from the present but also in a direct line from prehistory. To deny this would be to deny that the study of prehistory has any rational basis or scientific value. The prehistory of the Sahara is no longer a matter for individual research; it is now a collective enterprise, requiring team-work and money. It is tragic to see scientific work on the Sahara so abandoned, so neglected. The people responsible for this huge and harsh desert should make themselves responsible for providing the men to discover its secrets.

PLATE 23.1 *Flat notched axe from Gossolorum, Niger*

PLATE 23.2 *Cleaver from Ti-n-Assako, Mali*

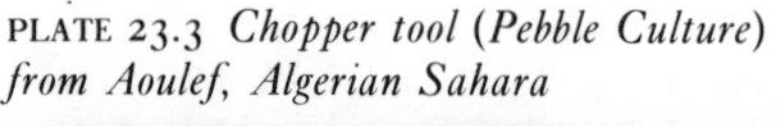

PLATE 23.3 *Chopper tool (Pebble Culture) from Aoulef, Algerian Sahara*

PLATE 23.4 *Chopper tool (Pebble Culture) from Aoulef, Algerian Sahara*

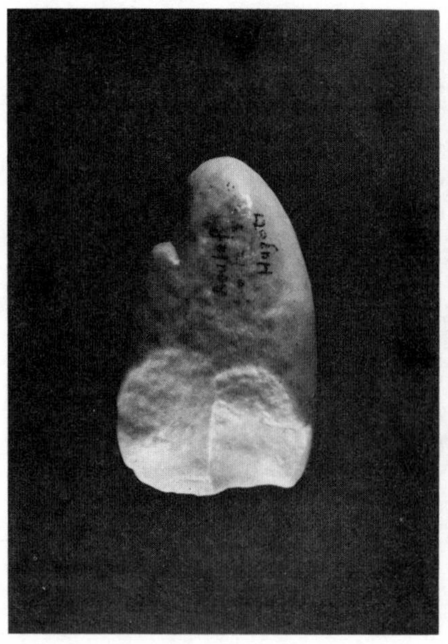

PLATE 23.5 *Lower Palaeolithic hand-axe from Tachenghit, Algerian Sahara*

PLATE 23.6 *Lower Palaeolithic cleaver from Tachenghit, Algerian Sahara*

PLATE 23.7 *Large bi-facial double point, Aterian Industry, from Timimoun, Algerian Sahara*

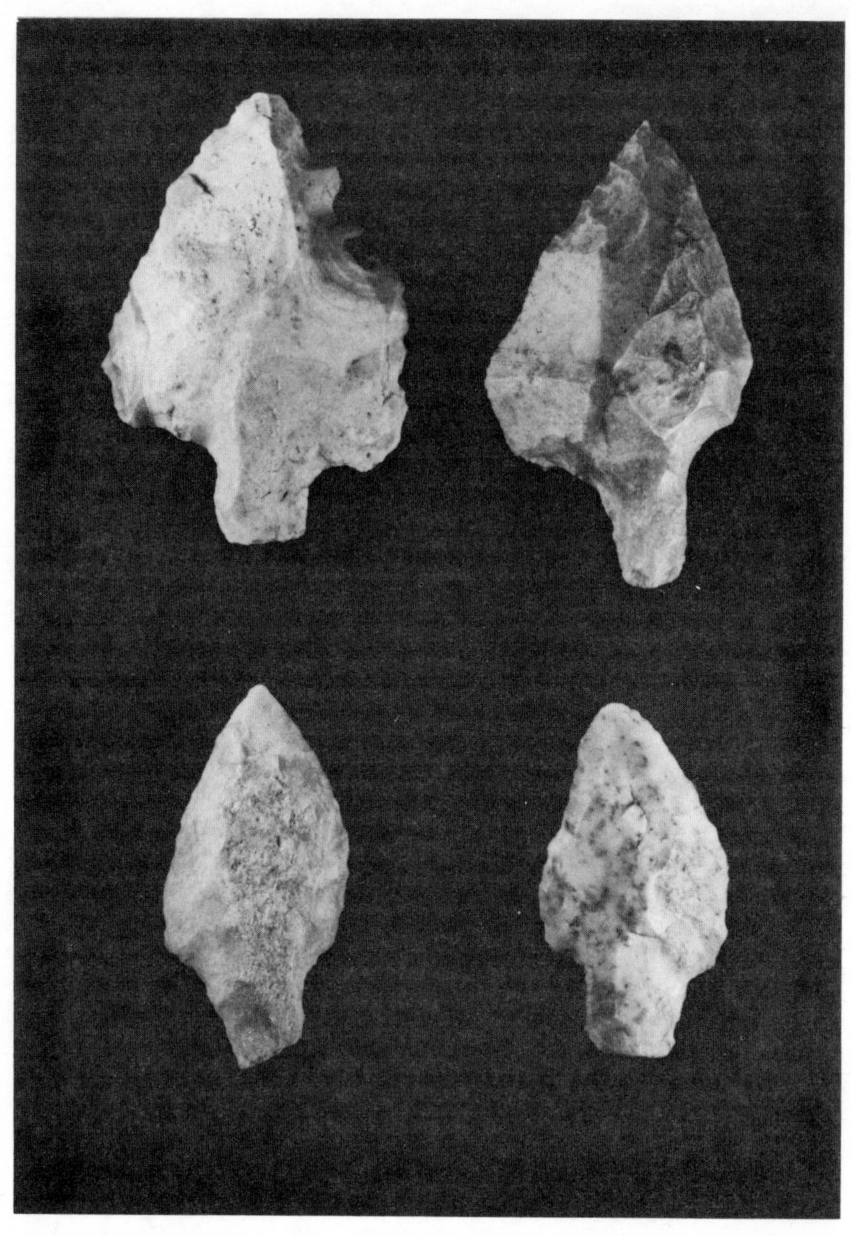

PLATE 23.8 *Aterian points from Aoulef, Algerian Sahara*

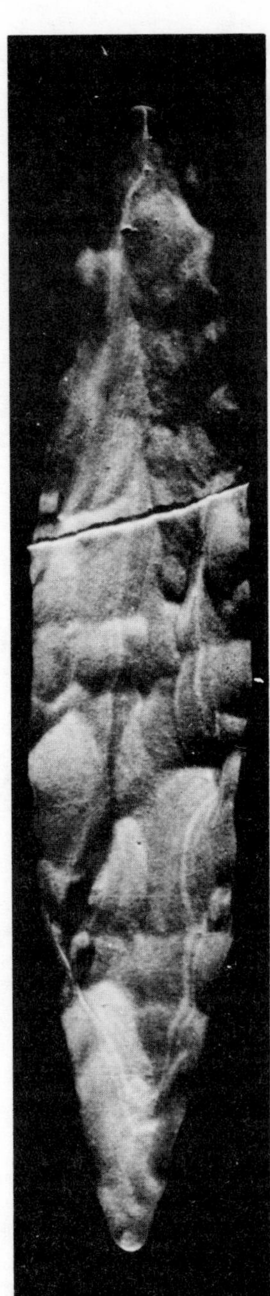

PLATE 23.10 *Neolithic pottery from Dhar Tichitt, Mauritania*

PLATE 23.9 *Aterian bi-facial double point from Adrar Bous V, Niger*

PLATE 23.11 *Neolithic arrow-heads from In Guezzam, Niger*

PLATE 23.12 *Neolithic grooved axe from Adrar Bous, Niger*

PLATE 23.13 *Neolithic polished axe from the Faya region, Chad*

The prehistory of West Africa

C. T. SHAW

Climate and environment

The main climatic and vegetation belts run east and west across the whole expanse of West Africa. The highest rainfall occurs near the coast, and the farther north and inland one goes, the less it becomes. The desert to the north is fringed along its southern edge by the dry Sahel strip; south of this comes the great savannah belt; between the savannah and the wet tropical rain forest which fringes the coast lies a zone of derived savannah which was once forest but which has been turned into savannah by the activities of man.

Rainfall in the area is markedly seasonal, falling predominantly from April to October (with peaks in July and October) in the south and from June to September in the north. These rains are carried on south-west winds which have gathered their moisture from the Atlantic. However the intertropical front runs east and west across West Africa, dividing the tropical maritime air mass formed over the south Atlantic from the dry continental air mass over the Sahara. The position of the front fluctuates with the seasons of the year; in January it is farthest to the south, with the consequence that the north-east trade winds from the dry northern air mass reach right down to the Guinea coast, bringing with them a dramatic fall in humidity.

An awareness of this weather and vegetation pattern is fundamental to the understanding of the prehistory and archaeology of West Africa: the location and extent of the different vegetation zones, and the position of the intertropical front, have varied at different times in the past, affecting the circumstances in which man was living in West Africa at different periods.

Set into these vegetation zones are a number of geographical features which make local modifications in the general pattern: the Futa Djalon and Guinea highlands, the Togo/Atakora chain, the Bauchi plateau and the Mandara/Cameroon highlands; the inland delta of the Niger and its great northward bend, Lake Chad, and the delta at the mouth of the Niger: there is a break between Ghana and Nigeria in the continuity along the coast of the tropical rainforest belt, which is known as the Dahomey gap.

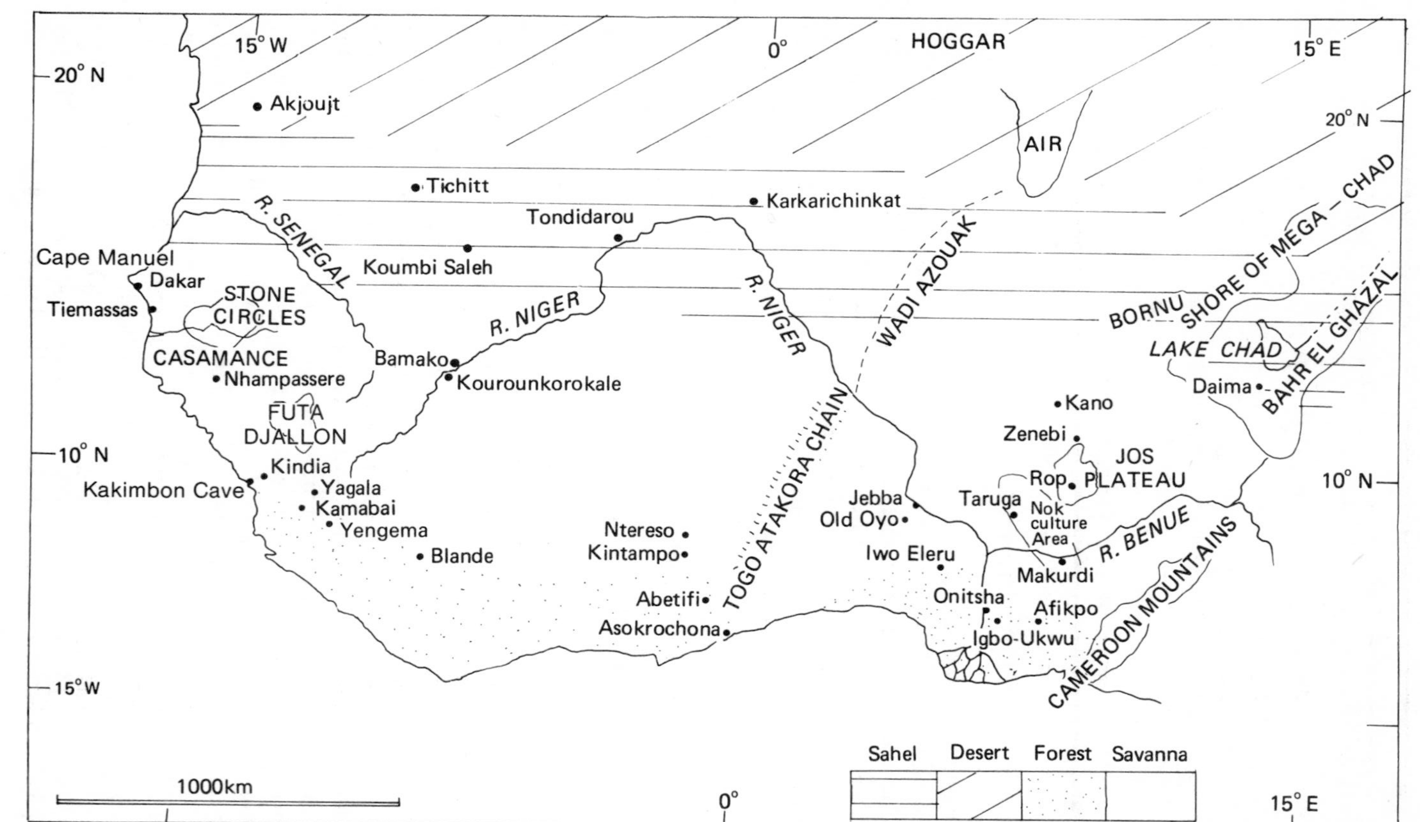

FIG. 24.1 *West Africa: vegetation zones*

Early man

Skeletal remains

West Africa has not so far produced remains of early forms of men or hominids such as have been found in eastern and southern Africa,[1] nor artefacts of correspondingly early date. [2] Can it be assumed that there were such beings in West Africa? Is our present lack of data due to the fact that these hominids were not living at the time in West Africa, or is it simply because the evidence has not yet been found? This is a question which it is impossible to answer at present but no research effort comparable to that in East Africa has yet been made in West Africa. It also has to be admitted that deposits of the right age appear to be scarcer in West Africa, and it is notorious that in the prevailing conditions of high humidity and soil acidity, preservation conditions are very much worse.[3] This fact is illustrated by data of a much later age: a distribution map of Africa plotting finds of skeletal remains of the Late Stone Age shows a complete blank in the Zaïre–West Africa area.[4] Yet since the compilation of that map, dated finds have been made in Nigeria and Ghana which show that the blank was indicative of a state of research, not of an absence of human occupation.[5] The same may then be true for the earlier period we are now considering,[6] and may also be true of a distribution map of the find places of vertebrate fossils of Lower and Middle Pleistocene age, which shows a similar blank.[7] As far as one can see, there must have been ecological conditions in certain parts of West Africa very similar to those which supported the Australopithecines of East Africa – but of course this does not mean that these areas in fact were occupied. There are many areas of tropical rainforest which could support gorillas today, but in fact they are only found in two circumscribed areas;[8] and in spite of some similarity of conditions, the West African savannah does not support the same collection of game types as East Africa, nor in the same density.[9]

One positive piece of evidence for thinking that early hominids were to be found in suitable areas of West Africa early in the Pleistocene is provided by the cranio-facial portion of a skull found 200 kilometres west-south-west of Largeau. It was named *Tchadanthropus uxoris*,[10] and was first thought to be

1. R. E. F. Leakey, 1973b.
2. M. Leakey, 1970.
3. J. D. Clark, 1968a, p. 37.
4. C. Gabel, 1966, p. 17.
5. C. T. Shaw, 1965b, 1969b; D. Brothwell and C. T. Shaw, 1971; C. Flight, 1968, 1970.
6. Y. Coppens, 1966b, p. 373.
7. ibid., p. 374
8. J. P. Dorst and P. Dandelot, 1970, p. 100.
9. ibid., pp. 213, 223.
10. B. G. Campbell, 1965, pp. 4, 9.

an Australopithecine[11] but was later regarded as more akin to *Homo habilis.*[12] The uncertainties in this case stem from the lack of secure dating and from the fact that the skull is only fragmentary. Further examination of the skull, with its combination of archaic and advanced characteristics, has suggested that it shows clear signs of evolving towards *Homo erectus,*[13] representing a more advanced stage of the hominids, and has cranial capacities ranging from 850 cc to 1300 cc. Once again, there are no examples of this form from West Africa, although specimens of this type, called *Atlanthropus mauritanicus,* have been found in Algeria.[14]

Artefacts

Although prehistoric man made tools of bone and wood as well as of stone, wood is rarely preserved, and soil conditions in West Africa militate against the survival of bone. Apart from utilized and roughly trimmed flakes, the earliest and simplest types of stone tools consist of pebbles or lumps flaked by percussion to form crude chopping and cutting tools with edges anything from 3 centimetres to 12 centimetres long; they are known as Oldowan-type tools, after Olduvai Gorge in Tanzania. Such tools are found in many places in Africa, and the early men who made them may well have spread over most of the savannah bushy grasslands of Africa. Examples of such tools are known from a number of places in West Africa,[15] but it is not at the moment possible to be sure if any of them genuinely date from the same period as the Oldowan industry of East Africa, which may be put in the period between 2 million and 0·7 million years ago. Careful investigation of pebble tools found along the Gambia river in Senegal demonstrated that some were likely to be of Neolithic origin and others to have derived possibly from the late stone age; there was no stratigraphical evidence for an industry of pre-Acheulian age.[16] So we can only be sure that pebble tools belong to an early period if they are independently dated by being found *in situ* in deposits which can be dated, either relatively or absolutely; palaeontology gives some relative dating for the Yayo deposits which produced *Tchadanthropus* but unfortunately there were no associated implements. From the evidence of fossil bones of the extinct *Hippopotamus imaguncula* which came from a depth of 58 metres in a well in Bornu,[17] it is likely that deposits of the Chad Basin contain palaeontological material of Pleistocene age – and as likely as

11. Y. Coppens, 1961.
12. Y. Coppens, 1965a, 1965b; H. B. S. Cooke, 1965.
13. Y. Coppens, 1966a.
14. C. Arambourg and R. Hofstetter, 1954, 1955; C. Arambourg, 1954, 1966.
15. O. Davies, 1961, pp. 1–4; 1964, pp. 83–91; R. Mauny, 1963; R. C. Soper, 1965, p. 177; H. J. Hugot, 1966b.
16. R. Mauny, 1968, p. 1283; C. Barbey and C. Descamps, 1969.
17. C. M. Tattam, 1944, p. 39.

not, archaeological material as well – but it lies under a mantle of later drift of great thickness.

Climatic changes

In Europe there were several different glaciations during the Quaternary, and the four principal ones were given the names of rivers in Germany. It is now realized, however, that whatever overall rhythm and pattern there may be in glacial phenomena, there are many local variations which have to be taken into account, with the result that local names are used for each particular region; the ensuing picture is one of much greater complexity but probably a lot nearer reality.[18]

The same kind of thing happened when early research workers in Africa found evidence in raised lake-levels, in erosions and in deposits of gravels which were taken to indicate that it dated from the Quaternary when the African climate was very much wetter than at present. Such periods of increased rainfall were christened pluvials. Since the concept of glacial periods was already evolved for the north temperate zones, what more natural than the idea that when there was a glacial period in Europe and North America there was a corresponding pluvial period in the warmer tropics?[19] In time, the idea of three, and then four, African pluvials became orthodox belief,[20] and it was supposed that they corresponded to the glaciations of the European ice age,[21] although an alternative theoretical scheme was put forward suggesting that one African pluvial corresponded to two northern glaciations.[22] That it was possible to put forward a view of this kind illustrates how almost non-existent was any true chronological correlation. In any case, geological correlations over wide distances should be based not on climates, but on rock formations. In addition, the evidence for pluvial events is somewhat equivocal when compared with that for glaciations, and has caused much confusion.[23] In time, the very evidence for four pluvials in Africa was called into question.[24]

West Africa has been no exception to this pattern of extrapolation and efforts have been made to use sequences derived from other parts of Africa to give meaning to data which are otherwise isolated or difficult to interpret.[25] More recently, however, two things have served to improve the scientific

18. R. F. Flint, 1971; B. W. Sparks and R. G. West, 1972.

19. E. J. Wayland, 1934, 1952.

20. L. S. B. Leakey, 1950; 1952, Resolution 14(3), p. 7; J. D. Clark, 1957, p. xxxi, Resolution 2.

21. E. Nilsson, 1952.

22. G. C. Simpson, 1957.

23. J. D. Clark, 1957, p. xxxi, Resolution 4; K. W. Butzer, 1971, pp. 312–15.

24. R. F. Flint, 1959b.

25. G. Bond, 1956, pp. 197–200; B. E. B. Fagg, 1959, p. 291; O. Davies, 1964, pp. 9–12; J. Pias, 1967.

approach for West Africa: an increase in the amount of relevant research,[26] and the emergence of a new theoretical framework for climatic change in Africa.[27]

We have no reliable geological or geomorphological information on West Africa bearing upon climatic change earlier than the period of the last glaciation of Europe. Study of Lake Chad has shown high lake-levels from 40 000 before our era.[28] This high lake is marked by the Bama ridge upon which Maiduguri stands, and which here runs north-west and south-east; both ends of this stretch then swing round to the north-east running up to enclose Largeau and the whole of the Bodele depression and Bahr el-Ghazal. The ridge, regarded as a lagoon bar rather than as the actual shore-line, may have taken 6000 years to form.[29] The ancient lake stood at a height of 332 metres above sea-level, compared with the present height of Lake Chad of 280 metres, and at times overflowed over the Bongor spillway and drained down the Benue. It seems therefore that during this wetter period in West Africa the forest is likely to have extended a good deal farther north than it does today, although whether as far as lat. 11°N[30] or the present 750 millimetre isohyet[31] it is impossible to be sure until we obtain confirmation from palynology.

Approximately coincident with the last maximum of the last glaciation in northern Europe, beginning from around 20 000 before our era, it appears that our West African area was much drier than at present. During this time the West African rivers were discharging into an ocean which was some 100 metres below its present level because so much water was locked up in the polar ice-sheets; thus the Benue cut a channel some 20 metres below present sea-level at Makurdi and deeper still at Yola, while the sunk channel of the Niger at Jebba lies 25 metres below sea-level and deeper than this at Onitsha.[32] The Senegal also flowed in a channel well below its present level, but at its mouth it was blocked by vast sand-dunes, as was also the course of the middle Niger. Lake Chad was dry at the time and sand-dunes formed over its floor and in parts of northern Nigeria where there is now more than 850 millimetres mean annual rainfall, indicating at the time less than 150 millimetres. Although only the events at the mouth of the Senegal and around Lake Chad have any kind of absolute dating attached to them, the other evidence fits best in terms of a generally dry period around 18 000 before our era. If sand dunes were forming at the latitude of Kano, the savannah and forest belts must have been pushed far to the south; in fact it is

26. *Association sénégalaise pour l'étude du Quaternaire*, 1966, 1967, 1969; K. Burke *et al.*, 1971; K. W. Butzer, 1972, pp. 312–51.

27. E. M. van Zinderen-Bakker, 1967.

28. M. Servant *et al.*, 1969; A. T. Grove and A. Warren, 1968; K. Burke *et al.*, 1971.

29. A. T. Grove and R. A. Pullan, 1964.

30. O. Davies, 1964.

31. O. Davies, 1960.

32. C. Voute, 1962; H. Faure and P. Elouard, 1967.

probable that most of the forest disappeared except in relict areas of the highest rainfall such as coastal Liberia, part of coastal Ivory Coast, the Niger Delta and the Cameroon mountains.

By 10 000 before our era conditions seem to have begun to get wetter; the Mali Niger overflowed over the Taoussasill, and Mega-Chad, as it has been called,[33] again had a vast extent; the sand-dunes formed in the previous dry period were reddened as a result of seasonally wetter conditions. Spreads of charcoal dated to the eleventh and seventh millennium before our era at Igbo-Ukwu may indicate bush fires and savannah-type vegetation surviving at this latitude to those dates.[34] During this period the forest would again have spread northwards from the relict areas near the coast where it had survived during the preceding dry period. The most satisfactory theory to relate the late Quaternary climatic events of West Africa with the events of northern Europe derives from evidence that is accumulating that changes in temperature were worldwide and that these caused a shift of the weather-belts on either side of the equator, modified by the shape of the large land and ocean masses.[35] When world temperatures fell, a glaciation resulted in northern latitudes and extended the polar anticyclone southwards; the weather zones beyond were compressed towards the equator, so that in West Africa the intertropical front was displaced from its present position southwards. This resulted in the dry north-east winds of the dry-season months blowing for a longer period and more strongly across West Africa, and the rain-bearing winds of the south-west 'monsoon' blowing more weakly and reaching less far during the rainy season. This would account for a dry period in West Africa roughly coinciding with a northern glacial period. At the same time it was wetter than at present in the northern Sahara because the storm tract from the Atlantic Ocean came in south of the Atlas mountains instead of passing north of them.

As world temperatures rose, the ice-sheets retreated northwards, so did the intertropical front, and the sea-levels returned to about their present level. It became drier in the northern Sahara as the Atlantic storm track moved northwards, but there was a sufficient reservoir of groundwater and of vegetation in the Sahara for the final desiccation to be delayed until after 3000 before our era. When it became too dry in the Sahara for the people living there to continue their way of life, naturally this had repercussions in the areas lying to the south.

The Stone Age

The terms Palaeolithic, epi-Palaeolithic and Neolithic are still applied to North Africa, but for a long time archaeologists in sub-Saharan Africa have

33. R. E. Moreau, 1963; M. Servant *et al.*, 1969.
34. C. T. Shaw, 1970, pp. 58, 91.
35. E. M. van Zinderen-Bakker, 1967.

found it more valid to use their own terminology, derived from the realities of the continent and not from a European system imposed from outside. This new terminology was officially endorsed by the Third Pan-African Congress on Prehistory twenty years ago. Hence the terms Early Stone Age, Middle Stone Age and Late Stone Age will be used.[36] The chronological boundaries of these divisions of the Stone Age in sub-Saharan Africa vary somewhat from area to area, but very roughly they may be thought of as 2 500 000–50 000 before our era for the Early Stone Age, 50 000–15 000 before our era for the Middle Stone Age and 15 000–500 before our era for the Late Stone Age. As new knowledge accumulates, such simple divisions and datings come to be modified and demand a more complex picture. The use of the term 'Neolithic' has come under increasing criticism when applied to sub-Saharan Africa, since it is ambiguous whether it indicates a period, a type of technology, or a type of economy or a combination of the three.[37]

The Early Stone Age in West Africa

The Acheulian

In eastern, southern and north-western Africa, the Oldowan industrial complex was succeeded by that known as the Acheulian, characterized by bifaces. These are tools of oval or pointed oval shape with a cutting edge all round carefully trimmed from both sides; one variety, known as a cleaver, has a straight transverse cutting edge. Although women and children probably still provided at least half the food intake by means of collecting wild fruit, nuts and roots, men now banded together in co-operative activities to hunt large game animals. The use of fire was known, at any rate by the end of Acheulian times. The type of early man responsible for making Acheulian implements, wherever this is known, was that called *Homo erectus*, with a brain size considerably less than that of modern man, but in other ways very similar in body form.

What are usually regarded as early types of bifaces (formerly called Chellean) are absent in the Sahara, but have been claimed for Senegal,[38] the Republic of Guinea,[39] Mauritania,[40] and Ghana, where they are said to be stratigraphically established in a rolled condition to the Middle Terrace[41]–whatever this means in relative chronological terms. The area of their distribution has been mapped[42] and this is said to indicate a colonization from the river Niger along the Atakora chain and the Togo hills.

36. J. D. Clark, 1957, p. xxxiii, Resolution 6.

37. W. W. Bishop and J. D. Clark (eds), 1967, pp. 687–899; C. T. Shaw, 1967, pp. 9–43; J. C. Vogel and P. B. Beaumont, 1972.

38. R. Corboil, 1951.

39. P. Créach, 1951a,b.

40. R. Mauny, 1955a.

41. O. Davies, 1964, pp. 86–91.

42. O. Davies, 1959.

The later stages of the Acheulian, marked by fine handaxes made with the advanced cylinder-hammer technique, are prolific in the Sahara north of about 16°N. Perhaps this distribution is to be correlated with the penultimate (Riss) glacial period in Europe – or possibly the earliest maximum of the last (Würm) glaciation; at such a time there would have been more rainfall in the northern Sahara and the desertic zone would have moved southwards and been unattractive for human occupation. An exception to this seems to have been the high ground of the Jos plateau, where the climate would not have been so arid and would have provided the open or lightly-wooded grasslands of the type favoured by Acheulian man. It therefore formed as it were a promontory of habitable land projecting southwards from Aïr and the main Saharan Acheulian area north of 16°N. There is a radio-carbon date of 'more than 39 000 years b.p.'[43] for material associated with Acheulian tools in the basal gravels filling in channels cut in a preceding wetter period.

At a time when Acheulian man favoured the Jos plateau, it is likely that the Fouta Djallon massif would also have been suitable for human occupation, and a certain amount of Acheulian material has been found in this area.[44] There is also a scatter of Middle and Late Acheulian deposits around and to the north of the upper Senegal river; this may be regarded as linking the Fouta Djallon area to the prolific sites of Mauritania.

Acheulian material has been recorded[45] in south-eastern Ghana and along the Togo/Atakora chain of hills, suggesting a possible route from the north which would have provided a favourable environment, but the penetration does not seem to have been very strong. No Acheulian material is firmly established stratigraphically in the area, and with small collections and individual pieces it is often very difficult to assign them with certainty to the Acheulian on typology alone, since so many of the forms overlap or are similar to those used in the succeeding Sangoan industries.[46]

The Sangoan

There are difficulties of definition over the Sangoan Industrial Complex.[47] Whether there is a true Sangoan in West Africa at all has been questioned.[48] In many parts of sub-Saharan Africa a complex of industries came into being, following the Acheulian, which retained some of the tool-kit of the latter, such as pick and biface forms, though the cleaver disappeared and spheroids became rare and there was a much greater emphasis on picks, often of a heavy and massive form. Choppers, often made of flaked pebbles, also occur.

43. G. W. Barendson *et al.*, 1965.
44. J. D. Clark, 1967b.
45. O. Davies, 1964; J. D. Clark, 1967b.
46. O. Davies, 1964, pp. 83–97, 114, 137–9.
47. J. D. Clark, 1971a.
48. B. Wai-Ogusu, 1973.

In West Africa, Sangoan material has a more southerly distribution than the Acheulian,[49] suggesting a new pattern of settlement. An industry from Cap Manuel at Dakar, which was formerly regarded as being Neolithic,[50] is now regarded as Sangoan,[51] or perhaps as a late development from it. The same can be said of some material collected from Bamako.[52] In Nigeria, Sangoan material is found particularly in the stretch of country south of the Jos plateau and north of the tropical rainforest, associated with river valleys. It also occurs in gravels at heights of 10–20 metres above modern river-level.[53] An industry from the Niger valley near Bussa which consists mostly of worked pebbles and is without picks is regarded on geological grounds as nevertheless being contemporary with the Sangoan.[54] A spread of Sangoan material down the Atakora-Togo chain and into southern Ghana has been reported.[55] Such material is rare in northern Ghana but fairly widespread in the south.

Elsewhere in Africa[56] the Sangoan is allocated to dates after 50 000 before our era and it has been suggested that the Sangoan Industrial Complex may represent a need to adapt to more wooded country in an increasingly arid period.[57] In West Africa there are no radio-carbon dates for a Sangoan industry; Sangoan material in the Asokrochona railway cutting in southern Ghana all occurred above Davies's Beach IV, which he equates with the Gottweig interstadial at the latest,[58] a stratigraphical position which does no more than give a *terminus post quem* which we should expect. If the gravels 10–20 metres above the Niger around Jebba were laid down when the river was graded to the upper Inchirian high sea-level,[59] the presence in them of unrolled Sangoan artefacts suggests a date of about 30 000 before our era, while the rolled specimens could be contemporaneous or older. It is possible that the southerly, riverine and woodland distribution of the Sangoan in West Africa represents a way of life adapted to dry conditions before 40 000 before our era after which Lake Chad began to fill up and spread. Perhaps the game which had formerly been hunted became scarcer and moved southwards, and the emphasis on picks may have indicated the need both to dig up roots and tubers and to dig pit-traps for animals which could no longer be so easily hunted in the open.

49. J. D. Clark, 1967b.
50. R. Corbeil *et al.*, 1948, p. 413.
51. O. Davies, 1964, p. 115; H. J. Hugot, 1964, p. 5.
52. O. Davies, 1964, pp. 113–14.
53. ibid., pp. 113–14; R. C. Soper, 1965, pp. 184–6.
54. R. C. Soper, pp. 186–8.
55. O. Davies, 1964, pp. 98, 100.
56. J. D. Clark, 1970c, p. 250.
57. J. D. Clark, 1959, p. 149.
58. O. Davies, 1964, pp. 23, 137–42.
59. H. Faure and P. Elouard, 1967.

The Middle Stone Age in West Africa

The term Middle Stone Age is used to describe a group of industrial complexes covering roughly the time span 35 000–15 000 before our era.

In West Africa, industries belonging to the Middle Stone Age have been identified with less certainty than in the rest of sub-Saharan Africa. Rare specimens of Lupemban type have been found in Ghana[60] and Nigeria[61] but none which give satisfactory stratigraphical indication of their date. On the Jos plateau and in the Lirue hills to the north of it, considerable collections of material characterized by the faceted butts of the prepared core technique have been found which have been classified as belonging to the Middle Stone Age,[62] stratified at Nok between the basal gravels containing Acheulian material and the later deposits containing the Nok culture.[63] They do not have affinities with the Lupemban industrial complex, but rather with Middle Palaeolithic industries of northern Africa of generalized Mousteroid type, and probably belonging to a more open savannah way of life. Comparable industries have been reported from Ghana and the Ivory Coast,[64] from Dakar[65] and from the central Sahara.[66] There is a radio-carbon date from a piece of wood from the deposits at Zenebi in northern Nigeria, one of the alluvial sites producing Mousteroid material, of 3485 ± 110 before our era, but the precise position of this piece of wood in relation to the stone artefacts is unrecorded, and the date is a good deal younger than would be expected for an industry of this type.[67]

An archaeological occurrence at Tiemassas, near the coast of Senegal, containing as it does among other things bifacially flaked projectile points in addition to Middle and Upper Palaeolithic type artefacts, was at first considered to represent a mixture of Neolithic and earlier elements.[68] More careful examination, however, showed that these bifacial points were an integral part of a stratified industry which did not contain other Neolithic elements, so that it is regarded as a type of Mousteroid which locally contains these elements and here replaces the Aterian of farther north.[69] The latter is an industrial complex belonging to the end of Middle Palaeolithic times in Algeria and extending southwards into the desert.

60. O. Davies, 1964, pp. 108–13.

61. Found on the surface in the Afikpo area by Professor D. D. Hartle and formerly in the collections of the University of Nigeria, Nsukka.

62. R. C. Soper, 1965, pp. 188–90.

63. B. E. B. Fagg, 1956a, pp. 211–14.

64. O. Davies, 1964, pp. 124–42; J. D. Clark, 1967b.

65. R. Corbeil *et al.*, 1948; R. Corbeil, 1951a,b; C. de Richard, 1955.

66. J. D. Clark, 1967b.

67. G. W. Barendson *et al.*, 1965.

68. T. Degan, 1956.

69. R. Guillot and C. Descamps, 1969.

Davies sees an extension of this industry into West Africa and calls it the Guinea Aterian,[70] but the evidence adduced is not convincing and is doubted by most workers.[71]

The Late Stone Age

Over most of Africa the Late Stone Age is characterized by the development of very small stone tools, called for that reason 'microliths'. These are tiny pieces carefully trimmed to be slotted into arrow shafts to form points and barbs, and to make other kinds of composite implements. They demonstrate that their makers were possessors of the bow and that hunting with it formed an important part of the economy.

At this point we become bedevilled by the word 'Neolithic', and its ambiguity of meaning; it is better avoided in Africa whenever possible, certainly in sub-Saharan Africa,[72] but one has to take account of the persistence of this usage for North Africa and the Sahara. Industries occur widely in the Sahara which have been termed Neolithic because of their tool-kit, and which, in the central area, date from the sixth millennium before our era. Conditions were moister than today, supporting a Mediterranean type of flora and cattle pastoralists who may or may not have been growers of cereal crops.[73] There is clear evidence for the advent of food-producers in Cyrenaica by 4800 before our era[74] but the Neolithic of Capsian tradition, widespread in north-west Africa following preceding epi-Palaeolithic cultures there, has now been shown to give no evidence of food production although it extends into the second millennium before our era.[75] At one time finds from Rufisque in Senegal were attributed to the Neolithic of Capsian tradition,[76] but they are probably best regarded as belonging to the general microlithic continuum of West Africa.[77] In addition to this occurrence near Dakar, this microlithic continuum, or Guinea Microlithic, is widespread in the eastern half of West Africa, but in the western half appears to be absent at the most southerly sites, in the area of Liberia, Sierra Leone and the Republic of Guinea. The first archaeological sites to be excavated in West Africa were a number of caves and rock-shelters in the southern part of the Republic of Guinea, some of which were dug into over seventy years ago.[78] In some there are bifacial pieces recalling forms earlier

70. O. Davies, 1964, pp. 116–23.

71. H. J. Hugot, 1966a.

72. W. W. Bishop and J. D. Clark (eds), 1967, p. 898, Resolution Q.; J. D. Clark, 1967a; C. T. Shaw, 1967, p. 35, Resolution 13; P. J. Munson, 1968, p. 11. Some authors do not share this opinion.

73. H. J. Hugot, 1963, pp. 148–51; F. Mori, 1965; G. Camps, 1969.

74. C. B. M. McBurney, 1967, p. 298.

75. C. Roubet, 1971.

76. R. Vaufrey, 1946; H. Alimen, 1957, pp. 229–33; O. Davies, 1964, p. 236.

77. H. J. Hugot, 1957; 1964, pp. 4–6; C. T. Shaw, 1971a, p. 62.

78. E. T. Hamy, 1900; P. Guébhard, 1907; L. Desplagnes, 1907a; E. Hue, 1912; R. Hubert, 1922; Abbé H. Breuil, 1931; R. Delcroix and R. Vaufrey, 1939; C. T. Shaw, 1944.

than the Late Stone Age, which have been regarded by some as hoes, and therefore as indirect evidence of agriculture. This possibility must certainly be borne in mind, as rice replaced yams as the staple crop in the western half of West Africa, and African rice, *Oryza glaberrima*, was probably domesticated in the area of the middle Niger Delta.[79] Flat, broad pieces of quartzite roughly chipped into shape are also regarded as hoes and as evidence of cultivation in Ghana,[80] but there are no clear associations or dates for these. The majority of the Republic of Guinea sites produced microliths, ground stone axes, grinding-stones and pottery, as did also a site in Guinea Bissau:[81] some of the Guinea sites had pottery, although in the Grotto de Kakimbon pottery is said to occur only in the upper level.[82] Excavations in the rock-shelter at Blande, in the south-east corner of the Republic of Guinea, also produced an industry with ground stone axes and pottery together with large bifacial tools reminiscent of the Kindia and Fouta Djallon caves, but without a microlithic element.[83] Microliths were similarly absent from the cave site of Yengema, in Sierra Leone, where the lowest level produced a small flake industry in quartz, compared by the excavator to the Ishangan of Lake Edward; middle-level bifacially flaked picks and hoes resembling some of the material from the caves in the Republic of Guinea and which the excavator assigns to a Lupemban industrial complex; and the upper level ground stone axes and pottery, from which there are two thermo-luminescent dates indicating the period 2000–1750 before our era.[84] A microlithic element is present, however, in two other rock-shelters excavated farther north in Sierra Leone at Yagala and Kamabai, with radio-carbon dates indicating a span of the late stone age here from 2500 before our era up to the seventh century of our era.[85]

It looks therefore, as if in this western part of West Africa there was some kind of Middle Stone Age tradition (which may also be present at Dakar and at Bamako) which survived comparatively unchanged in the most southerly sites and did not adopt or develop the microlithic technique; the reasons for this may well be ecological, since the microlithic technique is associated with a savannah zone economy in which hunting played an important part. If one plots the distribution of the sites without microliths (Conakry, Yengema, Blande) and draws a boundary between them and those with microliths (Kamabai, Yagala, Kindia, Nhampassere) one finds that this boundary runs very close to the boundary between the forest and the savannah. The technical innovations of ground stone axes and pottery subsequently arrived

79. R. Portères, 1962, pp. 197–9.
80. O. Davies, 1964, pp. 203–30.
81. A. de Mateus, 1952.
82. E. T. Hamy, 1900.
83. B. Holas, 1950, 1952; B. Holas and R. Mauny, 1953.
84. C. S. Coon, 1968.
85. J. H. Atherton, 1972.

in the area from the north. The date of the advent of these influences is in the middle of the third millennium before our era, which is just when the desiccation of the Sahara became widespread; it is therefore reasonable to connect the two events and see the influence of people moving out of the Sahara. Although we do not yet have the osteological evidence for it, these people probably also brought cattle with them, perhaps the stock ancestral to the Ndama breed of the Fouta Djallon, which developed an immunity to trypanosomiasis.

In most of the rest of West Africa, a microlithic continuum underlies and precedes the techniques of making pottery and ground stone axes, which appear to be grafted on to the microlithic tradition rather than to replace it.

At Kourounkorokale near Bamako a lower layer with coarse microliths and worked bone was stratified below an upper layer with more refined microliths, ground stone axes and pottery.[86] In Nigeria the rock-shelters at Rop,[87] on the Bauchi plateau, and at Iwo Eleru in the Western State, have provided microlithic levels without pottery and ground stone axes stratified below microlithic levels which do have them. At Iwo Eleru a radio-carbon date of 9200 before our era has been obtained from near the base of the lower level, and the transition to the upper seems to be a little after 3000 before our era.[88] At Mejiro Cave, Old Oyo, a microlithic industry was recovered which had no associated pottery, or ground stone axes, but the sample was small and it is undated.[89] In Ghana, the Bosumpra Cave at Abetifi produced an association of microlithic pottery and ground stone axes, but this also is undated.[90] There is a late facies of the Late Stone Age in Ghana which has been called the Kintampo Culture. Following an early phase with pottery and microliths, the Kintampo Culture has ground stone axes, stone armlets (known from Saharan Neolithic sites) and a peculiar type of hatched stone rubber. The early (Punpun) phase is dated to before 1400 before our era, and the later one has dwarf goats and domestic cattle of a breed closely resembling the West African Dwarf Shorthorn.[91] Even in southern Mauritania, microliths are present with pottery and ground stone axes in the earliest phase (Akreijit) of the Tichitt sequence at some date before 1500 before our era, but disappear in all subsequent phases.[92]

Along the northern margins of our area, in the Sahel zone immediately south of the Sahara desert, there was a somewhat different situation in the later part of the Late Stone Age, with adaptations to the local ecology evidenced in the material culture. At Karkarichinkat, north of Gao, cattle

86. G. Szumowski, 1956.

87. B. E. B. Fagg, 1944, 1972; E. Eyo, 1972a; A. Rosenfeld, 1972; A. Fagg, 1972a,b.

88. C. T. Shaw, 1969b.

89. F. Willett, 1962b.

90. C. T. Shaw, 1944.

91. O. Davies, 1962; 1964, pp. 239–46; 1967b, pp. 216–22; C. Flight, 1970; P. L. Carter and C. Flight, 1972.

92. P. J. Munson, 1968, 1970.

pastoralists lived on mounds above the level of the seasonal streams between 2000 and 1500 before our era and had pottery and a lithic equipment which included ground stone axes, Sahara-type bifacial arrow-heads (though not hollow-based ones)[93] and an occasional microlith; fishing was an important aspect of the economy, as is widely evidenced across the southern Sahara in late Neolithic times.[94] A somewhat similar situation obtained at Daima, in north-eastern Nigeria, a thousand years later, where cattle-keepers were probably also growing sorghum on the fertile clay lands left behind by the shrunken Lake Chad; while they had pottery, ground stone axes and a prolific bone industry they had no small lithic industry of any kind.[95]

A specialized adaptation to completely different ecological conditions occurred at the opposite end of our region along the southern margins of West Africa, on the Atlantic Coast. Here, Late Stone Age peoples were exploiting the abundant shellfish of the lagoons and estuaries, both for food and as bait for fishing, leaving behind huge mounds of shells. In the Ivory Coast such mounds have been shown to extend from 1600 before our era up to the fourteenth century of our era[96] and in Senegal one contained a ground axe made out of bone.[97] Those which have been examined in the Casamance are of post-stone age date.[98]

An assemblage with pottery, ground stone axes and a lithic industry without microliths was found at Afikpo in southern Nigeria, where radio-carbon dates give the time-span of the industry as from 3000–1 before our era.[99] In Fernando Po four main stages of a Late Stone Age complex have been recognized,[100] with pottery and ground stone axes, but no microliths; a radio-carbon date in the sixth century of our era was obtained for the earliest stage, which, if correct, puts the sequence very late; the waisted form of the axes shows affinities with similar ones from south-eastern Nigeria,[101] Cameroon and the Republic of Chad.[102]

To summarize: the Late Stone Age in West Africa can be divided into two phases: Phase I, beginning not later than 10 000 before our era, has two facies. Facies A has microlithic stone industries and is associated with hunting in the savannah; Facies B belongs to the forested area in the most south-westerly part of West Africa and is without microliths. Phase II, beginning soon after 3000 before our era, may be considered to have four facies: Facies A adds pottery and ground stone axes to microliths over most

93. R. Mauny, 1955b; A. Smith, 1974.
94. T. Monod and R. Mauny, 1957.
95. G. Connah, 1967, 1969, 1971.
96. R. Mauny, 1973; I. U. Olsson, 1973.
97. J. Joire, 1947; R. Mauny, 1957; 1961, pp. 156–62.
98. O. Linares de Sapir, 1971.
99. D. D. Hartle, 1966, 1968.
100. A. Martin del Molino, 1965.
101. R. A. Kennedy, 1960.
102. J. D. Clark, 1967a, p. 618.

of the savannah; Facies B, in the Sahel, has a fishing element in its economy, virtually no microliths, and a bone industry which includes harpoons, fish-hooks, and so on; Facies C is coastal, with an economy adapted to exploiting the resources of the lagoons and estuaries; Facies D is associated with a forest environment and has pottery and ground stone axes but no microliths.

When the cattle pastoralists of the Sahara first moved southwards in the third millennium before our era they not only encountered microlithic hunters to the south of them, but moved out of an area where flint was available into an area where arrow-points and barbs had been made of quartz or some other stone from which it is more difficult to make a bifacial arrow-head. So for the most part they seem to have adopted the microlithic technique of the indigenes, for tipping and barbing arrows, as they saw it was just as effective even if not so aesthetically pleasing to modern eyes; those who reached Ntereso in central Ghana in the second half of the second millennium before our era were exceptional in retaining their characteristic bifacial arrow-heads.[103]

If this southward movement of people out of the Sahara meant an infusion of population into the indigenous stock, it might have had little obvious influence on the physical type, since they were both negroid anyway.[104] If, as seems likely, the immigrants were speakers of proto-Nilo-Saharan, the small groups might well have lost their own languages and adopted the prevailing Niger-Congo language of the indigenes; only large groups, such as the ancestors of the Songhay, would have retained their own language.[105]

Food production

The change from dependence on hunting, fishing and gathering the fruits of the wild, to crop-raising and stock-keeping, is the most important step which man has taken in the last 10 000 years. This revolution did not take place in a single location and spread to the rest of the world, but there were a limited number of *foci* where such developments evolved. For Europe, western Asia and north-east Africa, the main focus was in the hill country of Anatolia, Iran and northern Iraq. Here were developed the cultivation of wheat and barley and the domestication of sheep, goats and cattle. Later, the techniques of food production were applied to the great river valleys of the Tigris/Euphrates, Nile and Indus, with the added techniques of drainage and irrigation.[106] By the fifth millennium before our era there were domesticated sheep and cattle in Egypt and cereals were being grown.[107] At

103. O. Davies, 1966a, 1967a; 1967b, p. 163; C. T. Shaw, 1969c, pp. 227–8.
104. M.-C. Chamia, 1968, D. Brothwell and C. T. Shaw, 1971.
105. J. H. Greenberg, 1963b.
106. G. Clark, 1969, pp. 70ff.; P. J. Ucko and G. W. Dimbleby (eds), 1969.
107. G. Caton-Thompson and E. W. Gardner, 1934; D. Seddon, 1968, p. 490; F. Wendorf *et al.*, 1970, p. 1168.

present we have evidence for domesticated cattle earlier than this in the central Saharan highlands, and some evidence, though slender, for cereal-growing.[108] The difficulty of starting up cereal agriculture in sub-Saharan Africa as a result of example from the Nile valley is that the crops anciently grown there, wheat and barley, are winter rainfall crops which can only be grown with difficulty south of the inter-tropical front in the summer rainfall area. What was necessary here was the domestication of suitable indigenous wild grasses, which gave rise to the African cultivated millets; the most important of these was *Sorghum bicolor* or Guinea corn, which was domesticated by the first half of the second millennium before our era in the area between the Sahara and the savannah, from the Nile to Lake Chad.[109] Other wild grasses were domesticated to become pearl millet and finger millet; African rice has already been mentioned.[110] Around Tichitt, in southern Mauritania, there is evidence for the use of the grain of local grasses, but around 1000 before our era, the proportion of pearl millet jumps from 3 per cent to 60 per cent.[111] In the moister zones of West Africa the important staple was the yam, of which more than one African variety was domesticated,[112] and although this may have taken place as long as 5000 years ago, we do not as yet have actual archaeological or botanical evidence for this; a long history of yam cultivation combined with the benefit of complementary food values from the nuts obtained from protected or tended oil-palms would help to account for the density of population in southern Nigeria.[113]

The development of food production, while a prerequisite for urbanization, does not automatically of itself lead to the growth of towns and cities. It seems that certain other circumstances have to be present, such as a build-up to a certain level of population pressure and a shortage of agricultural land.[114] In sub-Saharan Africa, the incidence of malaria increased as a result of agricultural clearing and the presence of larger settled communities, so that the increase in population following the adoption of agriculture was slower than it otherwise might have been;[115] and in most areas of sub-Saharan Africa there was not at the time a shortage of agricultural land.[116] Nevertheless, a sufficient agricultural basis had been established by the first millennium of our era to support such ancient kingdoms as Ghana, Mali, Songhay and Benin.

108. F. Mori, 1965; G. Camps, 1969.
109. J. M. J. de Wet and J. R. Harlan, 1971.
110. R. Portères, 1951b, 1958, 1972.
111. P. J. Munson, 1968, 1970.
112. D. G. Coursey, 1967, 1972.
113. C. T. Shaw, 1972, pp. 27–8; A. R. Rees, 1965.
114. M. C. Webb, 1968.
115. F. B. Livingstone, 1958; S. L. Wiesenfeld, 1967; D. G. Coursey and J. Alexander, 1968.
116. C. T. Shaw, 1971b, pp. 150–3.

The coming of metal

In spite of proposals a long time ago, on good methodological grounds, to abandon in Europe the three-age system of Stone Age, Bronze Age and Early Iron Age,[117] its very convenience has fostered its continued use. West Africa as a whole was hardly touched by the Bronze Age, but a facies of it reached down from Spain and Morocco to Mauritania, where nearly 130 copper objects have been found and where the rich source of Akjoujt was exploited; radio-carbon dates for this point to the fifth century before our era, and stray finds of flat copper arrow-heads have been made in Mali and in south-eastern Algeria.[118]

Why was there no bronze age in sub-Saharan Africa and why did ancient Egyptian civilization not use it more? The reasons are partly to do with the fact that the third millennium before our era, which was the time when metallurgy, writing, monumental building in stone, the use of the wheel and centralized government became firmly established in Egypt, was also the millennium of the final desiccation of the Sahara when people were moving out of it and when it could no longer serve as an indirect link between Egypt and West Africa. The link was not re-established until it was achieved with the help of the camel, some 3000 years later. Other reasons are connected with the later and slower build-up of an agricultural economy in West Africa, as described above. Some writers have sought to give dignity and lustre to West African history by trying to show connections with ancient Egypt, to enable West Africa to bask in its reflected glory.[119] This does not seem necessary.[120]

The Early Iron Age (from about 400 before our era to about 700 of our era)

Throughout the early part of the Iron Age there must have been many parts of West Africa which had no contacts with the outside, and in most cases such contacts as there were with the classical world were slender, sporadic and indirect.[121] Much has been made of Hanno's supposed voyage, but the account is probably a forgery.[122] Herodotus's account of the Carthaginians' silent trade for West African gold is almost certainly based on fact.[123] Indeed, there must have been some reason for contact with the outside world, since it was at the beginning of this period that a knowledge of iron

117. G. Daniel, 1943.
118. R. Mauny, 1951; R. Mauny and J. Hallemans, 1957; N. Lambert, 1970, 1971.
119. J. O. Lucas, 1948, C. A. Diop, 1955, 1960, 1962b.
120. C. T. Shaw, 1964a, p. 24.
121. R. C. C. Law, 1967; J. Ferguson, 1969; R. Mauny, 1970b, pp. 78–137.
122. G. C. Picard, 1971; R. Mauny, 1970; 1971, pp. 73–77.
123. Herodotus, 1964 edn, Book IV, p. 363.

reached West Africa. This was not just an importation of iron objects, but also of the knowledge of iron manufacture, which, since there was no previous knowledge of metallurgy at all, is most unlikely to have been an independent invention.[124] At Taruga, in central Nigeria, a number of iron-smelting sites have been excavated with radio-carbon dates from the fifth to the third century before our era.[125] Excavations in occupation mounds in the valley of the Niger also indicate the presence of iron by the second century before our era.[126] It seems most probable on present evidence that the knowledge of iron metallurgy reached West Africa, not from Meroe as has often been proposed,[127] but from the area of Carthaginian influence in North Africa, perhaps with the chariot-using Garamantes as the intermediaries; there are rock-engravings of chariots along the route connecting the Fezzan to the middle Niger bend.[128] Another chariot route is revealed by rock-paintings farther west, connecting Morocco and southern Mauritania, and perhaps it was the pressure of iron-using nomads (with the iron-pointed spear replacing the bow as the weapon most often depicted in the rock-engravings) which induced the Late Stone Age inhabitants of Tichitt (Akinjeir Phase) to fortify their villages from about the fifth/fourth centuries before our era.[129] The finds at Taruga were associated with terracotta figurines of the distinctive artistic style named after the Nigerian village of Nok where they were first discovered, as most of them have been, in the course of tin-mining.[130] Since they come from tin-bearing alluvial deposits, it is often only the more solid and resistant heads of whole figures which remain intact. It was difficult at first to know whether the other artefacts found in the gravels were all contemporaneous with the figurines or whether they represented a mixture of contemporaneous and older objects; for in addition to iron objects and iron-smelting draught-pipes, there were ground stone axes and smaller artefacts of late stone age character.[131] It now seems that the stone age material is older and represents an alluvial admixture.[132] At Taruga at any rate there was no stone age material, although at one of the rare Nok occupation sites, a ground stone axe was also found.[133] The Nok gravels produced dates which bracket the figurines between 500 before our era and 200 of our era, a time-span subsequently confirmed and made more precise by the Taruga radio-carbon dates by one from the occupation site

124. O. Davies, 1966b; C. T. Shaw, 1969c, pp. 227–8.
125. B. E. B. Fagg, 1968, 1969.
126. A. J. Priddy, 1970; D. D. Hartle, 1970; F. Yamasaki *et al.*, 1973, pp. 231–2.
127. G. Clark, 1969, p. 201.
128. R. Mauny, 1952a; H. Lhote, 1966; C. T. Shaw, 1969c, p. 229; C. Daniels, 1970, pp. 43–4; P. Huard, 1966.
129. R. Mauny, 1947; 1971, p. 70; P. J. Munson, 1968, p. 10.
130. B. E. B. Fagg, 1945, 1956b, 1959.
131. B. E. B. Fagg, 1956b.
132. C. T. Shaw, 1963, p. 455.
133. A. Fagg, 1972b.

referred to (third century before our era), and by a thermo-luminiscent date (620 ± 230 before our era).[134] The style of the Nok terracottas, although not uniform, represents remarkable artistic achievement, and some art historians have seen in them the ancestry of certain forms of the Yoruba art of 1000 years later and 640 kilometres away to the south-west.[135] Nok finds have been made in an elongated area some 480 kilometres long to the south and west of the Jos plateau.

In an area around the middle Gambia river in Senegal and the Gambia there is a district where there are large numbers of dressed stone pillars, isolated or arranged in circles; the most elaborate stones are double and resemble a lyre in shape. Excavations have been carried out which produced three radio-carbon dates in the seventh–eighth centuries and which suggested that they were funerary monuments. Tests on the old ground-surface below one of the monuments give two dates in the first century before our era and this provides a *terminus post quem* for its erection.[136] A remarkable collection of phalliform stone monuments at Tondidarou, in the middle Niger bend area, was plundered by the ignorant enthusiasm of twentieth-century diggers and administrators, with the result that we have little real knowledge of them; they may belong to the same period as the Senegambian monuments.[137]

By the end of the Early Iron Age, along the northern margin of West Africa, negroid people were in contact with the nomadic Berbers of the desert who were now equipped with camels and ferried West African gold north across the desert. By the end of the eighth century the fame of 'Ghana, the land of gold' had reached Baghdad.[138] These northern areas of West Africa were by now equipped with an agriculture and an iron technology, and were ready to embark on political development and the formation of states, to face the pressure from the northern nomads and to secure profitable control of the gold trade. Farther south, in northern Sierra Leone, the change to the use of iron does not appear to begin until the eighth century, and then not to have been abrupt.[139]

134. B. E. B. Fagg and S. J. Fleming, 1970.

135. W. Fagg and F. Willett, 1960, p. 32; F. Willett, 1960, p. 245; 1967, pp. 119–20, 184; 1968, p. 33; A. Rubin, 1970.

136. P. Ozanne, 1966; F. C. Beale, 1966; K. Cissé and G. Thilmans, 1968; B. M. Fagan, 1969, p. 150; G. Descamps, 1971.

137. A. M. L. Desplagnes, 1907a, pp. 40–1; E. Maes, 1924; R. Mauny, 1961, pp. 129–34; 1971a, pp. 133–6.

138. N. Levtzion, 1971, p. 120.

139. J. H. Atherton, 1972, 1973.

PLATE 24.1 *Industry of Cape Manuel, Senegal* (photo I. Diagne, Musée de l'IFAN)

PLATE 24.2 *Stone pendants (basalt) from the Neolithic site at Patte d'Oie* (photo I. Diagne, Musée de l'IFAN)

PLATE 24.3 *Neolithic 'Bel Air' pottery from the Diakité site, Senegal* (photo I. Diagne, Musée de l'IFAN)

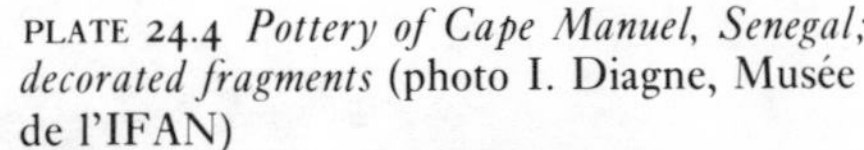

PLATE 24.4 *Pottery of Cape Manuel, Senegal; decorated fragments* (photo I. Diagne, Musée de l'IFAN)

PLATE 24.5 *Megalithic circle, Tiekène Boussoura, Senegal; the 'king's tomb' is visible in the foreground* (photo I. Diagne, Musée de l'IFAN)

PLATE 24.6 *'Bel Air' polished axes made of dolerite* (photo I. Diagne, Musée de l'IFAN)

PLATE 24.7 *Millstone made of volcanic rock, found on the Neolithic site of Ngor* (photo I. Diagne, Musée de l'IFAN)

PLATE 24.8 *Iron Age flat-bottomed pot* (photo I. Diagne, Musée de l'IFAN)

PLATE 24.9 *Bone smoothing tool, found on the Neolithic site at Cape Manuel* (photo I. Diagne, Musée de l'IFAN)

PLATE 24.10 *Anthropomorphic statue found on Thiaroye site, Senegal* (photo I. Diagne, Musée de l'IFAN)

Prehistory in the Nile Valley

F. DEBONO

Sudan, Nubia and Egypt, three very different areas linked only by a river, make up a unique valley. But it is hard to imagine today that the vast desert that encloses it on both sides once afforded (depending on climatic and environmental factors at the time in question) insurmountable barriers or communication links with the rest of Africa. The same physical factors also conditioned the way of life of the valley's earliest inhabitants in their never-ending struggle to adapt to hostile or favourable habitats.

In this context we propose to give a concise account of their long evolution from the origins of man to the glories of the Pharaonic period. Particular cultures at particular moments are already well known; in many other cases the incomplete nature of research on the one hand and an unduly classificatory approach to the results on the other have led to a piecemeal approach which may in future turn out to be artificial and sometimes even erroneous. There is certainly something implausible about the multiplication of 'types' sometimes only a few kilometres apart. Historians unhappy with this piecemeal approach have sought to group the identified 'types' together into broad chronological categories though some of these may in time themselves turn out to be defective or inadequate.

Oldowan[1]

This culture is characterized everywhere by worked pebbles (choppers). Recent discoveries bearing on the origins of man confirm the existence of the earliest human traces not only in other parts of Africa but also in the Nile valley. From 1949 onwards very early evidence of the presence of these hominids, in the shape of pebbles barely worked into crude tools, came to light at Nuri and Wawa, in the Sudan, but these isolated surface finds were not enough to amount to definite proof. It was not until 1971, following systematic research at Thebes, that it was possible to be certain on this point. Here the exploration of twenty-five alluvial deposits dating from the early Quaternary yielded a rich harvest of these primitive tools. The

1. This period takes its name from the finds at Olduvai Gorge (see Chapter 28 below); it was sometimes earlier known as the pre-Acheulian or Archaic Palaeolithic.

discovery in 1974 of three stratified sites containing worked pebbles (choppers) yielded a wealth of information and swept away the last lingering doubts. The worked-pebble strata were below the early Acheulian (Early Stone Age), which in its earliest levels is characterized in particular by trihedra. Very recently a hominid tooth was found in early alluvial strata in the Thebes mound, associated with choppers. It will be recalled that in about 1925 a similar sequence was found in alluvial strata at Abbassia, near Cairo; but at that time the worked pebbles were classified as eoliths. New light has most recently been thrown on this remote period as a result of our 1974 excavations at Adaima, in Upper Egypt (IFAO[2] Expedition): this is a new site that is still being studied, but is apparently similar to the previous ones.

The Early Stone Age[3]

This fine stone industry, characterized by thin-ended bifaces, occurs virtually throughout Africa. It may even have originated in Africa, starting from the worked pebbles of the previous period, and then have moved on to other parts of the world. Evidence of this civilization is found in the Nile valley with no apparent break from the Sudan to Egypt. It is better known in the northern Sudan, as the result of recent work, than farther south. The Lower Acheulian, illustrated by sometimes crude bifaces with somewhat wavy edges, is found at Atbara, Wawa and Nuri, together with worked pebbles. At the last-named site it develops with a transitional complex. The Middle and Upper Acheulian, which have been studied mainly in the north, are distinguished by the improvement in the workmanship and the appearance of Levalloisoid industries. These latter, which subsequently gave rise to the Levalloisian flaking technique, are to be seen also at Khor Abu Anja. While the Acheulian is met in other continents also, a Sangoan type, the final version of the Acheulian (which persisted for a long time), is peculiar to Africa. Hitherto found mainly in central and southern Africa, it is now beginning to be identified also in the Sudan, e.g. at Khor Abu Anja and Sai. Below Wadi Halfa it seems to lose several of its distinguishing features. A very few biface cleavers bevelled at the distal end apparently exist in the Sudan.

In Egyptian Nubia the Acheulian has been found on the old river terraces; a development is to be observed, based on the improvement of the technique; but its typological features are insufficiently known. In Egypt, on the other hand, the stratified sites at Abbassia, near Cairo, those we recently (1974) investigated at Thebes, and the old Nile terraces yield Acheulian industries in successive strata. After the Oldowan level, characterized by worked pebbles, comes an Acheulian containing trihedra, crude bifaces and also

2. Institut francais d'archéologie orientale.

3. This corresponds broadly to the Lower Palaeolithic, often known as the Acheulian, i.e. *c.* 600 000–*c.* 200 000 before our era.

worked pebbles. The next level yields more advanced bifaces and Levalloisoid (early Levalloisian) pieces. The Kharga site has superimposed strata of a more recent Acheulian, ending with the middle stone age. While the bifaces exhibit the classical shapes found elsewhere, examples are sometimes also found which have been reworked as cleavers at the distal end: this is at present the only type of cleaver known in Egypt. Also peculiar to Egypt are bifaces worked according to a technique similar to the so-called Victoria West technique, which itself preceded the classical Levalloisian flaking technique.[4] Other Sangoan-type bifaces, possibly more recent, are found almost as far as Cairo.

The Middle Stone Age[5]

Changes in the way of life led to the generalized use of the flake instead of the biface, and the latter soon became rare and then disappeared. These flakes with faceted heels, often made by the Levalloisoid technique already mentioned, came from a specially prepared core which produced flakes of predetermined shape. In some parts of Africa this procedure persisted until the Neolithic, which shows that at the time it was the result of very advanced technological thinking.

The Mousterian industry using the Levalloisian flaking technique has been little studied in the southern Sudan, though it probably occurs at Tangasi and in a more highly developed form at Abu Tabari and Nuri. On the other hand recent research in the north has established four distinct groupings. (1) *Nubian Mousterian* resembles the Mousterian of Europe, without being identical with it. There is a small proportion of Levalloisian flakes, and some Mousterian-type tools, poorly trimmed, comparable to Upper Palaeolithic types and in some cases with Acheulian bifaces (about 45 000–33 000 before our era). (2) *Denticulate Mousterian* also has only a few Levalloisian flakes and very few blades, whereas denticulate pieces abound. (3) *Lupemban Sangoan* exhibits an increase in Levalloisian flaking, together with bifaces, side-scrapers, notched and denticulate pieces, truncated flakes and biface points with foliate trimming. (4) *Khormusian* stretches from Jemai roughly as far as Dongola, and has a large number of trimmed Levalloisian flakes, some denticulate pieces and more rarely some burins; it has been dated by recent work at about 25 000–16 000 before our era, though these estimates have most recently been revised backwards to 41 490–33 800 before our era.

Compared with the northern Sudan, the data collected in Egyptian Nubia is inadequate. Early work by Sandford and Arkell established the predominance of the Levalloisian flaking technique, sometimes in an

4. A large flake is removed by percussion, usually on one of the sides but occasionally at one of the ends: the flake is then itself used as a tool.

5. This term broadly covers the Middle Palaeolithic, from *c.* 200 000 before our era.

Acheulian tradition. Recent research has reported it in 1962 at Afya and Khor Daoud. We ourselves detected it at Amada in 1962–3 in a pure Levalloisian form; and at Wadi Sebua we studied an industry no doubt belonging to the final phase of this period, associated with non-Levalloisian flakes including many burins.

The Aterian, the typical industry of the Maghrib and the southern Sahara, is distinguished by flakes with pronounced peduncular ends, and by the use of foliate trimming. No doubt starting with the Mousterian, it accidentally survived in some areas until the Neolithic. It has recently been identified in Egyptian Nubia in the Libyan desert north-west of Abu Simbel,[6] associated with a very rich fauna – white rhinoceros, large bovines, wild ass, two species of gazelle, antelope, fox, jackal, warthog, ostrich, an extinct species of dromedary, and tortoise. In Nubia the Aterian seems to be admixed with the Amadian, an industry of hybrid Mousterian-Levalloisian tradition. In Egypt it occurs in the pure state in the eastern oases of Siwa, Dakhla and Kharga: and it is found in the eastern desert at Wadi Hammamat. In the Nile valley itself it is scattered in small deposits at Thebes and Dara(?). It may have influenced the Hawarian in the following period at Esna and Thebes. It appears as microliths in the latter industry at Abbassia and Jebel Ahmar, near Cairo (from at least 44 000 before our era to at least 7000 before our era).

Despite the many remains of the Middle Stone Age cultures in Egypt, an exhaustive study of its tool-kit is nowhere near complete. Early work on the old terraces of the Nile valley and the Fayum afforded a general view of the civilization that existed at this period. Our recent excavations on the Thebes mound since 1971, under the auspices of Unesco, nevertheless throw new light. Stratified occurrences in geological deposits and in about a hundred sites of this period, arranged in successive chronological levels, already make it possible to sketch out the main lines of the development of this industry, which promises to be predominantly Levalloisian. All these lines of research converge to demonstrate the existence of an early 'Acheulian–Levalloisian' period, followed by another marked by massive cores which gradually become smaller and more refined. In a later phase lamellar flakes[7] show increasing traces of secondary retouching, suggestive of the Mousterian, as are the various tools. While these industries have features in common with others in Africa, we must mention one peculiarly Egyptian one that has never been reported elsewhere: this is the abundant so-called 'Jebel Suhan' industry, conspicuous for the use of cores flaked by the Levalloisian technique along two percussion planes, which were reworked after use to produce a concave scraper at one end. As regards the men of this period, at Silsila in 1952 we found two fragments of cranial

6. These finds date from 1976, and were made at Bir Tarfawi and Bir Sahara.

7. From this period onwards two flaking techniques are found: the classical Levalloisian, and the detaching of longish blades. Between the two many transitional forms exist.

bone probably dating from this period.[8] Investigation of them is not yet complete, but it has already revealed some archaic features together with other more recent ones. Work in progress on this may throw new light on the controversial question of the origins of African man in the Middle Palaeolithic; what little is so far known is derived from isolated finds in Cyrenaica, Morocco and Zambia.

The Late Stone Age

In Europe and other parts of Africa the transition from the preceding period to this one is in general marked by a sudden sharp break, in technological and sometimes also in human terms. This is not the case in the Nile valley. The difficulty of drawing sharp demarcation lines between one period and another makes the task of establishing chronological sequences a tricky one. From the preceding period onwards, evolution in response to localized habitats gave rise to new regional facies, adjusted to local conditions, but sometimes parallel. At the same time environmental changes seem to have altered the relationship between the inhabitants of the valley and their neighbours: old linkages break down and new alliances are forged. The list of cultural types now and recently identified gives an impression of great dispersion; but this is only an interim interpretation, until such time as more detailed analysis makes it possible to elucidate the linking features. These comments apply equally to the succeeding period, the Mesolithic.

This period has just been studied in the northern sector of the Sudan, and it exhibits two distinct industries: the Jemaian in the neighbourhood of Wadi Halfa, which has flakes, only a few of which are Levalloisian, and lightly retouched points, and is characterized by side-scrapers, end-scrapers, burins and denticulate pieces (*c.* 15 000–13 000 before our era); and the Sebilian, earlier reported at Kom Ombo in Egypt, which now appears in the Sudan at Stage I at Wadi Halfa. Its flakes with retouched truncations are struck from discoid or Levalloisian cores (*c.* 13 000–9000 before our era).

In Egyptian Nubia two industries are known: the Amadian, found by us at Amada (German Institute expeditions, 1963), which contains a variety of tools, mainly Levalloisian, associated with scourer-scrapers, awls, pieces made by the Kharga technique (see below) and occasional examples of foliate retouching reminiscent of the Aterian; and the Sebilian, identified by us at Sebua (IFAO 1964 expedition) in several places, which also belongs to Stage I, mixed with ordinary or Levalloisian flakes, a few scrapers and many burins. It probably exists also at Khor Daoud. As for the Gizan, this was identified near Cairo as long ago as 1938: it comprises some Levalloisian items, and the geometrical shapes of its flakes are thought to bear a

8. Information kindly supplied by P. Vandermeersch, of the Laboratory of Human Palaeontology, Faculty of Science, University of Paris VI, who was entrusted with the examination of this material.

resemblance to the Khormusian. The Hawarian (previously known as the epi-Levalloisian[9]), a microlithic industry, extends at least from Esna in Upper Egypt to the apex of the Delta and neighbouring areas (cf. Wadi Tumilat). Like the Sebilian, it shows Levalloisian technique (but without geometrical shapes), and comprises various stages and facies which are still the subject of study. It is characterized by the number of bipolar cores probably derived from the so-called 'Jebel Suhan' core already mentioned, which dates from the Middle Stone Age. Some of the cores, perhaps more recent, produced both flakes and lamellae with faceted ends at the same time, thus marking a transition to the smooth-heeled lamellae that predominate in the Late Stone Age and the Mesolithic. The Hawarian of Esna and Thebes is thought to betray Aterian influence, because of the occasional occurrence of foliate trimming and hybrid pieces. On the other hand peduncular microliths typologically associated with the Aterian are found in the Hawarian at Abbassia and Jebel Ahmar, near Cairo. These influences may conceivably be the result of raids by desert peoples into the valley. The Khargan (whose separate existence some prehistorians dispute) is more or less contemporary with the Hawarian: it occurs in Kharga oasis, with a Levalloisian Khargan preceding the pure form. It has Levalloisian flakes abruptly and seemingly shapelessly trimmed; and it occurs also in Karkur oasis, in Egypt, and at Qara and Thebes. At Esna (Upper Egypt) and Amada (Egyptian Nubia) it is associated with other industries.

Mesolithic

In the Nile valley this period in general differs from the previous one in that (except in cases of recurrence, survival, or duplication) flake industries are superseded by the production of microlithic blades and lamellae with faceted butts. Research in northern Sudan and southern Egyptian Nubia has unearthed a complex of industries which sometimes no doubt represent facies of a single culture.

The Halfian of Wadi Halfa (Khor Kussa) is thought to have been identified also north of Kom Ombo (Egypt): it perhaps represents a premature transition from the Levalloisian technique of the previous period to microlithic techniques using flakes or lamellae. The use of the so-called Ushtata retouching technique is thought to be an advanced technique that makes an appearance later with the Ibero-Maurusian in the Maghrib. The

9. This whole period was at first thought to have been characterized everywhere by the Sebilian. Research showed that the latter culture is in fact characteristic only of the Kom Ombo area; and thereafter a contemporary but distinct type was identified to which the term epi-Levalloisian was applied. After further discussion with other workers, the author rejected the idea of naming a culture solely on the basis of its techniques, preferring rather to name it after the place where it was first found. Thus the epi-Levalloisian became the Hawarian.

Halfian exhibits the successive use of backed flakes and lamellae, scrapers, burins and denticulate or scalloped pieces (*c.* 18 000–15 000 before our era).

The Ballanian, more recent at Wadi Halfa and Ballana, comprises truncated microliths, others with lightly retouched backs, truncated flakes, scrapers, burins, points and single- and double-sided cores (*c.* 14 000–12 000 before our era).

The Qadian, from Abka and Toshka in Nubia, comprises a tool-kit consisting initially of microlithic flakes and then of lamellae. It includes scrapers, round-backs, burins, truncated tools and points that later degenerate. The oval graves situated either within or outside the dwellings are covered over with flagstones: they reveal a people very similar to the Cromagnon of the Maghrib (*c.* 12 000–5000 before our era).

In Egypt the Arkinian, known from a single site near Wadi Halfa, is mainly a flake industry. It comprises end scrapers, backed and Ushtata-retouched lamellae, semi-circles, scalloped pieces and small pestles (*c.* 7400 before our era).

The El-Kabian near El-Kab has been identified in three successive occupation strata, one of which yielded what appears to be a rectangular polished bone palette (*c.* 5000 before our era).

The Shamakian, in the Wadi Halfa area, has multidirectional cores, and in its last phase exhibits geometrically shaped tools associated with cruder pieces. It may be an offshoot of the Capsian of the Maghrib (*c.* 5000–3270 before our era).

In Egypt we (and others after us) have studied the Silsilian in the Jebel Silsila area near Kom Ombo. It consists of three stages. Silsilian I has slightly retouched lamellae, sometimes tanged; irregular triangles, occasionally tanged; micro-burins; a few burins and scrapers; and a bone industry. The human remains appear to be of Cromagnon type (*c.* 1350 before our era). Silsilian II[10] has blades and long lamellae with discontinuous re-touching, sometimes tanged, burins and scrapers, and a bone industry (*c.* 12 000 before our era). Silsilian III, which is still under investigation, exhibits a profusion of lamellae, often little retouched, heating stones and a round hut, the earliest so far found in Egypt.

The Fakurian, studied in the Esna area, seems to be somewhat akin to the Ibero-Maurusian. It probably existed also at other places in Egypt (*c.* 13 000 before our era). This industry is characterized by delicate retouched lamellae, awls and darts.

The Sebilian, which retains the Levalloisian flaking technique, is characterized by flakes reduced to geometrical shapes and with their bases straightened. It is a southern industry in Egypt, occurring mainly in the Kom Ombo and Silsila sectors and at Darau, particularly in Stage II. It has

10. Called by P. E. Smith (1966b) after the Crocodile-god Sebek, the deity associated with this locality. Having also ourselves excavated this site, we suggest the term Silsilian II (from Jebel Silsila, in this area) as being more in accordance with the normal practice of naming cultures after place names.

been attested in Nubia, but is much rarer (and sometimes atypical) in the north. Our work at Silsila also yielded a bone tool-kit, grindstones and small pestles, and human remains which are still being examined (*c.* 11 000 before our era). The Sebilian is an interesting subject for discussion, since physico-chemical datings suggest a chronology which at first sight contradicts the technological data yielded by this culture. This is all the more remarkable seeing that the Sebilian is not far removed, either in time or space, from the Kakurian.

The Menchian (Silsila area) yields a stone industry somewhat akin to the Aurignacian of the Near East, a bone industry, small pestles, shiny-edged lamellae, personal adornments and human remains. The resemblance of certain new intermediate-type tools points to relative contemporaneity with Sebilian II.

The Lakeitian culture, identified by us in the eastern desert, is remarkable for heavily denticulate saws together with peduncular darts.

The Helwanian, which we identified in the neighbourhood of Helwan, south of Cairo, comprises four distinct phases. The first yields a profusion of blades and lamellae, sometimes slightly retouched in the Ushtata style. The second is distinguished by microliths consisting of scalene and isosceles triangles, segments of circles and micro-burins. The third has segments of circles; whilst the fourth and last has a new type of segments of circles with straight-line bases.

The Natufian, an industry from Palestine, is thought to have made a series of incursions into Egyptian territory. At Helwan a phase of this industry has been identified characterized by pieces with backs worked by crosswise retouching. On the other hand arrowheads with symmetrically notched bases, originally attributed to the Natufian, were found as long ago as 1876 at Helwan, where we ourselves found some more in 1936: and even more recently, in 1953, we found some in the northern part of the Eastern Desert (*c.* 8000–7000 before our era). They have since been found at El-Khiam and Jericho, in Palestine, and are known among specialists as 'El-Khiam points'. The hypothesis of incursions by the Natufian thus remains to be thoroughly checked.

Neolithic and Predynastic

This long period, covering roughly 2000 years (*c.* 5000–3000 before our era), is here analysed in detail. The *material* aspects of each of the 'cultures' or 'cultural horizons' that go to make it up are described in full; and the result is a compendium that is essential for an appreciation in its physical context of the slow evolution that must have taken place. Starting with groups of nomadic or semi-nomadic peoples, this led gradually to the formation of societies – either highly centralized, as in the case of Egypt, or as small independent principalities, as in the Nilotic Sudan. The *historical* development of these Neolithic and Predynastic societies is dealt with in

Chapter 28, pp. 706–29, of the present volume. The two accounts are thus complementary: they approach the problems from different angles. The cross-references needed to allow the reader to locate a given 'culture' described in the present chapter in the context of Chapter 28's more general account of the overall historical development of the 'cultural horizons' are given in footnotes.

This new period marks a decisive stage in the history of humanity. Once they had turned from nomadic or semi-nomadic to sedentary life, the men of the Nile created the main features of civilization as we know it today. A fixed habitat brought with it the use of pottery, the domestication and breeding of cattle, agriculture, and a host of tools to meet man's growing needs.

In the Sudan[11] the Khartoumian[12] is perhaps the earliest culture of this period. It is found in over a dozen localities spread over an enormous area, extending from Kassala in the east and over some 400 km of desert to the west, as far as Dongola in the north and almost to Abu Hijar on the White Nile in the south. Data from the excavations at Khartoum, in which we took part, furnish proof of a fixed habitat, namely, the use of wattle huts, the large-scale use of sophisticated pottery and the use of grindstones. The pottery, consisting of bowls, is characterized by incised 'wavy-line' and 'dotted-line' decoration. The abundant stone tools made of quartz, distinctly microlithic and geometrical, comprise a variety of types – half-circles and segments of circles, scalene triangles, rectangles, trapezes, scalloped flakes and awls. The half-circles and segments, retouched also on the cutting edges, show affinities with the Wiltonian and the Neolithic of Hydrax Hill in Zimbabwe. Tools made of a hard stone called rhyolite are larger than the quartz ones: they include flakes and plain blades, some of them with recut heels (scrapers), large half-circles and a few scrapers. Barbed bone harpoons, mostly single-edged, are also characteristic of the Khartoumian. There are also small stone pestles with a central cupule, grinders, hammerstones, discs with a central hole, a few grindstones, and sinkers for nets, probably of the same type as in the Fayum, at El Omari (Egypt) and in central southern Sahara. Personal adornments include disc-shaped beads made of ostrich eggshell, and a few drop earrings; red and yellow ochre were used for painting the body. The dead were buried in their dwellings, lying on their sides: they belonged to a black race, the earliest in Africa. In their lifetime they underwent ritual mutilation of the teeth, as practised among the Capsians and Ibero-Maurusians in the Maghrib and by Neolithic people in Kenya. This practice persisted for a long time in the Sudan and other parts of Africa. The fauna identified consisted mainly of buffalo, antelope, hippopotamus, wild cat, porcupine, mouse, crocodile and a large amount of fish (? *c.* 4000 before our era).

The Shaheinabian occurs at quite a number of sites scattered about south

11. See Chapter 28 below, pp. 720–1.

12. The 'Early Khartoum' of Chapter 28, p. 720. We prefer to retain the term 'Khartoumian' in case future discoveries reveal earlier phases.

of the Sixth Cataract. The excavations at Esh Shaheinab yielded items of a culture no doubt derived from the Khartoumian: its distinguishing features are a special pottery and the use of gouges and polished bone axes. The pottery consists of bowls, sometimes with 'dotted-line' decoration as in the Khartoumian: what sets it apart, however, is the smoothing of surfaces, the red slip used, the black edging and the incised triangle decoration. The stone tool-kit also comprises microlithic pieces, polished axes and barrel planes, and flat and convex sledgehammer heads. Bone harpoons persist, whilst mother-of-pearl fish-hooks make their appearance, as do amazonite and carnelian beads and the labrets that are still used to this day. Buffalo, antelope, giraffe and wart hog were hunted, and the dwarf goat was domesticated. There is no trace of light dwellings, but deep dug-out hearths are found. The Shaheinabian[13] has features in common with one of the stages of the Egyptian Fayumian, namely, the use of finishing tools, gouges, harpoons, sledgehammer heads, amazonite and dug-out hearths. The smoothed and black-edged pottery of Upper Egypt links it with the early predynastic in Egypt. Points in common with the western Sahara (Tibesti) are the amazonite, the gouges and the incised decoration on the pottery; and the dwarf goat is a point in common with the north-west. The Kadero site currently being excavated, which is of a later period, has yielded burials (*c.* 3500–3000 before our era). Excavations in progress (1976–7) at Kadada, in the Shendi area, are yielding a third, probably more recent, variant of the Shaheinabian, with burials associated with the living area. Its distinctive features seem to be polished stone axes, deeply ground, almost rhomboidal make-up palettes, pierced discs for a purpose so far unknown, cup-shaped vessels and child burials in jars.

The Abkian[14] of northern and southern Sudan, at least as far as Sai, is probably contemporary successively with the Khartoumian and the Shaheinabian; and may even have extended beyond the latter, going through three phases. One, with little pottery, is perhaps derived from the Qadian. Another comprised a range of pots with incised orifices and surface decoration in the form of zigzag incised lines and round or rectangular stippled patterns. Another had stone tools including awls made from flakes, sometimes double-ended, and lamellae, either plain or with retouched edges. Another again had black-edged pottery with red polished or ribbed surfaces, somewhat reminiscent of the Shaheinabian, the Nubian A-Group and predynastic Egypt (*c.* 3380–2985 before our era).

The post-Shamakian, found at only two sites, is characterized by micro-points, notched lamellae, lateral flakes and finishing tools, suggesting contacts with the Fayum and Kharga oases (*c.* 3650–3270 before our era).

The absence of the above-mentioned cultures or chronologically corresponding ones in Egyptian Nubia is to be explained either by a particular concatenation of environmental conditions, the rarity of sites, or

13. Sometimes called 'Khartoum Neolithic'.

14. Cf. the Abkian of Chapter 28, p. 721.

perhaps simply by incomplete exploration. On the other hand Egyptian Nubia, other peculiarities apart, shows a close affinity with the civilizations of the Egyptian Predynastic, and even seemingly with the Badarian.

Nagada I[15] occurs *inter alia* at Eneiba, Sebua, Shellal and Khor Abu Daoud (Nubia), the only site so far found with a living area equipped with provision stores.

Nagada II[16] occurs near Abu Simbel, and at Khor Daoud, Sebua, Bahan and Ohemhit. From the first dynasty onwards contacts between Egypt and Nubia slowed down. The Nubian industries developed where they were, keeping their prehistoric characteristics until the New Kingdom, under the names of Nubian A-Group[17], B-Group and C-Group.

In Egypt different geographical and environmental conditions brought into being two distinct cultural groups, which developed in parallel on Egyptian territory in the south and the north, preserving their cultural independence until the country was unified under the first dynasty. The use of copper is a secondary factor: it started in the south much earlier than in the north, because of the nearness of small deposits of the mineral sufficient for limited uses.

The southern cultural group (Upper Egypt)

The southern group appeared from the outset as an advanced civilization. It has been described on the basis of the study of many large cemeteries and a few remains of inhabited areas.

The Tasian, so far only summarily investigated and even questioned by some prehistorians, occurs in Middle Egypt at Tasa, Badari, Mustajidda and Matmar. Known from its cemeteries and some scanty remains of villages, it shows some original features unknown elsewhere. The pottery, mostly dark bowls, more rarely red or black-edged and sometimes with ribbed surfaces, is unusual because of the sharp angle between the straight or oblique upper portion and the narrow foot. The cup-shaped pots with incised or stippled decoration illustrate another original type, thoroughly African in character. The stone tools include in particular large polished axes of silicified limestone, scrapers, knives and awls. Rectangular make-up palettes, mainly of alabaster, rings, ivory bracelets and pierced shells make up the range of items concerned with personal adornment. There are also bone spoons and fish-hooks. As to the burials, graves are oval or rectangular, sometimes with a side niche containing a body lying on its side with its arms and legs drawn up, its head pointing to the south and its face turned to the west. The dead were provided with tools, pots and personal ornaments.

15. The 'Ancient Predynastic' of Chapter 28, pp. 714–15.
16. The 'Middle Predynastic' of Chapter 28, pp. 715–16.
17. See Chapter 28, pp. 722–4.

The Badarian,[18] a brilliant civilization, especially in Middle Egypt, occurs at Badari, Mustajidda, Matmar and Hamamia. Its unusual character is highlighted by the very fine pottery, which comprises vessels of various colours including red, brown, grey and red with black edging, often covered with finely incised lines, usually oblique. They are mainly narrow, keeled or wide-mouthed bowls. There are also basalt bowls and goblets, and ivory vessels. The insides are sometimes ornamented with incised plant motifs. The stone tool-kit includes biface cores with convex denticulate cutting edges, hollow-bottomed or bayleaf-shaped arrow-heads, and other lamellar tools. The bone or ivory ladles, combs, bangles, fish-hooks and figurines exhibit considerable artistic merit. The female and hippopotamus figurines had a ritual function. Personal adornments include quartz beads encased in cast copper, seashells, and rectangulat slate make-up palettes, often with a concavity at one end. Wheat, barley and flax were cultivated, cattle and sheep domesticated, and the gazelle, ostrich and tortoise hunted for food. The dwellings, simple light huts, have completely disappeared. The dead were buried in a doubled-up position in round, oval, or more rarely rectangular graves, usually lying on their sides with their heads pointing to the south and their faces turned to the west; they were provided for the after-life with the various items already mentioned. Disparate branches of this culture are probably to be detected in the eastern desert (Wadi Hammamat), at Armant (Upper Egypt), in the Adaima area (Upper Egypt) and perhaps even in Nubia.

Nagada I[19] is found in stratigraphy at Hamamia and Mustajidda below the Badarian, starting in Middle Egypt, in Nubia and even in the eastern desert (Wadi Hammamat). The smooth or polished red, brown or black pottery is distinct from that of the Badarian. A typical feature of Nagada I is the decoration on the pottery: it is no longer incised but painted in white on red vessels, and takes the form of geometrical designs, plant motifs and naturalistic compositions. The tubular stone pots, often of basalt with pierced handles, frequently end in a conical foot. The biface stone tools include arrow-heads with concave bases, lozenge-shaped and comma-shaped knives and others with U-shaped forked ends, polished axes, lamellar tools and conical and discoid sledgehammer heads. Make-up palettes, mainly of slate, are first lozenge-shaped and then take on animal shapes. The bone and ivory objects, which are in a new tradition, are ornamented, as are the combs and pins, with human or animal figures: they were used for magical purposes, but sometimes are also harpoons. The houses are light shelters enclosed by stockades, as identified at Mahasna. The use of copper is evidently on the increase. Provisions were kept in underground store-rooms, but also in pots, at Mustajidda and Deir El-Medineh. As to funerary customs, the dead were buried in rectangular graves

18. The 'Early Predynastic' of Chapter 28, pp. 713–14.

19. The 'Ancient Predynastic' of Chapter 28, pp. 714–15, sometimes known as the Amratian.

crouched on their sides, with their heads pointing to the south and their faces to the west; and there are examples of multiple burials and of the burial of dismembered corpses (*c.* 4000–3500 before our era).

Nagada II[20] is stratigraphically later than Nagada I at Hamamia, Mustajidda and Armant, and is found from the entrance to the Fayum at Gerza as far as southern Egyptian Nubia. The traditional Nagada I pottery develops by acquiring narrower orifices and pronounced rims. The white-decorated ware is superseded by pink pottery with brown decoration in the form of stylized symbolic motifs – spirals, boats, plants and figures with arms upraised. Also characteristic are the pot-bellied vessels with wavy handles, which later became tubular and then lost their handles in the early historical period. Pots made of various kinds of stone, often very sophisticated, mostly reproduce the shapes of the pink ceramic ware. The stone tools, many of them very advanced, include bifid knives with V-shaped ends and others with two cutting edges, one concave and the other convex, one of the faces having been first polished and then very neatly retouched. The handles are occasionally covered with gold leaf or a sliver of ivory. Sledgehammer heads are pear-shaped. The copper industry is more advanced, and produces points, pins and axes. Palettes are increasingly stylized, eventually becoming round or rectangular. Bone and ivory figurines also become excessively stylized. Burial practices show further refinement: the walls of the oval or rectangular graves are lined with wood, mud, or brick. Our recent excavations at Adaima (1974 IFAO expedition) found graves of a new type, shaped like bath-tubs, dating from the end of this civilization. The layout of grave-goods follows a standard pattern in this period: they are sometimes placed in side-chambers. Dismembered corpses are also sometimes reported, but multiple burials disappear. Moreover the directional placing of the dead is no longer uniform. Dwellings consist of round or partially round clay huts, flimsy shelters, and rectangular earthworks as at El-Amra (*c.* 3500–3100 before our era).

The northern cultural group (Lower Egypt)

The northern cultural group is quite distinct from the southern, mainly in the increased size of the inhabited areas, the monochrome pottery and the short-lived practice of burying the dead in the dwellings themselves.

Fayumian B,[21] still little known, has been studied north of Lake Fayum: it is thought to belong to a final Palaeolithic, or else to a pre-ceramic Neolithic. It comprises plain and microlithic lamellae with trimmed backs, bone harpoons and small pestles. Latest research has identified an intermediate stage between Fayumian B (the earliest) and Fayumian A (the more recent): this stage, which we propose to call Fayumian C, has gouges and stalked biface arrow-heads similar to those from the western

20. The 'Middle Predynastic' or Gerzean of Chapter 28, pp. 715–16.
21. See under Neolithic – Fayum B, Chapter 28, p. 709.

desert (Siwa oasis, in Libya), and constitutes a link with the Sahara. It is datable at *c.* 6500–5190 before our era.

Fayumian A[22] has been much more fully investigated so far as dwelling-places are concerned. It exhibits an ungainly type of monochrome pottery, smoothed or polished and red, brown or black, comprising bowls, goblets, cups, rectangular buckets, and vessels with feet or with bosses at the rim, as in the Badarian. The stone industry, which shows an advanced bifacial technique, comprises arrow-heads with concave or triangular bases, points, sickle-heads on straight wooden hafts, polished axes and one discoid sledgehammer head. There are bone pins, bradawls and points with peduncular bases. The crude make-up palettes are of limestone, or more rarely diorite. Seashells and pieces of eggshell and microcline (amazonite) were used for making strings of beads. Where the dwellings were, no trace of the presumably very flimsy shelters has survived, but there are many dug-out hearths similar to those at Shaheinab in the Sudan. Silos consisting of baskets sunk into the ground in groups near the dwellings will have been used for storing wheat, barley, flax and other goods. Pigs, goats, cattle, hippopotamus and tortoise were these people's food animals. No trace has yet come to light of their cemeteries, which were no doubt some distance away. This culture (*c.* 4441–3860 before our era) may have been contemporaneous with the Badarian.

The Merimdian[23] occupies a large inhabited area of more than 2 hectares west of the Delta. The excavations, incomplete and so far published only in brief preliminary reports, reveal three successive layers of archaeological debris tracing the development of a single culture down the ages. It is a culture all on its own, but typical of the northern group. The monochrome pottery, smoothed, polished or rough, comprises a variety of types, mainly bowls, goblets, dishes and jugs, but no rimmed vessels with narrow orifices. Specific forms include ladles like those of the Badarian, bowls with bosses like in the Badarian and the Fayumian, and footed pots as in the Fayumian. These pots are sometimes decorated with indented stippling on the rims, or with incised vertical lines, patterns in relief or a palm-leaf motif. There are a very few pots made of basalt or hard greenstone and ending in a Nagada I-type foot. The bifacial stone tool-kit contains the same types as the Fayumian. There is a globular or pear-shaped sledgehammer head; and there are carved bone and ivory bradawls, needles, awls, harpoons, spatulas and fish-hooks. Personal adornments include hair-pins, bracelets, rings, pierced shells and beads of various materials. It is worth mentioning two make-up palettes, a shield-shaped slate one and a granite one – both being materials imported from the south. The dwellings are initially well-spaced-out light oval huts supported by posts; then come sturdier ones set closer together; and lastly there are oval houses with walls made of lumps of clay stuck together, even forming the alignments of streets. Fayumian-type silos

22. The 'Early Predynastic' of Chapter 28, p. 714.
23. See Chapter 28, p. 714.

adjoin the huts, and are later superseded by jars sunk into the ground. The dead (though obviously not all of them) were buried without grave-goods in oval graves among the dwellings, apparently pointing towards their houses. Pigs, sheep, goats and dogs were domesticated, and the main animals hunted were the hippopotamus, crocodile and tortoise. There was also fishing. Developed between 4180 and 3580 before our era, this culture may have been contemporaneous with the Fayumian and have continued up to the beginning of Nagada I.

Omarian A,[24] another culture of the northern group, came to light near Helwan among the remains of a large inhabited area over three-quarters of a kilometre long at the entrance to Wadi Hof. Outbuildings associated with this prehistoric village stand on a plateau at the top of a steep cliff – the only example of its kind in Egypt. The excavations, carried out by ourselves and still unfinished, yielded a new material culture different from that of the south, as at Merimde and the Fayum. The fine-quality pottery, which though monochrome is of a more sophisticated style than that of the other two sites, comprises a great variety of types. The seventeen shapes of vessels – smoothed or polished, red, brown or black – include some with constricted openings, ovoid ones, goblet shapes, cylindrical ones, wide-mouthed or concave ones, conical ones and some jars. The only items resembling those from Merimde and the Fayum are the pots with bosses. Very occasionally calcite or basalt pots were used. The bifacial flint industry does not on the whole differ from those at the previous sites; but the blade industry exhibits some particular features that are new in Egypt. There are ridged-back knives curving towards the point, with a little handle at the base formed from a double notch: these may be relics of 'Natufians' who lived in the area during the previous period. There are also net-sinkers of a type met with in the Khartoumian, the Fayumian and north central Sahara, where a plentiful flake industry also exists. The high-quality bone industry exhibits the classical types: fish-hooks, however, are of horn. Personal adornments are more plentiful, and include gastropod shells from the Red Sea and beads made of ostrich eggshell, bone, stone and the backbones of fish. Fossil nummulites, pierced, served as drop earrings. Galena and resin were imported. Crude palettes for crushing ochre are made of limestone and quartzite. The fauna comprise bovines, goats, antelopes, pigs, hippopotamuses, a species of dog, ostriches, edible snails, tortoises and a large number of fish. Wheat, barley and flax were cultivated. The vegetation included the sycamore, date-palm, tamarisk and esparto grass. Dwellings were of two types: some ovoid, with the roof supported by posts, others round, larger, partly sunk into the ground, and characterized by grain silos everywhere. The dead were buried within the village, more crowded together than at Merimde; and by and large they were all positioned in the same way, in an earthenware jar with their heads pointing to the south and their faces to the west. One corpse, probably that of a chief, was holding a

24. See Chapter 28, p. 715.

wooden sceptre (the sceptre *Ames*) of a shape identified in the north from the Pharaonic period. This culture dates from ?*c.* 3300 before our era.

Omarian B[25] appears and develops at the beginning of Nagada I. It was identified by us east of the preceding site, and differs from it in the funerary practices and the industry. Thus the cemetery was quite separate from the inhabited area, and consisted of burials covered with stone cairns. There is no uniformity about the alignment of the bodies. The inhabited area is much smaller than that of Omarian A: but our researches are still far from complete. Whilst the pottery shows some features in common, the stone tool-kit is entirely different. Based on a flaking technique, it consists of small knives, small flat rounded scrapers and small tranches. Pending the resumption of our work, there is really no way of dating the site in relation to Omarian A.

The Maadian[26] came to light in a so far incomplete excavation of a large inhabited area adjoining two necropolises at Maadi, near Cairo, and also in our own excavation of a third necropolis discovered at Heliopolis, a suburb of Cairo. It is a culture quite unlike any other, does not chronologically directly follow the Omarian, and represents a secondary cultural grouping within the northern group. Its monochrome pottery, mostly smoothed and black or brown in colour, though occasionally red or coated with a white slip, is less fine than that of the Omarian. The commonest types are elongated ovoid vessels with pronounced rims, though there are also small globular-necked pots, often with indented stippled decoration. More characteristic are the pots with circular base-rings, reminiscent of the basalt pots of this type (which are also found here). Very rarely one comes across the brown-decorated pots of Nagada II (probably imported from the south). The pot-bellied vessels with wavy handles found in Nagada II and in Palestine also turn up, probably reflecting the continuation of longstanding cultural contacts between the Nile and Palestine. Likewise the tubular basalt pots are similar to those from Upper Egypt in Nagada I. A fine and plentiful stone flake industry appears in profusion, reworked into tools typical of this culture. Rarer, and perhaps also imported from Nagada I, are the U-shaped bifid knives. There is a dearth of personal adornments, though the few lozenge-shaped slate palettes also come from Nagada I: the others are of quartzite, or are mere flat flint nodules.

An important point is that the Maadian culture, for the first time in the Predynastic cultures of the north of the country, exhibits the use of copper, and on quite a large scale too. (The Fayumian, Merimdian and Omarian knew nothing about copper-working, though in Upper Egypt it was used in much earlier periods.) From the Badarian and particularly the Nagadian

25. Perhaps to be placed in the 'Late Predynastic' (also known as 'Late Gerzean') of Chapter 28, pp. 716–17, but the dating still remains uncertain.

26. Perhaps belongs, at any rate partly, to the 'Late Predynastic' or 'Late Gerzean' (see Chapter 28, pp. 716–17); but it may also be contemporary with the Middle Predynastic or Gerzean (see Chapter 28, pp. 715–16).

onwards, the people of the Nile valley worked the small deposits close at hand in the southern part of the eastern desert. Copper pins, chisels, gimlets, fish-hooks and axes have been found. At the same time there seems to have been some stock-piling of the mineral. At Maadi this metal was beginning to be of prime importance. In our view this is to be attributed to the Maadians' contacts at that time with the mineral deposits in Sinai: and this is confirmed by several features in common with the cultures to the east (in addition to the pottery, which as already mentioned is found also in Palestine, there are certain flint tools and manganese). The fauna comprise bovines, sheep, goats, pigs, hippopotamuses, tortoises and fish; and the plants include wheat, barley, castor-oil plant and esparto grass. The inhabited area yielded a large number of stakes driven into the ground, which might have made it possible to demonstrate the existence of oval huts and traces of rough shelters. More advanced rectangular huts have also been discovered, built of bricks as at Mahasna, and also underground ones with steps leading down to them. Jars sunk into the ground served as grain silos, and circular excavations turn out to be provision stores, often yielding pots as in the Nagadian. Cemeteries away from the villages contained round or oval, never rectangular, graves in which the corpses were doubled up on their sides, most commonly positioned with the heads facing south and their faces to the east: they were often provided with vessels. Gazelles, presumably sacred animals, were also buried in this cemetery, often with many vessels. In the necropolis at Heliopolis, on the edge of the cemetery, we unearthed a row of dogs, aligned at random and without grave-goods: they were presumably intended to act as watch-dogs, as in life.

This culture did not immediately follow the Omarian: it appeared at the end of Nagada I and went on developing until about the end of Nagada II in Upper Egypt.

The continuing use of stone in the Pharaonic period

Having outlined the various trends that formed a patchwork over the Egypt of the predynastic period, let us now summarize their main features and endeavour to account for the divergences between them and explain how they came to converge in the Pharaonic period.

References during the long history of the Pharaohs to two Egypts, north and south, having been united by the legendary Menes, founder of the first dynasty, are based on observable facts that go back to a very remote period of prehistory. Recent excavations are now seen to have confirmed the truth of this tradition and established that the partition between the north and the south existed as far back as the so-called 'Neolithic' stage. The differences were not merely a matter of geography but involved various aspects of human life: indeed, they gave rise to two independent main cultural groups, rooted in different geographical and environmental conditions. The southern group grew up along the narrow Nile corridor, hemmed in on either side by arid cliffs; the northern group took shape on the great fertile fan of the boundless Delta. The northern group exhibits several cultures, similar in their broad lines but differing in detail, and more or less immediately following one after another. The southern one, against a common background, shows much more marked differences than exist between the cultures of the north. These differences come out in the characters of the two main groups, which were later to combine to form Greater Egypt. Thus the north from the earliest stages displays outstanding progress in urban development: in the Fayum we find tiny hamlets, quite close to one another, and at Merimde a proper village covering nearly 2·25 hectares, including houses in rows. El Omari stretches for more than three-quarters of a kilometre, and Maadi for 1·6 kilometres. In the south, on the other hand, given the apparently small number of sites, very few remains of inhabited areas have survived.

Turning now to other evidence of man's way of life and accomplishments in Egypt during this period, pottery in the north, whether brown, black, or red, and despite progressive changes in shape, remains resolutely monochrome, with an almost complete lack of decoration. In the south, on the other hand, the distinctive features are the multiplicity of shapes and the very elaborate decoration, and of course the famous black-edged vessels. Though the pottery in the north is somewhat inferior, the same does not hold good for the flint industry, which shows an extraordinary improvement in workmanship – not that the finish of some pieces in the south does not reach a high standard. In the realm of pure art the north is completely poverty-stricken, in contrast with the great flowering in the south. This shows itself from the Badarian onwards in splendid bone, ivory and earthenware figures, and also in everyday objects such as combs, ladles, drop earrings, beautiful palettes for grinding cosmetics and carved green schist amulets.

Thus we see that there are big differences in many fields between the two parts of Egypt. We may say that whilst the north is more advanced in terms of the economy and of urbanization, the south achieved a very advanced level of artistic skill, foreshadowing the Pharaonic period. It was presumably the unification of these two different but complementary cultures that was responsible for the greatness of Egypt of the Pharaohs.

But the advent of the historical period, which saw the introduction of writing, the unification of Egypt under a single ruler, and progress in the technology of metal, nevertheless did not change certain features of the way of life of the Nile valley peoples. We refer in particular to the persistence of the use of flint, a highly efficient material abundant in the area, which continued throughout the Pharaonic period. Indeed, it is noteworthy that mastery of flint-working actually reached its peak under the early dynasties, as witness the superb so-called 'sacrificial' knives from the royal tombs at Abydos in Upper Egypt and Sakkara and Helwan near Cairo: the perfection of their workmanship and their great size are astonishing. Remains of dwellings from this period also yielded a complete set of domestic flint tools, only a very few copper objects being found at Hierakonpolis and El Kab in Upper Egypt and at Wadi Hammamat in the eastern desert. Among the Middle Kingdom remains of ancient Thebes at Karnak, recently unearthed, we found a great abundance of flint tools; and they are no different in manufacturing technique or range of types from those used during the upper Palaeolithic and Mesolithic. There are even many burins and some microliths. Moreover our systematic exploration since 1971 on the Thebes mound at Luxor has revealed that of 200 flint factories over half are not prehistoric at all, but date from the New Kingdom. They supplied the capital with large quantities of tools produced by a cruder technique than that of the Middle Kingdom: the output consisted almost entirely of knife-blades and sickle-heads, the latter still persisting into the Late Period.

At the time of the Pharaohs flint was not used only for household tools. Flint crescents were used to drill schist bracelets at Wadi Hammamat, these being a type of adornment used from the Early Historical Period up to the end of the Archaic Period. At the end of the third dynasty they were used at one stage for cutting up the blocks of stone for the step pyramid of the Pharaoh Soser at Sakkara. Soft stone vessels were hollowed out by means of these same tools in workshops in the Fayum, close to the calcite deposits, until the Old Kingdom. From the earliest dynasties until the end of the New Kingdom, Egyptian archers' arrows were tipped with flint stones. Those of the Pharaoh Tutankhamun (twenty-eighth dynasty) were made of glass, a luxury material as efficient as flint.

Pharaonic Egypt also used less fragile minerals than flint for making tools for particular purposes. Picks and mallets for work in mines and quarries, which had necks to take the hafts, were made of hard stones during the Old Kingdom, but were cruder and made of silicified limestones under the Middle and New Kingdoms. The Old Kingdom funerary hypogeums at Giza, near Cairo, the Middle Kingdom ones in Middle Egypt and the New Kingdom ones in the mound at Thebes were excavated and built with these crude stone implements.

In Egyptian Nubia and part of Sudanese Nubia, now under water, archaeological research had not gone far enough by the end of the rescue operations: and this deprives us permanently of much valuable information about the past of these areas, *inter alia* about the survival of the use of stone in the historical periods. But material retrieved from a Nubian C-Group village (Middle Kingdom) at Sebua has enabled us to identify a range of flint blades, lamellae and sickle-heads. The latter, no doubt imported from Egypt, are identical in every respect with those of the same period recently discovered at Karnak, as mentioned above. Moreover at Amada, another C-Group village also in Egyptian Nubia which we excavated some time ago, further proof is to be found of the stone age's survival into the age of metal. As at Sebua, there were flint blades, lamellae and sickle heads of

Egyptian origin: but in addition we discovered on the Amada site, cheek by jowl with this imported stone industry, tiny agate and carnelian transverse arrow-heads and polished hard-stone axes of local manufacture.

Turning to Sudanese Nubia, excavations at the Egyptian fortress of Mirgissa yielded weapons, as was to be expected. They dated from the twenty-eighth dynasty, and included arrows of the classical type, that is, tipped with stone heads of the type described above. What was new, however, was that the lance-points were not metal, as in Pharaonic Egypt at that period, but flint, of a perfect bifacial trim similar to that used in the Neolithic period. The revival of this technique was intended to reproduce as closely as possible the shape of metal lance-points; and the reason for reverting to a method of manufacture forgotten for thousands of years was presumably the difficulty of obtaining the metal (or ready-made lances) in this remote area at the time in question.

Conclusion

Having thus sketched a broad outline of the history of the first people to inhabit the Nile valley, it remains to take stock, assemble the solid evidence gained and point out the many large gaps that remain.

As regards the most remote periods, very recent discoveries confirm the presence of the most primitive known man, Oldowan, not only in South and East Africa but also in the northern part of the Nile valley. This we know from plentiful stone tools: but it would be desirable to continue research to fill in the palaeontological record, so far represented only by a solitary human tooth. Similar exploration of this period is called for in the Sudanese sector, for this is a point of contact with Ethiopia, where remarkable finds have been made for this period.

The typology of the stone tool-kit of the Early Stone Age has been thoroughly studied almost only in the Wadi Halfa area. The Thebes area has furnished data on one of the earliest phases. But there are manifold problems still to be solved, among them those concerning the races of man during this period.

Turning to the Middle Stone Age, stone tool evidence is there in plenty all along the Nile valley. Again, progress has been made in the Wadi Halfa area, which has improved our knowledge of the morphology of stone tools in that particular sector. The abundant harvest of finds from the Thebes mound is still being studied, and will make possible useful comparisons with the material from the south. The fragments of an occipital bone are still the only human remains so far unearthed. In the Libyan desert north-west of Wadi Halfa a stone tool-kit was found for the first time associated with fauna. Enormous areas of the Sudan still remain to be explored for this period.

The Aterian, which is almost contemporary, has also very recently been reported in the desert north-west of Abu Simbel. Associated with fauna, this industry from western North Africa spread very belatedly into this area. It would be interesting to see how it compares in date with other discoveries in Egypt, and whether it could have influenced typically Egyptian industries.

Turning to the Late Stone Age and the Mesolithic, only finds from well-defined sectors have yielded much new information. But it may be that in the absence of stratigraphical evidence there has been an undue tendency to coin new nomenclature on the strength of sometimes imperfectly worked out statistical studies and physico-chemical tests.

Definite progress has been made as regards the Neolithic (a term that has no precise meaning in Egypt) and the Predynastic along the Nile valley. The sites of the Egyptian southern cultural group have yielded a plethora of material, mainly from the cemeteries. Research on a wider scale is needed on the inhabited areas: this would yield fuller information on dwellings, everyday household pottery and stone tools.

The sites in northern Egypt have not been exhaustively dug because of the large areas they cover, and hence are only known from partial reports. Despite this they have furnished much fuller information than the contemporary sites in the south, as a result of investigations into both dwellings and cemeteries. It therefore seems desirable that exploration, which for various reasons has been suspended for some years in this northern part of Egypt, should be resumed in order to complete the picture.

Turning to Sudanese Nubia, several specific civilizations belonging to these periods have been painstakingly studied, the most representative so far being apparently the Khartoumian and the Shaheinabian. But an enormous amount of work still remains to be done, for dozens of sites have been located apparently relating to these cultures or to different phases, and await the attentions of excavators. The object of such investigation would of course be to help fit together the links in the chain of African history before the Pharaonic period.

PLATE 25.1 *Flint javelin heads from Mirgissa, Sudan; excavations led by J. Vercoutter* (French Archaeological Mission to the Sudan)

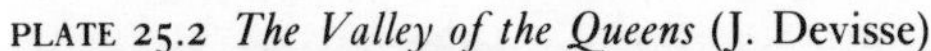

PLATE 25.2 *The Valley of the Queens* (J. Devisse)

26 African prehistoric art

J. KI-ZERBO

Introduction

As soon as man appears on the scene there are tools, but there is also art. The words *Homo faber, Homo artifex* hold good for African prehistory.

For thousands of years, prehistoric remains on this continent have been subjected to the depredations of man and the elements. Even in prehistoric times people sometimes perpetrated acts of destruction through ritual iconoclasm. Foreign troops, colonial settlers, tourists, oil men and indigenous inhabitants still engage in the depredations and 'bare-faced looting' to which L. Balout refers in his preface to the booklet produced as a guide to the exhibition on 'The Sahara before the desert'.[1]

By and large, prehistoric art is found mainly in the high plateaux and uplands of Africa. The mountain ranges, and the depressions, river basins and forest lowlands of the equatorial zone are far less rich in this respect.

In the areas where the largest number of finds occur, sites are mainly located in cliffs on the edges of the uplands, especially where they overhang the thalwegs of existing or fossil water courses. The two most important areas are the Sahara and southern Africa. In the zone bounded on the north by the Atlas mountains, on the east by the Red Sea, on the south by the tropical forest and on the west by the Atlantic, hundreds of sites have been found, containing tens or perhaps hundreds of thousands of engravings and paintings. Some of them are now known throughout the world, thanks to the work of French, Italian, English, American and, increasingly, African prehistorians. Examples are found in southern Oran and the Tassili N'Ajjer (e.g. Jabbaren, Sefar, Tissoukai and Djanet) in Algeria; in southern Morocco; in the Fezzan (Libya); in Aïr and Ténéré (Niger); in Tibesti

1. H. Lhote tells of the French troops in Algeria in 1954 who put a coat of oil paint over the magnificent elephant panel at Hadjra Mahisserat so as to be able to photograph it better. Others riddled with machine-gun bullets the near wall of the great scorpion carving at Garet Et-Taleb. At Beni Ounif the carved coping stones were taken down and used as building material; and so on. See H. Lhote, 1976. But even some scholars are not blameless: many pieces were cut up and shipped to Vienna by Emil Holub at the end of the nineteenth century.

(Chad); in Nubia; in the highlands of Ethiopia and in the Dhar Tichitt (Mauritania). The other main area is in the tapering part of southern Africa bounded by the Indian Ocean and the Atlantic which includes Lesotho, Botswana, Malawi, Zimbabwe, Namibia, Angola and the Republic of South Africa, with particularly significant finds in the Orange Free State, the Vaal river area and the Transvaal. There the paintings are in rock shelters and the engravings in the open. Caves like the Cango caves in the Cape Province are rare. There are few African countries in which traces of art (sometimes, admittedly, not prehistoric) have not been discovered, and exploration is far from complete.

As to why there should have been this flowering in the deserts and steppes, one reason is that at the period in question they were nothing of the kind. When they became so, this in itself, plus the dryness of the air, helped to preserve them and turn them into natural museums. In the Sahara, for instance, artefacts have been found that had lain undisturbed for thousands of years. As to why it should have occurred on the edges of the upland valleys, the reason is that these were the best habitats most easily defensible and within reach of water and game. For instance, in the Tassili, which consists of sandstone rocks overlaying the crystalline core of the Ahaggar mountains, with 500-metre cliffs to the south, the alternation of heat and cold (which is most marked at ground level) plus the surface runoff have eroded the base of the rocks, producing huge overhangs and shelters rising above the thalwegs of the rivers. One of the most impressive examples is the rock shelter at Tin Tazarift. Elsewhere, the tabular sandstone was carved and abraded by wind erosion into natural galleries which man was quick to make use of. Such is the environment so faithfully and vividly depicted in the masterpieces of African rock art.

Chronology and development

Dating methods and problems

The application of the stratigraphical method to the natural rock is often of little use here, since long exposure to the moist prehistoric climate caused deep leaching of the layers covering the shelter floors. Nevertheless, in southern Africa, engravings are sometimes found underneath paintings. Clues can be obtained from the debris of organic colouring matter which has fallen from the walls, into an undisturbed layer, but the disturbances, sometimes deliberate, which these layers have undergone make even relative dating from them a highly confusing business.

We sometimes resort to studying comparative colour changes in the patina of the paintings and the underlying rock. This method, which is appropriate because it takes account of the subject itself, starts from the assumption that the most recent patinas are those which are the clearest and which differ most from the natural rock. Patina formation in fact takes place gradually on all rocks, including white sandstone. It is a process analogous to laterization in which oxides and carbonates that have infiltrated in solution as a result of rain or humidity are brought to the surface by capillary action, and then as a result of evaporation form a solid crust which becomes darker with age. Comparison with the natural rock should thus theoretically provide a basis for comparative dating, but there are numerous pitfalls. Everything depends on the consistency of the rock, on whether or not it has been exposed to sun and wind, and so on. This method of dating can at best give only relative results.[2]

Sometimes it is possible to estimate the age of a picture from the fauna depicted in it, since not all types lived in the same major periods. *Bubalus,* for instance, is a very early species, now extinct and known only from its fossil remains. These animals could, however, quite well have been depicted as reminders of a bygone age. Nor, as we shall see, is style a reliable guide – far from it. In the beginning, it is true, observation seems to have been what mattered most, and the result was a characteristic semi-naturalistic approach. In addition, *Bubalus* carvings in the Sahara are in general earlier than the paintings. Buried artefacts bearing the same type of decoration as in the paintings are normally contemporary with them, but there is absolutely no universal rule about it. Another method sometimes used is relative dating on the basis of overlays, lines that obliterate other lines being the more recent. However, overlays are not by any means found everywhere and the weathering of the rock and the fading of the pigments often make interpretation risky and contradictory.[3]

There remains the radio-carbon method of dating, which of course is ideal, but it can only rarely be used, for the reasons mentioned above. One also has to be very cautious because paint debris could have been in contact with recent organic matter, or a charcoal fragment could have been the result of a fire caused by lightning. The number of such datings is nevertheless gradually growing. By way of example, charcoal from a deep layer at Meniet (Mouydir) in the central Sahara yielded a date of 5410 ± 300 b.p.

Politics may also become involved with dating. Thus Afrikaner observers are very loth to accept the very great age of Africa's indigenous artistic civilization, and tend to shorten its development by telescoping it or by mechanically applying methods of assessment used for European rock paintings. In this way, they put the Drakensberg paintings later than the

2. The shape of the groove in carvings degenerates in time, as a result of physical and chemical processes, from the original sharp V to a wide-mouthed V and then becomes flattened out, but these changes give only a very rough indication of age.

3. J. D. Lajoux, 1977, applied the latest photographic techniques to the paintings at Inahouanrhat (Tassili). Red figures appeared to have been painted over a greenish-brown masked woman but this turned out not to be entirely so. The woman's white ornaments had in fact been added later, over the red figures. Australian rock paintings (*wonjina*) are commonly repainted to freshen them up, the aborigines meanwhile telling legendary tales to conjure up rain. L. Frobenius also observed this practice among young people in Senegal.

seventeenth century, that is, long after the arrival of the Bantu. Now even if we disregard the fact that some South African rock art depicts fauna that dates from much earlier in this area, it seems hardly likely that the San would have waited for their wars with the Bantu to develop an art-form requiring at least a minimum of stability for its practice. We therefore need to re-examine the question of periods.

Periods

If we are to fit prehistoric art finds into an intelligible time scale, our first approach must be geological and ecological since the environment, for peoples without our technological adjuncts, was more of a constraint than it is today and both provided and imposed the general framework of existence. The biotope in particular conditioned the life of the species represented, including man himself, his techniques and his styles. Although it is true, as J. Ruffie puts it that 'man was originally a tropical animal' from Africa, the temperate conditions in the north after the end of the ice ages enabled the colonization of Europe to take place which culminated in the splendid flowering of rock art in underground galleries forty centuries ago. African rock art is much later. Admittedly some authors, such as E. Holm, consider that its origins go back to the Mesolithic, but in essence it dates from the Neolithic.[4]

It has become customary to call the major periods of rock art by the name of an animal which thus provides a typological reference point. Four major series are thus named after the *Bubalus*, the Ox, the Horse and the Camel.

The *Bubalus* (*Bubalus antiquus*) was a kind of enormous buffalo which, according to the palaeontologists, dates from the beginning of the Quaternary. It is depicted from the beginning of rock art (about 9000 b.p.) to around the year 6000. This period is also characterized by elephants and

4. The Sahara Neolithic is being put further and further back in the light of recent finds. A Neolithic pottery deposit in the Ahaggar has been radio-carbon dated to 8450 b.p., which makes it virtually contemporary with Near Eastern Neolithic. See also the dates suggested by D. Olderogge in Chapter 11 for the Nubian sites of Ballana (12050 b.p.) and Tochke (12550 b.p.). A rock shelter at I-n-Itinen, with paintings of oxen, has yielded food fragments. The earliest hearth has been radio-carbon dated from 4860 ± 250 b.p. In the Acacous massif (Libya), F. Mori found a fragment of fallen wall between two layers containing remains of hearths, with painting dating from the Ox period. The two layers having been dated, it materializes that the piece of wall goes back to 4730 b.p. (see H. Lhote, 1976, pp. 102 and 109). A date of 7450 b.p. has also been given for the middle Ox period at Acacous: cf. H. J. Hugot, 1974, p. 274. J. D. Clark has likewise reported a date of 6310 ± 250 b.p. from Solwezi (Zambia). On the other hand the date of 11250 ± 400 b.p. given in J. T. Louw's thesis for the Mattes Shelter (Cape Province) is regarded as precarious. At the extraordinary site of Ti-n Hanakaten, there are frescoes that can be correlated with a whole series of Neolithic and later levels containing skeletons, i.e. an easily datable human stratigraphy, even including an Aterian level (see 'Découverte exceptionnelle au Tassili', in *Archeologia*, 94, May 1976, pp. 28 and 59).

rhinoceroses. The ox is either *Bos ibericus* (or *brachyceros*), with short, stout horns, or *Bos africanus*, with a magnificent lyre-shaped pair of horns. It appears around the year 6000 b.p.

The horse (*Equus caballus*), sometimes pulling a chariot, makes its appearance about the year 6000 b.p.[5] The 'flying gallop' gait, whilst not realistic, is naturalistic on the western track from Morocco to the Sudan, whereas on the eastern 'road' from the Fezzan[6] it is highly stylized. By now we are well into the period of history when the hippopotamus disappears from rock paintings, no doubt denoting the end of perennial water. The camel brings up the rear of this historical caravan. Introduced into Egypt by the Persian conquest about 500 before our era it is common at about the beginning of the Christian era.[7]

For the purposes of prehistory, it is mainly the first two periods and the beginning of the Horse period that are of interest to us here since they cover the period of maximum activity in the vast area that was later to become the Sahara desert. Scholars obsessed with chronological divisions argue over the sub-periods to be established within the main periods, but discoveries are still being made and we must not be in too much of a hurry to affix rigid labels to whole sections of what is after all a largely unknown past. It is more a case, so to speak, of very ill-defined animal dynasties in the iconography, with a great deal of overlapping. For example the ram, classified as later than *Bubalus* and the elephant, sometimes seems to be contemporary with them. It appears on the same walls, portrayed by the same techniques and showing the same patina. Perhaps it was not yet domesticated, or kept in captivity for a religious purpose. Similarly, the great engraved oxen at Dider, in the Tassili (one of which is over 5 metres tall, with great lyre-shaped horns incorporating a symbol), seem to be contemporary with *Bubalus*. Some scholars place the ox wearing a pendant at Oued Djerat in the Bubalus period. Moreover, new animals increasingly appear on the scene, like the owls at Tan-Terirt, some forty of which coincide with the figures of oxen.

For areas other than the Sahara, the major periods are often later in date. They are defined by different criteria which also vary from author to author, especially as authors sometimes base their division into periods on techniques, genres and styles.[8]

5. The arrival of the horse in Africa is too often linked with that of the Hyksos in Egypt. On this point see J. Ki-Zerbo, 1978, p. 99.

6. On the 'chariot roads' see R. Mauny, 1961.

7. The camel nevertheless seems to have been known since the Pharaonic period. Cf. E. Demougeot, 1960, pp. 209–47.

8. In southern Africa, some authors distinguish two main periods on the basis of the shape of the groove, the attack technique (incision, hammering whether obvious or otherwise, polishing, and so on) and the fauna depicted. The first main period comprises two stages, and the second four.

Techniques, genres and styles

Techniques

Engravings

In general, where both exist, engravings are earlier than paintings, and the best engraving technique is found in the earliest periods. Engraving was done in the softer sandstone rocks, and in granite and quartzite as well, by means of a sharpened stone struck with a Neolithic hammerstone, specimens of which have been found near the carvings. With only this minimal equipment, the precision of the technique is brilliant. The elephant at Bardai (Chad) is delineated with a single light line. It is hardly more than a sketch, but it brings out the essentials. The elephants at In Galjeien (Mathendous) and In Habeter II, on the other hand, are deeply cut with a heavy lifelike line, and so is the rhinoceros at Gonoa (Tibesti). The groove is either V-shaped, or shaped like a U and taken down to a depth of about a centimetre. The notches were made either with a stone axe or a piece of very hard wood, damp sand possibly being used as an abrasive. Sometimes there is a combination of techniques with, for instance, delicate use of the hammer plus a V-shaped incision. Here and there, the preliminary marker-holes have left traces of roughness at the bottom of the groove. The final polishing was accompanied by light hammering. Making these engravings must sometimes have called for distinct athletic ability. At Oued Djerat, for instance, there is an elephant 4·5 metres high, and the beginnings of a rhinoceros 7·5 metres long.

In central and southern Africa, engravings with broadly incised outlines are thought to be associated with religious purposes, whilst delicately grooved engravings possibly denote an initiatory or instructional aim. Delicate effects are achieved by hollowing and highly polishing some surfaces between the outlines to represent the shades of animals' coats or their loads. This technique foreshadows the bas-reliefs of Pharaonic Egypt. Indeed, the figure is sometimes produced by engraving it entirely in intaglio, like a cameo. The natural rock is used very appositely. For instance, a giraffe is carved on an oblong block of diabase whose shape it exactly fits (western Transvaal). Similarly in the Leeufontein area, a rhinoceros is carved on a rock with a rough surface and angular ridges that precisely reproduce the animal's carapace. At Maretjiesfontein Hill (western Transvaal), a quagga has been engraved and stippled on a piece of diabase. Its lower jaw coincides with a slight bulge in the stone which vividly represents the reality. In the Transvaal Museum there is a splendid image of a male antelope whose mane is rendered by dotted stripes, while its frontal tuft is represented by delicately incised lines. The colours of the interior of the rock (blue) and its surface (red ochre) are used to perfection to bring out the contrasts. Another masterpiece of prehistoric African stone engravers is the group of giraffes at Blaka, with their spotted coats, their legs in such natural attitudes and even their waving tails. But technique tended on the whole to deteriorate. By the so-called Ox period, carvings are already often mediocre as, for instance, in the case of the giraffes at El Greiribat, produced by coarse heavy stippling.

Paintings

These should not be considered in isolation from engravings. At Tissoukai, for instance, there are outlines sketched on the walls, suggesting that the artists first engraved and then painted. Here again, artistic work sometimes called for feats of athletic prowess. At Oued Djerat there is a Horse period painting 8·5 metres long on a steeply sloping ceiling, and at some of the Tassili sites, such as Tissoukai, paintings begin nearly 4 metres from the ground, as though it was wished to avoid the lower levels within people's reach. This necessitated the use of crude ladders or even scaffolding. Paintings are either in monochrome or polychrome.[9] At lower Mertoutek, purple kaolin is used and in the shelter on the south face of Enneri Blaka, red ochre kaolin rather like blood. Elsewhere, a dazzling array of colours is to be found and cunning combinations of shades to recreate the appearance and balance of reality. This necessitated a quite complex associated technology and traces of workshops have been found. At I-n-Itinen, for instance, little flat grindstones have been dug up along with tiny grinders to reduce the rock to powder and also little bowls of pigment. The pigments have turned out to be very durable, and retain an amazing freshness and vividness to this day. The relatively extensive range of colours is based on certain basic tones such as red and brown, obtained from iron oxide ochres; white, obtained from kaolin, animal droppings, latex or zinc oxide; and black, extracted from charcoal, ground calcined bones, or from smoke and burnt fat. There are also yellow, green, violet and other colours. These ingredients were ground to a fine powder with a pestle and mortar, mixed together, and then made up with a liquid, perhaps milk, the casein in which is an excellent binder, dripping, or else white of egg, honey or cooked bone-marrow. This explains the brightness of the tints after all these thousands of years. The colours were applied with the fingers, with feathers, with straw or chewed wood spatulas, or with brushes made of animal hairs fixed to sticks with tendons. They were also sprayed on by squirting the liquid from the mouth. It was this last process that was responsible for the outlines of hands still to be seen on rock faces and which are a kind of authenticating signature on these masterpieces. Sometimes corrections are made without erasing the original lines: giving oxen with four horns, men with three arms, and so forth. Here again, the natural features of the rock are very cleverly used as for instance at Tihilahi, where a crevice in the rock becomes the water-hole where the herd is preparing to drink.[10]

9. In southern Africa, mainly monochrome paintings are found in the Transvaal and Namibia, whereas in Botswana, Griqualand and Natal, paintings tend to be polychrome.

10. Illustration, J. D. Lajoux, 1977, p. 151.

Jewellery

The art of jewellery calls for no less advanced techniques, in fact rather the reverse. Some beads are made from cornelian, an exceptionally hard stone. The techniques used by jewellers can be reconstructed by a study of the debris left at different stages of the work. First, flat discs were made by percussion flaking followed by grinding. Then a large needle, square in section, was chipped out of a flint core and used as a graving tool. Its point was driven into the centre of the disc on both sides in turn so as to produce two indentations back to back. Then the most delicate part of the job was to make two holes meet. For this, the flint stylus did duty as a twist drill, and with the help of some fine sand mixed with plant resin, the central hole was drilled right through. Other equally refractory stones such as amazonite, haematite and chalcedony were also worked, as were bone and ivory, to make pendants, bracelets and anklets. Pumice stone was used to polish them. At Ti-n-Hanakaten, some microdiorite drill bits were found among ostrich-eggshell beads.

Pottery

Clay for pottery was prepared with a binder made from cow dung. Pots were made by the coil method, that is, by taking a long rope of clay and coiling it round and round on itself, smoothing it meanwhile with the fingers and a smoothing-stick. The necks of pots are of various shapes: spiral, flared, slanted and lopsided. The firing must have been impeccable, to judge by the delicate shades ranging from pink to dark brown. Slip glazing was known, as was the vegetable glaze still used in Africa today for pottery and for varnishing or ornamenting the floors, walls and roofs of houses. The marvellous decorations were done with bone combs, fish-bones, and the imprint of ears of corn, rope or seeds, with enormous imagination and a great profusion of motifs. At Oued Eched, in northern Mali, potters' kilns grouped together in a place apart testify to the prestige of this craft, whose practitioners were no less skilled than their fellow-potters at Esh Shaheinab, in what is now the modern state of the Sudan.[11]

Sculpture

Sculpture is also represented usually in miniature like the ruminant lying down in the Oued Amazzar (Tassili), or an ox lying down at Tarzerouck (Ahaggar mountains). At Adjefou there is a little hare with its long ears laid back along its body; at Tamentit in the Touat, a striking head of a ram; at Ouan Sidi, in the Great Eastern Erg, a stone sculpture of a human figure; at Tabalbalet, a splendid stylized head of an owl; and at Ti-n-Hanakaten, clay figurines have been found representing stylized birds, women and cattle, one of which still has a pair of twigs in lieu of horns.

11. Cf. H. J. Hugot, 1974, p. 155.

Genres and styles

In broad terms, three main genres and styles may be distinguished in the Sahara, more or less coinciding with the periods mentioned above. The first is the archaic, monumental in size with symbolism overshadowing semi-naturalist representation. Man still seems to be suffering under the impact of his first shock at the might of the animal kingdom, which must be subdued – if necessary by magic. Two stages may be distinguished. The first is the *Bubalus* style, centred mainly on southern Oran, the Tassili and the Fezzan, with carvings characterized by acute observation. The subjects are usually large animals, often standing alone. The semi-naturalistic treatment, plain and austere, confines itself to essential outlines which are drawn with masterly skill. Examples are the rhinoceros and pelicans at Oued Djerat (Tassili), the elephant at Bardai (Chad) and the elephant at In Galjeien in the Oued Mathendous. The second stage is characterized by the presence of antelopes and moufflons, mostly painted. Men are everywhere, men with round heads. The treatment is still semi-naturalistic, sometimes symbolist; but the line is lively rather than austere, and may betray excitement and even pathos. Magic is not far away and can be sensed in the animal totems, masked men and ritual dances. Subjects do not stand alone. There are small pictures, but also continuous friezes and frescoes, the largest in the world. This style, which is centred in the Tassili, produces scenes depicting moufflons with powerful horns, and masked dancers as at Sefar (taken by J. Lajoux to be the eponymous site) and the priestess or White Lady of Ouanrhet.

The second main genre consists of naturalistic paintings and carvings of small subjects, either alone or in groups. The treatment is frankly descriptive. There is already a feeling that man is on the move and that he dominates and controls the cattle, dogs, sheep and goats. More colours are used. It is the Sahara of villages and encampments. The eponymous site is taken to be Jabbaren.

The third genre is stylized, symbolist or abstract. Earlier techniques are retained, but often deteriorate. There is, however, no general decline. The engraving in particular degenerates into blurred outlines, with dotting and rough stippling, but in painting the delicate line, though inferior in some respects to the strong, austere line of the earlier period, is better for catching movement, sometimes in three-quarter profile, and lends itself better to stylization and new forms of expression. For instance, the man at Gonoa (Saharan Chad) is outlined with an elegance reminiscent of a pen-and-ink drawing with eyes, pupils, hair, mouth and nose represented with almost photographic accuracy. The use of washes also makes possible the rendering of very subtle nuances, as in the case of the antelope calf at Iheren (Tassili), with its unsteady legs, coming to suck its mother while she almost tenderly lowers her head to it. This genre lends itself well to the stylizing of horses and chariots and subsequently of the dromedary, but it also lends itself to the stylization of man, who becomes two isosceles triangles as at Assedjen Ouan Mellen, or has nothing but a long neck where his head should be. The tendency is thus both to the mannerisms of pencil drawing and also to somewhat slapdash stylized geometrical representation which, by the end of the period, occurs alongside characters from the Numidian and the Tifinagh alphabets. It is evident from many details, such as Arab saddles with cantles, which are obviously later than the seventh century of our era, that such compositions fall well outside the realm of prehistory.

Some comments are called for on these genres which follow one another without sharp chronological dividing lines. The second stage of the archaic style, in particular, is heterogeneous and the ambling ox at Sefar bears no relation to the heads with masks and symbolic motifs. There are, in addition, certain stereotypes which straddle several genres and styles, such as the pictoral convention by which oxen are depicted with the head in profile and the horns full face, as at Ouan Bender. There are also stereotyped gestures and postures, like those of the herdsmen with one arm outstretched and the other akimbo. Lastly, there are very obvious regional motifs, such as the ram in southern Oran, and the spiral in the Tassili which does not appear in the Fezzan or southern Oran. On the other hand, sexual themes are particularly characteristic of the Fezzan and the Tassili.

Turning to other forms of art, we find that geometrical ornamentation on ostrich eggs occurs in jewellery in the upper Capsian, but it is above all to the Sudanic tradition of the Neolithic period that we owe the tools and weapons, the splendid mottled flint brooches polished with green and dark red, the pottery with wavy line decoration, and the Tichitt arrow-heads with their meticulously polished denticulations and their perfect triangular shape.

In other parts of Africa, the typology is still being worked out. In Namibia, for instance, one authority claims twenty different-coloured strata and styles, with four main stages: (a) a stage with large animals treated in an archaic style, without representations of human figures; (b) small panels with representations of human figures; (c) a monochrome stage with hunting scenes and lively ritual dances; and (d) a polychrome period in which the heights of artistry are reached, as in the Philipp Cave shelter (Damaraland) and the Brandberg paintings, which have been dated to the year 1500. Frobenius distinguished two main styles of rock art in southern Africa. In the southern part, from the Transvaal to the Cape and from the eastern Drakensberg to the coast of Namibia, he saw a naturalistic trend in which animals predominate, often treated individually and with consummate skill, the folds in a pachyderm's hide and the stripes on a zebra's coat being accurately rendered. But the style is stiff and cold, even though the paintings are in subtle polychrome, the colours being rubbed on with remarkable dexterity. There are set-piece hunting scenes, dances, processions and gatherings. From the central Transvaal to the Zambezi, on the other hand (i.e. Zambia, Zimbabwe and Malawi), the painting is in monochrome, essentially the red and ochre of iron oxides, sometimes verging on purple. The natural rock is granite, as against sandstone in the previous case. The technique is that of drawing, and is as realistic as the washes in the south, but it is not a mechanical type of realism. Landscapes are realistic but their representation reveals a tremendously fertile imagination.[12]

Man makes his appearance as broad-shouldered and wasp-waisted – in a word, wedge-shaped. Seen from in front, his limbs are depicted in profile, as in Egyptian bas-reliefs. In the south, in the hunting and battle scenes that are sometimes intermingled, the people are more natural, with more rounded limbs, whereas in the north we find solemn funeral scenes (perhaps royal obsequies) with people giving vent to poignant displays of grief. Animals, as for instance in the great cave at Inoro, file past not like a well-marshalled Noah's ark but like some weird bestiary. There are gigantic birds with beaks like crocodiles' jaws, giant elephants with crenellated backs, and two-headed animals. Sometimes myths, like that of rain, are elaborated. The background of these grotesque frescoes consists of landscapes, in which stylized rocks, botanically identifiable trees and lakes full of fish are comprehensibly arranged. This is the style in Zimbabwe, less animated than in the south, but fraught with stormy or poignant emotions. According to Frobenius, the wedge style was associated with a highly developed civilization, and we know that such civilizations existed in the Zimbabwe area. He also thought that this austere, angular style gave way to a more rounded, suppler, more mannered and more effeminate style as the societies degenerated.[13]

In Upper Volta the rock carvings in the north of the country (for example, at Aribinda) are semi-naturalistic or stylized, whilst in the south they tend to be geometrical. There are also paintings in the caves of the Banfora cliffs.

In the Central African Republic excavation has revealed sites with evidence of human occupation from before the Acheulian up to the iron age. Five centres of rock art have been identified: the Toulou shelter in the Ndele area, occupied from prehistoric times up to the present, with very early red stylized figures and white figures with their arms akimbo; the Koumbala shelter; and the sites with carvings at Mpatou Springs and Lengo (Mbomou). This tradition bears little relation to that of the Sahara, but rather more to the pictures found in East Africa and southern Africa.[14]

12. By and large, the representation of wild animals and animals in general is naturalistic for magical reasons since the picture must reproduce the object of the ritual as accurately as possible. Human figures, on the other hand, are often deliberately diagrammatical, since the point is to shield them from magical influences.

13. Cf. E. Haberland, 1973, p. 27.

14. Cf. R. de Bayle des Hermens, 1976.

Motives and meanings

The term 'petroglyph' has been coined for rock pictures. More than any other in fact, this kind of art is a sign language, that is, a bridge between reality and idea. It is a set of graphic symbols and to read it one needs a key.

When it comes to explaining it properly, the main drawback is our ignorance of the society that produced it. That is why it is important not to make over-hasty interpretations by omitting the descriptive stage in which the sign language itself is subjected to formal analysis. In very many instances, the actual description is already couched in descriptive terms. The ideal thing might be to adopt a statistical approach, collecting quantitative and qualitative data collected for as many pictures as possible, so as to allow of a comparative analysis.[15] This would make it possible to tell, for instance, whether the sign systems found in a particular number of pictures conformed to any general principle in either time or space. The more thorough the data compiled, the more plausible the reconstructed development pattern would be. In any event, hypotheses stemming from formal analysis of this kind would only be borne out if they tallied with the mass of data which goes to make up the whole social system in question. A prehistoric picture is, after all, only a minute component of an information macro-system, in other words, of a culture containing many other components. At this level of analysis, we begin to realize how complex a system of signs we need to grasp the real meaning of a work of art. Quite apart from this, a work of art may have a concealed meaning as well as its obvious one, for a sign is not only a sign of something but also a sign which means something to somebody and, as such, is a symbol. We have to graduate, therefore, from morphology to social syntax, and be capable of taking the step forward from the point where we make a straightforward comment on a purely representational picture, in which the meaning is plain, to that where we can decipher the coded message conveyed by an abstract picture. This is where reference to the cultural context is indispensable since the thing signified is represented differently in different cultures. The remoter a sign is from the object it denotes, the more culture-specific and the more significant it is. The same piece of onomatopoeia recurring in several languages is not characteristic of any one of them, for it merely reflects the same sound in nature, but the same is not true of a word in any given language. Great art collections may perhaps be regarded as transmitting stations sending out cultural messages, but the question then arises of what the receivers are. The transmitters may often have broadcast primarily for the benefit of those who set them up, as well as for their society as a whole, and we have not been left enough other remains to enable us to read and decipher their messages. In short, the problems and methods of

15. This quantitative approach might conceivably lend itself to computer analysis, subject to all the appropriate precautions. On this topic see the work of A. Striedter at the Frobenius Institute in Frankfurt, of which Professor Haberland is the Director.

artistic exploration must in the end come down to the description of the types of culture underlying these partial manifestations. If we can define the cultures that were their natural element, we can then attempt to reconstruct the historical framework into which they fitted.

This is why providing African rock paintings with captions such as 'Justices of the Peace', 'The White Lady', 'man pulling teeth', 'Josephine sold by her sisters', 'Martians', and suchlike, distort them from the outset, since they impose on them an interpretation of a single observer from another civilization with quite different symbols and codes.[16] African prehistoric art must be interpreted by reference to indigenous values and it is only when the local environment of time, space and culture fails to provide an answer to a problem that we are entitled to look elsewhere for the solution.

Having said this, I suggest that there are two main approaches to the interpretation of prehistoric art, the idealist approach and the materialist one. From the idealist standpoint this type of art is mainly an expression of the view of the world of the people who created this art. Only a knowledge of this view can provide an explanation of the subject-matter and also of its treatment. 'The art of southern Africa', writes Erik Holm, 'is seen in its true light if we regard it as the expression of religious fervour and the urge to transcend reality. This was the metaphysics of primitive man, and the animal figures are nothing but a mask to hide the true nature of man's aspirations. Rather than letting ourselves be drawn into controversy, let us rest content with the information supplied by myth. It is explicit enough.'[17]

Thus mythological and cosmological symbolism is the main key to an understanding of the world of rock art. Frobenius has brilliantly developed this proposition, although he also added sociological considerations. According to him, the lion at Leeufontein is carved on the east face of the rock so as to be lit up by the first rays of the sun, because it symbolizes the sun, whereas the rhinoceros faces west because it is the spirit of night and darkness. Another element to consider is that the rhinoceros, whose horns symbolize the crescent of the new moon, is considered in many African mythologies to have murdered the moon. Holm also speaks of the 'ritual uses' of caves in remote massifs. The cosmological legend which the German philologist Willem Bleek collected orally from the San in the nineteenth century led him to say that they 'do not distinguish between matter and spirit'. The Cape antelope drawn with atrophied limbs symbolizes the rising moon. When it is shown facing human figures, as in the Herenveen gallery (Drakensberg), the men are supposed to be worshipping it. The high-spirited, red-striped chamois symbolizes stormy weather; the praying mantis, lightning; and the elephant, rain clouds, as may

16. On this question see the pertinent comments of J. D. Lajoux, 1977, pp. 115ff. Without for a moment denying the Abbé Breuil's right to his sense of humour, nor his immense learning and his great services to the study of prehistory in general and African prehistory in particular, it must be said that he too often succumbed to this tendency.

17. E. Holm in 'L'art dans le monde. L'âge de pierre', pp. 183ff., 170ff., etc.

be seen at Mount St Paul (Drakensberg). This myth crops up again not only elsewhere in Africa (for example, at Philipp Cave, in Namibia, and Djebel Bes Seba and Ain Guedja in Algeria) but also on an ivory carving at La Madeleine in France.

The magnificent Cape antelope in the Transvaal Museum has a coat the colour of honey. This is thought simply to recall that the antelope was created by the praying mantis, the incarnation of the sun, and that the mantis smeared it with purest honey to make its coat glossy. The reason why the quagga is sometimes depicted without stripes, as at Nswatugi Cave in the Matopo mountains, Zimbabwe, is that originally the quagga had no stripes. It was only as a result of getting its back sunburnt that it acquired the burn marks on its coat, and so on. According to this view of things, all that would be needed in order to have a master-key to all the riddles of African rock art – 'timeless as myth' – would be a detailed knowledge of African pantheistic beliefs. This is surely a forlorn hope.

The supporters of the materialist approach, on the other hand, hold that prehistoric art, like all other kinds of art, is merely a reflection of the material conditions of life in a given society, an 'ideological' current and an instrument of that society's culture expressing a particular ecological and sociological balance and enabling man to preserve it or adjust it in his favour.

Each of these approaches seems incomplete by itself, and in my view a synthesis is called for. African prehistoric art unquestionably conveyed a social and educational message. The San, who nowadays are the people nearest to the life portrayed in rock art, say that their forefathers explained the San view of the world to them by means of the great picture-book of rock paintings. The education of peoples without a written language is primarily audiovisual, that is, it is based on sound and image, as may be seen in the initiation rites of young people in sub-Saharan Africa to this day. Petroglyphs are something similar. Nevertheless, myth is obviously not the whole explanation since, before myth can be produced, society itself must be produced and reproduced. Thus myth can be an ideal way of improving (or impairing) productive forces and the production relations. Holm suggests this himself when he quotes the case of the young San, 'convinced that his gleaming quartz arrowhead is a particle of the star to which he prays, as he sharpens his point: "You who never miss, you who are infallible, make me hit my quarry!".' This sentence is essentially utilitarian in scope – exactly the opposite of the idealist conclusion that the author draws from it. In order to survive, man marshals and mobilizes the universe. That is the function of myth, but I do not believe it is its only function. We must not let the trees of symbolism stop us seeing the wood of reality.[18]

18. From the historian's point of view there is sometimes much to be learnt from myths. Thus according to the San, the sun grew tired of being carried on the zebra's back, and deserted it to take refuge between the bull's horns. This takes us to the other end of the continent and depictions in Egypt, southern Oran and the Sahara of oxen bedecked with the solar disc. We may wonder whether the cow-goddess Hathor is not in fact the product of a pan-African myth.

The spiritual function can, in fact, sometimes exist independently, in which case it stops being a means and becomes an end in itself. Myth, after all, represents for man a way of understanding the universe by ordering it, that is, by rationalizing it in a particular way since mythology is not without a kind of inner logic. The spiritual purpose does exist even if it often carries a functional content. To portray a feared being is already to liberate oneself from it, and to keep it under one's eye is to overcome it. Is the almost tangible mineral silence investing the blind and secret stone passages at I-n-Itinen and Tissoukai expressive of remembered rites in sanctuaries and places of initiation, or of the hiding place of stolen livestock? Perhaps both. The people wearing animal masks, and the animals with discs, aureoles, rods, etc. on their heads,[19] often found together in southern Oran and at Oued Djerat, suggest the idea of people in an attitude of prayer before animals. Again, the three masked hunters at Djaret, apparently hemming in a buffalo carrying a disc, may possibly represent a scene of sympathetic magic. Since masks are still used by some African peoples, it might be preferable to base interpretations on this actual cultural material, rather than engaging in pure speculation. It would be found that the explanation is not always a religious one. To this day hunters in the Sahel zone wear a hornbill's head and bob it up and down in imitation of this bird so as to be able to creep up on an antelope on all fours and shoot their arrows at it from close range. Sometimes, however, the disproportion between method and result is so great that magic is strongly suggested, as when a masked man effortlessly drags a dead rhinoceros along on its back, in a carving at In Habeter, Libya. In some cases, fertility rites are clearly the motive of the figures who appear to be engaged in ritual intercourse (e.g. the coitus between a woman and a masked man, at Tin Lalan, Libya) or who are performing vigorous dances with protuberant phalluses. Fertility, in fact, was what mattered most, especially in the Sahara and the Namibia desert at the end of the prehistoric period, when all forms of life were in retreat before the relentlessly advancing drought. A hexagonal carnelian jewel from the Neolithic site at Tin Felki has been recognized by Hampaté Bâ as a fertility charm used to this day by Fulani women.[20] In this particular case the aesthetic motive is not to be dismissed either, for the men and women of the African Neolithic were *Homo sapiens* like ourselves, and they cannot be denied the species-specific pleasure we take in creating shapes simply for the pleasure of looking at them. The admiration we feel today at these works of art must have been still livelier when the pictures were quite fresh and the models for them abounded in the immediate neighbourhood. The little grinders for cosmetic powder and the amazonite, chalcedony and ostrich-eggshell beads at Ténéré, not to mention the supremely graceful lines of

19. See the famous examples of the ox at Maia Dib, Libya, and the ram at Boualem, Saharan Atlas.

20. The cross at Agadès or Iferouane perhaps evolved from the sign of Tanit, a female sex symbol.

the tanged axes, speak volumes for the aesthetic taste of the Africans of those days.

Examples abound of rough sketches abandoned as unsatisfactory. Again, many of the pictures are so exposed to the elements or the first chance passer-by that their secular character must be beyond all doubt. It was often folk art, in the sense also that there was probably a conscious sense of recording for posterity. Pleasure in recollection and the desire to perpetuate the memory of individual or group exploits is also one of the characteristics of our human species. Man is a born chronicler and the artists of prehistory are the first African historians, since they have left us a legible record of the successive stages of African man's relationship with his natural and social environment.

The burden of history, or art as a document

Let us consider to what extent African prehistoric art can be regarded as the illustrated edition of the first African history book.

In the first place, it constitutes a documentary film about the infrastructure of the first societies to live on our continent, for example, of their environment. This biotope can be observed directly in the objects found *in situ*, but it can equally well be deduced from the subject-matter of the pictures. A note of warning must be sounded because a pictorial representation is not necessarily an objective account of the actual surroundings. The artist may be recalling old memories, or portraying fantasies or dreams. In actual fact, however, the overwhelming weight of evidence agrees with the finding of geomorphological studies on the extent of prehistoric lakes and ancient water courses and puts the matter beyond doubt. H. Lhote has found hippopotamus bones at a site at Adrar Bous, radio-carbon dated to 5140 b.p., which confirms the historical accuracy of (for instance) the group of hippopotamuses depicted at Assadjen Ouan Mellen. Now this animal is an ecological indicator since it required perennial water in order to exist. The elephant which eats enormous quantities of vegetation daily is another indicator, and the Sahara of the prehistoric paintings must have been a great expanse of parkland with Mediterranean vegetation, traces of which have survived to this day. This environment gradually gave way to a Sudanic sahel biotope.[21] In the Horse and Chariot period, some representations of trees are found, such as palm-trees, no doubt indicating oases.

In southern Africa, the northern or 'Rhodesian' style is full of drawings of trees some of which are identifiable. Shelters in areas that are now desert are peopled with a teeming, varied fauna, like some latter-day Noah's ark or a zoo turned to stone. There are carvings of fish, tremendous shaggy wild animals like the extinct buffalo, with its enormous horns up to 3 metres

21. Cf. Y. and M. Via, 1974.

across, felines like the cheetah and the aardwolf, guenons and baboons (at Tin Tazarift), ostriches, owls, and so on. On all sides there are hunting scenes, reminders of the perennial duel between man and beast. These lively and sometimes violent scenes, where intelligence triumphs over brute force, are somewhat reminiscent of the hunters reported by Yoyotte in the Nile valley of Predynastic Egypt, with their phallic sheaths between their legs, their curved weapons and their false tails, which are in fact (as in tropical Africa to this day) animal skins worn crosswise over the shoulders. At Iheren there is a lion hunt in which the quarry is encircled by a ring of threatening lances. At Tissoukai, an onager that has been killed is about to be cut up. In the Nile valley, in Libya and throughout the Sahara there are innumerable representations of traps, demonstrating the manifold ingenuity of the men who adapted their techniques to the habits and habitats of the wild animals.[22]

This profusion of hunting scenes from the Nile to the Atlantic is vivid illustration of the existence of a whole hunting civilization. Even larger animals like the elephant did not escape, as witness the great hunting scenes at Upper Mertoutek. Traps are nearly everywhere associated with the symbols of hunters in a very original cultural pattern, which existed over almost the whole of Africa for tens of thousands of years until very late in the historical period, as the legend of Sundjata bears out.

These pictures also show the gradual transition from trapping animals or taking them into captivity, to feeding them and then to domesticating them. There is a man armed with a bow holding an animal on a leash, whilst at Tissoukai moufflon are being hunted with hounds. The lifelike saluki at Sefar, with its curly tail, was obviously the friend of desert man then as now. At Jabbaren there is a scene showing a man lying in wait for a wild animal. He is armed with a curved weapon, and there is another animal with its ears pricked behind him, seemingly domesticated. The varieties of oxen are depicted such as *Bos ibericus* with its short, stout horns in the south and *Bos africanus* with its great lyre-shaped horns at Taghit, Jabbaren and elsewhere. These animals sometimes have a pendant round their necks, as at Oued Djerat.

Then there are cattle with their horns splendidly worked, decorated and artificially twisted into a spiral, as at I-n-Itinen. The ass being hunted in the scene at Tissoukai is the same variety as had been domesticated since the Neolithic, where it is shown being ridden. There are also sheep and goats. Even boats are depicted, including one at Tin Tazarift shaped rather like the papyrus boats of the lakes and rivers of Chad and Nubia.

There are paintings at I-n-Itinen showing men bending down using

22. There are stockades and nets, trigger traps, ditches and pits, break-back traps, locking traps, tension traps and torsion traps, as at Dao Timni on the Niger-Chad border, where a giraffe is immobilized by a complicated tension mechanism which brings its head and neck right down to the horizontal. For details of the research done on this important subject, see P. Huard and J. Leclant, 1973, pp. 136ff.

angled tools, which are reminiscent of the harvest scenes with sickles of Pharaonic bas-reliefs. Again, paintings of women bending in the characteristic posture of people winnowing or gleaning suggest a Neolithic cereal cultivation in the Sahara, and this is borne out by the superabundance of grindstones and grinders which have been found.[23] Pollen studies carried out on samples from the Sahara nevertheless point the need for caution and what is depicted may have been no more than the gathering of wild crops. Besides, the demarcation line between growing little patches of food and agriculture properly so called is not an easy one to draw. At Battle Cave, San girls are depicted setting off food-gathering, their digging-sticks over their shoulders. Be that as it may, the sheer profusion of the rock art and of the tools and weapons found in vast areas of Africa, especially those that are now desert, gives an interesting idea of the population density in those areas. The quantity of artefacts sometimes suggests semi-industrial production, as for instance north-east of Béchar and in the Erroui Erg, and even (as reported by T. Monod) in the Madjouba (western Sahara).

African prehistoric art has also much to tell us about the clothing of the people of those days. As often happens in early civilizations, we find that the men were more decoratively dressed than the women – until the Ox period, when the situation seems to have been reversed.

Dressed in animal skins, bedecked with ornate head-bands or feather coats, they sport a variety of sometimes enigmatic insignia in the form of collars, armbands and bracelets. The women are often depicted in minimal garb, sometimes wearing the *lempe* (a strip of cotton material passing between the legs and tucked under a belt, with the loose ends falling at front and back) common among the girls of the Sudan. There are also loincloths, with various arrangements of the lower folds, clinging dresses; varieties of brassière and all kinds of head-dresses, including a crested one as at Jabbaren.

The home is often depicted schematically by hemispheres representing huts, in which furniture and also family scenes can be seen. The discoveries at the Tichitt cliffs (Mauritania), where 127 villages have so far been identified, show that Neolithic Africans were also builders. Perched on spurs forming the southward extension of the Dhar, these clusters of dry-stone buildings, each housing about 3000 people, often rest upon a substructure of Cyclopean masonry somewhat reminiscent of the *zimbabwes* of central and southern Africa. This type of architecture, which is remarkable for the period, is characterized by carved stone supporting pillars.[24]

The frescoes of African rock art thus afford us a glimpse of a whole society, and a very lifelike glimpse it is. At Takedetoumatine, for instance, buxom women looking as though they had been well fed on milk are sitting in front of the huts with their children, calves are carefully tethered in a row

23. Some of the finest are those brought back by the Berliet Ténéré expedition.
24. See H. J. Hugot's work on Tichitt in H. J. Hugot *et al.*, 1973.

to a rope, whilst men are busy milking the cows. It is an evening scene, bespeaking pastoral peace and quiet. We may wonder whether the number of women suggests polygyny. At Orange Springs and Nkosisana Stream (Natal), there are lifelike dancing scenes showing people, mostly women, clapping their hands in a group around masked dancers.

At Jabbaren, a woman is dragging her unwilling child along. At Sefar, a man is pulling on a calf's rope, which among some present-day Fulani herdsmen is still a holy object (*dangul*). The vast fresco at the Iheren shelter, one of the high points of prehistoric painting, shows finely caparisoned oxen, ridden by women in rich attire, passing by with waterskins hanging from their flanks. Some animals are lowering their heads to the water-hole, whilst a huge herd moves forward in stately fashion. Women in their finery are lounging outside their homes, and men with horse-tails have stopped, seemingly to greet them. Inside the huts various items of furniture are to be seen.

At I-n-Itinen there is a scene with notables in state attire and warriors in uniform, showing that society is beginning to develop along hierarchical lines. Archers in coats look as thouugh they are drawn up in squads under a commander. There is here even a suggestion of a police force.

In southern Africa, war scenes abound, telling of the succession of wars between the San and the Bantu.

But none of this interfered with love. There are many scenes showing that African prehistoric artists had no inhibitions about the sexual side of life. There are pictures of animals in rut, as on the west spur at Blaka, where two rhinoceroses are shown, one sniffing the other's sex organs. Elsewhere a he-goat is shown mounting a she-goat. There are naïve but realistic scenes of human intercourse in various positions, showing that man has not invented anything important in this field since distant times. Ahanna rock, in Oued Djerat (Tassili), portrays a whole scene of masked men with giant erect phalluses on the point of penetrating women lying in the posture of intercourse. All the details are shown. The great fresco at Tin Lalan (Acacous, Libya) is largely devoted to the same orgiastic theme (Hugot-Bruggman, No. 164). At Inahouanrhat there is a more prosaic scene showing coitus *a tergo*, whilst at Timenzouzine (Tassili), a couple in action is shown in the company of three other couples still on their feet, the not altogether serious show of resistance being offered by the women being rendered to perfection.

When we come to magic and religion, we are compelled to admit that many pictures still remain obscure, encapsulated in the mystery of myth. We do not know the meaning of the two-headed oxen or the oxen with two hermaphrodite bodies and but a single head to be seen at Oued Djerat, nor of the magnificently carved spirals associated with many animals, as with the *Bubalus* at Oued Djerat. This motif, also found on Guerze pottery, seems to be connected with hunting ritual or sympathetic magic, like the spiral of the snake Mehen from the Thinite period (first and second Egyptian dynasties).[25] Some scholars consider that the spiral symbolizes the continuity of life. As for the umbilical link to be seen between two people, as for instance one starting at the intersection of a woman's thighs and ending at the navel of a bowman out hunting, it seems as though it stands for a magical flux going from the mother (who is praying, with upraised hands) to her son, who is in a dangerous situation. Again, in southern Africa (Botswana), a rain-making animal sacrifice is shown being led across the country on a rope held by a procession of brisk-looking people. Sun motifs form part of the same religious background. There are some pictures, nevertheless, that are still obscure, but they will only ever be explained by reference to a genuinely African cultural and religious context. This is what happened with regard to a scene at Tin Tazarift, previously entitled 'conventionalized oxen'. Because their legs seemed to be reduced to stumps, it had been supposed that they were lying down, but A. Hampaté Bâ realized that in fact they had been led into the water as part of the *lotori* ceremony to celebrate the ox's aquatic origin. Next to this scene is an indecipherable finger motif in which Hampaté Bâ detected an allusion to the myth of the hand of the first herdsman, Kikala. This hand symbolizes the Fulani clans, the colours of oxen's coats and the four natural elements.[26]

In general, the development suggests a transition from magic, which was often associated with paroxysmal dances, to religion, as exemplified by a sequence in the great frieze at I-n-Itinen depicting the sacrifice of a sheep.

Influences and migrations

The tendency to explain all the features of African culture by the theory of outside influence must be rejected. This does not, however, mean denying any outside influence, but simply involves defining it carefully. Franco-Cantabrian rock art, which goes back about 40 000 years, is Palaeolithic and hence earlier than African prehistoric art. (Saharan Neolithic, on the other hand, is earlier than European Neolithic.)[27] There was thus a strong temptation to argue that the inspiration of artists on the African continent came from the north, and there was even talk of a Eurafrican art with its focal point in Europe – in fact, a sort of Hamitic theory in the field of African prehistoric art.

Now there is no truth in this at all. Quite apart from the fact that there is a difference of 15 000 years in the development of the two schools of art, it is accepted that the art of eastern Spain (which would have had to be the

25. See also the role of the snake in African cosmology.

26. We must admittedly be wary of automatically extrapolating modern myth and legend backwards in time in order to explain every detail of the symbols found in prehistory: cf. J. D. Lajoux, 1977.

27. The 'Saharan Neolithic goes back at least to the eighth millennium before our era, whereas not so long ago the accepted view was that it was later than North African, Egyptian and Near Eastern Neolithic'. H. Lhote, 1976, p. 227.

connecting link for any influence there was) has nothing in common with the art of southern Oran, the Tassili and the Fezzan. L. Balout has argued that there is no connection between North African prehistory and Spain in the Upper Palaeolithic. Moreover, the Capsian origin of the carvings of southern Oran and the Sahara is rejected by practically all authors. The real flowering of prehistoric art came from the Atlas, and its focal points are nothing if not African.

People have also wondered whether it was not from the east (that is, from the Nile valley) that this type of art radiated out to the interior of the continent. Now it is obvious that the art of the Egyptian Nile flourished much later than that of Saharan and Sudanic Africa. The Saharan representations of oxen with discs between their horns are much earlier than those of the cow-goddess Hathor. The hawk delicately carved on the sandstone plaque at Hammada el Guir is much earlier than the similar but smaller figures (the forerunners of Horus) on the lozenges of predynastic Egyptian tombs. The magnificent ram with a sphere at Bou Alem is much earlier than the ram of Amon, which only appears in Egypt in the time of the eighteenth dynasty. When André Malraux looked at the animal heads at Oued Djerat, he considered them to be 'forerunners of the Egyptian animal deities'. The same no doubt holds good for the bird-headed goddesses at Jabbaren. Semi-naturalism only appears in Egypt in the Gerzean period, and is derived from Saharan Ox period carvings. An example is the pictures at Oued Hammamat, which are in any case of inferior workmanship. The superb Egyptian-type boats depicted in the Sahara (for example, at Tin Tazarift) are no doubt simply Saharan-type boats. The silhouettes at Rhardes (Tissoukai), which supposedly portray the Hyksos, Pharaoh and Antinea with his head-dress supposedly representing the Pharaonic *pschent*, in my view need to be seen the other way round in terms of historical perspective. Of course Egypt had a tremendous influence on the interior of Africa, though no doubt it was limited, but what is even more certain is that the prehistoric civilization of the Sahara is earlier in time. It is also true that no obstacle except distance separated the peoples of the Ahaggar, Tassili and the Fezzan from the Nile valley, which was for a long time (until the drying-up of the Sahara) a rather unpleasant swampy area. It was only from the so-called 'historic' period onwards that Egyptian civilization achieved that splendour as a result of which (presumably on the principle of 'to him that hath shall be given') everything is now attributed to it. But where art and technology are concerned, the focal points were originally in the Sahara in the modern Republic of the Sudan, in East Africa and in the Near East. Moreover, the prehistoric Sahara owed much more to south-eastern influences than to those from the Near East. As for the contacts supposed to have taken place between southern Africa and the Sahara area, they do not seem to be based on solid evidence, although Frobenius drew attention to some analogies.[28] There has even been talk of a 'Magosian

28. Cf. E. Haberland, 1973, p. 74.

civilization', which according to Holm was almost pan-African, but nothing very clear emerges about it. Prehistoric works of art in southern Africa are in any case generally later than those in Africa north of the equator, even though the southern part of the continent was populated from an extremely early date.[29] As has already been stressed, it is quite wrong to put the great period of the paintings of the Drakensberg mountains in the seventeenth century of our era, that is, after the arrival of the Bantu. In any case, the painting of the south shows no stylistic affinity with the so-called 'round head' period in the Sahara, and seems related only to the Ox period. It is also distinguished by certain characteristic themes, such as abundant vegetation, landscapes with stylized representations of rocks, and funeral scenes. Be that as it may, comparative studies need to be pursued further and, above all, the general background to the history of African prehistoric *Homo sapiens* needs to be elucidated, before we can think of drawing arrows to mark the direction of artistic movements.

This remark applies with even greater force when we come to consider the 'races' responsible for this type of art. Indeed, to use the concept of race here at all is surely a misuse of the word.[30] It is questionable whether the few skeletons and bones that have been found are sufficient justification for the bold theories put forward concerning peopling by prehistoric 'races'. Nevertheless, an extremely complex demographic process has been mapped out by some authors as follows. After the initial peopling by indigenous 'Africans', Neanderthal people from the Near East supposedly migrated to Africa in two branches, one going as far as Morocco and the other to the East African highlands via the Horn of Africa. These were the Aterians of the Middle Palaeolithic. Subsequently, after a Mesolithic episode probably related to the Sebilian in Egypt, another wave of Cromagnon people arrived in North Africa. These included an Ibero-Maurusian strain and a Capsian strain. These groups presumably developed stone industries in their new habitat, giving rise in particular to the Capsian Neolithic tradition in (amongst other areas) the northern Sahara. Meanwhile a remarkable technological and artistic diversification was taking place in other centres. Particularly noteworthy was the powerful influence of the Sudanic and 'Guinean' Neolithic traditions, with secondary foci in Ténéré and on the Atlantic coast of northern Mauritania.[31] Some authors hold that the *Bubalus* period of rock art is to be attributed to ill-defined 'Mediterranean' people, white or half-caste according to different authors. The so-called

29. Cf. Chapter 20 of this volume, by J. D. Clark. Some authors have suggested that rock art spread from Zimbabwe to Namibia and the Cape, then to the Transvaal and the Orange Free State, and finally (for highly developed polychrome) again from Zimbabwe to Namibia: cf. A. R. Willcox, 1963.

30. The process of speciation referred to by J. Ruffié must have been largely reversed, particularly since the homogeneity of the Sahara as a habitat must have been conducive to interbreeding. See 'Theories on the "Races" and History of Africa', pp. 261–9 above.

31. Cf. H. J. Hugot, 1974, pp. 62ff.

'round head' period is attributed to 'negroids' whom some consider to have interbred with peoples from the Near East and who supposedly constitute the Sudanic Neolithic tradition. The Ox period was supposedly the work of the ancestors of the Fulani. Lastly, the influence of the so-called Guinean tradition, farther south, extended as far as the buildings of the Tichitt cliffs (Mauritania). The whole of this reconstruction, it must be said, remains highly precarious and gives too much weight to population movements from outside Africa. People even refer to 'the distinct African influence' in a Sahara rock picture. But above all, this reconstruction tends to equate concepts as different as race, ethnic group, life-style and culture. People refer to blacks, whites, Fulani, Africans, Capsians and Sudanic peoples without defining any of these terms – for obvious reasons. Lhote, for instance, rejects the idea of Capsian influence in the carvings of the *Bubalus* period,[32] yet he says that in the carvings at Oued Djerat 'there is not a single truly negroid profile. All those that can be made out are unquestionably caucasoid. We must therefore assume that these were whites, which is exactly the impression we get from looking at the figures in southern Oran and the Fezzan. What a pity, a South African colleague said to me one day, that they cannot speak!'[33]

It is on the strength of the same flimsy anthropometrical pointers that the 'round head' period is attributed to the blacks and the Ox period to the Fulani. The identification of races, however, is often based also on life-styles and cultures, which is a gross aberration. The people of the Sudanic Neolithic are defined as 'the ethnic group of the herdsmen-hunters from the east'. The 'delicate features, the herding methods, the women's crested headdresses and the men's plaits' are all that is needed to attribute all rock art exhibiting these features to the Fulani, and this despite the fact that the latter nowadays show no tastes of this kind, and have not even retained the memory of them, as for instance the San have. Also, this claim is made despite the fact that all the 'stages' and styles, as well as all physical types, overlap widely in the rock art. In almost any part of tropical Africa to this day it would be possible to assemble the whole range of profiles found in the Sahara paintings.[34] This also ignores the fact that a 'Fulani' painter may have portrayed masked dancers, just as a 'Negro' artist may perfectly well have depicted scenes of pastoral life, or have changed his heroes' and heroines' features, as some Senegalese painters do today. After all, the little San men often depict themselves as tall, slim and graceful, with hypertrophied anatomies. All art is convention, and nobody has ever seen a black people composed entirely of 'round heads'. Furthermore, it is questionable whether specialization

32. Cf. H. Lhote, 1976, p. 110.

33. ibid., p. 41.

34. P. V. Tobias also notes that all sizes and shapes of skull are to be found among the Khoi-Khoi of the Cape.

into pastoral and agricultural peoples was as sharply defined then as it is today.[35]

H. J. Hugot very rightly says of the Mauritanian Neolithic: 'When they arrived, the Black men of Tichitt had their oxen with them.' He says elsewhere that 'the middle pastoral period saw the arrival of the negroid elements. This was the great Ox period, with herds of oxen depicted in profusion.'[36] Pastoralism is thus not a sufficient criterion, nor are cranial indices nor subjective impressions of types of features. It is not 'races' that make history, and modern science does not include race among men's physical characteristics.[37] The 'white ladies' in African rock paintings, like the one in South Africa whose face only is white (reminding the Abbé Breuil of the frescoes at Knossos, and 'processions of prospectors from the Persian Gulf'), no doubt represent priests, hunters of African girls coming out of initiation ceremonies, just as they are to be seen today painted, with white kaolin, which denotes the death of a previous personality in order to acquire a new status.[38]

The authorship of the rock pictures in southern Africa is also a matter of some controversy. In this case, however, rather more is known about the general historical background, which is a matter first of relations between the Khoi-Khoi and the San and then between the Khoisan and the Bantu. There are many pictures depicting this historical movement. Statistical comparison of the hand imprints on rocks corresponds to the build of the San and so do the steatopygia and the semi-erect penis. The Saharan engravings of the Horse and Chariot period relate to historical times.

The question has been raised, on the other hand, whether the painters and the engravers were from different peoples, the former operating in the shelters and the latter on the hillsides. It seems not. The painters could not generally operate in the open, since if they did their works would have been washed away and lost. On the other hand, the dolerite or diabase of the *kopjes* was better material for engraving. It produced a nice contrast between the ochre of the patina and the grey or blue of the inside of the rock, which the limestone of the shelters did not. Besides, paintings and engravings are sometimes found in the same place, and there are some

35. 'It is remarkable that we know no reliable criterion for distinguishing between the men of the *Bubalus* period and those of the early pastoral period (Ox 1). Hence the existence of bovines, almost certainly domesticated, at the time of the fine naturalistic carvings means that livestock appeared on the scene relatively early.' T. Monod, Jan. 1951.

36. H. J. Hugot, 1974, pp. 225–74.

37. Cf. 'Theories on the "Races" and History of Africa', pp. 261–9.

38. Many authors consider that the 'White Lady' of Brandberg (reproductions of which are not faithful to the original) is in fact a young man, judging by the bow, the narrow hips and the prominent sex organ – as often found among the San, whose penis is semi-erect. As to colour, it should be noted that the face is not painted but represented by the natural rock. The body is pink from the feet up to the waist, and black above. In any case, colour is meaningless: we find red elephants, monkeys and women, and white men. Cf. A. R. Wilcox, 1963, pp. 43–5.

engravings that have been painted, as in the Tarkestad district. Again, the same aesthetic conventions are sometimes found in both categories of picture.

In the field of aesthetics proper, African prehistoric art is the source of inspiration for, and the brilliant introduction to, modern African art, whose roots have so far been very little studied. Prehistoric art comprises a wealth of styles, which can sometimes be traced almost step by step down to modern African art. The latter has borrowed much from Arab and European art, but there is also an ancient tradition whose roots are to be found in the rock shelters and prehistoric galleries. Painting is based on a few primary colours such as red ochre, white, black and yellow, with the addition of blue and green. To this day this range of colours turns up in masks and dancers' regalia.

It is an art characterized by observation, by an almost moving and sometimes reverent attention to real life. Carving and painting both show this, but in different ways. The ox at Augsburg (Botswana), only the front portion of which has survived, is delineated with an impeccable line that brings out the minutest anatomical details of the muzzle, eyes, ears and hair. The giraffe at Eneri Blaka is a remarkable piece of realistic engraving. The spots on the coat are rendered by hammered intaglio, with delicate shading to show the contours of the head, the zygomatic arches, the horns, the globulous eyes, the nostrils and the gleaming horn of the cloven hooves. The carving is true to life because of the masterly skill of the outline, which delineates the profile supremely well; because of the intaglio, which brings out the inner detail; but also because there is a giraffe foal too, leaning against its mother in a touchingly spontaneous attitude.

This vein of observation is also to be found in the fresco at Iheren, where a world of hurrying movement is kept distinct in all its details by impeccable sureness of line. There are sixteen giraffes, elegantly intermingled; parties of bedizened women travelling on their pack-oxen, and gazelles and antelopes (*dorcas, dama,* oryx and hartebeest) identifiable respectively by their slender horns and white coats, their swept-back horns and elongated heads. On the same panel, a newborn giraffe foal, still attached by its umbilical cord, is squatting and struggling to get its balance. A lion with a sheep in its claws is watching armed men who have set out in pursuit of it, whilst other sheep scamper away in terror. An ox is going to a pond to drink, which makes the frogs jump. This is the touching, variegated kaleidoscope of nature, with man the king in the role of intruder.

However, naturalistic detail never inhibits the bringing out of the essentials of composition by a technique which is rather like a sculptural approach to painting. Thus the principal character is depicted on a larger scale, overshadowing lesser characters who are relatively reduced in size like the tall masked hunters towering over wild animals, the huge Pharaoh laying his enemies low, or the *Oba* of Benin shown magnified in relation to his subjects.

This stress on the essential gives rise to symbolist forms, the antithesis of the baroque. Combined with a sculptural treatment, it produced the particular rhythms underlying both the *Bubalus* drawn with a crisp, simple line and the herd of oxen at Jabbaren, where we can almost hear the stamping of hooves, the snorting and the lowing (cf. Lajoux illustration).

It is everyday popular art, with a sense of humour that expresses the bittersweet ironies of life. It is also esoteric art, vibrating with the mystical fervour that impelled the painter or engraver, and as such it has yielded some of the gems of universal art, like the ram with a solar disc at Bualen, whose priestly posture is both an annunciation of the mystery and a call to meditation.[39] This dual approach well conveys the two sides of the modern African's make-up: spontaneous and almost casual in ordinary matters, solemn and mystical when caught up in the rhythm of a ritual dance.

African prehistoric art is not dead. It lives on, if only in the unchanging place names. For instance, a valley running into the Oued Djerat is called Tin Tehed, or 'place of the she-ass' and there is indeed a fine carving of an ass there. Issoukai-n-Afelia is reputedly haunted by spirits (*djinn*), perhaps because there is a horrifying animal figure, part-fowl, part-owl, with a colossal sex organ who peers over a pile of votive stones thrown there to propitiate it.

Africans are cut off from this art-form by distance, a barrier overcome only by scholars and experts from wealthy countries, and it deserves to be reintroduced into their lives, at least through the medium of school syllabuses.

It needs to be jealously protected from the various kinds of damage that threaten it daily, for it is a legacy without price.[40] A complete register should be compiled, to facilitate comparative study.

Prehistoric art offers many pointers to aspects of the life of early African man, from his physical environment to his loftiest feelings, and the image is sometimes a sign as eloquent as writing. The evidence is, of course, ambiguous, enigmatic, and needs to be supplemented from sources such as palaeontology, climatology, archaeology and oral tradition. But, even if it only shows us the tip of an iceberg, we should be justified in regarding prehistoric art as the continent's first history book, or as the projection on to the stone walls of rock shelters of a scenario for living which has long disappeared. It constitutes a monument where African man proclaims his desperate struggle to dominate nature and to attain to the boundless joy of creation and the ecstasy of God-knowing Man.

39. It is noteworthy that we find mention in the literature of two rams at the court of the Emperor of Mali in the fourteenth century, to protect the king from the evil eye. Rams have also been reported from other African courts, including Meroe, Akan (Ghana), Kuba (Zaïre) and Kanem (Chad).

40. In 1974 the Algerian government introduced regulations making the whole area of the Tassili paintings and carvings a national park.

PLATE 26.1 *Detail from the 'White lady' cave painting, South Africa* (A.A.A. Photo, Duverger)

PLATE 26.2 *'Serpent's track' cave painting* (A.A.A. Photo, Mauduit)

PLATE 26.3 *Engraving of rhinoceros, Blaka, Niger* (H. J. Hugot)

PLATE 26.4 *Engraving of an elephant, In Eker, Algerian Sahara* (H. P. C. Haan)

PLATE 26.5 *Bovine, Tin Rharo, Mali* (H. J. Hugot)

PLATE 26.6 *Gazelles, Blaka, Niger* (H. J. Hugot)

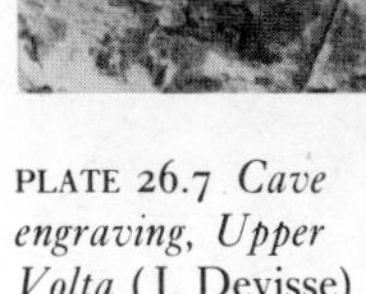

PLATE 26.7 *Cave engraving, Upper Volta* (J. Devisse)

PLATE 26.8 *Close-up of cave engravings, Upper Volta* (J. Devisse)

PLATE 26.9 *Erotic scene, Tassili* (P. Colombel)

PLATE 26.10 *Erotic scene, Tassili* (P. Colombel)

PLATE 26.11 *Cave painting, Tibesti, Chad* (Hoa-Qui)

PLATE 26.12 *Cave paintings, Tassili*
(A.A.A. Photo, Sudiez, Naud)

PLATE 26.13 *Cave paintings, Namibia* (A.A.A. Photo, Sudriez, Naud)

Origins, development and expansion of agricultural techniques

R. PORTÈRES[1] and J. BARRAU

Ideas about the origins of agriculture have for a long time been pervaded by some measure of ethnocentricity. The tendency was (and sometimes still is) to think that a 'Neolithic Revolution', as defined by Gordon Childe,[2] occurred in an agricultural and pastoral cradle in the Near East, and that this was not simply the birthplace for the cultivation of major cereals like wheat and barley and of animal husbandry (goats, sheep and later cattle), which are the very foundation of western material civilization, but also the genesis of civilization itself, at any rate so far as the Old World was concerned. It is no doubt true that archaeological research after the Second World War and especially during the last twenty years has to some extent modified this narrow and somewhat self-centred point of view. Recent research has confirmed the importance of the Fertile Crescent in the history of world agriculture,[3] but it has also thrown light on the role of other regions in this major change in the life of man, a change to the *production* of foodstuffs which previously had been merely *collected* from the natural environment. The result has been a clearer appreciation of the significance of agricultural inventions and plant domestication in America[4] and of the relatively earlier development of a cradle of agriculture in tropical south-

1. Note by Jacques Barrau: Roland Portères, Professor at the Musée national d'histoire naturelle de Paris, died on 20 March 1974. Entrusted by the International Scientific Committee for the Drafting of a General History of Africa with preparing this chapter on the origins and development of agricultural techniques, he had worked out an outline, but this was one of his last tasks. Taking this unfinished work of his and basing myself on his many published works, on his notes and on the numerous discussions that I had had with him on this subject, I have endeavoured to complete the task while remaining faithful to Portères's passionate interest in the fascinating character of Africa, of its regions, its peoples and its civilizations. While acknowledging its imperfections, I offer this contribution to his work as a tribute to the teacher and the friend who has done so much for a better understanding of the agriculture and the cultivated plants of the African continent.
2. V. G. Childe, 1954.
3. See, for example, R. J. Braidwood, 1960.
4. See, for example, R. S. MacNeish, 1964.

east Asia[5] and, lastly, of the contribution of Africa to the history of world agriculture.

Already, however, nearly half a century ago, the celebrated Russian agronomist and geneticist N. I. Vavilov[6] posited the existence of centres in Africa where cultivated plants could have originated, and later one of his assistants, A. Kuptsov,[7] demonstrated that such centres had, in fact, existed. A few years later, one of the authors of this chapter plotted in detail the situation and number of these centres of origin and described their role.[8]

However, colonialist prejudices, allied to ignorance about many African cultigens and, generally, about the prehistory of the continent, led to a long period when the participation of Africa in developing agricultural techniques and resources was either played down or disregarded altogether.

This situation has now radically changed and the last few years have seen the growth of a keen interest in the origins of African agriculture, witness, for example, the essays published in 1968 in *Current Anthropology*[9] and the large number of comments that they aroused. We must also mention the studies put together by J. D. Fage and R. A. Oliver[10] and, still more recently, the contribution of W. G. L. Randles to the history of Bantu civilization.[11] But before attempting a brief account of the state of our knowledge of the agricultural prehistory of Africa, we must describe the ecological setting into which it fitted.

Natural environments and the origins of African agriculture

It is obvious that the origins, development and diversity of agricultural techniques must be closely related to aspects of the natural environment such as the climate, the water resources, the geographical relief, the nature of the soil and of the vegetation, the types of plants originally utilized, and the nature of foodstuffs they yielded, and so on. However, these elements, important and even predominant as they are in the raising of plants and stock were not the sole agencies at work. There was also the influence of the prevailing cultures and civilizations.

Even in pre-agricultural times and when agriculture was just beginning, man had carried with him in his migrations implements, techniques, modes of understanding and interpreting the environment, and methods of

5. See J. Barrau, 1975.
6. N. I. Vavilov, 1951, pp. 1–6.
7. Cited by C. D. Darlington, 1963.
8. R. Portères, 1962.
9. O. Davies, 'The origins of agriculture in West Africa'; H. J. Hugot, 'The origins of agriculture: Sahara'; D. Seddon, 'The origins and development of agriculture in East and southern Africa'.
10. 1970.
11. 1974.

manipulating and using space. He also took with him a whole range of attitudes and of behaviour that had grown out of his relationships with nature in his original habitat. Thus, at a time when Europe was barely emerging from the Palaeolithic, the cultivation of plants and the raising of livestock were already established in the Near East, where the first cities were beginning to appear, and it was the Near East which introduced to a somewhat backward Europe those technical inventions which, with their attendant attitudes, made possible there also a 'Neolithic Revolution' based on agriculture and stock-breeding.

Similar migrations or exchanges took place in Africa, as elsewhere, as a result of population movements within Africa and between neighbouring continents.

It is essential, however, to grasp the implications both of the inventions of agriculture and stock-herding and of the domestication of plants and animals. Man passed from mere food *collecting* (gathering, hunting) to artificially *producing* (cultivating, rearing). Thus, progressively and partially, man began to free himself from the constraints of the ecosystems to which he belonged and in which, until he began to control agriculture and stock-raising, he led more or less the same passive or bio-cenotic life as other living organisms following the normal course of natural processes.

Thus the introduction of agriculture and stock-raising was a fundamental change which permitted human beings to adapt to various natural environments and made it possible to change biological processes in order to produce more or something different from what they would have done by themselves. Man's new role of cultivator and stock-breeder also caused very considerable changes in the natural environment as well as in quantity and quality of the food produced.

Nevertheless, in spite of his mastery over some elements of his natural environment, man was not able to free himself totally and immediately from all the constraints they imposed. We must therefore consider the environmental features which played an overriding role in agricultural prehistory and history in Africa, and so we need to sketch an environmental map of the continent. We find that it is divided into wide latitudinal bands which are ecologically distinct from each other and which lie symmetrically north and south of the equator.

As was pointed out by Randles (1974), some of these bands acted as barriers to north–south migrations. The barriers were the Sahara, the great equatorial rain forest, the Tanzanian steppe and the Kalahari desert. But other bands provided spaces, or convenient pockets, into which these currents or population movements could flow, for example, the northern and southern savannahs. Randles, however, also pointed out that none of the barriers were absolutely impenetrable; the Sahara and the great equatorial forest, for example, contain obvious evidence of some migration of peoples.

Latitude is not the sole factor roughly marking off the major ecological zones of Africa. Geographical relief and so also altitude enter into the picture

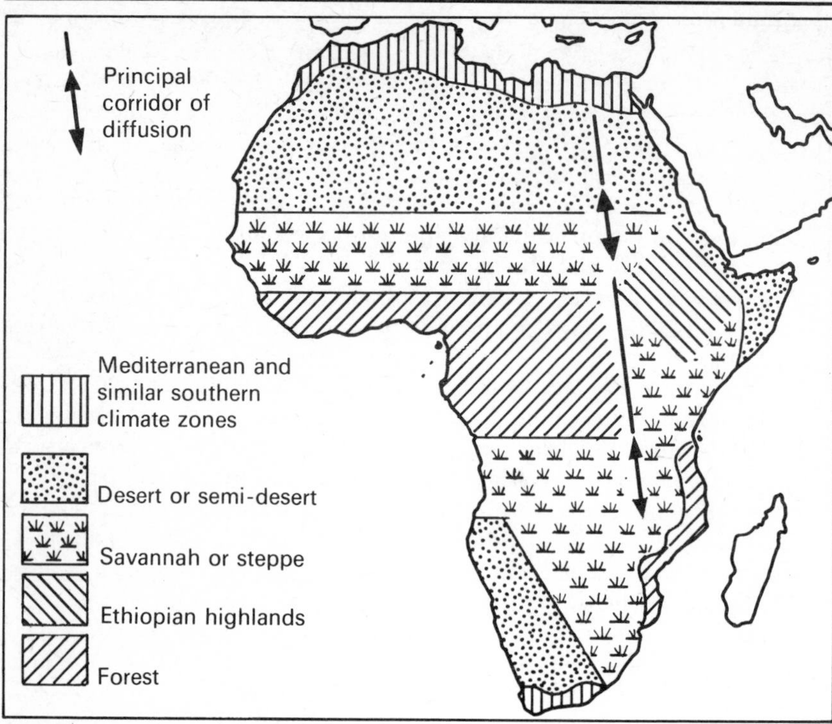

FIG. 27.1 *Latitudinal zoning of the African continent*

as well, witness the Zaïre–Nile axis which separates the East African highlands from the West African peneplain while the latter itself is bisected by a minor axis of up-thrust between Principe island and Chad.

There are therefore exceptions to this latitudinal zoning of the African continent, the most important of which is perhaps that of the highlands already mentioned extending, parallel to the Rift valley, from the north of Lake Victoria to the Munchinga hills and which, to cite Randles again, acted as a narrow and safe corridor through the equatorial barrier (Fig. 27.1). There is also the Ethiopian massif, the role of which in the origin of African cultivated plants will be described later.

If at this stage we put together the various elements of the picture, extremely summary though they may be, we can see Africa as consisting of an almost semicircular zone of savannah and steppe in the north, the east and the south enclosing a core of equatorial forest, and then still further north and south, two arid zones – the Sahara and the Kalahari – and lastly, to furthest north and furthest south, two narrow almost homo-climatic zones which, to simplify a great deal, could both be described as Mediterranean in climate even though there are certain ecological

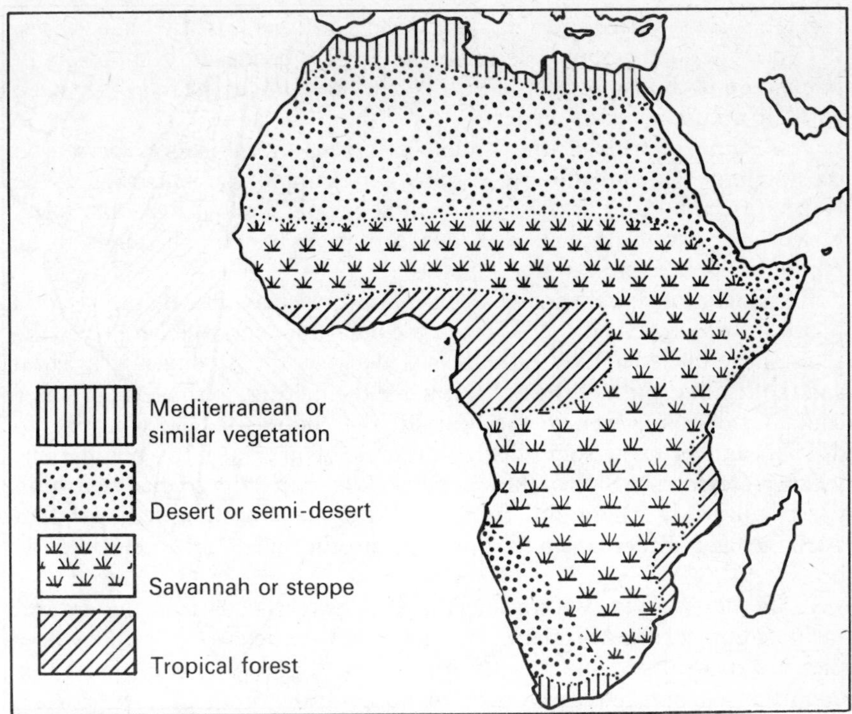

FIG. 27.2 *Ecosystems of the African continent*

peculiarities to be found in the extreme south of Africa (Fig. 27.2). Moving outwards, then, from the equatorial forest heart of Africa and leaving aside the coastal regions, we can draw a graph from the extremely humid to the extremely dry, from the generalized ecosystems of the tropical rain forest type to the more specialized ecosystems of the savannah, steppe and desert scrub types.[12]

With regard to deserts, and more specifically the Sahara, it may at this point be recalled, even though it is now a sufficiently well-known fact, that it was not always the desert that it is now. Agriculture and stock-raising were carried on there, and a number of writers[13] have suggested that cradles of agriculture and animal husbandry are to be found in the Sahara.

Returning, however, to our ecological map of Africa, we can assume that in pre-agricultural times food-gathering and hunting similar to those still used today by the Pygmies were practised in the generalized ecosystem of the great tropical rain forest, whose food resources, both animal and

12. For the terms 'specialized ecosystems' and 'generalized ecosystems', see D. Harris, 1969.

13. A. Chevalier, 1938; H. J. Hugot, 1968; J. J. Hester, 1968.

vegetable, are as varied and abundant as the constituents of their biocenoses.

Given the food resources available to Pygmy bands and the density of population in the forests, it is clear that they can obtain the food they need without undue effort or anxiety.

The same is true of the hunter-gatherers in the more specialized ecosystem of arid and sub-arid regions, for example, the Kung San of the Kalahari studied by J. B. Lee.[14] For these people the food available is less varied and, because of wide seasonal variations in rainfall, tends to be restricted to areas near water supplies.

Returning to Africa's pre-agricultural past, we may note that the humid phase known as the Makalian (5500–2500 before our era) which followed the Pleistocene made contacts rather easier between the Mediterranean coast and the regions south of the Sahara, while the increase in the level of water courses and lakes, even in the heart of the continent, helped fishing to develop and brought some degree of settlement among the populations which resorted to it. Both of these conditions favoured the gradual transition to agriculture.[15] Migrations from the Near Eastern and Mediterranean cradles of agriculture which took place at this time no doubt accelerated the process.[16]

From the end of the Pleistocene, that is, between 9000 before our era and the beginning of the Makalian, there seem to have been some places where the kind of food suitable for gathering grew in great abundance and this doubtless encouraged early man to concentrate in them. The forest-savannah borderland on the edges of the equatorial forest, the East African grassland plateaux, the waterside of lakes and major rivers, such as the Nile, as well as the coastal regions of the north and south come into this category.[17]

These transitional zones, and especially the forest-savannah borderland, possessed all the characteristics required for agricultural development and, much later, not surprisingly, for the growth of a number of African civilizations. Randles remarks in this connection that it is 'at the margins of the two savannahs (Sahel and forest fringes) that are to be found the most prestigious of the Bantu civilizations'.

We should now consider in some detail the possibilities for plant domestication that were available in Africa, for we must not forget that in the logic of ecology it is the plants which are the primary producers.

The African origin of some cultivated plants

It is only comparatively recently that interest has been focused on the origin

14. R. B. Lee, 1966.

15. For the relationship between this sedentarization of fishing communities and the origins of agriculture, see C. O. Sauer, 1952.

16. See J. D. Clark, 1970b.

17. ibid.

of cultivated plants. If the remarkable work by A. de Candolle, published in 1883, is excepted, it is only with the work of the Soviet geneticist N. I. Vavilov and his team beginning work soon after the October Revolution in 1917 that a global approach was made to this question of fundamental importance in the history of man, and that man's attempts to use his environment and its resources were studied.[18] Vavilov's point of departure was the variations observed in cultivated plants and, by combining a systematic analysis of botanical and phyto-geographical data with agro-botanical inventories and genetic studies, he and his assistants were able to point to eight regions where cultivated plants first emerged. These eight regions included three secondary centres, of more local importance. Only one of the main centres, the *Abyssinian,* is situated in Africa, though another, the *Mediterranean,* affects part of the African continent (North Africa and Egypt), and also shows affinities with the vastly important Near Eastern centre of origin where, as we have already said, the major cereals (wheats, barleys, ryes) appeared in addition to other cultivated plants.

With regard to Africa, Vavilov's conclusions represent a considerable change from those of Candolle, who recognized only three primary centres of origin for agriculture and the domestication of plants: China, South-East Asia (with an extension to Egypt) and America.

Vavilov's contribution to the understanding of the theory of the origin of cultivated plants was also of the highest importance, because he established the need to distinguish between a centre of primary mutation, where a very great diversity in any particular plant is combined with continuing dominant characteristics, and, on the other hand, sub-areas of secondary mutation which show many recessive characteristics which were masked in the centre of primary mutation.

When centres of mutation are found closely associated in the same area they are said jointly to constitute a 'cradle of agriculture', and its existence is usually an indication that a civilization has been at work for a long time, altering and domesticating the plants required by that society.

It is important to stress the point that the botanical place of origin of a cultivated plant species is not necessarily the same as the area in which it was first adapted by human intervention for man's own use. So, one often has to distinguish between the place of origin of the wild parent of a cultivated species and the place where the plant emerged in an altered form after being domesticated and subjected to selection by man. This last has a simple explanation. In the long years of plant-gathering a wild parent must have been frequently carried away from its original habitat.[19]

One of the present authors has been able to complete Vavilov's[20] picture by demonstrating that in addition to the Abyssinian centre and the African portion of the Mediterranean centre, there existed also a West African

18. For the enormous work of N. I. Vavilov, see op. cit., 1951.
19. See J. Barrau, 1962.
20. See R. Portères, 1950, 1951a.

centre and an East African one, this latter being possibly an extension into the equatorial highlands of the Abyssinian centre.[21]

We can summarize the situation as follows:

The Mediterranean centre. The African portion of this centre includes the group of cultivated plants now characteristic of Mediterranean regions, such as cereals, especially wheats and barleys, and leguminous plants with edible seeds (*Cicer*, *Lens*, *Pisum*, *Vicia*) which were also developed in the Near Eastern centre. We also find here common Mediterranean cultivated species such as the olive tree (*Olea europa* L.) and the carob or Mediterranean locust tree (*Ceratonia siliqua* L.). However, some of the plants are proper to Africa, like the argan tree (*Argania sideroxylon* Roem.) from Morocco which yields oil and gum. Egypt, whose links with the Near East are obvious and whose influence in agriculture and stock-breeding in North Africa is so important, belongs to this centre. In Egypt, and also Syria, the *berseem* or Alexandrian clover (*Trifolium alexandrinum* L.) was developed and proved of great economic importance. Although this African portion of the Mediterranean centre did not play a direct part in the development of agriculture in tropical Africa, it did profoundly influence the Sahara during the period when the climate there was favourable to cultivation and stock-raising.[22]

The Abyssinian centre has, in the cultivated species it produced, affinities with the *Near East centre* (wheats, barleys, leguminous plants like *Cicer*, *Lens*, *Pisum*, *Vicia*) and also with some found in African centres proper such as sorghum which will be dealt with later. It seems evident that plants originating in Asia passed into Africa through this centre. However, this Abyssinian centre also developed some characteristic cultivated species, among them the Arabian coffee shrub (*Coffea arabica* L.), the Abyssinian banana tree (*Musa ensete*, I.F. Gmelin) the *teff* grass (*Eragrostis abyssinica* Schrad.) and the *niger* with oleaginous seeds (*Guizotia abyssinica*, L.f. Cass.).

The East African centre is characterized by a number of varieties of sorghum including *Sorghum verticilliflorum* Stapf. and various penicilliary millets such as the *Eleusine coracana* Gaertn. and various sesames.

The West African centre. Here we find the origin of various types of sorghum deriving from *Sorghum arundinaceum* Stapf.; of penicilliary millet like *Pennisetum pychnostachyum* Stapf. and Hubb. and *P. gambiense* Stapf. and Hubb.; as well as digitary millets including *ibura* (*Digitaria ibura* Stapf.) and *fonio* (*D. excilis* Stapf.) and several rice varieties which will be referred to below.[23]

In this centre we can distinguish two main ranges of development, the tropical and the sub-equatorial. Within the tropical range there are several subdivisions (the Senegambian, the central Niger, the Chad-Nilotic), each of them producing characteristic cultivated plants, principally cereals but some tuberous (*Coleus dazo* Chev. especially) and some oleaginous such

21. See R. Schnell, 1957.
22. See J. D. Clark, 1970b and H. J. Hugot, 1968.
23. See R. Portères, 1962.

as *Butyrospermum parkii* (Don.) Kotschy (known to botanists also as *Vitellaria paradoxa* Gaertner). To the sub-equatorial range belong especially the yams (*Dioscorea cayenensis* Lamk., *D. dumetorum* Pax., *D. rotundata* Poir.), oleaginous plants (*Elaeis guineensis* Jacq., *Telfairia occidentalis* Hook. f.) and stimulants (*Cola nitida* A. Chev.). This centre actually extends itself into central Africa, as do the areas of diffusion of certain kinds of plants mentioned above (Cola, Coleus, Elaeis). The earth-pea or Bambara groundnut (*Voandzeia subterranea* Thon.) and the leguminous African geocarp (*Kerstingiella geocarpa* Harms.) also originated in the West African centre.

In the view of the present authors, there originally existed to the immediate east and south of the equatorial forest a belt with a complex of cultivated species similar to the one found in the West African centre and which roughly followed contours of the forest belt, skirting in the process the East African centre and thus practically co-extensive with the intensive gathering zone of the forest perimeter described above.[24]

All these considerations lead[25] us to suppose that a number of cradles of agriculture existed in Africa which we can list as follows (Fig. 27.3):

(1) *The Afro-Mediterranean cradle,* stretching from Egypt to Morocco, which influenced the development of agriculture and pastoralism in the Sahara and which also acted as a channel of exchange with the Near Eastern cradle through Egypt.

(2)(a) *The West African cradle,* with its tropical and sub-equatorial sectors.

(b) *The Nile-Abyssinian cradle* in the east, with two sectors: the Nilotic and the Abyssinian.

(3) *The Central African cradle.*

(4) *The East African cradle* to the east of the Central African cradle and extending west to Angola.

Further to the south, it appears that food gatherers, doubtless provided with adequate resources, but also protected by the aridity of the Kalahari, managed for a long time to resist the penetration of agriculture and pastoralism from the cradles described above and, more particularly, from the East African cradle.[26]

The concept of 'cradles of agriculture' has the disadvantage of suggesting that the prehistory and history of agricultural development proceeded in a patchwork pattern. However, in the light of what has already been said, we think it possible to present a more coherent general picture.

In the central core of forest, there was a generalized ecosystem out of which was developed a 'centre of horticulture' (a term which we think preferable to the unsatisfactory term 'centre of vegeculture' proposed by

24. See D. Seddon, 1968.
25. See R. Portères, 1962.
26. See D. Seddon, 1968.

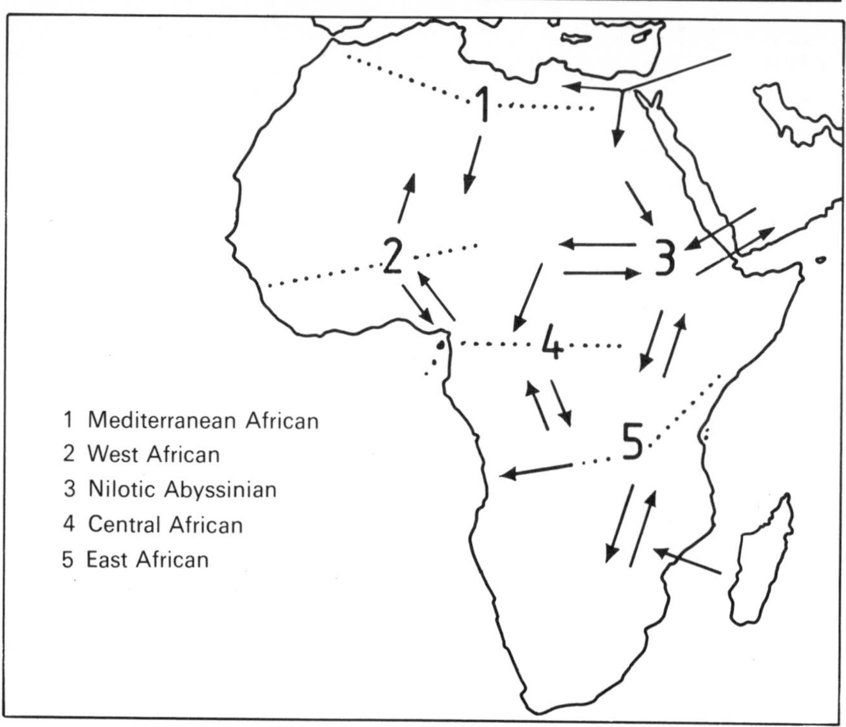

FIG. 27.3 *Cradles of African agriculture*

R. J. Braidwood and C. A. Reed[27]). But in the forest conditions, gathering was still sufficiently productive to allow this to continue. It should be noted that the range of plants from this centre which could usefully be domesticated was less wide than the range found in the wet tropical forest centres of Asia or America. Secondly, there was the savannah around forest fringes providing a more specialized ecosystem which became an agricultural centre for the cultivation of cereals, and which extended from West to East Africa and south towards Angola.

In North Africa along the Mediterranean the cultivation of cereals spread from Mesopotamia through Egypt. It also penetrated into the Sahara at a time when conditions were suitable, and this fact goes a long way towards explaining some diffusions towards the south of the present desert as well as others in the opposite direction from sub-Saharan Africa.

The influence of Mesopotamia can also be seen in the Ethiopian highlands, which however also share some affinities with the agricultural centre of the savannahs and steppes as well as possessing their own cultigenic characteristics.

A horticultural centre differs from a centre of agriculture in the

27. R. J. Braidwood and C. A. Reed, 1957.

preponderance of tuberous plants, and in the method of cultivation which belongs rather to the garden-orchard (the *hortus* of the forest and its borders) than to the field (the *ager* of the savannah and the steppe).

In the African continent as a whole, agricultural implements consisted principally of the hoe and the digging stick, with their variations, but a primitive plough introduced through Egypt and Ethiopia made an inroad into part of the centre of cereal cultivation.

The cultivation of sorghum and rice

In contrast to the horticultural centre of the generalized ecosystem of the forest belt, the African agricultural centre, within the relatively specialized ecosystem of savannah and steppe, is characterized first by the use of cultivated plants reproduced by the sowing of seeds and secondly by the importance of cereals in the food complex of the population.

Agricultural systems of this kind cultivated plants *en masse* as distinct from the cultivation of single plants that is characteristic of the horticulture found in the forest belt. The agricultural civilizations no doubt extended their cultivated fields at the expense of the forest as they came into contact with it in the course of their territorial expansion and this tended to increase the extent of the savannah. In ecological terms, these civilizations imposed some degree of specialization on ecosystems that were originally generalized in their nature and in this way subjected the natural environment to their techniques, or rather to their conception of what the environment should be. But there were failures as well as successes in this penetration of agriculture into the forest milieu: for example, cereals might have been abandoned in favour of food crops which were more characteristic of the forests and even – the possibility cannot be ruled out – the adoption of plant-gathering as the means of subsistence by savannah peoples normally agriculturists, who had been obliged to take to life in a forest environment.

The fact, however, remains that the cultivation of cereals is the main characteristic of steppe and savannah agriculture. Among these cereals one in particular – sorghum (*Sorghum* spp.) or great millet – appears as the characteristic cultigen throughout the area of this agricultural centre though other varieties of different origin are also found.

The origin of the various varieties of sorghum was for a long time the subject of conflicting views,[28] but it seems that the cereal sorghums did indeed originate in Africa and that in fact they did have a number of independent points of origin within the African agricultural centre. The wild variety *Sorghum arundinaceum* Stapf., which originated in the wet tropical zone running from Cape Verde to the Indian Ocean, gave rise to the group of sorghums cultivated in West Africa: *S. aterrimum* Stapf., *S. nitens* Snowd., *S. drummondii* Millsp. and Chase, *S. margaritiferum* Stapf., *S.*

28. See R. Portères, 1962.

guineense Stapf., *S. gambicum* Snowd., *S. exsertum* Snowd. The wild variety *S. verticilliflorum* Stapf., which originated in the area of East Africa from Eritrea to south-east Africa, gave rise to two groups of cultivated sorghums: the south-east African or the Kafir sorghums: *S. caffrorum* Beauv., *S. coriaceum* Snowd., *S. dulcicaule* (sweet sorghum), and the Chad-Nile type usually found from the Nigerian Sudan to Eritrea: *S. nigricans* Snowd. and *S. caudatum* Stapf. The wild variety *S. aethiopicum* Rupr., which originated in Eritrea and Ethiopia, gave rise to *S. rigidum* Snowd. found on the Blue Nile, *S. durra* Stapf. cultivated from Chad to India and in all semi-desert types of country, *S. cernuum* Host., *S. subglabrescens* Schw. and Asch. found in the Nilotic regions, and *S. nigricum* cultivated in the central Nigerian delta.

In the central River Niger sector of the tropical section of the West African cradle a special cultivated sorghum, *S. mellitum* Snowd. var. *mellitum* Snowd., is used for making an alcoholic drink[29] because of its rich sugar content. Other sorghums are also used for making 'millet beer'.

There are cross-relations between these various groups of cultivated sorghums, as is witnessed by the existence of *S. conspicuum* Snowd. (found from Tanganyika to Zimbabwe and Angola) and *S. roxburghii* Stapf. (found in Uganda, Kenya, Zimbabwe and South Africa), which seem to have arisen from crossing between sorghums, some of which were related to *S. arundinaceum* and others to *S. verticilliflorum*.

Of these sorghums, *S. durra* deserves to be noted because of its distribution over the whole area from the eastern Sudan to Asia Minor and India and from Mesopotamia to Iran and Gujarat.

Enough has been said to indicate the importance of these cereals in the plant economy of the agricultural centre of the African savannahs and steppes of Africa. Moreover, this importance transcends the limits of the continent since some types of sorghum domesticated here spread very early to other regions of the world.

So it would seem better to see Africa as having both a number of cradles of agriculture and a mosaic of centres where cultivated plants originated, some of which became of economic importance on a global scale. Africa was the source of other cultivated species, not least rice, which was developed from indigenous varieties. These varieties were found in the West African cradle and, more precisely, in the central River Niger sector, a centre of primary variation, and in the Senegambian sector, a secondary centre.

In classical times, Strabo had referred to the cultivation of rice in Africa and in the fourteenth centry Ibn Battuta mentioned that rice was produced on the Niger.[30] But this evidence was often ignored and it was for a long time believed that rice cultivation in Africa began with the introduction of Asian rice (*Oryza sativa* R.). It was only about 1914 that the existence

29. See R. Schnell, 1957.
30. ibid.

of a specifically African variety of rice was recognized (*O. glaberrima* Steudel). This has rigid, upright panicles and brown or red caryopses, a variety which can be gathered wild but which can also be cultivated and which seems to be related to the *O. breviligulata* A. Chev. and O. Roer found in much of the African tropics.

This African rice provides a good illustration of the theories of N. I. Vavilov. The Soviet agronomist and geneticist established that a wild parent plant required a very extensive territory if a cultivated species were to emerge. In the case of African rice there was a maximum possibility of variation with a preponderance of dominant characteristics in the central delta of the Niger (the primary centre) and a variety of species with recessive characteristics in upper Gambia and in Casamance (the secondary centre). Moving outwards, therefore, from the central delta of the Niger, the cultivated varieties of African rice spread in West Africa to the Guinea Coast. The gathering of the wild variety *O. glaberrima* was certainly an extremely ancient practice, and this wild cereal must have been plentiful in those relatively intensive food-gathering centres where conditions favoured the first domestication of plants. It may therefore be supposed that the domestication of African rice occurred at least as long ago as that of the other African cereals.

Later on, the cultivated rice varieties of Asia (*O. sativa*) were introduced into Africa – possibly from the eighth century onwards by the Arabs on the East African coast or possibly from the sixteenth century on by the Europeans on the western littoral.

Now that the origins of the various cultivated species discussed above have been established, and necessarily only a summary of them could be presented in this chapter, it seems clear that African agricultural civilizations were endogenous and based on plant resources deriving from local natural environments and without any necessary implication of influences from outside the continent.

Relations between Africa and Asia

It is perfectly true, as we have suggested, that diffusions from the Mesopotamian cradle of agriculture and pastoralism played an important role in the early history of agriculture in Africa. The zone stretching from Abyssinia via the Nile valley in Egypt to North Africa could be considered a part of the *palaeo-Mediterranean* domain defined by Haudricourt and Hedi (1943), but even here we find cultivated species which are properly speaking African, especially in Ethiopia but also in Egypt and North Africa.

More interesting but perhaps less known is the history of the contacts between Africa and Asia (beyond the Near East) in very early times. Africa gave to Asia a number of domesticated plants, as is clearly shown with the sorghums described above. But Africa also received from Asia not only the Near Eastern cultigens (wheats, barleys, and so on) but also plants transmitted from tropical South-East Asia. It does seem very probable that the bananas, the greater yam (*Dioscorea alata* L.), the taro (*Colocasia esculenta* L. Schott.) and possibly the sugar cane (*Saccarum officinarum* L.) arrived on African shores perhaps by way of south-western Arabia and East Africa, or perhaps brought in by early navigators landing on the coast of South-East Africa. Some of these cultivated plants native to Asia, notably the bananas, enabled agriculture to gain an easier foothold in the tropical forest regions of Africa.

A good example of this African-Asian exchange[31] is the case of the sorghums. In Asia, there exist today cultivated sorghums of African origin other than those already mentioned, especially, for example, *S. bicolor* Moench which seems to have originated through crossing cultigens deriving from *S. aethiopicum* on the one hand and on the other from the wild species *S. sudanense*. This *S. bicolor* may be linked in particular to the *S. dochna* Snowd. of India, Arabia and Burma, re-introduced into Africa in more recent times, the *S. miliforme* Snowd. of India recently introduced into Kenya, and the sorghums of East Africa. Yet another cultivated sorghum, *S. nervosum* Bess., seems related to *S. aethiopicum* and to *S. bicolor*, and it seems that the sorghums of Burma and also of China may, with others, be related to it.

Without going into the inevitably complex details of this genetic cocktail, we can simply state that there are plenty of indications of ancient contacts between the sorghums of Africa and those of Asia. Everything points to very old relationships and exchanges of plant material between the eastern parts of Africa and Asia. Certainly we know that in Africa, in precolonial times, there existed a number of cultivated plant species which had their origin in tropical South-East Asia.

We have already mentioned that it was perhaps easier for agriculture to gain a foothold in the African forest as a result of the appearance of cultivated species such as bananas and taro which had their origin in the wet, tropical forests of South-East Asia and the East Indies. It was from here that the early migrants set out for Madagascar and the East African coast, taking with them a number of their domesticated plants.

While Africa exchanged cultivated plants with the East in ancient times, it seems clear that Africa was Asia's debtor in the matter of domesticated animals. Some pig species of East Africa, for example, seem related to the *Suidae* domesticated in Asia. As C. C. Wrigley observes,[32] 'It is quite certain that animal husbandry did not develop independently in Africa south of the Sahara, where the fauna does not and did not include possible ancestors of the domestic cow, sheep or goat.' These species came in from Egypt via the Nile valley. However we should note that there is a good possibility that some of these animals had been domesticated in the African part of the palaeo-Mediterranean sphere. This seems particularly likely

31. See R. Portères, 1962.
32. C. C. Wrigley, 1970.

in the case of cattle since pre-Neolithic man seems to have hunted *Bos primigenius* and *B. brachyeros* in Egypt.

This brief account serves to show that Africa is far from having been dependent on development elsewhere for the elements of its agricultural and pastoral development. Africa was not, any more than Europe or Asia, closed to contributions from outside its borders and it is also true that its northern part belongs, as do Europe and Asia, to a Mediterranean sphere which formerly possessed a much greater ecological continuity than it does now. We have also seen that the African continent domesticated a certain number of indigenous plants which also benefited other parts of the world, such as a number of cultivated varieties of sorghum. And if in some parts of Africa gathering and hunting continued for a very long time to be the main type of subsistence, this was not due to lack of development but rather to the abundance and diversity of resources available in their natural state, which enabled man to live without much effort in their ecosystems rather than being obliged to try to transform them by means of domestication.

Conclusion

Side by side with food-gathering went that nascent form of agriculture which consists of assisting and favouring the development of a plant without being directly involved in its reproduction. This still happens with some food-yielding trees and shrubs, like the kola, shea-butter and the oil palm. But we also find on the African continent all the stages of horticultural and agricultural development. There is, in short, a very great range of traditional techniques of agriculture, including ingenious methods of preparing the land for the cultivation of rice, the use of fire, particularly for clearing the bush and fertilizing the soil, and also combinations of cultivation and stock-raising adapted to woodlands.

In effect, African agriculture began and developed in three principal centres or foci (Fig. 27.4). The first comprised North Africa from Egypt to Morocco and formed part of the Mediterranean sphere. This area was certainly influenced by developments in the Near Eastern cradle of agriculture and stock-raising, but it also without any doubt underwent developments specific to itself. The second comprised the belt of savannah and steppe peripheral to the forest heart of Africa. Here a cereal-producing agriculture (sorghum, millets) evolved. The third was composed of the forest and its fringes and was characterized by horticulture associated with food-gathering (and from this food-gathering it took some of its cultigens).

There were no insuperable barriers between these various centres: wheats, millets, sorghums are found next door to oasis cultivation; food plants deriving from the horticultural forest fringes are found in the fields of the savannah, and horticulture borrows plants from the specialized food-

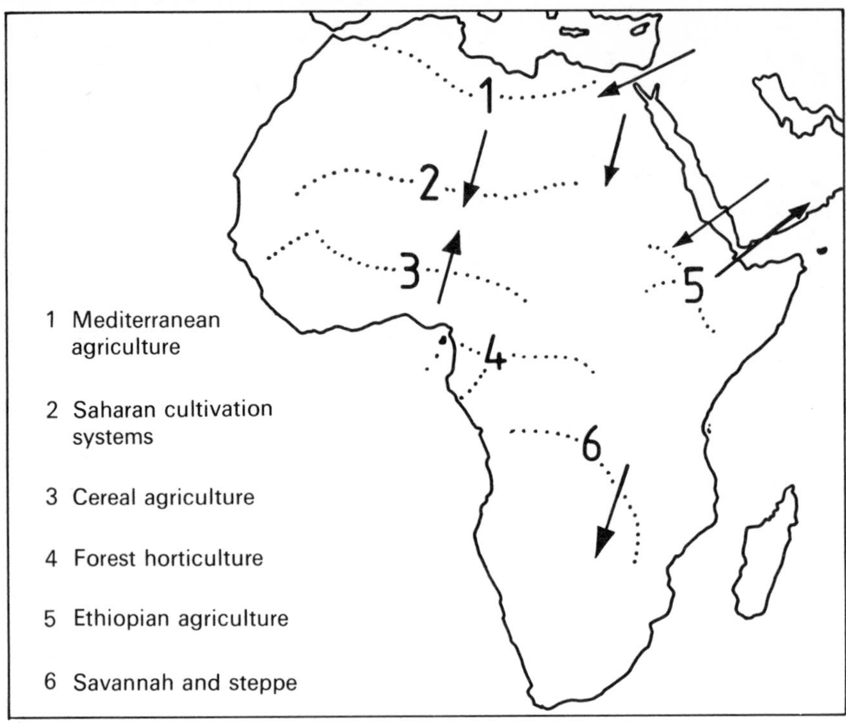

FIG. 27.4 *Geo-cultural sketch map of Africa*

gathering practised in the tropical forest. Ethiopia is another example whose economic crops include not only indigenous plants but some from the Mediterranean sphere, others from the agricultural centre of the savannah and the steppe and still others from Asia.

Of all these centres of agricultural development, the one that seems to be the most important is that of the savannahs and steppes and particularly those areas of it close by the forest or important water courses and lakes.

It is still difficult to date precisely African agricultural prehistory and history. Nevertheless, there are grounds for believing that the crucial period when the domestication of plants began was at the end of the Pleistocene, between 9000 and 5000 before our era. In this period, food-gathering increased and to some extent became specialized on the fringes of the central forest belt and around inland waters, and fishing was developed and led to some measure of settlement. In substance, the conditions favourable to domesticating plants appeared. We are at liberty to think, while waiting for archaeology to confirm or invalidate this opinion, that this occurred when, in the Fertile Crescent of the Near East, agricultural and pastoral foundations were being laid which, along with others, would become those of the civilizations of Europe.

PLATE 27.1 *Top-soil firing, Futa Djalon; Pita, Timbi-Madina* (photo R. Portères)

PLATE 27.2 *The* Soung *or spade of the Serer Gnominka, fishermen and rice growers of the islands of the 'Little Coast', Senegal. Used for tilling and ridging the heavy soil in the mangrove swamp rice fields, it corresponds to the* Kadyendo *of the Dyula Bayott of Casamance and the* Kofi *or* Kop *of the Baga of coastal Guinea* (photo R. Portères)

PLATE 27.3 *Cultivation of land, Kadyendo, by the Dyula of Oussouye (Casamance) in preparation for the re-planting of the rice beds* (photo R. Portères)

PLATE 27.4 *Artificial islands for the cultivation of rice in fields too low-lying for fresh water to drain away, Guinea-Bissau* (photo R. Portères)

PLATE 27.5 *Rice pits in hydromorphic soil subject to temporary swamping during the rainy season (implurium rice growing); Bayoyy village in Nyassa Casamance* (photo R. Portères)

28 Discovery and diffusion of metals and development of social systems up to the fifth century before our era

J. VERCOUTTER

In the general history of Africa the Nile valley plays a special part. Despite the difficulties – sometimes greatly exaggerated[1] – presented by the cataracts, the Nile, 6500 kilometres long, is a channel of north–south communication and transcontinental trade that should not be underestimated. Descending from the north, beyond the 16th parallel and the deserts of Baiyuda in the west and Butana in the east, the Nile valley gives access to a region of annual rains and to the great east–west route across Africa, stretching from the Atlantic to the Red Sea, through the valleys and depressions of the Niger and the Chad, the plateaux of Darfur and Kordofan, and the piedmont plains of the Atbara and Baraka. Thus to the advantages of a north–south line of communication running from the great equatorial lakes to the Mediterranean are added those of an east–west line, with the Nile Basin giving access to the basins of the Zaïre, the Niger and the Senegal.

So the vast area occupying the north-east corner of the continent is of primary importance for the early history of Africa. Unfortunately it has still not been properly explored archaeologically or historically. The lower part of the Nile valley, from the Second Cataract to the Mediterranean, is comparatively well known, thanks to the efforts of the archaeologists who have been investigating it since the beginning of the nineteenth century up to the present day. But such is not the case with the middle part of the valley, between the Second and the Sixth Cataracts, nor with the upper part, from Khartoum to the Great Lakes, nor, above all, with the desert areas on either side of the Nile and its tributaries, all practically untouched by archaeology and known to history only through hypotheses too often based on insufficient or even defective observation.

This chapter will be set out in an order that is both chronological and geographical. It will deal with two periods. The first extends from the Neolithic to the beginnings of the third millennium, when written evidence, and consequently history, appears in the lower Nile valley: proceeding from

1. On the cataracts and their real or imaginary difficulties, the most detailed work is still that of A. Chelu, 1891, pp. 30–73, which described each cataract and gives charts of the navigable channels.

the relatively better known to the unknown, or in other words from north to south, I shall set out what is known of the various civilizations which existed on the banks of the river. The second period runs from the early part of the third millennium up to the fifth century before our era, and, like the first period, proceeds geographically from the lower to the upper valley of the Nile.

From the Neolithic to the third millennium before our era

This period, covering roughly the two millennia from about 5000 to 3000 before our era, sees the appearance and diffusion of metal in the Nile valley, together with the appearance of the first social systems. From the historical point of view, therefore, it is one of the most important periods, if not *the* most important.

I shall recapitulate, briefly and without dwelling on the material aspect, the Neolithic cultures of the Nile valley already dealt with in Chapter 25, because it is difficult to speak of the dark age of proto-Nilotic history (from 3800 to 3000 before our era) without referring at the same time to the cultures that preceded it. In fact, all recent research both in Nubia and in Egypt has amply confirmed the fact that the appearance of metal does not constitute a break in the general evolution of North-East African civilizations: the cultures of the copper age are the direct and legitimate descendants of the Neolithic cultures, and it is often impossible, in the field, to tell a late Neolithic site from a Chalcolithic one. The first king of the Thinite dynasty in Egypt is the legitimate descendant of the chiefs of the last Neolithic ethnic groups, just as the great Pharaohs of the Theban period were the true heirs of the masters of the Memphian Empire.

The lower Nile valley (4500–3000 before our era[2])

The social organization one can see, or rather imagine, being established in the lower Nile valley in Egypt in about 3000 before our era unquestionably arose from the irrigation techniques that were necessary for the agricultural development of the valley. Man's possession of the valley began in the Neolithic, and continued to evolve up to the emergence of a unified monarchial system.

As Herodotus said, to be echoed by innumerable other writers: 'Egypt is the gift of the Nile.' From the beginning of the historical era, when the drying-up of the Sahara from the Atlantic to the Red Sea was in its last stages, Egypt could not have lived without the annual Nile flood.

2. On social development in Egypt prior to the Neolithic and Chalcolithic ages which witnessed the development of the first social systems, see the excellent survey by W. C. Hayes, 1965. This posthumous work, which was edited by K. C. Seele, has a complete chapter on social development in Egypt (Vol. 1, pp. 1–29), with an abundant analytical bibliography (pp. 29–41).

Without the alluvial deposits, the country would have been as much a desert as the Negev or as the Sahara itself. But the life-bestowing gift Egypt received from the river could also be a poisoned one. In year 3 of Osorkon III (754 before our era), the flood was so great no dyke could hold against it and 'all the temples of Thebes were like a swamp'; the High Priest of Amon had to implore the god to stay the rising of the waters. The same disaster occurred again in year 6 of Taharqa (683 before our era), when the whole valley 'was transformed into an ocean' – though to boost his own popularity the king represented the flood as a blessing from Heaven!

The flood is very variable: it tends to be too great or too small, rarely exactly right.[3] For example, between 1871 and 1900 three bad floods were recorded, three mediocre ones, ten good ones, eleven overabundant ones, and three that were dangerous. Out of thirty floods, only ten could really be considered satisfactory.[4]

So it might be said that the history of civilization in the Nile valley is the history of man's 'domestication' of the river. This process called for the building of dykes and earth banks or levees – some parallel and some at right angles to the course of the river. This made it possible to construct reservoirs or *hods* on either bank, to slow down or hold back the flooding and to extend it to land it would not have reached if left to itself.

This system was evolved through long experience, and could only be arrived at gradually.[5] To be really effective, the reservoirs needed to be planned methodically for the whole country, or at least over large areas. This meant a communal effort, only possible through previous agreement between a large number of people. This was the origin of the first social systems in the lower Nile valley: first came ethnic groups arranged around a provincial agricultural centre, then the joining together of several of these centres, which finally formed two larger political groupings, one in the north and the other in the south.[6]

The evidence available to us for the period from 5000 to 3000 before our era offers few clues as to the exact nature of the social system on which the occupation and cultivation of the lower Nile valley was based. The very term 'ethnic group', used above, is probably misleading. For there is no evidence to suggest that at that time the groups who had settled along the Nile valley were ethnically very different from each other, although it seems to be

3. On the dangers of flooding, cf. J. Besançon, 1957, pp. 78–84.

4. ibid., pp. 82–3; Bibliography, pp. 387–8.

5. To my knowledge, the general works of Egyptian irrigation do not examine the problems posed by the emergence and gradual development of irrigation in that country. The system as it existed is described in J. Besançon, op. cit., pp. 85–97 and in F. Hartmann, 1923, pp. 113–18. L. Krzyzaniak, 1977, draws a distinction between a natural irrigation period (ch. 1, pp. 52–123) and a controlled irrigation period (ibid., pp. 127–67). The latter is thought to have begun in the Gerzean (Nagada II), cf. ibid., p. 137, in about 3070 before our era plus or minus 290. With regard to this date, see H. A. Nordström, 1972, p. 5.

6. J. Vercoutter, 1967, pp. 253–7.

established that political or politico-religious groupings already existed. Our conclusions can be based only on the representations appearing on small votive offerings: make-up palettes and ceremonial clubs of magical or religious significance. This evidence reflects – and only very summarily – the situation at the very end of the period, the last few generations of the late fourth millennium.[7] It may, however, be assumed that the social system of which this evidence affords us a glimpse changed very little during the first two millennia of the period.

The beginning of written history coincides roughly with the fusing into a single system, under the authority of one king, of the political groupings of north and south. Such in outline is the history of the lower Nile valley from 5000 to 3000 before our era, characterized not only by the appearance of metal, really a minor phenomenon, but above all by man's taking over the whole Nile valley. This annexation involved not only the construction of dykes and reservoirs but also the levelling of the ground so that the water did not linger in the shallows and so that it could be channelled on to all the cultivable land in the valley. Without a doubt this represented a victory of the peasant over a nature that whatever anyone might say was basically hostile.

The Neolithic

Chapter 25 of this volume describes in detail the material features of the different cultures or cultural horizons forming the social development pattern of the cultures that are brought together under the general heading of Neolithic and Predynastic in the Nile valley in both Sudan and Egypt. In the pages that follow, our sole concern has been to shed light on the social aspects and the historical development of these cultures. In point of fact, in the Nile valley, Neolithic and Predynastic form a cultural continuum. To take only one example, the Badarian, analysed in detail in Chapter 25, p. 645, is only one stage in the development of a culture which started out from the Tasian (ibid., p. 644) and culminated in Nagada II (ibid., p. 646) and the pre-Thinite societies.

In other words, this chapter makes a synthesis of the facts analysed in Chapter 25. The two aspects of the issues raised are complementary to each other, and square brackets [ ] have been used to indicate the essential references which will make it easier for the reader to locate the detailed description of the cultures, which are only touched on in very general terms in this chapter.

The Neolithic period in Egypt is known only by a few sites, often not even contemporary with one another. The oldest is on the edge of the Fayum depression [= Fayumian B – Chapter 25, p. 646] in the west of the valley, in Middle Egypt.[8] In the north, there are sites at Merimde-Beni-Salame

7. On these problems see J.-L. de Cenival, 1973, pp. 49–57.

8. On the Neolithic of the Fayum, cf. W. C. Hayes, 1965, pp. 93–9 and 139–40, together with the comments of F. Wendorf, R. Said and R. Schild, 1970, pp. 1161–71.

[= Merimdian, Chapter 25, p. 647][9] on the edge of the desert on the west bank of the delta, about 48 kilometres north-west of Cairo; and at El Omari [= Omarian A and B, Chapter 25, pp. 648–9][10] near Helwan, not far from Cairo. In Middle and Upper Egypt there is one site at Deir Tasa south-east of Asyut and a couple of less important ones at Toukh and Armant-Gebelein in the region of Thebes.[11] Comparisons that might be made between these sites, to determine the nature and extension of the various aspects of Neolithic that they represent, are made more difficult by the fact that they are not contemporary. According to radio-carbon datings, the oldest site, Fayum A, goes back to 4400 before our era (± 180), then come Merimde-Beni-Salame, 4100 before our era (± 180) and El Omari, 3300 before our era (± 230), and finally Tasa, which dates from the end of the Neolithic.[12]

In other words, the excavated sites tell us something about the early Neolithic in the Fayum and the Delta, and about the late Neolithic to the south of the Delta and in Middle Egypt; but from 4000 to 3300 before our era, seven centuries, we know little or nothing about the general evolution of Egyptian Neolithic as a whole. The same is true of the region south of Middle Egypt. True, surface discoveries on the edge of the valley and in the desert have been numerous: they confirm the existence of what has been called the humid interval or Neolithic subpluvial[13] at the end of the sixth millennium, which marked a pause in the drying-up of the north-east African climate. But in the absence of systematic excavation these finds tell us little about the Neolithic cultures of which they are the survivors. The only really useful studies have been those based on the properly excavated sites already referred to. It is clear, then, what large tracts of time and space remain unexplored, and this is all the more regrettable in that it is generally admitted that the Neolithic Revolution came to Egypt from the Near East, the Fertile Crescent of Syria and Palestine, where it is attested a very long way back. The proto-Neolithic in Jericho has been dated at 6800, well before the Neolithic in the Fayum. But in order to prove that the Neolithic of the lower Nile valley, in particular of the Delta and Fayum, really came from Asia, one would need to have information from sites on the maritime edge and in the eastern part of the Delta up as far as Memphis. And these are precisely the gaps in our knowledge. The result is that the Asiatic origin of Egyptian Neolithic

9. On the Merimde-Beni-Salame site, cf. W. C. Hayes, ch. 1, pp. 103–16 and 141–3, and, with respect to ceramics, L. Hjalmar, 1962, pp. 3ff.

10. Cf. W. C. Hayes, 1965, pp. 117–22 and 143–4.

11. With regard to Upper Egypt, we unfortunately do not have the surveys and critical bibliography of W. C. Hayes, whose work *Most Ancient Egypt* remained uncompleted on the author's death (cf. ch. 1, p. 148, n. 1). Reference should be made to the survey of J. Vandier, 1952, pp. 166–80.

12. On the Tasian Neolithic, cf. G. Brunton, 1937, pp. 5–33. Cf. W. F. Libby, 1955, pp. 77–8, for the date.

13. K. W. Butzer, 1964, pp. 449–53, and G. Camps, 1974, p. 222.

remains a hypothesis.[14] This is a hypothesis which now needs to be supported, especially since archaeological investigations in the Sahara in the past decade have shown that the Neolithic there is also very old, particularly in the Ahaggar, where the Amekni site is almost contemporary with proto-Neolithic Jericho.[15] In point of fact, the dates of the Saharo-Sudanese Neolithic are all earlier than those of the Egyptian Neolithic, at least in respect of the currently dated sites of the Fayum and Merimde-Beni-Salame,[16] and of the Nubian Neolithic.[17] Moreover, if we again confine ourselves to the sources currently available, pottery may have appeared in Nubia at an earlier date than in Egypt.[18]

In view of the greater age of the Saharo-Sudanese Neolithic, at first sight there is nothing to rule out the possibility that the Neolithic of the Nile valley in both Egypt and Sudan descended from the African Neolithic. However, caution naturally must be exercised, owing to the considerable dearth of Neolithic sites in the lower Nile valley in Egypt and to the fact that only the banks of the river have been investigated in Nubia. The archaeology of the strip between the river valley and the eastern Sahara is still unexplored. Even so, the influences moving out from North Africa in the direction of Nubia in the Capsian and Ibero-Maurusian, and from central Africa likewise towards Nubia[19] in the Sebilian and Middle Palaeolithic, may have continued into the proto-Neolithic. Since the Delta was quite plainly a crossroads, it could have been the meeting-point of influences from both west and south and east and north-east.

As soon as the Neolithic makes its appearance in the lower Nile valley, a cultural differentiation is to be seen between the northern and southern groups. Both populations are cultivators and cattle-raisers who still practise fishing and hunting, but the material evidence they have left behind differs quite clearly according to the group it belongs to, in kind, quality and quantity. The same applies to certain customs.

In the north, the tighter grouping of the houses would suggest a social structure that was already quite ordered, and the dead are buried in the villages, as if they went on belonging to an organized community.[20] The

14. In studying the problem of the origins of the Predynastic Egyptian population, Mrs E. Baumgartel, writing in 1955, rejected the possibility of western, northern and eastern origins (cf. E. J. Baumgartel, 1955, p. 19). Recent archaeological work in the Sahara (cf. below) has shown that this view has to be qualified as regards the west, although it remains true of the east.

15. G. Camps, 1974, p. 224, and 1969. Amekni dates from 6700 before our era and the proto-Neolithic of Jericho from 6800 before our era.

16. H. A. Nordström, 1972, p. 5.

17. ibid., pp. 8, 16–17 and 251.

18. F. Wendorf, 1968, p. 1053. Pottery appeared in Nubia in the Shamarkian in 5750 before our era, but only in the Fayum in 6391 b.p., i.e. in about 4400 before our era.

19. ibid., p. 1055, Fig. 8.

20. H. Junker, 1930, pp. 36–47.

south, on the other hand, dug its tombs on the edge of the desert; the houses were more dispersed; its organization more closely based on the family. The differences between the northern and southern groups are also seen in their techniques: the craftsmen of the north have a finer method of working stone, and their stone vases introduce a technique that was to remain one of those most characteristic of ancient Pharaonic Egypt. As regards pottery, however, although the north shows a greater variety of form, the south has a better technique of production, with, in addition to black with white decoration, the remarkable red pottery with black border which the south in its turn bequeathed to ancient Predynastic Egypt, and which is one of the most characteristic industries of the Nile valley, both in Egypt and the Sudan.

So the Neolithic sees the emergence of two separate cultural groups, and perhaps two separate social systems. In space, one belongs to the area around Memphis, Fayum and the north-west edge of the Delta, and the other to Middle and Upper Egypt, between Asyut and Thebes.[21] This cultural difference, while not excluding points of contact between the two groups, grew more definite during the last centuries of the fourth millennium, then disappeared with the coming of a common civilization just before the appearance, in about 3000 before our era, of a unified monarchy in the Egyptian Nile valley.[22]

The Predynastic (*cf. pp. 646–50 above*)

The Predynastic period in Egypt is often referred to as the Eneolithic or Chalcolithic, as if the appearance of metal were a crucial event, a genuine turning-point, in the development of the valley. In actual fact, and this needs to be emphasized, there is no break between Neolithic and Eneolithic in the lower Nile valley. On the contrary, the line of development is clearly continuous. I therefore prefer to keep to the term *Predynastic* for these centuries about which we know little, but which are of cardinal importance in the history of Africa.

Metal made its appearance slowly in Egypt, and does not seem to have been brought by invaders. Reversing the order found in other civilizations, copper appears before gold,[23] although gold was more easily found in deposits not far from the valley. The first copper articles, very small in size, appear in the southern group, on the site at El Badari (which has given its name to the Badarian culture);[24] in the north, they are found at Demeh,

21. It will be noted that the northern group does not stretch as far as the sea. It is as continental as the southern group. Cf. J.-L. de Cenival, 1973, Map A, p. 50.

22. J. Vercoutter, 1967, pp. 250–3.

23. Cf. A. Lucas, 1962, pp. 199–200.

24. Cf. Chapter 25, p. 649–50. The Badarian civilization has often been studied. The basic work is still that of G. Brunton and G. Caton-Thompson, 1928, together with G. Brunton, 1948, ch. VI, pp. 9–12.

Kasr-Karoun and Khasmet-ed-Dib in the Fayum (this group of sites is called Fayum A to distinguish it from Neolithic Fayum or Fayum B).

There is some debate as to whether copper smelting originated in Egypt.[25] It may have been introduced from abroad, from the Near East, but in that case, only on a very limited scale, with a few individuals imparting the technique to the people of the valley. But the possibility of convergence cannot be ruled out: the people of the valley may have discovered copper for themselves at about the same time as it was discovered in the Fertile Crescent. It was, indeed, at the same period that the Badarian peoples, perhaps by accident, discovered blue enamel by heating grindstones or palettes on which eye make-up had been pounded – a cosmetic with a malachite base, malachite being an ore (green carbonate) of copper.[26] This would mean that the inhabitants of the valley simultaneously discovered copper, which they worked without smelting, and what is called Egyptian faïence or blue enamel, which they at once used for making beads.

But whether the discovery of metal came to Egypt from Asia or from within, its application was very limited, and stone tools continue to be the most common in both northern and southern groups. One thing that seems sure is that the discovery or diffusion of metal led to no change in social organization as evidenced by burials.

The Predynastic, from about 4000 to 3000 before our era, may be divided into four phases to help bring out the development of the Nile valley during a period which is still unfortunately very obscure. The phases are: early, ancient, middle and late.

During the *Early Predynastic* [= Badarian, Chapter 25, p. 645] the northern and southern groups continued to develop independently of one another. In the south, most of what we know about this phase comes from the site at El Badari, near Deir Tasa. Despite the fact that metal had made its appearance, Badarian[27] is still so close to Neolithic that it has sometimes been asked whether it is not merely a local variation of Tasian Neolithic. Study of skeletal remains has shown that the Badarians of the Predynastic were physically very close to the Egyptians living in the same area today. They still lived in oval huts, though these were slightly more comfortable than in the previous period, with woven mats, leather cushions and even wooden beds. The cult of the dead began to develop; the corpse was now placed in a wooden chamber within the oval grave and surrounded with grave-goods, food, jars and articles of everyday use. Like the people of the Tasian Neolithic, the Badarians grew flax and wove it into linen, as well as using leather obtained from hunting and from their own herds. They thus

25. Cf. A. Lucas, 1962, pp. 201–6. On the origin of copper smelting in the ancient Near East, cf. R. J. Forbes, 1964, pp. 16–23. The hieroglyph for copper was only recently decyphered, cf. J. R. Harris, 1961, pp. 50–62.

26. A. Lucas, 1962, p. 201.

27. On this civilization, the basic works are still those by G. Brunton, 1928, pp. 1–42; 1937, pp. 33–66; 1948, pp. 4–11.

practised a mixed economy, cultivation and animal husbandry still being supplemented by hunting and fishing. They went on making black-topped red ware and excellent and finely polished red pottery. The discovery of enamel made possible the manufacture of bright blue beads. Eye make-up was pounded up on palettes made of slate which were sometimes decorated, as were ivory combs. In this way, art gradually made its appearance.

In the north the Early Predynastic [= Fayumian A, Chapter 25, p. 647; the most recent level at Merimde-Beni-Salame may also belong to this Early Predynastic] is known to us through the Fayum A sites.[28] As in the Badarian, tools are made of flint much more often than of metal. The Fayum B potters produced vases with much more variety of shape than those of the Badarian, but their technique was less advanced. The northern craftsmen were superior again in the fine stone bowls and vases they carved, mostly out of black schist; but on the whole the two groups were very close, each representing the normal development of the Neolithic culture that had preceded it. There is no indication that, in either group, there were noticeable social differences between members of the community. In particular there do not seem to have been within the group any individuals who were substantially richer than others. Everything points to equality of social status between the different members of the community, regardless of their age or sex. This conclusion is, of course, based on the assumption that the cemeteries which are known and have been excavated belonged to the whole group under consideration; in other words, that no members of the community were buried outside these cemeteries on the basis of racial, religious or social discrimination of some kind.

Ancient Predynastic [= Nagada I, Chapter 25, p. 646] is unfortunately known only from sites in the south. It is also called Amratian, from the site of El Amrah[29] near Abydos, a good deal farther south than El Badari. Amratian corresponds also to what is still sometimes called Nagada I culture, following the nomenclature of Flinders Petrie which is used often in radio-carbon dating.

Amratian culture is the descendant, in time, of Badarian, though here again there is no discontinuity; on some sites the Amratian level is in direct contact with the Badarian. Amratian produced the same black-topped red ware as Badarian, but introduced pottery decorated with geometric and naturalistic designs painted in dull white on a red or red-brown ground; sometimes, more rarely, the decoration consists of white-filled hatchings on a black ground. The Amratian potter was more inventive than his predecessor, and created new, particularly animal, forms. The hunt still provided one of the main themes for naturalistic decoration, hippopotamus hunting being a special favourite. It seems, therefore, that in Ancient Predynastic the transition had not yet been completed between a social

28. G. Caton-Thompson and E. W. Gardner, 1934.

29. Cf. J. Vandier, 1952, pp. 231–2. The site was discovered in 1900. Work on it was published by D. Randall-MacIver and A. C. Mace, 1902, pp. 3–53.

system made up of more or less nomadic hunters and fishers to one based on villages or groups of sedentary cultivators and cattle raisers.

The characteristic weapon of the Amratian is a club, often carved out of hard stone in the shape of a truncated cone.[30] This fact is important, for weapons of this kind disappear completely after the Amratian, whereas a sign belonging to the hieroglyphic system of the historical period still uses it phonetically.[31] This means that the hieroglyphic system of writing must have begun to develop by the Amratian period, and thus in the Ancient Predynastic, about 3800 before our era according to radio-carbon dating.

Art continued to develop, with figurines of bearded men with phallic coverings, of dancing women and different kinds of animals. There were also more decorated palettes and combs with animal ornamentation.[32]

The Amratian sites between Asyut in the north and Thebes in the south include Nagada, Ballas, Hou and Abydos. The fact that there is no contemporary site in the north is all the more regrettable in that the Amratian shows distinct signs of contact between north and south: for example, Amratian grave-goods include stone vases the same shape as those found in the predynastic of the north. Nothing in the funeral customs indicates that there was a change in social organization between the Early Predynastic period and the Ancient Predynastic of the Amratian. These would still appear to be human communities composed of individuals enjoying equality even if they are under the authority of a single chief or of a group of individuals.

After being in existence for a century or perhaps less, Amratian culture gradually merged into a new and complex culture combining Amratian elements with others of undoubtedly northern origin. This mixed culture, the *Middle Predynastic* [= Nagada II, Chapter 25, p. 646, perhaps Omarian A – ibid., p. 648] or Gerzean (Nagada II according to Flinders Petrie terminology), is named after the site at Gerzeh[33] in Lower Egypt, near the Fayum, where it manifests itself most clearly. It has two forms, being purely Gerzean in the north and a combination of Amratian and Gerzean in the south.[34]

In the north this new culture centred on the area around Memphis, the Fayum and the southern edge of the delta. Northern Gerzean shows its originality above all in pottery, with buff-coloured vases made of material very different from that of the south. The decoration is naturalistic, in red ochre on a light ground, with new subjects such as mountains, ibexes, flamingoes, aloes, and particularly ships. Like the craftsmen of Fayum A

30. For this club, see W. M. F. Petrie, 1920, Plate XXVI and pp. 22–4.

31. A. H. Gardiner, 1957, p. 510, Table 1.

32. J.-L. de Cenival, 1973, pp. 16–21.

33. The village of Gerzen is situated at the latitude of the Fayum, hence well to the south of present-day Cairo. The predynastic site was excavated in 1911: cf. W. M. F. Petrie, E. Mackay and G. Wainwright, 1912.

34. J. Vercoutter, 1967, pp. 245–67, and J. Vandier, 1952, pp. 248–52 and 436–96.

whose successors they were, the Gerzeans made stone vessels, but as well as schist they also used harder stone like breccia, basalt, diorite and serpentine. The typical Gerzean weapon was a pear-shaped club[35] which was to become the royal weapon *par excellence* of early history, and was to survive, like the Amratian club, as one of the signs of hieroglyphic writing.[36]

There is also evidence of social and religious evolution. The dead are now buried in rectangular tombs, with their heads to the north and facing east instead of west as before. The ships so often represented on Gerzean pottery carry insignia on their prow in which it is hard not to see the ancestors of the symbols or standards of the *nomes* or provinces of Pharaonic Egypt.

Human groups were now, it seems, living together in associations much larger than those of family or village. The power arising from the new social organization made it possible to exploit the Nile valley better by means of irrigation, and the resulting increase in wealth was reflected in finer and more plentiful stone vessels and a greater number of tools and weapons made of copper: chisels, daggers, harpoons and axes. It cannot be by chance that grave jewellery now makes use of gold and semi-precious stones – lapis lazuli, chalcedony, turquoise, cornelian and agate. The art of statuary also advanced, and themes such as falcons' and cows' heads show that the Pharaonic religion was also there in embryo: Horus the Falcon and Hathor the Cow were already worshipped.

In the south the cultures which came after the Amratian of the Ancient Predynastic were strongly marked by Gerzean influences. The classic buff-coloured Gerzean pottery with red naturalistic decoration is found side by side with the traditional southern red ware with black rims or dull white decoration.

Influence in fact worked both ways between the two groups, and similarities are numerous at this period, for example in slate palettes for cosmetics, and in the making of flint knives, for which the technique had now reached its highest perfection. The two cultural groups were moving gradually towards complete fusion.

This fusion between north and south took place [= Omarian B and Maadian, Chapter 25, p. 649] in the *Late Predynastic* or late Gerzean, also sometimes called the Semainian.[37] We are now on the threshold of history, for this last phase may have been a very short one. If, faithful to traditional dates, we take 3000 before our era as the beginning of history, the Late Predynastic probably lasted no more than two or three generations at the most. A radio-carbon date from the Middle Predynastic shows it extending up to 3066 before our era, which leaves scarcely three-quarters of a century for the transition from the end of Middle Predynastic to the beginning of history. This beginning should probably be set a couple of

35. W. M. F. Petrie, 1920, Plate XXVI and pp. 22–4.

36. A. H. Gardiner, 1957, p. 510, Table 3.

37. The expression was coined by Flinders Petrie, 1939, pp. 55ff. Semaineh is a village in Upper Egypt near Qena. Cf. also J. Vercoutter, 1967, pp. 247–50.

hundred years later than it has been, but even if it is placed at 2800[38] that still leaves only just over 200 years for a phase which saw the exploitation of the Nile valley completed and the establishment of a social system headed by a monarchy ruling by divine right.

This phase is so close to the one which witnessed the appearance of written texts that attempts have been made to project evidence from the written documents on to the evidence from archaeology.[39]

The texts seem to suggest that at the beginning of the Late, if not at the end of the Middle, Predynastic, the most powerful town in the south was Ombos (in Egyptian, Noubet) near Nagada, right in the heart of Amratian culture. The town's god was Seth, an animal god whose exact nature is still debated: he has been variously identified as an anteater, a kind of pig, a giraffe, and a creature either mythical or extinct. The texts inform us that this southern god fought with a falcon god, Horus, worshipped in a village called Behdet which must have been in the Delta, i.e. in the area of Gerzean culture. Thus, at the end of the Middle Predynastic, Egypt would seem to have been divided into two social structures, one in the north dominated by Horus of Behdet, and the other in the south ruled over by Seth of Ombos. Once again the sources at our disposal do not, unfortunately, allow us to specify the nature of these social structures. The most that can be conjectured is the importance of a group chief, based on his magical and religious powers, which in the historical period was to be reflected in the divinity of the royal personage.[40] It might perhaps be taken that the chief of the community had practically unlimited powers over the individuals in that community but that the latter could, on the other hand, kill its chief upon occasion, if his magic powers had diminished (cf. A. Moret, *La Mise à mort du dieu en Egypte*).

According to the texts, the struggle between the two groups ended in the victory of the north over the south, after which a unified kingdom was set up centred on Heliopolis[41] near Cairo, i.e. some 65 kilometres north of the site at Gerzeh. In archaeological terms, this victory of north over south would correspond to the penetration of Gerzean culture into the Amratian area.

To continue this extrapolation of written evidence on to a period for which there are no texts, the Late Predynastic probably witnessed some social or political evolution, in both the northern and the southern groups. The political unity resulting from the victory of north over south, at the end of the Middle or the beginning of the Late Predynastic, is supposed to have lasted only a short while, after which each group resumed an independent existence. Following this, the political centre of the north shifted from Behdet, of which the exact position is unknown, to Buto in the western delta about 40 kilometres from the sea, where it has not been possible to

38. A. Scharff, 1950, p. 191.
39. The basic work still remains the outstanding essay by K. Sethe, 1930.
40. Cf. G. Posener, 1960.
41. K. Sethe, 1930, a hypothesis refuted by H. Kees, 1961, p. 43.

reach archaeological levels contemporary with the Predynastic. At the same time the political capital of the south moved from Ombos to El Kab (Nekheb, in ancient Egyptian), some 95 kilometres further south.[42] Thus the southern group became more southern and the northern more northerly.

At Buto they worshipped a cobra goddess, Wadjit, at El Kab they worshipped a female vulture. These two divinities were still protectors of the Pharaohs in the historical period and were to figure regularly in the royal coronation ritual.[43] Certain documents written nearly a thousand years later preserved the names of the rulers of these political groups at the end of the Late Predynastic, but very few of them have survived. But from that period on it seems certain that north and south were culturally united. In particular the god Horus, who originated in the north, was also worshipped in the south, and political leaders in both north and south looked on themselves as his servitors and supporters, with the title of Shemsu Horus.[44]

From the purely material point of view there is little difference between the civilization of the Middle and that of the Late Predynastic, but there was undoubted progress in both art and technique. The human figure became a frequent subject, and mural painting made its appearance at Hierakonpolis (Nekhen in ancient Egyptian), an important town on the west bank of the Nile, almost opposite El Kab.[45] Hierakonpolis became the cradle of the southern royalty which took up the struggle against the north in about 3000 before our era.

How long the struggle lasted it is impossible to say. It occupied all the end of the Late Predynastic, ending in the victory of the north over the south and the creation of a unified state covering the whole valley from El Kab to the Mediterranean. This state was to be ruled over by southern kings, from the region of This near Abydos,[46] who constituted the first two, or Thinite, dynasties. For this reason the brief Late Predynastic period is often known as the pre-Thinite.

Such pre-Thinite survivals as have come down to us have all been found at Hierakonpolis.[47] They consist chiefly of great votive palettes[48] made of slate inscribed with historical scenes, and big carved clubs made of limestone. Both kinds of document are illustrated with scenes which throw some light on the political and social system then operating in the lower Nile valley. The country was divided into provinces or human groups, each of

42. J. Vercoutter, 1967, pp. 248–9.

43. Cf. A. H. Gardiner, 1957, pp. 71–6.

44. On the *Shemsu horus*, cf. J. Vandier, 1952, pp. 129–30 and 635–6.

45. Hierakonpolis has produced a large number of Predynastic monuments, cf. B. Porter and R. L. B. Moss, 1937, pp. 191–9.

46. The site of the capital has not been discovered. The existence of a royal necropolis dating from this period (cf. W. M. F. Petrie, 1901) at Abydos, on the west bank of the Nile, suggests that the city was in the vicinity.

47. The site was explored in 1898: cf. J. E. Quibell, *Hierakonpolis* (London, 1900–2).

48. The finest items were collected by W. M. F. Petrie, 1953.

which had a symbol or standard that accompanied the king on great occasions.

Comparison of the insignia represented on the ships of Gerzean pottery and on pre-Thinite palettes and clubs with the emblems of the *nomes* or provinces on documents surviving from the historical period, shows that from the Gerzean period the social system in the lower Nile valley, north and south, developed in geographical and economic rather than in ethnic terms. The human group organized itself around a habitat and a divinity. This was the result of the agricultural imperatives imposed on both north and south by the Nile's flood cycle. A group could only survive and develop if it was sufficiently numerous and well organized to perform the work necessary to protect its land from flood, extend the cultivable area, and build up reserves against possible vagaries of the river. The organization was both agricultural and religious, for only the god could ensure the success of the work and hence the prosperity of the group. And this dual organization is the basic and permanent feature governing the social system of the lower Nile valley.

It is possible, however, that this system based on geographical distribution was superimposed on an older system that was ethnically or socially determined. This seems to be suggested by three Egyptian words which existed at the dawn of history and continued right through until the end of Egyptian civilization. These words – Pât, Rekhyt and Henememet[49] – seem to apply to three very large human groups. The Pâts were apparently the inhabitants of the upper valley, with Horus for their lord; the Rekhyts the people of the lower valley, conquered at the end of the Late Predynastic; and the Henememets, or People of the Sun, the inhabitants of the region in the east between the Nile and the Red Sea. This region, which was still inhabited in the Neolithic and Predynastic, is important for the economy of the Nile valley because it supplies its copper and gold. And it was this vast social and ethnic system that was, apparently, broken up into small geographical and agricultural units. The role of the monarchy was to be purely political. To begin with, it brought the provincial groups together into two large confederations, one in the north and the other in the south. Then, later, it unified the two confederations, by force, into one kingdom, thus making it possible to exploit the country as a whole more effectively. This second task was to belong to the first Thinite Pharaohs. And it is with them that we enter history.

The upper Nile valley (5000–3000 before our era)

The various lower valley cultures we have been examining go no further south than the region of El Kab. The region of Aswan and the First Cataract belongs to a different cultural area. From the ethnic point of view, the peoples of the upper valley of the Nile seem to have been close to those of the

49. A. H. Gardiner, 1947, Vol. I, pp. 98ff.–112ff.

southern group of the lower valley – the Badarians and Amratians. This comparison can probably be extended to apply to the neighbouring ethnic groups of the eastern Sahara, but the relevant anthropological studies are still too few to be conclusive.[50]

As we have seen, little is known about the Neolithic and Predynastic in Egypt because so few sites have been scientifically explored. This situation is worse still when it comes to the upper valley: only the northern part, between the First and Second Cataracts, has been comparatively well explored, and even here the results of the excavations carried out between 1960 and 1966 have not yet all been published.

From the Second Cataract down to the great equatorial lakes, such rare data as there are come to us from surface prospecting: very few sites indeed have actually been excavated. Hence our knowledge of the upper valley, both in time and space, is much more limited than our knowledge of the Egyptian part of the valley.

The Neolithic (c. *5000–3800 before our era*)[51]

The first indisputably Neolithic excavation was carried out in the neighbourhood of Khartoum. The culture it reveals, sometimes known as Khartoum Neolithic, is more generally called Shaheinab [Shaheinabian, Chapter 25, pp. 642–3].[52]

Shaheinab is a habitat site where the burial places have not been found, but the abundant evidence it has provided relating to everyday life shows that the Sudanese who lived there, though mainly hunters and fishermen, were also cattle raisers. The study of their pottery, which was decorated by means of a rotating rowel, indicates that they were probably the descendants of another, earlier Neolithic culture of which traces have been found on a site in Khartoum itself. This site, Early Khartoum [Khartoumian, Chapter 25, p. 642],[53] comprises tombs in which blacks were buried. If, as everything seems to show, Shaheinab really is a descendant of Early Khartoum, we should have to admit that at Esh Shaheinab we are in the presence of a black population composed of groups of fishermen and hunters whose victims included lions, buffalo and hippopotamuses as well as antelopes, gazelles, oryxes and hares: the bones of all these have been found in their homes. Their weapons consisted of polished axes and round-headed clubs, sometimes considered the ancestors of the Amratian club with its head like a truncated cone. They worked in wood and knew how to weave, but apparently preferred clothes of leather. Their civilization is sometimes called 'the gouge culture' because of the large number of gouges or hollow

50. Cf. O. V. Nielsen, 1970, *passim* and p. 22; Bibliography, pp. 136–9.

51. For the periods concerning us here, the work of F. Wendorf, 1968, and H. A. Nordström, 1972, should primarily be noted.

52. Cf. A. J. Arkell, 1953.

53. Cf. A. J. Arkell, 1949b.

chisels found on the site. Because of its very characteristic pottery it has been possible to show that the Shaheinab culture stretched not only eastward and westward (Ténéré and Tibesti) but also south of Khartoum along the White and Blue Niles. No clues have been found as to the social organization.

It would be interesting to know the connections between the Neolithic of Shaheinab and that of the lower Nile valley, especially the Fayum. But unfortunately there is no known site north of Khartoum, between the Sixth and Second Cataracts, to make such comparisons possible. Recent researches in Lower Nubia, north of the Second Cataract, seem to have shown that the Neolithic there is quite close to that of Shaheinab, but it is sufficiently different still for the British and American archaeologists who have studied it to call it the 'Khartoum Variant'.[54]

The transition in the upper Nile valley from Neolithic to Predynastic, and thus to Eneolithic, remains very obscure. A few graves found at the confluence of the White and Blue Niles may perhaps indicate the existence there of a culture influenced by the Nubian Predynastic, known as Group A (see below), but this culture cannot be dated accurately.

By the Second Cataract, however, an industry has recently been discovered called the Abkian, from Abka[44] [Abkian, Chapter 25, p. 643], the name of the site which best represents it. So far it is known only for its lithic industry and its pottery: the sites where it is found have not all been published yet. From what is known so far, it seems that this culture belonged to a people made up of fishermen and hunters, as at Shaheinab, but here hunting was less productive, perhaps because the climate had entered the drying-up phase that followed the humid period. For fishing the men of Abka appear to have used huge permanent traps, cleverly installed in the channels of the cataract when the waters were low, which held the fish prisoner when the flood receded. The Abkians supplemented their food supply by gathering wild fruit and plants. The building of traps, which consisted of stone walls sometimes of considerable dimensions, implies quite an organized social grouping. This culture is apparently unrelated to that of Shaheinab, which, in its nearby form of Khartoum Variant, seems to be both contemporary with and very distinct from it. The Abkian is probably a special form of Neolithic owing nothing to either north or south. On the other hand, it seems that it was from Abkian Neolithic that the Nubian Predynastic emerged.

The Predynastic (3800–2800 before our era)

When the Egyptian government decided, in 1907, to increase the height of the first Aswan Dam by more than 6 metres, thus flooding the whole of Lower Nubia from Shellal to Korosko, a systematic archaeological survey

54. F. Wendorf, 1968, pp. 768–90, and H. A. Nordström, 1972, pp. 9–10.

55. This industry is described in F. Wendorf, 1968, pp. 611–29; cf. also H. A. Nordström, 1972, pp. 12–16.

was made of the area that was to be inundated. The archaeologists involved, noting the differences between the Egypt they knew well and Nubia, adopted a temporary classification for the new cultures they discovered, distinguishing, according to relative dating, Group A, Group B, Group C, and so on.[56] Since then attempts have been made to work out a system based on that used for the lower Nile valley, in which, for example, Early Nubian and Middle Nubian would correspond to the Old and Middle Kingdom.[57] But it proved too difficult to make this system cover Nubia south of the Second Cataract as well as north of it, and the attempt has been abandoned for the time being. I shall therefore keep to the term Group A, which covers the Predynastic.

In time Group A[58] goes from the end of the Neolithic, around 3800 before our era, up to the end of the Old Egyptian Kingdom, around 2200 before our era. Within this period several phases may be distinguished: Early Group A, from about 3800 to 3200 before our era; Classical Group A, from about 3200 to 2800 before our era; and Late Group A (or Early Group B), from about 2800 to 2200 before our era. I shall consider only the first two of these phases.

Early Group A is the least well known.[59] It was in the course of the recent excavations in Sudanese Nubia, between 1960 and 1966, that it was noticed that the Eneolithic civilization of Group A directly succeeded that of Abkian Neolithic. We must therefore wait for the complete results of these excavations to be published before we can see exactly what is involved. In Lower Nubia, the site at Khor Bahan, south of Shellal, apparently belongs to this early phase, and seems to be contemporary with Gerzean, and thus with Egyptian Middle Predynastic. At this period, agriculture and cattle-raising, which are not found in Abkian civilization, are practised in Lower Nubia: the communities of farmers, using a technique peculiar to the upper Nile valley, built dams at low water, at right angles to the river, which slowed the current and stimulated alluvial deposits on the fields bordering the river, thus extending the area of cultivable land. Moreover, the bones of cattle and goats found in the tombs and no doubt the remains of burial sacrifice, suggest that these communities were semi-nomad. Since the fields were not adequate to feed large herds, we must imagine the people moving nomadically during part of the year over the neighbouring plateaux, which must then still have been steppe, as is shown by the presence of antelope and lion.

The discovery of objects made of copper on Early Group A sites raises the question of the diffusion of copper in the upper Nile valley. Like the

56. G. A. Reisner, 1910, pp. 313–32.

57. B. G. Trigger, 1965, pp. 67ff., and Fig. 1, p. 46.

58. Not all the reports on excavations carried out in Nubia in response to Unesco's appeal, and in Egypt and Sudan, have yet been published. For Group A, see H. A. Nordström, 1972, pp. 17–32.

59. H. A. Nordström, 1972, pp. 17–28 and *passim*.

Badarian peoples, the Group A Africans used malachite as eye make-up and ground it on quartz palettes; they also knew how to make Egyptian faïence. As there are copper ore deposits in Nubia which were exploited in very ancient times, it is very possible that the copper objects found on Early Group A sites (especially the needles) were of solely local manufacture.[60]

Imports from the north seem to have been limited to stone vessels made of alabaster, slate and breccia, and to raw materials such as flint, practically non-existent in Nubia but plentiful in Egypt. Pottery was still of the black-topped red ware type; it was made locally, and the technique was excellent. For tools and weapons the Group A people used stone and bone rather than metal: knives and clubs, identical in form with the Amratian, are made of flint or of diorite and basalt; needles, buckles and awls are usually of bone or ivory. Gold appears in jewellery. Slate palettes for cosmetics are probably inspired by those of Egypt, but there are some made of white quartz which are typical of Group A culture.[61]

After the still comparatively little-known Early Group A comes Classical Group A, which, to judge by the number of tombs and necropolises it has left behind, experienced what might be called a population explosion.[62] Very close materially to its predecessor, Classical Group A differs from it above all in the fact that it imported much more from the lower Nile valley. This has been interpreted as proof of active trade between the lower and upper Nile valleys. Pottery is still of superior quality and elegance, but many light-coloured Gerzean-type vases are also imported. These are utilitarian in type and were probably used for holding perishable goods, such as oil, imported in exchange for southern ivory and ebony.

Classical Group A culture continued to flourish up till about 2800 before our era, when it suddenly vanished almost completely, giving way to the very impoverished Late Group A culture (Early Group B).[63] This has been explained as the result of raids carried out by the Pharaohs of the first Thinite dynasty. Egyptian inscriptions of the period, discovered a little to the north of the Second Cataract, make this explanation very likely. At all events, we are now emerging from the prehistoric era.

To put in a nutshell the important but little-known period in which the Nile valley passed from Neolithic to the end of the Predynastic, we may say that in the lower valley it is characterized by the transition from a social system based on families or small groups of hunters and fishers, with a little animal husbandry and some agriculture limited to the banks of the river and the Fayum, to a complex system of sedentary peoples organized in villages and groups of villages, and practising irrigation and specialized agriculture. These villages were united, about 3000 before our era, under the authority

60. It will be noted that copper ore was already being smelted locally under the Ancient Kingdom, in particular at Buhen, cf. W. B. Emery, 1965, pp. 111–14.

61. F. Hintze, 1967, p. 44.

62. B. G. Trigger, 1965, pp. 74–5.

63. H. S. Smith, 1966, pp. 118–24.

of a Pharaoh or single ruler, who ruled over the lower Nile valley from the First Cataract to the Mediterranean.

What we witness in the upper Nile valley is the transition from groups of fishermen-hunters, practising animal husbandry to a very limited extent, to a system which, while it probably comprised semi-nomadic farmers and cattle raisers, also had geographical links with the river, where they dug channels at right angles to the Nile with the object of extending by irrigation the cultivable land at their disposal. The construction of these channels presupposes an extensive social organization, though here it was less ample in scope than in the lower Nile valley.

During this period, from 3300 before our era on, we see the use of copper spreading throughout the Nile valley. Although the origin of copper metallurgy remains little known and the subject of debate, it is not impossible that the technique of making copper was born, or reinvented, in the Nile valley.

The historical period, from 3000 to the fifth century before our era

By the time the first Egyptian texts appeared, around 3000 before our era, social systems seem to have been established throughout the Nile valley, and they were to show little further development. In the north we have a system of monarchy by divine right ruling over a population of individuals who were, in theory at least, equal before the king. In the south the system appears to be less rigid, and because nomadism or semi-nomadism still survived, an organization based largely on the family probably continued throughout almost all the period from 3000 to the fifth century before our era. It was only at the very end of the period that the part of the Nile valley which lay between the First Cataract and the confluence of the White and Blue Niles, and perhaps further south still, came to have a social system perhaps resembling that of the Egyptian part of the valley.

Because the social systems were so static during this period, their evolution can be very briefly stated. What I shall stress most are two cultural facts that characterize the period: the discovery and diffusion of bronze, and later of iron.

Evolution of the social systems

Our knowledge of social organization in the lower Nile valley is incomplete: so few legal and administrative documents survive. According to classical authors, including Herodotus and Strabo, Egyptian society was divided up into rigid castes. But this is certainly untrue, except perhaps as regards the military at the very end of the Pharaonic period. There never was a priestly class as Strabo maintains, and it is not even sure there was a class of slaves, in our sense of the word.[64] In fact the Egyptian social system of the historical period was very flexible. It was based on exploitation of the soil, on the development of the country, rather than on rigid law. As money was never used in Egypt, everyone, whatever his rank, had, in order to live, to belong to some organization that supplied him with food, clothing and shelter.

The simplest of these organizations was the family estate. Though the land belonged in theory to the Pharaoh, the right to cultivate it was sometimes bestowed on an individual, who might hand it down to his heirs.[65] From time immemorial there had been family estates of this kind, sometimes very small, where the head of the family shared out the income as he pleased, and the family, in the wide sense of the term, was entirely dependent on him. His only obligation was to meet the rights of the state: taxes, statute labour, bond service.

Side by side with the family estates, and on a much larger scale, were the religious and royal domains. The religious ones, especially from the eighteenth dynasty on (after 1580 before our era), were sometimes immensely wealthy. The estate of the god Amon included 81 322 men; 421 362 head of cattle; 433 gardens; 2393 square kilometres of fields; 83 boats; and 65 villages.[66] These possessions were in Upper and Lower Egypt, Syria-Palestine and Nubia. The royal estate was made up in the same way and scattered about the country, usually adjacent to a royal palace or funerary temple. Everyone necessarily belonged to some estate which supplied his needs in a very hierarchical fashion. Remuneration in kind varied widely according to occupation: a scribe's rations were more than those of a farmer or craftsman. The privileged could thus, in their turn, acquire servants and estates by selling not their office but some of the rewards attached to it.

Any individual who wanted to escape the restraints of the Egyptian social system had no solution but to run away. Deserters either fled to the west, to the edge of the desert, where they lived by raiding the farms in the valley, or else they went abroad, mostly to Syria and Palestine.[67]

The stability of the social system depended largely on the authority and energy of the central power – the king and the administration. When these were weak the functioning of the system could be gravely compromised. There might even be revolutions, as was the case between about 2200 and 2100 before our era, when the Pharaoh's authority was called in question

64. Cf. the pertinent comments of G. Posener in G. Posener, S. Sauneron and J. Yoyotte, 1959, s.v. 'Esclavage', p. 107.

65. J. Pirenne, 1932, pp. 206–11, and G. Posener, 1959, pp. 76 and 107.

66. J. H. Breasted, 1906, p. 97.

67. The most striking example of this is the case of Sinouhe who, because he was afraid of being involved in a palace plot, fled to Palestine. He had to ask the Pharaoh's pardon before he could return to Egypt. Cf. G. Lefebvre, 1949, 'L'Histoire de Sinouhé', pp. 1–25; bibliography of the different translations of the text, p. 4. See also W. K. Simpson, 1972, pp. 57–74.

and his favourites stripped of their possessions.[68] Local disorders sometimes occurred also, as when the artisans on the royal estate at Deir-el-Medineh went on strike in 1165 before our era because they had not received their monthly rations or the clothing due to them.

An individual's social position was not fixed once and for all. It might always be called in question, either at the king's whim or because of some duty unsatisfactorily performed. There are several references in Egyptian texts to the downgrading or dismissal of officials and their banishment back to the land.[69]

From about 1580 before our era onwards, the army occupies a special place in the Egyptian social system. To expel the Hyksos from Egypt and carry out their policy of raiding attacks on Nubia and Asia Minor, the Pharaohs had created what amounted to a professional army.[70] Soldiers were rewarded with gifts of land and agricultural estates which they could hand on to their heirs so long as these too pursued an army career. This system developed through the centuries to form, by the close of Egyptian history, a real military caste.

We still know very little about the social organization of the upper Nile valley. As we have seen, a social system was established by the end of the Predynastic period, at least in Lower Nubia, comprising sedentaries as well as nomads and semi-nomads, though we have no means of knowing whether the different groups lived communally or just side by side. The few Egyptian documents that allude to the political organization of the peoples south of the First Cataract suggest the existence of small, scattered groups all along the valley, under the authority of local hereditary chiefs.[71]

Archaeology has little to add to this. Animal husbandry was still an important economic factor in the upper Nile valley, and this probably encouraged the survival of family structures. From 1580 before our era, interference by Egypt certainly modified the existing system, or rather destroyed it. The Egyptian occupation of the lands south of Aswan soon led to their depopulation:[72] to support its Asiatic policy, Egypt exploited the upper valley to the utmost, and the inhabitants vanished, probably fleeing to the south and west, to areas still unknown to archaeology.

It was not until about 750 before our era that a properly organized kingdom, based on the Egyptian model, came into being under the leadership of Sudanese rulers from the region of Dongola. This kingdom, Napata, appears to have stretched from the confluence of the two Niles in the south up to, first, the Second Cataract and, later, the Mediterranean;

68. J. Vandier, 1962, pp. 213–20 and 235–7.

69. Notably in the decree of Nauri, where it was one of the common forms of punishment; cf. F. L. Griffith, 1927, pp. 200–8.

70. R. O. Faulkner, 1953, pp. 41–7.

71. G. Posener, 1940, pp. 35–8 and 48–62.

72. W. Y. Adams, 1964, pp. 104–9.

it also included Lower Nubia from 750 to 650 before our era.[73] Matriarchy played an important role, at least in the ruling family, but the documents are not numerous or explicit enough to tell us how the social system as a whole was organized.

The diffusion of metals

At the beginning of the historical period the precious metals, gold and silver, were, like copper, known and widely diffused throughout the Nile valley. The metallurgy of all three continued to develop after the third millennium; in the second millennium bronze, an alloy of copper and tin, appeared; iron appeared sporadically from 1580 before our era.

Most of the gold mines exploited by the Egyptians and the Nubians[74] were situated between the First and Third Cataracts. The Egyptians of the Middle Kingdom, prospecting for precious metals, reached and went beyond the Second Cataract. Under the New Kingdom, gold, used to 'buy' local alliances, played a major part in Egypt's Asiatic policy. Gold from the mines in Egypt and Nubia always contains a high proportion of silver,[75] and a distinction was made between white gold or electrum (in Egyptian, *hedji*) which contains at least 25 per cent of silver, and yellow gold (in Egyptian, *noub*. It is not impossible that the name Nubia comes from this word.) Gold was put to many uses in Egypt: for grave-goods, jewellery, even architecture – porches and rooms in temples, and the tips of obelisks, were often covered with sheets of gold.

The upper Nile valley used gold with the same profusion, though the systematic robbing of graves has allowed very few examples to survive. But we do have gold amulets, beads, hair ornaments, bracelets, rings and ear-rings. Grave-goods of the eighth century were also rich in gold and silver, as is seen at Nuri, below the Fourth Cataract, where, despite the thefts of long ago, many objects have been discovered.[76]

Copper and bronze can only be distinguished from one another by laboratory tests.[77] Bronze did not appear in the Nile valley until about 2000 before our era, and it was not until 1500 before our era that it was widespread, though it never replaced copper altogether. Bronze, an alloy of copper and tin, is stronger than copper as long as the proportion of tin is not too high, has a lower melting point, and is easier to cast.

Though Egypt did possess some deposits of tin, bronze was not discovered in the Nile valley. It seems to have been imported from Syria,[78] where it had been known since the beginning of the second millennium. In

73. H. V. Zeissl, 1955, pp. 12–16.
74. J. Vercoutter, 1959, pp. 128–33 and map, p. 129.
75. Cf. A. Lucas, 1962, pp. 224–34.
76. D. Dunham, 1955, *passim*.
77. A. Lucas, 1962, ch. 1, pp. 199–217 and 217–23.
78. ibid., pp. 217–18 and 255–7.

Egyptian alloys the proportion of tin varies from 2 per cent to 16 per cent. When the proportion of tin does not exceed 4 per cent bronze is harder than copper; when the proportion is higher than 4 per cent, bronze breaks easily and loses many of its advantages. This is probably why it never took the place of copper, which can be hardened considerably just by hammering.

Objects have been found in the upper valley, especially at Kerma, which if analysed to see whether they are of copper or bronze might tell us whether bronze had been adopted in the upper Nile valley by the second millennium. But they have not been analysed. However, objects made of copper – or bronze – are very numerous there, more so than in Egypt itself: 130 copper daggers have been found at Kerma for the period from about 1800 to 1700 before our era – more than for the whole of Egypt. At this period copper was used for toilet articles, especially mirrors, weapons, tools, vases, jewels and inlays for furniture. It was usually shaped by hammering, very rarely cast.

The number and quality of the objects found at Kerma[79] show that the upper valley played an important part in the diffusion of copper metallurgy in Africa from the second millennium on. The presence of copper mines in the basic geological complex of the Nile made the scope of this diffusion all the greater.

For a long time the Nile valley knew only meteoric iron.[80] It was not until the end of the eighth century before our era that smelted earth iron began to spread in the lower valley; a century later it was as commonly used as bronze and copper. At this period, in Egypt, iron was smelted and worked in centres of Greek influence.

The Nile valley occupies an important place in the diffusion of iron in Africa.[81] Iron may have been worked earlier in the upper valley than in the lower, which would explain why it is more frequently used under the twenty-fifth dynasty, which came originally from Dongola (about 800 before our era). But although the upper valley had both iron ore and forests to supply the charcoal necessary for working it, the use of iron did not become widespread[82] until the first century before our era, with the rise of the Meroitic civilization, between the Third and Fourth Cataracts. So the importance of the Nilotic culture of Napata in the diffusion of iron in Africa consists mainly in the fact that it was out of the Napatan culture that the civilization of Meroe emerged.

79. Cf. G. A. Reisner, 1923, ch. XXVI, pp. 176–205.

80. P. L. Shinnie, 1971, pp. 92–4.

81. Cf. A. Lucas, 1962, pp. 235–43.

82. The role which Meroe played in the dissemination of iron in Africa is not as obvious as used to be thought; cf. P. L. Shinnie, 1971, pp. 94–5, who also quotes B. G. Trigger, 1969, pp. 23–50. In point of fact, Meroe is not the only possible centre of dissemination. Iron may have spread from North Africa, via the caravan routes of the Sahara: cf. P. L. Shinnie, 1967, p. 168, with a reference to P. Huard, 1960, pp. 134–78, 1964, pp. 49–50.

PLATE 28.1 *Tomb of Huy, east wall, south side, after R. Lepsius* (*Egyptian Expedition*, vol x)

PLATE 28.2 *Tomb of Rekh mi-re at Thebes* (Metropolitan Museum of Art)

PLATE 28.3 *Copper statue of Pepi I* (*Old Kingdom*) (Cairo Museum)

PLATE 28.4 *Razor, Mirgissa* (French Archaeological Mission to the Sudan)

Conclusion: from nature in the raw to liberated humanity

J. KI-ZERBO

The preceding chapters amply demonstrate the major role Africa played at the dawn of human history. Placed today on the periphery of the technically developed world, Africa and Asia were in the forefront of progress for the first 15 000-odd centuries of world history, from the time of *Australopithecus* and *Pithecanthropus*. As we now know, Africa was the principal scene both of man's emergence as the royal species of the planet, and of the emergence of a political society. But this role of eminence in prehistory was to be replaced during the historical period of the last 2000 years by a 'law' of development hallmarked by exploitation and reduction to the role of a tool.

Africa, man's homeland?

Although there cannot be any absolute certainty in the matter, if only because the history of human origins, the hidden history of mankind, is not yet entirely exhumed, discoveries so far made point to Africa as one of the great, if not the principal, centre of man's development and this in spite of the fact that excavations are still only in the initial stages and that the acidity of African soils has consumed most fossil remains. *Kenyapithecus* (*Kenyapithecus wickeri*), considered by some to be the initiator of the human dynasty, appeared 12 million years ago. *Ramapithecus* of Asia is but one of its varieties which probably spread to India from Africa. But *Australopithecus* (*Australopithecus africanus* or *afarensis*) is incontestably the first hominid, the biped explorer of the savannahs of eastern and central Africa, casts from whose endocranium reveal a development of the frontal and parietal lobes of the brain indicative of an already advanced level of intellectual faculties. Thereafter came the Zinjanthropes and the variety bearing the prestigious name of *Homo habilis*, the first humans who represent a new leap upward in the progression towards the status of modern Man.

There follow the Archanthropes (Pithecanthropes and Atlanthropes), the Paleanthropes or Neanderthalians, and finally the *Homo sapiens* type (the Man of Elmenteita in Kenya, of Kibish in Ethiopia) of whom many authors have noted the frequently negroid features in the upper Aurignacian period.

Whether polycentrist or monocentrist, every scientist recognizes that it is in Africa that all the links are found in the chain connecting us with the most ancient hominids and prehominians, including those varieties which appear never to have developed beyond the stage of manlike creatures, and were unable to make the final step in evolution to rise to the stature and status of Adam. Furthermore, Africa is where the ancestors, or rather the supposed cousins, of man are still to be found. According to W. W. Howells, the 'apes of Africa, the gorilla and chimpanzee, are more closely related to man than is any of the three to the orangutang of Indonesia'.[1] And there is good reason why! Asia in its lower latitudes, and particularly Africa because of its remarkable extension into the southern hemisphere, escaped the discouraging climatic conditions of the northern zones. Thus Europe, covered by ice sheets during the 200000 years or so of the Kageran, offers no trace of early stone age implements, whereas the same period in Africa produced three successive varieties of progressively sophisticated palaeolithic tools. In fact, during this period the tropical latitudes had the advantage of a temperate climate that favoured the development of animal life. Indeed, in order to survey the influences that led to man's emergence, one must first consider the geographical and ecological environment. Thereafter, technology and, finally, social development must be taken into consideration.

The capacity to adapt to the environment

This was one of the most powerful factors affecting man's development from the time of his origins. The morpho-somatic characteristics of African populations were elaborated during that crucial period of prehistory. Thus the glabrous skin, its brown, coppery or black colour, the abundance of sweat-glands, the expanded nostrils and lips of many Africans, the curly, crisp or frizzy hair, all stem from tropical conditions. Melanin and frizzy hair, for example, protect from heat. Moreover, the adoption of an erect posture, which was a decisive step in man's development and which involved a modification of the pelvic girdle, was provoked, according to certain prehistorians, by the need to adapt to the geographical environment of the high grasses of the savannahs of the East African plateaux: it was always necessary to stand erect to see over them to stalk prey or flee from hostile beasts.

Other scientists (Alister Hardy, for example) consider the aquatic environment responsible not only for the appearance of life but also for human development. This is the view also of Mrs Elaine Morgan, in whose opinion the upright stance developed in Africa on the shores of the great lakes or the ocean because creatures which had dived into water to escape stronger monsters allergic to it had to stand with their heads out of water in order to breathe. She also ascribes to the aquatic surroundings certain

1. W. W. Howells, 1972, p. 5.

human characteristics such as their layer of sub-cutaneous fat, the retracted position of the female sex organs and the corresponding lengthening of the male sex organ, the fact that we are the only primates who weep, and so on.[2] All these biological adaptations gradually became hereditary and were transmitted as permanent features. Adaptation to the environment also dictated the style of the first human implements. Creighton Gabel holds that implements of the Capsian type are indigenous in origin, the style of the blades, gravers and scrapers being adapted to that remarkable material, obsidian.

The technological milieu

The technological milieu created by the African hominians was the second factor that enabled them to feel distinct from the rest of nature and later to dominate it.

It was because he was a *faber* (tool-maker) that man became *sapiens* (intelligent). With his hands freed from having to support his body, Man was able to relieve the muscles and bones of the jaw and cranium of numerous tasks. This both freed and increased the size of the brainpan, in which the motor-sensory centres developed. Furthermore, the hand confronts Man with the natural world. It is an antenna capturing an infinite number of messages, which in turn provoke the brain to develop the capacity to exercise judgement, in particular through the concept of appropriate means to achieve a given end (principle of identity and causality).

After having learnt to hew stone crudely by breaking it into parts of haphazard sizes (the Pebble Culture of Oldowan man), prehistoric African men progressed to a more conscious stage of creation. The stocks of stone tools in various stages of elaboration in vast workshops such as those near Kinshasa suggest that the finished object had been clearly conceived in his mind from the beginning, and was achieved flake by flake. As elsewhere, progress went from shaping tools by striking one stone against another, to shaping by means of a striker that was cylindrical and less hard (hammer of wood, bone, and so on) and, later still, by indirect percussion (through the use of a chisel) and, finally, by pressure for retouching, particularly on microliths.

Prehistoric man made constant advances in his mastery in creating implements, and from the beginning one recognizes in the changes of material, in the finishing of tools and weapons, that constant striving for greater efficiency and for adapting to increasingly complex ends which is the mark of intelligence and which frees man from the stereotypes of instinct. Thus the all-purpose Chellean pick gave way to the flake industries (Egypt, Libya, Sahara), then to the more specialized facies of the Aterian,[3] the

2. Alister Hardy, specialist in marine biology, quoted by E. Morgan, 1973, pp. 33–55.
3. From Bir el-Ater in Algeria.

Fauresmith,[4] the Sangoan,[5] the Stillbay[6] industries and finally to the still more refined forms of the Neolithic (Capsian, Wilton, Magosian, Elmenteitan). In Africa, more than elsewhere, it is impossible to plot exact chronological thresholds to measure precisely the transition from one stage to the next. For here, the various phases of prehistory seem to have overlapped, telescoped or coexisted for long periods. At the same stratigraphic level, one may find evidence of the Early Stone Age, much more advanced polished implements and even metal objects. Thus the Sangoan, which begins in the Early Stone Age, lingers till the end of the Neolithic. This progress, which is marked by continual exchanges and borrowings between techniques, takes on the form of waves of invention which occasionally overlap but on the whole form a general rising curve leading up to historical antiquity, after agro-pastoral techniques and the making of pottery had been mastered. The cultivation of wheat, barley and plants for textiles, such as the flax of Fayum, became widespread, as did the raising of domestic animals. Two principal centres of agricultural selection and exploitation doubtless exerted a marked and widespread influence as early as the sixth or fifth millennium: the Nile valley and the Niger bend. Sorghum, millet, certain varieties of rice, sesame, *fonio*, and farther south the yam, the *dâ* (*ibiscus esculentus*) planted for its leaves and fibres, the oil palm, the kola and possibly a particular variety of cotton were domesticated. In addition, the Nile valley profited by Mesopotamian discoveries, such as emmer wheat, barley, onions, lentils and peas, the melon and figs, whereas from Asia were introduced the sugar cane, other varieties of rice, and the banana, the latter doubtless through Ethiopia. The latter country, learning methods of cultivation from the peasants of the Nile valley, also developed the cultivation of coffee. The sites of Lake Nakuru and of the Njoro river in Kenya also suggest that the cultivation of cereal plants was undertaken.

Numerous plants domesticated during prehistory still persist to this day, sometimes in improved forms, as part of the African diet. Their use encouraged the settling and stabilizing of men, without which there can be no progress towards civilization. The true Neolithic, which did not develop in western Europe till between 3000 and 2000 before our era, began 3000 years earlier in Egypt. However, the pottery of Elmenteita (Kenya), which probably dates from 5000 before our era, suggests that knowledge of pottery reached the Sahara and Egypt from the uplands of eastern Africa. Pottery, a revolutionary innovation, accompanied the primitive accumulation of capital in the form of assets wrenched from nature by human industry.

With cooking began one of the most refined aspects of culture, enabling us to measure the qualitative progress achieved since *Homo habilis*, with

4. From Fauresmith in South Africa.
5. From Sango Bay on the western shore of Lake Victoria.
6. From Stillbay in the Cape Province.

his diet of leaves, roots and quivering flesh, in short, his hunting-gathering economy.

Qualitative changes

These qualitiative changes which confirmed and strengthened man's inherent natural gifts were possible only through exchanges with his fellows and through a social dynamic which fashioned the human being at least as much as the impulses from the deepest strata of his vitality, from the convolutions of his brain lobes or the interstices of his subconscious. Moreover, through aggressiveness, resulting in the violent elimination of the less strong, the social factor played a major role. Thus *Homo sapiens* must have eradicated Neanderthal man after a sort of world war which lasted several tens of thousands of years. But the social dimension also played a more constructive role: 'comparative studies of moulds made of the inner brain-case of *Paleanthropus* and *Homo sapiens* fossils show that, in the latter, the areas of the brain connected with purposeful labour, that is physical activity, speech and the regulation of the individual's social behaviour, underwent considerable changes'.[7]

Indeed, the need for social contact played a cardinal role in the acquiring of language, from the sound signals inherited from animal ancestors to articulated utterances variously combined as syllables. The phase of monosyllabic lallation sought to produce, as if by conditioned reflex, a given gesture, act or form of behaviour, or to call attention to a past or imminent event. In short, in the beginning, speech was essentially relation. At the same time, the lengthening jaw forced back the organs of the throat, thus lowering the point of attachment of the tongue. 'The air current was no longer directed straight at the lips, as with the apes, but had now to overcome various barriers, notably the tongue.'[8] Briefly, speech is a dialectical process between biology, technique and the mind dependent on the mediation of a group. With no echoing partner, no interlocutor, man would have remained mute. But, conversely, speech sets the social process in motion again, amplifies and refines it remarkably. Speech is such an invaluable acquisition that, in African magical or cosmogenic representations, it is recognized as having a hold over things. The Word is creative. Speech is also a carrier of progress. It is the vehicle for the transmission of knowledge, tradition or 'the heritage of the ears'. It is the capitalization of knowledge, raising man forever above the blind treadmill of instinct.[9] Speech was also the point of departure of social authority, i.e. of leadership and power.

7. V. P. Iakimov, 1972, p. 2.

8. Cf. V. Bounak, 1972, p. 69.

9. 'Is not language, which enabled man to conceptualize, memorize and retransmit the knowledge immediately apprehended in the experience of daily life, the most extraordinary product of the scientific potential of non-learned societies?' B. Verhaegen, 1974, p. 154.

Emergence of political societies

If *Homo sapiens* is a political animal, he became so during the prehistoric period. It is difficult to ascribe time-periods to the motive forces and stages of this process. But here again, production techniques and social relations must have played a major role.

Technical developments

The prehominids and prehistoric African man lived in herds, and later in bands, troops and teams organized for specific tasks, necessary for his survival and which could be performed only in a group.

The framework was a community which appeared with the first glimmers of human intelligence. There must always have been a rallying place, even if transitory, a point adapted for rest, defence and provisioning. The members of the troop must have assembled periodically around fires, set to guard against beasts, fear and the external darkness. In the Omo valley (Ethiopia), humble stone remains have been excavated which still outline the ground plan of the huts of the first hominids. The arrangement of the shelters gradually improves until we find Neolithic villages perched in advantageous positions sheltered from flooding and attack, but near some water source, for example, on the Tichitt-Walata escarpment (Mauritania). But it was for fishing and especially for hunting that the community expressed its purpose decisively. Our prehistoric ancestors could not slaughter animals stronger than themselves except through superior organization. They must have assembled to stalk beasts which they drove toward cliffs or ravines where some of their confederates were stationed below to finish them off. Near water-holes where big game swarmed in the dry season, they dug giant traps into which the animals fell. They thereupon had to finish off the beast, dismember it, transport the pieces – all jobs requiring a certain division of labour. This division increased in the Neolithic, owing to the further diversification of activities. A young man of the Early Stone Age had little choice. His orientation in life was restricted: gathering, hunting or fishing. But in the Neolithic, the choice was very much greater and implied a judicious division of labour as tasks became increasingly specialized: some for women and some for men, peasants and shepherds, shoemakers, tool-makers in stone, wood and bone, and soon blacksmiths.

Social relations

This new organization and the increasing efficiency of the implements it possessed enabled surpluses to be built up and allowed some of the group to escape the role of producers of goods and to devote themselves to services. Social relationships diversified as the groups became settled into the beginnings of a hierarchy. It was the time also when races were formed and localized, the most archaic being the Khoisan and the Pygmies. The tall Negro (Sudanic or Bantu) does not appear until later, as with Asselar man (Oued Tilemsi valley in Mali). It would appear that the Negro, who not long before had expanded into other continents,[10] acquired distinctive characteristics and developed triumphantly in Africa, his land of origin, beginning in the Sahara, whereas elsewhere he was driven back, as in Asia in the Dravidian retreat to the Deccan, or supplanted, as in Europe, by races better adapted to the harsh climatic conditions. This occurred also in North Africa before the pressure of the Mediterranean races. According to Furon, the statuettes of the Aurignacian feature an ethnic type that is negroid. Indeed, in the view of that author, 'the Negroid Aurignacians carry over into a civilization known as Capsian'.[11] As for Dumoulin de Laplante, he writes: 'At that point, a migration of Negroids of the Hottentot type, coming from southern and central Africa, is thought to have submerged North Africa ... and to have brought by force to Mediterranean Europe a new civilization, the Aurignacian.'[12] One must therefore conclude from this that, on the fringes of the black world, ancient crossbreedings account for populations with less pronounced negroid features, brashly dubbed the brown race: Fulani, Ethiopians, Somalis, Nilotes, and so on. A 'Hamitic' race has even been suggested.

A field in which an awakening social life is shown to us with unsurpassed vivacity is that of prehistoric African rock and plastic art. Africa having been the most important continent in prehistoric development, the one where the populations of hominids and then of hominians were the most ancient, numerous and inventive, it is not surprising that prehistoric African art should be by far the richest in the world and that, in its time, it should have imposed a dominance as considerable as Negro-African music in the world of today. Its vestiges are concentrated particularly in South Africa and eastern Africa, the Sahara, Egypt and the high plateau of the Atlas. This art was of course quite often the reflection of an individual's amazement at the animal life teeming around his shelter. But for the most part it is a social art centred on daily tasks, 'the working days' of the group: its clashes with beasts or hostile clans, its fears and terrors, its leisure and games, in short the high points of collective life. Animated and vibrant galleries or frescoes reflect in the mirror of rock walls the passions and bucolic life of the first human clans. This art, reduced to a quintessential technique, often reflects the spiritual concern and anguish of the group. It depicts spellbinding dances, cohorts of masked hunters, sorcerers hard at work, ladies with faces coated white (as is still done today in black Africa in initiation ceremonies), hurrying as though summoned to some mysterious appointment. Moreover,

10. Cf. 'Il y a 30,000 ans la race noire couvrait le monde', in *Science et Avenir*, October 1954, no. 92. Cf. also A. Moret, 1931, p. 19.

11. R. Furon, 1943, pp. 14–15.

12. P. Dumoulin de Laplante, 1947, p. 13.

with the passage of time, one feels a transition from magic to religion, thus also confirming the evolution of man towards political society since many early leaders were to be both chiefs and priests.

The mastery of food production in the Neolithic must have given rise to a sharp increase in population which in turn set migrations into motion; the characteristic dispersion of certain prehistoric workshops with stone artefacts of similar style attests to this. The radius both of forays and of permanent migrations increased with the efficiency of implements and weapons, facilitated by the fact that they were becoming less unwieldy. Africa is a continent where men have wandered about in every direction, as if drawn on by the immense horizons of that vast land.

The inextricable overlappings which an African ethnic map presents today make a jigsaw puzzle that would discourage a computer and are a result of this Brownian movement of peoples over a period of thousands of years. As far as can be judged, the initial migratory impetuses seem to have come from the 'Bantu' in the east and north-east and to have radiated west and north. Then, from the Neolithic onward, the general trend seems to have been a southward movement, as if under the repellent effect of the giant desert, that terrible ecological scarp henceforth imperiously bridging the continent. This ebb-tide to the south and east (Sudanese, Bantu, Nilotes, and so on) was to continue during the historical period into the nineteenth century, when its last waves died away on the coasts of the southern sea.

The caravan leader who, covered with amulets and bristling with weapons, led the clan towards progress or adventure, was the eponymous ancestor who propelled his people into history and whose name would pass through centuries, crowned with a halo of quasi-ritual veneration. Indeed, the migrations were essentially group phenomena, acts of a highly social character.

These migrations, prompted by successes (or failures) in the original environment, were ambiguous in their results. On the one hand, they assisted progress because their successive and convergent waves gradually ensured that the continent, if not mastered, was occupied, and through exchange they disseminated innovations in a sort of cumulative effect. But on the other hand, the migrations, by diluting the population over an enormous area, prevented human groups from reaching that threshold of concentration which human multitudes must achieve to excel in invention in order to survive. Dispersion over a wide geographical range increases the ascendancy of the environment, and it tended to pull back the first African clans to those dark origins whence man painfully struggled to maturity through the opaque crust of the unfeeling universe.

The historical movement

And so the thread of human evolution, whose direction and stages we have marked out all too briefly, shows us the prehistoric African laboriously wrenching himself free from nature and immersing himself by degrees in human society in the form of groups and primitive communities, now joining, now separating only to recombine in other forms, with a technology increasingly based on the use of iron implements or weapons, in marriages or confrontations that reverberated in history's first love songs and first clashes of weapons. But what strikes one about this upward progress is the continuation, throughout the historical period and into the very heart of the twentieth century, of communities originally born in prehistory.

Moreover, if the beginning of history is dated from the use of iron objects, it can be said that prehistory continued in a number of African regions until around the year 1000. As late as the nineteenth century, the productive forces and socio-economic relations of numerous African groups (and not only the palaeonegritic groups) were substantially no different from those of prehistory, save for the use of metal implements. Even in our own century, the hunting techniques of the Pygmies are the same as those of prehistoric Africans of thousands of years ago.

Obscured perhaps by the dazzling summit of Egyptian civilization and the glorious achievements of so many African kingdoms and empires, this weighty reality remains, giving body and texture to the development of African societies, and fittingly deserving to be stressed here.

To be sure, the sense of history has never implied a single direction on which all men have unanimously agreed. There are different conceptions of the sense of history. Marx and Teilhard de Chardin each have theirs. Africa has produced thinkers some of whom have elaborated profound visions of the means and destination of the movement of history. With St Augustine (354–430), the vision took a giant step forwards by breaking with the then-current cyclic concept of eternal repetition, and by professing that from original sin to the Last Judgement, an irreversible line exists, traced in its entirety by God's will, but along which each of us is saved or damned by his acts. And the past of the terrestrial City is studied only to detect in it the signs announcing the City of God.

For his part, Ibn Khaldun (1332–1406), while recognizing that Allah presided sovereignly over human destinies, is the founder of history as a science, based as it is on evidence verified by reason. 'One must put one's faith in the balance of one's own judgement, since any truth can be conceived by the intelligence.' Furthermore, he held that the object of that science is not merely to skim the surface of events: 'What is the advantage of relating the names of the wives of a former sovereign, the inscription engraved on his ring?' He studied particularly the modes of production and of life, social relationships, in short civilization (*al-umran al-bashari*). Finally, he elaborated, to explain the progression of history, a dialectical theory opposing the role of the equalitarian spirit of solidarity (*asabiyya*) to the dictatorship of the king, respectively in the rural or pastoral zones (*al-umran al-badawī*), and in the cities (*al-umran al-hadarī*).

Thus there is an incessant alternating transition from the *dominium* of the one form of civilization to that of the other, though the pattern is not cyclic, for it recurs each time at a higher level, resulting in a sort of upwards spiral of progress. By affirming that 'the differences in customs and institutions of the various peoples depend on the manner in which each of them provided for its subsistence', Ibn Khaldun formulated clearly, and several centuries in advance of Karl Marx, one of his main propositions regarding historical materialism. Having analysed the evolution of the western world with the vigour and the strength of synthesis for which he is renowned, Marx concerned himself in passing with alien modes of production. In 1859, in *Formen*, he formulated the concept of the 'Asiatic mode of production', one of the three forms of 'natural' agrarian communities founded on common ownership of the soil. The Asiatic mode of production, he considered, was characterized by the existence of basic village communities dominated by a state body collecting the surpluses produced by the peasants, who were subject not to individual slavery but to a 'general slavery', in which they were subjugated as a group. The rulers therefore possessed, along with the power of public office, a power of exploitation of the lower communities. This higher community allocated to itself the ultimate ownership of the land,[13] commercialized the surpluses, and undertook major public works, particularly of irrigation, to increase production, and in short exercised over the masses an authority described as 'oriental despotism'. However, the archaeological and anthropological knowledge acquired since Marx has shown that the development of certain societies does not necessarily correspond to either the five stages defined by Marx in *Das Kapital*, and laid down as unalterable doctrine by Stalin, or to the pre-capitalist variety of the 'Asiatic mode of production', taken by Marx to be a variant of the transition to the state in the case of non-European societies. In particular, and contingent on later monographic studies invalidating this proposition, an analysis of African structures fails to reveal the characteristics formulated by Marx for describing the succession of various modes of production.

So it is that in primitive communities, contrary to European experience (ancient and Germanic), where the private ownership of land developed from its common ownership, in Africa there is no sign of private ownership.[14] Aside from this remarkable characteristic, the first communities in Africa offer the same traits as those in the rest of the world. Likewise, the differences existing between African structures and the Asiatic mode of production are very marked. In African village

13. The higher unit is presented as the 'superior owner' or as 'the sole owner'. Indeed, 'at some points Marx stresses the fact that the State itself is the true owner of the soil, and at other points he noted the importance of the property rights of the village communities. There is doubtless no contradiction between these two tendencies.' J. Chesneaux, 1969, p. 29.

14. 'There is no private ownership of land, in the sense of Roman law or of the Civil Code.' J. Suret-Canale, 1964, p. 108.

communities, the higher authority, the state, was no more the owner of the land than were private individuals. Moreover, the state generally did not undertake any major public works. As for the power structure itself, considered as a superstructure, it does not come into any definition of modes of production, even though a power structure is an indication of the existence of classes. However, this structure in Africa does not have the characteristics of the 'oriental despotism' described by Karl Marx.[15] In spite of instances of sanguinary autocracy, the state authority in black Africa nearly always took the form of a limited monarchy within a framework of corporate bodies and customs, veritable unwritten constitutions, institutions most often inherited from an earlier organization or social stratification. Even when prestigious and efficient states such as the Empire of Mali, described with admiration by Ibn Battuta in the fourteenth century, spread over immense territories, their decentralization, adopted as a deliberate choice, allowed the basic communities to function with a very real measure of autonomy. In any event, since writing was generally little used and techniques of travel were still not very well developed, the sway of the capitals was always mitigated by distance. Distance also rendered very real the constant threat that subject peoples would evade any attempt at autocracy by running away.

Moreover, production surplus to the needs of the basic communities appears to have been modest in Africa, save where there was a state monopoly of precious commodities, such as gold in Ghana or Asante, ivory, salt, and so on. But even in such cases, the reciprocal services (security, justice, markets, and so on) provided by the chieftaincy must not be overlooked, nor the fact minimized that a good proportion of the taxes and levies was redistributed at the customary festivals, in accordance with the code of honour governing those obliged to live nobly.[16] This explains the lavish generosity of Mansa Musa the Magnificent, Emperor of Mali, at the time of his sumptuous pilgrimage in 1324.

As for production based on slavery, did it exist in Africa? Here again, the reply must be negative. In almost all the societies south of the Sahara, slavery played only a marginal role. Slaves, or more precisely captives, were nearly always prisoners of war. However, captivity did not reduce a man to

15. 'If by despotism is to be understood an absolute and arbitrary authority, the idea of an African despotism can only be rejected': ibid., p. 125. 'We do not believe there are any grounds for attempting to find in the organization of African states the duplication of a model borrowed from Asia; at most, a few superficial similarities might be noted': ibid., p. 122.

16. J. J. Maquet, after having noted that in the view of G. Balandier 'all things considered, the price that the holders of political power should pay is never fully acquitted', himself holds that the public services of rulers 'require no coercive power except in vast, heterogeneous and urban societies. Elsewhere, the lineal-relative network and its sanctions not imposed by force are sufficient ...' He therefore concludes: 'Except for redistribution, there was no economic counterpart for the surpluses that the rulers extracted from a traditional society.' J. J. Maquet, 1970, pp. 99–101.

the status of chattel, of property pure and simple in the sense defined by Cato. The African slave often enjoyed property rights. He was not exploited like an instrument or an animal. The prisoner of war, if he was not ritually sacrificed, as occasionally happened, was very rapidly integrated into the family whose collective property he became. He was a human addition to the family who within a short time enjoyed freedom by right or by circumstance. Captives used as foot soldiers sometimes enjoyed substantial advantages, and sometimes, as in Kayor, they were even part of the government in their capacity as commanders-in-chief. In Asante, to ensure national integration, it was strictly forbidden even to allude to the servile origin of anyone, and so a former captive might become a village chief. 'The condition of captive, although common in Africa ... did not imply the restricted role in production that characterizes a social class.'[17]

In places where slavery took on a massive and qualitatively different character, as in Dahomey, Asante and Zanzibar in the eighteenth and nineteenth centuries, the social structures involved stemmed from an already dominant mode of production, which was capitalism, and were in reality the result of external economic influences. Can this be regarded as the equivalent of the feudal mode of production? Hasty comparisons have led certain authors to qualify one African chieftaincy or another as 'feudal'.[18] However, here again, generally speaking, there was no private ownership or assignment of land, hence no fief. The land was an inalienable community asset, so much so that the group of conquerors who seized political power often left responsibility for the communal lands to their indigenous controller, the 'master of the land', the Mossi *teng-soba*, for example. Indeed, the authority of the aristocracy 'was exercised over goods and chattels and men, without affecting landed property itself, which was the prerogative of the autochthones'.[19] Moreover, the 'nobility' in Africa did not go in for trade. Nobility was always a birthright and no one could dispossess the holder of his rank.

Finally, one must take into account socio-economic structures such as the matrilineal family system which originally so strongly characterized African societies, at least before later influences like Islam or western civilization gradually introduced the patrilineal system. This social structure, so

17. J. Suret-Canale, 1964, p. 119. See also A. A. Dieng, 1974, for a penetrating and documented critique of the 'elastic' Marxist theses of Mahjemout Diop, 1971–2.

18. Even if one holds with J. J. Maquet, citing Bloch and Ganshof, that 'it is not the fief, but the relation between lord and vassal that is crucial', it is clear that the one cannot be entirely dissociated from the other. The 'feudalistic' relations that this author describes appear moreover to be rather peculiar to the interlacustrine societies, and were often established, as in Ankole or Buha, between members of the upper caste. Under these circumstances, is the institutional reality involved the same as that in Europe, for example?

19. Cf. V. Kabore, 1962.

important in defining the prominent role of women in the community, also had economic, political and spiritual consequences, since it played a remarkable role in the inheritance both of material wealth and of the rights to royal succession, as in Ghana. Uterine kinship appears to have come from the depths of African prehistory, at the time when permanent settlement during the Neolithic exalted the domestic functions of women, to the point where they became the central element in a social entity. Numerous practices stem from it, such as the 'joking relationship', brother-sister marriages, the bride-price paid to the parents of the future wife, and so on.

Given these conditions, how shall the characteristic evolution of prehistoric African societies be described? The first thing to note is that, during this period, Africa served in intercontinental relations as a pole and a central source for the invention and dissemination of techniques. But a subordinate and peripheral status rather quickly followed that exalted role, not only because of the conflict of internal factors mentioned above, but also because of the tapping of African resources and services without any adequate counterpart, in the form, for example, of an equivalent transfer of capital and techniques. This exploitation of Africa lasted several thousand years and had three peak periods. First, in antiquity, following the decline of Egypt, the Nile valley and the other Roman provinces in North Africa were exploited to become the granary of Rome. In addition to food, Africa supplied the Roman Empire with an enormous quantity of imports, including wild animals, slaves and gladiators, for the army, the palaces, the *latifundia* and the sanguinary games of the circus.

In the sixteenth century the sinister era of the slave trade began. Finally, in the nineteenth century, dependence took the form of territorial occupation and colonization. The simultaneous and complementary phenomena of capital accumulation in Europe and the rise of the industrial revolution could not be conceived of without the enforced contributions from Asia, the Americas and especially Africa.

Parallel to these phenomena, even during the centuries when external rapacity was not too pronounced (from antiquity to the sixteenth century), many internal contradictions in the African system itself constituted home-bred structural handicaps, which prevented any moves from within the societies towards more progressive structures. As J. Suret-Canale has shrewdly observed in respect of the Asiatic mode of production (but with even greater relevance to the case of Africa, including the colonial period): 'In this system, in fact, the sharpening of class exploitation, far from destroying the structures founded on collective ownership of the land, strengthened them: they constituted the framework within which the surpluses were drawn off, the very prerequisite of exploitation.' It was, of course, the basic communities which supplied the surpluses. The Africa of clans and villages which was still in existence was little given to private possession of land (a common asset as widespread and as precious, but also as free, as air), and was for a very long time ignorant of the acquisition of land as a source of conflicts between social groups. But that was not the only archaic social form found in Africa. The vicious circle of low level technology and production was at once the cause and the consequence of a dwindling population within a continental space that was virtually unlimited.

Natural obstacles impeded long-range commercial traffic which, as a result, never became widespread and too often concerned luxury products usually destined for the palaces. Indeed, without subscribing to the Plekhanovite notion of the 'geographical milieu', which is only one of the facets of the historical milieu, the ecological barriers mentioned in the Introduction to this volume must be taken into account. It should be noted that, wherever barriers to trade were overcome whether wholly or in part, as in the Nile valley and to a lesser degree in the Niger valley, social development blossomed as a consequence of an increase in population and private ownership.

Thus, in black Africa, apart from a few exceptions, there was neither slavery nor feudalism as these are understood in the West.[20] One cannot even say that there were African variations of these systems as their characteristic elements were missing. Does that mean that Africa was not subject to the general principles governing human evolution? Obviously not. But even if these principles are common to all humanity and even if we grant that the tenets of historical materialism are universally applicable, one should keep in mind the main points at issue which are, on the one hand, the similarities which can be observed between the productive forces and the relations of production and, on the other, the transition from a classless form of society to social forms of class conflict. So, the African situation should be analysed not by a return to the doctrines of Karl Marx, but rather in the light shed by his thought. If reason is universal, the role of scholars is to apply it to each of its practical manifestations.

In short, Africa presents a remarkably continuous indigenous mode of production similar to other 'primitive' communities but with fundamental differences, in particular its avoidance of private or state ownership.[21]

Then there was a gradual and sporadic transition toward state forms, themselves long immersed in the network of underlying pre-state relations, but gradually extricating themselves by internal impetus and external pressure from the matrix of destructurized primitive collectivism, and restructuring themselves on the basis of private property and the growth of the state, in a capitalist mode of production, first dominant, then monopolistic.

The colonial state was in fact created to administer the commercial

20. J. Chesneaux, 1969, p. 36: 'What appears well established is the quasi-impossibility of considering that pre-colonial African societies, except in rare instances, depend on a system of slavery or on feudalism properly so called.'

21. An avoidance not linked to a specific congenital status, nor to a different nature, but to an original historical milieu.

periphery of capitalism, before giving way in the middle of the twentieth century to an independent capitalist state. Alternatively, the transition was from a dominant community to a dominant colonial capitalism, and thereafter to a socialist type of development.

In any case, one fact in Africa compels recognition: since the structure of society has not changed for at least 500 years, and in spite of an increase in population, the productive forces have stagnated, though not to the exclusion of sporadic localized growths which usually failed to flourish. This stagnation did not exclude the extraordinary blossoming of art, nor the refinement of personal relations. It seems as if the Africans devoted the essence of their creative energy to these domains.[22] In short, the material civilization which originated in African and Asian tropical latitudes during prehistory radiated north as far as the European isthmus, where, by means of the conjunction of advanced technology and the accumulation of capital, it became established and, as it were, crystallized brilliantly. Will this planetary system be transformed from its western core, or from the periphery, re-enacting the role of the barbarians in the history of the Roman Empire? History will tell. What we can affirm is that the prehistory of Africa is the history of the development of a primate into a human being and later, the humanization of Nature by this agent-vector responsible for all progress – a long march wherein the balance between Nature and Man was gradually upset in favour of reason. There remained the balance or imbalance between the human groups both within the continent and outside. However, the more productive forces increase, the more antagonisms sharpen the edge of interested motives and the will to power. The liberation struggles which today are still raging in certain territories of Africa are both the indicator and the negation of the attempt to domesticate the continent within a system that might be called the 'African mode of under-production'. But from the earliest mumblings of *Homo habilis*, it was and is the same struggle for liberation, the same stubborn and irrepressible purpose to achieve higher things by freeing oneself from alienation, whether by nature or by Man.

In Africa, the creation, the self-creation of Man which began thousands of millennia ago still continues.

In other words, there is a sense in which the prehistory of Africa has not yet ended.

22. That is why, in defining any 'African mode of production' in the future, particular attention should be paid to the sociological, political and ideological institutions, with special reference to the analyses of A. Gramsci and N. Poulantzas.

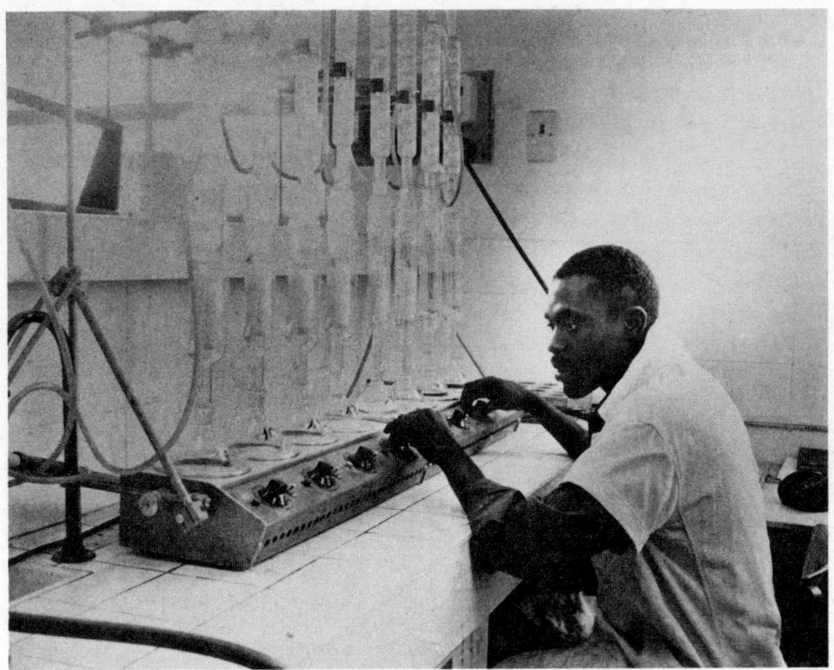

PLATE CONCL. 1 *Laboratory set up at Rosso Bithie for investigating the development of the delta of the River Senegal* (B. Nantet)

PLATE CONCL. 2. *Skull of* Australopithecus boisei, *Omo site* (photo J. Oster, Musée de l'Homme Coll.)

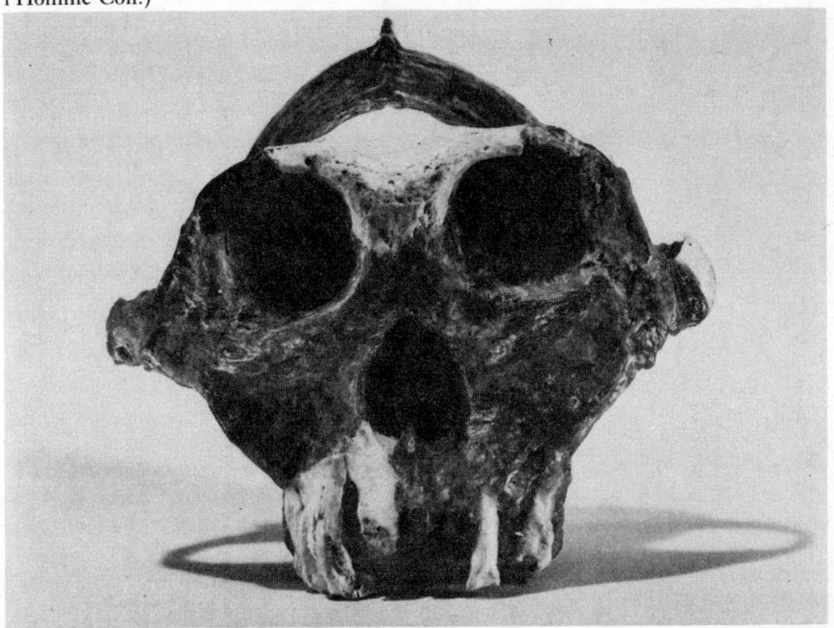

Members of the International Scientific Committee for the Drafting of a General History of Africa

The dates cited below refer to dates of membership.

Professor J. F. A. Ajayi
(Nigeria), from 1971
Editor Volume VI

Professor F. A. Albuquerque Mourao
(Brazil), from 1975

Professor A. A. Boahen
(Ghana), form 1971
Editor Volume VII

H. E. Boubou Hama
(Niger), 1971–8

H. E. Mrs M. Bull
(Zambia), from 1971

Professor D. Chanaiwa
(Zimbabwe), from 1975

Professor P. D. Curtin
(USA), from 1975

Professor J. Devisse
(France), from 1971

Professor M. Difuila
(Angola), from 1978

Professor H. Djait
(Tunisia), from 1975

Professor Cheikh Anta Diop
(Senegal), from 1971

Professor J. D. Fage
(UK), from 1971

H. E. M. El Fasi
(Morocco), from 1971
Editor Volume III

Professor J. L. Franco
(Cuba), from 1971

Mr M. H. I. Galaal
(Somalia), from 1971

Professor Dr V. L. Grottanelli
(Italy), from 1971

Professor E. Haberland
(Federal Republic of Germany), from 1971

Dr A. Habte
(Ethiopia), from 1971

H. E. Amadou Hampaté Bâ
(Mali), 1971–8

Dr I. S. El-Hareir
(Libya), from 1978

Dr I. Hrbek
(Czechoslovakia), from 1971

Dr A. Jones
(Liberia), from 1971

Abbé Alexis Kagame
(Rwanda), from 1971

Professor I. M. Kimanbo
(Tanzania), from 1971

Professor J. Ki-Zerbo
(Upper Volta), from 1971
Editor Volume I

M. D. Laya
(Niger), from 1979

Dr A Letnev
(USSR), from 1971

Dr G. Mokhtar
(Egypt), from 1971
Editor Volume II

Professor P. Mutibwa
(Uganda), from 1975

Professor D. T. Niane
(Senegal), from 1971
Editor Volume IV

Professor L. D. Ngcongco
(Botswana), from 1971

Professor T. Obenga
(People's Republic of the Congo), from 1975

Professor B. A. Ogot
(Kenya), from 1971
Editor Volume V

Professor C. Ravoajanahary
(Madagascar), from 1971

The late Dr W. Rodney
(Guyana), from 1979

The late Professor M. Shibeika
(Sudan), 1971–80

Professor Y. A. Talib
(Singapore), from 1975

Professor A. Teixeira da Mota
(Portugal), from 1978

Mgr T. Tshibangu
(Zaïre), from 1971

Professor J. Vansina
(Belgium), from 1971

Rt Hon. Dr E. Williams
(Trinidad and Tobago), 1976–8

Professor A. A. Mazrui
(Kenya)
Editor Volume VIII, not a
member of the Committee

Secretariat of the International Scientific Committee
Mr M Glélé, Division of Cultural Studies, Unesco, 1 rue Miollis, 75015 Paris

Biographies of Authors

INTRODUCTION J. Ki-Zerbo (Upper Volta); specialist in methods of teaching African history; author of a number of works dealing with black Africa and its history; Professor of History at the Centre d'Enseignement Supérieur, Ouagadougou; Secretary-General of the Conseil Africain et Malgache pour l'Enseignement Supérieur.

CHAPTER 1 J. D. Fage (UK); specialist in the history of West Africa; author and co-editor of a number of publications on African history; Pro-Vice-Chancellor at the University of Birmingham, and Director of the Centre of African Studies at that university.

CHAPTER 2 H. E. Boubou Hama (Niger); specialist in oral traditions; author of numerous works on the history of Niger and the Sudan region; former Director of the Centre Régional de Recherche et de Documentation sur les Traditions Orales et pour le Développement des Langues Africaines (CERDOTOLA).

CHAPTER 3 P. D. Curtin (USA); specialist on the history of the slave trade; author of numerous works on the subject; Professor of History at Johns Hopkins University.

CHAPTER 4 T. Obenga (People's Republic of the Congo); specialist in African languages; author of a number of articles on African history and of works on Africa in the ancient world; Professor at the Faculty of Letters of Marien N'Gouabi University.

CHAPTER 5 H. Djait (Tunisia); specialist in the medieval history of the Maghrib; author of numerous articles on the history of Tunisia; Professor at the University of Tunis.

CHAPTER 6 I. Hrbek (Czechoslovakia); specialist in African and Arab history; author of numerous works on the history of Africa; Professor, Head of the Arab and African Section, Institute of Oriental Studies, Prague.

CHAPTER 7 J. Vansina (Belgium); specialist in African history; author of numerous works on the history of Equatorial Africa; Professor of History at the University of Wisconsin (USA).

CHAPTER 8 A. Hampaté Bâ (Mali); specialist in oral traditions; author of numerous works on ancient African empires and African civilization.

CHAPTER 9 Z. Iskander (Egypt); specialist in Egyptian history; author of numerous works and articles on ancient Egypt; Director-General of Technical Affairs, Department of Antiquities.

CHAPTER 10 P. Diagne (Senegal); Doctor of Political and Economic Science; linguist; author of two works on African political power and on Wolof grammar; Assistant Professor at the University of Dakar.

CHAPTER 11 D. A. Olderogge (USSR); specialist in African social sciences; author of a number of works on Africa; member of the USSR Academy of Sciences.

CHAPTER 12 J. H. Greenberg (USA); linguist; author of numerous articles and works on anthropology and linguistics; Professor of Anthropology at Stanford University.

CHAPTER 13 S. Diarra (Mali); specialist in tropical geography; Professor of Geography at the University of Abidjan.

CHAPTER 14 A. Mabogunje (Nigeria); author of numerous works on the Yoruba; Professor of Geography at the University of Ibadan.

CHAPTER 15 J. Ki-Zerbo.

CHAPTER 16 R. Said (Egypt); physicist; Chairman of the Egyptian Geological Survey and Mining Authority.

CHAPTER 16 H. Faure (France); Doctor of Science; specialist in the geology of non-metropolitan France; author of works on the geology of West Africa; Lecturer at the University of Dakar and the University of Paris VI; Chairman of the Technical Committee on the Geology of the Quaternary at the Centre National de la Recherche Scientifique (CNRS).

CHAPTER 17 L. Balout (France); specialist in African prehistory; author of numerous works and articles on North Africa; former Director of the Muséum National d'Histoire Naturelle, Paris.

CHAPTER 17 Y. Coppens (France); specialist in prehistory; author of numerous works on the origin of mankind; Deputy Director at the Muséum National d'Histoire Naturelle, Paris.

CHAPTER 18 R. Leakey (UK); specialist in African prehistory; author of works on excavations relating to the origin of man in East Africa; Head of the International Louis Leakey Memorial Institute for African Prehistory, Nairobi.

CHAPTER 19 J. E. G. Sutton (UK); specialist in prehistory; author of numerous works and articles on African prehistory; former President of the Department of Archaeology at the University of Oxford.

CHAPTER 20 J. D. Clark (USA); specialist in African prehistory; author of numerous publications on the prehistory and ancient civilizations of Africa; Professor of History and Archaeology.

CHAPTER 21 R. de Bayle des Hermens (France); specialist in prehistory; author of numerous works and articles on African prehistory; engaged in research at the CNRS, Paris.

CHAPTER 21 F. Van Noten (Belgium); specialist in prehistory; author of works and publications on prehistory; Curator of the Royal Museum of Prehistory and Archaeology.

CHAPTER 22 L. Balout.

CHAPTER 23 H. J. Hugot (France); specialist in prehistory; author of numerous works on the natural history of the prehistoric and Quaternary periods; Deputy Director of the Muséum National d'Histoire Naturelle, Paris.

CHAPTER 24 C. T. Shaw (UK); author of numerous works on the prehistory of West Africa; Professor of Ancient History; Vice-President of the Pan-African Congress on Prehistory.

CHAPTER 25 F. Debono (UK); specialist in Egyptian prehistory; author of works on prehistoric research; research worker.

CHAPTER 26 J. Ki-Zerbo.

CHAPTER 27 R. Portères (France); devoted most of his life to African botanical research; former Professor at the Muséum National d'Histoire Naturelle, Paris; deceased.

CHAPTER 27 J. Barrau (France); author of numerous works on tropical plants; Deputy Director of the Laboratory of Ethno-botany and Ethno-zoology, Paris.

CHAPTER 28 J. Vercoutter (France); specialist in ancient history; author of numerous publications on ancient Egypt and its archaeology; Professor of History; Director of the Institut français d'Archéologie orientale, Cairo.

CONCLUSION J. Ki-Zerbo.

BIBLIOGRAPHY

The publishers wish to point out that while every effort has been made to ensure that the details in this Bibliography are correct, some errors may occur as a result of the complexity and the international nature of the work.

Abbreviations and List of Periodicals

AA *American Anthropologist*, Washington, DC
AARSC *Annales de l'Académie Royale des Sciences Coloniales*, Brussels
AATA *Art Archaeological and Technical Abstracts*, New York
ACPM *Annals of the Cape Provincial Museums*, Grahamstown
Actes 1er Coll. Intern. Archéol. Afr. *Actes du 1er Colloque International d'Archéologie Africaine*, Fort Lamy, 11–16 December 1966, Publications de l'Institut national tchadien pour les sciences humaines, Fort Lamy
Actes 2e Coll. Intern. LNA *Actes du second Colloque international de linguistique negro-africaine*, Dakar
Actes II Congr. PPEQ *Acts of the Second Pan African Congress of Prehistory and Quaternary Study*, Algiers, September–October 1952
Acts III PCPQS *Acts of the Third Panafrican Congress of Prehistory and Quaternary Studies*, Livingstone, 1955, London: Chatto & Windus, 1957
Actes III Congr. UISPP *Acts of the 3rd International Congress of Prehistoric and Protohistoric Sciences*, Zurich, 1950
Actes IV Congr. PPEQ *Actes du IV Congrès Panafricain de Préhistoire et de l'Etude du Quaternaire*, Leopoldville, 1959, Tervuren, 1962, AMRAC 40
Actes V Congr. PPEQ *Acts of the Fifth Pan African Congress of Prehistory and Quaternary Studies*, Tenerife, 1966
Actes VII Congr. PPEQ *Actes du VII Congrès panafricain de préhistorie et de l'étude du Quaternaire*, Addis Ababa, 1971
Actes VI Congr. UISPP *Acts of the 6th International Congress of Prehistoric and Protohistoric Sciences*, Rome, 1962
Actes IX Congr. UISPP *Acts of the 9th International Congress of Prehistoric and Protohistoric Sciences*, Nice, 1976
Actes 46e Congr. AFAS *Actes du 46e Congrès de l'Association Française pour l'Avancement des Sciences*, Montpellier, 1922
Actes Coll. Intern. Fer. *Actes du Colloque International. Le Fer à Travers les Ages; hommes et techniques*, Nancy, 3–6 October 1956, Annales de l'Est, Mémoire no. 16, Nancy, 1956
Acts IX INQUA Congr. *Acts of the 9th International Association Congress for Quaternal Research*, Christchurch, New Zealand
Acts XV Congr. IAAP *Acts of the 15th International Congress of Anthropology and Prehistoric Archaeology*, Paris, 1931
ADG *Abhandlungen der Deutschen Geographentags*
Africana *Africana Bulletin*, Uniwersytet Warszawski, Studium Afrykanistyczne, Warsaw
AG *Archaeologia Geographica*, Hamburg, West Germany
AGS *American Geographical Society*, New York
AHS *African Historical Studies*, Boston University, African Studies Center, Boston
AJHG *American Journal of Human Genetics*, American Society of Human Genetics, Chicago
AJPA *American Journal of Physical Anthropology*, American Association of Physical Anthropologists, Philadelphia
ALR *African Language Review* (now *African Languages*), International African Institute, London
ALS *African Language Studies*, School of Oriental and African Studies, London
AMRAC *Annales du Musée Royal d'Afrique Centrale*, Sciences humaines, Tervuren, Belgium
AMRCB *Annales du Musée Royal du Congo belge*
AN *African Notés*, University of Ibadan, Institute of African Studies, Ibadan, Nigeria
Annales *Annales, économies, sociétés, civilisations,* Paris
Ant. Afr. *Antiquités Africaines,* Editions du Centre National de la Recherche Scientifique, Paris
ASAE *Annales du Service des Antiquités de l'Egypte*, Cairo

ASAM *Annals of the South African Museum*, Cape Town
AT *Agronomie Tropicale*, Institut de Recherches Agronomiques Tropicales et des Cultures, Vivrières, Paris
BASEQUA *Bulletin de l' Association Sénégalaise pour l' étude du quaternaire de l'ouest africain*, Dakar-Fann, Senegal
BAUGS *Bulletin of the All Union Geographical Society*
BCEHS *Bulletin du Comité d'Etudes Historiques et Scientifiques de l'Afrique Occidentale Française*, Dakar
BFA *Bulletin of the Faculty of Arts*, Cairo
BGHD *Bulletin de Géographie Historique et Descriptive*, Comité des Travaux Historiques, Paris
BGSA *Bulletin of the Geological Society of America*, New York
BIE *Bulletin de l'Institut d'Egypte*, Cairo
BIEGT *Bulletin d'information et de liaison des Instituts d'Ethnosociologie et de Géographie Tropicale*, Abidjan
BIFAN *Bulletin de l'Institut Français (puis Fondamental) d'Afrique Noire*, Dakar
BIFAO *Bulletin de l'Institut Français d'Archéologie Orientale*, Cairo
BIRSC *Mémoires de l'Institut de Recherches Scientifiques du Congo*
BJBE *Bulletin du Jardin Botanique de l'Etat*, Brussels
BML *Bowman Memorial Lectures*, The American Geographical Society, New York
BNHSN *Bulletin of News of the Historical Society of Nigeria*, Ibadan
BSA *Bulletin de la Société d'Anthropologie de Paris*, Paris
BSAE *British School of Archaeology in Egypt and Egyptian Research Account*, London
BSOAS *Bulletin of the School of Oriental and African Studies*, London
BSERP *Bulletin de la Société d'Etudes et de Recherches Préhistoriques*, Les Eyzies, France
BSGC *Bulletin de la Société de Géographie Commerciale de Bordeaux*, Bordeaux, France
BSGF *Bulletin de la Société Géologique de France*, Paris
BSHNAN *Bulletin de la Société d'Histoire Naturelle d'Afrique du Nord*
BSL *Bulletin de la Société de Linguistique de Paris*, Paris
BSPF *Bulletin de la Société Préhistorique Française*, Paris
BSPM *Bulletin de la Société Préhistorique du Maroc*, Rabat
BSPPG *Bulletin de la Société Préhistorique et Protohistorique Gabonaise*, Libreville
BSRBAP *Bulletin de la Société Royale Belge d'Anthropologie et de Préhistoire*, Brussels
BSRBB *Bulletin de la Société Royale de Botanique de Belgique*, Brussels
BUPA *Boston University Papers on Africa*, African Studies Center, Boston University, 1967
CA *Current Anthropology*, Chicago
CAEH *Cahiers d'Anthropologie et d'Ecologie Humaine*, Paris
CDAPC *Companhia de Diamentes de Angola*, Lisbon
CEA *Cahiers d'Etudes Africaines*, Paris, Mouton
CHE *Cahiers d'Histoire Epytienne*, Cairo
CHM *Cahiers d'Histoire Mondiale*, Librairie des Méridiens, Paris
CJAS *The Canadian Journal of African Studies (Revue canadienne des études africaines)*, Canadian Association of African Studies, Department of Geography, Carleton University, Ottawa
CLAD *Centre de linguistique appliquée de Dakar*
CM *Cahiers de la Maboke*, Tervuren
Coll. CNRS *Colloques internationaux du Centre National de la Recherche Scientifique*, Paris
CORSTOM *Cahiers de l'Office de la Recherche Scientifique et Technique d'Outre-Mer*, Série sciences humaines, Paris
CRAS *Compte Rendu hebdomadaire des séances de l'Académie des Sciences*, Paris
CRSB *Compte rendu de la société de biogéographie*
EAJ *East Africa Journal*, East African Institute of Social & Cultural Affairs, Nairobi
Ecol. Monogr. *Ecological Monographs*
Econ. Bot. *Economic Botany*
GA *Geografiska Annaler*, Swedish Society of Anthropology and Geography, Stockholm
GJ *The Geographical Journal*, London
GSAB *Geological Society of America Bulletin*, Geological Society of America, Boulder, USA
GSAM *Geological Society of America Memoir*, Boulder, USA
L'Homme *L'Homme, cahier d'ethnologie, de géographie et de linguistique*, Paris
HT *Hesperis-Tamuda*, Université Mohammed V, Faculté de Lettres et des Sciences humaines, Rabat, Morocco
IJAHS *International Journal of African Historical Studies*, Boston University, African Studies Center, Boston

IJAL *International Journal of American Linguistics*, Linguistic Society of America, Chicago, USA
INEAC *Institut national pour l'étude agronemique du Congo belge*
IPH *International Association of Paper Historians*
IRS *Institut de recherches sahariennes* (*Université d'Alger*)
ISHM *Institut des sciences humaines du Mali*
JAF *Journal of American Folklore*, American Folklore Society, University of Texas, Austin, USA Washington, DC
JAH *Journal of African History*, CUP, London, New York
JAL *Journal of African Languages*, Hertford, England
JAOS *Journal of the American Oriental Society*, New Haven
JATBA *Journal d'Agronomie Tropicale et de botanique appliquée*
J. Afr. Soc. *Journal of the African Society,* London
JEA *Journal of Egyptian Archaeology*, Egypt Exploration Society, London
JEASC *Journal of the East African Swahili Committee*, Kampala
JHS *Journal Historique du Sokoto*
JHSN *Journal of the Historical Society of Nigeria*, Ibadan
JMAS *Journal of Modern African Studies*, CUP, London
JNS *Journal of Negro Studies*, Washington, DC
JRAI *Journal of the Royal Anthropological Institute of Great Britain and Ireland*, London
JRAS *Journal of the Royal Asiatic Society of Great Britain and Ireland*, London
JWAL *Journal of West African Languages*, University of Ibadan, Department of Linguistics & Nigerian Languages, Ibadan, Nigeria
Kush *Kush, Journal of the Sudan Antiquities Service,* Khartoum
LNR *Lagos Notes and Records*, University of Lagos, School of African Studies, Lagos, Nigeria
MAI *Mémoires de l'Académie des Inscriptions et Belles-Lett. es*, Paris
MAM *Mémoires de l' Académie Malgache,* Tananarive, Madagascar
Mém. Soc Ling. *Mémoires de la société linguistique*
MIRCB *Mémoires de l'Institut Royal du Congo Belge*, Brussels
MN *Masca Newsletter*, The University Museum, Philadelphia
MSB *Mémoires de la Société de Biogéographie*, Paris
NA *Notes Africaines*, Bulletin d'Information de l'IFAN, Dakar
OJS *The Ohio Journal of Science*, Ohio Academy of Science, Colombus, USA
OM *Oduma Magazine*, Rivers State Council for Arts and Culture, Port Harcourt, Nigeria
PA *Practical Anthropology* (now *Missiology*) American Society of Missiology, Pasadena, USA
PR *Polish Review*, Polish Institute of Arts & Sciences in America, New York
Proc. Burg Wart. Symp. *Proceedings of the Symposium held at Wartenstein, Austria, on the origin of African domesticated plants,* 1956
Proc. Conf. Cult. Ecol. *Proceedings of the Conference of Cultural Ecology*, Museum of Canada Bulletin
Proc. VII Congr. INQUA *Proceedings of the VIIth International Congress on Quaternary Studies*, Denver and Boulder, 1965
Proc. IX Congr. INQUA *Proceedings of the IXth International Association Congress for Quaternal Research*, Christchurch, New Zealand
Proc. III Intern. WAC *Proceedings of the IIIrd International West African Conference*, Ibadan, 1949
Proc. Sem. ASEWA *Proceedings of the Seminar on Application of Sciences in Examination of Works of Art*, Boston, Mass., 1958
PTRS *Philosophical Transactions of the Royal Society of London*, A: Mathematics and Physical Sciences, London
RA Revue Africaine, Journal des travaux de la société historique algérienne, Algiers
Rap. 12e CISH *Rapport du 12e Congrès international des sciences historiques*
RSO *Rivista degli studi orientali*, Scuola Orientale della Università di Roma, Rome
RE *Revue d'Egyptologie*, Paris
SAAAS *South African Association for the Advancement of Science*, Johannesburg
SAAB *South African Archaeological Bulletin*, Cape Town
SAJS *South African Journal of Science*, Johannesburg
SLLR *Sierra Leone Language Review*
SPPG *Société préhistorique et protohistorique gabonaise,* Libreville
SWJA *South Western Journal of Anthropology* (now *Journal of Anthropological Research*) University of New Mexico, Department of Anthropology, Albuquerque, New Mexico, USA
TGSSA *Transactions of the Geological Society of South Africa*, Johannesburg
THSG *Transactions of the Historical Society of Ghana*, Legon, Accra

TMIE *Travaux et Mémoires de l'Institut d'Ethnologie*, Université de Paris, Paris
Trav. CAMAP *Travaux du Centre d'Archéologie Méditerranéenne de l'Académie Polonaise des Sciences* (ed. K. Michalowski), Warsaw
Trav. IRS *Travaux de l'Institut de Recherches Sahariennes*, University of Algeria, Algiers
UJ *Uganda Journal*, Uganda Society, Kampala
WA *World Archaeology*, Henley on Thames, England
WAAN *West African Archaeological Newsletter*, Ibadan
WAJA *West African Journal of Archaeology*, Ibadan
WAR *West African Review*, Elder, Dempster & Co., London
ZES *Zeitschrift für Eingeboren in Sprachen*, Berlin
Z. Phon. *Zeitschrift für phonetik und allgemeine Sprach wissenschaft*

Adams, W. Y. (1964) 'Post-Pharaonic Nubia in the light of archaeology', *JEA*, 50. **(Chap. 28)**

Aguessy, H. (1972) 'Traditions orales et structures de pensée: essai de méthodologie, *CHM*, XIV, 2, pp. 269–97. **(Chaps 4, 7, 10)**

Aitken, M. J. (1961) *Physics and archaeology* (New York: Interscience Publishers). **(Chap. 9)**

Aitken, M. J. (1963) 'Magnetic location', in D. Brothwell and E. Higgs (eds), *Science in Archaeology* (London: Thames & Hudson), pp. 555–68. **(Chap. 9)**

Aitken, M. J. (1970) 'Dating by archaeomagnetic and thermoluminescent methods', *PTRS*, 269, 1193, pp. 77–88. **(Chap. 9)**

Akinjogbin, I. A. (1967) *Dahomey and its Neighbours, 1708–1818* (Cambridge: Cambridge University Press). **(Gen. Introd.)**

Alagoa, E. J. (1968a) 'The use of oral literacy data for history', *JAF*, 81. **(Chap. 7)**

Alagoa, E. J. (1968b) 'Songs as historical data. Examples from the Niger delta', *Research Review*, V, 1. **(Chap. 7)**

Alagoa, E. J. (1971) 'The Niger delta states and their neighbours, 1609–1800', in J. F. A. Ajayi and M. Crowder (eds), *History of West Africa* (London: Longman), Vol. I, pp. 269–303. **(Chap. 3)**

Alagoa, E. J. (1973) 'Oral tradition and archaeology. The case of Onyoma', *OM*, 1, 1. **(Gen. Introd., Chap. 4)**

Al-Alawi, ('Aidarus b, Al-Sharīf 'Alī al-'Aidarus al-Nadīrī al-'Alawī) (1374/1954–5) *Bughyat al-Amāl fī tarikh al-sumāl* (Mogadishu), in Arabic. **(Gen. Introd., Chaps 5, 6)**

al-Baydaq (1928) *Documents inédits d'histoire almohade* (tr. and ed. Lévi-Provençal) (Paris). **(Chap. 5)**

al-Shinqiti, A. (1910) *Al-Wasit fi tarajim Udaba Shinqit* (Cairo). **(Chap. 6)**

Alberti, L. (1811) *Description physique et historique des Cafres sur la côte méridionale de l'Afrique* (Amsterdam: Maaskamp). **(Chap. 6)**

Alexander, Sir J. E. (1967) *An Expedition of Discovery into the Interior of Africa* (New York: Johnson Reprint Corporation). **(Chap. 6)**

Alexandre, J. and Alexandre, S. (1968) 'Contribution à l'élaboration d'une stratigraphie du Quaternaire, basée sur les variations de climat dans une région du monde inter-tropical', *VIIe Congrès INQUA*, 7. **(Chap. 21)**

Alexandre, P. (1970) 'Afrique centre-équatoriale et centre-occidentale', in *Histoire Générale de l'Afrique Noire* ed. H. Deschamps, vol. 1 (Paris: PUF). **(Chap. 10)**

Alexseev, K. (1973) 'Sur la classification anthropologique de la population indigène de l'Afrique', *Les problèmes fondamentaux des études africaines* (Moscow). **(Chap. 11)**

Alimen, H. (1955) *Préhistoire de l'Afrique* (Paris: Boubée) tr. *The Prehistory of Africa* (London: Hutchinson), 1957. **(Chaps 13, 21–4, 28)**

Alimen, H. (1960) 'Découverte d'un atelier de l'acheuléen supérieur, en place, à la limite du 2e pluvial et du 3e pluvial dans les monts d'Ougarta (Sahara occidental)', *BSPF*, 57, pp. 421–3. **(Chap. 23)**

Alimen, H. (1962) 'Les origines de l'homme', *Bilan de la science* (Paris: Fayard), Conclusion.

Alimen, H. (1963) 'Considérations sur la chronologie du Quaternaire saharien', *BSGF*, 5, pp. 627–34. **(Chap. 13)**

Alimen, H. (1975a) 'Les isthmes hispano-marocains et sicilo-tunisiens aux temps acheuléens', *Anthropologie*, 79, 3, pp. 399–430. **(Chap. 22)**

Alimen, H. (1975b) 'Limite Pliocène-Quaternaire et définition du Quaternaire', *Prace o Plejstocie, Livre jubilaire du Prof. Rozycki* (Warsaw). **(Chap. 16)**

Alimen, H. (1976) 'Variations climatiques dans les zones désertiques de l'Afrique nord-équatoriale durant les quarante derniers millénaires', *Actes VII Congr. PPEQ*, Addis Ababa, pp. 337–47. **(Chap. 16)**

Alimen, H. and Chavaillon, J. (1956) 'Industrie acheuléenne in situ de l'oued Fares, dans les monts d'Ougarta (Sahara occidental)', *BSPF*, 53, pp. 202–14. **(Chap. 23)**

Alimen, H., Chavaillon, J. and Margat, J. (1965) 'Contribution à la chronologie préhistorique africaine. Essai de correlation entre les dépôts quaternaires du bassin Guir-Saoura (Sahara) et du bassin du Tafilat (Maroc)', *Congrès Préhistorique de France*, Monaco, 1959, pp. 161–267. **(Chap. 16)**

Allen, J. W. T. (1959) 'The collection of Swahili literature and its relation to oral tradition and history', *TNR*, 53, pp. 224–7. **(Chap. 6)**

Almagro-Basch, M. (1946) *Prehistoria del norte de Africa y del Sáhara Español* (Barcelona: Instituto de Estudios Africanos). **(Chap. 23)**

Amari, M. (1863) *I diplomi arabi del R. Archivo Fiorentino* (Florence). **(Chap. 5)**

Amer, M. (1935) 'The excavations in the prehistoric site at Maadi', *BFA*, II, pp. 176–8. **(Chap. 25)**

Amer, M. (1953a) 'Rizkana I. Excavations in the Wadi Digla', *BFA*, XV, pp. 97–100. **(Chap. 25)**

Amer, M. (1953b) 'Excavations in the Wadi Digla', *BFA*, XV, pp. 201–5. **(Chap. 25)**

Anciaux de Favaux, A. (1955) 'Les gisements préhistoriques de Kansenia', *Actes II Congr. PPEQ*, pp. 333–4. **(Chap. 21)**

Anciaux de Favaux, A. (1957) 'Une industrie sur galets speciale aux plateaux des Biano (Katanga, Congo Belge)', *Acts III PCPQS*, pp. 210–13. **(Chap. 21)**

Anciaux de Favaux, A. (1962) 'Evolution parallèle de deux ou plusieurs techniques au Paléolithique ancien et moyen sur les hauts plateaux Katangais. Fouilles 1960–61', *Actes VI Congr. UISPP*, III, pp. 230–5. **(Chap. 21)**

Anderson, B. (1870) *Narrative of a journey to Musardu, the capital of the western Mandingoes* (New York: Green). **(Chap. 6)**

Antoine, M. (1938) 'Notes de préhistoire marocaine, XIV: Un cône de résurgence du Paléolithique moyen à Tit-Mekil, près Casablanca', *BSPM*, 12. **(Chap. 23)**

Apter, D. E. (1955) *The Gold Coast in Transition* (Princeton, NJ: Princeton University Press). **(Chap. 3)**

Arab-Faqih (1897–1901) *Histoire de la conquête de l'Abyssinie (XVIe siècle)*, ed. R. Basset, 2 Vols (Paris: Leroux). **(Chap. 6)**

Arambourg, C. (1949) 'Sur la présence dans le Villafranchien d'Algérie de vestiges éventuels d'industrie humaine', *CRAS*, 229, pp. 66–7. **(Chap. 22)**

Arambourg, C. (1954) 'L'hominien fossile de Ternifine (Algérie)', *CRAS*, 239, pp. 293–5. **(Chap. 24)**

Arambourg, C. (1962) 'Etat actuel des recherches sur le Quaternaire en Afrique du Nord', *Actes IV Congr. PPEQ*, 40, pp. 255–77. **(Chap. 16)**

Arambourg, C. (1966) 'Aperçu sur les résultats des fouilles du gisement de Ternifine', *Actas V Congr. PPEC*, I, pp. 129–36. **(Chaps 16, 24)**

Arambourg, C. and Coppens, Y. (1967) 'Sur la découverte dans le Pléistocène inférieur de la vallée de l'Omo (Ethiopie) d'une mandibule d'Australopithécien', *CRAS*, 265, pp. 589–90. **(Chap. 17)**

Arambourg, C. and Coppens, Y. (1968) 'Découverte d'un Australopithécien nouveau dans les gisements de l'Omo (Ethiopie)', *SAJS*, 64, 2, pp. 58–9. **(Chap. 17)**

Arambourg, C. and Hofstetter, R. (1954) 'Découverte en Afrique du Nord de restes humains du Paléolithique inférieur', *CRAS*, 239, pp. 72–4. **(Chap. 24)**

Arambourg, C. and Hofstetter, R. (1955) 'Le gisement de Ternifine. Résultats des fouilles de 1955 et découvertes de nouveaux restes d'Atlanthropus', *CRAS*, 241, pp. 431–3. **(Chap. 24)**

Arambourg, C. and Hofstetter, R. (1963) 'Le gisement de Ternifine', *IPH Archives*, XXXII, Paris, Masson. **(Chap. 22)**

Arbousset, T. (1842) *Relation d'un voyage d'exploration* (Paris). **(Chap. 6)**

Arkell, A. J. (1949a) *The old stone age in the Anglo-Egyptian Sudan* (Khartoum: Sudan Antiquities Service, Occasional papers No. 1). **(Chap. 25)**

Arkell, A. J. (1949b) *Early Khartoum. An account of the excavations of an early occupation site carried out by the Sudan Government Antiquities Service, 1944–1945* (London: Oxford University Press). **(Chaps 23, 35, 28)**

Arkell, A, J. (1950) 'Gold Coast copies of fifth to seventh century bronze lamps', *Antiquity*, 24, pp. 38–40. **(Chap. 24)**

Arkell, A. J. (1953) *Shaheinab; An account of the excavation of a neolithic occupation site carried out for the Sudan Government Antiquities Service in 1949* (London: Oxford University Press). **(Chaps 23, 25, 28)**

Arkell, A. J. (1954) 'The late Acheulean of Esh Shaheinab', *Kush*, I, pp. 30–4. **(Chap. 23)**

Arkell, A. J. (1961) *History of the Sudan from the Earliest Times to 1821*, 2nd edn (London: Athlone Press). **(Chap. 28)**

Arkell, A. J. (1964) *Wanyanga, and an Archaeological Reconnaissance of the South-West Libyan Desert. The British Ennedi Expedition 1957* (London/New York: Oxford University Press). **(Chap. 23)**

Arkell, A. J. (1975) *Prehistory of the Nile Valley* (Handbuch das Orientalistik, VII, Vol. 2, pt A, no. 1, Leiden: Brill). **(Chap. 28)**

Arkell, A. J. and Sandford, K. S. (1933) *Palaeolithic Man and the Nile Valley in Nubia and Upper Egypt* (Chicago). **(Chap. 23)**

Armstrong, R. (1964) 'The use of linguistics in ethnogeography', in J. Vansina *et al.*, *The Historian in Tropical Africa* (London: Oxford University Press). **(Chap. 10)**

Armstrong, R. (1971) 'The collection of oral traditions in Africa', *AUA*, pp. 579–83. **(Chap. 7)**

Arnett, E. J. (1922) *The Rise of the Sokoto Fulani* (Kano). **(Chap. 6)**

ASEQUA (1964 and following years) *BASEQUA No. 1* and following. **(Chap. 16)**

ASEQUA (1966) 'Etat des recherches sur le Quaternaire de l'Ouest Africain, 1ère série', *BIFAN*, 28, pp. 371–429. **(Chap. 24)** (See *BASEQUA*.)

ASEQUA (1967) 'Etat des recherches sur le Quaternaire de l'Ouest Africain, 2ème série', *BIFAN*, A, 29, pp. 821–65. **(Chap. 24)** (See *BASEQUA*.)

ASEQUA (1969) 'Etat des recherches sur le Quaternaire de l'Ouest Africain, 3ème série', *BIFAN*, A, 31, pp. 210–83. **(Chap. 24)** (See *BASEQUA*.)

Atherton, J. H. (1972) 'Excavations at Kamabai and Yagala Rock Shelters, Sierra Leone', *WAJA*, 2, pp. 39–74. **(Chap. 24)**

Atherton, J. H. (1973) 'The Stone Age Iron Age transition in northeast Sierra Leone', *Underground West Africa*, 7. **(Chap. 24)**

Aubreville, H. (1949) *Climats – forêts, désertification de l'Afrique tropicale* (Paris: Société d'éditions géographiques, maritimes et coloniales). **(Chap. 13)**

Aubreville, H. (1962) 'Savanisation tropicale et glaciations quaternaires', *Andansonia*, 2, 1, p. 1684. **(Chap. 13)**

Ayache, G. (1961) 'Les archives marocaines', *HT*, 2. **(Chap. 6)**

Bâ, A. H. (1972) *Aspects de la civilisation africaine (personne, culture, réligion)* (Paris: Présence africaine). **(Chap. 8)**

Bâ, A. H. and Cardaire, M. (1957) *Tierno Bokar, le sage de Bandiagara* (Paris: Présence africaine). **(Chap. 8)**

Bâ, A. H. and Daget, J. (1962) *L'empire peul du Macina au XVIII*[e] *siècle* (Paris: Mouton). **(Chap. 8)**

Bâ, A. H. and Dieterlen, G. (1961) *Koumen, texte initiatique des pasteurs peul* (Paris: Mouton). **(Gen. Introd.)**

Ba, O. (1972) *Glossaire des mots étrangers passés en Pulaar du Fouta Toro* (Dakar: Centre de Linguistique appliquée de Dakar). **(Chap. 10)**

Babet, V. (1936) 'Note préliminaire sur un atelier de pierres taillées à Brazzaville (Afrique Equatoriale française)', *BSPF*, 33, pp. 153–5. **(Chap. 21)**

Bada, J. L., Schroeder, R. A., Protsch, R. and Berger, R. (1974) 'Concordance of collagen based radiocarbon and aspartic acid racemization ages', *AATA*, 11, 2. **(Chap. 9)**

Bailloud, A. (1966) 'L'évolution des styles céramiques en Ennedi', *Actes 1er Coll. Intern. Archéol. Afr.* **(Gen. Introd.)**

al-Bakri (1968) 'Routier de l'Afrique blanche et noire du Nord-Ouest' (Cordoue, 1068), trans. V. Monteil, *BIFAN*, B, 30, pp. 39–116. **(Chap. 24)**

Balandier, G. (1971) *Sociologie actuelle de l'Afrique noire* (Paris: PUF), 3rd edn. **(Gen. Introd., Chap. 15)**

Balandier, G. and Maquet, J. (1968) *Dictionnaire des civilisations africaines* (Paris: Hazan). **(Chap. 4)**

Balbi, A. (1826) *Atlas ethnographique du globe ou Classification des peuples anciens et modernes d'après leurs langues* (Paris: Rey et Gravies). **(Chap. 12)**

Ball, J. (1939) *Contributions to the geography of Egypt* (Cairo: Government Press, Bulâq). **(Chap. 16)**

Balout, L. (1952a) 'Pluviaux, interglaciaires et préhistoire saharienne', *Trav. IRS*, 8, pp. 9–21. **(Chaps 16, 23)**

Balout, L. (1952b) 'Du nouveau à l'Aîn Hanech', *BSHNAN*, 43, pp. 152–9. **(Chap. 22)**

Balout, L. (1954) 'Les hommes préhistoriques du Maghreb et du Sahara. Inventaire descriptif et critique', *Libyca*, II. **(Chap. 22)**

Balout, L. (1955a) in C. Arambourg and L. Balout, 'L'ancien lac de Tihodaîne et ses gisements préhistoriques', *Actes II Congr. PPEQ*, pp. 287–92. **(Chap. 23)**

Balout, L. (1955b) *Préhistoire de l'Afrique du Nord, essai de chronologie* (Paris: AMG). **(Chaps 12, 22, 23)**

Balout, L. (1958) *Algérie préhistorique* (Paris: AMG). **(Chap. 23)**

Balout, L. (1965) 'Le Moustérien du Maghreb', *Quaternaria*, 7, pp. 43–58. **(Chap. 22)**

Balout, L. (1967a) 'Procédés d'analyse et questions de terminologie dans l'étude des ensembles industriels du Paléolithique inférieur en Afrique du Nord', in W. W. Bishop and J. D. Clark (eds), *Background to Evolution in Africa* (Chicago/London: University of Chicago Press), pp. 701–35. **(Chap. 22)**

Balout, L. (1967b) 'L'homme préhistorique et la Méditerranée occidentale', *ROMM*, III, pp. 9–29. **(Chap. 22)**

Balout, L. (1968) 'L'art rupestre nord-africain et saharien. Etat de quelques problèmes', *Simposio internacional de arte rupestre* (Barcelona), pp. 257–64. **(Chap. 22)**

Balout, L. (1976) *Orientations nouvelles de la préhistoire maghrébine. In memoriam Pedro Bosch Gimpera, 1891–1974* (Mexico), pp. 99–113. **(Chap. 22)**

Balout, L. *et al.* (1967 onwards) Nine Collections of Papers published under the auspices of the PPEQ Congresses. **(Chap. 22)**

Balout, L., Biberson, P. and Tixier, J. (1967) 'L'Acheuléen de Ternifine, gisement de l'Atlanthrope', *Anthropologie*, 71, pp. 217–37. **(Chap. 22)**

Balout, L. and Roubet, C. (1970) 'Datation radiométrique de l'Homme de l'Aîn Dokkara et de son gisement. l'Escargotière du Chacal, région de Tébessa, Algérie', *Libyca*, 18, pp. 21–35. **(Chap. 22)**

Barber, E. J. W. (1974) *Archaeological decipherment. A Handbook* (Princeton: Princeton University Press). **(Chap. 4)**

Barbey, C. and Descamps, C. (1969) 'A propos des Pebble-tools de la Moyenne Gambie', *BIFAN*, A, 31, pp. 276–82. **(Chap. 24)**

Barbot, J. (1732) *A description of the Coasts of North and South Guinea* in Churchill and Awnsham (comp.), *A Collection of Voyages and Travels* (London). **(Chap. 1)**

Barendson, G. W., Deevey, E. S. and Gralemski, L. J. (1965) 'Yale natural radiocarbon measurements III', *Science*, 126, pp. 916–17. **(Chap. 24)**

Barrau, J. (1962) 'Les plantes alimentaires de l'Océanie, origines, distribution et usages', *Annales du Musée colonial de Marseille*, 7, III–IX, 275pp. **(Chap. 27)**

Barrau, J. (1975) 'L'Asie du Sud-est, berceau cultural?' *Etudes rurales*, pp. 53–6. **(Chap. 27)**

Barrow, J. (1801–3) *An Account of Travels into the Interior of Southern Africa in the Years 1797 and 1798*, 2 Vols (London). **(Chap. 6)**

Barry, B. (1974) 'La chronologie dans la tradition orale du Waalo. Essai d'interprétation', *Afrika Zamani*, 3, pp. 31–49. **(Chap. 4)**

Barth, H. (1857–8) *Travels and Discoveries in north and central Africa* (London), **(Chap. 1)**

Basch, M. A. and Gorbea, M. A. (1968) 'Estudios de arte rupestre nubio', *Memorias de la Misión arqueologica en Egypto*, 10 (Madrid). **(Chap. 23)**

Basset, R. (1894) *Etudes sur les dialectes berbères* (Paris: Leroux). **(Chap. 10)**

Basset, R. (1909–10) *Mission au Sénégal*, 3 Vols (Paris: Leroux). **(Chaps 6, 10)**

Battistini, R. (1967) *L'Afrique australe et Madagascar* (Paris: PUF). **(Chap. 13)**

Baulin, J. (1962) *The Arab role in Africa* (Baltimore: Penguin). **(Chap. 5)**

Baumann, H. (1936) *Schöpfung und Urzeit des Menschen in Mythus der afrikanischen Völker* (Berlin). **(Chap. 7)**

Baumann, H. and Westermann, D. (1940, 1948) *Völkerkunde Afrikas* (Essen) tr. *Les Peuples et les Civilisations de l'Afrique* (Paris: Payot) 1948, 1968. **(Gen. Introd., Chaps 1, 6, 10)**

Baumgartel, E. J. (1955) *The Cultures of Prehistoric Egypt*, rev. edn (London: Oxford University Press). **(Chap. 28)**

Bayle des Hermens, R. de (1967) 'Premier aperçu du Paléolithique inférieur en République Centrafricaine', *Anthropologie*, 71, pp. 135–66. **(Chap. 21)**

Bayle des Hermens, R. de (1969) 'Les collections préhistoriques de République Centrafricaine au Musée royal de l'Afrique centrale', *CM*, VII, pp. 27–40. **(Chap. 21)**

Bayle des Hermens, R. de (1971) 'Quelques aspects de la préhistoire en République Centrafricaine', *JAH*, XII, pp. 579–97. **(Chap. 21)**

Bayle des Hermens, R. de (1975) *Recherches préhistoriques en République Centrafricaine* (Laboratoire d'ethnologie et de sociologie comparative, Université de Paris, Série Recherches oubanguiennes no. 3, Paris: Klincksieck). **(Chap. 21)**

Bayle des Hermens, R. de (1976) 'A la découverte de la préhistoire en République Centrafricaine', *Archeologia*, no. 92 **(Chap. 26)**

Bayle des Hermens, R. de and Vidal, P. (1971) 'Deux datations sur la méthode du Carbone 14 des monuments mégalithiques de Bouar, RCA', *CM*, IX, pp. 81–2. **(Chap. 21)**

Beale, F. C. (1966) *The Anglo-Gambian Stone Circles Expedition 1964/65* (Bathurst: Government Printer). **(Chap. 24)**

Beattie, J. (1968) 'Aspects of Nioro Symbolism', *Africa*, 38, 4, pp. 413–42. **(Chap. 7)**

Beauchene, G. de (1963) 'La Préhistoire du Gabon', *Objets et Mondes*, Vol. III (Paris: Musée de l'Homme). **(Chap. 21)**

Bébey, F. (1969) *Musique de l'Afrique* (Collection Expressions, Horizons de France).

Beccari, C. (1905–17) *Rerum aethiopicarum scriptores occidentales inediti* (Rome). **(Chap. 1)**

Becker, C. H. (1968) 'Materialen zur Kenntnis des Islam in Deutsch Ost-Afrika', *INR*, LXVII. **(Gen. Introd., Chaps 5, 6)**

Beckingham, C. F. and Huntingford, G. W. B. (1954) *Some Records of Ethiopia 1593–1646* (London: Hakluyt Society). **(Chaps 1, 6)**

Behrensmeyer, A. K. (1975) 'The Taphonomy and paleoecology of Plio-Pleistocene vertebrate assemblages east of Lake Rudolf, Kenya', *Bull. Mus. Comp. Zool.* **(Chap. 17)**

Beidelman, T. (1970) 'Myth, legend and oral history: A Kaguru traditional text', *Anthropos*, 65, pp. 74–97. **(Chap. 7)**

Bello, M. (1951) *Infaqu' l-maysur*, ed. C. E. J. Whiting (London). **(Chap. 6)**

Benezet, A. (1772) *Some Historical Account of Guinea* (London). **(Chap. 1)**

Bequaert, M. (1938) 'Les fouilles de Jean Colette à Kalina', *AMRCB*, I, 2, pp. 29–88. **(Chap. 21)**

Bequaert, M. (1952) 'Fouilles à Dinga (Congo Belge)', *Actes II Congr. PPEQ*, pp. 317–53. **(Chap. 21)**

Bequaert, M. (1953) 'La préhistoire du Congo Belge et ses relations avec la préhistoire africaine sud-saharienne à l'Holocène', *BSRBAP*, LXIV, pp. 37–49. **(Chap. 21)**

Bequaert, M. and Mortelmans, G. (1955) 'Le Tshitolien dans le bassin du Congo', *AARSC*, II, 5. **(Chap. 21)**

Berg, F. (1968) 'The Swahili community of Mombasa 1500–1900', *JAH*, IX, pp. 35–56. **(Gen. Introd. Chaps 5, 6)**

Berger, R. (1970) 'Ancient Egyptian chronology', *PTRS*, 269, 1193, pp. 23–36. **(Chap. 9)**

Berggren, W. A. (1973) 'Correlation and calibration of late Pliocene and Pleistocene marine and continental biostratigraphies', *Acts IX INQUA Congr.* **(Chap. 16)**

Berque, J. (1957) *Histoire sociale d'un village égyptien au XXe siècle* (Paris: Mouton). **(Chap. 15)**

Berthier, H. (1933) 'Le cahier de l'écriture de Radama I', *MAM*, 36. **(Chap. 6)**

Besançon, J. (1957) *L'homme et le Nil* (Paris: Gallimard). **(Chap. 28)**

Biberson, P. (1961a) *Le cadre paléogéographique de la préhistoire du Maroc atlantique* (Rabat: Service des antiquités de Maroc). **(Chap. 22)**

Biberson, P. (1961b) *Le Paléolithique inférieur du Maroc atlantique* (Rabat: Service des antiquités de Maroc). **(Chap. 23)**

Biberson, P. (1965) 'Recherches sur le Paléolithique inférieur de l'Adrar de Mauritanie', *Actes V Congr. PPEQ*, pp. 173–89. **(Chap. 23)**

Biebuyck, D. and Mateene, K. C. (1971) *The Mwindo epic from the Banyanga (Congo Republic)* (Berkeley/Los Angeles: University of California Press). **(Chap. 7)**

Bird, J. (1888) *The Annals of Natal, 1495–1845* (Pietermaritzburg). **(Chap. 6)**

Birdsell, J. B. (1972) *Human evolution. An introduction to the new physical anthropology* (Chicago: Rand McNally). **(Chap. 4)**

Birot, P. (1970) *Les régions naturelles du globe* (Paris: Masson). **(Chap. 13)**

Bishop, W. W. (1965) 'Quaternary geology and geomorphology in the Albertine rift valley, Uganda', *GSAM*, 84, pp. 293–321. **(Chap. 21)**

Bishop, W. W. and Clark, J. D. (eds) (1967) *Background to Evolution in Africa* (Chicago/London: University of Chicago Press). **(Chaps 16, 19, 22, 23, 24, Concl.)**

Bishop, W. W. and Miller, J. A. (eds) (1972) *Calibration of hominoid evolution* (Toronto: University of Toronto Press). **(Chaps 16, 20)**

Bittner, M. (1897) *Capitel, die topographie des indischen Seespiegels Mohît* (Vienna). **(Chap. 6)**

Bivar, A. D. H. and Hiskett, M. (1962) 'The Arabic literature of Nigeria to 1804: a provisional account', *BSAOS*, XXV, 1. **(Gen. Introd., Chaps 5, 6)**

Blankoff, B. (1965) 'Quelques découvertes récentes au Gabon', *BSPPG*, I, 3, pp. 52–60. **(Chap. 21)**

Blankoff, B. (1966) 'L'état des recherches préhistoriques au Gabon', *Actes 1er Coll. Intern. Archéol. Afr.*, pp. 62–80. **(Chap. 21)**

Bleek, D. F. (1929) *Comparative Vocabularies of the Bushman Languages* (Cambridge: Cambridge University Press). **(Chap. 10)**

Bleek, W. H. I. (1851) *De nominum generibus, linguarum Africae australis, copticae, semiticarum, aliarumque sexualium* (Bonn: Marcus). **(Chap. 12)**

Bleek, W. H. I. (1862–9) *A Comparative Grammar of South African languages*, 2 Vols (Capetown: Juta/London: Trübner). **(Chaps 10, 12)**

Bloch, M. (1939) *La Société féodale, Vol. 1: La Formation des liens de dépendance* (Paris: Albin Michel). **(Chap. 1)**

Bloch, M. (1949) *Apologie pour l'histoire ou le Métier d'historien* (Paris: Colin). **(Chap. 7)**
Blundel, H. W. (1923) *The Royal Chronicle of Abyssinia, 1769–1840* (Cambridge: Cambridge University Press). **(Chap. 6)**
Blundel, H. W., Boaz, N. and Howell, F. C. (1977) 'A gracile hominid cranium from Upper Member G of the Shungura formation, Ethiopia', *AJPA*, 46, 1, pp. 93–108. **(Chap. 17)**
Boahen, A. A. and Webster, J. B. (1970) *The Growth of African Civilisation. West Africa since 1800* (London: Longman). **(Gen. Introd., Chap. 8)**
Bobo, J. (1956) 'Un ensemble de stations moustéro-atériennes aux environs de Djanet (Tassili des Ajjer)', *Libyca*, 4, pp. 263–8. **(Chap. 23)**
Bonatti, E. (1966) 'North Mediterranean climate during the last Würm glaciation', *Nature*, 209, 5027, pp. 985–7. **(Chap. 16)**
Bond, G. (1956) 'A preliminary account of the Pleistocene geology of the plateau Tia Fields region of northern Nigeria', *Proc. III Intern. WAC*, pp. 187–202. **(Chap. 24)**
Bonifay, E. (1975) 'Stratigraphie du Quaternaire et âge des gisements préhistoriques de la zone littorale des Alpes-Maritimes', *BSPF*, 72, 7, pp. 197–206. **(Chap. 16)**
Bonnefille, R. (1972) 'Associations polliniques actuelles et quaternaires en Ethiopie (vallées de l'Awash et de l'Omo)' thesis, 2 Vols (University of Paris). **(Chap. 16)**
Bonnefille, R. (1974) 'Etude palynologique de dépôts pliopléistocènes d'Ethiopie', *ASEQUA*, B, 42–3, pp. 21–2. **(Chap. 16)**
Bonnefille, R. (1976) 'Végétation et climats des temps oldowayens et acheuléens à Melka Kunturé (Ethiopie)', *L'Ethiopie avant l'histoire*, Vol. 1, pp. 55–71. **(Chap. 17)**
Bonnel de Mezières, A. (1920) 'Recherches sur l'emplacement de Ghana et de Tekrour', *MAI*, 13, 1, pp. 227–77. **(Chap. 24)**
Bonnet, A. (1961) 'La "Pebble Culture" in situ de l'Idjerane et les terrasses de piémont du Sahara central', *BSPF*, 58, pp. 51–61. **(Chap. 23)**
Bosman, W. (1967) *A New and Accurate Description of the Coast of Guinea*, eds J. D. Fage, R. E. Bradbury (London: Cass). **(Chap. 1)**
Boston, J. S. (1964) 'The hunter in Igala legends of origin', *Africa*, 34, pp. 118–20. **(Chap. 7)**
Boulle, M., Vallois, H. V. and Verneau, R. (1934) *Les Grottes paléolithiques des Bani Ségoual (Algérie)* (Paris: Masson). **(Chap. 22)**
Bounak, V. (1972) 'Du cri au langage', *Le Courrier* (August–September). **(Concl.)**
Bouyssonie, J., Breuil, H. *et al.* (1956) Musée du Bardo, collections préhistoriques, Planches, album no. 1 (Paris: AMG). **(Chap. 23)**
Bovier-Lapierre, P. (1925) 'Le Paléolithique stratifié des environs du Caire', *Anthropologie*, XXXV, pp. 37–46. **(Chap. 25)**
Bovill, E. W. (1933) *Caravans of the Old Sahara* (Oxford: Oxford University Press). **(Chap. 1)**
Boxer, C. R. (ed.) (1959) *The Tragic History of the Sea, 1589–1622* (Cambridge: Cambridge University Press). **(Chap. 6)**
Boyle, A. H. and Jeffreys, W. (1947) 'Speculative origins of the Fulany language', *The Language of Africa*, 17. **(Chap. 10)**
Bradbury, R. E. (1959) 'Chronological problems in the study of Benin history', *JHSN*, I, pp. 263–87. **(Chap. 24)**
Brahimi, C. (1970) *L'Ibéromaurusien littoral de la région d'Alger* (Paris: AMG). **(Chap. 22)**
Brahimi, C. (1972) *Initiation à la préhistoire de l'Algérie* (Algiers: SNED). **(Chap. 22)**
Braidwood, R. J. (1960) 'The agricultural revolution', *Scientific America* (September). **(Chap. 27)**
Braidwood, R. J. and Reed, C. A. (1957) 'The achievement and early consequence of food production; a consideration of the archaeological and natural historical evidence', *Cold Spring Harbor Symposium on Quantitative Biology*. **(Chap. 27)**
Brain, C. K. (1958a) 'The Transvaal Ape Man Bearing Cave Deposits', *Transvaal Museum Memoir* No. 11, Pretoria. **(Chap. 20)**
Brain, C. K. (1958b) *The Prehistory of Southern Africa* (London). **(Chap. 20)**
Brasio, A. D. (1952) *Monumenta missionaria africana*, 9 Vols (Lisbon: Agència Geral do Ultramar). **(Chap. 6)**
Braudel, F. (1969) *Ecrits sur l'histoire* (Paris: Flammarion). **(Gen. Introd.)**
Breasted, J. H. (1906) *Ancient Records of Egypt* (Chicago: University of Chicago Press), Vol. IV. **(Chap. 28)**
Breuil, Abbé H. (1931) *L'Afrique* (Paris: Cahiers d'Art). **(Chap. 24)**
Breuil, Abbé H. (1944) 'Le Paléolithique au Congo Belge d'après les recherches du docteur Cabu: VI; Plateau de Bena Tshitolo', *TRSA*, XXX, pp. 143–60. **(Chap. 21)**
Breuil, Abbé H. (1952) 'Les figures incisée et ponctuées de la grotte de Kiantapo (Katanga)', *AMRCB*, pp. 1–32. **(Chap. 21)**

Brézillon, M. N. (1969) *Dictionnaire de la préhistoire* (Paris: Larousse). **(Concl.)**
Brothwell, D. and Shaw, T. (1971) 'A late upper Pleistocene proto-West African Negro from Nigeria', *Man*, 6, 2, pp. 221–7. **(Chap. 24)**
Broutanoh, A. (1867) 'La tradition orale chez les Agni Ahali de Moronou', *BIEGT*. **(Chap. 7)**
Brown, E. J. P. (1929) *A Gold Coast and Asiatic Reader* (London). **(Chap. 1)**
Brown, G. (1941) *The Economic History of Liberia* (Washington, DC: Associated Publishers). **(Chap. 3)**
Browne, W. G. (1806) *Travels in Africa, Egypt and Syria from the year 1792 to 1798* (London: Cadell & Davies). **(Chap. 6)**
Bruce, J. (1813) *Travels to Discover the Source of the Nile*, 5 Vols (Edinburgh: Constable). **(Chap. 6)**
Brunschvig, R. (1942–7) 'Ibn 'Abd al-Hakam et la conquête de l'Afrique du Nord par les Arabes', *Annales de l'Institut d'études orientales d'Alger, VI*. **(Chap. 5)**
Brunton, G. (1928) in G. Brunton and G. Caton-Thompson, *The Badarian Civilisation and Predynastic Remains near Badari* (London: British School of Archaeology in Egypt). **(Chaps 25, 28)**
Brunton, G. (1937) *British Museum Expedition to Middle Egypt 1928–1929* [*Mostagedda*] *and the Tasian Culture* (London: Quaritch). **(Chaps 25, 28)**
Brunton, G. (1948) *British Museum Expedition to Middle Egypt 1929–1931* [*Matmar*] (London: Quaritch). **(Chaps 25, 28)**
Bryant, A. T. (1929) *Olden Times in Zululand and Natal, Containing Earlier Political History of the Eastern-Nguni Clans* (London/New York: Longman, Green). **(Chap. 6)**
Bucha, V. (1970) 'Evidence for changes in the earth's magnetic field intensity', *PTRS*, 269, 1193, pp. 47–55. **(Chap. 9)**
Bucha, V. (1971) 'Archaeomagnetic dating', in H. N. Michael and E. K. Ralph (eds), *Dating Techniques for the Archaeologist* (Cambridge, Mass.: MIT Press), pp. 57–117. **(Chap. 9)**
Buedel, J. (1958) 'Die Flaeschenbildung in den feuchten Troppen und die Rolls fossier solcher Flaeschen in anderen Klimazonen', *ADG*, pp. 89–121. **(Chap. 16)**
Bulck, G. van (1948) 'Les recherches linguistiques au Congo Belge', *MIRCB*. **(Chap. 10)**
Burke, K., Durotye, A. B. and Whiteman, A. J. (1971) 'A dry phase south of Sahara, 20 000 years ago', *WAJA*, I. **(Chap. 24)**
Burton, R. F. (1864) *A Mission to Gelele, King of Dahomey* (London). **(Chap. 1)**
Butler, J. (1967) *Boston University Papers on Africa. Prehistoric Populations in Africa*, II (Boston: Boston University Press). **(Concl.)**
Butzer, K. W. (1957) 'The last "pluvial" phase of the Eurafrican subtropics', *Les Changements de climats. Recherches sur la zone aride* (Paris: Unesco), 20, pp. 211–16. **(Chap. 13)**
Butzer, K. W. (1958–9) *Studien zum vor– und frühgeschichtlichen Landschaftswandel der Sahara*, (Mainz: Verlag der Akademie de Wissenschaften und der Literatur/Wiesbaden: Steiner). **(Chap. 23)**
Butzer, K. W. (1964) *Environment and Archaeology; An Ecological Approach to Prehistory*, 2nd edn 1972 (London: Methuen, Chicago: Aldine). **(Chaps 16, 24, 28)**
Butzer, K. W. and Hansen, C. L. (1968) *Desert and River in Nubia; Geomorphology and Prehistoric Environments at the Aswan Reservoir* (Madison: University of Wisconsin Press). **(Chap. 16)**
Butzer, K. W. and Isaac, G. L. (1976) *After the Australopithecines: Stratigraphy, Ecology and Culture, Change in the Middle Pleistocene* (The Hague: Mouton). **(Chap. 19)**
Butzer, K. W., Richardson, J. L. and Washbourknkamau, C. (1972) 'Radio-carbon dating of east African lake levels', *Science*, 175, pp. 1069–76. **(Chaps 16, 21)**
Butzer, K. W. and Thurber, D. L. (1969) 'Some late Cenozoic sedimentary formations of the lower Omo basin', *Nature*, 222, 5199, pp. 1132–7.
Bynon, J. (1970) 'The contribution of linguistics to history in the field of Berber studies', in D. Dalby (ed.), *Language and History in Africa*, op. cit. **(Chaps 6, 10, 15)**

Cabu, F. (1935a) 'Considérations sur la stratigraphie de gisements pléistocènes à outillage paléolithique de la région de Léopoldville', *BSRBAP*, 50, pp. 269–84. **(Chap. 21)**
Cabu, F. (1935b) 'Les industries préhistoriques de la cuvette centrale congolaise et leurs rapports avec la préhistoire générale', *BSRBAP*, 50, pp. 399–411. **(Chap. 21)**
Cadenat, P. (1957) 'Fouilles à Columnata. Campagne 1956–57. La nécropole', *Libyca*, V, pp. 49–81. **(Chap. 22)**
Cadenat, P. (1962) 'Sur l'extension de la civilisation capsienne vers l'Ouest', *BSPF*, 59, pp. 27–32. **(Chap. 22)**
Cadenat, P. (1970) 'Le columnatien, industrie épipaléolithique de l'Algérie', *BSERP*, 20, pp. 40–50. **(Chap. 22)**
Cadornega, A. de O. de (1940–2) *História general das guenas Angolanas* (Lisbon). **(Chap. 1)**
Cahen, D. (1975) 'Le site archéologique de la Kamoa (Région du Shaba, République du Zaïre). De l'âge de la pierre ancienne à l'âge du fer', *AMRAC*, 84. **(Chap. 21)**
Cahen, D. (1976) 'Nouvelles fouilles à la pointe de la Gombe (ex-pointe-de Kalina), Kinshasa, Zaïre',

Anthropologie, 80, 4, pp. 573–602. **(Chap. 21)**
Cahen, D. (1977) 'Vers une révision de la nomenclature des industries préhistoriques de l'Afrique centrale', *Anthropologie*, 81. **(Chap. 21)**
Cahen, D., Haesaerts, P. and Noten, F. Van (1972) 'Un habitat lupembien à Massango (Burundi). Rapport préliminaire', *Africa-Tervuren*, XVIII, pp. 78–80. **(Chap. 21)**
Cahen, D. and Martin, P. (1972) 'Classification formelle automatique et industries élithiques. Interprétations des hachereaux de la Kamoa', *AMRAC*, 76. **(Chap. 21)**
Cahen, D. and Moeyersons, J. (1977) 'Subsurface movements of stone artefacts and their implications for the prehistory of central Africa', *Nature*, 266, 5605, pp. 812–15. **(Chap. 21)**
Cahen, D. and Mortelmans, G. (1973) 'Un site tshitolien sur le plateau des Bateke (République du Zaïre)', *AMRAC*, 81, 46pp. **(Chap. 21)**
Cahen, D. and Noten, F. Van (1970) 'Des polissoirs dans la grotte de Mpinga (Burundi)', *Africa Tervuren*, XVI, 1, pp. 13–17. **(Chap. 21)**
Caley, E. R. (1948) 'On the application of Chemistry to Archaeology', *OJS*, XLVIII, pp. 1–8. **(Chap. 9)**
Caley, E. R. (1949) 'Validity of the specific gravity method for the determination of the fineness of gold objects', *OJS*, XLIX, pp. 76–92. **(Chap. 9)**
Campbell, B. G. (1965) 'The nomenclature of the Hominidae' (London: Royal Anthropological Institute, Occasional Paper no. 22). **(Chap. 24)**
Campbell, R. (1861) *A pilgrimage to my motherland, or Reminiscences of a Sojourn among the Egbas and Yorubas of Central Africa in 1859–60* (London: Johnson). **(Chap. 6)**
Camps, G. (1969) *Amekni, néolithique ancien du Hoggar* (Paris: AMG). **(Chaps 22, 23, 24, 28)**
Camps, G. (1974) *Les Civilisations préhistoriques de l'Afrique du Nord et du Sahara* (Paris: Doin). **(Chaps 22, 28)**
Camp-Fabrer, H. (1966) *Matière et art mobilier dans la préhistoire nord-africaine et saharienne* (Paris: Mémoires du Centre de Recherches Anthropologiques, Préhistoriques et Ethnographiques). **(Chaps 22, 23)**
Camp-Fabrer, H., Bouchud, J. *et al.* (1975) *Un gisement capsien de faciès sétifen Medjez II, El-Eulma* (*Algérie*) (Paris: CNRS). **(Chap. 22)**
Candolle, A. L. P. (1883) *L'Origine des plantes cultivées* (Paris: F. Alcan). **(Chap. 27)**
Caporiacco, L. di and Grazinzi, P. (1934) *Le pitture rupestri di Aīn Dòua* (*el-Auenàt*) (Florence: Coitipi dell'Istituto geografico militare). **(Chap. 23)**
Capot-Rey, R. (1953) *Le Sahara français* (Paris: PUF). **(Chap. 23)**
Caprille, Y. P. (1972) *Carte des langues du Tchad* (Paris: IGN). **(Chap. 10)**
Carr-Saunders, A. M. (1964) *World Population, Past Growth and Present Trends* (London: Cass). **(Chap. 14)**
Carré J. M. (1932) *Les voyageurs et écrivains français en Egypte, 1517–1840* (Cairo: Institut français d'archéologie orientale). **(Chap. 6)**
Carson, P. (1962) *Materials for West African History in the Archives of Belgium and Holland* (London; University of London). **(Chaps 6, 24)**
Carson, P. (1968) *Materials for West African History in French Archives* (London: Athlone Press). **(Chaps 6, 24)**
Carter, G. F. (1964) 'Archaeological maize in West Africa: a discussion of Stanton & Willet', *Man*, 64, p. 95. **(Chap. 24)**
Carter, P. L. and Flight, C. (1972) 'Report on the fauna from the sites of Ntereso and Kintampo Rock Shelter six in Ghana: with evidence for the practice of animal husbandry during the second millennium BC', *Man*, 7, 2, pp. 227–32. **(Chap. 24)**
Casalis, E. (1859) *Les Bassutos* (Paris). **(Chap. 6)**
Castanhoso, M. de (1548) *Historia das cousas que o muy esforçado capitão Dom Christouão da Gama fez nos reynos de Preste João* (Lisbon: Academia real dos sciencias). **(Chap. 6)**
Caton-Thompson, G. (1928) see Brunton, G. (1928).
Caton-Thompson, G. (1946) 'The Aterian industry: its place and significance in the Palaeolithic world', *JRAI*. **(Chap. 23)**
Caton-Thompson, G. (1952) *Kharga Oasis in Prehistory* (London: University of London). **(Chaps 23, 25)**
Caton-Thompson, G. and Gardner, E. W. (1934) *The Desert Fayum* (London: Royal Anthropological Institute of Great Britain and Ireland). **(Chaps 23, 24, 25, 28)**
Cavazzi de Montecudolo, G. A. (1687) *Istorica descrizione de tre regni Congo, Matamba et Angola, situati nell'Etiopia inferiore occidentale* (Milan: Stampe dell'Agnelli). **(Chap. 1)**
Celis, M. (1972) 'Gepolijst archeologisch stenen materiaal uit de Demokratische Republick van Zaïre', thesis (Gand: University of Gand). **(Chap. 21)**
Cenival, J.-L. de (1973) *L'Egypte avant les pyramides, 4ème millénaire*, Grand Palais, 29 May–

3 September 1973 (Paris: Editions des musées nationaux). **(Chap. 28)**

Cerulli, E. (1926) 'Iscrizioni e documente arabi per la Storia della Somalia', *Rivista degli studi orientali*, pp. 1–24. **(Chaps 3, 5, 6)**

Cerulli, E. (1931) *Documenti arabi per la storia dell' Etiopia*. **(Chap. 5)**

Cerulli, E. (1957) *Somalia, scritti vari editi ed inediti*, Vol. I (Rome: Istituto Poligrafico dello Stato P.V.). **(Chaps 5, 6)**

Chamard, P. (1969–70) *Le Bassin versant de la Sebkha de Chemchane* (*Adrar de Mauritanie*) (Dakar: Faculté de Lettres et de Sciences humaines). **(Chap. 23)**

Chamla, M.-C. (1968) 'Les populations anciennes du Sahara et des régions limitrophes: Etude des restes humains néolithiques et protohistoriques', *MCRAPE*, 9. **(Chaps 23, 24)**

Chamla, M.-C. (1970) *Les hommes épipaléolithiques de Columnata* (*Algérie occidentale*) (Paris: AMG). **(Chap. 22)**

Chamla, M.-C. (1973) 'Etude anthropologique de l'Homme capsien de l'Aïn Dokkara (Algérie orientale)', *Libyca*, XXI, pp. 9–53.

Chamot, E. M. and Mason, C. W. (1938) *Handbook of Chemical Microscopy*, 2nd edn (New York: Wiley/London: Chapman & Hall). **(Chap. 9)**

Champault, B. (1953) 'L'industrie de Tachenghit', *70ème Congr. AFSS*, Tunis, 1951. **(Chap. 23)**

Chasseloup Laubat, F. de (1938) *L'art rupestre au Hoggar* (*Haut Mertoutek*) (Paris: Plon). **(Chap. 23)**

Chavaillon, J. (1956) 'Quaternaire de la vallée du Guir (Sahara nord occidental)', *Comptes rendus sommaires des Séances de la Société géologie française*. **(Chap. 23)**

Chavaillon, J. (1958) 'Industrie archaïque du Paléolithique ancien en place dans les alluvions de l'oued Guir (Sahara nord occidental)', *BSPF*, 55, pp. 431–43. **(Chap. 23)**

Chavaillon, J. (1964) *Étude stratigraphique des formations quaternaires du Sahara nord-occidental, Colomb-Béchar à Reggane* (Paris: CNRS). **(Chap. 23)**

Chavaillon, J. (1973) 'Chronologie des niveaux paléolithiques de Melka-Kunturé (Ethiopie)', *CRAS*, 276, pp. 1533–6. **(Chap. 17)**

Chavaillon, J., Brahimi, C. and Coppens, Y. (1974) 'Première découverte d'Hominidé dans l'un des sites acheuléens de Melka Kunturé (Ethiopie)', *CRAS*, 278, pp. 3299–302. **(Chap. 17)**

Chavaillon, J., Chavaillon, N., Coppens, Y. and Senut, B. (1977) 'Présence d'hominidé dans le site oldowayen de Gomboré I à Melka Kunturé, Ethiopie', *CRAS*, 285, pp. 961–3. **(Chap. 17)**

Chelebi, E. (1938) *Seyahainume* (Istanbul). **(Chap. 6)**

Chelu, A. J. (1891) *De l'équateur à la Méditerranée; Le Nil, le Soudan, l'Egypte* (Paris: Chaix). **(Chap. 28)**

Chesneaux, J. (1969) *Le Mode de production asiatique* (Paris: Editions sociales), p. 29. **(Concl.)**

Chevalier, A. (1938) 'Le Sahara, centre d'origine des plantes cultivées', Société de Biogéographie, VI: *La Vie dans la région désertique Nord-tropicale de l'ancien monde* (Paris), pp. 309–22. **(Chap. 27)**

Childe, V. G. (1954) *What Happened in History?*, rev. edn (Harmondsworth: Penguin). **(Chap. 27)**

Cissé, K. and Thilmans, G. (1968) 'A propos de la datation des mégalithes sénégambiens', *NA*, 117, pp. 13–17. **(Chap. 24)**

Cissoko, S. M. (1966) *Histoire de l'Afrique occidentale* (Paris: Présence africaine). **(Gen. Introd.)**

Claridge, W. W. (1915) *History of the Gold Coast and Ashanti* (London). **(Chap. 1)**

Clark, G. (1969) *World Prehistory*, 2nd edn (Cambridge: Cambridge University Press). **(Chaps 19, 24)**

Clark, J. D. 'The Stone Age Cultures of Northern Rhodesia', *SAAB*.

Clark, J. D. (1957) *Third Panafrican Congress on Prehistory* (London: Chatto and Windus). **(Chap. 24)**

Clark, J. D. (1960) *The Prehistory of Southern Africa* (Harmondsworth: Penguin). **(Chaps 19, 21, 24)**

Clark, J. D. (1962) 'Vegetation patterns, climate and sands in north-east Angola', *Actes IV Congr. PPEQ*, pp. 151–66. **(Chap. 21)**

Clark, J. D. (1963a) 'Ecology and culture in the African Pleistocene', *SAJS*, 59, 7, pp. 353–66. **(Chap. 21)**

Clark, J. D. (1963b) 'Prehistoric cultures of north-east Angola and their significance in tropical Africa', *CDAPC*, 62. **(Chap. 21)**

Clark, J. D. (1964) *The Sangoan Culture of Equatoria: The implications of its stone equipment*. Instituto de Prehistoria y Argueologia, monographies, Barcelona, 9, pp. 309–25. **(Chap. 20)**

Clark, J. D. (1966) 'The distribution of prehistoric culture in Angola', *CDAPC*, 73. **(Chap. 21)**

Clark, J. D. (1967a) 'The problem of Neolithic culture in sub-Saharan Africa', in W. W. Bishop and J. D. Clark (eds), *Background to Evolution in Africa* (Chicago: University of Chicago Press), pp. 601–28. **(Chap. 24)**

Clark, J. D. (1967b) *Atlas of African Prehistory* (Chicago: University of Chicago Press). **(Chaps 19, 24)**

Clark, J. D. (1968a) 'Review of Oliver Davies's "The Quaternary in the Coastlands of Guinea"', *WAAN*, 13, 9, pp. 37–40. **(Chap. 24)**

Clark, J. D. (1968b) 'Further palaeo-anthropological studies in northern Lunda', *CDAPC*, 78. **(Chap. 21)**

Clark, J. D. (1969–74) *Kalambo Falls Prehistoric Site*, 3 Vols (Cambridge: Cambridge University Press). **(Chaps 19, 20, 21)**

Clark, J. D. (1970a) 'The prehistoric origins of African cultures', in J. D. Fage and R. A. Oliver (eds), *Papers in African Prehistory* (Cambridge: Cambridge University Press). **(Chap. 21)**

Clark, J. D. (1970b) 'The spread of food production in sub-Saharan Africa', in J. D. Fage and R. A. Oliver (eds) *Papers in African Prehistory* (Cambridge: Cambridge University Press). **(Chap. 27)**

Clark, J. D. (1970c) *The Prehistory of Africa* (London: Thames & Hudson). **(Chaps 14, 19, 20, 24)**

Clark, J. D. (1970d) 'African prehistory: opportunities for collaboration between archaeologists, ethnographers and linguists', *Language and History in Africa* (London: Cass). **(Chap. 15)**

Clark, J. D. (1971a) 'Problems of archaeological nomenclature and definition in the Congo basin', *SAAB*, XXVI, pp. 67–78. **(Chaps 21, 24)**

Clark, J. D. (1971b) 'Human Behavioural Differences in Southern Africa during the Later Pleistocene', *American Anthropologist*, Vol. 73, pp.1211–36. **(Chap. 20)**

Clark, J. D. and Haynes, C. V. (1969) 'An elephant butchery site at Mwanganda's village, Karonga, Malawi and its relevance for Palaeolithic archaeology', *WA*, 1, 3, pp. 390–411. **(Chap. 20)**

Clark, J. D. and Le Gros, W. E. (1967) *Man-apes or Ape-men? The Story of Discoveries in Africa* (New York). **(Chap. 20)**

Clark, J. D., Mawby, J. E. and Gautier, A. (1970) 'Interim report on Palaeoanthropological investigations in the Lake Malawi rift', *Quaternaria*, XIII, pp. 305–54. **(Chap. 20)**

Clark, J. D. and Zinderen-Bakker, E. M. van (1962) 'Pleistocene climates and cultures in north-eastern Angola', *Nature*, 196, 4855, pp. 639–42. **(Chap. 21)**

Clark, J. D. and Zinderen-Bakker, E. M. van (1964) 'Prehistoric cultures and Pleistocene vegetation at the Kalambo falls, Northern Rhodesia', *Nature*, 201, 4923, pp. 971–5. **(Chap. 21)**

Clarke, J. (1848) *Specimens of Dialects: Short Vocabulary of Languages and notes of countries and customs in Africa* (Berwick-on-Tweed: Cameron). **(Chap. 12)**

Clark-Howell, P., Kleindienst, M. R. and Keller, C. M. (n.d.) 'Isimilia. Preliminary report', *Proc. 4th PCPQS*. **(Chap. 19)**

CLIMAP (1974) 'Mapping the atmospheric and oceanic circulations and other climatic parameters at the time of the last glacial maximum about 17,000 years ago', Climatic Research Unit, School of Environmental Sciences, University of East Anglia (Norwich). **(Chap. 16)**

CNRS (ed.) (1974) 'Les Méthodes quantitatives d'étude des variations du climat au cours du Pléistocene', *Coll. CNRS*, no. 219. **(Chap. 16)**

Cockerell, T. D. A. (1907) 'A fossil tse-tse fly in Colorado', *Nature*, 76, 414. **(Chap. 14)**

Cockerell, T. D. A. (1909) 'Another fossil tse-tse fly', *Nature*, 80, 128. **(Chap. 14)**

Cockerell, T. D. A. (1919) 'New species of North American fossil beetles, cockroaches and tse-tse flies', *Proc. NS St. Nat. Mus.*, 54, pp. 301–11. **(Chap. 14)**

Coetze, J. A. and Zinderen-Bakker, E. M. van (1970) 'Palaeoecological problems of the Quaternary of Africa', *SAJS*, 66, pp. 78–84. **(Chap. 21)**

Cohen, D. W. (1972) *The historical tradition of Busoga, Mukama and Kintu* (Oxford: Clarendon Press). **(Chap. 3)**

Cohen, M. S. R. (1947) *Essai comparatif sur le vocabulaire et la phonétique du chamito-sémitique* (Paris: Champion). **(Chaps 10, 12)**

Cohen, M. S. R. (1958) *La grande invention de l'écriture et son évolution* (Paris: Imprimerie Nationale). **(Chap. 10)**

Cole, D. T. (1971) 'The history of African linquistics to 1945', in T. A. Sebeok (ed.) *Linguistics in South West Asia and North Africa* (1971) (The Hague: Mouton). **(Chap. 12)**

Cole, G. H. (1967) 'Nsongezi. Summary account', in W. W. Bishop and J. D. Clark (eds), *Background to Evolution in Africa*, pp. 481–528. **(Chap. 19)**

Cole, S. (1964) *The Prehistory of East Africa* (London: Weidenfeld & Nicolson). **(Chap. 19)**

Coleman, J. S. (1958) *Nigeria: background to nationalism* (Berkeley, Calif.: University of California Press). **(Chap. 3)**

Coles, J. M. and Higgs, E. S. (1969) *The Archaeology of Early Man* (London: Faber). **(Chap. 19)**

Colette, J. R. F. (1931) 'Industries paléolithiques du Congo Belge', *Actes XV Congr. I AAP*, pp. 285–292. **(Chap. 21)**

Colette, J. R. F. (1935) 'Complexe et convergences en préhistoire', *BSRBAP*, 50, pp. 49–192. **(Chap. 21)**

Commonwealth Arts Festival (1965) *Treasures from the Commonwealth*, Commemorative Catalogue (London: Royal Academy of Arts). **(Chap. 24)**

Connah, G. (1967) Progress report on archaeological work in Bornu, Northern History Research Scheme, Second Interim Report (Zaria). **(Chap. 24)**
Connah, G. (1969) 'Settlement mounds of the Firki – the reconstruction of a lost society', *Ibadan*, 26, pp. 48–62. **(Chap. 24)**
Connah, G. (1971) 'Recent contributions to Bornu chronology', *WAJA*, I, pp. 55–60. **(Chap. 24)**
Connah, G. (1972) 'Archaeology in Benin', *JAH*, 13, 1, pp. 25–38. **(Chap. 24)**
Conti Rossini, C. (1928) *Storia d'Etiopia* (Milan). **(Chap. 1)**
Cook, R. M. (1963) 'Archaeomagnetism', in D. Brothwell and E. Higgs (eds), *Science in Archaeology* (London: Thames & Hudson), pp. 59–71. **(Chap. 9)**
Cooke, C. K. (1969) 'A re-examination of the "Middle Stone Age" industries of Rhodesia', *Arnoldia*, 17. **(Chap. 4)**
Cooke, C. K. (1971) 'Excavation in Zombepata cave, Sipolilo district, Mashonaland, Rhodesia', *SAAB*, XXVI, pp. 104–27. **(Chap. 20)**
Cooke, H. B. S. (1958) 'Observations relating to Quaternary environments in east and southern Africa', *TGSSA*, Appendix to Vol. 61. **(Chaps 16, 21)**
Cooke, H. B. S. (1964) 'Pleistocene mammal faunas of Africa with particular reference to southern Africa', in F. C. Howell and F. Bourlière (eds), *African Ecology and Human Evolution* (London: Methuen), pp. 65–116. **(Chap. 20)**
Cooke, H. B. S. (1965) 'Tentative correlation of major Pleistocene deposits in Africa', *Wenner-Gren Symposium on the Origin of Man* (Chicago). **(Chap. 24)**
Cooke, H. B. S. (1972) 'Pleistocene chronology: long or short?', *Maritime Sediments*, 8, 1, pp. 1–12. **(Chap. 16)**
Coon, C. S. (1968) *Yengema Cave Report* (Philadelphia: University of Pennsylvania). **(Chap. 24)**
Copans, J. and Godelier, M. (1971) *L'Anthropologie, science des sociétés primitives?* (Paris: Editions Denoël). **(Gen. Introd.)**
Coppens, Y. (1960) 'Les cultures protohistoriques et historiques du Djourab', *Actes 1er Coll. Intern. Archéol. Afr.* **(Gen. Introd.)**
Coppens, Y. (1961) 'Découverte d'un Australopithéciné dans le Villafranchien du Tchad', *CRAS*, 252, pp. 3851–2. **(Chaps 23, 24)**
Coppens, Y. (1962) 'Découverte d'un Australopithéciné dans le Villafranchien du Tchad', *Coll. CNRS*, 104, pp. 455–9. **(Chaps 23, 24)**
Coppens, Y. (1965a) 'L'Hominien du Tchad', *CRAS*, 260, pp. 2869–71. **(Chaps 16, 24)**
Coppens, Y. (1965b) 'L'Hominien du Tchad', *Actes V Congr. PPEC*, I, pp. 329–30.**(Chaps 16, 24)**
Coppens, Y. (1966a) 'Le Tchadanthropus', *Anthropologia*, 70, pp. 5–16. **(Chap. 24)**
Coppens, Y. (1966b) 'Le gisement des vertébrés quaternaires de l'ouest africain', *BIFAN*, A, 27, pp. 373–81. **(Chap. 24)**
Coppens, Y. (1970a) 'Localisation dans le temps et dans l'espace des restes d'hominidés des formations plio-pléistocènes de l'Omo (Ethiopie)', *CRAS*, 271, pp. 1968–71. **(Chap. 17)**
Coppens, Y. (1970b) 'Les restes d'hominidés des séries inférieures et moyennes des formations plio-villafranchiennes de l'Omo en Ethiopie', *CRAS*, 271, pp. 2286–9. **(Chap. 17)**
Coppens, Y. (1971) 'Les restes d'hominidés des séries supérieures des formations plio-villafranchiennes de l'Omo en Ethiopie', *CRAS*, 272, pp. 36–9. **(Chap. 17)**
Coppens, Y. (1972) 'Tentative de zonation du Pliocène et du Pléistocène d'Afrique par les grands Mammifères', *CRAS*, 274, pp. 181–4. **(Chap. 16)**
Coppens, Y. (1973a) 'Les restes d'hominidés des séries inférieures et moyennes des formations plio-villafranchiennes de l'Omo en Ethiopie (récoltes 1970, 1971 et 1972)', *CRAS*, 276, pp. 1823–6. **(Chap. 17)**
Coppens, Y. (1973b) 'Les restes d'hominidés des séries supérieures des formations plio-villafranchiennes de l'Omo en Ethiopie (récoltes 1970, 1971 et 1972)', *CRAS*, 276, pp. 1981–4. **(Chap. 17)**
Coppens, Y. (1975a) 'Evolution des mammifères, de leurs fréquences et de leurs associations au cours du plio-pléistocène dans la basse vallée de l'Omo en Ethiopie', *CRAS*, 281, pp. 1571–4. **(Chap. 17)**
Coppens, Y. (1975b) 'Evolution des hominidés et de leur environnement au cours du plio-pléistocène dans la basse vallée de l'Omo en Ethiopie', *CRAS*, 281, pp. 1693–6. **(Chap. 17)**
Coppens, Y. *et al.* (1976) *Earliest Man and Environments in the Lake Rudolf Basin: Stratigraphy, Paleoecology, and Evolution* (Chicago: University of Chicago Press). **(Chaps 17, 18, 19)**
Corbeil, R. (1951a) 'Les récentes découvertes au Cap-Vert concernant la Paléolithique', *BIFAN*, B, 13, pp. 384–437. **(Chap. 24)**
Corbeil, R. (1951b) 'Mise en évidence d'industries lithiques anciennes dans l'extrême ouest sénégalais', *Comptes-rendus Conférence Internationale des Africanistes de l'Ouest I*, 2, pp. 387–90. **(Chap. 24)**
Corbein, R., Mauny, R. and Charbonnier, J. (1948) 'Préhistoire et protohistoire de la presque'ile

du Cap-Vert et de l'extrême ouest sénégalais', *BIFAN*, B, 10, pp. 378–460. **(Chap. 24)**
Cornevin, R. (1962) *Histoire de l'Afrique* (Paris: Payot). **(Chap. 5)**
Correia, E. A. de S. (1937) *História de Angola* (Lisbon). **(Chap. 1)**
Coupez, A. and Kamanzi, T. (1970) *Littérature de cour au Rwanda* (Oxford: Clarendon Press). **(Chap. 7)**
Coursey, D. G. (1967) *Yams* (London: Longman, Green). **(Chap. 24)**
Coursey, D. G. (1972) 'The origins and domestication of yams in Africa', *Proc. Burg. Wart. Symp. 56*. **(Chap. 24)**
Coursey, D. G. and Alexander, J. (1968) 'African agricultural patterns and the sickle cell', *Science*, 160, pp. 1474–5. **(Chap. 24)**
Courtois, C. (1955) *Les Vandales et l'Afrique* (Paris: AMG). **(Chap. 5)**
Creach, D. A. (1970) 'A tale type index for Africa', *Research in African Literatures* (Austin, Texas), I, 1, pp. 50–3. **(Chap. 7)**
Créach, P. (1951) 'Sur quelques nouveaux sites et quelques nouvelles industries préhistoriques d'Afrique occidentale française', *C-R Conf. Intern. des Africanistes de l'Ouest I*, 2, pp. 397–430. **(Chap. 24)**
Creach, S. A. (1852) *A Vocabulary of the Yoruba Language* (London: Seeleys). **(Chap. 12)**
Crone, G. R. (ed) (1937) *The Voyages of Cadamosto* (London: Hakluyt Society). **(Chap. 1)**
Crowther, S. (1885) *Journal of an Expedition up the Niger and Tshadda Rivers* (London). **(Chap. 16)**
Cugoano, O. (1787) *Thoughts and Sentiments on the Evil and Wicked Traffic of the Slavery and Commerce of the Human Species* (London). **(Chap. 6)**
Cuny, A. L. M. (1946) *Invitation à l'étude comparative des langues indo-européennes et des langues chamito-sémitiques* (Bordeaux: Bière). **(Chap. 10)**
Cuoq, J. (trans.) (1975) *Recueil des sources arabes concernant l'Afrique occidentale du VIIIe au XVIe siècle, Bilād al-Sūdān* (Paris: CNRS). **(Chap. 5)**
Curry, R. R. (1969) 'Chronologie glaciaire absolue de la Sierra Nevada, Californie, pour les derniers 2 700 000 ans' (thesis, University of Paris). **(Chap. 16)**
Curtin, P. D. (1960) 'Archives in tropical Africa: a reconnaissance', *JAH* I, i, pp. 129–47 **(Chap. 6)**
Curtin, P. D. (ed) (1967) *Africa Remembered* (Madison). **(Chap. 6)**
Curtin, P. D. (1968) 'Field techniques for collecting and processing oral data', *JAH*, IX, 3, pp. 367–85. **(Chap. 7)**
Curtin, P. D. and Vansina, J. (1964) 'Sources of the 19th century Atlantic slave trade', *JAH*, I. **(Chap. 6)**
Cuvelier, J. and Jadin, L. (1954) *L'Ancien Royaume du Congo d'après les archives romaines 1518–1640* (Brussels: Académie Royale des Sciences Coloniales). **(Chap. 6)**

Dahl, O. C. (1951) *Malgache et maanjan: une comparaison linguistique* (Oslo: Egede Institut). **(Chap. 12)**
Dain, A. (1961) 'Témoignage écrit et philologie', *L'Histoire et ses méthodes, Encyclopédie de la Pléiade* (Paris). **(Chap. 5)**
Dalby, D. (1965) 'The Mel languages: a reclassification of southern "West Atlantic"', *ALS*, 6, pp. 1–17. **(Chaps 10, 12)**
Dalby, D. (1966) 'Levels of relationship in the classification of African Languages', *ALS*. **(Chap. 10)**
Dalby, D. (1967) 'Survey of the indigenous scripts of Liberia and Sierra Leone', *ALS*, 8, pp. 1–51. **(Chap. 6)**
Dalby, D. (1970) 'Reflections on the classification of African Languages, with special reference to the work of Sigismund Wilhem Koelle and Malcolm Guthrie', *ALS*, XI. **(Chap. 12)**
Dalby, D. (1970) *Language and History in Africa* (New York: Africana Publishing Corporation; London: Cass). **(Chaps 10, 12)**
Dalby, D. (1977) *Language map of Africa and the adjacent islands*, provisional edn. (London: International African Institute) **(Chap. 12, appendix)**
Dalloni, M. (1934–5) *Mission au Tibesti (1930–1931)*, 2 Vols (Paris: Gauthier-Villars). **(Chap. 23)**
Dalloni, M. (1948) *Matériaux pour l'étude du Sahara oriental, région entre la Libye, le Tibesti et le Kaouar (Niger): géologie et préhistoire* (Algiers). **(Chap. 23)**
Dalloni, M. (1952) 'La station moustérienne de Retaïmia près d'Inkermann (Algérie)', *Actes II Congr. PPEQ*, pp. 419–27. **(Chap. 22)**
Dalloni, M., Dalrymple, G., Brent and Lanphere, Marvin A. (1969) *Potassium-Argon Dating. Principles, techniques and applications to geochronology* (San Francisco: Freeman). **(Chap. 4)**
Dalloni, M. and Monod, T. (1948) 'Géologie et préhistoire (Fezzan méridional, Kaouar et Tibesti); Mission scientifique du Fezzan (1944–45)', *Trav. IRS*, 6. **(Chap. 23)**
Dalton, G. (ed.) (1968) *Primitive, Archaic and Modern Economies, Essays of Karl Polanyi* (New York).

(Chap. 13)

Dalzel, A. (1793) *The History of Dahomy*. **(Chap. 1)**

Damas, D. (ed.) (1966) 'Ecological essays: proceedings of the conference of cultural ecology', *Museum of Canada Bulletin*, 230. **(Chap. 27)**

dan Fodio, A. (1963) *Tazyin al-waraqat*, ed. and trs. M. Hiskett (London). **(Chap. 6)**

Daniel, G. E. (1943) *The Three Ages: An essay on archeological method* (Cambridge: Cambridge University Press). **(Chap. 24)**

Daniels, C. (1970) *The Garamantes of Southern Libya* (Wisconsin, Mass.: Oleander Press). **(Chap. 24)**

Dapper, O. (1668) *Naukeurige Beschrijvinghe des Afrikaensche Gewesten* (Amsterdam: van Meurs).

Darlington, C. D. (1963) *Chromosome Botany and the Origins of Cultivated Plants*, 2nd edn (London: Allen & Unwin). **(Chap. 27)**

Davidson, B. (1959) *The Lost Cities of Africa* (Boston: Little, Brown). **(Gen Introd.)**

Davidson, B. (1965) *Old Africa Rediscovered* (London: Gollancz). **(Gen. Introd.)**

Davidson, B. (1967a) *The African Past* (Harmondsworth: Penguin). **(Gen. Introd.)**

Davidson, B. (1967b) *The Growth of African Civilisation: A history of West Africa 1000–1800* (London: Longman). **(Gen. Introd.)**

Davidson, B. (1968) *Black Mother; Africa: The years of trial* (London: Gollancz). **(Gen. Introd.)**

Davies, O. (1959) 'The distribution of Old Stone Age material in Guinea', *BIFAN*, B, 21, pp. 1–2. **(Chap. 24)**

Davies, O. (1960) 'The Neolithic revolution in tropical Africa', *THSG*, 4. **(Chap. 24)**

Davies, O. (1961) *Archaeology in Ghana; Papers* (Edinburgh: Nelson). **(Chap. 24)**

Davies, O. (1962) 'The Neolithic culture of Ghana', *Actes IV Congr. PPEQ*, 3, pp. 291–301. **(Chap. 24)**

Davies, O. (1964) *The Quaternary in the Coastlands of Guinea* (Glasgow: Jackson). **(Chap. 24)**

Davies, O. (1966a) 'The invasion of Ghana from the Sahara in the Early Iron Age', *Actas V Congr. PPEC*, 2, pp. 27–42. **(Chap. 24)**

Davies, O. (1966b) 'Comment on: J. Arkell, B. Fagan and R. Summers, "The Iron Age in sub-Saharan Africa"', *CA*, 7, pp. 470–1. **(Chap. 24)**

Davies, O. (1967a) 'New radiocarbon dates from Ghana', *ASEQAB*, 14–15, p. 28. **(Chap. 24)**

Davies, O. (1967b) *West Africa before the Europeans: Archaeology and prehistory* (London: Methuen). **(Chap. 24)**

Davies, O., Hugot, H. J. and Seddon, D. (1968) 'The origins of African agriculture', *CA*, 9, 5, pp. 479–504.

Davison, C. C. (1973) 'Glass beads in African Archaeology', *AATA*, 10, 2. **(Chap. 9)**

Davison, C. C., Giauque, R. D. and Clark, J. D. (1971) 'Two chemical groups of dichroic glass beads from West Africa', *Man*, 6, 4, pp. 645–9. **(Chap. 9)**

Day, M. H. and Leakey, R. E. F. (1973) 'New evidence for the genus Homo from East Rudolf, Kenya, I', *AJPA*, 39, pp. 341–54. **(Chap. 17)**

Day, M. H. and Leakey, R. E. F. (1974) 'New evidence for the genus Homo from East Rudolf, Kenya, III', *AJPA*, 41, pp. 367–80. **(Chap. 17)**

Day, M. H., Leakey, R. E. F., Walker, A. C. and Wood, B. A. (1975) 'New hominids from East Rudolf, Kenya, I', *AJPA*, 42, pp. 461–76. **(Chap. 17)**

Day, M. H., Leakey, R. E. F., Walker, A. C. and Wood, B. A. (1976) 'New hominids from East Turkana, Kenya', *AJPA*, 45, 3, pp. 369–436. **(Chap. 17)**

Dayrell, E. (1911) 'Further notes on Nsibidi signs with their meanings from the Ikom district, Southern Nigeria', *JRAI*, 41, pl. LXV–LXVII. **(Chap. 10)**

Deacon, H. J. (1970) 'The Acheulian occupation of Amanzi Springs, Uitenhage district, Cape province', *ACPM*, 8, 11. **(Chap. 20)**

Deacon, H. J (1972a) 'Wilton: an assessment after fifty years', *SAAB*, XXVII, 1–2, pp. 10–48. **(Chap. 20)**

Deacon, H. J. (1972b) 'A review of the post-Pleistocene in South Africa', *SAAB*, Goodwin series 1, pp. 26–45. **(Chap. 20)**

Debono, F. (1948a) 'Le Paléolithique final et le Mésolithique à Hélouan', *ASAE*, XLVIII, pp. 629–37. **(Chap. 25)**

Debono, F. (1948b) 'El-Omari', *ASAE*, XLVIII, pp. 562–8. **(Chap. 25)**

Debono, F. (1951) 'Expédition archéologique royale au Désert Oriental', *ASAE*, LI, pp. 59–91. **(Chap. 25)**

Debono, F. (1954) 'La nécropole prédynastique d'Héliopolis', *ASAE*, LII, pp. 625–52. **(Chap. 25)**

Debono, F. (1956) 'La civilisation prédynastique d'El Omari (Nord d'Hélouan)', *BIE*, XXXVII, pp. 331–9. **(Chap. 25)**

Debono, F. (1969) 'Le sentiment religieux à l'époque préhistorique en Egypte', *CHE*, XI, pp. 1–13. **(Chap. 25)**

Debono, F. (1970) 'Recherches préhistoriques dans la région d'Esna', *BIFAO*, LXIX, pp. 245–51. **(Chap. 25)**

Debono, F. (1971) 'Etude des dépôts de silex', *Graffiti de la Montagne Thébaine*, I, 2, pp. 32–50 (Cairo). **(Chap. 25)**

Debono, F. (1971) 'Prospection préhistorique (Campagne 1972–1973)', *Graffiti de la Montagne Thébaine*, I, 4 (Cairo). **(Chap. 25)**

Debono, F. (1975) 'Thèbes préhistorique, ses survivances à l'époque pharaonique', *Actes du XXIXe Congrès International des Orientalistes*, I. **(Chap. 25)**

Debono F. (1976a) 'L'homme oldowaien en Egypte', *BIE*. **(Chap. 25)**

Debono, F. (1976b) 'Survivances préhistoriques de l'usage du silex à l'époque pharaonique', *BIE*. **(Chap. 25)**

Degan, T. (1956) 'Le site préhistorique de Tiémassas (Sénégal), *BIFAN*, B, 8, pp. 432–61. **(Chap. 24)**

Delafosse, M. (1901) *Essai de manuel pratique de la langue mandé ou mandingue* (Paris: Leroux). **(Chap. 12)**

Delafosse, M. (1912) *Haut-Sénégal-Niger (Soudan français)* (Paris: Larose). **(Chaps 1, 10)**

Delafosse, M. (1914) 'Mots Soudanais du Moyen Age', *Mémoire de la Société de linguistique, Paris* 18. **(Chaps 10, 12)**

Delafosse, M. (1921), *Les Noirs de L'Afrique* (Paris). **(Chap. 1)**

Delafosse, M. (1924) 'Groupe sénégalo-guinéen', in A. Meillet and M. Cohen (eds), *Langues du Monde* (Paris: Champion). **(Chaps 10, 12)**

Delany, M. R. (1861) *Official Report of the Niger Valley Exploring Party* (New York: Hamilton). **(Chap. 6)**

Delcroix, R. and Vaufrey, R. (1939) 'Le Toumbien de Guinée Française', *Anthropologie*, 49, pp. 265–312. **(Chaps 23, 24)**

Delibrias, G., Guillier, M. T. and Labeyrie, J. (1974) 'Gif natural radiocarbon measurements VII', *Radiocarbon*, 16, 1, pp. 15–94. **(Chap. 21)**

Delivré, A. (1974) *L'histoire des rois d'Imerina: interprétation d'une tradition orale* (Paris: Klincksieck). **(Chap. 8)**

Demougeot, E. (1960) 'Le chameau et l'Afrique du nord romaine', *Annales*, 209–47. **(Chap. 26)**

Denis, J., Vennetier, P. and Wilmet, J. (1971) *L'Afrique centrale et orientale* (Paris: PUF). **(Chap. 13)**

Denninger, E. (1971) 'Use of paper chromatography to determine the age of albuminous binder and its application to rock paintings', *SAAAS*, 2, pp. 80–4. **(Chap. 9)**

Deny, J. (1930) *Sommaire des archives turques du Caire* (Cairo: Institut français d'archéologie orientale). **(Chap. 6)**

Descamps, G. (1971) *Sénégal, préservation et mise en valeur du patrimoine archéologique*, D: *Les mégalithiques du Sine-Saloum* (Paris: Unesco). **(Chap. 24)**

Deschamps, H. (1962) 'Pour une histoire de l'Afrique', in *Regards sur l'Afrique, Diogène*, 37, pp. 113–20.

Deschamps, H. (1964) *L'Afrique tropical aux XVIIe-XVIIIe siècles* (Paris: Centre de Documentation Universitaire). **(Introd.)**

Deschamps, H. (1969) *L'Afrique noire précoloniale*, 2nd edn (Paris: PUF). **(Introd.)**

Deschamps, H. (ed.) (1970–1) *Histoire générale de l'Afrique noire, de Madagascar et des archipels*, 2 Vols (Paris: PUF). **(Chap. 7)**

Desplagnes, A. M. L. (1907a) 'L'archéologie préhistorique en Guinée Française', *BSGC*, Bordeaux. **(Chap. 24)**

Desplagnes, A. M. L. (1907b) *Le plateau central nigérien. Une mission archéologique et ethnographique au Soudan français* (Paris: Larose). **(Chap. 21)**

Despois, J. and Raynal, R. (1967) *Géographie de l'Afrique du Nord-Ouest* (Paris: Payot). **(Chap. 13)**

Destaniq, E. (1911) 'Notes sur des manuscrits arabes de l'Afrique occidentale', *RA*. **(Chaps 5, 6)**

Deva, I. (1974) 'La tradition orale et l'étude des sociétés agricoles', *Diogène*, 85, pp. 123–42. **(Chap. 4)**

Diagne, P. (1972) *Teerebtanu ladab ci wālāf: anthropologie de littérature la wolof* (Dakar: IFAN). **(Chap. 10)**

Diagne, P. (1976) *Enquête linguistique* (Tchad: Unesco). **(Chap. 10)**

Diallo, T. (1968) 'Les institutions politiques du Fouta-Djallon au XIXème siècle', roneo (Dakar). **(Chap. 6)**

Diehl, C. (1969) *L'Afrique Byzantine. Histoire de la domination Byzantine en Afrique (533–709)*, 2nd edn. 2 Vols (New York: Franklin). **(Chap. 5)**

Dieng, A. A. (1974) *Classes sociales et mode de production esclavagiste en Afrique de l'Ouest* (Paris: Cahiers du Centre d'études et recherches marxistes, No. 114). **(Concl.)**

Dieng, A. A. (1978) *Hegel, Marx, Engels et les problèmes de l'Afrique noire* (Paris: Ed. Sankoré).

Dimbleby, G. W. (1963) 'Pollen analysis', in D. Brothwell and E. Higgs (eds), *Science in Archaeology*

(London: Thames and Hudson), pp. 139–49. **(Chap. 9)**
Diop, C. A. (1955) *Nations nègres et culture* (Paris: Présence africaine). **(Chaps 10, 24)**
Diop, C. A. (1959) *L'Unité culturelle de l'Afrique noire; Domaines du patriarcat et matriarcat dans l'antiquité classique* (Paris: Présence africaine).
Diop, C. A. (1960) *L'Afrique noire pré-coloniale; Etude comparée des systèmes politiques et sociaux de l'Europe et de l'Afrique noire, de l'antiquité à la formation des états modernes* (Paris: Présence africaine). **(Chap. 24)**
Diop, C. A. (1962a) 'Réponse à quelques critiques', *BIFAN*, B, 24, pp. 542–74. **(Chap. 24)**
Diop, C. A. (1962b) 'Histoire primitive de l'humanité: évolution du monde noir', *BIFAN*, B, 24, pp. 449–541. **(Chap. 24)**
Diop, C. A. (1973) *Introduction à l'étude des migrations en Afrique occidentale et centrale* (Dakar: IFAN). **(Chaps 6, 10)**
Diop, C. A. (1974) *Physique nucléaire et chronologie absolue* (Dakar/Abidjan: NEA). **(Chap. 4)**
Diop, M. (1971) *Histoire des classes sociales dans l'Afrique de l'ouest* (Paris: Maspero). **(Concl.)**
Doblhofer, E. (1959) *Le Déchiffrement des écritures*, trans. M. Bittebière (Paris: Arthaud). **(Chap. 4)**
Doize, R. L. (1938) 'Les boules de pierre et les pierres perforées des collections de préhistoire du Musée du Congo', *AMRAC*, 1, pp. 89–140. **(Chap. 21)**
Doke, C. M. and Cole, D. T. (1961) *Contributions to the History of African Linguistics* (Johannesburg: Witwatersrand University Press). **(Chap. 12)**
Doresse, J. (1971) *Histoire sommaire de la Corne orientale de l'Afrique* (Paris: Geuthner). **(Chap. 5)**
Dorize, L. (1974) 'L'oscillation pluviométrique récente sur le bassin du lac Tchad et la circulation atmosphérique générale', *Revue de géographie physique et de géologie dynamique*, 16, 4, pp. 393–420. **(Chap. 16)**
Dorson, R. M. (comp.) (1972) *African Folklore* (New York: Anchor Books). **(Chap. 8)**
Dorson, R. M. (1976) 'Oral literature, oral history and the folklorist', in R. M. Dorson, *Folklore and Fakelore* (Cambridge, Mass.: Harvard University Press), pp. 127–44. **(Chap. 8)**
Dorst, J. and Dandelot, P. (1970) *A Field Guide to the Larger Mammals of Africa* (London: Collins). **(Chap. 24)**
Drar, M. (1963) 'Flore du continent africain: région au nord du Sahara', *Enquête sur les ressources naturelles du continent africain* (Paris: Unesco), pp. 257–70. **(Chap. 13)**
Drioton, E. and Vandier, J. (1962) *Les Peuples de l'Orient Mediterranéen – L'Egypte*, 4th edn enlarged, 2 Vols (Paris: PUF). **(Chaps 5, 28)**
Droux, G. and Kelley, H. (1939) 'Recherches préhistoriques dans la région de Boko-Songho et à Pointe-Noire (Moyen-Congo)', *JSA*, 9, pp. 71–84. **(Chap. 21)**
Dubief, J. (1959) *Le Climat du Sahara* (Algiers: Institut des recherches sahariennes). **(Chap. 23)**
Du Bois, W. E. B. (1903) *The Souls of Black Folk, essays and sketches* (Chicago: McClurg). **(Gen. Introd.)**
Du Bois, W. E. B. (1939) *Black Folk, Then and Now: an essay in the history and sociology of the Negro race* (New York: Holt).
Dumoulin de Laplante, P. (1946–7) *Histoire générale synchronique* (Paris: Gallimard). **(Concl.)**
Dunbar, J. H. (1941) *The Rock-Pictures of Lower Nubia* (Cairo: Government Press). **(Chap. 23)**
Dunham, D. and Bates, O. (1950–63) *The Royal Cemeteries of Kush*, 5 vols.; El Nuri, vol. 2, 1955 (Cambridge, Mass.: Harvard University Press). **(Chap. 28)**
Dunhill, A. (1969) *The Pipe Book*, rev. edn (London: Barker). **(Chap. 24)**
Dupuis, J. (1824) *Journal of a residence in Ashantee* (London). **(Chap. 1)**
Duveyrier, H. (1864) *Les Touareg du Nord* (Paris: Challamel). **(Chap. 23)**
Duvigneaud, P. (1958) 'La végétation du Katanga et de ses sols métallifères', *Bulletin de la Société Royale de botanique de Belgique*, 90, 2, pp. 126–278. **(Chap. 21)**
Duyvendak, J. J. L. (1949) *China's Discovery of Africa* (London: Probsthain). **(Chap. 5)**
Duyvendak, J. J. L. (1973) 'Eastern African coast', *JRAS*, pp. 98–122. **(Introd., Chaps 5, 6)**

Eboué, F. (1933) 'Les peuples de l'Oubangui-Chari. Essai d'ethnographie, de linguistique et d'économie sociale', *Ethnographie*, 27, pp. 3–79. **(Chap. 21)**
Edwards, I. E. S. (1970) 'Absolute dating from Egyptian records and comparison with carbon-14 dating', *PTRS*, 269, 1193, pp. 11–18. **(Chap. 9)**
Egharevba, J. U. (1960) *A short history of Benin*, 3rd edn (Ibadan: Ibadan University Press). **(Chaps 1, 24)**
Ehret, C. (1968) 'Sheep and central Sudanic peoples', *JAH*, IX, 2, pp. 213–21. **(Introd.)**
El-Fasi, M. (1971) 'Berber, the sister language of Arabic' *Acts of the Academy of Cairo*. **(Chap. 12)**
El-Kettani, M. (1961) *L'Histoire et ses méthodes* (Paris: Encyclopédie de la Pléiade). **(Introd.)**

El-Kettani, M. (1968a) 'Les manuscrits de l'occident africain dans les bibliothèques du Maroc', *HT*, 9, 1, pp. 57–63. **(Introd.)**
El-Kettani, M. (1968b) 'Les sections d'archives et de manuscrits des bibliothèques marocaines', *HT*, 9, 3, pp. 459–68. **(Introd.)**
El-Tounsy, O. (1845) *Voyage au Darfour*, tr. Person (Paris). **(Chap. 6)**
Emery, W. B. (1961) *Archaic Egypt* (Harmondsworth: Penguin). **(Chap. 28)**
Emery, W. B. (1965) *Egypt in Nubia* (London: Hutchinson). **(Chap. 28)**
Emiliani, C. (1955) 'Paleoclimatological analysis of late Quaternary cores from the north-eastern Gulf of Mexico', *Science*, 189, 4208, pp. 1083–7. **(Chap. 16)**
Emphoux, J. P. (1970) 'La grotte de Bitorri au Congo-Brazzaville', *ORSTOM*, II, pp. 3–20. **(Chap. 21)**
Encyclopédie de l'Islam (1954), 2nd edn, ed. J. H. Kramers (Leiden: Brill). **(Introd., Chap. 5)**
Engelmayer, R. (1965) *Die Felsgravierungen im Distrikt Sayala Nubien* (Vienna: Böhlau). **(Chap. 23)**
Ennouchi, E. (1962) 'Un néandertalien: l'homme du Djebel Irhoud', *Anthropologie*, 66. **(Chap. 22)**
Erman, A. and Ranke, H. (1952) *La Civilisation égptienne*, trans. C. Mathieu (Paris: Payot). **(Chap. 28)**
Evans-Pritchard, E. E. (1939) 'Nuer time reckoning', *Africa*, 12, pp. 189–216. **(Chap. 7)**
Ewing, G. W. (1954) *Instrumental Methods of Chemical Analysis* (London: McGraw Hill). **(Chap. 9)**
Eyo, E. (1969) 'Excavation at Ile-Ife', *African Arts*, pp. 44–7. **(Chap. 24)**
Eyo, E. (1972a) 'Rop rock shelter excavations 1964', *WAJA*, 2, pp. 13–16. **(Chap. 24)**
Eyo, E. (1972b) 'New treasures from Nigeria', *Expedition*, 14, 2, pp. 1–11. **(Chap. 24)**
Eyo, E. (1974) 'Excavations at Odo-Ogbe Street and Lafogido, Ife, Nigeria', *WAJA*, 4. **(Chap. 24)**
Eyre, S. R. (1963) *Vegetations and Soils: A world picture* (London: Arnold). **(Chap. 14)**

Faegri, K. and Iversen, J. (1950) *Textbook of Modern Pollen Analysis* (Copenhagen: Munksgaard). **(Chap. 9)**
Fagan, B. M. (1969) 'Radiocarbon dates for sub-saharan Africa, VI', *JAH*, 10, pp. 149–69. **(Chap. 24)**
Fagan, B. M. and Noten, F. L. van (1971) *The Hunter-Gatherers of Gwisho, AMRAC*, 74. **(Chap. 21)**
Fage, J. D. (1961) 'Anthropology, botany and history', *JAH*, 2, 2, pp. 299–309.
Fage, J. D. (1962) *An Introduction to the History of West Africa*, 3rd edn (Cambridge: Cambridge University Press). **(Introd.)**
Fage, J. D. (1970) *An Atlas of African History* (London: Arnold).
Fage, J. D. (1970) *Africa Discovers Her Past* (London: Oxford University Press). **(Chap. 15)**
Fage, J. D. and Oliver, R. A. eds (1970) *Papers in African Prehistory* (*Journal of African History*) (Cambridge: Cambridge University Press). **(Concl.)**
Fagg, A. (1972a) 'Pottery from the rock shelter excavations of 1944 and 1964', *WAJA*, 2, pp. 29–38. **(Chap. 24)**
Fagg, A. (1972b) 'Excavation of an occupation site in the Nok valley, Nigeria', *WAJA*, 2, pp. 75–9. **(Chap. 24)**
Fagg, B. E. B. (1944) 'Preliminary report on a microlithic industry at Rop rock shelter, northern Nigeria', *Proceedings of the Prehistoric Society* (Cambridge), 10, pp. 68–9. **(Chap. 24)**
Fagg, B. E. B. (1945) 'A preliminary note on a new series of pottery figures from northern Nigeria', *Africa*, 15, pp. 21–2. **(Chap. 24)**
Fagg, B. E. B. (1956a) 'An outline of the Stone Age of the Plateau minesfield', *Proc. III Intern. WAC*, pp. 203–22. **(Chap. 24)**
Fagg, B. E. B. (1956b) 'The Nok culture', *WAR*, 27, pp. 1083–7. **(Chap. 24)**
Fagg, B. E. B. (1959) 'The Nok culture in prehistory', *JHSN*, 1, 4, pp. 288–93. **(Chap. 24)**
Fagg, B. E. B. (1962) 'The Nok terracottas in West African art history', *Actes IV Congr. PPEQ*, III, pp. 445–50. **(Chap. 24)**
Fagg, B. E. B. (1968) 'The Nok culture: excavations at Taruga', *WAAN*, 10, pp. 27–30. **(Chap. 24)**
Fagg, B. E. B. (1969) 'Recent work in West Africa: new light on the Nok culture', *WA*, 1, pp. 41–50. **(Chap. 24)**
Fagg, B. E. B. (1972) 'Rop rock shelter excavations 1944', *WAJA*, 2, pp. 1–12. **(Chap. 24)**
Fagg, B. E. B. and Fleming, S. J. (1970) 'Thermoluminescent dating of a terracotta of the Nok culture, Nigeria', *Archaeometry*, 12, pp. 53–5. **(Chap. 24)**
Fagg, W. (1963) *Nigerian Images* (London: Lund Humphries). **(Chap. 24)**
Fagg, W. and Willett, F. (1960) 'Ancient Ife: an ethnographical summary', *Odu*, 8, pp. 21–35. **(Chap. 24)**
Farag, N. and Iskander, Z. (1971) *The Discovery of Neferwptah* (Cairo: Government Printing Office). **(Chap. 9)**

Farine, B. (1963) *Sites préhistoriques gabonais* (Libreville: Ministère de l'Information). **(Chap. 21)**

Farine, B. (1965) *Recherches préhistoriques au Gabon, BSPPG*, I, 3, pp. 68–84. **(Chap. 21)**

Farine, B. (1967) 'Quelques outils principaux des divers faciès préhistoriques des districts de Ndjole et de Booué', *BSPPG*, pp. 22–36. **(Chap. 21)**

Farrand, W. R. (1971) 'Late Quaternary paleoclimates of the Eastern Mediterranean area in Late Cenozoic glacial ages', in K. K. Turekian (ed.), *The Late Cenozoic glacial ages* (New Haven: Yale University Press), pp. 529–64. **(Chap. 16)**

Faulkner, R. O. (1953) 'Egyptian military organisation', *JEA*, 39, pp. 32–47. **(Chap. 28)**

Faure, H. (1962) 'Reconnaissance géologique des formations sédimentaires postpaléozoîques du Niger oriental', thesis (University of Paris). **(Chap. 23)**

Faure, H. (1967) 'Evolution des grands lacs sahariens à l'Holocène', *Quaternaria*, 15, pp. 167–75. **(Chap. 16)**

Faure, H. (1969) 'Lacs quaternaires du Sahara', *Internationale Vereiningung für theoretische und angewandte Limnologie* (Stuttgart), 17, pp. 131–48. **(Chap. 16)**

Faure, H. and Elouard, P. (1967) 'Schéma des variations du niveau de l'océan Atlantique sur la côte de l'Ouest de l'Afrique depuis 40,000 ans', *CRAS*, 265, pp. 784–7. **(Chap. 24)**

Ferembach, D. (1970) *Les Cro-Magnoïdes de l'Afrique du Nord. L'Homme de Cro-Magnon* (Paris: AMG). **(Chap. 22)**

Ferembach, D., Dastugue, J. and Poitrat-Targowla, M.-J. (1962) *La nécropole épipaléolithique de Taforalt (Maroc oriental); étude de squelettes humains* (Rabat: Edita-Casablanca). **(Chap. 22)**

Ferguson, J. (1969) 'Classical contacts with West Africa', in L. A. Thompson and J. Ferguson (eds), *Africa in Classical Antiquity* (Ibadan: Ibadan University Press). **(Chap. 24)**

Fields, P. R., Milsted, J., Henricksen, E. and Ramette, R. W. (1971) 'Trace impurities in copper ores and artefacts', *Science and Archaeology*, pp. 131–43. **(Chap. 4)**

Filesi, T. (1962) *Le relazioni della Cina con l'Africa nel Medio-Evo* (Milan: Giuffrè). **(Chap. 5)**

Filipowiak, M. (1969a) 'L'expédition archéologique polono-Guinéenne à Niani en 1968', *Africana*, 11, pp. 107–17. **(Chap. 24)**

Filipowiak, M. (1969b) 'Discovering Niani', *Polish Review*, 4, 92, pp. 14–16. **(Chap. 24)**

Finnegan, R. (1970) *Oral Literature in Africa* (Oxford: Clarendon Press). **(Chap. 8)**

Fisher, H. J. (1972) 'He swalloweth the ground with fierceness and rage: the horse in the central Sudan', *JAH*, 13, 3, pp. 367–88. **(Chap. 24)**

Fisher, R. (1912) *Twilight tales of the black Bagansha* (London). **(Chap. 1)**

Flamand, G. B. M. (1902) 'Les pierres écrites (Hadjrat Mektoubat) du nord de l'Afrique et spécialement de la région d'In Salah', *Anthropologie*, 12, pp. 535–8. **(Chap. 23)**

Flamand, G. B. M. (1921) *Les pierres écrites (Hadjrat Mektoubat). Gravures et inscriptions rupestres du Nord-Africain* (Paris: Masson). **(Chap. 23)**

Fleming, H. C. (1969) 'The classification of West Cushitic within Hamito-Semitic', in D. F. McCall, N. R. Bennett and J. Butler (eds), *Eastern African History* (New York: Praeger), pp. 3–27. **(Chap. 12)**

Flight, C. (1968) 'Kintampo 1968', *WAAN*, 8, pp. 15–19. **(Chap. 24)**

Flight, C. (1970) 'Excavations at Kintampo', *WAAN*, 12, pp. 71–3. **(Chap. 24)**

Flinders-Petrie, W. M. *see* **Petrie, W. M. F.**

Flint, R. F. (1947) *Glacial Geology and the Pleistocene Epoch* (New York: Wiley; London: Chapman & Hall). **(Chap. 16)**

Flint, R. F. (1959a) 'Pleistocene climates in eastern and southern Africa', *BGSA*, 70, pp. 343–74. **(Chaps 16, 21)**

Flint, R. F. (1959b) 'On the basis of Pleistocene correlation in East Africa', *Geology Magazine*, V, pp. 265–84. **(Chaps 21, 24)**

Flint, R. F. (1971) *Glacial and Quaternary Geology* (New York: Wiley). **(Chaps 16, 24)**

Flutre, F. (1957) *Pour une étude de la toponymie de l'A.-O.F.* (Dakar: Publications de l'Université).

Fodor, I. (1966) *The Problems in the Classification of the African Languages* (Budapest: Centre for Afro-Asian Research of the Hungarian Academy of Sciences). **(Chap. 4)**

Foerster, R. (ed.) (1893) *Scriptores Physiognomonici* (Leipzig: Teubner). **(Chap. 11)**

Forbes, R. J. (1955–72) *Studies in Ancient Technology*, Vol. I (Leiden: Brill). **(Chap. 28)**

Ford, J. (1971) *The Historical Role of Tse-Tse* (Oxford: Clarendon Press). **(Introd.)**

Forde, C. D. (ed.) (1954) *African Worlds; studies in the cosmological ideas and social values of African peoples* (London: Oxford University Press). **(Introd.)**

Forde, C. D. (1956) *Efik Traders of Old Calabar* (London/New York: Oxford University Press). **(Chap. 6)**

Fortes, M. and Evans-Pritchard, E. E. (eds) (1958) *African Political Systems* (London: Oxford University Press). **(Gen. Introd.)**

Fosbrooke, H. A. (1950) 'Rock-paintings of north-central Tanzania', *TNR*, 29. **(Chap. 19)**

Foureau, F. (1883) 'Excursion dans le Sahara algérien', *L'Explorateur*, 16. **(Chap. 23)**
Foureau, F. (1903–5) *Documents scientifiques de la Mission saharienne, Mission Foureau-Lamy, d'Alger au Congo par le Tchad*, 3 Vols (Paris: Masson). **(Chap. 23)**
Fournier, F. (1963) 'Les sols du continent africain', *Enquête sur les ressources naturelles du continent africain* (Paris: Unesco), pp. 227–55. **(Chap. 13)**
Freeman, T. (1844) *Journal of Various Visits to the Kingdom of Ashanti, Dahomey and Abeokuta* (London). **(Chap. 6)**
Freeman-Grenville, G. S. P. (1958) 'Swahili literature and the history and archaeology of the East African coast', *JEASC*, 28, 2. **(Introd., Chaps 5, 6)**
Freeman-Grenville, G. S. P. (1959) 'Medieval evidences for Swahili', *JEASC*, 29, 1. **(Introd., Chaps 5, 6)**
Freeman-Grenville, G. S. P. (1960) 'East African coin finds and their historical significance', *JAH*, 1, pp. 31–43. **(Introd., Chaps 5, 6)**
Freeman-Grenville, G. S. P. (1962) *The East African Coast, select documents from the first to the earlier nineteenth century* (Oxford: Clarendon Press). **(Chaps 1, 6)**
Freeman-Grenville, G. S. P. (1962) *The Medieval History of the coast of Tanganyika* (Oxford: Clarendon Press). **(Chap. 6)**
Frobenius, L. (1912–13) *Und Afrika sproch* (Berlin, Charlottenburg), tr. R. Blind, *The Voice of Africa* (London: Hutchinson): **(Introd.)**
Frobenius, L. (1921–8) *Atlantis; Volksmärchen und Volksdichtungen Afrikas* (Jena). **(Chap. 1)**
Frobenius, L. (1937) *Ekade Ektab. Die Felsbilder Fezzans* (Leipzig: Harrassowitz). **(Chap. 23)**
Frobenius, L. (1949) *Mythologie de l'Atlantide, le 'Poseidon' de l'Afrique noir, son culte chez les Yorouba du Bénin* (Paris: Payot). **(Introd.)**
Frobenius, L. (1952) *Histoire de la civilisation africaine*, trans. H. Back and D. Ermont (Paris: Gallimard). **(Introd.)**
Frobenius, L. and Obermaier, H. (1923) *Hádschra maktuba, urzeitliche Felsbilder Kleinafrikas* (Munich: Wolff). **(Chap. 23)**
Froger, J. (1965) 'La machine électronique au service des sciences humaines', *Diogène*, 52, pp. 110–44. **(Chap. 4)**
Froude, J. A. (1888) *The English in the West Indies* (London; Longman; New York: Scribner). **(Chap. 1)**
Fuller, F. (1921) *A Vanished Dynasty: Ashanti* (London). **(Chap. 1)**
Furon, R. (1943) *Manuel d'archéologie préhistorique* (Paris: Payot). **(Concl.)**
Furon, R. (1958) *Manuel de préhistoire générale: géologie, biogéographie, archéologie préhistorique, évolution de l'humanité, les métaux et la protohistoire*, 4th edn (Paris: Payot). **(Concl.)**
Furon, R. (1960) *Géologie de l'Afrique* (Paris: Payot). **(Chap. 13)**
Fynn, N. F. (1950) *The Diary of Henry Francis Fynn*, eds J. Stuart and D. Malcolm (Pietermaritzburg: Shuter & Shooter). **(Chap. 6)**

Gabel, C. (1966) 'Prehistoric populations of Africa', *BUPA*, pp. 1–37. **(Chap. 15)**
Gabel, C. and Bennet, N. R. (1967) *Reconstructing African Culture History* (Boston, Mass.: Boston University Press). **(Chap. 15)**
Galton, F. (1891) *Narrative of an explorer in tropical South Africa*, 4th edn (London/New York: Ward Lock). **(Chap. 6)**
Gardiner, A. H. (1947) *Ancient Egyptian Onomastica* (London: Oxford University Press). **(Chap. 28)**
Gardiner, A. H. (1957) *Egyptian Grammar: Being an introduction to the study of hieroglyphs*, 3rd edn (London: Oxford University Press). **(Chap. 28)**
Gardner, J. V. and Hays, J. D. (1975) 'Eastern equatorial Atlantic: sub-surface temperature and circulation responses to global climatic change during the past 200,000 years', *GSAM*, 145. **(Chap. 16)**
Garlake, P. (1974) 'Excavations at Obalara's Land, Ife, Nigeria', *WAJA*, 4. **(Chap. 24)**
Gasse, F. (1975) 'L'évolution des lacs de l'Afar Central (Ethiopie et TFAI) du Plio-Pléistocène à l'Actuel', thesis, 3 Vols (Paris: University of Paris). **(Chap. 16)**
Gaudefroy-Demombynes, M. (1927) *L'Afrique moins l'Egypte* (Paris). **(Chap. 5)**
Gaussen, M. and J. (1965) 'Un atelier de burins à Lagreich-Néo. 1, Oued Tilemsi (Mali)', *Anthropologie*, 69. **(Chap. 23)**
Gautier, E. F. (1908) *Le Sahara algérien* (Paris: Colin). **(Chap. 23)**
Gautier, E. F. (1928) *Le Sahara* (Paris: Payot) 2nd edn 1946, 3rd edn. 1950. **(Chap. 23)**
Gautier, E. F. (1933) 'Deux centres d'influence mediterranéenne qui rendent intelligible l'Afrique occidentale', *BSGF*, pp. 71–2. **(Introd.)**

Gautier, E. F. and Reygasse, M. (1923) 'Découverte d'un outillage moustérien à outils pédonculés atériens dans le Tidikelt, oued Asriouel, région d'Aoulef Chorfa', *Actes 46e Congr. AFAS.* **(Chap. 23)**

Gautier, E. F. and Reygasse, M. (1934) 'Les monuments de Tin Hinan', *AARSC*, 7. **(Chap. 23)**

Gentner, W. and Lippolt, H. J. (1963) 'The potassium-argon dating of upper Tertiary and Pleistocene deposits', in D. Brothwell and E. Higgs (eds), *Science in Archaeology* (London: Thames and Hudson), pp. 72–84. **(Chap. 9)**

Germain, G. (1957) 'Qu'est-ce que le périple d'Hannon?' *Hesperis.* **(Chap. 5)**

Geus, F. (1976) *Rapport annuel d'activité 1975–76* (Khartoum: Service des Antiquités du Soudan). **(Chap. 28)**

Giegengack, R. F. (1968) 'Late Pleistocene history of the Nile valley in Egyptian Nubia', PhD dissertation (New Haven: Yale University). **(Chap. 16)**

Giglio, G. (1958) *L'Italia in Africa. Serie storice, Volume primo: Etiopia/Mar Rosso* (Rome). **(Chap. 6)**

Gilbert, E. W. (1932) 'What is historical geography?', *The Scottish Geographical Magazine*, 48, 3. **(Chap. 14)**

Girard, P. P. (1937) *Textes de droit romain*, 6th edn. **(Chap. 5)**

Glélé-Ahanhanzo, M. (1974) *Le Danxomé, du pouvoir Aja à la nation Fon* (Paris: Nutria). **(Chap. 10)**

Glover, T. R. (1977) *Rome and the Mediterranean* (London: Cambridge University Press). **(Chap. 5)**

Gobert, E. G. (1951–2) 'El-Mekta, station princeps du capsien', *Karthago*, 2. **(Chap. 22)**

Gobert, E. G. (1963) 'Bibliographie critique de la préhistoire tunisienne', *Cahiers de Tunisie*, 41–2, pp. 37–77. **(Chap. 22)**

Godée-Molsbergen, E. C. (1916–32) *Reizen in Zuid-Afrika in de Hollandse Tijd*, 4 Vols ('s-Gravenhage: Nijhoff). **(Chap. 6)**

Goeje, M. J. de (1879–94) *Bibliotheca Geographorum* (Leyden). **(Chap. 5)**

Goiten (1960) 'The Cairo Geniza as a source for Mediterranean social history', in *JAOS.* **(Chap. 5)**

Goiten (1967) *A Mediterranean Society: The Jewish Communities of the Arab World as Portrayed in The Documents of the Cairo Geniza* (Los Angeles: Economic Foundations), Vol. I. **(Chap. 5)**

Goodwin, A. J. H. and Riet Lowe, C. van (1929) 'The Stone Age cultures of South Africa', *ASAM*, 27. **(Chap. 20)**

Goody, J. (ed.) (1968) *Literacy in Traditional Societies* (Cambridge: Cambridge University Press). **(Chap. 7)**

Görög-Karady, V. (1966–72) 'Litterature orale africaine: bibliographie analytique (périodiques)', *CEA*, 21, VIII, pp. 243–501; 36, IX, pp. 631–66; 40, X, pp. 583–631; 45, XII, pp. 174–92. **(Chap. 7)**

Gourou, P. (1970) *L'Afrique* (Paris: Hachette). **(Chap. 13)**

Graft Johnson, J. C. de (1924) *African Glory* (London). **(Chap. 1)**

Graft Johnson, J. C. de (1928) *Towards Nationhood in West Africa* (London). **(Chap. 1)**

Graft Johnson, J. C. de (1929) *A Historical Geography of the Gold Coast* (London). **(Chap. 1)**

Grandidier, A., Charles-Roux, J., Delhorbe, C., Froidevaux, H. and Grandidier, G. (1903–20) *Collections des ouvrages anciens concernant Madagascar*, 9 Vols (Paris: Comité de Madagascar). **(Chap. 12)**

Gray, J. M. (1940) *A History of the Gambia* (London). **(Chap. 1)**

Gray, R. (1965) 'Eclipse maps', *JAH*, VI, 3, pp. 251–62. **(Chap. 7)**

Gray, R. (1968) 'Annular eclipse maps', *JAH*, IX, 1, pp. 147–57. **(Chap. 7)**

Gray, R. and Chambers, D. S. (1965) *Materials for West African History in Italian Archives* (London: Athlone Press). **(Chaps 6, 24)**

Graziosi, P. (1942) *L'arte rupestre della Libia* (Naples: Edizione della Mostra d'oltremare; Florence: Le Monnier). **(Chap. 23)**

Greenberg, J. H. (1948) 'The classification of African languages', *AA*, 10. **(Chap. 10)**

Greenberg, J. H. (1954) 'Etude sur la classification des langues africaines', *BIFAN*, B, XVI. **(Introd., Chaps 1, 10)**

Greenberg, J. H. (1957a) *Essays in Linguistics* (Chicago: University of Chicago Press). **(Chap. 10)**

Greenberg, J. H. (1957b) 'Nilotic, nilo-hamitic and Hamito-Semitic', *Africa*, 27, pp. 364–77. **(Chaps 10, 12)**

Greenberg, J. H. (1963a) 'Langues et histoire en Afrique', *Présence africaine*, 45, pp. 35–45. **(Chaps 10, 15)**

Greenberg, J. H. (1963b) 'The languages of Africa', *IJAL*, 29, 1, pp. 1–177. **(Chaps 1, 10, 12, 24)**

Greenberg, J. H. (1963c) 'History and present status of the Kwa problem', *Actes 2e Coll. Intern. LNA.*

Greenberg, J. H. (1966) *The Languages of Africa* (The Hague: Mouton). **(Chap. 12)**

Greenberg, J. H. (1971) *Language Culture and Communication* (Stanford, Calif.: Stanford University Press). **(Chap. 10)**

Greenberg, J. H. (1972) 'Linguistic evidence regarding Bantu origins', *JAH*, 13, 2, pp. 189–216. **(Chap. 12)**

Gregersen, E. A. (1967) 'Linguistic seriation as a dating device for loanwords with special reference to West Africa', *ALR*. **(Chap. 10)**

Gregersen, E. A. (1977) *Language in Africa: An Introductory Survey* (New York: Gordon & Breach). **(Chap. 12)**

Griaule, M. (1947) 'Mythe de l'organisation du monde chez les Dogon du Soudan', *Psyché*, 6, pp. 443–53. **(Chap. 8)**

Griaule, M. (1949) 'L'image du monde au Soudan', *JSA*, 19, pp. 81–7. **(Chap. 8)**

Griaule, M. (1952) 'Etendue de l'instruction traditionnelle au Soudan', *Zaïre*, 6, pp. 563–8. **(Chap. 8)**

Griaule, M. and Dieterlen, G. (1951) 'Signes graphiques soudanais', *L'Homme*. **(Chap. 10)**

Griaule, M. and Dieterlen, G. (1965) *Le renard pâle*, Vol. I: *Le Mythe cosmogonique* (Paris: Institut d'ethnologie). **(Chaps, 8, 15)**

Griffith, F. L. (1927) 'The Abydos decree of Seti I at Mauri', *JEA*, 13, pp. 193–208. **(Chap. 28)**

Grohmann, A. (1934–59) *Arabic Papiri in the Egyptian Library*. **(Chap. 5)**

Grohmann, A. (1955) *Einführung und Chrestomathie zur Arabischen Papyruskunde* (Praha). **(Chap. 5)**

Grove, A. T. and Pullan, R. A. (1963) 'Some aspects of the Pleistocene palaeogeography of the Chad Basin', *Viking Fund Publications in Anthropology*, 36, pp. 230–45.

Grove, A. T. and Pullan, R. A. (1964) 'Some aspects of the palaeogeography of the Chad Basin', in F. C. Howell and F. Bourlière (eds), *African Ecology and Human Evolution* (London), pp. 230–45. **(Chaps 16, 24)**

Grove, A. T., Street, F. A. and Goudie, A. S. (1975) 'Former lake levels and climatic change in the rift valley of southern Ethiopia', *GJ*, 141, 2, pp. 177–202. **(Chap. 16)**

Grove, A. T. and Warren, A. (1968) 'Quaternary landforms and climate on the south side of the Sahara', *GJ*, 134, pp. 194–208. **(Chap. 24)**

Gruet, M. (1954) 'Le gisement moustérien d'El Guettar', *Karthago*, 5. **(Chaps 22, 23)**

Gsell, S. (1920–8) *L'histoire ancienne de l'Afrique du Nord*, 8 Vols (Paris: Hachette). **(Chap. 5)**

Guébhard, P. (1907) 'Trois abris sous roche fouillés dans le Fouta--Djallon', *BGHD*, 3, pp. 408–20. **(Chap. 24)**

Guernier, E. L. (1952) *L'apport de l'Afrique à la pensée humaine* (Paris: Payot). **(Introd.)**

Guillain, M. (1848) *Documents sur l'histoire, la géographie et la commerce de l'Afrique orientale* (Paris). **(Chap. 1)**

Guillot, R. and Descamps, C. (1969) 'Nouvelles découvertes préhistoriques à Tiémassas (Sénégal)', *BIFAN*, B, 31, pp. 602–37. **(Chap. 24)**

Guitat, R. (1972) 'Présentation de pièces pédonculées d'El Azrag (Mauritanie)', *NA*, 135, pp. 29–33. **(Chap. 23)**

Guma, S. M. (1967) *The Form, Content and Technique of Traditional Literature in Southern Sotho* (Pretoria: Van Schaik). **(Chap. 7)**

Guthrie, M. (1948) *The classification of the Bantu Languages* (London/New York: Oxford University Press). **(Chap. 12)**

Guthrie, M. (1962) 'Some developments in the prehistory of the Bantu languages', *JAH*, 3, 2, pp. 273–82. **(Chap. 12)**

Guthrie, M. (1967) *Comparative Bantu; an introduction to the comparative linguistics and prehistory of the Bantu languages* (Farnborough: Gregg). **(Chap. 10)**

Guthrie, M. (1969) *Linguistics and History* (London). **(Chap. 10)**

Haberland, E. (ed.) (1973) *Leo Frobenius* (Wiesbaden: Steiner). **(Chap. 26)**

Hable-Sélassié, S. (1967) 'Source material for the ancient and medieval history of Ethiopia', Communication to the International Congress of Africanists, Dakar. **(Chap. 5)**

Hadjigeorgiou, C. and Pommeret, Y. (1965) 'Présence du Lupembien dans la région de l'estuaire', *BSPPG*, 1, 3, pp. 111–31. **(Chap. 21)**

Hair, P. E. H. (1965) 'The enslavement of Koelle's informants', *JAH*, 6. **(Chap. 6)**

Halk, P. (1972) 'Pour une localisation du Royaume de Gaoga', *JAH*, XIII, 4.

Halkin, L. E. (1963) *Initiation à la critique historique* (Paris: Colin). **(Introd., Chap. 15)**

Hall, E. T. (1965) 'Recent research at the Research Laboratory for archaeology and the history of art', *Proceedings of the Seminar on Applications of Science in Examinations of Works of Art,* Boston. **(Chap. 9)**

Hall, E. T. (1970) 'Analytical techniques used in archaeometry', *PTRS*, 269, 1195, pp. 135–41. **(Chap. 9)**

Halpern, J. W., Harris, J. E. and Barnes, C. (1971) 'Studying skulls in Egypt', *Research News* XXII, 1 (Ann Arbor: University of Michigan). **(Chap. 9)**
Hamet, I. (1911) *Chroniques de la Mauritanie sénégalaise* **(Paris). (Chap. 6)**
Hamilton, E. I. (1965) *Applied geochronology* (London/New York: Academic Press), pp. 47–79. **(Chap. 9)**
Hammen, T. van der (1974) 'The last glacial sequence on both sides of the Atlantic', *CLIMAP*, pp. 56–7. **(Chap. 16)**
Hamy, E. T. (1900) 'La grotte de Kakimbon à Rotoma près de Konakry', *CR 12 Congr. Intern. AAP*. **(Chap. 24)**
Hanotaux, G. and Martineau, A. (eds) (1931) *Histoire des colonies françaises*, 8 Vols (Paris). **(Chap. 1)**
Hardy, G. (1937) *Vue générale de l'histoire d'Afrique* (Paris). **(Chap. 1)**
Harlan, J. R. (1975) *Crops and Man* (Madison, Wis.: American Society of Agronomy). **(Chap. 27)**
Harlan, J. R., Wet, J. M. de and Stemler, A. B. L. (eds) (1976) *Origins of African Plant Domestication* (Paris/The Hague: Mouton). **(Chap. 27)**
Harley, G. W. (1950) Review of 'Masks as agents of social control in northeast Liberia', Peabody Museum, Harvard University, Vol. XXXII. **(Chap. 15)**
Harries, L. (ed. and trans.) (1962) *Swahili Poetry* (Oxford: Clarendon Press). **(Chap. 6)**
Harries, L. (1964) 'The Arabs and Swahili culture', *Africa*, XXXIV, pp. 224–9. **(Introd., Chaps 5, 6)**
Harris, D. (1969) 'Agricultural systems, ecosystems and the origin of agriculture', in P. J. Ucko and G. W. Dimbleby (eds), *The Domestication and Exploitation of Plants and Animals* (London: Duckworth). **(Chap. 27)**
Harris, J. R. (1961) *Lexicographical Studies in Ancient Egyptian Minerals* (Berlin: Akademie-Verlag). **(Chap. 28)**
Harrison Church, R. J. *et al.* (1966) *Africa and the islands* (London: Longman). **(Chap. 13)**
Harrison Church, R. J. (1969) *Africa and the Islands* (London: Longman). **(Chap. 13)**
Hartle, D. D. (1966) 'Archaeology in eastern Nigeria', *WAAN*, 5, pp. 13–17. **(Chap. 24)**
Hartle, D. D. (1968) 'Radiocarbon dates', *WAAN*, 9, p. 73. **(Chap. 24)**
Hartle, D. D. (1970) 'Preliminary report of the University of Ibadan's Kainji rescue archaeology project, 1968', *WAAN*, 12, pp. 7–19. **(Chap. 24)**
Hartmann, F. (1923) *L'Agriculture dans l'ancienne Egypte* (Paris: Librairies-Imprimeries réunies). **(Chap. 28)**
Hassan, F. A. and Wendorf, F. (1974) 'A Sibilian assemblage from El Elh', *Chronique d'Egypte*, 49, pp. 211–22. **(Chap. 25)**
Hau, E. (1959) 'Evidence of the use of pre-Portuguese written characters by the Bini', *BIFAN*, XXI. **(Chap. 10)**
Hay, R. L. (1976) *Geology of the Olduvai Gorge: A study of sedimentation in a semi-arid basin* (Berkeley, Calif.: University of California Press). **(Chap. 17)**
Hayes, W. C. (1964) *Most Ancient Egypt*, ed. K. C. Seele (Chicago: University of Chicago Press). **(Chap. 28)**
Hays, J. D., Saito, T., Opdyke, N. D. and Burckle, L. D. (1969) 'Pliocene-Pleistocene sediments of the Equatorial Pacific: their paleomagnetic, biostratigraphic and climatic record', *GSAB*, 80, pp. 1481–513. **(Chap. 16)**
Heintze, B. (1976) 'Oral traditions. Primary sources only for the collector', *History in Africa: A journal of method*, 3.
Heinzelin de Braucourt, J. de (1957) *Les fouilles d'Ishango* (Brussels). **(Chap. 21)**
Heinzelin de Braucourt, J. de (1963) 'Paleoecological conditions of the Lake Albert-Lake Edward rift', *Viking Fund Publications in Anthropology*, 36. **(Chap. 16)**
Heinzelin de Braucourt, J. de (1968) 'Geological history of the Nile Valley in Nubia', in F. Wendorf (ed.), *The Prehistory of Nubia* (Dallas: Fort Burgwin Research Center and Southern Methodist University Press). **(Chap. 16)**
Heinzelin de Braucourt, J. de, Brown, F. E. and Howell, F. C. (1971) 'Plio-Pleistocene formations in the lower Omo Basin (Southern Ethiopia)', *Quaternaria*. **(Chap. 16)**
Henige, D. P. (1971) 'Oral tradition and chronology', *JAH*, XII, 3. **(Chap. 7)**
Henige, D. P. (1974) *The Chronology of Oral Tradition: Quest for a Chimera* (Oxford: Clarendon Press). **(Chaps 2, 7)**
Herbert, E. W. (1973) 'Aspects of the use of copper in pre-colonial West Africa', *JAH*, 14, 2, pp. 179–94. **(Chap. 24)**
Herodotus (1964) *Histories*, Vol. 1, trans. George Rawlinson (London: Dent). **(Chaps, 1, 24)**
Herodotus, *Works*, trans. A. D. Godley 1920–4, 4 Vols (London: Heinemann).

Hervieu, J. (1969) 'Les industries à galets aménagés du haut bassin de la Benoué (Cameroun)', *BASEQUA*, 22, pp. 24–34. **(Chap. 21)**
Herzog, R. (1938) *Punt* (Glückstadt). **(Chap. 11)**
Hester, J. J. (1968) in 'Comments', *CA*, 9. **(Chaps 5, 27)**
Heusch, L. de (1972) *Le Roi ivre ou l'origine de l'Etat; mythes et rites bantous* (Paris: Gallimard). **(Chap. 7)**
Hiben, F. C. (1967) 'Lukuliro', *Archaeology*, XX, pp. 247–53. **(Chap. 19)**
Hiernaux, J. (1970) 'La Diversité biologique des groupes ethniques' *in Histoire générale de l'Afrique noire* (Paris: PUF). **(Introd., Chap. 11)**
Hiernaux, J. (1974) *Rapport sur le concept de race* (Paris: Unesco). **(Gen. Introd., Chap. 11)**
Higgs, E. S. (1970) 'Prehistoric economy in the Mount Carmel area of Palestine: site catchment analysis', *Proceedings of the Prehistoric Society*, 36. **(Chap. 20)**
Hill, P. (1963) *The migrant cocoa-farmers of Southern Ghana* (Cambridge: Cambridge University Press). **(Chap. 3)**
Hintze, F. (1951) 'Revue de l'essai comparatif sur le vocabulaire et la phonétique du chamito–sémitique de M. Cohen', *Z. Phon*, 5, pp. 65–87. **(Chap. 10)**
Hintze, F. (1955) 'Die sprachliche Stellung des Meroitischen', *Deutsche Akademie der Wissenchaften Veröff*, 26, pp. 355–72. **(Chap. 12)**
Hintze, F. and U. (1967) *Alte Kulturen im Sudan* (Munich: Callwey). **(Chap. 28)**
Hiob, L. (1681) *Historia Aethiopica* (Frankfurt). **(Chap. 6)**
Hirth, F. (1909–10) 'Chinese notices of East African territories', *JAOS*, 30. **(Chap. 5)**
Hiskett, M. (1957) 'Material relating to the state of learning among the Fulani before their jihad', *BSAOS*, 19. **(Chap. 6)**
Hjalmar, L. (1962) 'Die Merimdekeramik im Mittelmeermuseum', *Orientalia Suecana*, XI. **(Chap. 28)**
Hockett, C. F. and Ascher, R. (1964) 'The human revolution', *CA*, 5, 3. **(Chap. 4)**
Hodge, C. T. (1968) 'Afro-Asiatic 67', in *Language Sciences*, Indiana. **(Chap. 10)**
Hodgkin, T. (1956) *Nationalism in Colonial Africa* (London: Muller). **(Chap. 3)**
Hodgkin, T. (1966) 'The Islamic literary tradition in Ghana', in I. M. Lewis (ed.), *Islam in Tropical Africa* (London: Oxford University Press), pp. 442–60 **(Chaps 1, 6)**
Hofmann, I. (1967) *Die Kulturen des Nilstal von Aswan bis Sennar, vom Mesolithikum: bis zum Ende der Christischen Epoche* (Monographien zur Völkerkunde-Hamburgischen Museumfür Völkerkunde). **(Chap. 28)**
Hohenberger, J. (1956) 'Comparative Masai word list', *Africa*, 26, pp. 281–7. **(Chaps 12, 26)**
Holas, B. (1950) 'Notes préliminaires sur les fouilles de la grotte de Blandé', *BIFAN*, 12, pp. 999–1006. **(Chap. 24)**
Holas, B. (1952) 'Note complémentaire sur l'abri sous roche de Blandé (Guinée)', *BIFAN*, 14, pp. 1341–52. **(Chap. 24)**
Holas, B. and Mauny, R. (1953) 'Nouvelles fouilles à l'abri sous roche de Blandé (Guinée)', *BIFAN*, 15, pp. 1605–17. **(Chap. 24)**
Holm, E. (1961) 'The Rock Art of South Africa', in *The Art of the Stone Age* (London: Methuen).
Homburger, L. (1930a) 'Les dialectes copte et mandé', *BSL*, 3, 1. **(Introd.)**
Homburger, L. (1930b) 'Le bantou et le mandé', *BSL*, 135, 43. **(Introd.)**
Homburger, L. (1936) 'Le verbe en peul et en massaï', *Anthropologie*, 46. **(Introd.)**
Homburger, L. (1941) *Les langues négro-africaines et les peuples qui les parlent* (Paris: Payot). **(Introd., Chap. 12)**
Homburger, L. (1948–50) 'Eléments dravidiens en peul', *JSA*, 18, 2. **(Introd.)**
Homburger, L. (1958) 'La linguistique et l'histoire de l'Afrique', *BIFAN*, XX, 3, 4, pp. 554–61. **(Chap. 10)**
l'Honoré-Naber, S. L. (1931) *Reisebeschreibungen von deutschen Beamten und Kriegsleuten im Dienst der Niederländischen West und Ost indischen Kompanien 1602–1797*, 13 Vols (The Hague). **(Chap. 6)**
Hoore, J. L. d' (1964) *Soil Map of Africa, scale 1 to 5,000,000: Explanatory Monograph* (Lagos: Commission for Technical Cooperation in Africa). **(Chap. 13)**
Horton, J. A. B. (1868) *West African Countries and Peoples ... and a Vindication of African Race* (London: Johnson). **(Chap. 6)**
Houdas, O. (1899) *Sadhkirat an nisyan* (Paris). **(Chap. 6)**
Houdas, O. (ed. and trans.) (1964 revised.) *Documents arabes relatifs à l'histoire du Soudan: Tariqh-es-Soudan par Abderrahman ben Abdallah ben 'Imran ben' Amir es-Sa'di* (Paris: Maisonneuve). **(Introd.)**
Houdas, O. and Delafosse, M. (ed. and tr.) (1913) *Tarikh el-Fettach* (Paris: Leroux). **(Introd.)**
Houis, M. (1955) 'Problèmes linguistiques de l'ouest africain', *Guide bleu de 'l'Afrique occidentale Française.* (Paris: Hachette). **(Chap. 11)**

Houis, M. (1958) 'Quelques données de toponymie ouest africaine', *BIFAN.*

Houis, M. (1961) 'Mouvements historiques et communautés linguistiques dans l'ouest africain', *L'Homme*, I, 3, pp. 72–92. **(Chap. 11)**

Houis, M. (1971) *Anthropologie linguistique de l'Afrique noire* (Paris: PUF). **(Introd., Chaps 10, 11)**

Howell, F. C. and the editors of *Life* (1965) *Early Man* (New York: Time Inc.). **(Chap. 19)**

Howell, F. C. (1969a) 'Remains of Hominidae from Pliocene-Pleistocene formations in the lower Omo Basin, Ethiopia', *Nature*, 223, 20, pp. 1234–9. **(Chap. 17)**

Howell, F. C. (1969b) 'Hominid teeth from White Sands and Brown Sands localities, lower Omo Basin, Ethiopia', *Quaternaria*, XI, pp. 47–64. **(Chap. 17)**

Howell, F. C. (1972) 'Pliocene/Pleistocene Hominidae in Eastern Africa: absolute and relative ages', in W. W. Bishop and J. A. Miller (eds) *Calibration of hominoid evolution*, pp. 331–68. **(Chap. 16)**

Howell, F. C., Coppens, Y. and Heinzelin, J. de (1974) 'Inventory of remains of Hominidae from Pliocene-Pleistocene formations of the lower Omo Basin, Ethiopia (1967–1972)', *AJPA*, 40, 1, pp. 1–16. **(Chap. 17)**

Howells, W. W. (1972) '20 millions d'années pour faire un homme, les origines de l'homme', *Unesco Courrier*, August–September, pp. 4–13. **(Concl.)**

Hrbek, I. *Proceedings of the 12th International Congress of Historical Sciencies* (*Vienna, 1965*). (Horn, Austria: Berger) ed. H. L. Mikoletzky, V. (n.d.). **(Chap. 5)**

Hrbek, I., Kalous, M., Petráček *et al.* (1966) *Dějiny Afriky*, 2 Vols (Prague: Svoboda). **(Introd.)**

Huard, P. (1960) 'Contribution à l'étude anthropologique des Teda du Tibesti', *BIFAN*, B, XXII, 1–2, pp. 179–201. **(Chap. 28)**

Huard, P. (1963) 'Gravures rupestres de l'Ennedi et des Erdis', *BIRSC*, 2, pp. 3–39. **(Chap. 26)**

Huard, P. (1964) 'Un établissement islamique tchadien ouogayi', *BIFAN*, B, XXVI, 1–2. **(Chap. 28)**

Huard, P. (1966) 'Introduction et diffusion du fer au Tchad', *JAH*, 7, 3, pp. 377–407. **(Chap. 24)**

Huard, P. (1969) 'Aires ou origines de quelques traits culturels des populations pré-islamiques du Bas Chari, Logone', *Actes ter Coll. Intern. Archéol. Afr.*, pp. 179–224. **(Introd.)**

Huard, P. and Beck, P. (1969) *Tibesti, carrefour de la préhistoire saharienne* (Paris: Arthaud). **(Chap. 26)**

Huard, P. and Leclant, J. (1973) 'Figurations de chasseurs anciens du Nil et du Sahara', *RE*, 25. **(Chap. 26)**

Hubert, R. (1922) 'Objets anciens de l'Afrique occidentale', *BCEHS*, 5, pp. 382–99. **(Chap. 24)**

Hue, E. (1912) 'L'âge de la pierre au Fouta Djallon', *BSPF*, 2. **(Chap. 24)**

Hugot, H. J. (1955a) 'Du Capsien au Tidikelt', *Actes II Congr. PPEQ*, pp. 601–3. **(Chap. 23)**

Hugot, H. J. (1955b) 'Un gisement de pebble-tools à Aoulef', *Trav. IRS*, 13, pp. 131–49. **(Chap. 23)**

Hugot, H. J. (1957) 'Essai sur les armatures de pointes de flèches du Sahara', *Libyca*, 5, pp. 89–236. **(Chap. 24)**

Hugot, H. J. (ed.) (1962) *Documents scientifiques des missions Berliet-Ténéré, Tchad. 1959–60* (Paris: AMG). **(Chap. 23)**

Hugot, H. J. (1963) 'Recherches préhistoriques dans l'Ahaggar nord-occidental 1950–1957', *Mém. CRAPE.* **(Chaps 23, 24)**

Hugot, H. J. (1964) 'Etat des recherches préhistoriques dans l'Afrique de l'Ouest, 1964–1965', *WAAN*, 1, pp. 4–7. **(Chap. 24)**

Hugot, H. J. (1966a) 'Limites méridionales dans l'Atérien', *Actas V Congr. PPEC.* **(Chaps 22, 24)**

Hugot, H. J. (1966b) 'Présence d'un faciès archaïque du Paléolithique inférieur à Dakar', *BIFAN*, A, 28, pp. 415–16. **(Chap. 24)**

Hugot, H. J. (1967) 'Le Paléolithique terminal dans l'Afrique de l'ouest', in W. W. Bishop and J. D. Clark (eds), *Background to Evolution in Africa* (London/Chicago: University of Chicago Press pp. 529–56). **(Chap. 23)**

Hugot, H. J. (1970) *L'Afrique préhistorique* (Paris: Hatier). **(Chaps 21, 23)**

Hugot, H. J. (1974) *Le Sahara avant le désert* (Paris: Editions des Hespérides). **(Chaps, 25, 26)**

Hugot, H. J., Davies, O. and Seddon, D. (1968) 'The Origins of African Agriculture', *CA*, 9, 5. **(Chap. 27)**

Hugot, H. J. *et al.* (1973) 'Tichitt I, rapport scientifique', roneo, Paris. **(Chap. 23)**

Hugot, H. J. and Bruggmann, M. (1976) *Les gens du matin: Sahara, dix mille ans d'art et d'histoire* (Paris: La Bibliothèque des arts). **(Chap. 23)**

Huntingford, G. W. B. (1956) 'The "Nilo-Hamitic" languages', *SWJA*, 12, pp. 200–22. **(Chap. 12)**

Hunwick, J. O. (1962) 'Arabic manuscript material bearing on the history of the western Sudan', supplement, *BNHSN*, VII, 2, pp. 1–9. **(Introd., Chaps 5, 6)**

Hunwick, J. O. (1973) 'The mid-fourteenth century capital of Mali', *JAH*, 14, 2, pp. 195–208. **(Gen. Introd., Chap. 24)**

Huzayyin, S. A. (1936) 'Glacial and pluvial episodes of the diluvium of the old world', *Man*, 36, pp. 19–22. **(Chap. 23)**

Huzayyin, S. A. (1941) *The Place of Egypt in Prehistory: A correlated study of climates and cultures in the old world* (Cairo: Institut français d'archéologie orientale). **(Chap. 25)**

Iakimov, V. P. (1972) 'Deux grandes théories sur l'apparition des races', *Le Courrier* (August–September). **(Concl.)**

Ibn Battuta (1922) *Les Voyages*, ed. and tr. C. Defrémery and B. R. Sanguinetti (Paris). **(Chap. 1)**

Ibn Khaldun (1925–6) *Histoire des Berbères*, tr. M. G. de Slane (Paris). **(Chap. 1)**

Iliffe, J. (1969) *Tanganyika under German Rule, 1905–1912* (Cambridge: Cambridge University Press). **(Chap. 3)**

Inskeep, R. R. (1969) 'Some problems in relation to the Early Stone Age in South Africa', *SAAB*, XXIV, 3–4, pp. 174–81. **(Chap. 20)**

Irstarm, T. (1944) *The King of Ganda* (Uppsala). **(Chap. 1)**

Isaac, G. L. (1966) 'The geological history of the Olorgesailie area', *Proc. 5th PCPQS*, 2, pp. 125–44. **(Chap. 19)**

Isaac, G. L. (in press) 'East Rudolf', *Proc. 7th PCPQS*, 1977 **(Chap. 19)**

Isaac, G. L. (1971) 'The diet of early man: aspects of archaeological evidence from Lower and Middle Pleistocene sites in Africa', *WA*, 2, pp. 278–98. **(Chap. 20)**

Isaac, G. L., Leakey, R. E. F. and Behrensmeyer, A. K. (1971) 'Archaeological traces of early hominid activities, east of Lake Rudolf, Kenya', *Science*, 173, pp. 1129–34. **(Chap. 17)**

Isaac, G. L. and McCown, E. R. (eds) (1976) *Human Origins: Louis Leakey and the East African evidence* (Menlo Park, Calif.: Benjamin). **(Chap. 19)**

Isaacs, N. (1836–7) *Travels and Adventures in Eastern Africa*, 2 Vols (Cape Town: The Van Riebeeck Society). **(Chap. 6)**

Iskander, A. (1960) 'The scientific study and conservation of the objects and materials found in the discovery of the wooden boat at Giza', *The Cheops Boats*, pt 1 (Cairo: Antiquities Department of Egypt), pp. 29–61. **(Chap. 9)**

Iskander, A. (1961) 'Chemical identification of the samples found at the monastery of Phoebammon', in C. Bachatly (ed.), *Le Monastère de Phoebanmon dans la Thébaïde*, Vol. III (Cairo: Société d'archéologie copte). **(Chap. 9)**

Iskander, A. and Shaheen, A. E. (1964) 'Temporary stuffing materials used in the process of mummification in ancient Egypt', *ASAE*, LVIII, pp. 197–208. **(Chap. 9)**

Isnard, H. (1964) *Géographie de l'Afrique tropicale et australe* (Paris: PUF). **(Chap. 13)**

Isnard, H. (1966) *Le Maghreb* (Paris: PUF). **(Chap. 13)**

Ita, J. M. (1972) 'Frobenius in West African history', *JAH*, xiii, 4. **(Chap. 1)**

Jabavu, D. T. (1920) *The Black Problem*, papers and addresses on various native problems (Lovedale). **(Chap. 6)**

Jackson, J. G. (1820) *An Account of Timbuctoo and Hausa, Territories in the Interior of Africa* (London; reprinted 1967). **(Chap. 6)**

Jacquard, A. (1974) 'Distances généalogiques et distances génétiques', *CAEH*, pp. 11–124. **(Chap. 10)**

Janmart, J. (1953) 'The Kalahari sands of the Lunda (N-E Angola), their earlier redistribution and the Sangoan culture', *CDAPC*, 20. **(Chap. 21)**

Jason, H. (1959) 'A multidimensional approach to oral literature', *CA*, X, 5, pp. 413–26. **(Chap. 7)**

Jeffreys, M. D. W. (1963) 'How ancient is West African maize?', *Africa*, 33, pp. 115–31. **(Chap. 24)**

Johanson, D. C. and Coppens, Y. (1976) 'A preliminary anatomical diagnosis of the first Plio-Pleistocene hominid discoveries in the central Afar, Ethiopia', *AJPA*, 45, 2, pp. 217–34. **(Chap. 17)**

Johanson, D. C. and Taieb, M. (1976a) 'Pliocene hominid remains from Hadar, central Afar, Ethiopia', *Actes IX Congr. UISPP*, pp. 120–37. **(Chap. 17)**

Johanson, D. C. and Taieb, M. (1976b) 'Plio-Pleistocene hominid discoveries in Hadar, Ethiopia', *Nature*, 260, 5549, pp. 293–7. **(Chap. 17)**

Johnson, S. (1921) *The History of the Yorubas from the Earliest Times to the Beginning of the British Protectorate* (London: Routledge). **(Chaps 3, 10)**

Johnston, H. H. (1899, 1913) *A History of the Colonization of Africa by alien races* (London). **(Chap. 1)**

Johnston, H. H. (1919–22) *A Comparative Study of the Bantu and Semi-Bantu Languages*, 2 Vols (Oxford: Clarendon Press). **(Chap. 12)**

Joire, J. (1947) 'Amas de coquillages du littoral sénégalais dans la banlieue de Saint-Louis', *BIFAN*, 9, pp. 170–340. **(Chap. 24)**

Jones, D. H. (1949) *The Prehistory of Southern Rhodesia* (Cambridge: Cambridge University Press). **(Concl.)**

Jones, D. H. (1958) 'Report on the second conference of London on History and Archaeology in Africa', *Africa*, 28, 1. **(Concl.)**

Jones, D. J. (1970) 'Problems of African chronology', *JAH*, XI, 2, pp. 161–76. **(Chap. 7)**

Joubert, G. and Vaufrey, R. (1941–6) 'Le néolithique du Ténéré', *L'Anthropologie*, 50, 3–4, pp. 325–30. **(Chap. 23)**

Journaux, A. (1976) *L'Afrique* (Coll. Hatier) **(Chap. 14)**

Julien, C. A. (1931) *Histoire de l'Afrique du Nord* (Paris: Payot) rev. edn 1978. **(Chap. 5)**

Julien, C. A. (1944) *Histoire de l'Afrique* (Paris: PUF). **(Gen. Introd.)**

Julien, C. A. (1952) *L'Afrique du Nord en marche* (Paris: Julliard). **(Gen. Introd., Chap. 3)**

Junker, H. (1929–40) 'Vorlaüfiger Bericht über die Grabung der Akademie des Wissenschaften in Wien auf des neolitischen Siedlung von Merimde–Benisalame (Westdelta), in *Anzeiger des philosophist. Klasse des Akademie des Wissenschaften in Wien*, XCI–XVIII, pp. 156–248; V–XII, pp. 21–82; I–IV, pp. 82–6; XVI–XVIII, pp. 53–97; X, pp. 118–32; I–IV, pp. 3–25. **(Chaps 25, 28)**

Kabore, V. (1962) 'Le caractère féodal du système politique mossi', *CEA*, pp. 609–23. **(Concl.)**

Kagame, A. (1969) *Introduction aux grands genres lyriques de l'ancien Rwanda* (Butare: Editions universitaires du Rwanda). **(Chap. 7)**

Kagame, A. (1972) *Un abrégé de l'ethno-histoire du Rwanda* (Butare: Editions universitaires du Rwanda). **(Chap. 7)**

Kaiser, W. (1977) 'Zur inneren Chronologie des Nagadakultur', *AG*, 6. **(Chap. 28)**

Kalk, P. (1972) 'Pour une localisation du Royaume de Gaoga', *JAH*, xiii, 4, pp. 529–48. **(Gen. Introd.)**

Kamal, Y. (1926–51) *Monumenta cartographica Africae et Aegypti*, 16 vols (Cairo/Leyden). **(Chap. 5)**

Kamara, C. M. (1970) 'La vie d'El-Hadji Omar', *BIFAN*, B, 32, pp. 370–411. **(Chap. 3)**

Kardiner, A. and Preble, E. (1966) *Introduction à l'ethnologie* (Paris: Gallimard).

Kees, H. (1961) *Ancient Egypt. A Cultural Topography* (London: Faber). **(Chap. 28)**

Keller, C. M. (1970) 'Montagu cave: a preliminary report', *Quaternaria*, XIII, pp. 187–204. **(Chap. 20)**

Kennedy, R. A. (1960) 'Necked and lugged axes in Nigeria', *Antiquity*, 34, pp. 54–8. **(Chap. 24)**

Kensdale, W. E. N. (1955–8) *A Catalogue of the Arabic Manuscripts preserved in the University Library, Ibadan, Nigeria.* **(Introd., Chaps 5, 6)**

Kent, P. E. (1942) 'Pleistocene climates in Kenya and Abyssinia', *Nature*, 149, pp. 736–7. **(Chap. 21)**

Kent, R. K. (1970) *Early Kingdoms in Madagascar, 1500–1700* (New York: Holt, Rinehart & Winston). **(Chap. 3)**

Kesteloot, L. (1978) *Da Monzon de Ségou. Epopée Bambara*, 2 Vols (Paris: Nathan). **(Concl.)**

Khalatyanc, G. (1899) 'Armyanskiy pamyatnik XVII v.c. geografii Abissinii i Severnoy Afrike voonchsche' (A seventeenth century memoir on the geography of Ethiopia and North Africa in general), *Zemlevedeny*, 1–2. **(Chap. 6)**

Khalil, F. (1963) 'La faune du continent africain: taxonomie, écologie et zoogéographie', *Enquête sur les ressources naturelles du continent africain* (Paris: Unesco), pp. 285–325. **(Chap. 13)**

Khanykov, M. (1859) *Mélange asiatique* (St Petersburg). **(Chap. 6)**

Kilham, H. (1828) *Specimens of African Languages spoken in the Colony of Sierra Leone* (London). **(Chap. 12)**

Kiwanuka, M. S. H. (1967) 'Some reflections on the role of oral tradition in the writing of the pre-colonial history of Africa', *Acta Africana*, VI, 1, pp. 63–74. **(Chap. 4)**

Ki-Zerbo, J. (1957) 'Histoire et conscience nègre', in *Présence africaine*, 16, pp. 53–69. **(Introd.)**

Ki-Zerbo, J. (1964) *Le Monde africaine noir, histoire et civilisation*, (Paris: Hatier). **(Introd.)**

Ki-Zerbo, J. (1969) 'La tradition orale en tant que source pour l'histoire africaine', *Diogène*, 67, pp. 127–42. **(Introd.)**

Ki-Zerbo, J. (1978) *Histoire de l'Afrique noire*, 2nd edn (Paris: Hatier). **(Introd. Chaps 10, 13, 26)**

Klein, R. G. (1970) 'Problems in the study of the Middle Stone Age of South Africa', *SAAB*, XXV, pp. 127–35. **(Chap. 20)**

Klein, R. G. (1972a) 'Preliminary report of the July through September, 1970, excavations at Nelson Bay cave, Plettenberg Bay (Cape Province, South Africa)', *Palaeoecology of Africa*, 6, pp. 117–208. **(Chap. 20)**

Klein, R. G. (1972b) 'The late Quaternary mammalian fauna of Nelson Bay cave (Cape Province, South Africa): its implication for Negafaunal extinctions and environmental and cultural changes', *Quaternary Research*, II, 2, pp. 135–42. **(Chap. 20)**

Koechlin, J. (1963) 'Le flore du continent africain; région du sud du Sahara', *Enquête sur les ressources naturelles du continent africain* (Paris: Unesco), pp. 271–84. **(Chap. 13)**

Koelle, S. W. (1963) *Polyglotta Africana, or, A comparative vocabulary of nearly 300 words and phrases in more than 100 distinct African languages* (London: Church Missionary House). **(Chaps 6, 10, 12)**

Kohler, O. (1955) *Geschichte des Enforschung des nilotischen Sprachen* (Berlin). **(Chap. 10)**

Kolb, P. (1719) *Vollständige Beschreibung des afrikanischen Vorgebirges der Guten Hoffnung* (Nuremberg). **(Chap. 6)**

Kolthoff, I. M., Sandell, E. B., Meehan, E. J. and Bruckenstein, S. (1969) *Quantitative Chemical Analysis*, 4th edn (New York: Macmillan). **(Chap. 9)**

Kouyate, N. (1969–70) 'Recherches sur la tradition orale au Mali (Pays Manding)', Mém. de recherche non edité (Algeria: University of Algeria). **(Chap. 8)**

Kramers, H. (1938) 'L'Erythée décrite dans une source arabe du Xe siècle', *Atti* del xixe Congresso degli Orientalisti (Rome). **(Chap. 5)**

Krzyzaniak, L. (1972) 'Preliminary report on the first season of excavations at Kadero, Sudan', *Trav. CAMAP*. **(Chap. 25)**

Krzyzaniak, L. (1977) 'Early farming cultures on the lower Nile', *Trav. CAMAP*, 21. **(Chap. 28)**

Kubbel, L. E. and Matveiev, V. V. (1960 and 1965) *Arabskie istochniki po etnografii i istorii Africi yuzhnee Sakhary* (*Sources arabes pour l'ethnographie et l'histoire des peuples d'Afrique au sud du Sahara*) 2 Vols (Moscow). **(Introd., Chaps 3, 5)**

Kukla, G. J. and Matthews, R. K. (1972) 'When will the present inter-glacial end?', *Science*, 178, pp. 190–1. **(Chap. 16)**

Kuptsov, A. (1955) 'Geographical distribution of cultivated flora and its historical development', *BAUGS*, 87. **(Chap. 27)**

Labouret, H. (1946) *Histoire des Noirs d'Afrique* (Paris: Payot). **(Chap. 1)**

Lajoux, J. D. (1977) *Tassili N'Ajjer* (Paris: Chêne). **(Chap. 26)**

Lall, B. B. (1967) *Indian Archaeological Expedition to Nubia, 1962* (Cairo: Service des antiquités de l'Egypte). **(Chap. 25)**

Lamb, H. H. (1974) 'Remarks on the current climatic trend and its perspective', *WMO*, 421, pp. 473–7. **(Chap. 16)**

Lambert, N. (1970) 'Medinet Sbat et la protohistoire de Mauritanie occidentale', *AA*, 4, pp. 15–62. **(Chap. 24)**

Lambert, N. (1971) 'Les industries sur cuivre dans l'Ouest africain', *WAJA*, 1, pp. 9–21. **(Chap. 24)**

Lanfranchi, R. (1976) *Rapport des missions d'études et de recherches préhistoriques pour l'année scolaire 1975–76* (Brazzaville: Laboratoire d'anthropologie de l'Université de Brazzaville). **(Chap. 21)**

Laroui, A. (1970) *L'Histoire du Maghreb* (Paris: Maspero). **(Chap. 5)**

Lassort, A. 'L'écriture guerzée', *CR 1ère Conf. Afr. Ouest* (Dakar: IFAN). **(Introd.)**

Laude, J. (1966) *Les Arts de l'Afrique noire* (Paris: Le Livre de Poche). **(Introd.)**

Lauer, J. P. and Debono, F. (1950) 'Technique du façonnage des croissants de silex utilisés dans l'enceinte de Zozer à Saqqarah', *ASAE*, Vol. I, pp. 2ff. **(Chap. 25)**

Law, R. C. C. (1967) 'Contacts between the Mediterranean civilisations and West Africa in pre-Islamic times', *LNR*, 1, 1, pp. 52–62. **(Chap. 24)**

Law, R. C. C. (1971) 'The constitutional troubles of Oyo', *JAH*, XII, 1 **(Introd.)**

Lawson, A. C. (1927) *The Valley of the Nile* (Berkeley: Univ. California Press), 29, pp. 235–59. **(Gen. Introd., Chap. 16)**

Laya, D. (1972) *La Tradition orale: problématique et méthodologie des sources de l'histoire africaine* (Niamey: Centre régional de documentation pour la tradition orale). **(Chaps 7, 15)**

Leakey, L. S. B. (1949) 'Tentative study of the Pleistocene climatic changes and Stone Age culture sequence in north-eastern Angola', *CDAPC*, 4, 82pp. **(Chap. 21)**

Leakey, L. S. B. (1950) 'The lower limits of the Pleistocene in Africa', *Report on the XVIIIth International Geology Congress, 1948* (London), 9, pp. 62–5. **(Chap. 24)**

Leakey, L. S. B. (1952) *Proceedings of the Panafrican Congress on Prehistory* (Oxford: Blackwell). **(Chap. 24)**

Leakey, L. S. B. (1965) *Olduvai Gorge, 1951–61: Fauna and Background* (Cambridge: Cambridge University Press). **(Chap. 17)**

Leakey, L. S. B. (1968) 'Bone-smashing by a late Miocene hominid', *Nature*, **(Chap. 17)**

Leakey, L. S. B. (1970) *Stone Age Africa; An outline of prehistory in Africa* (New York: Negro University Press). **(Chap. 19)**

Leakey, L. S. B. (1971) *The Stone Age cultures of Kenya colony*, repr. (London: Cass). **(Chap. 19)**

Leakey, L. S. B. and M. D. *et al.* (1965–71) *Olduvai gorge*, Vols I–III (Cambridge: Cambridge University Press), more vols in preparation. **(Chaps 18, 19, 20)**

Leakey, L. S. B. and M. D. (1971) *Olduvai Gorge – Excavations in Beds I and II, 1960–1963* (Cambridge: Cambridge University Press). **(Chap. 17)**

Leakey, M. D. (1970) 'Early artefacts from the Koobi Fora area', *Nature*, 226, pp. 228–30. **(Chaps 17, 24)**
Leakey, M. D., Hay, R. L., Curtis, G. H., Drake, R. E., Jackes, M. K. and White, T. D. (1976) 'Fossil hominids from the Laetolil beds', *Nature*, 262, pp. 460–6. **(Chap. 17)**
Leakey, R. E. F. (1970) 'New hominid remains and early artefacts from northern Kenya', *Nature*, 226, pp. 223–4. **(Chap. 17)**
Leakey, R. E. F. (1971) 'Further evidence of lower Pleistocene hominids from East Rudolf, North Kenya', *Nature*, 231, pp. 241–5. **(Chap. 17)**
Leakey, R. E. F. (1972) 'Further evidence of lower Pleistocene hominids from East Rudolf, North Kenya, 1971', *Nature*, 237, pp. 264–9. **(Chap. 17)**
Leakey, R. E. F. (1973a) 'Evidence for an advanced Plio-Pleistocene hominid from East Rudolf, Kenya', *Nature*, 242, pp. 447–50. **(Chaps 17, 24)**
Leakey, R. E. F. (1973b) 'Further evidence of lower Pleistocene hominids from East Rudolf, North Kenya, 1972', *Nature*, 242, pp. 170–3. **(Chaps 17, 18)**
Leakey, R. E. F. (1973c) 'Skull 1470', *Natural Geographic*, 143, pp. 818–29. **(Chaps 17, 18)**
Leakey, R. E. F. (1974) 'Further evidence of lower Pleistocene hominids from East Rudolf, North Kenya, 1973', *Nature*, 248, pp. 653–6. **(Chaps 17, 18)**
Leakey, R. E. F., Butzer, K. W. and Day, M. H. (1969) 'Early *Homo sapiens* remains from the Omo river region of south-west Ethiopia', *Nature*, 222, 5199, pp. 1137–43. **(Chap. 17)**
Leakey, R. E. F. and Isaac, G. L. (1972) 'Hominid fossils from the area east of Lake Rudolf, Kenya: photographs and a commentary on context', in S. L. Washburn and P. Dolhinow (eds), *Perspectives on Human Evolution*, Vol. 2 (San Francisco: Holt, Rinehart & Winston), pp. 129–40. **(Chaps 17–18)**
Leakey, R. E. F., Mungai, J. M. and Walker, A. C. (1971) 'New australopithecines from East Rudolf, Kenya', *AJPA*, 35, pp. 175–86. **(Chap. 17)**
Leakey, R. E. F., Mungai, J. M. and Walker, A. C. (1972) 'New australopithecines from East Rudolf, Kenya, II', *AJPA*, 36, pp. 235–51. **(Chap. 17)**
Leakey, R. E. F. and Walker, A. C. (1973) 'New australopithecines from East Rudolf, Kenya, III', *AJPA*, 39, pp. 205–22. **(Chap. 17)**
Leakey, R. E. F. and Wood, B. A. (1973) 'New evidence for the genus *Homo* from East Rudolf, Kenya, II', *AJPA*, 39, pp. 355–68. **(Chap. 17)**
Leakey, R. E. F. and Wood, B. A. (1974a) 'A hominid mandible from East Rudolf, Kenya', *AJPA*, 41, pp. 245–50. **(Chap. 17)**
Leakey, R. E. F. and Wood, B. A. (1974b) 'New evidence for the genus *Homo* from East Rudolf, Kenya, IV', *AJPA*, 41, pp. 237–44. **(Chap. 17)**
Lebeuf, J. P. (1956) 'La civilisation du Tchad', *Proc. III Intern. WAC*, pp. 293–6. **(Chap. 24)**
Lebeuf, J. P. (1962a) *Archéologie tchadienne; les Sao du Cameroun et du Tchad* (Paris: Hermann). **(Chap. 24)**
Lebeuf, J. P. (1962b) 'Caractères particuliers de la recherche historique en Afrique', *Revue de psychologie des peuples.* **(Chap. 15)**
Lebeuf, J. P. (1969a) 'Essai de chronologie sao', *Actes 1er Coll. Intern. Archéol. Afr.*, pp. 234–41. **(Chap. 24)**
Lebeuf, J. P. (1969b) *Carte archéologique des abords du lac Tchad au 1/300 000* (Paris: CNRS). **(Chap. 24)**
Leclant, J. (1956) 'Le fer dans l'Egypte ancienne, le Soudan et l'Afrique', *Actes Coll. Intern. Fer.*, pp. 83–91. **(Chap. 28)**
Lee, D. N. and Woodhouse, H. C. (1970) *Art on the Rocks of Southern Africa* (Cape Town: Purnell). **(Chap. 26)**
Lee, R. B. (1966) 'The !Kung Bushman subsistence: an input/output analysis', in D. Damas (ed.), *Contributions to Anthropology: Ecological Essays, Proc. Conf. Cult. Ecol.*, Ottawa 1966 (published Ottawa 1969), p. 230. **(Chap. 27)**
Lee, R. B. (ed.) (1968) *Man the Hunter* (Chicago: Aldine). **(Chap. 19)**
Lefebvre, G. (1949) *Romans et contes égyptiens de l'époque pharaonique* (Paris). **(Chap. 28)**
Lefebvre, H. (1974) *La Production de l'espace* (Paris: Anthropos). **(Chap. 15)**
Le Gros-Clark, W. E. (1972) *The Fossil Evidence for Human Evolution*, 2nd edn (Chicago: University of Chicago Press). **(Chap. 18)**
Leiris, M. and Delange, J. (1967) *Afrique noire, la création plastique* (Paris: Gallimard). **(Introd.)**
Lenz, O. (1884) *Timbuktu*, 2 Vols (Leipzig: Brockhaus). **(Chap. 23)**
Leo Africanus (1956) *Description de l'Afrique*, tr. A. Épaulard (Paris). **(Chap. 1)**
Lepsius, C. R. (1863) *Standard Alphabet for Reducing Unwritten Languages and Foreign Graphic Systems to a Uniform Orthography in European Letters* (London: Williams & Norgate). **(Chap. 12)**

Lepsius, C. R. (1880) *Nubische Grammatik mit einer Einleitung über die Völker und Sprachen Afrika's* (Berlin: Hertz). **(Chaps 10, 12)**

Leroi-Gourhan, A. (1943) *L'Homme et la matière, Evolution et Techniques, Vol. 1* (Paris: Albin Michel). **(Concl.)**

Leroi-Gourhan, A. (1945) *Milieu et technique, Evolution et Techniques, Vol. 2* (Paris: Albin Michel). **(Concl.)**

Leroi-Gourhan, A. (1969) *Sur le 'mode de production asiatique'* (Paris: Editions sociales). **(Concl.)**

Leroi-Gourhan, A. (1974) 'Analyses polliniques, préhistoire et variations climatiques quaternaires' – in 'Les méthodes quantitatives d'étude des variations du climat au cours du Pleistocène', *Coll. CNRS*, 219, pp. 61–6.

Leroy, P. (1953) 'La préhistoire à Brazzaville et dans le Moyen Congo', *Liaison*, 31, pp. 39–43. **(Chap. 21)**

Leslau, W. (1949) 'Revue d'essai comparatif sur le vocabulaire et la phonétique du chamito-sémitique', *LG*, 25. **(Chap. 10)**

Leslau, W. (1963) *Etymological Dictionary of Harari* (Berkeley, Calif.: University of California Press). **(Chap. 11)**

Le Tourneau, R. (1954) 'Les archives musulmanes en Afrique du Nord', *Archivum*, 4. **(Chap. 6)**

Le Vaillant, F. (1790) *Travels from the Cape of Good Hope into the Interior Parts of Africa* (London: W. Lane). **(Chap. 6)**

Lévi-Provençal, E. (1922) *Les historiens des Chorfa. Essai sur la Littérature Historique et Biographique au Maroc du 16e au 20e Siècle* (Paris). **(Chap. 6)**

Lévi-Provençal, E. (1954) *Arabica.* **(Chaps 5, 10, 12)**

Levtzion, N. (1968) 'Ibn-Hawqual, the Cheque and Awdaghost', *JAH*, 9, 2, pp. 223–33. **(Chap. 24)**

Levtzion, N (1968) *Muslims and Chiefs in West Africa* (Oxford). **(Chap. 1)**

Levtzion, N. (1971) 'The early states of the western Sudan to 1500', in J. F. A. Ajayi and M. Crowder (eds), *History of West Africa*, Vol. I (London: Longman), pp. 120–37. **(Chap. 24)**

Lewicki, T. (1961) *Les Historiens biographes et traditionalistes des Ibadites*, Folia orientalia, 3 (Krakow). **(Chap. 6)**

Lewicki, T. (1969) *Arabic external sources for the history of Africa to the south of the Sahara* (Warsaw, Krakow, Wroclaw). **(Chap. 5)**

Lewicki, T. (1971) 'The Ibâdites in Arabia and Africa', *CHM*, XII, 1, pp. 51–130. **(Chap. 5)**

Lewicki, T. (1971) *Perspectives nouvelles sur l'histoire africaine.* A report of Dar-es-Salaam congress. **(Chap. 5)**

Lewin, S. Z. (1968) 'The conservation of limestone objects and structures', *Study of Weathering of Stones*, ICOMOS (Paris), pp. 41–50. **(Chap. 9)**

Lhote, H. (1958) *The Search for the Tassili frescoes*, trans. A. H. Porodrick (London: Hutchinson). **(Chap. 23)**

Lhote, H. (1966) 'La route des chars de guerre libyens, Tripoli–Gao', *Archéologia*, 9, pp. 28–35. **(Chap. 24)**

Lhote, H. (1970) 'Les gravures rupestres du Sud Oranais', *MCRAPE*, XVI, 208pp. **(Chap. 22)**

Lhote, H. (1976) *Vers d'autres Tassili: nouvelles découvertes au Sahara* (Paris: Arthaud). **(Chap. 26)**

Lhote, H. and Kelley, H. (1936) 'Gisement acheuléen de l'Erg d'Admer (Tassili des Ajjers)', *JSA*, 6, pp. 217–26. **(Chap. 23)**

Libby, W. F. (1955) *Radiocarbon Dating*, 2nd edn (Chicago: University of Chicago Press). **(Chaps 9, 28)**

Libby, W. F. (1970) 'Radiocarbon dating', *Phil. Trans. Roy. Soc.*, Vol. A, 269, no. 1193, pp. 1–10.

Libra, L. (1963) 'I Cinesi e l'Africa orientale', *Africa*, 18. **(Chap. 5)**

Lichtenstein, H. (1811) *Reisen in südlichen Afrika, in den jahren 1803, 1804, 1805 und 1806*, 2 Vols (Berlin: Salfeld). **(Chaps 6, 12)**

Linares de Sapir, O. (1971) 'Shell Middens of Lower Casamance and problems of Diola protohistory', *WAJA*, 1, pp. 23–54. **(Chap. 24)**

Linington, R. E. (1970) 'Techniques used in archaeological field surveys', *Phil. Trans. Roy. Soc.*, Vol. A, 269, no. 1193, pp. 89–108. **(Chap. 9)**

Livingstone, D. (1957) *Missionary Travels and Researches in South Africa* (London: Murray). **(Chap. 6)**

Livingstone, D. A. (1967) *Postglacial Vegetation of the Ruwenzori Mountains in Equatorial Africa* (Durham, NC). **(Chap. 16)**

Livingstone, F. B. (1958) 'Anthropological implications of sickle cell gene distribution in West Africa', *AA*, 60, 3, pp. 533–62. **(Chap. 24)**

Lo, A. (1934) *Bindoum Cholofol ti arab toubab* (St Louis). **(Chap. 10)**

Lods, A. (1950) *Les Prophètes d'Israël et les débuts du Judaïsme* (Paris). **(Chap. 5)**

Lofgren, O. (1936–50) *Arabische Texte zur Kenntnis der Stadt Aden im Mittelalter*, 3 vols (Leipzig–Uppsala). **(Chap. 6)**

Lombard, J. (1935) 'Quelques remarques sur le Quaternaire de l'Afrique tropicale équatoriale', *JSA*, V, pp. 175–80. **(Chap. 21)**

Lovejoy, P. E. (1979) *Indigenous African Slavery* (Studies Conference, University of Waterloo, Ontario)

Lucas, A. (1962) *Ancient Egyptian materials and industries*, 4th edn, revised and enlarged by J. R. Harris (London: Arnold) **(Chaps 9, 28)**

.**Lucas, Sir C. P.** (1887–1923) *Historical Geography of the British Colonies*, 15 Vols. **(Chap. 1)**

Lucas, J. O. (1938) 'Der hamitische Gehalt der Tschadchamistischen Sprachen', *ZES*, 28, pp. 286–99. **(Chap. 12)**

Lucas, J. O. (1948) *The Religion of the Yorubas in Relation to the Religion of Ancient Egypt* (Lagos: CMS Bookshop). **(Chap. 24)**

Lucas, S. A. (1967) *L'Etat traditionnel luba*, pt. 2: *Mythe et structure politique luba – Problèmes sociaux Congolais* (Kinshasa). **(Chap. 7)**

Ludolf, H. (1681) *Historia Aethiopica* (Frankfurt). **(Chap. 16)**

Lukas, J. (1936) 'The linguistic situation in the Lake Chad area of central Africa', *Africa*, 9, pp. 332–49. **(Chap. 10)**

Lynch, H. R. (1967) *Edward Wilmot Blyden: Pan-Negro Patriot, 1832–1912* (London: Oxford University Press). **(Chap. 6)**

Macaulay, T. B. (1971) 'Minute on Indian education of February 2, 1835', in P. D. Curtin (ed.), *Imperialism* (New York: Harper & Row). **(Chap. 3)**

McBurney, C. B. M. (1967) *The Haua Fteah (Cyrenaica) and the Stone Age of South East Mediterranean* (Cambridge: Cambridge University Press). **(Chap. 24)**

McBurney, C. B. M. and Hey, R. W. (1955) *Prehistory and Pleistocene Geology in Cyrenaican Libya* (Cambridge: Cambridge University Press). **(Chap. 23)**

McCall, D. F. (1964) *Africa in Time-Perspective* (Boston: Boston University Press). **(Chap. 15)**

MacGaffey, W. (1974) 'Oral tradition in central Africa', *IJAHS*, VII, pp. 417–26. **(Chap. 8)**

MacGregor, J. K. (1909) 'Some notes on Nsibidi', *JRAI*, 39, pp. 215, 217, 219. **(Chap. 10)**

McIntyre, A *et al.* (1974) 'The Climap 1700 years BP North Atlantic map', *CLIMAP*, pp. 41–7.

McIntyre, A. *et al.* (1975) 'Thermal and oceanic structures of the Atlantic through a glacial – interglacial cycle', *Proceedings of the WMO/IAMAP Symposium on long-term climatic fluctuations, Norwich*, no. 421, pp. 75–80.

MacMichael H. A. (1922) *A History of the Arabs in the Sudan*, Vol. II (Cambridge). **(Chap. 6)**

MacNeish, R. S. (1964) 'Ancient mesoamerican civilisation', *Science*, 143. **(Chap. 27)**

Maes, E. (1924) 'Notes sur les pierres taillées de Tundidarou', *BCEHS*, pp. 31–8. **(Chap. 24)**

Mahabava, J. (1922) *The Colour Bar in South Africa* (Lovedale). **(Chap. 6)**

Maitre, J. P. (1971) 'Contribution à la préhistoire de l'Ahaggar. I, Tefedest central', *MCRAPE*, XVII. **(Chap. 23)**

Malcolm X (1967) *On Afro-American History* (New York: Merit Publishers). **(Introd.)**

Maley, J. (1973) 'Mécanisme des changements climatiques aux basses latitudes', *PPP*, 14, pp. 193–227. **(Chap. 16)**

Mallams, Hassan, Shuaibu (1952) *A Chronicle of Abuja*, trs. F. L. Heath (Ibadan). **(Chap. 6)**

Malowist, M. (1969) *Europa i Afryka Zachodnia w dobie wczesnej ekspansji kolonialnej* (Warsaw: Państwowe Wydawnictwo Naukowe). **(Introd.)**

Manessy, G. (1971) 'Les langues Gurma', *BIFAN*. **(Chap. 11)**

Manso, P. (1877) *Historia da Congo, Documentos* (Lisbon). **(Chap. 6)**

Mantran, R. (1964) *Inventaire des documents turcs du Dar-el-Bey, Tunis.* (Paris: PUF). **(Chap. 6)**

Maquet, J. J. (1961) 'Une hypothèse pour l'étude des féodalités africaines', *CEA*, 6, 11, pp. 292–314. **(Chap. 15)**

Maquet, J. J. (1970) *Pouvoir et société en Afrique* (Paris: Hachette). **(Concl.)**

Maret, P. de (1977a) 'Premières datations pour les haches polies associées à la céramique au Bas-Zaïre', *Actes IX Congr. UISPP.*

Maret, P. de (1977b) 'Bribes, débris et bricolage', *Coll. CNRS, L'expansion Bantu* **(Chap. 21)**

Maret, P. de, Noten, F. van and Cahen, D. (1977) 'Radiocarbon dates from central Africa: a synthesis', *JAH*, XXVIII, 4. **(Chap. 21)**

Marin, P. (1972) 'Classification formelle automatique et industries lithiques. Interpretation des hachereaux de la Kanoa', *AMRAC*, 76. **(Chap. 21)**

Marin, P and Moeyersons, J. (1977) 'Subsurface movements of stone artefacts and their implications for the prehistory of Central Africa', *Nature*, 256, pp. 812–5. **(Chap. 21)**

Marin, P. and Mortelmans, G. (1973) 'Un site tshitolien sur le plateau des Bateke (Republique de Zaïre)', *AMRAC*, 81. **(Chap. 21)**

Marliac, A. (1973) 'Prospection archéologique au Cameroun', *CORSTOM*, X, pp. 47–114. **(Chap. 21)**

Marrou, H. L. (1954) *De la connaissance historique* (Paris: Seuil). **(Introd., Chaps 5, 6)**

Martin, B. G. (1969). 'Kanem, Bornu and the Fazzan; notes on the political history of a trade route', *JAH*, 1, pp. 15–27. **(Introd.)**

Martin, B. G. (1969) 'Mai Idris of Bornu and the Ottoman Turks, 1576–8', in S. M. Stein (ed). *Documents from Islamic Chanceries, Series 2* (Oxford). **(Chaps 5, 6)**

Martin, D. and Yannopoulos, T. (1973) *Guide de recherches – l'Afrique noire* (Paris: Colin). **(Chap. 15)**

Martin del Molino, A.(1963) 'Secuencia cultural en el Neolitico de Fernando Poo', *Trabajoz de prehistoria, seminaria de historia primitiva, del hombre de la universidad de Madrid*, XVII. **(Chaps 21, 24)**

Martins, R. (1976) 'A estaçào arqueológica da antiga Banza Quibaxe', *Contribucoes para o estudo da anthropologia portuguese* (Coimbra), IX, 4, pp. 242–306. **(Chap. 21)**

Marty, P. (1927) *Les chroniques de Oualata et de Nema* (Paris: Geuthner). **(Chap. 6)**

Marx, K. (1972) *Contribution à la critique de l'économie politique* (Paris: Editions sociales). **(Concl.)**

Marx, K. and Engels, F. (1952) *Formen* (Berlin: Dietz). **(Concl.)**

Marx, K. and Engels, F. (1968) *L'Idéologie allemande* (Paris: Editions sociales). **(Concl.)**

Masatoshi, N. and Roy Coudhury, A. R. (1974) 'Genetic variation within and between the three major races of man', *AJHG*, 26, 421. **(Chap. 11)**

Mas-Latrie, L. (1866) Traités de paix et de commerce et documents divers concernant les relations des chrétiens avec les arabes d'Afrique septentrionale au moyen-âge; Supplément, 1872 (Paris). **(Chap. 5)**

Mason, R. J. (1962) *Prehistory of the Transvaal* (Johannesburg: Witwatersrand University Press). **(Chap. 20)**

Massaquoi, M. (1911) 'The Vaî people and their syllabic writing', *JAS*, pp. 10–40. **(Introd.)**

Massoulard, E. (1949) 'Préhistoire et protohistoire d'Egypte', *TMIE*, 111. **(Chap. 28)**

Mateus, A. de (1952) 'Nota preliminar acerca da estaçào prehistórica de Nhampasseré', *CRCIAO*, IV, pp. 375–86. **(Chap. 24)**

Mauny, R. (1947) 'Une route préhistorique à travers le Sahara', *BIFAN*, 9, pp. 341–57. **(Chap. 24)**

Mauny, R. (1947) 'L'ouest africain chez ptolémée', *Actes de la IIe Conférence Internationale des Africanistes de l'ouest, Bissau*. **(Chap. 5)**

Mauny, R. (1951) 'Un âge de cuivre au Sahara Occidental?', *BIFAN*, 13, 1, pp. 168–80. **(Chap. 24)**

Mauny, R. (1952a) 'Essai sur l'histoire des métaux en Afrique occidentale', *BIFAN*, 14, pp. 545–95. **(Chap. 24)**

Mauny, R. (1952b) *Glossaire des expressions et termes locaux employés dans l'Ouest africain* (Dakar: IFAN). **(Chap. 10)**

Mauny, R. (1955a) 'Contribution à l'étude du Paléolithique de Mauritanie', *Actes II Congr. PPEQ*, pp. 461–79. **(Chap. 24)**

Mauny, R. (1955b) 'Les gisements Néolithiques de Karkarichinkat', *Actes II Congr. PPEQ*, pp. 616–19. **(Chap. 24)**

Mauny, R. (1957) 'Buttes artificielles de coquillages de Joal-Fadioute', *NA*, 7, 75, pp. 73–8. **(Chap. 24)**

Mauny, R. (1960) 'Reviews of Cheikh Anta Diop's "Nations nègres et cultures" and "L'Afrique noire précoloniale"', *BIFAN*, B, 22, pp. 544–5. **(Chap. 24)**

Mauny, R. (1961) *Tableau géographique de l'Ouest africain au Moyen Age, d'après les sources écrites, la tradition orale et l'archéologie* (Dakar: IFAN). **(Chaps 5, 24, 25, 26)**

Mauny, R. (1963) 'Contribution à la préhistoire et la protohistoire de la région de Kédougou (Sénégal oriental)', *BSA*, 5, 11, pp. 113–22. **(Chap. 24)**

Mauny, R. (1965) 'Les problèmes des sources de l'histoire de l'Afrique noire . . .', XIIth International Congress of Historical Studies, Vienna, II: *Rapports*, Histoire des Continents. **(Chap. 5)**

Mauny, R. (1968) 'Commentaires sur "West Africa before the Europeans" par Oliver Davies', *BIFAN*, B, 30, pp. 1283–4. **(Chap. 24)**

Mauny, R. (1970) 'Le périple d'Hannon, un faux célèbre concernant les navigations antiques', *Archéologia*, 37, pp. 78–80. **(Chap. 24)**

Mauny, R. (1971a) *Les Siècles obscurs de l'Afrique noire* (Paris: Payard). **(Chaps 5, 24)**

Mauny, R. (1971b) 'The Western Sudan', in P. L. Shinnie (ed.) *The African Iron Age* (Oxford: Clarendon Press) pp. 66–87. **(Chap. 24)**

Mauny, R. (1973) 'Datation au carbonne 14 d'amas de coquillages des lagunes de Basse Côte d'Ivoire', *WAJA*, 3, pp. 207–14. **(Chap. 24)**

Mauny, R. and Hallemans, J. (1957) 'Préhistoire et protohistoire de la région d'Akjoujt (Mauritanie)', *Acts III PCPQS*, pp. 248–61. **(Chap. 24)**

Mazrui, A. A. (1969) 'European exploration and Africa's self discovery', *JMAS*, 7, 4. **(Chap. 6)**
Mazrui. S. A. (1944) *Tarikh al-Mazari.* Arabic MS. in photostat in the possession of G. S. P. Freeman-Grenville. **(Gen. Introd., Chaps 5, 6)**
Mbiti, J. (1967) 'Afrikaanse begrippen van tijd, geschiedenis en de dood', *Africa*, 21, 3, pp. 78–85. **(Chap. 7)**
Meek, C. K. (1931) *Tribal Studies in Northern Nigeria*, 2 Vols (London: Paul, Trench, Trubner). **(Chap. 10)**
Meillassoux, C. (1972) 'L'itinéraire d'Ibn Battuta de Walata à Mali', *JAH*, 13, 3, pp. 389–95. **(Chap. 24)**
Meillassoux, C. (ed.) (1975) *L'Esclavage en Afrique précoloniale* (Paris: Maspero), 17 studies. **(Concl.)**
Meillassoux, C. (1975) *Femmes, greniers et capitaux* (Paris: Maspero)
Meillassoux, C. (1977) *Terrains et théories* (Paris: Anthropos)
Meinhof, C. (1904) *Linguistische Studien in Ost Africa* (Berlin: MSOS). **(Chap. 10)**
Meinhof, C. (1906) *Grundzüge einer vergleichenden Grammatik der Bantusprachen* (Berlin: Reimer). **(Chap. 10)**
Meinhof, C. (1912) *Die Sprachen der Hamiten* (Hamburg: Friederichsen). **(Chaps 10, 12, 19)**
Meinhof, C. (1919–20) 'Afrikanische Wörtezin Orientalischer Litteratur', *ZES*, 10, pp. 147–52. **(Chap. 12)**
Meinhof, C. (1932) *An Introduction to the Phonology of the Bantu Languages* (Berlin: Reimer). **(Gen. Introd., Chap. 10)**
Meknasi, A. (1953) *Sources et bibliographies d'histoire marocaine du XVI*[e] *à la première moitié du XXe siècle* (Rabat). **(Chap. 6)**
Menghin, O. and Amer, M. (1932 and 1936) *The Excavations of the Egyptian University in the Neolithic site at Maadi. First and Second Preliminary Reports* (Cairo: Misr-Sokkar and Government Press). **(Chap. 25)**
Mercier, P. (1966) *Histoire de l'anthropologie* (Paris: PUF). **(Gen. Introd.)**
Merivale, H. (1861) *Lectures on colonization and colonies* (London: Longman). **(Chap. 1)**
Metcalfe, G. E. (1964) *Great Britain and Ghana; Documents of Ghana History, 1807–1957* (London: Nelson). **(Chap. 6)**
Michael, H. N. and Ralph, E. K. (1970) 'Correction factors applied to Egyptian radiocarbon dates from the era before Christ', *Nobell Symposium 12*, pp. 109–20. **(Chap. 9)**
Migeod, F. W. (1911) *The Languages of West Africa* (London: Paul, Trench, Trubner). **(Chap. 10)**
Miller, J. C. (1976) *Kings and Kinsmen; Early Mbundu States in Angola* (Oxford: Clarendon Press) **(Chap. 8)**
Miller, S. (1972) 'A new look at the Tshitolian', *Africa-Tervuren*, XVIII, 3–4, pp. 86–9. **(Chap. 21)**
Minette de Saint Martin (1914) 'Note sur une collection préhistorique saharienne', *RA*. **(Chap. 23)**
Miquel, A. (1976) *La Géographie humaine du monde musulman jusqu'au milieu du 11e siècle*, 2 Vols (Paris/The Hague: Mouton/De Gruyter). **(Chap. 5)**
Mischlish, A. and Lippert, J. (1903) *Beiträge zur Geschichte der Haussastaaten* (Berlin: MSOS). **(Gen. Introd., Chaps 5, 6)**
Moeyersons, J. (1975) 'Evolution paléogéographique du site de la Kamon', *AMRAC*, 84, pp. 18–46. **(Chap. 21)**
Moeyersons, J. (1977) 'The behaviour of stones and stone implements buried in consolidating and creeping Kalahari sands', *Earth Surface Processes* (Leeds). **(Chap. 21)**
Moffat, R. (1842) *Missionary Labours and Scenes in Southern Africa* (London: Snow). **(Chap. 6)**
Moffat, R. (1945) *The Matabele Journals of Robert Moffat, 1829–1860*, ed. J. P. R. Wallis (London: Chatto & Windus). **(Chap. 6)**
Mohammadou, A. and E. (1971) 'Un nouveau manuscrit arabe sur l'histoire du Mandara', *Revue camerounaise d'histoire*, 1 (October), pp. 130–55.
Mokhtar, H. and Heymowski, A. (1965–6) *Catalogue provisoire des manuscrits mauritaniens en langue arabe préservés en Mauritanie* (Nouakchott/Stockholm). **(Gen. Introd., Chaps 5, 6)**
Molema, S. M. (1920) *The Bantu, past and present* (Edinburgh: Green). **(Chap. 6)**
Moniot, H. (1962) 'Pour une histoire de l'Afrique Noire', *Annales*. **(Chap. 15)**
Moniot, H. (1965) 'Les sources orales dans le problème des sources de l'histoire de l'Afrique noire jusqu'à la colonisation européene', *Rap. 12e CISH*, II, pp. 198–208. **(Chap. 15)**
Monod, T. (1932) 'L'Adrar Ahnet. Contribution à l'étude d'un district saharien', *TMIE*, 19. **(Chap. 23)**
Monod, T. (1932) *Contribution à l'étude archéologique d'un district Saharien* (Paris: Larose). **(Concl.)**
Monod, T. (1945) 'La structure du Sahara atlantique', *Trav. IRS*, 3, pp. 27–55. **(Chap. 23)**
Monod, T. (1951) 'Peintures rupestres du Zernmour français au Sahara occidental'. *BIFAN*, 1.

Monod, T. (1957) 'Découverte de nouveaux instruments en os dans l'Ouest africain', *Acts III PCPQS*, pp. 242–7. **(Chap. 24)**

Monod, T. (1958) 'Majâbât al-Koubrâ. Contribution à l'étude de "l'empty quarter" ouest saharien', *Mém. IFAN*, 52. **(Chap. 23, Concl.)**

Monod, T. (1961) 'The late Tertiary and Pleistocene in the Sahara and adjacent southerly region with implications for primate and human distribution', *Symposium, 15, African ecology and human evolution.* **(Chap. 23)**

Monod, T. (1963) 'The late Tertiary and Pleistocene in the Sahara and adjacent southerly regions', in F. C. Howell and F. Bourlière (eds), *African ecology and human evolution* (New York: Viking Fund Publications in Anthropology). **(Chaps 16, 23)**

Monod, T. (1969) 'Le "Macden Ijäfen": une épave caravanière ancienne dans la Mâjâbat al-Koubrâ', *Actes 1er Coll. Intern. Archéol. Afr.*, pp. 286–320. **(Chap. 24)**

Monod, T. and Mauny, R. (1957) 'Découverte de nouveaux instruments en os dans l'Ouest africain', *Acts III PCPQS*. **(Chap. 24)**

Montagu, M. F. A. (1952) *Man's Most Dangerous Myth – The Fallacy of Race* (New York: Harpers and Brothers.)

Monteil, C. (1929) 'Les empires du Mali', *BCEHS*, 12, pp. 291–447. **(Chap. 1)**

Monteil, V. (1965) 'Les manuscrits historiques arabo-africains', *BIFAN*, B, XXXVII. **(Gen. Introd., Chap. 6)**

Montfrans, H. M. Van (1971) *Palaeomagnetic Dating in the North Sea Basin* (Rotterdam: Prince NV). **(Chap. 16)**

Moodie, D. (ed.) (1960) *The Record; or A Series of Official Papers Relative to the Conditions and Treatment of the Native Tribes of South Africa* (Amsterdam: Balkema). **(Chap. 6)**

Moorsel, H. van (1959) *Esquisse préhistorique de Léopoldville* (Léopoldville: Musée de la vie indigène). **(Concl.)**

Moorsel, H. van (1968) *Atlas de préhistoire de la plaine de Kinshasa* (Kinshasa: Publications université Lovanium). **(Chap. 21)**

More, B. (1969) 'Contribution du Libéria à la science de la communication par écrit', *Symposium du festival panafricain d'Alger.* **(Introd.)**

Moreau, R. E. (1963) 'Vicissitudes of the African Biomas in the late Pleistocene', *Proceedings of the Zoological Society of London*, 141, pp. 395–421. **(Chap. 24)**

Morel, J. (1953) 'Le capsien du Kahnguet el Mouhaâd', *Libyca*, 1, pp. 103–19. **(Chap. 22)**

Moreno, M. (1940) *Manuale di Sidamo* (Rome: Mondadori). **(Chap. 10)**

Moret, A. (1931) *Histoire de l'Orient* (Paris: Les Presses Universitaires de France) 2nd edn. 1950. **(Concl.)**

Morgan, E. (1973) *La Fin du Surmâle* (Paris: Calmann-Lévy), trans. G. Fradier, *The Descent of Woman* (New York: Stein and Day; London: Souvenir Press) **(Concl.)**

Morgan, W. B. and Pugh, J. C. (1969) *West Africa* (London: Methuen). **(Chap. 14)**

Mori, F. (1965) *Tadrart Acacus: Arte rupestre e culture del Sahara preistorico* (Turin: Einaudi). **(Chaps 23, 24)**

Moritz, B. (1892) *Sammlung arabischer Schriftstücke aus Zanzibar und Oman, mit einem Glossar* (Stuttgart: Spemann). **(Gen. Introd., Chaps 5, 6)**

Morner, N. A. (1973) 'Climatic changes during the last 35,000 years as indicated by land, sea, and air data', *Boreas*, 2, pp. 33–53. **(Chap. 16)**

Morner, N. A. (1975) 'Eustatic amplitude variations and world glacial changes', *Geology*, 3, pp. 109–10. **(Chap. 16)**

Morrison, R. B. and Wright, H. E. J. (eds) (1968) 'Means of correlation of Quaternary successions', *Proc. VII Congr. INQUA*, 8. **(Chap. 16)**

Mortelmans, G. (1952a) 'Les dessins rupestres gravés, ponctués et peints du Katanga, Essai de synthèse', *AMRCB*, pp. 33–55. **(Chap. 21)**

Mortelmans, G. (1952b) *Contribution à l'étude des cultures pre-Abbevilliennes à galets taillés du Katanga: le site Mulundwa 1* (Brussels: Publications de la Société Royale Belge d'anthropologie et de préhistoire). **(Chap. 21)**

Mortelmans, G. (1952c) 'Les industries à galets taillés (Pebble Culture) du Katanga', *Actes II Congr. PPEQ*, pp. 295–8. **(Chap. 21)**

Mortelmans, G. (1953a) 'La Pebble Culture africaine, source des civilisations de la pierre', *BSRBAP*, LXV. **(Chap. 21)**

Mortelmans, G. (1953b) 'Vue d'ensemble sur le Quaternaire du bassin du Congo', *Actes III Congr. UISPP*, pp. 114–26. **(Chap. 21)**

Mortelmans, G. (1957a) 'Le Cennozoïque du Congo Belge', *Acts III PCPQS*, pp. 23–50. **(Chap. 21)**

Mortelmans, G. (1957b) *La préhistoire du Congo Belge* (Brussels: Revue de l'Université de Bruxelles). **(Chap. 21)**

Mortelmans, G. (1957c) 'The early Pebble Culture of Katanga', *Acts III PCPQS*, pp. 214–16. **(Chap. 21)**

Mortelmans, G. (1959) 'Préhistoire et protohistoire du Bas-Congo Belge, une esquisse', *Volume de Homenagem ao Prof. Doutor Mendes Corrêa* (Porto: Sociedade Portuguesa Anthropologia e Ethnologia), pp. 329–44. **(Chap. 21)**

Mortelmans, G. (1962) 'Vue d'ensemble sur la préhistoire du Congo occidental', *Actes IV Congr. PPEQ*, pp. 129–64. **(Chap. 21)**

Mortelmans, G. and Monteyne, R. (1962) 'Le Quaternaire du Congo occidental et sa chronologie', *Actes IV Congr. PPEQ*, pp. 97–132. **(Chap. 21)**

Moscati, S. (1964) *An Introduction to the Comparative Grammar of the Semitic Languages* (Wiesbaden: Harrassowitz). **(Chap. 10)**

Mukarovsky, H. G. (1966) 'Ueber die Stellung der Mandesprachen', *Anthropos*, 61, pp. 679–88. **(Chap. 12)**

Muller, D. K. (1923) *Die Geschichte der erstern Hottentotenmission 1737–1744* (Herrnhut). **(Chap. 6)**

Muller, F. (1853) *Geographi Graeci Minores* (Paris). **(Chap. 5)**

Muller, F. (1863) *Die Musik-sprache in Zentral Africa* (Vienna). **(Chap. 10)**

Muller, F. (1867) *Reise der österreichischen Fregate 'Novara' um die Erde in den Jahren 1857, 1858, 1859. Linguistischer Teil* (Vienna: Staatsdruckerei). **(Chap. 12)**

Muller, F. (1876–84) *Grundriss der Sprachwissenschaft*, 4 Vols (Vienna: Hölder). **(Chap. 12)**

Munson, P. J. (1968) 'Recent archaeological research in the Dhar Tichitt region of south-central Mauretania', *WAAN*, 10, pp. 6–13. **(Chaps 23, 24)**

Munson, P. J. (1970) 'Corrections and additional comments concerning the "Tichitt Tradition"', *WAAN*, 12, pp. 47–8. **(Chap. 24)**

Murdock, G. P. (1959) *Africa: Its Peoples and their Culture History* (New York: McGraw Hill). **(Introd., Chaps 3, 10, 12)**

Murray, G. W. (1920) 'The Nilotic languages, a comparative essay', *JRAI*. **(Chap. 10)**

al-Murshidi, Hamid bin Al-Hasan b. Hamid Bá Fajin (1937) *A History of the Walis of Lamu* (Arabic text with draft trans.). **(Gen. Introd., Chaps 5, 6)**

Muzur, A. and Nosek, E. (1974) 'Metal examination of iron objects from Niani', *AATA*, 11, 1. **(Chap. 9)**

Myint Hla, U. (1964) *The Economics of the Developing Countries* (London: Hutchinson). **(Chap. 3)**

Nachtigal, G. (1879–89) *Sahara und Sudan* (Berlin, Leipzig). **(Chap. 1)**

National Academy of Sciences, Washington, DC (1975) 'Understanding climatic change. A program for action', *United States Committee for the Global Atmospheric Research Program* (Washington). **(Chap. 16)**

Nei Masatoshi and Roy Coudhury, A. R. (1974) 'Genetic variation within and between the three major races of man', *AJHG*, 26. **(Chaps 10, 11)**

Nenquin, J. (n.d.) *Inventaria archaeologica africana* (Belgium: Tervuren). **(Concl.)**

Nenquin, J. (1957–8) 'Opgravingen te Sanga' (Fouilles à Sanga), *Gentse Bijdragen tot de Kunstgeschiedenis er de Oudheidkunde*, XVIII, pp. 289–311. **(Chap. 21)**

Nenquin, J. (1963) *Excavations at Sanga, 1957: The Protohistoric Necropolis* (Belgium: Tervuren). **(Chap. 21)**

Nenquin, J. (1967) 'Contribution to the study of the prehistoric cultures of Rwanda and Burundi', *AMRAC*, 59. **(Chaps 19, 21)**

Newbury, C. W. (1965) *British Policy towards West Africa; Select Documents, 1786–1874* (Oxford: Clarendon Press). **(Chap. 6)**

Newbury, P. E. (1899) *The Amherst Papyri* (London). **(Chap. 5)**

Newman, P. and Ma, R. (1966) 'Comparative Chadic: phonology and lexicon', *JAL*, 5, 3, pp. 218–51. **(Chaps 10, 12)**

Newton, A. P. (1922–3) 'Africa and historical research', *J. Afr. Soc.*, 22 **(Chap. 1)**

Niane, D. T. (1960a) 'Recherches sur l'Empire du Mali', *Etudes africaines* (Conakry). **(Chap. 7)**

Niane, D. T. (1960b) *Soundjata; ou, L'épopée mandingue* (Paris: Présence africaine). **(Chaps 3, 7)**

Niane, D. T. (1970) 'Notes sur les fouilles de Niani, ancienne capitale du Mali', *WAAN*, 12, pp. 43–6. **(Chap. 24)**

Nielsen, O. V. (1970) *Human Remains: Scandinavian Joint Expedition to Sudanese Nubia*, Vol. 9 (Stockholm: Scandinavian University Books) **(Chap. 28)**

Nilsson, E. (1931) 'Quaternary glaciations and pluvial lakes, in British East Africa', *GA*, 13, pp. 249–349. **(Chap. 16)**

Nilsson, E. (1940) 'Ancient changes of climate in British East Africa and Abyssinia: a study of ancient lakes and glaciers', *GA*, XXII, 1–2, pp. 1–79. **(Chaps 16, 21)**
Nilsson, E. (1949) 'The pluvials of East Africa: an attempt to correlate pleistocene changes of climate', *GA*, XXXI, 1–4, pp. 204–11. **(Chap. 21)**
Nilsson, E. (1952) 'Pleistocene climatic changes in East Africa', *Proc. II PCPQS*, pp. 45–55. **(Chap. 24)**
Nketia, J. H. (1975) *History and the Organisation of Music in West Africa* (Legon: University of Ghana, Institute of African Studies). **(Gen. Introd.)**
Nordström, H. A. (1972) *Neolithic and A-group sites: Scandinavian Joint Expedition to Sudanese Nubia*, Vol. 3 (Uppsala: Scandinavian University Books). **(Chaps 25, 28)**
Norris, E. (1841) *Outline of a Vocabulary of a Few of the Principal Languages of Western and Central Africa* (London: Parker). **(Chap. 12)**
Norris, T. H. (1968) *Shinqiti Folk Literature and Songs* (Oxford). **(Chap. 6)**
Noten, F. van (1968a) 'Note sur l'âge de la pierre récente dans la région des lacs Mokoto (Kivu, Congo)', *BSRBAP*, 79, pp. 91–101. **(Chap. 21)**
Noten, F. van (1968b) *The Uelian. A culture with a neolithic aspect, Uele-Basin (N.E. Congo Republic)* (Tervuren: Musée royal de l'Afrique centrale). **(Chap. 21)**
Noten, F. van (1969) 'A ground axe from Burundi', *Azania*, IV, p. 166. **(Chap. 21)**
Noten, F. van (1971) 'Excavation at Nunuama cave', *Antiquity*, XLV, 177, pp. 56–8. **(Chap. 21)**
Noten, F. van (1973) 'Mystificatic en archeologie in Noord-Zaïre (Mystification et Archéologie au N. Zaïre)' *Africa-Tervuren*, XIX, 4, pp. 97–102. **(Chap. 21)**
Noten, F. van and E. (1974) 'Het Ijzersmelten bij de Madi (La fonte du fer chez les Madi)', *Africa-Tervuren*, XX, 3–4, pp. 57–66. **(Chap. 21)**
Noten, F. van (1977) 'Excavations at Matupi cave', *Antiquity*, LI, 201, pp. 35–40. **(Chap. 21)**
Noten, F. van (1978) 'The early iron age in the interlacustrine region', *JAH*, XIX, 1. **(Chap. 21)**
Noten, F. van, Cahen, D., Maret, J. de, Moeyersons, J. and Roche, E. (in press) *The Archaeology of Central Africa* (Graz: Akademische Druck-u. Verlagsanstalt). **(Chap. 21)**
Noten, F. van and Hiernaux, J. (1967) 'The Late Stone Age industry of Mukinanira, Rwanda', *SAAB*, 22, IV, pp. 151–4. **(Chap. 21)**

Oakley, K. P. (1961) *Man the Tool-maker*, 5th edn, British Natural History Museum. **(Chap. 19)**
Obenga, T. (1970) 'Méthodologie en histoire africaine: sources locales', *Africa*, XXV. **(Gen. Introd.)**
Obenga, T. (1973) *L'Afrique dans l'antiquité – Egypte Pharaonique – Afrique noire* (Paris: Présence africaine). **(Chap. 10)**
O'Brien, T. P. (1939) *The Prehistory of Uganda Protectorate* (Cambridge: Cambridge University Press). **(Chap. 21)**
Olabiyal, J. (1968) *Remarques sur l'état actuel des recherches linguistiques au Dahomey* (Paris: Présence africaine). **(Chap. 10)**
Olderogge, D. (1966) 'Ecritures méconnues de l'Afrique noire', *Le Courrier* (Unesco). **(Chap. 10)**
Olderogge, D. (1971) 'Astrakhanee v Tombuktu v 1821g' (A man from Astrakhan in Timbuktu in 1821), *Afrikana/Afrikankiy etnograficheskiy sbornik*, VII (Leningrad). **(Chap. 6)**
Olderogge, D. and Potekin, I (1954) *Les Peuples de l'Afrique* (Moscow). **(Gen. Introd.)**
Oliver, R. (1966) 'The problem of the Bantu expansion'. *JAH*, 7, 3. **(Chap. 12)**
Oliver, R. (1973) 'African studies in London, 1963–1973', *Proc. III Intern. WAC* (unpublished paper). **(Chap. 3)**
Olsson, I. U. (1973) 'The radiocarbon dating of Ivory Coast shell mounds', *WAJA*, 3, pp. 215–20. **(Chap. 24)**
Onde, H. (1963) 'La géographie régionale et le monde africain', *Genève-Afrique*, II, 2, pp. 149–62. **(Chap. 4)**
Organ, R. M. (1968) *Design for Scientific Conservation of Antiquities* (London: Butterworth). **Chap. 9)**
Orhonlu, C. (1972) 'Turkish archival sources about Ethiopia', *Proc. 4th ICES*. **(Gen. Introd., Chaps 5, 6)**
Orlova, A. S. (1967) *Histoire de l'Afrique au XIXe siècle et au début du XXe siècle* (Moscow: Institut d'Afr. de l'URSS). **(Gen. Introd.)**
Oussedik, O. (1972) 'Les bifaces acheuliens de l'Erg Tihodaïne: analyse typométrique', *Libyca*, 20. **(Chap. 22)**
Ozanne, P. (1964) 'Notes on the later prehistory of Accra', *JHSN*, 3, 1, pp. 3–23. **(Chap. 24)**
Ozanne, P. (1966) 'The Anglo-Gambian stone circles expedition', *WAAN*, 4, pp. 8–18. **(Chap. 24)**

Ozanne, P. (1969a) 'The diffusion of smoking in West Africa', *Odu*, n.s., 2, pp. 29–42. **(Chap. 24)**
Ozanne, P. (1969b) 'A new archaeological survey of Ife', *Odu*, 3, 1, pp. 28–45. **(Chap. 24)**
Ozanne, P. (1971) 'Ghana', in P. L. Shinnie, *The African Iron Age* (Oxford: Clarendon Press), pp. 36–65. **(Chap. 24)**

Padmore, G. (1961) *Panafricanisme ou Communisme?* (Paris: Présence africaine). **(Gen. Introd.)**
Pager, H. L. (1971) *Ndedema* (Graz: Akademische Druck).
Pager, H. (1975) *Stone Age and Magic* (Graz: Akademische Druck).
Palmer, H. R. (1928) *Sudanese Memoirs*, 3 Vols (Lagos: Government printer). **(Chaps 1, 5, 6)**
Palmer, H. R. (1929) *History of the First Twelve Years of the Reign of Mai Idris Alooma* (Lagos). **(Chap. 6)**
Palmer, H. R. (1936) *The Bornu, Sahara and Sudan* (London). **(Chap. 6)**
Pankhurst, R. K. P. (ed.) (1966) *The Ethiopian Royal Chronicles* (Addis Ababa: Oxford University Press). **(Chap. 6)**
Parenko, P., Parenko, R. P. and Hebert, J. (1962) 'Une famille ethnique; les Gan, les Padoro, les Dorobe, les Komono', *BIFAN*, B, I, XXIV, pp. 3, 4 and 6. **(Chap. 15)**
Parkington, J. and Poggenpoel, C. (1970) 'Excavations at De Hangen, 1968', *SAAB*, XXVI, pp. 3–36. **(Chap. 20)**
Patterson, J. R. (1926) *Kanuri Songs* (Lagos: Government printer). **(Chap. 6)**
Paulme, D. (1956a) *Les Sculptures de l'Afrique Noire* (Paris: PUF). **(Gen. Introd.)**
Paulme, D. (1956b) *Parures africaines* (Paris: Hachette). **(Gen. Introd.)**
Paulme, D. (1960) *Les Civilisations africaines* (Paris: PUF). **(Gen. Introd.)**
Payddoke, E. (1963) *The Scientist and Archaeology* (London: Phoenix House). **(Chap. 9)**
Pédelaborde, P. (1970) *Les Moussons* (Paris: Colin). **(Chap. 16)**
Peet (1920) *The Mayer Papyri* (London). **(Chap. 5)**
Peet (1930) *The Great Tomb-Robberies of the Twentieth Egyptian Dynasty*, 2 vols (Oxford). **(Chap. 5)**
Pelletier, A. and Goblot, J.-J. (1973) *Materialisme historique et histoire des civilisations* (Paris: Editions sociales) 2nd edn. **(Concl.)**
Pender Cutlip, P. (1972) 'Oral traditions and anthropological analysis: some contemporary myths', *Azania*, VII, pp. 3–24. **(Chap. 8)**
Pender Cutlip, P. (1973) 'Encyclopedic informants and early interlacustrine history', *IJAHS*, VI, pp. 468–79. **(Chap. 8)**
Perlman, I. and Isaro, F. (1969) 'Pottery analysis by neutron activation', *Archaeometry*, 11, pp. 21–52. **(Chap. 8)**
Perret, R. (1937) 'Une carte des gravures rupestres et des peintures à l'ocre de l'Afrique du Nord', *JSA*, VII, 71, pp. 107–23. **(Chaps 8, 23)**
Perrot, C. (1974) 'Ano Aseman: mythe et histoire', *JAH*, XV, pp. 199–212. **(Chap. 8)**
Person, Y. (1962) 'Tradition orale et chronologie', *CEA*, 7, II, p. 3. **(Chap. 7)**
Person, Y. (1963) 'Classe d'âges et chronologie', *Latitudes*, special no. **(Chap. 15)**
Person, Y. (1968–70) *Samori. Une révolution dyula*, 3 Vols (Dakar: IFAN). **(Chap. 3)**
Petrie, W. M. F. (1901) *The Royal Tombs of the First Dynasty* (London). **(Chaps 9, 28)**
Petrie, W. M. F. (1920) *Prehistoric Egypt* (London: British School of Archaeology in Egypt). **(Chaps 23, 28)**
Petrie, W. M. F. (1921) *Corpus of Prehistoric Pottery and Palettes* (London: British School of Archaeology in Egypt). **(Chap. 23)**
Petrie, W. M. F. (1939) *The Making of Egypt* (London: The Sheldon Press; New York: Macmillan). **(Chaps 25, 28)**
Petrie, W. M. F. (1953) 'Ceremonial slate palettes', *BSAE*, LXVI. **(Chaps 25, 28)**
Petrie, W. M. F., Mackay, E. and Wainwright, G. (1912) *The Labyrinth, Gerzeh and Mazghuneh* (London: School of Archaeology in Egypt). **(Chap. 28)**
Peyrouton, M. (1966) *Histoire générale du Maghreb* (Paris: Michel). **(Gen. Introd.)**
Philips, J. (1828) *Researches in South Africa*, 2 Vols (London). **(Chap. 6)**
Phillipson, D. W. (1976) 'The early iron age in eastern and southern Africa: a critical re-appraisal', *Azania*, XI, pp. 1–23. **(Chap. 21)**
Pias, J. (1967) 'Chronologie du dépôt des sédiments tertiaires et quaternaires dans la cuvette tchadienne', *CRAS*, 264, pp. 2432–5. **(Chap. 24)**
Picard, G. C. (1971) 'Le Périple d'Hannon n'est pas un faux', *Archéologia*, 40, pp. 54–9. **(Chap. 24)**
Pigafetta, F. and Lopez, D. (1965) *Description du royaume de Congo et des contrées environnantes* (Rome, 1591), trans. and annot. by Willy Bal (Louvain: Nauwelaerts). **(Chaps 1, 4)**
Piotrovsky, B. (1967) 'The early dynasty settlement of Khor-Daoud', *Campagne internationale de*

l'Unesco pour la sauvegarde des monuments de la Nubie (Cairo: Service des antiquités de l'Egypte). **(Chap. 25)**

Pirenne, J. (1932) *Histoire des Institutions et du droit privé de l'ancienne Egypte* (Brussels: Fondation égyptologique Reine Elisabeth). **(Chap. 28)**

Piveteau, J. (1973) *Origine et destinée de l'homme* (Paris: Masson). **(Chap. 18)**

Plaatje, S. T. (1916) *Native Life in South Africa before and since the European War and the Boer Rebellion* (London: King). **(Chap. 6)**

Plaatje, S. T. (1930) *Mhudi: an epic of South Africa native life a hundred years ago* (South Africa: Lovedale). **(Chap. 6)**

Plenderleith, H. J. (1962) *The Conservation of Antiquities and Works of Art; Treatment, Repair, and Restoration* (London: Oxford University Press). **(Chap. 9)**

Ploey, J. De (1963) 'Quelques indices sur l'évolution morphologique et paléoclimatique des environs du Stanley-Pool (Congo)', *Studia universitatis Lovanium*, 17. **(Chap. 21)**

Ploey, J. De (1965) 'Position géomorphologique, génèse et chronologie de certains dépôts superficiels au Congo Occidental', *Quaternaria*, VII, pp. 131–54. **(Chap. 21)**

Ploey, J. De (1968) 'Quaternary phenomena in the western Congo', *Proc. VII Congr. INQUA*, 8, pp. 500–18. **(Chap. 21)**

Ploey, J. De (1969) 'Report on the Quaternary of the western Congo', *Palaeoecology of Africa, the surrounding islands and Antarctica*, IV, pp. 65–8. **(Chap. 21)**

Poirier, J. (1969) *Histoire de l'ethnologie* (Paris: PUF). **(Gen. Introd.)**

Polotsky, H. (1964) *Egyptians at the Dawn of Civilisation*, in The World History of the Jewish People, Series I. **(Chap. 10)**

Pommeret, Y. (1965) 'Notes préliminaires à propos du gisement lupembien et néolithique de Nodjobé', *Mém. SPPG*, II. **(Chap. 21)**

Pommeret, Y. (1966a) 'Principaux types d'outils de tradition forestière (Sangoen-lupembien-tchitolien) découverts à Libreville', *BSPPG*, II, 4, pp. 29–47. **(Chap. 21)**

Pommeret, Y. (1966b) 'Les outils polis au Gabon', *BSPPG*, II, 6, pp. 163–79. **(Chap. 21)**

Pond, W. P. *et al* (1938) *Prehistoric habitation sites in the Sahara and North Africa* (Logan Museum Beloit College: Wisconsin), pp. 17–21. **(Chap. 23)**

Porter, B. and Moss, R. L. B. (1927) *Topographical Bibliography of Ancient Egyptian Hieroglyphic Texts, Reliefs and Paintings* (Oxford: Clarendon Press). **(Chap. 28)**

Portères, R. (1950) 'Vieilles agricultures de l'Afrique intertropicale', *AT*, pp. 9–10. **(Chap. 27)**

Portères, R. (1951a) 'Géographie alimentaire, berceaux agricoles et migrations des plantes cultivées en Afrique intertropicale', *CRSB*, pp. 239–40. **(Chap. 27)**

Portères, R. (1951b) '*Eleusine coracana Gaertner*', céréale des humanités pauvres des pays tropicaux', *BIFAN*, 23, pp. 1–78. **(Chap. 24)**

Portères, R. (1958) 'Les appellations des céréales en Afrique', *Journal d'Agriculture Tropicale et de Botanique Appliquée*, 5. **(Chap. 24)**

Portères, R. (1960) 'La monnaie de fer dans l'Ouest africain au XIXe siècle', *Recherche africaine*, 4. **(Chap. 15)**

Portères, R. (1962) 'Berceaux agricoles primaires sur le continent africaine', *JAH*, 3, 2, pp. 195–210. **(Chaps 14, 24, 27)**

Portères, R. (1972). 'Le millet coracan ou Finger Millet', *Proc. Burg Wart. Symp. 56*. **(Chap. 24)**

Posener, G. (1934) Catalogue des ostraca liératiques littéraires de Deir el-Médineh (Cairo). **(Chap. 5)**

Posener, G. (1940) *Princes et pays d'Asie et de Nubie* (Brussels: Fondation égyptologique Reine Elisabeth). **(Chap. 28)**

Posener, G. (1951) *RE* VI, pp. 27–48. **(Chap. 5)**

Posener, G. (1960) 'De la divinité de Pharaon', *CSA*, 15. **(Chap. 28)**

Posener, G., Sauneron, S. and Yoyotte, J. (1959) *Dictionnaire de la Civilisation Egyptienne* (Paris: Hazan), trans. *A Dictionary of Egyptian Civilisation*, A. Macfarlane (London: Methuen). **(Chap. 28)**

Posnansky, M. (1969) 'The prehistory of East Africa', in B. A. Ogot and J. A. Kieran (eds), *Zamani, A Survey of East Africa* (Nairobi/London: Longman) pp. 49–68. **(Chap. 19)**

Posnansky, M. (1971) 'Ghana and the origins of West African trade', *Africa Quarterly*, II, pp. 110–25. **(Chap. 24)**

Présence africaine (1971) *Perspectives nouvelles sur l'histoire africaine* (Paris). **(Chap. 5)**

Priddy, A. J. (1970) 'An iron age site near Yelwa, Sokoto Province: preliminary report', *WAAN*, 12, pp. 20–32. **(Chap. 24)**

Prins, A. H. J. (1953) *East African Age-Class Systems* (Groningen: Wolters). **(Chap. 15)**

Prins, A. H. J. (1958) 'On Swahili historiography', *JEASC*, LXXVIII, 2. **(Chaps 5, 6)**

Pritchard, J. C. (1855) *The Natural History of Man*, 2 Vols, 4th edn (London: Ballière). **(Chap. 12)**

Quezel, P. Pons (1957) *Première étude palynologique de quelques paléo-sols sahariens* (Algiers: Institut de Recherches Sahariennes). **(Chap. 4)**

Rabie, H. (1972) *The Financial System of Egypt* (London/New York: Oxford University Press). **(Chap. 5)**

Radcliffe-Brown, A. R. and Forde, D. (eds) (1960) *African Systems of Kinship and Marriage* (London/New York: Oxford University Press). **(Gen. Introd.)**

Ralph, E. K., Michael, H. N. and Han, M. G. (1973) 'Radiocarbon dates and reality', *MN*, 9, 1, pp. 1–20. **(Chap. 9)**

Ramendo, L. (1963) 'Les galets aménagés de Reggan (Sahara)', *Libyca*, II, pp. 43–74. **(Chap. 22)**

Randall-MacIver, D. and Mace, A. C. (1902) *El Amrah and Abydos, 1899–1901* (London). **(Chap. 28)**

Randles, W. G. L. (1958) *South East Africa and the Empire of Monomatapa as shown on selected printed maps of the sixteenth century* (Lisbon). **(Chap. 6)**

Randles, W. G. L. (1974) 'La civilisation bantou, son essor et son déclin', *Annales*, 29, 2. **(Chap. 27)**

Ranger, T. O. (1962) 'Emerging themes of African history', *International Congress of African Historians*, Dar es Salaam. **(Chap. 15)**

Ranger, T. O. (1967) *Revolt in Southern Rhodesia, 1896–97; A Study in African Resistance* (London: Heinemann). **(Chap. 3)**

Rattray, R. S. (1923) *Ashanti* (Oxford: Clarendon Press). **(Chap. 24)**

Reed, C. H. (1964) 'Natural history study of Karkur oasis, Libyan desert', *Postilla-Peabody Museum*, 84. **(Chap. 25)**

Reed, C. H. (1965) 'A human frontal bone from the late pleistocene of the Kom-Ombo plain', *Man*, 95, pp. 101–4. **(Chap. 25)**

Reed, C. H. (1967) *Preliminary Report on the Archaeological Research of the Yale University Prehistoric Expedition to Nubia, 1962–1963* (Cairo: Service des antiquités de L'Egypte). **(Chap. 25)**

Rees, A. R. (1965) 'Evidence for the African origin of the oil palm', *Principes*, 9, pp. 30–6. **(Chap. 24)**

Reindorf, C. C. (1895) *History of the Gold Coast and Asante* (Basle). **(Chap. 3)**

Reiniseh, L. (1891) *Die Kunama-Sprache in Nordost-Afrika* (Vienna). **(Chap. 10)**

Reisner, G. A. (1910–27) *Archaeological Survey of Nubia, Report for 1907–1908*, Vol. I (Cairo: National Printing Dept). **(Chap. 28)**

Reisner, G. A. (1923) *Excavations at Karma* (Cambridge, Mass.: Harvard African Studies). **(Chap. 28)**

Renan, E. (1855) *Histoire générale et système comparé des langues sémitiques* (Paris: Calmann-Lévy). **(Chaps 1, 2)**

Revue de Géographie Physique et de Géologie Dynamique (1976) *Oscillations climatiques au Sahara depuis 40 000 ans*, special number (Paris: Masson). **(Chap. 16)**

Reygasse, M. (1922) 'Note au sujet de deux civilisations préhistoriques pour lesquelles deux termes nouveaux me paraissent devoir être employés', *Actes 46e Congr. AFAS*, pp. 467–72. **(Chap. 23)**

Reygasse, M. (1923) 'Découverte d'outillage moustérien à outils pédonculés atériens dans le Tidikelt, Oued Asriouel, région d'Aoulef Chorfa', *Actes 46e Congr. AFAS*, pp. 471–2. **(Chap. 23)**

Rhodenburg, H. (1970) 'Mosphodynamische Activitäts und Stabilitätszeiten statt Pluvial und Interpluvialzeiten', *Eiszeitalter und Gegenwart*, 21, pp. 81–96. **(Chap. 21)**

Rhodenburg, H. and Sabelberg, U. (1969) 'Zur Randschaftsökologisch-Bodengeo graphischen und klimagenetisch – Geomorphologischen Stellung des westliche Mediterrangebietes', *Göttinger Bodenkundlige Berrichte*, 7, pp. 27–47. **(Chap. 16)**

Rhotert, H. (1952) *Libysche Felsbilder* (Darmstadt: Wittich). **(Chap. 23)**

Richard, Abbé (1869) 'Sur la découverte de silex taillés dans le sud de l'Algérie', *Matériaux pour l'histoire primitive de l'homme*, 4, pp. 74–5. **(Chap. 23)**

Richard, C. de (1955) 'Contribution à l'étude de la stratigraphie de Quaternaire de la Presqu'île du Cap Vert (Sénégal)', *BSPF*, 52, pp. 80–8. **(Chap. 24)**

Richardson, J. L. and Richardson, A. E. (1972) 'History of an African rift lake and its climatic implication', *Ecological Monograph*, 42, pp. 499–534. **(Chap. 16)**

Rightmire, G. P. (1974) *Comments on Race and Population History in Africa* (New York). **(Chap. 11)**

Robert, D. (1970a) 'Les fouilles de Tegdaoust', *JAH*, 11, 4, pp. 471–93. **(Chap. 24)**

Robert, D. (1970b) 'Report on the excavations at Tegdaoust', *WAAN*, 12, pp. 64–8. **(Chap. 24)**

Robert, D., Robert, S. and Devisse, J. (1970) *Tegdaoust I, Recherches sur Aoudaghost* (Paris: AMG). **(Chap. 24)**

Roberts, A. (1967) 'Oral traditions of the peoples of Tanzania', *EAJ*, 12, pp. 23–5. **(Chap. 7)**

Roberts, A. (1968a) *Recording East Africa's Past: A brief guide for the amateur historian* (Nairobi: East African Publishing House). **(Chap. 7)**

Roberts, A. (1968b) 'Oral tradition through the sieve: notes and comments on the second conference on Tanzania's oral history', *EAJ*, pp. 35–8. **(Chap. 7)**
Roberts, A. (1968c) *Tanzania before 1900* (Nairobi: East African Publishing House). **(Chap. 3)**
Roche, E. (1963) *L'Epipaléolithique marocain* (Lisbon). **(Chap. 22)**
Roche, E. (1975) 'Analyse palynologique du site archéologique de la Kamoa', in D. Cahen, *Le Site archéologique de la Kamoa (Région du Shaba, République du Zaïre). De l'âge de la pierre ancienne à l'âge du fer* (Tervuren: Musée royal de l'Afrique centrale). **(Chap. 21)**
Rodier, J. (1963) 'Hydrologie du continent africain', *Enquête sur les ressources naturelles du continent africain* (Paris: Unesco), pp. 185–226. **(Chap. 13)**
Roget, M. (1924) *Le Maroc chez les auteurs anciens.* **(Chap. 5)**
Rognon, P. (1974) 'Modifications naturelles du cycle hydrométéorologique depuis 10,000 ans. Leur utilisation pour la prévision climatique à long terme', in *Influence des activités de l'homme sur le cycle hydrométéorologique 13e Journée de l' hydraulique, Société Hydrotechnique française* **(Chap. 16)**
Rosenfeld, A. (1965) *The Inorganic Raw Minerals of Antiquity* (London). **(Chap. 14)**
Rosenfeld, A. (1972) 'The microlithic industries of Rop Rock Shelter', *WAJA*, 2, pp. 17–28. **(Chap. 24)**
Rotberg, R. I. (ed.) (1971) *Africa and its Explorers: Motives, Methods and Impact* (Cambridge, Mass.). **(Chap. 6)**
Rotberg, R. I. and Mazrui, A. A. (eds) (1970) *Protest and Power in Black Africa* (New York: Oxford University Press). **(Chap. 3)**
Rotberg, R. I. and Roubet, C. (1968) 'Nouvelles observations sur l'Epipaléolithique de l'Algérie orientale. Le gisement de Koudiat Kifene Lahda', *Libyca*, 16, pp. 55–101. **(Chap. 22)**
Rotberg, R. I. and Roubet, C. (1972) 'The microlithic industries of Rop rock shelter', *WAJA*, 2, pp. 17–28. **(Chap. 24)**
Rotberg, R. I. and Roubet, C. (in press) 'Une économie pastorale pré-agricole en Algérie orientale. Le néolithique de tradition capsienne. L'exemple de l'Aurès'. **(Chap. 22)**
Rotberg, R. I. and Roubet, F. E. (1966) 'Présentation comparative d'un gisement côtier, des environs de Berard, à l'ouest d'Alger', *Congrès de préhistoire français, Ajaccio*, pp. 109–28. **(Chap. 22)**
Roubet, C. (1968) *Le Gisement du Damous el Ahmar* (Paris: AMG). **(Chaps 21, 22)**
Roubet, C. (1971) 'Sur la définition et la chronologie néolithique de tradition capsienne', *Anthropologie*, 75, pp. 553–74. **(Chaps 22, 24)**
Rouch, J. (1953) *Contribution à l'histoire des Songhay* (Dakar). **(Chap. 5)**
Rubin, A. (1970) 'Review of Phillip Allison's "African Stone Sculpture" and Franck Willett's "Ife in the History of West African Sculpture"', *Art Bulletin*, 72, 3, pp. 348–54. **(Chap. 24)**
Ruffié, J. (1976) *De la biologie à la culture* (Paris: Flammarion). **(Chap. 11)**
Ruffié, J. (1977) 'Génétique et anthropologie', *Science et vie* (Paris), no. 120. **(Chap. 11)**
Ryder, A. F. C. (1965a) *Materials for West African History in Portuguese Archives* (London: Athlone Press). **(Chaps 6, 24)**
Ryder, A. F. C. (1965b) 'A reconsideration of the Ife-Benin relationship', *JAH*, 6, 1, pp. 25–37. **(Chap. 24)**

Saberwal, S. (1967) 'The oral tradition, periodization and political system', *CJAS*, I, pp. 157–62. **(Chap. 7)**
Sacid, H. (n.d.) *History of Sokoto*, trs. C. E. J. Whiting (Kano). **(Chap. 6)**
Said, R. (in press) *The Geological Evolution of the River Nile.* **(Chap. 16)**
Saleh, S. A., George, A. W. and Helmi, F. M. (1972) 'Study of glass and glass-making processes at Wadi-El-Natrum, 1st part. Fritting crucibles, their technical features and temperature employed', *Studies in Conservation*, Journal of the International Institute for the Conservation of Museum Objects (London), 17, pp. 143–70. **(Chap. 9)**
Samb, A. (1971) 'Langues négro-africaines et leurs emprunts à l'arabe', *NA*. **(Chap. 10)**
Sampson, C. G. (1968) *The Middle Stone Age Industries of the Orange River Scheme Area* (Bloemfontein: National Museum). **(Chap. 20)**
Sancho, I. (1781) *Letters of the late I. Sancho, an African ... to which are prefixed memoirs of his life*, 2 Vols (London). **(Chap. 6)**
Sander, E. R. (1969) 'The Hamitic hypothesis, its origin and function in time perspectives', *JAH*, X, 4, pp. 521–32. **(Gen. Introd., Chap. 12)**
Sandford, K. S. and Arkell, W. J. (1929) 'Palaeolithic man and the Nile-Fayum divide', Oriental Institute Publication, 10 (Chicago University Press). **(Chap. 23)**
Sandford, K. S. and Arkell, W. J. (1933) *Palaeolithic Man and the Nile Valley in Nubia and Upper Egypt, with some notes upon a part of the Red Sea littoral; A study of the regions during Pliocene and Pleistocene times* (Chicago: Chicago University Press). **(Chap. 23)**

Sapir, D. (1973–4a) *Linguistics in Sub-Saharan Africa* (Paris: Mouton). **(Chap. 10)**
Sapir, D. (1974b) 'West Atlantic: an inventory of the languages, their noun class systems, and consonant alterations', in T. A. Sebeok (ed.), *Current Trends in Linguistics*, Vol. VII (Paris/The Hague: Mouton). **(Chap. 12)**
Sauer, C. O. (1952) 'Agricultural origins and dispersion', *BML*, 2. **(Chap. 27)**
Saunders, A. M. C. (1964) *World Population: past growth and present trends* (London). **(Chap. 14)**
Sauvaget, J. (1946) *Historiens arabes* (Paris; Maisonneuve). **(Gen. Introd.)**
Sauvaget, J. (1961) *Introduction à l'histoire de l'Orient Musulman* (Paris). **(Chap. 5)**
Savage, G. (1967) *The Art and Antique Restorers' Handbook* (London: Barrie & Rockliff). **(Chap. 9)**
Savary, P. (1966) 'Monuments en pierres sèches du Fasnoun', *MCRAPE*, 6. **(Chap. 23)**
Sayce, R. U. (1933) *Primitive Arts and Crafts* (Cambridge: Cambridge University Press). **(Chap. 24)**
Sayre, E. V. and Meyers, P. (1971) 'Nuclear activation applied to materials of art and archaeology', *AATA*, 8, 4, pp. 115–50. **(Chap. 9)**
Schapera, I. (1933) *The Early Cape Hottentots described in the writings of Olfert Dappr, 1668, Willem Ten Rhyne, 1668, and Johannes Guliemus de Grevenbroek, 1695* (Cape Town: Van Riebeeck Society). **(Chap. 6)**
Scharff, A. and Moorgat, A. (1950) *Ägypten und Vorderasien im Altertum* (Munich: Bruckmann). **(Chap. 28)**
Scheub, H. (1975) *The Ntsomi: A Xhosa Performing Art* (Oxford: Clarendon Press). **(Chap. 7)**
Schlözer, A. L. von (1781) in **Eichhorn, J. G.** (1777–86) *Repertorium für Biblische und Morgenländische Litteratur* (Leipzig), part VIII. **(Chap. 12)**
Schmitz, A. (1962) 'Les Muhulu du Haut-Katanga meridional', *BJBE*, XXXII, 3. **(Chap. 21)**
Schmitz, A. (1971) 'La végétation de la plaine de Lubumbashi', *Publ. INEAC*, 113, pp. 11–388. **(Chap. 21)**
Schnell, R. (1957) *Plantes alimentaires et vie agricole de l'Afrique noire* (Paris: Larose). **(Chap. 27)**
Schollar, I. (1970) 'Magnetic methods of archaeological prospecting – advances in instrumentation and evaluation techniques', *PTRS*, 269, 1193, pp. 109–19. **(Chap. 9)**
Sebeok, T. A. ed (1963–74) *Current Trends in Linguistics* (Paris/The Hague: Mouton). **(Chaps 10, 12)**
Seck, A. and Mondjannagni, A. (1967) *L'Afrique occidentale* (Paris: PUF). **(Chap. 13)**
Seddon, D. (1968) 'The origins and development of agriculture in east and southern Africa', *CA*, 9, 5, pp. 489–94. **(Chaps 24, 27)**
Seligman, C. G. (1930) *Races of Africa* (London: Butterworth). **(Chap. 10)**
Servant, M. (1973) 'Séquences continentales et variations climatiques: évolution du bassin du Tchad au Cénozoïque supérieur', *CORSTOM*. **(Chap. 16)**
Servant, M. (1974) 'Les variations climatiques des régions intertropicales du continent africain depuis la fin du Pléistocène', in *13e Journée de l'hydraulique, Société hydrotechnique française*. **(Chap. 16)**
Servant, M., Servant, S. and Delibrias, G. (1969) 'Chronologie du Quaternaire récent des basses régions du Tchad', *CRAS*, 269, pp. 1603–6. **(Chap. 24)**
Sethe, K. H. (1930) *Urgeschichte und älteste Religion der Ägypter* (Leipzig: Deutsche morgenländische gesellschaft). **(Chap. 28)**
Seydou, C. (ed.) (1977) *La Geste de Ham-Bodedio ou Hama le Rouge* (Paris: Colin). **(Chap. 2)**
Shaked, S. (1964) *A Tentative Bibliography of Geniza Documents* (Paris, The Hague: Etudes Juives).
Shaw, C. T. (1944) 'Report on excavations carried out in the cave known as Bosumpra at Abetifi, Kwahu, Gold Coast Colony', *Proceedings of the Prehistoric Society* (Cambridge), 10, pp. 1–67. **(Chap. 24)**
Shaw, C. T. (1960) 'Early smoking pipes: in Africa, Europe and America', *JRAI*. **(Chap. 24)**
Shaw, C. T. (1961) *Excavation at Dawu* (Edinburgh: Nelson). **(Chap. 24)**
Shaw, C. T. (1962) 'Chronology of excavation at Dawu', *Man*, 72, p. 217. **(Chap. 24)**
Shaw, C. T. (1963) 'Field research in Nigerian archaeology', *JHSN*, 2, 4, pp. 449–64. **(Chap. 24)**
Shaw, C. T. (1964a) *Archaeology and Nigeria* (Ibadan: Ibadan University Press). **(Chap. 24)**
Shaw, C. T. (1964b) 'Smoking in Africa', *SAAB*, 19, 75, pp. 75–6. **(Chap. 24)**
Shaw, C. T. (1965a) 'Spectrographic analyses of the Igbo and other Nigerian bronzes', *Archaeometry*, 8, pp. 86–95. **(Chap. 24)**
Shaw, C. T. (1965b) 'Akure excavations: stone age skeleton 9000 BC', *AN*, 3, pp. 5–6 **(Chap. 24)**
Shaw, C. T. (1967) 'Terminology', *WAAN*, 7, pp. 9–43. **(Chap. 24)**
Shaw, C. T. (1969a) 'Further spectrographic analyses of Nigerian bronzes', *Archaeometry*, 11, pp. 85–98. **(Chap. 24)**
Shaw, C. T. (1969b) 'The Later Stone Age in the Nigerian forest', *Actes 1er Coll. Intern. Archéol. Afr.*, pp. 364–74. **(Chap. 24)**
Shaw, C. T. (1969c) 'On radiocarbon chronology of the Iron Age in sub-Saharan Africa', *CA*, 10, pp. 226–31. **(Chap. 24)**

Shaw, C. T. (1970a) 'The analysis of West African bronzes: a summary of the evidence', *Ibadan*, 20, pp. 80–9. **(Chap. 24)**
Shaw, C. T. (1970b) *Igbo-Ukwu: An Account of Archaeological Discoveries in Eastern Nigeria*, 2 Vols (London: Faber, for the Institute of African Studies, University of Ibadan). **(Chap. 24)**
Shaw, C. T. (1971a) 'The prehistory of West Africa', in J. F. A. Ajayi and M. Crowder (eds), *History of West Africa*, Vol. 1 (London: Longman). **(Chap. 24)**
Shaw, C. T. (1971b) 'Africa in prehistory: leader or laggard?' *JAH*, 12, 1, pp. 143–53. **(Chap. 24)**
Shaw, C. T. (1972) 'Early crops in Africa: a review of the evidence', *Proc. Burg Wart. Symp. 56*. **(Chap. 24)**
Shaw, C. T. (1973) 'Trade and the Tsoede bronzes', *WAJA*, 3, pp. 233–8. **(Chap. 24)**
Shaw, F. (1906) *A Tropical Dependency* (London). **(Chap. 1)**
Shayyal (1958) *Majmu'at al-Watha'iq al-Fatimiyya* (Cairo). **(Chap. 5)**
Shelton, A. K. (1968) 'Causality in African thought; Igbo and other', *PA*, 15, 4, pp. 157–69. **(Chap. 7)**
Shepperson, G. and Price, T. (1958) *Independent African; John Chilembwe and the Origins, Setting and Significance of the Nyasaland Native Rising of 1915* (Edinburgh: Edinburgh University Press). **(Chap. 3)**
Shibeika, M. (1947) *Ta'rīkh muluk al-Sudan* (Khartoum). **(Chap. 6)**
Shinnie, P. L. (1967) *Meroe: a Civilization of the Sudan* (New York: Praeger; London: Thames & Hudson). **(Chap. 28)**
Shinnie, P. L. (1971) *The African Iron Age* (Oxford: Clarendon Press). **(Chaps 24, 28)**
Shumovskiy, T. A. (1957) *Tri neizvestyne lotsii Akhmada ibn Majida* (Three unknown pilot books of Aktumed ibn Majida) (Moscow). **(Chap. 6)**
Sibrava, V. (ed.) (1975) *Quaternary Glaciations in the Northern Hemisphere* (Prague: Unesco). **(Chap. 16)**
Silva Rego, A. da (1949–58) *Documentaçao para a história das missões do Padroada Português do Oriente* (Lisbon). **(Chap. 6)**
Simpson, G. C. (1957) 'Further studies in world climate', *JRMS*, 83, pp. 459–85. **(Chap. 24)**
Simpson, W. K. (ed.) (1972) *The Literature of Ancient Egypt. An Anthology of Stories, Instructions and Poetry*, trans. R. D. Faulkner, E. F. Wente and W. K. Simpson (New Haven/London). **(Chap. 28)**
Singer, R. (1958) 'The Rhodesian, Florisbad and Saldanha skulls', in G. H. R. von Hoenigswald (ed.), *Neanderthal Centenary* (Utrecht), pp. 52–62. **(Chap. 20)**
Singer, R. and Wymer, J. (1968) 'Archaeological investigations at the Saldanha skull site in South Africa', *SAAB*, XXV, pp. 63–74. **(Chap. 20)**
Singh, G. (1973) 'Late Quaternary changes in vegetation and climates in the arid tropics of India', *Acts IX INQUA Congr.* **(Chap. 16)**
Slane, M. de (1911) Description de l'Afrique septentrionale (Paris). **(Chap. 5)**
Smith, A. (1974) 'Preliminary report of excavations at Karkarichinkat, Mali, 1972', *WAJA*, 4. **(Chap. 24)**
Smith, H. F. C. (1958) 'Source material for the history of the western Sudan', *JHSN*, 1, 3, pp. 238–48. **(Chaps 5, 6)**
Smith, H. F. C. (1961) 'Arabic manuscript material bearing on the history of the western Sudan: a seventeenth century writer of Katsina', *BNHSN*, VI, 1. **(Chaps 5, 6)**
Smith, H. S. (1966) 'The Nubian B-group', *Kush*, XIV, pp. 69–124. **(Chap. 28)**
Smith, P. E. (1966a) 'The late Paleolithic of northern Africa in the light of recent researches', *AA*, 68, pp. 326–55. **(Chap. 25)**
Smith, P. E. (1966b) 'New prehistoric investigation at Kom-Ombo', *Zephyrus*, XVII. **(Chap. 25)**
Smith, P. E. (1967) 'New investigations in the late Pleistocene archaeology of the Kom-Ombo plain', *Quaternaria*, IX. **(Chap. 25)**
Soga, T. B. (1929) *Intlalo ka Xosa* (Lovedale). **(Chap. 6)**
Soga, J. H. (1930a) *The South-Eastern Bantu* (Johannesburg). **(Chap. 6)**
Soga, J. H. (1930b) *Ama-Xhosa: Life and Customs* (Johannesburg). **(Chap. 6)**
Sommer, F. (1953) *Man and Beast in Africa* (London: Jenkins). **(Chap. 14)**
Soper, R. C. (1965) 'The Stone Age in northern Nigeria', *JHSN*, 3, 2, pp. 175–94. **(Chap. 24)**
Souville, G. (1958–9) 'La pêche et la vie maritime au Néolithique en Afrique du nord', *BAM*, 3, pp. 315–44. **(Chap. 22)**
Souville, G. (1973) *Atlas préhistorique du Maroc* (Paris: CNRS Etudes d'antiquités africaines). **(Chap. 22)**
Sow, A. I. (1968) *Chroniques et récits du Fouta Djalon* (Paris: Klincksieck). **(Chap. 6)**

Sowunmi, M. A. (1973) 'A preliminary palynological study in the Rivers State', *OM*, I, 1, pp. 13–14. **(Chap. 4)**

Sparks, B. W. and West, R. G. (1972) *The Ice Age in Britain* (London: Methuen). **(Chap. 24)**

Sparrman, A. (1789) *A Voyage to the Cape of Good Hope, towards the Antarctic Polar Circle, round the World, and to the Country of the Hottentots and Caffres, from the year 1772 to 1776*, ed. V. S. Forbes, rev. trans. J. and I. Rudner (Cape Town: Van Riebeeck Society) 1975–7. **(Chap. 6)**

Stainer, X. (1899) 'L'âge de la pierre au Congo', *AMRAC*, III. **(Chap. 21)**

Stanton, W. R. and Willett, F. (1963) 'Archaeological evidence for changes in maize type in West Africa: an experiment in technique', *Man*, 63. **(Chap. 24)**

Stigand, C. H. (1913) *The Land of Zinj* (London). **(Chap. 1)**

Streel, M. (1963) *La végétation tropophylle des plaines alluviales de la Lufira moyenne* (Liège: FULREAC). **(Chap. 21)**

Stross, F. H. and O'Donnell, A. E. (1972) *Laboratory Analysis of Organic Materials* (USA: Addison-Wesley), Module 22. **(Chap. 9)**

Strouhal, E. (1976) *Problems of Study of Human Races* (Prague). **(Chap. 11)**

Struever, S. (ed.) (1971) *Prehistoric Agriculture* (New York: American Museum Sourcebooks in Anthropology). **(Chap. 4)**

Stuvier, M. and Suess, H. E. (1966) 'On the relationship between radiocarbon dates and true sample ages', *Radiocarbon*, 8, pp. 534–40. **(Chap. 9)**

Suret-Canale, J. (1964) 'Les sociétés traditionnelles en Afrique tropicale et le concept de mode de production asiatique', *Pensée*, 117, pp. 21–42. **(Concl.)**

Suret-Canale, J. (1968) *Afrique noire occidentale et centrale*, Vol I: *Géographie, civilisations, histoire* (Paris: Editions sociales). **(Gen. Introd., Chap. 13)**

Suret-Canale, J. (1969) Preface to *Sur le mode de production asiatique*, Centre d'études et de recherches marxistes (Paris: Editions Sociales).

Swadesh, E. (1966a) 'A preliminary glottochronology of Gur', *JWAL*. **(Chap. 10)**

Swadesh, E. (1966b) 'Glottochronology', *JWAL*, III. **(Chap. 10)**

Szumowski, G. (1956) 'Fouilles de l'abri sous roche de Kourounorokale', *BIFAN*, B, 18, pp. 462–508. **(Chap. 24)**

Taieb, M. (1974) 'Evolution quaternaire du bassin de l'Awash (Rift éthiopien et Afar)', 2 Vols, thesis (University of Paris). **(Chap. 17)**

Taieb, M., Coppens, Y., Johanson, D. C. and Kalb, J. (1972) 'Dépôts sédimentaires et faunes du Plio-Pléistocène de la basse vallée de l'Awash (Afar central, Ethiopie)', *CRAS*, 275, pp. 819–22. **(Chap. 17)**

Taieb, M., Johanson, D. C. and Coppens, Y. (1975) 'Expédition internationale de l'Afar, Ethiopie (3e campagne, 1974), découverte d'Hominidés plio-pléistocène à Hadar', *CRAS*, 281, pp. 1297–300. **(Chaps 17, 18)**

Taieb, M., Johanson, D. C., Coppens, Y. and Aronson, J. L. (1976) 'Geological and paleontological background of Hadar hominid site, Afar, Ethiopia', *Nature*, 260, 5549, pp. 289–93. **(Chaps 16, 17)**

Taieb, M., Johanson, D. C., Coppens, Y., Bonnefille, R. and Kalb, J. (1974) 'Découverte d'hominides dans les séries plio-pléistocènes d'Hadar (bassin de l'Awash, Afar, Ethiopie)', *CRAS*, 279, pp. 735–8. **(Chap. 17)**

Talbot, P. A. (1923) *Life in Southern Nigeria: the magic, beliefs and customs of the Ibids Tribe* (London: Macmillan), pp. 448–64. **(Chap. 10)**

Tardits, C. (1962) '*Religion, épopée, histoire* – notes sur les fonctions latentes des cultes dans les civilisations du Bénin', *Diogène*, 37. **(Chap. 15)**

Tattam, C. M. (1944) *A Review of Nigerian Stratigraphy*, annual report of the geological survey of Nigeria, 1943 (Lagos: Government printer). **(Chap. 24)**

Tauxier, H. (1882) 'Les deux rédactions du périple d'Hannon', *RA*, pp. 15–37. **(Chap. 5)**

Tauxier, L. (1942) *Histoire des Bambara* (Paris). **(Chap. 1)**

Teilhard de Chardin, P. (1954) 'Les recherches pour la découverte des origines humaines en Afrique au sud du Sahara', *Anthropologie*. **(Concl.)**

Teilhard de Chardin, P. (1955) *Le Phenomène humain* (Paris: Senil), p. 203. **(Chap. 22)**

Teilhard de Chardin, P. (1955) 'L'Afrique et les origines humaines', *Revue des questions scientifiques*. **(Concl.)**

Teilhard de Chardin, P. (1956) *Le Groupe zoologique humain* (Paris: Albin Michel). **(Chap. 15)**

Theal, G. M. (1898–1903) *Records of South-Eastern Africa*, 9 Vols (London). **(Chap. 6)**

Theal, G. M. (1897–1905) *Records of the Cape Colony*, 36 Vols (London). **(Chap. 6)**

Thomassey, P. and Mauny, R. (1951) 'Campagne de fouilles à Koumbi Saleh', *BIFAN*, 13, 1, pp. 438–62. **(Chap. 24)**

Thomassey, P. and Mauny, R. (1956) 'Campagne de fouilles à Koumbi Saleh (Ghana?)', *BIFAN*, B, 18, pp. 117–40. **(Chap. 24)**

Thompson, L. ed. (1969) *African Societies in Southern Africa* (London: Heinemann). **(Gen. Introd., Chap. 24)**

Time-Life Books (1972) *The Missing Link – Emergence of Man*, Series 3. **(Chap. 19)**

Tixier, J. (1957) 'Le hachereau dans l'Acheuléen nord africain. Notes typologiques', *CR XV Congr. Préhist. Fr.*, pp. 914–23. **(Chaps 22, 23)**

Tixier, J. (1958–9) 'Les pièces pédonculées de l'Atérien', *Libyca*, 6, 7, pp. 127–57. **(Chap. 22)**

Tixier, J. (1963) 'Les industries lithiques de l'Aïn Fritissa', *BAM*, 3, pp. 107–247. **(Chap. 22)**

Tixier, J. (1963) *Typologie de l'épipaléolithique du Maghreb* (Paris: AMG). **(Chap. 22)**

Tobias, P. V. (1967a) *Olduvai Gorge – The Cranium and Maxillary Detention of Australopithecus (Zinjanthropus) boisei* (Cambridge: Cambridge University Press). **(Chap. 17)**

Tobias, P. V. (1967b) 'Cultural hominization among the earliest African Pleistocene hominids', *Proceedings of the Prehistoric Society* (Cambridge), 33, pp. 367–76. **(Chap. 20)**

Tobias, P. V. (1968a) 'Middle and Early Upper Pleistocene members of the genus Homo in Africa', *Sonderdruck aus Evolution und Hominization* (Stuttgart: Kurth), pp. 176–94. **(Chap. 20)**

Tobias, P. V. (1968b) *Man's Past and Future.* Fifth Raymond Dart Lecture (Johannesburg: Witwatersrand University Press). **(Chap. 20)**

Tobias, P. V. and Coppens, Y. (1976) 'Les plus anciens hominidés', *Actes IX Congr. UISPP.* **(Chap. 17)**

Tricart, J. (1956) 'Tentative de corrélation des périodes pluviales africaines et des périodes glaciaires', *CRSGF*, pp. 164–7. **(Chap. 16)**

Trigger, B. G. (1965) *History and Settlement in Lower Nubia* (New Haven: Yale University Publications in Anthropology), 69. **(Gen. Introd., Chap 28)**

Trigger, B. G. (1965) 'Meroitic and Eastern Sudanic, a linguistic relationship?' *Kush*, 12, pp. 188–94.

Trigger, B. G. (1969) 'Meroe and the African iron age', *AHS*, II. **(Chap. 28)**

Tschudi, J. (1955) *Nordafrikanische Felsmalereien* (Florence: Sansoni). **(Chap. 23)**

Tucker, A. N. (1940) *The Eastern Sudanic Languages* (London: Oxford University Press). **(Chap. 10)**

Tucker, A. N. (1948) *Distribution of the Nilotic and Nilo-Hamitic Languages of Africa* (London: Oxford University Press). **(Chap. 10)**

Tucker, A. N. and Bryan, M. A. (1966) *Linguistic Analysis: the non-Bantu Languages of North-Eastern Africa* (London/New York/The Cape: Oxford University Press). **(Chaps 10, 12)**

Turekian, K. K. (ed.) (1971) *The Late Cenozoic glacial ages* (New Haven: Yale University Press). **(Chap. 16)**

Turner, L. D. (1955) 'The odyssey of a Zulu warrior', *JNH*, 40, 4. **(Chap. 6)**

Twiesselmann, F. (1958) *Les ossements humains du gîte mésolithique d'Ishango, Mission J. de Heinzelin de Braucourt en 1950* (Brussels: Institut des parcs nationaux du Congo belge). **(Chap. 21)**

Ucko, P. J. and Dimbleby, G. W. (eds) (1969) *The Domestication and Exploitation of Plants and Animals* (Chicago: Aldine). **(Chap. 24)**

Ucko, P. J. and Dimbleby, G. W. (1970) 'The history of Africa', *CHM*, XII, 4, pp. 527–605. **(Chap. 15)**

Ucko, P. J. and Dimbleby, G. W. (1972) 'Les origines de l'homme', *Unesco Courier*, August–September, special issue. **(Concl.)**

Unesco (1965) L'Art de l'ecriture.

Unesco (1973) *Recueil sélectif de textes en arabe provenant d'archives marocaines* by Professor Mohammed Ibrahim El Kettani (Paris). **(Introd.)**

Unesco (1974) *Colloque sur le peuplement de L'Egypte ancienne et le déchiffrement de l'écriture meroïtique* (Cairo, 28 January–3 February). **(Introd.)**

Urvoy, Y. (1936) *Histoire des populations du Soudan central* (Paris). **(Chap. 1)**

Urvoy, Y (1941) 'Chroniques du Bornou', *Journ. Société des Africanistes*, II, **(Chap. 6)**

Urvoy, Y. (1949) *Histoire du Bornou* (Paris). **(Chap. 1)**

US National Report (1971–4, publ. 1975) American Geophysical Union, 15th General Ass. International Union of Geology and Geophysics, Grenoble, *Review of Geophysics and Space Physics*, 13, 3. **(Chap. 16)**

Vajda, G. (1950) 'Contribution à la connaissance de la littérature arabe en Afrique occidentale', *JSA*, XX, pp. 229–37. **(Chaps 5, 6)**

Vandier, J. (1952) *Manuel d'archéologie égyptienne* (Paris: Picard). **(Chap. 28)**

Vandier, J. and Drioton, E. (1962) *Les Peuples de l'ouest Méditerranéen, II, l'Egypte* (Paris: PUF). **(Chap. 28)**

Vansina, J. (1961) *De la tradition orale; essai de méthode historique* (Tervuren: Mémoire no. 36 du Musée Royal d' Afrique Centrale). **(Gen. Introd., Chap. 7)**

Vansina, J. (1971) 'Once upon a time: oral traditions as history in Africa', *Daedalus*, 100, 2, pp. 442–68. **(Chap. 7)**

Vansina, J. (1973) *The Tio kingdom of the Middle Congo, 1880–1892* (London: Oxford University Press). **(Chap. 3)**

Vansina, J. (1974) 'Comment: traditions of Genesis', *JAH*, XV, pp. 317–22. **(Chap. 8)**

Vansina, J., Mauny, R. and Thomas, L. V. eds (1964) *The Historian in Tropical Africa* (London: Oxford University Press). **(Gen. Introd., Chap. 15)**

Vaufrey, R. (1938) 'L'âge de l'art rupestre nord africain', *Ipek*, Berlin, 12, pp. 10–29. **(Chap. 23)**

Vaufrey, R. (1939) *L'Art rupestre nord-africain* (Paris: Institut de paléontologie humaine), Mem. 20. **(Chap. 23)**

Vaufrey, R. (1946) 'Le Néolithique de tradition capsienne au Sénégal', *Rivista di sciencia prehistorica* (Rome). **(Chap. 24)**

Vaufrey, R. (1949) 'Le Néolithique paratoumbien, une civilisation agricole primitive du Soudan', *JEA*, 35. **(Concl.)**

Vaufrey, R. (1953) 'L'âge de la pierre en Afrique, exposé synoptique', *JSA*, XXIII, pp. 103–38. **(Concl.)**

Vaufrey, R. (1955 and 1969) *Préhistoire de l'Afrique*, I: *Le Maghreb*; II: *Au nord et à l'est de la Grande forêt* (Paris: Masson). **(Chaps 22, 23)**

Vavilov, N. I. (1935) *Bases théoriques de la sélection des plantes*, I: *Sélection générale* (Moscow/Leningrad). **(Chaps 14, 27)**

Vavilov, N. I. (1951) 'The origin, variation, immunity and breeding of cultivated plants; selected writings', trans. K. Staar, *Chronica Botanica*, 13, pp. 1–6. **(Chap. 27)**

Vedder, H. (1938) *South-West Africa in Early Times* (Oxford; reprinted London 1966). **(Chap. 6)**

Vercoutter, J. (1959) 'The gold of Kush', *Kush*, VII, pp. 120–53. **(Chap. 28)**

Vercoutter, J., Bottero, J. and Cassin, E. (1967) *The Near East, the early civilizations* (New York: Delacorte). **(Chap. 28)**

Verhaegen, B. (1974) *Introduction à l'histoire immédiate* (Gembloux: Duculot). **(Introd., Chap. 15, Concl.)**

Vermeersch, S. (1976) 'L'épipaléolithique dans la vallée du Nil', *Actes IX Congr. UISSP*. **(Chap. 25)**

Via, Y. and M. (1974) *Sahara, milieu vivant* (Paris: Hatier). **(Chap. 26)**

Vidal, O. E. (1852) in S. A. Crowther, *A Vocabulary of the Yoruba Language* (London: Seeleys). **(Chap. 12)**

Vidal, P. (1969) *La civilisation mégalithique de Bouar. Prospections et fouilles 1962–1966* (Paris: Didot). **(Chap. 21)**

Vignard, E. (1923) 'Une nouvelle industrie lithique: le Sébilien', *BIFAO*, 22, pp. 1–76. **(Chap. 23)**

Voegelin, C. F. and F. M. (1973) *Index of the World's Languages* (Washington, DC). **(Chap. 12)**

Vogel, J. C. and Beaumont, P. B. (1972) 'Revised radiocarbon chronology for the Stone Age in South Africa', *Nature*, 237, pp. 50–1. **(Chaps 20, 24)**

Voute, C. (1962) 'Geological and morphological evolution of the Niger and Benue valleys', *Proc. IV PCPQS*, 1, pp. 189–207. **(Chap. 24)**

Wainwright, G. A. (1949) 'Pharaonic survivals between Lake Chad and the west coast', *JEA*, 35, pp. 170–5. **(Chap. 24)**

Wai-Ogusu, B. (1973) 'Was there a Sangoan industry in West Africa?', *WAJA*, 3, pp. 191–6. **(Chap. 24)**

Wai-Ogusu, B. (1974) 'Pleistocene man in Africa with special reference to West Africa', *JHSN*, 7, 2, pp. 357–68. **(Chap. 24)**

Ward, W. E. F. (1948) *A History of the Gold Coast* (London). **(Chap. 1)**

Watts, A. D. (1926) 'The early hunters and explorers in South West Africa', thesis (University of Cape Town). **(Chap. 6)**

Wayland, E. J. (1929) 'Rift valleys and Lake Victoria', *CR XVe CIG*, II, pp. 323–53. **(Chaps 21, 24)**

Wayland, E. J. (1934) 'Rifts, rivers and rains and early man in Uganda', *JRAI*, 64, pp. 332–52. **(Chaps 21, 24)**

Wayland, E. J. (1952) 'The study of past climates in tropical Africa', *Proc. 1st PCPQS*, pp. 59–66. **(Chap. 24)**

Webb, M. C. (1968) 'Carneiro's hypothesis of limited land resources and the origins of the state: a

Latin Americanist's approach to an old problem', *South Eastern Latin Americanist*, 12, 3, pp. 1–8. **(Chap. 24)**

Webster, J. B. and Boahen, A. A. (1967) *The Revolutionary Years: West Africa since 1800* (London: Longman).

Welmers, W. E. (1973) *African Language Structures* (Berkeley, Calif.: University of California Press). **(Chap. 12)**

Wendorf, F. (ed.) (1965) *Contributions to the Prehistory of Nubia* (Dallas: Fort Burgwin Research Center and Southern Methodist University Press). **(Chap. 23)**

Wendorf, F. (1968) *The Prehistory of Nubia* (Dallas: Fort Burgwin Research Center and Southern Methodist University Press). **(Chaps 16, 28)**

Wendorf, F., Laury, R. L., Albriton, C. C., Schild, R., Haynes, C. V., Damon, P. E., Shafiquillah, M. and Scarborough, R. (1974) 'Dates for the Middle Stone Age of East Africa', *Science*, 187, pp. 740–2. **(Chap. 16)**

Wendorf, F., Said, R. and Schild, R. (1970) 'Egyptian prehistory: some new concepts', *Science*, 169, pp. 1161–71. **(Chaps 24, 28)**

Wendorf, F. and Schild, R. *Late Paleolithic stratigraphy in the Lower Nile Valley of Egypt* (unpublished).

Wendt, W. E. and Reed, C. H. (1966) 'Two prehistorical archaeological sites in Egyptian Nubia', *Postilla*, 102, pp. 1–46. **(Chap. 25)**

Werner, A. (1915) *The Language-Families of Africa* (London: Society for Promoting Christian Knowledge). **(Chap. 12)**

Werner, A. (1930) *Structure and Relationship of African Languages* (London/New York: Longman, Green). **(Chap. 12)**

Werner, A. E. A. (1970) 'Analysis of ancient metals', *PTRS*, 269, 1193, pp. 179–85. **(Chap. 9)**

Westcott, R. W. (1957) 'Did the Yoruba come from Egypt?', *Odu*, 4. **(Chap. 24)**

Westermann, D. (1911) *Die Sudansprachen, eine sprachvergleichende Studie* (Hamburg: Friederichsen). **(Chap. 12)**

Westermann, D. (1927) *Die westlichen Sudansprachen und ihre Beziehungen zum Bantu* (Berlin: Mitteilungen des Seminars für Orientalische Sprachen). **(Chap. 12)**

Westermann, D. (1952) *Geschichte Afrikas* (Cologne). **(Chap. 1)**

Westphal, E. O. J. (1962) 'On classifying Bushman and Hottentot languages', *ALS*, III, pp. 30–48. **(Chap. 11)**

Westphal, E. O. J. (1966) 'The non-Bantu languages of southern Africa', in A. N. Tucker and M. A. Bryan (eds), *Linguistic Analyses* (London: Oxford University Press). **(Chap. 12)**

Wet, J. M. J. de, and Harlan, J. R. (1971) 'The origin and domestication of sorghum-bicolor', *Economic Botany*, 25, pp. 128–35. **(Chap. 24)**

Wheatley, P. (1964) *The Land of Zanj: Exegetical Notes on Chinese Knowledge of East Africa prior to AD 1500* (London: Liverpool Essays). **(Chap. 5)**

Wickens, G. E. (1975) 'Changes in the climate and vegetation of the Sudan since 20,000 BP', *C-R VIII Reunion ABIFAT*, pp. 43–65. **(Chap. 16)**

Wiercinsky, K. (1965) 'The analysis of racial structure of early dynastic populations in Egypt', *Materialow practical anthropologicanich*, 72. **(Chap. 11)**

Wieschoff, H. A. (1943) *The Zimbabwe–Monomotopa culture* (Menasha). **(Chap. 1)**

Wiesenfeld, S. L. (1967) 'Sickle cell trait in human biological and cultural evolution', *Science*, 157, pp. 1134–40. **(Chap. 24)**

Wiet, G. (1960) *Journal d'un bourgeois du Caire* (Paris). **(Chap. 6)**

Wilcox, A. R. (1963) *The Rock Art of South Africa* (Johannesburg: Nelson). **(Chap. 26, Concl.)**

Wilks, I. (1956) 'Tribal history and myth', *Universitas*, 2–3. **(Gen. Introd.)**

Wilks, I. (1961) 'Begho and the Mande', *JAH*, 2, pp. 25–34. **(Chap. 24)**

Wilks, I. (1963) 'The growth of islamic learning in Ghana', *JHS*, 2, 4, pp. 409–17. **(Chaps 1, 6)**

Wilks, I. (1975) 'Do Africans have a sense of time?', *IJAHS*, VIII, 2. **(Chap. 2)**

Willett, F. (1960) 'Ife and its archaeology', *JAH*, 2, pp. 231–48. **(Chaps 15, 24)**

Willett, F. (1962a) 'The introduction of maize into west Africa: an assessment of recent evidence', *Africa*, 32, pp. 1–13. **(Chap. 24)**

Willett, F. (1962b) 'The microlithic industry from Old Oyo, western Nigeria', *Actes IV Congr. PPEQ*, 2, pp. 261–72. **(Chap. 24)**

Willett, F. (1964) 'Spectrographic analysis of Nigeria bronzes', *Archaeometry*, 7, pp. 81–93. **(Chap. 24)**

Willett, F. (1966) 'On the funeral effigies of Owo and Benin, and the interpretation of the life-size bronze heads from Ife', *Man*, 1, pp. 34–45. **(Chap. 24)**

Willett, F. (1967) *Ife in the History of West African Sculpture* (London: Thames & Hudson). **(Chap. 24)**

Willett, F. (1968) 'New light on the Ife–Benin relationship', *African Forum*, 3, 4; 4, 1. **(Chap. 24)**
Willett, F. (1969) 'New radiocarbon dates from Ife', *WAAN*, 11, pp. 23–5. **(Chap. 24)**
Williams, M. A. J. (1966) 'Age of alluvial clays in the western Gezira, Republic of the Sudan', *Nature*, 211, pp. 270–1. **(Chap. 16)**
Williams, M. A. J. (1975) 'Late Pleistocene tropical aridity; synchronous in both hemispheres?' *Nature*, 253, 5493, pp. 617–18. **(Chap. 16)**
Williams, M. A. J., Clark, J. D., Adamson, D. A. and Gillespie, R. (1975) 'Recent Quaternary research in central Sudan', *BASEQUA*, 46. **(Chap. 16)**
Willis, R. G. (1964) 'Tradition, history and social structure in Ufipa', *Africa*, 34, 4, pp. 340–51. **(Chap. 7)**
Wilson, A. C. and Sarich, V. M. (1969) 'A molecular timescale for human evolution', *PNAS*, 63, 4, pp. 1088–93. **(Chap. 20)**
Wilson, M. and Thompson, L. eds (1969–71) *The Oxford History of South Africa*, 2 Vols (Oxford: Clarendon Press). **(Chap. 3)**
Wilson, W. A. A. (1966) 'Temme and the West Atlantic Group', *SLLR* (Indiana), 2, 26–9. **(Chap. 10)**
Winkler, H. A. (1937) *Völker und Völkerbewegungen im vorgeschichtlichen Oberägypten im Lichte neuer Palsbilderfunde* (Stuttgart). **(Chap. 23)**
Winkler, H. A. (1939) *Rock Drawings of Southern Upper Egypt*, 2 Vols (London: Egypt Exploration Society). **(Chap. 23)**
Winston, D. (1960) 'Greenberg's classification of African language', *ALS*, 7. **(Chap 12)**
Wollin, G., Ericson, D. B. and Wollin, J. (1974) 'Geomagnetic variations and climatic changes 2,000,000 BC – 1970 AD', *Coll. CNRS*, 219, pp. 273–88. **(Chap. 16)**
World Meteorological Organisation (1975) 'WMO/IAMAP Symposium on long-term climatic fluctuations', *Proc. Norwich, WMO*, no. 421. **(Chap. 16)**
Wrigley, C. C. (1970) 'Speculations on the Economic Prehistory of Africa', in J. D. Fage and R. Oliver (eds), *Papers in African Prehistory* (*Journal of African History*) (Cambridge: Cambridge University Press). **(Chap. 27)**
Wymer, J. J. and Singer, R. (1972) 'Middle Stone Age occupational settlements on the Tzitzikama coast, eastern Cape Province, South Africa', in P. J. Ucko, R. Tringham and G. W. Dimbleby (eds), *Man, Settlement and Urbanism* (London: Duckworth), pp. 207–10. **(Chap. 20)**

Yamasaki, F., Hamada, C. and Hamada, T. (1973) 'Riken natural radiocarbon measurements VII', *Radiocarbon*, 14, 1, pp. 223–38. **(Chap. 24)**
Yilbuudo, J. T. (1970–1) 'Tradition orale', Mémoire, *Séminaire de Koumi, Haute Volta.*
York, R. N. (1973) 'Excavations at New Buipe', *WAJA*, 3, pp. 1–189. **(Chap. 24)**
Young, W. J. (1958) 'Examination of works of art embracing the various fields of science', *Proceedings of the Seminar on Application of Sciences in Examination of Works of Art* (Boston), pp. 18–19. **(Chap. 9)**
Yoyotte, J. (1954) see Posener, Sauneron, Yoyotte, op. cit. **(Chap. 28)**
Yoyotte, J. (1956) 'L'Egypte ancienne', in *Histoire Universelle* (Paris: Pléiade). **(Chap. 5)**

Zahan, D. (1963) *La Dialectique du verbe chez les Bambara* (Paris). **(Chap. 8)**
Zaki, A. and Iskander, Z. (1942) 'Ancient Egypt cheese', *ASAE*, XLI, pp. 295–313. **(Chap. 9)**
Zeissl, H. V. (1955) 'Athiopen und Assyrer in Ägypten', *Ägyptologische Forschungen*, 14 (Glügstadt/Hamburg/New York: Augustin). **(Chap. 28)**
Zeuner, F. E. (1950) *Dating the Past* (London: Methuen). **(Chap. 16)**
Zeuner, F. E. (1959) *The Pleistocene Period, its Climate, Chronology and Faunal Successions* (London: Hutchinson). **(Chaps 16, 21)**
Ziegert, H. (1967) *Dor el Gussa und Gebel ben Ghnema* (Wiesbaden: Steiner). **(Chap. 23)**
Zinderen-Bakker, E. M. van (ed.) (1975) *Paleoecology of Africa*, Vols 1–9. **(Chap. 16)**
Zinderen-Bakker, E. M. van (1967) 'Upper Pleistocene and Holocene Stratigraphy and Ecology on the basis of vegetation changes in Sub-Saharan Africa', in W. W. Bishop and J. D. Clark (eds), *Background to Evolution in Africa* (Chicago: Chicago University Press), pp. 125–47. **(Chap. 24)**

General Index

Abbevillian industry, 499, 570
Acheulian industry, 335, 419, 463, 496–505: in Central Africa, 540–2, 555–6; foodstuffs, 337; hominid fragments, 406, 445; in Kamasian pluvial, 537; in Nile Valley, 371, 635–6, 637; in North Africa, 570–572; in Sahara, 592–3; in West Africa, 618–19; widespread, 465, 468
African Glory (Johnson), 39
African Studies Association (North America), 70
Afrikaans language, 307
Afro-Asiatic language family, 299, 300–2
Agau languages, 301
agriculture, *see* animal husbandry, cultivation, plant
air photography, 224
Ajami language, xxi, 130; script, 6
Al-Muhit (Ibn Majid), 125
al-Wafibi-l-Wafayat (Safadī), 111
allele, 261, 269
Alpine system, 367, 372: of Maghrib, 318
Amharic Chronicle (Menelik II), 120
Amharic language, 28, 242, 254, 293: documents, 121
Amirian industry, 419, 571
analyse acculturiste, 247
ancestor: theme of single, 158; worship, 44, 172
Anfatian industry, 419, 572
animal husbandry, 342, 481, 700: Neolithic, 689; in Nile Valley, 724, 726; origin, 480, 528, 687; in Rift Valley, 480; in Sahara, 602–3, 622, 625, 626
animal resources, *see* fauna
animism, 49, 51, 62, 201, 357
Ansāb al-Ashrāf, 101
Antarctic ice sheet, 378, 392
anthropology, 15–16, 35–7: biological factors, 22; functional, 61, 349; palaeo-, 274, 276; physical, 354–5; semantic, 248–9
anthroponymy, 12, 247, 248
anticyclones, tropical, 322–3
aquatic tradition, *see* fishing
Aramaic language, 301
Archaeological Research Laboratory, Oxford University, 226
archaeology, 350–1: dependence on written sources, 34; East African record, 457; search for origins of man, 34; substantiates oral tradition, 161, 164; techniques, 206–31; terminology, 465
archaeomagnetic investigations, 222–3
archaeometry: aims, 212–17; analytical techniques, 207–12; dating, 217–18, 221–3; presentation of results, 208; testing authenticity, 215–17
Archanthropes, 730
archives, 6: editions or catalogues, 137; governmental, 138; guides to, 136–7
Arctic ice sheet, 378, 392
Ari-Banna languages, 302
aridification, 378, 385
Arkinian industry, 640
art, African, 11, 351, 358: prehistoric, 656–81, 736
art, Capsian, 578, 597, 604
art, hunter, *see* rock art
art, rock, *see* rock art
Aterian industry, 371, 419, 515, 677, 732; Guinea, 622; for hunting, 593; in Nile Valley, 637, 653; in North Africa, 568, 573–4, 621; in Sahara, 592, 593–5
Atlanthropus, 419, 568, 571, 572: *mauritanicus*, 614
Atlas of African Prehistory, 499
atomic absorption analysis, 207, 210–211
Aurignacian industry, 419, 573, 641, 730, 736
Australopithecines, 401, 404–5, 555: dating, 407, 412, 415, 468; their discovery, 405–11, 489, 490; sites, 494; South African fossils, 415, 489, 493
Australopithecus, 265, 405, 420, 443, 446–7; *africanus*, 274, 447, 490, 491, 730; *boisei*, 446; *gracilis*, 407, 408, 411, 444, 446; *habilis*, 407, 408; *robustus*, 407–8, 409, 411, 444, 446, 491, 493
Awija language, 301
Azilian industry, 575

Baghirmian language, 242
Baka language, 12
Bambata industry, 518: mesolithic in Zimbabwe, 335
Bamum script, 6, 79, 114, 136
beads, 476, 663: Akori glass, 217; ostrich shell, 561, 642, 663
Bellum Civile (Caesar), 97
Bellum Jugurthinum (Sallust), 97
Benue-Congo languages, 303, 304, 305, 314
Berliet-Tenere expedition, 587, 592
Berlin Corpus, 98
Biber ice sheet, 372, 375
Bibliotheca Teubneriana, 97
blood-groups, 263–4, 355
blue, Egyptian, 214, 713
Bohairic language, 301
Bonn Byzantine Collection, 98
Book of Kings, 94–5
Book of Roger (Al-Idrīsī), 110
botany, 693; palaeo-, 75–6
brass, 210, 212

bronze, 210, 212: age, 628; in Nile Valley, 724, 727
Brunhes epoch, 360, 375
Bubalus, 658: period of art; 659; style, 664
Bubi language, 285
Bulom language, 283
Burg Wartenstein Symposium (1965), 570
burials, 517, 576
Bustana s-Seyahe (Shirwani), 126

Calabrian magnetic event, 360, 420
Cambridge History of the British Empire, The (CHBE), 33
Cambridge Modern History, The, 33
camels, 26, 77, 630: period of art, 659, 660
CAMES (Conseil Africain et Malgache pour l'Enseignement Supérieur), 68
Canaanite languages, 301
Capsian industry, 420, 732: developed, 576, 577; -Elmenteitan, 481; Kenya, 335, 479, 482; in North Africa, 568, 574, 576–8, 711
Caravans of the Old Sahara (Bovill), 39
carbon-14 dating, *see* radiocarbon dating
caste, notion of, 184–7
Castelperronian industry, 573
Catarrhina, 401, 420
caucasoids, 245, 267
caves, *see* rock-shelters
Cenozoic age, 359, 367, 420, 487: climate, 392, 397
Chaka (Mofolo), 356
Chalcolithic period, 707, 712
Chari-Nile languages, 305
Chavuma industry, 511
Chellean industry, 370, 420, 593, 618, 732
Chipeta industry, 506
chromatographic analysis, 207
Chronicles of the Wars of Amda Sion, 28
chronology: climatic, 388–90; distortion, 157–8; framework, 359–99; oral, 155, 157–60; use of several sources, 17–19, 349–50, 354
circumcision: impassivity at, 189; sacrificial hen at, 178; smith performs, 183
Clactonian industry, 420, 570
click languages, 273, 281, 283, 306, 478
CLIMAP (Climatic Long-Range Interpretation, Mapping and Prediction), 379
climate: chronological stages of African, 379–88; cosmic factors in, 322; deterioration, 360; events of Pleistocene, 359, 360, 367; evolution, 7; factor in progress, agriculture, 5*n*, 688; variations, 398, 437, 611; zonality, 321–6
Climatic Long-Range Interpretation, Mapping and Prediction (CLIMAP), 379
climatic system: causes of changes in, 376; changes, 473; changes in Central Africa, 553–5; changes in West Africa, 615–17; definition, 376
climatology, 377–8: chronology, 372; mechanisms of global, 376–7; palaeo-, 318–19, 355, 359–61, 363
coasts, African, 321: influence on climate, 324; marine currents, 323; navigation, 579
coinage: cowries as, 351; iron, 358
Collection des Universités de France, 97
Collection G. Bude, 97
'Collignon horizon', 574, 576
colonial history, 33–4, 39, 59, 60, 68: French, 40
colonialism, 742, 743–4: correspondence from administration, 135; effect on ethnology, 14; effect on names, 20; Eurocentric bias, 54–5; false frontiers of, 21; prejudices against African cultigens, 688
Comité d'Etudes Historiques et Scientifiques de l'AOF, 40
Condition Humaine, La (Malraux), 356
Congress of Africanists, Accra (1962), 70
Congress of Black Writers and Artists, Paris (1956) and Rome (1959), 65
Conseil Africain et Malgache pour l'Enseignement Supérieur (CAMES), 68
conservation: of rock art, 657; techniques, 227–31
copper: belt of Zaire and Zambia, 333–334; confusion with bronze, 212, 727; localized, 336; in Nile Valley, 644, 649–50, 712, 719, 722, 724; in Nubia, 723; production leads to expansion, 285; in West Africa, 628
Coptic language, 242, 301: writing, 254
cosmic rays, 227
crafts, 180–7, 351
Cromagnons, 575–6, 640, 677
Cromerian period, 375
crops, 700: grain, 275, 337; marks, 224; rice, African, 698–9
cultivation, plant, 338, 626–7, 733: in art, 673; dating, 702; in Fertile Crescent, 275; Neolithic, 689; origins, 687, 692–7; in Sahara, 602–603; simultaneous with animal domestication, 77, 481; in West Africa, 623, 626–7
Cushitic languages, 243, 301–2

Dabban industry, 515
dating methods, 217–24, 354: absolute, 73; of climatic events, 372; radiometric, 372, 375; of rock art, 657–9; value to anthropology, 274
De Bello Vandalico (Procopius), 98
deciphering, 78, 234
deformation, skeletal, 355
deglaciation, 383, 388
Deir el Fakhuri subpluvial, 371
demography, *see* population
Demotic Chronicle, 95
demotic writing, 78, 251
dental mutilation: Capsian, 576, 578; Khartoumian, 642
Description de l'Egypte, 118
desert: climates, 325–6; wild-life, 340
dieli caste, 173, 187–92
Dishna subpluvial, 371
Djokocian industry, 558
Documents sur l'histoire, la géographie et le commerce de l'Afrique orientale (Guillain), 32
domas, 172–7, 192–6
domestication, animal, 77, 341–2, 700, 733: in art, 672; Egyptian, 603, 626, 700; in Fertile Crescent, 275; in Sahara, 603, 627. *See also* animal husbandry
Donatism, 98
Donau glaciation, 372, 375
drums, 151, 352

Ebers Papyrus, 214
Eburonian event, 375
eclipses: to establish chronology, 17, 160
Ecole des Langues Orientales Vivantes, 270

Ecole Supérieure des Lettres, Dakar, 40
ecology, 4, 7: barriers, 743; changes caused by agriculture, 689, 697; plant and animal, 398; setting for origins of agriculture, 688–92
economies, African, 62–3: West African agricultural, 628
education: development of universities, 40–1; European character, 55; Islamic oral, 197; traditional African oral, 175, 178–9, 184, 193–196; in West Africa, 38
Eemian interglacial, 390, 500
Egyptian language, 242, 300–1: knowledge essential for historical study, 78–80; Pharaonic, 239; scripts, 78
Egyptology, 78–80, 97
'elassolithic', 576
electrical resistivity surveying, 225–6
embalming materials, 214
emission spectrometry, 207, 210
endogamy, 184
Eneolithic (Chalcolithic or predynastic), 712, 721
English language: creolized (Krio), 307; literature, 114; in South Africa, Zimbabwe, Liberia, 307
engravings, 656, 661–2: dating of Saharan, 658; under paintings, 657
environments, bioclimatic, 326–31
Eocene age, 318, 335, 401–2, 421
eoliths, theory of, 417, 418
epi-Levalloisian industry, *see* Hawarian industry
equatorial and sub-equatorial belts: climates, 324–5, 361–6
equatorial forest, *see* forest, equatorial
erosion, 318: wind, 367
Esmeraldo (Pereira), 17
Esquisses Sénégalaises (Boilat), 134
ethnodemographic map, Soviet, 309
ethnography, 270, 353: Eurocentric, 349
ethno-linguistics, 248–9
ethnology, 13–15, 37–8: palaeo-, 568
European: documents on Islamic Africa, 109; literature on Africa, 115, 126–9; travellers in North Africa, 31, 118
evolution, doctrine of, 272, 349
excavation methods, 457–8, 568

faïence, Egyptian, 216, 713, 723
Fakurian industry, 640
Fath-al-Sahkur (al-Bartayili), 130
fatwas, 92, 108, 109
fauna, 340–4, 601, 637
Fauresmith industry, 421, 462, 475, 505–8, 733
fertility rites, 670
Fields of Gold (Mas'ūdī), 107
fire: bush in West Africa, 617, 701; causes colour change in soil, 458; in East Africa, 472; -eaters association, 192; evidence of, 501; use dates from lower Palaeolithic, 338, 415, 618
fishing, 7, 341, 475, 479, 480, 481, 692, 735: in Mid and East Africa, 481–4, 625
flora: Neolithic in Sahara, 601
folk-motif: indexes, 147
food production, 7, 626–7, 737: beginning of, 687, 689
foodstuffs, 76, 337, 456, 733: cereals, 697
forests, equatorial, 4, 330, 336–7: barrier to migrations, 689; 'centre of horticulture', 695, 696–7, 701; fluctuation of boundaries, 362, 530; wild game in, 341
fossils, dating of, 490; evidence for hominids, 487; formation, 437, 439, 454
Fragmenta historicorum graecorum, 98
Fragmentation Belt, 312
Franco-Cantabrian rock art, 675
Fula language, 304
Fulfulde language, 130, 131, 195, 239, 240, 246
Funj Chronicle, 119
Futūh al-Buldān (Balādhurī), 101
Futuk Misr wa-l-Maghrib (Ibn Abd-al-Hakam), 101

Galla language, 301
Gamblian pluvial epoch, 361, 362, 369, 421: in Central Africa, 531, 538, 553
gaolos class, 195
Gauss epoch, 360
Gbeya language, 305
Ge'ez language, 28, 29, 293
genealogists, 151: oral tradition, 157, 187, 189, 194–6
genetic drift, 261, 269
Geniza documents, Cairo, 108
Geographical History of Africa, A (Leo Africanus), 26
Geography (Ptolemy), 99
geography, historical: economic aspects, 333–47; physical aspects, 4, 74, 316–32, 359
geology, 7, 74, 316–20, 355, 362
geomagnetic time scale, 360
German: Africanist studies, 270–5; Institute expeditions (1963), 638
Geschichte Afrikas (Westermann), 37
Gigantopithecus: *bilaspurensis*, 404; *blacki*, 404
Gilbert epoch, 360
Gilbert Vieillard Collection, 130
Gilsa event, 375
glacial epochs, 359–60, 365, 371–8, 438
glass, 7: -fritting crucibles, 215; volcanic, 335
Glossarium Comparativum Linguarum Totius Orbis, 294
glottochronology, 237–8
gold: determining presence of in artefacts, 209; in Kush, Sudan, Zimbabwe, 332; in Nile Valley, 712, 719, 727; not exploited in Baule, 183–4; Nubian, 332, 727; in South Africa, Ghana and Zaïre, 334; trade, 334; West African, 628, 630
Gonja Chronicle (*Kitab al-Ghunja*), 28
Gottweig interstadial, 620
Grapes of Wrath, The (Steinbeck), 356
grasslands, 330–1: contribute to mobility, 339; extension of, 339, 554–5, 697; rich in game, 336, 340–341; suitable for agriculture, 692, 696, 701
grindstones, 476, 517, 597, 603, 605
griots, African, 82, 143, 152, 249: French idea, 168, 191
Guide to the Sources of the History of Africa, xxi, 137
Guirian wet episode, 369, 371
Gujerati language, 308
Günz glaciation, 359, 360, 372, 375, 421
Gur language (or Voltaic), 283, 304
Gwelo industry, 506

Hadiths, 144
haematology, *see* blood-groups
hagiography, 111
Halfian industry, 639–40
Hamitic languages, 242–3, 246, 273–4, 297: first use of name, 294
Hamitic myth, 21, 35–6, 245–7, 272–274, 296, 297, 736: in art, 675; in physical anthropology, 355
handaxes, 362, 421, 472, 496: related to *Homo sapiens*, 447
harmattan, 377

Hawarian industry (formerly epi-Levalloisian), 637, 639
Hebrew language, 301
hieratic writing, 78, 94, 251
hieroglyphic writing, 78, 94, 251
Histoire Générale (ed. Glotz), 34
Historia mundi: Ein Handbuch der Weltgeschichte, 34
historical studies, 55–8: analytical field, 60; elitism in, 58; Eurocentric, 54, 58; and linguistics, 233–55; parochialism, 55; weakness of linear approach, 348–9, 357; world perspective, 55, 56, 70
historiography: African, 25–42, 54–71, 114–15; Arab, 116; principles of research, 16–23; South African, 124
history, African, 2, 3: African consciousness of, 19, 43–53, 54, 233; decolonized, 40, 59; European viewpoint, 30, 127, 129; static fallacy, 61; study developed, 41; in tropical Africa, 67
history, total, 357, 358: as symphonic discipline, 23, 348
History of Angola (Correia), 30
History of Dahomy, The (Dalzell), 30, 128
History of the Berbers (Ibn Khaldun), 16, 109, 110
History of the Colonization of Africa by Alien Races, A (Johnston), 36
History of the Gambia (Gray), 40
History of the Gold Coast (Ward), 40
History of the Gold Coast and Asante (Reindorf), 38, 134
History of the Gold Coast and Ashanti (Claridge), 40
Holocene period, 359, 360, 421: population increase of early, 526; subpluvial, 361
Hominidae family, 400, 401, 440, 442–443
hominids, 421: earliest in Africa, 73, 487, 489; early way of life, 491–3; effect of glaciations, 371; in Nile Valley, 634–5, 637–8; from South Africa, 439
hominization: general problems, 400–419; glossary, 419–26; prehistorian's attitude to, 412–13
Homo, genus, 400, 401, 409, 411, 421, 443: adaptive abilities, 731–2; compared with Australopithecines, 491; stone tools, 440
Homo erectus, 265, 407, 409–10, 411, 444–5: fossils, 499; handaxes, 445, 468, 591, 618; in North Africa, 572; in Sahara, 591–3; use of fire, 472, 556
Homo faber, 412, 414, 421, 656, 732
Homo habilis, 265, 407, 408, 409, 421, 446, 730; distinct from Australopithecines, 444, 491; tools, 468, 493, 555, 591
Homo loquens, 415
Homo neanderthalensis, 265, 274, 423
Homo rhodesiensis, 441, 502, 516
Homo sapiens, 265, 274, 412, 414, 422, 730: emergence, 734; endocranial volume, 445; middle stone age, 472, 516; related to handaxe, 447; *sapiens*, 460, 473, 516, 517; today, 441–2
horse, 77: period of art, 659, 660
hunter art, *see* rock art
hunter-gatherers, 456, 458–9, 478: in Central Africa, 559–62; change to production, 687, 689; of middle Pleistocene hominids, 505; present day, 691–2
hunting, 337, 341, 455, 481, 735: in early Holocene, 526; by early hominids, 493; first use of bow and arrow, 476; new methods in late stone age, 520; regional specialization, 473; related to microlithic, 623; scenes in rock art, 672; school of initiation, 187
hydrological network, 326–9
hydronymy, 247, 248

IARE (International Afar Research Expedition), 398, 406
Ibero-Maurusian industry, 422, 568, 573, 574–6, 599, 639; influence from North Africa, 711; people, 677
ideographic systems, 253
Idfu pluvial, 370, 371
IFAO (Institut français d'archéologie orientale) expedition (1974), 635, 638, 646
Ifitah al-Da'wa (Qadi Nu'man), 106
Imbo Zabantsundu (*Voice of the Black People*), 123
Indo-European languages, 292
infra-red survey, 207, 215
initiation schools, 173, 357, 736: concept of education, 178, 187
INQUA (International Association for Quaternary Research), 360
Institut des Musées Nationaux, Zaïre, 550
Institut français d'archéologie orientale (IFAO), 635, 638, 646
Institut Français d'Afrique Noire, 40
Instructions for King Merikere, 92
interdisciplinarity, 16–19, 73, 75, 85, 348–58, 440: method, 355–8; problems, 348–50
International Afar Research Expedition (IARE), 397, 406
International African Institute: Seminar on the historian in tropical Africa, Dakar (1961), 60
International Association for Quaternary Research (INQUA), 360
International Council of Archives: guides, 6, 136–7
International Institute for Conservation of Historic and Artistic Works, London, 228
intertropical convergence zone (ITCZ), 377
Iraqw languages, 282
iron: meteoric or man-made, 213, 728; in Nile Valley, 724, 727, 728; ore in Sierra Leone, Liberia and Guinea, 334; technology, 7, 285, 336, 738; trade, 332, 334
Iron Age, Early, 628–30
irrigation system, of Nile, 707–8, 716, 724
Isidigimi, 123
Islam, 62, 196–7: first age, written sources, 100–6; second age, written sources, 108–11; schools, 196
isotopes, radioactive, 73
al-Istibsār, 109
Italian documents, 108
ITCZ (intertropical convergence zone), 377

Jaramillo event, 375
'Jebel Suhan' industry, 637, 639
Jemaian industry, 638
jewellery, African, 663
Journal of Negro History, 66
Jurassic sandstones, 318

Kafuan industry, 418, 422, 535: in Central Africa, 539; supposed, 415
Kageran pluvial, 361, 369, 371, 422, 731: in Central Africa, 531, 535–7, 553
Kakurian industry, 641
Kamasian pluvial, 361, 369, 422; in Central Africa, 531, 537–8, 553
Kamil (Ibn al-Athīr), 109
Kanjeran pluvial, 361, 369, 422, 531

Kano Chronicle, 28
Kanuri language, 12, 131
keepers of the tombs, 151
Kenyapithecus: *Africanus*, 403, 404; 'bone bashing', 418; *wickeri*, 403, 404, 730
Keremian industry, 576
Kharijīte treatises, 108
Khitat (Maqrīzī), 109
Khormusian industry, 636, 639
Kikongo language, 140
Kilwa Chronicle, 28, 132
king, 45, 83, 725
King of Ganda, The (Irstam), 37
kinship structures, 349: dominance in intermarriage, 16
Kiswahili language, 132, 236, 239
Kitāb al-Ghunja, 130
Kitāb al-Ibar (Ibn Khaldūn), 16, 109, 110
Kombewa technique, 571
Kordofanian languages, 302–3, 305
Kristelian industry, 576
Kulturkreislehre, 298
Kwa languages, 304

lacustrine areas: pluvial eras, 362–4, 371, 383, 439, 481
Lakeitian industry, 641
land: African ownership, 184, 739, 742–3; ownership in Egypt, 725
Land of Zinj, The (Stigand), 39
languages, 233: African description, 297; classification, 234–6, 240, 314; divergence, 281, 284, 310; families, 281–5, 292–308, 312–13; listing, 241–2; relationships between, 234, 310, 313–14
Latin alphabet, 114
law: Roman texts, 97; written sources, 108
lead: testing for in ceramics, 208
leather-workers, 186–7
Leopoldian Neolithic industry, 558, 564
Leopoldvillean, 553
Levallois technique, 422, 505, 510, 513: in Central Africa, 542, 557; in Nile Valley, 635, 636; in North Africa, 571; in Sahara, 593
Levalloisian industry, 422, 570: in Nile Valley, 635
Limba language, 303
Lingala language, 239
linguistics: basic unity of African languages, 268; classification, 292–308; comparative, 81, 235, 310; data as source material, 139–40; ethnocentric ideology, 241, 244–7; and ethnocultural relations, 238–47; historical, 81, 235; and history, 11–13, 80–1, 233–55, 352; history of African, 293–300; map of Africa, 281, 309–15; need for methodological precautions, 241, 247; no correlation with racial distribution, 281, 353
literacy, African, 57–8
literary sources, 26, 91, 92: Turkish, 116, 125; unpublished, 6
locust, 343–4
Loeb Classical Library, 97
Lupemban industry, 337, 442: in Central Africa, 543–5, 557, 560; forest culture, 538; lance-heads, 475; in West Africa, 621, 623. *See also* Sangoan-Lupemban tradition
Lupembo-Tschitolian, 545

Maanyan language, 307
Madārik ('Iyādh), 111
Magdalenian industry, 574
māghāzī works, 101
magic, 171, 354, 674
magnetochronological scale, 372
magnetometers, 222, 226
magnetostratigraphy, 372
Mahdiyya records, 120
Makalian subpluvial, 361, 423, 692: in Central Africa, 531, 538, 553
Makhadma subpluvial, 371
Malagasy languages, 13, 293, 295
maps, 138
marabouts, 197
Masālik al-Absār (al-'Umarī), 110
Masālik wa'l-Mamālik (Al-Bakrī), 110
masks: in art, 670; Bobo, 351
materials, 212, 213–14, 228, 454
matrilineal societies, 48, 741–2: dynasties, 159
Matuyama epoch, 360, 375, 500
Mazzerian pluvial, 368, 371, 423
Mbandaka language, 239
Mbugu language, 302
Mechta El-Arbi man, 575
megaliths, 548, 564
Meganthropus (*Homo erectus*), 407: *javanicus*, 411
Mehri language, 301
Mel languages, 283, 303
Memoirs of the Reign of Bossa Ahadee (Norris), 30
memory, in oral societies, 167, 195, 197, 199–201, 250
Menchian industry, 641
Meroitic script, 11, 252, 307
Mesolithic period, 335, 337, 423: in Nile Valley, 639–41; use of term, 466, 595
metallographic examination, 214
metallurgy: Bantu, 285; copper, 724, 728; Late Stone Age, 528; in Nile Valley, 651, 727; in West Africa, 629
metals: coming of, 628; diffusion, 727–728; impurities in ancient, 216; in Nile Valley, 707, 712
methodology, 1–23: in interdisciplinarity, 355–8; in oral chronology, 157–60; of oral tradition, 143; of prehistory, 452–60; tools, 72
microliths, 524–5, 527, 559–61, 595, 622
microscopic examination, 208–9
migration, 21, 737: and anthropological problems, 276–81; cause of cultural diffusion, 463, 515; causes, 339, 342, 344–5; currents and agriculture, 689; and ethnic differentiations, 270–6; Kuba concept, 156; and linguistic differentiations, 246, 281–6
Mindel glaciation, 359, 372, 375, 423, 571
Minean inscriptions, 301
mineral resources, 332, 333–6
Miocene epoch, 369–70, 403, 423, 440, 487
Mission to Gelele, King of Dahomey (Burton), 32
missionaries, 29, 62, 128
mongoloids, 267
monogeny, theory of, 413
monophyletism, 73
monsoons, 321, 377
Monumenta Germaniae Historica (*Auctores antiquissimi*), 98
mortars, 218, 230–1
mosquito, malarial, 343
Mousterian tradition, 371, 423, 519, 557; denticulate-, 636; in Nile Valley, 636, 637; in North Africa, 568, 572–3; Nubian-, 636; in West Africa, 621
Mousterian-Aterian industry, 572–4
'Mozhafferian geography', 111
Mudawwana (Sahnūn), 108
music: court, 11; modern Negro-African, 736; North African, early, 517; studies, 352
musicians, 187, 192

mutation, 269, 277: in plants, 693
myth, 669–70: effect on concept of time, 43–5, 200; in oral tradition, 156; in rock art, 666, 668; symbiosis of man, 180

Nakasasa industry, 511
Nakuran subpluvial, 361, 423: in Central Africa, 531, 538, 553
names: family, 189; power of, 9–10, 19–20, 142
narratives, 146, 150: art of storyteller, 199–200; formulae, 145, 150; stock theme, 147; variants, 148, 153, 162
Natufian industry, 641
Natural History (Pliny), 95, 96
Ndolian industry, 558, 559
Neanderthal man, 423, 441, 572, 574, 677, 730
Nebraskan glaciation, 360
negroes, 32: term, 268
negroids, 267, 277, 516: term, 268
Neolithic era, 423, 453: dating, 274, 601; in East Africa, 479–81; Khartoum, 479, 596; pluvials in, 369; subpluvial, 710; use of term, 465–6
Neolithic industries: in Central Africa, 547–8; coastal, 599, 604–5; in Nile Valley, 641–4; in North Africa, 568, 578–80; 'Revolution', 687, 689, 710; in Sahara, 596–605, 659, 711
Neolithic of Capsian tradition (NTC), 574, 577, 578–80, 677; in Sahara, 597–9, 604, 622
Neolithic of Sudanese tradition, 596–597, 603, 665, 711
neutron activation analysis, 207, 211
New Cambridge Modern History, The, 33
Niger–Congo language family, 299, 302, 303–5, 626
Niger–Kordofanian language family, 302–5
Nilo–Saharan language family, 300, 305–6, 483, 626
Noahite language family, 296
Novellae (Justinian), 95, 99
Nsong-a-Lianja (epic), 279
NTC (Néolithique de tradition capsienne), 578, 579
Nubian writing, 254
Numidian alphabet, 664
Nzako diamond workings, 543

obsidian, 213, 334, 423, 476, 579
oceans: rise of levels, 383–5, 386; temperature, 379–80; in upper Pleistocene, 391
Old Testament, 413
Oldowan industry, 406, 411, 413, 414, 417–18, 424, 463, 468, 493–6, 732: in Central Africa, 539–40; Developed, 496, 502; in Nile Valley, 634–5, 653; note on name, 466; tools, 447, 460, 466
Oligocene age, 400, 402, 424
onomastics, 247
oral traditions, 7–11, 142–65, 160, 161, 166: causality in, 156; collection, 42, 162–3, 197–9, 202; contamination, 162–3; definition, 142, 143–4, 167–8; evaluation, 144–8, 160–2; and linguistics, 249–50; literature, 234; living example, 166–203, 249; mental framework, 153–7; problem of distortion, 150–1, 161; publication, 163–4; social framework, 148–53; spatial concepts in, 155–6; time conceptions, 82, 154–5, 200; use in African history, 60, 81–2, 350, 351; values, roles in, 154
Oreopithecus, 401, 404: *bambolii*, 404
Osteodontokeratic industry, 410, 413, 414, 415–17, 424, 492
ostracon, 94
Ougartian pluvials, 369, 371, 424
Ox: period of art, 659, 660
Oxford History of Africa, 67

paintings, rock, *see* rock art
Palaeanthropus, 734
Palaeolithic period, 335, 337, 338, 424, 453; bifacial tools of, 593; in North Africa, 574–80; term in Europe, 465
palaeomagnetism, 222, 359: reversal timescale, 490
palaeontology: animal, 568, 572; human, 73, 400–1, 439, 442, 446, 487
Palaeozoic era, 367, 424
palynology, 375, 458, 602; palaeo-, 76
Papuan language, 296
papyri, 94, 95, 100
Paranstralopithecus, 407
Paranthropus, 407, 424
pastoralism, *see* animal husbandry
patina, 216: conservation, 230: of paintings, 657
Patrologia Graeca (Migne), 98
Patrologia Latina (Migne), 98
Pebble culture, *see* Oldowan industry
pebbles, 410: in Acheulian, 335; circles, 411, 467, 518; split and trimmed, 414–15, 466, 467
Periplus of Hanno, 96, 99
Periplus of the Erythraean Sea, 26, 95
Peuples et Civilisations, Histoire Générale, 34
Phanerozoic era, 367
Philosophy of History (Hegel), 30–1
phonetic writing, 253
physics, nuclear, 73
pigments, 517: identification, 216, 662; minerals for, 335; used by Capsians, 604
Pithecanthropines, 274, 409, 417: Javanese, 409
Pithecanthropus, 406, 424, 572
Platyrrina, 401, 424
Pleistocene period, 424: chronology of upper, 390–2; climatic events of, 359, 360, 367, 489; dating of limits, 221, 360; humid era of upper, 383, 439; hyperarid lower, 320, 383; tools, 447, 500
Plesanthropus, 407
Pliocene period, 320, 424: climatic changes, 489; dating of, 221, 360; fossils from, 487; pluvial, 370; threshold of technology, 447
pluvial epochs, 361–5, 368–71, 439, 615
poems, 145, 150: epic, 8–11, 145–6, 150, 352
pollen analysis, 225: in Afar, 391; in Central Africa, 554; in Fertile Crescent, 275; in Shungura formation, 396
Polyglotta Africana (Koelle), 244
Pomongwan industry, 524
Pongidae, 424, 440, 487
population: concentration, 5; dispersion, 737; growth, 340, 473, 627; race, 262–9
potassium-argon dating, 73, 220–1, 372, 462
pottery, 663: determination of trace elements, 213; earliest firing, 479; early use of, 442; home-drawing role, 483; thermoluminescence of, 217, 223–4; value of finds, 7; wavy-lined, 480, 482, 642
Pragmateia (Polybius), 97
pre-Cambrian, 318, 424, 552: rocks in Sahara, 367
pre-Cretaceous age, 334
prehistory, African, 350: attitude to hominization, 412–19; progress of Saharan research, 586–8
Présence Africaine, 40, 65
Primary period, 318

Primates, 400: comparative biochemistry of, 487; ecology, 460; Prosimian, 400, 401; Simian, 400, 401; societies, 459; variety listed, 402
Propliopithecus, 400
Propyläen Weltgeschichte, 34
Punic period, 96

Qadian industry, 640, 643
Qatabanian inscriptions, 301
Qawānīn al-dawāwīn (Mammāti), 109
Quaternary period, 318, 367, 401*n*: chronology of Sahara, 588*n*; climatic variations, 371–2, 378, 531; glaciations, 372–5, 615; late, 363; in North Africa, 568; transgressions, 375

Rabat man, 572
race: concept of, 355; forming of types, 281; 'Indigenous African', 517; migration theories of, 276–81; morphological approach, 262; related to rock art, 677–9; standardization process, 265; theories, 261–9
racemization, 221, 500
radiocarbon dating, 73, 218–20, 275, 372, 490, 508
radiography, 209
rainfall mechanism, 322–4, 344
Ramapithecus, 400, 401, 425, 487, 730: *punjabicus*, 403, 404; *wickeri*, 487
Rasā'il (al-Qādhi al-Fādhil), 111
religions, African, 62, 351; evidence of belief in after-life, 517; priests, 151; written sources, 108
Rhodesian man, 221, 441
Riss glaciation, 359, 360, 371, 372, 375, 425, 571
ritual, 171, 174–5, 184: chants, 180
rivers, 327–9
Riyādh (Mālikī), 111
rock art, 662: in Central Africa, 548–9; in Central Tanzania, 456, 478; dating of South African, 218, 657–9; earliest, 528; educational role, 669; as historical source, 671–675; in North Africa, 579; periods of, 659–60; 'petroglyphs', 667; in racial identification, 355; in Sahara, 274, 275, 603, 656, 677; in South Africa, 274, 280, 459, 528, 656, 657; stereotypes, 665
rock-shelters, 476, 526
Roman law texts, 97
Royal Chronicle (Lebna Dengel), 120

Sabaean writing, 254, 301
sacrifices, 44
Sahara und Sudan (Nachtigal), 32
salt mines, 332
Sangoan industry, 462, 465, 506, 508, 516, 733: in Central Africa, 542–3, 557; forest culture, 538; in Nile Valley, 635; in West Africa, 619–20; widespread, 475
Sangoan-Lupemban tradition, 366, 371, 425, 475, 479: in Nile Valley, 636
Saourian pluvial, 369, 371, 425
saponification solvent extraction, 207
Sara language, 242
savannah, *see* grasslands
scarification; facial, 21; bodily, 358
Scriptorum classicorum Bibliotheca Oxoniensis, 97
sculpture, African, 663; terracotta figurines, 629, 630
Sebilian industry, 638, 640, 641, 711: 111, 595
Secondary period, 318
sedimentology, 318, 359, 398
Semainian industry, 716
semantic anthropology, *see* ethnolinguistics
semantics, 236–7
Semitic language family, 294, 301
Sequence Dating System, 224
Serer language, 237, 239, 240, 246
serology, 75, 263
sexual themes in art, 674
Shaheinabian industry, 642–3, 720
Shahri language, 301
Shamakian industry, 640
shell middens, 604, 625
Sidi Abderrahmane (Casablanca Man), 572
silver, 727
Sinanthropines, 425: at Choukoutien, 415, 417; *pekinensis*, 572
Sinat al-Hājib Ja'far, 101
Sivanpithecus, 406
slavery, 740, 741: trade, 5, 30, 347, 742
smiths, 182–3, 185
Smithfield industry, 524, 526
SOAS (School of Oriental and African Studies), London, 69, 270
social systems: age group, 51, 159; in Nile Valley, 724–7; political, 735–7
Société Africaine de Culture: *Présence Africaine*, 40
Société Préhistorique et Protohistorique Gabonaise, 550
sociology, 55, 83–4, 353

soils, 329–30, 345–7: acidity, 531, 550, 730; analysis, 224–5, 458; cultivable nature of, 688; fertility, 345; movements, 565; in West Africa, 614
Some Historical Accounts of Guinea (Benezet), 30
sorghum, 697–8, 700
sources, archaeological, 6–7
sources, written: classification, 90–1; critical approach necessary, 106, 108, 127–8; external, 124–9; from 15th century, 114–40; internal, 129–34; inventory: pre-Islamic, 94–100; inventory: first Islamic age, 100–8; inventory: second Islamic age, 108–11; modern, 123–4; periodization problem, 88–90; pre-15th century, 87–112; primary, 114, 134–40; types, 92–3; uneven distribution, 5–6, 116. *See also* literary sources
specific gravity determination, 209
spectrophotometric analysis, 207
speech: bond between man and, 167, 175; as creative power, 170–1; dialectalization, 250; and history, 233, 734; in magic, 171–2; power of, 9, 142; rhythm, 171–2
states, emergence of, 339, 740
steppe lands, 331
stock raising, *see* animal husbandry
stone, 335, 650–3
Stone Age: chronology and classification, 460–84; Early, 460, 466–72, 618–20, 635–6; in East Africa, 452–455; Late, 460, 476–9, 524–9, 622–6, 638–9; Middle, 460, 472–5, 508–24, 621–2, 636–8; variant technologies, 462; in West Africa, 617–618
stone monuments: deterioration, 228; recommendations for restoration, 230–1; surface treatment, 229–30; in West Africa, 630
Storia d'Ethiopia (Conti Rossi), 34
stratigraphy, 372, 458: bio-, 372; chrono-, 372, 375, 396, 569; climato-, 376–7; dating from, 462; litho-, 372, in Sahara, 588*n*
Studies in Conservation, 288
Subh al-A'shā (Qalqashansī), 109
succession, royal, 158–9, 353
Sudanic language families, 297: Central, 306; Eastern, 295, 306; Western, 295, 297, 299
Sufi shaykhs, 197
Siyar (Wisyānī), 108

Sundjata Fasa, 47, 146, 672
Sūrah al-Ardh, 106
Swahili language, 13, 239: historical writings in, 28, 132
symbolism: cosmological and mythological in art, 668; of loom, 171, 181; sexual, of smithy, 182; of spirals, 674–5
symposia on conservation of stone monuments, 229
Symposium on the Peopling of Ancient Egypt and the Deciphering of the Meroitic Script, Cairo (1974), 40, 80, 243
synchronisms, 160

Tabaqāt works, 108, 111, 119
Tafineq writing, 254
Tale of the Castaway, 80
Taouirirtian pluvial, 369
tarīkhs, 101, 106
Ta'rīkh al-Fattāsh, 27, 38, 50, 129, 350
Ta'rīkh al-Sūdān (al-Sa'di), 27, 38, 50, 129
Ta'rīkh Say (Ibn Adwar), 130
Tchadanthropus uxoris, 613, 614
Tebessan industry, 577
techniques, historical, *see* methodology
Telanthropus, 407, 411, 425; *capensis*, 409
Tenerean industry, 599, 605, 677
Tensiftian industry, 425, 572
Tertiary period, 318, 401*n*
Theodosian Code, 95
thermal analysis, 207
thermo-remnant magnetism (trm), 222
thermoluminescence testing, 217, 223–4
Tifinagh alphabet, 665
Tigriniya language, 254
time, African concepts of, 18–19, 43–53
tin: localized, 336; mining, 629; in Nile Valley, 727; testing for, 208; in Zaïre and Nigeria, 334
tools, 447–8: Australopithecine types, 494; biface, 420; blades, 476, 515; bone, 547, 604; disc-core technique, 505, 510, 513; earliest bone and stone, 410–11, 452, 466, 614; flake, 473, 504, 593; hafted, 473, 476, 517; Heavy-Duty variant, 506; -kits, 454–5; micro-blade technology, 517; not peculiar to man, 414; polished, 563, 603; stone, 335, 440, 445, 492, 569; use by man, 413, 414, 415–19; wooden, 337, 500, 501
Topographia Christiana (Cosmas Indicopleustes), 95
toponymy, 12, 99, 139, 247, 248
trade: ecological barriers to, 743; on Red Sea and Indian Ocean, 25–6; across Sahara, 353; watershed in 15th century, 89, 90
Trade of Guinea (Sundstrom), 37
transmission, of oral tradition, 143–4, 162: authenticity, 174–80, 199; break in, 202; chain of informants, 144, 167, 170, 177; eye-witness testimony, 143; frequency, 152; by mnemotechnical means, 151
Travels and Discoveries in North and Central Africa (Barth), 32
Travels to Discover the Source of the Nile (Bruce), 31
tropical and subtropical zones, 325, 366–71
tsetse fly, 342–3
Tschitolian industry, 426, 479, 525: in Central Africa, 538, 546–7, 557, 560
Twi language, 239
Twilight Tales of the Black Baganda (Fisher), 39

ultra-violet light examination, 215
Unesco: conference on race as social myth, 265–6; excavation of Thebes mound, 637; fosters African need of history, 41–2; International Scientific Committee, xxi, xxii, xxv, 3
universities: development of African, 40–1, 64–71; French in Africa, 65
Ushtata technique, 639, 640, 641

Vai script, 79, 114, 136, 252, 254
Van Riebeeck Society of Cape Town, 122
Vanished Dynasty: Ashanti (Fuller), 39
vegetal resources, 336–40
Vienna Corpus, 98
Villafrancian pluvial, 73, 360, 368, 371, 392, 426, 569
volcanic activity, 318, 367
Völkerkunde (Baumann), 37
Volta–Congo language family, 314
Vsemirnaja Istorija (*World History*), 34

Waqd records, 108
wars, African: in art, 674; and religion, 354
water resources, 344–5
weavers, 7, 181–2, 185–6
wet chemical analysis, 207, 210
Wilton industry, 426, 465, 478, 733: microlithic element, 479, 524, 525; -Tschitolian, 562
women, 47–8
wood-workers, 185, 186
words: divine origin, 168–70; power, 19, 175, 181; significance, 352–3; translation of unknown, 212
writing, African systems: Egyptian, 79–80, 251, 651, 715; inter-relationships, 79, 250–5; technique of transcription, 7, 251–2; West African, 254
Wulāt Misr wa Qudhatuhu (Kindī), 101
Würm glaciation, 359, 360, 366, 372, 375, 379, 426, 573

X-ray diffraction analysis, 207
X-ray fluorescence, 207, 211

Zande language, 305
Zimbabwe-Monomotapa Culture (Weischoff), 37
Zindj languages, 282
Zinjanthropus, 73, 221, 407, 730
Zuhur al-Basatin (Moussa), 131

Index of Persons

Abdanī, 111
Abidin Shirwani, Zain al-: *Bustana s-Seyahe*, 126
Abraham, D. P., 9
Abu al-Fida, 26
Abu Makhrama: *Chronicle of the Fortress of Aden*, 125
Abu Zakariyā, 111
Acton, Lord, 33
Africanus, Leo, 100: *A Geographical History of Africa*, 26, 124
Agathias, 99
Al-, al-. For personal names with this prefix, *see under* following element.
Alexseev, K., 263
Alexandre, J. and S., 553
Ali, Alfa, 197
Ali, Sidi, 125
Alimen, H., 368, 569, 571
Almeida, M. de, 29
Amina, 48
Amo, A. W., 132
Anciaux de Favaux, P., 534, 546
Ankermann, 272
Antoine, M., 573
Appian, 96
Arambourg, C., 73, 274, 369, 405, 569, 570
Aristodemus, 95
Arkell, A. J., 480, 636
Askiya (of Songhay), 135
Augustine, St, 98, 738
Ayyashi, al-, 117

Bâ, Amadou Hampâté, 143, 670, 675
Baba, Ahmad, 130
Babet, J., 534
Bada, J., 500
Baghdadi, 111
Bakary Dian, 9
Bakrī, al-, 26, 350: *Masālik wa'l-Mamālik*, 110
Balandier, G., 349
Balawi, 111
Ball, J., 364
Balout, L., 656
Banzoumana, 173, 190
Bartayili, Muhammad al-: *Fath-al-Sahkur*, 130
Barth, H., 128: *Travels and Discoveries in North and Central Africa*, 32
Basi, Saa, 249
Basset, R., 241
Bates, E., 254
Baumann, H.: *Völkerkunde*, 37
Bayle des Hermens, R. de, 355, 534, 550, 556, 563
Beauchène, G. de, 534
Bacquaert, M., 534
Beidelman, T., 156
Belime, 201
Benezet: *Some Historical Accounts of Guinea*, 30
Biberson, P., 418, 568, 569, 571
Bishop, W. W., 553
Blaeu, W., 139
Blankoff, B., 534
Bleek, W. H. I., 238, 240, 295, 668
Blyden, E. W., 38, 133
Boilat, Abbé: *Esquisses Sénégalaises*, 134
Bokar, T., 197
Boston, J. S., 154
Boule, 570
Boury N'Diaye, Al, 354
Bovill, E. W.: *Caravans of the Old Sahara*, 39
Bowdich, T. E., 31
Boyd, 263, 268
Brain, C. K., 409
Braudel, F., 5
Breasted, J. H., 275
Breuil, Abbé H., 413, 415, 534
Brown, E. J. P., 39
Bruce, J.: *Travels to Discover the Source of the Nile*, 31
Brunschwig, H., 65
Bryan, M. A., 284
Buedel, J., 366
Bukele, Momolu Duwela, 136
Burton, R.: *Mission to Gelele, King of Dahomey*, 32
Butzer, K. W., 363, 364, 369, 553

Cabu, F., 534, 541
Cadamosto, 28
Caesar, Julius: *Bellum Civile*, 97
Cahen, D., 534, 558, 565
Calame-Griaule, 349
Camps, G., 573
Candolle, A. de, 693
Capitein, Jacobus, 132
Casely-Hayford, J. E., 39
Cassiodorus, 98
Cavalli-Sforza, L., 264
Cavazzi, de Montecudolo, 29, 164, 252
Chamzashe, G., 123
Chavaillon, J., 368, 406, 411, 569
Cheops, 214
Chephren, 227
Claridge, W. W.: *History of the Gold Coast and Ashanti*, 40
Clark, Sir George, 33
Clark, J. D., 534, 550, 553, 556, 560
Clark-Howell, P., 73
Clarke, R., 409
Coetzef, J. A., 554
Cohen, M., 281
Colette, J. R. F., 534, 544, 550, 558, 564, 565
Conti Rossi, C.: *Storia d'Ethiopia*, 34
Cooke, H. B. S., 553
Coppens, Y., 73, 405
Corippus, 98
Cornevin, R., 65
Correia, Silva: *History of Angola*, 30
Cosmas Indicopleustes, 26: *Topographia Christiana*, 95
Cugoana, O., 133
Cyprian, 98

Da Monzon, king of Segou, 8, 9
Dakodonu (Dokodonu), king: récade, 252
Dalzell, A.: *The History of Dahomy*, 30, 128
Danquah, J. B., 39
Dapper, O., 29
Darci, Ahmad al-, 117
Darjīnī, 111
Dart, R., 34, 405, 414, 415–17
Darwin, C., 32, 266, 274, 437
David, N., 534
Dayfallah, Wad.: *Tabaqat*, 119
de Graft Johnson, J. W.: *African Glory*, 39

Delafosse, M., 14: glottochronology, 238; language classification, 235, 298
Dembo, A., 173
Deschamps, H., 65
Devisse, J., 82
Dhahabī, 109
Dieterlen, G., 253
Dike, K. O., 41, 64
Dimashqî, 111
Diodorus Siculus, 95, 96
Diop, C. A., 282
Dixon, 262
Doize, R. L., 534
Dolgopoljskij, 243
Dorize, L., 377
Drexel, A., 298
Droux, G., 534
Dubois, W. E. B., 66
Duke, A., 133
Dupois, J., 32
Duvigneaud, P., 554

Eboué, F., 534
Ehrlich, C., 64
Emphoux, J. P., 559
Equiano, O., 133
Essa, A., 173
Evans-Pritchard, E. E., 14

Fage, J. D., 64, 358
Farine, B., 534
Farrand, W. R., 391
Fisher, R.: *Twilight Tales of the Black Baganda*, 39
Flint, R. F., 365, 553
Frobenius, Leo, 14, 37–8, 272: on rock art, 665, 666, 668
Froude, J. A., 33
Fu Kiau, 143
Fulgentius, St, 98
Fuller, Sir Francis: *A Vanished Dynasty: Ashanti*, 39

Gabel, C., 732
Gasse, F., 378, 383
Georgius Cyprius, 99
Gervais, 404
Gezo, king: récade, 252
Ghalbun, Muhammad, 117
Giegengack, R. F., 369
Glass, B., 265
Glélé, king: récade, 251, 252
Glélé, M., 83
Gobert, E. G., 572, 575
Goody, J., 150
Gosaas, N., 249
Gqoba, W. W., 123
Gray, Sir John: *History of the Gambia*, 40
Greenberg, J. H.: on Bantu, 12; on genetic language classification, 283, 292, 299–308, 314
Gregory the Great, Pope, 99
Griaule, M., 253
Grove, A. T., 364
Guillain, M.: *Documents sur l'histoire, la géographie et le commerce de l'Afrique orientale*, 32
Guillen, N., 66
Guthrie, M., 12, 284

Hama, B., 143
Hamet, I., 119
Hamidun, Mukhtarwuld, 119
Hanotaux, G., 33
Hansberry, W. L., 66
Hansen, C. L., 369
Hargreaves, J. D., 64
Hassan ibn Muhammad al-Wuzza'n, al-, *see* Africanus, Leo
Hatshepsut, Queen, 80
Hayford, J. E. Casely-, 39
Hegel, G. W. F., 272: *Philosophy of History*, 30–1
Heinzelin, J. de, 366, 369, 550, 561
Herkhuf, 80, 278
Herodotus, 25, 93, 95, 99, 707
Hervieu, J., 534
Hiernaux, J., 266
Himyari, 111
Holm, E., 659
Homburger, L., 298
Homer, 93
Honea, 273
Hor-'Aha, king, 212
Horton, J. A. B., 32, 38, 133–4
Houis, M., 349
Howell, F. Clark, 73, 405, 409
Hugot, H. J., 569, 574
Hunwick, J. O., 130
Hürzeler, Johannes, 404
Hydatius, 98

Ibn Abd-al-Hakam: *Futūk Misr w-al-Maghrib*, 101
Ibn Abī Zar', 109
Ibn Adwar: *Ta'rīkh Say*, 130
Ibn al-Athīr: *Kamil*, 109
Ibn al-Faqīh, 107
Ibn al-'Idhārī, 109, 110
Ibn as-Saghīr, 108
Ibn Battuta, 26, 110: on Mali, 77, 351, 740; his place names, 6
Ibn Hawqal: *Kitāb surat al-ard*, 107
Ibn Iyas, 118
Ibn Jubayr, 111
Ibn Khaldūn, 26–7, 93, 116, 738–9: *History of the Berbers*, 16; *Kitāb al-Ibar*, 109, 110
Ibn Khurdādhbah, 107
Ibn Majid, Ahmad, 124: *Al-Muhit*, 125
Ibn Mbeng, 249
Ibn Othman, 117
Ibn Raziq, Salil: *History of the Imams and Sayyids of Oman*, 125
Ibn Sa'īd al-Gharnātī: *Geography*, 110
Ibn Shariyar, Buzurg, 107
Idrisi, al-, 26: *Book of Roger*, 110
Irstam, Tor: *The King of Ganda*, 37
Isaac, G. L., 405
Isesi, Pharaoh, 278
Iwa, 173, 190
'Iyādh: *Madārik*, 111

Jabarti, Al-, 118
Jabawu, J. T., 123
Jahiz, 93
Janmart, J., 534
Johanson, D. C., 406, 491
Johnston, Sir Harry, 284: *A History of the Colonization of Africa by Alien Races*, 36
Jones, William, 293
Jousse, Marcel, 11
Juba II: notices, 96, 99
Justinian: Code, 99; *Nouvellae*, 95

Kagwa, A., 39, 160
Kamal, Y.: *Monumenta Cartographica Africae et Aegypti*, 139
Kamara Moussa, C.: *Zuhur al-Basatin*, 131
Katwinkel, 539
Kelley, H., 534
Kent, P. E., 553
Khayyat, Khalifa b.: *Tarikh*, 101
Khuwarizmī, 106
Ki-Zerbo, J., 65
Kiewiet, C. W. de, 34
Kindī: *Kitāb Wulāt Misr wa Qudhatuha*, 101
Koelle, S. W., 35, 235, 240: *Polyglotta Africana*, 244; on Vai writing, 254
Koenigswald, Von, 409
Kolb, P., 279
Koullel, 198
Kwarizmi, 93

Labriola, A., xix

Lacroix, 534
Landman, 263
Larsen, L. Kohl, 405
Latif, 173, 198
Lawson, A. C., 364
le Hérisse, 252
Le Roy, P., 534
Leakey, L. S. B., 34, 362, 482, 553; on blade tools, 479; on *Hominidae*, 403, 405, 418, 441; in Kenya, 457; on Olduvai, 539
Leakey, M. D., 405, 466
Leakey, R. E. F., 405
Lebna Dengel, Emperor: *Royal Chronicle*, 120
Lepsius, R., 295, 296
Leroi-Gourhan, A., 353
Lévi-Strauss, C., 15, 62, 349
Lewontin, R. C., 264
Lhote, H., 671
Linnaeus, 265, 266, 268
Linschoten, Van, 139
Livingstone, D., 265, 378, 388
Livy, 96
Lombard, J., 534
Lopez, D., 29
Lubbock, 272
Lucas, Sir Charles P., 33
Ludolf(us), Job, 29, 293
Lueji, 48
Lushan, 273

M'Bow, Amadou-Mahtar, 65
McBurney, C. B. M., 573
McGaffey, W., 154
Mackenzie, J., 20
Macmillan, W. M., 34
Mago, 96
Mai Idris (of Bornu), 135
Maley, J., 377
Malīkī: *Riyādh*, 111
Malinowski, B., 14, 37, 61
Malraux, André, 676: *La Condition humaine*, 356
Mamadou Gaolo, 195
Mammāti: *Qawānīn al-dawāwīn*, 109
Manessy, G., 284
Manethon, 25
Mannūnī, 106
Mansa Musa, Emperor of Mali, 740
Maqrīzī: Khitat, 109
Maret, P. de, 559
Margat, 368
Marinus of Tyre, 99
Marliac, A., 534
Marx, K., 15, 84, 738: *Das Kapital*, 739
Mas'ūdī, al, 26: *Fields of Gold*, 93, 107
Mauny, R., 65
Meinhof, C., 240, 245, 273, 297
Menander, 95
Menelik II, 120
Menes, 650
Merivale, H., 33
Meyerowitz, E. L. R., 39
Mgnoki, 123
Migeod, F. W., 253
Migne, J. P.: *Patrologia Graeca*, 98; *Patrologia Latina*, 98
Milankovitch, 554
Miller, S., 560
Moeyersons, J., 553, 554
Mofolo: *Chaka*, 356
Molom Gaolo, 195
Mommsen: *Monumenta Germaniae Historica, Auctores Antiquissimi*, 98
Moniot, H., 148
Monod, T., 368, 673
Monteil, C., 39, 199
Moorsel, H. van, 534, 550
Morgan, L. H., 272
Moriano, L., 293
Morice, 135
Morner, N. A., 378
Mortelmans, G., 534, 535, 550, 560
Movius, H., 418
Muhallabī, 107
Müller, F., 295, 296–7
Murdock, G. P., 37
Mveng, Père Engelbert, 65

Nachtigal, G.: *Sahara und Sudan*, 32
Narmer: palette, 251, 252
Nasiri al-Slawi, al-, 117
Nazimpaka Yubi III, king, 44
Nefer-Ka-Re (Pepi II): letter, 80, 278
Neferwptah, 213–14
Nenquin, J., 550, 556, 562
Newton, A. P., 32–3
Nilsson, E., 362, 366, 553
Njoya, Sultan (of Bamum), 136
Nkrumah, K., 70
Norris: *Memoirs of the Reign of Bossa Ahadee*, 30
Noten, F. van, 534, 559
Nuwayrī, 109, 110

O'Brien, T. P., 553
Obenga, T., 241
Olderogge, D. A., 65, 252
Oliver, R., 40, 65
Osei Tutu, 47
Osorkon III, 708
Paez, P., 29
Pallary, 574
Palmer, H. R., 13, 14, 36
Patterson, B., 73, 405
Pedelaborde, P., 377
Pepi II: letter, 80, 278
Pereira, P.: *Esmeraldo*, 17
Petrie, Sir W. M. Flinders, 714
Philocorus, 95
Pigafetta, F., 29
Pliny the Elder, 25, 93: *Natural History*, 95, 96
Ploey, J. de, 553
Plutarch, 96
Polinard, E., 534
Polybius, 93, 95, 96, 97, 99
Pommeret, Y., 534
Poseidonius, 99
Price-Mars, 65
Procopius, 93: *De Bello Vandalico*, 98
Prosper Tiro, 98
Pseudo-Scylax, 99
Ptolemy, Claudius, 26, 93, 95, 96: *Geography*, 99
Pullan, R. A., 364

Qaa', king, 219
Qādhī al-Fādhil, al-: *Rasā'il*, 111
Qadi Nu'man: *Ifitah al-Da'wa*, 106
Qalqashansi: *Subh al-A'shā*, 109
Quaque, Philip, 133

Radama I, king, 133
Radcliffe-Brown, A. R., 14, 37
Ramendo, L., 418, 569
Randles, W. G. L., 139, 689
Raqīq, al-: *Tārīkh*, 106
Reickstedt, 262
Reindorf, C. C.: *A History of the Gold Coast and Asante*, 38, 134
Reubeni, D., 119
Rhodenburg, H., 554
Richardson, J. L. and A. E., 378
Riet Lowe, R. Van, 414, 418
Robert, D., 82
Robert, S., 82
Roche, E., 410, 554
Roubet, C., 579
Rudin, H. R., 66
Ruffie, J., 261, 659

Sa'di, al-: *Tarikh al-Sudan*, 129
Safadī: *al-Wafibi-l-Wafayat*, 111
Safaqusi, Maqdish al-, 117
Sahnūn: *Mudawwana*, 108
Said, R., 365, 369, 372
Sallust, 96: *Bellum Jugurthinum*, 97

Sancho, Ignatius, 133
Sandford, K. S., 636
Sarbah, J. M., 38
Sauneron, S., 243
Saxon, E., 575
Schild, R., 369
Schlegel, A. W., 13
Schleicher, A., 13
Schmitz, A., 554, 555
Schwarz, 272
Schwidejzky, 263
Scipio Aemilianus, 97
Seeley, J. R., 33
Seligman, C. G., 273: *Races of Africa*, 35, 245–6
Servant, M. and S., 378, 383
Sforza, L. Cavalli-, 264
Shabayni, Abd-al-Salam, 125
Shaka, 47, 49
Shammākhī, al-, 111, 117
Shapera, 279
Shaw, F., 36
Shinqiti, Ahmad al-, 119
Simons, 403
Sine, D., 173, 198
Soga, T., 123
Soh, S.-A., 130
Sonni Ali, 46, 47
Soser, Pharaoh, 652
Spannus, 273
Stainier, X., 534, 550
Steinbeck, J.: *The Grapes of Wrath*, 356
Stephen, J., 33
Stewart, J. M., 314
Stigand, C. H.: *The Land of Zinj*, 39
Stow, 272
Strabo, 25, 95, 96
Streel, M., 554
Stuhlmann, Fr., 272
Sundstrom, L.: *The Trade of Guinea*, 37
Suret-Canale, J., 742
Swadesh, E., 238

Tacitus, 96
Taharqa, 708
Taieb, M., 406
Tait, D., 358
Talbot, P. A., 79
Tamghruti, al-, 117
Tauxier, L., 40
Taylor, R., 272
Taylor, W., 246
Teilhard de Chardin, P., 412, 415, 738
Tetry, 414
Thompson, L., 67
Tijani, 111
Tilimsani, Muhammad al-, 117
Tixier, J., 571, 573, 575
Tobias, P. V., 405, 409
Trevor-Roper, H., 31*n*, 41
Tucker, A. N., 284
Tunisi, al-, 125
Tutankhamun, 213, 652
Twiesselmann, F., 562

Ubri, 21
Ufrani, al-, 117
'Umarī, al-, 6, 26, 110: *Masālik al-Absār*, 110
Urvoy, Yves, 36

van der Hammen, T., 379
Vansina, J., 65
Vaufrey, R., 573, 576, 578–9
Vavilov, N. I., 693
Vedder, 280
Victor Vitensis, 98

Wahab Gaolo, 195
Ward, W. E. F.: *History of the Gold Coast*, 40
Warga, 126
Watt, 150
Wayland, E. J., 417, 418, 539, 542, 546
Wendorf, F., 369
Westermann, D., 235, 297, 315: *Geschichte Afrikas*, 37
Westphal, E. O. J., 282
Wickens, G. E., 378
Wieschoff, H. A.: *The Zimbabwe-Monomotapa Culture*, 37
Williams, M. A. J., 378, 379
Wilson, M., 67
Wisyānī, 111: *Siyar*, 108
Wolberg, D. F., 415
Woodson, C. G.: *Journal of Negro History*, 66
Wrigley, C., 64

Ya'qūbī, Al Biruni: *Tārīkh, Buldān*, 107
Yâqût, 111
Yoyotte, J., 672

Zarkashi, Al-, 117
Zayyanı, al-, 117
Zboïnsky, 534
Zeuner, F. E., 553
Zinderen Bakker, E. M. van, 378, 388, 554
Zuhrī, al-, 111

Index of Places

Abbassia, 635, 637, 639: pluvial, 370–1
Abay, Lake, 383, 391
Abidjan: University, 68
Abka, 640, 721: industry of, 643, 721
Abomey, 11, 251
Aboukir, 570
Abu Simbel, 644
Abu Tabari, 636
Abuja, 131
Abydos, 715: sacrificial knives, 651
Abyssinia: centre of agriculture, 693, 694, 695
Acacus: negroid skeleton, 274, 275
Accra: Congress of Africanists (1962), 70
Adaima, 635, 645, 646
Adamawa, 135: languages, 305; mountains, 552
Addis Ababa, 403
Adjefou, 663
Admer Erg, 592: Aterian, 595
Adrar Bous, 599, 600, 602, 671: culture of, 594, 595
Afalou-bou-Rhummel, 576
Afar lakes, 383, 385, 388
Afikpo, 625
Africa: exploitation, 742; image through the ages, 2; liberation struggles, 744; origin of man in, 275, 413; origin of name, 1*n*; problem of break in transmission, 201–2

Africa, Central: cradle of agriculture, 695; peopling of, 555–6; prehistory, 530–66
Africa, East: cradle of agriculture, 694, 695; geology, 318, 361–3; prehistory, 452–84
Africa, North: geology, 318; prehistory, 568–80; written sources, 25, 66, 116–20
Africa, Republic of South: rock art, 657; universities, 41; written sources, 121–4
Africa, Southern: geology, 318; historical studies, 67; prehistory, 487–529
Africa, West: cradle of agriculture, 628, 694, 695; geology, 318; prehistory, 611–30; written sources, 99–100
Afya, 637
Agordat, 480
Ahaggar, 275, 367: Aterian, 594; rock art, 579
Ahanna rock, 674
Aïn Boucherit, 569
Aïn Brimba, 569
Aïn Dokkara, 578
Aïn Fritissa, 570
Aïn Guedja, 669
Aïn Hanech, 569
Aïn Metkerchem, 572
Aïn Mhrotta (Kairouan), 572
Aïr, 367: rock paintings, 656
Akjoujt, 628
Akkad, 275: cuneiform language, 301
Al-Kharja, 636
Algeria: Aterian, 594; rock paintings, 656; war, 41
Amada, 637, 638, 639, 652: industry, 637, 638
Amanzi, 503
Amba Farit, 366
Ambile, 543
Amekni, 710
America, North: African studies in, 69–70
Amra, El-, 646, 714; industry, 714–715
Angola, 280: European history of, 28, 29; prehistory, 534; rock art, 657
Aoulef, 591, 592
Aphrodite, 100
Api, 564
Apollo II Rock-Shelter: earliest paintings, 528
Arak, 592
Aribinda, 666
Armant, 645, 646; -Gebelein, 710; pluvial, 370, 371
Ashanti (Asante), 47, 151, 740, 741
Ashmunayn, 100
Asia: agricultural relations with Africa, 699–701
Asokrochona, 620
Assadjen Ouan Mellen, 665, 671
Asselar: man, 277, 736
Aswan Dam, 721
Atakora hills, 611, 618, 619
Atbara, 635
Ater, Mount, 367
Atlantic Ocean: coast, 625; temperatures, 379
Atlas mountains, 320, 365, 367: rock paintings, 274, 676
Augsburg (Botswana), 680
Awash river, 363

Badari, (El-), 644, 645, 712: industry, 644, 645, 709, 713
Bafour, 185: tradition, 188
Baguirmi, 131
Bahan, 644
Bahr el-Gebel, 364
Bahr-el-Ghazal, 4, 327, 364, 616
Ballana, 275, 640: industry, 640
Ballas, 715
Bamako, 620
Bandiagara, 251
Banfora: paintings, 666
Baol, 252
Bardai: elephant, 661, 664
Baringo, Lake, 406
Batalimo, 547, 563
Bateke plateau, 546, 560
Battle Cave, 673
Bauchi plateau, 611
Baule: divinity of gold, 183–4
Behdet, 717
Beni Abbes, 592
Benin, 11, 627: artists, 351, 680
Benue river, 616
Bidzar, 549
Bijago Islands: language, 304
Bitorri, 551: Cave, 559
Blaka, Enneri, 662, 680: giraffes, 661, 674
Blande, 623
Blue Nile, 365, 721
Bodele, 363, 616
Bodo, 409
Bône, 570
Border Cave, 516
Borkou: rock art, 549
Boskop, 516
Bosumpra Cave, 624
Botswana: rock paintings, 657
Bou Alem, 676
Bouar, 548, 564
Brandberg: paintings, 218, 665
Broken Hill, Zambia; Rhodesian man, 221, 441
Broukkou, 589, 593
Bualen, 681
Buhen: temple, 228
Buru, 563
Burundi, 550: polished tools, 563
Bushveld, 334
Bussa, 620
Buto, 717
Buvuma Island, 525

Cairo: mummies in Museum, 209; Registry, 109; Unesco symposium (1974), 40, 80, 243
Calola, 549
Cameroon, 534: mount, 318
Cana: battle (1892), 48
Cango Caves: rock art, 657
Cape of Good Hope, 318: Dutch colony, 121
Cap Manuel, 620
Cape Hangklip, 503
Cape Macchia, 503
Capeletti Grotto, 579
Casamance river, 625
Cave of Hearths, Makapan, 503, 511, 518, 519
Central African Republic, 534
Ceuta: Portuguese at, 89
Chad basin, 74–5, 327: fossil man, 591; Lake, 341, 363, 364, 611, 616; language, 242, 243; in Pleistocene, 363–5, 383
Champlain, 570
Chebket Mennouna, 592
Chemeron, 406
Chesowanja, 446
Chetma (Biskra), 570
Chillalo, Mount, 366
Chotts, 576
Clairfontaine, 570
Columnata, 575, 576: sickles, 578
Conakry, 623
Congo, People's Republic of the, 534
Congo dia Vanga, 547
Copenhagen: Royal Library, letters in, 135
Cornelia, 502
Crescent Island, 481
Cyrenaica, 367, 573, 622

Dahomey, 30, 611, 741: bas reliefs, 250, 252
Daima, 625
Dakar: Ecole Supérieure des Lettres, 40; IFAN Library, 130; Pan-African Prehistoric Conference (1967), 403, 565, 570; Seminar on the historian in tropical Africa (1961), 60; University, 68
Dakhla oasis, 637
Damara Systems, of Namibia, 334
Danxome (Dahomey), 83
Dar-es-Salaam: Seminar on a new view of African history (1965), 60
Darau, 637, 640
Darfur: Sultan of, 136
De Hangen, 527
Deir El-Medineh, 645, 726
Deir Tasa, 710
Demeh, 712
Dider: engraved oxen, 660
Dimba, 564: Cave, 559
Dinga, 560
Djaret (Djerat), 656, 670
Djebel Bes Seba, 669
Djebel Idjerane, 589
Djebel Irhoud, 572
Djebel Mela, 549
Djidjelli, 570
Dogon: caves, 19
Dongola, 728
Dongorongo, 9
Doornlaagte, 502
Drakensberg: Herenveen gallery, 668; Mount St Paul, 669; paintings, 218, 528, 658–9, 677

Edward, Lake, 341, 479
Efik, 79
Egypt, 626, 628: Acheulian, 635; agriculture in, 694, 695; evolution of social systems, 724–7; Neolithic, 654, 710; Ottoman, 118; pottery, 651; predynastic, 712; two cultural groups, 644; unification, 650, 651; written sources, 94–5
Egypt, Lower (Delta), 646–50, 707–719: Neolithic in, 709–12; predynastic, 712–19
Egypt, Upper, 644–6, 719–24: Neolithic in, 720–1; predynastic, 721–4
Ekker, 592
El Beyed, 592
El Greiribat: giraffes, 662
El-Guettar, 572
El-Kab (Eg. Nekheb), 640, 652, 718: industry, 640
El-Khiam, 641
El-Ma El-Aboid, 570, 571
Elandsfontein, 502
Elgon, Mount, 365
Elmenteita, Lake, 362: industry, 733; man, 730
Eneiba, 644
Ennedi, 17: Neolithic in, 275; rock art, 549
Errouri Erg, 673
Esh Shaheinab, 480, 592, 596, 605: excavation data, 643, 720; pottery, 663
Esna, 637, 639, 640
Ethiopia, 110: coffee, 733; European history of, 28, 29; succession, 354; written sources, 120–1
Ethiopian highlands, 365: rock paintings, 657; role in agriculture, 690, 696
Eyasi, Lake, 280

Faid Sonar, 578
Fayum, 637: A industry, 647, 713, 714; B industry, 646, 714; C industry, 646; Neolithic in, 710, 711; papyri from, 100; Primates discovered, 402
Fernando Po (Poo), island, 285, 563, 625
Fertile Crescent, 275, 687, 702
Fezzan: Aterian, 595; rock paintings, 656, 664, 665
Florisbad, 516: Peat I, 511
Fort Ternan, 403, 443, 487
Fouarat, 569
Fourah Bay College, Sierra Leone, 41
Fouta Djallon (Futa Djallon), 130, 611, 619: caves, 623
France, African studies in, 69
Funj kingdom, 119
Futa Toro, 130

Gabon, 564: prehistory, 534
Gafsa, 576
Gambia river, 630
Gamble's Cave, 482: blade industry, 362, 479
Ganoa: rhinoceros, 661
Gao empire, 350
Garusi (or Laetotil), 405, 406, 408, 444, 446
Gerzeh, 715: culture, 676, 715–16, 717
Ghana, kingdom, 155, 346, 613, 627: land of gold, 630, 740; royal succession, 742
Giza, 652: industry, 638; Sphinx, 229
Godebra, 480
Gold Coast: universities, 40
Gombe, 511, 558, 564
Gondwana, 316
Gonoa, 661, 664
Gossolorum, 600
Great Britain: African studies in, 69
Great Dike, 334
Great Escarpment, 320
Gregory Rift valley, 335
Guinea, 28–9: Bissau, 623; highlands, 611; Neolithic, 597, 605; rock-shelters, 622; Upper, 51
Guna, Mount, 366
Gundu, Mount, 549
Gwandu, 135
Gwelo Kopje, 502
Gwisho, 561, 562: Springs, 337

Hadar: palaeoanthropological fragments, 406, 410, 444, 446, 491; sedimentary formations, 397
Hamamia, 645, 646
Hamburg: Colonial Institute, 270
Hammada el Guir, 676
Harrar, 280
Hau Cave, 559
Heliopolis, 649, 650, 717
Helwan, 641, 648, 651: industry, 641
Hierakonpolis (Eg. Nekhen), 652, 718
Hou, 715
Howiesons Poort, 515, 517
Huambo plateau, 552
Hydrax Hill, 642

I-n-Itinen, 662, 670, 672, 674, 675
Igbo-Ukwu, 617
Iheren, 664, 672, 674, 680
Imakassen: gazelle sculpture, 604
In Afaleh, 569
In Galjeien: elephants, 661, 664
In Habeter, 670
Inahouanrhat, 674
Indian Ocean, 25, 321
Inoro, 666
Isanghila rapids, 547
Isangho, 482, 547, 551: industry, 561–562, 623
Ischkeul, Lake, 569
Isimila, 468, 472, 500
Issoukai-n-Afelia, 681
Ituri, 279, 563
Ivory Coast, 625
Iwo Eleru, 624

Jabbaren, 656, 664, 672, 673, 674, 676, 681

Java, 409, 411, 445
Jebba, 616
Jebel Ahmar, 637, 639
Jebel Silsila, 640
Jenne, 129, 130
Jericho, 641, 710
Jos plateau, 619, 621

Kabwe (Broken Hill), 502, 503: skull, 515–16
Kabylian coast, 570
Kadada, 643
Kadero, 480, 643
Kafu valley, 539
Kaka, Mount, 366
Kakimbon, Grotto de, 623
Kakontwe, 546
Kalahari desert, 4, 689
Kalambo, 551, 556: Chipeta industry, 506; Falls, 472, 500, 511; Rubble I, 518
Kalina, 542: industry, 558; Pointe, 544
Kalkbank, 518
Kamabai, 623
Kamoa, 551, 553, 554, 556, 562: river, 541
Kanam, 443
Kanapoi, 406, 408
Kanem, 107
Kanjera, 441, 516
Kano, 131, 616
Karar, Lake, 570
Kariandusi, 472
Karkarichinkat, 624
Karkur oasis, 639
Karnak, 652
Karoo, 318, 334, 489, 502
Karouba, 573
Kasaï, 541, 560: basin, 537, 563
Kasr-Karoun, 713
Katsina, 131
Kayor, 741
Kenya, Mount, 320, 365: glaciation, 554
Keringet Cave, 480
Kerma, 728
Kerzas, 592
Kharga, 593, 643; Amadian, 637; Aterian, 595; industry, 638, 639
Khartoum, 642: Gordon College, 40; Neolithic industry, 642, 720; 'Variant', 721
Khasmet-ed-Dib, 713
Khenchela, 577
Khor Abu Anja, 635
Khor Bahan, 722
Khor (Abu) Daoud, 637, 638, 644
Kiantapo Cave, 549
Kibish, 730: formation, 516
Kifan bel Ghomani, 572
Kilimanjaro, Mount, 318, 320, 365
Kilwa: Sultan of, 135
Kindia, 623
Kinshasa, 328, 543, 546, 553, 560, 732: language, 239
Kintampo: culture, 624
Kisale, Lake, 9
Kisese Rock Shelter, 525
Kiumbala, 549
Kivu, Lake, 552
Kizala, Lake, 161
Kjourab, 363
Klassies river, 511, 519
Klip river, 499
Klipplaatdrif, 499
Kom Ombo, 638, 640
Kongo, kingdom of, 83, 140
Kono, 543
Koobi Fora, 446
Korotoro, 490
Kotoko: language, 131
Koudiat Khifene Lahda, 576
Koulikoro, 172
Koumbala shelter, 666
Koumbi-Saleh, 9, 161, 350
Kournari, 9
Kourounkorokale, 624
Kromdraai cave, 405, 407, 491, 494
Krugersdorp, 490
Kuku, 107
Kumasi, 31: Arab chancery, 135
Kunta, 196
Kwango, 547, 560

La Madeleine, 669
La Mouillah, 575, 577
Laetolil (Garusi), 405, 406, 408, 444, 446
Lalla, 576
Largeau, 613, 616
Lascaux: *homo sapiens*, 414
Leeufontein: lion, 668; rhinoceros, 661
Lengo, 549, 666
Leopard's Hill Cave, 524
Leptis Magna: Roman temple, 228
Lesotho: rock paintings, 657
Liberia College, Monrovia, 41
Libyan desert, 593: Aterian, 637
Limpopo: paintings dated, 218
Lions Cave, Swaziland, 518
Lirue hills, 621
Livingstone, 499
Loanga, 81
Lobaye, 547
Lobi: circular ruins, 353
Lochard, 502
Logone river, 364
London: Anthropological Society (later Royal Anthropological Institute), 32; School of Oriental and African Studies (SOAS), 69, 270; University, Bedford College, 405–6
Lothagam, 406, 408, 443: hominid jaw fragment, 73
Lovanium: University, 41
Lubu, 81, 82
Lubumbashi: University, 68
Luembe river, 543
Luena river, 541
Lukanda, 525
Lukeino, 406
Lukuliro, 472
Luembe Basin, 541
Lunda, 543, 554, 556, 560
Luxor, 214, 224, 652
Lwandjili, 81, 82

Maadi, 649, 650, 651: industry, 649
Macina, 135, 198, 327
Madagascar: history, 133; migration to, 700; revolt (1947), 41
Madjouba, 673
Magadi, Lake, 363
Magaliesberg, 502
Maghrib: prehistory, 568–80; written sources, 96–9
Magosi, 546; industries, 423, 479, 513, 545, 546, 676–7, 733
Mahasna, 645
Maiduguri, 616
Makapan Limeworks, 490, 491
Makapansgat Cave, 405, 407, 408, 410, 415
Makerere College, Kampala, 40
Makurdi, 616
Malawi, 494: rock art, 657
Mali, empire, 27, 110, 155, 351, 357, 627, 740
Mandara, 131, 611: language, 131
Mansourah (Constantine), 570
Maretjiesfontein Hill: quagga, 661
Masanga, 557
Mataria, 214
Matmar, 644, 645
Matupi, 551, 566: Cave, 561
Mauritania: Aterian, 594; history, 119; Neolithic industry, 677, 679
Mazer, 592
Mdaga, 85

Mediterranean: climates, 326, 331, 391–2; cradle of agriculture, 692–5; ecological continuity with Africa, 701
Mejiro Cave, 624
Melka Kunturé (or Kontoure), 406 409, 411, 447, 499: platform at, 467
Memphis, 710, 715: empire, 707
Meniet, 597, 601, 602, 658
Merdjouma, 595
Merimde, 648: -Beni-Salame, 709, 711; industry, 647
Meroe, 629, 728
Mertoutek, 662, 672
Mesopotamia: influence on agriculture, 696, 733
Micoque, 423, 593
Mirgissa, 653
Modjokerto, 409
Mokoto lakes, 562
Montagu, 503: Cave, 515, 518
Morocco: Acheulian on Atlantic coast, 570; archives, 116; Aterian in, 594; independence (1955), 41; rock paintings, 656
Moscow: Patrice Lumumba University, 68
Mose, 553
Mossel Bay, 517, 518
Mouka plateau, 534
Moussanda, 553, 559
Mozambique: languages, 293
Mpatou, 549: Springs, 666
Mufo, 506
Mukinanira, 562
Mumbwa, 516
Munyama Cave, 525, 551
Mustajidda, 644, 645, 646
Mwanganda, 501
Mwela rocks, 337

Nagada, 715: I, 644, 645, 714; II, 644, 646, 709, 715
Nairobi: Pan African Congress of Prehistory (1947), 558
Naivasha, Lake, 362, 363
Nakuru, Lake, 341, 362, 363, 479, 482, 733
Namib desert, 510
Namibia: rock art, 657, 665; scrapers from, 524
Napata, kingdom, 726–7, 728
Narosura, 481
Nata river, 518
Natron, Lake, 405, 407
Nelson's Bay Cave, 525
Nenniet, 592
Ngoere river, 542
Ngorongoro, 480
Ngorora, 406, 443
Ngovo Cave, 564
Ngwane: rock art, 657
Nhampassere, 623
Niani: iron objects, 210
Niger river, 328, 611, 733
Nigeria, 613: universities, 40
Nile river, 327, 328: fishing, 341; variable floods, 708, 719
Nile valley, 706: climatic changes in, 369–71; fertility, 346; prehistory, 634–54; social systems, 707, 708, 711–12
Njarassi, 516
Njoro River Cave, 480, 733
Nkosisana Stream, 674
Nok: culture, 621; terracotta figurines, 629
Nsongezi, 472, 539
Nswatugi Cave, 669
Ntadi-ntadi Cave, 564
Ntereso, 626
Nubia, 711: Egyptian industries, 635, 637; rock paintings, 657
Nubia, Lower: flooding of, 721; Neolithic organic remains, 275, 711
Nuri, 634, 635, 636, 727

Ohemhit, 644
Okovango Basin, 327
Olduvai Gorge: *Hominidae* specimens, 405, 407, 408, 409, 446, 491, 499, 516; magnetic event, 360, 362; sedimentary formations, 393; *Zinjanthropus* remains, 73, 221. *See also* Oldowan industry
Olorgesailie, 472
Omari, El, 651, 710: A industry, 648, 715; B industry, 649, 716
Ombos (Eg. Noubet), 717
Omo river, 363: chopping tool, 418; palaeontological sites, 405, 406, 408, 409, 410, 442; sedimentary successions, 393; valley, 73, 735
Onitsha, 616
Oppermansdrif, 502
Oran: rock paintings in South, 656, 664, 665
Orange Free State: rock art, 657; scrapers from, 524
Orange Springs, 674
Orangea I site, 518
Ouagadougou kingdom, 353, 354
Ouan Bender, 664
Ouan Sidi, 663
Ouanrhet: White lady, 664
Oued Akarit, 572
Oued Amazzar, 663
Oued Djebbana, 573
Oued Djerat, 662, 664, 670, 672, 676: elephant, 661; ox with pendant, 660
Oued Eched, 663
Oued Hammamat, 676
Oued Mellah, 570
Oued Tilemsi, 736
Ouzidane, 570
Oweinat massif, 367
Oxford University: Archaeological Research Laboratory, 226
Oyo kingdom, 48, 160

Pacific Ocean, 380
Palestine, 641
Paris: Centre d'Etudes Africaines, 69; (National Museum of Natural History) expedition (1932–3), 405
Peer's Cave, 516
Peninj, 446
Philipp Cave, 665, 669
Pondoland, 525

Qara, 639
Qattara, 367

Red Sea, 25: hills, 367
Redeyef (Gafsa), 570
Reggan, 569
Retaïmia, 572
Rhardes, 676
Rhodesia, *see* Zimbabwe
Rif mountains, 320
Rift Valley, 4, 439; aquatic tradition in, 484; geology, 318, 320; stratigraphy, 393
Rio Muni, 550
Rooidam, 505, 506
Rop: rock shelters, 624
Rudolf, Lake, *see* Turkana, Lake
Rufisque, 622
Ruwenzori, Mount, 365, 366, 552
Rwanda, 550: Sangoan industry in, 475

S'Baïkia, 570: tools, 592
Sabaluka ridge, 365
Sabratha, 228
Sahara, 319, 585: aquatic civilization in, 482; as barrier to migration, 689; chronology of climatic variation, 378; chronology of industries, 588, 622; climatic changes of, 366–369, 586; cradle of agriculture,

Sahara—*cont.*
602–3, 691; filter of Mediterranean influence, 319; humid era, 331, 336, 368, 377; prehistory, 585–605; written sources, 99–100
Sahel, 5, 377, 624
Sai, 635
Saldanha: skull, 515, 516
Sakkara, 214, 651, 652
Salo plateau, 539
Samo, 357
Sanga, 557
Sangha valley, 4
Sango Bay, 542
Sansanding Dam, 201
Saoura river basin, 368–9, 569, 591: Aterian, 594
Saqqara, 214, 651, 652
Sebua, 638, 644, 652
Sefar, 656, 664, 665, 674: saluki, 672
Segou, 9
Semien mountains, 365–6
Semliki river, 366
Senegal river, 616, 618, 625
Shaba, 539: copperbelt, 333; gravel terraces, 537; polished tools, 563; rock art, 549
Shambe, 364
Shari river, 364
Shellal, 644
Sherda, 592
Shungura formation, 393
Shungwaya, 139
Sidi Mansour de Gafsa, 572
Sidi Zin (Le Kef), 570, 572
Sierra Leone, 630: Fourah Bay College, 41
Silet: bull sculpture, 604
Silsila, 637, 640, 641: industry, 640
Sinai: copper, 650
Sirikwa, 161
Siwa, 637
Skildergat, 516
Sokoto: Caliphate, 135
Songhai kingdom, 129, 305, 627
Soqotra island: language, 301
Stanley Pool, 543, 546
Stellenbosch, 499
Sterkfontein caves, 405, 407, 408, 490; stone tools, 493, 494, 499
Still Bay, 546: industry, 425, 465, 473, 545, 546, 733
Sudan, 635, 642
Sudd basin, 363, 364–5
Suez isthmus, 320
Sumer, 275
Swartkrans Cave, 405, 407, 409, 491: faunal remains, 492; stone tools, 493, 494, 499

Tabalbalet, 663
Tabelbala, 571, 592
Table de Jaatcha, 579
Tachenghit, 571, 592, 593
Tademaït, 595
Taforalt, 576
Takedetoumatine, 673
Tamar Hat, 575
Tamentit, 633: ram sculpture, 604
Tamla, 570
Tan-Terirt: owls, 660
Tana, Lake, 362
Tanganyika, Lake, 557
Tangasi, 636
Tanzania, 689: rock paintings, 456, 478; Sangoan industry, 475
Taoussasill, 617
Tarforalt, 572
Taruga, 629
Tarzerouck, 663
Tasa, 644, 710: industry, 644, 709, 713
Tassili N'Ajjer, 657: frescoes, 664; Neolithic remains, 274, 275; rock art, 17, 579, 603, 656, 665
Taudenit, 586
Taung, 405, 407, 490, 491
Teffassasset river, 591
Tegdaoust, 82
Tekrur empire, 155
Tell mountains, 320
Ténéré, 599, 670: rock paintings, 656
Téré, 543
Ternifine, 568, 570, 571
Tete: hieroglyphic inscription, 252
Thebes, 634, 637, 653: Hawarian, 639; hominid tooth, 635
This, 718
Three Rivers, 499
Ti-n-Assako, 602
Tiaga, 543
Tibesti, 367: rock paintings, 656
Tichitt, 602, 624, 627, 629: arrow heads, 665; Dhar, 600–1, 657; stone pillars, 673
Tidikelt, 594
Tiemassas, 621
Tiguelguemine, 589
Tihilahi, 662
Tihodaïne, 592, 595
Timbrourine, 593
Timbuktu, 129, 130: Ahmed Baba Centre, 6
Timenzouzine, 674
Tin Felki, 670
Tin Lallan, 670, 674
Tin Hanakaten, 663
Tin Tazarift, 657, 672, 675
Tin Tehed, 681
Tissoukai, 656, 662, 670, 672
Tit Mellil, 570
Togo hills, 611, 618, 619
Tondidarou, 630
Toshka, 275, 640
Toukh, 710
Toulou, 549, 666
Transvaal, 492, 493: Museum, 661, 669; rock art, 657; scrapers from, 524
Tripolis, 117
Tshangula Cave, 525; industry, 515
Tuinplaats, 516
Tunisia: Aterian, 594; history, 117
Turkana, Lake (Rudolf), 341, 363, 405, 408, 418, 482: East, 396; fossil cranium, 491; tools and habitation sites, 447, 460, 472
Twin Rivers, 511

Ubangi river, 563: valley, 4
Uele Basin, 279, 547, 563
Uganda: local historians, 39; Sangoan industry, 475
Um Ruwaba, 364
Umgazana Cave, 525
Usno formation, 396

Vaal river, 494, 499: rock art, 657
Vereeniging, 499
Verwoerd Dam, 505
Victoria, Lake, 363: Sangoan industries in, 475; West I technique, 537, 541; West II technique, 636

Waday, 131
Wadi Eched, 595
Wadi-El-Natrun, 215
Wadi Halfa, 638, 639, 640, 653
Wadi Hammamat, 213, 637, 645, 652
Wadi Hof, 648
Wadi Kharit, 368
Wadi Saoura, 368
Wadi Sebua, 637
Wadi Tumilat, 639
Wanzarba, 48
Washington: National Academy of Science, 376
Wawa, 634: Acheulian, 635
White Nile, 365, 721
Windsorten, 505
Wonderboompoort, 502

Yacut, 26
Yagala, 623
Yatenga, 353
Yayo, 614
Yemen: origin of name, 13
Yengema, 623
Yola, 616
Zafila Basin, 539
Zaïre river, 327, 328: basin, 4, 327, 475, 479, 530; European history of Lower, 28; prehistoric industries, 539–45; tools, 534
Zambezi: European history of, 28, 29; river, 327, 494
Zambia: copperbelt, 333
Zanzibar, 741
Zenebi, 621
Zimbabwe (Rhodesia): frescoes, 666; gold mines, 350; historical studies in, 67
Zombepata Cave, 519, 525
Zumri: Aterian, 595

Index of Ethnonyms

Akan, 240: calendar, 52*n*
Amazons, 48
Antiliban, 301
Arabs, 276: correspondence, 135–6; language, 129, 239, 242, 301; script, 114
Asante, 47, 151, 350; Asantehenes, 135

Bafulero, 45
Baga, 237
Bambara, 10: -Dyola language, 239; hieroglyphs, 79, 250, 251; tradition of the Komo, 168–70, 177, 179–80
Bantu, 238, 240, 529: expansion linked with iron, 17, 285; language family, 293, 295, 304–5; languages, 12, 249, 281, 284–5; relations with Khoisan, 679
Banyoro, 45
Bariba, 84
Basari, 237
Bassa, 136
Bauti, 342
Beja: language, 301
Berbers, 110, 630: Azilian industry, 575; languages, 300
BergDama, 529
Biiru, 151
Buganda, 160
Bushmen, 516

Cape Khoi, 122
Cerko, 46, 48*n*, 49
Chaouis, 579

Dagomba, 353
Dinka, 278
Dogon: healing powers, 187; hieroglyphs, 79, 250, 251; nominalism, 142; Sigi ritual, 152
Dorobo, 459
Duala, 239
Dyola, 357
Dzing, 281

Embu, 148, 157
Ethiopians, 736

Falasha (Ethiopian Jews), 301
Fang: song fables, 146
Fulani, 9, 10, 240, 674: animal husbandry, 342; Bororo ceremonies, 189; fertility charm, 670; genealogy, 195; jihad, 131; languages, 237, 239; tradition (of Gueno and Kiikala), 170, 179–80

Galla, 148, 280
Gan: kings, 354
Garamantes, 629
Gouro, 10, 149
Guanches: language, 300
Guerze (Kpelle), 136: pottery, 674
Gurma, 253
Gurmanche, 240

Hadza, 459
Hadzapi, 280: languages, 281
Hatsa, 306
Hausa, 27: languages, 12, 239, 242, 302; writings, 28, 131
Herero, 122
Hilali, 90
Hottentots, 736
Hutu, 143, 343
Hyksos, 726

Ibo, 234: common altar, 357; language, 239; Nsibidi ideography, 253
Ife, 210, 253
Igala, 153
Imbangala, 160

Kaguru, 155
Khoi-Khoi, 279, 280, 529: languages, 281, 294, 296; pastoralists, 528; relations with San, 679
'Khoisan', 279, 283, 736: language family, 300, 306–7, 478; relations with Bantu, 679
Kikuyu: Gicandi ideographical system, 79; legend about iron, 45
Kirdi, 350
Kissi, 358
Koba, 237
Kongo, 154, 234
Konianke, 358
Konkomba, 358
Koulango: pottery, 353
Kouranko, 358
Kpelle (Guerze), 136: pottery, 674
Kuba, 151, 154, 155: sculpture, 11
Kung San, 692
Kusase, 353
Kwadi, 280: languages, 281

Lebu, 239
Lobi: Dyoro secret society, 357
Loma (Toma), 136, 358: script, 79
Lunda, 48

Macinanke, 198
Malinke, 47
Mande, 240, 248, 283, 356: languages, 303; Marka tradition, 195; traditional classes, 185
Mandingo, 47: Mansas, 250
Mangbetu: lengthening of skull, 355
Masai, 148, 342, 481: language, 306
Mbochi, 81
Mboon, 152
Mende, 136: coinage, 358; script, 79

Merina, 133: language, 307
Meru, 148
Mongo, 279
Mossi, 43, 45, 240: succession, 353

Nachikufan, 337: industry, 520
Nama, 122: tradition, 173
Naron, 282
Nsibidi: language, 136; pictograms, 79, 251, 253
Nubian: A-Group, 643, 644, 721, 722, 723; B-Group, 644, 722, 723; C-Group, 480, 644, 652, 722
Nyangatom (Bumi), 75

Ogboni, 151
Otavi, 280, 282
Ova Tjimba, 529

Peoples of the Sea, 603
Portuguese, 126, 285: creolized language, 308
pygmies, 350, 736: hunter-gatherers, 691–2; theories on, 273, 276, 278, 738

Rwanda, 44

Safen, 237
Sandawe, 282, 306
San, 122, 529: cosmological legend, 668, 669; hunter art, 478; hunter-gatherers, 459; languages, 279, 281, 294; relations with Khoikhoi, 679; theories on, 273, 279–81
Sao, 7, 85
Senianke, 49
Senufo, 21, 357
Shilluk, 45: language, 306
Shona, 9, 152
Siddi: in India, 276
Somali, 736: language, 301
Somono, 186
Songhay, 46, 47, 626: language, 45, 239
Susu, 234

Tehenu, 277
Teke (Tio), 149, 155
Temehu Libyan, 277
Temne, 237
Tio (Teke), 149, 155
Toma (Loma), 136, 358: script, 79
Tonga, 149
Tuareg, 254, 342
Tukulor, 248
Turkana, 75
Tutsi, 142, 343
Twa, 529

Vili, 82

Wolof, 278: language, 12, 239

Xhosa, 152: history, 123

Yoruba: art, 630; language, 239; priests' writing, 251

Zaghawa, 107
Zandj, 107
Zarma, 46: language, 45
Zulu: oral traditions, 123; war (1879), 123

Index of Dynasties

Abbasid, 89
Almohad, 92, 110: letters, 108, 109
Almoravid, 90: letters, 108, 109
Ashanti, 135, 151, 350
Ayyubid, 90, 93, 109

Bornu, 12, 135, 136, 614: chronicles, 131

Egyptian, Pharaonic, 650–3

Fatimid, 89, 100, 106, 108

Hafsid, 92

Idrissid, 135
Ifriqiyan, 106

Mamluk, 93, 108

Ottoman: archives, 116

Ramessid, 94
Rustamid, 108

Sa'di, 117
Saite, 95
Sassanid, 100
Sherifian, 117
Songhay, 28, 45, 125

Thinite, 707, 718, 723

Umayyad, 89

Zirids, 90